Social Security Disability Practice

Volume Two

Thomas E. Bush

2nd Edition

Managing Editor: Jim Pawell

 **James** Publishing

Contact us at (866) 72-JAMES or www.jamespublishing.com

Related Texts

Medical Issues in Social Security Disability
Social Security Issues Annotated
Social Security Disability Advocate's Handbook
Social Security Disability Medical Tests

www.JamesPublishing.com or (866) 72-JAMES

This publication is intended to provide accurate and authoritative information about the subject matter covered. It is sold with the understanding that the publisher does not render legal, accounting or other professional services. If legal advice or other expert assistance is required, seek the services of a competent professional.

Persons using this publication in dealing with specific legal matters should exercise their own independent judgment and research original sources of authority and local court rules.

The publisher and the author make no representations concerning the contents of this publication and disclaim any warranties of merchantability or fitness for a particular purpose.

We view the publication of this work as the beginning of a dialogue with our readers. Periodic revisions to it will give us the opportunity to incorporate your suggested changes. Call us at (866) 72-JAMES or send your comments to:

Revision Editor
James Publishing, Inc.
3505 Cadillac Ave., Suite P-101
Costa Mesa, CA 92626

First Edition, 3/85
Revision 1, 3/86
Revision 2, 8/87
Revision 3, 8/88
Revision 4, 6/89
Revision 5, 6/90

Second Edition, 2/92
Revision 1, 4/93
Revision 2, 3/94
Revision 3, 3/95
Revision 4, 2/96
Revision 5, 4/97
Revision 6, 4/98
Revision 7, 7/99
Revision 8, 5/00

Revision 9, 6/01
Revision 10, 5/02
Revision 11, 5/03
Revision 12, 7/04
Revision 13, 10/05
Revision 14, 12/06
Revision 15, 12/07
Revision 16, 12/08
Revision 17, 12/09
Revision 18, 12/10
Revision 19, 12/11
Revision 20, 12/12
Revision 21, 12/13
Revision 22, 12/14
Revision 23, 11/15
Revision 24, 4/17

Summary of Contents

Preface: How to Use This Book and Other Tips for Improving Your Social Security Disability Practice

VOLUME 1

1. Initial Client Contact

2. Prehearing Procedure

VOLUME 2

3. The Hearing

4. Following a Favorable Decision

5. Appeals Council

6. Federal Court Review

7. Attorney's Fees

Detailed Contents

VOLUME 1

Preface: How to Use This Book and Other Tips for Improving Your Social Security Disability Practice

1. Initial Client Contact

2. Prehearing Procedure

VOLUME 2

3. The Hearing

4. Following a Favorable Decision

5. Appeals Council

6. Federal Court Review

7. Attorney's Fees

Appendices

Index

Preface

How to Use This Book and Other Tips for
Improving Your Social Security Disability Practice

Learn the Five-Step Sequential Evaluation Process. The five-step Social Security disability sequential evaluation process provides the framework for most arguments to the Social Security Administration about your client's disability. This book is organized around the five-step process. *See* §§110-119 and 20 C.F.R. § 404.1520. Take time to learn how the five steps work. Because the process is *sequential*, if a claimant can be found *not disabled* at any step other than step three, the claimant does not get to proceed to the next step.

Read the First Three Chapters. If you are new to Social Security disability law, sit down and read the first three chapters of this book. This should give you a reasonably good grasp of the unique and often peculiar rules governing this area of practice. You can peruse the other chapters and appendices later, as issues come up.

Use the Forms With Care. This book is absolutely filled with useful forms. The residual functional capacity forms, in particular, are great time savers. You may copy these forms directly out of the book or utilize Digital Access to adapt them for your word processing program. But beware, forms may need to be modified to address the specific issues in a particular case. A form cannot cover every possible situation. For example, a properly completed interview form will always have comments written in the margins about your client's case.

All of the forms in this book are in use in the author's office, but we are constantly modifying them for individual cases. Sometimes we like a modification so much, we incorporate it into the form. If you make any especially useful modifications, we would appreciate a copy so we can publish improvements.

Check Out the Charts. The charts provide useful summaries of disability concepts. The chart at §121.1 summarizes rules from the Medical Vocational Guidelines. From this chart you can quickly determine what exertional limitations a claimant must have in order to win a disability case. The chart at §135 summarizes differences between the Social Security disability and SSI programs. The chart at §271.1 shows how particular limitations affect ranges of work, and the chart at §349.6 summarizes the different standards for transferability of skills for different ages and exertional levels. The author keeps a copy of this chart in his briefcase for use in questioning vocational experts at hearings.

Do Not Neglect the Appendices. There is a wealth of material in the appendices. The author often begins research on disability issues with Appendix 1, an index to Social Security Rulings. Appendix 8 is an excerpt from the manual given by SSA to medical experts to prepare them to testify. Reading this manual may help prepare you to cross-examine a medical expert. Appendices 4 and 7, excerpts from manuals given by SSA to vocational experts, are required reading when you are preparing to cross-examine a vocational expert (even though they were published by SSA years ago). Appendix 5 is the complete list of unskilled sedentary occupations from the current edition of the *Dictionary of Occupational Titles*. (There are so few of these occupations that vocational experts tend to come up with other jobs which they will testify that they know from "experience" to be unskilled sedentary occupations.) Appendix 9 is a 2007 law review article by Professor Robert E. Rains which tackles the ethical issue that haunts all social security disability practitioners: Must you submit an adverse medical report?

You Will Need Basic Reference Materials. This book provides a place to start. It cannot be used successfully without also reading the regulations and rulings themselves. You can order from the Superintendent of Documents a hard copy of 20 C.F.R. Parts 400-499, which in many circumstances is easier to use than the Internet version. You will also need access to Social Security Rulings and Acquiescence Rulings since 1981, a good medical dictionary and a medical textbook, all of which can be found on the Internet. *See* Appendix 2.

About the Author

Thomas E. Bush has represented Social Security disability claimants since 1977 when he spent a year as a VISTA attorney with the Milwaukee Indian Health Board. At the end of 1977, he opened his own law office. Since then his law practice has concentrated more and more on Social Security disability representation. At present, Bush practices almost exclusively in this area.

Bush received his law degree from the University of Wisconsin where he also did graduate work in Chinese history. He has regularly written and spoken about Social Security disability issues to other lawyers, advocacy groups and the general public. Two brochures he has written, "Social Security Disability and SSI Claims–Your Need for Representation" and "Preparing for Your Social Security Disability or SSI Hearing," are in use all over the country.

A member of the National Organization of Social Security Claimants' Representatives (NOSSCR) since 1980, he served on the Board of Directors from 1988 to 2001. He was the President of NOSSCR for the 1997-98 term.

He may be reached at Thomas E. Bush, S.C., 310 W. Wisconsin Avenue, Suite 930E, Milwaukee, WI 53203, (414) 765-9333.

Chapter 3

The Hearing

---

§300   The ALJ Hearing

An administrative law judge (ALJ) hearing, which is much less formal than a court hearing, is non-adversarial. That is, there is no lawyer representing the Social Security Administration who appears to present SSA's side. Indeed, SSA claims that it doesn't have a "side." The agency views its role as providing benefits to those claimants who are disabled and denying benefits to those who are not. It is the ALJ's job, as a neutral fact-finder working for a neutral agency, to inquire fully into the issues and find the claimant disabled if the claimant meets the requirements for disability set forth in the Social Security Act, regulations and rulings.

For the most part, during the years since the 1979 effective date of the Medical-Vocational Guidelines, most ALJs have fulfilled the neutral fact-finder role most of the time. There are times, though, when ALJs as a group, influenced by what SSA officials in the past have called the "adjudicative climate," find fewer claimants disabled. "Adjudicative climate" refers to the total influence on ALJs not only from SSA but also from public opinion, the media, politicians' speeches, hearing testimony before the House Social Security Subcommittee, academic papers, think tank publications, etc. When the adjudicative climate turns against claimants for disability benefits, ALJs as a group find fewer claimants disabled even without SSA changing the rules for disability adjudication. We are currently in one of those times. ALJ allowance rates have dropped from 63% in 2008 to 45% in 2014 and 2015. *See* §156.

Michael Astrue, the former SSA Commissioner, explained the declining ALJ allowance rate was a result of increased applications from people who did not meet the disability standard. Instead of being disabled, these claimants applied for disability because they were out of work as a result of the recession of 2007 - 2009. While there may be a kernel of truth in this position that could account for some reduction in the ALJ allowance rate, it is impossible to attribute the steadily dropping ALJ allowance rate to a recession-driven increasing number of bad disability claims. While most disability lawyers agree that they have seen more bad cases in recent years, virtually all disability lawyers say that today it is much more difficult to have disabled claimants with good claims found disabled by ALJs than it was in 2008.

The decline of overall ALJ allowance rates has occurred at a time when individual ALJ statistics are readily available on SSA's website as a result of President Obama's Open Government Initiative. So we not only have available to us the overall ALJ allowance rates statistics, but we can also track the allowance rates of individual ALJs. Individual ALJ disposition data for the past few years appears on SSA's website. Start at http://

www.socialsecurity.gov/open/data/. See http://www.disabilityjudges.com, which uses SSA data to calculate the national allowance rate, individual ALJ allowance rates, allowance rates by state and by hearing office.

Before the Open Government Initiative, ALJs themselves could not readily obtain their own statistics. Now it is easy for an ALJ to find his or her own allowance rate and the allowance rates of other ALJs. Many observers wanted to know whether the ready availability of ALJ disposition data would affect the allowance rates of outlier ALJs on both ends of the spectrum—ALJ's who were extremely generous in awarding benefits and ALJs who were extremely stingy. The thought was that when an individual ALJ discovered that his or her allowance rate deviated significantly from the mean, the ALJ would make adjustments in approach to bring his or her allowance rate more in line with other ALJs. This seems to have worked only for formerly high-paying ALJs, whose allowance rates have tended toward the mean. It does not appear to have affected the low paying ALJs.

A study of ALJ disposition data shows that there is a group of low-paying outlier ALJs who find disabled an astonishingly small number of claimants. Such outliers may have always existed—we may not have known how many ALJs found so few claimants disabled, but it is more likely that this is a recent phenomenon. Some observers attribute this phenomenon to opening the ALJ corps in recent years to lawyers who in their careers never represented an actual human client, e.g., SSA staff attorneys, OGC attorneys and other government attorneys. Other observers say this phenomenon is driven by political ideology.

It always mattered which judge was assigned to a claimant's case. Within the group of reasonable ALJs, the ones in the middle of the bell curve, some are harder to convince than others. As a lawyer for claimants, you need to pay attention to these differences and provide more evidence of disability to reasonable ALJs who are harder to convince. As for the unreasonable outliers, you need to start building your case for appeal as soon as you discover that a low-paying outlier is assigned to your client's case. As a rule, cases involving low paying outlier ALJs present great issues for appeal because it is generally impossible to actually follow the claimant-oriented disability law and find so few claimants disabled.

In the past when a low paying outlier ALJ was assigned to a client's case, some lawyers advised clients to withdraw the request for hearing and file a new application — hoping that a different ALJ would be assigned the next time the client's case got to the hearing level. SSA hated this practice and changed its rules in 2013 so that the same ALJ would be assigned next time around. HALLEX I-2-1-55 E. Indeed, SSA goes to great lengths to avoid giving a claimant any opportunity to change ALJs. SSA will not tell which ALJ is assigned before the deadline expires for objecting to a video hearing so that the choice cannot be based on the identity of the ALJ. See §304.2. Even a change of residence to outside the hearing office service area does not always work to get a new ALJ assigned. See HALLEX I-2-0-70 C. and I-2-3-10 A.1.

Because recusal is at the discretion of the ALJ, 20 C.F.R. § 404.940, your client is pretty much stuck with the ALJ who is initially assigned. While some lawyers make it a practice to ask low paying outliers to recuse themselves, the real audience for such a request may be the federal court. Although the issue of an ALJ's refusal to grant a request for recusal can be presented to the Appeals Council, the Appeals Council will do nothing if the only argument is that the ALJ typically finds only a ridiculously small number of claimants disabled.

When preparing a case for any ALJ, your job as the claimant's attorney is to gather and submit medical records, medical opinions and other documentary evidence at least five working days before the hearing (and after the hearing, if allowed by the ALJ), present witnesses' testimony at the hearing and examine witnesses called by the ALJ (cross-examining them, if necessary), and present the claimant's case in its best light to show that the claimant is disabled under the law. It is part of your job to avoid treating the ALJ as an adversary, even when you are arguing that the ALJ is wrong about the law or facts. In fact, opportunities to present an argument to an ALJ arise more often with the very good judges, the ones who will tell you when they have a problem with a particular aspect of your client's case. They tell you this in order to give you the opportunity to argue for your client's position. Even with judges who are more difficult to convince, it is counterproductive to treat a judge as an adversary.

The claimant may appear in person before the ALJ or by video teleconferencing, though a claimant is not required to appear by video if the claimant does not want to. See §304.2. At a hearing before an ALJ, evidence may be received even though it would not be admissible in court under the rules of evidence used by courts. You must inform the ALJ about or submit evidence no later than five business days before the hearing. 20 C.F.R. § 404.935(a). If you are having trouble getting particular evidence, you can ask the ALJ to issue a subpoena for the evidence as long as you do so at least ten business days before the hearing. 20 C.F.R. § 404.950(d)(2). But note that merely informing the ALJ about the evidence at least five business days before the hearing fulfills the requirements of the five day rule. 20 C.F.R. § 404.935(a).

Vocational experts (VEs) or medical experts (MEs) may testify, appearing in person, by video teleconferencing, or sometimes by telephone. VEs testify in about three quarters of all hearings. MEs testify in somewhat fewer than 15 percent. Such experts are supposed to be neutral, too, unlike, for example, experts in worker's compensation or personal injury cases, where everyone expects the experts to take sides. One might make a good argument that neutrality by medical experts is achieved within limits set by their own backgrounds and preconceptions (just like all of us) and any constraints imposed on medical experts by the ALJs who they appear before. Of course, when a medical expert appears who is used to testifying for insurance companies in worker's compensation cases, your client is not likely to get much help on the case from the ME. Although an ME's testimony alone can win a case for a claimant (by demonstrating that the claimant's impairments meet or equal an impairment found in SSA's Listing of Impairments), it is less likely that an ME's testimony will be the sole reason a claimant loses. On dealing with ME testimony, see §§330 to 337.

A vocational expert's testimony, on the other hand, can be the sole reason a claimant loses a disability case. Although VEs also view themselves as neutral, neutrality is not the issue. VEs have been given a nearly impossible role by SSA, one that is at the very edge of their expertise. A vocational expert's real expertise usually involves job placement for people with physical or mental limitations. VEs' jobs often include encouraging employers to accommodate disabilities, which SSA says is not relevant to the disability determination process because SSA is concerned with how jobs are ordinarily performed in the economy, not with whether an employer might be willing to alter job duties to accommodate a limitation. See §344.1 and section II.D of SSR 11-2p. SSA expects a VE to have expertise with the Dictionary of Occupational Titles, which most VEs have stopped using in their regular jobs because it is outdated. And SSA expects a VE to be able to tell an ALJ how many jobs exist in the economy for people with certain limitations, which is not something they do much at all in their regular jobs and requires a lot of guess work.

Most VEs view their role as giving the ALJ options—that is, they provide a basis for a denial decision and a basis for a favorable decision. VEs say they help ALJs find the line between who is disabled and who is not. It is a rare VE, however, who will challenge an ALJ's preconceived notion about a case.

If the VE draws the line correctly between those who are disabled and those who are not, your job is to make sure your client is on the disabled side of the line. This is not something done by cross-examining a VE. This is done by presenting convincing evidence about your client's residual functional capacity. If the ALJ does not include enough limitations in hypothetical questions to the VE, your job is to ask additional questions that include all your client's limitations so that the line can be drawn between the disabled and not disabled. If the VE draws the line incorrectly, you must deal with that VE testimony (through cross examination or obtaining a rebuttal VE opinion) in order to redraw the line. *See* §§340 through 349.10.

Sometimes at the conclusion of a hearing, an ALJ will issue an oral bench decision setting forth findings of fact and conclusions of law establishing that your client is disabled. Then, within a few days, your client will receive a short summary of the decision, which is the official favorable decision from which benefits are paid. *See* §361.

Otherwise, after the hearing, a full written decision will be issued by the administrative law judge. Although ALJs have no time limits for issuing decisions, because of the backlog at hearing offices, ALJs are under pressure from SSA to issue decisions expeditiously. Most ALJs do so, though a few do not.

When an ALJ does not issue a bench decision at the hearing, the ALJ usually will not tell you whether your client won or lost. Sometimes, though, it is obvious—such as when an ALJ stops a hearing without taking testimony from a vocational expert after a medical expert testifies that your client's impairment meets or equals an impairment found in the Listing of Impairments.

§301   Prehearing Orders

Your job as the claimant's attorney is to comply, to the degree possible, with any prehearing order issued by the ALJ—following the basic rule of this informal administrative area of practice: It is best to get along with the ALJ. Do the best you can to follow a prehearing order while, at the same time, protecting your client's rights.

§302   Hearing Issues

If you object to the issues to be addressed at your client's hearing, you are required to submit your objection "in writing at the earliest possible opportunity, but no later than five business days before the date set for the hearing." 20 C.F.R. § 404.939. *See* §289.

The issue in most disability claims is whether your client is disabled. When there is a date last insured that runs before the date of the hearing, the issue becomes: Was your client disabled on or before the date last insured?

The issues for a hearing include all issues that were not decided in the claimant's favor in the initial or reconsideration determinations. Thus, when the claimant appeals a partially favorable reconsideration determination seeking an earlier onset date, the ALJ is not supposed to consider whether the claimant might not be disabled at all unless evidence causes the ALJ to question the matter. If so, the ALJ must provide notice of a new issue. 20 C.F.R. § 404.946 provides:

(a) *General.* The issues before the administrative law judge include all the issues brought out in the initial, reconsidered or revised determination that were not decided entirely in your favor. However, if evidence presented before or during the hearing causes the administrative law judge to question a fully favorable determination, he or she will notify you and will consider it an issue at the hearing.

(b) *New issues—*

(1) *General.* The administrative law judge may consider a new issue at the hearing if he or she notifies you and all the parties about the new issue any time after receiving the hearing request and before mailing notice of the hearing decision. The administrative law judge or any party may raise a new issue; an issue may be raised even though it arose after the request for a hearing and even though it has not been considered in an initial or reconsidered determination. However, it may not be raised if it involves a claim that is within the jurisdiction of a State agency under a Federal-State agreement concerning the determination of disability.

(2) *Notice of a new issue.* The administrative law judge shall notify you and any other party if he or she will consider any new issue. Notice of the time and place of the hearing on any new issues will be given in the manner described in §404.938, unless you have indicated in writing that you do not wish to receive the notice.

The HALLEX states that in addition to where new evidence raises a question about an issue decided favorably to the claimant, if the favorable determination from which the claimant appealed is based on an error of law, the ALJ will consider it even where there is no new evidence. HALLEX I-2-2-1. In both circumstances, the HALLEX requires that advance notice be given to inform the claimant that a new issue will be considered at the hearing. In practice, if a new issue comes up during a hearing, the ALJ will offer you the option of waiving advance notice or the ALJ will reschedule the hearing for a future date so that proper notice can be issued before the hearing.

On rare occasions, you may get involved in a disability claim in which the state agency did not develop the medical evidence or consider whether or not the claimant was disabled. Instead, a denial was issued that had nothing to do with whether or not the claimant was disabled—for example, a step-one denial was issued because a claimant was working or an SSI claimant's assets or income exceeded the limits for the SSI program, *etc*. The issue in such a case involves the matter that formed the basis for the denial decision.

The question such a case raises about the issues is the following: Once the ALJ resolves the immediate issue in the claimant's favor, can the ALJ then address whether or not the claimant is disabled? Because the state agency has not addressed the issue of disability, based on 20 C.F.R. § 404.946(b), many ALJs and attorneys might say, "No, this is within the jurisdiction of the state agency." But this is not what the HALLEX says. HALLEX I-2-2-10 says that under these circumstances if the ALJ is prepared to issue a wholly favorable decision, the ALJ can do so, raising disability as a new issue in the case. HALLEX I-2-2-10 provides:

> An issue is "new" if it has not been previously adjudicated. When an ALJ has jurisdiction to do so, he or she may agree to adjudicate a new issue(s) raised by a party to the hearing, or may adjudicate a new issue(s) on his or her own initiative.

> When raising a new issue(s), an ALJ must notify all parties, in writing, about the new issue(s) at any time after receiving the request for hearing and before mailing a decision. *See* 20 CFR 404.946 and 416.1446. The ALJ may also raise a new issue(s) if, on the record during the hearing or in a writing the ALJ associates with the record, the claimant waives the right to advance notice of the new issue(s).

> However, an ALJ may not raise a new issue(s) if it involves a claim that is within the jurisdiction of a State agency under a Federal-State agreement concerning the determination of disability, unless the ALJ is issuing a fully favorable decision on the issue of disability. If the ALJ does not intend to issue a fully favorable decision and there is a disability claim within the jurisdiction of the State agency, the ALJ will rule on the issues within his or her jurisdiction and dismiss the request for hearing with respect to the issue(s) within the State agency's jurisdiction. The ALJ will then return the claim(s) file to the State agency for action on the issue(s) within its jurisdiction.

Example 1.

> An ALJ is adjudicating a claim for supplemental security income based on disability. The claim was previously denied because of the claimant's excess income and there is no medical evidence in the file. The ALJ is prepared to rule favorably on the excess income issue, but cannot issue a fully favorable decision on the issue of disability because the medical record has not been developed. The ALJ cannot raise the disability issue as it is "new." The ALJ must rule only on the excess income issue and return the claim file to the State agency for action on the disability issue.

Example 2.

> An ALJ is adjudicating a claim for supplemental security income based on disability. The claim was previously denied because of the claimant's excess income but there is medical evidence in the file. The ALJ is prepared to rule favorably on the excess income issue and find the claimant disabled, but at a date later than the claimant alleges. The ALJ cannot raise the disability issue because, although it is "new," the decision about disability would not be fully favorable. The ALJ must rule only on the excess income issue and return the claim file to the State agency for action on the disability issue. (NOTE: If the ALJ had found disability as of the claimant's alleged onset date, the ALJ could have issued a fully favorable decision.)

If you have a case like this, you need to gather all the medical evidence and ask the ALJ to address the new issue of whether your client is disabled. This is a situation in which the claimant cannot lose. The ALJ will either issue a fully favorable decision or send the case back to the state agency. The ALJ cannot issue a decision finding your client not disabled.

§302.1   Hearing Issues in Court Remand Cases

To determine hearing issues after a court remand, review both the court's remand order and the remand order of the Appeals Council. Look to see if the Appeals Council issued a standard order that vacated the prior decision and ordered the ALJ to offer the claimant "the opportunity for a hearing." HALLEX I-4-3-101. Such an order requires *de novo* consideration of the claim that is not inconsistent with the order of the court. Issues at the remand hearing are not much different from the issues at the first hearing.

When the Appeals Council does not issue a standard order there are a range of possible issues, some more subtle than others.

Sentence Six Remands

When a case is remanded under sentence six of 42 U.S.C. § 405(g), the court retains jurisdiction of the claim. Sentence six remands include those for consideration of new evidence. In new evidence cases, the Appeals Council will vacate the prior hearing decision and require that a new decision be issued considering the new evidence. If the date last insured is before the date of the prior decision, unless the court orders a new hearing, the Appeals Council will not order the ALJ to offer the claimant the opportunity for a hearing. *See* HALLEX I-4-3-101, footnote 1.

Cases are also remanded under sentence six when the recording of a hearing is inaudible or lost or an exhibit file is lost. In these situations, the case is remanded for a *de novo* hearing and the issuance of a new decision. *See* HALLEX I-4-3-102.

When a case is remanded under sentence six, SSA says the claim cannot be dismissed because the "statute precludes dismissal of a sentence six remand in a court remand case." HALLEX I-2-8-18 A. Thus, if a claimant fails to appear for a hearing or even if a claimant requests dismissal, an ALJ cannot dismiss the claim. Instead, the ALJ must issue a decision. HALLEX I-4-4-60 A.2. Such a decision usually adopts the prior final decision of the Commissioner. HALLEX I-2-4-5, Note; HALLEX I-2-8-18 A. However, the HALLEX instructs an ALJ not to adopt the prior final decision where "the court has held that the claimant is in fact disabled and has remanded the case to the Commissioner to determine the onset of disability or if the ALJ determines that the claimant's appearance is not necessary to issue a favorable decision. In such a case, the ALJ will develop the record and comply with the court's order." HALLEX I-2-8-18 A, Note.

Sentence Four Remands

Most cases are remanded by the court under the fourth sentence of 42 U.S.C. § 405(g) because the decision is not supported by substantial evidence or the decision contains legal errors. HALLEX I-4-4-60 provides:

> When a court remands a case to the Commissioner under sentence 4, the court remand includes a judgment that terminates the civil action. This places the case back within the

administrative review process and the procedures provided for in the Commissioner's regulations apply. The regulations at 20 CFR 404.983 and 416.1483 provide that if the AC remands the case, the procedures explained in 20 CFR 404.977 and 416.1477 will be followed. In turn, cases remanded to an ALJ are handled under the procedures in 20 CFR 404.944 ff and 416.1444 ff. Because the case is now handled under the same regulatory scheme as an initial request for hearing, the provisions of 20 CFR 404.957 and 416.1457 (Dismissal of a Request for Hearing before an Administrative Law Judge) are available (consistent with the terms of the particular court order) to the same extent as in an initial claim.

The HALLEX provides that after a federal court remands a case to SSA, when remanding the case to an ALJ, the Appeals Council generally vacates the final decision of the Commissioner. That is, the Appeals Council vacates the earlier decision that was appealed to federal court. "When the Appeals Council vacates a final decision of the Commissioner, the ALJ must consider all pertinent issues *de novo*." HALLEX I-2-8-18 A.

20 C.F.R. § 404.983, which deals with cases remanded by a federal court, provides that 20 C.F.R. § 404.977, which deals with cases remanded by the Appeals Council, applies to the case. Thus, the same procedures apply as when the Appeals Council remands a case that has never been to federal court. 20 C.F.R. § 404.983, the court remand regulation, specifically provides: "Any issues relating to your claim may be considered by the administrative law judge whether or not they were raised in the administrative proceedings leading to the final decision in your case." 20 C.F.R. § 404.977(b) provides: "The administrative law judge shall take any action that is ordered by the Appeals Council and may take any additional action that is not inconsistent with the Appeals Council's remand order." In other words, in the hearing on remand, you can raise any issue you want, and so can the ALJ, as long as it is not inconsistent with the court's or Appeals Council's remand order. Thus, even though the court's remand order was based on problems with vocational expert testimony, you can present evidence about the claimant's RFC (*e.g.*, take the treating doctor to testify) in order to convince the ALJ to make a different RFC finding on remand.

ALJs have been known to take the position that they will do what the court orders, *e.g.*, address a particular vocational issue, but beyond that the claimant must provide new evidence to "reopen" the prior decision. As a statement of law, this is dead wrong. Because the earlier decision has been vacated, there is no reopening to be done. Although the law allows an ALJ after *de novo* consideration of the claim to adopt the earlier decision (with modifications required by the federal court), adopting the earlier decision is not required. Indeed, it would be error to adopt the earlier decision without giving *de novo* consideration to the entire claim. As a piece of practical advice, though, if you're trying to change an ALJ's mind about something, you are probably going to need some new evidence.

The issues on remand are not limited to the period of time covered by the prior ALJ decision, unless, of course, the date last insured came before the date of the prior ALJ decision. "For initial entitlement cases, vacating a final decision reactivates the application. Accordingly, the ALJ must decide the remanded issues through the date of the new hearing decision or through the date that insured status expired, because the prospective life of the application will continue until the ALJ issues a final decision following the court remand." HALLEX I-2-8-18 A.

In a Notice of Proposed Rule Making, 72 Fed. Reg. 61222 (2007), SSA explained its current policy as follows:

> When cases are remanded for further proceedings, either from a Federal court or the Appeals Council, our current rules allow ALJs and the Appeals Council to consider changes in the individual's condition after the date of the first ALJ decision on the claim, such as an increase in severity of the claimant's original impairment(s) or the development of a new impairment. Under our current rules, for example, when the Appeals Council grants an individual's request that it review the decision made by an ALJ and finds reasons to reverse that decision and remand the case for further proceedings, it has typically "vacated" the decision of the ALJ. As a result, we consider the case during the subsequent proceedings on remand as if the earlier ALJ's decision had not been issued. This same situation may arise where a Federal court remands a case for further proceedings. In practical terms, this approach allowed individuals to continue to submit evidence freely throughout the subsequent proceedings or to attempt to establish an onset of disability even after the date of the first hearing decision.

When the ALJ decision that was appealed to federal court was issued after the date last insured, unless the court orders a hearing, the Appeals Council may not order the ALJ to hold a hearing. *See* HALLEX I-4-3-101. But the Appeals Council will vacate the earlier hearing decision, which requires that the ALJ consider the matter *de novo*.

Sometimes, because of the language of the court's order, the Appeals Council will not totally vacate the prior decision. HALLEX I-4-4-1 provides:

> Occasionally, a court will affirm a decision in part through the date when issued while reversing and remanding the balance of the decision for additional proceedings (e.g., reconsidering a treating physician's opinion, obtaining vocational expert testimony, etc.). In these cases, including Title II claims having a date last insured in the past, the AC may vacate the prior hearing decision, but only to the extent not affirmed by the court.

Subsequent Applications

Although SSR 11-1p severely restricted a claimant's ability to file a new claim after July 27, 2011 while an earlier claim is pending at the Appeals Council, *see* §507, there are many subsequent applications in the pipeline. In addition, nothing restricts a claimant's right to file a new application while an earlier claim is pending in federal court. Thus, although they may be seen less frequently, SSR 11-1p did not do away with subsequent claim issues.

When there is a subsequent application that was denied at the initial or reconsideration levels of administrative review, that subsequent claim is treated as a duplicate claim, whether or not the subsequent claim is still pending. The claims are supposed to be consolidated. The subsequent claim denial has no *res judicata* effect. The fact that the subsequent claim was denied has no bearing on the current claim other than that the file now contains one or more state agency doctor RFC opinions that say the claimant is not disabled.

When a subsequent application is denied by an ALJ decision and becomes final because the time for appeal to the Appeals Council or to federal court has run out, that claim has *res judicata* effect. That is, it stands as an impediment to the claimant being found disabled during the time covered by the subsequent ALJ decision. Thus, an additional issue is injected into the case that was remanded by the federal court: is there new evidence or a new issue so that *res judicata* does not apply? *See* HALLEX I-4-2-101 I.B.

When a subsequent claim is successful, there is an impact on the issues in the remanded claim. If the Appeals Council affirms the finding in the subsequent claim that the claimant is disabled, the issues on remand are constricted so that it is necessary to address only the time period not covered by the subsequent favorable decision. If the Appeals Council directs the ALJ on remand to consider reopening the subsequent finding that the claimant is disabled, another issue is placed squarely before the ALJ. If the Appeals Council does not address the subject in its remand order, SSA says it is up to the ALJ's discretion whether or not to reopen the subsequent claim. *See* §507.3.

§303 *Before the Hearing*

Electronic Disability Folder

If your client's case uses an electronic disability folder, and SSA has granted you online access to your client's electronic files (*see* § 178.5), you must review the hearing exhibit file before the hearing from your office. At the hearing, the hearing office will not provide you with access to your client's electronic folder from one of SSA's computers and it won't provide you with a CD-ROM containing all exhibits. *See* § 201.3. Hearing offices do not provide Wi-Fi access to the Internet.

From your office, check the electronic file to make sure everything you submitted has been entered as exhibits and either write down the exhibit numbers (for ease of referring to particular exhibits at or after the hearing) or download the latest edition of the hearing exhibits. Look to see if there are any surprise exhibits— exhibits you have never seen before. Although it is rare that a medical exhibit will be obtained by the hearing office and entered as an exhibit after you last obtained a copy of the electronic hearing exhibit file, it does happen. More often, shortly before the hearing you will find that there is a new exhibit in the D section that shows your client's income after the alleged onset date, or maybe it will show that your client received unemployment compensation benefits. You need to go over such things with your client before the hearing.

Practice Tip

Take a laptop along to the hearing containing the entire hearing exhibit file. Or download the latest edition of the hearing exhibit file to a CD-ROM, which you will take to the hearing and view on an SSA computer in the hearing room. Store your notes about hearing exhibits electronically and, with your laptop or the hearing room computer, use those files at the hearing.

Paper Files

When you arrive for a hearing, you will be allowed to review the original paper hearing exhibit file. You will have obtained a copy of this file at some point before the hearing and reviewed it long before the day of the hearing. On the day of the hearing, your job is to make sure everything you submitted has been entered as an exhibit, obtain exhibit numbers, and look for surprise exhibits.

The one advantage of a paper file is that it is the same file the ALJ uses. If you see any post-it notes or flags sticking out from the file, pay special attention because they may have been put there by the ALJ. If so, reviewing the flagged records may give you an idea of the ALJ's initial impression of your client's case. If the ALJ has flagged all the best evidence, you can rest easy. If the ALJ has flagged all the worst evidence, the flags provide you with a checklist of critical issues to be addressed at the hearing.

Video Hearings

When you appear for a video hearing in a case involving a paper file, you will not be given the opportunity to review the file because it is with the ALJ. Otherwise, video hearings for cases with an electronic file are the same as in person hearings with an electronic file. You must have reviewed the file before going to the hearing office and take along a laptop computer or a CD-ROM containing the hearing exhibit file for your use at the hearing.

In All Cases

Just before the hearing, you need to answer any last-minute questions from your client, do what you can to allay your client's fears about the hearing, and remind your client about any crucial issues. If you have not done so before, talk to any witnesses about their testimony. As a rule, it is a bad idea to try to conduct full hearing preparation with your client just before the hearing. That needs to be done earlier. *See* § 292. Although it is best to spend a few minutes on the telephone with any witnesses before the day of the hearing, *see* § 295, it is possible to prepare a lay witness to testify in a few minutes just before the hearing.

§304 *Hearing Procedure*

The regulations do not describe hearing procedure in much detail. They provide that "[a]t the hearing, the administrative law judge looks fully into the issues, questions [the claimant] and the other witnesses, and subject to the provisions of § 404.935: Accepts as evidence any documents that are material to the issues." 20 C.F.R. §404.944. "Subject to the provisions of § 4 04.935," the ALJ "may receive evidence at the hearing even though the evidence would not be admissible in court under the rules of evidence used by the court." 20 C.F.R. § 404.950(c). Witnesses will testify under oath and the ALJ will allow parties to question witnesses. 20 C.F.R. § 404.950(e). The ALJ "may decide when the evidence will be presented and when the issues will be discussed." 20 C.F.R. § 404.944.

The "provisions of § 404.935," referred to in §§ 404.944 and 404.950(c), require that each "party must make every effort to ensure that the administrative law judge receives all of the evidence and must inform us about or submit any written evidence, as required in § 404.1512, no later than 5 business days before the date of the scheduled hearing." If you do not, the ALJ may "decline to consider or obtain the evidence" unless one of the exceptions applies in 20 C.F.R. § 404.935(b). These exceptions, in effect, require you to show that the failure to submit evidence was not your fault.

Each ALJ conducts a hearing somewhat differently from every other ALJ. An individual ALJ may use different procedures when conducting a hearing involving an unrepresented claimant than those used in a hearing when a very experienced attorney is representing the claimant. Adjustments may be made based on the experience of the attorney. For example, the length and content of opening statements by ALJs vary greatly, as does the degree to which an ALJ questions the claimant, and whether the ALJ questions the claimant before or after the claimant's attorney asks questions. Some ALJs ask witnesses to remain in the waiting room while the claimant testifies; others do not.

There are, however, broad similarities in the way disability hearings are conducted around the country because, to one degree or another, individual ALJs follow procedures set forth in HALLEX guidelines. *See* HALLEX Chapter I-2-6.

§304.1 ALJ's Opening Statement

In a typical hearing, the administrative law judge will open the record, state who is present and note that you are representing the claimant. The ALJ may ask you or your client to verify that fact on the record. Most ALJs will make some effort at the beginning of the hearing to put your client at ease. The following may be part of an opening statement by the ALJ:

1. A statement of the de novo nature of the hearing and that the ALJ is not part of the office that previously denied the claim.
2. An explanation that a recording of the proceeding is being made and that the official record of the case will consist of oral testimony and documents admitted into evidence of record.
3. A description of the manner in which the hearing will be conducted including:
   a. one person will testify at a time;
   b. witnesses will be examined under oath and may be cross-examined;
   c. the strict rules of evidence used in court will not be applied;

d. a reasonable time will be allowed to present oral argument or to file briefs about the facts and law material to the case.
4. A procedural history of the claim.
5. A statement of the issues.
6. A brief description of the documents that are proposed as exhibits, an inquiry whether there are any objections to those exhibits, and admission of exhibits after ruling on objections.

Some ALJs ask if you will waive reading of the procedural history and statement of the issues. Unless there is some unusual issue in the case, experienced attorneys always agree to waive it.

§304.2 Video Hearings

Other than some SSA bureaucrats who claim that they are "efficient," no one likes video hearings. Not the ALJs, not the experts, not the attorneys, least of all the claimants. Claimants generally like the opportunity to tell their stories to ALJs in person, but claimants generally do not find the same satisfaction with video hearings. To overcome claimant resistance, SSA tries to encourage claimants to accept video hearings by sending them a brochure that explains the advantages of having a video hearing. It is a short brochure. It tells claimants, "Except for the equipment, a video hearing is no different than a hearing at which you appear in person." This statement is true only if one accepts the proposition that the video equipment does not fundamentally change the nature of the interaction between the claimant and the ALJ. Instead of being in person, immediate and three dimensional, the hearing is remote and two dimensional. The single advantage of a video hearing is that the claimant may get the hearing sooner.

SSA has set up five National Hearing Centers, located in Albuquerque, Baltimore, Chicago, Falls Church and St. Louis, which are designed to hold only hearings by video. Other hearing offices have an increasing proportion of video hearings.

20 C.F.R. § 404.936(c) provides, "The administrative law judge will determine that your appearance, or the appearance of any other party to the hearing, be conducted by video teleconferencing if video teleconferencing equipment is available to conduct the appearance, use of video teleconferencing to conduct the appearance would be more efficient than conducting the appearance in person, and the administrative law judge determines that there is no circumstance in the particular case that prevents the use of video teleconferencing to conduct the appearance." While a claimant has veto power over

an appearance by video, in mid-2014 SSA made it more difficult to exercise this veto by setting a 30-day time limit for objecting.

When the hearing office sends a claimant the "acknowledgment letter" saying that the request for hearing has been received, SSA will notify the claimant that his or her hearing may be held by video unless the claimant objects within 30 days of the date of the acknowledgement letter. HALLEX I-2-0-20 B. The acknowledgment letter, of course, is sent long before an ALJ is assigned, which was SSA's goal in setting up this procedure – there will be no opportunity to change ALJs. If a claimant objects to appearing by video within 30 days of the date of the notice, the claimant will be allowed to have an in-person hearing as long as the claimant's "residence does not change while your request for hearing is pending." 20 C.F.R. § 404.936(d). If the claimant misses the deadline for objecting to a video hearing, the claimant must show good cause for missing the deadline. 20 C.F.R. § 404.936(d)(2) and HALLEX I-2-0-21 D.

HALLEX I-2-0-21 A. provides that "if a claimant established a change in residence while the request for hearing is pending, an administrative law judge (ALJ) will determine how the claimant appears, regardless of whether the claimant previously objected to appearing at the hearing by VTC. Generally, the ALJ will honor the claimant's request not to appear by VTC even when a claimant changes residences if there is no additional delay or other reason not to schedule the claimant for an in person hearing."

On the other hand, HALLEX I-2-0-70 C. provides that if a claimant, who has not objected to a hearing by video teleconferencing (VTC), moves to the jurisdiction of another hearing office, the hearing office "will generally not transfer the case. Rather, using the instructions in HALLEX I-2-3-10 A.1., the ALJ will schedule the claimant's appearance by VTC whenever possible."

In a typical video hearing where the ALJ is in one location and the claimant is in another, sometimes an ALJ will use a vocational or medical expert who is in the same location as the ALJ. Other times an expert will be in the same location as the claimant. While there are hearings in which only the expert appears by video, more often, the expert testifies by telephone. See §304.3. There have also been hearings in which only the claimant's attorney appears by video. Who is allowed to appear by video is left to the discretion of the ALJ.

The advent of electronic hearing exhibit files has reduced problems associated with obtaining copies of the hearing exhibit file for a video hearing. Online access to your client's hearing exhibit file virtually eliminates the problem. See §178.5. But when your client's hearing exhibit file is paper, a video hearing presents a serious logistical problem. It is very difficult to get a copy of the entire paper hearing exhibit file early enough to obtain and submit new evidence and develop the issues in time for the scheduled hearing. Additional problems arise on the day of the hearing because the hearing exhibit file is with the ALJ. You will have no opportunity to review hearing exhibits just before the hearing. See §303. You may ask that an updated exhibit list and any new exhibits submitted by SSA since the time you copied the file be faxed to you a day or so before the hearing. If you do not receive such things by the time of the hearing, it is necessary to ask the ALJ at the beginning of the hearing to provide you with exhibit numbers for all exhibits you submitted and to describe any other exhibits added to the file after you copied it.

When you prepare your client to testify at a video hearing, be sure to advise your client that after you go into the hearing room before the actual hearing starts, although you won't be able to hear what is being said in the room where the ALJ sits, the ALJ may very well be able to hear everything being said in the room where the claimant is. Tell your client not to say anything in the hearing room before the hearing starts or after the hearing ends.

§304.3   Telephone Testimony by Expert Witnesses

Because of a shortage of vocational and medical experts who can appear in person at hearings, more and more ALJs are taking testimony by telephone from expert witnesses. Lawyers sometimes object to telephone testimony from experts because of the difficulty cross-examining a witness over the telephone. It is within an ALJ's discretion to require the expert to testify in person based on such an objection, but few experts have been required to testify in person only because an attorney complained about the difficulty of cross-examining the expert over the telephone. HALLEX I-2-3-12 A.3. offers little guidance to ALJs for dealing with objections to the manner of appearance at the hearing by a witness. 20 C.F.R. § 404.936(c)(2) provides:

(2) The administrative law judge will determine whether any person other than you or any other party to the hearing, including a medical expert or a vocational expert, will appear at the hearing in person, by video teleconferencing, or by telephone. If you or any other party to the hearing objects to any other person appearing by video teleconferencing or by telephone, the administrative law judge will decide, either in writing or at the hearing, whether to have that person appear in person, by video teleconferencing, or by telephone. The administrative law judge will direct a person, other than you

or any other party to the hearing if we are notified as provided in paragraph (e) of this section that you or any other party to the hearing objects to appearing by video teleconferencing, to appear by video teleconferencing or telephone when the administrative law judge determines:

> *(i) Video teleconferencing or telephone equipment is available;*

> *(ii) Use of video teleconferencing or telephone equipment would be more efficient than conducting an examination of a witness in person, and;*

> *(iii) The ALJ determines there is no other reason why video teleconferencing or telephone should not be used.*

Note that the difficulty experienced by claimants' attorneys in cross-examining a witness over the telephone is not listed as a consideration for the ALJ in deciding whether to have a witness testify by telephone over a claimant's objection. The emphasis is on administrative efficiency.

20 C.F.R. § 404.938(b) requires that the Notice of Hearing include the information that a witness will appear by telephone.

§304.4 Persons Present in the Hearing Room

A Social Security disability hearing is private. The people present will be the ALJ, the judge's assistant (usually a part-time outside contractor) who runs the recording equipment, the claimant, claimant's attorney and any witnesses. Observers may be present only with the permission of the claimant and the ALJ. HALLEX I-2-6-50.

Many ALJs allow witnesses to remain in the hearing room during the claimant's testimony. Some ALJs have all witnesses come into the hearing room and then ask them to leave immediately after completing opening statements and procedural matters. Other ALJs ask witnesses to remain in the waiting area until it is time for their testimony. ALJs who follow the practice of excluding witnesses, sometimes referred to as sequestering witnesses, claim that witnesses who do not hear other testimony may be more credible.

Sometimes a claimant requests that a witness not be present when the claimant is testifying. ALJs have no difficulty accommodating such a request.

Practice Tip

As a rule, in mental impairment cases, it is better not to have the claimant in the hearing room when the claimant's family and friends are testifying. Claimants with mental impairments can become upset with the sort of testimony you must elicit in such a case. Witnesses also seem to give better testimony when the claimant is not present because they tend to be more relaxed and candid than when they are worrying about how the claimant is going to take each remark.

So, in mental impairment cases, arrange in advance with the claimant and the witnesses that the claimant will leave the room when the witnesses testify. Explain this to the ALJ at the beginning of the hearing. Since the claimant has a right to be present, the ALJ may want to ask a few questions to make sure the claimant is leaving the hearing room voluntarily. Before the hearing, explain to the claimant that the ALJ may ask such questions.

§304.5 Making Your Own Recording of the Hearing

If you to want make your own recording of a hearing, granting such a request is within an ALJ's discretion. You will probably be allowed to do so as long as your recording of the hearing does not interfere with the conduct of the hearing. HALLEX I-2-6-52 D.

You may want your own copy of a hearing recording when:

- You want to prepare an extensive post-hearing brief.
- You want the treating doctor, if necessary, to be able to comment on the testimony of a medical expert.
- You want your own vocational expert to hear the testimony of the VE called by the ALJ so that you can submit a rebuttal opinion after the hearing.

If, as frequently happens, you don't know you need your own recording of the hearing until you are well into the hearing or after the hearing, if you have ERE access to your client's electronic folder, a copy of the hearing recording should be available for download shortly after the hearing. If you do not have ERE access or your client's file is not electronic, you may ask the hearing office to make you a copy of the official recording. A copy of the recording is available to you under both the Freedom of Information Act and the Privacy Act, 5 U.S.C. §§ 552(a)(3) and 552(a)(d). Note, however, that SSA uses an uncommon format for its recordings. Unless hearing office personnel convert the recording to one of the more common formats, you will need to download and install on your computer FTR's The Record Player audio player from the following site: http://community. fortherecord.com/ index.php?/page/playerdownload.

If a denial decision is issued and you cannot download a copy of the recording yourself, you may obtain a copy of the recording from the Appeals Council. *See* §516.

§304.6 Objections to ALJ's Questions

Do not treat the ALJ as an adversary. Always be tactful and polite.

In contrast to trial practice, the only reason for objecting to an ALJ's question is to educate the ALJ or the witness. Objections are not necessary to protect your client's appeal rights. No Circuit Court of Appeals has required an objection submitted before a witness answers a question in order to preserve an issue for appeal. If you do not object at the time the question is asked, at some point during the hearing or in a legal brief submitted following the hearing, bring the issue to the attention of the ALJ as tactfully as possible.

Lawyers schooled in the adversarial process often find it difficult not to interpose objections to clearly objectionable questions asked by, for example, an inexperienced ALJ. But before you say anything, ask yourself this: Will you be able to present your objection in such a way as to achieve the goal of educating, but not alienating, the ALJ? Will you be able to correct the problem with follow-up questions to the witness or later in a brief?

§305 Objections to Exhibits

Whether the hearing is in person or by video, the ALJ will ask for objections to exhibits. Just because the ALJ asks doesn't mean you necessarily need to offer an objection. Although some attorneys make a practice of always objecting to state agency physician RFC evaluations, a general objection is unlikely to result in the ALJ ruling that such exhibits are not admitted into evidence. ALJs are required by 20 C.F.R. § 404.1527(e)(2) to consider the opinions of state agency doctors and ALJs are required by SSR 96-5p to address these opinions in their decisions.

Some lawyers say that specific objections to state agency doctor RFC opinions help sensitize the ALJ to particular issues such as when there are questions about the state agency doctor's qualifications (*e.g.*, a gynecologist rendering an opinion in an orthopedic case), lack of medical support for the opinion, or lack of explanation for the opinion. However, these are not objections to the admissibility of the exhibit; they are

arguments about the weight, and the ALJ is likely to tell you so.

If you find medical records in the exhibit file that do not belong to your client, these are clearly objectionable and inadmissible. You need to make sure that such records are taken out of your client's hearing exhibit file.

§305.1 Unsigned "Reports of Contact" With Physicians

Watch for unsigned "reports of contact" with doctors and with doctors' staff. These are the most objectionable documents to creep into hearing exhibit files. Such "reports of contact" with physicians, even the signed ones, are notoriously unreliable. *See* §221.

State agency physicians (and sometimes non-physician disability examiners) often telephone treating (and sometimes consultative) physicians with questions and prepare a "report of contact" concerning their conversations with the doctors. (Sometimes you will find "reports of contact" concerning conversations with a member of a doctor's staff purporting to recite the contents of medical records.) Standard procedure requires the state agency to send such "reports of contact" to the physician for signature. If the "report of contact" that appears in the hearing exhibit file is not signed by the physician whose views it purports to represent, it should not be made a hearing exhibit. It is not reliable evidence. Object to it.

§305.2 Denial of Right to Cross-Examine Authors of Adverse Medical Reports

If your argument against the admissibility of the state agency physician RFC evaluation is based on a denial of your client's right to cross-examine the author of an adverse medical report, a legitimate complaint, you must have requested that the ALJ subpoena the state agency physician at least ten business days in advance of the hearing. *See* §§222 and 284. Such requests, however, are routinely denied. Requests to subpoena the author of a consultative physician report, on the other hand, are not always denied. *See* §§223 and 284.

In the Fifth Circuit, pursuant to *Lidy v. Sullivan*, 911 F.2d 1075 (5th Cir. 1990) (adopted as an acquiescence ruling, AR 91-1(5)), claimants have an absolute right to subpoena and cross-examine an examining physician who is the author of an adverse report. According to AR 91-1(5), "when a claimant requests, prior to the closing of the record, that a subpoena be issued for the purpose of cross-examining an examining physician, the adjudicator *must* issue the subpoena." Emphasis in original. The reasoning of *Lidy* is based on *Richardson v. Perales*, 402 U.S. 389, 402 (1971), which upheld the use of unsworn hearsay reports from doctors "when the claimant has not exercised his right to subpoena the reporting physician and thereby provide[s] himself with the opportunity for cross-examination of the physician." However, the rationale of the *Lidy* acquiescence ruling, AR 91-1(5), does not extend to state agency doctors who never examined a claimant. Thus, even in the Fifth Circuit, a claimant does not have the right to subpoena a state agency doctor.

SSA's position is that a claimant does not have an absolute right to question the author of any adverse report that is added to the exhibit file before the hearing. In circuits other than the Fifth, according to SSA, a claimant's representative must not only demonstrate the need to ask questions of the author of the report, but must also explain why interrogatories are not sufficient. This SSA position is based on 20 C.F.R. § 404.950(d)(2), which calls for a party requesting a subpoena to "indicate why these facts could not be proven without issuing a subpoena." Current instructions provide that an Administrative Law Judge may deny the claimant's request to subpoena an individual if the claimant fails to show that the evidence or testimony he or she wishes to obtain from the individual is essential, or that the evidence or testimony cannot be obtained in any other way. *See* HALLEX I-2-5-78.

However, SSA recognizes a right to subpoena the author of an adverse post-hearing report. *See* §358.

§305.3   Consultative Physician Reports

You may object to consultative physician reports that do not comport with the requirements of 20 C.F.R. §§ 404.1519n and 404.1519p. 20 C.F.R. § 404.1519n(e) requires that a report be signed by the examining physician himself. Signature stamps are not good enough. However, POMS DI 22510.015C.1. accepts electronic signatures as valid. A report not signed by the doctor cannot be used to make a decision that is not fully favorable to the claimant. 20 C.F.R. § 404.1519o(b).

20 C.F.R. § 404.1519n(b) and (c) state requirements for the content of a report of a consultative examination, and 20 C.F.R. § 404.1519p sets forth standards for reviewing a consultative examination. These sections may provide the basis for an objection to the admissibility of a consultative report. For example, 20 C.F.R. § 404.1519n(b) requires the report to "reflect [the claimant's] statement of . . . symptoms, not simply the medical source's statements or conclusions." To many attorneys, failure to mention a claimant's symptoms is a bellwether of a biased consultative report.

Although the report should include a statement about the claimant's ability to do work-related activities, the absence of such a statement does not make the report incomplete. 20 C.F.R. § 404.1519n(c)(6). *See also* 20 C.F.R. § 404.1513(b)(6).

§306   Claimant Representative's Opening Statement

Although some do, most ALJs do not ask for an opening statement by a claimant's attorney. Thus, if you want to give an opening statement, request the opportunity. Your request is unlikely to be denied. Where the issues are obvious and the ALJ has already read the hearing exhibits, an opening statement may not be necessary. But in those cases hinging on difficult or unusual issues or when it is important to sensitize the ALJ to a change of the claimant's position, be sure to request the opportunity to give an opening statement. For example, where your client is no longer disabled and is asking for a finding of a "closed period" of disability (that is, the claimant was disabled for 12 or more months in the past but has now improved to the point that he is capable of working), explain this to the ALJ in an opening statement. The ALJ will appreciate having this information before questioning the claimant about current symptoms which are irrelevant if the claimant is no longer disabled.

Your client, too, may find an opening statement helpful. For example, in cases involving a "date last insured" issue (that is, where the claimant's insured status has lapsed and the claimant must prove disability as of some date in the past to qualify for any disability benefits), a concept difficult for some claimants to grasp, an opening statement may have the beneficial effect of keeping your client's attention focused on the crucial issue.

Similarly, it may happen that on the day before the hearing you spent an hour explaining to a 50-year-old claimant clearly capable of sedentary work that all he must prove to win his case is that he is limited to sedentary work. By the end of that hour you thought he understood this issue. But after the ALJ stated in his opening statement that the claimant must prove that he is "incapable of doing any kind of substantial gainful work that exists in significant numbers in the economy," he looks bewildered. A brief opening statement explaining that you're going to prove that the claimant is limited to sedentary work may remind him of your talk the day before and point his testimony toward the proper issue.

Opening statements also may be useful for educating medical and vocational experts about the claimant's case. But don't overdo it. A paragraph or two is usually sufficient. Keep an opening statement, if you give one, brief and to the point.

§307   Order of Testimony

After witnesses are sworn, the claimant is usually questioned first. The ALJ may conduct extensive examination of the claimant and then turn the questioning over to you; or the ALJ may expect you to develop the claimant's testimony. Thus, both you and the claimant need to be prepared. An outline for claimant's testimony is provided in §§310 to 319.

Your questioning should be to the point. It should not be repetitious. If you have clearly proved a point by one witness, do not put on another witness to prove it again, particularly if the point is a minor one. *See* §§320 to 328 concerning lay witness testimony. At the same time, however, brevity should not go to the extreme that it jeopardizes your client's case.

Expert witnesses called by the administrative law judge are usually put on last and questioned first by the ALJ. The vocational expert usually follows the medical expert.

Every once in a while, an ALJ may ask if you have any objection to the ALJ questioning the medical expert at the beginning of the hearing. Usually this is a good sign. It may mean that the ALJ has reason to believe that the medical expert is going to testify that your client's impairment meets a Listing, whether based on the ALJ's knowledge of the case and how the medical expert has testified in other cases or whether it is based on an off-the-record conversation between the ALJ and the medical expert (a prohibited practice that is rumored to occur rather frequently), usually it is best not to object. Sometimes, though, your own knowledge of the individual ALJ and medical expert coupled with your analysis of your client's case, may lead you to a conclusion that it is best for your client's case if testimony is taken in the normal order. If so, explain in detail why you think it is important for the medical expert to hear your client's testimony before the medical expert testifies. That is, make, in effect, an offer of proof in which you explain what your client will say in testimony. Then, even if the ALJ overrules your objection (since the ALJ has discretion to "decide when the evidence will be presented," 20 C.F.R. § 404.944), you have accomplished the goal of putting your client's position in front of the medical expert before the medical expert testifies.

§308   Claimant's Experts

On those rare occasions that a claimant's attorney calls a physician or a vocational expert to testify at a hearing, they usually testify following the claimant's other witnesses.

However, if you have witnesses who are pressed for time and you call this problem to the ALJ's attention, the ALJ will usually let you take a witness out of order.

Don't overlook the value of presenting your experts as rebuttal witnesses. You may present an expert's testimony during your case in chief and recall the expert for rebuttal; or you may present the expert's testimony solely as rebuttal, after the testimony of a medical or vocational expert called by the ALJ. Although rebuttal is not mentioned in the Social Security Regulations, the Administrative Procedure Act provides that a party is entitled "to submit rebuttal evidence." 5 U.S.C. § 556(d).

When you are going to be calling an expert or any other witness whose testimony may be time consuming, the ALJ will appreciate being notified of this in advance so that the ALJ can adjust the hearing schedule. The party whose hearing is scheduled with the same ALJ immediately after your client's hearing will appreciate the courtesy also.

§309   Burden of Proof

SSA says that lawyers schooled in traditional adversarial litigation often do not understand the burden of proof in a disability case. Here is SSA's explanation, which was published in commentary in the Federal Register, 68 Fed. Reg. 51154-51155 (2003), when SSA revised regulations concerning determining residual functional capacity:

> Under the Act and §§ 404.1512 and 416.912 of our regulations, you generally have the burden of proving your disability. You must furnish medical and other evidence we can use to reach conclusions about your impairment(s) and its effect on your ability to work on a sustained basis. Our responsibility is to make every reasonable effort to develop your complete medical history. That includes arranging for consultative examinations, if necessary, and making every reasonable effort to get medical reports from your own medical sources. We are responsible for helping you produce evidence that shows whether you are disabled.

> Our administrative process was designed to be nonadversarial. (*See* §§ 404.900(b) and 416.1400(b) of our regulations; *Richardson* v. *Perales,* 402 U.S. 389, 403 (1971); *Sims* v. *Apfel,* 120 S. Ct. 2080, 2083-85, 2086 (2000).)

In addressing burdens of proof, it is critical to keep in mind that we are using a term in our nonadversarial administrative process that describes a process normally used in adversarial litigation. 'Burdens of proof' operate differently in the disability determination process than in a traditional lawsuit. In the administrative process, the burden of proof generally encompasses both a burden of production of evidence and a burden of persuasion about what the evidence shows. (*Director, OWCP v. Greenwich Collieries*, 512 U.S. 267, 273 (1994) (citing *Powers v. Russell*, 30 Mass. 69, 76 (1833).) You shoulder the dual burdens of production and persuasion through step 4 of the sequential evaluation process. (*See Bowen v. Yuckert*, 482 U.S. 137, 146 n.5 (1987).)

Although you generally bear the burden of proving disability throughout the sequential evaluation process, there is a limited shift in the burden of proof to us 'only if the sequential evaluation process proceeds to the fifth step ....' *Bowen v. Yuckert, id.* When the process proceeds to the fifth step, this means that you have demonstrated the existence of a severe impairment(s) resulting in an RFC that prevents the performance of past relevant work. When we decide that you are not disabled at step 5, this means that we have determined that there is other work you can do. To make this finding, we must provide evidence that demonstrates that jobs exist in significant numbers in the national economy that you can do, given your RFC, age, education, and work experience. In legal terms, this is a burden of production of evidence.

This burden shifts to us because, once you establish that you are unable to do any past relevant work, it would be unreasonable to require you to produce vocational evidence showing that there are no jobs in the national economy that you can perform, given your RFC. However, as stated by the Supreme Court, 'It is not unreasonable to require the claimant, who is in a better position to provide information about his own medical condition, to do so.' *Bowen v. Yuckert, id.* Thus, the only burden shift that occurs at step 5 is that we are required to prove that there is other work that you can do, given your RFC, age, education and work experience. That shift does not place on us the burden of proving RFC.

When the burden of production of evidence shifts to us at step 5, our role is to obtain evidence to assist in impartially determining whether there are a significant number of jobs in the national economy you can do. Thus, we have a burden of proof even though our primary interest in the outcome of the claim is that it be decided correctly. As required by the Act, the ultimate burden of persuasion to prove disability, however, remains with you.

The ALJ makes factual findings based on a preponderance of the evidence. 20 C.F.R. § 404.953(a). See also 20 C.F.R. § 404.929. A "*[p]reponderance of the evidence* means such relevant evidence that as a whole shows that the existence of the fact to be proven is more likely than not." 20 C.F.R. § 404.901.

§310   Claimant's Testimony

This section is presented in outline/checklist form so that you can use it at a hearing to make sure all of the issues are covered, whether the ALJ questions your client first or you conduct the direct examination of the claimant. Needless to say, not all questions will be relevant to your client's case nor will the answers to many relevant questions measurably add to your client's case. You will need to focus your client's testimony on his individual limitations. Use this section to make sure you don't forget anything important, not as an outline for testimony to be followed point by point.

§311   *Background, Age, Education and Vocational Training*

- Name, address, Social Security number.
- Date of birth, age today, age at onset of disability.
- Highest grade completed in school.
  If did not complete high school:
  - Did you get a G.E.D.?
  If not fluent in English:
  - Where were you born?
  - What language did you grow up speaking?
  - Where were you educated?
  - When did you come to the United States?
  - What language is spoken at your home today?
  - Who reads the mail at your house?
  - Are you able to read in another language?
  In mental retardation and similar cases:
- Did you attend regular classes or special education classes?
- How well did you do in school?

- If an 8th grade reading level is average, would you say that you're at least an average reader?

If less than an average reader:
- Can you read and understand a newspaper?
- Can you "read or write a simple message such as instructions or inventory lists"? *See* 20 C.F.R. § 404.1564(a)(1) definition of illiteracy.

If illiterate:
- Who does your reading for you?
- How have you handled job applications?
- How did you get a driver's license?
- How have you managed to deal with SSA forms?
- Can you multiply and divide/add and subtract/make change?
- Describe any vocational training; was it completed? When?
- Describe any on-the-job training. When?
- Describe any training in the military. When?

§312   Work Experience

For work to be "past relevant work" it must have been "done within the last 15 years, lasted long enough for you to learn to do it, and was substantial gainful activity." 20 C.F.R. § 404.1565(a) and *see also* SSR 82-62. Thus, for all work during 15 years prior to date of adjudication or prior to last date insured if that date is earlier [*see* 20 C.F.R. § 404.1565(a)]:

1. Job background information:
   - Name of employer
   - Approximate dates of employment
   - Name of job
   - Job duties
   - Full-time or part-time
   - Length of employment
   - Did you do this job long enough to learn the job and develop "the facility needed for average performance"? (SSR 82-62)
   - Earnings (relevant to SGA issue and in assessing skill level)
   - Why did you leave this job?
   - Before you left this job, did your impairment cause you to miss work, do a poor job, change job duties, change hours of work, etc.?
2. Exertional level:
   - Heaviest weight lifted/carried
     - How often did you lift/carry this much?
     - What objects weighed this much?
     - How far did you carry them?
   - Average weight lifted/carried
     - How often?
     - What objects?

- How far?
- How much sitting and standing/walking in an eight-hour working day?
- Did the nature of this job allow you to sit, stand or walk as you chose?
- How much bending? Any crawling, climbing, balancing?
- How much manipulative ability was required?
3. Environmental limitations:
   - Describe work environment: temperature, wetness, humidity, noise, vibration, fumes, odors, dusts, gases, hazards (*e.g.*, machinery, heights).
4. Skill level:
   - How long did it take to learn to do this job?
   - Describe machines, tools and equipment used.
   - Describe any technical knowledge or skill used on this job.
   - Describe any writing or completing reports.
   - How much independent judgment was required?
   - Describe any supervisory responsibilities: how many people? Did you complete work evaluations? Have any hiring/firing responsibilities?
5. Stress level:
Where stress tolerance is an issue:
   - What was it about this job that you found stressful? *e.g.*, speed, precision, complexity, deadlines, working within a schedule, making decisions, exercising independent judgment, working with other people, dealing with the public (strangers), dealing with supervisors, being criticized by supervisors, simply knowing that work is supervised, monotony of routine, getting to work regularly, remaining at work for a full day?
6. Meeting the claimant's burden of proof:
   - Why can't you do this job now?
Or, if no longer insured for Title II:
   - Why couldn't you do this job as of [the date last insured]?

§313   Medical History

Medical history is established by the medical records. Most ALJs have read the medical records and taken notes on them for use at the hearing. Thus, detailed testimony about medical history is not necessary in most cases. There is no need to establish through the claimant's testimony the date of his back surgery when the operative report is a medical exhibit; and it is unnecessary to develop testimony about the extent of the claimant's suffering at his lowest points such as immediately before or after surgery. Because of the requirement that a claimant be disabled for 12 months, it is the plateaus, not the valleys or peaks, which are most important in a Social Security disability case.

Often you may want to use the medical history to establish a time frame for the claimant's testimony about the plateaus. If so, do it as quickly as possible with leading questions. For example:

Q: You injured your back at work on January 15th, 2011, didn't you?

Q: And you never went back to work after that, did you?

Q: Your condition continued to get worse, you had numerous medical tests which found a ruptured disc, and you had surgery on May 15, 2011, didn't you?

Q: During the summer of 2011 you recovered from the immediate aftereffects of surgery, didn't you?

Q: And wouldn't you say that as of September 15th of 2011, the day your doctor told the worker's compensation insurance carrier that your condition had plateaued, your symptoms then were pretty much the same as they are now?

Caveat: Do not get carried away with leading questions. Do not use them to establish a fact which is controverted. Never use leading questions when asking about symptoms.

The degree to which you go into medical history depends on the nature of your client's case. Cases in which more development of medical history is useful include those involving virtually every known treatment for pain, unusual impairments, unusual treatment or especially cryptic medical records where testimony from the claimant will educate the ALJ. In cases where the acute phase is unusually long, where the claimant's medical history involves a series of peaks and valleys with few plateaus, or in any case where better sense can be made from the medical records after hearing the claimant's description of his ordeal, spend time going through medical history. In such cases use a combination of leading questions (to avoid the claimant fumbling over the medical details which already appear in the record) and encouraging the claimant to provide a full description of his symptoms and response to treatment.

§314   Current Treatment

While, as a rule, testimony about past medical treatment should be kept to a minimum, a claimant's testimony about current, on-going treatment should be fully developed, and any lack of ongoing treatment should be fully explained. Ask:
• Names of those treating claimant now
• Their specialties
• Length of relationship
• Frequency of treatment
• Which condition does this doctor, therapist, etc. treat?

• What treatment does he provide?
• How much has this treatment helped?
• What medication do you take now? How much do you take each time you take it? How often do you take it? Are there any side-effects? How much does it help and for how long?
• If no regular treatment/medication, why not?

Caveat: Try to avoid building your case with the question: What has your doctor told you about this? Or what has your doctor said your limitations are? Use these questions only as a last resort in cases where you've been unable to obtain a medical report from the doctor and then only after careful questioning of your client before the hearing concerning his understanding of what the doctor said, when he said it and the circumstances under which he said it.

§315   Physical Symptoms

In a physical impairment case, your client's description of his symptoms is the most important part of his hearing testimony. It is the severity of these symptoms, after all, which keep your client from working. If he can give a credible, vivid description of his symptoms, he has taken one giant step toward winning his case. He must be well-prepared. *See* §292, *supra*.

As a general rule, when questioning a claimant about his symptoms, keep a low profile. Let the claimant talk. Never ask leading questions about symptoms. Construct your examination concerning symptoms to get your client talking and then interfere as little as possible with his description of his symptoms. Draw your models not so much from the way lawyers examine plaintiffs in personal injury court cases, but rather from the way the best television and radio journalists get people talking.

The way you ask about symptoms differs from client to client and it is done differently by every lawyer, according to the individual lawyer's personality. Thus, what follows is a checklist to be used to make sure that the claimant has covered everything. It is a rare claimant who will need to be asked so many specific questions. Most claimants will describe their conditions vividly and completely, in a way which addresses most of the symptom issues, if they are well-prepared prior to the hearing.

§315.1 Pain

Where pain is an issue, you will want to inquire about the factors identified in 20 C.F.R. § 404.1529(c)(3):
1.   Pain:

• nature	• location	• onset
• duration	• frequency	• radiation
• intensity	• precipitating factors	• aggravating factors

2.   Medication:
- type   • dosage
- effectiveness • adverse
                  side-effects
3.   Treatment other than medication
4.   Functional restrictions
5.   Daily activities.

Where there are multiple symptoms/ impairments/ parts of the body affected, it works best to ask for a list. (Example: Tell us where you have pain in your body. Tell us what medical problems you have.) Then go back and request additional details, exploring each item one at a time.

Description:

1. Tell us about the pain in your [part of body affected].

2. What happened to cause you to have this pain?

3. How long have you had the pain?

4. Has there been any significant period since it started that the pain was in remission?
- What caused the period of remission, *e.g.*, medication, surgery, physical therapy, etc.?
- How long did the remission last?

5. What does the pain feel like?

6. Is it tender to touch?

7. Does it limit the amount you can bend the affected joint? How much?

8. Is the quality of the pain always the same **or** is it sometimes different? If so, how and when is it different?

9. Show us where this pain is located. [Attorney then states, for example, "Let the record reflect that the claimant is pointing to his low back at the beltline."]

10. Is this pain constant or does it come and go?

11. If it comes and goes:
- How often does it come?
- How long does it last?
- How many hours per day/days per month do you have this pain?
- What sorts of things bring on this pain?
- What relieves it?

12. Do you have muscle spasms?

13. How severe is your pain? If we use a ten-point scale with ten being the most severe pain you've ever had, how would you rank the pain you've been telling us about?

14. Is it always of the same intensity? If not, how often is it at each intensity?

15. What increases the intensity of your pain?
- Is it affected by movement, activity, staying in one position, environmental conditions or stress?

16. Does the pain ever radiate, such as going down one of your legs? If so:

- Which leg?
- What route does it travel? Be specific.
- What does it feel like when it goes down your leg?
- How often does this happen?

17. Is there any numbness or pins-and-needles feeling associated with this pain?

18. Are there any other symptoms associated with this pain, such as redness, swelling, heat, stiffness, crepitus (crackling noise heard when joint moves), muscle weakness, muscle atrophy, fatigue, appetite loss, weight loss?

Treatment:

1. How often do you see your doctor?
- What does your doctor do for you?

2. How is the pain affected by medication?
- Do you have side effects from pain medication such as drowsiness, dizziness, lack of concentration, slow reflexes, nausea?

3. What treatment other than medication have you tried, such as transcutaneous nerve stimulator (TENS unit), physical therapy, massage, "back school" (training in back exercises and mechanics), bio-feedback, hypnosis, psychological therapy, chiropractic manipulation, acupuncture, Hubbard tank, traction, exercises, injections, pain clinic?
- How much have these things helped?

4. What home remedies have you tried, such as hot baths, heating pads, ointments?
- How much have these things helped?

5. Is the pain helped by limiting your activities, lying down, shifting positions frequently, sitting in a special chair, etc.?

Resulting Restrictions:
- How has this pain affected your life?
- Do you use assistive devices? (For example, cane, brace, cervical collar, special door handles, gripping devices, bathtub or shower bars, special chair.)
- Are your daily activities affected (including relationship with others, sleep, hobbies, etc.)? *See* §319, *infra*.
- Are you irritable, depressed, worried, anxious, have difficulty concentrating, or remembering? *See* mental symptoms, §316, *infra*.
- How has the pain affected your capacity for work? *See* mental and physical residual functional capacity, §§317-318, *infra*.

§315.2 Shortness of Breath

1. What brings on shortness of breath?
- Cardiac chest pain
- Lung congestion

- Asthma
- Weather chances
- Allergies
- Speaking
- Exertion
- Lying down
- Hyperventilation
- Stress
- Panic attacks.

2. Describe how it feels when you are short of breath.

3. How many pillows do you use when you sleep?

4. How many stairs can you climb before you become short of breath and have to stop?

5. How fast do you walk?

6. How far can you walk before you become short of breath and have to stop?

7. Are you bothered by dust, fumes, gases? If so, to what degree do you need to be in a clean environment?

8. How often do you wheeze?

9. How often do you have lung infections?

10. How often do you have acute episodes of breathing problems?
- What brings on these acute episodes?
- How long does each episode last?
- What are your symptoms during acute episodes?

11. How often would you miss work because of your breathing problems?

12. If you were at work, would you need to take unscheduled breaks? If so, do you expect that this would occur daily, weekly, several times per month? Would you need to sit down or recline?

§315.3 Fatigue

1. When did you begin feeling fatigued?

2. Did fatigue come on gradually or all at once?

3. Describe your fatigue.

4. Is it the same as being weak? physically tired? lacking energy?

5. Is it the same as being drowsy or sleepy?

6. When you are fatigued, how would you describe your level of motivation to do anything?

7. Is your fatigue associated with a lack of patience?

8. What things make your fatigue worse?
- Physical activity
- Stress
- Heat
- Depression.

9. Give specific examples of things that worsen your fatigue.
- How much physical activity will bring on fatigue?

- Give examples of stressful things that you think made your fatigue worse in the past.
  - How much heat brings on the fatigue?
  - Will a hot bath make you fatigued?

10. Is fatigue affected by the time of day? What time of day is worse? What time of day is better?

11. What things make your fatigue better?
- Rest
- Sleep
- Positive experiences.

12. How well do you sleep?

13. How long do you need to rest for your fatigue to get better so that you can get up and do something?

§316 Mental Symptoms

Sometimes in mental impairment cases, the *way* your client goes about answering (or not answering) questions about his symptoms is more important than what he says. For this reason, beware of over-preparing such a claimant to testify. Allow the ALJ to see your client in his unvarnished state.

In some cases it will be necessary to rely primarily on family and friends of your client for development of testimony concerning mental symptoms. Most people with mental impairments, however, are used to talking to therapists about their symptoms. Thus, try to ask questions of your client in the same way that a sympathetic therapist would ask them.

§316.1 Use DSM-IV as an Outline for Questioning

As an outline for questioning, use symptoms listed in the "diagnostic criteria" for your client's particular mental impairment found in the American Psychiatric Association's DIAGNOSTIC AND STATISTICAL MANUAL OF MENTAL DISORDERS (Fourth Edition), known as DSM-IV. These DSMIV "diagnostic criteria" are similar to the "A criteria" for the appropriate mental impairment found in §12 of the Listing of Impairments. But the DSM-IV "diagnostic criteria" contain more information about symptoms from which you can develop questions. As a simple example, compare the requirement of "thoughts of suicide" found in the criteria for "affective disorders," §12.04A.1.h. in the Listing of Impairments, with the "diagnostic criteria" for "major depressive episode" from DSM-IV: "recurrent thoughts of death (not just fear of dying), recurrent suicidal ideation without a specific plan, or a suicide attempt or a specific plan for committing suicide."

Be sure to translate psychiatric terms into ordinary language. For example, instead of asking about "paranoid thinking" (Listing, of Impairments §12.04A.l.i.), ask: "Do you ever feel that people want to harm you?" "Do you ever feel that people are plotting against you?" "Do you ever feel that people are trying to trick you?" "Do you ever feel that people are talking about you behind your back?" "Do you ever feel that people are trying to control you?" "Do you ever feel that someone is following you?" "Do you ever feel that someone is watching you?"

Follow up any affirmative response to a question about psychiatric symptoms with: "Tell us about it." Try to get your client talking freely about his symptoms.

§316.2 Stress

Whenever stress tolerance is at issue, establish through your client's testimony the specific kinds of things that he finds stressful. SSR 85-15 states that the "reaction to the demands of work (stress) is highly individualized and mental illness is characterized by adverse responses to seemingly trivial circumstances." See §247, supra, in which the section of SSR 85-15 concerning stress and mental illness is quoted in its entirety. Ask for a lot of examples of stressful things, and ask for a description of what happens to him when he is under stress; e.g., panicky feeling, terror, a feeling of impending doom, fight or flight response, trembling, shaking, palpitations, chest pain, shortness of breath, smothering feeling, choking, feeling faint, unsteady, sweaty, nausea, stomach ache, numbness, tingling, hot flashes, chills, hallucinations, flashbacks, fear of dying, fear of going crazy, fear of doing something uncontrolled. etc.

Here is a list of some demands of work which some people find stressful:
- speed
- precision
- complexity
- deadlines
- working within a schedule
- making decisions
- exercising independent judgment
- completing tasks
- working with other people
- dealing with the public (strangers)
- dealing with supervisors
- being criticized by supervisors
- simply knowing that work is supervised
- getting to work regularly
- remaining at work for a full day
- fear of failure at work.

SSA often takes the position that routine repetitive work constitutes low stress work. But many people

find one or more of the following aspects of such work to be stressful:
- monotony of routine
- little latitude for decision-making
- lack of collaboration on the job
- no opportunity for learning new things
- underutilization of skills
- lack of meaningfulness of work.

§317 Mental Residual Functional Capacity

The following may be used as a checklist for developing testimony concerning mental RFC. It is an expansion of the basic mental work-related activities which appear at 20 C.F.R. § 404.1545(c):

1. Understanding, carrying out, and remembering simple instructions:
- remember locations and work-like procedures
- understand and remember very short and simple instructions
- carry out very short and simple instructions
- maintain concentration and attention for extended periods (the approximately 2-hour segments between arrival and first break, lunch, second break and departure)
- perform activities within a schedule
- maintain regular attendance
- be punctual within customary tolerances
- sustain an ordinary routine without special supervision
- work in coordination with or proximity to others without being unduly distracted by them
- complete a normal workday and workweek without interruptions from psychologically based symptoms
- perform at a consistent pace without an unreasonable number and length of rest periods.

2. Use of judgment:
- make simple work-related decisions
- be aware of normal hazards and take appropriate precautions.

3. Responding appropriately to supervision, coworkers, and usual work situations:
- ask simple questions or request assistance
- accept instructions
- respond appropriately to criticism from supervisors
- get along with coworkers or peers without unduly distracting them or exhibiting behavioral extremes.

4. Dealing with changes in a routine work setting:
  • respond appropriately to changes in a routine work setting.

§318   Physical Residual Functional Capacity

The following outline for questioning about physical capacity deals with the most common physical RFC issues. For a list of additional postural, manipulative, visual, communicative and environmental limitations, *see* the Physical RFC Assessment Form, Form SSA-4734-U8, reproduced at §207.2 of this book.

Be sure to preface your questioning of the claimant concerning his RFC with the explanation that you are interested in his best estimate of his capacity to do these activities on a day-to-day basis, 8 hours per day, 5 days per week, approximately 50 weeks per year in a regular work setting. Encourage your client to volunteer examples of his limitations when answering RFC questions.

§318.1 Sitting

1. Do you have any problem with sitting?
2. How long can you sit:
  • continuously in one stretch?
  • total during an eight-hour working day (with normal breaks)?
3. When you sit, can you sit:
  • without squirming?
  • without leaning on elbows?
  • at a desk:
    —in an armless office chair?
    —in an office chair with arms?
    —on a backless stool?
  • at a bench:
    —on a high backless stool?
    —on a high stool with a back?
  • in a work-like position:
    —with your arms extended?
    —with hands available to manipulate objects?
    —with neck slightly bent forward?
4. If pain limits your sitting tolerance, describe:
  • changes in the pain:
    —onset
    —the way the pain feels (type or quality of pain)
    —radiation
    —intensity
  • how you try to control the pain:
    —shifting position in chair?
    —leaning?
    —getting out of the chair?

5. If you must get out of the chair:
  • how long can you sit before getting up?
must you:
    —stand?
    —walk?
    —lie down?
  • how long is it before you can resume sitting?
6. When you sit is it necessary for you to elevate a leg? If so,
  • which leg?
  • why?
  • how long must you elevate it?
  • how high?
7. When you get up from sitting:
  • do you need help getting up?
  • do you have difficulty standing when you first get up?
    —Why? *e.g.*, dizziness, stiffness, pain?
    —How long does this problem last?
8. What happens if you try to sit too long?
9. Give examples of sitting; limitations:
  • driving or riding in a car
  • sitting at the dining room table:
    —eating
    —paying bills
  • watching a movie
  • watching television
  • doing crafts
  • fishing
10. Have you had to give up or limit any hobbies because of your problem with sitting?

§318.2 Alternate Sitting, Standing and Walking

1. Can you alternate sitting with standing? If so:
  • how often do you need to stand?
  • how long must you stand before resuming sitting?
  • can you work at a bench while standing?
    —does it depend on the height of the bench?
  • can you get through an eight-hour working day alternating sitting and standing? If not, how many hours total?
2. Is it necessary for you to alternate periods of sitting with periods of walking?
  • why?
  • how often do you need to walk?
  • how long, must you walk before you can resume sitting?
  • can you get through an eight-hour working day alternating sitting and walking? If not, how many hours total?

§318.3 Standing

1. Do you have any problem with standing?
2. How long can you stand:
   • continuously in one stretch?
   • total during an eight-hour working day?
3. When you stand, can you stand:
   • without, for example, moving away from a machine?
   • without leaning against something?
   • in a work-like position:
     —with your arms extended?
     —with hands available to manipulate objects?
     —with neck slightly bent forward?
4. What happens if you try to stand too long?
5. Examples of standing limitations:
   • Waiting in line
   • standing at the stove to cook
   • doing dishes at the sink
   • waiting for a bus.

§318.4 Walking

1. Do you have any problem with walking?
2. How long/how far can you walk:
   • continuously in one stretch without stopping to rest?
   • total during an eight-hour working day?
3. Can you walk:
   • without an assistive device?
   • at a normal speed?
4. What happens if you try to walk too far?
5. Do you have any problem keeping your balance on a slippery or moving surface?
6. Examples of walking limitations:
   • walking the aisles at a grocery store
   • walking around the neighborhood

§318.5 Lifting and Carrying

1. Do you have any problem with lifting or carrying?
2. How much can you lift or carry:
   • if you only had to do it for up to one-third of a work day?
   • if you had to do it from one-third to two-thirds of a work day?
3. What is the heaviest thing you encounter in your daily life that you can still lift and carry?
4. Describe how you lift/carry these objects.
5. What sorts of things that you encounter in your daily life can you no longer lift and carry?
6. What happens when you try to lift or carry too much?

§318.6 Postural Limitations

1. Describe any difficulty:
   • bending at the waist
   • twisting
   • stooping (bending the spine)
   • kneeling (bending the legs)
   • crouching (bending both the spine and the legs)
   • climbing stairs
   • climbing a ladder
   • other climbing
   • crawling.
2. Can you do these activities:
   • up to one-third of a working day?
   • from one-third to two-thirds of a working day?
3. What happens if you overdo any of these activities?

§318.7 Manipulative Limitations

1. Are you left or right-handed?
2. Describe any difficulty using your hands and arms for:
   • reaching all directions, including overhead
   • handling objects (gross manipulation)
   • fingering (fine manipulation)
   • feeling
   • pushing or pulling
   • twisting the wrists
   • working with hand tools, *e.g.*, screwdrivers, pliers.
3. Do you have any problem with dropping things?
4. Do your hands ever shake? go numb? have a pins and needles sensation?
5. How well can you perform the following?
   • opening a jar
   • opening a door
   • buttoning clothes
   • picking up coins
   • writing
   • washing the dishes.
6. Can you do repetitive hand activities for most of an eight-hour working day?

§318.8 Traveling

1. How did you get to this hearing today?
2. How often have you left your home during the past (month) (year)?
3. When you go out:
   • Where do you go?

- Do you usually go alone?

4. If you usually have someone with you when you go out, why don't you go alone?

5. Do you have emotional problems when you leave your home alone?

- If so, describe the feelings you have and why it is difficult to leave your home alone.

6. Do you have a driver's license?

- If no, have you ever had a driver's license?
- Why don't you have one now?

7. Do you have any special restrictions on your driver's license? For example:

- glasses
- times of day,
- speed,
- distance?

8. Do you have a handicapped parking permit?

9. Do you have regular access to an automobile?

- Does it have a standard or automatic transmission?
- Does it have power or regular brakes and steering?

10. How is driving different for you now than before your health problems became severe?

11. How often do you drive?

12. How long (or far) can you tolerate driving before you have to stop and rest?

- How long must you rest?

13. What is the greatest distance (or longest time) you have driven in the last year?

- Did you have to stop during this trip?
- How many times and for how long?

14. Describe any difficulties with:

- getting into or out of a car;
- turning your head from side to side;
- looking behind you when you drive in reverse;
- sitting while you drive;
- using your legs while driving;
- using your arms or hands while driving
- vision.

15. Do you have emotional problems while driving? For example,

- mental confusion?
- nervousness or fear?
- getting lost?
- difficulty keeping your concentration and attention?

16. Are you taking any medications:

- which affect your driving
- about which you have been warned that you should not drive while taking them?
- If so, what are these medications?

17. If you have problems driving, how do you get around?

18. Do you have problems being a passenger in a car, either physically (*e.g.*, getting in and out, prolonged sitting) or emotionally (*e.g.*, paranoia, anxiety)?

19. Do you ride the bus or use any other public transportation?

- If so, how often?

20. Do you have difficulties taking a bus, such as:

- walking to the bus stop?
- standing waiting for the bus?
- climbing the steps into the bus?
- sitting on the bus?
- standing on the bus?
- Have you ever fallen while on a bus?

21. Do you have any emotional problems riding buses?

- If a bus is crowded, do you feel anxious or paranoid?

22. Have you ever gotten lost or missed your stop while riding a bus?

- What happened?
- How often has this happened?

§318.9 Good Days/Bad Days

If your capacity widely varies:

- Categorize your days, for example:
—good days/bad days
—good days/so-so days/bad days.
- Describe each kind of day.
- What are you capable of doing on each kind of day?
- Would you be going to work on a bad day?
- How many of each kind of day do you have in a month?

§319   Daily Activities

§319.1   Background and General Description

1. Do you live in an apartment, a house, a duplex, a condo, a mobile home?

- does your house have one story or two?
- is your bedroom upstairs or downstairs?
- how many rooms?

2. What do you do on an average day?

3. Describe your day for us from the time you get up in the morning until you go to bed at night.

4. Give us some examples of things you do differently now than you used to do.

§319.2   Activities of Daily Living

How are the following things handled at your house?

- cooking
- doing the dishes
- grocery shopping
- cleaning
  —dusting
  —straightening up
  —taking out the garbage
  —making beds
  —changing bed sheets
  —vacuuming
  —floor mopping
  —bathroom cleaning
  —laundry
- watching children
- yard work
  —grass cutting
  —gardening
  —snow shoveling
- home repairs
- paying bills/handling finances
- going to the post office
- taking public transportation
- obtaining a telephone number from phone directory or directory assistance.

§319.3　Social Functioning and Leisure Activities

1. How often do you visit:
   - family members
   - friends
   - neighbors?
2. Do you initiate contacts or do they?
3. Do you have any problem getting along with:
   - family
   - friends
   - neighbors
   - store clerks
   - landlords
   - bus drivers?
4. How often do you go to church?
5. Do you participate in any organizations?
6. Do you play cards? Other games?
7. Do you attend sports events?
8. Do you go to movies?
9. Do you go out to eat?
10. Do you have any hobbies?
11. How often do you read the newspaper
12. Do you watch television news programs?
13. Do you keep up with current events?

§319.4　Personal Care

1. Do you have any problem, need any assistance or reminders with:
   - dressing
   - buttoning clothes
   - tying shoelaces
   - bathing
   - combing/fixing hair
   - shaving
2. Do you get dressed every day?

§319.5　Examples of Limited Activities

1. How much time do you spend daily doing the following:
   - sitting in your favorite chair—describe the chair
   - watching television
   - reading
   - talking on the telephone
   - sleeping
   - lying down?
     —Where do you go to lie down (*e.g.*, bed, couch, recliner)?
2. How often do you drive a car?
3. How often do you go out of the house?
4. When you begin a household task, do you complete it in a timely manner? If not, give examples.
5. Are there any hobbies you have been forced to give up because of your impairment?

§320　Lay Witnesses

Sincere, straightforward lay testimony, or lack of it, can well be the deciding factor in a disability claim, even where expert medical testimony is used. No disability claim under the Social Security Act, except in the most unusual circumstances, should go to hearing without it. In arranging for the testimony of lay witnesses, keep in mind a few basic points.

§321　Limit the Number of Witnesses

Do not bring in the whole community to testify. Select a few witnesses who can corroborate and, where possible, add to your client's testimony. The use of cumulative lay testimony will unnecessarily lengthen the hearing, quite possibly irritate the administrative law judge and, in any event, make it possible for him to lose sight of essential details in a welter of unneeded information.

§322   Screen Witnesses and Pick the Best

Screen your witnesses carefully. Eliminate, so far as possible, those who have difficulty in expressing themselves, those who do not really want to testify, those who do not have good firsthand knowledge of some aspect of the case, and those who have an exaggerated opinion of themselves and their cleverness.

The most common lay witnesses are the claimant's spouse, adult children (sometimes minor children), other relatives, and close friends. Often such close family members and friends are the only people with whom the claimant has contact; and frequently, depending on the demeanor, candor, ability to offer vivid description, etc., of the individual witnesses, one could not expect to find better witnesses than close family and friends. But, sometimes ALJs tend to view such people as less objective than neighbors, former employers or co-workers, and other associates, such as members of the same church or union, or members of hobby groups or professional groups. Therefore, depending on the issues in your client's case, ask the claimant and his family about possible witnesses who are outside of the claimant's immediate circle of family and close friends and who, therefore, might be properly characterized as more objective.

§323   Prepare Witnesses But Do Not Rehearse Testimony

Interview your witnesses ahead of time, by phone, if an in-person interview is not possible. The preliminary interview should be devoted to selecting the best witnesses and to telling them, using the guidelines given here and those you develop independently, how their testimony can be most effective.

Do not rehearse the witnesses. It is almost impossible to rehearse a witness so that his testimony does not appear to be rehearsed and consequently entitled to less weight. Rehearsed testimony tends to be trite and stilted, to add unneeded details and, quite often, to overlook valuable information that might be elicited through spontaneous testimony.

§324   Seek Testimony From Observation; Avoid Conclusory Testimony

The best possible testimony from lay witnesses emphasizes their observations and minimizes their conclusions. Limit the testimony of your lay witnesses to those matters such people would reasonably be familiar with. Testimony from a layman, for instance, that your client suffers from emphysema, grand mal epilepsy, or arachnoiditis is simply a restatement of what someone else has told him and adds little to your case, particularly if other evidence from better sources shows the witness to be in error.

In a similar vein, it is probably better not to let your lay witnesses testify that your client is "disabled," "totally disabled," "permanently disabled," or anything of a similar nature. Disability under the Social Security Act is not premised on total disability or permanent disability and the use of those terms may well cloud your presentation, particularly if the entire evidence shows that your client is disabled but that the disability is not, in fact, either total or permanent. If a witness does use such terminology, by all means get into the record a statement from him as to what he means and on what he premises his conclusion. Then relate the testimony to your theory of the claimant's case, e.g., that he cannot do anything more than sedentary work, etc.

Here are some sample questions:

Walking:
• In the last few years, have you observed the claimant having any difficulty walking? Describe what you have observed.
• Expressed in terms of city blocks, how far would be a long way for the claimant to walk without stopping to rest? How long will the claimant need to rest?

Arms and Hands:
• Has the claimant had any difficulty using his or her arms or hands? Describe what you have observed.
• Does the claimant drop things? What things? How often have you observed this?

Pain:
• Does the claimant appear to be in pain?
• About how much of the time is he or she in pain?
• How do you know the claimant is in pain?

Fatigue:
• Does the claimant seem to get worn out easily? What would be a good example (other than walking) of an activity that would wear the claimant out? How long does the claimant then need to rest?

Pace:

- Is the speed or pace at which the claimant does things any different from the speed or pace at which normal people do things? What is the difference?
- Expressed as a percentage, about what percentage of a normal person's pace is the claimant's pace?

Mental/Emotional:

- Have you noticed any mental or emotional changes in the claimant? *E.g.*, depression, crying spells, panic attacks, social withdrawal, problems with memory, attention span, or concentration. How often? How long do these problems last?

§325   Corroborative Testimony

Sometimes the goal of using lay testimony is simply corroboration of the claimant's testimony. If your goal is corroboration, consider doing it this way:

Q: How often do you have the opportunity to observe the claimant?

A: Every day.

Q: You have been present throughout the claimant's testimony, haven't you?

A: Yes.

Q: If I were to ask you the same questions that you heard asked of the claimant, would your answers be the same or essentially the same as the answers given by the claimant?

A: Yes.

Q: From your observations of the claimant, has he testified truthfully here today?

A: Yes he has.

Occasionally this testimony is all you need. Usually, however, you will couple such corroborative testimony with additional observations or anecdotes from the witness.

§326   Before and After Testimony

A common approach is to elicit "before" and "after" testimony, testimony which compares the claimant's condition before his disability started with how he functions now.

If a wife testifies that her husband, the claimant, has emphysema, is disabled, and that they need the money, she has not helped your cause very much. If she testifies that she has known her husband for 28 years and has been married to him for 26 years, that he has always been a hard worker and a good provider, that he is now distraught because he can no longer provide for the family, and that because of his illness she has had to go to work, she has made a start.

If she then testifies as to his impairments, as observed by her, and indicates how they limit his actions, particularly those having to do with work functions, and verifies his medical regimen, she is being helpful. If, in addition, she then describes in graphic detail that he keeps her awake most of the night with his continuous coughing, that he appears to have difficulty lifting a gallon of milk from the refrigerator, that he recently tried to pick up a two-year-old grandchild and dropped him, that he quit smoking last year and uses an intermittent positive pressure breathing machine regularly in addition to taking prescribed medication and still has difficulty breathing after walking to the mailbox, 50 feet from their front door, she has gone a long way toward making your case.

§327   Anecdotal Testimony

The following examples further illustrate the difference between strong and weak lay testimony. The best examples provide detailed testimony about a specific incident observed by the witness—an anecdote which represents many other such incidents.

§327.1   Seizures

Weak: Mr. Jones [the claimant] has epilepsy. [This is a conclusion, quite likely based on what someone has told the witness who, being a layman, not a doctor, may be surprised before the end of the hearing to learn that the claimant suffers from an organic brain syndrome instead of epilepsy.]

Strong: My son suffers from grand mal epilepsy according to his doctor, and Mr. Jones' actions are almost the same as my son's. He has what appears to be seizures, falls down, bites his tongue, loses consciousness, and loses control of his bladder. When he recovers, after 25 minutes or so, he appears to be in a daze and has trouble speaking. He sleeps for a couple of hours and then appears to be all right. I have seen this happen maybe a dozen times in the last two years. [These observations will go far to convince the administrative law judge that the claimant suffers from a serious seizure disorder, regardless of the label placed on it.]

§327.2   Breathing Impairment

Weak: Mr. Smith has emphysema.

Strong: Mr. Smith sits in a chair by the window most of the day. The phone is maybe 20 feet away. When his wife is not there and he has to answer the phone when I call, he is gasping for breath after walking even that short distance and has to rest for a minute after saying, "Hello." [Here the witness has furnished not a conclusion ("emphysema") but observations from which the administrative law judge can conclude that the claimant has a severe breathing impairment. The exact label to be placed on the impairment (emphysema, bronchitis, asthma, allergy, tuberculosis) is not important at this point, and can be supplied by the administrative law judge after all the evidence is in.]

§327.3   Pain

Weak: My husband is disabled by his pain.

Strong: From what I have seen since my husband came home from the hospital, he appears to be in almost constant pain; he is up and down all night, groans in his sleep, and never appears to be comfortable. His doctor told him to take up to four pain tablets a day, but he never takes less than six. Then he takes a dozen or so aspirin on top of that. He has lost his appetite and 15 pounds. Our social life is nonexistent. He doesn't drive anymore, or even ride in a car when he doesn't have to, since he says it hurts too much. I do all the grocery shopping and do the yard work because I'm convinced he hurts too bad to do it. He always did those things before he was hurt. We don't go to church anymore because he says he can't sit still that long.

§328   Interference With Work

Graphic descriptions of impairments and of how they affect work-related activities are invaluable. Testimony from your lay witnesses should cover all pertinent facts of the case: the claimant's home life, work, hobbies, business and professional activities, and even, where appropriate, his religious activities. Curtailment or restriction of almost any activity can be related to your client's impairments, and then to his ability to work.

§328.1   Coworker Testimony

Weak: Mr. Brown was disabled even while he was working at the plant with me.

Strong: I worked with Mr. Brown for six years. He always did his share of the work until he was hurt. In the last year he was there, I saw him faint twice and took him to the emergency room at the hospital on one occasion. The foreman gave him a lighter job, where he wouldn't have to lift over five pounds and wouldn't have to work around moving machinery. All of us pitched in and did part of his work for him. He was absent one or two days a week toward the last. I understand he is retired now on disability.

Weak: Mrs. Jones can't do her housework.

Strong: Mrs. Jones has always been a meticulous housekeeper. However, during the past year, she has simply let the housework go. I do the laundry for her and the vacuuming. When I visit her, she is usually resting on the couch or in bed. I have seen her try to cook dinner and drop a pan full of hot food. She drops dishes a lot. Once, when I was there, she fainted while she was cooking dinner and fell across the stove.

Weak: Operating a power sewing machine in a clothing factory is hard work; Mrs. Smith can't do it anymore.

Strong: I sat next to Mrs. Smith at the sewing factory and we operated power sewing machines. We were required to sit all day, except for one 30 minute lunch break and two 15 minute coffee breaks. We were required to use both hands and one foot to perform the necessary sewing operations and had to lift and carry up to 20 pounds of finished garments. We had a quota to make. It required good eyesight and good coordination. If she can't do all those things, she can't do the work.

Weak: As personnel manager for the XYZ Company, I can say that Mrs. Brown is too disabled to do her former work, even though she tried.

Strong: As personnel manager for the XYZ Company, I am familiar with the work Mrs. Brown did. She worked as a hand sander, finishing pieces of furniture. This required her to stand for eight hours a day, with the usual breaks, to bend, stoop, work in awkward positions, and to lift up to 30 pounds. She was often absent due to her illness and once we had to shut down the assembly line due to her absence. Our records show that during the last six months she worked for us, she was absent for 31 whole days and went home early on 16 occasions. Her work was satisfactory when she was there, but she was absent so much we had to let her go. Reports from her doctor indicated that she was absent due to treatment for a nervous condition.

§328.2   Company Disability

Weak: As personnel manager, I think Mr. Jones is entitled to Social Security disability benefits since he is already drawing disability retirement from our company.

Strong: As personnel manager, I help make disability determinations for persons who file for disability benefits under our company plan. Under our policy, a person is considered disabled if he is unable to do his usual work or comparable work in the plant because of his impairments, for a period of at least six months.

Under that definition, Mr. Jones has been found by us to be disabled.

§330   The Government's Medical Expert

Medical experts are sometimes called by ALJs to testify in disability hearings. Part of the criteria for selection of a medical expert is that he must not have conducted a consultative examination of the claimant and he must not have acted as the claimant's treating physician. Medical experts are not examining physicians. Their opinions are based upon the medical records and testimony presented at the hearing.

Medical experts were formerly called medical advisors and some regulations and Social Security Rulings still use the term "medical advisor." Hearing offices were instructed in an administrative memorandum issued in 1989 to refer to a medical doctor or psychologist called by a ALJ to at a disability hearing as a "medical expert" because this term more accurately described the doctor's function. *See also* SSR 96-6p, footnote 2.

The role of a medical expert is simply to provide medical expertise to assist the ALJ in grappling with complicated medical issues. Although they are often viewed by claimants' attorneys as experts hired by the other side to testify against claimants, analogous to physicians retained by a worker's compensation insurance carrier to defeat or minimize an injured employee's claim, in theory, anyway, they are supposed to be neutral experts who are not expected by the Social Security Administration to favor one side or the other. The degree to which the reality reflects the theory varies.

One of the worst things a claimant's attorney can do is to treat the medical expert as a hostile witness—even when the medical expert actually is a hostile witness. Treating the medical expert as hostile is self-fulfilling. It is the surest way to turn him into a hostile witness if he is not already. And even when you really are dealing with a hostile medical expert, a snarling cross-examination is likely to alienate the ALJ, to bring out all of the ALJ's protective instincts.

Be well prepared whenever a medical expert has been called to testify. Try to anticipate the questions the ALJ will ask and, based on your knowledge of your client's case, try to work out answers to these questions supported by the opinion of the treating physician or by medical treatises. Work around a truly hostile medical expert by holding the record open and submitting a well-supported letter from the claimant's treating physician addressing the issues raised by the medical expert's testimony.

For general preparation to deal with medical expert testimony, read the Medical Expert Handbook prepared by the Office of the Chief Administrative Law Judge. *See* Appendix 9, which reprints pages 8-36 of this useful manual.

§331   *Purpose of Medical Expert Testimony*

If a medical expert is going to be called to testify at your client's hearing, a notice to this effect will be sent to you along with the notice of hearing. When you get a notice indicating that a medical expert is going to testify, it means that the ALJ (or perhaps a member of his staff) has reviewed the hearing exhibits and concluded that the case involves:

1. a complicated medical issue which a medical expert may assist the ALJ in understanding [*see Richardson v. Perales*, 402 U.S. 389, 408 (1971)];

2. a question of meeting the Listings;

3. a question of equaling the Listings [*see* 20 C.F.R. § 404.1526(b)];

4. a mental impairment and the ALJ feels he needs a medical expert's help in completing the required psychiatric review technique form [*see* 20 C.F.R. § 404.1520a(d)(1)(ii)];

5. a question of residual functional capacity;

6. an "onset date" which must be "inferred" from the medical evidence (*see* SSR 83-20); or

7. a question of failure to follow prescribed treatment (*see* SSR 82-59).

HALLEX I-2-5-34 mentions calling a medical expert to address the issue of whether or not there are inadequacies in the medical evidence requiring additional medical evidence to be obtained. It is rare that this would be the only reason that an ALJ called a medical expert to testify. However, when a medical expert is called to testify for some other reason, he is often asked this question by the ALJ.

When you look carefully at the range of issues an ME may be called to testify about and compare the medical issues in your client's case, you may have a good idea why the ALJ called a medical expert. Do not necessarily assume that a medical expert's presence at a hearing means that the ALJ has prejudged your client's case negatively. Indeed, it could mean that the ALJ suspects that your client's impairment equals a Listed impairment. Before an ALJ may find that a claimant's impairments equal a Listing, the ALJ is required by SSR 96-6p to obtasin the opinion of a medical expert. Or it could mean that the ALJ thinks that your client is disabled, but because of the nature of your client's impairment, the ALJ is unsure of the date disability began.

§332   Procedure

Normally the medical expert testifies after the claimant and his other witnesses have testified. Medical expert testimony is usually taken before the testimony of a vocational expert, if a VE has been called by the ALJ to testify. Indeed, in many cases in which a medical expert testifies that a claimant's impairments meet or equal a Listed impairment, thus justifying a finding of disabled at step three of the sequential evaluation process, the ALJ will stop the hearing without taking the testimony of a vocational expert concerning issues at steps four and five of the sequential evaluation process.

Medical experts testify more often in mental impairment cases than in cases involving any other single impairment. For this reason we provide below at §333 an example of an ALJ's direct questioning of the medical expert in a mental impairment case. This is from a set of questions actually in use by ALJs; however, as far as we know, there is no officially sanctioned set of questions for direct examination of a medical expert. Instead, questions are developed by individual ALJs and shared. ALJ questioning of MEs concerning physical impairments generally follows the same format.

§333   ALJ's Direct Examination of Medical Expert in a Mental Impairment Case

1. Please state your name, occupation, and business address.

2. In conjunction with your appearance at this hearing today, you have been asked to provide a resume. Is this resume a true and accurate reflection of your professional qualifications?

    Counsel, do you have any objections to Dr. _____'s qualifications?

3. Prior to the hearing you were provided with a copy of the claimant's medical records as well as a copy of the Listing of Impairments contained in Appendix 1, Subpart P, Social Security Regulations No. 4. Have you reviewed these materials?

    And have you been present throughout the claimant's testimony today?

    And have you and I had any discussions prior to today's hearing concerning the merits of the claimant's case?

    Do you understand that your role here today is that of a neutral expert?

4. Are there any significant conflicts or deficiencies in the medical record?

    If so, please explain. (What, if any, examinations, laboratory tests, or procedures would you recommend to resolve any conflicts or remedy deficiencies in the record?)

    Are there any questions that you would like to ask the claimant concerning his/her condition?

    Counsel, do you have any objection to Dr. _____ questioning the claimant directly?

    (ME provided an opportunity to question the claimant.)

5. Dr. _____, I am now handing to you a Psychiatric Review Technique Form. [Editor's note: A copy of this form appears at §243.1, supra.] Under the Social Security Laws and Regulations, I must complete a Psychiatric Review Technique Form in every case that comes before me where the claimant alleges, or there is evidence which indicates, that the claimant suffers from a mental impairment. I now ask that you direct your attention to Part B of the Medical Summary section of the form which is on page 1. Part B lists eight different categories of mental impairments, cited as sections 12.02 through 12.09. If it is your opinion that the claimant suffers from a mental impairment or impairments, under which category or categories do you believe the mental impairment(s) would be best classified? (In cases where there appears to be a conflict as to the correct diagnosis of a claimant's mental impairment, the ME should be questioned as to his reasons for concluding that the claimant's mental impairment is given one diagnosis as opposed to another.)

6. Please turn to Part III of the Psychiatric Review Technique Form, "Documentation of Factors that Evidence the Disorder," which begins on page 3. Part III of the Psychiatric Review Technique Form corresponds with the paragraph A criteria of the mental listings under Social Security Regulations. Please direct your attention to (ALJ cites the applicable sections based on the ME response to question No. 5). In your opinion, does the claimant satisfy the paragraph A criteria of section _____? Please provide specific references from the record and/or the claimant's testimony which, based on your expertise in the area of mental illness and mental impairments in general, persuade you that the paragraph A criteria are met.

    (If the ME testifies that the paragraph A criteria are not met, no further questioning relative to the Mental Listings is required unless the claimant or his attorney elicits testimony from the ME which the ALJ believes raises the possibility that the paragraph A criteria may be met, then questioning should continue as follows.)

7. I now ask that you turn with me to Part IV of the Psychiatric Review Technique Form, "Rating of Impairment

Severity." This part of the Psychiatric Review Technique Form corresponds with the paragraph B criteria of the Mental Listings under Social Security Regulations. The paragraph B criteria are used to determine the degree of functional limitation which results from the claimant's mental impairment. Please rate the degree of functional limitation which you believe the claimant exhibits secondary to his mental impairment under the paragraph B criteria. Again, please give specific references from the record and/or the claimant's testimony which persuade you as to the degree of limitation from which the claimant suffers.

(Where the ME has testified that the claimant has a mental impairment coming under sections 12.03 or 12.06 of the Listings "schizophrenic, paranoid and other psychotic disorders" and "anxiety-related disorders," the ME should be questioned concerning his/her opinion concerning the evidence in the claimant's case and the paragraph C criteria of the applicable Listings section.)

8. (Where the ME testimony concerning the degree of functional limitation which results from the claimant's mental impairment reflects that the claimant has an impairment which meets the requirements of a listed impairment, the following question should be posed to the ME.)

In your medical judgment, when is the earliest date that the claimant's mental impairment caused the degree of functional limitation to which you have testified that the claimant suffers? In so answering, please indicate on what evidence you rely in arriving at the date which you have chosen. Also, please indicate if the record, in your opinion, demonstrates periods when the degree of functional limitation has been less than or more than the degree to which you testified in answer to the previous question.

9. (Where the ME has provided testimony which indicates that, in his/her opinion the claimant does not suffer from an impairment which meets the severity of a listed mental impairment, the following question should be posed to the ME.)

From your testimony thus far, it appears that you believe that the claimant suffers from a mental impairment. However, your testimony concerning the degree of functional limitation which results from the claimant's mental impairment indicates that the claimant does not suffer from a mental impairment of Listing-level severity. Based on this, please give your opinion as to the claimant's ability to perform the following nonexertional aspects of basic work activities using the terms "poor or none," "fair," "good" and "unlimited or very good."

a. Ability to tolerate normal work stresses

b. Ability to relate to coworkers

c. Ability to relate to supervisors

d. Ability to deal with changes in a routine work setting

e. Ability to interact appropriately with the public

f. Ability to use judgment

g. Ability to maintain concentration/attention

h. Ability to understand, carry out, and remember complex instructions

i. Ability to understand, carry out, and remember simple instructions.

§334 *Critique and Objections to ALJ's Direct Examination*

The sample direct examination is fairly complete. It deals with all of the issues except that it does not address the question of equaling the Listings, a subject difficult to put into form questions. We deal with this problematic issue below at §336.

In this sample direct examination, the ALJ gives the claimant's attorney two opportunities to object—to the medical expert's qualifications and to direct questioning of the claimant by the medical expert. The opportunity to object to the medical expert's qualifications is drawn from courtroom procedure when an expert witness testifies. However, because in actual practice there are so few objections to a medical expert's qualifications (and even fewer which are upheld), many ALJs fail to ask for objections. If you have an objection, consider taking it to the ALJ in advance of the hearing so that if your objection is sustained, a different medical expert can be scheduled to testify.

The opportunity to object to a medical expert questioning the claimant is apparently based on the lack of any regulatory authority for allowing someone not a party to question a witness. *See* 20 C.F.R. § 404.950(e). An objection on this basis will result in the ALJ asking the medical expert what questions he has. The ALJ will then repeat the medical expert's questions to the claimant if they are relevant. Given this alternative, it is unlikely that an attorney would want to object. If you do not object to allowing the medical expert to ask questions, you still may object to particular questions asked by a medical expert.

By far the most objectionable question asked by the ALJ in the sample direct examination is the one concerning residual functional capacity. The ALJ asks the medical expert to assess mental RFC using terms which are not defined in the question: "poor or none," "fair," "good," and "unlimited or very good." Apparently the ALJ has drawn these terms from a form titled Medical Assessment of Ability to Do Work-Related Activities (Mental), a copy of which appears at §245.3, *supra*. It is not uncommon, for example, that a psychiatrist or a psychologist used to dealing with psychiatric in-patients would rank as fair or good a claimant's ability to relate to supervisors if the medical expert thought the claimant was ready for sheltered work. Using the definitions stated on the form, a person who could relate only to special supervisors found in a sheltered work setting should be ranked "poor or none" because he has "no useful ability to" relate to supervisors "on a day-to-day basis in a regular work setting."

Whether to object to the ALJ's question or to wait for cross-examination depends on your assessment of how the ALJ will respond to an interruption as well as how difficult it will be to get the medical expert to use a different definition of the terms on cross-examination. If you decide to say something at the time of the question, do not say, "I object to the form of the question." Instead, say, "Excuse me, judge. Just so that I understand this question, are you using those terms the way they're used in the mental medical assessment form? If so, could you read through the definitions so that I've got them fresh in my mind?"

§335 *Meeting the Listings*

Do not assume that testimony by a medical expert that your client's impairment does not meet the Listings closes the issue. Make sure that the medical expert has considered all of the evidence, including testimony at the hearing; and always investigate the possibility that the medical expert has construed the Listings too narrowly. Inquire into the medical expert's interpretation of the Listings by having him define the terms in the Listings or describe a hypothetical individual who meets the Listings. Then have him assume a different definition of the Listing and inquire whether your client's impairment meets the Listing using this definition. (There are, of course, sections of the Listing of Impairments which are not subject to much interpretation; however, when such sections are at issue, ALJs tend to call medical experts to testify much less frequently.)

§336 *Equaling the Listings*

The regulations state that a claimant's impairment(s) will be found "medically equivalent to a listed impairment in [A]ppendix 1 if it is at least equal in severity and duration to the criteria of any listed impairment." 20 C.F.R. § 404.1526(a). SSA says that it can find medical equivalence in three ways:

> (1)(i) if you have an impairment that is described in [A]ppendix 1, but—

> (A) You do not exhibit one or more of the findings specified in the particular [L]isting, or

> (B) You exhibit all of the findings, but one or more of the findings is not as severe as specified in the particular [L]isting.

> (ii) We will find that your impairment is medically equivalent to that [L]isting if you have other findings related to your impairment that are at least of equal medical significance to the required criteria.

(2) If you have an impairment(s) that is not described in [A]ppendix 1, we will compare your findings with those for closely analogous listed impairments. If the findings related to your impairment(s) are at least of equal medical significance to those of a listed impairment, we will find that your impairment(s) is medically equivalent to the analogous [L]isting.

(3) If you have a combination of impairments, no one of which meets a [L]isting (see § 404.1525(c)(3)), we will compare your findings with those for closely analogous listed impairments. If the findings related to your impairments are at least of equal medical significance to those of a listed impairment, we will find that your combination of impairments is medically equivalent to that [L]isting.

[20 C.F.R. § 404.1526(b).]

When evaluating whether a Listing is equaled, SSA will consider "all evidence in [the claimant's] case record about [the claimant's] impairment(s) and its effects on [the claimant] that is relevant to this finding"; SSA, however, will not consider vocational factors—age, education and work experience. 20 C.F.R. § 404.1526(c). Although SSA reserves the right to determine equivalence, it says it will consider the opinion of a treating doctor on the issue of equivalence, even though it gives no special weight to that opinion because of its source. 20 C.F.R. § 404.1527(d)(2). SSA says that it "will not substitute [a claimant's] allegations of pain or other symptoms for a missing or deficient sign or laboratory finding to raise the severity of [the claimant's] impairment(s) to that of a listed impairment." 20 C.F.R. § 404.1529(d)(3). It is SSA policy that before an ALJ or the Appeals Council may find that an impairment is medically equivalent to a Listed Impairment, the ALJ or Appeals Council must seek the opinion of a medical expert (ME). SSR 96-6p. Note, however, that because the ALJ "or Appeals Council is responsible for deciding the ultimate legal question whether a listing is met or equaled," SSR 96-6p, the ALJ or Appeals Council can accept or reject that opinion. *See also* 20 C.F.R. § 404.1526(e). In other words, an ME can testify that your client's condition does not equal any Listed impairment, but the ALJ may nevertheless find that the Listings are equaled.

Read to the medical expert the definition of medical equivalence and explain the three circumstances under which equivalence may be found. Then, ask the following:
• What is the closest section of the Listing of Impairments to the claimant's impairment(s)?
• Doctor, conjure up in your mind an image of a hypothetical person whose impairment minimally

meets that section of the Listings. Do you think that the claimant's disability is as severe as the disability of this hypothetical person?

§337   *Residual Functional Capacity Testimony*

Consider this: If the ALJ does not open up the Residual Functional Capacity (RFC) issue, why should you? Often ALJs call a medical expert only for help in understanding the Listings. If the medical expert testified that your client's impairment does not meet the Listings, you can still win your client's case based on the treating physician's opinion about RFC. So why ask the medical expert any questions about RFC? It is true that sometimes a medical expert will help the claimant's case. He could testify that the claimant has an extremely limited RFC. But how do you know in advance whether he will help or harm the case? He could testify that the state agency physician's RFC assessment is reasonable.

If the RFC issue has not been broached by the ALJ in his direct examination of the medical expert, do not directly ask the medical expert to state his opinion about the claimant's RFC. Instead, if you are determined to get into this issue, approach it this way:
• The claimant has a medical condition that could produce the *type* of symptom he alleges, doesn't he? That is, the condition could produce [pain, etc.], couldn't it?
• Considering the differing individual tolerances for [pain etc.], do you think that the claimant's medical signs and findings show a condition that could produce the limitations described by the treating physician [or by the claimant]?

If the issue of RFC has been opened and damaging testimony is received from the medical expert, you have two choices: 1) wade into the issue with cross-examination; or 2) ask the claimant's treating physician to respond.

The reality of RFC evaluations is this: For every diagnosis and set of medical findings there is a range of possible RFCs because of differing individual tolerances for pain, for example. Some people are limited very little by their impairments. Many people are moderately limited by an impairment. Others, including many who apply for disability benefits, are severely limited. The RFCs of malingerers may fall outside the range of possible RFCs created by a medical impairment.

A medical expert who has read your client's medical records and listened to his testimony can really tell only if your client's alleged RFC falls outside of the range of possible RFCs for his impairment. He can do little more. Many medical experts will agree with this.

When a medical expert states a specific RFC, he does one of three things: 1) he accepts as reasonable the alleged RFC, the RFC stated by the treating physician; 2) he simply states an RFC of an "average man" with the claimant's impairments; or 3) he rejects the alleged RFC because he doesn't find the claimant credible and states an RFC which he thinks is appropriate.

Cross-examination of a medical expert on the issue of RFC is filled with pitfalls. If you can show on cross-examination that the medical expert was using an "average man" standard, you have helped your client's case. But it is hard to tell from the way RFC testimony is given whether the medical expert is using an average man standard or is assessing credibility. And if he is assessing credibility, on cross-examination you may find that this assessment is a reflection of improper bias and a usurpation of the ALJ's role (*e.g.*, "this man lacks motivation to work"); or you may find that the medical expert will state valid medical reasons for doubting your client's testimony about his RFC.

The medical expert may agree that the best way to assess work capacity is in a work situation. If so, in an appropriate case consider asking that the ALJ order a workshop evaluation at SSA expense.

§340 The Government's Vocational Expert

Vocational experts testify at the request of SSA in many more Social Security disability hearings than do medical experts. In fiscal year 2012 vocational experts testified in 75% of hearings compared to 14% for medical experts. The presence of VEs at hearings has been growing in recent years while the percentage of hearings with medical expert testimony has declined a little over the years. The growing presence of VEs at disability hearings is not a good thing for disabled claimants or for the lawyers who represent them. When a VE testifies, an element of unpredictability is introduced into a disability hearing that potentially could lead to similarly situated claimants receiving different outcomes. It is up to the claimant's lawyer to see to it that this does not happen—a heavy burden.

To understand why VEs testify so often today at disability hearings, it is necessary to look at how the Medical-Vocational Guidelines have been reinterpreted over the years by SSA and the courts. The Guidelines, which took effect in 1979, were designed and promulgated to reduce the need for vocational expert testimony in disability hearings. They were designed to treat similarly situated claimants the same and encourage consistency of decision making among different ALJs. In the early years, the presence of a VE at a disability

hearing meant that the ALJ had reviewed the hearing exhibits and concluded that the claimant could not do past work, at least not as the claimant actually performed it, and that the case was not one in which benefits could be granted or denied using the Medical-Vocational Guidelines alone to direct the outcome of the case. It may have meant that the ALJ identified a specific vocational issue that needed to be addressed by VE testimony. Today, it no longer means much of anything about an ALJ's view of a case when a VE is called to testify. Most ALJs call VEs in virtually all of their cases involving adult disability.

The Medical-Vocational Guidelines were designed not only to dictate the outcome of cases where a claimant exactly met a vocational profile described in the Guidelines, but they were also supposed to provide a framework for decision making in other cases as well, a framework that could be applied often by a decision maker without the assistance of a VE (although sometimes VE testimony was necessary for framework analysis). But over the years, ALJs and the Social Security Administration have transformed framework analysis.

At the same time, when no VE testified at a hearing, we lawyers have done such a good job of obtaining remands from the Appeals Council or federal court that more and more ALJs have concluded that if they are going to deny benefits, they may as well call a VE to testify at the first hearing. Indeed, from an institutional perspective, the primary purpose of vocational expert testimony is to meet SSA's burden of proof in denying benefits to a disability claimant. Using a VE's testimony, an ALJ can conclude that jobs exist in significant numbers within the claimant's capacity for working even if the original interpretation of the *framework* of the Medical-Vocational Guidelines would call for a different result. Thus, some ALJs use the Medical-Vocational Guidelines to find a claimant disabled only when a claimant's vocational factors *exactly match* a Medical-Vocational Rule in the Guidelines.

The Medical-Vocational Guidelines were designed to address the fundamental issues created by the Social Security Act, which provides that a claimant "shall be determined to be under a disability only if his physical or mental impairment or impairments are of such severity that he is not only unable to do his previous work but cannot, *considering his age, education and work experience*, engage in any other kinds of substantial gainful work which exists in the national economy . . . *in significant numbers . . . .*" 42 U.S.C. § 423(d)(2)(A), emphasis added. The Medical-Vocational Guidelines answer the question whether jobs exist in significant numbers for certain combinations of residual functional capacity (RFC), age, education and work experience, and the Guidelines set the parameters for assessing the impact of age, education and work experience in those cases where the rules themselves do not direct a conclusion whether a claimant is or is not disabled. In essence, the broad structure of the Medical-Vocational Guidelines was designed to address the issue of whether a claimant of a certain age, education and work experience with a certain residual functional capacity can be expected to adjust to other work; that is, whether jobs exist in significant numbers for certain combinations of RFC, age, education and work experience. Age is second in importance only to RFC as a vocational factor, but age doesn't affect work adjustment until a claimant is 50 years old (or, if illiterate or unable to communicate in English, 45 years old). 20 C.F.R. § 404.1563(b). It is only in conjunction with age that education and work experience affect the ability to adjust to new work.

Younger Claimants

For a younger claimant (under age 50 or under age 45 if illiterate or unable to communicate in English), the job of the vocational expert today is to determine how many jobs (positions) the claimant is capable of doing based on the claimant's residual functional capacity. If the claimant is capable of performing a "significant number" of jobs, he or she is not disabled. Education and work experience do not matter for younger claimants. *See* 20 C.F.R. § 404.1563(c) and the Medical-Vocational Guidelines. It is the decision-maker's job to determine what a "significant number" is. Over the years, ALJs have found an ever decreasing number of jobs to be "significant" when deciding cases for younger claimants and the federal courts have concluded, in effect, that as long as an ALJ said the number was significant, it must be significant.

In SSR 83-12, on the other hand, the decision maker was instructed "to decide whether the full range of sedentary work is significantly compromised." The medical-Vocational Guidelines say there are approximately 200 unskilled sedentary occupations. Rule 201.00(a). The actual count of sedentary unskilled occupations is 137 based on the 1991 Dictionary of Occupational Titles (DOT), the last edition. Whether you view it as 200 or 137, the full range of sedentary unskilled work is a tiny occupational base out of the 12,761 occupations in the DOT. It is reasonable to say that any significant compromise of such a small occupational base means a claimant is disabled. A mid-1980s letter from an SSA official to Attorney Carl Weisbrod stated that there was a significant compromise of the sedentary occupational base if a claimant was capable of performing only 15 percent of unskilled sedentary occupations that appear in the Dictionary of Occupational Titles. It is unlikely that any ALJ would apply the 15 percent rule today. Indeed, it is unlikely that many ALJs would inquire if the sedentary

occupational base was significantly compromised or even think about the issue in those terms. ALJs no longer look at occupations to assess the extent of erosion of the claimant's occupational base. ALJs today want to know how many jobs (individual positions) exist. ALJs generally like to have the numbers of positions for at least three DOT occupational titles.

For the emphasis on number of jobs, ALJs cite Rule 201.00(h)(3) of the Medical-Vocational Guidelines and SSR 96-9p. But neither Rule 201.00(h)(3) nor SSR 96-9p directs the ALJ to obtain a number of jobs from a VE and then use discretion to decide if that number is "significant." They both call for a much more sophisticated analysis.

Rule 201.00(h)(3) of the Medical-Vocational Guidelines provides:

> (3) Nevertheless, a decision of "disabled" may be appropriate for some individuals under age 45 (or individuals age 45-49 for whom rule 201.17 does not direct a decision of disabled) who do not have the ability to perform a full range of sedentary work. However, the inability to perform a full range of sedentary work does not necessarily equate with a finding of "disabled." Whether an individual will be able to make an adjustment to other work requires an adjudicative assessment of factors such as the type and extent of the individual's limitations or restrictions and the extent of the erosion of the occupational base. It requires an individualized determination that considers the impact of the limitations or restrictions on the number of sedentary, unskilled occupations or the total number of jobs to which the individual may be able to adjust, considering his or her age, education and work experience, including any transferable skills or education providing for direct entry into skilled work.

In SSR 96-9p, SSA acknowledged that "a finding of 'disabled' usually applies when the full range of sedentary work is significantly eroded," but, in an example of bureaucratic doublespeak, SSA warned that "the mere inability to perform substantially all sedentary unskilled occupations does not equate with a finding of disability. There may be a number of occupations from the approximately 200 occupations administratively noticed, and jobs that exist in significant numbers, that an individual may still be able to perform even with a sedentary occupational base that has been eroded." Nevertheless, SSR 96-9p states:

> Whether the individual will be able to make an adjustment to other work requires adjudicative judgment regarding factors such as the type and

extent of the individual's limitations or restrictions and the extent of the erosion of the occupational base; i.e., the impact of the limitations or restrictions on the number of sedentary unskilled occupations or the total number of jobs to which the individual may be able to adjust, considering his or her age, education, and work experience, including any transferable skills or education providing for direct entry into skilled work. Where there is more than a slight impact on the individual's ability to perform the full range of sedentary work, if the adjudicator finds that the individual is able to do other work, the adjudicator must cite examples of occupations or jobs the individual can do and provide a statement of the incidence of such work in the region where the individual resides or in several regions of the country.

SSR 96-9p also provides this guidance for questioning a vocational expert:

> The vocational resource may be asked to provide any or all of the following: An analysis of the impact of the RFC upon the full range of sedentary work, which the adjudicator may consider in determining the extent of the erosion of the occupational base, examples of occupations the individual may be able to perform, and citations of the existence and number of jobs in such occupations in the national economy.

Claimants Over Age 50

The role of the vocational expert in assessing the ability of a claimant over age 50 to adjust to new work has also changed since the Medical-Vocational Guidelines first took effect in 1979. In its original conception, if the Medical-Vocational Guidelines did not directly dictate the outcome of the claimant's case, it was necessary to determine the extent of erosion of the claimant's occupational base caused by medical limitations, a task for which VE testimony was often essential. For example, let's say a claimant who is age 50 has a high school education and an unskilled work background at the medium exertional level. He has no sitting limitations but because of his impairments is capable of standing and walking for only about 20 minutes at a time, a total of no more than 4 hours out of an 8-hour working day; and, although he is capable of lifting up to 20 pounds occasionally, he is capable of lifting only a few pounds frequently.

The Medical-Vocational Guidelines say that a claimant with the same age, education and work experience will be found disabled if limited to sedentary work (that is, he would be found disabled despite the capacity to

perform a full range of sedentary occupations) pursuant to Rule 201.12; but if he were capable of a full range of light work, Rule 202.13 of the Medical-Vocational Guidelines directs that he be found not disabled.

According to Social Security Ruling 83-12, an ALJ will need to consult a vocational expert "where the extent of the erosion of the occupational base is not clear" and the claimant's exertional capacity falls between two rules from the Medical-Vocational Guidelines that dictate opposite conclusions. That is, if the light occupational base for our hypothetical claimant "is significantly reduced . . . it could . . . justify a finding of 'Disabled.'" When the claimant's exertional limitations are somewhere "'in the middle' in terms of the regulatory criteria for exertional ranges of work, more difficult judgments are involved as to the sufficiency of the remaining occupational base to support a conclusion as to disability."

Using these rules, a vocational expert's testimony could be taken without ever getting into the issue of how many jobs exist in the economy within this claimant's capacity. The vocational expert could say that this claimant's exertional capacity is significantly reduced in terms of the definition of light work, that relatively few light occupations could be done by this claimant. Out of 1,571 unskilled light occupations in the Dictionary of Occupational Titles, only a handful could be done because most light occupations require frequent lifting of 10 pounds, the ability to stand and walk for prolonged periods and the ability to stand and walk for 6 hours out of an 8-hour working day. Thus, this claimant would be found disabled using Rule 201.12 from the Medical-Vocational Guidelines, the rule pertaining to a capacity for sedentary work. The issue of whether a significant number of jobs exist in the economy is addressed by the structure of the Medical-Vocational Guidelines, a structure based on DOT occupations which provides the framework for evaluating the factors affecting capability for adjustment to other work—exertional capacity, age, education and work experience.

In recent years, most decision-makers say that when the Medical-Vocational Guidelines are not directly applicable, the role of the vocational expert in assessing the case of a claimant over age 50 is to offer an opinion about the number of jobs in the economy that the claimant is capable of performing within the framework of the Medical-Vocational Guidelines. In our example of a 50-year-old claimant who would be found disabled if limited to sedentary work, an ALJ may ask for numbers of jobs only for light occupations. Then, it is up to the ALJ to determine whether this is a "significant number." Although ALJs tend to take an "I know a significant number when I see one" approach, the regulations require "full consideration to all relevant facts in accordance with the definitions and discussions under vocational considerations," 20 C.F.R. § 404.1569, and "full consideration must be given to all of the relevant facts in the case in accordance with the definitions and discussions of each factor in the appropriate sections of the regulations, which will provide insight into the adjudicative weight to be accorded each factor." Medical-Vocational Guidelines, Rule 200.00(e)(2). One does not often see decisions that assess whether the number of jobs is significant considering age, education or work experience or assessing a claimant's ability to adjust to other work as is required by these rules.

The original framework of the Medical-Vocational Guidelines provides a useful tool to be used by a lawyer for figuring out who ought to be found disabled. Indeed, before you invest years in a case, it might be a good idea to test the case using these rules. *See* §348 *ff*. But don't expect to win on this basis. You'll probably have to find some other way to win the case.

Numbers Testimony

At the same time that ALJs are finding ever decreasing numbers of jobs to be "significant," they are finding these numbers "significant" in relation to an ever increasing region. Instead of asking VEs to provide numbers of jobs in the region where the claimant lives, many ALJs ask for state-wide numbers or national numbers. Indeed, an ALJ training video in April 2013 provided this "tip":

> With very rare exceptions, an estimate of the number of jobs nationally is sufficient; there is no need for testimony on the number of jobs regionally.

> This is so because 20 CFR Sections 404.1566 and 416.966 say there must be a significant number of jobs in the region where the claimant lives OR in several other regions of the country.

> National numbers almost always embrace several regions, so the national number of jobs will be sufficient.

The Social Security Act says that "'work which exists in the national economy' means work which exists in significant numbers either in the region where such individual lives or in several regions of the country." 42 U.S.C. § 423(d)(2)(A). Note that the Act does not call for anyone to assess whether there are a significant number of jobs in the national economy. Instead, it looks like Congress intended that a "region" be the area within commuting distance from a claimant's home. But because Congress did not want differing results for someone who lives in a remote area compared to

someone who lives in a metropolitan area, it added "several regions of the country."

When SSA promulgated the Medical-Vocational Guidelines in 1978, it noted that Congress "'believes it is desirable that disability determinations be carried out in as realistic a manner as possible, and that theoretical capacity in a severely impaired individual can be somewhat meaningless if it cannot be translated into an ability to compete in the open labor market.'" 43 Fed. Reg. 55350 (November 28, 1978). "Where occupations are named that a claimant can do, the citations are meant to show that the individual has a meaningful vocational opportunity despite the limiting effects of his or her impairment(s) . . . ." 43 Fed. Reg. 55361 (November 28, 1978). In other words, to justify turning down a claimant, there must be a significant number of jobs in the area where the claimant lives that are within the claimant's remaining capacity for work so that the claimant has a meaningful vocational opportunity.

This is not to say that whether there is a "meaningful vocational opportunity" is ever an issue in an individual case. It is not. It specifically does not matter whether "work exists in the immediate area in which [the claimant] lives"; "a specific job vacancy exists"; or the claimant would be hired. 20 C.F.R. § 404.1566(a) (1) – (3).

SSA's system for determining disability has evolved in practice to place heavy emphasis on vocational experts' numbers testimony. This is ironic because while vocational experts do have some expertise in assessing vocational opportunities, they have virtually no expertise in assessing how many jobs exist for a particular RFC. SSA has no current studies showing how many unskilled jobs there are at various exertional levels or for various commonly seen RFCs, such as the RFC for alternate sitting and standing. *See* §§348.4 and 348.9. Indeed, there is no government source for the numbers of unskilled jobs anywhere in the United States. The best source of jobs data is from the U.S. Census Bureau, which many VEs do not use, and it is a rare vocational expert who uses Census Bureau data correctly. The methodology used by most vocational experts for the number of unskilled jobs barely rises to the level of an educated guess. If the case were in federal court, such an opinion will not meet the requirements for expert testimony set forth in *Daubert v. Merrell Dow Pharmaceuticals, Inc.*, 509 U.S. 579 (1993), and *Kumho Tire Co. v. Carmichael*, 526 U.S. 137 (1999). *See Donahue v. Barnhart*, 279 F.3d 441, 446 (7th Cir. 2002).

DOT

SSA expects vocational experts to identify some DOT job titles that are within a claimant's residual functional capacity and provide numbers of jobs existing in the economy for these occupations that appear in the Dictionary of Occupational Titles, which was the basis for SSA's regulatory definitions of exertional levels, skill levels and transferability of skills. The DOT formed the foundation of the Medical-Vocational Guidelines. According to SSR 00-4p, "Occupational evidence provided by a VE . . . generally should be consistent with the occupational information supplied by the DOT." Yet, because the DOT is so outdated—it was last updated in 1991— conflicts with it are inevitable, providing abundant fodder for cross-examination. If the ALJ does not ask the VE to provide DOT job titles and DOT codes, you should. *See* §§346 – 346.9.

Giving the ALJ Options

VEs sometimes say that their job is to give an ALJ options. Usually an ALJ will ask the VE a series of hypothetical questions that add more and more limitations. Because the initial hypothetical questions have few limitations, a VE invariably will opine that the hypothetical claimants described by those questions are capable of performing many jobs or perhaps a past relevant job, thus providing the basis for a finding of no disability for such hypothetical claimants. As more limitations are added, the number of jobs that the hypothetical claimants are capable of performing goes down, perhaps to zero, which provides the basis for a finding of disability.

In most cases where you deal with a reasonable vocational expert and a reasonable ALJ, the real winning issue is the claimant's residual functional capacity, not the VE's testimony. Your job is to convince the ALJ that the claimant's actual RFC is the one described in a hypothetical question to which the VE answered that there were few or no jobs. Minimal cross-examination of the VE may be all that is necessary. You need to make sure that the VE is asked questions that include all of your client's limitations and that the VE did not make any unwarranted assumptions. When a VE testifies that there are a lot of jobs existing in the economy in answer to a particular hypothetical question, you need to make sure that the VE is not over reaching.

Indeed, when you're dealing with a reasonable VE and a reasonable ALJ, you need to be very careful with any cross-examination. VE issues have become such fertile ground for remands, especially by federal courts, that lawyers are often tempted to launch cross-examination of the VE solely for the purpose of creating an issue requiring remand just in case the ALJ disagrees about the claimant's RFC. But such cross-examination can backfire. It can tick off even the most reasonable ALJ, who will undoubtedly view it as an aggravating waste of time, and might even inspire the ALJ to turn down your

client's case either because you have obfuscated the real issue (RFC) or because the ALJ wants to teach you a lesson about wasting his or her time.

But when you're dealing with an unreasonable vocational expert who bends over backwards to find jobs that hypothetical claimants can do, including past relevant work (*see* §§347 – 347.4), or the VE finds transferable work skills where none exist (*see* §§349 – 349.10), it is your job to cross-examine the VE. Although VE testimony presents many potential issues for cross-examination, you must be well prepared. This book will help you prepare, but there is only so much that a book can do. Preparing to cross-examine a vocational expert often requires knowledge of the way that VE has testified in the past. Many VEs, for example, have favorite jobs that they cite in case after case. Start keeping a list of such jobs and learn about them. You may find a basis for challenging particular jobs.

Some very organized attorneys keep files on every VE they have ever dealt with in disability hearings. Each file contains notes of testimony of the individual VE at many hearings. Some ambitious attorneys have even been known to send clerks to the federal district court to copy VE testimony from federal court transcripts. Such files make great fodder for cross-examination.

Although you will find in this book many sample questions to ask vocational experts, the questions are intended as examples provided more as food for thought than as templates for real world cross-examination. In the real world of working lawyers who appear before ALJs worried about whether the next hearing will begin on time, time constraints usually call for a tightly focused cross-examination rather than a broad ranging inquiry into all possible aspects of a case. Sometimes the best approach is to lay a foundation of doubt in the ALJ's mind by asking the VE a few well-chosen questions, perhaps requesting DOT titles and DOT codes. Then ask to hold the record open to submit additional evidence after you look up the DOT occupations cited by the VE to see if there are any conflicts with the VE's testimony. Or submit a rebuttal report from a VE you hired who thoroughly addresses vocational issues.

Needless to say, when a vocational expert testifies at your client's hearing, if you are properly prepared, you will discover that you have many more cross-examination questions than most ALJs have patience to listen to.

Practice Tips

1. Understand vocational issues, the exertional and non-exertional requirements of jobs and the job market.

2. Know the sources of jobs data administratively noticed by SSA, 20 C.F.R. § 404.1566(d), and understand that not one of these publications provides numbers of unskilled jobs in the economy.

3. Know the VE and the ALJ.

4. Try new approaches all the time. If you use the same approach to cross-examining an individual VE more than a very few times, it may not work. In fact, it may backfire.

5. As a rule, a friendly approach works better than slash and burn cross-examination. At the least, always start with questions that will yield answers on which you and the VE will agree.

6. Don't overlook the possibility of submitting a rebuttal opinion from a well-respected vocational expert.

7. Because of their usefulness in cross-examining errant VEs, portions of the 1984 VE Self Study Guide and the Vocational Expert Handbook, published by the Office of Disability Adjudication and Review in June 2011, are reproduced as Appendices 4 and 8 of this book, respectively. Although these two appendices deal with the same issues, there are sufficient differences in the two documents to make reading both of them useful in preparing to cross-examine a vocational expert.

8. The experience, knowledge, ability, understanding of the VE role, and the prejudices of individual VEs vary widely. In the unlikely event that you discover a genuine vocational issue in a case where no vocational expert has been scheduled to testify, you are presented with a golden opportunity: hire your own VE to testify or provide a written opinion. It is rarely wise to suggest that the ALJ call a VE to testify. Vocational experts are assigned to testify in rotation. If you have a choice, do not settle for potluck.

§341   Vocational Issues

There are a limited number of vocational issues in a disability case. They are:

1.   What are the physical and mental demands of a claimant's past relevant work as the claimant performed it?

It is unlikely that a vocational expert would be called to answer only this question. SSR 82-62 provides that "statements by the claimant regarding past work are generally sufficient for determining the skill level, exertional demands and nonexertional demands of such work." But when a vocational expert is present at the hearing, the VE is usually asked to describe the claimant's past relevant work. The regulations provide that a "vocational expert or specialist may

offer relevant evidence within his or her expertise or knowledge concerning the physical and mental demands of a claimant's past relevant work, either as the claimant actually performed it or as generally performed in the national economy. Such evidence may be helpful in supplementing or evaluating the accuracy of the claimant's description of his past work." 20 C.F.R. § 404.1560(b)(2).

2.   What are the physical and mental demands of the claimant's former job as generally required by employers throughout the national economy?

This issue comes up where a claimant is unable to do any past job as the claimant actually performed it, but a past job involved functional demands and job duties significantly in excess of those generally required for that job by other employers. The claimant will be found not disabled if he or she retains the capacity to perform the job as *ordinarily* required by employers throughout the national economy. *See* SSR 82-61 and §347.2.

3.   Can the claimant meet the demands of the claimant's previous work, either as the claimant actually performed it or as generally performed in the national economy?

The regulations provide that "a vocational expert or specialist may offer expert opinion testimony in response to a hypothetical question about whether a person with the physical and mental limitations imposed by the claimant's medical impairment(s) can meet the demands of the claimant's previous work, either as the claimant actually performed it or as generally performed in the national economy." 20 C.F.R. § 404.1560(b)(2).

4.   Does the claimant have skills that are transferable to a significant range of work?

The issue of transferability of work skills is a complicated one made relevant in some cases by the Medical-Vocational Guidelines. The issue is decisive for relatively few claimants since, even if it is determined that there are no transferable skills, younger claimants may be denied benefits based upon the capacity for unskilled work. In those cases involving claimants age 50 and over where transferability matters, there are different standards based on age for determining whether or not skills are transferable. *See* §349.

5.   Is the claimant capable of performing other work? Do jobs exist in significant numbers within the claimant's RFC considering age, education and work experience? That is, is vocational adjustment possible to other work? This issue includes the questions: **For a literate, English speaking claimant under age 50, how many jobs are available to a claimant with a particular residual functional capacity? For the rest, how much of the claimant's occupational base has been eroded by his or her impairments?**

These issues come up when the Medical-Vocational Guidelines do not direct a conclusion that the claimant is or is not disabled. For the Medical-Vocational Guidelines to be used, a claimant's RFC, education and work experience must coincide with the criteria of one of the rules in the Guidelines. Where there is no close fit between a claimant's characteristics and the Medical-Vocational Guidelines, the Guidelines must be used as a framework for determining the interaction of the claimant's remaining occupational base with the other factors affecting capability for occupational adjustment— age, education and work experience. *See* §348.

§342   Proper ALJ Questions to VE

Most SSA advice for questioning VEs appears in ALJ training materials. The HALLEX provides only a little information.

HALLEX I-2-6-74 provides:

C. Questioning the VE

The ALJ will ask the VE questions designed to elicit clear and complete information. The claimant and the representative have the right to question the VE fully on any pertinent matter within the VE's area of expertise. However, the ALJ will determine when they may exercise this right and whether questions asked or answers given are appropriate.

The ALJ will also ensure the following during questioning of the VE:

• If the VE's replies are ambiguous or overly technical, the ALJ will follow up with specific questions in order to obtain a response that is understandable to the average person.

• The ALJ will not permit the VE to respond to questions on medical matters or to draw conclusions not within the VE's area of expertise. For example, the VE may not provide opinions regarding the claimant's residual functional capacity or the resolution of ultimate issues of fact or law.

• The ALJ will not ask or allow the VE to conduct any type of vocational examination of the claimant during the hearing.

• If the VE bases certain testimony on an assumption, the ALJ will ask the VE to clearly describe the assumption on the record.

D. Hypothetical Questions

The ALJ may use hypothetical questions to elicit the VE's opinion about whether a person with the physical and mental limitations imposed by the claimant's medical impairment(s) can meet the demands of the claimant's previous work, either as the claimant actually performed it, or as generally performed in the national economy, or any other work in the national economy (and the availability of such work).

E. Conflicts With the Dictionary of Occupational Titles

Before the ALJ may rely on a VE's testimony to support a disability decision, the ALJ must inquire on the record whether there are any conflicts between occupational evidence the VE provided and information contained in the *Dictionary of Occupational Titles* (DOT), including its companion publication, the *Selected Characteristics of Occupations Defined in the Revised Dictionary of Occupational Titles* (SCO), published by the U. S. Department of Labor. The ALJ must identify and obtain a reasonable explanation for any such conflict. The ALJ also must explain in the decision how he or she resolved any identified conflict. See Social Security Ruling 00-4p: *Titles II and XVI: Use of Vocational Expert and Vocational Specialist Evidence, and Other Reliable Occupational Information in Disability Decisions.*

ALJs sometimes ask improper questions of a VE. Before we discuss the improper questions (*see* §343), it is useful to outline the proper questions ALJs ask. They are:

1. What are the skill and exertional levels of the claimant's past job as the claimant actually performed it?

2.   What are the skill and exertional levels of the claimant's past job as generally required by employers throughout the country?

3. Assuming that the claimant is capable of [describe hypothetical RFC findings, etc.], is the claimant capable of returning to past relevant work?

4. [Where the issue of transferability of skills is critical] If the claimant has the following residual functional capacity: [insert RFC], and the claimant is incapable of performing his skilled (or semi-skilled) past relevant work, does the claimant have any acquired skills that are transferable to some other skilled or semi-skilled work?

If yes,

• list the transferable skills;

• identify the jobs to which these skills transfer; and

• state the number of these jobs in the local and national economy.

5. [Where the Medical-Vocational Guidelines do not direct a conclusion of whether the claimant is or is not disabled] Assuming that the claimant is unable to

perform the prior work of [insert description of PRW], that the claimant has no transferable work skills, that the claimant's educational level is [insert educational level], and that the claimant's residual functional capacity is [insert hypothetical RFC], is the claimant capable of performing other work?

If yes,

• identify the jobs; and
• state the number of these jobs in the regional and national economies.

§343   Improper ALJ Questions to VE

Former Chief Administrative Law Judge Frank Cristaudo, who has spoken at training sessions for ALJs and for private attorneys, says that it is improper for an ALJ to ask a VE a hypothetical question that does not state limitations in terms of specific, work-related functional abilities. For example, Judge Cristaudo states that it is improper to ask a hypothetical question that includes a limitation to "low stress work" without explaining what sort of work that is. Likewise, any RFC that uses the uses the word "moderate," without explaining its meaning, is improper. "Moderate," after all, can mean anything from slightly more than "not severe" to almost Listing level severity. Descriptions of capacity that include the words fair, low, often, mild, excessive, repetitive, reasonable, or unreasonable may be improper because they do not describe specific, work-related functional abilities. *See* "Phrasing Hypothetical Questions to Vocational Experts Training Guide: Manipulative Limitations, Mental Impairment Limitations, SSR 00-4p," Appendix 6.

The most interesting list of improper ALJ questions to a vocational expert appears in a draft document not intended for publication without SSA approval, titled "Vocational Expert Manual: The Use, Questioning, and Testimony of Vocational Experts," written by Judge Cristaudo before he became Chief Administrative Law Judge. Judge Cristaudo's draft Vocational Expert Manual contains this list of improper questions to VEs, which we provide here as food for thought in edited form (some citations and examples have been omitted):

1. Asking VE if the claimant is credible or disabled.

2. Asking VE to determine the claimant's residual functional capacity (RFC) (i.e., by asking VE hypothetical question with non-functional RFC component).

a. Example, asking VE to assume claimant has "moderate pain and fair ability to concentrate" without including the specific

work-related limitations imposed by those symptoms.

b. If VE asked a non-functional hypothetical, VE should seek clarification of functional limitations before answering.

3. Asking VE for a medical opinion.

4. Asking VE if a "significant number of jobs exist" instead of asking VE to identify the approximate number of jobs which exist. ALJ, not VE, decides whether the number identified is a "significant number." SSR 83-12 states that VE provides "a statement of the incidence of such jobs."

5. Asking VE about factors not permitted by 20 C.F.R. § 404.1566(c) to be considered in deciding whether an individual is disabled: Inability to get work; lack of work in the local area; hiring practices of employers; cyclical economic conditions; whether job openings exist; whether claimant would actually be hired to do work the claimant could otherwise do; and claimant does not wish to do a particular type of work.

6. Asking VE whether claimant could compete with unimpaired individuals for available employment.

7. Asking VE whether claimant could perform in a specific occupation with the same degree of efficiency or productivity as individuals with less severe or no impairments.

8. Asking VE questions already answered the Medical-Vocational Guidelines or other regulation or ruling. SSR 83-5a.

a. Example: Asking VE to assume claimant able to perform full range of sedentary or light work when transferability of work skills is not an issue. *Hogg v. Shalala*, 45 F.3d 276 (8th Cir. 1995).

b. Example: Asking VE about effect on occupational base of the claimant's non-exertional impairments when Appendix 2 directs conclusion claimant is disabled based on exertional limitations alone. SSR 83-14; Section 200.00(e)(2) of Appendix 2.

9. Asking VE a hypothetical question which does not include all of the claimant's limitations established by the record, when the VE's response to the hypothetical is the basis for the decision.

10. Asking VE to name specific employers that have the alternative occupations identified by the VE. *Hardaway v. HHS*, 823 F.2d 922, 928 (6th Cir. 1987).

11. Asking VE to identify total number of all jobs in region or nation so that percentage of such jobs which the claimant can perform may

be determined; whether there are a significant number of jobs the claimant is able to perform is relevant, not whether the claimant is able to perform a significant percentage of all jobs which exist. *Hall v. Bowen*, 837 F.2d 272, 275 (6th Cir. 1988); *Martinez v. Heckler*, 807 F.2d 771, 775 (9th Cir. 1986); *Lee v. Sullivan*, 988 F.2d 789 (7th Cir. 1993); and "Evaluating Work Which Exists in the National or Local Economy: Significant Number of Jobs or Erosion of the Occupational Base?" *OHA Law Journal*, Vol. 4, No. 2, Fall 1994.

12. Asking VE to identify the number of "occupations" the claimant is able to perform without also asking the VE to identify the number of "jobs" in those occupations, or asking VE whether the number of occupations the claimant is able to perform is significantly eroded without asking VE to identify the approximate number of jobs which exist in those remaining occupations. *OHA Law Journal*, Vol. 4, No. 2, Fall 1994.

13. Asking VE hypothetical inquiries whether an employer would or could be required to make accommodations (as required by the Americans with Disabilities Act of 1990) that would allow return to a prior job or performance of "other work" would not be appropriate "because our assessment must be based on broad vocational patterns rather than on any individual employer's practices." We consider only the functional demands and duties of jobs as actually performed by the claimant in the past or as customarily performed in the national economy. June 23, 1993, memorandum from Associate Commissioner; *Eback v. Chater*, 94 F.3d 410 (8th Cir. 1996).

14. Asking the VE a hypothetical which includes a residual functional capacity based on non-functional medical reports (unless limitations are obvious to layperson). *Gordils v. HHS*, 921 F.2d 327 (1st Cir. 1990).

Judge Cristaudo's list is fairly representative of thinking within the Social Security Administration that the issue in step 5 of the sequential evaluation process is whether the claimant is capable of performing a significant number of jobs, not whether the claimant's occupational base has been eroded. Indeed, the concept of "erosion" is in disfavor in many parts of SSA.

Nevertheless, whether an ALJ *should ask* questions about erosion of the occupational base and whether a claimant's attorney *is allowed to ask* about it are two different issues. Since evaluating erosion of the occupational base as a way of determining what is a significant number of jobs appears in the regulations and rulings, it is hard to make the case that a claimant's attorney should not be allowed to ask such questions. Likewise, although it may not be proper for an ALJ to ask a VE to name specific employers that have the alternative occupations identified by the VE, it is proper for a claimant to ask this question as part of cross-examination.

§344 Improper VE Testimony

The VE Handbook, p. 8, Appendix 8, provides this advice to vocational experts: "Give complete answers to the questions you are asked, and do not volunteer information." They are expected to testify "only on vocational issues and only on those vocational issues which are relevant to the requirements of the statute, regulations and rulings." The *VE Self Study Guide*, p. 21, Appendix 4. Vocational experts are provided with citations to the vocational regulations and directions for finding them on SSA's website. *VE Handbook*, pp. 41-42, Appendix 8. They are given a list of the most important Social Security Rulings on vocational issues. See *VE Handbook*, pp. 42-44, Appendix 8. See also §271. The *VE Self Study Guide*, p. 21, Appendix 4, provides the following specific examples of improper testimony. A VE is not to:

a. Provide his or her own evaluation of the medical evidence. This is to be provided by the ALJ in the form of one or more hypothetical questions with similar rights extended to the claimant;

b. State whether the claimant is a proper candidate for vocational rehabilitation;

c. State whether a claimant can compete with unimpaired individuals for available employment;

d. State whether job vacancies exist or whether the claimant would be hired for existing jobs;

e. State whether a claimant can perform in a specific occupation with the same degree of efficiency or productivity as individuals with less than severe or no impairments;

f. State whether the claimant is or is not disabled.

An additional example of improper VE testimony occasionally seen in a Social Security disability case is where a VE raises the issue of job modification to accommodate a disability. The issue in a Social Security disability case is whether jobs *exist* within a claimant's RFC, not whether a job can be *modified* to accommodate a disability. Job modification is a "hire-ability" issue, not a disability issue. The Americans with Disabilities Act, 42 U.S.C. §12101, is not to the contrary.

It is SSA's position that the Americans With Disabilities Act, 42 U.S.C. § 12101, does not apply to the vocational issues presented by the disability sequential evaluation process. SSR 11-2p provides: "When we determine whether a person can do other work that exists in significant numbers in the national economy, we do not consider whether he or she could do so with accommodations, even if an employer would be required to provide reasonable accommodations under the Americans with Disabilities Act of 1990." According to a memorandum dated June 2, 1993, from the Associate Commissioner of the Office of Hearings and Appeals, at step four, "hypothetical inquiries about whether an employer would or could make accommodations that would allow return to a prior job would not be appropriate." Likewise, at step five, "[w]hether or how an employer might be willing (or required) to alter job duties to suit the limitations of a specific individual would not be relevant because [SSA's] assessment must be based on broad vocational patterns (as established by the various vocational sources discussed in 20 C.F.R §§404.1566(d) and 416.966(d)) rather than on any individual employer's practices." This memorandum which appears at §344.1 is also reprinted in *Social Security Forum*, Vol. 15, No. 7, July 1993, p. 8. The memorandum is quoted in *Eback v. Chater*, 94 F.3d 412 (8th Cir. 1996),

which rejected a vocational expert's testimony based on an assumption that employers would be willing to make accommodations under the ADA.

Some vocational experts seem to take so much to heart the admonitions listed above that they fail to consider valid issues. This is useful to keep in mind when cross-examining a VE. For example, although it may be irrelevant that a claimant cannot perform an occupation with the same degree of productivity as an unimpaired person, it is certainly relevant that a claimant cannot meet reasonable production standards.

The irrelevant "hire-ability" issue often blends into the relevant capability issue. For example, a VE is not supposed to answer a question involving the issue of work absences if the VE is asked whether or not a claimant would be hired if the claimant had an impairment that would cause the claimant to miss two workdays per month. However, you certainly may ask and a VE must answer questions about job attendance requirements:

• Can an employee who will be missing an average of at least two days of work per month meet customary standards for job attendance?

• Is an employee capable of sustaining employment if his impairment or treatment causes him to miss an average of two workdays per month?

§344.1   Americans With Disabilities Act—Associate Commissioner's Memorandum

June 2, 1993
Memorandum to: Headquarters Executive Staff
                Administrative Appeals Judges
                Regional Chief Administrative Law Judges
                Administrative Law Judges
                Supervisory Staff Attorneys

From: Associate Commissioner

Subject: Americans with Disabilities Act of 1990
          (Pub. L. 101-336)—INFORMATION

We have received several inquiries about the Americans with Disabilities Act (ADA) of 1990 (Pub. L. 101-336) and its potential effect on the evaluation of disability under the Social Security Act. The questions asked concern whether the ADA has (or will have) any effect on the vocational issues we assess at steps four and five of the sequential evaluation process.

The ADA addresses the major areas of discrimination faced day-to-day by people with "disabilities." It provides a national mandate for the elimination of this discrimination and enforceable standards addressing such situations. In assessing the effect of this important legislation, it should be noted that the ADA defines "disability" in relation to the ability to perform what it describes as "major life activities." Consequently, the term is not synonymous with "disability" as defined in the Social Security Act.

Title I of the ADA addresses discrimination in employment and provides that employers must make "reasonable accommodations" for individuals with disabilities (as defined in the ADA). As explained in the Equal Employment Opportunity Commission's implementing regulations, reasonable accommodations are changes in the work environment or in the way things are customarily done that either: (1) ensure equal opportunity in the job application process, (2) allow individuals with disabilities to perform the essential functions of positions held or desired, or (3) provide benefits and privileges of employment equal to those enjoyed by employees without disabilities (see 29 CFR Part 1630).

The Social Security Act, its implementing regulations, and the Social Security rulings currently contain guidelines to evaluate situations that might arise involving employer accommodations. These guidelines also apply to situations involving employer accommodations made as a result of Title I of the ADA. The following sections address some of the specific areas that may be of concern.

PAST WORK ACTIVITY INVOLVED EMPLOYER ACCOMMODATIONS

The regulations at 20 CFR sections 404.1565 and 416.965 address whether work activity is vocationally relevant, including situations in which an individual's previous work activity was performed under special circumstances (e.g., with ADA-related accommodations or some other special considerations). If the work was done within the relevant past, lasted long enough for the claimant to learn it, and was substantial gainful activity (SGA), the work is considered to be past relevant work (PRW). (For purposes of determining whether such work was SGA, the regulations at 20 CFR sections 404.1571 through 404.1575 and 416.971 through 416.975 also include provisions for assessing work performed under special conditions. These same rules would also apply in resolving employer accommodation questions raised at step one of the sequential evaluation process.)

EMPLOYER ACCOMMODATIONS THAT WOULD ALLOW PERFORMANCE OF PRW

The fact that an individual may be able to return to a past relevant job, provided that the employer makes accommodations, is not relevant to the issue(s) to be resolved at the fourth step of the sequential evaluation process. A finding of ability to do past relevant work is only appropriate if the claimant retains the capacity to perform either the actual functional demands and job duties of the particular past relevant job he or she performed or the functional demands and job duties of the occupation as generally required by employers throughout the national economy (see Social Security Ruling 82-61). Consequently, hypothetical inquiries about whether an employer would or could make accommodations that would allow return to a prior job would not be appropriate.

EMPLOYER ACCOMMODATIONS ALLOW VOCATIONAL ADJUSTMENT TO OTHER WORK

When we evaluate an individual's capacity to make a vocational adjustment to other work at the fifth step of the sequential evaluation process, we consider his or her ability to do work that exists in significant numbers in the national economy (i.e., either in the region where he or she lives or in several other regions of the country). We do not consider isolated jobs that exist only in very limited numbers or in relatively few locations. Consequently, the fifth-step assessment is based on the functional demands and duties of jobs as ordinarily required by employers throughout the national economy, and not on what may be isolated variations in job demands (regardless of whether such variations are due to compliance with anti-discrimination statutes of other factors). Whether or how an employer might be willing (or required) to alter job duties to suit the limitations of a specific individual would not be relevant, because our assessment must be based on broad vocational patterns (as established by the various vocational sources discussed in 20 CFR sections 404.1566(d) and 416.966(d)) rather than on any individual employer's practices. To support a fifth-step finding that an individual can perform "other work," the evidence (e.g., vocational expert testimony) would have to show that a job, which is within the individual's capacity because of employer modifications, is representative of a significant number of other such jobs in the national economy.

In summary, we must remember that the ADA and the disability provisions of the Social Security Act have different purposes, and have no direct application to one another. Employer accommodations for "disabled" workers are not new (although the legislative mandate to provide them is), and our current policies and procedures address the evaluation of such accommodations.

As the SSA component responsible for disability policy matters, the Office of Disability is closely following implementation of the ADA and will continue to assess the need for any disability policy changes. We will, of course, keep you informed of future developments.

Field personnel who have questions should contact their Regional Office. Regional Office personnel should contact the Division of Field Practices and Procedures in the Office of the Chief Administrative Law Judge. Headquarters personnel should contact the Division of Policy, Planning, and Evaluation. Since this is an evolving area, we would welcome communications raising new issues, identifying dilemmas, or expressing concerns or suggestions on the OHA/ADA interface.

Daniel L. Skoler

§345 Prepare Your Own Hypothetical Questions for the VE

Before the hearing, outline one or more hypothetical questions to ask the vocational expert. Base the elements of the hypothetical questions on the claimant's limitations that are documented by medical evidence, reports from treating physicians and any reasonable inferences about RFC that you can draw from the medical evidence. Start with a fairly conservative position. If there is more than one treating physician, there may be a range of choices. Important factors frequently get left out of descriptions of RFC done by physicians. You may fill these things in from the claimant's description of capacity for working, but be careful to make sure that the claimant's description is consistent with the medical evidence.

State your hypothetical questions in terms of specific, work-related functional abilities. As much as possible, use descriptions of capacity that appear in the Dictionary of Occupational Titles or its companion volume, Selected Characteristics of Occupations Defined in the Revised Dictionary of Occupational Titles. Avoid vague terms such as low stress, moderate, fair, often, mild, excessive, repetitive, reasonable, or unreasonable. Try to describe how often a claimant is capable of doing a particular activity in terms of never, occasional, frequent or constant as those terms are defined by the DOT. See §346.1.

Note, though, that there may be ambiguity when something can be done less than one-third of the day. If something can be done 15% of the day and you describe the claimant as capable of the activity "occasionally," the VE will assume that the claimant can do the activity one-third of the day. If you say the claimant can "never" do the activity, which means 0% of the day, the ALJ will think you're exaggerating your client's limitations. Thus, instead of trying to choose between "never" and "occasional," use a percentage of the day when something can be done less than one-third of the time.

Do not put all of your eggs into the "claimant's description" basket. Some ALJs ask a VE two questions: an extremely conservative one and a question in which the VE is asked to assume that everything the claimant says is true. Then when the VE identifies numerous jobs in answer to the first question and no jobs in answer to the second, a decision may be issued finding the claimant's description not credible.

For this reason, you may want to ask medically sound, hypothetical questions describing RFCs between the extremes defined by the ALJ's two questions. You may be able to convince the ALJ that, even if the ALJ does not accept everything the claimant says, the RFC described in your hypothetical question is reasonable and incorporates all of the claimant's medically determinable impairments. Or you may be able to ask for reversal rather than remand by the Appeals Council or federal court if you elicit the right response from a VE to a hypothetical question describing a well-documented RFC.

§346 Use of Dictionary of Occupational Titles (DOT)

The most valuable tool for cross-examining a VE about specific jobs is the DICTIONARY OF OCCUPATIONAL TITLES (DOT), Fourth Edition, Revised 1991. This two volume set, which contains brief descriptions of 12,741 occupations, should be in the library of every Social Security disability practitioner. There is a close link between the DOT and Social Security regulations. The DOT provide the definitions of exertional and skill levels in the regulations; and the grids, the individual charts based on exertional levels in the Medical-Vocational Guidelines, are based on the numbers of unskilled DOT occupational titles at each level of exertion.

Vocational experts are expected to be familiar with the DOT. See 20 C.F.R. §§ 404.1566-1569, the VE Handbook, Appendix 8 of this book, and the VE Self Study Guide, Appendix 4 of this book. It is SSA policy that SSA will rely on the DOT and other publications identified in the regulations, 20 C.F.R. § 404.1566(d), even though the DOT, last revised in 1991, is out of date. The Department of Labor stopped revising the DOT, replacing it with the O*Net, which has virtually no useful information for disability determination using the sequential evaluation process. See the O*Net at www.doleta.gov/programs/onet. However, in 2012 SSA entered into an agreement with the Department of Labor's Bureau of Labor Statistics to develop an updated Occupational Information System (OIS) for use in disability determinations. The new OIS may utilize aspects of the O*Net that can be adapted for SSA's purposes. The new OIS does not have a projected completion date. Some observers say it may be ready later this decade, but that may depend on funding for what is likely to be a complicated and time-consuming task.

In the meantime, SSA has told decision-makers that when making disability decisions, they are not to rely on the O*Net. See Disability Determination Services Administrators' Letter No. 507, dated June 30, 1999, from the Office of Disability and the memorandum from the Associate Commissioner for the Office of Hearings and Appeals dated December 3, 1999, "Current Status of the Dictionary of Occupational Titles (DOT) and Occupational Information Network (O*Net)—Information."

The O*NET does not classify jobs according to the same exertional levels used by the Social Security Administration and the O*NET uses a different approach to skill level. SSR 00-4p provides, "SSA adjudicators may not rely on evidence provided by a VE . . . if that evidence is based on underlying assumptions or definitions that are inconsistent with our regulatory policies or definitions."

In addition, SSR 00-4p provides that if vocational expert testimony conflicts with the DOT about the way a particular job is performed, the ALJ must obtain a reasonable explanation and set forth in the decision how the conflict was resolved.

DOT contains the following, among other things:

1. A listing of most of the jobs in the national economy as of 1991;

2. A description of the duties and requirements of those jobs;

3. An indication of the physical demands strength rating of the jobs;

4. The reasoning, mathematical, and language development required for the jobs;

5. The specific vocational preparation time (training time) required for the jobs.

You will discover that having a copy of the DOT alone is not sufficient. Additional information about particular job requirements is necessary, especially where one deals with the difficult issues of transferable work skills or the impact of manipulative or vision limitations. Companion volumes to the DOT and computer programs are available that compile job characteristics, such as those listed in the chart in §346.6, for each job found in the DOT. These resources use the same Department of Labor information from which the DOT itself is drawn. Consult SELECTED CHARACTERISTICS OF OCCUPATIONS DEFINED IN THE REVISED DICTIONARY OF OCCUPATIONAL TITLES, published by the Department of Labor in 1993; THE TRANSITIONAL CLASSIFICATION OF JOBS, by Janet Field and Timothy Field, published by Elliot and Fitzpatrick, Inc., 2004; or THE SPECIFIC OCCUPATION SELECTOR MANUAL, Fifth Edition, 2008, published by U.S. Publishing. *See* Appendix 2 for information about obtaining these resources.

§346.1   *Physical Exertion Levels*

According to 20 C.F.R. § 404.1567, the classification of physical exertion levels used by SSA is the same as in the DICTIONARY OF OCCUPATIONAL TITLES, but note that the work levels published by the Department of Labor in the DOT and its related volumes have changed since 20 C.F.R. § 404.1567 was first published. The work levels stated in 20 C.F.R. § 404.1567, which coincides with earlier editions of the DOT and SELECTED CHARACTERISTICS, published in 1981, may be summarized as follows:

Exertional Level	Requires Occasional Lifting and Carrying of a Maximum of	Requires Frequent Lifting/ Carrying of
Sedentary	10 lbs.	Small objects
Light	20 lbs.	Up to 10 lbs.
Medium	50 lbs.	Up to 25 lbs.
Heavy	100 lbs.	Up to 50 lbs.
Very Heavy	Over 100 lbs.	Over 50 lbs.

Sedentary jobs involve sitting; walking and standing are required occasionally. When walking or standing are involved to a significant degree, the job is classified as light even when the weight lifted is negligible. A job is also classified as light when it involves sitting most of the time with a degree of pushing and pulling of arm and/or leg controls.

The 1991 revised edition of the DOT uses different definitions of exertional levels, which recognizes that constant lifting increases the exertional level. These newer definitions, which are acknowledged by SSA at POMS DI 25001.001B.21, may be useful in cases where your client's past relevant work required constant lifting.

Level	Occasionally	Frequently	Constantly
Sedentary	up to 10 lbs.	negligible	N/A
Light*	up to 20 lbs.	up to 10 lbs.	negligible
Medium	20 to 50 lbs.	10 to 25 lbs.	up to 10 lbs.
Heavy	50 to 100 lbs.	25 to 50 lbs.	10 to 25 lbs.
Very Heavy	greater than 100 lbs.	greater than 50 lbs.	greater than 20 lbs.

Occasionally: activity or condition exists up to 1/3 of the time.

Frequently: activity or condition exists from 1/3 to 2/3 of the time.

Constantly: activity or condition exists 2/3 or more of the time.

*The definition of Light Work used in the 1991 Revision includes the following notation:

Even though the weight lifted requirements may be a negligible amount, a job should be rated Light Work:

(1) when it requires walking or standing to a significant degree; or

(2) when it requires sitting most of the time but entails pushing and or pulling of arm or leg controls; and/or

(3) when the job requires working at a production rate pace entailing the constant pushing and/or pulling of materials even though the weight of those materials is negligible. NOTE: The constant stress and strain of maintaining a production rate pace, especially in an industrial setting, can be and is physically demanding of a worker even though the amount of force exerted is negligible.

In POMS DI 25001.001B.82, SSA explained the "strength factors of work" as follows:

- Lifting, carrying, standing, walking, sitting, pushing, and pulling.
- This factor is defined by one of five levels: Sedentary, Light, Medium, Heavy, and Very Heavy. Most jobs require workers to expend energy to some extent. The amount can be affected by the worker's body position and the frequency of the repetition of the task.
- A worker in an awkward crouching position may experience as much difficulty exerting five pounds of force as when exerting thirty pounds at waist height while standing.
- A worker who continuously lifts, pushes or pulls 15-pound objects or carries them over long distances may exert as much physical effort as when lifting, pushing, pulling or carrying 30-pound objects over short distances on a frequent basis.
- In determining strength level, job analysts review body position, weight/force, and controls (hand/arm and foot/leg).

§346.2 DOT Specific Vocational Preparation and Skill Level

Social Security regulations define unskilled work as work that a person can usually learn to do in 30 days. 20 C.F.R. § 404.1568(a). The DOT sets forth training time for jobs called "specific vocational preparation" or SVP, which is the time it takes to develop the facility for average performance on the job. The different SVP levels correspond to SSA's definitions of unskilled, semi-skilled and skilled work in the following chart. We also provide the number of DOT titles per SVP level.

SSA Skill Level	SVP Level	Time	Number of DOT Titles
Unskilled	1	Short demonstration	191
Unskilled	2	Anything beyond short demonstration up to and including one month	2934
Semi-skilled	3	Over one month up to and including 3 months	2199
Semi-skilled	4	Over 3 months up to and including 6 months	1637
Skilled	5	Over 6 months up to and including 1 year	1205
Skilled	6	Over 1 year up to and including 2 years	1328
Skilled	7	Over 2 years up to and including 4 years	2055
Skilled	8	Over 4 years up to and including 10 years	1146
Skilled	9	Over 10 years	46

In POMS DI 25001.001.B.79., SSA explained SVP as follows:

The amount of time required by a typical worker to:
- Learn the techniques,
- Acquire the information, and
- Develop the facility needed for average performance of a job.

An individual may acquire SVP in a school, military, institutional or vocational environment through such settings as:
- Vocational training,
- Apprenticeship training,
- In plant training,
- On-the-job training,
- Essential experience in other jobs.

A 4-year college degree is equal to 2 years of SVP. Each year of graduate school is equal to 1 year of SVP.

If an individual has past work with a high SVP level, it may be appropriate to consider the length of the work, as well as the claimant's education when determining if work was done long enough to be relevant.

EXAMPLE: An RN has an SVP of 7 which would mean that this job is generally learned in about 2-4 years. If the nurse has a 4-year college degree, which counts for 2 years of SVP, and 2 years of nursing experience, the adjudicator would determine that the claimant did the job long enough to learn it unless there was evidence to the contrary.

Except in cases involving transferable skills, you will find that you are most concerned with unskilled jobs—those with an SVP 1 or 2. There are relatively few SVP 1 occupations found in the DOT. Here are the numbers of SVP 1 and SVP 2 DOT titles by exertional level. Also included are the numbers of semi-skilled and skilled DOT occupational titles by exertional level.

Exertional Level	SVP 1	SVP 2	Total Unskilled	Total SVP 3-9	Total by Exertional Level
Sedentary	6	131	137	1260	1397
Light	107	1464	1571	4747	6318
Medium	50	917	967	2803	3770
Heavy	25	400	425	739	1164
Very Heavy	3	22	25	67	92
Total	191	2934	3125	9616	12741

Based on Selected Characteristics of Occupations Defined in the Revised Dictionary of Occupational Titles, p. A-2.

§346.3 Example of the Use of the DOT: Nurse Assistant

Nurse Assistant is an occupation found in the work histories of many Social Security disability claimants. As a demonstration of how to use the DOT, let us see what we can learn about this occupation. You will find the pages pertinent to this demonstration in §346.4, and Appendix 3 of this volume. (Appendix 3 contains an appendix to the DOT with the current definitions of terms, something that is useful to have at your fingertips during a hearing.)

The DOT contains an "Alphabetical Index of Occupational Titles," located at the end of volume two. This is where we will start our search. At page 1327 (see §346.4), the following entry is found:

NURSE ASSISTANT (medical ser.) 355.674-014

The DOT code number has a specific meaning, which is explained in the introduction to the DOT. For example, the first three digits identify the occupational group. The middle three digits reflect different levels of complexity in dealing with data, people and objects—the lower the digit, the more complex. The DOT number will be used in the next step to find the job description.

The front part of volume one, beginning at page 1, contains a listing of job descriptions arranged in numerical order according to the DOT code. Location of particular numbers is made easy by the listing (much as in a telephone directory) of code numbers at the top of each page. DOT code number 355.674-014 is found at

page 258. See §346.4. There you will find a description of the duties of a nurse assistant, and the "definition trailer" for that job:

355.674-014 NURSE ASSISTANT (medical ser.) alternate titles: nurse aide

Performs any combination of following duties in care of patients in hospital, nursing home, or other medical facility, under the direction of nursing and medical staff. Answers signal lights and bells, or intercom system to determine patients' needs. Bathes, dresses, and undresses patients. Serves and collects food trays and feeds patients requiring help. Transports patients using wheelchair or wheeled cart, or assists patients to walk. Drapes patients for examinations and treatments, and remains with patients, performing such duties as holding instruments and adjusting lights. Turns and repositions bedfast patients, alone or with assistance, to prevent bedsores. Changes bed linens, runs errands, directs visitors, and answers telephone. Takes and records temperature, blood pressure, pulse and respiration rates, and food and liquid intake and output, as directed. Cleans, sterilizes, stores, prepares, and issues dressing packs, treatment trays, and other supplies. Dusts and cleans patients' rooms. May be assigned to specific area of hospital, nursing home, or medical facility. May assist nursing staff in care of geriatric patients and be designated Geriatric Nurse Assistant (medical ser.). May assist in providing medical treatment and personal care to patients in private home settings and be designated Home Health Aide (medical ser.).

GOE: 10.03.02 STRENGTH: M GED: R3 M2 L2 SVP 4: DLU: 89

You now know what a nurse assistant does. By decoding the definition trailer (in italics), you can immediately know the physical demands of the job, the language or mathematics development (education and other training time) required, how long it takes to learn the job, and the last time this definition was updated. The definitions for these codes are found at page 1009, volume two, of the DOT, which is reprinted in Appendix 3 of this book.

The GUIDE FOR OCCUPATIONAL EXPLORATION (GOE) code number, useful in comparing similar jobs, is 10.03.02; and the strength factor (STRENGTH) for the job is M or medium. The general education development (GED) for this job is 3 for reasoning, 2 for mathematical development, and 2 for language development. The specific vocational preparation (SVP) is 4, and the job description data were last updated in 1989.

Medium work is defined at page 1013 of the DOT, Appendix 3. It is work that requires the following:

> Exerting 20 to 50 pounds of force occasionally, and/or 10 to 25 pounds of force frequently, and/or greater than negligible up to 10 pounds of force constantly to move objects. Physical demand requirements are in excess of those for Light Work.

The GED for this job is as follows:

> Reasoning 3:
> Apply commonsense understanding to carry out instructions furnished in written, oral or diagrammatic form. Deal with problems involving several concrete variables in or from standardized situations.

> Mathematical Development 2:
> Add, subtract, multiply, and divide all units of measure. Perform the four operations with like common and decimal fractions. Compute ratio, rate, and percent. Draw and interpret bar graphs. Perform arithmetic operations involving all American monetary units.

> Language Development 2:
> Reading: Passive vocabulary of 5,000-6,000 words. Read at a rate of 190-215 words per minute. Read adventure stories and comic books, looking up unfamiliar words in dictionary for meaning, spelling, and pronunciation. Read instructions for assembling model cars and airplanes. Writing: Write compound and complex sentences using cursive style, proper end punctuation, and employing adjectives and adverbs. Speaking: Speak clearly and distinctly with appropriate pauses and emphasis, correct pronunciation, variations in word order, using present, perfect, and future tenses.

The specific vocational preparation (SVP) for this job is 4. This means that to perform this job a person must have over 3 months, up to and including 6 months, of training in vocational education, apprenticeship training, in-plant training, on-the-job training, or essential experience in other jobs.

From this information, you can determine whether this job qualifies as past relevant work. Remember, past relevant work must last long enough for the claimant to learn how to do it. It takes three to six months to learn to do the nurse assistant job. For claimants who have a nurse assistant job in their work background but did the job for six months or less, you may argue that they never learned to do this job. Thus, it is not past relevant work.

In addition, from the above description of this job, you may be able to develop an explanation of why your client cannot return to it, *e.g.*, inability to lift 50 pounds, inability to stand and walk for extended periods, inability to tolerate frequent job duty changes and emergencies, *etc.*

You also may be able to use this information in cross-examining a vocational expert on the issue of transferable work skills. In fact, as you can see from the job description, most of the tasks performed by a nurse assistant are things that people do for themselves in their daily lives. Thus, having had a job in which these same things are done may not provide a former nurse assistant with any special advantage over unskilled workers in the job market. *See* §349.7.

§346.4   Pages From DOT

355.667-010

355.667-010 MORGUE ATTENDANT (medical ser.)
Prepares bodies, specimens of human organs, and morgue room to assist PATHOLOGIST (medical ser.) in postmortem examinations: Places body in compartment tray of refrigerator or on autopsy table, using portable hoist and stretcher. Lays out surgical instruments and laboratory supplies for postmortem examinations. Washes table, storage trays, and instruments, sharpens knives, and replaces soiled linens. Records identifying information for morgue file. Releases body to authorized person. May close post mortem incisions, using surgical needle and cord. May fill cranium with plaster. May feed, water, and clean quarters for animals used in medical research. May prepare preserving solutions according to formulas. May preserve specimens and stain slides. May photograph specimens.
GOE: 02.04.02 STRENGTH: M GED: R3 M2 L2 SVP: 4 DLU: 77

355.674-010 CHILD-CARE ATTENDANT, SCHOOL (personal ser.)
Attends to personal needs of handicapped children while in school to receive specialized academic and physical training: Wheels handicapped children to classes, lunchrooms, treatment rooms, and other areas of building. Secures children in equipment, such as chairs, slings, or stretchers, and places or hoists children into baths or pools. Monitors children using life support equipment to detect indications of malfunctioning of equipment and calls for medical assistance when needed. Helps children to walk, board buses, put on prosthetic appliances, eat, dress, bathe, and perform other physical activities as their needs require.
GOE: 10.03.03 STRENGTH: M GED: R3 M1 L2 SVP: 2 DLU: 81

355.674-014 NURSE ASSISTANT (medical ser.) alternate titles: nurse aide
Performs any combination of following duties in care of patients in hospital, nursing home, or other medical facility, under direction of nursing and medical staff: Answers signal lights, bells, or intercom system to determine patients' needs. Bathes, dresses, and undresses patients. Serves and collects food trays and feeds patients requiring help. Transports patients, using wheelchair or wheeled cart, or assists patients to walk. Drapes patients for examinations and treatments, and remains with patients, performing such duties as holding instruments and adjusting lights. Turns and repositions bedfast patients, alone or with assistance, to prevent bedsores. Changes bed linens, runs errands, directs visitors, and answers telephone. Takes and records temperature, blood pressure, pulse and respiration rates, and food and fluid intake and output, as directed. Cleans, sterilizes, stores, prepares, and issues dressing packs, treatment trays, and other supplies. Dusts and cleans patients' rooms. May be assigned to specific area of hospital, nursing home, or medical facility. May assist nursing staff in care of geriatric patients and be designated Geriatric Nurse Assistant (medical ser.). May assist in providing medical treatment and personal care to patients in private home settings and be designated Home Health Aide (medical ser.).
GOE: 10.03.02 STRENGTH: M GED: R3 M2 L2 SVP: 4 DLU: 89

355.674-018 ORDERLY (medical ser.)
Performs any combination of following tasks, as directed by nursing and medical staff, to care for patients in hospital, nursing home, or other medical facility: Bathes patients and gives alcohol rubs. Measures and records intake and output of liquids, and takes and records temperature, and pulse and respiration rate. Gives enemas. Carries meal trays to patients and feeds patients unable to feed themselves. Lifts patients onto and from bed, and transports patients to other areas, such as operating and x-ray rooms, by rolling bed, or using wheelchair or wheeled stretcher. Sets up equipment, such as oxygen tents, portable x-ray machines, and overhead irrigation bottles. Makes beds and collects soiled linen. Cleans rooms and corridors. Bathes deceased patients, accompanies body to morgue, and places personal belongings in mortuary box. Administers catheterizations and bladder irrigations. Accompanies discharged patients home or to other institutions.
GOE: 10.03.02 STRENGTH: H GED: R3 M2 L2 SVP: 4 DLU: 86

355.674-022 RESPIRATORY-THERAPY AIDE (medical ser.)
Performs any combination of following tasks to assist personnel in Respiratory Therapy Department: Cleans, disinfects, and sterilizes equipment used in administration of respiratory therapy. Examines equipment to detect worn tubes, loose connections, or other indications of disrepair, and notifies supervisor of need for maintenance. Starts equipment and observes gauges measuring pressure, rate of flow, and continuity to test equipment, and notifies supervisor of malfunctions. Assists in preparation of inventory records. Delivers oxygen tanks and other equipment and supplies to specified hospital locations. Assists in administration of gas or aerosol therapy as directed by RESPIRATORY THERAPIST (medical ser.) 076.361-014 and prescribed by physician.
GOE: 10.03.02 STRENGTH: M GED: R3 M3 L3 SVP: 4 DLU: 88

355.677-014 TRANSPORTER, PATIENTS (medical ser.) alternate titles: escort, patients
Escorts or transports patients within hospital or other medical facility: Determines patient name, destination, mode of travel, time, and other data, following written or oral instructions. Directs or escorts incoming patients from admitting office or reception desk to designated area. Carries patient's luggage. Assists patient in walking to prevent accidents by falling, or transports nonambulatory patient, using wheelchair. Transports patient, alone or with assistance, in bed, wheeled cart, or wheelchair to designated areas within facility during patient stay. Delivers messages, mail, medical records, and other items.

GOE: 10.03.03 STRENGTH: M GED: R2 M1 L2 SVP: 2 DLU: 88

355.687-014 GRAVES REGISTRATION SPECIALIST (military ser.)
Collects and identifies remains of deceased military personnel, both buried and unburied, and evacuates bodies to rear area for burial activities: Searches battlefields and other areas for unburied dead and for isolated and unmarked graves. Exhumes bodies of buried dead. Examines immediate area for identification items, such as dog tags, watches, and similar personal effects, and transports remains and personal effects to rear area. Takes fingerprints, skeletal x rays, and prepares teeth chart to aid in identifying remains. Examines remains, removes personal effects, and records property inventory on designated forms. Records identity of remains including name, military unit, location, and cause and date of death. Indicates location of temporary graves on map, sketch, or overlay for purposes of future recovery.
GOE: 02.04.02 STRENGTH: V GED: R2 M2 L2 SVP: 3 DLU: 77

357   BAGGAGE HANDLERS

This group includes occupations concerned with carrying bags for passengers in train, bus, marina and airplane terminals; checking baggage and calling taxicabs; pushing wheelchairs for invalids; and connecting marine utilities to boats for customers. Occupations concerned with handling of baggage for guests of hotels and related establishments are included in Group 324.

357.477-010 BAGGAGE CHECKER (air trans.; motor trans.) alternate titles: luggage checker
Receives and returns baggage to passengers at motorbus or airline terminals: Prepares and attaches baggage claim checks. Stacks baggage on specified carts or conveyors. Returns baggage to patrons on receipt of claim check. May receive, weigh, and bill parcels for express shipment by bus. May weigh baggage and collect excess weight charge. May complete baggage insurance forms, determine rate from schedule and collect charge from customer.
GOE: 09.05.03 STRENGTH: M GED: R3 M2 L2 SVP: 3 DLU: 77

357.677-010 PORTER (air trans.; motor trans.; r.r. trans.) alternate titles: porter, baggage; redcap
Carries baggage for passengers of airline, railroad, or motorbus by hand or handtruck, to waiting or baggage room, onto train or bus, or to taxicab or private automobile. Performs related services, such as calling taxicabs, directing persons to ticket windows and rest rooms, and assisting handicapped passengers upon their arrival or departure. May clean terminal floors; wash walls, windows and counters; and dust furniture. When employed in airline terminal, is designated Skycap (air trans.).
GOE: 09.05.03 STRENGTH: M GED: R2 M1 L2 SVP: 2 DLU: 77

358   CHECKROOM, LOCKER ROOM, AND REST ROOM ATTENDANTS

This group includes occupations concerned with serving clients of checkrooms, locker rooms, or rest rooms. Includes storing apparel or valuables, issuing claim checks and returning items on demand; providing towels or soap; and over-seeing children in shower or rest rooms of schools and institutions.

358.137-010 CHECKROOM CHIEF (any industry)
Supervises and coordinates activities of workers engaged in storing guests' wearing apparel, parcels and other articles in checkrooms of establishment. Reviews printed schedule of activities to determine services needed. Assigns work schedules and keeps time records of personnel. Receives customers' complaints concerning quality of service and rectifies or instructs workers to rectify complaints. Submits reports of unclaimed or lost articles to hotel security department. Performs duties as described under CHECKROOM ATTENDANT (any industry).
GOE: 09.05.03 STRENGTH: L GED: R3 M2 L3 SVP: 5 DLU: 77

358.677-010 CHECKROOM ATTENDANT (any industry)
Stores wearing apparel, luggage, bundles, and other articles for patrons of an establishment or employees of business establishment, issuing claim check for articles checked and returning articles on receipt of check. May be designated according to article stored as Baggage Checker (any industry); Coat Checker (any industry); Hat Checker (any industry); Stand-By (motion picture); Wrap Checker (any industry).
GOE: 09.05.03 STRENGTH: L GED: R2 M2 L2 SVP: 2 DLU: 77

358.677-014 LOCKER-ROOM ATTENDANT (personal ser.) alternate titles: cage clerk; dressing-room attendant; locker attendant; locker-room clerk; personal attendant; suit attendant
Assigns dressing room facilities, locker space or clothing containers, and supplies to patrons of athletic or bathing establishment: Issues dressing room or locker key. Receives patron's clothing-filled container, furnishes claim check, places container on storage shelf or rack, and returns container upon receipt of claim check. Issues athletic equipment, bathing suit, or supplies, such as soap and towels. May arrange for valet services, such as clothes pressing and shoeshining. May collect soiled linen and perform cleaning tasks, such as mop dressing room floors, wash shower room walls and clean bathroom facilities. May collect fees for use of facilities, equipment, or supplies. May pack athletic uniforms and equipment for individual or team out-of-town sporting events. May attend to needs of athletic team in team clubhouse and be designated

ALPHABETICAL INDEX OF OCCUPATIONAL TITLES

NEUTRALIZER (soap & rel.) 558.585-034
Neverslip Stitcher (boot & shoe) 690.682-082
new-account interviewer (clerical) 205.367-014
new-business clerk (insurance) 209.687-018
NEW-CAR GET-READY MECHANIC (automotive ser.; retail trade) 806.361-026
NEW-CAR INSPECTOR (motor trans.) 919.363-010
News Agent (r.r. trans.) 291.457-014
News Analyst (radio-tv broad.) 131.067-010
News Anchor (radio-tv broad.) 131.262-010
NEWS ASSISTANT (radio-tv broad.) 209.367-038
NEWSCASTER (radio-tv broad.) 131.262-010
news information resource manager (library) 100.167-038
NEWS LIBRARIAN (library) 100.167-038
news library director (library) 100.167-038
NEWSPAPER CARRIER (retail trade) 292.457-010
newspaper deliverer (retail trade) 292.457-010
NEWSPAPER-DELIVERY DRIVER (wholesale tr.) 292.363-010
newspaper library manager (library) 100.167-038
newspaper-press-operator apprentice (print. & pub.) 651.362-034
newsperson (print. & pub.; radio-tv broad.) 131.262-018
newsperson (radio-tv broad.) 131.262-010
NEWSWRITER (print. & pub.; radio-tv broad.) 131.262-014
nib adjuster (pen & pencil) 733.687-042
Nib Assembler (pen & pencil) 733.685-010
NIBBLER OPERATOR (any industry) 615.685-026
NIB FINISHER (pen & pencil) 705.684-050
NIB INSPECTOR (pen & pencil) 733.687-058
Nickel Cleaner (any industry) 709.687-010
NICKEL-PLANT OPERATOR (smelt. & refin.) 519.362-010
Nickel Plater (electron. comp.) 500.684-026
Nickel Plater (electroplating) 500.380-010
NICKER (boot & shoe) 690.685-298
nicker and breaker (nonfer. metal) 614.684-014
NICKING-MACHINE OPERATOR (cutlery-hrdwr.) 609.682-026
nick setter (cutlery-hrdwr.) 609.682-026
NIGHT AUDITOR (hotel & rest.) 210.382-054
Night Baker (hotel & rest.) 313.381-010
night cleaner (any industry) 599.684-010
night cleaner (hotel & rest.) 323.687-018
night-clerk auditor (hotel & rest.) 210.382-054
Night-Court Magistrate (government ser.) 111.107-014
Night Guard (any industry) 372.667-034
NIGHT-PATROL INSPECTOR (fabrication, nec) 824.683-010
nipper (any industry) 932.664-010
Nipple-Machine Operator (machine shop) 604.682-014
NITRATING-ACID MIXER (chemical) 550.585-030
NITRATOR OPERATOR (chemical) 558.382-046
nitric-acid-concentrator operator (chemical) 559.682-062
NITROCELLULOSE OPERATOR (chemical) 553.684-014
NITROGLYCERIN DISTRIBUTOR (chemical) 559.664-010
NITROGLYCERIN NEUTRALIZER (chemical) 558.685-050
Nitroglycerin-Nitrator Operator, Batch (chemical) 558.382-046
NITROGLYCERIN-SEPARATOR OPERATOR (chemical) 551.685-102
NITROGLYCERIN SUPERVISOR (chemical) 559.132-038
Nock Applier (toy-sport equip.) 795.687-014
NODULIZER (cement) 579.685-034
Noise-Abatement Engineer (profess. & kin.) 019.081-018
NONDESTRUCTIVE TESTER (profess. & kin.) 011.261-018
NOODLE-CATALYST MAKER (chemical) 559.685-126
NOODLE MAKER (food prep., nec) 529.385-010
NOODLE-PRESS OPERATOR (food prep., nec) 520.662-010
normalizer (heat treating) 504.682-010
normalizing-equipment tender (rubber goods) 559.685-066
Notched-Blade Loader (cutlery-hrdwr.) 701.687-018
notcher (glass products) 673.685-070
NOTCH GRINDER (glass products) 673.685-070
Notching-Press Operator (any industry) 615.682-014
Notch-Machine Operator (rubber goods) 690.680-010
NOTEREADER (clerical) 203.582-078
Nougat-Candy Maker (sugar & conf.) 529.361-014
Nougat-Candy-Maker Helper (sugar & conf.) 520.685-050
Nougat Cutter, Machine (sugar & conf.) 521.685-102
Novelty-Balloon Assembler And Packer (rubber goods) 920.587-018
novelty-candy maker (fabrication, nec) 739.684-010
novelty-candy maker (sugar & conf.) 520.687-018
Novelty-Chain Maker (jewelry-silver.) 700.684-022
novelty dipper (dairy products) 529.482-014
novelty maker (paper goods) 794.684-022
NOVELTY MAKER I (dairy products) 529.482-014
NOVELTY MAKER II (dairy products) 529.482-018
Novelty-Printing-Machine Operator (textile) 652.382-010
Novelty-Twister Tender (textile) 681.685-130
NOVELTY WORKER (dairy products) 524.686-014
NOZZLE-AND-SLEEVE WORKER (nonfer. metal) 514.684-018

NOZZLE TENDER (nonfer. metal) 512.685-014
Nozzle Worker (mine & quarry) 939.684-014
Nub-Card Tender (textile) 680.686-018
NUCLEAR-CRITICALITY SAFETY ENGINEER (profess. & kin.) 015.067-010
Nuclear-Decontamination Research Specialist (profess. & kin.) 015.021-010
NUCLEAR ENGINEER (profess. & kin.) 015.061-014
NUCLEAR-FUELS RECLAMATION ENGINEER (profess. & kin.) 015.061-026
NUCLEAR-FUELS RESEARCH ENGINEER (profess. & kin.) 015.061-030
Nuclear Logging Engineer (petrol. & gas) 010.261-022
NUCLEAR MEDICAL TECHNOLOGIST (medical ser.) 078.361-018
nuclear plant control operator (utilities) 952.362-022
Nuclear-Plant-Instrument Technician (utilities) 710.281-030
NUCLEAR-PLANT TECHNICAL ADVISOR (utilities) 015.167-010
Nuclear-Powerplant Mechanic (utilities) 631.261-014
Nuclear-Powerplant-Mechanic Helper (utilities) 631.684-010
Nuclear-Powerplant Supervisor (utilities) 631.131-010
NUCLEAR-TEST-REACTOR PROGRAM COORDINATOR (profess. & kin.) 015.167-014
Nuclear-Waste-Process Operator (any industry) 955.382-014
Nuclear Weapons Mechanical Specialist (government ser.) 632.261-018
NUMBERER AND WIRER (textile) 689.587-010
NUMERICAL-CONTROL DRILL OPERATOR, PRINTED CIRCUIT BOARDS (electron. comp.) 606.382-018
Numerical Control Machine Machinist (machine shop) 600.280-022
NUMERICAL-CONTROL-MACHINE OPERATOR (machine shop) 609.362-010
NUMERICAL CONTROL MACHINE SET-UP OPERATOR (machine shop) 609.360-010
NUMERICAL-CONTROL ROUTER OPERATOR (aircraft mfg.; electron. comp.) 605.382-046
Numerical-Control-Wire-Preparation-Machine-Tender (aircraft mfg.) 728.685-010
NUMISMATIST (profess. & kin.) term
nurse (medical ser.)   see NURSE, PROFESSIONAL
nurse aide (medical ser.) 355.674-014
NURSE ANESTHETIST (medical ser.) 075.371-010
NURSE ASSISTANT (medical ser.) 355.674-014
nurse, certified (medical ser.)   see NURSE, PROFESSIONAL
nurse, children's (domestic ser.) 301.677-010
Nurse, College (medical ser.) 075.124-010
NURSE, CONSULTANT (medical ser.) 075.127-014
nurse, first aid (any industry) 354.677-010
NURSE, GENERAL DUTY (medical ser.) 075.364-010
NURSE, HEAD (medical ser.) 075.137-014
Nurse, Infants' (domestic ser.) 301.677-010
NURSE, INFECTION CONTROL (medical ser.) 075.127-034
NURSE, INSTRUCTOR (medical ser.) 075.124-018
nurse, licensed (medical ser.)   see NURSE, PROFESSIONAL
NURSE, LICENSED PRACTICAL (medical ser.) 079.374-014
NURSE-MIDWIFE (medical ser.) 075.264-014
NURSE, OFFICE (medical ser.) 075.374-014
NURSE, PRACTICAL (medical ser.) 354.374-010
NURSE PRACTITIONER (medical ser.) 075.264-010
NURSE, PRIVATE DUTY (medical ser.) 075.374-018
NURSE, PROFESSIONAL (medical ser.) term
nurse, registered (medical ser.)   see NURSE, PROFESSIONAL
Nursery Laborer (agriculture) 405.687-014
NURSERY SCHOOL ATTENDANT (any industry) 359.677-018
NURSE, SCHOOL (medical ser.) 075.124-010
nurse, special (medical ser.) 075.374-018
nurse, staff (medical ser.) 075.364-010
NURSE, STAFF, COMMUNITY HEALTH (medical ser.) 075.124-014
nurse, staff, industrial (medical ser.) 075.374-022
NURSE, STAFF, OCCUPATIONAL HEALTH NURSING (medical ser.) 075.374-022
NURSE, SUPERVISOR (medical ser.) 075.167-010
NURSE, SUPERVISOR, COMMUNITY-HEALTH NURSING (medical ser.) 075.127-026
NURSE, SUPERVISOR, EVENING-OR-NIGHT (medical ser.) 075.127-030
nurse supervisor, industrial nursing (medical ser.) 075.137-010
NURSE, SUPERVISOR, OCCUPATIONAL HEALTH NURSING (medical ser.) 075.137-010
Nursing Home Administrator (medical ser.) 187.117-010
NUT-AND-BOLT ASSEMBLER (nut & bolt) 929.587-010
NUT CHOPPER (can. & preserv.; food prep., nec; sugar & conf.) 521.686-046
nut-dehydrator operator (can. & preserv.) 523.685-066
NUT FORMER (nut & bolt) 612.462-014
NUT GRINDER (can. & preserv.) 521.685-234
Nut Orchardist (agriculture) 403.161-010
nut picker (can. & preserv.) 521.687-086
NUT-PROCESS HELPER (can. & preserv.) 529.486-010
nutrition aide (government ser.) 195.367-022
nutrition consultant (any industry) 199.251-010

§346.5   Example of the Use of Materials that Supplement the DOT: Surveillance-System Monitor

Surveillance-System Monitor is an example of a sedentary, unskilled job which appears in the DOT. It is a job that you may hear about from VEs, even though this job may not exist at all, let alone in significant numbers. This job, by the way, is the one unskilled sedentary occupation which requires no reaching, handling, or fingering; see chart in §346.6.

To demonstrate the sort of information available in resources supplementing the DOT (and on the off chance your client's capacity to do this particular job ever becomes a crucial issue in his case) we provide this discussion.

The DOT provides:

379.367-010 Surveillance-System Monitor (government ser.)

Monitors premises of public transportation terminals to detect crimes or disturbances, using closed circuit television monitors, and notifies authorities by telephone of need for corrective action. Observes television screens that transmit in sequence views of transportation facility sites. Pushes hold button to maintain surveillance of location where incident is developing, and telephones police or other designated agency to notify authorities of location of disruptive activity. Adjusts monitor controls when required to improve reception, and notifies repair services of equipment malfunctions.

GOE 04.02.03. STRENGTH: S GED: R3 M1 L3 SVP: 2 DLU 86

The definition trailer tells us that this job is rated *R3 M1 L3* on the scale of general educational development (GED). R3 means that a worker in a Surveillance-System Monitor position must be capable of sufficient *reasoning* to apply common sense understanding to carry out instructions furnished in written, oral, or diagrammatic form. The worker must deal with problems involving several concrete variables in or from standardized situations. *Mathematical Development* at level 1 requires the ability to add and subtract two-digit numbers, and to multiply and divide 10's and 100's by 2, 3, 4, and 5. *Language Development* at level 3 requires the ability to read novels, magazines, and encyclopedias. The worker must be able to read safety rules and instruction manuals; have the skills to write reports and essays with proper format, punctuation, spelling, and grammar, using all parts of speech; and possess the ability to speak before an audience with poise, voice control, confidence, and proper English. *See* Appendix 3.

As you can see, the DOT provides useful information about this job; but if you evaluate this job using SELECTED CHARACTERISTICS OF OCCUPATIONS DEFINED IN THE REVISED DICTIONARY OF OCCUPATIONAL TITLES, CLASSIFICATIONS OF JOBS or a similar resource that gives the full range of Department of Labor coding for the job, you will discover even more useful information. You will find the following: this job requires frequent talking, hearing, and near visual acuity. A surveillance-system monitor must have the temperament to perform "repetitive or short cycle work." According to the REVISED HANDBOOK FOR ANALYZING JOBS, performing "repetitive or short cycle work" involves "performing a few routine and uninvolved tasks over and over again according to set procedures, sequence, or pace with little opportunity for diversion or interruption." A surveillance-system monitor must also work under specific instructions and deal effectively with people. Intelligence, that is, the ability to understand instructions and underlying principles, reasoning, and the ability to make judgments, must be equal to that found in the middle third of the population. This intelligence requirement is a significant difference from most sedentary unskilled work, 90 percent of which can be performed by individuals who are well below average. *See* the chart in §346.6. Likewise, verbal skills, the ability to understand meanings of words and the ideas associated with them and then use them effectively, must be equal to the middle third of the population, also a significant difference from most unskilled sedentary work. *See* §346.6.

If surveillance system monitor is offered in response to a hypothetical question that includes an allowance for being off task up to, say, 10% of the day, ask how long a person would keep this job if he or she were missing 10% of the events being monitored.

If a VE ever seriously suggests that your client is not disabled because your client is capable of performing this job, ask the VE how many surveillance-system monitor positions exist exactly as described in the DOT. Note that this job was analyzed by the Department of Labor as it exists in government service, specifically in government operated mass transit systems. Does your local area contain a government operated light rail system? How many surveillance-system monitor positions exist in that system? Notice how narrowly defined the equipment use is for this job.

If the VE responds that similar positions exist, ask if similar positions require the use of a radio, or if the worker must monitor alarm systems. Don't many similar positions require the worker to keep track of the names and locations of other security personnel? If these additional requirements are present, doesn't this become a semi-skilled job with an SVP higher than 2, rather than an unskilled job with an SVP of 1 or 2? *See* Dispatcher Radio (government ser.), DOT 379.362-010, SVP 4. Similarly, the inclusion of other security duties, such as patrolling on foot, using a ladder to adjust or maintain camera equipment (rather than the monitor), or working with others to restrain intruders, will take this job out of the sedentary category.

When cross-examination does not obtain concessions from the VE, it may be necessary to retain your own vocational expert to provide an opinion. Several attorneys in different cities have commissioned labor market surveys, not one of which has demonstrated that the security monitor position exists in large numbers. These surveys have discovered that most security guards whose jobs include watching video monitors also include other duties that either take the job out of the sedentary range or out of the unskilled category. For example, many such guards are deliberately assigned other duties at various intervals because their employers found that the guards' attention began to wander after only a couple of hours of watching video monitors. In addition, it is good security practice to randomly rotate job duties and locations to make it more difficult for a crooked security guard working with an accomplice to be involved in theft, *etc*. Also, even for those jobs that primarily involve watching monitors, many employers require security guards to assist with the apprehension of suspects and many require the guards to make rounds. Computer operation skills are often required. The ability to provide customer service to individuals experiencing a crisis and to work under high stress was required in many such positions.

A vocational expert report prepared for the author is included as a sample to show what can be done in such a report. The author provided to VE Keith Moglowsky a list of places where SSA VEs had testified at hearings that unskilled sedentary Surveillance-System Monitors were employed. The result of VE Moglowsky's investigation appears at §346.5.1.

§346.5.1   Sample Vocational Expert Report Re: Surveillance System Monitor

ampbell & associates, llc

1166 Quail Court, Suite 305, Pewaukee, WI 53072
262.695.6100 * * * 262.695.6102 (fax)

November 24, 2014

Attorney Thomas E. Bush
Bush Law Office
310 West Wisconsin Avenue, Suite 930E
Milwaukee, WI 53203

RE: SURVEILLANCE SYSTEM MONITOR
       OUR FILE NUMBER: 15459-KM

Dear Attorney Bush:

You have requested that I conduct labor market research and provide a professional opinion regarding surveillance-system monitor positions as defined by the U.S. Department of Labor.[1] When conducting my research, I also relied upon data from the **O-Net**, Wisconsin Department of Workforce Development/ U.S. Bureau of Labor Statistics **Occupational Employment Statistics (OES)**, the **Specific Occupation Selector Manual** which provides "crosswalks" for census, **SOC**, and **DOT** codes, as well as **Occupational Employment Quarterly II (OEQ)**. The last two sources are from U.S. Publishing, a private firm not affiliated with the U.S. government. However, their data sources include the Department of Labor's **OES**, Unemployment Statistics, as well as the **DOT**.

The position of surveillance system monitor (379.367-010) is defined by the **DOT** as an unskilled Sedentary job, with an SVP of 2. The job description is as follows:

> Monitors premises of public transportation terminals to detect crimes or disturbances, using closed circuit television monitors, and notifies authorities by telephone of need for corrective action: Observes television screens that transmit in sequence views of transportation facility sites. Pushes hold button to maintain surveillance of location where incident is developing, and telephones police or other designated agency to notify authorities of location of disruptive activity. Adjusts monitor controls when required to improve reception, and notifies repair service of equipment malfunctions.

This **DOT** job title corresponds with Census code 395 and SOC code 33-9099 for protective service workers, all other. There are five **DOT** titles under this **SOC** code,

---

[1] U.S. Department of Labor, Employer & Training Administration, **Dictionary of Occupational Titles (DOT), 4th Edition, Revised 1991**

Page 2
November 24, 2014
THOMAS E. BUSH
RE: SURVEILLANCE SYSTEM MONITOR

but surveillance system monitor is the only one that is Sedentary and unskilled. Three others are light occupations; one is medium.

Numbers of jobs in the economy are gathered by the states' workforce development agencies and are provided to the US Department of Labor, Bureau of Labor Statistics which compiles them by **SOC** code. There is no official government source for numbers of jobs by individual **DOT** title or by exertional level and skill level. Only U.S. Publishing in its **OEQ** attempts to provide an estimate of the number of jobs by exertional and skill level. But its numbers must be viewed with skepticism because of its methodology.

U.S. Publishing arrives at its estimate of the number of unskilled Sedentary jobs by assuming that jobs are evenly distributed among **DOT** occupations, which is an assumption that rarely corresponds to the real world. To arrive at the number of unskilled Sedentary jobs in a particular **SOC** code, U.S. Publishing divides the total number of jobs in the **SOC** code by the total number of **DOT** occupations in that **SOC** code and then multiplies by the number of Sedentary unskilled occupations in the **SOC** code. Although sometimes U.S. Publishing makes a minor adjustment to the total number of unskilled Sedentary jobs in an **SOC** code, it makes no effort to identify **DOT** occupations that no longer exist, which ought to be the threshold issue, considering how long ago various **DOT** titles were last updated.

The first quarter 2014 **OEQ** for the state of Wisconsin, **OEQ** estimates that there were 1,472 protective service workers, with 299 working in an unskilled Sedentary capacity. For the Milwaukee metro area, it is estimated there were 65 persons out of a total of 302 respectively. Thus, the numbers were boosted slightly compared to strict application of the formula. Note that because surveillance-system monitor is the only unskilled sedentary occupation in this **SOC** code, these numbers constitute U.S. Publishing's estimate of how many surveillance-system monitor jobs there are in the Milwaukee metro area and the state of Wisconsin.

However, my opinion is that this occupation, surveillance-system monitor, as described in the **DOT** no longer exists. My opinion is based on the fact that this occupation was last updated in the **DOT** in 1986, as well as the **DOT** description of this occupation, which places it under the Government Services category with which I am familiar. I also spoke with our state Department of Transportation regarding surveillance/security positions at the Milwaukee Intermodal Station. See below.

You have informed me that while vocational experts in Social Security disability cases usually agree that unskilled Sedentary surveillance system monitor jobs no longer exist in the government services industry, they often testify that a similar position exists in other industries. That is, they testify that there are unskilled Sedentary jobs in which workers watch video monitors similar to the surveillance-system monitor occupation described in the **DOT** but working in industries such as security, gambling or retail. You have asked me to assess this assertion.

•   •   •   •   •   •   •   •

Page 3
November 24, 2014
THOMAS E. BUSH
RE: SURVEILLANCE SYSTEM MONITOR

The description of surveillance-system monitor is different in many facets, when compared to that of a gaming surveillance officer or gambling monitor (343.367-014), and that of a retail security guard (372.667-034). These latter two positions fall under Census code 392. The first falls under **SOC** code 33-9031, gaming surveillance officers and gaming investigators. The other one falls under **SOC** code 33-9032, security guards.

Gambling monitor is a Light skilled position, with an SVP of 7.

Security Guard positions range from unskilled to semiskilled with SVP ranging from 2 to 4, and Light to Medium strength demands. The only unskilled occupation listed is for an airline security representative (372.667-010), which has drastically changed since the September 11 terrorist attacks. Persons in this position are federal employees under the TSA. Through my work with the U.S. Department of Labor, Office of Workers Compensation Programs, I am certain this position is now a Heavy skilled job.

All other **SOC** and census code titles are categorized as semiskilled. Armored car guard and driver positions are Medium, with the rest having Light physical demands. A retail security officer would be categorized as Light semiskilled work under these occupational publications.

In an effort to find out if there are any unskilled surveillance system monitor positions in industries other than government services, I conducted labor market research using Wisconsin Department of Workforce Development's Job Center of Wisconsin website for the entire state, in addition to immediate areas of border states including Illinois, Iowa, Minnesota, and Michigan. I also searched other employment websites for the entire United States. Contact was initiated with several employers as outlined below, to obtain actual information regarding prerequisite hiring requirements, physical demands, and job duties for these occupations.

I recognize that finding no job openings does not prove that the occupation does not exist, though if I found even one Sedentary unskilled surveillance system monitor job opening, it would prove that the job does exist. I found no job openings.

I also contacted employers to obtain actual information regarding hiring requirements, physical demands and job duties for occupations similar to the surveillance system monitor described in the **DOT**.

        •   •   •   •   •   •   •   •

Potawatomi Casinos
Surveillance Operator I

Unlike security officers here, surveillance operators are employees of the Forest County Potawatomi Tribe and not the casino. Persons working in this position regularly spend time at a workstation in an office environment watching video,

Page 4
November 24, 2014
THOMAS E. BUSH
RE: SURVEILLANCE SYSTEM MONITOR

completing reports and daily logs, and communicate with others via two-way radio. I was informed that surveillance operators are also on the gaming floor. A high school diploma is required with a post-secondary degree or prior experience in gaming operations, with specific knowledge of Indian gaming preferred. One needs prerequisite computer skills in order to operate equipment and to write reports. There is significant ongoing training for this position. Physical requirements include up to 20 pounds lifting, regular sitting, standing, and walking, use of the hands and fingers, 20/20 corrected color vision, ability to be exposed to moderate to loud noise levels, and tolerate exposure to heavy tobacco smoke when on the gaming floor. There are no openings at the present time.

Ho-Chunk Nation
Surveillance Agents

Ho-Chunk Nation has casinos in Madison, Nekoosa, Tomah, Wisconsin Dells, and Wittenberg. One must have a high school diploma or equivalent for this position. At least one year of experience in surveillance/security or military is preferred. Agents report status of all surveillance equipment and follow preventative maintenance schedules. They must be willing to learn different types of prosecuting alternatives within local, state, and federal authorities. One must possess ability to acquire working knowledge of investigative techniques and undercover operations through tribal-related casino courses. Applicants also must be bondable, have 20/20 eyesight with no color blindness and be physically able to attend all courses in both surveillance and security departments. Job duties and physical demands involve primarily sitting and observing video in close quarters, but may involve substantial standing, walking, and climbing, when performing preventative maintenance on cameras and other equipment. There are openings in Madison and Wisconsin Dells.

Oneida Casinos
Surveillance Officer

I was informed that this job is primarily sedentary, working in close quarters in a confined area, but physical requirements also require lifting up to 25 pounds occasionally. There can be some walking, exposure to high noise levels, as well as second-hand smoke when on the gaming floor or in other public areas. This job would be considered skilled, as at least two years experience in law enforcement, criminal justice, police science, table games, work as a slot technician, and/or any combination of experience are required. A closely related Associate degree is preferred. One must also be able to type 30 wpm, have report writing skills, and experience in using business computers, working in a Windows environment, specifically MS Word. There is additional training and education required, such as learning how to operate surveillance and video equipment, Class II and Class III in house casino games, and obtaining Oneida certification on reporting child abuse and neglect.

Page 5
November 24, 2014
THOMAS E. BUSH
RE: SURVEILLANCE SYSTEM MONITOR

Target Corporation
Security Surveillance

Their security personnel do sit and watch security monitors, but are also required to walk the retail floor to surveil potential suspects, as well as apprehend alleged shoplifters as they are leaving the store. They will hire persons with no prior experience. There is a six week initial training period, and then ongoing training after that. One has to have basic computer skills, as there is an element of report writing required for each incident. Also noteworthy, is that they do have sit-down only security surveillance system monitors at their regional centers, that have network access to all of their stores. This is a skilled position with significant prior experience being required. The closest center is located in the Chicago metro area.

Wal-Mart
Asset Protection Associates

While their personnel sit and watch security monitors, they are primarily walking around performing their job duties on the sales floor. In addition to surveilling, they are also required to apprehend suspected shoplifters as they are leaving the store. Other duties include safety/prevention, making sure fire exits are clear, checking fire extinguishers, and that spill kits are fully stocked. While prior experience is preferred it is not required, they will hire the right candidate. One needs to have basic computer skills for report writing and a clear criminal background. The training program is typically six weeks or more, depending on prior education and experience.

Sears/K-Mart
Loss Prevention Associates

They have openings at numerous locations around the metro area for loss prevention associates. One is primarily walking the retail floor, surveilling suspected shoplifters. They do have to attempt apprehension of suspected shoplifters as they are leaving, but have a "non-contact" policy. Associates are to ask for the merchandise back and if a shopper refuses, then the authorities are contacted. Duties involve observing surveillance monitors occasionally, but this is not done the majority of the time. There is also a large aspect of safety to this position. Associates walk around to ensure that other employees are wearing proper protective gear, such as back braces in the merchandise pickup area or eyewear in the automotive department. They also look out for any tripping/falling hazards, picking things up off the floor, and using a mop bucket to pick up any spills for example. They assist in the merchandise pick-up area with larger/heavier items when needed. Some prior criminal justice education or retail asset protection background is preferred, but applicants with no prior experience will be considered. There is a 60 to 90 day initial training period in order to get certified. Basic computer skills are needed for report writing purposes.

Page 6
November 24, 2014
THOMAS E. BUSH
RE: SURVEILLANCE SYSTEM MONITOR

J.C. Penney
Loss Prevention Specialist

Specialists are typically working on the sales floor, but do spend time observing surveillance cameras. However, Specialists alternate doing this and working on the sales floor each day. A loss prevention background is preferred for these positions, but not required. There is a 60 day minimum training period. To successfully complete training, one has to actually witness and physically participate in an apprehension from start to finish. One also needs to have basic computer skills to write reports, use software, and have writing skills. Other job duties involve addressing safety concerns such as cleaning up debris on the floor, ensuring that wet floors and entrance areas are mopped up, and that employees are engaging in safe lifting and other work practices for example. There is also a remote center where there are surveillance system monitors in Fort Worth, Texas where this is their only job duty but the job is not unskilled.

Shopko
Loss Prevention Investigator

Loss prevention investigators observe CCTV monitors, but regularly spend time on the retail floor conducting surveillance and monitoring for internal theft, detaining suspected shoplifters. They also perform checks on fire and alarm systems, set-up and maintain surveillance cameras and equipment, and monitor reports for override and cash handling inconsistencies. Investigators provide employee theft and shoplifting awareness training to other staff in the stores. There is a comprehensive training program for new hires. A high school diploma is required and at least one year of prior retail loss prevention, and/or prior coursework in criminal justice, police science or security administration. There is regular sitting, standing, and walking, light lifting, and climbing ladders when setting up/maintaining equipment. Prior computer skills are required to write reports and operate equipment.

Menards
Security Officers

Menards actually sub-contracts security services from several regional vendors. Regardless, officers spend a substantial portion of the work day on the retail floor posing as shoppers to surveil suspected shoplifters, confronting and apprehending suspects when necessary. I was informed they are also working as gate guards, stationed at the entrance/exit of the outdoor products/lumber yard. They ensure customers are leaving the yard with the proper type and amount of merchandise. Some time is spent watching surveillance monitors occasionally. Officers have to write incident reports as needed. This job requires significant standing and walking, with light lifting. One needs to have good vision and hearing. Gate guards occasionally have to bend and reach in order to move and count merchandise leaving the yard. No prior experience is required, but one must have a high school diploma and a clean criminal record. Officers need to have the ability to write detailed incident reports. There is an initial training period of at least 30 to 60 days.

Page 7
November 24, 2014
THOMAS E. BUSH
RE: SURVEILLANCE SYSTEM MONITOR

Wisconsin Department of Transportation
Security Positions

I inquired with this state agency that oversees the Milwaukee Intermodal Station. Security positions are contracted out through a private company. I was informed however, that job duties involve watching surveillance monitors, but this is a small part of the job. There is significant standing and walking, while making rounds inside and outside the facility. Through this facility, the Amtrak Railroad Police also provide law enforcement, as well as the TSA.

The Milwaukee Intermodal Station also houses the Statewide Traffic Operations Center. This office monitors 300 DOT cameras across Wisconsin. The main function is to help ensure free traffic flow. Persons working in this position are primarily seated in an office work station. Job duties include interfacing with multiple software modules, typing messages on overhead highway alert signs, adjusting ramp meter timings, and updating software packages. I was informed that one needs to have above average communication and computer software skills as a prerequisite for employment.

•   •   •   •   •   •   •   •

From the above employer contacts, it is quite clear that surveillance positions working in the casinos are skilled, consistent with the occupational sources cited earlier. This is based upon prerequisite experience requirements and/or the amount of training involved for a typical worker to learn techniques, acquire information, and develop skills needed for average performance in this position. It would appear this would be more so the case presently when compared to the **DOT** job description for gambling monitor (343.367-014), which was last updated in 1977. There have been substantial advancements in electronic surveillance technology and other security techniques since.

Physically, these jobs would appear to fall under the Light physical demand category. At the Potawatomi Casinos, persons walk the casino floors conducting surveillance, in addition to working in the office. One has to be able to lift a maximum of 20 pounds.

At Ho-Chunk Casinos around the state, surveillance agent jobs are primarily Sedentary, sitting operating video and surveillance equipment. However, Light physical demands may be required when performing preventative maintenance of cameras and other equipment, as well as participating in security officer training.

Likewise, at Oneida Casinos, job duties are primarily Sedentary, but do involve standing and walking in public areas of the casino, as well as the ability to lift a minimum of 25 pounds.

The retail security officer positions would be considered semiskilled to skilled. While little to no prior experience is required for most of these jobs, there is an initial training period of approximately 60 days, if not longer, depending on one's prior

Page 8
November 24, 2014
THOMAS E. BUSH
RE: SURVEILLANCE SYSTEM MONITOR

experience level. Shopko requires at least one year of prior related experience or education.

Physically, all of these retail security positions would have at least Light physical demands. Officers are standing and/or walking a significant part of the workday, while on the retail floor conducting surveillance, and engaging in safety activities. Some of them require ladder climbing to set-up and maintain equipment.

At the Milwaukee Intermodal Station, while it appears that the traffic operations personnel work in a Sedentary capacity, based on the description I was provided, their job duties are clearly skilled. While I obtained only brief information regarding station security/surveillance positions, it appears that these have Light physical demands.

In conclusion, I was unable to find any surveillance system monitor positions that are Sedentary and unskilled in any industry. Therefore, it is my professional opinion not only that this occupational title no longer exists in the labor market as described in the **DOT**, but also that there are no similar Sedentary unskilled positions existing in the economy.

I hope you find this information helpful. If you have any questions or require any additional contacts, please do not hesitate to contact me.

Sincerely,

CAMPBELL & ASSOCIATES, LLC

Keith M. Moglowsky, M.S., C.R.C., L.P.C.
Vocational Consultant

KM/all

§346.6   The DOT and Sedentary Work

When the Medical-Vocational Guidelines were promulgated to take effect in 1979, administrative notice was taken of "approximately 200 unskilled sedentary occupations...which may be performed after a short demonstration or within 30 days." Rule 201.00(a). The current (1991) edition of the DOT has 137 unskilled sedentary occupations. *See* Appendix 5, for a list. SSA says that the regulatory estimate of approximately 200 sedentary unskilled occupations remains valid "because some of the 137 occupations in the current edition of the DOT comprise more than one of the separate occupations of which we take administrative notice." SSR 96-9p, footnote 5.

Whether there are 137 occupations or whether some occupational titles can be divided up to make approximately 200 separate occupations, the relative scarcity of unskilled sedentary work has significant implications for those Social Security disability claimants (literate claimants under age 50 and illiterate claimants under age 45) who must prove, to be found disabled, that they are incapable of performing sedentary work. They must prove that they are incapable of performing jobs they *probably* will never get in any case. *See* Bose, et al., "Misuse of Occupational Information in Social Security Disability Cases," *Rehabilitation Counseling Bulletin*, December 1986, at 83. U.S. Publishing data show that unskilled sedentary occupations constitute only about one-half of one percent of all jobs in the United States.

With an occupational base this small, what happens when there is any significant erosion? How much does this tiny sedentary occupational base need to be reduced before one can say that the remaining jobs do not exist in significant numbers?

The following chart shows how many of the 137 sedentary unskilled occupations found in the Revised Fourth Edition of the DOT remain available to a claimant when certain additional limitations are present. (The information for this chart was provided by the late Dr. Brent C. Evans, CVE, CWA, of Hales Comers, Wisconsin. Dr. Evans obtained the data using OASYS software developed by VERTEK, Inc., Bellevue, Washington.)

This chart reveals, as one might expect, that if a claimant has the limitation of never climbing, there is no impact on the sedentary occupational base because the definition of "sedentary" already precludes climbing activities. Accordingly, 137 occupations remain available to that claimant. On the other hand, if an individual is capable of handling objects only *occasionally*, the sedentary base is reduced from 137 occupations to just three.

The three occupations that can be done by someone who can handle objects only occasionally are: election clerk, DOT 205.367-030; call-out operator, DOT 237.367-014; and surveillance-system monitor, DOT 379.367-010. These three occupations also do not require reaching or fingering more than occasionally. Thus, a person who is limited to reaching, handling and fingering only occasionally can do these same three occupations. If a person has no restrictions on handling and fingering but reaching is limited to the occasional level, our search of the DOT found four occupations: the three listed above plus: bonder, semiconductor, DOT 726.685-066.

Effect of Certain Limitations on the Unskilled Sedentary Occupational Base

Physical Demands   **Number of Occupations Remaining**

	Never	Occasionally	Frequently
Climbing	137		
Balancing	137		
Stooping	131		
Kneeling	137		
Crouching	135		
Crawling	137		
Reaching	1	4	96
Handling	1	3	95
Fingering	19	38	113
Feeling	126		
Talking	127		
Hearing	127		
Tasting/Smelling	137		
Near Acuity	25	29	118
Far Acuity	135		
Depth Perception	94		
Accommodation (focus of eye)	107	114	132
Color vision	118	135	
Field of vision	135		

Note: Reaching, Handling & Fingering taken as a group at the occasional level yields only 3 occupations.

Aptitudes

	Level 5, the lowest level of ability, 0 to 10% of the population	Level 4, below average, 11 to 33% of the population
G: General Learning Ability	0	123
V: Verbal	5	129
N: Numerical	59	134
S: Spacial Perception	12	122
P: Form Perception	2	93
Q: Clerical Perception	75	122
K: Motor Coordination	0	67
F: Finger Dexterity	1	62
M: Manual Dexterity	0	51
E: Eye-Hand-Foot Coordination	123	135
C: Color Discrimination	117	
K: Motor Coordination	No	No
F: Finger Dexterity	occupations	occupations
M: Manual Dexterity	for this	for this
E: Eye-Hand-Foot Coordination	cluster.	cluster.

Temperaments

		Occupations remaining for an individual with *no* temperament for this kind of work
A	Working ALONE or apart in isolation	137
D	DIRECTING, controlling or planning work of others	137
E	EXPRESSING personal feelings	137
I	INFLUENCING people in their opinions, attitudes or judgments	137
J	Making JUDGMENTS and decisions	137
P	Dealing with PEOPLE	132
R	Performing REPETITIVE or short cycle work	**8**
S	Performing effectively under STRESS	137
T	Attaining precise set limits, TOLERANCES, and standards	**96**
U	Working UNDER specific instructions	**96**
V	Performing a VARIETY of duties	136

General educational development (GED), a measure of the formal and informal education and skill in reasoning, math and language "which are required of the worker for satisfactory job performance," according to Vol. 2, Appendix C.III of the DOT (reprinted at Appendix 3 of this book), has important effects on the sedentary base. *See* the scale of GED at page 1010, Vol. 2 of the DOT, Appendix 3 of this book. This educational measure is not aimed at a specific vocational goal, but is general in nature, and this includes elementary, high school, college, and self-study. There is a progression of development from the lowest level (1) to the highest level (6), although unskilled sedentary work has no GED level higher than 3.

At the lowest level (1), *reasoning* requires commonsense understanding to carry out simple one or two-step instructions, *math* requires simple addition, subtraction and multiplication, and *language* requires recognition of 2,500 English words, reading at 95-120 words per minute. Ability to write and speak simple sentences in English is also required.

At level 3, *reasoning* includes the application of commonsense understanding to carry out instructions furnished in written, oral, or diagrammatic form. A worker must deal with problems involving several concrete variables in or from standardized situations. Math requires algebra, geometry, and the ability to calculate discounts, interest, profit and loss, commission, markup, ratio and proportion, and selling price. *Language* includes the ability to read a variety of novels, magazines, safety rules, and instructions in the use and maintenance of shop tools and equipment. *Language* also includes the skills necessary to write reports and essays with proper format, punctuation, spelling and grammar, while using all parts of speech. At level 3, a worker must be able to speak in public before an audience, with poise, in correct English, and with a well-modulated voice.

When GED is examined without consideration of any other limitations, the number of sedentary unskilled occupations defined in the Dictionary of Occupational Titles is reduced from 137 occupations as follows:

Level of General Educational Development (from 1 to 6)

Reasoning	1	1	3	3
Math	1	3	1	3
Language	1	3	3	1
Number of Remaining Occupations	**46**	**46**	126	**97**

§346.7 Some Popular Jobs Which Are Not Sedentary Unskilled Jobs in the DOT

Sedentary Security Guard

The list of unskilled sedentary occupations, Appendix 5, is useful in cross-examining VEs who reach outside the list for examples of unskilled sedentary work. The printed version of the unskilled sedentary occupation list is organized according to the DOT code number. (The version on Digital Access is in Excel spreadsheet format, which can be sorted according to different parameters; but this is usually easier to do after you return to your office.)

Ask the VE for the DOT code of the job that the VE is testifying about. With this code, it is easy to check the printed list on the spot. For example, the job of "stationary security guard" is a favorite of some VEs. You won't find this occupation on the list as a sedentary job. The DOT has only one sedentary unskilled job within the GOE 04.02 (security services) category, and that is surveillance-system monitor. See §346.5. If you check a resource such as SELECTED CHARACTERISTICS OF JOBS DEFINED IN THE REVISED DOT, you will find only four light jobs with an SVP of 2 (there are none with an SVP of 1) listed under the security services category, 04.02. These jobs are airline security representative, parking enforcement officer, chaperon, and school bus monitor. All of the rest of the security services jobs have an SVP higher than 2. Indeed, because SSA's own definition of semi-skilled work includes the example of "guarding," 20 C.F.R. § 404.1568(b), one wonders why any security jobs are classified as unskilled. See §346.8, for some specific questions that may be useful in cross-examining VEs on this issue.

Cashier II

The job identified in the DOT as Cashier II, 211.462-010, GOE 07.03.01, is sometimes offered by VEs as an example of an unskilled sedentary job; but it is a light job. In fact, in the past Cashier II was classified as sedentary work. The 1991 DOT, however, states that Cashier II is classified as a light job. Reclassification of Cashier II from sedentary to light removed the only job from the sedentary unskilled category that existed in truly large numbers.

There is no unskilled job in the DOT with cashier in its title. Selected Characteristics does not show any unskilled sedentary cashiers in GOE 07.03.01. There are no unskilled sedentary cashiers in the census code containing Cashier II—Census Code 472, SOC Occupation 41-2011, Cashiers.

Telephone Solicitor

Telephone Solicitor (any ind.), 299.357-014, GOE 08.02.08, is a sedentary job with an SVP of 3 according to the definition trailer. It has reasoning, math, and language development levels of 3. There are no sedentary unskilled sales jobs listed in the DOT, Appendix 5.

Receptionist

The job of Receptionist (clerical), 237.367-038, has an SVP of 5 according to the definition trailer, GOE number 07.04.04. There is, however, one unskilled job listed under this GOE number which relates to "reception and information giving." This job is Telephone-Quotation Clerk (finan. inst.), 237.367-046. Note that it has reasoning and language development levels of 3.

VEs often do not differentiate the different receptionist positions identified by the DOT when testifying that thousands of receptionist jobs exist in the local economy. Insist that they give you the number of *unskilled* jobs that fall into the receptionist category, that is, the number of Telephone-Quotation Clerks in financial institutions.

Four other sedentary jobs with an SVP of 2 fall within the broader category of GOE 07.04. These are:
• Charge Account Clerk (DOT 205.367-014, reasoning 3, math 2, language 3),
• Order Clerk (food and beverage) (DOT 209.567-014, reasoning 3, math 2, language 2),
• Election Clerk, (DOT 205.367.030, reasoning, 3, math 2, language 2), and
• Scoreboard Operator (DOT 349.665-010, reasoning 3, math 2, language 3).

Each of these jobs has a reasoning level of 3 and two of them also have a language level of 3. Two of these jobs do not exist in significant numbers, and, even if they did, the jobs of election clerk and scoreboard operator are usually part time. How many elections per year could an election clerk supervise? Would this provide more than one or two days of work per year? How often would a scoreboard operator work? How many scoreboards are operated professionally in your job market? How often are games played when those scoreboards are in operation?

Information Clerk

Information clerk is a popular job with some VEs. Although the job identified in the DOT as "Information

Clerk (clerical)," 237.367-022, is a sedentary job, it has an SVP of 4; the job identified as "Information Clerk (motor trans.; r.r. trans.; water trans.)," 237.367-018, is an unskilled job but it is light. Census Code 540, SOC Occupation 43-4171, "Receptionists and Information Clerks," which includes both of these jobs, contains only one sedentary unskilled job, "Telephone-Quotation Clerk (finan. inst.)," 237.367-046, described above under receptionist.

General Office Clerk

Clerk, General (clerical), 209.562-010, is not a sedentary unskilled job. It is a light semi-skilled job. Census Code 586, "Office Clerks, General," SOC Occupation 43-9061, contains three unskilled sedentary DOT titles: Election Clerk, 205.367-030; Cutter-and-Paster, Press Clippings, 249.587-014; and Document Preparer, Microfilming, 249.587-018. Election clerk is, of course, a part-time job. How much cutting and pasting or microfilming goes on in today's digital world is a question for cross-examination.

File Clerk

File Clerk I (clerical), 206.387-034, and File Clerk II (clerical), 206.367-014, are both light semi-skilled jobs (SVP 3). Census Code 526, "File Clerks," SOC Occupation 43-4071, contains no sedentary unskilled jobs.

Bookkeeping, Accounting & Auditing Clerks

A VE who looks only at the title of Census Code 512, "Bookkeeping, Accounting, and Auditing Clerks," SOC Occupation 43-3031, might list this as a significant category of sedentary unskilled jobs. This census code includes only one unskilled sedentary DOT title—Parimutuel-Ticket Checker (amuse. & rec.), 219.587-010. Most Parimutuel-Ticket Checker jobs are likely to be part time since racetracks have most customers on weekends and in evenings.

Hand Packager

The job of "hand packager" is another example of a sedentary unskilled job offered by some VEs. In fact, the job identified by the DOT as Packager, Hand (any ind.), 920.587-018, is of medium exertion although it does have an SVP of 2. Its GOE number is 06.04.38. Of the 49 occupations listed under GOE number 06.04.38, only two are classified as sedentary by the DOT—however, these are not hand packaging jobs. A Carding-Machine Operator (trim. & embroid.), 681.685-030, "tends machines that winds binding, rickrack, and braid on paperboard cards. . ." and is a machine tending, not a hand packaging, job. The other

job, Bander, Hand (tobacco), 920.687-030, "wraps trademark band around cigars: Moistens or applies paste to tip end of band and presses ends of band together around cigars. Places banded cigars aside for further processing." This is an assembly job, not a packaging occupation. *See* Appendix 5.

The only other unskilled sedentary jobs that might qualify as packaging jobs are Ampoule Sealer in the pharmaceutical industry, 559.687-014, GOE 06.04.34, Census Code 964, the job duties of which are to seal "ampoules filled with liquid drug products, preparatory to packaging"; and Stuffer, in the toy—sporting equipment industry, 731.685-014, GOE 06.04.34, Census Code 880, which is a machine tender position. A Stuffer tends a machine that blows filler into stuffed toy shells.

Inspector

Some VEs say that there are many unskilled sedentary inspector jobs. If you look at the alphabetical index to the DOT, you will find nearly two pages of different jobs identified as "inspector," virtually all of which have higher exertional or higher skill levels than sedentary unskilled jobs, according their definition trailers. In fact, there are only two unskilled sedentary occupations in the DOT in which the word "inspector" appears in the title. *See* Appendix 5. These are Dowel Inspector in the wood-working industry, 669.687-014, GOE number 06.03.02, and Film Touch-Up Inspector in the electronics components industry, 726.684-050, GOE number 06.03.04.

There are, however, twelve other sedentary unskilled jobs categorized under the "Quality Control" heading 06.03. Examples of such jobs are Weight Tester in the paper and pulp industry, Nut Sorter, and Button Reclaimer. *See* Appendix 5. These jobs appear in Census Code 874, "Inspectors, Testers, Sorters, Samplers, and Weighers."

Self-Service Gas Station Attendant

Another favorite job of some VEs is self-service gas station attendant. (It is also sometimes offered as an example of an unskilled job in which one can alternate sitting and standing.) This job is identified in the DOT as Automobile-Self-Serve-Service-Station Attendant, 915.477-010. You won't find it on the list of unskilled sedentary jobs. The definition trailer classifies it as a semi-skilled (SVP 3) light job, GOE code 09.04.02.

If you are told that this job has changed since the DOT was written, a proposition with which you will agree if you read the DOT definition, note that according to the Definition Trailer, this definition has not changed since 1981. The Department of Labor changed the classification of many jobs in the 1991 edition of the DOT, but self-service gas station attendant was not one of them. This job remained as a semi-skilled (SVP 3) light job in the 1991 Revised Edition. *See* §346.9 for some specific questions on this job. On the issue of the alternate sitting and standing RFC, *see* §§348.4 and 348.9.

Modern self-serve gas stations frequently offer a variety of groceries and other convenience items. Many jobs at these stations are covered by Cashier II, which is alternately titled Cashier, self-service Gasoline (automotive ser.). The Cashier II job is a light job, as indicated above. Keep in mind that such jobs usually include lifting and carrying cartons of stock, stocking and cleaning shelves, setting up displays, unloading delivery trucks, and shoveling snow and ice from the entrance walkway. When these real world tasks apply, the job may cease to be a light job. Be sure to ask about these other job duties that may make the job a hybrid of two or more jobs properly classified as medium work.

§346.8   Use of the DOT in Cross-Examining a Vocational Expert

1. Have the VE Provide Information from the DOT.

Some VEs make a practice of writing down DOT, GOE or Census Code numbers when doing their research. (Indeed, some VEs know these codes by heart because they always identify the same jobs.) Others do not have these numbers at their fingertips. If you are going to use the DOT in your cross-examination, write the ALJ to request that the VE be prepared to provide this information at the time of testimony.

In general, for all jobs discussed, including past relevant work, ask the VE for:
- DOT number
- GOE number
- Census Code number
- SVP
- physical demands
- environmental conditions
- reasoning development
- mathematical development
- language development

2. Establish that the claimant (as described in the hypothetical question) cannot perform the job as described in the DOT.
- The DOT classifies this job as light, doesn't it?
- Light work involves walking or standing to a "significant degree," doesn't it? This is usually considered to be about six hours out of an eight-hour working day, isn't it?
- This job also involves a mathematical development level of [*e.g.*, 3] which requires: [read definition from page 1011 of Vol. 2 of the DOT, reproduced in Appendix 3 of this book]. The claimant's educational background isn't this high, is it?

3. When the VE responds that actually the job is performed differently than it is described in the DOT, ask a series of questions addressing this issue: How does the VE know?
- How do you know the DOT is wrong about how this job is performed?
- How many job site inspections have you done?
- In what parts of the country?
- What companies did you visit?
- When did you do these job site inspections?
- How long did you spend observing this particular job?

4. Sedentary Security Guard
- There is no sedentary security guard position in the DOT, is there?
- How long do you claim that this sedentary security guard position has existed?
- So, it isn't because of its newness that this job was not included in the 1991 edition of the DOT, is it?
- If this job were listed in the DOT, would it be listed with the other security guard positions?
- Are you aware that SSA's definition of semi-skilled work, 20 C.F.R. § 404. 1568(b), includes the example of "guarding equipment, property, materials, or persons against loss, damage or injury?" You have classified this job as unskilled, haven't you? Can you cite any source materials that classify a sedentary security guard job as unskilled?
- The claimant is not physically fit, is he? Isn't being physically fit a job requirement for security services? Doesn't this requirement appear in the introductory paragraph to security services in SELECTED CHARACTERISTICS OF OCCUPATIONS DEFINED IN THE REVISED DOT?
- Because of his impairments, the claimant would not be able to react quickly in emergencies, would he?
- The security guard position described in the DOT, 372.667-034, says that the security guard "apprehends or expels miscreants." Isn't this a function of any security guard, including the one you describe? If so, that requires more than sedentary work capacity, doesn't it? If not, what is it that this security guard is guarding against?
- A security guard must be capable of operating a fire extinguisher, must he not? How much do such fire extinguishers weigh?
- A security guard must be capable of moving a person out of harm's way in an emergency, must he not?

5. Self-Service Gas Station Attendant

• This job is described as having an SVP of 3, isn't it?
• This means that it takes more than 30 days to develop the facility needed for average performance, doesn't it?
• Products such as oil, antifreeze and windshield washer solution are sold at all self-service gas stations, aren't they?
• Isn't it part of the attendant's job duties to stock the shelves? How much does a case of oil weigh?
• If it isn't part of the attendant's job, who stocks the shelves?

6. Cashier

• Isn't it correct that there is only one sedentary cashier job identified in the DOT?
• Isn't that job Order Clerk (food and beverage) in the hotel and restaurant industry, DOT # 209.567-014?
• Isn't it true that in *most* restaurants and hotels, the people that perform the function of taking telephone orders (for room service and carry out) also have other duties?
• Don't these other duties indicate that the worker is performing a job at the light (or heavier) level?
• Wouldn't it be only in the very largest hotels and carry out restaurants that a sedentary order clerk job exists?
• Doesn't this mean that there are very few of these jobs? *See* §348.8 for an approach to dealing with VE testimony about the number of sedentary cashier jobs.

§346.9   *Submit a Rebuttal Opinion*

If a vocational expert insists that an occupation appears in the DOT as a sedentary unskilled job when, in fact, it does not, you need only ask the ALJ to take administrative notice of how the job is classified in the DOT. But what do you do when the VE concedes that the job is listed differently in the DOT, but the VE says that he or she knows from personal experience that there really are many such jobs that are sedentary and unskilled?

Here is one approach: Submit a well-reasoned opinion from another vocational expert that relies on the DOT as well as that expert's expertise to say that the jobs cited by the VE who testified at the hearing do not exist in significant numbers.

In some circuits, attorneys may be tempted to rely on the DOT alone because some cases have been read as saying that where a VE testifies contrary to the DOT, the DOT is controlling. *See, e.g., Bjornholm*

v. Shalala, 39 F.3d 888, 890 (8th Cir. 1994); *Young v. Secretary*, 957 F.2d 386, 392-393 (7th Cir. 1992); *Campbell v. Bowen*, 822 F.2d 1518, 1523 (10th Cir. 1987); *Williams v. Shalala*, 997 F.2d 1494, 1500 (D.C. Cir. 1993); and *Mimms v. Heckler*, 750 F.2d 180, 186 (2d Cir. 1984). However, these cases tend to deal with unexplained variances between the VE's testimony and the DOT—certainly something to keep in mind when cross-examining the VE. The more questions you ask, the more opportunity the VE will have to explain his or her position.

At the other extreme is *Conn v. Secretary*, 51 F.3d 607, 610 (6th Cir. 1995), which seems to say that any VE opinion, no matter how it conflicts with the DOT, may be substantial evidence. Other cases have held that a supported VE opinion contrary to the DOT could be relied upon by the ALJ. *See, e.g., Johnson v. Shalala*, 60 F.3d 1428, 1435 (9th Cir. 1995), and *Logan v. Shalala*, 882 F.Supp. 755, 764 (C.D. Ill. 1995). This, in fact, is SSA's position as stated in SSR 00-4p, which provides:

> Occupational evidence provided by a VE . . . generally should be consistent with the occupational information supplied by the DOT. When there is an apparent unresolved conflict between VE . . . evidence and the DOT, the adjudicator must elicit a reasonable explanation for the conflict before relying on the VE . . . evidence to support a determination or decision about whether the claimant is disabled. At the hearings level, as part of the adjudicator's duty to fully develop the record, the adjudicator will inquire, on the record, as to whether or not there is such consistency.

> Neither the DOT nor the VE . . . evidence automatically "trumps" when there is a conflict. The adjudicator must resolve the conflict by determining if the explanation given by the VE . . . is reasonable and provides a basis for relying on the VE . . . testimony rather than on the DOT information.

Submitting a rebuttal VE opinion gives the ALJ the opportunity to rely on that VE's well-reasoned and supported opinion rather than the opinion of the VE who testified at the hearing.

There may be other sources for rebuttal evidence. Some attorneys have obtained affidavits from local employers that contradicted the VE's testimony at the hearing. Others have submitted job surveys. Sometimes the Occupational Employment Quarterly from U.S. Publishing (*see* Appendix 2 for ordering information) can be used in rebuttal.

§347   Past Relevant Work

There are two common problems that can be created by a VE's testimony concerning your client's past relevant work. First, the VE can say that a person with the limitations described is capable of performing the claimant's past relevant work. Second, the VE could say that the exertional level of the claimant's past occupation, as generally required by employers throughout the national economy, is less than the level at which the claimant performed this job.

One other past relevant work issue arises in a few cases. When this comes up, VE testimony can help the ALJ conclude that past work is not "relevant."

§347.1   Make Sure the Prior Job Really Was Relevant Work

Make sure that the claimant's past jobs actually qualify as relevant work. In order to qualify:

1.   The job must have been performed within:

a. 15 years prior to adjudication; or

b. if insured status has lapsed, 15 years prior to the date last insured.

2.   The job must have been "substantial gainful activity."

a. The job must involve doing significant physical or mental activities; and

b. it must have been done at the SGA level. *See* 20 C.F.R. §§ 404.1574-1575. (Note that part-time work performed at the SGA level qualifies. SSR 96-8p, footnote 2.)

3.   The job must have lasted long enough for the claimant to develop the facility needed for average performance. *See* 20 C.F.R. § 404.1565(a) and SSR 82-62.

Beware of comparing this last requirement to the DOT concept of "specific vocational preparation" (SVP), the length of time it takes an average worker to develop average facility in a job. To develop average facility to do an unskilled job, it generally takes 30 days or less. Does this mean that an unskilled job held by a worker for 30 days ten years ago will qualify as relevant work?

Generally, SSA does not treat such brief work experience as relevant.

20 C.F.R. § 404.1565(a) states that a claimant who has "worked only 'off-and-on' or for brief periods of time during the 15-year period" may be considered to have no relevant work experience. *See also* SSR 82-62. Neither the regulation nor the ruling is specific about the minimum duration of relevant work. An informal SSA rule of thumb requires that unskilled work be done for three months or more to be considered relevant. Many ALJs use a three- to six-month standard.

Semi-skilled and skilled jobs must be done for a longer period to be vocationally relevant.

"*Work experience* means skills and abilities . . . acquired through work" which show the type of work a claimant may be expected to do. 20 C.F.R. § 404.1565(a). SSR 82-63, stating a rule applicable to claimants age 55 and over who have no relevant work experience, finds the rule applicable when "the work activity performed within this 15-year period does not (on the basis of job content, recency, or duration) enhance present work capability." These principles ought to apply to all circumstances.

Ask the vocational expert:

- On the basis of job content, recency and duration, how does [a particular job] enhance the claimant's present work capability?
- As a result of [a particular job], does the claimant have any greater skills and abilities than a person with no work experience?
- How does [a brief job] show the type of work an individual may be expected to do?

The vocational expert's answers may lead to a brief sedentary or light job being found not relevant, even if that job was done for a longer time than the informal SSA rule of thumb usually allows.

§347.1.1 Relevant Work Period

POMS DI 25001.001B.65. explains that the "relevant work period" is the "period for which a claimant's past work can be considered past relevant work (PRW)." It provides a useful table showing the "most common scenarios of the relevant work period":

TYPE OF CLAIM	RELEVANT PERIOD
Title II Disability Insurance Benefits (DIB) – Date Last Insured (DLI) in the future	Within the 15 years before adjudication*
Title II DIB – DLI in the past	Within the 15 years before DLI
Title II Widow or Widower, or Surviving Divorced Spouse (DWB) Prescribed Period (PP) not expired	Within the 15 years before adjudication *
Title II DWB – PP expired	Within the 15 years before expiration of the PP
Title II or Title XVI Residual Functional Capacity (RFC) projected to a future date.	Within the 15 years before the projected date is reached
Title II Full Retirement Age (FRA) in the past	Within the 15 years before FRA
Title II Childhood Disability Beneficiaries (CDB) – Initial claim filed before age 22	Within the 15 years before adjudication*
Title II CDB – Initial claim filed after age 22, no relevant work after age 22	Within the 15 years before age 22
Title II CDB – Reentitlement Claim, 7 year period applies and ended in the past	Within the 15 years before the end of the reentitlement period
Title II CDB – Reentitlement Claim, 7 year period applies and has not yet ended, or 7 year period does not apply	Within the 15 years before adjudication*
Title XVI Adult	Within the 15 years before adjudication*
Title II or Title XVI Continuing Disability Review (CDR)	Within the 15 years before CDR adjudication**
Appeal of Title II or Title XVI CDR medical cessation	Within the 15 years prior to the initial CDR medical cessation determination**
Any type of claim - closed period of disability ***	Within the 15 years before the end of the closed period

* Indicates the date we adjudicate the claim at the initial, reconsideration, administrative law judge levels or for Appeals Council decisions. (*See* 20 CFR 404.1565 and 416.965.) The date of adjudication is not frozen at the initial determination but is the date of determination or decision at any level of review.

** DI 28005.015A.7 provides that in CDR cases we will not count work performed during the current period of disability as PRW or as work experience. However, SGA done during a current period of disability may change an individual's vocational outlook for the purposes of applying collateral estoppel to a new claim. *See* EM-01204 and DI 27515.001 for additional information on potential adoption cases involving work activity.

*** A closed period of disability is one in which the claimant was unable to engage in substantial gainful activity for a continuous period of at least 12 months, but by the time the determination or decision is made, improvement has occurred and the claimant is no longer disabled.

§347.2 The Functional Demands and Job Duties of the Occupation as Generally Required by Employers Throughout the National Economy

If a claimant's prior job qualifies as past relevant work, check the DOT to see how this job is classified. If the DOT exertional level is consistent with your client's description of the job, you should not have a problem with VE testimony on the issue of past relevant work. VE testimony contrary to the DOT on the exertional level of a job is rare; and when it happens, it should not control the outcome of your client's case. SSR 82-61 states that the DOT "can be relied upon—for jobs listed in the DOT—to define the job as it is *usually* performed in the national economy." *Also see* SSR 00-4p.

If a VE testifies contrary to the DOT, you may submit pages from the DOT in rebuttal; or you may establish from the VE's testimony the exertional level of the job in the DOT. Once this is established, consider whether you need anything more, in light of the fact that Social Security Rulings are binding. If you decide to proceed with cross-examination, focus on this issue: How does the VE know the DOT is wrong about how this job is required by employers to be performed *throughout the national economy*? *See* §346.8.

In those cases where the DOT appears to say that your client's job was light while your client describes it as medium, first make sure you have the right job. Don't rely simply on the job title, as given to you by your client. Also, make sure you've got the right industry.

Watch for hybrid jobs. The job done by your client may look like a combination of two jobs which appear in the DOT, one classified as medium and the other classified as light. But your client has done neither of these jobs. Your client has done a different job, one which includes elements of two jobs which appear in the DOT. On composite jobs *see* SSR 82-61 and *Paige v. Bowen*, 695 F. Supp. 975, 981 (N.D. Ill. 1988).

In those instances in which it appears to you that your client's former job did involve functional demands significantly in excess of those generally required by employers throughout the economy, consult with your own vocational expert prior to the hearing to make sure. This, of course, changes the nature of what you have to prove in your client's case.

§347.3 When a VE Testifies That a Claimant Can Do His Former Job as He Performed It

There are four possibilities when a VE testifies in response to an ALJ's hypothetical question that a claimant can do his or her past relevant work: 1) the claimant really can do this job; 2) the ALJ's hypothetical

question does not include all of the claimant's limitations; 3) the VE doesn't understand the limitations stated in the hypothetical question; or 4) you may be dealing with a hostile VE. (A hostile VE is one who has made up his or her mind that the claimant can work, so that no matter what elements are included in a hypothetical question, the VE will answer that the claimant can do a past job or can do a lot of other jobs.)

If the first possibility applies, the claimant loses the case. If the second possibility explains the VE's answer, the solution is simple: propose a hypothetical question to the VE including all of the claimant's limitations. If neither of the first two possibilities appear to apply, you must determine whether the VE simply doesn't understand the limitations stated by the ALJ or if the VE is refusing to apply them—the hostile VE. Ask this:

- Are there some abilities that are so essential to competitive employment that without them the claimant would be unable to work?

Then, take what the VE says, *e.g.*, reliability, regular attendance, the ability to deal with routine work stress, etc., to fashion a line of questioning coupled with the elements of the ALJ's hypothetical question. Also, ask this:

- Assuming that everything that you heard the claimant testify to today is true, do you think the claimant is capable of performing past work?

If the VE testifies that the claimant cannot do a past job if one assumes everything the claimant said is true, don't stop there. There are two possible approaches to take to find out more. First, try some different hypothetical questions suggesting limitations somewhere in between those described in the ALJ's hypothetical question and the claimant's testimony. Keep changing elements of the hypothetical question until you can determine what aspects are crucial. Second, compare specific parts of the ALJ's hypothetical question to the claimant's former job duties. For example, didn't the claimant's former job involve occasionally lifting up to 30 lbs.? Didn't the ALJ ask you to assume that this hypothetical individual was incapable of lifting over 20 lbs.?

§347.4 A Past Job Need Not Exist

SSA's position is that if a claimant is capable of performing a particular past relevant job, the claimant is not disabled. SSA will not look at the issue of whether that past job exists at all, let alone whether it exists in significant numbers. This position was upheld by the United States Supreme Court in *Barnhart v. Thomas*, 540 U.S. 20 (2003).

§348 Using the Grids as a Framework for Decision-Making

If a claimant cannot do past work, the sequential evaluation of disability moves on to step five at which residual functional capacity, age, education and work experience are considered to determine if a claimant can do other work. These factors must be considered under the Social Security Act, which provides that a claimant "shall be determined to be under a disability only if his physical or mental impairment or impairments are of such severity that he is not only unable to do his previous work but cannot, *considering his age, education and work experience*, engage in any other kinds of substantial gainful work which exists in the national economy . . . *in significant numbers . . . .*" 42 U.S.C. § 423(d)(2)(A) (emphasis added). Prior to the effective date of the Medical-Vocational Guidelines,

> the Secretary relied on vocational experts to establish the existence of suitable jobs in the national economy. After a claimant's limitations and abilities had been determined at a hearing, a vocational expert ordinarily would testify whether work existed that the claimant could perform. Although this testimony often was based on standardized guides, see 43 Fed. Reg. 9286 (1978), vocational experts frequently were criticized for their inconsistent treatment of similarly situated claimants . . . . To improve both the uniformity and efficiency of this determination, the Secretary promulgated medical-vocational guidelines . . . .

> These guidelines relieve the Secretary of the need to rely on vocational experts by establishing through rulemaking the types and numbers of jobs that exist in the national economy. They consist of a matrix of the four factors identified by Congress—physical ability, age, education, and work experience—and set forth rules that identify whether jobs requiring specific combinations of these factors exist in significant numbers in the national economy. Where a claimant's qualifications correspond to the job requirements identified by a rule, the guidelines direct a conclusion as to whether work exists that the claimant could perform.

Heckler v. Campbell, 461 U.S. 458, 461-462, 103 S.Ct. 1952, 76 L.Ed.2d 66 (1983).

The Medical-Vocational Guidelines have three major implications for vocational expert testimony:

First, the Medical-Vocational Guidelines are binding and where they are directly applicable, they may not be rebutted by VE testimony. SSR 83-5a.

Second, the Medical-Vocational Guidelines themselves create a category of cases in which VE testimony is often necessary—those cases in which transferability of skills is a critical issue. *See* §349.

Third, where the Medical-Vocational Guidelines are not directly applicable, a vocational expert may be called to testify about jobs that a claimant can still do despite his or her impairments; however, even in those cases the Medical-Vocational Guidelines must be used as a framework for decision-making.

The situations in which the Medical-Vocational Guidelines are not directly applicable and do not direct a conclusion as to whether a claimant is or is not disabled occur when a claimant's RFC, age, education and work experience do not coincide with the corresponding criteria of a rule in the grids. This happens, generally, in the following circumstances:

1. The claimant's RFC falls between ranges of work (Rule 200.00(d) and SSR 83-12);

2. The case involves a combination of exertional and nonexertional impairments (Rule 200.00(e)(2) and SSRs 83-12 and 83-14);

3. The case involves solely nonexertional impairments (Rule 200.00(e)(1) and SSR 85-15); or

4. The case involves a literate claimant under age 50 or an illiterate or non-English speaking claimant under age 45 who is incapable of performing a full range of sedentary work (Rule 201.00(h) and SSRs 83-12, 83-14 and 96-9p).

SSA says that vocational expert testimony is not necessary in all cases where the Medical-Vocational Guidelines are to be used as a framework. According to SSA:

> In those claims where a person comes very close to meeting the criteria of a grid rule directing a finding of not disabled because it is clear that the additional nonexertional limitation(s) has very little effect on the exertional occupational base, we may rely on the framework of the grid rules to support a finding that the person is not disabled without consulting a vocational expert or other vocational resource. On the other hand, an additional nonexertional limitation may substantially reduce a range of work to the extent that an individual is very close to meeting a grid rule which directs a conclusion of disabled. Particular nonexertional limitation(s) may significantly erode or may have very little effect on the occupational base of jobs an individual can perform.

AR 01-1(3). *See also,* SSR 83-14.

In *Sykes v. Apfel*, 228 F.3d 259, 273 (3d Cir. 2000), the Third Circuit Court of Appeals required SSA to produce "the testimony of a vocational expert or other similar evidence" before it may use the framework of the grids to deny a claim. SSA's position, even as stated in AR 01-1(3), the acquiescence ruling in which SSA agreed to follow *Sykes* in the Third Circuit, is that it does not necessarily have to consult a vocational expert in all framework cases even in the Third Circuit. Instead, SSA says that it can use a Social Security ruling for guidance in determining the degree of erosion of the occupational base in a particular case and simply cite the ruling in the denial decision without ever giving the claimant advance notice and the opportunity to respond.

Sykes, however, seems to hold to the contrary: "On remand, if the ALJ intends to rely on official notice rather than additional vocational evidence to establish that Sykes's nonexertional impairment does not diminish his occupational base for light work, the ALJ must provide notice to Sykes that he intends to notice that the lack of binocular vision causes no diminution in the occupation base and give Sykes an opportunity to respond." *Sykes v. Apfel*, 228 F.3d 259, 273 (3d Cir. 2000). Thus, it is hard to see how SSA really has acquiesced in *Sykes. See* AR 01-1(3).

When a claimant under age 45 is *both* illiterate *and* unable to communicate in English, testimony of a vocational expert is required in the Fifth Circuit. *See* AR 86-3(5) in which SSA acquiesced in *Martinez v. Heckler,* 735 F.2d 795 (5th Cir. 1984).

§348.1   Erosion of the Occupational Base

As we explained in §340, SSA's use of the Medical-Vocational Guidelines as a framework has changed since the Guidelines were first promulgated. Today, SSA calls it using the Guidelines as a framework when an ALJ does little more than obtain numbers of jobs from a vocational expert (within the context of the Medical-Vocational Guidelines) and simply asserts that the total number of jobs is "significant."

Those few ALJs who actually use the Medical-Vocational framework as originally intended know better than to use the phrase "erosion of the occupational base" in their decisions, especially when no VE testifies. Use of the phrase is an invitation for an Appeals Council remand. Here is how such an ALJ actually deals with the classic situation where a claimant's RFC falls between two rules that dictate opposite results, but the claimant's RFC is much closer to the RFC for the lower rule, the one that dictates that the claimant is disabled. If the VE suggests jobs at the higher exertional level, the ALJ may encourage the VE to reconsider, to say that the claimant is really only capable of performing jobs at the lower RFC. Then the ALJ will apply the lower grid rule to find

the claimant disabled. It will look like the framework wasn't used at all.

Use of the original approach to the framework of the Medical-Vocational Guidelines has become a theoretical method of analysis used by many lawyers and some ALJs to figure out which claimants, who do not fit exactly into the Medical-Vocational Guidelines, are disabled. Then they will find some other way to see to it that such claimants are actually found disabled. Although an argument founded on original framework analysis is unlikely to win at the administrative level or in federal court, to fully understand this area of law, you must understand the Medical-Vocational Guidelines and original framework analysis.

The Medical-Vocational Guidelines, in essence, constitute an "administrative evaluation which determines whether a work adjustment" to other work is possible for an individual described by one of the rules in the grids. SSR 83-10 states:

> In each instance, the issue [of work adjustment] is decided based on the interaction between the person's occupational base as determined by RFC with his or her age, education and work experience.

> The ultimate question in the medical-vocational evaluation of the capability to do other work is whether work that an individual can do functionally and vocationally exists in the national economy. Whether work exists in the national economy for any particular individual depends on whether there are a significant number of jobs (in one or more occupations) with requirements that the individual is able to meet, considering his or her remaining physical and mental abilities and vocational qualifications.

> The occupational base that is determined to be available based on RFC alone consists of a full range of occupations, each of which represents numerous jobs in the national economy. Where a rule indicates that a work adjustment is expected, a reasonable opportunity exists for adjusting to work other than that previously performed . . . . Conversely, where the rules determine that a work adjustment is not expected, no reasonable opportunity exists for adjusting to substantial work.

Where the Medical-Vocational Guidelines are not directly applicable, they are required to be used as a framework for decision-making. The Medical-Vocational Guidelines "provide an overall structure for evaluation of those cases in which the judgments as to each factor [RFC, age, education, work experience] do not coincide with those of any specific rule." Rule 200.00(d). Adjudicators are instructed to use the grids as a "frame of reference" (Rule 200.00(d)) or a "framework for consideration" (Rule 200.00(e)(2)).

Use of the Medical-Vocational Guidelines as a "framework" for decision-making as originally intended is easiest to grasp in cases involving an exertional impairment. This is discussed in the introduction to the Medical-Vocational Guidelines, Rule 200.00, but it is most clearly set forth in Social Security Rulings 83-12 and 83-14, especially in the concept of "erosion of the occupational base," the shrinking of the numbers of occupations available for a particular claimant because of the claimant's specific impairments.

When an exertional impairment is involved, one does not have to begin the evaluation of the occupational base with the broad world of work, that is, work at all exertional levels from sedentary through very heavy work. Instead, one can start by examining the occupational base closest to the claimant's exertional RFC and then evaluate how much this occupational base has been eroded by the claimant's additional impairments. There are three occupational bases consisting of unskilled occupations of which administrative notice was taken in 1978 for the three grid tables: 2,500 medium, light and sedentary occupations; 1,600 light and sedentary occupations; and 200 sedentary occupations. The occupational base of higher RFCs is assumed to include that of the lower RFC occupations unless there are reasons to exclude some or all of the occupations at the lower RFC. (Note that the 1991 DOT has fewer sedentary and more light occupations. *See* §348.5. But these are differences not relevant to our theoretical discussion here.)

Let us take as an example a 52-year-old claimant with a back condition who is capable of standing and walking for six hours out of an eight-hour working day but is capable of sitting for only two hours out of a working day. He is capable of frequently lifting 10 pounds and occasionally lifting up to 15 pounds with his left arm. His right arm has been amputated. His past relevant work is unskilled medium work. He has a high school education.

The exertional limitations of our hypothetical claimant put him closest to Rule 202.13 from the light grid which requires a finding of not disabled. If he were limited to sedentary work, on the other hand, he would be found disabled pursuant to Rule 201.12.

The occupational base which we first must examine in evaluating this case is that consisting of 1,600 unskilled light and sedentary occupations represented by a capacity for a full range of both sedentary and light work. But there are several ways that this light and

sedentary occupational base has been eroded for the claimant described above:

1. Because he cannot sit for six hours out of an eight-hour working day and has manipulative limitations, he is not capable of performing the 200 sedentary occupations. This, in itself, reduces (erodes) the occupational base to 1,400 jobs. This erosion can be determined without VE assistance because these limitations are addressed by SSRs 83-10, 83-12 and 96-9p.

2. His inability to lift more than 15 lbs. (rather than the 20 lbs. maximum lifting required by the regulatory definition) will further erode the remaining light occupational base. The extent of this erosion is a question for a VE.

3. His manipulative limitations will cause further erosion of the light occupational base. The degree of erosion is also a question for a VE; but note the profound effect that manipulative limitations have on the light occupational base. *See* §§348.1.1 and 348.1.2.

Let us say for the sake of illustration that, because of all the limitations, a VE testifies that the 1,600 light and sedentary occupations represented by the light grid are eroded to approximately 200 occupations, each one representing numerous jobs in the national economy: a total of perhaps hundreds of thousands of jobs in the national economy.

Does this mean these jobs are present in "significant numbers" in the national economy so that our hypothetical claimant can be found not disabled?

Note that the sedentary occupational base is considered to be 200 occupations. If our hypothetical claimant were limited to sedentary work, he would be found disabled pursuant to Rule 201.12, which, in essence, is an administrative finding that 200 is not a significant number of occupations for vocational adjustment to be possible for someone of the same age, education and work experience as our hypothetical claimant. Thus, because the remaining occupational base of our hypothetical claimant is equal to the occupational base represented by the full range of sedentary work, he should be found disabled. (This, in effect, is the conclusion of the POMS, which notes that loss of use of an upper extremity would "reduce the total number of unskilled occupations within the person's RFC to a little more than the number represented by the full range of sedentary work." POMS DI 25020.005A.5.b.)

Many ALJs today will work it out that the claimant described above will be found disabled. Some ALJs will think in terms of original framework analysis to come to this conclusion.

The ALJs who want to conclude that such a claimant is not disabled will try to rely on VE numbers testimony. You may be able to punch holes in such testimony. (*E.g.*, the DOT does not address one arm work; there may be conflicts between VE testimony and the DOT; reaching, handling and fingering arguably should be considered to be at the "occasional" level because there are only half as many arms to do it—and there are few such occupations—*see* §348.1.2; the VE probably can cite no valid studies; VE numbers testimony is probably hogwash, etc.) By appealing, you may eventually win such a case, perhaps with a different ALJ.

Note, though, the same holes can be punched in VE testimony when you're dealing with a younger claimant, but the end result after appeals is that even ALJs who think in terms of original framework analysis would find such a claimant *not* disabled. *See also* SSR 87-11c, which adopted as a Social Security ruling *Odle v. Secretary of Health and Human Services*, 788 F.2d 1158 (6th Cir. 1985). Thus, as you can see, understanding original framework analysis helps you pick your spots.

§348.1.1 Chart: Analysis of the Light Occupational Base

The following chart shows how many of the 1,571 unskilled light occupations found in the Revised Fourth Edition of the Dictionary of Occupational Titles remain available to a claimant when particular additional limitations are present. (The information for this chart was provided by Anne Repaci, M.S., CRC, Vocational Directions, Milwaukee, Wisconsin, who used OASYS software developed by VERTEK, Inc., Bellevue, Washington.)

The chart reveals, for example, that for someone unable to climb, there are still 1,520 out of 1,571 light unskilled occupations available. The greatest impact on the light occupational base occurs when reaching, handling or fingering are impaired. For example, only 8 unskilled light occupations are available to someone who can never reach. If a person can reach only occasionally, there are 36 occupations available. If a person can never reach, handle or finger, there are only six occupations available. Because of the significance of these manipulative limitations, we provide lists of the DOT job titles for the manipulative limitations with the greatest impact on the unskilled light occupational base at §348.1.2.

The total number of light unskilled occupations is 1,571.

Physical Demands	Never	Occasionally	Frequently
Climbing	1520		
Balance	1551		
Stooping	1244		
Kneeling	1528		
Crouching	1459		
Crawling	1566		
Reaching	**8**	**36**	1266
Handling	**6**	**37**	1260
Fingering	**410**	**819**	1465
Feeling	1427		
Talking	1440		
Hearing	1399		
Tasting/Smelling	1566		
Near Acuity	**471**	682	1472
Far Acuity	1518		
Depth Perception	1069		
Accommodation	1288		
Color Vision	1224		
Field of Vision	1545		
Reaching Handling = As a group Fingering	**6**	**29**	1259

Aptitudes	Level 5	Level 4
General Learning Ability	**0**	1472
Verbal Aptitude	**29**	1512
Numerical Aptitude	**487**	1531
Spatial Aptitude	**83**	1465
Form Perception	**29**	1185
Clerical Aptitude	**740**	1504
Motor Coordination	**7**	982
Finger Dexterity	**13**	1103
Manual Dexterity	**2**	**520**
Eye-Hand-Foot Coordination	1264	1529
Color Discrimination	1206	1531

Temperaments/Situations	Occupations remaining for individual with no temperament for this kind of work
Working ALONE or apart in physical isolation from others	1571
DIRECTING, controlling or planning work of others	1571
EXPRESSING personal feelings	1571
INFLUENCING people in their opinions, attitudes or judgments	1571
Making JUDGMENTS and decisions	1376
Dealing with PEOPLE	1385
Performing REPETITIVE or short cycle work	**113**
Performing effectively under STRESS	1571
Attaining precise set limits, TOLERANCES, and standards	915
Working UNDER specific instructions	1571
Performing a VARIETY of duties	1382

NOISE

Quiet	**26**
Moderate	**762**
Loud	1571

GED

	Level 1	Level 2	Level 3	
Reasoning	**391**		Language	1
1513	1569		3	3
Mathematics	1386		1	
1565	1571			
Language	1198		Remaining Jobs	**391**
1549	1570		**391**	1386
			1198	

Taken as a group:

Reasoning	1
1	3
3	
Mathematics	1
3	1
3	

§348.1.2   Chart: Unskilled Light Occupations —Manipulative Limitations

The following lists of light occupations were derived from the analysis of the light occupational base that appears at §348.1.1. For example, one list shows the six light occupations in the DOT that do not require *any* handling of objects. Note that when a claimant is limited to "occasional handling" or "occasional reaching," that claimant can perform occupations that require no handling or no reaching. Thus, the lists of occupations labeled occasionally include occupations that do not require the activity at all.

HANDLING—OCCASIONALLY

DOT Code	Occupational Title	Industry	SVP
159.647-022	Show Girl	Amusement and Recreation	2
222.687-046	Protective-Clothing Issuer	Chemical	2
241.367-038	Investigator, Dealer Accounts	Financial Institutions	2
249.366-010	Counter Clerk	Photofinishing	2
295.357-018	Furniture-Rental Consultant	Retail Trade	2
295.467-014	Boat-Rental Clerk	Amusement and Recreation	2
299.647-010	Impersonator, Character	Any Industry	2
299.687-014	Sandwich-Board Carrier	Any Industry	1
342.357-010	Weight Guesser	Amusement and Recreation	2
342-657-010	Barker	Amusement and Recreation	2
344.677-014	Usher	Amusement and Recreation	2
349.667-014	Host/Hostess, Head	Amusement and Recreation	2
349.677-018	Children's Attendant	Amusement and Recreation	2
352.667-014	Parlor Chaperone	Hotel and Restaurant	2
353.367-022	Page	Radio and TV Broadcasting	2
359.367-010	Escort	Personal Service	2
359.567-014	Tanning Salon Attendant	Personal Service	2
359.667-010	Chaperon	Personal Service	2
359.677-030	Research Subject	Any Industry	1
363.686-010	Flatwork Finisher	Laundry and Related	2
371.567-010	Guard, School-Crossing	Government Services	2
372-667-042	School Bus Monitor	Government Services	2
429.587-010	Cotton Classer Aide	Agriculture	2
520.687-066	Blending-Tank Tender Helper	Canning and Preserving	2
521.685-386	Scaling Machine Operator	Canning and Preserving	2
524.687-022	Bakery Worker, Conveyor Line	Bakery Products	2
529.687-126	Kosher Inspector	Dairy Products	2
569.686.046	Laminating-Machine Offbearer	Wood Products, NEC	2
573.685-038	Burner	Brick, Tile, Nonclay Refractories	2
590.685-042	Ironer	Button and Misc. Notions	2
659.685-026	Mill Stenciler	Steel Work	2
669.685-102	Groover-and-Striper Operator	Wood Products, NEC	2
679.685-018	Thermal-Surfacing-Machine Operator	Stonework	2
728.685-010	Wire Preparation Machine Tender	Any Industry	2
754.685-014	Assembly-Machine Tender	Fabricated Plastic Products	2
921.685-046	Fruit Distributor	Agriculture	2
922.687-038	Coal Sampler	Utilities	2
961.667-014	Stand-In	Motion Picture	2

REACHING—OCCASIONALLY

DOT Code	Occupational Title	Industry	SVP
153.367-010	Clocker	Amusement and Recreation	2
221.667-010	Work-Ticket Distributor	Knitting	2
222.387-074	Shipping-and-Receiving Weigher	Clerical and Kindred	2
241.367-038	Investigator, Dealer Accounts	Financial Institutions	2
249.366-010	Counter Clerk	Photofinishing	2
295.357-018	Furniture-Rental Consultant	Retail Trade	2
295.467-014	Boat-Rental Clerk	Amusement and Recreation	2
299.647-010	Impersonator, Character	Any Industry	2
299.687-014	Sandwich-Board Carrier	Any Industry	1
342.357-010	Weight Guesser	Amusement and Recreation	2
342-657-010	Barker	Amusement and Recreation	2
344.677-014	Usher	Amusement and Recreation	2
349.667-014	Host/Hostess, Head	Amusement and Recreation	2
349.677-018	Children's Attendant	Amusement and Recreation	2
352.667-014	Parlor Chaperone	Hotel and Restaurant	2
353.367-022	Page	Radio and TV Broadcasting	2
359.367-010	Escort	Personal Service	2
359.567-014	Tanning Salon Attendant	Personal Service	2
359.667-010	Chaperon	Personal Service	2
359.677-030	Research Subject	Any Industry	1
372-667-042	School Bus Monitor	Government Services	2
429.587-010	Cotton Classer Aide	Agriculture	2
520.687-066	Blending-Tank Tender Helper	Canning and Preserving	2
521.685-386	Scaling Machine Operator	Canning and Preserving	2
524.687-022	Bakery Worker, Conveyor Line	Bakery Products	2
529.687-126	Kosher Inspector	Dairy Products	2
529.687-186	Sorter, Agricultural Produce	Agriculture	2
569.686.046	Laminating-Machine Offbearer	Wood Products, NEC	2
573.685-038	Burner	Brick, Tile, Nonclay Refractories	2
590.685-042	Ironer	Button and Misc. Notions	2
659.685-026	Mill Stenciler	Steel Work	2
669.685-102	Groover-and-Striper Operator	Wood Products, NEC	2
679.685-018	Thermal-Surfacing-Machine Operator	Stonework	2
712.684-050	Inspector, Surgical Instruments	Instruments and Apparatus	2
735.687-026	Racker	Jewelry, Silverware, Plated Ware	2
921.685-046	Fruit Distributor	Agriculture	2
961.667-014	Stand-In	Motion Picture	2

REACHING, HANDLING, FINGERING—OCCASIONALLY

DOT Code	Occupational Title	Industry	SVP
241.367-038	Investigator, Dealer Accounts	Financial Institutions	2
249.366-010	Counter Clerk	Photofinishing	2
295.357-018	Furniture-Rental Consultant	Retail Trade	2
295.467-014	Boat-Rental Clerk	Amusement and Recreation	2
299.647-010	Impersonator, Character	Any Industry	2
299.687-014	Sandwich-Board Carrier	Any Industry	1
342.657-010	Barker	Amusement and Recreation	2
344.677-014	Usher	Amusement and Recreation	2
349.677-014	Host/Hostess, Head	Amusement and Recreation	2
349.677-018	Children's Attendant	Amusement and Recreation	2

352.667-014	Parlor Chaperone	Hotel and Restaurant	2
353.367-022	Page	Radio and TV Broadcasting	2
359.367-010	Escort	Personal Service	2
359.567-014	Tanning Salon Attendant	Personal Service	2
359.667-010	Chaperon	Personal Service	2
359.677-030	Research Subject	Any Industry	1
372.667-042	School Bus Monitor	Government Services	2
429.587-010	Cotton Classer Aide	Agriculture	2
520.687-066	Blending-Tank Tender Helper	Canning and Preserving	2
521-685-386	Scaling Machine Operator	Canning and Preserving	2
524.687-022	Bakery Worker, Conveyor Line	Bakery Products	2
529.687-126	Kosher Inspector	Dairy Products	2
569.686-046	Laminating-Machine Offbearer	Wood Products, NEC	2
573.685-038	Burner	Brick, Tile, Nonclay Refractories	2
590.685-042	Ironer	Button and Misc. Notions	2
659.685-026	Mill Stenciler	Steel Work	2
669.685-102	Groover-and-Striper Operator	Wood Products, NEC	2
679.685-018	Thermal-Surfacing-Machine Operator	Stonework	2
921.685-046	Fruit Distributor	Agriculture	2
961.667-014	Stand-In	Motion Picture	2

HANDLING—NEVER

DOT Code	Occupational Title	Industry	SVP
342.657-010	Barker	Amusement and Recreation	2
349-667-014	Host/Hostess, Head	Amusement and Recreation	2
352.667-014	Parlor Chaperone	Hotel and Restaurant	2
359.667-010	Chaperon	Personal Service	2
372.667-042	School Bus Monitor	Government Services	2
529.687-126	Kosher Inspector	Dairy Products	2

REACHING—NEVER

DOT Code	Occupational Title	Industry	SVP
153.367-010	Clocker	Amusement and Recreation	2
221.667-010	Work-Ticket Distributor	Knitting	2
342.657-010	Barker	Amusement and Recreation	2
349-667-014	Host/Hostess, Head	Amusement and Recreation	2
352.667-014	Parlor Chaperone	Hotel and Restaurant	2
359.667-010	Chaperon	Personal Service	2
372.667-042	School Bus Monitor	Government Services	2
529.687-126	Kosher Inspector	Dairy Products	2

REACHING, HANDLING, FINGERING—NEVER

DOT Code	Occupational Title	Industry	SVP
342.657-010	Barker	Amusement and Recreation	2
349-667-014	Host/Hostess, Head	Amusement and Recreation	2
352.667-014	Parlor Chaperone	Hotel and Restaurant	2
359.667-010	Chaperon	Personal Service	2
372.667-042	School Bus Monitor	Government Services	2
529.687-126	Kosher Inspector	Dairy Products	2

§348.2 Basic Rules for Using the Medical-Vocational Guidelines as a Framework for Evaluating Cases Involving Exertional Impairments

The basic rules for using the Medical-Vocational Guidelines as a framework appear in SSR 83-12:

1. If the individual's exertional capacity falls between two rules which direct the same conclusion, a finding of "Disabled" or "Not disabled," as appropriate, will follow.
   a. As an example, where an exertional RFC is between the sedentary and light exertional levels and a finding of "Disabled" is indicated under both relevant rules, a finding of "Disabled" will follow. Even the complete occupational base (light) would not represent significant work for the individual.
   b. As a second example, where an exertional RFC is between medium and light work, and both relevant rules direct a conclusion of "Not disabled," the occupational base is clearly more than what is required as representing significant numbers of jobs because even the rule for less exertion directs a decision of "Not disabled."
2. If the exertional level falls between two rules which direct opposite conclusions, i.e., "Not disabled" at the higher exertional level and "Disabled" at the lower exertional level, consider as follows:
   a. An exertional capacity that is only slightly reduced in terms of the regulatory criteria could indicate a sufficient remaining occupational base to satisfy the minimal requirements for a finding of "Not disabled."
   b. On the other hand, if the exertional capacity is significantly reduced in terms of the regularity definition, it could indicate little more than the occupational base for the lower rule and could justify finding of "Disabled."
   c. In situations where the rules would direct different conclusions, and the individual's exertional limitations are somewhere "in the middle" in terms of the regulatory criteria for exertional ranges of work, more difficult judgments are involved as to the sufficiency of the remaining occupational base to support a conclusion as to disability. Accordingly,

V[ocational] S[pecialist] assistance is advisable for these types of cases.

§348.3 Using the Medical-Vocational Guidelines for Evaluating Impairments of Claimants Under Age 50

SSR 83-12 describes the need for VE testimony when a claimant younger than age 50 is unable to perform a full range of sedentary work:

Another situation where V[ocational] S[pecialist] assistance is advisable is where an individual's exertional RFC does not coincide with the full range of sedentary work. In such cases, equally difficult judgments are involved. Rather than having two rules which direct either the same or opposite conclusions, the decision-maker would have only one relevant rule and would have to decide whether the full range of sedentary work is significantly compromised.

A V[ocational] S[pecialist] can assess the effect of any limitation on the range of work at issue (e.g., the potential occupational base); advise whether the impaired person's RFC permits him or her to perform substantial numbers of occupations within the range of work at issue; identify jobs which are within the RFC, if they exist; and provide a statement of the incidence of such jobs in the region in which the person lives or in several regions of the country.

a. Where an individual's impairment has not met or equal[ed] the criteria of the Listing of Impairments at an earlier step in the sequence of adjudication but the full range of sedentary work is significantly compromised, section 201.00(h) of Appendix 2 provides that a finding of "Disabled" is not precluded for even younger individuals. (The examples in that section are of significantly restricted occupational bases.)
b. Where a person can perform all of the requirements of sedentary work except, for example, a restriction to avoid frequent contact with petroleum-based solvents, there is an insignificant compromise of the full range of sedentary work. Technically, because of the restriction, this person cannot perform the full range of sedentary work. However, this slight compromise within the full range of sedentary work (i.e., eliminating only the very few sedentary jobs in which frequent exposure to petroleum-based solvents would be required) leaves the sedentary occupational base substantially intact. Using the rules as a framework, a finding of "Not disabled" would be appropriate.

Consideration of restrictions less clear in their effect than in the examples cited will require a more detailed review of the impact of the particular limitations on the performance of the full range of sedentary work. The assistance of a V[ocational] S[pecialist] will usually be required in assessing the extent of the reduced work capabilities caused by the limitations. The particular examples set out above illustrate cases in which nonexertional impairments impinge upon the full range of sedentary work. Using the rules as a framework, the same principles may be applied to determine whether there has been a significant compromise in those instances where additional exertional limitations impinge on the full range of sedentary work.

For literate, English-speaking claimants under age 50, the real issue, indeed, the only issue, is whether jobs exist in significant numbers considering residual functional capacity. *See* SSR 96-9p. Education and work experience, no matter how limited, have been determined by the framework of the Medical-Vocational Guidelines to have no significant impact on work adjustment for this group of claimants. Nevertheless, there are RFCs that have been recognized by SSA to be so limited as to rule out all work. *See* the chart at §271.1, §§260 *et seq.*, and *see* SSR 96-9p.

Opinions on the meaning of "significant numbers" vary. For the most part, however, ALJs take an "I know a significant number when I see one" approach. In support of decisions denying benefits, some administrative appeals judges and ALJs have cited circuit court decisions which have, in effect, affirmed denials of benefits based on the existence of ridiculously small numbers of jobs, numbers so small that one can virtually be certain that no seriously impaired claimant will ever find a job opening if so few jobs exist. When you are dealing with a decision maker who ascribes to this school of thought, you cannot rest easy until you have ruled out virtually all potential jobs.

§348.4 The RFC of Alternate Sitting and Standing

The RFC for alternate sitting and standing is virtually a case study of how using the Medical-Vocational Guidelines as a framework has evolved to find fewer and fewer claimants with this RFC disabled. At first, SSR 83-12 provided a basis for finding disabled most claimants with this RFC, even those under age 50. VE testimony was necessary only in "cases of unusual limitation of ability to sit or stand":

In some disability claims, the medical facts lead to an assessment of RFC which is compatible with the performance of either sedentary or light work except that the person must alternate periods of sitting and standing. The individual may be able to sit for a time, but must then get up and stand or walk for a while before returning to sitting. Such an individual is not functionally capable of doing either the prolonged sitting contemplated in the definition of sedentary work (and for the relatively few light jobs which are performed primarily in a seated position) or the prolonged standing or walking contemplated for most light work. (Persons who can adjust to any need to vary sitting and standing by doing so at breaks, lunch periods, etc., would still be able to perform a defined range of work.)

There are some jobs in the national economy—typically professional and managerial ones—in which a person can sit or stand with a degree of choice. If an individual had such a job and is still capable of performing it, or is capable of transferring work skills to such jobs, he or she would not be found disabled. However, *most jobs have ongoing work processes which demand that a worker be in a certain place or posture for at least a certain length of time to accomplish a certain task. Unskilled types of jobs are particularly structured so that a person cannot ordinarily sit or stand at will.* In cases of unusual limitation of ability to sit or stand, a V[ocational] S[pecialist] should be consulted to clarify the implications for the occupational base.

[Emphasis added.]

SSR 96-9p acknowledges that the RFC for alternate sitting and standing erodes the sedentary occupational base but notes that the "extent of the erosion will depend on the facts in the case record, such as the frequency of the need to alternate sitting and standing and the length of time needed to stand." SSR 96-9p notes, in effect, that it may be "especially useful" to consult a vocational expert to determine if the individual is able to make adjustment to other work, a practice followed by many ALJs when confronted with this RFC prior to the promulgation of SSR 96-9p. Thus, SSR 96-9p makes inoperative the SSR 83-12 recommendation that a vocational expert be consulted only in cases of "unusual limitation of ability to sit or stand."

Whenever a VE testifies about the RFC for alternate sitting and standing, it is virtually assured that the VE will identify a number of jobs that the ALJ may find "significant." Nevertheless, many VEs treat this RFC as essentially within the sedentary occupational base. Such VEs say that it is easier to stand up on a sedentary job than it is to sit down on a light job. Thus, even though many claimants with this RFC lose when they are under age 50, they are found disabled as soon as they reach age 50.

But there are also VEs who say the RFC for alternate sitting and standing is in between sedentary and light work. The concept of erosion of the occupational base would require finding such a claimant disabled at least at age 50, since it is hard for a VE to make a credible argument that the occupational base of a claimant who must alternate sitting and standing is larger than the unskilled sedentary occupational base (200 occupations). But consider what happens when an ALJ uses the current mechanistic interpretation of framework. When an ALJ says to the VE, "Just tell me about the numbers of light jobs that can be done alternating sitting and standing," recognize that the ALJ is thinking about denying your 50-year-old client's case. If the VE comes up with any number of jobs that can be deemed "significant," your client will be denied benefits until age 55. It does not matter to many ALJs that your client's occupational base of 1,600 light and sedentary DOT occupations (according to Rule 202.00(a) of the Guidelines), millions and millions of jobs, has been eroded to a relatively small number of occupations. As long as the number of jobs your client can do can be deemed "significant," your client will lose.

For run-of-the-mill alternating sitting and standing cases, you may be tilting at windmills to try to convince most ALJs that merely the requirement of alternating sitting and standing requires that a claimant under age 50 be found disabled. When your client is over age 50, though, you may be able to get some traction. *See* §348.9 for questions to ask a VE on the alternate sitting and standing RFC.

Nevertheless, when a client tells you that he must alternate sitting and standing, there may be much more going on. He may need to walk around from time to time, a requirement that is much more difficult to accommodate than standing up from time to time. He may not be able to alternate sitting and standing all day long; he may need periods of lying down. He may have so many bad days, he would be unable to sustain work. He may have problems with attention and concentration that are serious enough to prevent holding a regular job. There are many possibilities that must be investigated.

Practice Tip

The RFC for alternate sitting and standing appears so frequently that it is worthwhile to hire a vocational expert to prepare a general report on the issue, a report that can be submitted in many different clients' cases. A sample report by Dr. Brent C. Evans follows. (Attachments have been omitted.) In the author's office, we still use this report despite the fact that it was written in 1995. When we use it, we attach it to a more recent report by a different VE that says all of the points made by Dr. Evans in 1995 are still valid.

December 1, 1995

Mr. Thomas E. Bush
Attorney at Law
161 West Wisconsin Avenue, Suite 4162
Milwaukee, WI 53203

Re: Alternate sitting, standing and walking jobs

Dear Mr. Bush:

You have asked me to provide a vocational expert's perspective on the Social Security Administration's policy regarding jobs that allow a worker to alternately sit, stand and walk. You provided me with a copy of a part of Social Security Ruling 83-12 that addresses this issue and a copy of POMSI DI 25020.005A.7. Let me first answer your primary question and then address additional issues.

Does the requirement that a worker alternately sit and stand significantly compromise the sedentary occupational base?

Yes. The POMS points out that the need to alternately sit and stand may significantly impinge on all ranges of work. This conclusion, explained in SSR 83-12, coincides with my experience. There are no medium or heavy occupations that can accommodate this limitation because, simply, there is no opportunity to sit down on such jobs. There are only a few light jobs in isolated occupations that will accommodate this limitation.

Some unskilled sedentary bench assembly occupations which, according to SSA, make up 85 percent of the sedentary occupational base, will allow a degree of alternate sitting and standing. I estimate that one-half of these occupations could be performed by an average worker who periodically shifts from sitting to standing. Other bench assembly occupations cannot be performed because the work processes won't accommodate such position changes. Of those jobs that the work processes will allow position changes, many cannot be performed because they are not performed at a "bench." They are performed at desk height. (It is impossible to do assembly work at desk height while standing up.) Thus, only one-third or fewer of unskilled sedentary jobs can be performed by someone who periodically alternates sitting and standing during the workday. There is a significant compromise of the sedentary occupational base even if we were to add those few light jobs that would accommodate this limitation.

Additional Factors

Things that will affect the number of jobs a person could do with this limitation include the following:

1. Maximum length of time a worker can sit or stand;
2. Whether the worker must change position at will;
3. Whether walking is required; and
4. The degree to which concentration and attention are affected.

How long must a worker be in a "certain posture" to accomplish work tasks?

If one has to change position more frequently than about once every thirty minutes, productivity will drop. As noted in SSR 83-12, a worker must be in a certain "posture for at least a certain length of time to accomplish a certain task" because of the "ongoing work processes." That certain length of time, in my opinion, is about 30 minutes.

Many people with back problems need to shift position more frequently than every 30 minutes. They need to shift when their back demands it. That is, in the words of SSR 83-12, they need a job that allows them to "sit or stand at will." This means that they must shift position unpredictably. It is certainly true, as pointed out in SSR 83-12, that "unskilled types of jobs are particularly structured so that a person cannot ordinarily sit or stand at will." In fact, the unpredictability of required position change is vocationally more important than the average length of time a person can sit or stand.

How long must a worker be in a "certain place" to accomplish work tasks?

SSR 83-12 describes an individual who "may be able to sit for a time, but then must get up and stand or walk for awhile before returning to sitting." Standing is easier to accommodate on the bench assembly jobs described above than is walking. A requirement of any significant walking at unpredictable intervals reduces the number of unskilled jobs to virtually zero. A walking requirement takes a worker away from his work station. This relates to the reference in SSR 83-12 that a worker must be "in a certain place" for "at least a certain length of time to accomplish a certain task." A worker cannot be away from the work station very often. Most factory jobs allow a worker a 15 minute break in the morning, a 15 minute break in the afternoon, and one-half hour for lunch. There is only a little additional leeway available on some jobs that will allow an additional five minute "bathroom break" every hour; but here I believe we're talking about a tolerant employer. Anyone who must walk so frequently that it cannot be accommodated on regular breaks or at lunch would not be capable of performing any of the bench assembly jobs.

Security Guard Jobs

There are no sedentary unskilled security guard jobs described in the current edition of the Dictionary of Occupational Titles. Nevertheless, there may be a few security guard jobs that are unskilled, which are essentially sedentary and which require that rounds be made. This job does not exist in significant numbers; but, even if it did exist in significant numbers, rounds are required at set times, not when a worker feels like he must take a walk. The unskilled security guard jobs that will accommodate this limitation do not exist.

Concentration and Attention

The matter of the degree to which concentration and attention are affected is not addressed in SSR 83-12 and the POMS; however, this issue is often present whenever a worker must frequently alternate positions. That is, we are not only dealing with posture and place, the physical manifestations of an impairment. We are also dealing with an issue that involves whether or not a worker can get his mind off his back pain and keep it on his work. It is common that such an impaired worker cannot maintain attention for the two hours necessary to do most jobs.

"Unusual limitation of ability to sit or stand"

SSR 83-12 refers to the need to seek a vocational expert opinion "in cases of unusual limitation of ability to sit or stand." You have asked my opinion about what this means. It seems to me that it is unusual when an impairment requiring alternate positioning does not include walking. That is, it's unusual when simply alternating sitting and standing will accommodate such an impairment. It is also unusual when an impairment requiring frequent position changes does not also include problems with concentration and attention.

I know of no study of the issue of alternate sitting, standing and walking which quantifies the jobs of which a worker with such limitation is capable. The Dictionary of Occupational Titles, Fourth Edition, Revised 1991, does not specifically address such a limitation nor do the computer programs based on Department of Labor materials. These sources, however, do demonstrate the relative scarcity of unskilled sedentary occupations. I enclose a list of the 137 sedentary unskilled occupations. It is from this list that we draw the relatively few occupations that will accommodate this limitation.

My opinion is based on the above sources, my training, experience, and observation of jobs. I note that my opinion is also supported by the Social Security Administration's position on this issue as stated in SSR 83-12 and POMS DI 25020.005A.7, copies of the relevant portions of which are attached to this letter.

I also enclose a copy of my resume.

Respectfully,

Dr. Brent C. Evans

Dr. Brent C. Evans, CVE, CWA
Diplomate, ABVE
President, VOC-EVAL Associates, Inc.

BCE/krn

§348.5   *Using the Medical-Vocational Guidelines as a Framework for Evaluating Solely Nonexertional Impairments*

These days, in cases where claimants have solely nonexertional impairments, many ALJ denial decisions may not even mention using the Medical-Vocational Guidelines as a framework. Or they might pay lip service to the framework of Medical-Vocational Guidelines Rule 204.00, which deals with heavy or very heavy work and amounts to saying nothing more than that the claimant has no exertional impairments. The real basis of denial decisions in such cases is that vocational experts testified that the claimants could do a number of jobs, which ALJs deemed to be "significant."

How are age, education and work experience considered in such cases? What if a claimant is 55 years old, has a limited education and an unskilled work background? How will these vocational adversities be taken into account? The answer from many within SSA is that age, education and work experience are included in hypothetical questions to the VE. So the VE considered them when giving the number of jobs the hypothetical claimant could perform.

The real answer to how age, education and work experience are considered in such nonexertional impairment cases is that they are not considered at all. They are not considered because by and large the Medical-Vocational Guidelines are not used as a framework when dealing with nonexertional impairment cases.

Although Rule 200.00(e) of the Medical-Vocational Guidelines provides that the Guidelines "do not direct factual conclusions of disabled or not disabled for individuals with solely nonexertional types of impairments," the same rule provides that the "determination as to whether disability exists shall be based on the principles in the appropriate sections of the regulations, giving consideration to the rules for specific case situations in this appendix 2." Thus, the Medical-Vocational Guidelines are supposed to be used as a framework.

Using the Medical-Vocational Guidelines as a framework in cases involving solely nonexertional impairments is discussed in SSR 85-15, which provides for consideration of erosion of the claimant's occupational base, an approach now out of favor within SSA:

Given no medically determinable impairment which limits exertion, the first issue is how much the person's occupational base—the entire exertional span from sedentary work through heavy (or very heavy) work—is reduced by the effects of the nonexertional impairment(s). This may range from very little to very much, depending on the nature and extent of the impairment(s). In many cases, a decisionmaker will need to consult a vocational resource....

The second issue is whether the person can be expected to make a vocational adjustment considering the interaction of his or her remaining occupational base with his or her age, education, and work experience. A decisionmaker must consider sections 404.1562-404.1568 and 416.962-416.968 of the regulations, section 204.00 of Appendix 2, and the table rules for specific case situations in Appendix 2. If, despite the nonexertional impairment(s), an individual has a large potential occupational base, he or she would ordinarily not be found disabled in the absence of extreme adversities in age, education, and work experience. (This principle is illustrated in rules 203.01, 203.02, and 203.10 and is set out in SSR 82-63, PPS79, Medical-Vocational Profiles Showing an Inability to Make an Adjustment to Other Work.) The assistance of a vocational resource may be helpful.

The examples provided in SSR 85-15 are generally fairly obvious, occurring at the two extremes of the spectrum. SSR 85-15 notes that even persons with a large occupational base may be found disabled because of adversities of age, education, and work experience. It gives the following example:

Example 3: Someone who is closely approaching retirement age, has a limited education or less, worked for 30 years in a cafeteria doing an unskilled job as a "server," almost constantly dealing with the public, and now cannot because of a severe mental impairment, frequently deal with the public. In light of the narrowed vocational opportunity in conjunction with the person's age, education, lack of skills, and long commitment to the particular type of work, a finding of disabled would be appropriate; but the decision would not necessarily be the same for a younger, better-educated, or skilled person. (Compare sections 404.1562 and 416.962 of the regulations and rule 203.01 of Appendix 2.)

Note that Rule 203.01 directs a finding of disabled for someone who is limited to medium work, is 60 years old, has a marginal or no education and an unskilled or no work background, despite having an occupational base of the administratively noticed 2,500 sedentary, light and medium occupations.

Two examples presented by SSR 85-15 of individuals of advanced age are useful for understanding the use of the Medical-Vocational Guidelines as a framework for evaluating solely nonexertional impairments:

Example 4: Someone who is of advanced age, has a high school education and did skilled work as manager of a housing project can no longer, because of a severe mental impairment, develop and implement plans and procedures, prepare budget requests, schedule repairs or otherwise deal with complexities of this level and nature. Assuming that, in this case, all types of related skilled jobs are precluded but the individual can do work which is not detailed and does not require lengthy planning, the remaining related semi-skilled jobs to which skills can be transferred and varied unskilled jobs, at all levels of exertion, constitute a significant vocational opportunity. A conclusion of "not disabled" would be appropriate. (Compare rules 201.07, 202.07, and 203.13 of Appendix 2.)

Example 5: Someone who is of advanced age, has a limited education, and did semi-skilled work as a first-aid attendant no longer has the mental capacity to work with people who are in emergency situations and require immediate attention to cuts, burns, suffocation, etc. Although there may be very few related semi-skilled occupations to which this person could transfer work skills, the large occupational base of unskilled work at all levels of exertion generally would justify a finding of not under a disability. (This is consistent with rules 203.11-203.17 of Appendix 2.)

As can be seen from these examples, using the Medical-Vocational Guidelines as a framework for analysis of solely nonexertional impairments involves reasoning by analogy. The regulations and rulings on this subject offer little guidance on how to draw analogies between erosion of the occupational base caused by nonexertional impairments and the rules stated in the Medical-Vocational Guidelines. No regulation or ruling describes how to use a vocational expert's testimony to assist in drawing these analogies.

SSA offered an approach to this problem in the POMS and then withdrew it during the first decade of the 21st century, replacing it with advice to cite at least three specific occupations "with an affirmative statement (based on the County Business Patterns, census records or other data) that such jobs exist in

significant numbers in the national economy." Here is how the now withdrawn POMS DI 25025.001 C.4 said to approach the problem:

It is first necessary to approximate the size of the remaining occupational base at all exertional levels (sedentary—very heavy).

Then it is necessary to compare the approximated occupational base to the number of occupations represented by the Appendix 2 tables (sedentary—medium) to determine the appropriate table(s) to be used.

The rule(s) in the table(s) selected that correspond to the person's age, education level and previous work experience, provide guidance as to the proper decision of disabled or not disabled.

NOTE: Based upon administrative notice taken in the disability regulations:

The number of occupations represented by the sedentary exertional table is approximately 200.

The total number of occupations represented by the light exertional table is approximately 1,600 (i.e., approximately 200 unskilled sedentary and 1,400 unskilled light occupations).

The total number of occupations represented by the medium exertional table is approximately 2,500 (i.e., approximately 200 unskilled sedentary, 1,400 unskilled light and 900 unskilled medium occupations).

In cases involving solely nonexertional impairments, according to SSR 85-15, the potential occupational base is the entire exertional span from sedentary through heavy (or very heavy) work. The Medical-Vocational Guidelines do not give any numbers of occupations for those above the medium level and neither did the POMS. However, analysis of Department of Labor data gathered for the Revised Fourth Edition of the Dictionary of Occupational Titles yields the following breakdown of unskilled occupations by exertional level, which we include here for the sake of providing a complete picture:

Exertional Level	Total Unskilled DOT Titles
Sedentary	137
Light	1571
Medium	967
Heavy	425
Very heavy	25
Total	3125

Consider a 55-year-old with nonexertional limitations, a limited education and unskilled work background. To apply the Medical-Vocational Guidelines as a framework, you must use the disfavored concept of erosion of the occupational base. You first figure out how many unskilled occupations such a 55-year-old claimant is capable of performing. Then you use that number to determine which exertional grid to apply as a framework. Say the claimant is capable of performing about 1,500 occupations, which is in the range of the number of light and sedentary occupations to which Table No. 2, the light grid, of the Medical-Vocational Guidelines applies. (Rule 202.00(a) says there are 1,600 separate sedentary and light unskilled occupations. The actual number from the DOT is 1,708 occupations.) Thus, you use as a framework Rule 202.01 from the light exertional grid to find the claimant disabled. If the claimant is capable of performing significantly more occupations than that represented by the light grid, it will be necessary to use as a framework Rule 203.11 from medium exertional grid, which will find the claimant not disabled.

In the real world, although they will not use the methodology described above, many ALJs, perhaps a majority, will instinctively come up with a way to find disabled a 55-year-old claimant with solely nonexertional limitations who cannot perform one-half of all unskilled occupations. Age 55, after all, "significantly affects a person's ability to adjust to other work." 20 C.F.R. § 404.1563(e).

But many other ALJs will simply ask the VE how many jobs this claimant can perform and then find the claimant not disabled because the claimant can perform a "significant number" of jobs. Your challenge is to figure out how to prevent this result. Arguments founded on assessing erosion of the claimant's occupational base will not work with an ALJ determined to deny the claim, will not work at the Appeals Council and, so far, have not worked in federal court. *See*, for example, *Fast v. Barnhart*, 397 F.3d 468 (7th Cir. 2005).

Although the erosion approach, despite its elegance, will not work, the significant numbers approach is wrong whenever age, education and work experience have a significant impact on a claimant's ability to work. The regulations and ruling still require use of the Medical-Vocational Guidelines as a framework. Although no one knows exactly what it means to use the Guidelines as a framework without using the erosion concept, it is clear that age, education and work experience must be considered in cases with nonexertional impairments.

The hypothetical question asked the VE included the claimant's age. To see how the VE weighed age, ask the VE if the number of jobs would be different if the claimant were age 40 instead of age 55. You may be able to demonstrate that the VE did not reduce the number of jobs for the claimant's age and that therefore age was not considered by the VE. You may also be able to show that education and work experience were not considered either.

Also address the issue of vocational adjustment. Vocational adjustment is, after all, the concept underlying the determinations in the grids of whether jobs exist in significant numbers considering a person's age, education, and work experience. For example, you may ask a VE: Would this claimant with [describe nonexertional impairments] have more difficulty, the same difficulty or less difficulty adjusting to different work than a person with solely an exertional impairment who [describe individual who meets a particular rule in the Medical-Vocational Guidelines]? If the VE responds that the claimant would have the same difficulty or more difficulty adjusting to different work as someone who is found disabled by the grids, this can form the basis for your argument that the claimant ought to be found disabled, too.

It is not necessarily inconsistent for a VE to state, in response to a hypothetical question from the ALJ, that a claimant with a mental impairment is *capable* of many jobs but, in response to a question about vocational adjustment, to state that the claimant would have greater difficulty *adjusting* to other work than someone who is found disabled by the grids. Part of the apparent inconsistency may arise out of the way the original hypothetical question was asked and answered. For example, people who are depressed may be arguably *capable* of a job (that is, they can lift an object and carry it from point A to point B over and over during a workday), but they may have great difficulty *adjusting* to work. (That is, they have difficulty getting to work every day. If anything unusual comes up, they become stressed. They have difficulty adjusting to dealing with new people, etc.) Thus, in any case involving mental impairments, be sure to ask some questions about vocational adjustment.

Also, depression, and other mental impairments such as somatoform disorders, may limit exertion, a fact which is recognized by SSRs 85-15 and 96-8p. If you can use a mental impairment to establish the equivalent of an exertional impairment, it simplifies the task of using the grids as a framework for decision-making.

§348.6 Court Decisions on Framework Analysis

There are only a few court decisions that discuss the issue of analysis of disability using the Medical-Vocational Guidelines as a framework. *Cooper v. Sullivan*, 880 F.2d 1152 (9th Cir. 1989), is a leading case. Mrs. Irene Cooper was of advanced age (55 and over), had a high school education and an unskilled work background. She was found by an ALJ to be not disabled by her nonexertional manipulative impairment. The ALJ relied on a VE's testimony that although Mrs. Cooper was not capable of returning to her past work as a stock clerk, she was capable of performing several jobs including crossing guard, self-service station operator and cashier, and gate tender.

The ALJ found that the Medical-Vocational Guidelines did not apply to Mrs. Cooper's nonexertional impairment and that jobs within her RFC existed in significant numbers. The Court of Appeals, however, concluded that Mrs. Cooper's restrictions were the result of both exertional and nonexertional impairments. The court applied Rules 201.04 and 202.04 of the Medical-Vocational Guidelines to find Mrs. Cooper disabled, stating that:

> where application of the grids directs a finding of disability, that finding must be accepted by the Secretary. That is so whether the impairment is exertional or results from a combination of exertional and nonexertional limitations. Here, the testimony of the Secretary's own witness establishes that the combination of Mrs. Cooper's exertional and nonexertional impairments limits her to at most light work. Applying the grids to Mrs. Cooper's case results in a finding of disability.

Cooper v. Sullivan, 880 F.2d 1152, 1157 (9th Cir. 1989).

The court then addressed the issue of vocational adjustment:

> Moreover, we note that the ALJ erred when he disregarded the assumptions which underlie the grids. Based on the vocational expert's testimony, the ALJ concluded that Mrs. Cooper was not disabled because "[c]onsidering the types of work which the claimant is still functionally capable of performing in combination with her age, education and work experience, *she can be expected to make a vocational adjustment to work which exists in significant numbers in the national economy*." (Emphasis added). However, the regulations stress that the most difficult problem that a claimant such as Mrs. Cooper faces is that of adapting to a new job. Indeed, that is the reason that the grids direct the conclusion that claimants like Mrs. Cooper are disabled. "[F]or individuals of advanced age [i.e., age 55 or older] who can no longer perform vocationally relevant past work and who have a history of unskilled work experience . . . the limitations in vocational adaptability represented by functional restriction to light work warrant a finding of disabled". *Id.* at §202.00(c). Just as the ALJ may not disregard the grids' conclusion of disability, he also may not disregard the assumptions which

underlie the grids.

Cooper v. Sullivan, 880 F.2d 1152, 1157-1158 (9th Cir. 1989).

Another Ninth Circuit case, *Swenson v. Sullivan*, 876 F.2d 683, 688 (9th Cir. 1989), interpreted "the regulations to require the Secretary to reject vocational testimony that is inconsistent with the grids' overall framework." In that case, the VE testified that the jobs he identified as within the claimant's RFC existed in fewer numbers than did jobs for a person who would be found disabled under the grids.

For an example of a case remanded by a court for VE testimony to assess the extent of erosion of the occupational base, *see DeFrancesco v. Bowen*, 867 F.2d 1040, 1045 (7th Cir. 1989).

For an example of a case which discusses the erosion issue in some detail and finds that the ALJ was correct in using the grids as a framework without calling a VE to testify, because the claimant's capacity for the full range of light work was not significantly reduced, *see Ortiz v. Secretary*, 890 F.2d 520 (1st Cir. 1989).

In *Fast v. Barnhart*, 397 F.3d 468 (7th Cir. 2005), the Seventh Circuit rejected the sort of framework analysis outlined in this book in favor of a finding of "significant numbers" in an ALJ decision.

§348.7   Questions to the Vocational Expert Laying a Foundation for Argument Concerning Using the Grids as a Framework

Demonstrate That the VE Did Not Consider Age, Education and Work Experience

- You have identified _____ jobs (positions) in the national/local economy within the claimant's RFC. If this claimant were 10 years younger, does that change the number of jobs? If the claimant had a different educational background, would that change the number of jobs?

The Vocational Adjustment Approach

- Would this claimant with [describe nonexertional impairments] have more difficulty, the same difficulty or less difficulty adjusting to different work than a person with solely an exertional impairment who [describe individual who is found disabled by a particular rule in the Medical-Vocational Guidelines]?

Erosion of the Occupational Base

As a rule, arguments founded on demonstrating erosion of the claimant's occupational base will fail. If you are so intrepid that you want to try to set this issue up for testing in federal court, you will need to establish a foundation for it with VE testimony.

The Medical-Vocational Guidelines provide the number of occupational titles for the unskilled sedentary, light and medium occupational bases. VEs, however, often testify in terms of job groups (*e.g.*, packaging jobs, bench assembly jobs) rather than occupational titles; and they usually give numbers of jobs or positions in the local and national economy. Before you can draw any analogies from the VE's testimony, some translation is necessary. Thus, you must either obtain from the VE the number of occupational titles in the claimant's remaining occupational base or translate the concepts of the Medical-Vocational Guidelines into the frame of reference used by the VE.

Translate into the Language of the Grids the VE's Testimony About the Number of Jobs the Claimant Can Do

• What percentage of the 1,600 light and sedentary occupations identified in the Medical-Vocational Guidelines is the claimant still capable of performing?

Or, if the VE has identified a small number of jobs:

• What are the DOT occupational titles of the unskilled jobs that you have identified as within the claimant's RFC?

• Thus, there are a total of _____ occupational titles that you have found to be within the claimant's RFC. Is that right?

In argument to the ALJ, compare the number of occupational titles given you by the VE to the 200 unskilled sedentary/1,400 light/900 medium occupations of which administrative notice was taken. Draw analogies from the Medical-Vocational Guidelines to argue that the appropriate occupational base is significantly compromised.

Or Translate the Grids into the VE's Frame of Reference

• You have identified _____ jobs (positions) in the national/local economy within the claimant's RFC. Tell us how many unskilled medium/unskilled light and unskilled sedentary jobs there are in the same area.

With these numbers, you will be able to draw analogies from the grids, including possibly that the full range of work at the appropriate level is significantly compromised.

§348.8   *Questions for Vocational Expert About Numbers of Sedentary Unskilled Jobs Within Claimant's RFC*

Vocational expert testimony about the numbers of sedentary unskilled jobs within a claimant's RFC existing in the economy is frequently hogwash. VEs often refer to jobs with a higher exertional requirement or a higher skill level. They make no effort to sort out

how many jobs are part time. They tend to testify about numbers of jobs based on faulty assumptions with little or no support for their conclusions other than their own "personal experience" which, as a rule, does not include counting the numbers of particular sedentary unskilled jobs.

If you plan on cross-examining a vocational expert about numbers of jobs, ask the ALJ at least ten business days before the hearing to send the VE a subpoena *duces tecum*. A sample letter requesting the issuance of a subpoena *duces tecum* along with an attachment listing the required documents appears at §348.8.1. It is essential to preserve the issue for appeal, that you ask for underlying data and the vocational expert's reasoning backing up the opinion. *Donahue v. Barnhart*, 279 F.3d 441, 446 (7th Cir. 2002). According to the Seventh Circuit Court of Appeals in a leading case, the data and reasoning must be available on demand. *McKinnie v. Barnhart*, 368 F.3d 907, 911 (7th Cir. 2004).

There is no source of official information that provides actual numbers of unskilled sedentary jobs. States gather data about numbers of jobs for use of their unemployment compensation agencies; but state data based on the Occupation Employment Statistics (OES) system is even harder to use than that gathered by the federal government and it is not standardized nationwide. It does not break down the number of full time unskilled sedentary jobs.

The United States Bureau of the Census gathers data about numbers of jobs grouped by census codes, which were changed for the 2000 census. The current census codes are based on codes from the Standard Occupational Classification (SOC) system, which eventually will be used by all federal statistical agencies to classify workers into occupational categories for the purpose of collecting data. The Specific Occupation Selector Manual, Fourth Edition, from U.S. Publishing, lists the DOT occupational titles in each SOC code and census code. It also provides for each individual DOT title information that supplements the DOT, such as that which appears in the chart at §346.6, *e.g.*, how often during the workday reaching, handling or fingering is required to do the job.

Many census codes include more than one Standard Occupational Classification code. Each census code includes numerous occupations related by broad job similarities, not by SVP, skill or exertional level. For example, Census Code 512, SOC Occupation 43-3031, "Bookkeeping, Accounting and Auditing Clerks," contains 27 DOT occupational titles, only one of which is an unskilled sedentary job—Parimutuel-Ticket Checker, 219.587-010. Census code data from the U.S. Census Bureau will show the grand total jobs in Census Code 512, a reliable number, but it will not break down the numbers of jobs by skill or exertional level. Analysis is necessary by someone familiar with the local job market to make an estimate of the number of unskilled sedentary jobs in Census Code 512. How many Parimutuel-Ticket Checker jobs there are in your area depends, of course, on how many race tracks are nearby. Once you come up with an estimate of the total number of Parimutuel-Ticket Checker jobs, the number will need to be reduced to account for the fact that many, if not most, of these jobs are part time evening and weekend jobs.

There are several census codes that one might guess would contain unskilled sedentary DOT occupational titles; but they do not. For example, census code 775 applies to "Miscellaneous Assemblers and Fabricators," and includes the following SOC Occupations: 51-2091, "Fiberglass Laminators and Fabricators"; 51-2092, "Team Assemblers"; 51-2093, "Timing Device Assemblers, Adjusters and Calibrators"; and 51-2099, "Assemblers and Fabricators, All other." Included in census code 775 are 45 DOT occupational titles, none of which is an unskilled sedentary job. Census Code 835, "Tailors, Dressmakers & Sewers," contains no unskilled sedentary occupation. Likewise, there are no sedentary unskilled occupations in Census Code 836, "Textile Bleaching and Dyeing Machine Operators and Tenders."

Census Code 392, "Security Guards and Gaming Surveillance Officers," which includes SOC Occupations 33-9031, "Gaming Surveillance Officers and Gaming Investigators," and 33-9032, "Security Guards," includes 10 DOT occupational titles, none of which are sedentary. Census Code 472 applies to cashiers, SOC Occupations 41-2011 and 41-2012. Included in census code 472 are 19 DOT occupational titles, only 7 of which are unskilled—none of which is an unskilled sedentary job. Census Code 975, "Material Moving Workers, All Other," contains no unskilled sedentary occupational title.

Twenty-one individual census codes, like Census Code 512 discussed above, contain only one unskilled sedentary occupational title. Five census codes contain two unskilled sedentary DOT occupations; and two census codes have three unskilled sedentary occupations. See Appendix 5 of this book, which identifies the 137 sedentary unskilled DOT occupations by census code. The following chart shows which census codes contain so few sedentary unskilled occupations:

There are 5 unskilled sedentary occupations in Census Code 871, "Cutting Workers," and there are 5 unskilled sedentary DOT occupations in Census Code 865, "Crushing, Grinding, Polishing, Mixing, and Blending Workers." There are 10 unskilled sedentary DOT titles in Census Code 881, "Painting Workers," out of hundreds of occupational titles. There are 12 unskilled sedentary DOT titles among the hundreds of DOT titles in Census Code 895, "Helpers—Production

Census Codes With Three or Fewer Unskilled Sedentary DOT Titles			
Census Code	Census Code Title	DOT Title and Number	Total DOT Titles in Census Code
272	Athletes, Coaches, Umpires & Related Workers	Scoreboard Operator, 349.665-010	30
395	Lifeguards & Other Protective Service Workers	Surveillance-System Monitor, 379.367-010	8
511	Billing & Posting Clerks & Machine Operators	Telegraph Service Rater, 214.587-010	40
512	Bookkeeping, Accounting and Auditing Clerks	Parimutuel-Ticket Checker, 219.587-010	27
523	Credit Authorizers, Checkers, and Clerks	Call-Out Operator, 237.367-014	4
531	Interviewers, Except Eligibility and Loan	Charge-Account Clerk, 205.367-014	6
535	Correspondence & Order Clerks	Order Clerk, Food and Beverage, 209.567-014	14
540	Receptionists and Information Clerks	Telephone Quotation Clerk, 237.367-046	14
551	Couriers and Messengers	Tube Operator, 239.687-014	7
560	Production, Planning and Expediting Clerks	Weave-Defect-Charting Clerk, 221.587-042	61
582	Word Processors and Typists	Addresser, 209.587-010	8

Census Code	Census Code Title	DOT Title and Number	Total DOT Titles in Census Code
	Census Codes With Three or Fewer Unskilled Sedentary DOT Titles		
586	Office Clerks, General	Election Clerk, 205.367-030; Cutter-and-Paster, Press Clippings, 249.587-014; Document Preparer, Microfilming, 249.587-018	73
772	Electrical, Electronics and Electromechanical Assemblers	Stem Mounter, 725.684-018	61
795	Cutting, Punching, & Press Machine, Setters, Operators & Tenders—Metal & Plastic	Clearance Cutter, 615.685-014; Press Operator, Pierce and Shave, 715.685-050	74
800	Grinding, Lapping, Polishing & Buffing Machine Tool Setter & Operators	Polisher, Eyeglass Frames, 713.684-038; Smoother, 733.685-026	73
822	Other Metal, Plastic, Milling, Planning Workers & Operators & Tenders	Bonder, Semiconductor, 726.685-066; Tapper, Bit, 739.685-046	69
826	Printing Machine Operators	Ink Printer, 652.685-038	87
832	Sewing Machine Operators	Window-Shade-Ring Sewer, 692.685-254; Sack Repairer, 782.687-046	128
835	Sewers, Hand	Umbrella Tipper, Hand, 739.684-162	21
840	Textile Cutting Machine Setters, Operators & Tenders	Label Pinker, 585.685-062	35
842	Textile Winding, Twisting, and Drawing Out Machine Setters, Operators and Tenders	Carding-Machine Operator, 681.685-030	73
872	Extruding, Forming, Pressing and Compacting Machine Setters, Operators and Tenders	Laminator I, 690.685-258	162
880	Packaging & Filling Machine Operators & Tenders	Stuffer, 731.685-014	74
886	Cleaning, Washing, & Metal Pickling Equipment Operators & Tenders	Washroom Operator, 529.665-014	26
913	Drivers/Sales Workers & Truck Drivers	Escort-Vehicle Driver, 919.663-022	28
962	Laborers & Freight, Stock & Material Movers, Hand	Leaf Tier, 529.687-138	48
963	Machine Feeders and Offbearers	Plastic-Design Applier, 690.686-046; Toggle-Press Folder-and-Feeder, 690.686-066; Clip-Loading-Machine Feeder, 694.686-010	291
964	Packers and Packagers, Hand	Ampoule Sealer, 559.687-014; Bander, Hand, 920.687-030	59

Workers." There are 14 unskilled sedentary DOT titles among the hundreds of DOT titles in Census Code 874, "Inspectors, Testers, Sorters, Samplers, and Weighers." There are 54 unskilled sedentary DOT occupational titles in Census Code 896, "Other Production Workers Including Semiconductor Processors," which contains more than 1,800 DOT titles. These numbers appear broadly consistent with SSA's estimate that "[a] pproximately 85 percent of these jobs are in the machine trades and benchwork occupational categories." Rule 201.00(a) of the Medical-Vocational Guidelines.

While the number of jobs in a census code provided by the Census Bureau is a reliable number, there is no other source for national numbers; and no source breaks down the numbers according to skill and exertional level. Can a vocational expert work from the census code numbers to estimate the number of unskilled sedentary jobs in that census code? What methodology would be used to do this? Isn't it more likely that a reasonable estimate can be made when there are many sedentary unskilled jobs contained in a particular census code?

U.S. Publishing provides estimates of the numbers of unskilled jobs at various exertional levels by census code. But it recognizes the limitations of its data. U.S. Publishing's website, www.occustats.com/references.html, includes the following explanation:

> The Dictionary of Occupational Titles (DOT) is a publication of the U.S. Department of Labor. It provides job descriptions and worker requirement information for 12,741 individual jobs found in the national economy. All DOT titles have been assigned a corresponding Census Code by the National Crosswalk Service Center in Des Moines, Iowa. U.S. Publishing has published a crosswalk for the Census and DOT. It is called the Specific Occupation Selector (SOS) manual and shows all DOT codes and titles grouped by Census Codes. When using the Occupational Employment Quarterly in conjunction with the SOS Manual to estimate the number of individuals employed in a specific DOT job, local knowledge of the labor market should be used. No government agency reports employment by specific DOT codes.

U.S. Publishing provides numbers of unskilled sedentary occupations by assuming that the numbers of jobs within a particular census code are distributed roughly proportionately to the total number of occupational titles that make up that census code. This assumption underlies the Occupational Employment Quarterly from U.S. Publishing, a customized printout that can be ordered for virtually any geographic area in the country or for the entire United States. See Appendix 2 for ordering information. It shows total employment by census code for the selected area, numbers of unskilled and semi-skilled jobs within the census code by exertional level, and the total number of skilled jobs within the census code.

A good vocational expert would use the Occupational Employment Quarterly as a starting place, recognizing the assumptions underlying the numbers, and make adjustments to arrive at an even better estimate of the number of unskilled sedentary jobs in the local or national economy. For example, the one unskilled sedentary job in census code 913 is Escort-Vehicle Driver, 919.663-022, a job with primary duties of driving a vehicle equipped with warning lights and signs to escort trucks hauling mobile homes on public thoroughfares. The Occupational Employment Quarterly assumes that the 28 DOT titles in census Code 913, of which only one is sedentary, exist in roughly equal numbers. This is an assumption that a good vocational expert would examine carefully.

Indeed, U.S. Publishing publishes a pamphlet titled "Data Usage Sources and References" in which it sets forth the limitations of its data. It admits that it "cannot tell how many are employed in each DOT job within [a census] code." It states that to use the data it provides correctly "to estimate the number of individuals employed in a specific DOT job, local knowledge of the labor market along with common sense should be used." A similar warning appears on the Occupational Employment Quarterly itself.

It is possible, and sometimes fruitful, to start your examination about numbers of jobs at the point where the judge asks you if you have any questions about the vocational expert's qualifications. The sample voir dire questions included below, as well as many of the other questions in this section, are based on an approach taken by Attorney A. Robert Kassin, a careful student of vocational issues. Attorney Kassin recommends that if you do not question the VE concerning qualifications, that you ask to reserve your right to question the VE concerning qualifications after the VE testifies.

After the VE testifies, the first approach for cross-examining a VE about numbers of jobs is to try to weed out those jobs that do not fit your client's RFC or require a higher skill level. See §346.6. Then focus on the numbers issue.

What research did the VE do? What sources did the VE consult? Did the VE bring along any excerpts from the vocational source? If so, ask to look at it.

Did the numbers come directly from this source? Or did the VE have to make calculations of numbers of jobs based on information in the vocational source? If so, how was the calculation done? What was the methodology? What assumptions were made?

If the answers to where the numbers come from is essentially "personal experience," ask some questions about how the VE's experience can lead to estimates of numbers of jobs in the area.

Here are some sample questions:

Voir Dire on Qualifications for Determining Numbers of a Particular Occupational Title in an Area
• Will you be able to state with a reasonable degree of professional certainty the number of jobs in this area for a particular DOT occupational title?
• Do you have any training in determining the number of jobs in the local economy for a particular DOT occupational title?
    • Please describe your training.
• Are you familiar with methods for determining how many jobs there are in the local economy with a particular DOT occupational title?
• What are the guidelines for determining how many jobs there are in a job market area for a particular DOT occupational title?
• Are there certain procedures to be followed in making such determinations?
    • Please describe those procedures.
• If your goal is to determine how many jobs there are in an area with a particular DOT occupational title but which are performed differently than the occupation is described in the DOT, such as sedentary jobs that allow alternate sitting and standing, how do you go about determining this?
• Do you have any experience in determining how many jobs there are in the local economy for a particular DOT occupational title?
    • Please summarize that experience.
• Your work is primarily as a rehabilitation counselor, is that correct?
• Would it be fair to say that basically you are involved in determining whether specific jobs exist in which a particular individual can be placed?
• Would it be fair to say that job placement seldom requires you to determine a reasonably exact number of such types of jobs in a certain area?
• Would it be fair to say that no part of your job as a rehabilitation counselor is involved in determining how many jobs there are within particular DOT occupational titles that exist in a local labor market?
• Would it be fair to say that you rely upon other sources for those determinations?

After VE Testimony About Numbers of Jobs— Introductory Questions
• Would you agree that the numbers of jobs you listed as being available are merely rough estimates and that

you really can't say for sure how many of any particular jobs exist in this area?
• What did you base your testimony on?
• Where did you obtain this information?
• Could you show it to me?
• Are you familiar with the methodology and documentation used by your source in its compilation of the data on which you rely? Describe the methodology.
• Are you familiar with the limitations on the use of the data suggested by the compiler of your source of information? What are those limitations?
• Is any of your testimony today based upon surveys that you have personally conducted? Which part of your testimony? What were the surveys? When did you conduct them? Could you please provide me with a copy of each survey?
• Is any of your testimony today based on surveys that other persons have conducted? (Same questions as above.)

General Questions
• Do you have knowledge of the availability of jobs in the area?
    • How did you derive this information?
• Do you understand that the Dictionary of Occupational Titles is considered an authoritative source by the SSA?
• Are you aware how the Dictionary of Occupational Titles classifies jobs as far as strength requirements?
    • What are the classifications?
• Does the DOT have codes to designate which positions are entry level? Sedentary?
    • What are those codes? [VE should say that it is an SVP of 1 or 2; and "S."]
• What does an SVP of 1 or 2 mean? [Should be up to 30 days preparation.]
• What does an SVP of 3 mean?
• A job with an SVP of 3 would not be an entry level position as defined by the Social Security Administration, is that correct? Did your answer state only the number of entry level jobs available? Didn't your answer include some SVP 3 jobs?
• What are the DOT numbers for the specific jobs you said existed? According to the DOT, what SVP level do those jobs have? Do those jobs have SVP levels of 1 or 2? Do they have an exertional level of "S"?

If Source Is Occupational Employment Quarterly From U.S. Publishing
• In fact, doesn't the Occupational Employment Quarterly only *authoritatively* report the numbers of jobs for a census code number?
• How many census code numbers are there? [About 470.]
• How many DOT code numbered jobs are there? [12,741.]

- So, on an average, each census code number would contain 27 individual DOT job titles?
- Isn't it true, then, that U.S. Publishing arrives at the number of SVP 1 and 2, sedentary jobs, by dividing the total number of jobs in any particular census code by the number of DOT occupational titles with that census code number and then multiplying by the number of sedentary unskilled jobs?
- It assumes that all the DOT occupations within a census code exist in roughly equal numbers, doesn't it?
- So basically, it makes an estimate of the number of actual jobs that exist for any particular DOT occupational title, doesn't it?
- What is the census code number for the job you listed?
- How many DOT occupational titles does it contain?
- Isn't it true that the total number of people employed for a certain census code is shown in the second column of the Occupational Employment Quarterly?
- This is the number of jobs reported by the Bureau of the Census, isn't it?
- It includes jobs with SVPs higher than 2, doesn't it?
- The Occupational Employment Quarterly shows the total number of unskilled jobs by exertional level, doesn't it?
- Do you know what the relationship is between the number shown as total sedentary unskilled jobs and the total number currently employed for this census code?
- Doesn't it appear that U.S. Publishing took the total number of jobs for a census code and divided by the number of DOT job titles, then multiplied by the number of sedentary unskilled DOT job titles to arrive at its estimate of unskilled sedentary jobs?
- Census code data on which U.S. Publishing relies includes part time jobs, doesn't it?
- Have you reduced the numbers you have given us to account for part time jobs? If we want to know only how many full time jobs there are, what would your estimate be?
- Do you know that U.S. Publishing, on its website, www.occustats.com/references.html, states: "Part-time participation in the labor force occurs over a large range depending on the occupation. Occupations like retail sales clerks and waiters and waitresses are on the high end of the range, while professional and technical occupations are on the low end. The mean for all occupations is 18%"?
- You say there are thousands of sedentary unskilled hand packaging jobs in the national economy; and you base this number on data from U.S. Publishing, which in turn bases its numbers on Census Code 964? Is that right?
- What are the unskilled sedentary DOT titles in Census Code 964?
- Isn't it true that the sedentary unskilled occupations in Census Code 964 are Ampoule Sealer, 559.687-014, and Bander, Hand, 920.687-030? Have you investigated these jobs? Without investigating these two jobs, how can you give us an estimate of how many of them exist in the national economy? Are cigar trademark bands still put on by hand? Are ampoules still sealed by hand? If you do not know the answers to these questions, how can you estimate the number of these jobs in the economy?

Where the VE Claims Not to Use DOT Definitions for Jobs

You stated that the jobs you identified as meeting the requirements of hypothetical question #___ are not as defined in the DOT.
- What is your source for the numbers of these jobs?
- How does that source define these jobs?
- What does the source say are the weight requirements of each job?
- What does the source say are the stress requirements?
- What does the source say is the amount of walking, standing, sitting?
- If you don't know how the source defines the jobs, then how do you know whether the jobs listed meet the requirements of hypothetical question #___ as far as weight, standing, walking, sitting, etc.?

§348.8.1 Form: Request for Subpoena Duces Tecum to Vocational Expert With Attachment

_____

Administrative Law Judge

_____

_____

_____

           RE: Disability Claim of _____

                  SSN: _____

                  Date of Hearing: _____

Request for Subpoena Duces Tecum to Vocational Expert   _____

                               Address: _____

                                             _____

Dear Judge _____:

A vocational expert (VE) has been retained by the Social Security Administration to testify at the upcoming hearing in this case.

Please issue a Subpoena Duces Tecum to the vocational expert to insure that the VE brings to the hearing documents upon which the expert may rely in forming opinions during the course of the hearing.

The availability of the requested documents is reasonably necessary for a full presentation of the case. 20 C.F.R. § 404.950(d)(1). It is particularly important in a case involving a step 5 analysis where the burden of proof is on the Commissioner that these documents be available to demonstrate the existence of significant numbers of jobs.

It has been my experience that vocational experts often testify about numbers of jobs that exist in the region where the claimant resides for various occupations but fail to adequately identify the statistical source for those opinions. The regulations permit vocational experts to rely upon various sources of statistical information including U.S. Census data, Department of Labor data, County Business Patterns, etc. However, unless the vocational expert brings the documents to the hearing, it is not possible to adequately understand the basis for the vocational expert's conclusions or cross-examine the expert.

I also request that the vocational expert bring to the hearing all labor market surveys performed by the vocational expert upon which the VE plans to rely in forming opinions about the number of jobs that may exist for specific occupations in the labor market. If the vocational expert has performed such job analysis or job surveys, that documentation should exist and should be available as a basis for cross-examination.

Finally, I request that the vocational expert bring to the hearing all professional articles or other publications that explain, discuss or report how the availability of various jobs or occupations are affected by a variety of limitations. These limitations are generally outlined in Social Security Ruling 96-9p and I believe that the limitations may be part of a hypothetical question posed to the vocational expert.

I object to the vocational expert testifying about the number of jobs that may exist in the labor market unless the VE produces valid, reliable data of some sort to support such testimony. I object to any VE opinion based on the VE's personal experience unless the VE provides a foundation demonstrating a valid, reliable methodology supporting that opinion as required by Daubert v. Merrell Dow Pharmaceuticals, Inc., 509 U.S. 579 (1993), and Kumho Tire Co. v. Carmichael, 526 U.S. 137 (1999).

Please issue this subpoena with the enclosed attachment identifying the documents that the vocational expert should bring to the hearing. The cost of issuing the subpoena, witness fees and mileage should be paid by the Social Security Administration. See 20 C.F.R. § 404.950(d)(3)&(4).

Sincerely,

Enclosure

cc: Vocational Expert
     Client

ATTACHMENT TO SUBPOENA DUCES TECUM
1.   All statistics, statistical summaries, reports, or compilations upon which you typically rely in forming
         opinions about the number of jobs that exist in the region where the claimant resides.
2.   All documents that describe the methodologies used by the publishers and/or compilers of the documents
         described in Item No. 1 above.
3.   All labor market surveys performed by you or other vocational professionals upon which you rely in
         forming opinions about the number of jobs that may exist for specific occupations in the labor market.
4.   All job analyses prepared by you on behalf of employers upon which you rely in forming opinions about
         the number of jobs that exist in the labor market.
5.   Any compilation of job descriptions or job summaries (other than the Dictionary of Occupational Titles)
         that are incorporated by reference into any of the statistical summaries, reports or compilations identified in
         item #1 above.
6   Any published articles or labor market surveys that describe the vocational impact of manipulation
         limitations, sitting limitations, standing limitations, and reaching limitations on the unskilled sedentary and
         light occupational base. Any published articles or labor market surveys that describe the vocational impact
         of psychological, cognitive, or emotional limitations on the occupational base.
7.   Copies of any data summaries, work sheets, or "crib sheets" that the vocational expert has prepared in
         anticipation of testifying in Social Security hearings which identify occupations and numbers of jobs in
         those occupations.

§348.9   Questions for the Vocational Expert About the RFC for Alternate Sitting and Standing

- Are the jobs that you have identified as allowing alternate sitting and standing classified as light or sedentary jobs by THE DICTIONARY OF OCCUPATIONAL TITLES?
- For the jobs that are classified as light, can't we assume that they require standing and walking for approximately six hours out of an eight-hour working day?
- If you contend that the DOT is wrong in classifying these jobs as light, how many of these jobs have you personally observed? When? Where? Did you observe these jobs in different parts of the country? How long did you observe them?
- The DOT doesn't address the question of opportunity to alternately sit or stand, does it?
- So, the only evidence we have about the existence of jobs which allow alternate sitting and standing is your observations of jobs?
- The opportunity to sit on a light job depends on the availability of chairs or stools provided by employers, doesn't it?

- Employees usually cannot provide their own chairs, can they?
- You're not contending, are you, that *all* employers provide chairs for the jobs you've identified but which the DOT classifies as light?
- Thus, we're dealing with some percentage of these jobs where stools or chairs are provided, aren't we?
- Tell us for what percentage of these jobs the employers provide stools or chairs; and tell us how you know this.
- Isn't it a fact that some of these jobs that we've been talking about are performed at desk height? If so, tell us what percentage of these jobs are performed at desk height versus bench height; and tell us how you know this.
- And isn't it also true that if the work station is at desk height, approximately 29 inches, most people are going to find it very uncomfortable to stand and work while bent over the desk?
- It is true, isn't it, that one normally has more opportunity to stand up when doing a job which is classified as sedentary than one has to sit down when doing a light job?
- But if one is doing a job which is classified as sedentary, it is most likely done at a work station which is at desk height, isn't it?

- If one is doing a job at bench height, what kind of chair is usually provided?
- Do most of these chairs have lumbar support? Is the lumbar support adjustable? Are the chairs adjustable in height? If not, how high is the seat from the floor? Do most of these chairs have hard seats or cushioned seats? Do these chairs have arm rests?
- What height is a bench placed at? Are benches at standard height?
- The height of most benches is not adjustable, is it?
- The benches are set at a height for an average person, aren't they?
- To work while standing at a bench of standard height, a person taller than average must bend over more, mustn't he? A person shorter than average must reach more?
- For the job where there is an opportunity to sit or stand, that opportunity is for the most part dictated by the work process, isn't it?
- Don't you agree with Social Security Ruling 83-12 that "most jobs have ongoing work processes which demand that a worker be in a certain . . . *posture* for a certain length of time to accomplish a certain task"?
- Reading SSR 83-12 is part of a vocational expert's training, isn't it?
- Aren't you told as part of your training to be a vocational expert that you are "expected to testify only on vocational issues and only on those vocational issues which are relevant to the requirements of the statute, regulations and rulings"?
- Do you agree with the statement in Social Security Ruling 83-12 that "unskilled types of jobs are particularly structured so that a person cannot ordinarily sit or stand at will"?
- You do agree, don't you, with the statement from SSR 83-12 that "most jobs have ongoing work processes that require a worker to be in a certain place . . . for at least a certain length of time to accomplish a certain task"?
- This means simply that a worker has to spend a certain length of time at the work station in order to do his work, doesn't it?
- The jobs you have identified as allowing alternate sitting and standing don't allow a worker to walk around whenever he feels the need, do they?
- For the jobs you have identified, what is the maximum amount of time out of every hour that a worker could be away from the work station that would be acceptable and would still allow a worker to meet normal production standards?
- Some jobs do, in fact, require walking, don't they? This is also dictated by the work process, isn't it? If the worker is required by the work process to walk but

his impairment dictates that he must sit, he won't be fulfilling his job duties, will he?
- If the work process requires that a worker either stand or sit, but his impairment requires that he do the opposite, he won't be able to fulfill his job duties, will he?
- From your work with impaired workers, you understand, don't you, that shifting positions isn't dictated by the clock?
- It is dictated by the way the person feels, isn't it?
- You interpreted the ALJ's question literally as involving x number of minutes sitting followed by x number of minutes standing, etc., didn't you?
- So if we change the hypothetical question to emphasize the unpredictable nature of the length of time the claimant may sit or stand, does that change your answer?
- What is the minimum amount of time a worker must remain in a certain posture (either standing or sitting) to accomplish the job tasks?
- If we change the hypothetical question to include the requirement for significant walking at unpredictable intervals during a working day, how would that affect your opinion about the number of jobs the claimant can do?
- From your experience dealing with impaired workers, it is most common, isn't it, that the requirement to shift positions comes unpredictably?
- In fact, it is unusual that someone's impairment would allow a shift of position by the clock, isn't it?

§349   *Transferable Skills*

The issue of transferable skills comes up in cases involving a few categories of claimants under the Medical-Vocational Guidelines. All of these claimants are incapable of performing their past relevant work. They are over age 50 and limited to sedentary work or over age 55 and limited to light work. These claimants will be found disabled or not disabled based upon whether or not they have acquired skills in past semiskilled or skilled work which are transferable to a significant range of other semiskilled or skilled work.

Do not lose sight of the fact that the transferability concept is part of the issue of vocational adjustment. The drafters of the Medical-Vocational Guidelines decided that individuals over age 50 with an unskilled work background who are unable to do their past work would not be able to adjust to sedentary unskilled work. It was also decided that individuals over age 55 with an unskilled work background who are unable to do their past work would not be able to adjust to unskilled light work. It is appropriate to use these benchmarks of vocational adjustment to unskilled sedentary and light work in assessing the vocational adjustment required for an individual who must take up a new line of semiskilled or skilled work after age 50.

It is also appropriate to inquire how well someone over age 55 with a skilled work background will adjust to a significantly lower level semiskilled job.

§349.1   Definition of Skill

SSR 82-41 provides:

A skill is knowledge of a work activity which requires the exercise of significant judgment that goes beyond the carrying out of simple job duties and is acquired through performance of an occupation which is above the unskilled level (requires more than 30 days to learn). It is practical and familiar knowledge of the principles and processes of an art, science or trade, combined with the ability to apply them in practice in a proper and approved manner. This includes activities like making precise measurements, reading blueprints, and setting up and operating complex machinery. A skill gives a person a special advantage over unskilled workers in the labor market.

In POMS DI 25001.001B.74, SSA explained skill as follows:

For disability program purposes is:
- Experience and demonstrated proficiency with work activities in particular tasks or jobs.
- Can only be gained through doing past relevant skilled or semi-skilled work. Cannot be gained from unskilled work.
- Cannot be gained through volunteer work or hobbies.
- Cannot be gained through education.

§349.2   No Skills Develop From Unskilled Work Nor May Skills Be Transferred to Unskilled Work

SSR 82-41 states that "[s]kills are not gained by doing unskilled jobs, and a person has no special advantage [over unskilled workers in the labor market] if he or she is skilled or semiskilled but can qualify only for an unskilled job because his or her skills cannot be used to any significant degree in other jobs."

§349.3   Skills vs. Traits

Work skills and worker traits are frequently confused. A worker trait is an innate aptitude or ability while a skill must be acquired. SSR 82-41 states: "It is the acquired capacity to perform the work activities with facility (rather than the traits themselves) that gives rise to potentially transferable skills." The Vocational Expert Handbook, p. 32, Appendix 8, provides this explanation:

We distinguish "skills" from worker "traits." Traits are inherent qualities that a worker brings to the job, such as good eyesight or good eye-hand coordination. When an ALJ asks you whether a claimant has a "skill," you must be careful not to confuse the two terms. For example, the traits of coordination and dexterity may be contrasted with a skill in the use of the hands or feet for the rapid performance of repetitive work tasks. It is the acquired capacity to perform the work activities with facility that gives rise to potentially transferable skills.

The VE Self-Study Guide, p. 15, Appendix 4, provides the following charts to illustrate the difference between skills and traits:

Skills	Traits
• Reading blueprints	• Ability to comprehend blueprints
• Operating a machine by using foot pedals	• Eye, hand, foot coordination
• Guarding a payroll delivery	• Can maintain alertness

Occupation	Skills	Traits
Arts Musician	Play a piece of music by ear without notes	Good sense of pitch and fine finger coordination
Science Lab Researcher	Identify particular bacteria found in a culture	Acute vision among other traits
Craft/Trade Machinist	Cuts material within certain tolerances	Fine perception of size and shape

§349.4   Skills Acquired vs. Skills Transferable

Vocational expert and ALJs often confuse acquired skills with transferable skills. Acquired skills are those skills which a claimant gained from his past work. In order to prepare for a hearing, VEs are advised in the VE Self-Study Guide, p. 14, Appendix 4, *infra,* to make a list of skills acquired by a claimant in past work. It is from such a list that a VE may determine if any skills are transferable—that is, may be used in particular jobs within the claimant's residual functional capacity. "Transferability means applying work skills which a person has demonstrated in vocationally relevant past jobs to meet the requirements of other skilled or semiskilled jobs." SSR 82-41. *See also* 20 C.F.R. § 404.1568(d)(1).

Sometimes an ALJ, without stating any limitations, will ask a vocational expert, "Does this claimant have any transferable skills?" It may be that the ALJ meant, "Does this claimant have any acquired skills?" Or perhaps this is a way of asking if the claimant's past work was skilled or semi-skilled. But this question, as asked, cannot be answered without the ALJ first stating the claimant's limitations such as, "Does this claimant have any skills transferable to sedentary work?" Some skills, for example, may be transferred from a medium job to a light job, but the same skills may not be transferred from a medium job to a sedentary job. The transferability of some skills may be prevented by nonexertional impairments. Indeed, the transferability of most skills may be prevented by many mental impairments. SSR 82-41 states that if an impairment "does not permit acquired skills to be used, the issue of transferability can be easily resolved."

§349.5   *Determining Transferability*

The regulations note that there are degrees of transferability "ranging from very close similarities to remote and incidental similarities among jobs." A complete similarity is not necessary for transferability. 20 C.F.R. § 404.1568(d)(3). Nevertheless, transferability does depend "largely on the similarity of occupationally significant work activities among different jobs." 20 C.F.R. § 404.1568(d)(1).

> 20 C.F.R. § 404.1568(d)(2) provides:
> Transferability is most probable and meaningful among jobs in which—
> (i)   The same or a lesser degree of skill is required;
> (ii)   The same or similar tools and machines are used; and
> (iii)   The same or similar raw materials, products, processes, or services are involved.

SSR 82-41 states that "people are not expected to do more complex jobs than they have actually performed."

The regulations provide that "when skills are so specialized or have been acquired in such an isolated vocational setting (like many jobs in mining, agriculture, or fishing) that they are not readily usable in other industries, jobs, and work settings, we consider that they are not transferable." 20 C.F.R. § 404.1568(d)(3). Examples given of jobs in such industries in SSR 82-41 are placer miners, bee-keepers and spear fisherman. SSR 82-41 notes that a VE's assistance may be required "for less obviously unusual occupations in isolated vocational settings."

The VE Self-Study Guide, p. 27, Appendix 4, advises VEs to research transferability of skills as follows:

> In testifying on transferability of skills, VEs should rely first and foremost on their own personal knowledge obtained through training and experience. In addition, the DOT and ancillary texts can be of great value. For example, the SELECTED CHARACTERISTICS OF OCCUPATIONS DEFINED IN THE DICTIONARY OF OCCUPATIONAL TITLES (1981) groups all occupations into one of the 12 interest groups and a further breakdown into 66 work-groups. The work-groups are selected on the basis of similar adaptabilities and capabilities.
>
> These work-groups are broken down further into specific occupations showing the industry in which they are found, the strength factor, environmental conditions, math and reading skill requirements and Specific Vocational Preparation (SVP). Thus, after identifying the work-group of the claimant's prior occupation, the VE can then ascertain which occupations in the same or related workgroup, if any, are compatible with the hypothesized medical restrictions and involve use of the same or similar tools and machines, raw materials, products, processes or services as the prior occupation.
>
> The 6-digit GOE subgroup (within the 4-digit GOE work group) which contains the claimant's prior occupation is the place to begin research. If related occupations are not found here or in other subgroups of the pertinent work-group, reference should be made to other work-groups which have a connection with the prior occupations, since insufficient research could lead to an improper conclusion that transferability of skills does not exist.

§349.6   *Different Standards of Transferability for Different Ages*

As a claimant gets older, the standard for finding that skills are transferable becomes more stringent, making it easier to show that he has not transferable skills. The following chart identifies the transferability standards.

Note that Rule 201.00 of the Medical-Vocational Guidelines, the rule pertaining to the sedentary grid, fails to mention transferability to semiskilled work. On the other hand, the rule pertaining to the light grid, Rule 202.00, specifically refers to transferability to both semiskilled and skilled work. The sedentary grid itself draws attention to this issue for those claimants over age 55 by footnote 1 to the grid which refers the reader to Rule 201.00(f), quoted above.

Most ALJs say that the reference in Rule 201.00(f) only to skilled sedentary work is an oversight by the drafters. It is apparent that a drafting error does exist either in the rule or in the grid table itself. The "previous work experience" column of the sedentary grid table refers to transferability *from* a semiskilled work background, something which makes little sense if transferability is limited to skilled work (since skills developed from semiskilled work are not transferable to skilled work). It is clear that the official SSA position is that there may be transferability *to* semiskilled or skilled sedentary work for those over age 55 because SSR 82-41 discusses transferability to semiskilled sedentary clerical positions. *See also, Burton v. Secretary of Health & Human Services*, 893 F.2d 821, 824 (6th Cir. 1990) which affirmed a finding of transferability of skills to semiskilled work for a person over age 55.

Age	RFC	Transferability Standard	Rule
50-54	Sedentary	"special skills or experience relevant to sedentary work" and "skills that are readily transferable to a significant range of skilled work"	201.00(c)
	Light & Medium	Irrelevant. Will be found not disabled based on capacity to do unskilled work	201.00(e)
55-59	Sedentary	"In order to find transferability of skills to skilled sedentary work . . . , there must be very little, if any, vocation adjustment required in terms of tools, work processes, work settings, or the industry." "[J]ob duties of their past work must be so closely related to other jobs which they can perform that they could be expected to perform these other identified jobs at a high degree of proficiency with a minimal amount of job orientation."	201.00(f)
	Light	Skills "readily transferable to a significant range of semi-skilled or skilled work."	SSR 82-41
	Medium	Irrelevant	202.00(c) and (e)
60-64	Sedentary & Light	"[T]here must be very little, if any, vocational adjustment required in terms of tools, work processes, work settings, or the industry." "[J]ob duties of their past work must be so closely related to other jobs which they can perform that they could be expected to perform these other identified jobs at a high degree of proficiency with a minimal amount of job orientation."	201.00(f) 202.00(f)
	Medium	Irrelevant.	SSR 82-41

§349.7 Examples of Jobs Discussed in SSR 82-41

Lower Level of Semiskilled Work

SSR 82-41 states that "the content of work activities in some semiskilled jobs may be little more than unskilled." Many jobs at the lower end of semiskilled work give the worker "very little vocational advantage over an unskilled person" and therefore provide no transferable skills. Examples are:
• Chauffeur
• Some sewing machine operators
• Room service waiter

Higher Level of Semiskilled Work

• Nurse aide

"The only duties which suggest transferable skills are those related to 'nurse' rather than 'aide'.... However, these occasional or incidental parts of the overall nurse aide job, which are a small part of a higher skilled job (nurse), would not ordinarily give a meaningful vocational advantage over unskilled work. The extent of such duties, however, may vary with individual nurse aides." SSR 82-41.
• Clerical jobs

A semiskilled general office clerk, *e.g.*, an administrative clerk, "doing light work, does typing, filing, tabulating and posting data in record books, preparing invoices and statements, operating calculators, etc. "These clerical skills may be readily transferable to such semi-skilled sedentary occupations as typist, clerk-typist and insurance auditing control clerk." SSR 82-41.

Clerical skills also "have universal applicability across industry lines," thus, "transferability of skills to industries differing from past work experience can usually be accomplished with very little, if any, vocational adjustment where jobs with similar skills can be identified as being within an individual's RFC." SSR 82-41.

Therefore, these skills meet the standard for transferability after age 55.

Skilled Work

• Professional
• Administrative
• Managerial

Job skills for professional, administrative and managerial types of jobs have universal applicability across industry lines and may be transferred to different industries "with very little, if any, vocational adjustment where jobs with similar skills can be identified as being within an individual's RFC." SSR 82-41.
• Carpenter

SSR 82-41 gives an example of a hypothetical case analysis of a carpenter, age 57, whose job was determined to be medium skilled work involving study of blueprints, sketches or building plans for constructing, installing, and repairing structures and fixtures of wood and wallboard using saws, planes and other tools. He was limited to light work. No light jobs were found in the construction industry but several semiskilled light jobs were found in other industries which involved tools, raw materials and activities similar to carpentry. Examples of such jobs are: cabinet assembler, hand shaper, and rip and groove machine operator in the furniture industry; box repairer in the wooden box industry; and grader in the woodworking industry. Such jobs are found to exist in significant numbers.

If the carpenter were age 60 or older it would be found that the carpentry skills cannot be transferred with very little, if any, vocational adjustment required in terms of tools, work processes, work settings or the industry. Thus, the carpenter would be found disabled at age 60 but not before.

If this carpenter were limited to sedentary work, he would be found disabled at age 50 because there are "few occupations performed in the seated position which utilize the specific work skills learned and used in construction carpentry." Thus, there would be no transferable work skills.

§349.8 A Significant Range of Work

For benefits to be denied based upon the presence of transferable skills, the Medical-Vocational Guidelines require that skills be transferable to "a significant range" of semiskilled or skilled work. Rule 202.00(e). This formulation is not further defined; but note that for every rule which directs a finding of not disabled because of the presence of transferable skills, there are corresponding rules which find disabled 1) a person with the same RFC and vocational factors who has no transferable skills and 2) a person with the same RFC, age and education who has an unskilled work background. Thus, the range of semiskilled or skilled work to which the claimant's skills are transferable must be so significant as to justify treating the claimant differently from others of his age and education.

In *Lounsburry v. Barnhart*, 468 F.3d 1111, 1117 (9th Cir. 2006), an ALJ found that the claimant had transferable skills to one light occupation, which represented 65,855 jobs in the national economy. The ALJ found this to be a significant number of jobs. The Ninth Circuit rejected the notion that one occupation constituted a "significant range of work." *But see Tommasetti v. Astrue*, 533 F.3d 1035, 1043-1044 (9th Cir. 2008), which found that transferable skills to one sedentary occupation (100,000 jobs nationally) was a significant range of work. Although the structure of the Medical-Vocational Guidelines would allow for a smaller number of occupations to constitute a significant range of work at the sedentary level, it is hard to see how one sedentary occupation makes a significant range of semi-skilled or skilled work.

When there are transferable skills, the person's job base is considered to be the unskilled jobs of which administrative notice was taken in the Medical-Vocational Guidelines *plus* the semiskilled or skilled jobs to which the claimant's skills transfer. SSR 83-10. Thus, the significance of the range of semiskilled and skilled work must be evaluated in relation to the unskilled job base.

The argument outlined below may be presented to the ALJ, who must determine if the jobs cited by the VE constitute a "significant range" of skilled or semiskilled work.

Make sure the foundation for this argument to the ALJ is laid by the VE's testimony. Where it appears there may be a finite number of occupations to which the claimant's skills are transferable, don't let the VE stop with a few "examples." Ask for DOT and GOE numbers. Press the VE to take a stand about how many different occupational titles are involved.

But don't ask the VE his opinion about whether these jobs constitute a "significant range" of skilled or semiskilled work. His opinion on this score doesn't matter anyway. It is the ALJ's job to determine this.

Here is the argument: Say the VE testifies that there are four light low-level (SVP 3) semiskilled occupations to which the claimant's skills may be transferred. This 55-year-old claimant who is limited to light work would be found *disabled* if his work background were unskilled despite having an occupational base of 1,600 separate sedentary and light occupations. *See,* for example, Rule 202.04. Why shouldn't the result be the same when his occupational base has been increased only to 1,604? *Cf.* Rules 202.06 and 202.07.

This argument becomes even stronger if the claimant cannot do several unskilled occupations. Even including the four semiskilled jobs, his occupational base would be less than the occupational base of others found disabled by the grids. Why should he be found not disabled only because he has skills transferable to four low-level semiskilled occupations?

As one moves up the skill ladder, of course, skills are transferable to a wider range of semiskilled and skilled work. And as more and more skills are involved, vocational adjustment becomes easier, despite the adversity of age.

§349.9   *Questions for the Vocational Expert About Transferable Skills*

- What is a skill?
- What is the difference between a skill and a worker trait?
- Can skills be developed from unskilled work?
- What is the difference between acquired skills and transferable skills?
- You would agree, wouldn't you, that a person's RFC may prevent the transferability of skills?
- Explain how residual functional capacity affects transferability.
- Would you agree that a house painter's painting skills are not transferable if he has severe allergic reactions to paint fumes? That a watchmaker's skills would not be transferable if he has hand tremors? That a construction machine operator's skills would not be transferable if he has a back impairment that will not permit jolting? That a craftsman's skills would not be transferable if his impairment has caused him to lose eye-hand coordination? That a business executive's skills would not be transferable if he has suffered brain damage which notably lowers his IQ? [All examples appear in SSR 82-41.]
- List the claimant's transferable skills.
- Isn't transferability of the claimant's skill of [identify skill] prevented by [describe aspect of claimant's RFC that prevents transferability]?
- [A particular skill identified by the VE] doesn't give the claimant a special advantage over an *unskilled* worker in the labor market, does it?
- Is it your opinion that this skill can be transferred to unskilled work?
- What are the DOT *and* GOE numbers of each job you have identified to which the claimant's skills are transferable?
- According to the DOT, what is the "specific vocational preparation" (SVP) of the claimant's past relevant work?
- What is the SVP of each job you have identified to which the claimant's skills are transferable? [These SVPs must be equal to or lower than those of the claimant's past relevant work.]
- How did you go about researching what occupations to which the claimant's skills might be transferable?
- Did you use SELECTED CHARACTERISTICS OF OCCUPATIONS DEFINED IN THE DICTIONARY OF OCCUPATIONAL TITLES in your research?
- Can I see your research notes?
- When you were doing this research, what medical restrictions did you assume that the claimant had?

Skills Readily Transferable

• [A particular skill identified by the VE] is not a *special* skill which is *readily* transferable to sedentary work, is it?

• [A particular skill identified by the VE] is not a skill which is *readily* transferable to light work, is it?

• How long do you think it will take for the claimant to establish *an average degree of proficiency* in each of the jobs you have identified to which the claimant's skills are transferable?

Very Little, If Any, Vocational Adjustment

• Identify the following used in the claimant's past relevant work and for each job to which you have concluded the claimant's skills are transferable:

—tools
—machines
—raw materials
—products
—processes
—services

• For the jobs you have identified to which the claimant's skills may be transferred, how much vocational adjustment is required in terms of tools, work processes, work settings or the industry?

• How long do you think that it will take for the claimant to establish *a high degree of proficiency* in each of the jobs you have identified to which the claimant's skills are transferable?

§349.10 Nine Stages of Transferability of Work Skills Analysis

The following, which is based on 20 C.F.R. §§ 404.1568 and 416.968 and SSR 82-41, was part of ALJ training in 2013 about dealing with vocational expert testimony:

STAGE 1	Determine whether transferable work skills are even required (Appendix 2, Subpart P, Regulations No. 4 and SSRs 82-63 and 85-15). If transferable skills are not required for a legally sufficient decision, the transferability of work skills analysis should be ended. If transferable work skills are required, proceed with the following analysis.
STAGE 2	The work activity from which the "skills" were acquired must meet the three-part "past relevant work (PRW)" test (recency, duration and substantial gainful activity) and must be semi-skilled or skilled, **not unskilled.**
STAGE 3	The specific transferable work skills (not aptitudes or traits) and the PRW (i.e., not hobbies, life experiences, etc.) from which the skills were acquired must be identified.
STAGE 4	The occupations to which the work skills are transferable must be semi-skilled or skilled, **not unskilled.**
STAGE 5	The specific occupations to which the work skills are transferable must be identified.
STAGE 6	The occupations to which the work skills are transferable must be within the claimant's residual functional capacity (RFC).
STAGE 7	The occupations to which the work skills are transferable must require the transferable work skills, but no additional work skills.
STAGE 8	If the claimant is age 55 or older (advanced age) and limited to sedentary work, or age 60 or older (close to retirement age) and limited to light or sedentary work, for the work skills to be transferable there must be a "very little, if any, vocational adjustment required in terms of tools, work processes, work settings, or the industry" (Sections 201.00(f) & 202.00(f), Appendix 2, Subpart P, Regulations No. 4).

STAGE 9	The decision must include rationale and "Finding" for each stage of the above analysis as appropriate.

§350   Concluding the Hearing and Closing the Record

§351   Closing Argument by Claimant's Representative

20 C.F.R. § 404.949 provides the claimant or representative with the right to appear and make oral argument "to state [the claimant's] case." (Written statements must be submitted "no later than 5 business days before the date set for the hearing. 20 C.F.R. § 404.949.) HALLEX I-2-6-76 provides:

During a hearing, an ALJ will provide the claimant and appointed representative, if any, reasonable time to present oral argument. Absent special circumstances, the ALJ will not fix a time limit on oral argument prior to the presentation of arguments. The ALJ will ensure all oral arguments are recorded and made a part of the record.

After all hearing testimony has been presented, the ALJ will:
- Offer the claimant and appointed representative, if any, the opportunity to make a final oral argument at the hearing; and
- If necessary, address assertions made during final oral argument by the claimant or appointed representative, if any, if the argument varies sharply with the evidence of record or if the argument raises new and relevant issues.

Closing argument at the hearing is often unnecessary, as when a medical expert testifies that a claimant exhibits a Listed Impairment or a vocational expert responds to the ALJ's only hypothetical question that such a person cannot perform any work. In cases where the claimant's testimony made the claimant's position perfectly clear, especially when the claimant's position is supported by the opinion of a treating doctor, closing argument may also be unnecessary. In other cases, a brief closing argument can be an effective tool in representing a claimant for Social Security disability benefits. Your goal is to show that a preponderance of the evidence supports your client's claim. See 20 C.F.R. §§ 404.901 and 404.953.

The best closing arguments offer a clear, concise statement emphasizing your theory of the case and the evidence in favor of your client. It should explain or minimize any evidence that appears to be against the claimant, especially if the ALJ has indicated a concern about a particular issue.

A closing argument may refer the ALJ to a grid rule or section of the medical Listings that directs a finding of "disabled." A closing argument may be particularly appropriate if the rationale for a favorable decision is not obvious; for example, the claimant's occupational base for sedentary work has been significantly eroded by bilateral manual dexterity restrictions or an I.Q. in the 70s.

Sometimes the closing argument is the best place to address vocational issues. If the vocational expert testified that your client can do a particular past job, but the claimant's earnings on that job did not rise to the substantial gainful activity level (thus disqualifying the job as past relevant work under SSA's rules), closing argument is a much better place to address this issue than cross-examination of the VE.

In the appropriate case, have a quotation from a Social Security Ruling ready to read to the ALJ, particularly if it is a principle that is often ignored in denial decisions. For example, if there is medical evidence showing that your client's orthopedic difficulty is aggravated by obesity, read the ALJ the following excerpt from Social Security Ruling 02-1p: "The combined effects of obesity with other impairments may be greater than might be expected without obesity. For example, someone with obesity and arthritis affecting a weight-bearing joint may have more pain and limitation than might be expected from the arthritis alone." Thus, you may point out that the limitations claimed by your client are consistent with SSA's experience in other cases.

In the appropriate case, run through the factors stated in SSR 16-3p, pointing out all those things that lead to a conclusion that your client's testimony about symptoms is credible.

Since so many ALJs are disinclined to find alcoholics disabled, when you have an alcoholic client, closing argument may be the best place to discuss the law concerning whether alcoholism is "material." Point out that the test is whether stopping drinking would restore the claimant's ability to work. Explain how the evidence shows that alcoholism is not material.

Because the administrative law judge is allowed to evaluate the claimant's appearance, attitude, demeanor, and testimony at the hearing, urge that the ALJ do so and point out those things that are favorable, *e.g.,* the claimant's apparent sincerity, obvious forgetfulness, emotional instability, monosyllabic replies, obvious lack of education, mental retardation, shortness of breath, need to stand during the hearing, or whatever else is important. In effect, closing argument can be used to put the ALJ's observations on the record. At the least, it gives you the opportunity to discuss the ALJ's observations with the ALJ. Note that the ALJ is supposed to tell you if your oral argument assertions "vary sharply with the evidence." HALLEX I-2-6-76.

If you have done your job, you will have (1) given the administrative law judge reason to hold for your client, and (2) indicated to the ALJ the arguments and strategy that must be overcome in the decision if the ALJ wishes to deny benefits and have the decision stand up. Show the impossibility of overcoming those arguments and suggest that the only reasonable decision is one in favor of your client.

A closing argument is most helpful if it is brief. If it cannot be made within a few minutes, or if you are awaiting additional evidence before closing the record, it may be best to request an opportunity to submit a post-hearing memorandum.

§352   ALJ's Closing Statement

HALLEX I-2-6-78 provides:

> Before closing the hearing, the administrative law judge (ALJ) will remind the claimant that he or she must inform the ALJ about or submit, in its entirety, all evidence known to him or her that relates to whether he or she is blind or disabled. See 20 CFR 404.1512 and 416.912. If the claimant has a representative, then the ALJ will remind the representative that he or she must help the claimant obtain the information that the claimant must submit. See 20 CFR 404.1512, 404.1740, 416.912, and 416.1540. The ALJ must ask the claimant and the representative if they are aware of any additional evidence that relates to whether the claimant is blind or disabled.

NOTE:

> Evidence generally does not include a representative's analysis of the claim or oral or

written communications between a claimant and his or her representative that are subject to the attorney-client privilege, or that would be subject to the attorney-client privilege if a non-attorney representative was an attorney. See 20 CFR 404.1512(b)(2) and 416.912(b)(2).

If the claimant and the representative have no additional evidence to submit or to inform the ALJ about and the ALJ determines that no additional evidence is needed, the ALJ will state on the record that the hearing and record are closed. In addition, the ALJ will advise the claimant and the representative that he or she will issue a written decision setting forth the findings of fact and the conclusions of law.

If the claimant or representative have additional evidence to submit, or the ALJ determines that additional evidence is needed (e.g., a consultative examination or an updated medical report), the ALJ will inform the claimant and representative (if any) that the record will remain open after the hearing to allow time to submit or obtain the additional evidence. If the claimant and representative intend to submit additional evidence, the ALJ will decide how long to leave the record open. If the ALJ intends to obtain additional evidence, the ALJ will advise the claimant and the representative that, before the ALJ issues a decision, the ALJ will give them an opportunity to examine the evidence, provide comments, object to the evidence, refute the evidence by submitting other evidence, or, if needed, request a supplemental hearing. For specific proffer instructions, see Hearings, Appeals and Litigation Law (HALLEX) manual I-2-7-1. The claimant and representative may voluntarily waive their right to examine the evidence. If they voluntarily waive this right, the ALJ will indicate such waiver on the record. For more information about the waiver, see HALLEX I-2-7-15.

NOTE:

> Before relying on the above, review HALLEX I-2-6-78 online for changes necessitated by the requirement that all evidence be submitted 5 business days before the hearing.

§353   Post-Hearing Development

The best approach to post-hearing development is to avoid it altogether. If you are allowed to hold the record open to submit additional evidence, it not only delays issuing the decision but it also creates the possibility that the new evidence will raise issues that the ALJ will be unable to resolve in your client's favor. ALJs generally dislike holding the record open because it makes considerable additional work in reviewing the exhibits again in light of the new evidence.

It is not a good sign when an ALJ, on the ALJ's own initiative, holds the record open for a consultative examination, interrogatories to a vocational or medical expert, or for some other additional evidence. It means that you didn't provide the ALJ with enough evidence to win your client's case on the day of the hearing. It is seldom a good idea to suggest that the ALJ obtain answers to interrogatories, a consultative examination or other evidence after the hearing. If you know that such information is needed, why not obtain it yourself before the hearing? The advantage of having such things paid for by the Social Security Administration is outweighed by the risks involved in random selection of experts paid at government contract rates.

Nevertheless, there are times when a record must be held open by the claimant's attorney or when an ALJ cannot be dissuaded from seeking a post-hearing expert opinion. There are also times when an ALJ requests a post-hearing brief or when you realize at the hearing that a post-hearing brief is necessary to convince the ALJ that your position is correct.

§354   *Close the Record*

A good calendaring system is important for keeping track of deadlines for submitting evidence or a brief that the ALJ allowed you to hold the record open to submit; and it is important for your relations with the ALJ to close the record as soon as possible.

§355   *Consultative Exam Ordered by ALJ*

HALLEX I-2-5-20 describes the procedures that an ALJ must follow for requesting the State Agency to arrange a consultative examination (CE) or medical test. Consistent with 20 C.F.R. § 404.1519h, the HALLEX indicates a preference that the treating physician or psychologist conduct the evaluation. HALLEX I-2-5-20 C. provides:

> The ALJ usually will not need to specify a particular medical source to conduct a CE or test. Because SSA considers a claimant's treating source(s) to be the primary source of medical information about a claimant's impairment, the State agency will, if possible, select a treating

source who is qualified, equipped, and willing to perform the CE or test for the amount allowed under its fee payment schedule.

> An ALJ may request that the State agency use a particular nontreating medical source or other medical source to conduct a CE or test only if the Appeals Council or a court has so ordered.

> An ALJ may request that the State agency not use a particular treating, nontreating, or other medical source to conduct a CE or test if he or she has a good reason. If an ALJ requests a State agency to use or not use a particular treating or nontreating medical source to conduct a CE or test, the ALJ must:

> • Provide the medical source's name, address, and telephone number, and explain the reason(s) for the special request; and
> • Place a copy of the special request in the CF.

> The State Agency may decline to use a particular treating, nontreating, or other medical source to conduct a CE or test if it has a good reason, e.g., the medical source has a history of not providing timely or complete reports. When the State Agency declines to use a particular treating, nontreating or other medical source, the reason should be provided in writing to the ALJ or HO.

20 C.F.R. § 404.1519j provides rules for a claimant or representative objecting to a particular physician or psychologist. It notes that a good reason may be that a doctor has previously given an opinion adverse to the claimant. It also says that if the allegation is that the doctor "lacks objectivity" in general, the examination will be changed to avoid delay, and the doctor will be investigated. However, if there has been a previous investigation of the particular doctor and the doctor's reports "conformed to [SSA's] guidelines," the examination will not be rescheduled.

In an initial entitlement case, if a claimant fails to attend a consultative examination or provide requested evidence, the ALJ must determine whether the claimant had good cause for the failure. If there is good cause, the State Agency should be directed to reschedule the consultative examination. If not, the ALJ must decide the case without the benefit of the consultative examination. 20 C.F.R. §§ 404.1516 and 404.1518. If the case involves a mental impairment, the ALJ must consider the mental impairment in determining if there was good cause for the failure to attend the consultative exam or provide the requested evidence; and the ALJ is supposed to try to obtain the evidence from some other source, including consulting a medical expert. HALLEX I-2-5-24. In an initial entitlement case, failure to attend a consultative examination cannot be a basis for denial of the claim.

In a continuing disability review (CDR) case, on the other hand, failure to attend a consultative examination or provide requested evidence without good cause can constitute separate grounds for finding that the disability ended. 20 C.F.R. §§ 404.1518 and 404.1579(e)(2).

In both CDR and initial entitlement cases, when an ALJ finds that a claimant did not have good cause for failure to provide evidence or attend a consultative examination, the documents supporting such a finding are to be sent to the claimant's representative for comment. HALLEX I-2-5-24. In neither an initial entitlement nor a CDR case, however, can failure to attend a consultative examination constitute grounds for dismissal of the claimant's request for hearing. HALLEX I-2-5-24. *See also* 20 C.F.R. § 404.957. A decision on the merits is required.

§356   Post-Hearing Interrogatories to Medical or Vocational Expert

HALLEX discusses obtaining vocational (VE) or medical expert (ME) opinions following the hearing, in sections that are essentially identical except for the examples why expert opinion may be necessary after the hearing. HALLEX I-2-5-40 offers only this example for why a medical expert opinion may be needed after the hearing: "evidence produced during the hearing may suggest the claimant's impairment(s) medically equal a listing."

Two examples are provided in HALLEX I-2-5-56 for why vocational expert opinion may be necessary after a hearing:
* The claimant may establish the existence of another severe impairment that requires VE testimony to evaluate step 5 of the sequential evaluation process.
* Evidence submitted after the hearing indicates that the claimant's functional limitations differ from the hypothetical questions presented to the VE at the hearing.

HALLEX I-2-5-30 B notes, "Generally, it is preferred that an ALJ obtain an ME or VE opinion at the hearing, regardless of the expert's manner of appearance (i.e., in-person, by video teleconferencing (VTC), or by telephone). Obtaining testimony at a hearing, rather than through interrogatories, is preferred because it allows the ALJ, claimant, and representative, if any, the opportunity to ask the ME or VE any questions material to the issues, including questions that arise for the first time during the hearing."

HALLEX I-2-5-40 (for medical experts) and HALLEX I-2-5-56 (for vocational experts) identify three factors to be weighed by the ALJ in determining whether to obtain the medical or vocational expert opinion in live testimony in a supplemental hearing, or in response to written interrogatories:
1. Whether and when an ME or VE is available to testify in person, by telephone or by video teleconference;
2. The feasibility of scheduling a hearing at a remote hearing site and the availability of an ME or VE at that location; and
3. The potential for delays if the ALJ schedules a supplemental hearing.

If the ALJ decides to use interrogatories rather than question a medical or vocational expert at a supplemental hearing, the ALJ is directed by HALLEX I-2-5-42 B and I-2-5-57 B to "phrase each question in a way that will not suggest any specific conclusion." Note that HALLEX does not provide for sending interrogatories to the representative or claimant prior to sending them to the expert. But the answers to the interrogatories must be sent to the representative or claimant after they are received unless the claimant waived the right to examine the evidence and appear at a supplemental hearing. HALLEX 1-2-5-44 and I-2-5-58. See §357.

When you know the ALJ is planning to send interrogatories to an expert, if you have access to the claimant's electronic folder on the ERE, you will likely be able to see what the ALJ has sent to the expert around the time the interrogatories are sent.

§357   Proffer to Attorney

According to HALLEX I-2-7-1, whenever an ALJ receives evidence from someone other than the claimant or claimant's representative, "and proposes to admit the evidence into the record, the ALJ must proffer the evidence, *i.e.*, give the claimant and representative the opportunity to examine the evidence and comment on, object to, or refute the evidence by submitting other evidence, requesting a supplemental hearing, or if required for a full and true disclosure of the facts, cross-examining the author(s) of the evidence."

When the claimant has knowingly waived the right to examine the evidence (something which no represented claimant would ever do), or the ALJ plans to issue a fully favorable decision, this rule does not apply. HALLEX I-2-7-1 B. Thus, no news is usually good news. If the time that you should have received the evidence from the ALJ is long past, it probably means that the ALJ is going to issue a favorable decision. You may find the new evidence on the ERE. HALLEX I-2-7-30 A states that along with the evidence, the ALJ must send a proffer letter that provides the following information::
* A time limit to object to, comment on, or refute the proffered evidence, and to submit a

written statement as to the facts and law that the claimant believes apply to the case in light of the evidence submitted;

- A time limit to submit written questions to the author(s) of the proffered evidence;

- When applicable (see HALLEX I-2-7-1), an opportunity to exercise his or her right to request a supplemental hearing, including the opportunity to cross-examine the author(s) of any posthearing evidence; and

- The opportunity and a description of the procedures for requesting a subpoena to require the attendance of witnesses or the submission of records.

If the representative proposes additional interrogatories to the expert, the HALLEX notes that the "ALJ must allow a claimant to propose additional interrogatories" to the VE or ME." HALLEX I-2-5-44 B and I-2-5-58 B. The ALJ must rule on any such request.

§358 Right to Cross-Examine Authors of Adverse Post-Hearing Reports

When SSA secures an expert opinion after a hearing, HALLEX recognizes that a claimant has the right to a supplemental hearing to cross-examine the expert. "If the claimant requests a supplemental hearing, the ALJ must grant the request, unless the ALJ receives additional documentary evidence that supports a fully favorable decision." HALLEX I-2-5-44 B and I-2-5-58 B. At a supplemental hearing, pursuant to HALLEX I-2-5-40 and I-2-5-56 the ALJ "will direct the expert to appear by video teleconferencing (VTC) or telephone when:
"• VTC or telephone equipment is available;
"• Use of VTC or telephone equipment would be more efficient than conducting an examination of a witness in person; and
"• There is no other reason VTC or telephone should not be used."
This policy is also clearly stated by SSA in AR 91-1(5), which acquiesced in *Lidy v. Sullivan*, 911 F.2d 1075 (5th Cir. 1990), when explaining how *Lidy* differed from SSA policy:

SSA has interpreted *Richardson v. Perales* to mandate the issuance of a subpoena only when it is shown that the testimony sought is "reasonably necessary for the full presentation of a case."

Therefore, SSA's policy is that a claimant's right to a subpoena is qualified.

Social Security Administration Regulations at 20 CFR 404.950(d) and 416.1450(d) state that when the claimant requests a subpoena, he or she must "state the important facts that the witness or document is expected to prove; and indicate why these facts could not be proven without issuing a subpoena." These sections also state that the Administrative Law Judge may issue a subpoena, "[w]hen it is reasonably necessary for the full presentation of a case."

Current instructions provide that an Administrative Law Judge "may deny the claimant's request to subpoena an individual if the claimant fails to show that the evidence or testimony he or she wishes to obtain from the individual is essential, or that the evidence or testimony cannot be obtained in any other way." *An exception to this policy is made when securing expert medical opinion after a hearing. These instructions state that if the claimant objects to the use of interrogatories and requests a supplemental hearing, the Administrative Law Judge must grant the request in such event.*

As indicated above, the Fifth Circuit has held that in the Social Security hearings process the right to a subpoena for the purposes of cross-examining an examining physician is absolute.

[Emphasis added.]

§359 Rebuttal Evidence and Argument

The requirement that you submit or inform the ALJ about all evidence applies to prehearing submissions. It does not apply to rebuttal evidence or to written rebuttal arguments. The introductory commentary to the five-day rule regulation published at 81 Fed. Reg. 90991 (2016) stated:

[I]f an ALJ introduces new evidence at or after a hearing, the claimant could use the exception in 20 CFR 404.935(b)(3) and 416.1435(b)(3) to submit rebuttal evidence. The claimant could also rebut evidence introduced at or after the hearing by submitting a written statement to the ALJ. As previously mentioned, we added language to 20 CFR 404.949 and 416.1449 to clarify that the

5-day requirement applies only to pre-hearing written statements, not to post-hearing written statements.

Thus, if an ALJ tells you that holding the record open after the hearing for rebuttal evidence or a brief is not allowed under the five-day rule, the ALJ is wrong. Submit your brief or rebuttal evidence anyway.

§360 ALJ Decision and After

§361 Bench Decision

Sometimes at the conclusion of a hearing, an ALJ will issue an oral bench decision setting forth findings of fact and conclusions of law establishing that your client is disabled. Then, within a few days after the hearing, the claimant will receive a short written decision that incorporates the oral decision by reference stating only the date of application and the date of onset found by the ALJ. This is the official favorable decision from which benefits are paid.

The bench decision procedure is based on 20 C.F.R. § 404.953(b), which provides:

> (b) *Fully favorable oral decision entered into the record at the hearing.* The administrative law judge may enter a fully favorable oral decision based on the preponderance of the evidence into the record of the hearing proceedings. If the administrative law judge enters a fully favorable oral decision into the record of the hearing proceedings, the administrative law judge may issue a written decision that incorporates the oral decision by reference. The administrative law judge may use this procedure only in those categories of cases that we identify in advance. The administrative law judge may only use this procedure in those cases where the administrative law judge determines that no changes are required in the findings of fact or the reasons for the decision as stated at the hearing. If a fully favorable decision is entered into the record at the hearing, the administrative law judge will also include in the record, as an exhibit entered into the record at the hearing, a document that sets forth the key data, findings of fact, and narrative rationale for the decision. If the decision incorporates by reference the findings and the reasons stated in an oral decision at the hearing, the parties shall also be provided, upon written request, a record of the oral decision.

In the past, HALLEX I-2-8-13 encouraged claimants and representatives to submit a proposed checksheet that contains "proposed decisional rationales and proposed findings of fact and conclusions of law in any case which is proper for a bench decision." In the past HALLEX I-5-1-17 also stated that the ALJ "may adopt and use a proposed checksheet if it is properly formatted (*i.e.*, is in the format of the checksheet at Attachment 1)." This language was removed from both HALLEX provisions in 2014 but SSA's website, www.socialsecurity.gov/appeals/otr.html?, encourages claimants' representatives to submit a proposed checksheet. See §286 about prehearing briefs and proposed decisions. We provide a copy of the checksheet at §286.3.

A bench decision may be issued only in an initial adult Social Security disability or SSI case; a claim for benefits as a disabled widow, widower, or surviving divorced spouse; or a child's SSI claim. Thus, a bench decision may not be issued in claims of disabled adult children under Title II, SSI "age-18 redeterminations," continuing disability reviews, and closed period of disability cases. Also, if drug addiction or alcoholism is an issue in the determination of disability, the bench decision procedure may not be used. HALLEX I-5-1-17.

When an ALJ issues a bench decision, the ALJ is supposed to explain on the record that the ALJ could still change his or her mind after the hearing, in which case a full written decision will be issued that discusses "any changes in the findings and reasons as stated at the hearing." If the ultimate decision is going to be less than wholly favorable, the claimant or representative will be given the opportunity to comment on any changes to the decision and "the ALJ will proffer such changes and their supporting exhibits of record to the claimant or representative." HALLEX I-5-1-17 III.B. Some ALJs read this notice at the beginning of the oral bench decision (which is the procedure contemplated by the HALLEX). Some give you a written document containing this information and ask you to waive the reading of it. And some simply ask if you will waive reading of this notice, which is called different things by different ALJs, thus creating potential confusion about what it is you are being asked to waive. Make sure you understand. Try not to allow any waiver to be interpreted as affecting your opportunity to comment on changes to the decision in that rare circumstance where the ALJ decides not to issue a fully favorable decision.

When an ALJ changes his or her mind after issuing an oral bench decision, note that the checksheet is supposed to remain as an exhibit. HALLEX I-5-1-17 III.A.

§362   Writing a Favorable Decision at the Request of the ALJ

Sometimes an ALJ will ask a claimant's attorney to write a favorable decision. It is hard to say no to such a request. It is something that you ought to do at least once. It gives you the opportunity to view the system from an ALJ's perspective. As soon as you realize how professionally embarrassing it would be for a decision you wrote to be remanded by the Appeals Council on own motion review, which has been known to happen to claimants' attorneys, you will want to review several Social Security Rulings, particularly the 1996 Process Unification Rulings—SSRs 96-1p through 96-9p, looking carefully not at the requirements for issuing a denial decision (as you have undoubtedly done in the past), but rather at the requirements for issuing a fully favorable decision.

After you prepare a draft, go back and look at it with a critical eye. Try to view it from the perspective of an administrative appeals judge. You will realize that the ALJ's job is not an easy one. It is not easy to write a review-proof favorable decision.

§370   *Res Judicata*, Administrative Finality and Reopening

Frequently Asked Questions

1.   Does the time limit for reopening run from the application date or the date of the final (last) decision in a case?

Neither. The time limit runs from the date of the notice of the initial denial determination, which is the *first* denial issued after an application is filed. It does not run from the last denial issued on an application, nor does it run from the date of the application itself. 20 C.F.R. § 404.988. *See* §371..

2.   What tolls the time limit?

The time limit is tolled if a claimant makes an express or implied request for reopening within the time limit. *See* HALLEX I-2-9-20 A.

3.   Does the decision about reopening have to be made within four years or is it enough just that the request for reopening is made within the time limit?

Only the request for reopening must be made within the time limit. HALLEX I-2-9-20 A. Don't be misled by 20 C.F.R. § 404.991a, which provides that SSA may revise a decision if it began an investigation within the time limit, diligently pursued that investigation, and revised the decision "as promptly as the circumstances

permitted." SSA is presumed to have diligently pursued the investigation if it revises the decision within six months from the date the investigation began. These rules apply only where SSA revises a decision to make it less favorable to a claimant. Where SSA revises a decision to make it more favorable to a claimant, the "diligent pursuit" rules do not apply. *See* 20 C.F.R. § 404.991a(a)-(b).

4.   If there are two applications with final decisions within the time limit for reopening, can you reopen the first one or are you limited to reopening only the second??

HALLEX refers to reopening "multiple" prior decisions. *See* §371 and HALLEX I-2-9-20 B.

5.   Is the claimant entitled to a hearing on the issue of reopening?

No. If reopening is the only issue, there is no legal right to a hearing. A request for hearing may be dismissed on the grounds that *res judicata* applies. 20 C.F.R. § 404.957(c)(1). If a claimant has something important to say in a case, put it in an affidavit and argue that a hearing is necessary to address the issue raised by the claimant. *See* §377.

6.   To invoke the reopening rules, does the claimant have to have a good reason for failing to appeal?

No. No inquiry is necessary into a claimant's reasons for failing to appeal an earlier denial to address the issue of whether there is good cause for reopening. If there is good cause for reopening, *e.g.*, "new and material evidence is furnished," the case should be reopened. 20 C.F.R. § 404.989(a). The claimant's reasons for not appealing are irrelevant if reopening for good cause is the issue.

Sometimes, though, you can resurrect a claim without using the reopening rules. If the issue is whether there is good cause for missing the deadline to appeal an earlier denial, then the reasons the claimant failed to appeal may be very important, especially if a *pro se* claimant lacked the mental capacity for understanding the procedures for requesting review or if an SSA notice misinformed the claimant about appeal rights, etc. *See* §§374.2 and 378.

7.   If the claimant submits new evidence for the purpose of reopening an earlier claim, must the claimant have a good reason for failing to submit that evidence originally?

No. Nothing in the regulations, rulings, HALLEX or POMS imposes that requirement.

8. If the time limit for reopening has already expired before the representative got into the case, is it still possible to reopen the case?

It still may be possible. It depends on whether you can construe a new application as an implied request for reopening within the time limit. *See* §376.

9. If an ALJ dismisses a hearing on the issue of reopening, is it worth appealing to the Appeals Council?

It depends on the case, of course, but do not assume that the Appeals Council won't address the reopening issue. *See* §§370.3 and 509.

10. Is court review of refusal to reopen ever possible?

As a rule, court review is possible in only three circumstances. First, where SSA refuses even to consider a claimant's timely and well-supported request for reopening, a claimant may invoke mandamus jurisdiction to force SSA to address the issue. Second, where you can make the argument that refusal to reopen amounted to a due process violation or other constitutional error, there may be federal court jurisdiction. Third, where there was implied or *de facto* reopening of the earlier claim resulting in a new denial, there is federal court jurisdiction. *See* §§377-378.

11. What impact does Disability Service Improvement (DSI) have on the reopening rules?

If you're in a state where DSI rules apply, *see* §150.1; reopening rules from 20 C.F.R. §§ 404.987 to 404.996, as described in §§370 to 379, usually apply. The exception to this is when a claimant seeks reopening of a final decision that is issued after a hearing. Here, the time limit for reopening for good cause is six months from the date of the final decision and SSA will not find that "new and material evidence" is a basis for good cause. 20 C.F.R. § 405.601(b). Otherwise, new and material evidence is a basis for reopening initial and reconsideration determinations.

12. If an ALJ decision fails to address reopening but finds an onset date within the previously adjudicated period, has the earlier application been reopened?

This may be construed as a reopening by the payment center. If all of the requirements for reopening are met in an ALJ decision, the payment center is supposed to reopen an initial or reconsideration determination and pay benefits based on the earlier application even when the ALJ decision does not explicitly address reopening. POMS DI 42010.025B.2. The payment center thus acts as a check on the ALJ, but this cuts both ways. If an ALJ decision specifically, but erroneously, reopens an earlier decision (*e.g.*, reopening outside the time limit), the payment center has directions to pay benefits based on the current application and prepare a memorandum to ODAR for clarification of the reopening issue. POMS DI 42010.025B.1.

13. Do the limitations on reopening stated in the regulations apply to reopening by SSA?

Yes. The reopening rules apply to circumstances where SSA wants to reopen a favorable determination or decision. When SSA intends to reopen a claim, it is required to give the claimant notice and an opportunity to object. See §§ 531 and 542. When you receive such a notice, make sure the component of SSA doing the reopening has jurisdiction. See §375. Make sure reopening was begun within the time limit allowed in the regulations. Make sure the regulations provide a basis for reopening and that the stated basis is in accordance with the facts. For example, if SSA says it is reopening for "good cause" within the meaning of 20 C.F.R. § 404.988, make sure there really is "good cause." See §373.

§370.1 Overview

All denials of disability benefits become final if not appealed. Nevertheless, a claimant may later request reopening of a final denial determination or decision if certain requirements are met. 20 C.F.R. §§ 404.987 -- 404.996 and 416.1487 -- 416.1494. According to POMS DI 27501.005B.1. a., other than when SSA itself request reopening, reopening will be considered when:

a. A party to the determination or decision requests (or impliedly requests) reopening by:
   • writing SSA or the DDS;
   • writing a third party (e.g., a congressman); or
   • filing a new claim (e.g., a denied claimant files a subsequent claim and alleges an onset of disability in the period adjudicated by the prior denial determination or decision).

It works best to request reopening of an earlier application in conjunction with a current application either by letter to SSA or by making sure the claimant alleges an onset date within the period adjudicated in the prior claim. If you merely request reopening by letter when no current application is pending, reopening can be denied by SSA without providing the right to appeal. Denial of a request for reopening is not an initial determination that comes with appeal rights. 20 C.F.R.

§ 404.903(l). A new application, even one that will be denied as *res judicata*, provides more appeal rights.

Fortunately for claimants, reopening most commonly arises in the circumstance where the Social Security Administration is the most generous—when there is a later application that cannot be denied as *res judicata* coupled with a request to reopen the denial of an earlier claim. When the request to reopen the earlier denial is granted, the claimant will be paid benefits pursuant to the earlier application, thus perhaps resulting in several years of back benefits paid to the claimant.

Last Denial on Earlier Claim Comes Before Date Last Insured

In the most common case where a claimant requests reopening, reopening is quite straightforward. SSA's policy allows and, indeed, encourages reopening an earlier denial when 1) reopening is requested in conjunction with a new application and 2) the earlier denial comes before the date last insured. A lawyer's job in this kind of case is to:

- make sure that the earliest possible application is reopened;
- take care that the reopening issue is raised within any time limit; and
- see to it that other conditions are met, for example, by finding new evidence.

The difficulty of reopening, as we shall see, depends on the sequence of events and the length of time between them. In cases involving reopening issues, it is useful to draw a timeline to help visualize this sequence. The following timeline illustrates the common situation in which the last denial on the first application comes *before* the date last insured. Here reopening is easier because the claimant has the right to file a new application.

8/1/08	—Onset date
1/2/10	—First application
6/1/10	—Initial denial
9/1/10	**—Reconsideration denial**
12/31/13	*—Date last insured*
1/31/14	—Second application

(In this example it doesn't matter if the date last insured is 9/30/10, so long as it's after the reconsideration denial of 9/1/10.)

Last Denial on Earlier Claim Comes After Date Last Insured

But where a claimant wants to reopen a denial issued *after* the claimant's date last insured, major efforts at resuscitation are required. The following timeline (in which only the date last insured is different from the timeline above) illustrates this situation:

8/1/08	—Onset date
1/2/10	—First application
6/1/10	—Initial denial
6/30/10	*—Date last insured*
9/1/10	**—Reconsideration denial**
1/31/14	—Second application

The date last insured is a pivotal point. It is the date by which the claimant must become disabled in order to be eligible for Social Security disability benefits. If a claimant becomes disabled after the date last insured (for example, if the date last insured were 6/30/08 on the above timeline), the claimant will not be eligible for Social Security disability benefits. For more information about insured status, *see* §§131 and 204.

When a denial issued after a claimant's date last insured becomes final (because the claimant failed to appeal or lost all appeals), SSA's policy is to discourage the claimant from later filing a new Social Security disability application (the "Second application" shown in the timeline above). If the claimant insists on filing the application, it likely will be denied on the grounds of administrative *res judicata*. Although reopening within applicable time limits is a possibility, such cases are a lawyer's nightmare. An ALJ may dismiss the case without a hearing. 20 C.F.R. § 404.957(c)(1). SSA's stingy application of the reopening rules and knee jerk application of the doctrine of administrative *res judicata* frequently obstruct reopening these cases, despite many federal court decisions that emphasize "that more significance should be placed on fairness in the administrative process than on the finality of administrative judgments." *See*, for example, *Purter v. Heckler*, 771 F.2d 682, 693 (3d Cir. 1985), and *Lyle v. Secretary of Health & Human Services*, 700 F.2d 566, 568 n. 2 (9th Cir. 1983).

Harder yet is the situation where reopening is impossible but obtaining a favorable decision on a current application is not. Suppose a claimant's application for Social Security disability benefits was denied after the date last insured more than four years ago and the claimant did not appeal. Now there is new evidence showing that the claimant has been disabled since the onset date alleged in the first application:

8/1/08	—Onset date
1/2/10	—First application
6/1/10	—Initial denial
6/30/10	*—Date last insured*
9/1/10	—Reconsideration denial
1/31/15	—Second application

Because the time limit for reopening based on new evidence runs out four years after the date of the initial denial (this is 6/1/14 in the timeline above, well before the date the second application was submitted), many would incorrectly say that nothing can be done. Although it is too late to reopen the reconsideration denial in order to be paid benefits under the first application, this claimant can be found disabled from the onset date used in the first application; but the claimant will be paid only under the current application. *See* SSR 68-12a, HALLEX I-3-9-40 C.3. and 20 C.F.R. § 404.995. This is a difficult case, not because the law says it cannot happen, but because of the way the doctrine of administrative *res judicata* is applied in practice. ALJs are often so quick to invoke *res judicata* to dismiss such a case that they fail to carefully examine the new evidence. It may be necessary to take the case up to the Appeals Council, which may take a less pressured approach to evaluating the new evidence. Appeal of these cases to federal court, though, is fraught with the same problems as trying to appeal a case involving a refusal to reopen.

§370.2 Res Judicata *and Administrative Finality Compared*

There is perhaps no area of Social Security disability law more confusing than the concepts of administrative *res judicata* and administrative finality. But there is also no area where good lawyering makes a bigger difference in the amount of benefits obtained by your client.

In practice many administrative *res judicata* and administrative finality issues appear to overlap. But *res judicata* focuses on facts and issues; administrative finality focuses on the application and dates of denial. Both doctrines address whether the denial has become final. Careful examination of those circumstances where these two distinct doctrines do not coincide is well worth the effort. It often uncovers an approach that may make the difference between winning and losing or may yield thousands of dollars of additional benefits for your client.

Res judicata, translated literally as "a thing decided," effectively means that once an issue is decided it does not need to be decided again. Largely a creature of the common law, *res judicata* is mentioned in the Social Security disability regulations only once—at 20 C.F.R. § 404.957(c)(1). It provides that an ALJ may dismiss a request for hearing or refuse to consider an issue under the doctrine of *res judicata* where:

1) there has been a previous denial;
2) about the same claimant's rights;
3) under the same subpart of the regulations;
4) on the same facts;
5) on the same issues; and
6) the previous denial has become final.

In other words, a denial by SSA to which the doctrine of administrative *res judicata* applies bars later consideration of the matters decided. So, when a later claim is filed, the doctrine of *res judicata* precludes SSA from considering whether the claimant was disabled back through the date of the last denial on the earlier claim. But *res judicata* is not a total bar if that denial came *before* the claimant's date last insured, since there is still an unadjudicated period that must be addressed. That is, the earlier denial did not decide whether the claimant was disabled from the day after the reconsideration denial through the date last insured. In the timeline below, the unadjudicated period runs from 9/2/10 through 12/31/10.

8/1/08	—Onset date
1/2/10	—First application
6/1/10	—Initial denial
9/1/10	—Reconsideration denial
9/2/10	—Unadjudicated period
12/31/10	*—Date last insured*
1/31/15	—Second application

However, when the earlier denial comes after the date last insured, there is no unadjudicated period. The doctrine of *res judicata* prohibits SSA from considering whether the claimant was disabled at any time.

8/1/08	—Onset date
1/2/10	—First application
6/1/10	—Initial denial
6/30/10	*—Date Last Insured*
9/1/10	—Reconsideration denial
1/31/14	—Second application

A *res judicata* denial will likely be issued by the local office in such a case. POMS DI 27516.001C. provides: "The notice in a *res judicata* case informs the claimant that the decision reached on the prior application applies and the only appeal available is on the question of whether the same person, facts and issues were present in both the prior and subsequent claims for the same period."

Note that if the facts are different, for example, if there is new evidence showing that a condition was more severe than originally thought, *res judicata* does not apply. Similarly, if the issues are different, for example, if there has been a change in the law that would lead to a different result, *res judicata* does not apply. These results flow from the common law definition of *res judicata* as described in 20 C.F.R. § 404.957(c)(1), which is completely separate and distinct from the reopening rules found at 20 C.F.R. §§ 404.987 *et seq.*

The reopening rules, 20 C.F.R. §§ 404.987 *et seq.*, are used to obtain relief from the strictures of administrative finality. The doctrine of administrative finality, in contrast to the doctrine of administrative *res judicata*, is entirely a creature of regulation. Administrative finality is not mentioned in the Social Security Act. The general principle of administrative finality is stated at 20 C.F.R. § 404.987(a), which provides that a claimant who does not request further review within the allowed time frame loses the "right to further review and that determination or decision becomes final." This regulation also provides that a determination or decision "may" nevertheless be reopened and revised by SSA if certain conditions are met. The most important condition for reopening, as we shall see, is the presence of new and material evidence. New and material evidence allows reopening of a Social Security disability claim within four years. *See* 20 C.F.R. §§ 404.988(b) and 404.989(a)(1). In fact, if there is new and material evidence and if the time limit is met, the final denial on an earlier application "must" be reopened and the claimant must be paid pursuant to the earlier application. HALLEX I-2-9-1 B. Potentially, this could add several years to the back benefits that the claimant receives.

Although it is seldom explicitly stated in a reopening decision, new and material evidence also plays a role in eliminating the *res judicata* problem, as stated above. Thus, whenever a case is reopened, new and material evidence has two different functions: under the doctrine of administrative finality, it provides "good cause" for reopening an earlier application required by the reopening regulations, 20 C.F.R. § 404.989(a)(1); and by presenting new facts, it simultaneously removes the common law *res judicata* bar to revisiting the earlier claim. Although this particular distinction may appear at first trivial, it is extremely important for Social Security disability lawyers to understand what happens when something, usually the time limit, makes reopening impossible: There is still a *res judicata* issue to be addressed!

When new and material evidence is discovered more than four years after initial denial of a Social Security disability claim, the doctrine of administrative finality will foreclose reopening of the earlier application under the reopening rules. But the time limits (and other requirements) in the reopening regulations do not apply to the doctrine of administrative *res judicata*. Because there is new and material evidence, *res judicata* cannot bar a finding of onset in the earlier adjudicated period.

Therefore, although the claimant cannot be paid on the earlier application, the claimant can be paid on the current application. *See* SSRs 68-12a and 86-16a. *See also* HALLEX I-3-9-40 C.3. and 20 C.F.R. § 404.995.

Similarly, the two doctrines diverge where there is a change of legal interpretation or administrative ruling on which an earlier decision was based. Administrative *res judicata* cannot apply because the issues are different. However, 20 C.F.R. § 404.989(b), a part of the reopening regulations, restricts the effects of such changes by providing that SSA "will not find good cause to reopen your case if the only reason for reopening is a change of legal interpretation or administrative ruling upon which the determination or decision was made." Thus, although the earlier claim cannot be reopened, because *res judicata* does not apply, a hearing typically must be held and a decision using the new legal interpretation must be issued on the merits. If, following such a hearing, the ALJ issues a favorable decision, the claimant will be entitled to benefits only under the current application. *See* SSR 63-41 and HALLEX I-2-4-40 K, Note 1. (Of course, nothing prevents the ALJ from also finding the necessary facts for reopening the earlier decision on some basis other than a change in legal interpretation or administrative ruling; but this is a separate issue to be addressed under the reopening regulations, 20 C.F.R. §§ 404.987 *et seq.*)

§370.3   *"Reopening is Discretionary"*

A commonly held misconception is that if a request for reopening is denied, nothing can be done because reopening is "discretionary." This does not mean that reopening is at the whim of the decision maker, nor does it mean that it is pointless to appeal a reopening issue to the Appeals Council. **"Reopening is at the discretion of SSA and is not a right afforded to the claimant upon request, even if the claimant makes the request within one year of the notice of the initial determination. However, in all cases it is SSA's policy to honor the request to review the case to see if reopening applies**. SSA informs the claimant if we decide not to reopen and why (GN 04001.090)." POMS GN 04001.001D.3, emphasis in original. Although the reopening regulations state that a denial "may" be reopened, reasons for denying reopening must be related to the facts and law in the claimant's case. If the facts and law warrant it, it is SSA policy to reopen. HALLEX I-2-9-1 B. states: "An ALJ must reopen a determination or decision if the conditions and timeframes for reopening are met (as explained in HALLEX I-2-9-30, I-2-9-40, and I-2-9-60), the ALJ has jurisdiction over the issue, and the facts and evidence of the particular case warrant reopening."

"It is SSA's policy to revise a determination if reopening applies and the evidence shows the prior determination was incorrect." POMS GN 04001.001D.4. Note.

An ALJ's failure to reopen a claim can and ought to be appealed to the Appeals Council. See §§509 and 531. Although reopening is not something over which federal courts usually have jurisdiction, federal courts do have mandamus jurisdiction to compel SSA to fully consider new evidence submitted in conjunction with a request to reopen. See *Burnett v. Bowen*, 830 F.2d 731, 736-741 (7th Cir. 1987). Furthermore, federal courts have jurisdiction when the failure to reopen results in a constitutional violation such as the denial of due process. *Califano v. Sanders*, 430 U.S. 99, 109 (1977).

§371   The Time Limit

Both Social Security disability and SSI cases may be reopened within 12 months of the date of the initial determination "for any reason." 20 C.F.R § 404.988(a) and § 416.1488(a). Note that the time limit runs from the date of the initial determination. It does not run from the date of the application nor does it run from the date of the last denial, though, in effect, it is that last denial that is reopened. (When the last denial is reopened, the application that spawned it is also reopened. Thus, ALJs, lawyers, and this book sometimes refer to "reopening an application" as a shorthand reference for a "request to reopen the last denial of a particular application which thereby reopens the application itself.")

To calculate the time limit, look at the notice of initial determination, that is, the first denial a claimant receives after filing an application. See 20 C.F.R. § 404.988, and *cf.* 20 C.F.R. § 404.900(a)(1). Calculate the time from the initial determination until the date of the claimant's express or implied request to reopen or, when reopening is at the initiation of SSA, the date SSA first takes action to reopen. HALLEX I-2-9-20 A. But to determine whether you have new evidence, look at the evidence in SSA's possession when it issued its last, most recent denial—an initial or reconsideration determination, an ALJ or Appeals Council decision. HALLEX I-2-9-40 C.1. and I-3-9-40 C.1

SSI cases may be reopened for good cause within two years of the date of the initial determination. 20 C.F.R. § 416.1488(b). Social Security disability cases, however, have a four-year time limit for reopening for good cause. 20 C.F.R. § 404.988(b). Here is a timeline illustration:

8/1/08	—Onset date
1/2/10	—First application
6/1/10	—Initial denial
9/1/10	—Reconsideration denial
12/31/13	—Date last insured
1/31/14	—Second application and request for reopening

Reopening is requested within four years of 6/1/10.

It is possible to successfully reopen denials on more than one application within the time limit. For example, if a Social Security disability claimant received two initial denials on two different applications within the past four years, the claimant can request reopening of final denials of both applications when the third application is adjudicated. But SSA says that reopening may not be "piggy backed" or "stacked." That is, when a case within the four-year period is reopened, this action cannot be used to reach back beyond the four-year limit to reopen an even earlier denial. HALLEX I-2-9-20 B and I-3-9-20 B.

Nevertheless, using reopening of one application to reach back an additional four years to reopen an even earlier application, also called the "domino" theory, has been accepted by at least four U.S. district courts. See *Gallegos v. Shalala*, No. 93-Z-310 (D. Colo. August 3, 1994), CCH Unempl. Ins. Rep. §14,176B; *Gonzales v. Secretary*, No. 84-1771-M (D. N.M. November 25, 1988), CCH Unempl. Ins. Rep. §16,034A; *Brunckhurst v. Heckler*, No. C-84-2084-WAI (N.D. Cal. October 15, 1985), CCH Unempl. Ins. Rep. §16,644; and *West v. Heckler*, No. CIV-82-006-GLO-RMV (D. Ariz September 30, 1983). The argument in favor of the domino theory is that in the process of reopening an application, SSA also necessarily reopens an implied or explicit request to reopen an even earlier application. Nothing in the regulations appears to prevent application of the domino theory. The argument on the other side springs from the bureaucratic urge for bright lines in establishing administrative finality.

§372   Reopening for "Any Reason" Within Twelve Months

What sort of reason is necessary to reopen within the 12-month time limit? Assertions that the 12-month rule established a right of reopening (*e.g.*, reopening for no reason other than that the claimant desires it), are regularly rejected by SSA and were rejected by the Fourth Circuit Court of Appeals in *Monger v. Bowen*, 817 F.2d 15 (4th Cir. 1987), published as SSR 88-1c. POMS says: "Reopening within 12 months is not 'automatic.' A request to reopen within 12 months can be denied if there is no reason to revise the prior determination or decision." POMS DI 27505.001A.1. Thus, some reason is necessary, but the reason does not have to rise to the level of "good cause."

While it is best for you to state a reason that the denial issued within the 12-month time limit ought to be reopened, note that HALLEX I-2-9-30 provides a basis for arguing that failure to state a reason cannot be grounds for denial of reopening: "This does not mean the claimant has to submit a reason for revising the prior determination or decision. Rather, the ALJ must evaluate whether the record demonstrates a reason for revising the prior determination or decision."

HALLEX provides no examples of "any reason" for reopening within 12 months. The only example of "any reason" that appears in POMS is a change in SSA policy. POMS DI 27505.020B.1. Note that in contrast to other reopening situations in which a claimant is paid pursuant to rules applicable to the earlier application, when reopening is because of a change of policy, the claimant, as a rule, will not be paid earlier than the effective date of the policy change except when there is a change in disability criteria, e.g., a change in the Listing of Impairments. When there is a change in disability criteria, it usually applies to the entire period at issue.

Whenever you are involved in a case within 12 months of the notice of initial denial of an earlier application, request reopening. Demonstrate that the earlier denial was wrong. Fundamental fairness to the claimant may add to the weight of your argument that the earlier application ought to be reopened. Sometimes a claimant's reasons for failing to appeal may add to your argument.

§373 Reopening for Good Cause

Social Security disability claims may be reopened within four years and SSI claims within two years where there is "good cause." 20 C.F.R. § 404.988(b) and 20 C.F.R. § 416.1488(b). Good cause is defined in 20 C.F.R. § 404.989(a) as existing where:

1) New and material evidence is furnished;
2) A clerical error in the computation or recomputation of benefits was made; or
3) The evidence that was considered in making the determination or decision clearly shows on its face that an error was made.

(The parallel SSI regulation, 20 C.F.R. § 416.1489(a), is identical except that (2) refers simply to a clerical error with no reference to computation of benefits.)

When there is a clerical error or error on the face of the evidence, 20 C.F.R. § 404.989(a) functions to set a time limit of four years for SSA to reopen a Social Security disability beneficiary's case to make a decision adverse to the claimant's interest. On the other hand, a decision

that is "fully or partially unfavorable" to a claimant can be reopened at any time when there is clerical error or error that appears on the face of the evidence. 20 C.F.R. § 404.988(c)(8). Thus, from a Social Security disability claimant's perspective, the four-year time limit applies only to one issue—whether there is new and material evidence.

The parallel SSI regulation is quite different. 20 C.F.R. § 416.1488(c), which provides for reopening at any time, does not provide for unlimited reopening by claimants for clerical error or error on the face of the evidence. Thus, SSI claimants may ask to reopen on these grounds only within the two-year time limit applicable to reopening for good cause. 20 C.F.R. § 416.1488(b).

Both the Social Security disability and the SSI regulations provide that good cause will not be found if the only reason for reopening is a change in legal interpretation or administrative ruling. 20 C.F.R. §§ 404.989(b) and 416.1489(b). But a change in legal interpretation or administrative ruling can form the basis for reopening within 12 months of the date of the notice of initial determination. See §372. A change in legal interpretation or administrative ruling also makes *res judicata* inapplicable. See §378.

§373.1 New and Material Evidence

HALLEX I-2-9-40 C offers the following definition and examples of new and material evidence:

1. Definition

To satisfy the regulatory standard for reopening, evidence is "new and material" when:

- The evidence is not part of the claim(s) record as of the date of the ALJ decision or determination;
- The evidence is relevant, i.e., involves or is directly related to issues adjudicated in the prior decision or determination;
- The evidence relates to the period on or before the date of the decision or determination; and,
- The evidence shows that the decision or determination is contrary to the weight of the evidence.

NOTE:

The weight of the evidence is defined as the balance or preponderance of evidence. See HALLEX I-3-3-6 C Note. In other words, the weight of the evidence means it is "more likely than not" that the totality of evidence, including the additional evidence, would change the action, findings, or conclusion.

Examples:
- New medical evidence shows that the claimant's impairment met an impairment listed in Appendix 1, Subpart P, during the previously adjudicated period and that an allowance based on the prior application is warranted.
- New medical evidence shows that an original medical prognosis did not prove to be accurate, and that an allowance based on a prior application is warranted; e.g., the prior adjudicator believed that the claimant's broken hip would be healed within 12 months, but later medical evidence shows that the broken hip had not healed sufficiently within 12 months to permit the claimant to return to substantial gainful activity.

2. Effect of New and Material Evidence
- It may not always warrant a different conclusion.
- It may produce a significant change in a factor of entitlement that warrants a revision of a prior unfavorable determination or decision, but does not change the ultimate unfavorable determination or decision.

EXAMPLE:

An ALJ found that a 30 year-old claimant for disability insurance benefits was illiterate, unskilled, could no longer perform his heavy labor job due to his back impairment but had the residual functional capacity to perform light work. The ALJ issued a decision finding that the claimant was not disabled pursuant to Rule 202.16. The ALJ's decision became final and binding when the claimant did not appeal to the Appeals Council. Two years later, the claimant requests that the ALJ reopen the hearing decision and submits evidence that establishes he was limited to sedentary work during the period at issue. Even though the claim will still be denied under Rule 201.23, if the reopening time limit criteria are met, the ALJ may reopen the prior hearing decision, issue a revised decision and provide the claimant with appeal rights.

Note that the above example calls for the ALJ to reopen a claim only to deny it again on a somewhat different basis. Although a decision that reopens and revises an earlier decision, and denies the claim again can be appealed to federal court, such decisions are rare. More often, one sees a dismissal order denying a request to reopen either by ignoring or attempting to explain away new evidence. This more common type of order can and should be appealed to the Appeals Council

because it is an abuse of discretion; but without a claim of a constitutional violation, the possibilities for appeal to federal court are limited.

New evidence can come in many forms. It is not just a medical report or test results that SSA didn't receive at the time the earlier application was adjudicated. It could be evidence concerning an impairment that wasn't alleged at the time of the earlier application such as a mental impairment (which is frequently not alleged by a claimant whose disability is primarily physical). It could even be new opinion evidence, such as a report prepared today by the claimant's doctor, which convincingly demonstrates that the claimant's RFC at the time of the earlier application was much more restricted than SSA previously concluded.

When seeking a route for reopening, it is also important to bear in mind that the claimant's testimony may constitute new evidence. If the claimant did not appeal a prior denial to the ALJ level, the claimant has not had the opportunity to describe limitations and explain the impact of the impairments on the claimant's life. The claimant hasn't been able to tell an ALJ about the severity of symptoms. The claimant's description may not appear anywhere in the evidence supporting the prior claim. If not, the claimant's testimony is new evidence. That a claimant's testimony may constitute new and material evidence is acknowledged in HALLEX. *See* HALLEX I-2-4-40 M, which discusses the procedure for holding a hearing for the limited purpose of determining if testimony from the claimant, a treating physician or some other witness might constitute new and material evidence. *See also* §377.

§373.2   *Clerical Error*

HALLEX I-2-9-40 D, which applies to ALJ actions, and HALLEX I-3-9-40 D, which applies to Appeals Council actions, offer this explanation of clerical error:

> A clerical error is a mathematical error, misapplication of benefit tables, etc., which resulted in an incorrect payment of a monthly benefit or an incorrect lump-sum death payment. It ordinarily occurs in the computation or recomputation of benefits.

Slightly different language appears in the Social Security disability and SSI regulations, 20 C.F.R. § 404.989(a)(2) and § 416.1489(a)(2). The SSI regulation appears broader because it isn't limited to computation of benefits..

In Social Security disability cases, the regulation sets a time limit for SSA to reopen for the purpose of taking away benefits granted as a result of clerical error. In contrast, where a Social Security disability claimant fails to receive the correct amount of benefits because of clerical error, the claim can be reopened at any time under 20 C.F.R. § 404.988(c)(8).

§373.3   *Error on Face of Evidence*

POMS GN 04010.020A provides this definition:

> An error on the face of the evidence exists where it is **absolutely clear** that the determination or decision was incorrect. That is, based on all the **evidence in the file and** any evidence of record anywhere **in SSA** at the time the determination or decision was made, it is unmistakably certain that the determination or decision was incorrect.

Emphasis in original.

If correcting an error on the face of the evidence results in a more favorable outcome for the claimant, the decision may be reopened at any time. 20 C.F.R. §404.988(c)(8). It is only when correcting such an error leads to a less favorable result that there is a four-year time limit for Social Security disability cases. 20 C.F.R. §§404.988(b) and 404.989(a)(3). *See also* POMS GN 04010.020 B.

HALLEX I-2-9-40 E and HALLEX I-3-9-4 E provide:

> Error on the face of the evidence is an obvious error which clearly causes an incorrect determination or decision. The following are examples of "error on the face of the evidence":
> - The adjudicator relied on the wrong person's medical report or earnings record.
> - In a Title II only claim, onset of disability was established after the claimant last met the special earnings requirements.
> - Benefits in a cessation case were terminated as of the month disability ceased, rather than being terminated as of the close of the second month following the month in which disability ceased.
> - Evidence in the possession of SSA at the time the determination or decision was made clearly shows that the determination or decision was incorrect.

Example:

While a claim was being processed, the claimant submitted a medical report to the Social Security field office which would have resulted in a different conclusion. However, the medical report was not associated with the claim file until after the determination or decision became final.

NOTE: Under title II, an ALJ may generally only reopen a determination or decision which is otherwise final within 4 years from the date of the notice of the initial determination. However, if a determination or decision was fully or partially unfavorable to the claimant due to an error that appears on the face of the evidence that was considered when the determination or decision was made, the ALJ can reopen at any time. See 20 CFR 404.988(c)(8) and HALLEX I-2-9-60 A.8.

Error on the face of the evidence also includes an error of law. *See* SSR 85-6c and HALLEX I-5-3-17, Note 5. But a decision that was "reasonable on the basis of the evidence in the file and on the statute, regulations, instructions, precedents, etc., existing at the time" the decision was made will not be reopened on the grounds that there is an error on the face of the evidence merely because a different rule of law would now be applied or because there has been a change in the law. POMS GN 04010.020 C. When there is a change in the law, consider whether a claim can be reopened under the "any reason" 12-month time limit discussed at §372. Also, check to see if Congress or a federal court has provided that the change in the law will have retroactive effect. POMS GN 04001.110.

§374   *Reopening at Any Time*

Under 20 C.F.R. § 404.988(c), a decision may be reopened at any time when:
(1) It was obtained by fraud or similar fault (*see* §416.1488(c) of this chapter for factors which we take into account in determining fraud or similar fault);
(2) Another person files a claim on the same earnings record and allowance of the claim adversely affects your claim;
(3) A person previously determined to be dead, and on whose earnings record your entitlement is based, is later found to be alive;
(4) Your claim was denied because you did not prove that a person died, and the death is later established—
   (i) By a presumption of death under § 404.721(b); or
   (ii) By location or identification of his or her body;
(5) The Railroad Retirement Board has awarded duplicate benefits on the same earnings record;
(6) It either—
   (i) Denies the person on whose earnings record your claim is based gratuitous wage credits

for military or naval service because another Federal agency (other than the Veterans Administration) has erroneously certified that it has awarded benefits based on the service; or

(ii) Credits the earnings record of the person on which your claim is based with gratuitous wage credits and another Federal agency (other than the Veterans Administration) certifies that it has awarded a benefit based on the period of service for which the wage credits were granted;

(7) It finds that the claimant did not have insured status, but earnings were later credited to his or her earnings record to correct errors apparent on the face of the earnings record (section 205(c)(5)(C) of the Act), to enter items transferred by the Railroad Retirement Board, which were credited under the Railroad Retirement Act when they should have been credited to the claimant's Social Security earnings record (section 205(c)(5)(D) of the Act), or to correct errors made in the allocation of wages or self-employment income to individuals or periods (section 205(c) (5) (G) of the Act), which would have given him or her insured status at the time of the determination or decision if the earnings had been credited to his or her earnings record at that time, and the evidence of these earnings was in our possession or the possession of the Railroad Retirement Board at the time of the determination or decision;

(8) It is fully or partially unfavorable to a party, but only to correct clerical error or an error that appears on the face of the evidence that was considered when the determination or decision was made;

(9) It finds that you are entitled to monthly benefits or to a lump sum death payment based on the earnings of a deceased person, and it is later established that:

(i) You were convicted of a felony or an act in the nature of a felony for intentionally causing that person's death; or

(ii) If you were subject to the juvenile justice system, you were found by a court of competent jurisdiction to have intentionally caused that person's death by committing an act which, if committed by an adult, would have been considered a felony or an act in the nature of a felony;

(10) It either—

(i) Denies the person on whose earnings record your claim is based deemed wages for internment during World War II because of an erroneous finding that a benefit based upon the internment has been determined by an agency of the United States to be payable under another Federal law or under a system established by that agency; or

(ii) Awards the person on whose earnings record your claim is based deemed wages for internment during World War II and a benefit based upon the internment is determined by an agency of the United States to be payable under another Federal law or under a system established by that agency; or

(11) It is incorrect because—

(i) You were convicted of a crime that affected your right to receive benefits or your entitlement to a period of disability; or

(ii) Your conviction of a crime that affected your right to receive benefits or your entitlement to a period of disability is overturned.

Except for clerical error and error on the face of the evidence (20 C.F.R. § 404.988 (c)(8)), the regulatory provisions allowing for reopening at any time are, for the most part, useful to SSA, not claimants. Certain claimants might use 20 C.F.R. § 404.988(c)(4) and (7) in the unusual circumstances described by those subsections. Lawyers sometimes find themselves looking at this regulation when SSA is in the process of reopening a beneficiary's claim to take away benefits.

§374.1   Fraud or Similar Fault

When a determination or decision is obtained by fraud or similar fault, it may be reopened at any time. 20 C.F.R. § 404.988(c)(1). Note that fraud or similar fault is the only basis for reopening an SSI determination or decision at any time. 20 C.F.R. § 416.1488(c). The SSI regulation, which is cross-referenced in 20 C.F.R. § 404.988(c)(1), says that in determining whether a decision was obtained by fraud or similar fault, SSA "will take into account any physical, mental, educational, or linguistic limitations (including any lack of facility with the English language) which you may have had at the time." "Similar fault" is like fraud only without the intent to defraud. Similar fault occurs when SSA is misled by incorrect or incomplete information provided by the claimant or representative. To prove "similar fault," SSA does not have to show intent to defraud but it does have to show that the person committing the fault knew the information, which is material to the decision or determination, was false or incomplete. *See* SSR 16-2p.

According to HALLEX I-2-9-65 A, "Fraud or similar fault may be perpetrated by a claimant or any other person (e.g., a representative, interpreter, medical provider, or a Social Security Administration (SSA) employee). For reopening purposes, it is not necessary that the other person have any direct relationship to the claimant or be acting on behalf of the claimant." Thus, reopening at a claimant's request because of fraud or similar fault perpetrated by a consultative examiner or vocational expert is not out of the question.

§374.2   SSR 91-5p: Good Cause for Missing the Deadline to Appeal Because of Mental Incapacity

20 C.F.R. § 404.988(c) describes most circumstances where reopening is allowed at any time, but one of the most important is not listed in this regulation. Social Security Ruling 91-5p provides, in effect, for reopening at any time when there is evidence that a *pro se* claimant who didn't have a hearing on the earlier application lacked the mental capacity to understand the procedures for requesting review. SSR 91-5p directs SSA decision makers to find good cause in these cases for missing the deadline to appeal a denial under 20 C.F.R. § 404.911, a different approach from using the reopening rules to accomplish the same end. *See* §158.

This situation also is an exception for finding *res judicata because the earlier denial did not become final*. Adjudicators are instructed to consider inability to read or write, lack of facility with the English language, limited education, and any mental or physical impairment that limits the claimant's ability to do things for himself or herself. They are also instructed to "resolve any reasonable doubt in favor of the claimant." SSR 91-5p. HALLEX I-2-4-40 E provides the following:

1. When an ALJ Addresses Mental Competence

    An ALJ must address and resolve in the decision or dismissal the issue of whether a claimant lacked the mental competence to pursue the appeal when:

    - the ALJ considers the application of administrative finality or administrative *res judicata* to a determination or decision made on a prior application;

    - there is evidence that a claimant lacked the mental capacity to timely request review of an adverse determination, decision, dismissal, or review by a federal district court; and

    - the claimant had no one legally responsible for prosecuting the claim.

    If the claimant satisfies the substantive criteria, the time limits in the reopening regulations do not apply. In that situation, regardless of how much time has passed since the prior administrative action, the claimant can establish good cause for extending the deadline to request review of that action. If the ALJ finds that good cause exists, he or she will extend the time for requesting review and take the action that would have been appropriate had the claimant filed a

timely appeal. In that instance, administrative finality and administrative *res judicata* will not apply.

NOTE:

> **Social Security Ruling (SSR) 91-5p** contains a full discussion of the policy we apply in determining whether good cause exists in claims involving mental incapacity.

Note that the ALJ may find against the claimant without a hearing addressing the issue of competency, except in the Fourth Circuit, where a hearing on the competency issue is mandatory. *See* AR 90-4(4) adopting *Culbertson v. Secretary of Health & Human Services*, 859 F.2d 319 (4th Cir. 1988), and *Young v. Bowen*, 858 F.2d 951 (4th Cir. 1988). HALLEX, however, does not explain how an ALJ, outside the Fourth Circuit, can decide this issue without a hearing.

§375   Jurisdiction to Reopen

Time limits for reopening are set by the regulations. In addition, if there is reopening to be done, either at the request of the claimant or by SSA on its own, SSA has a set of rules that appear in HALLEX and POMS that determine who has jurisdiction to reopen. The general rule is best stated by POMS DI 27501.005B.3: "An SSA or DDS component at the same or higher adjudicative level may reopen an administratively final determination or decision, when reopening is appropriate." There is a corollary to this rule: A decision maker can reopen a determination or decision from a lower level of administrative review only if the case is properly before the decision maker. *See* HALLEX I-2-9-1 B. and I-3-9-5.

The Appeals Council, in conjunction with reviewing an ALJ decision, can reopen and deny an application that was submitted to SSA and favorably decided *after* the date of the application currently being appealed. HALLEX I-3-9-5 A. Although effective July 28, 2011, SSR 11-1p changed SSA's policy of allowing new applications to be filed without permission while an earlier claim is pending at the Appeals Council, the new policy had no impact on the Appeals Council's jurisdiction to reopen a subsequent claim. Thus, the Appeals Council has jurisdiction to reopen a subsequent claim filed before the effective date of the new policy. It has jurisdiction to reopen a subsequent claim filed with the permission of the Appeals Council. And after remand of a claim by the federal court to SSA, when the Appeals Council is processing the federal court remand order, it has jurisdiction to reopen a subsequent claim filed when the earlier claim was pending in federal court. See HALLEX I-1-10-30 and I-3-9-5.

Decision makers at the initial and reconsideration level do not have jurisdiction to reopen an earlier ALJ denial decision. POMS DI 27501.005B.3. At these levels, local office personnel make a determination of whether *res judicata* applies. If it does, a *res judicata* denial is issued. Only if local office personnel determine that *res judicata* does not apply do they then forward the claim to the state agency to be evaluated by a disability examiner and physician. POMS DI 27516.001. Thus, it is not surprising that few requests to reopen are granted at the initial and reconsideration stages.

An ALJ has jurisdiction to reopen a determination made at a lower level of review where another claim is pending before the ALJ. But if the Appeals Council denied the other claim in a decision, the ALJ must refer the request to reopen to the Appeals Council. HALLEX I-2-9-5, I-2-9-6, and I-3-9-5. Note that if the Appeals Council simply denied review, an ALJ still has jurisdiction over the claim because the final decision was made at the ALJ level. See HALLEX I-2-9-5 B.2. Note.

The Appeals Council has primary jurisdiction to reopen and revise any decision of the Appeals Council itself unless the decision is pending in federal court. HALLEX I-3-9-5 C. It may reopen denials from other levels of the administrative appeals system only when the "case is properly before" the Appeals Council on the basis of a request for review, a subsequent application, the Appeals Council's own motion review or "other appropriate jurisdiction." HALLEX I-3-9-1 B. and I-3-9-5. The Appeals Council "also has authority to reopen and revise any final determination or decision in which an ALJ has primary jurisdiction, but will generally do so only if the particular circumstances allow the AC to act more expeditiously than an ALJ." HALLEX I-3-9-5 B.

A federal court's affirmation of a prior decision does not affect the Social Security Administration's jurisdiction to reopen it. SSR 67-22 and HALLEX I-2-9-5 A, Note 2. However, if the earlier claim is still pending in federal court, the earlier decision of the Social Security Administration has not yet become final and binding. Thus, there is no jurisdiction to reopen.

§376   *Implied Request for Reopening*

HALLEX I-2-9-10 B. provides:

> A claimant might not expressly request that an ALJ reopen and revise a final determination or decision, but may submit additional evidence or information that implies he or she is requesting reopening and revision of a prior determination or decision. Usually, this occurs when a claimant alleges an onset date of disability within a previously adjudicated period or, after the ALJ issues a decision, the claimant sends the ALJ new

and material evidence that relates to the earlier period at issue. (See HALLEX I-2-9-40 C for the definition of new and material evidence.) When a claimant submits information that implies a request for reopening, the ALJ will first determine whether he or she has jurisdiction to reopen and revise the prior determination or decision. See HALLEX I-2-9-5.

> An ALJ must reopen a determination or decision if the conditions and timeframes for reopening are met (as explained in HALLEX I-2-9-30, I-2-9-40, and I-2-9-60), the ALJ has jurisdiction over the issue, and the facts and evidence of the particular case warrant reopening.

The concept of an implied request for reopening, discussed in *Purter v. Heckler*, 771 F.2d 682, 695 (3d Cir. 1985), is crucially important where, by the time you get involved in the case, the two- or four-year time limit has already run out. A request for reopening at that point must be denied as untimely. Thus, you need to look to see if the claimant took some action or made a statement within the time limit that can be construed as an implied request for reopening. But don't limit yourself to looking only at the onset date alleged in the application.

Many times you will find that the onset date alleged in the application was provided, not by your client, but by a Social Security claims representative. Often the alleged onset date chosen by the claims representative is the day after the last denial of an earlier application (which is the earliest date SSA may find to be the onset date without reopening the earlier application).

Are there other ways the claimant's application can be construed as a request for reopening the earlier one? The Disability Report that the claimant completes, Form SSA-3368, may help. The form contains this question: "When did you become unable to work because of your illnesses, injuries or conditions?" If the claimant's answer to this question is the same as the alleged onset date in the earlier application, this form may constitute the implied request for reopening. One may also argue that an uncounseled claimant's right to reopen should not be lost because of the action of a claims representative in choosing an onset date that is meaningless to the claimant. Careful review of the file may uncover other arguments.

If the claimant is still within the two- or four-year time limit to request reopening based on new evidence, it is best to make the request for reopening in writing, pointing out the new evidence.

§377 *Res Judicata* **Dismissals**

Res judicata applies if the parties, facts and issues are the same in the current application as they were in an earlier denial. When the claimant still has insured status after a denial, there will always be facts and issues pertaining to the unadjudicated period to be determined in a later application, even though the issue of whether the claimant was disabled through the date of the last denial decision may be barred by the doctrine of administrative *res judicata*.

Since there is no date last insured in SSI cases, there is no *res judicata* problem for determining disability in an SSI case. The issue is always whether or not the claimant is disabled at any time from the date of the SSI application through the date of the decision.

But in a Social Security disability claim, when the date last insured is before the date of the earlier denial, that earlier denial has finally determined that the claimant is not disabled through the date last insured. There is no unadjudicated period. The entire current application can be denied based on *res judicata*. Indeed, the regulations provide that the ALJ may dismiss a request for hearing if the doctrine of *res judicata* applies. 20 C.F.R. § 404.957(c)(1). *See also* HALLEX I-2-4-40. Thus, even though the claimant requests reopening of the earlier denial, there is no right to a hearing on the issue, something that usually comes as a complete surprise to claimants and sometimes to representatives. Nothing in the regulations or HALLEX calls for advance notice that a request for hearing will be dismissed unless new evidence is provided. Nothing calls for the ALJ to request a brief before dismissing the request for hearing. Instead, a notice of dismissal may arrive at your office even before you have had a chance to review SSA's file.

Practice Tip

Whenever the earlier denial that you want reopened comes after the date last insured, make your record in writing to the ALJ soon after the request for hearing is filed. Explain the new evidence. Explain both why it is new (by summarizing the evidence SSA had in its possession at the time of the last denial) and why it is material (by showing that it changes the outcome of the case). Explain why reopening is appropriate. If the claimant has something significant to say in testimony, summarize it in an affidavit and submit it to the ALJ.

Some ALJs will hold a hearing to determine whether a claimant's testimony constitutes new evidence rather than deny the claimant the right to a hearing on *res judicata* grounds if the claimant never had a hearing on the earlier application. These ALJs think it is unfair to a claimant to deny on *res judicata* grounds all opportunity for a hearing. Indeed, some attorneys point to this language in the Social Security Act as supporting the proposition that denials below the hearing level should not be given *res judicata* effect: "The findings and decision of the Commissioner of Social Security after a hearing shall be binding upon all individuals who were parties to such hearing." 42 U.S.C. § 405(h). Nevertheless, this is not SSA's interpretation of the Act and several courts have found neither a constitutional violation nor a violation of the Social Security Act in such denials. *See*, for example, *Harper v. Secretary of HHS*, 978 F.2d 260, 264 (6th Cir. 1992); *Rogerson v. Secretary of Health & Human Services*, 872 F.2d 24, 29 (3d Cir. 1989); *Taylor v. Heckler*, 765 F.2d 872, 876 (9th Cir. 1985); and *McGowen v. Harris*, 666 F.2d 60, 65 (4th Cir. 1981). The minority view is represented by *Dealy v. Heckler*, 616 F. Supp. 880, 887-888 (W.D. Mo. 1984); *Aversa v. Secretary of Health & Human Services*, 672 F. Supp. 775, 777-778 (D.N.J. 1987); and *Delamater v. Schweiker*, 721 F.2d 50, 53 (2d Cir. 1983).

When a hearing is held to determine if the claimant's testimony constitutes new evidence, special language is inserted in the Notice of Hearing indicating the limited purpose of the hearing and notifying the claimant that if additional testimony does not warrant revision of the earlier denial, the current request for hearing "will be dismissed on the basis of administrative *res judicata*." HALLEX I-2-4-40 M.1.c. When the ALJ dismisses the request for hearing under these circumstances, the ALJ is supposed to "include in the dismissal order a discussion of the testimony at the hearing and the ALJ's rationale." HALLEX I-2-4-40 M.2. In short, when an ALJ does not find grounds for reopening in this circumstance, SSA wants ALJs to issue clear dismissal orders so that a claimant cannot later argue that there was implied or *de facto* reopening of the earlier claim resulting in a denial that can be appealed to federal court. *See*, for example, *McGowen v. Harris*, 666 F.2d 60 (4th Cir. 1981); *Purter v. Heckler*, 771 F.2d 682 (3d Cir. 1985); *Wolfe v. Chater*, 86 F.3d 1072, 1079-1080 (11th Cir. 1996); and *Schmidt v. Callahan*, 995 F. Supp. 869, 880 (N.D. Ill. 1998).

If the ALJ does not dismiss a request for hearing on the grounds of *res judicata* and the case thereafter properly ends up before the Appeals Council, it is SSA's position that the Appeals Council has authority to vacate the ALJ's decision and dismiss the request for hearing. HALLEX I-3-3-9 B. *See Ellis v. Schweiker*, 662 F.2d 419, 420 (5th Cir. 1981); *Johnson v. Sullivan*, 936 F.2d 974, 976 (7th Cir. 1991); *Harper v. Secretary of HHS*, 978 F.2d 260, 264 (6th Cir. 1992), adopted as SSR 95-2c; and *Tobak v. Apfel*, 195 F.3d 183, 187-188 (3d Cir. 1999).

§378 Circumstances Where *Res Judicata* Does Not Apply

If the decision maker cannot determine the applicability of *res judicata* because the prior claim cannot be located, *res judicata* cannot be applied. POMS DI 27516.005D. Note. That is, if the decision maker cannot determine what evidence was considered in the prior claim, it may be impossible to determine if the facts of the current claim are the same. Sometimes, though, it may be possible to determine this without the entire prior file. For example, the decision itself may provide enough information to conclude that *res judicata* should be applied.

Res judicata applies only if the current claim involves 1) the same parties, 2) the same facts, and 3) the same issues. For disability determination issues, other potential parties tend to stand in the same shoes as the claimant. Thus, they are not considered to be different parties. HALLEX I-2-4-40 I.

The same principles for determining if evidence is new and material are applied in the *res judicata* context as are applied for reopening. *See* §373.1. Note that when a claimant alleges a new impairment, the claimant is making a two-pronged attack on *res judicata*. One prong introduces evidence not yet considered, that is, evidence regarding the new impairment. The other prong introduces a new issue. The new issue is whether the additional impairment causes limitations that, in conjunction with the limitations from the claimant's other impairments, make the claimant disabled.

POMS DI 27516.001B presents this summary:

- A subsequent Title II claim may be denied using the legal principle of *res judicata* when a previous determination or decision denying a prior Title II claim

- has become final (no timely appeal); and

- denied the prior claim through the date the nondisability requirements for entitlement were last met (i.e., date last insured (DLI) for Disability Insurance Benefits (DIB); ending date of the prescribed period for Disabled Widow's or Widower's Benefits (DWB); or

attainment of age 22 for Childhood Disability Benefits (CDB)); and

- considered the same facts and issues for the same period.

Ensure that all of the following conditions are met before using *res judicata* as the basis for denial:

- the law or regulations pertaining to the alleged disabling condition have not changed (to determine the applicability of *res judicata* see DI 27516.010–Disability Determination Services (DDS) Medical Evaluation Criteria);

- the subsequent claim presents no new facts or issues which were not considered in making the prior determination or decision (such as an unadjudicated period);

- an onset of a significant new impairment during the previously adjudicated period is not alleged; and

- the claimant does not allege that he or she failed to timely appeal an adverse initial or reconsideration Title II determination because of good faith reliance on incorrect, incomplete, or misleading information given by SSA or the disability determination services (DDS) regarding the effects of reapplying instead of appealing (for additional information, see Social Security Ruling (SSR) 95-1p);

- the claimant does not allege nor does the evidence support a failure by the claimant to timely appeal the previous adverse determination, decision, or dismissal because of the claimant's mental incapacity (for additional information, see SSR 91-5p).

NOTE: The application of *res judicata* only applies to Title II claims, *i.e.*, the current application must be Title II and the prior claim must be Title II. This procedure does not apply for Title XVI claims.

Note that SSA specifically includes the situations involved in SSRs 91-5p and 95-1p as exceptions to the applicability of *res judicata*. Note also that whenever a change in the law makes it easier for a claimant to be found disabled, *res judicata* does not apply because there is a new issue. This includes when a change in the Listing of Impairments sets less restrictive standards. POMS DI 27516.010F, which is reproduced below, contains a list of such less restrictive Listings.

F. Changes to the listing of impairments that affect the application of res judicata

Subsequent claims involving the listings shown below should not be denied based on *res judicata* if the determination or decision on the prior claim was made before the date of the listing change.

NOTE: If a listing for a particular impairment is not in the table below, a less restrictive change was not made to the listing of impairments and a subsequent claim involving the impairment may be denied based on *res judicata*, absent new facts or issues.

Impairments/Listings Involved	Date of Change	Explanation and Action
Musculoskeletal System (1.00)		
All musculoskeletal disorders	02/19/02	We so extensively revised the musculoskeletal listings in 2002 that, while they are not, in general, less restrictive than the prior listings, the "issues" are different and include the use of functional criteria to indicate listing-level severity. **If the prior claim was denied before 02/19/02,** prepare a new determination for all subsequent claims involving a musculoskeletal impairment.
Special Senses and Speech (2.00)		
All hearing impairments	08/02/10	We revised the listings for hearing impairments by removing the requirement for testing with hearing aids and replacing listings 2.08 and 102.08 with new listings 2.10 and 102.10, respectively. **If the prior claim was denied before 08/02/10,** prepare a new substantive determination for all subsequent claims involving hearing loss.
Vision	04/29/13	If the prior claim was denied before 04/29/2013, prepare a new substantive determination for all subsequent claims involving vision.
Respiratory System (3.00)		
All respiratory disorders	10/07/16	We revised the listings for respiratory disorders. While the listings are not, in general, less restrictive, we added new criteria. **If the prior claim was denied before 10/07/16,** prepare a new substantive determination for any subsequent claim involving a respiratory impairment.

Impairments/Listings Involved	Date of Change	Explanation and Action
Cardiovascular system (4.00)		
All cardiovascular disorders	02/10/94	We revised the cardiovascular listings so extensively that, while they are not, in general, less restrictive, the "issues" are different. **If the prior claim was denied before 02/10/94,** prepare a new determination for all subsequent claims involving a cardiovascular impairment.
Cardiovascular disorders: chronic heart failure; ischemic heart disease; peripheral arterial disease	04/13/06	We revised the adult listings for chronic heart failure (4.02), ischemic heart disease (4.04), and peripheral arterial disease (4.12). While the listings are not, in general, less restrictive, we added new criteria or revised existing criteria to reflect technological improvements. **If the prior claim was denied before 04/13/06,** prepare a new substantive determination for all subsequent claims involving chronic heart failure, ischemic heart disease, or peripheral arterial disease.
Digestive System (5.00)		
Any digestive disorder	12/18/07	**If the prior claim was denied before 12/18/07,** prepare a new substantive determination for all subsequent claims involving any digestive disorder.
Hematological Disorders (7.00)		
All hematological disorders	05/18/15	We so extensively revised the hematological disorders listings in 2015 that, while they are not, in general, less restrictive than the prior listings, the "issues" are different and include the use of functional criteria to indicate listing-level severity. **If the prior claim was denied before 05/18/15,** prepare a new determination for all subsequent claims involving a hematological disorder impairment.

Impairments/Listings Involved	Date of Change	Explanation and Action
Skin Disorders (8.00)		
All skin disorders	07/09/04	We revised the listings for evaluation of skin disorders. We added new listings and included a specific time requirement for most listings, which is less restrictive. **If the prior claim was denied before 07/09/04,** prepare a new substantive determination for all subsequent claims involving skin disorders.
Congenital Disorders That Affect Multiple Body Systems (10.00)		
Non-mosaic Down syndrome in an individual age 18 or older	6/19/00	We added listing 10.06 for non-mosaic Down syndrome. **If the prior claim was denied before 06/19/00,** prepare a substantive determination for all subsequent claims involving an individual aged 18 or older with non-mosaic Down syndrome.
Neurological (11.00)		
Amyotrophic lateral sclerosis (ALS)	08/28/03	We revised the listing criteria for evaluating ALS under listing 11.10. We will find disability with medical evidence showing that the claimant has ALS. **If the prior claim was denied before 08/28/03,** prepare a new substantive determination for all subsequent claims involving ALS.
All neurological disorders except for ALS	9/29/16	We comprehensively revised the listings for evaluating neurological disorders. We added new listings, removed 3 listings and included new functional criteria for most listings. If the prior claim was denied before 09/29/16, prepare a new substantive determination for all subsequent claims involving a neurological disorder other than ALS.

Impairments/Listings Involved	Date of Change	Explanation and Action
Mental Disorders (12.00)		
Mental Disorders	08/28/85	We extensively revised the mental disorders listings. These changes included severity criteria that are less restrictive. **If the prior claim was denied before 08/28/85,** prepare a new substantive determination for all subsequent claims involving a mental disorder.
Mental disorders: Organic mental disorders; schizophrenic, paranoid and other psychotic disorders; affective disorders; somatoform disorders; personality disorders	09/20/00	We revised the listings for the evaluation of these disorders. While these listings are not, in general, less restrictive, we: • added new paragraph C criteria for organic mental disorders (12.02) and affective disorders (12.04); • revised the paragraph C criteria for schizophrenic, paranoid, and other psychotic disorders (12.03); and • revised the paragraph B criteria for somatoform disorders (12.07) and personality disorders (12.08), changing the requirement for three "marked" limitations to two. **If the prior claim was denied after 08/28/85 but before 09/20/00,** prepare a new substantive determination for all subsequent claims involving these mental disorders.
Cancer (13.00)		
Malignant neoplastic disease of the lungs	01/06/86	We revised the listing for evaluating malignant lung tumors (13.13) to reflect advances in medical knowledge regarding the expected course of squamous cell carcinoma and other histologic (tissue) types of carcinoma. This change has less restrictive criteria for evaluating these tumors. **If the prior claim was denied before 01/06/86,** prepare a substantive determination on any subsequent claim involving squamous cell and other histologic types of carcinoma.
Malignant neoplastic disease of the esophagus	01/06/86	We revised the listing for evaluating tumors located in the lower half of the esophagus (13.16) to remove the requirement for metastatic disease. **If the prior claim was denied before 01/06/86,** prepare substantive determination on subsequent claim involving a tumor located in the lower half of esophagus if the prior claim was denied before 01/06/86.

Impairments/Listings Involved	Date of Change	Explanation and Action
Cancer (13.00)		
Malignant neoplastic disease of the gallbladder	01/06/86	We revised the criteria for evaluation of carcinoma of the bile ducts to require less extension of the tumors. This change is less restrictive. **If the prior claim was denied before 01/06/86,** prepare a substantive determination on the subsequent claim involving carcinoma of the bile ducts if the prior claim was denied before 01/06/86.
Malignant neoplastic disease of the penis	01/06/86	We added new listings to provide standards for tumors of the penis and vulva. (The listing for tumors of the penis was 13.29 from 01/06/86 to 07/08/04. It was renumbered to 13.26 beginning 07/09/04.) **If the prior claim was denied before 01/06/86,** prepare a substantive determination on the subsequent claim involving tumors of the penis.
• Malignant neoplastic disease of: soft tissue of the head and neck; skin; breast; skeletal system; lungs; small intestine; kidneys, adrenals, or ureters; female genital tract • Malignant neoplastic disease treated by bone marrow or stem cell transplantation • Leukemia • Multiple myeloma • Primary site unknown after appropriate search	12/15/04	We revised the listings for these disorders (13.02C, 13.02E, 13.03A, 13.03B2, 13.06, 13.07, 13.10A, 13.11D, 13.14A, 13.17A, 13.21A, 13.23, 13.27, and 13.28). While these listings are not, in general, less restrictive, we added criteria to recognize the length and debilitating effects of treatment for some malignancies. We also: • added criteria for other types of tumors that have a similar prognosis as those already in the listings; • revised the criteria for multiple myeloma to clarify that this listing includes all listing-level manifestations of the disease; and • added criteria for tumors for which the site of origin cannot be determined. **If the prior claim was denied before 12/15/04,** prepare a new substantive determination for all subsequent claims involving these malignant neoplastic diseases.
Malignant neoplastic diseases of: skin; thyroid gland; breast; lungs; female genital tract	11/5/09	We have revised the listings for these disorders (13.03B, 13.09C, 13.10B, 13.14C, 13.23C, 113.09C). While these listings may not, in general, be less restrictive, we added criteria to recognize the length and debilitating effects of treatment for some malignancies. We also added criteria for evaluating malignant neoplastic diseases of the skin, thyroid gland, and breast. If the prior claim was denied before 11/5/09, prepare a new substantive determination for all subsequent claims involving these malignant neoplastic diseases.
Cancer	07/20/15	We have revised the listings and added some new listings for these disorders and renamed the body system "Cancer" (13.02, 13.03, 13.05, 13.06, 13.10, 13.12, 13.13, 13.15, 13.16, 13.17, 13.18, 13.20, 13.22, 13.23, 13.24, 13.29, 113.05, 113.06 and 113.13, 113.29). While these listings may not, in general, be less restrictive, we added criteria to recognize the unfavorable prognoses and length and debilitating effects of treatment for some malignancies. If the prior claim was denied before 7/20/15, prepare a new substantive determination for all subsequent claims involving these malignant neoplastic diseases.

Impairments/Listings Involved	Date of Change	Explanation and Action
Immune System Disorders (14.00)		
Immune system disorders	07/02/93	We added a separate body system with accompanying listings for immune system disorders (14.00). We incorporated impairments that were previously contained in the multiple body system listings (10.00). Many of these listings include the use of restriction of function to indicate listing-level severity. In addition, they include a listing for human immunodeficiency virus (HIV) infection; however, the standards for documentation have been expanded to permit both definitive and clinical documentation of HIV infection and to include specific manifestations of HIV infection seen in women and children. **If the prior claim was denied before 07/02/93,** prepare a substantive determination for all subsequent claims involving an immune system disorder.
Systemic lupus erythematosus (SLE)	02/19/02	We revised the musculoskelatal system listings. This change affected the listing for SLE because it includes a cross-reference to the musculoskeletal listings. While the revised musculoskeletal listings are not, in general, less restrictive, the criteria are different and include the use of functional criteria to establish listing-level severity. **If the prior claim was denied before 02/19/02,** prepare a new substantive determination for all subsequent claims involving SLE with joint involvement.
Inflammatory arthritis	02/19/02	We extensively revised the listings for the evaluation of inflammatory arthritis. While the revised listings are not, in general, less restrictive, the criteria are different and include the use of functional criteria to establish listing-level severity. **If the prior claim was denied before 02/19/02,** prepare a new substantive determination for all subsequent claims involving inflammatory arthritis.
All immune system disorders except human immunodeficiency virus (HIV) infection	06/16/08	We revised the listings for these disorders by either making them less restrictive or making major changes that result in the listing criteria being significantly different. For example, in some listings, we added functional criteria to indicate listing-level severity. **If the prior claim was denied before 06/16/08,** prepare a new substantive determination for all subsequent claims involving these immune system disorders listings.

There are additional situations recognized by HALLEX or published as Social Security Rulings or Acquiescence Rulings where *res judicata* does not apply because of a change in the law. *See*, for example, SSR 63-41, which dealt with a change in the law pertaining to disability insured status. Where there is a mentally impaired *pro se* claimant who lacked the mental capacity to understand the procedures for requesting review, neither *res judicata* nor the limitations imposed by administrative finality apply. SSR 91-5p. A somewhat broader rule applies in the Fourth Circuit, which requires that an evidentiary hearing be held in all cases where a claimant raises the issue. AR 90-4(4). *See* §374.

Congress determined that *res judicata* would not apply if a claimant was misled by an SSA employee or by a notice issued after July 1, 1991, which provided incorrect, misleading or incomplete information about the consequences of reapplying for benefits instead of appealing. 42 U.S.C. § 405(b)(3). Prior to the time Congress acted, SSA had sent denial notices to claimants that said, usually in all capitals, "IF YOU DO NOT REQUEST A HEARING WITHIN THE PRESCRIBED TIME PERIOD, YOU STILL HAVE THE RIGHT TO FILE ANOTHER APPLICATION AT ANY TIME."

This notice, of course, fails to mention possible loss of benefits in all cases; but it is most misleading for those whose insured status has already run out. Their new claims will be denied by the doctrine of administrative *res judicata*.

Although you are unlikely to find this language in a denial notice issued after July 1, 1991, you may find it in denials issued before that date—something which is not covered by the statute. Nevertheless, for those in the Ninth Circuit, Acquiescence Ruling 92-7(9), adopting *Gonzalez v. Sullivan*, 914 F.2d 1197 (9th Cir. 1990), provides that denials containing such language will not be given *res judicata* effect and that the time limits for reopening would not apply. Several courts outside the Ninth Circuit have come to similar conclusions. *See*, for example, *Dealy v. Heckler*, 616 F. Supp. 880 (W.D. Mo. 1984); *Aversa v. Secretary of Health & Human Services*, 672 F. Supp. 775 (D.N.J. 1987); and *Butland v. Bowen*, 673 F. Supp. 638 (D. Mass. 1987).

SSR 95-1p attempts to limit the impact of *Gonzalez v. Sullivan* for those outside the Ninth Circuit by recasting the issue as a failure to timely appeal. The ruling provides that a claimant must demonstrate that, "as a result of the [misleading] notice, he or she did not timely request ... review. The mere receipt of a notice covered by this Ruling will not, by itself, establish good cause [for missing the deadline to appeal]." SSR 95-1p also provides that, absent evidence to the contrary, SSA will presume that all initial and reconsideration notices issued between August 31, 1997 and March 1, 1990 denying Title II claims contained the misleading language. The ruling lists factors for the decision maker to consider in making a determination whether the language in the notice misled a claimant. These factors include the claimant's explanation of the meaning of the notice and how that understanding influenced the claimant's actions, the claimant's mental condition, education level, facility with the English language, and how much time elapsed before the claimant filed a subsequent claim. SSR 95-1p also provides that, normally, attorney representation at the time of receipt of the erroneous notice would bar a claimant from relief under the ruling. Non-attorney representation, however, is a factor for consideration.

The reason many claimants fail to request a hearing is simply that they become discouraged with the prospect of ever being found disabled by an agency that has already denied them twice. (Indeed, many people think that increasing claimant discouragement to deter further appeals is a primary function of the reconsideration step.) SSR 95-1p may make it difficult for discouraged claimants to reopen earlier applications based on the language in the denial notice. Nevertheless, SSR 95-1p begs the question in the most egregious circumstance—where the misleading notice comes after the date last insured telling a claimant about "the right to file another application at any time." In this situation, SSA will apply *res judicata* when the claimant files a new application, making this "right" meaningless.

Outside the Ninth Circuit, if your goal is simply reopening an earlier application based on misleading language, SSR 95-1p may prove to be an impediment. You will have to show, in effect, that the claimant did not know that he would lose benefits if he or she failed to appeal rather than filing a new application at a later date. Loss of benefits may not come as a surprise to many claimants. But even the best-educated claimants are taken entirely off guard when SSA applies *res judicata* to bar filing of a new application. Most claimants in this situation, had they known the implications of failing to appeal, certainly would have done so. Since this issue rises to the level of a due process violation, *res judicata* should not work to bar the claimant from filing a new application.

There are also class action decisions on various issues around the country, which provide that *res judicata* will not apply under certain circumstances. To see if a class action decision applies in your area, search the POMS. A POMS search can be conducted most efficiently from the NOSSCR website, www.nosscr.org/research-advocates.

§379　Res Judicata or Administrative Finality Invoked by Claimants

A concept related to *res judicata*, collateral estoppel, is sometimes used by claimants to obtain additional benefits when they are awarded benefits under one title of the Social Security Act but denied benefits under another. 20 C.F.R. § 404.950(f) provides:

> Collateral estoppel—issues previously decided. An issue at your hearing may be a fact that has already been decided in one of our previous determinations or decisions in a claim involving the same parties, but arising under a different title of the Act or under the Federal Coal Mine Health and Safety Act. If this happens, the administrative law judge will not consider the issue again, but will accept the factual findings made in the previous determination or decision unless there are reasons to believe it was wrong.

Claimants or beneficiaries also may invoke the doctrines of administrative finality and *res judicata*. For example, SSA's attempt to retroactively terminate disability benefits was found to be barred after the claimant invoked *res judicata* in *Dugan v. Sullivan*, 957 F.2d 1384 (7th Cir. 1992).

Nevertheless, in cases involving initial determination of disability, the utility of these doctrines on behalf of claimants is narrow. *Lively v. Secretary of Health & Human Services*, 820 F.2d 1391 (4th Cir. 1987), illustrates the most common situation in which a disability claimant has tried to use *res judicata* against SSA. *Lively's* first application was denied (using Rule 202.10 of the Medical-Vocational Guidelines) two weeks before his 55th birthday on the grounds that he had the residual functional capacity for light work. As of age 55, however, *Lively* should have been found disabled using Rule 202.02; but, without finding any improvement in his condition, the ALJ on the second application found that *Lively* was capable of work at any exertional level. The Fourth Circuit Court of Appeals applied *res judicata* to the first decision. It required SSA to produce new evidence showing that *Lively's* RFC was different than it was in the first decision.

SSA adopted *Lively* as an acquiescence ruling, AR 92-2(4), and applied it whenever a claimant filed a later application in the Fourth Circuit. SSA required the claimant to produce new evidence that his or her condition was different than it was at the time the first application was denied. One such case, *Albright v. Commissioner of the SSA*, 174 F.3d 473 (4th Cir. 1999), involved a denial at step 2 of *Albright's* earlier application on the grounds that *Albright's* impairment was not severe in 1991. A second application was denied by an ALJ in October 1994 applying AR 92-2(4) on the grounds that there was no new evidence showing that *Albright's* impairment was severe.

The Fourth Circuit held in *Albright* that SSA had interpreted *Lively* too broadly. It drew a distinction between *Lively's* situation, which involved a claim that he was disabled two weeks after the earlier denial, and *Albright's* situation, where the relevant period exceeded three years. In response, SSA rescinded the acquiescence ruling pertaining to *Lively* and adopted *Albright* as an acquiescence ruling, AR 00-1(4). This ruling noted that SSA would consider the prior finding as evidence in the later case and give it appropriate weight in light of all relevant facts and circumstances such as whether the facts on which the prior finding was based were subject to change over time, the likelihood of such a change and the extent to which evidence not considered in the first claim provides a basis for making a different finding in the later claim. The ruling noted that SSA would give greater weight to a prior finding when it is close in time, such as a few weeks as in *Lively*, than when it is more remote, such as when it is more than three years as in *Albright*.

In narrowing *Albright's* application even further, AR 00-1(4) applies only to findings of a claimant's residual functional capacity or other finding at a step of the sequential evaluation process. In a footnote, SSA explained that the rule of *Albright* does not apply to "subsidiary findings," such as credibility findings. AR 00-1(4), note 5.

The Sixth Circuit Court of Appeals relied on *Lively* in *Drummond v. Commissioner of Social Sec.*, 126 F.3d 837 (6th Cir. 1997), a case with similar facts, to hold that "[a]bsent evidence of an improvement in a claimant's condition, a subsequent ALJ is bound by the findings of a previous ALJ." This case was adopted as AR 98-4(6). In *Dennard v. Secretary of HHS*, 907 F.2d 598 (6th Cir. 1990), adopted as AR 98-3(6), the issue was whether *res judicata* should be applied to a prior ALJ's finding about the exertional level of past relevant work. The court held that unless new evidence or changed circumstances provided a basis for a different finding, SSA must adopt the prior finding.

There is a similar line of cases in the Ninth Circuit. *See*, for example, *Lyle v. Secretary of Health & Human Services*, 700 F.2d 566 (9th Cir. 1983); and *Booz v. Secretary of Health & Human Services*, 734 F.2d 1378, 1379-1380 (9th Cir. 1984). The Ninth Circuit rule explicitly increases a claimant's burden of proof in all cases involving a later application. It requires a claimant whose RFC was determined in the first proceeding to produce new evidence that shows a different RFC in the second proceeding, even when the date last insured comes after the last denial on the earlier application. *See*,

Chavez v. Bowen, 844 F.2d 691 (9th Cir. 1988), which was adopted as Acquiescence Ruling 97-4(9).

SSA's general policy, applicable in circuits where there is no acquiescence ruling to the contrary, is to provide a *de novo* hearing on a second application when there is still an unadjudicated period. Although under SSA's general policy that the earlier denial is not considered "evidence" that must be rebutted, most ALJs nonetheless treat it as a factor for consideration. ALJs often follow the earlier decision; that is, *de novo* hearings often yield similar results. Still, an ALJ can and sometimes does come to a different conclusion than that arrived at in the earlier denial, even when there is no new evidence.

§380 Deceased Claimants

A Social Security disability claim does not usually end with a claimant's death. An SSI claim, on the other hand, may end unless there exists one of the few eligible individuals who can receive the claimant's SSI benefits.

Practice Tip

To obtain the medical records concerning the claimant's death (and any earlier records which you have not yet obtained), it will be necessary for you to have a consent form signed by the person authorized under state law to allow access to the claimant's medical records. A consent form signed by the claimant is not valid after he dies. Procedures differ depending on whether the claimant dies before or after the hearing and whether he or she dies before or after a favorable decision is issued. If the claimant dies before the hearing, a party eligible to receive the deceased's benefits must be substituted. HALLEX I-2-1-50. Individuals who may be substituted in a Social Security disability case are listed in order of priority in §381, SSI substitute parties are identified in §382. Parties are substituted using form HA539, Notice Regarding Substitution of Party Upon Death of a Claimant, §383. In a Social Security disability case, in the unusual situation where there is no substitute party (because either a claimant has no heirs or no one is interested in pursuing the claim), the ALJ may dismiss the request for hearing. This dismissal may be vacated within 60 days if a substitute party comes forward. HALLEX I-2-4-35.

In an SSI claim, if none of the few possible substitute parties are available, the ALJ will dismiss the request for hearing unless the claimant signed an interim assistance agreement. If so, the claim will proceed to a decision. HALLEX I-2-4-35 A.2 and I-2-8-37 C. However, the request for hearing will be dismissed even if someone who cannot be

an SSI substitute party wants SSA to issue a decision so that the claimant will be found eligible for Medicaid (Title 19). The HALLEX suggests that such a person be referred to the state agency which administers Medicaid so that the Title 19 claim can be pursued there. HALLEX I-2-4-35 A.2.

In both Social Security disability and SSI cases, if the case has been remanded by a federal court, the ALJ cannot dismiss the request for hearing. HALLEX I-2-4-35 A. Note 1. If a hearing has already been held and the record is complete, the ALJ is instructed to proceed with issuing the decision in both Social Security disability and SSI claims. HALLEX I-2-8-37 B.

If a claimant dies after he is found disabled but before he is paid all benefits due, SSA will pay the appropriate beneficiaries. Individuals eligible to receive the benefits usually are asked to complete form SSA-1724, Claim for Amounts Due in the Case of a Deceased Beneficiary, §384, *infra*.

Practice Tip

According to HALLEX I-1-2-19, if a valid fee agreement has been submitted and the claimant dies before SSA issues a favorable decision, the fee agreement will be approved. Thus, it isn't necessary to have a substitute party sign and submit a new fee agreement. But if no one is eligible to receive the back benefits, that is, if a substitute party never turns up, there will be no back benefits to be paid from which a lawyer will be paid. Therefore, it is in the lawyer's self-interest to make sure there is a substitute party.

§381 Social Security Disability Substitute Parties

A party may be substituted for a claimant if that party is entitled to receive all or part of the claimant's payment if the case is won. The statute, 42 U.S.C. §404(d), and regulations, 20 C.F.R. § 404.503(b), provide the following order under which eligibility to receive payment is determined:

1. To the spouse of the claimant if (a) living in the same household at the time of death, or (b) entitled to a monthly benefit on the same earnings record as the claimant for the month of death.

2. To the children of the claimant entitled to monthly benefits on the same earnings record as the claimant for the month of death. (If there is more than one entitled child, payment is made in equal parts to each child.)

3. To the parent or parents of the claimant entitled to monthly benefits on the same earnings record as the claimant for the month of death. (If there is more than one entitled parent, payment is made in equal parts to each parent.)

4. To a spouse who does not meet the requirements of (1).

5. To children who do not meet the requirements of (2).

6. To parents who do not meet the requirements of (3).

7. To the legal representative of the claimant's estate.

§382   SSI Substitute Parties

For an adult SSI claimant, only the claimant's spouse is eligible to receive payments and then only if the spouse was living in the same household as the claimant at any time during the month of death or the preceding six months. 20 C.F.R. § 416.542(b)(1).

If the claimant is a disabled child, payment will be made to a parent who was living in the same household with the child at any time during the month of death or the preceding six months. 20 C.F.R. § 416.542(b)(2).

§383 Form: Notice Regarding Substitution of Party Upon Death of Claimant (HA-539)

SOCIAL SECURITY ADMINISTRATION | Form Approved
OMB No. 0960-0288

NOTICE REGARDING SUBSTITUTION OF PARTY UPON DEATH OF CLAIMANT

OFFICE OF HEARINGS AND APPEALS

NOTE: Please read the **PRIVACY ACT/ PAPERWORK ACT** statement on reverse and the statements below. Then print, write, or type your response to the statements in the space provided below. If you need additional space, attach a separate page to this form.

NAME OF DECEASED CLAIMANT	CLAIM FOR

WAGE EARNER'S NAME *(Leave blank if same as above)*	SOCIAL SECURITY NUMBER

I have been informed that the claimant had requested a hearing but died before action on the request was completed. I understand that the deceased claimant's request for hearing will have to be dismissed unless an eligible person is substituted. My relationship to the deceased claimant is:

☐ Widow/Widower

☐ Surviving Divorced Spouse

If you have checked either of the above boxes and have in your care the deceased's child (children) who is (are) under the age 16 or disabled, check here ☐

☐ Child

☐ Disabled Child

☐ Parent

☐ Administrator/Executor of Estate

☐ Other (Describe) _____

Check *either* **1.** or **2.**

1. ☐ I wish to be made a substitute party and to proceed with the hearing requested by the deceased. Check *either* a. or b.

   a. ☐ I want to come to the hearing in person.

   b. ☐ I do not want to come to the hearing in person, and I request a decision be made without a hearing.

2. ☐ I do not wish to proceed with the hearing requested by the deceased, and I ask that the request for hearing be dismissed.

SIGNATURE *(First Name, Middle Initial, Last Name)*	DATE *(Month, Day, Year)*

PRINT OR TYPE FULL NAME	AREA CODE AND TELEPHONE NUMBER

MAILING ADDRESS *(Number and Street Address, P.O. Box or Rural Route)*

CITY, STATE, AND ZIP CODE

Form HA-539 (06-2015) UF (06-2015)   Page 1   CLAIMS FOLDER

PRIVACY ACT NOTICE
Collection and Use of Personal Information

Sections 205(a), 702, 1631(e)(1)(A) and (B), and 1869(b)(1) and (c), as amended, authorizes us to collect the information requested on this form. The information you provide will be used to make a decision on this claim. Your response is voluntary. However, failure to provide the requested information may prevent an accurate and timely decision on any claim filed, or could result in the loss of benefits.

We rarely use the information provided on this form for any purpose other than for determining entitlement to Social Security benefits. We may, however, disclose the information provided on this form in accordance with approved routine uses of the Privacy Act (5 U.S.C. § 552a(b)), which include but are not limited to the following:

1. To enable an agency or third party to assist Social Security in establishing rights to Social Security benefits and/or coverage;

2. To make determinations for eligibility in similar health and income maintenance programs at the Federal, State, and local level;

3. To comply with Federal laws requiring the disclosure of the information from our records; and,

4. To facilitate statistical research, audit, or investigative activities necessary to assure the integrity of SSA programs.

We may also use the information you provide when we match records by computer. Computer matching programs compare our records with those of other Federal, State, or local government agencies. Information from these matching programs can be used to establish or verify a person's eligibility for Federally-funded or administered benefit programs and for repayment of payments or delinquent debts under these programs.

A complete list of routine uses for this information is contained in our System of Records Notice 60-0089 (Claims Folders System). Additional information regarding this form and our other system of records notices and Social Security programs are available from our Internet website at www.socialsecurity.gov or at your local Social Security office.

Paperwork Reduction Act Statement - This information collection meets the requirements of 44 U.S.C. § 3507, as amended by section 2 of the Paperwork Reduction Act of 1995. You do not need to answer these questions unless we display a valid Office of Management and Budget control number. We estimate that it will take about 5 minutes to read the instructions, gather the facts, and answer the questions. **SEND OR BRING THE COMPLETED FORM TO YOUR LOCAL SOCIAL SECURITY OFFICE. You can find your local Social Security office through SSA's website at www.socialsecurity.gov. Offices are also listed under U. S. Government agencies in your telephone directory or you may call Social Security at 1-800-772-1213 (TTY 1-800-325-0778).** *You may send comments on our time estimate above to: SSA, 6401 Security Blvd, Baltimore, MD 21235-6401. Send only comments relating to our time estimate to this address, not the completed form.*

§384   Form: Claim for Amounts Due in the Case of a Deceased Beneficiary (SSA-1724)

Social Security Administration   OMB No. 0960-0101

CLAIM FOR AMOUNTS DUE IN THE CASE OF A DECEASED SOCIAL SECURITY RECIPIENT

PRINT NAME OF DECEASED	SOCIAL SECURITY NUMBER OF DECEASED
If the deceased received benefits on another person's record, print name of that worker	NAME OF THE WORKER

The deceased may have been due a Social Security payment at the time of death. The Social Security Act provides that amounts due a deceased may be paid to the next of kin or the legal representative of the estate under priorities established in the law. To help us decide who should receive any payment due, please **COMPLETE THIS ENTIRE FORM** and **RETURN** it to us in the enclosed envelope.

This claim for the amounts due from the Social Security Administration is being made on behalf of the family or the estate of

_____ who died on _____ day of _____   _____
    (name of deceased)   (month)   (year)

and who lived in the state of _____ .

PRINT NAME OF APPLICANT	RELATIONSHIP TO DECEASED (Widow, Son, Legal Representative, etc.)

THE FOLLOWING ARE THE NEXT OF KIN OR LEGAL REPRESENTATIVE OF THE DECEASED NAMED ABOVE:

1.	NAME OF SURVIVING WIDOW(ER) (Please print. **If none, state "NONE"**)	ADDRESS OF SURVIVING WIDOW(ER) (Please print house number, street, apt. number, P.O. Box, rural route, city, state, and ZIP code)
	ENTER SOCIAL SECURITY NUMBER(S) OF WIDOW(ER) NAMED ABOVE.	
	WAS THE WIDOW(ER) NAMED ABOVE LIVING IN THE SAME HOUSEHOLD WITH THE DECEASED AT THE TIME OF DEATH?	☐ YES If "YES", then SKIP items 2,3,4,5 and SIGN at bottom of page 2. ☐ NO
	WAS HE OR SHE ENTITLED TO A MONTHLY BENEFIT ON THE SAME EARNINGS RECORD AS THE DECEASED AT THE TIME OF DEATH?	☐ YES If "YES", then SKIP items 2,3,4,5 and SIGN at bottom of page 2. ☐ NO (Go on to item 2)

2.	ENTER NUMBER OF LIVING CHILDREN OF THE DECEASED. INCLUDE ADOPTED CHILDREN AND STEPCHILDREN; INCLUDE GRANDCHILDREN AND STEP-GRANDCHILDREN IF THEIR PARENTS ARE DISABLED OR DECEASED; OR IF THEY HAVE BEEN ADOPTED BY THE SURVIVING SPOUSE OF THE DECEASED. IF NONE OF THE ABOVE, SHOW "NONE" AND GO ON TO ITEM 4.	**NUMBER**

PRINT NAME AND COMPLETE ADDRESS OF EACH CHILD
Remarks -(If you need more space for explaining any answers to the questions, attach a separate sheet.)

NAME OF CHILD	ADDRESS OF CHILD (Include house number, street, apt. number, P.O. Box, rural route, city, state, and ZIP code)
RELATIONSHIP TO DECEASED (Grandchild, stepchild, etc.)	SOCIAL SECURITY NUMBER OF CHILD
NAME OF CHILD	ADDRESS OF CHILD (Include house number, street, apt. number, P.O. Box, rural route, city, state, and ZIP code)
RELATIONSHIP TO DECEASED (Grandchild, stepchild, etc.)	SOCIAL SECURITY NUMBER OF CHILD

<table>
<tr><td>3.</td><td>If any child listed in item 2 has a different name from that given at birth, attach a separate sheet with the following information: Child's Present Name, Name Given At Birth, and a brief explanation for the difference (e.g. Marriage or Court Order).</td></tr>
</table>

4.	ENTER NUMBER OF LIVING PARENTS OF THE DECEASED (Include adopting parents and stepparents. **If none, show "None"**) IF THERE ARE NO LIVING PARENTS, GO ON TO ITEM 5.	**NUMBER**

PRINT NAME AND COMPLETE ADDRESS OF EACH PARENT

NAME OF LIVING PARENT	ADDRESS OF LIVING PARENT (Include house number, street, apt. number, P.O. Box, rural route, city, state, and ZIP code)
ENTER SOCIAL SECURITY NUMBER OF PARENT NAMED	
NAME OF LIVING PARENT	ADDRESS OF LIVING PARENT (Include house number, street, apt. number, P.O. Box, rural route, city, state, and ZIP code)
ENTER SOCIAL SECURITY NUMBER OF PARENT NAMED.	

5.	**LEGAL REPRESENTATIVE OF THE DECEASED'S ESTATE (Skip this item if relatives are listed in 1, 2, or 4.)**

NAME OF LEGAL REPRESENTATIVE (Please print)	ADDRESS OF LEGAL REPRESENTATIVE (Please print house number, street, apt. number, P.O. Box, rural route, city, state, and ZIP code.)

NOTE: If you are applying as legal representative, please submit a certified copy of your letters of appointment.

I declare under penalty of perjury that I have examined all the information on this form, and on any accompanying statements or forms, and it is true and correct to the best of my knowledge.

SIGNATURE OF APPLICANT

SIGNATURE (First name, middle initial, last name)	DATE (Month, day, year)	TELEPHONE NUMBER (Include area code)

MAILING ADDRESS (House number and street, apt. number, P.O. Box, or rural route)

CITY	STATE	NAME OF COUNTY	ZIP CODE

Direct Deposit Payment Address (Financial Institution)

Type of Account	Nine Digit Routing Number
☐ Checking ☐ Savings	
Account Number	

WITNESSES ARE REQUIRED ONLY IF THIS APPLICATION HAS BEEN SIGNED BY MARK (X) ABOVE. IF SIGNED BY MARK (X), TWO WITNESSES TO THE SIGNING WHO KNOW THE APPLICANT MUST SIGN BELOW GIVING THEIR FULL ADDRESSES.

SIGNATURE OF WITNESS	SIGNATURE OF WITNESS
ADDRESS (House number and street, city, state, and ZIP code)	ADDRESS (House number and street, city, state, and ZIP code)

Form **SSA-1724-F4** (01-2010) EF (10-2012)   Page 2

PRIVACY ACT NOTICE

Section 204 (d) of the Social Security Act, as amended, authorizes us to collect this information. We will use this information to help us determine the beneficiary's payment.

Furnishing us the information is voluntary. However, failing to provide us with all or part of the requested information may prevent us from making an accurate and timely decision on your claim, which may result in the loss of payments.

We rarely use the information you supply for any purpose other than for determining problems in Social Security programs. However, we may use it for the administration and integrity of Social Security programs. We may also disclose information to another person or to another agency in accordance with approved routine uses, which include, but are not limited to the following:

1)   To contractors and other Federal agencies, as necessary, for the purpose of assisting the Social Security Administration in the efficient administration of its programs;

2)   To comply with Federal laws requiring the release of information from Social Security records (e.g., to the Government Accountability Office and Department of Veteran's Affairs);

3)   To make determinations for eligibility in similar health and income maintenance programs at the Federal, State, and local level; and,

4)   To facilitate statistical research, audit, or investigatory activities necessary to assure the integrity and improvement of Social Security programs.

We may also use the information you provide in computer matching programs. Matching programs compare our records with records kept by other Federal, State, or local government agencies. We use the information from these matching programs to establish or verify a person's eligibility for federally-funded and administered benefit programs and for repayment, incorrect payments or delinquent debts under these programs.

A complete list of routine uses for this information is available in our Privacy Act Systems of Records Notices, 60-0089, Claims Folder Systems, and 60-0090, Master Beneficiary Record. These notices, additional information regarding our programs and systems, are available on-line at www.socialsecurity.gov or at any local Social Security office.

Paperwork Reduction Act Statement - This information collection meets the requirements of 44 U.S.C. § 3507, as amended by section 2 of the Paperwork Reduction Act of 1995. You do not need to answer these questions unless we display a valid Office of Management and Budget (OMB) control number. We estimate that it will take about 10 minutes to read the instructions, gather the facts, and answer the questions. *Send only comments relating to our time estimate above to:* SSA, 6401 Security Blvd., Baltimore, MD 21235-6401.

§390   Hearing Checklist

§391   At the Hearing

1. Note any exhibits to which you intend to object; offer objections at the proper time.

2. Ask the ALJ to amend onset date, to request benefits for a closed period, or to reopen an earlier application, as appropriate.

3. Ask the ALJ to set a timeframe for submitting any additional evidence about which you informed the ALJ at least five business days before the hearing.

4. In a complicated or unusual case, ask the ALJ to allow you to give an opening statement.

5. Present your case in terms of the Social Security Act, regulations, and pertinent court cases from your jurisdiction.

6. Avoid cumulative evidence; when you have completed your case, quit.

7. If necessary, ask to hold the record open so that you may submit rebuttal evidence or a brief.

8. Make your closing statement.

9. Be professional and respectful, but not fawning or obsequious.

§392   After the Hearing

1. If the ALJ indicated how he was going to decide the case, discuss it with your client to make sure he understood.

2. Explain to your client that even in those cases in which the ALJ indicates which way he is going to rule, the decision will not be forthcoming immediately.

3. If the record was left open to submit a brief or additional evidence, as soon as you return to your office from the hearing, enter the due date in your calendaring system.

4. File your post-hearing brief.

5. If the record was left open for you to submit additional evidence, as the due date approaches, contact the source of this evidence to make sure it will be provided on time.

6. If the due date arrives and you still do not have the additional evidence, request an extension from the ALJ; don't wait for the ALJ to contact you.

7. Send in the additional evidence with a letter telling the ALJ that the record is now complete and the case is ready fordecision.

(This page intetntionally left blank.)

Chapter 4

Following a Favorable Decision

§400 Check the Decision and Contact Your Client

When you receive any favorable decision, check it against your file to make sure it really is "fully favorable." Don't rely on the cover sheet of the decision. Sometimes a cover sheet will identify a partially favorable decision as fully favorable and vice versa. If the decision is less than fully favorable, that is, it fails to give the claimant everything for which the claimant asked and to which the claimant is entitled, you will need to evaluate the appeal possibilities. *See* §508, *infra*, on appealing the partially favorable decision. But before you launch an appeal, make sure that the problem you perceive with the decision is not the product of a simple error by someone in the hearing office. It is not uncommon for an error to appear in a decision which, if caught early, can be corrected before the error affects receipt of benefits without a formal appeal. If you wait, sometimes a simple error can turn into a monumental delay. For this reason, it is imperative that all decisions be reviewed carefully when you receive them.

A typographical error in the final paragraph of the decision, known as the "decisional paragraph," concerning the onset date or sometimes even the date of application can result in your client getting an incorrect amount of back benefits. Such errors can also delay payment of benefits. The error may be caught just as a payment center is getting ready to pay benefits, causing the payment center to request an amended decision from the ALJ before processing payment. Or worse yet, the payment center may refer a case to the Appeals Council "because it contains a clerical error affecting the outcome of the claim." 20 C.F.R. § 404.969(b)(2).

If, for example, the body of the decision consistently discusses one onset date but the decisional paragraph states another date, the decisional paragraph contains a typographical error that can be corrected simply by bringing it to the attention of the ALJ. It is not reasonable to assume that the error will be caught when back benefits are calculated and an order is issued to pay benefits, called "effectuating" the decision by SSA. And if the error is detected at the payment center, payment will be held up while the ALJ is contacted for clarification.

Something as seemingly minor as an incorrect claimant's address on the face of the decision has been known to delay receipt of back benefits for months in Title II cases. If the check for back benefits is sent to a wrong address, it may be returned to the Treasury. It may be a long time before it is reissued.

Section 401, *infra*, is a checklist for making sure there are no errors affecting benefits and to trigger further action as required. Section 402 contains a worksheet for identifying payment and attorney fee issues and summarizing actions taken. In §431, *infra*, is a worksheet for calculating back benefits to double-check SSA's calculations.

§401 Favorable Decision Checklist

1. Check the claimant's address. *See* §408, *infra*, if the address is wrong.
2. Check the date of application recited in the decisional paragraph.
   a. Does the file contain an application that corresponds to that date?
   b. Was there an earlier protective filing date that should have been used? *See* §205.1 of this book on protective filing date.
      i. Title II cases: protective filing date matters only if a claimant became disabled more than 17 months before the date of application.
      ii. SSI cases: protective filing date frequently matters. (It doesn't matter for applications filed after August 22, 1996 when the protective filing date is in the same month as the actual application date or when a claimant becomes disabled after the actual filing date.)
   c. Did the ALJ overlook a request to reopen an earlier application? Note that a request to reopen can be implied. *See* §376, *supra*.
3. Check date of onset of disability in the decisional paragraph.
   a. Is it the same as the onset date alleged in the claimant's application?
   b. Did the ALJ overlook a request to amend the onset date to a date different from that alleged in the application?
   c. If the onset date in the decisional paragraph is different from that alleged, does it represent a deliberate finding or a typographical error? Does it coincide with the discussion in the body of the decision?
4. If the decision is not fully favorable, calendar it for 45 days to evaluate appeal to the Appeals Council. *See* §508, *infra*.
5. If the decision contains any errors that may affect payment, immediately request that the ALJ issue an amended decision. *See* §409, *infra*.
6. Calculate the date of entitlement to benefits. *See* §432, *infra*.
7. Check your client's earnings record to find out the PIA, which is the benefit amount. *See* §205.4, *supra*, and §433 of this book.
8. Check your file to see if your client has children who will be entitled to auxiliary benefits. If so, advise your client to see that applications are submitted. *See* §435, *infra*.

9. In a case involving applications for both Social Security disability and SSI benefits, evaluate whether it is to your client's advantage to withdraw the SSI application. *See* §411 *et seq., infra.*

10. In a Title II case where no SSI application was ever filed but where the claimant might, in fact, be eligible for SSI during the five month waiting period, consider whether an SSI application can be submitted now using the Title II application date as the SSI application protective filing date. *See* §410, *infra.*

11. Check your file to determine if there is a long-term disability insurer involved. With your client's permission, send the L.T.D. carrier a copy of the decision.

12. Telephone your client.

13. Send your client a letter explaining payment issues, *etc. See* §§403, 404 and 404.1 for samples. **Caution**: These samples will not apply to every case. They are designed for cases involving wholly favorable decisions where the "fee agreement process" for obtaining approval of the attorney's fee applies. They will need to be edited to apply to other circumstances. In addition, the samples in §§404 and 404.1 may need changing because of state variations in the SSI and Medicaid programs. Note that §404 deals with a claim where your client receives ongoing Social Security disability *and* SSI benefits. Section 404.1 deals with the common situation where SSI stops after back benefits are paid because the monthly amount of Social Security disability benefits is too high for continuing SSI eligibility.

14. If there is SSI involved, send the Social Security office a reminder letter that you'd like copies of all SSI notices. *See* §405 for a sample. A reminder to the Social Security office that the "fee agreement process" applies along with a request that the SSI fee be paid by SSA is included in the sample letter in §405. Strike the second paragraph of this letter if the "fee agreement process," in fact, does not apply, but include a reminder that attorney fees need to be withheld from SSI back benefits and paid after you obtain approval of your fee petition.

15. If you filed your fee agreement before the date of the favorable decision intending that the "fee agreement process" apply to approval of your fee, you should receive, along with the decision, an order approving or disapproving the fee agreement. If you get an order disapproving the fee agreement, *see* §707, *infra,* regarding appeal. If you do not get an order at all, this oversight can be corrected. Immediately send the ALJ a letter about this. *See* the sample letter, §406, *infra.*

16. If you're going to file a fee petition, send the ALJ a Notice of Intent to File Fee Petition. *See* §407, *infra,* for a sample.

17. Calendar the case for follow-up with your client:

a. 30 days in Title II cases to see if your client has heard anything about payment.

b. 15 days in SSI cases to see if the Social Security office has contacted your client about updating financial information.

§402   Form: Favorable Decision Summary/Worksheet

Client: _____ SSN:_____

Decision Date:_____ □ Fully Favorable   □ Partially Favorable

Issues:_____

ALJ Name & Address: _____

Date of Application: T.2:_____   SSI:_____

Date of Onset: Found: _____   Alleged:_____

Date of Termination: Found: _____   Alleged:_____

First month of benefits: T.2: _____   SSI: _____

Medicare Begins: _____

PIA: $ _____   Family Maximum: $ _____

Family Maximum minus PIA: $ _____

□ Auxiliaries   Auxiliary applications dated: _____   □ WC/PDB Offset

□ SSI 1/3 reduction   □ SSI couple   □ Withdraw SSI Withdrawal filed: _____

□ TANF   □ General Assistance   □ Interim Assistance Agreement

□ Fee Petition Process   □ Notice Of Intent To File Fee Petition sent

Fee Agreement: □ Approved   □ Disapproved   □ Appealed/Date: _____

□ Ignored   □ Reminder Sent/Date: _____

Attorney Expenses: $ _____

Social Security Office Address: _____

LETTER NUMBER	SENT TO	DATE SENT
	Client	
	Social Security Office	
	ALJ	

L.T.D. Carrier: _____   n Decision copy sent

Decision errors/other issues _____

§403   Sample: Letter to Title II Claimant After Receipt of Favorable Decision

Date   SSD Only—Fully Favorable
                                               $6,000 Limit/ 25% Fee

                                               Insert the following in text:

Client Name   T.2 Date of Entitlement
Address   Amount of Monthly Benefit
City/State/Zip   Medicare Eligibility Date
                                               Example Year & Medicare Premium
Re: Social Security Disability Decision   Amount of Expenses

Dear [Client's Name]:
    Congratulations on winning your Social Security disability case.
    This letter attempts to answer some of the common questions that people have after receiving a favorable Social Security disability decision. I suggest that you keep it for a reference.

Do I have to do anything such as visit the Social Security Office or complete some forms in order to get paid?
    No. The Social Security Administration (SSA) will process your claim and send you your benefits automatically. But if you have children who were under age 18 (or under age 19 and still in high school) at any time after your "date of entitlement," it will be necessary to put in an application for them to receive benefits; but your own benefits will still be processed automatically.

How long will it take for SSA to pay me?
    As a rule, it takes a month or so for back benefits to be paid and monthly benefits to begin in a Social Security disability case in which no SSI application was ever filed. (When there is SSI involved it takes considerably longer.) But these are only general rules. In some cases, it takes as long as 3 months for back benefits to be paid. When it takes more than 90 days for back benefits to be paid in a Social Security disability case, it may mean that there has been a bureaucratic mix-up somewhere in the system.

If 90 days pass from the date of the decision and I am still not paid my back benefits, is there anything that can be done to speed up payment?
    It is possible that I may be able to do something if you are not paid after 90 days. Be sure to telephone me to let me know you haven't gotten paid after about three months. It may be necessary at that point to contact the payment center, which usually works better than simply telephoning the toll-free number or contacting the local office.

How far back will my benefits go?
    Your benefits should begin with the month of _____, _____. This is the "date of entitlement" in your case. Many people ask why benefits don't begin on the date they were found disabled. Social Security disability benefits never begin on the date one is found disabled because of the waiting period of five full calendar months. Another rule limits payment of back benefits to 12 months before the date of the application. Therefore, your benefits begin either 12 months before the date of application or five full months after the date you were found to be disabled, whichever is later.

What will the amount of my monthly benefits be?
    The amount of your first month's benefits will be $_____, according to information we obtained from your Social Security file. However, SSA may recalculate your benefit amount before it pays you. If SSA recalculates, it may come up with a higher benefit amount because, for example, all of your earnings might not have been posted when the original calculation was made. Also, there are cost of living increases which are applied every December.

Will I receive a notice from SSA explaining my benefits?
    Yes. That notice is usually called a Notice of Award. This notice will show the "date of entitlement" and the amounts of benefits for all months of back benefits. It will show the total amount of benefits to be paid to you. It will show the

amount of benefits withheld for direct payment of attorney's fees. It may also give you information about your Medicare eligibility and monthly Medicare premium. It may also give you some information about when to expect a "continuing disability review."

When will I get the Notice of Award?

The Notice of Award will come around the time that your past-due benefits are directly deposited into your bank account. The Notice of Award often comes after you receive your past-due benefits.

I have not signed up for direct deposit. Should I do that now?

Yes. In fact, beginning in March 2013, SSA requires direct deposit of disability benefits. You can sign up by contacting your local Social Security office.

Another option instead of direct deposit to a bank account is that SSA will allow you to receive your benefits using a Direct Express Debit MasterCard. At your request, SSA will open a Direct Express Debit MasterCard account for you and pay your benefits to that account every month. This card can be used wherever you can use a debit MasterCard.

Are there any problems with direct deposit?

Direct deposit is a great convenience. It is very dependable. SSA usually has people sign up for direct deposit at the time they apply for benefits. We have noticed that once in a while people forget that they signed up for direct deposit and they keep looking for a check in the mail when the money has already been deposited to their bank account.

Worse yet, sometimes people close the bank account that they told SSA they wanted to use for direct deposit. If this is your situation, you need to deal with this right away. It might be necessary for you to go to the Social Security office to update SSA on your current account information.

If I get paid first, should I wait until I receive the Notice of Award before I spend my past-due benefits?

There is no problem with using the money. But it is best that you not spend it all until you receive the Notice of Award so that we can make sure that attorney's fees were withheld and that you have not been overpaid.

Why would there be a problem if I were overpaid?

If you are paid too much, SSA almost always figures it out eventually. Then, after you have already spent all of the money, it will send you a letter demanding that you repay the overpayment. If you do not have the money to repay the full amount of the overpayment, SSA may threaten to cut off your benefits until the overpayment is recouped. Usually, however, it will accept a more reasonable reduction of your monthly benefits. However, this is still a hassle and you may have trouble making ends meet during the time that your benefits are reduced. Under some circumstances it may be possible to get repayment of all or part of the overpayment waived; but this is not something to count on.

When will my regular monthly benefits begin?

Usually regular monthly benefits begin the month after you receive your past-due benefits, although occasionally people get their regular monthly benefits first. Your benefits will arrive on the second, third or fourth Wednesday of the month, depending on what day of the month you were born. The current monthly deposit will pay benefits for the previous month. Thus, for example, the deposit in February will pay January's benefits.

Will I be eligible for Medicare?

Medicare eligibility begins after you have received 24 months of Social Security disability benefits. Therefore, your Medicare eligibility begins in _____, _____. Please note that to receive Part B of Medicare (which pays for doctor visits), you pay a premium that will be deducted from your Social Security disability monthly benefits. For example, the Medicare premium for [year] is $_____ per month, though individuals with incomes greater than $80,000 per year and couples with incomes greater than $160,000 per year pay more.

Disabled people with relatively low income and assets may be eligible for other programs that pay for medical expenses not covered by Medicare and/or pay the Medicare premium for you. To find out if you are eligible for any such programs, you need to check with your county welfare department.

If you have health insurance coverage already, you need to figure out how Medicare works with your health insurance. Many health insurance policies state that Medicare is to provide the primary coverage with your present health insurance paying only for what Medicare doesn't cover. You need to check with your health insurance company when you get your Medicare card.

The cover sheet of the favorable decision says that the Appeals Council may review the decision "on its own motion." What does this mean?

In a very small number of cases the Appeals Council in Falls Church, Virginia, will decide on its own to take away benefits awarded by the decision of the administrative law judge. If it is going to do this, the Appeals Council will almost always send you a notice within 60 days of the date of the judge's decision. (In an extremely small number of cases the Appeals Council will reverse a decision after the 60 days have run.) I doubt if the Appeals Council is going to do this in your case; but if it happens, we will deal with it even if it means fighting SSA in federal court.

I understand that I should not spend all of my back benefits until we figure out if attorney's fees were withheld. Does it happen very often that attorney's fees are not withheld?

No. Not at all. It does happen once in a while, though.

How much is the attorney's fee?

Our contract calls for your attorney's fee to be *25%* of past-due benefits paid on your account, including any benefits paid to your family up to $6,000.00.

What's the difference between attorney's fees and expenses?

In addition to the fee, our contract calls for you to pay me back for medical records or reports, *etc.*, that I paid for in your case. SSA will not pay for these things nor will it send an attorney any money for such expenses out of a claimant's funds.

Were there any expenses in this case?

Expenses owed are $_____. I am enclosing with this letter a bill for these expenses. I am not expecting you to pay this bill until you receive your past-due benefits. However, I will appreciate prompt payment as soon as you are paid.

Will attorney's fees be paid around the same time that I get my back benefits?

Yes. If SSA withheld more than the amount of the fee, it will pay you the excess amount withheld shortly after that.

Will I have to pay taxes on the Social Security disability benefits I receive?

Probably not; but this depends on the amount of your total income. Most people won't have to pay taxes on their Social Security disability benefits. Couples whose combined incomes exceed $32,000 and individuals with income exceeding $25,000 will pay income tax on a portion of their Social Security disability benefits. IRS has an odd way of figuring out total income for this rule. The IRS uses adjusted gross income as reported on Form 1040, plus one-half of the total Social Security benefits received for the year, plus non-taxable interest.

Single people with incomes over $34,000 and married people with incomes over $44,000 pay tax on a higher percentage of their Social Security disability benefits.

Here's an odd thing: People whose Social Security benefits are reduced because of the worker's compensation offset or offsets for other public disability benefits must count the amount of Social Security benefits not paid when determining taxability of their benefits. But if a child receives benefits on a parent's account, those benefits count only for determining if the child must pay taxes on Social Security benefits received.

If you fall into the group of people who may be taxed on Social Security disability benefits only because you received a large check for past-due benefits during the year, you still may not have to pay tax on your Social Security benefits. The IRS has set up a way to recalculate your back benefits and consider them received in the year you should have gotten them rather than in the current year. Ask the IRS for a copy of Publication 915.

Those people whose Social Security disability benefits end up being taxable should note that a portion of the attorney's fee may be deductible; but this depends on the "2% of adjusted gross income" ceiling on miscellaneous itemized deductions. Those people who have to repay a long term disability insurance carrier because of receipt of Social Security disability benefits may get special tax relief. They should ask the IRS for Publication 525.

SSA is supposed to send you a Form 1099 by February 1st of the year after your back benefits are paid. If you will have to pay taxes on your Social Security disability benefits, be sure to compare the information on the Form 1099 with the information on your Notice of Award. The Form 1099s from SSA are often wrong. You will need to bring any errors to the attention of your tax preparer. For this reason it is important for you to keep track of how much you actually receive from SSA.

Tax law is very complex. Because this office does not handle tax matters, please talk to a tax specialist if you have any questions about taxes on your Social Security benefits.

What is a "continuing disability review"?

SSA is required periodically to review the cases of all people who are receiving disability benefits. Usually cases are reviewed every three years; but some cases are reviewed more often. Sometimes the decision will direct SSA to conduct a review at a certain time. Often the Notice of Award will tell you when to expect a review.

What will I have to do for a "continuing disability review"?

You will be asked to complete a form about your medical treatment, any vocational training or work and how your condition has changed since the time you were found eligible for disability benefits.

What if SSA finds that my disability has ceased but I'm still not able to work?

The notice, which you will receive from SSA following a "continuing disability review," will explain your appeal rights. Read this notice carefully. If you appeal within ten days of the date you receive the notice, your benefits will continue during your appeal. So be sure to act quickly.

Is there anything that I can do now to help insure that my benefits will continue?

The very best thing you can do is to continue seeing your doctor. A lot of people with long-term chronic medical problems stop seeing their doctors because no treatment seems to help. This is a mistake for two reasons. First, it means that when SSA conducts a review, no medical evidence will exist to show that your condition is the same as it was when you were first found disabled. Second, and perhaps even more importantly, doctors recommend that even healthy people after a certain age periodically have a thorough physical examination. This is even more important for people who already have chronic medical problems.

Is SSA going to make it as difficult to keep my benefits as it did to get them in the first place?

No. Not at all. The disabilities of the vast majority of people are found to continue at the initial evaluation. Few people have their benefits stopped.

Is there anything I can do to make dealing with SSA easier?

You shouldn't expect as many problems dealing with SSA while receiving benefits as you had trying to get benefits in the first place. Sometimes, though, some people have problems. Here are some things you can do to try to minimize the hassle:

- Keep all decisions, letters, and notices you receive from SSA in a safe place.
- Read everything you get from SSA. The booklets that come with award letters and notices are well written and informative.
- When reading the booklets you receive from SSA, pay special attention to the kind of information you are required to report to the Social Security Administration. Report promptly and in writing and keep a copy with your Social Security papers.
- Don't necessarily believe everything they tell you at the SSA 800 number. If you have an important issue to take up with SSA, sometimes it is better to go to your local Social Security Office.

And if I can answer any other questions you have now or in the future, please do not hesitate to telephone me. Sincerely,

[Name of Attorney]
Enclosure

[Note: When there are no expenses, delete the question and answer pertaining to expenses and the reference to Enclosure. When there are expenses, be sure to enclose the bill.]

§404   Sample: Letter to Concurrent Claimant After Receipt of Favorable Decision

Date

> Concurrent—Fully Favorable
> On-going SSI Benefits
> $6,000 Limit/ 25% Fee
>
> Insert the following in text:
>
> SSI Date of Entitlement

Client Name   T.2 Date of Entitlement
Address   Amount of Monthly Benefit
City/State/Zip   Medicare Eligibility Date

> Example Year & Medicare Premium

Re: Social Security Disability/SSI Decision   Amount of Expenses

Dear [Client's Name]:

Congratulations on winning your Social Security disability/SSI case.

This letter attempts to answer some of the common questions that people have after receiving a favorable decision from the Social Security Administration (SSA). I suggest that you keep it for future reference.

What's the difference between the Social Security disability and SSI disability programs?

Both programs require that you be disabled; but benefits are calculated differently for the two programs. SSI is a federal welfare program. As such, there is a limit on the amount of "assets" you may have in order to receive any payment at all. Also, the monthly amount of SSI benefits depends on your income from all sources, including the amount of your Social Security disability benefits.

Social Security disability, on the other hand, is similar to an insurance program. You are eligible for Social Security disability benefits because you are disabled and because you paid Social Security taxes.

All SSI benefits are processed at your local Social Security Office. Social Security disability benefits for most people are processed in Baltimore, Maryland. Benefits of those people who are over age 55 are processed in regional payment centers.

Do I have to do anything such as visit the Social Security Office or complete some forms in order to get paid?

Yes. Payment of your SSI benefits will require that you update your financial information at the Social Security Office. You will be contacted by the Social Security Office soon. If your financial situation is not complicated, you may be able to handle this on the telephone.

On the other hand, payment is automatic for your Social Security disability benefits. If you have children who were under age 18 (or under age 19 and still in high school) at any time after your "date of entitlement," it will be necessary to put in an application for them to receive benefits; but your own benefits will still be processed automatically.

How long will it take for SSA to pay me?

Your regular monthly benefits should start in one to two months (or so). However, it may take several additional months for all of your back benefits to be paid. This is because you will be first "overpaid" SSI. The reason for the SSI overpayment is that SSA usually calculates your SSI benefits without counting the amount of your Social Security disability benefits. The SSI "overpayment" then will be deducted from your past-due Social Security disability benefits. (Nevertheless, the total amount of benefits from both programs should be the same as if the offset were not involved.) Even if you are not overpaid SSI, the payment center will hold up payment of your past-due Social Security disability benefits to see if you will be overpaid SSI. All of these bureaucratic maneuvers take several months, possibly six months. It will be necessary for you to be patient.

If six months pass from the date of the decision and I am still not paid all of my back benefits, is there anything that can be done to speed up payment?

It is possible that I may be able to do something if you are not paid after six months. Be sure to telephone me to let me know you haven't gotten paid after about six months.

How far back will my benefits go?

Your Social Security disability benefits should begin with the month of _____, _____. This is the "date of entitlement" in your case. Many people ask why Social Security disability benefits don't begin on the date the ALJ found that they became disabled. Social Security disability benefits never begin on the date one becomes disabled because of the waiting period of five full calendar months. Another rule limits payment of back benefits to 12 months before the date of the application. Therefore, your benefits begin either 12 months before the date of application or five full months after the date you were found to be disabled, whichever is later. Your Social Security disability benefits may be subject to the "SSI offset," that is, where SSA deducts the SSI overpayment that I mentioned above.

Your SSI benefits work somewhat differently. You won't be paid SSI benefits prior to the date of your SSI application; but there is no five month waiting period with SSI. You will be paid SSI from the first of the month after you applied as long as you were disabled then. Otherwise you will be paid SSI from the first of the month after you became disabled. In your case, your SSI benefits will begin on _____.

What will be the amount of my monthly Social Security disability benefits?

The amount of your first month's benefits will be $_____ according to the information we obtained from SSA. This number, however, may be subject to revision by SSA for numerous reasons. It is a preliminary calculation which was made at the time that you filed your application for disability benefits. At that time all your earnings might not have been posted. There are other reasons including simply a calculation error (the calculation is very complicated) which may account for the difference between the number that appears in my file and the amount that you actually end up receiving, although the difference is not usually very great. In addition, there will be cost of living increases which will be applied every December.

How much will my monthly SSI benefits be?

This depends on the amount of your income, marital status and living arrangement. SSA uses complicated formulas to figure out the amount of SSI benefits. It is so complicated, I suggest that we let SSA figure it out first. Then I will double-check their calculations.

Will I receive notices from SSA explaining my benefits?

Yes. For Social Security disability benefits you should receive a Notice of Award and a Benefit Information Notice. The first notice will show the "date of entitlement," the amounts of benefits for all months of back benefits, and the amount withheld for direct payment of attorney's fees. Usually a second notice will show the total amount of benefits to be paid to you. It will also show the amount of the "SSI offset." The notices may give you information about your Medicare eligibility. They may also give you some information about when to expect a "continuing disability review." You will also get an SSI notice that shows a monthly breakdown of benefits and a separate notice showing the amount of attorney fees that will be paid out of your SSI benefits.

When will I get the notices?

Notices will start arriving in about a month or so. You will get a total of four or more notices over the next several months. Often it happens that a person gets a payment before he or she receives the notice explaining it.

When will I get my benefits?

You may get monthly benefits from both programs directly deposited to your bank account before you get any back benefits. You will get an SSI back benefits payment before you get your Social Security disability back benefits. As a rule, an SSI payment for back benefits will come shortly after you get the Social Security disability notice explaining your Social Security disability benefits. If your SSI back benefits are greater than three times the monthly federal SSI benefit rate, your SSI back benefits will be paid in up to three installments paid six months apart—unless you're not going to be eligible for on-going SSI monthly payments, in which case SSA will pay SSI back benefits all at once. After all SSI back benefits are paid, any remaining Social Security disability back benefits will be released.

Is there any way to convince SSA not to pay the SSI back benefits in installments six months apart?

Yes. Social Security regulations say that the amount of the first and second installment payments may be increased by the amount of outstanding debt for food, clothing, shelter, or medically necessary services, supplies or equipment, or medicine, or current or anticipated expenses in the near future for medically necessary services, supplies or equipment, or medicine, or for the purchase of a home. So if you have debts or you want to buy a home, be sure to tell SSA.

I have not signed up for direct deposit. Should I do that now?

Yes. In fact, beginning March 2013 SSA requires direct deposit of disability benefits. You can sign up by contacting your local Social Security office.

Another option instead of direct deposit to a bank account is that SSA will allow you to receive your benefits using a Direct Express Debit MasterCard. At your request, SSA will open a Direct Express Debit MasterCard account for you and pay your benefits to that account every month. This card can be used wherever you can use a debit MasterCard.

Are there any problems with direct deposit?

Direct deposit is a great convenience. It is very dependable. SSA usually has people sign up for direct deposit when they apply for benefits. We have noticed that once in a while people forget that they signed up for direct deposit and they keep looking for a check in the mail when the money has already been deposited to their bank account.

Worse yet, sometimes people close the bank account that they told SSA they wanted to use for direct deposit. If this is your situation, you need to deal with this right away. It might be necessary for you to go to the Social Security office to update SSA on your current account information.

If I get direct deposit of benefits before I get the notice explaining my benefits, should I wait until I receive the notice before I spend the money?

No. There is no need to wait. But don't spend it all until you receive the notice so that we can make sure that attorney's fees were withheld and that you have not been overpaid.

Why would there be a problem if I were overpaid?

If you are paid too much, SSA almost always figures it out eventually. Then, after you have already spent all of the money, it will send you a letter demanding that you repay the overpayment. If you do not have the money to repay the full amount of the overpayment, SSA may threaten to cut off your monthly benefits until the overpayment is recouped. Usually, however, it will accept a more reasonable reduction of your monthly benefits. However, this is still a hassle and you may have trouble making ends meet during the time that your benefits are reduced. Under some circumstances it may be possible to get repayment of all or part of the overpayment waived; but this is not something to count on.

Should I telephone my representative whenever I get a notice?

It is not necessary to telephone me when you get the first Social Security disability notice. I almost always get copies of those. But I would appreciate it if you'd telephone me or my secretary when you get the second Social Security disability notice, the one that tells how much SSA is deducting from your back Social Security disability benefits because you received SSI. I don't always get copies of those notices. We may ask you to send us a copy.

I would also appreciate it if you'd telephone me or my secretary when you first hear from SSI so that I can be sure that I am on SSA's list for receiving copies of SSI notices. Despite the fact that I am asking for copies from the Social Security Administration, I sometimes am not sent copies of SSI notices by SSA. I need copies in order to double-check their calculations. I may have to ask you to make copies of these for me.

Will I receive my regular monthly benefits on the first of each month?

Your regular monthly SSI benefit will arrive in your bank account on the first of each month. The SSI deposit is intended to pay you for the current month. Social Security disability benefits, on the other hand, arrive in your bank account on the third of the month, and they pay benefits for the previous month. Thus, for example, the deposit on February 3rd will pay January's benefits.

Why do you advise getting a savings account that pays interest quarterly rather than monthly or daily?

If interest is paid quarterly on a bank account and it is $20.00 or less, it is generally not counted as income to be deducted from your SSI benefits. Be sure to keep your interest payment to $20.00 or less, otherwise all of the payment counts.

Won't a savings account affect my eligibility for SSI?

You will be allowed nine months to spend your checks for back benefits. After that, in order to continue to receive SSI benefits, you won't be allowed to have more than $2,000 in assets (with some exceptions) if you are single and $3,000 in assets (with some exceptions) if you are married.

What are the exceptions to the asset limit?

SSA has a list of assets that don't count against your asset limit. In other words, you can own these things and still be eligible for SSI. Here are the most significant things on the list:

1. Your home. It can have any value; but if you move out and rent out the house, it becomes an asset and is counted.
2. Household goods of any value if they are used on a regular basis or used for household maintenance. Thus, furniture, appliances, dishes, cooking utensils, electronic equipment such as a stereo, computer or a television, lawn care equipment, *etc.* do not count as an asset.
3. Personal effects that are ordinarily worn or carried by someone, including a claimant's own wedding and engagement rings, are not counted as an asset. Also not counted as an asset are "articles otherwise having an intimate relation to the individual." Thus, for example, if you save your grandmother's diamond as a keepsake, even though you never wear your grandmother's diamond, it will not be counted as an asset because it has an "intimate relation" to you; but if you are a gem collector, the value of your gem collection counts.
4. Household goods and personal effects required because of your physical condition, such as wheel chairs, hospital beds, *etc.*
5. One car of any value will not be counted if you use the car for your transportation or the transportation of someone in your household.
6. If life insurance has a face value not exceeding $1,500, its cash surrender value won't be counted as an asset.
7. Term insurance, that is, life insurance which does not have any cash surrender value.
8. Burial insurance.
9. Burial spaces.
10. Burial funds up to $1,500 (as long as you don't use the exclusion of $1,500 face value life insurance).

However, if you are holding anything as an investment, it probably counts as an asset.

Will I be eligible for Title 19?

Yes. Title 19 (Medicaid) eligibility is automatic once you've been found eligible for SSI. You will receive a Title 19 card in the mail. Title 19 eligibility should begin three months before SSI eligibility begins but usually your Title 19 card is just back dated to the date when your SSI began. If you have some significant medical bills from within three months of your date of SSI eligibility and your Title 19 card doesn't go back far enough, telephone me.

Will I be eligible for Medicare?

Medicare eligibility begins after you have received 24 months of Social Security disability benefits. Therefore, your Medicare eligibility begins in _____, _____. Because you are eligible for Title 19, it will work out that the Medicare premium is paid by the state.

The decision cover sheet says that the Appeals Council may review the decision "on its own motion." What does this mean?

In a very small number of cases the Appeals Council in Falls Church, Virginia, which is the body to which appeals from ALJ decisions go, will decide on its own to take away benefits awarded by the decision. If it is going to do this, the Appeals Council almost always will send you a notice within 60 days of the date of the decision. (In an extremely small number of cases the Appeals Council will reverse a decision after the 60 days have run.) I doubt if the Appeals Council is going to do this in your case; but if it happens, we will deal with it even if it means fighting SSA in federal court.

I understand that I should not spend all of my back benefits until we figure out if attorney's fees were withheld. Does it happen very often that attorney's fees are not withheld?

No. Not at all. It does happen once in a while, though.

How much is the attorney's fee?

Our contract calls for your attorney's fee to be 25% of past-due benefits paid on your account, including any benefits paid to your family, up to $6,000.

Will the fee be withheld from my benefits and paid to my representative by SSA?

Yes. SSA will withhold attorney fees from Social Security disability back benefits and from SSI back benefits.

What's the difference between attorney's fees and "expenses"?

In addition to the fee of 25% of past-due benefits, our contract calls for you to pay me back for medical records or reports, *etc.*, that I paid for in your case. SSA will not pay for these things, nor will it send an attorney any money for such expenses out of a claimant's funds.

Were there any expenses in this case?

Expenses were $_____. I am enclosing a bill for these expenses with this letter. I am not expecting you to pay this bill until your first payment of back benefits. However, I will appreciate prompt payment as soon as you receive your first payment of back benefits.

When will SSA pay attorney's fees?

The notice concerning your back Social Security disability benefits will explain about attorney's fees and give you and the ALJ the right to object to the fee. The payment of attorney fees from the Social Security disability part of your case will be sent out around the time the Social Security disability notice is sent. Any payment for attorney fees from back SSI benefits will be sent out shortly after that.

[See §419 to determine if SSI recalculation after payment of Title II attorney fees will increase the amount of SSI back benefits due the claimant. If not, strike the next questions and answer.]

Is there anything else I ought to know about attorney's fees?

Yes. SSA should recalculate your SSI benefits after attorney fees and expenses are paid. This recalculation increases the amount of your SSI benefits. Although SSA is supposed to do this automatically, SSA may need to be reminded. When you pay us back for expenses, be sure to tell SSA how much you paid. This will be worked into the calculation, too, to increase your SSI benefits.

What is a "continuing disability review"?

SSA is required periodically to review the cases of all people who are receiving disability benefits. Usually cases are reviewed every three years; but some cases are reviewed more often. Sometimes the decision will direct SSA to conduct a review at a certain time. Often the Notice of Award will tell you when to expect a review.

What will I have to do for a "continuing disability review"?

You will be asked to complete a form about your medical treatment, any vocational training or work and how your condition has changed since the time you were found eligible for disability benefits.

What if SSA finds that my disability has ceased but I'm still not able to work?

The notice that you will receive from SSA following a "continuing disability review" will explain your appeal rights. Read this notice carefully. If you appeal within ten days of the date you receive the notice, your benefits will continue during your appeal. So be sure to act quickly.

Is there anything that I can do now to help insure that my benefits will continue?

The very best thing you can do is to continue seeing your doctor. A lot of people with long-term chronic medical problems stop seeing their doctors because no treatment seems to help. This is a mistake for two reasons. First, it means that when SSA conducts its review, no medical evidence will exist to show that your condition is the same as it was when you were first found disabled. Second, and perhaps even more importantly, doctors recommend that even healthy people after a certain age periodically have a thorough physical examination. This is even more important for people who already have chronic medical problems.

Is SSA going to make it as difficult to keep my benefits as it did to get them in the first place?

No. Not at all. The disabilities of the vast majority of people are found to continue at the initial evaluation. Few people have their benefits stopped.

Is there anything I can do to make dealing with SSA easier?

You shouldn't expect as many problems dealing with SSA while receiving benefits as you had trying to get benefits in the first place. Sometimes, though, some people have problems. Here are some things you can do to try to minimize the hassle:

- Keep all decisions, letters, and notices you receive from SSA in a safe place.
- Read everything you get from SSA. The booklets that come with award letters and notices are well written and informative.
- When reading the booklets you receive from SSA, pay special attention to the kind of information you are required to report to the Social Security Administration. Report promptly and in writing and keep a copy with your Social Security papers.
- Don't necessarily believe everything they tell you at the SSA 800 number. If you have an important issue to take up with SSA, sometimes it is better to go to your local Social Security Office.

And if I can answer any other questions you have now or in the future, please do not hesitate to telephone me.

Sincerely,

[Name of Attorney]
Enclosure

[Note: When there are no expenses, delete the question and answer pertaining to expenses and the reference to Enclosure. When there are expenses, be sure to enclose the bill.]

§404.1 Sample: Letter to Concurrent Claimant After Receipt of Favorable Decision — SSI Stops

Date   Concurrent—Fully Favorable
                                                  SSI Stops
                                                  $6,000 Limit/ 25% Fee

                                                  Insert the following in text:

                                                  SSI Date of Entitlement
Client Name   T.2 Date of Entitlement
Address   Amount of Monthly Benefit
City/State/Zip   Medicare Eligibility Date
                                                  Example Year & Medicare Premium
Re: Social Security Disability/SSI Decision   Amount of Expenses

Dear [Client's Name]:
    Congratulations on winning your Social Security disability/SSI case.
    This letter attempts to answer some of the common questions that people have after receiving a favorable
decision from the Social Security Administration (SSA). I suggest that you keep it for future reference.

What's the difference between the Social Security disability and SSI disability programs?
    Both programs require that you be disabled; but benefits are calculated differently for the two programs. There
are also differences in the way the two programs are operated. SSI is a federal welfare program. As such, there is
a limit on the amount of "assets" you may have in order to receive any payment at all. Also, the monthly amount
of SSI benefits SSA will pay you depends on your income from all sources, including the amount of your Social
Security disability benefits. In your case, it appears that your Social Security disability benefits will be great enough
to disqualify you from receiving on-going SSI benefits. But you'll get some SSI back benefits.
    Social Security disability, on the other hand, is similar to an insurance program. You are eligible for Social
Security disability benefits because you are disabled and because you paid Social Security taxes.
    All SSI benefits are processed at your local Social Security Office. Social Security disability benefits for most
people are processed in Baltimore, Maryland. Benefits of those people who are over age 55 are processed in regional
payment centers.

Do I have to do anything such as visit the Social Security Office or complete some forms in order to get paid?
    Payment of your SSI benefits will require that you update your financial information at the Social Security
Office. You will be contacted by the Social Security Office soon. If your financial situation is not complicated, you
may be able to handle this by telephone and mail.
    For your own Social Security disability benefits, payment is automatic. However, if you have children who
were under age 18 (or under age 19 and still in high school) at any time after your "date of entitlement" it will be
necessary to put in an application for them to receive Social Security auxiliary benefits.

How long will it take for SSA to pay me?
    Your regular monthly benefits should start in one to two months (or so). However, it may take several
additional months for all of your back benefits to be paid. This is because SSA will "overpay" SSI benefits. The
reason for the SSI overpayment is that SSA calculates your SSI benefits without counting the amount of your
Social Security disability benefits. Then the SSI "overpayment" will be deducted from your past-due Social
Security disability check. These bureaucratic maneuvers take several months, as much as five or six months. It
will be necessary for you to be patient.

Will the SSI back benefits be paid in installments?
    No. SSA has a rule that says when SSI back benefits are greater than 3 months of the maximum SSI benefit rate,
the back benefits will be paid in installments six months apart. But another rule says that if you are not going to be
eligible for ongoing monthly SSI payments, which appears to be your situation based on information we received
from SSA about your Social Security disability benefit rate, it will not be necessary for SSI back benefits to be paid

in installments six months apart. Nevertheless, it is possible that SSA will first send you a letter saying that your SSI back benefits will be paid in installments and then pay you the rest shortly after that.

If six months pass from the date of the decision and I am still not paid all of my back benefits, is there anything that can be done to speed up payment?

If six months pass and you are still not paid everything, it is possible that I may be able to do something. Be sure to telephone me to let me know you haven't been paid after about six months from the date of your decision.

How far back will my benefits go?

Your Social Security disability benefits should go back to the month of _____, ____. This is the "date of entitlement" in your case. Many people ask why benefits don't begin on the date the ALJ found that they became disabled. Social Security disability benefits never begin on the date one becomes disabled because of the waiting period requirement of five full calendar months. Another rule limits payment of back benefits to 12 months before the date of the application. Therefore, your Social Security disability benefits begin either 12 months prior to the date of application or five full months after the date you became disabled, whichever is later. Your Social Security disability benefits may be subject to the "SSI offset," that is, where SSA deducts the SSI overpayment that I mentioned above. The total amount of benefits from both programs should be the same as if the offset were not applied, however.

Your SSI benefits work somewhat differently. You won't be paid SSI benefits prior to the date of your SSI application; but there is no five month waiting period with SSI. You will be paid SSI from the first of the month after you applied as long as you were disabled then. Otherwise you will be paid SSI from the first of the month after you became disabled. In your case, your SSI benefits will begin on _____; however, you are really only entitled to SSI through the month of your Social Security disability "date of entitlement."

What will the amount of my Social Security disability benefit be?

The amount of your first month's benefits will be $_____ according to the information we obtained from SSA. This number, however, may be subject to revision by SSA for numerous reasons. It is a preliminary calculation which was made at the time that you filed your application for disability benefits. At that time all your earnings might not have been posted. There are other reasons including simply a calculation error (the calculation is very complicated) which may account for the difference between the number that appears in my file and the amount that you actually end up receiving, although the difference is not usually very great. In addition, there will be cost of living increases which will be applied every December.

How much will my monthly SSI benefit be?

This depends on the amount of your income, marital status and living arrangement. SSA uses complicated formulas to figure out the amount of SSI benefits. It is so complicated, I suggest that we let SSA figure it out first. Then I will double-check their calculations.

As I noted above, it appears that your Social Security disability benefits are high enough to disqualify you from receiving on-going SSI benefits. However, you are eligible for SSI during the five month waiting period during which no Social Security disability benefits are payable. Nevertheless, SSA may pay SSI to you for additional months and then take this money back out of your Social Security disability benefits.

Will I receive a notice from SSA explaining my benefits?

Yes. For Social Security disability benefits you may receive a Notice of Award and a Benefit Information Notice. The first notice will show the "date of entitlement," the amounts of benefits for all months of back benefits and the amount of benefits withheld for direct payment of attorney's fees. Usually a second notice will show the total amount of benefits to be paid to you and the amount of the "SSI offset." The notices may also give you information about your Medicare eligibility and monthly Medicare premium. SSA may give you some information about when to expect a "continuing disability review." You will also get an SSI notice which will show a monthly breakdown of back benefits and another SSI notice that says you will not be eligible for ongoing monthly benefits because the amount of your Social Security disability payment is too high.

When will I get the notices?

Notices will start arriving in about a month or so. You will get a total of three or four over the next several months.

Should I telephone my lawyer when I get a notice?

It is not necessary to telephone me when you get the first Social Security disability notice. I almost always get copies of those. But I would appreciate it if you'd telephone me or my secretary when you get the second Social Security disability notice, the one that tells how much SSA is deducting from your back Social Security disability benefits because you received SSI. I don't always get copies of those notices. We may ask you to send us a copy.

I would also appreciate it if you'd telephone me or my secretary when you first hear from SSI so that I can be sure that I am on SSA's list for receiving copies of SSI notices. Despite the fact that I am asking for copies from the Social Security Administration, I sometimes am not sent copies of SSI notices by SSA. I need copies in order to double-check their calculations. I may have to ask you to make copies of these for me.

When will I get my benefits?

You may get your monthly Social Security disability benefits first by direct deposit to your bank account. You will get your SSI back benefits before you get the Social Security disability back benefits. As a rule, the SSI back benefits will come shortly after you get the Social Security disability notice explaining those benefits. The Social Security disability notice will say that your Social Security disability back benefits will be held until SSA figures out if you are going to receive SSI benefits. After all SSI back benefits are paid, any remaining Social Security disability back benefits will be released.

I have not signed up for direct deposit. Should I do that now?

Yes. In fact, beginning March 2013 SSA requires direct deposit of disability benefits. You can sign up by contacting your local Social Security office.

Another option instead of direct deposit to a bank account is that SSA will allow you to receive your benefits using a Direct Express Debit MasterCard. At your request, SSA will open a Direct Express Debit MasterCard account for you and pay your benefits to that account every month. This card can be used wherever you can use a debit MasterCard.

Are there any problems with direct deposit?

Direct deposit is a great convenience. It is very dependable. SSA usually has people sign up for direct deposit when they apply for benefits. We have noticed that once in a while people forget that they signed up for direct deposit and they keep looking for a check in the mail when the money has already been deposited to their bank account.

Worse yet, sometimes people close the bank account that they told SSA they wanted to use for direct deposit. If this is your situation, you need to deal with this right away. It might be necessary for you to go to the Social Security office to update SSA on your current account information.

If I get direct deposit of benefits before I get the notice explaining my benefits, should I wait until I receive the notice before I spend the money?

No. There is no need to wait. But don't spend it all until you receive the notice so that we can make sure that attorney's fees were withheld and that you have not been overpaid.

Why would there be a problem if I were overpaid?

If you are paid too much, SSA almost always figures it out eventually. Then, after you have already spent all of the money, it will send you a letter demanding that you repay the overpayment. If you do not have the money to repay the full amount of the overpayment, SSA may threaten to cut off your monthly benefits until the overpayment is recouped. Usually, however, it will accept a more reasonable reduction of your monthly benefits. Nevertheless, this is still a hassle and you may have trouble making ends meet during the time that your benefits are reduced. Under some circumstances it may be possible to get repayment of all or part of the overpayment waived; but this is not something to count on.

Will I be eligible for Title 19?

Yes, but only for past months. Title 19 (Medicaid) eligibility is automatic once you've been found eligible for SSI. You will receive a Title 19 card in the mail which will cover those months for which you are paid SSI. Because you won't receive any SSI monthly checks in the future, you won't have ongoing Title 19 eligibility as a result of receiving SSI. You may want to check with your county Department of Social Services to see if you might be eligible for Title 19 in the future.

Will I be eligible for Medicare?

Medicare eligibility begins after you have received 24 months of Social Security disability benefits. Therefore, your Medicare eligibility begins in _____, _____. Please note that to receive Part B of Medicare (which pays for doctor visits), you pay a premium that will be deducted from your Social Security disability monthly benefits. For example, the Medicare premium for [year] is $_____ per month. Disabled people with relatively low income and assets may be eligible for other programs that pay for medical expenses not covered by Medicare and/or pay the Medicare premium for you. To find out if you are eligible for any such programs, you need to check with your county welfare department.

The decision cover sheet says that the Appeals Council may review the decision "on its own motion." What does this mean?

In a very small number of cases the Appeals Council in Falls Church, Virginia, which is the body to which appeals from ALJ decisions go, will decide on its own to take away benefits awarded by the decision. If it is going to do this, the Appeals Council almost always will send you a notice within 60 days of the date of the decision. (In an extremely small number of cases the Appeals Council will reverse a decision after the 60 days have run.) I doubt if the Appeals Council is going to do this in your case; but if it happens, we will deal with it even if it means going to federal court.

How much is the attorney's fee?

Our contract calls for your attorney's fee to be 25% of the total back benefits paid on your account, including any benefits paid to your family. This includes SSI benefits. However, my fee will not be greater than $6,000.

Will attorney's fees be withheld from my benefits and paid to my attorney by SSA?

Yes. SSA will withhold attorney fees from Social Security disability back benefits and from SSI back benefits.

Is there a difference between attorney's fees and "expenses"?

Yes. In addition to the fee of 25% of past-due benefits up to $6,000, our contract calls for you to reimburse me for expenses in your case.

Were there any expenses in this case?

Expenses were $_____. I am enclosing a bill for these expenses with this letter. I am not expecting you to pay this bill until you receive back benefits. However, I will appreciate prompt payment as soon as you receive your first payment of back benefits.

When will SSA pay attorney's fees?

The notice concerning your back Social Security disability benefits will explain about attorney's fees and give you and the ALJ the right to object to the fee. The attorney fees payment from the Social Security disability part of your case will be sent out around the time the Social Security disability notice is sent. Any payment of attorney fees from back SSI benefits will be sent out shortly after that.

Is there anything else I ought to know about attorney's fees?

Yes. In your case, SSA should recalculate your SSI benefits after attorney fees and expenses are paid. This increases the amount of your SSI benefits. Although SSA is supposed to do this automatically, SSA may need to be reminded. When you pay us back for expenses, be sure to tell SSA how much you paid. This will be worked into the calculation, too, to increase your SSI benefits.

What is a "continuing disability review"?

SSA is required periodically to review the cases of all people who are receiving disability benefits. Usually cases are reviewed every three years; but some cases are reviewed more often. Sometimes the decision will direct SSA to conduct a review at a certain time. Often the award letter will tell you when to expect a review.

What will I have to do for a "continuing disability review"?

You will be asked to complete a form about your medical treatment, any vocational training or work and how your condition has changed since the time you were found eligible for disability benefits.

What if SSA finds that my disability has ceased but I'm still not able to work?

The notice that you will receive from SSA following a "continuing disability review" will explain your appeal rights. Read this notice carefully. If you appeal within ten days of the date you receive the notice, your benefits will continue during your appeal. So be sure to act quickly.

Is there anything that I can do now to help insure that my benefits will continue?

The very best thing you can do is to continue seeing your doctor. A lot of people with long-term chronic medical problems stop seeing their doctors because no treatment seems to help. This is a mistake for two reasons. First, it means that when SSA conducts its review, no medical evidence will exist to show that your condition is the same as it was when you were first found disabled. Second, and perhaps even more importantly, many doctors recommend that even healthy people after a certain age periodically have a thorough physical examination. This is even more important for people who already have chronic medical problems.

Is SSA going to make it as difficult to keep my benefits as it did to get them in the first place?

No. Not at all. SSA used to do this; but several years ago Congress stepped in and established a new standard for continuing disability reviews under which the benefits of the vast majority of people are found to continue without SSA making the review into a big deal.

In general, is dealing with the Social Security Administration going to be difficult?

As a rule, it is not. Sometimes, though, some people have problems. Here are some things you can do to try to minimize the hassle:

- Keep all decisions, letters, and notices you receive from SSA in a safe place.
- Read everything you get from SSA. The booklets that come with Award Letters are well written and informative.
- When reading the booklets you receive from SSA, pay special attention to the kind of information you are required to report to the Social Security Administration. Report promptly and in writing and keep a copy with your Social Security papers.
- Don't necessarily believe everything they tell you at the SSA 800 number. If you have an important issue to take up with SSA, sometimes it is better to go to your local Social Security Office.

If I can answer any other questions you have now or in the future, please do not hesitate to telephone me.

Sincerely,

[Name of Attorney]
Enclosure

[Note: When there are no expenses, delete the question and answer pertaining to expenses and the reference to Enclosure. When there are expenses, be sure to enclose the bill.]

§404.2 Sample: Letter to SSI-Only Claimant After Receipt of Favorable Decision

Client Name
Address
City/State/Zip

Re: SSI Decision

Dear [Client's Name]:

SSI-Only—Fully Favorable
$6,000 Limit/ 25% Fee

Insert the following in text:
SSI Date of Entitlement
Amount of Monthly Benefit
Amount of Expenses

Congratulations on winning your SSI case.

This letter attempts to answer some of the common questions that people have after receiving a favorable SSI decision from the Social Security Administration. I suggest that you keep it for a reference.

Do I have to do anything such as visit the Social Security Office or complete some forms in order to get paid?

Payment of your SSI benefits will require that you update your financial information at the Social Security Office. You will be contacted by the Social Security Office soon. If your financial situation is not complicated, SSA may let you handle this by phone and mail. If you haven't heard from the Social Security Office in about two weeks, please call me and I will try to speed things up.

How long will it take for SSA to pay me?

Your regular monthly benefits should start in one to two months (or so). Sometimes it takes an additional month or two for some back benefits to be paid. But if back benefits are being paid for more than three months, SSA will pay benefits in up to three installments six months apart.

If three months pass from the date of the decision and I am still not paid any of my back benefits, is there anything that can be done to speed up payment?

If three months pass and you are still not paid any back benefits, it is possible that I may be able to do something. Be sure to telephone me to let me know you haven't been paid after about three months from the date of your decision.

How far back will my benefits go?

Your SSI benefits will begin on _____. SSA will pay SSI from the first of the month after a claimant meets all requirements to get SSI. These requirements are (1) you file an application, (2) you are disabled, (3) you meet the income and asset requirements of the program.

How much will my monthly SSI benefits be?

This depends on the amount of your income, marital status, and living arrangement. As a rule, people who are not married, live in their own household, and have no other income will receive $_____ per month. If an SSI recipient is married and living with a non-working spouse who is not also eligible for SSI benefits, the SSI recipient gets the same amount. But where there is other income, such as income from a working spouse, or where a spouse also is getting SSI, it gets really complicated how to figure the amount of benefits. It is so complicated, I suggest that we let SSA figure it out first. Then I will double-check their calculations.

Will I receive a notice from SSA explaining my benefits?

You will get an SSI notice that shows a monthly breakdown of back benefits, one or more notices about how much SSA is paying out of your back benefits and when SSA will pay, and a separate notice showing the amount of attorney fees that will be paid out of your SSI benefits.

When will I get the notices?

Notices will start arriving in about a month or so. You may get a number of notices over the next several months. Sometimes it happens that a person gets a payment by direct deposit before he or she receives the notice explaining it.

Should I telephone my representative whenever I get a notice?

Yes. Social Security is not really good about sending me copies of SSI notices, despite the fact that I am requesting copies. So I would appreciate it if you'd telephone me or my secretary whenever you hear from SSI. I need copies of these notices in order to double check SSA's calculations. I may have to have you make copies for me.

I have not signed up for direct deposit. Should I do that now?

Yes. In fact, beginning March 2012 SSA requires direct deposit of all SSI benefits. You can sign up by contacting your local Social Security office.

Another option instead of direct deposit to a bank account is that SSA will allow you to receive your benefits using a Direct Express Debit MasterCard. At your request, SSA will open a Direct Express Debit MasterCard account for you and pay your benefits to that account every month. This card can be used wherever you can use a debit MasterCard.

Are there any problems with direct deposit?

Direct deposit is a great convenience. It is very dependable. SSA usually has people sign up for direct deposit when they apply for benefits. We have noticed that once in a while people forget that they signed up for direct deposit and they keep looking for a check in the mail when the money has already been deposited to their bank account.

Worse yet, sometimes people close the bank account that they told SSA they wanted to use for direct deposit. If this is your situation, you need to deal with this right away. It might be necessary for you to go to the Social Security office to update SSA on your current account information.

If I get a direct deposit of benefits before I get the notice explaining the benefits, should I wait until I receive the notice before I spend the money?

No. There is no need to wait. People often get direct deposit of **SSI back benefits before the notice that explains the benefits.** We recommend that you deposit this money in an interest bearing savings account that pays interest quarterly.

Why do you advise getting a savings account that pays interest quarterly rather than monthly or daily?

If interest is paid quarterly on a bank account and it is $20.00 or less, it is generally not counted as income to be deducted from your SSI benefits. Be sure to keep your interest payment to $20.00 or less, otherwise <u>all</u> of the payment counts.

Won't a savings account affect my eligibility for SSI?

You will be allowed nine months to spend your back benefits. After that, in order to continue to receive SSI benefits, you won't be allowed to have more than $2,000 in assets (with some exceptions) if you are single and $3,000 in assets (with some exceptions) if you are married.

What are the exceptions to the asset limit?

SSA has a list of assets that don't count against your asset limit. In other words, you can own these things and still be eligible for SSI. Here are the most significant things on the list:

1.   Your home. It can have any value; but if you move out and rent out the house, it becomes an asset and is counted.
2.   Household goods of any value if they are used on a regular basis or used for household maintenance. Thus, furniture, appliances, dishes, cooking utensils, electronic equipment such as a stereo, computer or a television, lawn care equipment, etc. do not count as an asset.
3.   Personal effects that are ordinarily worn or carried by someone, including a claimant's own wedding and engagement rings, are not counted as an asset. Also not counted as an asset are "articles otherwise having an intimate relation to the individual." Thus, for example, if you save your grandmother's diamond as a keepsake, even though you never wear your grandmother's diamond, it will not be counted as an asset because it has an "intimate relation" to you; but if you are a gem collector, the value of your gem collection counts.
4.   Household goods and personal effects required because of your physical condition, such as wheel chairs, hospital beds, etc.
5.   One car of any value will not be counted if you use the car for your transportation or the transportation of someone in your household.
6.   If life insurance has a face value not exceeding $1,500, its cash surrender value won't be counted as an asset.
7.   Term insurance, that is, life insurance which does not have any cash surrender value.

8.   Burial insurance.
9.   Burial spaces.
10. Burial funds up to $1,500 (as long as you don't use the exclusion of $1,500 face value life insurance). However, if you are holding anything as an investment, it probably counts as an asset.

Will SSA pay all the back benefits at once?
Unfortunately, no. SSA pays in three installments six months apart. The first two installments will be equal to three times the federal SSI monthly benefit. The third installment will be the rest.

Is there any way to convince SSA not to pay the SSI back benefits in installments six months apart?
Yes. Social Security regulations say that the amount of the first and second installment payments may be increased by the amount of any outstanding debts for food, clothing, shelter, or medically necessary services, supplies or equipment, or medicine, or current or anticipated expenses in the near future for medically necessary services, supplies or equipment, or medicine, or for the purchase of a home. So if you have debts or you want to buy a home, be sure to tell SSA.

Will I be eligible for Title 19?
Yes. Title 19 (Medicaid) eligibility is automatic once you've been found eligible for SSI. You will receive a Title 19 card in the mail. Title 19 eligibility should begin three months before SSI eligibility begins but usually your Title 19 card is just back dated to the date when your SSI began. If you have some significant medical bills from within three months of your date of SSI eligibility and your Title 19 card doesn't go back far enough, telephone me.

The decision cover sheet says that the Appeals Council may review the decision "on its own motion." What does this mean?
In a very small number of cases the Appeals Council in Falls Church, Virginia, which is the body to which appeals from ALJ decisions go, will decide on its own to take away benefits awarded by the decision. If it is going to do this, the Appeals Council almost always will send you a notice within 60 days of the date of the decision. (In an extremely small number of cases the Appeals Council will reverse a decision after the 60 days have run.) I doubt if the Appeals Council is going to do this in your case; but if it happens, we will deal with it even if it means fighting SSA in federal court.

I understand that I should not spend all of my back benefits until we figure out if attorney's fees were withheld. Does it happen very often that attorney's fees are not withheld?
No. Not at all. It does happen once in a while, though.

How much is the attorney's fee?
Our contract calls for your attorney's fee to be 25% of back benefits, up to $6,000.

Will the fee be withheld from my benefits and paid to my representative by SSA?
Yes. SSA will withhold attorney fees from SSI back benefits.

What's the difference between attorney's fees and "expenses"?
In addition to the fee of 25% of past-due benefits, our contract calls for you to pay me back for medical records or reports, etc., that I paid for in your case. SSA will not pay for these things, nor will it send an attorney any money for such expenses out of a claimant's funds.

Were there any expenses in this case?
Expenses were $_____. I am enclosing a bill for these expenses with this letter. I am not expecting you to pay this bill until you receive a payment of back benefits. However, I will appreciate prompt payment as soon as you receive your first payment of back benefits.

What happens if I am overpaid?
If you are paid too much, SSA almost always figures it out eventually. Then, after you have already spent all of the money, it will send you a letter demanding that you repay the overpayment. If you do not have the money to repay the full amount of the overpayment, SSA may threaten to cut off your monthly benefits until the overpayment is paid back. Usually, however, it will accept a more reasonable reduction of your monthly benefits. Nevertheless, this is still a hassle

and you may have trouble making ends meet during the time that your benefits are reduced. Under some circumstances it may be possible to get repayment of all or part of the overpayment waived; but this is not something to count on.

What is a "continuing disability review"?
SSA is required periodically to review the cases of all people who are receiving disability benefits. Usually cases are reviewed every three years; but some cases are reviewed more often. Sometimes the decision will direct SSA to conduct a review at a certain time. Sometimes the award letter will tell you when to expect a review.

What will I have to do for a "continuing disability review"?
You will be asked to complete a form about your medical treatment, any vocational training or work and how your condition has changed since the time you were found eligible for disability benefits.

What if SSA finds that my disability has ceased but I'm still not able to work?
The notice that you will receive from SSA following a "continuing disability review" will explain your appeal rights. Read this notice carefully. If you appeal within 10 days of the date you receive the notice, your benefits will continue during your appeal. So be sure to act quickly.

Is there anything that I can do now to help insure that my benefits will continue?
The very best thing you can do is to continue seeing your doctor. A lot of people with long-term chronic medical problems stop seeing their doctors because no treatment seems to help. This is a mistake for two reasons. First, it means that when SSA conducts its review, no medical evidence will exist to show that your condition is the same as it was when you were first found disabled. Second, and perhaps even more importantly, doctors recommend that even healthy people after a certain age periodically have a thorough physical examination. This is even more important for people who already have chronic medical problems.

Is SSA going to make it as difficult to keep my benefits as it did to get them in the first place?
No. Not at all. The disabilities of the vast majority of people are found to continue at the initial evaluation. Few people have their benefits stopped.

What if I work part-time while I'm receiving benefits? Will this cause my benefits to stop?
It depends on how much you make. We have a several-page memo on this subject. If you'd like a copy, please ask a member of our office staff to send you one.

Is there anything I can do to make dealing with SSA easier?
You shouldn't expect as many problems dealing with SSA while receiving benefits as you had trying to get benefits in the first place. Sometimes, though, some people have problems. Here are some things you can do to try to minimize the hassle:
- Keep all decisions, letters, and notices you receive from SSA in a safe place.
- Read everything you get from SSA. The booklets that come with award letters and notices are well-written and informative.
- When reading the booklets you receive from SSA, pay special attention to the kind of information you are required to report to the Social Security Administration. Report promptly and in writing, and keep a copy with your Social Security papers.
- Don't necessarily believe everything they tell you at the SSA 800 number. If you have an important issue to take up with SSA, sometimes it is better to go to your local Social Security Office.

And if I can answer any other questions you have now or in the future, please do not hesitate to telephone me.
Sincerely,

[Name of Attorney]
Enclosure

[Note: When there are no expenses, delete the question and answer pertaining to expenses and the reference to Enclosure. When there are expenses, be sure to enclose the bill.]

§405   Sample: Letter to Social Security Office Requesting Copies of SSI Notices

LETTER TO SS OFFICE
CONCURRENT CASE

Date

Social Security Office
Address
City/State/Zip

Re: [Client]_____
      SSN: _____

Dear Social Security Office:

I represented [client] at an administrative hearing in a claim for concurrent benefits in which we received a favorable decision from an ALJ dated _____. An Appointment of Representative form should appear in this claimant's file. Please see to it that I get copies of all SSI notices concerning this case as required by 20 C.F.R. § 416.1515.

Please note that we also received approval of our fee agreement. Therefore, please send us a notice concerning the amount of the SSI fee, and please withhold and pay the fee from our client's back benefits as appropriate.

Sincerely,

_____
[Name of Attorney]

cc: [Client]

§406 Sample: Letter to ALJ re: Failure to Issue Order Approving or Disapproving Fee Agreement

Date

[Judge's Name]
Administrative Law Judge
Office of Disability Adjudication and Review, SSA
Address
City/State/Zip

Re: Claimant: [Client]
      SSN:

Dear Judge

I have received a copy of the fully favorable decision in the case of   [Client's Name]   dated   [date]   ;
however, I did not receive a copy of your order approving my fee agreement with my client so that the "fee
agreement process" will apply to approval of attorney's fees in this case. I assume this was an oversight.

If the order was issued, please send me a copy. If the order was not issued, please issue the order as soon as possible.
I understand that instructions to hearing offices about the fee agreement process state that an order may be issued
after a favorable decision is mailed.

I filed my fee agreement with SSA on   [date]   . I enclose a copy of the fee agreement and a copy of my transmittal
letter.

                                                    Sincerely,

                                                    _____
                                                    [Name of Attorney]

cc: Client

§407 Sample: Notice of Intent to File Fee Petition

Date

[Judge's Name]
Administrative Law Judge
Office of Disability Adjudication and Review, SSA
Address
City/State/Zip

Re: Notice of Intent to File Fee Petition
      Claimant: _____[Client]_____
      SSN: _____

Dear Judge _____:

On ____[date]____, you issued a decision finding the above claimant to be disabled. As soon as the determination is made of the total amount of past-due benefits due my client, I will file a request for approval of my fee. I give this notice in compliance with 20 C.F.R.
§ 404.1730(c)(1), which requires that I give you notice of intent to file a fee petition within 60 days of the date of the notice of favorable decision.

In a concurrent case such as this one, determination of the full amount of past-due benefits usually takes longer than 60 days. I have explained this to my client, and I have also explained that in such cases the Social Security Administration may "overpay" SSI past-due benefits and then recoup this "overpayment" by reducing the Social Security disability past due benefits, thus complicating the calculation of attorney's fees.

                                 Sincerely,

                                 _____

                                 [Name of Attorney]

§408　　The Bad Address Problem

When the ALJ decision is sent to a claimant's *former* address, no significant problem is created. If a forwarding order is on file, the post office will forward the claimant's mail. SSA, of course, must be notified of the new address. The claimant can contact his or her Social Security office about the address change. There is little need for a lawyer's involvement.

But when the address which appears on the ALJ decision is an undeliverable address, or, worse yet, simply a wrong address, the problem can be serious and surprisingly difficult to correct in a Social Security disability case. The Social Security disability check for back benefits is usually sent automatically to the address which appears on the decision. If the claimant's check for back benefits is delivered to an address where no one knows the claimant and an unauthorized person is able to cash it, it may be months before the check is replaced.

When you find a bad address on the face of the decision, you can head off this problem in three ways. First, contact the hearing office immediately and insist that a notice be sent to the payment center informing it of the correct address. Second, because the notice may not be associated with the file before the back benefits are released, discuss the problem with a supervisor at the claimant's Social Security office. Suggest that the supervisor contact the payment center by telephone. Third, telephone the payment center yourself.

If the worst happens, it may help in getting the check replaced quickly that a supervisor at the Social Security office is already involved. It is possible for SSA to issue a replacement check without waiting for a full-fledged investigation of the missing check by the Secret Service, though SSA employees may advise you to the contrary. Ask for the check to be replaced as a "critical payment."

Note: Because SSI payment is processed at the local Social Security office usually after another interview of the claimant, it is likely that the claims representative will notice the wrong address and correct it. But, to be sure, advise your client to tell the claims representative about the wrong address on the decision.

§409　　Amending the Decision

The regulations pertaining to reopening decisions, particularly 20 C.F.R. § 404.987(b), which allows a claimant to ask that a decision be revised, permit a request that the ALJ correct an error or oversight by issuing a revised decision.

Under 20 C.F.R. § 404.988, a decision may be reopened within 12 months, four years, or with no time

limit, depending on the circumstances. The time limits begin running not from the date on the ALJ decision that you want reopened, but rather from the *date of the initial determination*, that is, the date of the initial denial. Thus, the twelve-month time limit which provides for reopening for any reason may have already lapsed by the time the ALJ decision is issued.

If this occurs, you may use the four-year time limit which provides for reopening for "good cause." The definition of good cause in 20 C.F.R. § 404.989(a)(3) includes the situation where the "evidence that was considered ... clearly shows on its face that an error was made." Even the rule that allows for reopening at any time may be used if the problem is clerical error or error that appears on the face of the evidence. 20 C.F.R. § 404.988(c)(8).

In practice, the vast majority of ALJs are not concerned with the procedural niceties of the reopening regulations. Most will not question their authority to correct errors in their decisions. The issue is usually the selection of an appropriate tactful approach rather than the technical application of a particular subsection of the reopening regulations. It usually works best to telephone the hearing assistant to explain any error you find in the decision, and then to follow up with a letter requesting that the ALJ correct the error.

§410　　Peculiar Problems in Concurrent Cases

In many concurrent cases, that is, cases involving both a Social Security disability (Title II) application and an SSI application, the SSI application is little more than a nuisance that adds nothing to a claimant's benefits. *See* §411. Occasionally an SSI application will actually reduce a claimant's recovery. *See* §§415-416.

Sometimes, though, there are Title II cases in which you wish an SSI application had been submitted. This happens most often when the claimant was found disabled later than alleged. If there had been an SSI application, a claimant, who meets the income and asset requirements of the SSI program, would get benefits during the five-month waiting period when no Social Security disability benefits are payable.

It might not be too late. Fairly frequently, SSA makes a mistake that allows an SSI application to be submitted using the date of the Social Security disability application as a protective SSI application filing date. SSA's rules provide that when a claimant files a Social Security disability application, that application is to be treated as an inquiry about SSI. 20 C.F.R. § 416.350(b). The date of the Social Security disability application is used to establish an SSI application date for a claimant who actually files an SSI application within 60 days of a notice that SSA is required to send the claimant explaining the need to file an application. *See* 20 C.F.R. § 416.345(d). Many times, however, this notice, called a "close-out letter," is never sent by SSA.

In cases where no "close-out letter" is sent to the claimant, the claimant can go back to SSA after winning the case and ask that an SSI application be taken with the date of filing, which is the date of the Social Security disability application. If no "close-out letter" is sent to the claimant, the SSI filing protection remains open indefinitely. *See* POMS GN 00201.005F, SI 00601.027, and SI 00601.037.

Sometimes even when SSA did send a "close-out letter," it may be possible to argue that an SSA employee gave the claimant misinformation about potential eligibility for SSI benefits. *See* 20 C.F.R. § 416.351. If so, an SSI application may be submitted using the date the misinformation was given as the date of filing. 20 C.F.R. § 416.351(b).

Once in a great while you will see a case that is the mirror image of the situation described above. If a case was processed only as an SSI claim even though the claimant actually had insured status for Title II benefits, there is an easy fix. An SSI application is supposed to be treated by SSA as an application for all other possible benefits. POMS GN 00204.027 and SI 00601.035.

§411 The Odd Way That SSA Processes SSI When There Are Concurrent Applications

SSI is a welfare program. SSI eligibility depends on (1) disability, (2) assets, and (3) monthly income. Receipt of a favorable decision in a concurrent case disposes of the first issue. The fact that an SSI application was processed at all usually (but not always) means that SSA investigated your client's assets (a maximum of $2,000 for an individual, $3,000 for an individual and spouse) and found that your client qualifies, at least as of the date of the application. The third issue, income, is crucial in a concurrent case—a case involving both Social Security disability and SSI benefits.

The Social Security Administration counts income month-by-month from virtually all sources, whether this income is earned or unearned, in cash or in-kind. SSA uses formulas that reduce the SSI benefit because of this other income and if the result reaches zero, SSA finds the claimant ineligible for the month in question because of excess income. As a rule, SSA counts income when it is actually received by the claimant. Treatment of past-due Social Security disability benefits, however, is an exception to this rule. Social Security disability back benefits are *ultimately* counted month-by-month

when they *should have been* received beginning with the month of entitlement. But, as we shall see, SSA adds a complicating twist to how it counts Social Security disability benefits.

It is SSA policy that in all concurrent cases, when SSA first calculates payment of SSI back benefits, it does not take into account the fact that Social Security disability benefits will be paid for the same months. That is, SSA pretends that the claimant is not going to be eligible for any Social Security disability payments. SSA does this, it says, to insure that a claimant's outstanding medical bills will be paid by T.19 (Medicaid), which is linked to SSI eligibility in most states. SSI is paid in full, without reference to the fact that the claimant is also going to receive Social Security disability benefits for the months being processed, often in an amount large enough to entirely disqualify the claimant for SSI. Thus, all or part of the SSI payment is actually an overpayment. Then SSA recoups the SSI overpayment out of the claimant's past-due Social Security disability benefits. 20 C.F.R. §§ 404.408b and 416.1123(d)(1).

SSA takes its time doing this. The first calculation of SSI back benefits takes a month or two. It takes another couple of months or so for the calculation to be done again, this time including the Social Security disability benefits so that SSA can figure out how much to deduct from the claimant's past-due Social Security disability benefits—sometimes referred to as the "SSI windfall offset" or just the "SSI offset"—which is the amount of the overpayment of SSI benefits.

Although SSA will start paying monthly Social Security disability benefits, SSA's rules provide that no past-due Title II benefits will be paid until SSI is processed. Sometimes the payment center puts payment of past-due Title II benefits on hold for months waiting for the SSI calculation even when there is no pending SSI application. Since payment personnel won't listen to a claimant's attorney when you tell them there is no SSI claim pending (and they don't find the fact that the ALJ did not mention an SSI claim in the favorable decision to be proof that an SSI claim does not exist), you need to contact the local office whenever you receive a Title II Notice of Award that wrongly says payment of past-due benefits is held up by a pending SSI claim. Ask local office personnel to contact the payment center.

Your job as the claimant's lawyer, which includes seeing to it that the claimant receives all benefits due as a result of winning the claimant's disability case, is complicated by the fact that for Title II purposes, SSA treats your representation as ending when you are paid. In a case paid under the "fee agreement process" (*see* §§700 to 719 of this book), you're likely to be paid your fee around the time the Notice of Award is issued, which is long before the claimant will receive his or her past due Title II benefits in a concurrent case. When past due Title II benefits are finally paid, SSA sends the claimant a letter that states how much was deducted from the claimant's back benefits because of the SSI offset, but SSA will not send you a copy of this letter. For this reason, after winning a concurrent case, our letters to the claimant ask that the claimant call when the second Social Security disability letter is received. *See* §§404 and 404.1.

Although it is unusual for SSA to make a mistake calculating the SSI offset, you're likely to get questions about it from your clients, many of whom have the impulse to appeal when they get a much smaller Title II back benefit than they were expecting. You need to be able to explain the SSI offset to such clients.

It is useful to make a ballpark estimate of the claimant's back benefits when you get the favorable decision. This way, you'll be able to tell the claimant approximately what to expect; you'll be able to estimate your attorney fee; and when you receive the award letters, the only cases that you will need to look at closely to determine if the claimant was correctly paid are those that differ significantly from your estimate. You will also be able to identify the total offset cases, those cases where the claimant's benefits are not increased at all by processing an SSI application.

Make an estimate of your client's *net* potential maximum SSI benefit, that is, the amount of SSI that your client would receive if your client's Social Security disability benefits were counted when SSI was calculated in the first place. Use the maximum SSI benefit for the year in question (since you can always adjust later if the claimant receives a reduced SSI benefit rate). The net potential maximum SSI benefit divided by four is the maximum possible SSI attorney fee. The amount you come up with can also be subtracted from the grand total SSI actually paid. The result is the amount of the SSI offset, which will be deducted later by SSA from the claimant's past-due Title II benefits.

To do this calculation, you must look specifically at SSI eligibility during the five-month waiting period, §412. Review your client's monthly income, including Social Security disability benefits for past months to determine if your client is going to be eligible for any SSI, §413. Review the next several sections of this book for the basic rules about SSI. You may use the worksheet at §431 if you find it more helpful than using the back of an envelope.

If you come to the conclusion that your client is not going to receive a net increase as a result of the SSI application, you may have the impulse to withdraw the SSI application. But before you do this, consider whether your client might be paid a state SSI supplement that is not recouped with the SSI offset, §414. Examine the possibility that SSI eligibility will be created after

payment of attorney fees, §419, and consider whether your client will have outstanding medical bills paid by T.19 (Medicaid).

Look at the link to Medicaid in your state and consider whether your client has any outstanding medical bills incurred during the relevant period (beginning about three months before the date of the SSI application up to the last month of SSI benefits) that will be paid by Medicaid if your client is found entitled to fleeting SSI eligibility. Even if SSA takes every penny of SSI back, your client will be ahead if medical bills are paid.

§412   Check for SSI Eligibility During the Five-Month Waiting Period During Which No Social Security Disability Benefits Are Payable

If your client applied for SSI during any time within six months after the month your client became disabled, your client may be eligible for SSI during the five-full-month waiting period before payment of Social Security disability benefits commences. During this period, there will be no deduction from SSI based on the amount of your client's Title II benefits.

Social Security disability payments are counted for SSI purposes in the month they would have been received. Since a Social Security disability payment received in one month is actually a payment for the previous month, your client won't actually receive payment for the Title II month of entitlement, the first month of benefits, until the next month. Therefore, the five-full-month waiting period turns into six months without a Social Security disability check.

Thus, full SSI may be paid from the SSI month of entitlement (usually the first month after the date of the SSI application) through the month of Title II entitlement.

Practice Tip

You'll see many cases where your client is eligible for SSI only during the Title II waiting period. In a simple case with no welfare recoupment, it is easy to figure out how much SSA is going to deduct as the SSI offset from your client's past due Title II benefits: All SSI paid except the SSI paid during the Title II waiting period. The formula is:

Total SSI paid
Minus   SSI paid during Title II waiting period
Equals   SSI Windfall Offset

In such a simple case, it is easy to figure out maximum attorney fees from the SSI, too. It is 25% of the SSI paid during the Title II waiting period.

§413   Determining SSI Eligibility After the Five-Month Waiting Period

Here is the formula for SSI eligibility outside the five-month waiting period:

If the Title II monthly benefit plus any other countable income received by your client is greater than or equal to the Federal SSI benefit rate, plus any federally administered state supplement plus $20, then your client is not eligible for SSI for the month in question. This formula must be applied for every month of potential SSI eligibility.

When the Federal SSI benefit rate, plus any federally administered state supplement, plus $20 (which we will call the SSI sum) is greater than the Title II benefit amount, the maximum potential net monthly SSI payable can be determined by subtracting the Title II benefit from the SSI sum. This result times the number of months of back SSI (outside the Title II waiting period) plus any SSI payable during the Title II waiting period represents a ballpark estimate of your client's maximum net SSI. Subtract the result from the total SSI paid to get the approximate amount of the SSI offset. Divide the maximum net SSI by four to get the approximate maximum potential SSI attorney fee.

Note, though, the above method may yield only a ballpark estimate. After using receipt of Social Security disability benefits to determine whether the claimant is eligible at all in the current month, as a rule, SSA does not count Social Security disability benefits in the month they are received. Instead, SSA counts these benefits two months later. A major exception to this rule occurs when Social Security disability benefits are received in the first month SSI benefits are paid. If this happens, which it does whenever the Title II month of entitlement is earlier than the SSI month of entitlement, in effect, SSA ends up counting the Social Security disability benefits in the current month. *See* §428. Unless the exception applies, actual SSI back benefits paid to the claimant will be greater than the ballpark estimate. Also, the ballpark estimate of the SSI offset may be low because SSA may deduct attorney fees. *See* §419. Nevertheless, ballpark estimates have their place, especially when you are dealing with a program as complicated as SSI.

When your client is going to be eligible for both Social Security disability and SSI (that is, where the Social Security disability benefit is less than the total SSI plus $20), here's a shortcut calculation for a ballpark estimate of the maximum back benefits from both Social Security disability and SSI. The following calculation is subject to the same warnings stated above and may yield a low estimate some of the time:

	Federal SSI benefit rate
Plus	Federally administered state supplement
Plus	$20.00
Equals	Monthly benefit from both programs

Times	Number of months of back benefits
Equals	Total potential back benefits from both programs

Divide by four for the total attorney fee from both programs

§414   Consider the State Supplement

SSI, a federal welfare program with a nationwide uniform monthly benefit amount, is supplemented by most states. Thus, total payment differs from state to state. Many states administer their own supplements to certain categories of SSI eligible individuals. Another group of states have federally administered supplements. *See* POMS SI 01415.001 *ff.*

You need to understand how the system works in your state to determine whether your client's Social Security disability benefit amount is large enough to disqualify your client for SSI payments. Generally, your client will not be eligible for SSI if your client's Social Security disability benefit amount plus any other countable income is equal to the federal SSI benefit amount plus the federally administered state supplement, if any, plus $20. For example, in 2016, the federal SSI benefit rate for an individual is $733. If there is also a federally administered supplement of $100 and your client's only other income is from Social Security disability benefits, it is only if your client receives $853 or more in monthly Social Security disability benefits that your client becomes ineligible for SSI. When an offset calculation is done, the total amount of the check paid by the federal government, that is, including the federally administered state supplement, will be deducted from your client's Social Security disability back benefits.

When there is a state administered supplement to SSI, the calculations work differently. A state administered supplement doesn't increase the amount of income a claimant can have from all sources. To be eligible for SSI, a claimant's income must be less than the federal benefit rate plus $20. If a state supplement is paid when initial SSI eligibility is determined before counting the amount of Social Security disability benefits, this supplement is not recouped by SSA as part of its offset calculation.

Federally administered state supplements are included in SSI attorney fees; state administered supplements are not. SSA says that an attorney can charge a claimant a fee out of a state administered supplement and that the fee is not subject to the provisions of 42 U.S.C. § 406(a) that require a fee to be approved by SSA. This fee would need to be collected directly from the claimant after the claimant receives the state supplement payment. Most attorneys do not bother to charge a fee out of an SSI state supplement.

§415   *The Impact of Welfare Recoupment*

Most states have "interim assistance agreements" with SSA. Under the terms of these federal-state agreements, welfare benefits (usually called general assistance or general relief, not including Temporary Assistance to Needy Families payments) paid by the state during the pendency of an SSI application are recouped out of back SSI. 20 C.F.R. §§ 416.1901, *et seq*. SSA reimburses the state out of the claimant's back SSI benefits. This must be done with the "consent" of the claimant who is required to sign an authorization as a condition of receiving assistance. 20 C.F.R. § 416.1904.

Curiously, however, interim assistance agreements and the authorizations signed by claimants do not apply to past-due Social Security disability benefits. These benefits remain protected from state garnishment by the anti-assignment provisions of the Social Security Act.

If you determine that your client is not going to be eligible for any SSI benefit and your client withdraws the SSI application, this will preclude welfare reimbursement under the interim assistance agreement and result in substantially more in-pocket benefits for your client.

Even when your client is entitled to some back SSI payment, for example, where eligibility is limited to the five-month waiting period for Title II benefits, your client may be financially better off withdrawing the SSI application. There is no way to arrange for SSA to pay your client the amount of SSI benefits to which your client is actually entitled, that is, benefits limited to the five-month waiting period. Instead, SSA will pay SSI from the month after the date of the SSI application to the present time. It will reimburse the state and ultimately send the balance to your client; and your client will have a huge SSI windfall offset deducted from back Title II benefits. Nothing requires your client to pursue an SSI application, especially when to do so would result in receiving less benefits than if your client had never applied for SSI.

It is SSA policy that attorney fees from the SSI part of the case are calculated before the state is repaid for interim assistance. When there isn't enough money left after the state is reimbursed to pay the full SSI attorney fee, SSA will direct the attorney to collect the balance of the attorney fee from the claimant.

§416   *The Strange Case of the SSI Eligible Couple*

One of the most surprising results of an SSI benefit calculation occurs where your client's spouse is already receiving SSI benefits and your client has been found disabled in a concurrent case. Like some welfare recoupment situations, your client may receive much more back benefits by withdrawing the SSI application

rather than allowing it to be processed; but withdrawing the SSI application will have an adverse effect on the spouse's SSI benefits and Medicaid eligibility, factors that must be considered. This strange case is better understood if we use an illustrative case. We will use SSI benefit amounts for 2016 and assume that the couple lives in the author's home state of Wisconsin, which does not have a federally administered state supplement; but the Wisconsin state supplement to a couple of $130.43 will be paid directly by the state.

Let us say for purposes of illustration that for the past 10 months your client's wife has been receiving the SSI benefit for a disabled person living in her own household. She received $733 per month. She also received a state supplement of $83.78 per month from the state of Wisconsin. Her husband, your client, has just been found disabled in a concurrent case. He has a PIA (Social Security disability benefit rate) of $900 per month and, for the sake of a simplified example, let us assume that there are 10 months of retroactive benefits to be paid under each program.

Based on his PIA of $900 and entitlement to 10 months of back benefits, it looks like your client ought to receive past-due Social Security disability benefits of $9,000. He won't get nearly this much if his SSI application is processed. Here is why:

SSA treats disabled couples as a unit. There is a special benefit amount for them. In 2016, it is $1,100 per month. To calculate current benefits, SSA will treat your client's $900 Social Security disability benefit as unearned income and apply the $20 per month exclusion, reducing it to $880 which is subtracted from the couple's benefit amount of $1,100, to give a couple's benefit of $220, which is then split between the two of them. Henceforth, each will receive $110 in SSI benefits. The total amount that the disabled SSI couple will receive, then, is $1,250.43 per month. He will get his $900 monthly Social Security disability check, and the couple will get $220 in SSI from the federal government and $130.43 from the state of Wisconsin.

But let us look at what happens when back SSI benefits are calculated: Without looking at the fact that your client is going to get $900 per month in Social Security disability benefits, SSA will start the calculation with the monthly SSI disabled couple's benefit rate of $1,100. But, SSA will say, this couple has already received a monthly SSI payment of $733. Thus, your client will receive the difference between the couple's rate, $1,100, and the amount his wife received at the time, $733. Your client will receive $367 per month, totaling $3,670 in back SSI benefits for 10 months.

Then, when the SSI offset is calculated for the purpose of paying past-due Social Security disability benefits, SSA will look at the total amount of SSI benefits received by the couple during the 10-month period, $10,480.

She received: $733 x 10 months = $7,330
He received: $367 x 10 months = $3,670
Total $1,100 $11,000

If the couple has unearned income (in this case Social Security disability benefits), $20 per month of that unearned income will be disregarded. Here is how SSA approaches the question of what would happen if the couple received $900 per month in unearned income:

Title 2 benefit: $900.00
minus disregarded: – 20.00
Countable income: $880.00 x 10 months
                      = $8,800.00

Since the couple has received everything to which it is entitled, the amount of the overpayment is the excess countable income of $8,800 during the 10-month period. In effect, SSA will treat everything except the $20 per month disregarded amount as an overpayment. The couple's total monthly payment to which it is entitled will come out to $1,120, the SSI rate for an eligible couple plus $20.

Therefore, $8,800 will be deducted from your client's past-due Social Security disability benefits. He will be paid the remaining $200. In short, the total amount of back benefits he will receive from both federal programs will be $3,870 ($200 in past-due Social Security disability benefits plus $3,670 in back SSI benefits). He will also receive 10 months difference between the Wisconsin state supplement for a couple, $130.43, and that for an individual, which was already paid—$83.78 per month. This comes out to $46.55 per month or $465.50 over 10 months. Thus, the grand total received will be $4,335.50.

If he withdraws his SSI application, he will receive Social Security disability past-due benefits of $9,000 instead of $4,335.50, a net gain of $4,664.50. But there will be an impact on his wife's SSI when the past-due benefits are received.

Spouse to spouse deeming rules, whereby part of the income of one spouse is counted against another, operate to make her SSI benefit $220 per month, the same amount the disabled couple would receive, during months that he receives $900 in Social Security disability benefits. 20 C.F.R. § 416.1163. When the back benefits of $9,000 are received, this amount will be treated as income to your client in the month it is received and a large portion of it will be deemed to his wife. 20 C.F.R. § 416.1123(d). Receipt of this money by your client will make your client's wife ineligible for SSI for the month

it is received and for all later months that the couple's assets exceed $3,000.

Your client's wife will not be able to take advantage of the rule that for six months after receipt of Social Security disability past due benefits, such benefits will not be counted for SSI asset purposes. 20 C.F.R. § 416.1233. Therefore, your client will have to quickly spend at least $6,000 of his $9,000 past-due benefit to reduce his assets to the $3,000 couple asset limit.

Once the assets are at $3,000, your client and his wife can reapply for SSI.

Whether withdrawing his SSI application and taking his spouse off of SSI for a month or more is worth it depends on the amount of money at stake. If your client's Social Security disability benefit amount is low, this clearly is not prudent, especially when you include in your calculation the month or more that your client's spouse may not be eligible for SSI.

Where there is not going to be any continuing SSI couple's eligibility (which would result from a monthly Social Security disability benefit amount of $1,120 in our example), processing your client's SSI application will have the effect of simply reducing his grand total back benefit by the amount of the SSI that his wife was paid during all months covered by his past-due benefits. Since the wife is losing her SSI benefits anyway, it is hard to see a downside to withdrawing the SSI application.

§417   What Is the Lawyer's Duty to Advise Withdrawing an SSI Application?

If there is no welfare recoupment involved (and no SSI recoupment as in the couple's situation) and your calculation shows that your client is not going to be eligible for SSI anyway, withdrawing the SSI application results in administrative savings for SSA, your client does not have to provide updated financial information to SSA, and your client may possibly receive the Social Security disability past-due benefits earlier (although this is not something to count on). There are no other reasons to withdraw the SSI application. The amount of benefits your client receives is the same, even if your client is overpaid SSI and that overpayment is recouped out of past-due Social Security disability benefits. There is no effect on attorney fees because attorney fee withholding is calculated before the SSI offset is determined in all cases except for ones that have gone to federal court.

But what about withdrawing the SSI application where there is going to be welfare recoupment or recoupment of SSI benefits paid to a spouse? At the least, an attorney must advise the client of the consequences and implications of withdrawing an SSI application and let the client make up his or her own mind.

§418   Form: Request for Withdrawal of Application (SSA-521)

SOCIAL SECURITY ADMINISTRATION		TOE 420	Form Approved OMB No. 0960-0015

REQUEST FOR WITHDRAWAL OF APPLICATION

Do not write in this space

IMPORTANT NOTICE - This is a request to cancel your application. If we approve it, the decision we made on your application will have no legal effect. You will forfeit all rights attached to an application, including the rights of appeal. You will have to return any payment we made to you or anyone else on the basis of that application. You must then reapply if you want a determination of your Social Security rights at any time in the future. Any subsequent application may not involve the same retroactive period. We intend for you to use this procedure only when your decision to file has resulted, or will result, in a disadvantage to you. Your local Social Security office will be glad to explain whether, and how, this procedure will help you.

NAME OF WAGE EARNER, SELF-EMPLOYED INDIVIDUAL, OR ELIGIBLE INDIVIDUAL	SOCIAL SECURITY NUMBER

IF DIFFERENT, PRINT YOUR NAME (*First name, middle initial, last name*)	YOUR SOCIAL SECURITY NUMBER

TYPE OF BENEFIT YOU WANT TO WITHDRAW	DATE OF APPLICATION	IF APPLICABLE, DO YOU WANT TO KEEP MEDICARE BENEFITS? ☐ Yes ☐ No

I hereby request the withdrawal of my application, dated as above, for the reasons stated below. I understand that (1) this request may not be cancelled after 60 days from the mailing of notice of approval; and (2) if a determination of my entitlement has been made, there must be repayment of all benefits paid on the application I want withdrawn, and all other persons whose benefits would be affected must consent to this withdrawal. I further understand that the application withdrawn and all related material will remain a part of the records of the Social Security Administration and that this withdrawal will not affect the proper crediting of wages or self-employment income to my Social Security earnings record.

Give reason for withdrawal. *(If you need more space, use the reverse of this form.)*

1. ☐ I intend to continue working. (I have been advised of the alternatives to withdrawal for applicants under full retirement age and still wish to withdraw my application.)

2. ☐ Other (Please explain fully): _____

_____

_____

☐ Continued on reverse

SIGNATURE OF PERSON MAKING REQUEST

Signature (*First name, middle initial, last name*) (*Write in ink*)	Date (*Month, day, year*)
SIGN HERE ▶	Telephone Number (*include area code*)

Mailing Address (*Number and Street, Apt. No., P.O. Box, or Rural Route*)

City and State	ZIP Code	Enter Name of County (if any) in which you now live

Witnesses are required ONLY if this request has been signed by mark (X) above. If signed by mark (X), two witnesses to the signing who know the person making the request must sign below, giving their full addresses.

1. Signature of Witness	2. Signature of Witness
Address (*Number and Street, City, State and ZIP Code*)	Address (*Number and Street, City, State and ZIP Code*)

FOR USE OF SOCIAL SECURITY ADMINISTRATION

☐ APPROVED	☐ NOT APPROVED BECAUSE ➡	☐ BENEFITS NOT REPAID	☐ CONSENT(S) NOT OBTAINED	☐ OTHER (*Attach special determination*)

SIGNATURE OF SSA EMPLOYEE	TITLE ☐ CLAIMS AUTHORIZER ☐ OTHER (*Specify*)	DATE

Form **SSA-521** (10-2012) EF (10-2012)
Destroy Prior Editions

Additional Remarks: _____

_____

_____

_____

_____

_____

_____

_____

_____

_____

Privacy Act Statement

Collection and Use of Personal Information

Sections 202 (a), 205 (a), and 1872 of the Social Security Act, as amended, authorize us to collect this information. The information you provide will be used to cancel your application for benefits.

The information you furnish on this form is voluntary. However, failure to provide the requested information may cause continued consideration of your benefits claim.

We rarely use the information you supply for any purpose other than for cancelling an application. However, we may use it for the administration and integrity of Social Security programs. We may also disclose information to another person or to another agency in accordance with approved routine uses, which include but are not limited to the following:

1. To enable a third party or an agency to assist Social Security in establishing rights to Social Security benefits and/or coverage;

2. To comply with Federal laws requiring the release of information from Social Security records (e.g., to the Government Accountability Office and Department of Veterans' Affairs);

3. To make determinations for eligibility in similar health and income maintenance programs at the Federal, state and local level; and

4. To facilitate statistical research, audit or investigative activities necessary to assure the integrity of Social Security programs.

We may also use the information you provide in computer matching programs. Matching programs compare our records with records kept by other Federal, state, or local government agencies. Information from these matching programs can be used to establish or verify a person's eligibility for Federally funded or administered benefit programs and for repayment of payments or delinquent debts under these programs.

Additional information regarding this form, routine uses of information, and our programs and systems, is available on-line at www.ssa.gov or at your local Social Security office.

Paperwork Reduction Act Statement - This information collection meets the requirements of 44 U.S.C. § 3507, as amended by Section 2 of the Paperwork Reduction Act of 1995. You do not need to answer these questions unless we display a valid Office of Management and Budget control number. We estimate that it will take about 5 minutes to read the instructions, gather the facts, and answer the questions. SEND OR BRING THE COMPLETED FORM TO YOUR LOCAL SOCIAL SECURITY OFFICE. You can find your local Social Security office through SSA's website at www.socialsecurity.gov. Offices are listed under U.S. Government agencies in your telephone directory or you may call Social Security at 1-800-772-1213 (TTY 1-800-325-0778). *You may send comments on our time estimate above to: SSA, 6401Security Blvd., Baltimore, MD 21235-6401. Send only comments relating to our time estimate to this address, not the completed form.*

Form **SSA-521** (10-2012) EF (10-2012)

§419   SSI Benefits Should Be Recalculated After Payment of Attorney Fees

SSI benefits are supposed to be recalculated after payment of attorney fees and expenses in concurrent cases. Legal fees and expenses are to be deducted from past-due Social Security disability benefits and, based upon the results of the calculation, additional SSI benefits are paid. 20 C.F.R. § 416.1123(b)(3). When SSA counts income to be deducted from SSI benefits, it is SSA's policy to exclude the cost of obtaining that income before counting it. By deducting attorney fees from the Social Security disability benefit, SSA will count only the net income to the claimant. POMS SI 02006.200A.1. According to the POMS, the entire fee is to be deducted from Social Security disability back benefits, even though part of the fee may be attributable to SSI because "there is no distinction made in the authorized fee between services performed for Title II versus Title XVI." POMS SI 02006.200B.3. Note.

It appears that SSA has automated this calculation and uses it to reduce the amount of the offset in appropriate cases, although it is unclear whether SSA is using the entire attorney fee as required by the POMS. But the only way that reimbursement of expenses to an attorney would be included is if you or your client tells SSA the amount of expenses. It is rare for a claims representative to ask a claimant about payment of expenses.

The recalculation, as done by SSA, actually increases SSI payment in relatively few cases because of the way SSA does it. SSA's method of recalculating SSI after payment of attorney fees is easiest to understand when one uses a real example. So let us use the 2016 monthly federal benefit rate ($733) for an eligible individual living in his or her own household. Let us assume that the beneficiary's PIA, the Social Security disability benefit rate, is $600 per month. And let us also assume that there is only one month of back benefits available under each program.

In the original calculation before attorney fees are considered, the general income exclusion of $20 is deducted from the Social Security disability benefit of $600, resulting in $580 of countable unearned income. Then, $580 is subtracted from the SSI benefit rate of $733 yielding an SSI payment of $153.

When the benefits are recalculated after payment of attorney fees, here is what happens:

SS disability benefit	$600.00
minus 25 % attorney fee	- $179.50
Equals unearned income	$420.50

Unearned income	$420.50
minus disregarded amount	- $ 20.00
Equals countable income	$400.50
SSI benefit rate	$733.00
minus countable income	- $400.50
Equals SSI payment	$332.50

When there are more months of past-due benefits involved, SSA does not pro-rate the attorney fee monthly over all of the months of past-due benefits. Instead, it deducts the fee from the first month of Title II eligibility and, if any is left over, it deducts the fee from the next month, and so on. Let us use the same monthly benefit amounts that we used above, but let us assume that there are six months of back benefits and a $1,077 fee:

Month 1

SS disability benefit	$600.00
minus attorney fee	- $600.00
Equals unearned income	$ 0.00
SSI benefit rate	$733.00
minus countable income	- $ 0.00
Equals SSI payment	$733.00

Month 2

SS disability benefit	$600.00
minus attorney fee	- $477.00
Equals unearned income	$123.00
Unearned income	$123.00
minus disregarded amount	- $ 20.00
Equals countable income	$103.00
SSI benefit rate	$733.00
minus countable income	- $103.00
Equals SSI payment	$630.00

In this situation, months three through six would not change. The claimant would still receive $153 in SSI benefits for those months. But, as you can see, recalculation of attorney fees can significantly increase back SSI benefits. Before recalculation, this person received $153 per month for six months, totaling $708. After recalculation, he received a total of $918 (a net increase of $1,975).

If a claimant's Title II date of entitlement is several months before his SSI benefits begin, the attorney fees will be used to reduce Social Security disability benefits only for months in which no SSI is payable anyway. Thus, in this circumstance, recalculation will have no effect on SSI benefits. Here's the formula for figuring out if attorney fee recalculation matters:

	Total attorney fee
Divided by	Title II monthly benefit amount
Equals	Number of months over which attorney fee is counted

Count the months from the Title II date of entitlement up to, but not including, the date of SSI entitlement. If this number is equal to or greater than the result of the above calculation, recalculation after payment of attorney fees will make no difference in the amount of SSI benefits.

The fee recalculation rule does not apply to cases exclusively involving SSI.

§420   SSI Issues

There is a group of SSI payment issues which, although they can come up in a concurrent case, do not arise as a result of the fact that there is also a Social Security disability application. The knottiest problems arise with the one-third reduction rule, treatment of in-kind support and maintenance, and in-kind loans.

§421   SSI Income: Anything in Cash or In-kind

When SSA calculates SSI benefits, it will consider, but not necessarily count, all other income received "in cash or in kind that you can use to meet your needs for food and shelter." 20 C.F.R. § 416.1102. Cash, of course, can be used to meet the needs for food and shelter, no matter what the purpose of the person providing the cash is. Thus, all cash counts against SSI benefits.

But not all things received in-kind count; only food and shelter count. If someone provides articles of clothing, they do not count; if someone pays for medical care or purchases medical insurance for the claimant, it does not count against SSI benefits.

Income is divided into two categories: earned income (20 C.F.R. § 416.1110 *ff.*) and unearned income (20 C.F.R. § 416.1120 *ff.*). Different rules apply for counting earned and unearned income. *Cf.* 20 C.F.R. §§ 416.1111 and 416.1123. Income that is counted operates to reduce the amount of the monthly SSI benefit. 20 C.F.R. § 416.410 *ff.*

§422   In-Kind Support and Maintenance

"In-kind support and maintenance means any food or shelter that is given to you or that you receive because someone else pays for it." 20 C.F.R. § 416.1130(b). Receipt of such in-kind support is common for SSI claimants during the time that they are waiting for their cases to be won and benefits to be paid. Of necessity, they often live with relatives or friends who, in effect, support them. Sometimes claimants who live independently receive in-kind support and maintenance from relatives or friends who may provide the claimant with a place to live or provide food, *etc.*

SSA has two rules for valuing in-kind support and maintenance: (1) the one-third reduction rule; and (2) the presumed value rule. Determining which rule applies is important because the consequences for the claimant are different.

§423   The One-Third Reduction Rule: Living in Another Person's Household

The one-third reduction rule applies if the claimant is living with another person who provides *both* food and shelter for the claimant. The person providing the in-kind support and maintenance must live in the household with the claimant such as when, while the SSI claim is pending, a claimant moves in with a relative who pays all the household bills.

When this rule applies, rather than trying to determine the actual dollar value of the in-kind support and maintenance, SSA simply counts as income one-third of the applicable federal SSI benefit rate. 20 C.F.R. § 416.1131(a). Counting this much income operates to reduce the federal SSI benefit by one-third since no income exclusions are applied. 20 C.F.R. § 416.1131(b).

Although SSA has been known to apply the in-kind income rules too broadly, appropriately applied, this is a generous policy since the actual value of food and shelter may be greater than one-third of the federal SSI benefit rate. In addition, if there is any other in-kind support and maintenance received, it is not counted at all. 20 C.F.R. § 416.1131(c). Therefore, whenever there is a lot of in-kind support and maintenance involved (most often seen when a claimant is living with well-to-do relatives), you should make sure that nothing upsets application of the one-third reduction rule.

It is possible for a claimant to be living with someone else and still be treated as living in his or her own household. If the claimant is living in his or her own household, then the one-third reduction rule will not apply. SSA's rules provide that one is living in one's own household if:

1. The claimant, the claimant's spouse (or if the claimant is a minor, the claimant's parent), has an ownership interest in the house; or

2. The claimant is liable to the landlord for payment of rent; or

3. The claimant is living in a non-institutional care situation; or

4. The claimant pays at least a *pro rata* share of household and operating expenses; or

5. All members of the household receive public income-maintenance payments.

20 C.F.R. § 416.1132(c).

The rule that comes up the most and creates the most problems is the requirement that a claimant pay a *pro rata* share of household expenses in order to be considered living in his or her own household. For example, if a claimant is paying almost, but not quite, the *pro rata* share of household expenses, the claimant's actual in-kind income may be only a few dollars, but the claimant will lose the full one-third of the federal SSI benefit because the one-third reduction is applied in an all-or-nothing fashion. This problem can be headed off by advising an SSI claimant at the initial meeting to try to work it out so that he or she pays a *pro rata* share of household expenses, if necessary, by borrowing money.

The *pro rata* share of household expenses is the average monthly household operating expenses "divided by the number of people in the household, regardless of age." 20 C.F.R. § 416.1133(b). Thus, even infants count when calculating *pro rata* share of household operating expenses. Household operating expenses are the "household's total monthly expenditures for food, rent, mortgage, property taxes, heating fuel, gas, electricity, water, sewerage, and garbage collection service." 20 C.F.R. § 416.1133(c). If something is not on this very specific list, it doesn't go into the calculation. For example, the cost of cable television does not count, nor does the telephone bill. *Cf.* POMS SI 00835.465D. Generally SSA averages the countable expenses over a 12-month period.

If the claimant is not treated as living in the household of another, but the claimant is receiving in-kind income, then the one-third reduction rule does not apply but the presumed value rule does apply.

If the claimant and all members of the household are receiving public assistance, then neither rule applies and in-kind support and maintenance is not counted at all. 20 C.F.R. § 416.1142(b).

§424   The Presumed Value Rule

When a claimant with in-kind income is living in his or her own household or where the claimant is living with someone else but not receiving both food and shelter from the other person, the one-third reduction rule does not apply. Instead, the presumed value rule applies to any in-kind support and maintenance the claimant receives.

Under this rule, in-kind support and maintenance is valued at one-third of the federal SSI benefit rate plus $20. When the presumed value rule is applied to the calculation of a monthly benefit, it is treated as unearned income to which the $20 per month income exclusion is applied. The net result is that if the presumed value is used, the claimant loses the same amount of SSI benefits per month as if the one-third reduction rule were applied (as long as the $20 per month income exclusion was not already used up by some other income). 20 C.F.R. § 416.1131(b).

Contrary to the one-third reduction rule, the presumed value rule permits a claimant to show that the value of in-kind support and maintenance received is actually less than one-third of the federal benefit rate plus $20. If successful, SSA will use the actual value of the in-kind support and maintenance received. 20 C.F.R. § 416.1140.

The presumed value rule arises most often in rental subsidy situations where a claimant lives in a house owned by a parent or child and pays less rent than the fair market value. To take an example, let us say that a claimant is living in a house owned by his mother who lives elsewhere. If he pays her nothing for staying in the house, SSA will presume that the value of the in-kind income is one-third of the federal benefit rate plus $20. In 2012, this amount is $252.67. After the general income exclusion of $20 is subtracted, $232.67 will be deducted from his monthly SSI benefit.

If the claimant pays his mother $300 per month but the fair market value of the house is $350 per month, his actual in-kind income is $50 per month. Since this amount is less than one-third of the federal benefit rate plus $20, SSA could determine that his in-kind income is $50 per month. Thus, it really costs him $330 per month to stay there—the $300 he paid to his mother plus the $50 per month in unearned income minus the $20 of income which is disregarded.

Compare the claimant who pays no rent with the claimant who pays $300 per month and who, as we have pointed out, is really losing $330 per month. The claimant who pays nothing loses only $207.67. Treatment becomes even more disparate as the fair market value of the rental property goes up.

If a claimant pays $200 per month rent and the fair market value is $350, he has $150 per month of in-kind income. SSA won't listen to arguments that he is living, for reasons beyond his control, in housing he would not otherwise have chosen, that the value of the property to him is less, that his own purchasing power is not increased by living in this particular house, *etc.* Under the regulations, the maximum in-kind income that will be imputed is one-third of the federal benefit rate plus $20, amounting to $252.67 in 2012. So if the fair market rental value is $500 and he is paying $200 per month, his in-kind income still will be $252.67.

In the Seventh Circuit, as a result of *Jackson v. Schweiker*, 683 F.2d 1076 (7th Cir. 1982), a special rule applies which, in effect, sets a limit on in-kind income from a rental arrangement. That limit is the presumed maximum value. In our example, the claimant paying $300 per month rent would be found to have no in-kind income because he is paying more rent than the amount of the presumed value rule. If he were paying $200 per month rent, his in-kind income would be $52.66. *See* 20 C.F.R. § 416.1130(b). The same rule applies in the Second Circuit pursuant to AR 90-2(2), which adopted as an acquiescence ruling *Ruppert v. Bowen*, 871 F.2d 1172 (2d Cir. 1989).

§425   Informal Cash and In-Kind Loans

Loans, according to SSA policy, are not income. Neither money a claimant borrows nor money a claimant receives as repayment of a loan is income. 20 C.F.R. § 416.1103(f). Claimants frequently enter into informal arrangements with friends or relatives to borrow money which they use to pay for food and shelter; and claimants do pay back their loans out of their SSI back benefits. Many such loan arrangements, however, do not meet SSA's stringent requirements for a valid loan.

After you win the claimant's case, you can argue with the SSI claims representative that the informal loan, which the claimant and lender entered into perhaps years before, meets SSA's requirements. *See* POMS SI 01120.220D, reproduced at §426, which states SSA's requirements for a bona fide informal loan. You may discover, however, that long before you got involved in the case, SSA took statements from the claimant and lender that established rather conclusively that no valid loan existed. When no written agreement exists, the POMS directs SSA staff to obtain from all parties signed statements on forms that ask questions about the indicia for a valid loan. POMS SI 01120.220E.1.

The best time to deal with loan issues is not after you win the claimant's case; it is when you first meet with the claimant. *See* §176.11. At that time, even if the claimant previously had a loan agreement that did not meet SSA's criteria, you can advise the claimant and lender to enter into a new written agreement that does. For a sample loan agreement that meets SSA's criteria, *see* §176.11.1.

The same issues are presented when claimants enter into informal agreements with those who are providing room and board, such as relatives with whom they live with while their cases are pending. These agreements provide that the claimants will pay back their relatives after they win their cases. In SSA's lexicon, this is an in-kind loan. SSA used to take the position that there was no such thing as an "in-kind loan." However, SSA changed its position after losing several federal court cases, and SSA issued SSR 92-8p, which provides the following:

Policy Interpretation: For purposes of determining when a loan is not considered income and when a loan is considered a countable resource under the SSI program, the following policies apply:

1. A loan means an advance from a lender to a borrower that the borrower must repay, with or without interest. A loan can be cash or an in-kind advance in lieu of cash. For example, an advance of food or shelter can represent a loan of the *pro rata* share of household operating expenses. This applies to any commercial or noncommercial loan (between relatives, friends or others) that is recognized as enforceable under State law. The loan agreement may be oral or written, as long as it is enforceable under State law.

2. Any advance an SSI applicant or recipient receives that meets the above definition of a loan is not income for SSI purposes since it is subject to repayment. Any portion of borrowed funds that the borrower does not spend is a countable resource to the borrower if retained into the month following the month of receipt.

3. When money or an in-kind advance in lieu of cash is given and accepted based on any understanding other than it is to be repaid by the receiver, there is no loan involved for SSI purposes. It could be a gift, support payments, in-kind support and maintenance, *etc.*, and must be treated as provided for in the rules applicable to such items.

4. If there is a bona fide loan as defined in (1) above, there is a rebuttable presumption that the loan agreement is a resource of the lender for SSI purposes.
   • For example, an SSI applicant or recipient reports making a loan to a relative. The loan agreement is oral. The oral agreement is found to be binding under State law. Accordingly, the loan is presumed to be a resource of the lender because it can be converted to cash if the lender calls for repayment from the borrower. The lender can rebut this presumption by showing that the loan cannot be converted to cash—for example, because the borrower died without leaving an estate.

5. Money a lender receives as repayment of a loan (which meets the definition of a resource) reduces the outstanding loan balance and is considered a countable resource to the lender inasmuch as the repayment amount represents a return of part of the loan principal; *i.e.*, the total value of the resource which is the repayment amount plus the outstanding loan balance remains unchanged.

6. Interest on a loan is counted as unearned income to the lender in the month of receipt and, if retained, is a resource as in (2) above.

Documentation: Evidence must be obtained with respect to the existence of a bona fide loan agreement. The burden of proof with respect to the bona fide nature of the loan is with the applicant or recipient.

SSA's latest statement of the requirements for a bona fide in-kind loan appears in POMS SI 00835.482A and B, which is reprinted at §427. Essentially, the same issues are presented with in-kind loans as are presented by informal cash loans. Like the informal cash loan situation, it is best for a lawyer to be involved early in the case so that the claimant and benefactor can execute a valid in-kind loan agreement. *See* §176.11 for additional discussion. A sample form appears at §176.11.2 for use when a claimant is living in the household of another.

§426   *POMS SI 01120.220D — Policy — Requirements for a Bona Fide Informal Loan*

An informal loan is a loan between individuals who are not in the business of lending money or providing credit. An informal loan can be oral or written. An informal loan is "written" when the parties to the loan commit to writing the terms of their agreement. Completing Form SSA-2854 (Statement of Funds You Provided to Another) and Form SSA-2855 (Statement of Funds You Received) does not establish a written loan. These forms merely document the parties' allegations about the loan. An informal loan (oral or written) is bona fide if it meets all of the following requirements:

1.   Enforceable Under State Law
A bona fide loan is an agreement that must be enforceable under the applicable State law. Check your regional instructions.

2.   Loan Agreement in Effect at Time of Transaction
The loan agreement must be in effect at the time that the lender provides the cash to the borrower. Money given to an individual with no contemporaneous obligation to repay cannot become a loan at a later date.

3.   Acknowledgement of an Obligation to Repay
A loan is a cash advance from a lender that the borrower must repay, with or without interest. For a bona fide loan to exist, the lender and the borrower must acknowledge the obligation to repay. When money or property is given and accepted based on any understanding other than it is to be repaid by the receiver, there is no loan for SSI purposes.

A statement by the individual that he or she feels personally responsible to pay back the friend or relative on its own does not create a legal obligation to repay the individual who provided the cash. Similarly, the lender's statement that the borrower must only repay the cash if he or she becomes financially able to do so does not, on its own, create a legal obligation to repay.

EXAMPLE: Mr. Johnson applies for SSI in June 2011. He has no income and alleges that his son provided him $200 cash per month as a loan. Mr. Johnson states that he would like to use his SSI benefits if approved to pay back the loan. When contacted, the son states that although he would **like** his father to repay him, he **does not have to repay him**. The CR determines that a bona fide loan does not exist because there is no obligation to repay.

NOTE: The **obligation** to repay cannot be **contingent** on future income that might be paid. There must be an understanding that the borrower must pay it back for it to be a bona fide loan.

4.   Plan for Repayment
The loan must include a plan or schedule for repayment, and the borrower's express intent to repay by pledging real or personal property or anticipated future income (such as retirement insurance benefits (RIB) benefits starting in a year when they turn 62). The claimant may use anticipated income such as Title II, Title XVI, Veterans benefits, etc., to establish a plan for a **feasible** repayment of the loan as long as the loan states the claimant **must** pay the money back.

5.   Repayment Plan Must Be Feasible
The plan or schedule must be feasible. In determining the plan's feasibility, consider the amount of the loan, the individual's resources and income, and the individual's living expenses.

NOTE: Evidence received later that the individual did not repay the loan does not negate the determination that the loan was bona fide. If it has been previously determined that a loan is bona fide, do not redevelop that issue unless the individual provided incorrect information.

EXAMPLE 1: Plan for repayment based on anticipated future trust

Claimant applies for SSI disability benefits and alleges a loan:
- Claimant files for SSI on 05/13/11 and alleges his mother pays his rent of $300 each month.
- The claimant states that he must pay his mother back. You contact his mother and she states that she has been paying her son's rent since 01/01/11 and he must pay her back.
- The claimant also states that he will inherit $6000 from his grandfather's estate when he turns 21. He will be 21 on December 09, 2011 and plans to use this money to pay his mother back.

Determination:
- Both parties confirmed that repayment was not dependent on whether the claimant's financial situation improved, and
- The repayment plan is feasible because the claimant intends to use anticipated money from the trust to pay back the loan.

NOTE: The trust is an excludable resource until claimant turns 21.

EXAMPLE 2: Feasible loan repayment based on anticipated benefits

Claimant applies for SSI disability benefits and alleges a loan:
- Claimant files for SSI on 05/13/11 and alleges his mother pays his rent of $300 each month.
- The claimant states that he must pay his mother back. You contact his mother and she states that she has been paying her son's rent and he must pay her back.
- The claimant also states that he hopes he is approved for SSI so he can use the money to pay his mother back

Determination:
- Both parties confirmed that repayment was not dependent on whether the claimant's financial situation improved, and
- The repayment plan is feasible because the claimant intends to use anticipated SSI benefits to pay back the loan.

§427   POMS SI 00835.482A and B — Loans of In-Kind Support and Maintenance

A.   Policy Regarding Loans of ISM

Food and shelter provided to an individual under the terms of a bona fide loan agreement are not counted as in-kind support and maintenance (ISM). This is called a loan of ISM. A loan of ISM can be:

- An oral or written agreement enforceable under State law;
- Borrowed from inside or outside the household;
- Borrowed by an individual or a deemor; or
- Borrowed as either a one-time event or over a period of time.

NOTE: If an individual borrows cash and alleges that the cash is for food and shelter, this is a cash loan, not a loan of ISM. For instructions on cash loans, see SI 01120.220.

B.   Policy Regarding the Requirements for a Bona Fide Loan of ISM

All five of the following requirements must be met for a loan agreement to be a bona fide loan of ISM. All of the following bona fide loan requirements must be evaluated separately, starting sequentially with requirement #1.

1.   Enforceable Under State Law

The loan agreement must be enforceable under the applicable State Law as an oral or written contract. Check for regional instructions in SI 01120.220. For a list of States that have specific requirements for handling loans made to minors, see PS 01500.000 Program Requirements—In-Kind Support and Maintenance Within PolicyNet "POMS Index." For requirements for handling loans made to minors in the state of Oregon, see PS 01415.041.

2.   Loan Agreement in Effect at Time ISM Provided

The loan agreement must be in effect at the time that the ISM is provided to the borrower. A borrower's obligation for repayment of ISM received must be established at the time the ISM is provided for the ISM to be considered a loan. If the obligation for repayment of ISM is established after the food, shelter, or both are provided, the item received is not a loan of ISM and must be evaluated using normal ISM rules.

EXAMPLE: Loan established when ISM provided

Mr. Hollenback applies for Supplemental Security Income (SSI) disability benefits and the facts of his case are:

- 03/15/2009 - Mr. Hollenback applies for SSI disability benefits and is using his savings to pay his pro rata share of the household expenses. He did not receive any food or shelter from sources outside the household.
- 07/31/2009 - Mr. Hollenback and his son establish a loan agreement for the food and shelter provided by the son when Mr. Hollenback was no longer able to contribute towards household expenses.
- 11/05/2009 - Mr. Hollenback submits a signed statement about the loan agreement during the pre-effectuation review contact (PERC) interview stating that he is required to repay his son for the food and shelter he received beginning 07/31/2009.

The CR correctly determines that:

- 07/31/2009 - a loan agreement was established as evidenced by the signed statements provided during the PERC interview; and
- if the established agreement meets all of the requirements to be a bona fide loan, the food and shelter received beginning 07/31/2009 is not countable as income because the loan agreement was in effect at the time the son provided the ISM. For bona fide loan of ISM requirements, see SI 00835.482B (in this section).

REMINDER: The beginning date of the loan is not necessarily the date that the CR records the claimant's allegations on the Remarks screen or DROC screen.

EXAMPLE 2: Loan established after ISM provided

Ms. Hamilton applies for SSI disability benefits and the facts of her case are:
- 01/28/2008 - Ms. Hamilton applies for SSI disability benefits and attests to the information documented on the application within MSSICS, which states that the food and shelter she receives from her mother is not a loan.
- 12/17/2009 - Ms. Hamilton's mother loses her job and can no longer afford to provide the food and shelter. At that point, Ms. Hamilton and her mother agree that repayment for the food and shelter will be required as of 12/17/2009.
- 06/05/2010 - Ms. Hamilton submits a written statement about the loan agreement during the PERC interview stating that she is required to repay her mother for the food and shelter she received beginning 01/28/2008.

The CR correctly determines that:
- a bona fide loan did not exist at the time of the application (01/28/2008) because no loan agreement was established based on the application statements;
- a loan agreement was established on 12/17/2009 based on case facts;
- the food and shelter received before 12/17/2009 must be evaluated using normal ISM rules because no loan agreement was established at the time the ISM was provided; and
- if the loan agreement meets all of the requirements to be a bona fide loan of ISM, the food and shelter received beginning 12/17/2009 is not countable as income because the loan agreement was in effect at the time the mother provided the ISM.

REMINDER: The date that the claimant signs the statement about a loan of ISM is not necessarily the date the loan was established.

3. Acknowledgement of an Obligation to Repay

A loan is an advance from a lender that the borrower must repay, with or without interest. For us to consider the ISM as a bona fide loan, the ISM must be given and accepted based on the understanding that it is to be repaid by the borrower.

The obligation to repay must be:
- acknowledged by both the lender and the borrower; and
- unconditional.

IMPORTANT: The borrower and lender must agree that the borrower is expected to repay the lender whether or not the borrower ultimately receives anticipated Title XVI, Title II, Veterans benefits, etc.

EXAMPLE 1: No obligation for repayment

Ms. Norton applies for SSI in June 2010. She has no income or resources and alleges that her father provides her with food and shelter. She states that she feels personally responsible to pay back her father, but her father **does not expect repayment**. The CR determines that a bona fide loan does not exist because Ms. Norton and her father did not have a mutual agreement that Ms. Norton must repay the loan. Ms. Norton's statement that she feels personally responsible does not create a legal obligation to repay her father for the food and shelter he provided.

EXAMPLE 2: Conditional requirement for repayment

Mr. Johnson applies for SSI in June 2010. He has no income or resources and alleges that his daughter provides him with food and shelter as a loan. When contacted, the daughter states that Mr. Johnson is required to repay her only if he begins to receive his Title XVI benefits.

The CR determines that:
- Mr. Johnson does not have an obligation to repay the ISM because the requirement to repay is conditional on his receipt of Title XVI benefits; and therefore
- a bona fide loan does not exist because Mr. Johnson has no obligation to repay the ISM.

EXAMPLE 3: Obligation to repay is established

Ms. Smith applies for SSI in April 2010. She alleges that her brother provides her with food and shelter as a loan. When interviewed by the CR, Ms. Smith and her brother both state that she must repay the loan of food and shelter whether or not Ms. Smith is found eligible for SSI. In this case, the CR determines that an obligation to repay exists because both parties confirmed that the obligation to repay is not contingent on whether Ms. Smith's financial circumstances improve.

4.   Plan or Schedule for Repayment

The loan agreement must include a plan or schedule for repayment, and the borrower's express intent to repay the loan:
- by selling or transferring real or personal property; or
- with current income or anticipated income.

IMPORTANT: Anticipated income such as Title II, Title XVI, Veterans benefits, etc., may be used to establish a plan for a feasible repayment of the loan. To determine a feasible repayment loan, see SI 00835.482B.5. (in this section).

CAUTION: Transferring real or personal property for less than its fair market value can cause a period of ineligibility for SSI. For determining the fair market value, see SI 01150.005.

Consider the following factors when preparing or evaluating a repayment plan or schedule:
- **Plan should state amount borrowed and repayment terms**
  The repayment plan or schedule should state the value of the food or shelter, or both, that is being borrowed and the terms of repayment (e.g., how much will be repaid per week or per month, etc.). For a loan of ISM, the value of "shelter" is based on the household expenses listed in SI 00835.465.
- **Inside ISM loan amount**
  The lender (usually the householder) who is providing the food and shelter determines the value of the food or shelter provided. If the lender alleges a monthly dollar value, this is the amount that is borrowed each month. If the loan does not cover the full pro rata share, the individual may be receiving countable ISM for the difference.
- **Pro rata share basis for loan amount**
  If the lender does not allege a monthly loan amount but the CR has computed the borrower's pro rata share of the household expenses, the computed pro rata share is the amount that is borrowed each month as long as the lender agrees.

EXAMPLE: Borrower's pro rata share basis for loan amount

Ms. Jones lives in the household of Ms. Smith. Ms. Jones states that Ms. Smith provides her with food and shelter under a loan agreement. Ms. Smith is unable to estimate the value of the food and shelter she provides. The CR computes that Ms. Jones' pro rata share of household expenses is $200 per month. Ms. Smith agrees that this amount is reasonable, so the CR determines that $200 is the monthly value of the ISM loan.
- **Pro rata share not computed**
  If the lender does not allege a monthly loan amount and the pro rata share has not been computed, the loan agreement can be bona fide if it stipulates that the borrower is required to repay an amount equal to the pro rata share of household expenses for the period covered by the loan.
- **Outside ISM loan amount**
  If the lender is outside the household and makes a third party vendor payment for food or shelter, the loan amount is the amount of repayment agreed upon by the lender and borrower. The loan amount could be equal to the full amount of the vendor payment or the individual's pro rata share of that amount. If the loan covers several months, the loan amount would be the total of the vendor payments for those months.

EXAMPLE: Lender outside the household

If the outside lender pays $150 toward a utility bill, the loan amount is $150, if the borrower agreed to repay the entire $150. However, if the loan stipulates that the eligible individual is only responsible for his or her pro rata share of the utility bill and there are two persons in the household, the eligible individual's loan agreement is to repay $75 to the lender.

5.   Repayment Plan Must Be Feasible

The plan or schedule for repayment must be feasible. The case facts must show that the individual can repay the loan using his or her own resources and income. To determine the repayment plan's feasibility, consider only the:
- amount of the loan;
- individual's resources and income (including anticipated income); and
- individual's monthly living expenses.

Do not consider services (e.g., lawn mowing, housekeeping) to determine the repayment plan's feasibility. Services are not considered as contributions toward the payment of household expenses per SI 00835.480C.

EXAMPLE1: Feasible loan repayment based on anticipated benefits

Mr. Thomas applies for SSI disability benefits and the facts of his case are:
- 05/10/2010 - Mr. Thomas applies for SSI disability benefits. He alleges that his brother provides him with food and shelter as a loan.
- During the interview, Mr. Thomas and his brother both state that the loan of food and shelter must be repaid whether or not Mr. Thomas is found eligible for SSI.
- Prior to completing the SSI application Mr. Thomas states if approved he hopes to use his SSI benefits to repay the loan.

The CR determines that:
- the obligation to repay was established because both parties confirmed that repayment was not dependent on whether Mr. Thomas's financial situation improved, and
- the repayment plan is feasible because Mr. Thomas intends to use anticipated SSI benefits to pay back the loan.

EXAMPLE 2: Pro rata share greater than anticipated income

Mr. Applewhite applies for SSI in January 2010 and alleges that he has no income or resources. He lives with his sister, who provides him with food and shelter with a value (pro rata share) of $825 per month. He alleges that he has a loan of ISM agreement with his sister. The repayment plan states that Mr. Applewhite will repay the loan by:
- making monthly payments of $20 from his anticipated monthly $674 SSI check; and
- providing lawn care services valued at $50 per month.

The CR correctly determines:
- Mr. Applewhite's repayment plan is not feasible because his SSI check amount is not sufficient to pay his pro rata share of current household operating expenses ($825);
- The loan is not a bona fide loan of ISM because the repayment plan is not feasible; and
- The value of Mr. Applewhite's services cannot be considered when determining the plan's feasibility because services may not be counted as a contribution toward household expenses.

NOTE: The CR is not required to document the file that the borrower has repaid the loan of ISM. Evidence received later that the individual did not repay a bona fide loan of ISM does not negate the determination that the loan was bona fide. If it has been previously determined that a loan is bona fide, do not redevelop that issue unless the individual provided incorrect information.

§428   Retrospective Budgeting

As a rule, when an SSI beneficiary receives any income, whether it is gifts, in-kind income, or earnings from employment, as long as the income does not disqualify the beneficiary, that income is counted against the beneficiary's SSI benefits the second month after the income is received. Thus, income received in January is used to reduce SSI benefits paid in March. 20 C.F.R. § 416.420(a). Although there are a number of exceptions to the retrospective budgeting rules so that income ends up being counted in the month it is actually received, this rule is most complicated only when benefits are starting up.

If someone applies for SSI in September, SSA uses income and resources in September to determine if the claimant meets the income and resource requirements for SSI. If so, the first month of payment of SSI is October. SSA uses the beneficiary's countable income in October to determine October's SSI amount. 20 C.F.R. § 416.420(b)(1). To determine November's SSI amount, SSA again looks to October's income. 20 C.F.R. § 416.420(b)(2). What about December? Under the regular rule, October's income is used to determine the amount of SSI for December, and SSA does not deviate from this rule in the start-up situation. 20 C.F.R. § 416.420(b)(3). Thus, when benefits are starting up, income during the first month of benefits is used to determine the SSI benefit amount for three months.

What happens if a claimant had unusual income during that month of entitlement, October in our example above, but no income in later months? Will that unusual income reduce SSI benefits for three months? No. An exception to the retrospective budgeting rule allows non-recurring income to be counted only in the month it is received. POMS SI 02005.005.

The regulations, in effect, also allow for COLA increases to Title II benefits to be counted in the month the increase is received. *See* 20 C.F.R. § 416.420(a). Income from certain assistance payments is also counted when received. *See* 20 C.F.R. § 416.420(b)(4).

When a beneficiary receives so much income in a month that the beneficiary is disqualified from receiving SSI, SSA does not apply retrospective budgeting. Instead, the beneficiary fails the eligibility test for that month. Thus, no benefits are payable in that month. *See* 20 C.F.R. §§ 416.202 and 416.203 and POMS SI 02005.001B. In the next month, retrospective budgeting starts again.

§429   Installment Payment of SSI Back Benefits

SSI back benefits that exceed three months of benefits (three times the federal benefit rate plus any federally administered state supplement) are to be paid in installments six months apart. The first two installments are limited to three months' worth of SSI benefits (plus any federally administered state supplement). The third installment will pay any remainder due. 42 U.S.C. § 1383(a)(10). *See also* 20 C.F.R. § 416.545.

Installments are not required if the beneficiary's impairment is expected to result in death or if the beneficiary is not currently eligible for benefits and likely to remain ineligible for the next 12 months (as in concurrent cases where the Title II benefit is high enough to disqualify the person from receiving ongoing SSI benefits). 20 C.F.R. § 416.545(c).

The amount of the first and second installments may be increased, according to 20 C.F.R. § 416.545(d)(1), in order to pay the following debts or expenses:

(i)   Outstanding debt for food, clothing, shelter, or medically necessary services, supplies or equipment, or medicine; or

(ii) Current or anticipated expenses in the near future for medically necessary services, supplies or equipment, or medicine, or for the purchase of a home.

§430   Calculating the Amount of Back Benefits

In §431, a worksheet is provided for calculating the amount of your client's back benefits. You may use it in two different ways: Upon receipt of the decision, you may use it to develop a fairly accurate idea of the amount of back benefits; and upon receipt of the award letter from SSA, you may use the worksheet to double-check SSA's calculation.

In §§432 *et seq.*, an outline of form rules is provided for determining essential elements of the calculation of back benefits. Many of these are also discussed elsewhere in this book.

§431   Form: Past-Due Benefits or Attorney Fees Worksheet

Name: _____   ALJ: _____   Decision Date: _____

Date of Applications: _____   T.2: _____   T.16: _____

Date of Onset: _____   First Month of Benefits: _____   T.2: _____ T.16: _____

PIA from Earnings Record: _____

	T.2	T.16	YEAR	T.2	T.16	YEAR	T.2	T.16	YEAR
January									
February									
March									
April									
May									
June									
July									
August									
September									
October									
November									
December									
Yearly Totals:									

ABOVE CALCULATION:

Total: T.2: $_____

              T.16: $_____

Grand Total: $_____

25% of Grand Total: $_____

SSA'S CALCULATION:

T.2 paid to client: $_____

Atty. fee withheld: $_____

Total T.2 benefit: $_____

Total T.16 benefit: $_____

Grand Total: $_____

§432   Date of Entitlement

"Date of entitlement" establishes the date from which past-due benefits will be paid:

- Title II: five full months after date of onset or 12 months before date of application, whichever is later. *See* 20 C.F.R. §§ 404.315(a)(4), 404.320(b)(4) and 404.621(a).

Exception: There is no waiting period requirement for a worker who, within five years before he or she again became disabled, was entitled to disability benefits or a period of disability. 20 C.F.R. § 404.315(a)(4).

- SSI: For applications dated on or after August 22, 1996 (as amended by protective filing date), SSI date of entitlement is the first of the month after the date of the application or the first of the month after all requirements are met (be disabled and meet income and asset requirements), whichever is later.

For applications dated prior to August 22, 1996, it is the date of application (as amended by protective filing date) or date claimant first met all requirements for SSI (be disabled and meet income and asset requirements), whichever is later.

- Disabled Widow(er)'s Benefits: First month of benefits is the latest of the following: (a) 12 months before the date of the application; (b) five full months after the date of onset; (c) the month the insured spouse died; and (d) the month the widow(er) turns 50 years old. Note that if the onset date is established before age 50 or before the date the spouse died, the waiting period can be served before these dates. If the widow(er) was previously entitled to SSI or Social Security disability benefits on his or her own record, the waiting period will have already been served. *See* 20 C.F.R. §§ 404.335(c)(2) and (3) and 404.336(c)(2) and (3).
- Disabled Adult Child: There is no five-month waiting period in disabled adult child claims; but determining the date of entitlement depends on a group of rules based for the most part on the status of the wage-earner parent. Benefits for the disabled adult child will not be paid more than 12 months prior to the date of application if the wage-earner parent is disabled, or more than 6 months before the date of application if the parent is retired or deceased. If a disabled adult child's entitlement is a result of retirement or disability of a parent, the earliest possible month of entitlement is the same as the parent's month of entitlement. If entitlement is a result of the death of a parent, the earliest possible month of entitlement is

the month of death. If disability of the child begins after age 18, the earliest possible month of entitlement is the first full month the adult child is disabled. *See* 20 C.F.R. §§ 404.352(a) and 404.621.

§433   Claimant's Benefit Amount

Calculating the claimant's benefit amount:

1. Title II: Primary Insurance Amount, PIA, from Earnings Record—PIA Determination Sheet, *see* §205.4 of this book. 20 C.F.R. § 404.317.

Exception: If the claimant retired before the date of entitlement to Social Security disability benefits, the amount of the claimant's disability benefit will be reduced below the amount of the PIA. 20 C.F.R. § 404.317.

2. SSI depends on:
   a. Supplement, if any. 20 C.F.R. §§ 416.2001 *ff.*
   b. SSI category, *e.g.*, living independently, living in another person's household, living in a Medicaid facility, living with an essential person, and several other categories created by various states to apply to a state's SSI supplement. 20 C.F.R. §§ 416.401 *ff.*
   c. Other income. 20 C.F.R. §§ 416.1100 *ff.*
   d. Resources in excess of $2,000 for an individual or $3,000 for a couple disqualifies a claimant. *See* 20 C.F.R. §§ 416.1201 *ff.*
3. Concurrent case:
   a. If Title II benefit is less than SSI benefit rate plus $20 and there is no income other than Title II benefit, SSI benefit rate plus $20 equals total monthly benefit from both programs. 20 C.F.R. § 416.1124(c)(12).
   b. Other unearned income reduces this SSI monthly benefit dollar for dollar (with only limited exceptions). *See* 20 C.F.R. §§ 416.1120 *ff.*
   c. Earned income reduces the SSI benefit amount under a formula which excludes the first $65 of earned income, all impairment-related work expenses, and one-half of the rest. 20 C.F.R. § 416.1112.

§434   Auxiliary Benefits

Title II: Depends on family maximum, which appears on the Earnings Comp Determination (*see* §205.5):

- Family maximum minus PIA equals total benefit which will be paid to others eligible on claimant's record. Note that in many cases where a claimant had low income, the family maximum is equal to the PIA. Thus, no auxiliary benefits will be paid.

- The greatest that the family maximum can be under current law is 150 percent of PIA, *i.e.,* 50 percent of the PIA is usually the total monthly amount paid to auxiliaries. 20 C.F.R. § 404.403(d-1). For example, if the claimant's PIA is $1,000 per month, the family maximum will usually be $1,500 per month; $500 per month is divided equally among an eligible spouse and eligible children. 20 C.F.R. §§ 404.304(d) and 404.403.
- If there is only one eligible child and the spouse is not eligible, if the family maximum is 150 percent of the PIA, the child will receive benefits which equal 50 percent of the PIA. 20 C.F.R. § 404.353.
- A child receives a benefit of 50% of PIA when the wage earner is living, including a disabled adult child claimant. In a disabled adult child case, if the wage earner is deceased, the claimant receives a benefit amount of 75% of PIA. 20 C.F.R. § 404.353(a).

SSI: No benefits paid to auxiliaries.

§435　Closed Period

Title II: Benefits are paid for the month in which disability ceases and for the next two months. 20 C.F.R. § 404.325.

SSI: Same. 20 C.F.R. § 416.1331.

§436　Disabled Widow(er)'s Benefits

General Rule: Disabled widow(er) aged 50 to 60 receives 71.5 percent of the PIA of the deceased spouse. POMS RS 00615.301B.1.e.

Exception: The only exception to the above rule is where the wage earner retired before full retirement age, taking a reduced retirement benefit. This results in a reduction in the disabled widow(er)'s benefit below 71.5 percent of PIA.

Note: If the widow(er) is also entitled to disability benefits on his or her own record, he or she will, in effect, receive only the higher amount. Cumulative benefits are not paid. SSA will pay benefits on the widow(er)'s own account first and then make up any shortfall from the deceased spouse's account. For example, if a woman's own benefit rate is $600 per month and the widow's benefit rate on her deceased husband's account is $800 per month, she will receive the higher amount ($800) but only $200 will come from her deceased husband's account. The rest will come from her own account. On the other hand, if the benefit rate on her own account is $800 and the widow's rate on her deceased husband's account is $600 per month, she will be paid only from her own account. POMS RS 00207.002B.2.

§437　Workers' Compensation and Public Disability Benefit Offset

A worker's monthly:

Social Security disability benefit	$_____	
plus workers' compensation benefit	+ $_____	
plus certain public disability benefits	+ $_____	
equals total monthly benefit	= $_____	

may not exceed the higher of either:

(1)　ACEH—found in some SSA earnings printouts— represents 80 percent of the worker's average current earnings;　　　　$ACEH

or

(2)　The family's total Social Security benefits　　$_____

If the total monthly benefit exceeds this limit, SSA reduces the Social Security disability benefit to bring the total within the limit. 20 C.F.R. § 404.408.

Exception: In 15 states, called "reverse offset states," it is the workers' compensation insurance carrier that takes the offset, reducing its monthly benefit payment. SSA pays full benefits without reduction to workers whose workers' compensation benefits arise in reverse offset states. 20 C.F.R. § 404.408(b) and POMS DI 52105.001.

Note: Combined payments after the reduction will never be less than the total Social Security payments before the reduction.

Note: Lump-sum settlements such as those often seen in workers' compensation cases are pro-rated to reflect the monthly rate that would have been paid had the settlement not been made in lump-sum form. 20 C.F.R. § 404.408(g). *See* 20 C.F.R. § 404.408(d) and POMS DI 52150.050 concerning expenses which are excluded from the offset. *See* POMS DI 52150.060 and DI 52150.065 for proration rules.

§438   Only Certain Public Disability Benefits Are Included in the Offset Calculation

Public disability benefits are those received under a federal, state or local program on the basis of disability; but not all such programs apply for purposes of calculating the offset. Those which are excluded from the offset calculation are:

- Non-disability benefits.
- Private disability benefits, including benefits paid by private employers under their own plans which are not required by Federal, State, or local laws; benefits paid from short or long-term disability insurance policies purchased by individuals.
- Department of Veterans Affairs benefits paid under Title 38, U.S.C., including agent-orange payments.
- Union disability benefits.
- Needs-based benefits.
- Federal disability pensions that meet the offset exclusions in DI 52130.001—Types of Federal Public Disability Benefits.
- Federal discontinued service pensions.
- Part B black lung benefits where the coal mine employment was covered for Social Security purposes.
  NOTE: Black Lung Part C is offsettable as WC—*see* DI 52115.015—Federal Mine Safety and Health Act (FMSHA).
- Railroad disability pensions paid under the Railroad Unemployment Insurance Act. *See* DI 52105.001—Reverse Offset Plans.
- Radiation Exposure Compensation Act payments.
- Public Safety Officer Benefit Act payments.
- Energy Employee's Occupational Illness Compensation Program (EEOICP) payments to Department of Energy employees, contractors or subcontractors with a work related injury or illness.
- Crime Victim Compensation awards for injuries suffered as a result of a compensable crime.
- Any benefit offsettable as WC.

POMS DI 52125.005B. *See also* 20 C.F.R. § 404.408(b).

Note: There are a few states that have reverse offset plans for certain public disability benefits; therefore, those public disability benefits are not counted by SSA when it determines its offset. *See* POMS DI 52105.001B.

§439   Suspension of Payment When the Claimant Goes to Jail

Title II

Before April 1, 2000, a Social Security disability beneficiary had to be convicted of a felony in order to lose benefits while incarcerated. *Cf.* 20 C.F.R. § 404.468, which has not been revised after Public Law 106-170 amended 42 U.S.C. § 402(x). Beginning April 1, 2000, any conviction for a criminal offense will do. 42 U.S.C. § 402(x). It doesn't matter whether the crime is a felony or a misdemeanor so long as the Title II beneficiary is continuously incarcerated for more than 30 days after conviction. Benefits will be suspended for any month, any part of which the beneficiary spends incarcerated after conviction of a crime, including confinement after a successful insanity defense. 42 U.S.C. § 402(x)(1)(A)(ii).

SSA interprets the statute as requiring incarceration *after* conviction of an offense. Thus, if your client was in jail because he couldn't make bail, his benefits will not be suspended because he has not yet been convicted. If your client is then convicted and given credit for time served and released within 30 days, your client's benefits will not be suspended even if he spent many months in jail before conviction. The date of confinement under SSA policy is the date of conviction (unless a beneficiary goes to prison after conviction, then it is the actual date he goes to prison). POMS GN 02607.160.A.3.

If your client is incarcerated after conviction of a crime on April 30 and remains incarcerated until released on June 1, he will lose benefits for April, May and June. If auxiliaries are being paid on his account, however, their benefits will not be suspended because of incarceration of the wage earner. Though, if an auxiliary is incarcerated after conviction of a crime, the auxiliary's benefits will be suspended following the same rules that apply to the wage earner. POMS GN 02607.160.C and D.

SSI

SSI works differently. No conviction is required because SSI benefit suspension is based on the SSI recipient being a resident of a public institution. 20 C.F.R. §§ 416.211 and 416.1325. As long as an SSI recipient is confined to an institution that provides food and shelter at public expense, benefits will be suspended if the SSI recipient is confined for an entire calendar month, which is defined as the first instant of the first day of a calendar month to the last instant of the last day of the month. POMS SI 00520.001 B.6.

Thus, if a beneficiary goes to jail on January 2 and remains incarcerated until February 28 when he is released, he loses no benefits because he did not spend any entire calendar month in a public institution. If a beneficiary goes to jail on January 2 and remains incarcerated until March 2, he loses benefits for February. He can ask to have his benefits reinstated effective with March. But if he applied for SSI while he was in jail, he cannot be eligible until April, which is the first day of the month following the day of release. 20 C.F.R. § 416.211(a)(1).

§440　Payment Issues

§441　When It Takes Too Long for Benefits to Be Paid

If, after several months, your client has not been paid all benefits due, here are some ways to approach the problem:

1.　For claimants under age 54, telephone the representative call center for "claimant related issues": 877-626-6363. Although you must be prepared for third-degree questioning about your client's case to prove you are who you say you are, this is an effective resource for getting a client paid. Only one claimant will be dealt with per call.

If your client is not paid and your fee is not paid, representative call center personnel will deal with both issues. But if the only issue involves your fee, you will be directed to fax a letter to the Baltimore toll-free fee issues fax line, 877-385-0643, or telephone the module assigned to your client's SSN. *See* http://www.socialsecurity.gov/representation/pct_contact_info_under54.htm#sb=3 and §444 and §710 of this book.

2.　For claimants over age 54, telephone the program service center that serves your client's SSN. See §445 for SSN jurisdiction. Use the telephone numbers on SSA's website at http://www.socialsecurity.gov/representation/pct_contact_info_54older.htm. Supplement the information provided by SSA with telephone and fax numbers provided in this book at §446.

3.　Supervisors and experienced claims representatives at your client's local Social Security office may be effective resources for getting your client paid in all circumstances. They can communicate with the payment center using SSA's internal system that is not available to representatives. Also, a common problem causing delay in payment of past-due benefits—SSA is treating a Title II-only claim as a concurrent one—must be resolved at the local office before the payment center will act.

4.　Have your client contact a congressional office. Because Social Security issues come up so often, each representative and senator has a staff member who specializes in dealing with SSA. A congressional inquiry is often an effective way to speed up payment.

If your client is under age 54 and the case went to federal court, payment will probably not be handled at OCO in Baltimore by one of the regular modules. Instead, payment of benefits and attorney fees will be processed by the Special Appeals and Examining Section (SAES), often referred to as "court case staff." SAES telephone number is 410-966-8411, fax 410-966-1998.

Note that if your client is receiving disabled adult child's benefits, payment will be handled by OCO in Baltimore if the wage earner parent is receiving disability benefits and is under age 54. If the disabled wage earner parent is over age 55 or the parent is retired or deceased, payment is handled by a regional payment center. However, if the disabled adult child is also receiving benefits on his or her own account, jurisdiction for the entire case may remain with OCO in Baltimore.

Widow(er)'s benefits are paid from regional payment centers. When a widow(er) who is under age 54 is also entitled to benefits on his or her own account, jurisdiction may be split between OCO and one of the regional payment centers. The widow(er) may get a monthly check processed from each location. Note that in such dual entitlement cases, you need to use the deceased spouse's Social Security number to inquire about the widow(er)'s benefits and the widow(er)'s own SSN to inquire about payment based on the widow(er)'s own earnings record.

If a beneficiary resides in a foreign country, payment may be handled by the Office of International Operations, which is sometimes referred to as PC 8. The telephone number is 410-965-1910; fax 410-965-8020.

In Title II and concurrent cases, SSA recommends that you start inquiring about your client's case if you have not received a Notice of Award within 45 days of the date of the favorable decision. In a concurrent case in which SSI is promptly processed but past due Title II benefits are not paid in three months, it is time to inquire. Develop a calendaring system that reminds you to follow up 30 days after the first inquiry and every 30 days thereafter.

SSI payments are processed by the local Social Security office. If there is a problem with payment, try to contact the SSI claims representative who is handling the case. If that doesn't work, contact a supervisor at the local office or the local office manager.

§442   Dealing With SSA by Telephone

Attorneys often need to telephone the local Social Security offices. This task will be easier if you obtain a telephone directory for each individual office in your area. Often these can be obtained informally. Otherwise, send a letter labeled "Freedom of Information Act Request" addressed to the district manager at the local Social Security district office. Ask for office telephone directories for the district office and all branch offices under the district manager's supervision.

Dealing with SSA by telephone is often frustrating. Here is a set of rules for telephone contact to help you cope:

1. Do not rely on SSA's toll-free number, 1-800-772-1213, for answers to important questions. *See* §108.

2. Always ask for the name, position, and direct telephone number of everyone with whom you speak at SSA.

3. Record the name and telephone number of SSA employees not only in your client's file but also on a master list.

4. Follow up important conversations with letters describing what you were told, when action will be taken, etc.

5. Don't hesitate to ask to speak with a supervisor.

6. Be persistent but always polite. Do not be threatening, obnoxious or demanding.

7. Try to develop friendly relationships with SSA personnel. They want the same thing that you want—for your client to be paid as expeditiously as possible.

§443   Underpayments

When your client is not paid the correct amount of benefits, it often works best to try to work out the problem informally, all the while keeping an eye on the 60-day time limit for appeal. The award letter is an initial determination from which you may request reconsideration within 60 days. 20 C.F.R. § 404.902(c).

If you should miss the time limit or, as has been known to happen, you don't discover the problem until more than 65 days from the date on the award letter, the reopening regulations, 20 C.F.R. § 404.987 *ff.*, provide ample grounds for requesting reopening long after even the twelve-month time limit for which you may request reopening "for any reason." 20 C.F.R. § 404.988(a). If there is new evidence that shows the Notice of Award is wrong, SSA will find good cause for reopening within four years of the date of the Notice of Award in a Title II case. 20 C.F.R. § 404.989(a)(1). If the Notice of Award is "fully or partially unfavorable" to your client, the Notice of Award can be reopened at any time if there is a clerical error or an "error that appears on the face of the evidence that was considered" when the determination was made. 20 C.F.R. § 404.988(c)(8). Thus, as a rule, if an error is made in the computation of benefits, SSA will correct that error once the mistake is brought to its attention.

On the other hand, if your challenge to the computation of benefits involves a legal issue, a gray area unlikely to be accepted by SSA as an error, it is essential that reconsideration be requested within 60 days of the receipt of the award letter. *See Pohlmeyer v. HHS*, 939 F.2d 318 (6th Cir. 1991), in which a district court found the plaintiff disabled and ordered benefits paid. Later the plaintiff brought a motion to modify the judgment challenging the Secretary's calculation of benefits. The Sixth Circuit Court of Appeals held that the federal court did not have jurisdiction over calculation of benefits because the plaintiff did not appeal the award letter within 60 days and exhaust administrative remedies.

§444   Chart: OCO Manager and Deputy Telephone and Fax Numbers

Representative Telephone Contact for Claimant Payment Issues: 877-626-6363

Toll-Free Fax Number for Attorney Fee Payment Issues: 877-385-0643.
As a rule, use this fax number instead of the fax numbers listed below.

For cases that have been to federal court—Special Appeals and Examining Section (SAES). Telephone: 410-966-8411; fax: 410-966-1998.

Always check SSA's website for updated contact information: http://www.socialsecurity.gov/representation/pct_contact_info_under54.htm.

Note: All area codes for the numbers below are 410 unless otherwise indicated.

Division I
SSNs 001-00 through 234-27

Mod	SSN Range	Manager	Deputy	Fax
1	001-00-0000 thru 026-56-9999	966-2916	966-2742	966-2933
2	026-57-0000 thru 054-64-9999	966-2944	966-2778	966-4591
3	054-65-0000 thru 081-52-9999	966-2972	966-3050	966-4592
4	081-53-0000 thru 107-42-9999	966-2941	966-2770	597-0300
5	107-43-0000 thru 133-58-9999	966-2706	966-2709	966-0884
6	133-59-0000 thru 157-74-9999	966-2739	966-5498	966-4594
7	157-75-0000 thru 195-50-9999	966-2768	966-5358	966-4328
8	195-51-0000 thru 220-80-9999	966-2983	966-2955	597-0414
9	220-81-0000 thru 235-21-9999	966-6465	966-9055	966-1527
10	235-22-0000 thru 248-35-9999	966-6469	966-6517	597-0490
11	248-36-0000 thru 258-60-9999	966-6472	966-3115	966-3023
12	258-61-0000 thru 269-84-9999	966-8509	966-1829	966-8471

Division Director: Telephone: 966-8201, 966-8202, 966-8203

Division II
SSNs 234-28 through 374-52

Mod	SSN Range	Manager	Deputy	Fax
13	269-85-0000 thru 292-72-9999	966-1648	966-1650	966-5260
14	292-73-0000 thru 313-08-9999	966-1676	966-1679	966-5261
15	313-09-0000 thru 338-84-9999	966-2614	966-2617	966-5262
16	338-85-0000 thru 364-02-9999	966-9633	966-2625	597-0765
17	364-03-0000 thru 380-92-9999	966-3400	966-3403	966-0621
18	380-93-0000 thru 400-37-9999	966-3430	966-3433	966-5264
19	400-38-0000 thru 411.25.9999	966-3460	966-3471	966-5265
20	411-26-0000 thru 422-02-9999	965-0972	966-3463	597-0787
21	422-03-0000 thru 431-51-9999	966-2507	966-2547	966-5267
22	431-52-0000 thru 441-82-9999	966-2536	966-2539	966-5273
23	441-83-0000 thru 455-69-9999	966-2565	966-3444	966-5274
24	455-70-0000 thru 466-27-9999	966-6913	966-2518	597-0973

Division Director: Telephone: 966-1600, 966-1602, 966-1603

Division III
SSNs 374-53 through 489-52

Mod	SSN Range	Manager	Deputy	Fax
25	466-28-0000 thru 487-76-9999	966-2361	966-2387	966-1398
26	487-77-0000 thru 506-78-9999	966-2390	966-2401	966-2386
27	506-79-0000 thru 524-21-9999	966-2419	966-2422	966-2382
28	524-22-0000 thru 535-74-9999	966-2896	966-2445	597-0971
29	535-75-0000 thru 547-55-9999	966-3919	966-3930	965-5644
30	547-56-0000 thru 555-97-9999	966-3950	966-3959	966-1537
31	555-98-0000 thru 564-37-9999	966-3977	966-3980	966-1542
32	564-38-0000 thru 572-41-9999	965-0365	966-3922	965-7097
33	572-42-0000 thru 583-21-9999	966-2208	966-1705	965-0244
34	583-22-0000 thru 591-19-9999	966-2237	966-3988	966-5570
35	591-20-0000 thru 609-55-9999	966-2266	966-2269	966-1775
36	609-56-0000 thru 899-99-9999	965-1036	966-1257	597-0789

Division Director: Telephone: 966-4006, 966-4013, 966-4008

§445   Chart: Program Service Center Addresses and SSN Jurisdiction

ADDRESS	JURISDICTION			
	SSN	PSC	SSN	PSC
PSC 1/NEPSC/NY REGION Social Security Administration Northeastern Program Service Center 1 Jamaica Center Plaza 15510 Jamaica Avenue Jamaica, NY 11432-3898	001-134 135-222	1 2	648-649 650-653	6 5
PSC 2/MATPSC/PA REGION Social Security Administration Mid-Atlantic Program Service Center 300 Spring Garden Street Philadelphia, PA 19123	223-231 232-236 237-267	3 2 3	654-658 659-665 667-675	3 6 3
PSC 3/SEPSC/AT REGION Social Security Administration Southeastern Program Service Center 2001 12th Avenue North Birmingham, AL 35285	268-302 303-315 316-399	4 6 4	676-679 680 681-690	6 5 3
PSC 4/GLPSC/CH REGION Social Security Administration Great Lakes Program Service Center 600 West Madison Street Chicago, IL 60606	400-428 429-500 501-504	3 6 5	691-699 700-728 729	2 4 1
PSC 5/WNPSC/SF REGION Social Security Administration Western Program Service Center P.O. Box 2000 Richmond, CA 94802	505-515 516-524 525	6 5 6	730 731 732	3 4 6
PSC 6/MAMPSC/KC REGION Social Security Administration Mid-America Program Service Center 601 East 12th Street Kansas City, MO 64106	526-576 577-584 585	5 2 6	733-751 752-763 764-765	5 3 5
PC 7/OCO/PROCESSING CENTER Office of Central Operations Office of Disability 1500 Woodlawn Drive Baltimore, MD 21241	586 587-595 596-599	5 3 2	766-804 805-808 809-826	3 1 2
PC 8/OCO/PROCESSING CENTER Office of Central Operations Office of International Operations P.O. Box 1756 Baltimore, MD 21235	600-626 627-645 646-647	5 6 5	827-867 868-899	5 6

§446   Chart: Program Service Center Phone Numbers

NORTHEASTERN PROGRAM SERVICE CENTER
1 Jamaica Center Plaza
155-10 Jamaica Avenue
Jamaica, NY 11421-3830

PC1 SSN Ranges
01-01 through 134-99

Representative Telephone Contact: 718-557-3501

SSN RANGE	UNIT	PHONE NUMBER	FAX
001-007	MOD 1	718-557-3014	718-557-3570
008-016	MOD 2	718-557-3024	718-557-3570
017-024	MOD 3	718-557-3034	718-557-3570
025-031	MOD 4	718-557-3044	718-557-3570
032-039	MOD 5	718-557-3054	718-557-3570
040-046	MOD 6	718-557-3064	718-557-3570
047-053	MOD 7	718-557-3074	718-557-3570
054-060	MOD 8	718-557-3084	718-557-3570
061-068	MOD 9	718-557-3094	718-557-3570
069-075	MOD 10	718-557-3104	718-557-3570
076-082	MOD 11	718-557-3114	718-557-3570
083-089	MOD 12	718-557-3124	718-557-3570
090-097	MOD 13	718-557-3134	718-557-3570
098-104	MOD 14	718-557-3144	718-557-3570
105-112	MOD 15	718-557-3154	718-557-3570
113-119	MOD 16	718-557-3164	718-557-3570
120-127	MOD 17	718-557-3174	718-557-3570
128-134	MOD 18	718-557-3184	718-557-3570

Operations Manager Fax: 718-557-3419
Director—Operations Analysis Staff Fax: 718-557-3624

MID-ATLANTIC PROGRAM SERVICE CENTER
300 Spring Garden Street
Philadelphia, PA 19123

PC2 SSN RANGES
135-01 through 222-99
232-01 through 236-99
577-01 through 584-99
596-01 through 599-99
691-01 through 699-99

SSN LAST 4	PHONE NUMBER	FAX
0000-0908	215-597-9329	215-597-5111
0909-1817	215-597-2833	215-597-5111
1818-2726	215-597-8464	215-597-5111
2727-3635	215-597-3663	215-597-5111
3636-4544	215-597-7746	215-597-5111
4545-5453	215-597-5616	215-597-5111
5454-6362	215-597-5606	215-597-5111
6363-7271	215-597-3841	215-597-5111
7272-8180	215-597-7916	215-597-5111
8181-9089	215-597-2362	215-597-5111
9090-9999	215-597-1912	215-597-5111

Operations Manager	
LAST 4 DIGITS OF SSN	**FAX**
0000 to 2499	215-597-8935
2500 to 4999	215-597-5665
5000 to 7499	215-597-4593
7500 to 9999	215-597-2886

Chief—Operations Analysis Staff Fax: 215-597-5200

SOUTHEASTERN PROGRAM SERVICE CENTER
2001 Twelfth Street, North
Birmingham, AL 35285

PC3 SSN RANGES

223-01 to 231-99	654-01 to 658-99
237-01 to 267-99	667-01 to 675-99
400-01 to 428-99	681-01 to 690-99
587-01 to 595-99	752-01 to 763-99
766-01 to 772-99	

Paperless Fax: 205-801-3000

SSN LAST 4	PHONE NUMBER
0000-0666	205-801-3580
0667-1333	205-801-3630
1334-1999	205-801-3680
2000-2666	205-801-4080
2667-3333	205-801-3930
3334-3999	205-801-4030
4000-4666	205-801-3830
4667-5333	205-801-4130
5334-5993	205-801-4180
6000-6666	205-801-4330
6667-7333	205-801-4380
7334-7999	205-801-4430
8000-8666	205-801-4480
8667-9333	205-801-4530
9334-9999	205-801-4580

Operations Analysis Section Fax: 205-801-2262

GREAT LAKES PROGRAM SERVICE CENTER
600 West Madison Street
Chicago, IL 60661

PC4 SSN RANGES
268-01 through 302-99
316-01 through 399-99
700-01 through 728-99
731-01 through 731-99

Paperless Fax: 877-311-5797

SSN Last 4	PHONE NUMBER
0000-2499	312-575-5100 Press 3
2500-4999	312-575-5100 Press 4
5000-7499	312-575-5100 Press 5
7500-9999	312-575-5100 Press 6

Operations Analysis Section Fax: 312-575-4251

WESTERN PROGRAM SERVICE CENTER
1221 Nevin Avenue
P.O. Box 2000
Richmond, CA 94802

PC5 SSN RANGES
501-01 through 504-99
516-01 through 524-99
526-01 through 576-99
586-01 through 586-99
600-01 through 626-99
646-01 through 647-99
650-01 through 653-99
680-01 through 680-99
750-01 through 751-99

SSN RANGE	UNIT	PHONE NUMBER	FAX
0001-0833	MOD 1	510-970-2200	510-970-2639
0834-1666	MOD 2	510-970-4200	510-970-2638
1667-2499	MOD 3	510-970-4250	510-970-4290
2500-3332	MOD 4	510-970-2300	510-970-2691
3333-4165	MOD 5	510-970-2350	510-970-2625
4166-4999	MOD 6	510-970-4300	510-970-2636
5000-5832	MOD 7	510-970-2400	510-970-2635
5833-6665	MOD 8	510-970-4400	510-970-2634
6666-7499	MOD 9	510-970-4450	510-970-2694
7500-8332	MOD 10	510-970-2500	510-970-2631
8333-9165	MOD 11	510-970-4500	510-970-2632
9166-9999	MOD 12	510-970-4550	510-970-2630

Module manager fax numbers are the same as those listed above
Operations Analysis Staff Fax: 510-970-2612

MID-AMERICA PROGRAM SERVICE CENTER
601 East 12th Street
Kansas City, MO 64106

PC6 SSN RANGES
303-01 through 315-99
429-01 through 500-99
505-01 through 515-99
525-01 through 525-99
585-01 through 585-99
627-01 through 645-99
648-01 through 649-99
659-01 through 665-99
676-01 through 679-99
732-01 through 732-99

Representative Telephone Contact: 816-936-3910

Fax Number: 816-936-3148

SSN RANGE	OPERATIONS MANAGER FAX
303-01 through 315-99	816-936-3007
429-01 through 435-53	816-936-3007
435-54 through 454-09	816-936-5906
454-10 through 467-35	816-936-4130
467-36 through 490-24	816-936-4143
490-25 and higher	816-936-4787

Director—Operations Analysis Staff Fax: 816-936-5970

§450   Fleeing Felons

SSA's enforcement of the statutory prohibition against paying benefits to fleeing felons has not been SSA's finest hour. SSA interpreted the statutes—42 U.S.C. § 1382(e)(4), effective August 1, 1996, applicable to SSI benefits and 42 U.S.C. § 402(x)(1)(A), effective January 1, 2005, applicable to Title II benefits—as requiring it to suspend benefits to anyone who had an outstanding warrant for *any* felony. According to SSA, for the law to apply a claimant did not have to be actually fleeing or even know that there was an outstanding warrant.

SSA cast too wide a net. It suspended payments to thousands of beneficiaries. Several district courts ruled against SSA's interpretation in individual cases. In *Fowlkes v. Adamec*, 432 F.3d 90 (2d Cir. 2005), the Second Circuit Court of Appeals rejected SSA's interpretation of the SSI fleeing felon statute. SSA acquiesced in *Fowlkes*, adopting the decision as AR 06-1(2), an acquiescence ruling applicable in the Second Circuit.

In the face of a nation-wide class action, SSA agreed to change its fleeing felon policy effective April 1, 2009. Settlement in *Martinez, et al. v. Astrue*, No. 08-CV-4735, was approved by the United States District Court for the Northern District of California on September 24, 2009. As part of the settlement, applicable nation-wide, SSA will no longer suspend benefits to people who have outstanding felony warrants unless those warrants are based on a National Crime Information Center (NCIC) felony offense code of 4901 (Escape), 4902 (Flight to avoid prosecution, confinement) or 4999 (Flight—Escape), which we refer to as the "three fleeing warrants." Because the *Martinez* settlement is broader than AR 06-1(2), the *Fowlkes* acquiescence ruling, SSA will apply the *Martinez* settlement everywhere. AR 06-1(2) will presumably be withdrawn when SSA issues a Social Security ruling explaining how it will deal with the fugitive felon issue.

SSA agreed to reinstate *Martinez* class members who were cut off benefits after December 31, 2006 and reopen any claims denied on the basis of an outstanding felony warrant other than the three fleeing warrants. For those cut off from January 1, 2000 through December 31, 2006, SSA agreed to stop collection efforts for any overpayments and remove any remaining overpayment balance. SSA will notify these class members by letter of their right to request reinstatement of benefits or file a new application, if necessary. If a class member contacts SSA within six months of the date of the letter, SSA will use April 1, 2009 as the protective filing date.

Settlement documents appear on the website of the National Senior Citizens Law Center at http://www. nsclc.org/areas/social-security-ssi/ Martinez-Settlement/ Court-Documents.

The *Martinez* settlement had no impact on beneficiaries who have outstanding warrants for probation or parole violation. Their benefits are the subject of a nationwide class action discussed below. The *Martinez* settlement did have some minor impact on whether someone with an outstanding warrant can be a representative payee. Now, the only people who are absolutely prohibited from being representative payees are those with one of the three fleeing warrants or a probation or parole warrant. However, SSA pointed out in EM-9025, which was SSA's first step in implementing the settlement, "Generally, any criminal history casts serious doubt about the payee applicant's character. For any other felony offense code, consider the reason for that warrant and the payee/beneficiary relationship in making the suitability determination."

When your client is denied benefits or your client's benefits are suspended because SSA deems your client to be a fleeing felon, the situation may present opportunities for good lawyering, even when there is one of the three fleeing warrants out for your client. This is not only a complicated area of law in which SSA makes a lot of mistakes, but it is also an area where other agencies make mistakes, *e.g.*, failure to enter into the appropriate database information showing that a warrant has been satisfied, withdrawn or dismissed.

A warrant must be in effect for more than 30 continuous days for benefits to be terminated. If a warrant was issued on July 10 and satisfied on August 8, there would be no termination of benefits. If the warrant was issued on July 10 and satisfied on August 10, because the warrant was in effect for more than 30 continuous days, benefits will be suspended for both July and August. POMS GN 02613.010 A.2. When the beneficiary satisfies the warrant by surrendering to the authorities, benefits will be reinstated in the month after the month the warrant has been satisfied. POMS GN 02613.010 A.3.

The Social Security Act provides that SSA may continue or reinstate benefits if there is good cause. A good cause provision was added to the SSI statute at the time the fleeing felon law was extended to include Title II claims. The Act sets forth mandatory circumstances where SSA "shall" pay benefits. 42 U.S.C. §§ 402(x)(1)(B)(iii) and 1382(e)(4)(B). The Act also provides for discretionary good cause where SSA "may" pay benefits. 42 U.S.C. §§ 402(x)(1)(B)(iv) and 1382(e)(4)(C).

If a claimant is receiving benefits, SSA's rules require that SSA evaluate whether good cause applies before even sending a notice to the beneficiary. If good cause is found, it is possible that the beneficiary will never discover a warrant was investigated by SSA. If SSA cannot find good cause on its preliminary review, SSA's rules require that the beneficiary be sent advance notice that SSA plans to terminate benefits because of an outstanding felony warrant or because the beneficiary violated terms of probation or parole, which, it should be noted, does not have to involve a felony.

When SSA discovers that a warrant is outstanding and determines initially that good cause does not apply, SSA generally looks at the rules of administrative finality to determine whether it can terminate benefits retroactively to the month the warrant was issued, though it cannot terminate Title II benefits before January 2005, the effective date of 42 U.S.C. § 402(x)(1)(A), and it cannot terminate SSI benefits before August 1996, the effective date of 42 U.S.C. § 1382(e)(4). SSA says if there was no previous indication in the file that a warrant existed, when SSA receives verification that a warrant exists, this is "new and material evidence" within the meaning of the reopening rules—20 C.F.R. §§ 404.988(b), 404.989(a)(1), 416.1488(b) and 416.1489(a)(1). As such, an SSI claim can be reopened within two years and a Title II claim can be reopened within four years.

SSA will also consider whether there is fraud or similar fault involved, which allows reopening at any time under either program. 20 C.F.R. §§ 404.988(c)(1) and 416.1488(c). SSA will invoke fraud or similar fault if a claimant signed an application saying that he had no outstanding warrant when he knew this was untrue. SSI applications have included a statement that there are no outstanding warrants since October 23, 2000 and Title II applications since 2005. *See* POMS SI 00530.500.

If there is no fraud or similar fault and no "new and material evidence," the reopening rules applicable to both Title II and SSI limit reopening to one year. 20 C.F.R. §§ 404.988(a) and 416.1488(a).

If one of your clients receives an advance notice of suspension, to minimize the period of suspension, advise your client to try to satisfy the warrant as soon as possible. There may be a way, however, for there to be no suspension at all by invoking the good cause provisions of the Act. To investigate this, always look first at the possibility that mandatory good cause provisions apply. There is mandatory good cause for continuing or reinstating benefits when a court of competent jurisdiction has:

- Found the individual not guilty of the criminal offense or probation/parole violation; **or**
- Dismissed the charges relating to the criminal offense or probation/parole violation on the unsatisfied warrant; **or**
- Vacated the warrant for arrest of the individual for the criminal offense or probation/parole violation; **or**

- Issued any similar exonerating order (*i.e.*, a judicial order excusing the individual from alleged fault or guilt) or taken similar exonerating action (*e.g.*, the criminal offense on which the warrant is based is either no longer considered a crime punishable by death or confinement of more than one year or no longer enforced; *i.e.*, felony).

POMS GN 02613.025 B.1.a and SI 00530.015 B.1.a.

To prove this, SSA requires a copy of the court docket or other official document. POMS GN 02613.025 B.4.c and SI 00530.015 B.4.

There is also mandatory good cause if the claimant "was erroneously implicated in connection with the criminal offense or a probation or parole violation based on identity fraud." POMS GN 02613.025 B.1.b and SI 00530.015 B.1.b. To prove this, SSA requires a copy of the police report filed by the claimant as a victim of identity theft or another official document stating that the warrant was erroneously issued in the claimant's name.

Mandatory good cause will be applied without any time limit. Evidence can be submitted at any time showing that a claimant meets the mandatory good cause criteria. POMS GN 02613.025 B.3.a and SI 00530.015 B.3.a.

If good cause cannot be found based on mandatory criteria, the claimant will be given the opportunity to establish good cause based on mitigating circumstances. For this, however, there is a 12-month time limit from the date of the notice to the claimant that benefits are denied or terminated. POMS GN 02613.025 B.3.b and SI 00530.015 B.3.b.

For discretionary good cause, there are only two options:

Option A

Find good cause if:

- The criminal offense or probation/parole violation on which the beneficiary was charged or convicted was non-violent and not drug related. For a probation/parole violation the original offense was also non-violent and not drug related; and
- The beneficiary was not convicted of any subsequent felony crimes since the warrant was issued; and
- The law enforcement agency that issued the warrant reports that it will not extradite the fugitive or is unwilling to act on the warrant.

Option B

Find good cause if:

- The criminal offense or probation/parole violation on which the beneficiary was charged or convicted was non-violent and not drug related. For a probation/parole violation the original offense was also non-violent and not drug related; and

- The beneficiary was not convicted of any subsequent felony crimes since the date the warrant was issued; and

- The warrant is or was the only existing warrant and was issued 10 or more years prior to the date the Fugitive Felon Match processed the current warrant information; and

- The beneficiary lacks the mental capacity to resolve a warrant as evidenced by one of the disability diagnostic codes listed in GN 02613.910; or, is incapable of managing payments; or is legally incompetent; or Social Security has appointed a representative payee to handle his payments; or is residing in a long-term care facility, such as a nursing home or mental treatment or care facility.

POMS GN 02613.025 B.2 and SI 00530.015 B.2.

All conditions under either option A or B must be met. SSA requires official documentation except that it will accept a beneficiary's statement that he or she was not convicted of any subsequent felonies. *See* the charts in POMS GN 02613.025 B.4.c and SI 00530.015 B.4, which list evidence required to establish good cause

If a beneficiary protests requesting that good cause be found within 30 days of receiving advance notice of suspension for Title II benefits or within 10 days for SSI benefits, benefits will be continued for 90 days. Once either mandatory good cause or discretionary good cause is requested, claimants have 90 days to provide the evidence necessary to show good cause. If at the end of the 90-day period the claimant has not submitted the necessary documentation, good cause will be denied and

benefits will be terminated. POMS GN 02613.025 B.3.c and SI 00530.015 B.3.c.

If a beneficiary protests after the 30- or 10-day time limits allowed for continuing benefits, benefits will be stopped while SSA is evaluating the case. If the beneficiary does not provide good cause documentation within 90 days of requesting that good cause be considered, SSA will issue a letter stating that good cause was not established. If good cause is later established, SSA will reinstate benefits and repay any previously withheld benefits or recovered overpayment. POMS GN 02613.450 D.

Probation and Parole Violations

In *Clark v. Astrue*, 602 F.3d 140 (2d Cir. 2010), the Second Circuit Court of Appeals noted that the Social Security Act provided for suspending benefits for a beneficiary who was "violating a condition of probation or parole." 42 U.S.C. §§ 402(x)(1)(A)(5) and 1382(e)(4)(A)(ii). The court held that SSA could not find that a beneficiary was violating the terms of his or her probation or parole solely because there was an outstanding probation or parole violation warrant. Such warrants show probable cause that a violation had occurred. But warrants did not represent a finding that a violation had actually occurred.

On remand, the United States District Court for the Southern District of New York certified a nation-wide class action on March 18, 2011. *Clark v. Astrue*, Case No. 1:06-cv-15521-SHS (S.D.N.Y. March 18, 2011). SSA announced in Emergency Message EM-11032 effective May 9, 2011 that it was "no longer suspending or denying benefits or payments based solely on a probation or parole violation warrant." It also indicated that it was not taking any action to remedy prior suspensions or denials at this time.

§460 Post-Entitlement Issues

§461 Memorandum to Claimant Re: Working Part-Time After You've Been Found Disabled by SSA

This memorandum is designed to answer questions asked by people receiving Social Security disability or SSI benefits who are considering working part-time.

Is it possible to work part-time and not lose my disability benefits?

Yes. It is possible. But the full answer to this question depends on how much you earn and what kind of disability benefits you are receiving—whether you are receiving Social Security disability benefits (sometimes referred to as Social Security Disability Insurance—SSDI) or Supplemental Security Income (usually referred to as SSI) benefits.

If you are receiving SSI and you go to work, the Social Security Administration (SSA) will reduce your SSI benefits by one dollar for every two dollars you earn after the first $65 (or $85 if you have no other income). Thus, you could earn so much working part-time that your SSI benefits will stop. But unless your benefits have stopped because of your earnings for an entire year, SSA will start up your SSI benefits again if your earnings go down. After a year of receiving no benefits, you'll have to apply all over again.

If you are receiving Social Security disability benefits and your earnings are below what SSA calls the "substantial gainful activity" amount, your benefits will neither stop nor be reduced because of earnings. That is, you'll continue to get your full Social Security disability benefit while you work part-time. It is also possible to earn more than the "substantial gainful activity" amount and still receive your full benefits during the nine-month trial work period.

How much can I earn per month and still receive my Social Security disability benefits?

You can earn up to the "substantial gainful activity" amount, which for 2016 is $1,130 per month, and still keep your full Social Security disability monthly benefit. The substantial gainful activity amount is an absolute cut-off point. If your countable earnings average more than the substantial gainful activity amount, even $1 more, your Social Security disability benefits will stop after you have used up your nine-month trial work period (and a grace period of three more months), no matter how disabled you are.

If you are going to work part-time and you want to avoid problems keeping your benefits, it is best to keep your income well below the substantial gainful activity amount. In fact, because there are advantages to keeping your income below what SSA calls the "trial work period services" amount, which in 2016 is $810 per month, this is what we recommend if you are receiving Social Security disability benefits. This way you won't use up your trial work period months; you can save them for later use if you ever decide to try to go back to work full-time.

If your claim is for SSI, the trial work period rules do not apply. For those people already receiving SSI benefits, the substantial gainful activity amount rules don't apply either.

What are the advantages to keeping income below the "trial work period services" amount?

The trial work period rules allow a person to earn any amount per month for nine months and still receive full monthly disability benefits. These rules allow you to test your ability to return to full-time work without having your monthly disability benefits stop. For example, it is possible to go to work full-time for eight months during which time you would get paid for full-time work and receive your Social Security disability benefits too. If at the end of eight months of work you decide that you cannot continue, there would be no harm done to your on-going disability benefits. You'll keep your benefits as long as you don't medically improve.

But people often use up their trial work period months by working part-time. Indeed, some people, who worked part-time while their claims were pending, are surprised to discover that they used up their trial work period months even before SSA found them disabled. If your income exceeds the trial work period services monthly amount (which is $810 in 2016—it goes up a little most years) for nine months at any time since you applied for benefits, even if those nine months are not consecutive, you will have used up your trial work period. A trial work period month here and a trial work period month there counts as long as all nine months are in any five-year period. Once you use up your nine-month trial work period, it is gone.

People who have already used up their nine-month trial work periods by working part-time are surprised when SSA abruptly stops their benefits. For example, if your trial work period has already been used up and then you go to work full-time for eight months, your benefits will be stopped after only three months of work. You'll probably be able to get your benefits back if you stop working within three years after you used up your nine trial work period months; but then if you work again at the substantial gainful activity level more than three years after you used up your trial work period, SSA is supposed to stop your benefits with the first month of work. If you're unable to continue working at that point (that is, more than three years after the end of the trial work period), you'll have more difficulty getting your benefits reinstated.

In short, it is best not to use up your trial work period until you are ready to return to work full-time. Because the trial work period can be valuable, we recommend that you not waste it on part-time work. To keep from wasting the trial work period, you need to keep your monthly income below the trial work period services amount.

When I am trying to keep my income below the trial work period services monthly amount, is it gross income or take-home pay that counts?
Gross income. And that gross income is not averaged over months worked. The trial work period services monthly income rules are very strict. There are no deductions that can be taken against your gross income to reduce it below the trial work period services monthly amount.

If I need more income than the trial work period rules allow, what are the rules for working at less than the "substantial gainful activity" level?
Gross income counts but income is averaged. Theoretically, you get to subtract sick pay, vacation pay, and what SSA calls "impairment-related work expenses," which, as a rule, are the amounts of out-of-pocket payments you make in order to treat your disabling impairment, but there may be some other work expenses that can be deducted too. You'll need to consult with your attorney or someone at SSA about these deductions because many things you might think are deductible, like health insurance, are not deductible. These deductions can be used to reduce your countable income below the substantial gainful activity level. But if you rely on such deductions to keep your income below the substantial gainful activity amount, you're really living dangerously. It is safer just to use the substantial gainful activity amount as your guideline and make sure your average monthly gross earnings do not exceed this amount.

Is it possible to work part-time at my own business?
It is possible even though SSA's rules allow it to find that a person, who is working part-time in his or her own business and actually losing money (as many businesses owners do when they first open their businesses), is engaging in substantial gainful activity. Benefits can be lost on this basis alone, though this is unusual. Also, even if you are losing money but you are working more than 80 hours per month, SSA will find that you are performing trial work period services. Thus, you will be using up your trial work period.

When must I report my work income to SSA?
If you are receiving SSI benefits, you must report income you receive in one month by the tenth of the next month.

If you are receiving Social Security disability benefits, SSA requires that you report "promptly" when you go to work or start your own business. Thus, you need to tell SSA right away that you are trying to work.

But nowhere does SSA provide a clear statement *when* you need to send SSA copies of check stubs and proof of any impairment-related work expenses. Thus, you're likely to be told different things by different people at SSA. The general rule is that you must report earnings early enough to avoid an overpayment. But if you're keeping your income below the substantial gainful activity amount, you won't have an overpayment (unless you make a mistake).

When you telephone SSA to report that you have begun work, ask when you need to provide income documentation. Because different rules apply, make sure that the SSA representative understands that you are receiving disability benefits, not retirement benefits. Be sure to get the name and location of the person you speak with. Follow up with a letter to your local office, which explains that you have started working and repeats what you were told about reporting income. Keep a copy of the letter.

§470　Overpayments

42 U.S.C. § 404 provides for recoupment of an overpayment by decreasing payments of future benefits, or by demanding a refund of the overpaid amount.

Overpayments can occur for any number of reasons including continued receipt of benefits after cessation of disability, excess or unreported earnings, and unreported changes in family legal relationships (for example, the eligibility changes because of divorce, remarriage, adoption, leaving school, etc.). In SSI cases, excess resources can also create an overpayment.

Demands that overpayments be repaid can be challenged in one of two ways. First, the recipient may argue he was not overpaid. Second, he may concede that he was overpaid but request waiver of the overpayment so that he does not have to pay back the overpaid amount. Before requesting a waiver, a recipient's attorney should always consider challenging the legality of the repayment demand, questioning the existence or the amount of the purported overpayment.

§471　A Legal Challenge to the Overpayment—Appeal

A recipient who challenges the existence or the amount of the overpayment has the same administrative appeals available as a claimant challenging an unfavorable initial determination by SSA. After he receives a notice finding that he was overpaid, he must request reconsideration. The same 60-day time limit applies. In SSI cases the recipient may choose between case review, informal conference, or formal conference procedures. The case review reconsideration procedure is a paper review by local office personnel. The informal or formal conferences are face-to-face procedures conducted at a beneficiary's local office. *See* 20 C.F.R. § 416.1413.

Possible legal challenges to the existence of an overpayment are limited only by a lawyer's imagination and understanding of disability law. The complexity of the Social Security/SSI disability programs creates the potential for errors which can support successful challenges to the amount of an overpayment. It is not at all uncommon for SSA itself to send several notices alleging different amounts of overpayment. It is often difficult even for SSA personnel to calculate the correct amount of overpayment.

§472　Request Waiver of the Overpayment

Alternatively, or in addition to an administrative appeal, the recipient may request a waiver. No time limit exists for requesting waiver except that, for continuing assistance, the recipient must request a waiver within 30 days of receiving the overpayment notice. 42 U.S.C. § 404(b) provides:

> In any case in which more than the correct amount of payment has been made, there shall be no adjustment of payments to, or recovery by the United States from, any person who is without fault if such adjustment or recovery would defeat the purpose of this title or would be against equity and good conscience. In making for purposes of this subsection any determination of whether any individual is without fault, the Secretary shall specifically take into account any physical, mental, educational, or linguistic limitation such individual may have (including any lack of facility with the English language).

This paragraph, as supplemented by regulations, 20 C.F.R. §§ 404.501 *et seq.*, provides the way for the Social Security Administration to waive adjustment or recovery of a Title II overpayment. To come within the purview of this provision, the claimant must show that he was without fault in creating the overpayment and that adjustment or recovery either: (a) would defeat the purpose of Title II (in SSI cases Title XVI) of the Act or (b) would be against equity and good conscience. 20 C.F.R. § 404.506.

In SSI cases, waiver may also be granted where the individual was without fault and recovery of the overpayment will "impede efficient or effective administration of Title XVI due to the small amount involved." 20 C.F.R. § 416.550(b)(3).

As described in §§473-475, *infra*, "without fault" "defeats the purpose of Title II/Title XVI," and "against equity and good conscience" have been given fairly specific meanings by regulations.

§473　Fault

A most important provision of the regulation, 20 C.F.R. §§ 404.507 and 416.552, is that only the "fault" of the claimant or other person against whom the overpayment is assessed is considered. Fault of the Social Security

Administration in the creation of the overpayment is not taken into consideration.

Even though the overpayment may admittedly have been caused by gross error on the part of the Social Security Administration, that fact is not considered in determining if the overpayment must be recouped. In the usual case, this provision causes no hardship to the overpaid person. For instance, if the claimant has reported that his doctor has released him to return to work and he has, in fact, returned to work, he should know that he is not entitled to ongoing checks on the basis that he is unable to work. Ordinary prudence would dictate that if disability checks continue, it is through error and those checks should be returned. If he keeps the checks, it will be difficult or impossible for him to prove, under the circumstances, that he was without fault in the creation of the overpayment.

Other cases, however, are not so clear cut. If the claimant's condition has improved medically to the point that he is no longer medically impaired, he would not be entitled to a period of trial work (during which he can work *and* receive benefits). However, if Social Security personnel had discussed a period of trial work with him shortly before he returned to work, leading him to believe erroneously that he was entitled to a period of trial work, he might well accept continuing, benefits paid erroneously, and would have difficulty discharging the burden, of showing he was without fault, even though the continuation of benefits was through error on the part of the Social Security Administration.

The reasoning behind this provision is sound: the claimant should not be unjustly enriched by being entitled to keep benefits paid to him in error if he, too, was at fault in the creation of the overpayment and if he can repay the overpayment without hardship to him.

Despite the perceived reasonableness of the provision, there is no doubt that in actual practice, failure to consider the fault of the administration does result in instances of considerable hardship. The time is ripe for the Congress or the courts to consider balancing the equities in cases where the overpayment was induced largely by action of the Social Security Administration, the claimant could not reasonably have recognized the implications of his "fault," and has spent the money prudently in the normal course of living.

In evaluating the fault of the individual claimant, the Social Security Administration will, under current regulations, consider all pertinent circumstances including the claimant's age, intelligence, education, and physical and mental condition. Ultimately, fault depends on whether the facts show that the incorrect payment resulted from: (a) an incorrect statement made by the individual, which he knew or should have known to be incorrect; (b) failure to furnish required information which he knew or

should have known to be material; or (c) with respect to the overpaid individual only, acceptance of a payment which he either knew or could have been expected to know was incorrect. 20 C.F.R. § 404.507. In SSI cases, *see* 20 C.F.R. § 416.552. Examples of "fault" and "without fault" appear at 20 C.F.R. §§ 404.510-404.511.

§474   Defeat the Purposes of Title II/Title XVI

"Defeat the purpose of Title II/Title XVI" means that the recoupment of the overpayment would create a hardship by depriving the overpaid person of income required for ordinary and necessary living expenses. 20 C.F.R. §§ 404.508 and 416.553. These expenses include fixed living expenses such as food, clothing, rent and similar items, medical, hospitalization and other such expenses, expense for the support of others for whom the individual is legally responsible and (an important provision little used by claimants and their attorneys) other miscellaneous expenses that may reasonably be considered part of the individual's standard of living. Thus, adjustment or recovery of the overpayment will defeat the purpose of Title II of the Act in situations where the person from whom recovery is sought needs all his current income to meet current ordinary and necessary living expenses. 20 C.F.R. § 404.508. SSA assumes that collection of an overpaid amount will cause a hardship if the overpaid person is a recipient of SSI. 20 C.F.R. § 416.553(b).

§475   Against Equity and Good Conscience

"Against equity and good conscience" means that the individual, because of the overpayment, relinquished a valuable right (*e.g.*, in a retirement case, the person retired from his usual work, only to find that the notice of entitlement to Social Security benefits was erroneous) or changed his position for the worse (*e.g.*, a widow, having been awarded benefits for herself and her daughter, entered the daughter in college because the monthly benefits made this possible and then learned, after a year, that her husband had not been insured, there being no other funds to discharge the financial obligations incurred for the daughter to go to college). 20 C.F.R. § 404.509(a)(1). *Cf.* 20 C.F.R. § 416.554 which applies the same principles to SSI examples.

It is also against equity and good conscience to recover the overpayment from someone who was living in a separate household from the overpaid person at the time of the overpayment, and did not receive the overpayment. 20 C.F.R. § 404.509(a)(2).

§476   *Overpayment Recovery Questionnaire*

Information necessary for a determination whether recovery or adjustment of the overpayment may be waived is listed on Form SSA-632, Request for Waiver and Recovery Questionnaire, *see* sample §477, *infra*. This form is often filled out before an attorney enters the case. However, if the claimant's representative is retained during the early stages of the claim for repayment of an overpayment, great care should be exercised in completing, the form.

At the hearing level, the information on this form is not binding on the ALJ, but it may be given great weight. The practitioner who wishes to assist his client to the maximum extent possible will be sure, by going over the subject several times with his client, that all expenses are listed, entered into the record and described in testimony.

§477   Form: Request for Waiver of Overpayment Recovery or Change in Repayment Rate (SSA-632)

SOCIAL SECURITY ADMINISTRATION

Form Approved
OMB No. 0960-0037

Request For Waiver Of Overpayment Recovery Or Change In Repayment Rate

We will use your answers on this form to decide if we can waive collection of the overpayment or change the amount you must pay us back each month. If we can't waive collection, we may use this form to decide how you should repay the money.

Please answer the questions on this form as completely as you can. We will help you fill out the form if you want. If you are filling out this form for someone else, answer the questions as they apply to that person.

FOR SSA USE ONLY	
ROAR Input	☐ Yes
	☐ No
Input Date	
Waiver	☐ Approval
	☐ Denial
SSI	☐ Yes ☐ No
AMT OF OP $	
PERIOD (DATES) OF OP	

1. A. Name of person on whose
       record the overpayment occurred: _____

    B. Social Security Number: _____

    C. Name of overpaid person(s) making this request and his or her Social Security Number(s):

2. Check any of the following that apply. (Also, fill in the dollar amount in B, C, or D.)

    A. ☐ The overpayment was not my fault and I cannot afford to pay the money back and/or it is
         unfair for some other reasons.

    B. ☐ I cannot afford to use all of my monthly benefit to pay back the overpayment. However I can
         afford to have $_____ withheld each month.

    C. ☐ I am no longer receiving Supplement Security Income (SSI) payments. I want to pay back
         $_____ each month instead of paying all of the money at once.

    D. ☐ I am receiving SSI payments. I want to pay back $_____ each month instead of
         paying 10% of my total income.

Form SSA-632-BK (08-2014) ef (08-2014)   Page 1
Destroy Prior Editions

SECTION I - INFORMATION ABOUT RECEIVING THE OVERPAYMENT

3. A. Did you, as representative payee, receive the overpaid benefits to use for the beneficiary?

    ☐ Yes   ☐ No (Skip to Question 4)

    B. Name and address of the beneficiary

    C. How were the overpaid benefits used?

4. If we are asking you to repay someone else's overpayment:

    A. Was the overpaid person living with you when he/she was overpaid? ☐ Yes ☐ No

    B. Did you receive any of the overpaid money? ☐ Yes ☐ No

    C. Explain what you know about the overpayment AND why it was not your fault.

5. Why did you think you were due the overpaid money and why do you think you were not at fault in causing the overpayment or accepting the money?

6. A. Did you tell us about the change or event that made you overpaid? If no, why didn't you tell us? ☐ Yes ☐ No

    B. If yes, how, when and where did you tell us? If you told us by phone or in person, who did you talk with and what was said?

    C. If you did not hear from us after your report, and/or your benefits did not change, did you contact us again? ☐ Yes ☐ No

7. A. Have we ever overpaid you before? ☐ Yes ☐ No

    If yes, on what Social Security number?

    B. Why were you overpaid before? If the reason is similar to why you are overpaid now, explain what you did to try to prevent the present overpayment.

Form **SSA-632-BK** (08-2014) ef (08-2014)   Page 2

	FOR SSA USE ONLY
SECTION II - YOUR FINANCIAL STATEMENT	NAME:
	SSN:

You need to complete this section if you are asking us either to waive the collection of the overpayment or to change the rate at which we asked you to repay it. Please answer all questions as fully and as carefully as possible. We may ask to see some documents to support your statements, so you should have them with you when you visit our office.

EXAMPLES ARE:

- Current Rent or Mortgage Books
- Savings Passbooks
- Pay Stubs
- Your most recent Tax Return

- 2 or 3 recent utility, medical, charge card, and insurance bills
- Cancelled checks
- Similar documents for your spouse or dependent family members

Please write only whole dollar amounts-round any cents to the nearest dollar. If you need more space for answers, use the "Remarks" section at the bottom of page 7.

8. A. Do you now have any of the overpaid checks or money in your possession (or in a savings or other type of account)? ☐Yes Amount: _____
☐No Return this amount to SSA

B. Did you have any of the overpaid checks or money in your possession (or in a savings or other type of account) at the time you received the overpayment notice? ☐Yes Amount: _____
☐No Answer Question 9.

9. Explain why you believe you should not have to return this amount.

ANSWER 10 AND 11 ONLY IF THE OVERPAYMENT IS SUPPLEMENTAL SECURITY INCOME (SSI) PAYMENTS. IF NOT, SKIP TO 12.

10. A. Did you lend or give away any property or cash after notification of the overpayment? ☐Yes (Answer Part B)
☐No (Go to question 11.)

B. Who received it, relationship (if any), description and value:

11. A. Did you receive or sell any property or receive any cash (other than earnings) after notification of this overpayment? ☐Yes (Answer Part B)
☐No (Go to question 12.)

B. Describe property and sale price or amount of cash received:

12. A. Are you now receiving cash public assistance such as Supplemental Security Income (SSI) payments? ☐ Yes (Answer B and C and See note below)
☐ No

B. Name or kind of public assistance   C. Claim Number

IMPORTANT: If you answered "YES" to question 12, DO NOT answer any more questions on this form. Go to page 8, sign and date the form, and give your address and phone number(s). Bring or mail any papers that show you receive public assistance to your local Social Security office as soon as possible.

Form **SSA-632-BK** (08-2014) ef (08-2014)   Page 3

Members Of Household

13. List any person (child, parent, friend, etc.) who depends on you for support AND who lives with you.

NAME	AGE	RELATIONSHIP (If none, explain why the person is dependent on you)

Assets - Things You Have And Own

14. A. How much money do you and any person(s) listed in question 13 above have as cash on hand, in a checking account, or otherwise readily available? $ _____

B. Does your name, or that of any other member of your household appear, either alone or with any other person, on any of the following?

TYPE OF ASSET	OWNER	BALANCE OR VALUE	PER MONTH	SHOW THE INCOME (interest, dividends) EARNED EACH MONTH. (If none, explain in spaces below. If paid quarterly, divide by 3).
SAVINGS (Bank, Savings and Loan, Credit Union)		$	$	
		$	$	
CERTIFICATES OF DEPOSIT (CD)		$	$	
INDIVIDUAL RETIREMENT ACCOUNT (IRA)		$	$	
MONEY OR MUTUAL FUNDS		$	$	
BONDS, STOCKS		$	$	
TRUST FUND		$	$	
CHECKING ACCOUNT		$	$	
OTHER (EXPLAIN)		$	$	
	TOTALS	$	$	Enter the "Per Month" total on line (k) of question 18.

15. A. If you or a member of your household own a car, (other than the family vehicle), van, truck, camper, motorcycle, or any other vehicle or a boat, list below.

OWNER	YEAR/MAKE/MODEL	PRESENT VALUE	LOAN BALANCE (if any)	MAIN PURPOSE FOR USE
		$	$	
		$	$	
		$	$	

B. If you or a member of your household own any real estate (buildings or land), OTHER than where you live, or own or have an interest in, any business, property, or valuables, describe below.

OWNER	DESCRIPTION	MARKET VALUE	LOAN BALANCE (if any)	USAGE-INCOME (rent etc.)
		$	$	
		$	$	
		$	$	
		$	$	

Form SSA-632-BK (08-2014) ef (08-2014) Page 4

Monthly Household Income

If paid weekly, multiply by 4.33 (4 1/3) to figure monthly pay. If paid every 2 weeks, multiply by 2.166 (2 1/6). If self-employed, enter 1/12 of net earnings. Enter monthly TAKE HOME amounts on line A of question 18 also.

16. A. Are you employed?   ☐ YES (Provide information below)   ☐ NO (Skip to B)

Employer name, address, and phone: (Write "self" if self-employed)	Monthly pay before deduction (Gross) $
	Monthly TAKE-HOME pay (NET) $

B. Is your spouse employed?   ☐ YES (Provide information below)   ☐ NO (Skip to C)

Employer(s) name, address, and phone: (Write "self" if self-employed)	Monthly pay before deduction (Gross) $
	Monthly TAKE-HOME pay (NET) $

C. Is any other person listed in Question 13 employed?   ☐ YES   Name(s)   ☐ NO (Go to Question 17)

Employer(s) name, address, and phone: (Write "self" if self-employed)	Monthly pay before deduction (Gross) $
	Monthly TAKE-HOME pay (NET) $

17. A. Do you, your spouse or any dependent member of your household receive support or contributions from any person or organization?   ☐ YES (Answer B)   ☐ NO (Go to question 18)

B. How much money is received each month? $ _____ (Show this amount on line (J) of question 18)   SOURCE

BE SURE TO SHOW **MONTHLY AMOUNTS** BELOW - If received weekly or every 2 weeks, read the instruction at the top of this page.

18.

INCOME FROM #16 AND #17 ABOVE AND OTHER INCOME TO YOUR HOUSEHOLD	YOURS	√	SPOUSE'S	√	OTHER HOUSEHOLD MEMBERS	√	SSA USE ONLY
A. TAKE HOME Pay (Net) (From #16 A, B, C, above)	$	☐	$	☐	$	☐	
B. Social Security Benefits		☐		☐		☐	
C. Supplemental Security Income (SSI)		☐		☐		☐	
D. Pension(s) (VA, Military, Civil Service, Railroad, etc.) TYPE		☐		☐		☐	
TYPE		☐		☐		☐	
E. Public Assistance (Other than SSI) TYPE		☐		☐		☐	
F. Food Stamps (Show full face value of stamps received)		☐		☐		☐	
G. Income from real estate (rent, etc.) (From question 15B)		☐		☐		☐	
H. Room and/or Board Payments (Explain in remarks below)		☐		☐		☐	
I. Child Support/Alimony		☐		☐		☐	
J. Other Support (From #17 (B) above)		☐		☐		☐	
K. Income From Assets (From question 14)		☐		☐		☐	
L. Other (From any source, explain below)		☐		☐		☐	
REMARKS TOTALS	$		$		$		

GRAND TOTAL $ _____
(Add 3 total blocks above)

Monthly Household Expenses

If the expense is paid weekly or every 2 weeks, read the instruction at the top of Page 5. Do NOT list an expense that is withheld from income (Such as Medical Insurance). Only take home pay is used to figure income.

Show "CC" as the expense amount if the expense (such as clothing) is part of CREDIT CARD EXPENSE SHOWN ON LINE (F).	$ PER MONTH	SSA USE ONLY
19. A. Rent or Mortgage (If mortgage payment includes property or other local taxes, insurance, etc. DO NOT list again below.)		
B. Food (Groceries (include the value of food stamps) and food at restaurants, work, etc.)		
C. Utilities (Gas, electric, telephone)		
D. Other Heating/Cooking Fuel (Oil, propane, coal, wood, etc.)		
E. Clothing		
F. Credit Card Payments (show minimum monthly payment allowed)		
G. Property Tax (State and local)		
H. Other taxes or fees related to your home (trash collection, water-sewer fees)		
I. Insurance (Life, health, fire, homeowner, renter, car, and any other casualty or liability policies)		
J. Medical-Dental (After amount, if any, paid by insurance)		
K. Car operation and maintenance (Show any car loan payment in (N) below)		
L. Other transportation		
M. Church-charity cash donations		
N. Loan, credit, lay-away payments (If payment amount is optional, show minimum)		
O. Support to someone NOT in household (Show name, age, relationship (if any) and address)		
P. Any expense not shown above (Specify)		
EXPENSE REMARKS (Also explain any unusual or very large expenses, such as medical, college, etc.)	TOTAL $	

Income And Expenses Comparison

20. A. Monthly income (Write the amount here from the "Grand Total" of #18.) $ _____

    B. Monthly Expenses (Write the amount here from the "Total" of #19.) $ _____

    C. Adjusted Household Expenses   +$25 _____

    D. Adjusted Monthly Expenses (Add (B) and (C)) $ 25.00 _____

21. If your expenses (D) are more than your income (A), explain how you are paying your bills.	FOR SSA USE ONLY	
	☐ INC. **EXCEEDS** ADJ EXPENSE	$ +
	☐ INC **LESS THAN** ADJ EXPENSE	$ −

Financial Expectation And Funds Availability

22. A. Do you, your spouse or any dependent member of your household expect your or their financial situation to change (for the better or worse) in the next 6 months? (For example: a tax refund, pay raise or full repayment of a current bill for the better-major house repairs for the worse).   ☐ YES (Explain on line below)   ☐ NO

    B. If there is an amount of cash on hand or in checking accounts shown in item 14A, is it being held for a special purpose?   ☐ NO (Amount on hand)   ☐ NO (Money available for any use)   ☐ YES (Explain on line below)

    C. Is there any reason you CANNOT convert to cash the "Balance or Value" of any financial asset shown in item 14B.   ☐ YES (Explain on line below)   ☐ NO

    D. Is there any reason you CANNOT SELL or otherwise convert to cash any of the assets shown in items 15A and B?   ☐ YES (Explain on line below)   ☐ NO

Remarks Space – If you are continuing an answer to a question, please write the number (and letter, if any) of the question first.

Form SSA-632-BK (08-2014) ef (08-2014)   Page 7   (MORE SPACE ON NEXT PAGE)

REMARKS SPACE (Continued)

PENALTY CLAUSE, CERTIFICATION AND PRIVACY ACT STATEMENT

I declare under penalty of perjury that I have examined all the information on this form, and on any accompanying statements or forms, and it is true and correct to the best of my knowledge. I understand that anyone who knowingly gives a false or misleading statement about a material fact in this information, or causes someone else to do so, commits a crime and may be sent to prison, or may face other penalties, or both.

SIGNATURE OF OVERPAID PERSON OR REPRESENTATIVE PAYEE

SIGNATURE (First name, middle initial, last name) (Write in ink)

SIGN
HERE

DATE (Month, Day, Year)

WORK TELEPHONE NUMBER IF WE MAY CALL YOU AT WORK (Include area code)

HOME TELEPHONE NUMBER (Include area code)

MAILING ADDRESS (Number and street, Apt. No., P.O. Box, or Rural Route)

CITY AND STATE	ZIP CODE

ENTER NAME OF COUNTY (IF ANY) IN WHICH YOU NOW LIVE

Witnesses are required ONLY if this statement has been signed by mark (X) above. If signed by mark (X),two witnesses to the signing who know the individual must sign below, giving their full addresses.

SIGNATURE OF WITNESS	SIGNATURE OF WITNESS
ADDRESS (Number and street, City, State, and ZIP Code)	ADDRESS (Number and street, City, State, and ZIP Code)

Form **SSA-632-BK** (08-2014) ef (08-2014)   Page 8

Privacy Act Statement
Collection and Use of Personal Information

Sections 204, 1631(b), and 1879, of the Social Security Act, as amended, authorize us to collect this information. We will use the information you provide to determine whether we can waive collection of your overpayment or adjust the amount you repay each month.

Furnishing us this information is voluntary. However, failing to provide us with all or part of the information may affect the processing of this form and an accurate, timely decision of whether to waive collection of your overpayment or to change your repayment rate.

We rarely use the information you supply us for any purpose other than to make a determination regarding overpayment recovery and repayment rate changes. However, we may use the information for the administration of our programs including sharing information:

1. To comply with Federal laws requiring the release of information from our records (e.g., to the Government Accountability Office and Department of Veterans Affairs); and,
2. To facilitate statistical research, audit, or investigative activities necessary to ensure the integrity and improvement of our programs (e.g., to the Bureau of the Census and to private entities under contract with us).

A complete list of when we may share your information with others, called routine uses, is available in our Privacy Act System of Records Notices 60-0094, entitled, Recovery of Overpayments, Accounting and Reporting/Debt Management System. Additional information about this and other system of records notices and our programs are available online at www.socialsecurity.gov or at your local Social Security office.

We may share the information you provide to other health agencies through computer matching programs. Matching programs compare our records with records kept by other Federal, State or local government agencies. We use the information from these programs to establish or verify a person's eligibility for federally funded or administered benefit programs and for repayment of incorrect payments or delinquent debts under these programs.

Paperwork Reduction Act Statement - This information collection meets the requirements of 44 U.S.C. § 3507, as amended by section 2 of the Paperwork Reduction Act of 1995. You do not need to answer these questions unless we display a valid Office of Management and Budget control number. We estimate that it will take about 2 hours to read the instructions, gather the facts, and answer the questions. *Send only comments relating to our time estimate above to: SSA, 6401 Security Blvd, Baltimore, MD 21235-6401.*

§478   Adjustment or Recovery of Overpayment

Even though "without fault" is established and expenses are shown to equal or even exceed income, SSA may still insist on adjustment or recovery if some of the expenses are for nonessentials (*e.g.*, cable television) or if the expenses include monthly payments which will be completed shortly (*e.g.*, a final car payment will be due next month) or where the expenses include continuing gifts, for instance, to grandchildren whose parents are working and able to support them.

Overpayment notices are notorious for inadequate communication of the details of the claimed overpayment. Notices have been known to give one figure as the amount of overpayment at the beginning of a paragraph and another figure at the end of the same paragraph. Some notices are so incomprehensible that you might truthfully argue that they do not contain enough information to permit an effective refutation of the contention that an overpayment has been made and must be repaid.

Certainly, it is not unreasonable for a claimant or his representative to demand the exact basis for the assessment of the overpayment, as well as the exact amount of the alleged overpayment, together with a showing of how that amount was determined.

Even when the notice adequately states the overpayment claim, the issues are sometimes not supported by the file of proposed exhibits selected for the hearing. This file should contain documents supporting each element of the alleged overpayment. If it does not, the representative has several unsatisfactory alternatives: He may insist that the demand for overpayment is too uncertain to allow defense, a position not likely to succeed except in the most extreme case; he may go to the hearing with no clear understanding of the evidence in support of the claim against his client, which the conscientious representative tries to avoid; or he may wade through the claims file in an effort to ascertain the basis for the allegations of overpayment—a time-consuming process, though often a rewarding one.

Even if the ultimate decision regarding overpayment is adverse to the claimant (*i.e.*, it is determined that he was not without fault in the creation of the overpayment, or if he was not without fault, adjustment or recovery of the overpayment would not be against equity and good conscience and would not defeat the purpose of Title II/Title XVI and therefore cannot be waived), certain actions may still be taken to ease the burden placed on him for repayment. For example, if benefits are still payable to him, the amount of the overpayment may be recouped from those benefits. In most cases SSA demands immediate refund of the full amount of the overpayment. If it is not forthcoming, the entire amount of benefits is withheld until the overpayment is recouped, unless the claimant requests, because of hardship, that a lesser amount be withheld each month. Such requests are usually granted. In the SSI program, no more than 10 percent of the recipient's total monthly income can be withheld, unless the recipient agrees. 20 C.F.R. § 416.571.

If a recipient is not currently receiving Social Security or SSI benefits, overpayments may be used to offset future benefits when and if eligibility is reestablished.

Title II overpayment may not be recouped against SSI, and vice versa, unless the recipient agrees. 20 C.F.R. § 416.570.

§479   Compromise Payment

If benefits are no longer payable, installment repayment may be worked out.

Under the Federal Claims Collection Act of 1966, an amount less than the total owed may be accepted by the Social Security Administration as a compromise settlement. Such settlements are discretionary, and are not available where the claimant is still alive and there is indication of fraud, the filing of a false claim, or misrepresentation. 20 C.F.R. § 404.515.

Overpayments may be discharged in bankruptcy. *See In re Neavear*, 674 F.2d 1201 (7th Cir. 1982).

§480   Continuing Disability Review and Termination of Eligibility for Disability Benefits

Although SSA doesn't always hold to this schedule, the eligibility of most recipients of Social Security disability and SSI disability benefits—that is, recipients whose improvement is considered possible—is supposed to be reviewed every three years. 42 U.S.C. § 421(i). These investigations are called "continuing disability reviews" or CDRs. People with permanent impairments such as amputations or retardation are subject to review every seven years. Claimants with impairments such as fractures that are likely to improve may be scheduled for review within 6 to 18 months of approval of the claim. 20 C.F.R. § 404.1590(d).

Although CDRs strike fear in the hearts of disability benefit recipients, more than 90 percent of such reviews find that the recipient's disability continues.

The Social Security Disability Benefit Reform Act of 1984, Public Law 98-460, provided recipients with three important safeguards: (1) benefit continuation pending appeal; (2) face-to-face reconsideration hearings; and (3) the medical improvement standard. Since then Congress has sought ways to encourage those who still qualify for disability benefits to return to work, passing various work incentive legislation, while at the same time urging SSA to remove from the disability rolls those who no longer qualify as disabled or worse, those who never should have been found disabled in the first place. The result is a complicated patchwork of incentives and disincentives for beneficiaries to work.

In sections 480 through 489, we're going to examine the medical improvement standard and look at how SSA evaluates whether a beneficiary's disability is continuing. At §489.1 we provide a sequential evaluation diagram for determining, once a recipient's disability is found to continue, whether drug abuse or alcoholism is material. In sections 490 through 495, we'll address what happens when a recipient of Social Security disability benefits returns to work. Section 496 deals with working SSI recipients, who are dealt with very differently.

Most recipients who appeal cessation notices receive continuing benefits. Since no past due benefits accumulate, attorney's fees for the appeal are not withheld or paid directly to the attorney by SSA. Although the attorney and client can make arrangements for payment of a fee that does not invoke the fee agreement process and will require a fee petition in order for the attorney to be paid, most termination cases are handled by legal services offices.

Even attorneys who do not handle termination cases find it useful to know the rudiments of the benefit continuation and medical improvement provisions. Former clients who were awarded benefits need to be assured that there is no reason to panic when they are notified that their eligibility is being reviewed. A former client may need help and a referral to a legal services office if the former client receives a cessation notice.

Also, the medical improvement review standard applies in initial entitlement cases in which a client receives a partially favorable ALJ decision granting a closed period of disability but not finding the claimant currently disabled. The ALJ must justify the finding that the claimant is not currently disabled under the medical improvement review standard. See SSR 02-1p, note 2; SSR 02-2p, note 4; and POMS DI 28005.001 D.1.b.

Sometimes lawyers refer to the medical improvement review standard as putting the burden on SSA to show medical improvement. Although SSA must find that there was medical improvement, such reference to a "burden," a term that does not appear in the statute or regulations in this context, can be misleading. A recipient is required to cooperate with SSA and provide information or attend consultative examinations if requested. Non-cooperation alone can be the basis for finding that disability ended. 20 C.F.R. § 404.1594(e) (2). The statute also explicitly provides that there is no

presumption of continuing disability: "Any determination made under this section shall be made on the basis of the weight of the evidence and on a neutral basis with regard to the individual's condition, without any initial inference as to the presence or absence of disability being drawn from the fact that the individual has previously been determined to be disabled." 42 U.S.C. § 423(f).

Continuing disability reviews are addressed in the regulations in five different contexts: for widow(er)s applicable to determinations before January 1991—20 C.F.R. § 404.1579—which is only of historical interest; for blind beneficiaries—20 C.F.R. § 404.1586—which is straightforward; for Title II beneficiaries (including widow(er)s beginning January 1991)—20 C.F.R. § 404.1594; for SSI children—20 C.F.R. § 416.994a—which is beyond the scope of this book; and for SSI adults—20 C.F.R. § 416.994. We will address only those regulations pertaining to Title II and SSI adults.

§481   Benefit Continuation

If a recipient's eligibility for disability benefits is terminated after a CDR, benefits will cease two months after the recipient is sent a cessation notice in the usual case.

The notice will inform the recipient that he or she has 60 days to request reconsideration of the decision to terminate benefits. But reconsideration must be requested within 10 days of receiving the termination notice if the recipient wishes benefits to continue pending the reconsideration determination. Since SSA presumes that recipients receive Social Security notices 5 days after the notices are dated, recipients, in effect, have 15 days from the date on the face of the cessation notice to file a request for reconsideration along with a request for continuation of benefits. If a recipient elects to receive continuing benefits, Medicare and Medicaid as well as auxiliary benefits for the recipient's children and spouse, if any, will also continue pending the reconsideration determination.

If the request for benefit continuation is filed later than the 10-day period provided by the regulations, 20 C.F.R. §§ 404.911 or 416.1411 will be used to determine whether good cause exists for failure to timely request benefit continuation. See 20 C.F.R. §§ 404.1597a(f)(2) and (g)(3) and §§ 416.996(c)(2) and (d)(2).

Similarly, if a recipient receives a reconsideration determination affirming the cessation of benefits, the reconsideration notice will inform the recipient of the right to request an ALJ hearing within 60 days, but if the recipient wants benefits continued pending the ALJ decision, a hearing must be requested within 10 days of receiving the reconsideration determination. See 20

C.F.R. §§ 404.1597a(g)(1) and 416.996(d)(1). If the recipient requests continued benefits pending an ALJ decision but did not request continuing benefits while SSA reconsidered the initial cessation determination, Social Security disability benefits will begin effective the month of the reconsideration determination. *See* 20 C.F.R. §§ 404.1597a(g)(2) and 416.996(d).

Continuing benefits are supposed to stop with payment for the month before the month of the unfavorable ALJ decision. 20 C.F.R. §§ 404.1597a(b)(3)(i) and 416.996(a)(2). But if the case is appealed further and ultimately remanded by an order of the Appeals Council that vacates the ALJ decision, continuing benefits are available again pending a new decision by an ALJ. 20 C.F.R. §§ 404.1597a(i) and 416.996(e).

SSA takes the position that if Social Security disability benefits are terminated due to a recipient's performance of substantial gainful activity (as opposed to a determination that the impairments are no longer disabling or never were disabling), it will not continue benefits during appeal. POMS DI 12027.015. However, recipients may elect to continue benefits in concurrent cases even if termination is due to performance of SGA. *See* 20 C.F.R. §§ 404.1597a(b), 416.996(f) and 416.1336 and POMS DI 12027.007A.3.

If continued benefits are received during an appeal which ultimately proves unsuccessful, SSA says that it will ask for repayment of the continued benefits. However, SSA says that waiver of repayment of the overpayment will be considered as long as the determination was appealed in good faith. "It will be assumed that such appeal is made in good faith and, therefore, any overpaid individual has the right to waiver consideration *unless* such individual fails to cooperate in connection with the appeal, *e.g.*, if the individual fails (without good reason) to give us medical or other evidence we request, or to go for a physical or mental examination when requested by us, in connection with the appeal." 20 C.F.R. §§ 404.1597a(j)(3) and 416.996(g)(2). In practice, waivers are freely granted since a recipient who appeals in good faith is without fault and such a recipient usually cannot afford to repay the overpaid benefits.

§482 Face-to-Face Reconsideration Hearings

In cessation cases, SSA's regulations provide for a face-to-face reconsideration hearing with a disability examiner, usually held at a local Social Security office. 20 C.F.R. §§ 404.914-918, 416.1414-1418. The disability examiners are not ALJs. They are state agency employees responsible for determining eligibility at the initial and reconsideration levels. Examiners do not need to be attorneys.

Face-to-face reconsideration hearings are generally less formal than ALJ hearings. However, procedural rights such as representation, issuance of subpoenas, presentation of witnesses, submission of new evidence, and so forth are available. If a recipient waives the right to appear at the hearing, the disability examiner will issue a written reconsideration determination based on the information in the case file.

Attorneys who represent recipients at the reconsideration stage generally prepare for a face-to-face reconsideration hearing in the same manner required to prepare a case for an ALJ hearing.

§483 The Continuing Disability Review Evaluation Process — Overview

42 U.S.C. §§ 423(f) and 1382c(a)(5) provide that the Commissioner shall not terminate a person's disability benefits unless, subject to various exceptions, there is substantial evidence that the person's medical condition has improved and he or she is now able to engage in substantial gainful activity (SGA).

Application of the medical improvement review standard is accomplished by following an eight-step sequential evaluation process for Title II that begins (like the five-step sequential evaluation process for initial claims) with "Are you engaging in substantial gainful activity?" 20 C.F.R. § 404.1594(f). In SSI continuing disability review cases, there are only seven steps because the issue of engaging in substantial gainful activity is not included. 20 C.F.R. § 416.994(b)(5). We address the details of engaging in substantial gainful activity in sections 490 to 493 of this book in Title II cases and section 496 in SSI cases.

The second step of the Title II sequential evaluation process (the first step for SSI), which addresses whether the recipient's impairments meet or equal an impairment found in the current Listing of Impairments, is actually a shortcut that allows SSA to avoid the issue of whether there has been medical improvement. At this step SSA evaluates all impairments, including impairments that arose after the individual was originally found disabled. After all, SSA says, if an individual's impairments currently meet or equal the Listings, what is the point of figuring out whether there has been medical improvement in the original impairment? Benefits will be continued anyway. *See* POMS DI 28005.015 A.2.

It is only after SSA addresses whether all current impairments meet or equal the current Listings that SSA addresses the issue of medical improvement set forth in the statute. The medical improvement standard generally requires that there be evidence that (1) there has been medical improvement of the recipient's impairments, (2) the medical improvement is related to the ability to work and (3) the recipient is now able to engage in substantial gainful activity.

In order to determine if the recipient is capable of engaging in SGA, the sequential evaluation process looks very similar to the sequential evaluation process for initial disability determinations except that the step considering whether all the recipient's impairments meet or equal the Listings has already been addressed. *See* §484.

§484   Chart: CDR Evaluation Process Summary Chart From POMS DI 28005.010

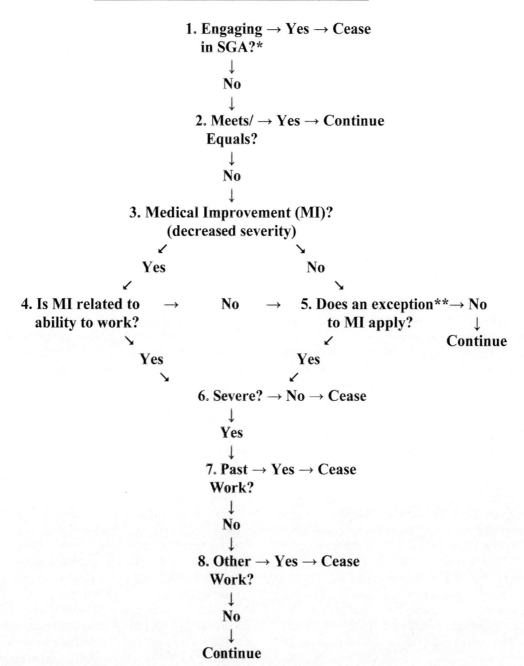

CDR Evaluation Process Summary Chart

1. Engaging → Yes → Cease
   in SGA?*

   No

2. Meets/ → Yes → Continue
   Equals?

   No

3. Medical Improvement (MI)?
   (decreased severity)

   Yes   No

4. Is MI related to   →   No   →   5. Does an exception** → No
   ability to work?   to MI apply?   ↓

   Yes   Yes   Continue

6. Severe? → No → Cease

   Yes

7. Past → Yes → Cease
   Work?

   No

8. Other → Yes → Cease
   Work?

   No

   Continue

*Subject to TWP and EPE provisions. In Title XVI cases, *see* section 1619 provisions.

**Group II exceptions are not controlled by sequence, and may result in cessation at any point.

§485   Points of Comparison and Cessation Month

To make an initial medical improvement determination, the regulations require SSA to compare two points in time, the "current" date and the date of the most recent prior decision finding that the recipient was disabled. The most recent prior decision of disability may be the date the recipient was first found to be disabled or the date of some intervening favorable determination pursuant to a CDR. 20 C.F.R. §§ 404.1594(b)(7) and 416.994(b)(1)(vii).

At the time of the continuing disability review, SSA tells state agency adjudicators to assess the case based only on the recipient's current condition (with certain exceptions applicable whenever the termination date is not the date of the CDR determination—see §485.1). Thus, adjudicators are not concerned with figuring out if the recipient has been continuously disabled. Instead, for the most part, state agency adjudicators are allowed to ignore evidence that there may have been a time when the recipient was receiving benefits but was possibly not disabled. POMS DI 28005.210 B.3. State agency adjudicators are directed to look at the recipient's condition at the time they are evaluating the case—the recipient's truly current condition.

If medical improvement is found, unless improvement was obvious at a specific date in the past, 20 C.F.R. § 404.1594(g)(1), or the recipient's doctor was on record saying the recipient could return to work and there is no substantial conflict between the physician's statement and the recipient's statements about the recipient's own awareness of his or her own capacity for work, 20 C.F.R. § 404.1594(g)(9), SSA does not concern itself with determining if medical improvement could possibly have occurred earlier than the time SSA evaluates the case. SSA simply finds that the recipient's disability ended at the time of evaluation. The cessation date is the date of the notice informing the recipient that he or she is no longer disabled. 20 C.F.R. § 404.1594(g)(2). For a full list of exceptions, see §485.1. See also SSR 82-66.

What "current" comparison point do you use when a termination case is appealed? Do you use the date the recipient's impairments were found by the state agency to be no longer disabling (usually the CDR date)? Or can you use today's date, e.g., the date you represent your client at the reconsideration or ALJ hearing? It is the rule in all cases, both Title II and Title XVI, that the adjudicator on appeal must look at whether the state agency determination was correct. Thus, the termination date is the "current" comparison point date on appeal. On appeal, the adjudicator's first job is to figure out if the termination determination was correct.

If the adjudicator determines on appeal that the termination determination was *not* correct, the adjudicator is supposed to consider the possibility that the recipient's disability ended later. The adjudicator is supposed to consider the entire time period up to the time of the adjudicator's determination or decision. If the adjudicator determines that the recipient's disability never ended, then, of course, benefits continue.

What happens if the termination determination was correct but, because of worsening of the recipient's long-standing impairments or new impairments that arose later, the recipient becomes disabled again by the time of the reconsideration, ALJ hearing or appeal to the Appeals Council? This is a question that SSA had some difficulty answering. It wasn't until 2013 in SSR 13-3p that SSA established a consistent nation-wide policy applicable to both Title II and Title XVI cases. SSR 13-3p provides:

> If the adjudicator determines the initial medical cessation determination was correct, he or she will then determine whether the beneficiary has again become disabled at any time through the date of his or her determination or decision because of a worsening of an existing impairment or the onset of a new impairment, if all other requirements for establishing a period of disability, including the duration and insured status requirements are met.

If SSA finds the beneficiary is entitled to an additional period of disability, it will treat an appeal of a termination determination as a protective filing for a new application for disability benefits.

SSR 13-3p also provides: "If the beneficiary's disability has medically ceased, the determination or decision must specifically address the initial cessation determination and the beneficiary's eligibility (or ineligibility) for a new a period of disability through the date on which the appeal determination or decision is being made, or, if earlier, through the date last insured."

If a termination ALJ decision is appealed to the Appeals Council, the Appeals Council approaches the case in the usual way. That is, it considers whether the ALJ decision is supported by substantial evidence or is legally insufficient. The Appeals Council will not consider new evidence that shows, for example, worsening after the date of the ALJ decision. If the Appeals Council remands the case, on remand the ALJ will consider the entire period from the initial termination determination through the date of the date of the ALJ decision on remand. However, in the unlikely event that Appeals Council takes jurisdiction of the case and decides to issue its own decision, in theory the Appeals Council will consider the beneficiary's condition up through the date of the Appeals Council decision.

§485.1 Chart: Cessation Month POMS DI 28005.205

A. Setting the cessation month

To set the cessation month in cases where disability ended, use the table in DI 28005.205C. Do not use this table in reopenings.

B. Cessation month procedure

The cessation month generally coincides with the month of the notice. Find retroactive cessation only in the situations outlined in DI 28005.205C, items 2-8, in this section.

C. Cessation month table

Use the following table to determine the cessation month in CDR cases:

	If Cessation Is Based On:	Find That Disability Ended in the Month:	Reference:
1.	ANY SITUATION NOT COVERED BY 2-8 BELOW (most cessations)	The cessation notice is mailed to the individual (general rule).	DI 28005.205B.
2.	REPORT OF EARLIER MEDICAL CESSATION	The treating physician told the individual of regained capacity to engage in substantial gainful activity (SGA), or, in a Title XVI child case, told the child's representative payee that the child could return to normal activities.	DI 28005.205D.1.
3.	CLEAR-CUT CESSATION (return to work in a medical improvement expected case)	The individual returns to full-time work with no significant medical restrictions.	DI 28030.035
4.	FAILURE TO COOPERATE	The individual fails, without good cause, to do what the Social Security Administration (SSA) or the Disability Determination Services (DDS) has requested and the individual was aware that he or she had to cooperate and the repercussions of failing to do so.	DI 28075.005F; DI 25205.020 for Title XVI child cases
5.	WHEREABOUTS UNKNOWN	SSA first knew that the individual's whereabouts are unknown but not earlier than the month a continuing disability issue arose. NOTE: Title XVI benefits are suspended rather than ceased.	DI 28075.005 F.5.
6.	FAILURE TO FOLLOW PRESCRIBED TREATMENT	The evidence clearly establishes the individual's unjustified failure to follow prescribed treatment.	DI 23010.005
7.	WORK ACTIVITY ONLY	The individual first engages in SGA following completion of any applicable trial work period. DDSs do not decide this issue. Do not cease Title XVI cases on this basis.	DI 28050.001 DI 28075.600 SI 02302.001
8.	RECOVERY PRIOR TO INITIAL ALLOWANCE DECISION (closed period cases)	Shown by the evidence.	DI 25510.001

D. Determining cessation months

1. Report of Earlier Medical Cessations

The following situations involve the setting of earlier cessation months.

a. Find retroactive cessation in cases where there is no doubt that the individual was aware that he or she was able to work. Alternatively, in a Title XVI child case, there is no doubt that the child's representative payee (or the child, if the child is his or her own payee) was aware that the child could return to normal activities, but failed to report this change. That is, find retroactive cessation only if:

- the individual (or Title XVI child's representative payee) reports that at an earlier date the treating source informed the individual that he or she had regained the capacity to return to work or, in a Title XVI child case, had informed the child's representative payee that the child could return to normal activities; or

- the treating source voluntarily reports the individual was informed at an earlier date that he or she had the capacity to return to work or, in a Title XVI child case, the child's representative payee was informed that the child could return to normal activities.

b. Set cessation as of the month the individual was made aware he or she had regained capacity to engage in SGA or, in a Title XVI child case, the child's representative payee was made aware that the child could return to normal activities.

c. Do not set this type of retroactive cessation date if:

- o there is substantial conflict between statements from the treating source and the individual (or, in a Title XVI child case, the treating source and the child's representative payee) concerning the individual's awareness of capacity to work, or the child's ability to return to normal activities; or

- o inadequate (or no) objective medical evidence supports the statement from the treating source establishing the retroactive cessation date.

2. Cessation Month in Error Exception Cases

In cessations that rely on the error exception to medical improvement (MI), do not find retroactive cessation unless the conditions for reopening the prior decision are met.

3. Cessation Month in Low Birth Weight (LBW) Infant Cases

For LBW infants who are found no longer disabled, establish the cessation month no earlier than the month the baby attains age 1.

§486   Is There Medical Improvement?

Regulations define "medical improvement" as "any decrease in the medical severity of your impairment(s)." The decision that there has been a decrease in medical severity "must be based on changes (improvement) in the symptoms, signs and/or laboratory findings ... associated with your impairment(s)." 20 C.F.R. §§ 404.1594(b)(1) and 416.994(b)(1)(i). When addressing the issue of medical improvement, SSA will consider only the impairments that the individual had at the time of the most recent favorable decision, and will not consider those impairments which developed since that time. (Newly developed impairments, in fact, are considered before the issue of medical improvement is addressed when it is determined whether the recipient's current impairments meet or equal an impairment found in the Listing of Impairments; and newly developed impairments are also considered at a later step in the analysis.)

Although the adult Title II regulations contain no explicit requirement that the medical improvement be significant, such a requirement appears in the medical improvement regulations pertaining to SSI children:

"Although the decrease in severity may be of any quantity or degree, we will disregard minor changes in your signs, symptoms, and laboratory findings that obviously do not represent medical improvement and could not result in a finding that your disability has ended." 20 C.F.R. § 416.994a(c). According to POMS DI 28010.020 A.1., "This guidance applies to adults as well as children." Thus, medical improvement must be more than minor.

The POMS directs decision-makers to ignore any changes within the standard error of measurement for the particular test. POMS DI 28010.020B.1.a. In the obesity ruling, SSR 02-1p, SSA says that weight loss of less than 10 % of initial body weight is too minor to result in a finding of medical improvement. But, SSA says, weight loss of at least 10% of initial body weight that is maintained for 12 months is not minor. SSR 02-1p #12.

Also, pursuant to a provision that does appear in the adult CDR regulations, if the impairment is subject to temporary remission, a temporary improvement will not warrant a finding of medical improvement. 20 C.F.R. §§ 404.1594(c)(3)(iv) and 416.994(b)(2)(iv)(D).

§487   Is Medical Improvement Related to Ability to Work?

Once SSA has decided that medical improvement has occurred, it will then determine whether the improvement is related to ability to work. To make this determination, SSA will compare the person's residual functional capacity (RFC) at the time of the most recent favorable decision with a current RFC based on only those impairments which were present at the time eligibility was most recently approved. You can imagine the difficulties in comparing, let's say, the RFC of a person found disabled years ago due to a back impairment, subsequently develops diabetes with neuropathy in his feet and legs and now has arthritis in one knee as well. In the meantime, however, the range of motion in his back has improved. By looking at the back alone, one might find an improved RFC. And that is what state agency adjudicators are supposed to do at this step; but then they come back again later in the analysis to evaluate the RFC when considering all impairments.

If, for some reason, the RFC assessment does not appear in the file pertaining to the comparison point decision (because an RFC was never done or it was lost), SSA will reconstruct the RFC by finding the highest RFC consistent with a finding of disability. 20 C.F.R. §§ 404.1594(c)(3)(iii) and 416.994(b)(2)(iv)(C).

What happens in those cases where a claimant's impairment was originally found to meet the Listings? There will not be an RFC assessment done at the time of the comparison point determination. In those cases, if the Listing is the same and the claimant no longer meets that Listing (or another current Listing—this is evaluated at step 2 of MIRS, see §483), SSA simply assumes that medical improvement is related to the ability to work and moves on to the next step in the evaluation. 20 C.F.R. §§ 404.1594(c)(3)(i) and 416.994(b)(2)(iv)(A).

However, if the Listing which the claimant's impairment was originally found to have met or equaled has been changed or no longer exists, SSA will evaluate under the original Listing to determine if medical improvement is related to the ability to work. If the individual's impairment still meets or equals the original Listing, medical improvement will be found not related to the ability to work, and benefits will be continued. 20 C.F.R. §§ 404.1594(c)(3)(i) and 416.994(b)(2)(iv)(A). See also SSR 02-1p #11, which deals with obesity, the most prominent example of a Listing that has been removed.

If no medical improvement is found or medical improvement is found not related to ability to work, the inquiry stops and the disability is found to continue as long as none of the exceptions to medical improvement discussed in the next section applies.

§488   Exceptions to Medical Improvement

If no medical improvement is found or medical improvement is found not related to ability to work, before the recipient's disability is found to continue, the decision maker must look to see if any exception to medical improvement applies. There are two groups of exceptions, which are referred to in the regulations as the first group of exceptions to medical improvement, 20 C.F.R. §§ 404.1594(d) and 416.994(b)(3), and the second group of exceptions to medical improvement, 20 C.F.R. §§ 404.1594(e) and 416.994(b)(4).

First Group of Exceptions to Medical Improvement

The purpose of the first group of exceptions to medical improvement is stated in the regulations: "These exceptions to medical improvement are intended to provide a way of finding that a person is no longer disabled in those limited situations where, even though there has been no decrease in severity of the impairment(s), evidence shows that the person should no longer be considered disabled or never should have been considered disabled." 20 C.F.R. §§ 404.1594(d) and 416.994(b)(3). If one of the first group of exceptions applies, after determining that there is no medical improvement or that medical improvement is not related to ability to work, instead of finding that disability continues, SSA continues with the CDR sequential evaluation process to determine if the recipient is capable of engaging in substantial gainful activity.

The first group of exceptions in the Social Security disability regulations contains five specific items: (1) where advances in medical or vocational therapy or technology increases a recipient's ability to work; (2) the individual has completed vocational therapy; (3) on the basis of new and improved diagnostic techniques, the individual's impairment is determined not to be as disabling as it was considered to be at the time of the most recent prior favorable decision; (4) where the prior decision granting benefits was clearly an error; and (5) where the recipient is working at the substantial gainful activity level. 20 C.F.R. § 404.1594(d). The adult SSI regulations include only the first four exceptions. 20 C.F.R. § 416.994(b)(3). (We discuss working at the substantial gainful activity level in this book at §490 and following.) If one of this first group of exceptions applies, SSA must continue the analysis to determine the recipient's current ability to work. 20 C.F.R. §§ 404-1594(f)(5) and 416.994(b)(5)(v).

Vocational Therapy

In fact, the first group of exceptions is not as widely applicable as it may appear at first glance because the exceptions themselves have exceptions and limitations. Even the most widely applicable exception, the one you need to warn your client about, itself has exceptions and qualifications. This is the provision dealing with completion of vocational therapy. Consider this: Say your 55-year-old client who has a medium work background was originally found disabled because he was limited to sedentary work as a result of obesity. If he successfully goes to vocational school and learns to do a specific sedentary job, it is this exception that will cause his benefits to be terminated at a continuing disability review even though he has not medically improved and even though he cannot find a job. 20 C.F.R. § 404.1594(d)(2), example 1, and § 416.994(b)(3)(ii), example 1.

Note, though, that the vocational school has to prepare the claimant for a specific type of job. Broad general education such as a technical school associate degree in business does not qualify because a "broad, general training program does not significantly affect [a recipient's] ability to transfer directly to skilled work." POMS DI 28020.150 F.3.

An exception to the vocational therapy exception occurs when the recipient's impairment was originally found to meet the Listing of Impairments and the recipient has not improved. POMS DI 28020.150 E. provides that the vocational therapy exception will not be applied when the earlier decision found that the claimant's impairments met the Listings. This rule applies whether or not the prior Listing still exists (because meeting the Listings under the regular 5-step sequential evaluation process for determining disability establishes that a claimant is disabled without considering vocational factors).

There also is an exception to the vocational therapy exception when a recipient is currently eligible for SSI benefits based on section 1619 or eligible for section 1619 in the past 12 months. POMS DI 28020.150 E. On section 1619, *see* §496.

Advances in Medical or Vocational Therapy

It is hard to determine the applicability of the exception that applies to advances in medical or vocational therapy or technology that increases to a recipient's ability to work (without decreasing the medical severity of the claimant's impairment). In fact, SSA acknowledged in the regulation itself that this exception has very limited application. 20 C.F.R. §§ 404.1594(d)(1) and 416.994(b)(3)(i). Indeed, before this exception may be applied, the state agency is required to submit an explanation to the Regional Office Center for Disability, which undoubtedly discourages its use. POMS DI 28020.100 C.2.

New or Improved Diagnostic or Evaluative Techniques Show Impairments Not as Disabling as They Were Considered to Be

When substantial evidence shows that based on new or improved diagnostic or evaluative techniques the recipient's impairments are not as disabling as they were considered to be at the time of the most recent favorable decision, SSA requires that the new or improved diagnostic or evaluation techniques "must have become generally available after the date of our most recent favorable medical decision." 20 C.F.R. §§ 404.1594(d)(3), 416.994(b)(3)(iii). The regulation calls for SSA to publish a list of new or improved diagnostic or evaluative techniques in the *Federal Register*. 20 C.F.R. §§ 404.1594(d)(3)(ii)(B), 416.994(b)(3)(iii)(B)(2). The table of contents of the list appears at POMS DI 33535.000. The list contains no new or improved diagnostic or evaluative techniques that have become generally available since October 1984.

Prior Decision Was Wrong

When substantial evidence indicates that the prior decision finding the recipient disabled was wrong, an exception to medical improvement applies. According to SSA, a prior determination will be found in error only if: (1) substantial evidence shows on its face that the prior determination should not have been made; (2) crucial evidence, which was missing at the time of the prior evaluation, becomes available and shows that had it been available at the time of the earlier determination, the finding of disability would not have been made; or (3) substantial new evidence refutes the conclusions that were based on the prior evidence. "Substantial evidence must show that had the new evidence (which relates to the prior determination) been considered at the time of the prior decision, the claim would not have been allowed or continued. A substitution of current judgment for that used in the prior favorable decision will not be the basis for applying this exception." 20 C.F.R. §§ 404.1594(d)(4)(iii) and 416.994(b)(3)(iv)(C).

SSA says that the exception for error will not be applied retroactively unless the conditions for reopening the prior decision are met under 20 C.F.R. §§ 404.988 or 416.1488. 20 C.F.R. §§ 404.1594(d)(4)(iv) and 416.994(b)(3)(iv)(D).

It is SSA policy that error can be found in any prior decision, not just the comparison point decision. However, SSA cautions decision makers not to begin review of the comparison point decision (or any other decision) with the intent of finding an error. POMS DI 28020.350.

Second Group of Exceptions

If one of the second group of exceptions applies, benefits are terminated without further inquiry. That is, there is no inquiry whether the recipient can now engage in substantial gainful activity. This second group of exceptions includes the situation where the favorable decision was obtained by fraud. In the fraud situation, SSA can also reopen the claim under the reopening rules found in the regulations. *See* 20 C.F.R. §§ 404.1594(e)

(1) and 416.994(b)(4)(i). When there is fraud, a prior decision can be reopened at any time. 20 C.F.R. §§ 404.988(c)(1) and 416.1488(c).

The second group of exceptions also includes the situation where the recipient fails to cooperate with SSA (by, for example, refusing to provide requested information or failing to attend a consultative examination). *See* 20 C.F.R. §§ 404.1594(e)(2) and 416.994(b)(4)(ii). In addition, the second group of exceptions applies if SSA cannot locate the recipient, 20 C.F.R. §§ 404.1594(e)(3) and 416.994(b)(4)(iii), or if the recipient fails without good cause to follow prescribed treatment which would be expected to restore the ability to work. 20 C.F.R. §§ 404.1594(e)(4) and 416.994(b)(4)(iv). If one of these second group exceptions applies, the recipient's Title II disability will be found to have ended. 20 C.F.R. §§ 404.1594(f)(5) and 416.994(b)(5)(v). However, if SSA cannot locate an SSI recipient, instead of finding that the recipient's disability ends as is done when a recipient is receiving Title II benefits, SSA will suspend SSI benefits. 20 C.F.R. § 416.994(b)(4)(iii).

§489   When Medical Improvement Is Found Related to Ability to Work

If medical improvement is found to be related to a recipient's ability to work, the inquiry does not stop. The severity of all current impairments must be analyzed, including those that may not last 12 months. 20 C.F.R. § 404.1598. RFC must be assessed based on all current impairments, and the issue whether or not a claimant is capable of past relevant work must be addressed. However, past relevant work does not include any job performed by the recipient during the current period of entitlement. 20 C.F.R. §§ 404.1594(i)(1) and 416.994(b)(8)(i). Past relevant work would include only those jobs performed in the 15 years prior to adjudication. 20 C.F.R. § 404.1560(b)(1), SSR 82-62. If the individual cannot perform past relevant work, then it must be considered whether the recipient, considering age, education and work experience, can do other work. 20 C.F.R. §§ 404.1594(f)(8) and 416.994(b)(5). In short, after considering whether there is medical improvement and whether it is related to ability to work, the analysis turns to the last two steps of the CDR process, which are identical to the last two steps of the five-step sequential evaluation process for determining initial entitlement to disability benefits.

As with the sequential evaluation process for determining initial entitlement to disability benefits, a proper determination of residual functional capacity is essential. The regulations provide useful advice for determining the current residual functional capacity of an individual who has been receiving disability benefits for years:

(ii) Many impairment-related factors must be considered in assessing your functional capacity for basic work activities. Age is one key factor. Medical literature shows that there is a gradual decrease in organ function with age; that major losses and deficits become irreversible over time and that maximum exercise performance diminishes with age. Other changes related to sustained periods of inactivity and the aging process include muscle atrophy, degenerative joint changes, decrease in range of motion, and changes in the cardiac and respiratory systems which limit the exertional range.

(iii) Studies have also shown that the longer an individual is away from the workplace and is inactive, the more difficult it becomes to return to ongoing gainful employment. In addition, a gradual change occurs in most jobs so that after about 15 years, it is no longer realistic to expect that skills and abilities acquired in these jobs will continue to apply to the current workplace. Thus, if you are age 50 or over and have been receiving disability benefits for a considerable period of time, we will consider this factor along with your age in assessing your residual functional capacity. This will ensure that the disadvantages resulting from inactivity and the aging process during a long period of disability will be considered. In some instances where available evidence does not resolve what you can or cannot do on a sustained basis, we will provide special work evaluations or other appropriate testing.

20 C.F.R. §§ 404.1594(b)(4)(ii)-(iii) and 416.994(b)(1)(iv)(B)-(C).

According to the POMS, "a considerable period of time" for receiving benefits in the paragraph above is 7 years. POMS DI 28015.310 D. & I. The POMS directs decision makers to count from the onset date when considering how long an individual has been receiving disability benefits. POMS DI 28015.310 J.

The POMS cautions decision makers against finding large increases in residual functional capacity since the comparison point decision if there are only relatively minor changes in symptoms, signs and laboratory findings. "This would represent substitution of current judgment for that of the prior adjudicator, and would (essentially) represent a reassessment of prior RFC (which is prohibited per DI 28015.315)." POMS DI 28015.320 A.2.b.

If disability is found to continue after applying the medical improvement standard's sequential evaluation process, SSA will then proceed to apply additional steps in some cases to evaluate whether drug addiction or alcoholism is a contributing factor material to the finding of disability. The test, which appears at 20 C.F.R. § 404.1535, is whether the recipient would still be disabled if he or she stopped using drugs or alcohol. The test is applied in this situation by asking if there would be medical improvement if the recipient stopped using drugs or alcohol and then, in effect, marching through the medical improvement sequential evaluation process again to evaluate the impact of this hypothetical improvement. *See* §489.1.

§489.1 Chart: Is DAA Material? From POMS DI 28005.040

For a more detailed discussion of the DAA process see DI 28005.045B.
NOTE: Follow the CDR evaluation process shown in DI 28005.010 to determine if disability continues before proceeding to step 1 of the following chart.

.

1. Disability continues? → No → Cease

↓

Yes

↓

2. Medical evidence of DAA? → No → Continue

↓

Yes

↓

3. Medical Improvement if DAA stopped? → No → Continue*

↓

Yes

↓

4. Medical Improvement related to the ability to work? → No → Continue*

↓

Yes

↓

5. Severe? → No → Cease**

↓

Yes

↓

6. Past work? → Yes → Cease**

↓

No

↓

7. Other work? → Yes → Cease**

↓

No

↓

Continue*

* DAA not material
** DAA material

§490   Cessation of Benefits Because of Performance of Substantial Gainful Activity

The principles of cessation of benefits because of performance of substantial gainful activity are easy to state: When a recipient returns to work and performs substantial gainful activity, benefits will stop. Whether benefits stop right away or whether benefits stop after completion of a nine-month trial work period and whether benefits will resume again if the recipient stops performing SGA depends on whether SSA finds that the recipient medically improved to the point that he or she is no longer disabled.

The regulations, though, are confusing because SSA refers to cessation based on work activity without medical improvement and cessation based on medical improvement the same way—disability ends.

The possibility of cessation of benefits based on performance of substantial gainful activity appears as step one of the CDR sequential evaluation process, 20 C.F.R. § 404.1594(f)(5): "(1) Are you engaging in substantial gainful activity? If you are (and any applicable trial work period has been completed), we will find disability to have ended (*see* paragraph (d) (5) of this section)." Note that any applicable trial work period must have been completed. *See* §491. Note also the cross reference to paragraph (d)(5), which is part of the first group of exceptions to medical improvement, 20 C.F.R. § 404.1594(d)(5), which provides:

> (5) *You are currently engaging in substantial gainful activity.* If you are currently engaging in substantial gainful activity before we determine whether you are no longer disabled because of your work activity, we will consider whether you are entitled to a trial work period as set out in § 404.1592. We will find that your disability has ended in the month in which you demonstrated your ability to engage in substantial gainful activity (following completion of a trial work period, where it applies). This exception does not apply in determining whether you continue to have a disabling impairment(s) (§ 404.1511) for purposes of deciding your eligibility for a reentitlement period (§ 404.1592a).

Recall that you get to the first group of exceptions only after it is determined that the recipient's impairment either did not improve or the medical improvement was not related to the recipient's ability to work. Since this is a sequential evaluation process, it is legitimate to ask how does one proceed past step one? If the recipient is working after completion of the trial work period, isn't that the end of the inquiry? The regulations and SSA's own diagram of the CDR sequential evaluation process—*see* §484—indicate that the inquiry stops when it is determined that the recipient is engaging in SGA after completion of the trial work period. So why do we need an exception (paragraph (d)(5)) that calls for benefits to stop because of working even when there is no medical improvement?

If the working recipient did not medically improve, the exception found in 20 C.F.R. § 404.1594(d)(5) provides, in effect, that even though the recipient is still disabled, benefits may be stopped for performance of substantial gainful activity after completion of any applicable trial work period. It is confusing that SSA calls this a finding that "disability has ended in the month in which you demonstrated your ability to engage in substantial gainful activity." This section also provides an important qualification, which attempts to clear up the confusion: "This exception does not apply in determining whether you continue to have a disabling impairment(s) (§ 404.1511) for purposes of deciding your eligibility for a reentitlement period (§ 404.1592a)."

Pursuant to 20 C.F.R. § 404.1511(a), a disabling impairment is one that "would result in a finding that you are disabled under § 404.1594. In determining whether you have a disabling impairment, earnings are not considered." Thus, 20 C.F.R. § 404.1511(a) provides the basis for skipping step one of the sequential continuing disability review process and 20 C.F.R. § 404.1594(d)(5) provides the basis for stopping benefits for someone who continues to be disabled after completion of the trial work period and is therefore eligible for a reentitlement period.

See §494 for discussion of the reentitlement period.

§491   Is Recipient Eligible for Trial Work Period?

A disabled individual receiving disability insurance benefits, child's benefits based on disability, or widow's or widower's or surviving divorced spouse's benefits based on disability (but not SSI) is generally entitled to a trial work period. 20 C.F.R. § 404.1592(d)(1). That is, the individual is eligible to test his or her ability to return to work for nine months, not necessarily consecutive, during which time full benefits continue. None of the situations where a person is not entitled to a trial work period found in 20 C.F.R. § 404.1592(d)(2) are applicable to someone who has already been found disabled and is receiving benefits.

Lawyers like to argue that any recipient of disability benefits, even one who has medically improved, ought to be eligible for a nine-month trial work period. It certainly would simplify the concept if this were true. Although the general rule is that if a recipient's impairment is not expected to improve, SSA will not conduct a continuing disability review until the completion of the nine-month trial work period, the regulations recognize some possibilities for a recipient not being entitled to a full nine-month trial work period. First, if a recipient's impairment was expected to improve and that recipient returns to work with no significant medical limitations and acknowledges to SSA that medical improvement has occurred, SSA may find that the recipient's disability ended in the month the recipient returned to work. 20 C.F.R. § 404.1591. Thus, such a person is not entitled to a nine-month trial work period.

Second, a trial work period can end when "new evidence, other than evidence relating to any work you did during the trial work period, shows that you are not disabled" even though the full nine-month trial work period has not been completed. 20 C.F.R. § 404.1592(e)(3). Thus, a crucial issue is whether SSA will conduct a continuing disability review before the nine-month trial work period has been completed. *See* §492.

It is also possible for a recipient to have used up the trial work period more or less without noticing. Recipients who have done some part-time work, as so many do these days while waiting for a hearing to be held, may find that although the work was well below the substantial gainful activity level, it counts for trial work. After the date of application and after the five-month waiting period, any month in which a claimant earns over a certain amount constituting "services" for trial work period purposes, qualifies as a trial work period month, even if those months of work are also determined to be unsuccessful work attempts and even if the recipient's income did not constitute substantial gainful activity.

The "services" amount, which was $200 during the years 1990 through 2000 and was raised to $530 per month beginning in 2001 and indexed annually after that, remains well below the substantial gainful activity level. 20 C.F.R. § 404.1592(b). For example, for 2016, the trial work period services amount is $810 per month while the substantial gainful activity amount is $1,030. *See* Appendix 12 for the trial work period services monthly amounts and SGA amounts for years after 2001.

For self-employed recipients, whether work constitutes "services" is determined by looking at both income and the number of hours worked. If income exceeds the "services" amount used for recipients employed by other people, then the work for that month constitutes "services." But even if a self-employed recipient does not earn this much, as long as he or she is working enough hours in a month, the month counts as a services month. Beginning with the year 2001, to constitute "services" a self-employed person must work more than 80 hours. From 1990 through 2000, if the self-

employed person worked more than 40 hours, the work met the definition of "services." 20 C.F.R. § 404.1592(b)(2).

Once the recipient performs "services" for 9 months in what SSA calls a rolling 60-month period, the trial work period is used up. 20 C.F.R. § 404.1592(e)(2). To determine whether the 9 months of work fall within the 60-month rolling period, take the last month that qualifies as a services month and count backward in time for 60 months. If during that 60-month period there are 9 months of trial work, the trial work period ends. POMS DI 13010.035D.

Although a recipient is entitled to only one trial work period during a period of disability, the recipient can actually have more than nine months of trial work if the months are spaced widely enough apart so that nine of them do not fall in any 60-month period.

The services amount is not subject to impairment-related work expenses deductions. POMS DI 10520.015A.2.a. "Services" are counted in the month the services were performed rather than in the month the recipient was paid. POMS DI 10505.005 C.1.d. Sick pay and vacation pay arguably should not be counted. *Cf.* 20 C.F.R. § 404.1592(b) and POMS DI 10505.010 C. As a rule, the "services" amount may not be averaged. POMS DI 10505.015 B. But when income is from commissions and a monthly income cannot be determined, it is permissible to average them over the months worked. POMS DI 13010.060 B.1.

§492   Will SSA Conduct Medical Review During Trial Work Period?

A trial work period ends after a recipient performs services in nine months during a rolling period of 60 months. 20 C.F.R. § 404.1592(e)(2). But it can also end earlier. According to 20 C.F.R. § 404.1592(e)(3), it can end:

> (3) The month in which new evidence, other than evidence relating to any work you did during the trial work period, shows that you are not disabled, even though you have not worked a full 9 months. We may find that your disability has ended at any time during the trial work period if the medical or other evidence shows that you are no longer disabled. *See* § 404.1594 for information on how we decide whether your disability continues or ends.

Note that in order for the trial work period to end and benefits to be terminated before the nine months of trial work are used up, SSA must have new evidence of improvement other than evidence relating to the work done by the recipient. This provision is meant as a work incentive. It is SSA's way of providing that the work itself won't be used against the recipient.

For SSA to discover new evidence of improvement, it must conduct a continuing disability review. In fact, return to work is a trigger for a continuing disability review. According to 20 C.F.R. § 404.1590(b), SSA will start a continuing disability review under the following circumstances:

(5) Substantial earnings are reported to your wage record;
(6) You tell us that—. . .
(ii) You have returned to work;
(7) Your State Vocational Rehabilitation Agency tells us that—. . .
(ii) You are now working;
(8) Someone in a position to know of your physical or mental condition tells us any of the following, and it appears that the report could be substantially correct: . . .
(iii) You have returned to work;

In other words, if the recipient reports that he has returned to work (which is required reporting, 20 C.F.R. § 404.1588(a)(2), enforced by potential criminal penalties, 42 U.S.C. § 408) or if anyone else reports that the recipient has returned to work, the regulations provide that SSA will conduct a continuing disability review. Although SSA provides the trial work period as an incentive for recipients to return to work, the specter of a continuing disability review operates as a distinct disincentive for return to work.

In order to increase the incentive for returning to work, 20 C.F.R. § 404.1590(i) establishes an exception for those who have received disability benefits for at least 24 months. For such recipients SSA will not start a medical continuing disability review based *solely* on a report of work activity. The POMS calls this "protection from medical review based on work activity." POMS DI 13010.012.

Nevertheless, although recipients of disability benefits who have received benefits for 24 months are protected from SSA *initiating* a continuing disability review solely because of work activity, such recipients are subject to regularly scheduled medical CDRs and medical CDRs that are initiated for other reasons. 20 C.F.R. § 404.1590(i)(3). POMS DI 13010.012A Note provides:

"If a beneficiary qualifies for protection from medical review based on work activity,

he or she will still undergo regularly scheduled medical CDRs, and to any other medical CDRs that are initiated for a reason(s) other than the beneficiary's work activity, unless the individual is "using a ticket" under the Ticket to Work program."

If SSA erroneously starts a medical continuing disability review solely because of work activity for a recipient who received 24 months of benefits, SSA will vacate any medical cessation determination as long as it receives information about its error within 12 months of the date of the cessation determination. 20 C.F.R. § 404.1590(i)(5).

SSA also says that for those recipients who have received benefits for 24 months, it will not consider the activities performed in the work done by the recipient during the current period of entitlement based on disability if the activities support a finding that disability has ended. But SSA will consider the work activities if they support a conclusion that disability continues. 20 C.F.R. § 404.1594(i)(2). For those not subject to protection from continuing review because they have received benefits for 24 months, at the conclusion of the trial work period, SSA will consider whether the work performed during the trial work period shows that the disability has ended. 20 C.F.R. § 404.1592(a). *See also* POMS DI 13010.060E.

If someone is participating in the ticket-to-work program described at 20 C.F.R. §§ 411.100 to 411.730, SSA will not begin a continuing disability review during the period in which the recipient is using the ticket. 20 C.F.R. § 411.165.

There is one other major exception. When a recipient is participating in an "appropriate program of vocational rehabilitation services, employment services, or other support services as described in § 404.327(a) and (b)," 20 C.F.R. § 404.316(c)(1)(i), continuing disability reviews do not matter. Benefits may be continued after the impairment is no longer disabling. This program is referred to in the POMS as Section 301 payments because it was established in Section 301 of the Social Security Disability Amendments of 1980 (P.L. 96-265), 42 U.S.C. § 425(b). It is explained in POMS DI 14505.010A as follows:

Eligibility for payments under Section 301 applies to:
• Individuals receiving title II benefits based on disability, including Disability Insurance Benefits (DIB), Disabled Widow(er)'s Benefits (DWB), Childhood Disability Benefits (CDB), career railroad workers and/ or Railroad Retirement Board annuitants; and

- Individuals receiving title XVI benefits based on disability or blindness, including age 18 recipients whose disability is determined to have ended because of an age-18 redetermination.

An individual receiving title II or title XVI benefits based on disability or blindness must have been medically ceased or been determined to be ineligible due to an age 18 redetermination and meet all of the following requirements:

- The individual participates in an appropriate program of Vocational Rehabilitation (VR) services, employment services, or other support services;
- The individual began participating in the program before the month his or her disability or blindness ceased;
- The individual's participation in the program continues through the 2-month grace period after cessation; and
- We determined that the individual's completion of the program, or continuation in the program for a specified period-of-time, will increase the likelihood that the individual will not return to the disability or blindness benefit rolls.

Section 301 payments to the individual and any auxiliaries, including Medicare, Medicaid, and State Supplementation (where applicable), will continue until one of the following things happen:

a. the individual completes the program;
b. the individual stops participation in the program for any reason (excluding temporary interruptions as defined in DI 14505.010D); or
c. we determine that continued participation in the program will no longer increase the likelihood that the individual will not return to the disability or blindness benefit rolls.

The Office of Disability Operations (ODO) will make the determinations regarding initial and continuing eligibility under this provision after the Disability Determination Services (DDS) determines that disability or blindness has ceased as described in DI 14510.003.

§493   At Conclusion of Trial Work Period

Consider this case. Suppose a recipient with a high school education and a medium unskilled work background who was 49 when he was found disabled returns to work at a full-time sedentary job with earnings above the substantial gainful activity level. Let's say he worked 11 months by the time SSA evaluates his case. After the 9-month trial work period is over, monthly benefits will end when the claimant performs substantial gainful activity. Since he is performing SGA in the tenth

month of work, the tenth month of work is the month disability is found to have ceased. He is paid for that month and the next two months. 20 C.F.R. § 404.325.

SSA refers to this as finding that "disability ceased" under 20 C.F.R. § 404.1594(f)(1), step one of the CDR evaluation process. This is not a finding that the claimant no longer has a disabling impairment or that the claimant has medically improved. It is a finding only that the claimant is engaging in SGA after the end of the trial work period. *See* 20 C.F.R. § 404.1594(d)(5).

To determine if the claimant is performing SGA after the trial work period is over, unsuccessful work attempt rules apply, impairment-related work expenses (IRWEs), sick pay and vacation pay may be deducted, and income will be averaged to make sure the claimant is performing SGA. 20 C.F.R. § 404.1592a(a)(1).

After working for 9 months, disability ends because of performance of substantial gainful activity pursuant to step one of the CDR process. 20 C.F.R. § 404.1594(f)(1). This determination made at the local office is not a medical determination. The local office considers only whether it is appropriate to stop benefits because of the recipient's income, not whether he has medically improved.

For someone who has not yet received 24 months of benefits, SSA still has to determine whether or not the recipient continues to meet the "disability requirements of the law," that is, whether there has been medical improvement. A continuing disability review is required by 20 C.F.R. § 404.1590(b)(4) when a recipient returns to work and successfully completes a period of trial work. Thus, the state agency considers steps of the CDR process other than step 1.

But if the recipient has already received 24 months of benefits by the time the continuing disability review is begun, SSA will not conduct a continuing disability review. 20 C.F.R. § 404.1590(i). Since there will be no continuing disability review to find the recipient's medical disability has ended, it will be considered to continue.

Let us say that our hypothetical recipient (who has not yet received 24 months of benefits) has medically improved. There is both a decrease in medical severity as shown by symptoms, signs, and laboratory findings and an increase in his functional capacity from a medical point of view so that he is now determined to be capable of sedentary work. Since his past work was medium, he is not capable of performing past relevant work. (The sedentary job he is currently doing does not count as past relevant work. 20 C.F.R. § 404.1594(i)(1).) Since he is now over 50, Rule 201.12 of the Medical-Vocational Guidelines requires a finding that his disability continues.

How does SSA consider the work done in the trial work period after it is over? That is, will SSA use the work activity itself as evidence that a recipient is no longer medically disabled? The trial work period regulation says that SSA will not consider the work performed during the trial work period as showing that disability has ended until the recipient has performed nine months of trial work. But then SSA will consider that work. 20 C.F.R. § 404.1592(a). This makes no difference in our example of a 50-year-old recipient doing sedentary work. But if he were doing light work and SSA used the work to determine his residual functional capacity, he could be found not disabled pursuant to Rule 202.13 of the Medical-Vocational Guidelines.

But if a recipient has received benefits for 24 months before a continuing disability review is begun, SSA will not consider the work if it supports a finding that disability has ended; SSA will consider the work activity if it supports a finding that disability continues. *See* 20 C.F.R. § 404.1594(i)(2), which acts as an exception to 20 C.F.R. § 404.1592(a).

If the recipient is self-employed, there is a work incentive provision that applies if the recipient has received benefits for 24 months before a continuing disability review is begun. Recall that SSA, which is notoriously suspicious of self-employed people, uses three tests to determine if a claimant for disability benefits who is self-employed is working at the SGA level. Test one: Does the recipient provide significant services to the business *and* receive monthly income at the SGA level? If so, the recipient is performing SGA; but if the answer to test one is no, SSA considers tests two and three. 20 C.F.R. § 404.1575(a)(2)(i). SSA considers whether the work is comparable to that of unimpaired individuals in the community who are in a similar business as their means of livelihood—test two. 20 C.F.R. § 404.1575(a)(2)(ii). And SSA considers whether the *value* of the claimant's work to the business is clearly at the minimum SGA level—test three. 20 C.F.R. § 404.1575(a)(2)(iii). Although we try to show that the self-employment tests do not grant decision makers as much leeway as they appear to at first blush—*see* §176.3 of this book—test two and especially test three do appear to give decision makers a degree of latitude that tends to exasperate claimants' attorneys.

Once a self-employed recipient has received 24 months of benefits, SSA essentially applies only test one to determine if the self-employment is SGA. That is, SSA compares the self-employed recipient's countable income to the SGA amount, *e.g.*, $940 per month in 2008. If the recipient is not earning more than this amount, the work is not SGA. Even if the recipient is earning more than the SGA amount in a particular month but the recipient is not rendering significant services to the business in the particular month, the work will not be considered SGA. 20 C.F.R. § 404.1575(e) (3). SSA will also not consider the services performed

in work when it evaluates whether there was medical improvement unless the particulars of the work activity support a finding that disability continues. 20 C.F.R. § 404.1594(i)(2).

If the recipient is found to have medically improved, the recipient will not be eligible for resuming benefits during the reentitlement period if the recipient reduces income below the SGA level (*see* §494), or for expedited reinstatement (*see* §495) or Medicare continuation. On Medicare continuation, *see* POMS DI 28055.001, DI 28075.635 and HI 00820.025.

§494   *Extended Period of Eligibility/ Reentitlement Period*

As we have seen, once it is determined that the recipient is performing SGA after the trial work period is over, disability is found to cease because of performance of SGA. The recipient is paid for the first month of SGA and the next two months, whether or not the recipient does SGA in the next two months. 20 C.F.R. §§ 404.401a and 404.1592a(a)(2). Whether the recipient is paid benefits in the months after those three months depends on whether the recipient is actually performing SGA in those months and whether the recipient continues to have a disabling impairment.

For 36 months counting from the end of the trial work period, which is called the "reentitlement period" in the regulations and referred to as the "extended period of eligibility" (EPE) in the POMS, benefits will not be paid for any month in which the recipient is performing substantial gainful activity. Benefits will be paid for any month in which the recipient is not performing SGA as long as the recipient continues to have a disabling impairment. 20 C.F.R. § 404.1592a(a).

Benefits are not averaged for this determination, IRWEs may not be deducted, and unsuccessful work attempt rules do not apply. During the reentitlement period, payment is accomplished without a new application—an excellent arrangement for recipients experiencing starts and stops in their efforts to return to work. 20 C.F.R. § 404.1592a(a)(2)(i).

What happens after the 36-month reentitlement period is over? This depends on whether the recipient worked at the SGA level during the reentitlement period. If a recipient is found to be working at the SGA level at any time during the 36-month reentitlement period, SSA will find that the claimant's *entitlement* to disability benefits terminates with the very first month of SGA *after* the end of the reentitlement period. 20 C.F.R. § 404.1592a(a)(3). This is easiest to understand if we use examples. Assume that a claimant began working and never stopped—that is, the claimant worked in consecutive months at the

SGA level throughout the 9-month trial work period, the 36-month reentitlement period and beyond. If this was the work pattern, actual payment of the claimant's monthly benefits would stop with the 12th month of work (nine months of trial work plus three months after that), which would also happen to be the third month of the reentitlement period in this example. But entitlement to disability benefits does not end for another two and three-quarter years, even though the claimant is not getting paid during this time. *See* 20 C.F.R. § 404.325, Example 1 and POMS DI 13010.210. This rather technical "entitlement" that existed during the intervening months is the claimant's right to contact SSA to have benefits paid for any month the recipient's income drops below the SGA level.

If a recipient did not work at the SGA level at all during the 36-month reentitlement period after the end of the trial work period, that is, benefits were paid during this entire time, SS:

> will apply all of the relevant provisions of §§ 404.1571-404.1576 including, but not limited to, the provisions for averaging earnings, unsuccessful work attempts, and deducting impairment-related work expenses to determine whether your disability ceased because you performed substantial gainful activity after the reentitlement period. If we find that your disability ceased because you performed substantial gainful activity in a month after your reentitlement period ended, you will be paid benefits for the month in which your disability ceased and the two succeeding months. After those three months, your entitlement to a period of disability or to disability benefits terminates (*see* §§ 404.321 and 404.325).

20 C.F.R. § 404.1592a(a)(3). *See also* POMS DI 13010.210.

If the recipient worked enough at the beginning of the 36-month reentitlement period to have benefits cease because of performance of SGA, and then stops working during the reentitlement period, the recipient's benefits will resume and continue beyond the 36-month reentitlement period until the very first month the recipient performs SGA. For this determination, income is not averaged and unsuccessful work attempt rules do not apply, though IRWEs may be deducted and subsidies or special consideration by the employer may be considered. POMS DI 13010.210 D. Benefits will stop with the first month the claimant's earnings, after appropriate deductions, exceed the SGA amount; and they do not resume if, for example, the very next month the claimant stops working again. Entitlement has terminated with that first month of SGA after the end of the 36-month reentitlement period. 20 C.F.R. § 404.325.

Consider the consequences of using up the trial work period. Note that the 36-month reentitlement period does not begin until the nine-month trial work period ends. Thus, if a claimant never uses up the trial work period, the 36-month reentitlement rules never kick in. Note that even if the claimant never works during the 36-month extended period of eligibility, and starts working after the 36 months have passed, the claimant's entitlement to disability benefits will end once it is determined that the claimant is performing SGA. At least for this SGA determination, though, all of the rules for evaluating a recipient's work apply including unsuccessful work attempt rules and the rules for averaging earnings.

Because there are significant consequences for using up the trial work period, in our memorandum to recipients about working part time after they have been found disabled, we recommend that they keep their income below the trial work services amount. *See* §461.

§495   *Expedited Reinstatement*

If a recipient, whose benefits were terminated because of the performance of SGA, stops working after the end of the reentitlement period, that recipient can request "expedited reinstatement," referred to as EXR in the POMS, for 60 months after entitlement is terminated because the claimant returned to work at the SGA level. To qualify for expedited reinstatement, an individual must:

(1) Not be performing SGA in the month he or she applies for EXR;

(2) Be unable to work at the SGA level due to his or her medical condition;

(3) Have his or her current medical impairment be the same as or related to the original impairment; and

(4) Be under a disability based on application of the medical improvement review standards set forth in 20 C.F.R. § 404.1594.

See 20 C.F.R. §§ 404.1592b through 404.1592f.

§496   *Working SSI Recipients*

For SSI, there is no trial work period, no reentitlement period and no expedited reinstatement. In addition, 20 C.F.R. § 416.994 makes no mention of performance of SGA as a consideration in determining if disability has ended. Compare the evaluation steps for finding medical improvement in the SSI rules, 20 C.F.R. § 416.994(b)(5), with the steps for finding medical improvement in the Title II case, 20 C.F.R. § 404.1594(f). *See also* 42 U.S.C. § 1382h, known as Section 1619 of the Social Security Act.

Section 1619(a) provides that the SGA rules do not apply to SSI recipients as long as they continue to have a disabling impairment. (The SGA rules apply for initially determining if an SSI claimant is disabled.) To be eligible for monthly benefits under section 1619(a), an SSI recipient must continue to meet the asset and income rules of the SSI program. Monthly SSI benefits will be reduced in accord with the rules for working beneficiaries. *See* 20 C.F.R. §§ 416.260 to 416.267, and 416.1111.

SSA will reduce SSI benefits by one dollar for every two dollars earned after the first $65 (or $85 if there is no other income). 20 C.F.R. §§ 416.1110 to 416.1112. Thus, it is possible to earn so much working part-time that the SSI benefits will be suspended. 20 C.F.R. § 416.1323(a). But unless the benefits have stopped because of earnings for an entire year, SSA will start up the benefits again if earnings go down. 20 C.F.R. § 416.1323(b). After a year of receiving no benefits, a new application is required. 20 C.F.R. § 416.1335. *See* POMS SI 02302.006 B.

Chapter 5

Appeals Council

§500 Appeals Council: The Decision to Appeal

§501 The Final Step of Administrative Review

When benefits are denied by an ALJ decision, the final administrative appeal is to the Appeals Council, the main office of which is located in Falls Church, Virginia, a suburb of Washington, D.C. From 2008 to 2011, annual receipts of Requests for Review filed by claimants grew dramatically—up 14.5% in fiscal year 2009, up 20.3% in 2010 and up 34.7% in 2011—to the point where the Appeals Council received 173,332 Requests for Review in fiscal year 2011 compared to 93,454 in 2008. In 2012 and 2013, the number of Requests for Review leveled off with 173,849 in 2012 and 172,492 in 2013. In 2014 the number of Requests for Review dropped to 155,352. In 2015, there were 149,437 Requests for Review.

The Executive Director of the Office of Appellate Operations, which includes more than 1,250 support personnel for the Appeals Council, acts as the Deputy Chair of the Appeals Council. The Deputy Chair, along with an Assistant Deputy Chair, is responsible for day-to-day operation of the Appeals Council. Although the Executive Director/Deputy Chair is sometimes referred to informally as the "head" of the Appeals Council, the Deputy Commissioner for the Office of Disability Adjudication and Review is the titular Chair of the Appeals Council.

The Appeals Council has about 75 administrative appeals judges (AAJs) and more than 40 appeals officers. The Appeals Council is organized into 7 Disability Program Divisions, 1 Quality Review Division, and 1 Civil Action Division. Within these divisions there are 33 disability program branches, a Retirement and Survivors Insurance (RSI) branch, 4 quality review branches, and an attorney fee branch. The disability program branches handle claimants' disability appeals. The RSI branch handles appeals not involving disability issues in retirement, survivor, and SSI cases. The quality review branches handle own motion review. Each branch has at least one administrative appeals judge assigned to it along with one or two appeals officers. In addition to branches in Falls Church, there are several branches in two locations in Baltimore near SSA's Office of Central Operations. Another group of branches is located in the Crystal City area of Alexandria, Virginia. All branches use the Falls Church mailing address.

Five branches, known as court case preparation and review branches (CCPRBs), handle court cases. When a claimant files a case in federal court, one of these branches prepares a certified transcript that is filed in court. The CCPRBs are generally the clearinghouse for *all* cases going to and coming back from court, including appeals from ALJ decisions after court remand. The CCPRBs also act on most requests for voluntary remand from the Office of General Counsel. Assignment of cases to four of these branches is based on the circuit in which the district court is located. A fifth branch handles overflow work.

An administrative appeals judge in one of the disability program branches, acting alone, cannot reverse or remand an ALJ decision. To reverse or remand a case, the first judge assigned to the case, known as the "A judge," must conclude that the case is appropriate for the Appeals Council to review. The case then passes to a second judge, known as the "B judge." Both the A and the B judges are chosen using an assignment system based on the claimant's Social Security number and on the judicial circuit where the claimant resides, which allows judges to specialize in the law of particular circuits. If the A and B judges do not agree, a C judge is appointed using a rotation system among division chief administrative appeals judges. The C judge votes to break the tie. *See* 20 C.F.R. §422.205(b). While two votes are required to reverse or remand a case, the signature of only one judge is needed to deny review. Review also may be denied by one of the appeals officers, attorneys who are members of the Appeals Council but who are not judges and who have no authority to reverse or remand a case. An appeals officer has signature authority only in those cases for which there are appeal rights. 20 C.F.R. §422.205(c). Appeals officers therefore do not act in cases involving dismissal.

If the Appeals Council decides that issuing a partially favorable decision is the appropriate course, it will give the claimant and attorney notice and the opportunity to argue against this result.

In addition, in a tiny but apparently increasing number of cases, the Appeals Council will reverse the ALJ decision and issue a new (and theoretically better reasoned) denial decision, which the Appeals Council calls a correcting decision. When it intends to do this, the Appeals Council will give the claimant and attorney notice and the opportunity to submit arguments contesting this course of action.

The stated purpose of the Appeals Council is to ensure that the law, regulations and binding policies of the Social Security Administration are followed, and to promote consistent decision-making among ALJs. Most claimants' attorneys say that this purpose has never been fully achieved—that the Appeals Council has always upheld too many wrong decisions; but in recent years, a time when ALJs are turning down more and more disabled claimants, the Appeals Council has abdicated its responsibilities to claimants by emphasizing productivity over following the law. It has increasingly denied review. In FY 2010, the Appeals Council granted review in 24.94% of its dispositions; in FY 201 24.43%; in FY 2012 21.16%; in FY 2013 18.98%; and 16.12% in FY 2014. Because the number of cases dealt with by the Appeals Council is so much greater than the number of cases that are appealed to the federal courts, in 2012 the Appeals Council found disability or remanded nearly five times the number of claimants' cases remanded or paid by the federal courts—about 34,000 cases compared to about 7,000 cases. In 2014 the Appeals Council granted review in 26,167 cases compared to 8,768 court remands.

The Appeals Council can be frustrating to deal with. It often turns down good cases, cases involving truly disabled claimants who received erroneous ALJ decisions for unfathomable reasons. Indeed, when it turns down an appeal, the Appeals Council's official policy is not to offer an explanation. From 1995 to 2012, the Appeals Council operated under a *temporary* directive that suspended a HALLEX requirement that denial notices contain specific responses to arguments why the ALJ decision is wrong. In 2012, this policy was made permanent. See HALLEX I-3-5-15 A. When arguments are submitted, it is Appeals Council policy to say that the arguments have been considered, but that they do "not provide a basis for changing the ALJ's decision." HALLEX I-3-5-15 B.

Although the overall chances of winning a remand or reversal from the Appeals Council at first glance look to be quite limited, the odds for good cases that are well-briefed may not be as bad as they look. Lawyers who choose their cases carefully and spend the time necessary to develop arguments and write good briefs report receiving remands or reversals from the Appeals Council far more often than is reflected in the overall statistics. The purpose of this chapter is to help you increase your odds of success at the Appeals Council. But if you have a good case that is turned down by the Appeals Council, remember, the federal courts reverse or remand about one-half the cases that come before them.

§502   Should You Appeal?

Never appeal a bad case. Both you and the Appeals Council have better things to do than deal with cases involving claimants who do not meet SSA's disability standard. When you have a disabled client, though, you are faced with a difficult choice after receiving an ALJ denial decision. To obtain disability benefits for your client you must appeal or have your client file a new application. Your client generally cannot do both.

But see §507.1. That is, your client cannot file a new application until the appeal to the Appeals Council is concluded. *See* §507.2.

If your client is genuinely disabled, appealing may be the best route to obtaining benefits. Begin with an assessment of whether your client is disabled. But be aware this is *not* the issue at the Appeals Council where substantial evidence and legal error are the threshold issues for success. This recommendation is based on the idea that if you understand your client's disability and you understand Social Security regulations and rulings (which were designed to yield correct decisions), you can usually find a pretty good argument that the ALJ decision failed to follow the law. *See* §504. Or you can find new evidence of disability. *See* §524.

To avoid tilting at windmills, though, you need to look carefully at your client's case and your predilection to believe your client. Although Social Security disability lawyers have never been studied, when social scientists or psychologists have looked at lawyers in other areas they have found lawyers to be overconfident in their predictions of outcomes. *See*, for example, Goodman-Delahunty, *et al.*, "Insightful or wishful: Lawyers' ability to predict case outcomes," *Psychology, Public Policy, and Law*, Vol 16(2), May 2010, 133-157.

If you start your analysis not with whether your client is disabled but rather with whether there are legal errors in the ALJ decision that might require a remand, you could end up wasting a lot of time. You may get the case remanded for another hearing. But you very well may ultimately lose. Do not let legal errors in the ALJ decision divert your attention from your client's disability.

If your client is genuinely disabled and the denial decision can be attributed to the bad luck of drawing a low paying ALJ, you may be tempted by the new application option. A remand to the same ALJ is likely to lead to the same result. You may need two remands and the assignment of a different ALJ to win the case. But how likely is it that the state agency will find your client disabled on a new application? How likely is it that the ALJ denial decision will taint the analysis of the state agency? Before electronic files were the norm, although the state agency could see there had been an ALJ denial decision, the state agency usually did not see the decision itself. Now it is easy for state agency examiners to look at the decision online, conclude that their co-workers were right about this claim the first time around, and deny the new application.

When a second application gets to the ALJ hearing level, success is not assured even for a genuinely disabled claimant. Many ALJs view second applications as almost morally wrong because they contribute to the hearing backlog. Your genuinely disabled client may not have an easy time being found disabled on a second application.

Although this is a subject about which lawyers argue over the best course, the author is in the camp that says for a genuinely disabled claimant, appealing is better than a new application. Nevertheless, there may be differences depending on where you are in the country—different state agencies, different ALJ personnel, different federal courts and different circuit law. You need to examine these issues for yourself. Note, though, that in the 4th, 6th and 9th circuits, the analysis may tilt even more strongly toward appealing because of some acquiescence rulings, which apply a presumption that the claimant's RFC remains as it was when the denial decision was issued. *See* AR 97-4(9), AR 98-4(6) and AR 00-1(4).

The decision whether to appeal is even more agonizing when your client's disability is less clear. The author often is in favor of appeal, but these are tough decisions. The decision is easy in cases in which the date last insured has already passed before the date of the ALJ denial decision. Appeal is your client's only hope. In this situation you need to investigate whether a new SSI claim can be pending at the same time your client's Title II claim is pending at the Appeals Council. *See* §507.

There are a few unwinnable cases, though. There are a few cases of disabled claimants where ALJs did such good jobs writing denial decisions that the Appeals Council will certainly deny the appeals. Such cases are usually not good cases for federal court review. When you have such a case, it is important to advise your client of the prognosis for appeal. The only possible alternative is to file a new application. *See* §506. Maybe with your help on a new application, a better case can be built.

If you recommend against an appeal that the claimant wants to pursue, the claimant may file a Request for Review of Hearing Decision with the help of local Social Security office personnel. Tell the claimant that you have taken the case as far as you are willing to take it; the claimant is now on his or her own; remind the claimant of the time limit; and send the claimant to the local office.

What about those cases in which the claimant has received a partially favorable decision? Because the Appeals Council may give more review than you request, these cases present some particularly knotty strategic and ethical problems which are discussed at §508.

§503 Exhaustion of Administrative Remedies

When a claimant simply requests review by the Appeals Council, the claimant has exhausted administrative remedies—a prerequisite for filing the claimant's case in federal court. Nothing more is required. No arguments are required to be made to the Appeals Council, though, of course, a claimant or attorney has the right to present an argument. *See* 20 C.F.R. §404.967 *ff.* Except in a case remanded by a federal court, *see* §560, Social Security regulations impose no requirements about the content or quality of arguments to be presented to the Appeals Council.

In *Sims v. Apfel*, 530 U.S. 103 (2000), the Supreme Court decided that a judicially created issue exhaustion rule was not appropriate for non-adversarial Social Security proceedings. The Court pointed out that under the regulations, the Appeals Council, not the claimant, has primary responsibility for identifying and developing the issues. 530 U.S. at 112. Thus, you are not required to raise arguments to the Appeals Council that you may want to raise later in federal court.

Nevertheless, good lawyering requires that you address all significant issues in your client's case and explain why the Appeals Council should find your client disabled or remand your client's claim for another hearing. Although there are examples of unrepresented claimants (and even some represented ones) whose cases are remanded or paid by the Appeals Council based on a Request for Review that does little more than say the ALJ decision is wrong, most observers say cases that are not well-briefed at the Appeals Council get short shrift. They are likely to end up in the 75 percent of cases that are denied by the Appeals Council with little more than a form letter.

§504 Develop a Legal Theory for the Appeal

The best arguments for successful Appeals Council review are those in which you show that the ALJ decision 1) failed to follow a Social Security regulation or ruling *and* 2) is not supported by substantial evidence *and* 3) the claimant is disabled. An argument *only* that the claimant is disabled—without showing how the ALJ decision is faulty—is likely doomed.

The Appeals Council will not even look at the issue of whether a claimant is disabled until after it concludes that the ALJ decision is not supported by substantial evidence, is legally erroneous, or that there was an abuse of discretion by the ALJ. *See* §523. If the

Appeals Council concludes that the decision is faulty, unless it also concludes there is at least a good chance the claimant is disabled, the Appeals Council could conclude the error was harmless. *See* §505. Sometimes in this situation, though, depending on the magnitude of the error in the ALJ decision, the Appeals Council will conclude that the case cannot be defended in federal court. Thus, it may rewrite the ALJ denial decision to make it more defensible or it may remand the case for another hearing.

The first thing you need to do is find a good legal argument that the ALJ decision is erroneous. Evaluate the decision using the sequential evaluation process to develop a legal theory for the appeal. The following questions are offered as food for thought, not as an all-inclusive outline for appeal issues. Use them to help find the weakest points in the ALJ's rationale.

At each step ask:
- Is the ALJ decision substantially supported by the evidence?
- Does the medical evidence really say what the decision claims it says?
- Does the decision give even minimal reasons for its conclusions? 20 C.F.R. §404.953(a).
- Does the decision "reconcile any significant inconsistencies," particularly between its findings and opinions from all medical sources, including nonexamining state agency reviewers? SSR 86-8.
- Does the decision explain why evidence supporting a finding of disability was rejected?
- Does the decision rely on evidence that was not "offered at the hearing or otherwise included in the record"? 20 C.F.R. §404.953(a). *See also* 42 U.S.C. §405(b)(1).
- Does the decision cite medical texts or medical publications, which were not proffered to the claimant, as the authority for resolving any issue? HALLEX I-2-8-25 A.

If the claim is denied wholly or in part at Step 1 (substantial gainful activity), ask:
- Did the decision mechanically find SGA based on the amount of earnings without considering testimony or other evidence (material to outcome) of subsidized earnings or impairment-related work expenses? SSR 83-33, SSR 84-26.

If the claim is denied at Step 2 (no severe impairment) or a particular impairment is found to be non-severe, ask:
- Did the decision apply the standard in SSR 85-28, "that the impairment(s) would not have more than a minimal effect on the performance of basic work-related functions"? *See also* SSR 96-3p.
- Did the decision correctly determine based on medical signs and laboratory findings that there was no medically determinable mental impairment? SSR 96-4p.
- Did the decision correctly apply the special evaluation technique required by 20 C.F.R. §404.1520a when it found that a medically determinable mental impairment was not severe?
- Did the decision find no severe impairment based on the medical evidence alone, without considering the credibility of symptoms, in the face of evidence of medically determinable impairments that could reasonably be expected to produce the pain or other symptoms alleged? SSRs 96-3p, 96-4p and 96-7p.

At Step 3 (meets or equals Listing of Impairments), ask:
- If a mental impairment is alleged, did the decision apply the special evaluation technique required by 20 C.F.R. §404.1520a?
- Does the decision set out a boilerplate conclusion that no listings are met or equaled without addressing a colorable interpretation of the evidence that a particular listing is met or equaled?

In evaluating the weight given to medical opinions from treating sources, ask:
- Does the decision evaluate and explain the weight given to all medical opinions that are inconsistent with its findings?
- Is there a treating source medical opinion in the file that is well-supported by medically acceptable clinical and laboratory diagnostic techniques and is not inconsistent with other substantial evidence in the case record? If so, it must be given controlling weight. SSR 96-2p.
- Is there a treating source medical opinion in the file which is not entitled to controlling weight (because it is not "well-supported" or is inconsistent with other evidence) that may be entitled to deference and should have been adopted by the ALJ? Does the ALJ decision end its evaluation of this opinion with a conclusion only that the opinion cannot be given controlling weight? SSR 96-2p.
- Does the ALJ require more than that the medical opinion be "well-supported"? Does the ALJ, in effect, require that the medical opinion be "fully supported" by medically acceptable clinical and laboratory diagnostic techniques? Note that SSR 96-2p provides that for a medical opinion to be "well-supported by medically acceptable clinical and laboratory diagnostic techniques, it is not necessary that the opinion be fully supported by such evidence."
- Does the decision weigh the medical source statement under the rules set out in 20 C.F.R. §404.1527? "The regulations provide progressively more rigorous tests for weighing opinions as the

ties between the source of the opinion and the individual become weaker. For example, the opinions of physicians or psychologists who do not have a treatment relationship with the individual are weighed by stricter standards, based to a greater degree on medical evidence, qualifications, and explanations for the opinions, than are required of treating sources." SSR 96-6p.

- If the decision concluded that the opinion of a state agency doctor was entitled to more weight than that of the treating doctor, was the state agency doctor's opinion "supported by evidence in the case record, considering such factors as the supportability of the opinion in the evidence including any evidence received at the administrative law judge and Appeals Council levels that was not before the State agency, the consistency of the opinion with the record as a whole, including other medical opinions, and any explanation for the opinion provided by the State agency medical or psychological consultant"? SSR 96-6p.

- Does the decision give "good reasons" for the weight given to a treating source's opinion? 20 C.F.R. §404.1527(c)(2). Are these reasons "supported by the evidence in the case record" and is the decision "sufficiently specific to make clear to any subsequent reviewers the weight the adjudicator gave to the treating source's medical opinion and the reasons for that weight"? SSR 96-2p.

- Does the decision take into account opinions from sources who are not "acceptable medical sources"? Except for questions about the existence of a medically determinable impairment, opinions from medical professionals such as nurse practitioners "may outweigh the opinion of an 'acceptable medical source'" and are to be weighed under criteria effectively identical to those that apply to opinions from acceptable medical sources. SSR 06-03p.

- Does the ALJ decision evaluate decisions on disability by other governmental and nongovernmental agencies? "These decisions, and the evidence used to make these decisions, may provide insight into the individual's mental and physical impairment(s) and show the degree of disability determined by these agencies based on their rules." SSR 06-03p.

In examining the decision's evaluation of symptoms, see note below and ask:

- Does the decision apply the two-step process for evaluating symptoms? First, the ALJ must determine whether there is an underlying medically determinable impairment that could reasonably be expected to produce the claimant's symptoms. This inquiry "does not involve a determination as to the intensity, persistence, or functionally limiting effects of the symptoms." 20 C.F.R. § 404.1529(b). Intensity, persistence and limiting effects of a claimant's pain is considered at the second step. 20 C.F.R. §404.1529(c). *See* the discussion at §§250-255.

- Does the decision misstate or distort the claimant's testimony?

- Does the decision fail to address evidence consistent with the claimant's statements about symptoms, particularly for the areas listed in 20 C.F.R. §404.1529(c)?
  1. The individual's daily activities;
  2. The location, duration, frequency, and intensity of the individual's pain or other symptoms;
  3. Factors that precipitate and aggravate symptoms;
  4. The type, dosage, effectiveness, and side effects of any medications the individual takes or has taken to alleviate pain or other symptoms;
  5. Treatment, other than medication, the individual receives or has received for relief of pain or other symptoms;
  6. Any measures other than treatment the individual uses or has used to relieve pain or other symptoms (e.g., lying flat on his or her back, standing for 15 to 20 minutes every hour, or sleeping on a board); and
  7. Any other factors concerning the individual's functional limitations and restrictions due to pain or other symptoms.

- Does the decision "contain specific reasons for the weight given to the individual's symptoms"? Is it "consistent with and supported by the evidence"? And is it "clearly articulated so the individual and any subsequent reviewer can assess how the adjudicator evaluated the individual's symptoms"? SSR 16-3p. Or is it instead rationalized with boiler plate statements?

- If the level or frequency of treatment is inconsistent with the level of complaints or if the individual is not following treatment as prescribed, does the ALJ draw inferences from this "without considering possible reasons he or she may not comply with treatment or seek treatment consistent with the degree of his or her complaints"? SSR 16-3p. SSR 16-3p provides examples of reasons an individual may not have pursued treatment including: structuring daily activities to minimize symptoms to a tolerable level; failure to take prescribed medication because side effects are less tolerable than the symptoms; symptoms may have plateaued; inability to afford treatment; advice by medical source that there is no further effective treatment that can be prescribed; or medical treatment may be contrary to the tenets of the claimant's religion.

- Did the ALJ consider the consistency of the claimant's statements? SSR 16-3p provides: "If an individual's various statements about the intensity, persistence, and limiting effects of symptoms are consistent with one another and consistent with the objective medical evidence and other evidence in the record, we will determine that an individual's symptoms are more likely to reduce his or her capacities for work-related activities..."

Note: The evaluation of symptoms is deficient in probably a majority of ALJ decisions. But perhaps for fear of opening the floodgates, as long as symptoms are addressed at all in the ALJ decision (unless it is totally crazy), the Appeals Council is unlikely to remand a case because of such errors alone. Nevertheless, arguments about symptom evaluation add to the weight of your Appeals Council arguments and, if nothing else, may signal to the Appeals Council that you're likely to be able to convince a federal court to remand the claimant's case.

In evaluating the decision's assessment of residual functional capacity (RFC), ask:

- Does a fair reading of the medical records support the ALJ's conclusions about RFC?
- Did the ALJ "make every reasonable effort to ensure that the file contains sufficient evidence to assess RFC"? SSR 96-8p.
- Does the decision provide "an assessment of an individual's ability to do sustained work-related physical and mental activities in a work setting on a regular and continuing basis"? 20 C.F.R. §404.1545(b) and (c). A "'regular and continuing basis' means 8 hours a day, for 5 days a week, or an equivalent work schedule." SSR 96-8p.
- Is the RFC assessment "based on all of the relevant evidence in the case record, including information about the individual's symptoms and any 'medical source statements'—i.e., opinions about what the individual can still do despite his or her impairment(s)—submitted by an individual's treating source or other acceptable medical sources"? SSR 96-8p.
- Does the RFC assessment "consider the limiting effects of all . . . impairment(s), even those that are not severe"? 20 C.F.R. §404.1545(e) and SSR 96-8p.
- Was the combination of impairments addressed?
- Was the impact of obesity addressed in the decision? SSR 02-1p provides: "The combined

effects of obesity with other impairments may be greater than might be expected without obesity."
- Is the RFC assessment based on all the relevant evidence in the record such as the following items listed in SSR 96-8p?
  1. Medical history,
  2. Medical signs and laboratory findings,
  3. The effects of treatment, including limitations or restrictions imposed by the mechanics of treatment (e.g., frequency of treatment, duration, disruption to routine, side effects of medication),
  4. Reports of daily activities,
  5. Lay evidence,
  6. Recorded observations,
  7. Medical source statements,
  8. Effects of symptoms, including pain, that are reasonably attributed to a medically determinable impairment,
  9. Evidence from attempts to work,
  10. Need for a structured living environment, and
  11. Work evaluations, if available.
- Does the RFC assessment "include a narrative discussion describing how the evidence supports each conclusion, citing specific medical facts (e.g., laboratory findings) and nonmedical evidence (e.g., daily activities, observations)"? SSR 96-8p.
- Do the "objective" test results relied upon by the ALJ decision tell one very much about RFC? Note that 20 C.F.R. § 404.1529(c)(3) states that "symptoms sometimes suggest a greater severity of impairment than can be shown by objective medical evidence alone" and that "symptoms, such as pain, are subjective and difficult to quantify."
- Is there a medical opinion linking the "objective" evidence relied upon by the ALJ to the conclusion about RFC?
- Is the ALJ qualified to draw conclusions from the objective evidence on which the decision relies?
- Does the decision "explain how any material inconsistencies or ambiguities in the evidence in the case record were considered and resolved"? SSR 96-8p.
- Does the RFC assessment assess the claimant's work-related abilities on a function-by-function basis? SSR 96-8p. (Only after assessment on a function-by-function basis "may RFC be expressed in terms of the exertional levels of work," e.g., sedentary. SSR 96-8p.)
- Is non-exertional capacity expressed in terms of work-related functions? SSR 96-8p.

- In cases where inability to tolerate certain kinds of work stress is alleged, does the decision make a specific finding concerning the aspects of work the claimant himself or herself finds stressful, or is the decision based on an implicit assumption that anyone can do generic "low stress" work? *Cf.* SSR 85-15.
- If the decision finds that the claimant must alternate sitting and standing, is the RFC assessment "specific as to the frequency of the individual's need to alternate sitting and standing"? SSR 96-9p.
- If the claimant has environmental restrictions, does the RFC assessment "specify which environments are restricted and state the extent of the restriction"? SSR 96-9p.

Concerning past relevant work, ask:

- Is there a specific finding concerning the physical and mental requirements of past relevant work? 20 C.F.R. §404.1560(b) and SSR 82-62. If there is no specific finding, is there evidence contrary to the decision's implicit findings about the demands of the past relevant work?
- If there are significant nonexertional limitations, how was it determined that the claimant can do past relevant work?
- Does the decision use the RFC assessment for a function-by-function comparison with the functional demands of an individual's past relevant work as he or she actually performed it and then, if necessary, as the work is generally performed in the national economy? SSR 96-8p. *See also* SSR 96-9p.
- Is the work which the ALJ decision classified as past relevant work:
  1. work done within the past 15 years;
  2. work which lasted long enough for the claimant to learn to do it; and
  3. work which was substantial gainful activity? 20 C.F.R. §404.1565(a).

At Step 5 of the sequential evaluation process, ask:

- Does the ALJ decision correctly apply the Medical-Vocational Guidelines?
- Do the claimant's vocational characteristics accurately fit the categories set forth in the Medical-Vocational Guidelines?
- If the claimant's characteristics do not exactly fit the Medical-Vocational Guidelines, is the deviation little enough that the Guidelines may still be applied without the assistance of a vocational expert?
- How does the ALJ decision deal with the claimant's nonexertional limitations?
- Did the ALJ obtain a vocational expert's opinion concerning the impact of significant nonexertional limitations?

- Does one of the hypothetical questions to the vocational expert address the RFC ultimately found by the ALJ to be the claimant's RFC?
- Did the ALJ properly apply the concept of using the Medical-Vocational Guidelines as a framework for decision-making?
- Did the ALJ correctly deal with the complicated issue of transferable work skills? Does the decision identify acquired work skills? Does the decision identify the semiskilled or skilled jobs within the claimant's RFC to which the claimant's acquired work skills transfer? Did the decision apply the correct standard of transferability for the claimant's age? *See* §§349-349.9.
- Did the ALJ inquire at the hearing whether there was consistency between the vocational expert's testimony and the *Dictionary of Occupational Titles* (DOT)? SSR 00-4p.
- Did the vocational expert rely on any underlying assumptions that are inconsistent with SSA regulatory policies or definitions? SSR 00-4p.
- Did the decision provide a reasonable explanation resolving any conflicts between the vocational expert's testimony and the DOT? SSR 00-4p.

In closed period cases ask:

- Did the ALJ decision apply the medical improvement standard? SSR 02-1p, note 2; SSR 02-2p, note 4.
- Is sufficient rationale with reference to supporting medical evidence provided for the date of medical improvement?
- Did the decision consider or apply provisions regarding trial work period and extended period of eligibility? *See* §§490 to 494.

Practice Tips

If your argument is that the ALJ failed to accord due process to the claimant, before you research Constitutional law, look at HALLEX. In many instances, HALLEX provides a short cut to a due process analysis. If the ALJ decision violates a specific requirement of HALLEX, base your primary argument on HALLEX but also point out that the ALJ's action constitutes a denial of due process.

If you prevail at the Appeals Council, the Council will probably send the claimant's case back to the same ALJ for a new hearing. Start thinking about your strategy for another hearing early. Ask yourself: How is this case going to be won if the Appeals Council remands it for a new hearing with the same ALJ?

§505　The Harmless Error Rule

A harmless error is an error in a decision that does not affect the outcome of the case. No statute, regulation, or ruling states that the Appeals Council will apply a harmless error rule when evaluating claimants' appeals. No statute, regulation or ruling articulates the test for harmless error. Although there is a statement in SSR 82-13 (and HALLEX I-3-6-1 C) that says, in effect, a harmless error rule applies to own motion review ("The Appeals Council will not ordinarily review a hearing decision where the end result would remain unchanged unless there is a compelling need to do so") the test for harmless error is not described.

Nevertheless, the Appeals Council certainly applies a harmless error rule to claimants' appeals. And what is more, it applies the rule differently at different times. When the adjudicative climate turns against claimants, the Appeals Council applies the harmless error rule vigorously so that many errors are found to be harmless. At other times, the Appeals Council finds fewer errors to be harmless and therefore vacates more ALJ decisions.

There are many ways to state a test for harmless error with subtle and sometimes not so subtle differences. The test has been articulated as "a significant chance that but for the error the agency might have reached a different result." *NLRB v. American Geri-Care, Inc.* 697 F. 2d 56, 64 (2d Cir. 1982). For the now defunct Decision Review Board, SSA proposed but never adopted a regulation that stated the test should be whether "there is a reasonable probability that the error, alone or when considered with other aspects of the case, changed the outcome of the decision." 72 Fed. Reg. 61234 (2007). The Ninth Circuit Court of Appeals has held that "where the ALJ's error lies in a failure to properly discuss competent lay testimony favorable to the claimant, a reviewing court cannot consider the error harmless unless it can confidently conclude that no reasonable ALJ, when fully crediting the testimony, could have reached a different disability determination." *Stout v. Commissioner, Soc. Sec. Admin.*, 454 F.3d 1050, 1056 (9th Cir. 2006).

In short, we know the Appeals Council applies a harmless error test, but we do not know precisely the standards of that test. Therefore, we need to argue it in general terms: whether the defect in the decision affects the outcome of the case. If it does, the error is not harmless. This is important to keep in mind when writing an Appeals Council brief. It is your job to demonstrate why the errors you point out in the ALJ decision, if corrected, could lead to your client being found disabled.

If a decision is not supported by substantial evidence, it is usually easy to show that the error is harmful. There are two problems with substantial evidence arguments, though. First, reasonable minds may differ on what is substantial. This is sometimes a close call. Second, what happens if the evidence cited by the ALJ is not substantial, but other substantial evidence in the record supports the ALJ's conclusion? This problem is implicitly addressed at HALLEX I-3-3-4 B.1, which directs the analyst to consider evidence cited in the ALJ decision and evaluate the entire record. One note to this HALLEX provision refers to the harmless error rule. The other says "it may be appropriate for the AC to issue a corrective decision." (A "corrective decision" is one in which the Appeals Council rewrites the denial decision to make it better.) To attempt to head this off, do not stop with an argument simply that a particular finding is not supported by substantial evidence. Show how the decision's unsupported finding cannot be read as obvious from the evidence.

An argument that the ALJ decision contains a legal defect, on the other hand, can be clear cut: the ALJ decision failed to do something required by a regulation or ruling. But even here unless you show how correcting the legal error could lead to a finding that the claimant is disabled, the Appeals Council may find even such a legal defect to be harmless error.

§506　Starting Over With a New Application

Recommend filing a new application instead of appealing to the Appeals Council only in unusual circumstances. If you're sure the claimant's case will be denied by both the Appeals Council and federal court, you must ask yourself why a new application might be successful. If it is a case where a new application might have a chance, won't an appeal have a chance, too? You may think that if evidence in a case can support both sides of an issue, a different ALJ might decide the crucial issue in the claimant's favor. You may think you might be able to convince a different ALJ to reopen the earlier claim. But there is a tendency of one ALJ to follow a preceding ALJ's decision, and reopening is seldom a sure thing. Without reopening the earlier claim, your client will lose back benefits up through the time of the prior ALJ decision.

Because of the length of time it takes to get a decision from the Appeals Council or federal court, some attorneys, motivated by their client's dire financial straits, have made a practice of recommending filing a new application instead of appealing. This is good advice only if it works, and often it doesn't work because of the phenomenon of copycat ALJ denial decisions. If it doesn't work, the claimant may be labeled as a chronic disability seeker after two ALJ denials, thus further decreasing the claimant's chances of ever winning benefits in the future.

Many of these claimants would have received benefits if their attorneys had pursued their first denial decision through the Appeals Council and, if necessary, into federal court. A remand from the Appeals Council or federal court often makes a claimant's chances of winning benefits at an ALJ hearing better than they would be if the claimant filed a new application. An appeal and remand often improves a claimant's strategic position. This is reflected in SSA's statistics that consistently show a small but significant difference in reversal rates for remanded cases compared to the overall average. For example, the overall percentage of favorable decisions issued by ALJs from 2001 through 2004 ranged from 61.0% to 61.7%. During the same period, the percentage of favorable decisions after Appeals Council remand ranged from 65.0% to 67.6%. After court remand, favorable decisions ranged from 66.5% to 69.0%.

Sometimes, it does make sense to file a new application instead of appealing when you think the claimant will lose the appeal and the claimant is turning 50, 55, or 60—ages where it becomes easier to win disability benefits. This is especially true if the ALJ denial decision establishes a residual functional capacity that actually calls for a finding of disabled at the higher age level. Although only three circuits (4th, 6th and 9th) apply a presumption that the claimant's RFC remains as it was when the denial decision was issued, when a claimant reaches the higher age level in this circumstance, it creates a pretty good case on the facts everywhere. *See* AR 97-4(9), AR 98-4(6) and AR 00-1(4).

If you think the claimant may win a remand from the Appeals Council, but you expect that on remand the ALJ will find the claimant disabled only as of the time when the claimant reached the higher age category, you may have to decide the course of action based on whichever path might be fastest.

On a new application, no matter what date prior to the ALJ decision the claimant alleges as the onset date, SSA will use the day after the date of the ALJ denial decision as the recommended alleged onset date. If the claimant's insured status lapsed before this date, SSA will use the doctrine of administrative *res judicata* to deny a new Title II application. While it is theoretically possible to reopen a prior application based on new evidence or other grounds, (*see* §§370 *ff.*), reopening a prior application is not necessarily easy. And it is difficult to obtain judicial review of the reopening issue if the request for reopening is turned down. *See Califano v. Sanders*, 430 U.S. 99 (1977). Thus, if the denial

decision came after the date last insured, it is essential to appeal.

If you have one of those cases where it is best to start a new application rather than appeal, beware of advice from SSA claims representatives. If your client goes to the local office to file a new application within 60 days of the ALJ denial decision, it is possible that a claims representative may try to convince your client to appeal. Prepare your client for this possibility.

§507 Subsequent Claims: New Application Filed While Earlier Claim Is Pending at the Appeals Council or in Federal Court

SSA has always allowed a claimant to file a new application once the Appeals Council denied review even if the earlier claim was pending in federal court. *See* §507.2. From December 30, 1999 through July 27, 2011, SSA allowed a claimant to file a subsequent application while an earlier application was pending at the Appeals Council. Effective July 28, 2011, SSR 11-1p changed this policy. New applications can no longer be filed while an earlier claim is pending at the Appeals Council without the express permission of the Appeals Council. *See* §507.1. Otherwise, the claimant has a choice: new application or appeal. The claimant cannot do both. If the claimant wants to file a new application, the claimant has the option of requesting to withdraw the Request for Review and file a new claim after the Appeals Council dismisses the claim pending before it. See HALLEX I-3-4-3.

An exception to this rule allows filing a new application under a different title of the Social Security Act or for a different type of benefits under the same title. SSR 11-1p. In other words, if a claimant has a Social Security disability claim pending at the Appeals Council, the claimant should be able to file a Title II Disabled Widower's Benefit (DWB) claim. If a claimant with a Title II claim pending at the Appeals Council wants to file an SSI claim, SSA's new policy indicates that this will be allowed. *See* SSR 11-1p and the July 29, 2011 Memorandum from Patricia Jonas, Executive Director, Office of Appellate Operations, reprinted in the NOSSCR *Social Security Forum*, Vol 33, No. 8, August 2011, pp. 19-21. *See also* the Emergency Message EM-11052 REV 2 (effective 9/26/2011), reprinted in the NOSSCR *Social Security Forum*, Vol 33, No. 9, September 2011, pp. 12-16.

SSA has always allowed filing a subsequent claim if the prior claim involved a continuing disability review (CDR) under any title or an SSI age 18 redetermination.

For a few years, there will be cases in the pipeline in which claimants filed subsequent claims before the effective date of SSR 11-1p. We address Appeals Council procedures for dealing with such cases in §507.3.

§507.1　SSR 11-1p: Permission Required to File New Application While the Earlier Application Is Pending at the Appeals Council

Under what circumstances is the Appeals Council likely to allow filing a subsequent claim while the earlier claim is pending at the Appeals Council? A July 29, 2011 memorandum from Patricia Jonas, the Executive Director of the Office of Appellate Operations, reprinted in the NOSSCR *Social Security Forum*, Vol 33, No. 8, August 2011, p. 19, explained when a new application would be allowed:

> If the claimant has (1) additional evidence that shows a new critical or disabling condition, and (2) tells us that he or she wants to file a new claim based on the evidence, we may permit the filing of a new disability claim before we complete our action on the request for review. The exception only applies when a prior claim is at the Appeals Council level, and the Appeals Council permits the filing of a new application. These requests will be centrally handled through the Executive Director's office.

Note that there must be additional evidence showing a *new* critical or disabling condition with an onset after the date of the ALJ decision. When you submit evidence of a new *critical* condition, request not only the opportunity to file a new application but also that the Appeals Council expedite action on the Request for Review. Indeed, if a case meets SSA's definition of "critical," the Appeals Council is supposed to expedite. *See* HALLEX I-1-10-1 C.

When there is evidence of a new *disabling* condition with an onset after the date of the ALJ decision, the issue, of course, is: how disabling does it have to appear for the Appeals Council to grant the right to file a new application? This is going to be determined on a case by case basis. Thus, what sort of evidence you submit and what you point out to the Appeals Council may matter.

Perhaps equally important as the quality of the new evidence and the quality of your argument is how you go about getting the Appeals Council's attention. Although in the past this has not been easy, the Appeals Council has promised to be more responsive. There are three ways to approach getting

the Appeals Council's attention when your client has a new disabling condition. First, it is possible to ask someone at the local office to be your intermediary in dealing with the Appeals Council to obtain permission for the claimant to file a new application. Deliver new evidence to the local office. Obtain a commitment from local office personnel that they will upload the new evidence to the claimant's electronic file and that they will ask the Appeals Council for permission to file a new application. *See* Emergency Message EM-11052 REV 2 (effective 9/26/2011), reprinted in the NOSSCR *Social Security Forum*, Vol 33, No. 9, September 2011, pp. 12 - 16.

Second, telephone the Public Inquiries staff at the Appeals Council, *see* §515.1, request a bar code, and submit the new evidence electronically yourself. Call back to Public Inquiries staff a few days later to make sure that the request for permission to file a new application is being handled by the Executive Director's office.

Third, consider taking the case directly to the Appeals Council ombudsman. *See* §515.3.

Whatever route you take for getting the Appeals Council's attention, be sure to follow up to make sure the request has not run off track. You cannot just submit a request for the claimant to be allowed to file a new application (with supporting new evidence) and expect that it will be processed.

No longer will a claimant be able to file a new application merely as a way of hedging bets if the case pending at the Appeals Council is turned down. During the 11.5 years the former policy was in effect, many lawyers advised filing a new Title II application about 17 months after the date of the ALJ denial decision. (If the onset date is found to be the day after the ALJ denial decision, such a Title II application—which pays benefits 12 months prior to the date of application— would obtain all possible benefits.) Bet hedging new applications will no longer be possible.

What about the situation where a claimant turns 50 or 55 while the claim is pending at the Appeals Council and would be found disabled under the RFC finding in the ALJ denial decision based on application of a different rule from the Medical-Vocational Guidelines? In this situation many lawyers in the past would recommend a subsequent application. Is there any way to protect the right to file so that no potential benefits are lost?

SSR 11-1p itself suggests how to obtain a protective filing date as of the date of the Request for Review. SSR 11-1p points out that under 20 C.F.R. §§404.976(b) and 416.1476(b), if you submit new evidence that does not pertain to the period of time on or before the date of the ALJ decision, that evidence is supposed to be returned to you with a letter that gives the claimant the right to file a new claim using the date of the Request for Review as the protective filing date. Thus, in some circumstances it may be necessary to gather additional evidence and submit it to the Appeals Council solely for the purpose of obtaining a protective filing date as of the date of the Request for Review.

§507.2   Subsequent Application Pending Before SSA While Earlier Application Is Pending in Federal Court

After the Appeals Council turns down a Request for Review, the agency will allow a subsequent application to be filed and proceed through all levels of administrative review even if the earlier claim is pending in federal court. There is one significant limitation on the new application: the new application will not be allowed to establish an onset date earlier than the day after the prior ALJ denial. HALLEX I-2-8-16.

Also, an ALJ cannot reopen the application currently pending in federal court because SSA, in effect, treats that application as still open—the ALJ decision on that application is not binding until federal court review is finished. 20 C.F.R. §404.955(b). ALJs have instructions that they are not to reopen an application that is being reviewed in federal court. HALLEX I-2-9-5 B.

If a claimant loses in federal court before a new application gets to an ALJ decision (i.e., the case is no longer pending in federal court), an ALJ has the authority to reopen the earlier application based on the reopening regulations. SSR 67-22. Also, HALLEX I-2-9-5 A, Note 2, states that a "court's affirmation of the prior decision does not affect the ALJ's jurisdiction to reopen and revise the prior decision."

If a claimant is found disabled on a subsequent application while an earlier application is pending in federal court, SSA's instructions to the Appeals Council, which plays a supervisory role even while a case is pending in court, describe four points where evaluation of a subsequent application could come up: first, when a new court case is filed; second, when there is a request from the government's attorney for a voluntary remand; third, when the federal court case is remanded by the court; and fourth, after a new final decision is issued by an ALJ following court remand. At these points, the Appeals Council must determine if there is an allowance on a subsequent application, obtain information about that allowance to determine if the two outcomes can "co-exist," evaluate whether the new evidence submitted in connection with the new

claim could be used to find the claimant disabled on the first claim, or consider reopening the subsequent allowance. HALLEX I-4-2-101.

If the federal court remands the claim pending before it, unless the federal court restricts SSA's options, the Appeals Council may take any action it could have taken if the case were pending on a Request for Review. It may: (1) use a subsequent allowance to find the claimant disabled on the first application; (2) affirm the subsequent allowance when it remands the first application to an ALJ, or (3) address the issue of reopening the allowance on the subsequent application. HALLEX I-4-2-101 II.C.2.

If a claimant receives a favorable decision on a subsequent application during the pendency of a federal court action, you may be able to use this favorable decision to advantage in the federal court action even though, strictly speaking, the fact that the claimant was found disabled after the date of the ALJ decision is arguably not relevant to the federal court action. The issues in federal court are: (1) whether substantial evidence supports SSA's decision that the claimant is not disabled up to and including the date of the ALJ decision; and (2) whether SSA committed legal error in denying the claim. Thus, something that happened after the date of the ALJ decision has no direct bearing on the case. Nevertheless, although it is theoretically correct to say that "the possibility of drawing two inconsistent conclusions from the evidence does not prevent an administrative agency's finding from being supported by substantial evidence," *Consolo v. Federal Maritime Commission*, 383 U.S. 607, 620 (1966), when SSA actually draws two inconsistent conclusions from the evidence, it is likely to get the attention of a federal judge, especially when SSA finds the claimant disabled on the subsequent application on the day after the ALJ decision on the earlier claim.

While a finding on a later application that the claimant was disabled on the day after the ALJ decision on the earlier application, without more, will not convince a federal court to rule in a plaintiff's favor, generally there is more. In fact, SSA has made the inconsistency between the two decisions a crucial factor when deciding whether it should voluntarily request remand, an issue it examines when a new court case is filed and when it receives a request for voluntary remand from the attorney representing SSA in the federal court action.

SSA instructs Appeals Council analysts to consider whether the outcomes in the two cases can "co-exist." For example, when a claimant is found disabled on the subsequent application based on an impairment that did not exist at the time of the ALJ denial on the first application, the two outcomes can co-exist. Likewise, when a claimant is found disabled simply because he got older and fell into a new age category under the grids, the two outcomes can co-exist. HALLEX I-4-2-101 II.A.2.a. If the two outcomes can co-exist, a subsequent allowance would not cause SSA to voluntarily request that the case pending in federal court be remanded. HALLEX I-4-2-101 II.A.2. and II.B.2.

But, for example, where the state agency violates SSA's rules by setting an onset date before the date of the ALJ denial decision, the two outcomes cannot co-exist. HALLEX I-4-2-101 II.A.2.b. This can form the basis for a voluntary remand at the time the action is filed or in response to a request for voluntary remand from SSA's litigation attorney. HALLEX I-4-2-101 II.A.2. and II.B.2. Indeed, when the state agency finds the claimant disabled before the date of the ALJ denial decision, the Appeals Council views it as imperative that something be done about this conflict because of the violation of SSA's rules. The state agency determination will have to be reopened, but, even so, in conjunction with its evaluation of the case after the case is remanded by the federal court, the Appeals Council could find that the state agency had such significant new evidence in its possession at the time of the determination on the subsequent application that the Appeals Council will issue a fully favorable decision on the first application.

Where the ALJ denied the claim under a rule from the light grid and that claimant's impairment is found to meet the Listings on the day after the ALJ decision, HALLEX says the two outcomes cannot co-exist. HALLEX I-4-2-101 II.A.2.b. Indeed, Appeals Council insiders say that in most situations a denial decision and a "day after allowance" cannot co-exist.

In federal court you may argue that a finding of disability on a second application, which does not invade the period adjudicated by the final decision on the first application, has limited the issue before the court to eligibility during the closed period not covered by the new application. Ask the court to remand the case for consideration of disability during a closed period from the date of onset alleged in the first application to the date of onset found by SSA on the second application. Arguably, such a remand order would deprive the Appeals Council of its SSA-assigned jurisdiction over the subsequent application because the periods covered do not overlap; and potentially, reopening the subsequent application could bring the Appeals Council into direct conflict with the federal court's order, something that the Appeals Council would probably want to avoid. But beware: the articulation of the Appeals Council's jurisdiction contains more than a bit of probably deliberate fuzziness. "The Appeals Council has primary jurisdiction to consider reopening and revising of . . . any initial determination, or reconsidered determination, if the case is properly before the AC on the basis of request for review, a subsequent application, own motion review, or other appropriate jurisdiction." HALLEX I-3-9-5 A. And however unlikely this is to happen in actual practice, if the Appeals Council does not have jurisdiction to reopen, the Appeals Council could refer the matter to the component of SSA that has jurisdiction.

The most difficult problem with pursuing a new application during the pendency of a federal court action arises when the new application is denied by an ALJ decision. Then the claimant must fight on two fronts; there are administrative and federal court appeals pending simultaneously. In the unlikely event that SSA's attorney in the federal court action finds out about the fate of the subsequent application, the SSA attorney may have the same impulse you would have if the situation were reversed—to try to use the denial decision to advantage in federal court. Although a subsequent ALJ denial decision is not directly relevant to SSA's argument in court, SSA's attorney may simply point out, perhaps in a footnote, that SSA looked at the claimant's condition again and the claimant is *still* not disabled. Or, if remand looks inevitable, the attorney could ask to limit remand to consideration of a closed period.

What happens if the federal court action is remanded for a new hearing but the claimant did not appeal denial of the second application? Is denial of the second application *res judicata*? Here is SSA's answer to this question: "When SSA has denied a subsequent claim through the hearing level, that otherwise binding ALJ decision (20 CFR §§404.955 and 416.1455) may need to be reviewed consistent with applicable reopening regulations, when deciding the prior claim(s) remanded by the court." But if the subsequent claim has been denied at the initial or reconsideration level, the two claims will be consolidated "if the subsequent claim is made duplicate or now involves an overlapping time period. This will apply whether or not a request for hearing is pending on the subsequent claim(s)." HALLEX I-4-2-101 I.B.

In other words, when there is a federal court remand, SSA treats as binding an ALJ denial decision on a subsequent application, but it does not treat an initial or reconsideration determination as binding. Instead, it treats an initial or reconsideration denial simply as part of a duplicate claim to be consolidated with the first claim on remand. It is hard to see, though, why 20 C.F.R. §§404.905 and 404.921 do not also make initial or reconsideration denials binding, thus raising this question: Could SSA change its interpretation? Could SSA in the future require that an initial or reconsideration denial determination on the subsequent application be reopened before an ALJ can issue a fully favorable decision on remand of the first application? Although this is something to worry about, we will approach the problem based on the current interpretation.

Because of the horrible, though largely theoretical, possibility that an ALJ denial of the second application may preclude anything more than an award for a closed period on the first application remanded by the federal court, you and your client need to consider whether you want to take the subsequent application as far as an ALJ hearing decision, especially if it looks like that decision is going to be a denial. At any time before an ALJ decision is issued, even after the hearing is held, you can ask to withdraw the request for hearing. 20 C.F.R. §404.957(a). Dismissal of the request for hearing makes the reconsideration determination final; and under the current interpretation, SSA does not require that this determination be reopened before an ALJ can issue a fully favorable decision on remand of the first claim.

You also need to consider how significant the problem would be if you received an ALJ denial decision on the subsequent application. In practice, when putting together a case for a remand hearing, one can usually find something to point to as new evidence to be used as part of an argument for reopening the ALJ denial decision on the subsequent application for good cause under 20 C.F.R. §404.988(b). But if the two- or four-year time limits for reopening for good cause have expired under 20 C.F.R. §§404.988(b) and 416.1488(b), what then? In fact, despite HALLEX's reference to the reopening rules in the standard remand order, HALLEX I-4-2-101 I.B, reopening is not the real issue for claimants in this circumstance at all. Claimants seek reopening in order to get paid on an earlier application. From the claimant's perspective, it is unnecessary for a later application to be reopened. After all, the claimant already has an earlier application pending—the one remanded by the federal court. The real issue is whether *res judicata* applies to the denial on the subsequent application. *Res judicata* is a separate concept from reopening. *See* §370.2. *Res Judicata* has no time limit. *Res judicata* applies only when the same facts and the same issues are present currently and in the previous decision. *See* 20 C.F.R. §404.957(c)(1). If there is new evidence, then the facts are different and *res judicata* does not apply, even if it has been more than four years since the decision on the subsequent application. SSR 68-12a.

Thus, a final ALJ denial decision on the subsequent application may not be an insurmountable hurdle. Nevertheless, by appealing the ALJ denial decision on the subsequent application, you keep your options open. After all, you could ultimately lose the first application and win the second after appeal.

But if you choose to appeal an ALJ denial decision on a subsequent application, how far are you going to take the appeal? If the Appeals Council turns down the Request for Review on the subsequent application, are you prepared to take the denial of the subsequent application to federal court so that the two claims are pending in federal court at the same time?

An even more interesting question, though largely a hypothetical one, is whether it could ever be necessary to consider taking the second claim to federal court while the first claim is being remanded. One would think that if the second claim is still alive when the first is remanded by the federal court, the second claim ought to be treated as moot or simply as a duplicate claim with no practical impact on the case other than the files being consolidated, but this is not SSA's position if there has been an ALJ decision. Or, one would think, if the second claim is pending at the Appeals Council on a Request for Review when the first claim is remanded by the federal court, the two claims ought to simply be consolidated and remanded together. Although this is generally what happens in practice, HALLEX contemplates the possibility of a different result.

According to HALLEX I-4-2-101 II.C.b.ii., if the case pending in federal court is remanded when a Request for Review on a subsequent claim is pending at the Appeals Council, the two claims will be acted upon at the same time. "If the AC denies review in the subsequent claim, it will issue a standard denial notice. An AC remand in the prior claim (following court remand) will acknowledge the decision on the subsequent claim and direct the ALJ to consider that decision if necessary, consistent with applicable reopening regulations, when deciding the claim remanded by the court." HALLEX I-4-2-101 II.C.b.ii. Under SSA's rules, though, a claim pending in federal court cannot be reopened by an ALJ. Even though there is little likelihood of ever having to face such a case in practice, whether you would conclude that it would be advantageous to take the subsequent claim to federal court may depend on the facts and legal issues in the two claims and your strategy for the hearing on remand of the first claim.

§507.3   Pipeline Cases

Although beginning July 28, 2011 a claimant will not be able to file a new application while a previous claim is pending at the Appeals Council, there are many cases in the pipeline in which new applications were filed before July 28, 2011. For this reason we include the following discussion:

The new application will be processed through the initial and reconsideration stages, and if denial determinations are issued, a claimant may request a hearing. But, unless someone at a hearing office makes a mistake, a request for hearing on the new application will not be acted upon until after the Appeals Council acts on the first application.

If a claimant is found disabled at the initial or reconsideration stage on the subsequent application, the state agency determination cannot reopen the application pending at the Appeals Council. The claimant will be paid with an onset date established no earlier than the day after the ALJ denial decision on the earlier application; and the Appeals Council is supposed to be notified electronically so that the Appeals Council can determine if the electronic folder contains new evidence that sheds light on the application pending at the Appeals Council. "The Appeals Council will expedite its action on the Request for Review in this situation." HALLEX I-5-3-17 I.B.

Sometimes a claimant will request a hearing on a subsequent application favorable determination in which the onset date is found to be the day after the earlier ALJ denial decision. This is an onset date appeal, which is actually an appeal of the state agency's failure to reopen the application that is pending at the Appeals Council. Because it is SSA's position that the state agency has granted all relief to which the claimant is entitled, the Office of the Chief Administrative Law Judge issued a memo dated December 18, 2002 directing that such onset date appeals on subsequent applications be dismissed and the file be sent to the Appeals Council. The memo stated, "As the only issue before the ALJ is the denial of reopening by the State agency, which is not an initial determination with appeal rights, there are no due process violations."

Whenever the Appeals Council finds that new evidence submitted for the second application shows that the claimant may have been disabled at the time relevant to the first application, it can grant review on the first application and use the new evidence as a basis to issue a fully favorable decision, propose a partially favorable decision, or remand the case for another hearing on the first application, which directs the ALJ to consider on remand only the time before the subsequent favorable determination. HALLEX I-5-3-17 III.B.2, Example 1, a.

If there is no new evidence and the Appeals Council agrees with the award of benefits on the second application, and if there is no other basis for granting review, the Appeals Council will turn down the Request for Review on the first application and not disturb the subsequent favorable determination. Or it could grant the Request for Review on some other basis and remand the case for reevaluation of whether the claimant was disabled during the time before the claimant was found disabled on the second application. HALLEX I-5-3-17 III.B.2, Example 1b.

What happens if the Appeals Council concludes that the state agency decision finding the claimant disabled on the new application is wrong? It is SSA's policy that the Appeals Council must consider whether the new application can be reopened under 20 C.F.R. §§404.988 or 416.1488. HALLEX I-5-3-17 I.B. If the second application can be reopened, it will be consolidated with the first application on which the Appeals Council will grant the Request for Review. The consolidated cases will be remanded for another hearing.

The Appeals Council can reopen a subsequent application for reasons similar to those for which a claimant can request reopening. It can reopen for "any reason" as long as it does so within 12 months of the date of the notice of initial determination. 20 C.F.R. §§404.988(a) and 416.1488(a). If it is more than 12 months from the date of the notice of initial determination by the time the Appeals Council gets to the case, a common occurrence even though Appeals Council policy is to expedite cases involving subsequent favorable determinations, the Appeals Council must find "good cause" to reopen if it is within four years of the date of the notice of initial determination in a Title II case or two years in an SSI case. 20 C.F.R. §§404.988(b) and 416.1488(b). When the two- or four-year time limits have already run, the Appeals Council's options for reopening are limited to "fraud or similar fault" and a few other possibilities in Title II cases seldom actually seen in practice. See 20 C.F.R. §§404.988(c) and 416.1488(c).

According to HALLEX, "evidence already in the record on which the ALJ decision is based is not 'new' and would not satisfy" the "good cause" requirement for reopening based on "new and material evidence" under 20 C.F.R. §404.989(a)(1). HALLEX I-5-3-17 III.B.2, Example 1, note 5. Since it is unlikely that there would be new evidence showing that the claimant was not disabled submitted with the Request for Review, the Appeals Council will not be able to use new evidence as the basis for reopening in most circumstances. Thus, this basis for finding good cause, the most common basis used when a claimant is seeking reopening, will not ordinarily be available to the Appeals Council. See 20 C.F.R. §§404.989(a)(1) and 416.1489(a)(1). SSA acknowledges that such reopenings will be "rare." HALLEX I-5-3-17 III.B.2, Example 1, note 5. Instead, the Appeals Council must consider whether the evidence clearly shows on its face that the subsequent favorable determination was erroneous. 20 C.F.R. §404.989(a)(3).

Appeals Council policy is to find "error on the face" if there is an error of law such as when the state agency establishes an onset date before the day after the ALJ denial decision on the first application. HALLEX I-5-3-17 III.B.2, Example 1, note 8. Or the Appeals Council may find "error on the face" if the state agency did not consider all the evidence in SSA's possession when it made its determination (i.e., the state agency did not have the evidence that was before the ALJ) and the evidence "clearly shows on its face that an error was made." *See* 20 C.F.R. §§404.989(a)(3) and 416.1489(a)(3). HALLEX I-5-3-17 III.B.2, Example 1, note 5.

When the Appeals Council proposes to reopen a subsequent application, it gives notice that it intends to grant the Request for Review, reopen the second application and remand the consolidated cases for another hearing. The Appeals Council gives the claimant's attorney the opportunity to object. Be assured that if the Appeals Council gives notice of reopening within 12 months of the date of the notice of initial determination, objection is likely to be futile. But if the Appeals Council is using the "good cause" provision to reopen a subsequent application when the notice of initial determination is dated more than 12 months before (and less than 4 years in a Title II case or less than 2 years in an SSI case), carefully examine the Appeals Council's position. It could be on shaky ground. A carefully thought out objection might cause the Appeals Council to back off reopening.

If the Appeals Council concludes that the subsequent favorable determination is wrong but it has no basis for reopening it and it finds no basis for granting the Request for Review on the first application, the Appeals Council's instructions are to deny the Request for Review. HALLEX I-5-3-17 III.B.2, Example 1, c.ii. How carefully the Appeals Council will look for a basis for reopening the subsequent application may depend on its conclusion whether the favorable and denial decisions can "co-exist." Agency insiders say that when the ALJ decision directly conflicts with a favorable determination on a subsequent application, e.g., the ALJ used a rule from the light grid to deny the claim and the state agency found the claimant to meet the Listings on the day after the ALJ decision, the Appeals Council fears that the ALJ denial of the first application will not be defensible in federal court. But, for example, where a claimant is found disabled on a subsequent application with an onset date set as of the date of a stroke that occurred after the date of the ALJ denial decision on the first application, the two outcomes can co-exist. See the discussion of co-existing contrary outcomes in HALLEX I-4-2-101 II.A.2. *See also* HALLEX I-5-3-17 III.B.2, Example 1, c, note 4.

HALLEX makes clear that it is the Appeals Council's job to evaluate the favorable determination on the subsequent application and include in any remand order specific directions whether or not the ALJ is to address the period of time during which the claimant was found disabled in the subsequent application. HALLEX I-5-3-17 III.B.2. But what happens if an Appeals Council remand order fails to address the issue of the favorable determination on the subsequent application? Should the Appeals Council be asked to issue a revised order of remand? Is it SSA policy that the ALJ is then supposed to determine whether the subsequent allowance should be reopened? A memorandum from the Chief ALJ dated May 21, 2003 answered these questions. The memorandum stated that it should not be necessary for the Appeals Council to issue a revised order of remand and, it said, the "ALJ may also determine if the subsequent allowance should be reopened in accordance with the applicable regulations." The memorandum is published in *Social Security Forum*, Vol 26, No. 1, January 2004, pp. 8-9.

If the state agency does not find the claimant disabled on the subsequent application and the claimant requests a hearing, the case file is supposed to be forwarded to the hearing office where it will sit until the Appeals Council acts on the appeal of the first application. The Appeals Council will not request that the subsequent application file be sent to it. It will presume that the second application file contains no new evidence relevant to the case before the Appeals Council. HALLEX I-5-3-17 I.C.

If new evidence is submitted to the hearing office, which makes it appear that a favorable decision is appropriate on the new application, ALJs have instructions to formally remand the case to the state agency pursuant to 20 C.F.R. §404.948(c). HALLEX I-5-3-17 I.C. and II.D. Thus, if you submit such new evidence to the hearing office on a subsequent application, ask for formal remand to the state agency. This is likely to be much faster than waiting for the Appeals Council to decide the Request for Review on the prior application.

If the Appeals Council remands the case that is before it, the two cases will be consolidated for hearing. Indeed, even if the new application is still pending at the state agency when the Appeals Council remands the first application, the second application is supposed to be treated as a duplicate claim. That is, the state agency is supposed to stop working on the claim and the claim file is supposed to be forwarded to the hearing office to be consolidated with the earlier case. POMS DI 20101.025F.

If the Appeals Council turns down the appeal on the first application, a hearing may be held on the second application. HALLEX I-5-3-17 II.F.

§508   Appealing the Partially Favorable Decision

Where you disagree with the onset date found by the ALJ or the grant by the ALJ of a closed period of disability, you are presented with a dilemma. If you appeal, there is risk that the Appeals Council may find that your client never was disabled. SSA takes the position that if the Appeals Council grants review in response to a claimant's request, the entire case is open to review, so that any finding of the ALJ may be changed. The cover sheet attached to all ALJ decisions gives notice that if the claimant appeals, the Appeals Council will "consider all of [the ALJ] decision, even the parts with which you agree. . . . Requesting review places the entire record of your case before the Council. Review can make any part of [the ALJ] decision more or less favorable or unfavorable to you."

When faced with a case in which you want review only on a limited issue, it is important to analyze the strengths and weaknesses of your client's entire case. How likely is the Appeals Council to decide the appealed issue in your client's favor? How likely is the Appeals Council to take away what you have already won for the claimant? How likely are you to get relief from the federal court?

Onset Date Appeals

When you appeal a partially favorable decision to the Appeals Council and run the risk that the Appeals Council will determine that the claimant never was disabled, be sure to explain this risk to your client. Although in the usual case this risk is minimal, unless there are substantial additional back benefits available in an onset date appeal, your client may not view it as worth taking even a small risk by requesting review. This is a cost-benefit analysis. If the Appeals Council takes benefits away from the claimant, even if you ultimately win benefits back, the claimant could be without benefits for years while the case is fought in federal court and on remand. And, of course, the claimant may ultimately lose. All this must be explained to the claimant so that the claimant can make an informed decision about appeal. If the claimant wants to go forward with the appeal and the worst happens, you do not want to be in the position of having your client say you never explained the risks. Thus, repeating your explanation about risk in a letter to the claimant is essential.

It is also possible to successfully appeal a nominally fully favorable decision in which the claimant agreed to a later onset date or closed period. Amend the onset date or state that the claimant continues to be disabled in the Request for Review. Such appeals, though, present an awkward ALJ-relations problem for the lawyer who agreed to the amended onset date or closed period at the hearing. If a client decides after the hearing that amending the onset date alleging a closed period was a bad idea and wants to appeal, it may be best to refer the client to another lawyer.

The passage of time helps perspective whenever you're dealing with an onset date appeal. Thus, it is a bad idea to appeal immediately after you receive an ALJ decision. Such cases should be calendared for 11th hour appeals. That is, wait until 45 days or so have passed since the date of the ALJ decision. Then look at the case again. It may look different both to you and to your client. Your client may also have been paid back benefits by that time so you won't need to worry that an appeal might stop the payment center from processing payment of your client's back benefits. (This is something lawyers worry about that probably does not actually happen in real life.)

Closed Period Cases

Where an ALJ finds a closed period of disability but the claimant remains unable to work, doing nothing is generally not an option. It is best to view the closed period problem as initially presenting two choices: request review by the Appeals Council or file a new application. There are ALJ closed period decisions that are legally sufficient and so well-reasoned that it would be a bad idea to appeal them. If you're not appealing your client's case, then you need to consider the timing of a new application. It may be best to wait a while, especially if your client is heavily involved in ongoing treatment.

In the 4th, 6th, and 9th circuits, filing a new application is less attractive than elsewhere. The prior closed period can be used against the claimant, in effect applying a presumption of continuing nondisability to the period of time after the date of the ALJ decision. You'll need some new evidence showing that the claimant's impairments are worse than when the ALJ looked at the claim. *See* Acquiescence Rulings 97-4(9), 98-3(6), 98-4(6) and 00-1(4).

In other circuits, the prior ALJ closed period decision does not have the same effect. Evaluation of whether a claimant is disabled during a period of time not covered by an ALJ decision is *de novo*.

Deciding whether to appeal or file a new application requires consideration of the potential strength of your client's arguments on appeal (and after remand). To find a closed period of disability, an ALJ must apply medical improvement rules. SSR 02-1p, note 2; SSR 02-2p, note 4; POMS DI 28005.001 D.1.b. Medical improvement rules are so complicated (*see* §§480-489) that ALJs make more than the usual number of mistakes when applying them. Thus, there are often strong legal arguments to raise at the Appeals Council to show that the closed period finding is legally deficient. The Appeals Council has been known to reverse and award continuing benefits in such cases. Depending on the facts of the case, a remand based on failure to follow medical improvement rules may place enough constraints on how an ALJ must decide the case on remand to ensure that a fully favorable decision is issued. Worsening of your client's condition with the passage of time also may increase the likelihood that the ALJ will issue a fully favorable decision on remand.

If you file a new application instead of appealing, how will the state agency view the strength of your client's new application? This is a new application which, as pointed out above, in most circuits involves *de novo* review of the claim. Thus, the state agency will not review the claim under the medical improvement standard.

If you file a new application instead of appealing, your client may lose many months of back benefits that could be obtained with a successful appeal. Whether months of potential back benefits are lost depends on the cessation date (the date the claimant's disability was found to have ceased by the ALJ decision) and the date of the ALJ decision itself. The claimant is paid for the month disability ceased and the next two months. Months after that up until the month after the date of the ALJ closed period decision are potentially lost. Because the state agency cannot reopen an ALJ decision, it will not be able to find your client disabled any earlier than the day after the date of the ALJ closed period decision. Thus, a new application cannot obtain benefits from the time benefits stopped until the month after the ALJ decision unless the new application is appealed to the hearing level where an ALJ reopens the earlier closed period decision.

When an ALJ decision is dated no later than the end of the second calendar month after the date disability was found to have ceased, there would be no potential benefits lost by filing a new application instead of appealing. But the proximity of the two dates could be a sign of ALJ over reaching, which could make for a successful appeal. Stingy ALJs, when faced with overwhelming evidence of disability, have been known to scour recent records looking for any sign of improvement, whether it is sustained or not, and find cessation of disability based on flimsy evidence. Such cases make for good appeals. They also may be good cases for filing new applications.

As a rule, though, there is an advantage to waiting as long as possible after the date of the ALJ closed period decision before filing a new application. In a Title II case, you can wait 13 months from the date of the ALJ decision without losing any potential benefits. Waiting this long provides a better longitudinal perspective for the state agency to determine that your client is disabled after the date of the ALJ decision, thus increasing the likelihood that the state agency will find your client disabled.

Waiver of Overpayment

Although it is small consolation for a client who loses all benefits as a result of an appeal to the Appeals Council, if asked, SSA will likely waive recovery of any overpayment. Although this precise scenario does not appear to be discussed in POMS, there are some analogous situations where SSA waives recovery of an overpayment or, as in the case of interim benefits paid, directs that such benefits are not an overpayment. *See* POMS GN 02250.325 "Waiver of Recovery After Administrative Change of Position"; and POMS DI 42010.205B.5, "Interim Benefits in Cases of Delayed Final Decisions—Title II."

§509 Appealing Denial of Reopening Request

The same considerations as those described in §508 apply when you consider appealing a claim in which an ALJ issued a fully favorable decision on the current claim but failed to address a reopening issue or refused to reopen a prior decision. Nevertheless, there may be somewhat less risk because of the Appeals Council's position on the regulatory basis for such an appeal. Success on such an appeal produces more back benefits than a run-of-the-mill onset date appeal. Thus, the cost-benefit analysis usually tilts in favor of such an appeal.

When the only issue on appeal is the failure to address reopening or the correctness of the ALJ's refusal to reopen an earlier decision, the Appeals Council does not treat such an appeal as an appeal of the favorable decision on the current claim under 20 C.F.R. §404.970. If it did, the current claim would be in front of the Appeals Council to reverse or modify as it sees fit. Instead, the Appeals Council treats such a reopening appeal as pertaining only to the application on which you are requesting reopening, not the application that was before the ALJ. In other words, although this may look like an appeal, it is merely a reopening request under the reopening regulations. 20 C.F.R. §§404.987 and 404.988.

Thus, if the Appeals Council thinks there is something wrong with the ALJ favorable decision itself, because that claim is not before the Appeals Council, the Appeals Council must find some regulatory authority to touch it. The Appeals Council must use its own motion review authority under 20 C.F.R. §404.969 or apply the reopening regulations to the favorable ALJ decision.

When the ALJ fails to address a reopening issue, it's easier to get the Appeals Council's attention. HALLEX I-3-9-10 A. Note provides: "Under 20 CFR 404.903(l) and 416.1403(a)(5), if the adjudicator at the initial, reconsideration, or hearing level concluded that the criteria for reopening were not met, the claimant has no right to request review of the reopening action. If the prior adjudicator did not address a reopening issue, the AC will evaluate whether a basis for granting review is present (see HALLEX I-3-3-1)." But even when there is no "right to request review," you can still ask the Appeals Council to address reopening because the ALJ decision, which said the criteria for reopening were not met, was not supported by substantial evidence, was based on legal errors or an abuse of discretion.

An ALJ's legal errors when addressing reopening help to get the Appeals Council's attention but they usually do not go to the heart of the reopening issue at the Appeals Council. To take an example, let's say the ALJ decision refused to reopen because the claimant did not have a good reason for failing to appeal the denial determination on the first application—an erroneous reason for refusing to reopen that has been known to appear in ALJ decisions. This presents a deceptively easy argument for appeal to the Appeals Council (because a good reason for failing to appeal is not part of the reopening criteria for good cause. *See* 20 C.F.R. §404.989). Although the Appeals Council may agree that the ALJ's rationale for refusing to reopen is wrong, this doesn't address the reopening issue. You're still going to have to convince the Appeals Council that reopening the earlier application is appropriate under the reopening regulation, 20 C.F.R. §404.987.

For discussion of the substantive issues involved in requesting reopening by the Appeals Council, *see* §531.

§510 Requesting Review by the Appeals Council

§511 Time Limit for Requesting Appeals Council Review

The time limit for requesting review by the Appeals Council is the same as the time limit for the other layers of administrative review: 60 days from receipt of the ALJ decision and, unless there is some other showing, that decision will be presumed received five days after the date on the face of the decision. Thus you are allowed 65 days from the date on the ALJ decision to request review. Note, however, that a 30-day time limit applies if the ALJ denial decision has been issued following a federal court remand. *See* §560.

The regulation states that one must "file" the Request for Review within the 60-day time limit. 20 C.F.R. §404.968(a). Ordinarily SSA uses the date the Request for Review is received by any Social Security Administration office as the date of filing. But if using the date the Request for Review is actually received would result in loss of a claimant's rights, SSA considers the date of postmark on the Request for Review to be the date that it is "filed." If the postmark is unreadable or missing, SSA considers a Request for Review timely filed if received by the 70th day after the date of the ALJ decision. HALLEX I-3-1-1 D. In one case where the Request for Review was deposited in a mailbox on the 60th day but postmarked a day later, a court adopted a "date of mailing" rule. *Dietsch v. Schweiker*, 700 F.2d 865 (2d Cir. 1983). This court decision is consistent with SSA policy which states that it will consider other evidence of when a Request for Review was mailed. HALLEX I-3-1-1 D. Pursuant to a provision of the Social Security Act, 42 U.S.C. §416(j), when the period for requesting the next appellate step ends on a Saturday, Sunday, legal holiday or any other day when federal employees do not work under a statute or executive order, the period is extended to include the next full workday. 20 C.F.R. §§404.3(b) and 416.120(d). *See also* HALLEX I-3-1-1 D., POMS GN 03101.010A and *Monferrato v. Schweiker*, 700 F.2d 869 (2d Cir. 1983).

This time limit is important. It is treated as nearly absolute by the Appeals Council, and an untimely Request for Review will be dismissed. The Appeals Council might not grant an extension for requesting review; and possibilities for federal court review of the extension issue are very limited. *See* §513.

Unrepresented claimants have a tendency to contact attorneys at the last minute. You need to know the last possible time for requesting review for these new clients. For continuing clients, your calendaring system should trigger submission of the Request for Review well in advance of the deadline.

A Request for Review by the Appeals Council may be mailed to any Social Security office or to the Appeals Council itself at 5107 Leesburg Pike, Falls Church, VA 22041-3255. 20 C.F.R. §404.968(a)(2). The Request for Review also can be faxed to a local office or directly to the Appeals Council at 703-605-7101 or 703-605-7201. POMS GN 03104.100B.3.

The regulation requires filing only a "written request" (20 C.F.R. §404.968(a)), but to be sure that SSA recognizes your appeal for what it is, the better practice is to use the official form, HA-520-U5 titled Request for Review of Hearing Decision/Order, a copy of which follows. Although there are places for signatures of the claimant and representative on the Request for

Review, SSA does not require that the Request for Review be signed. POMS GN 03104.100B.3 and GN 03104.200C.2. You may obtain a pdf copy of this form on SSA's website, www.socialsecurity.gov.

Practice Tips

Faxing the Request for Review to one of the Appeals Council's main fax numbers—703-605-7101 or 703-605-7201—has the advantage of instant gratification. You can print a fax confirmation that shows the Request for Review was filed. POMS GN 03104.100B.3 says that the Appeals Council will accept a faxed Request for Review. Be sure that your fax machine is set to display a header showing the date of transmission. And be sure it prints a confirmation that shows the claimant's name and SSN, the Appeals Council fax number, and that the fax went through.

Appeals Council officials have cautioned against trying to appeal by faxing a Request for Review to one of the Appeals Council branches using a fax number found at HALLEX I-3-0-7, which is the basis for this book's §515.2. Because of staffing changes, branches are no longer set up to efficiently handle processing a faxed Request for Review. If you fax the Request for Review to the Appeals Council branch, although you will win the argument that you "filed" the Request for Review "at one of our offices," 20 C.F.R. §404.968(a)(2), your client's case may be delayed if the Request for Review is not properly processed.

Worse yet is attempting to fax a Request for Review into a claimant's electronic folder using a hearing level bar code. According to Appeals Council officials, an appeal cannot be filed electronically at this time. See *Social Security Forum,* Vol. 35, No. 5, May 2013, p. 3 and www.ssa.gov/appeals/reps/Appt_Rep_Guide_Req_AC_Review_Submit_Evidence.pdf

The Appeals Council has been known to lose copies of Requests for Review that are faxed to it. To avoid arguments about whether you timely appealed your client's case, consider this: Although you cannot appeal by filing the Request for Review electronically, you can submit a copy of the Request for Review electronically (using a hearing-level barcode) after you have faxed it to one of the Appeals Council's main fax numbers. Electronically file a copy of the fax confirmation, too.

If you mail the Request for Review, send the official form directly to the Appeals Council by certified mail, return receipt requested, early enough so that the stamp on the return receipt is within 60 days of the date of the ALJ decision. Pin the certified mail slip to a bulletin board to be removed only when the return receipt arrives. An old slip still on the bulletin board flags a problem.

If your cover letter asks the Appeals Council for an extension to submit evidence or a brief, the Appeals Council advises putting such requests in bold font. Put any such requests on the Request for Review, too. If the cover letter is your brief to the Appeals Council, be sure to refer to it on the Request for Review.

§512   Form: Request for Review of Hearing Decision (HA-520)

SOCIAL SECURITY ADMINISTRATION/OFFICE OF DISABILITY ADJUDICATION AND REVIEW	Form Approved OMB No. 0960-0277

REQUEST FOR REVIEW OF HEARING DECISION/ORDER
(**Do not** use this form for objecting to a <u>recommended</u> ALJ decision.)

(Either mail the signed original form to the Appeals Council at the address shown below, or take or mail the signed original to your local Social Security office, the Department of Veterans Affairs Regional Office in Manila, or any U.S. Foreign Service Post and keep a copy for your records.)

See Privacy Act Notice

1. CLAIMANT NAME	CLAIMANT SSN - -
2. WAGE EARNER NAME, IF DIFFERENT	3. CLAIMANT CLAIM NUMBER, IF DIFFERENT - -

4. I request that the Appeals Council review the Administrative Law Judge's action on the above claim because:

_____

_____

ADDITIONAL EVIDENCE

If you have additional evidence submit it with this request for review. If you need additional time to submit evidence or legal argument, you must request an extension of time in writing now. This will ensure that the Appeals Council has the opportunity to consider the additional evidence before taking its action. If you request an extension of time, you should explain the reason(s) you are unable to submit the evidence or legal argument now. If you neither submit evidence or legal argument now nor within any extension of time the Appeals Council grants, the Appeals Council will take its action based on the evidence of record.

IMPORTANT: WRITE YOUR SOCIAL SECURITY NUMBER ON ANY LETTER OR MATERIAL YOU SEND US. IF YOU RECEIVED A BARCODE FROM US, THE BARCODE SHOULD ACCOMPANY THIS DOCUMENT AND ANY OTHER MATERIAL YOU SUBMIT TO US.

SIGNATURE BLOCKS: You should complete No. 5 and your representative (if any) should complete No. 6. If you are represented and your representative is not available to complete this form, you should also print his or her name, address, etc. in No. 6.

I declare under penalty of perjury that I have examined all the information on this form, and on any accompanying statements or forms, and it is true and correct to the best of my knowledge.

5. CLAIMANT'S SIGNATURE	DATE	6. REPRESENTATIVE'S SIGNATURE	DATE
PRINT NAME		PRINT NAME ☐ ATTORNEY ☐ NON-ATTORNEY	
ADDRESS		ADDRESS	
(CITY, STATE, ZIP CODE)		(CITY, STATE, ZIP CODE)	
TELEPHONE NUMBER ( ) -	FAX NUMBER ( ) -	TELEPHONE NUMBER ( ) -	FAX NUMBER ( ) -

THE SOCIAL SECURITY ADMINISTRATION STAFF WILL COMPLETE THIS PART

7. Request received for the Social Security Administration on _____ by: _____
   (Date)   (Print Name)

(Title)	(Address)	(Servicing FO Code)	(PC Code)

8. Is the request for review received within 65 days of the ALJ's Decision/Dismissal?   ☐ Yes   ☐ No

9. If "No" checked: (1) attach claimant's explanation for delay; and
                      (2) attach copy of appointment notice, letter or other pertinent material or information in the Social Security Office.

10. Check one:
   ☐ Initial Entitlement
   ☐ Termination or other

   APPEALS COUNCIL
   OFFICE OF DISABILITY ADJUDICATION AND
   REVIEW, SSA
   5107 Leesburg Pike
   FALLS CHURCH, VA 22041 - 3255

11. Check all claim types that apply :
   ☐ Retirement or survivors   (RSI)
   ☐ Disability-Worker   (DIWC)
   ☐ Disability-Widow(er)   (DIWW)
   ☐ Disability-Child   (DIWC)
   ☐ SSI Aged   (SSIA)
   ☐ SSI Blind   (SSIB)
   ☐ SSI Disability   (SSID)
   ☐ Title VIII Only   (SVB)
   ☐ Title VIII/Title XVI   (SVB/SSI)
   ☐ Other - Specify: _____

Form **HA-520-U5** (07-2011) ef (07-2011)
Destroy Prior Editions

TAKE OR SEND ORIGINAL TO SSA AND RETAIN A COPY FOR YOUR RECORDS

Privacy Act Statement

Request for Review of Hearing Decision/Order

Sections 205(a), 702, 1631 (e)(1)(a) and (b), and 1869(b)(1) and (c) of the Social Security Act and Public Law 106-169 (sections 809(a)(1) and 251 (a)), as amended, authorize us to collect this information. The information you provide on this form is used to complete our claims process. Your response is voluntary. However, failure to provide all or part of the requested information may affect the continued processing of your claim.

We rarely use the information provided on this form for any purpose other than for the reasons explained above. However, we may use it for the administration and integrity of Social Security programs. We may also disclose information to another person or to another agency in accordance with approved routine uses, which include but are not limited to the following:

1. To enable a third party or an agency to assist Social Security in establishing rights to Social Security benefits and/or coverage;
2. To comply with Federal laws requiring the release of information of Social Security records (e.g., to the Government Accountability Office, the General Services Administration, the National Archives and Records Administration, and the Department of Veterans Affairs);
3. To make determinations for eligibility in similar health and income maintenance programs at the Federal, State, and local level; and,
4. To facilitate statistical research, audit, and investigative activities necessary to ensure the integrity and improvement of Social Security Programs.

We may also use this information in computer matching programs. Computer matching programs compare our records with those of other Federal, State, or local government agencies. Information from these matching programs can be used to establish or verify a person's eligibility for Federally-funded or administered benefit programs and for repayment of payments of delinquent debts under these programs.

A complete list of routine uses for this information is available in Systems of Records Notices entitled, Administrative Law Judge Working File on Claimant Cases (60-0005), Storage of Hearing Records: Tape Cassettes and Audiograph Discs (60-0006), and Hearing Office Tracking System of Claimant Cases (60-0010), Social Security Administration, Office of Disability Adjudication and Review. These notices, additional information about this form, and information regarding our programs and systems are available online at www.socialsecurity.gov or at your local Social Security Office.

Paperwork Reduction Act Statement - This information collection meets the requirements of 44 U.S. C. § 3507, as amended by section 2 of the Paperwork Reduction Act of 1995 . You do not need to answer these questions unless we display a valid Office of Management and Budget (OMB) control number. We estimate that it will take about 10 minutes to read the instructions, gather the facts, and answer the questions. *You may send comments on our time estimate above to: SSA 6401 Security* Blvd., *Baltimore, MD 21235-6401. Send only comments relating to our time estimate to this address, not the completed form.*

Form **HA-520-U5** (07-2011) ef (07-2011)

§513   Extension of Time to Request Review

If a claimant does not meet the 60-day deadline for filing a Request for Review, you may ask that the time for requesting review be extended. The rules are the same for missing the deadline for filing a Request for Review as they are for missing the deadline for any other level of review, *see* §158, except that it is the Appeals Council that must determine whether good cause exists for failure to timely appeal. Thus, when you send a Request for Review to the Appeals Council, enclose a letter explaining why the Request for Review is untimely. Depending on the circumstances, an affidavit from the claimant may be included. If the Appeals Council finds "good cause" for the delay in requesting review, it will extend the time limit. 20 C.F.R. §404.968(b).

"Good cause" for missing a deadline for requesting review is described in 20 C.F.R. §404.911. According to that regulation, the Appeals Council will consider circumstances preventing a timely appeal, whether any SSA action misled the claimant and whether the claimant failed to understand the requirement of timely appeal. 20 C.F.R. §404.911(a). 20 C.F.R. §404.911(b) provides nine examples of good cause for missing a deadline. These nine examples are:

1. You were seriously ill and were prevented from contacting us in person, in writing, or through a friend, relative or other person.
2. There was a death or serious illness in your immediate family.
3. Important records were destroyed or damaged by fire or other accidental cause.
4. You were trying very hard to find necessary information to support your claim but did not find the information within the stated time periods.
5. You asked us for additional information explaining our action within the time limit, and within 60 days of receiving the explanation you requested reconsideration or a hearing, or within 30 days of receiving the explanation you requested Appeals Council review or filed a civil suit.
6. We gave you incorrect or incomplete information about when and how to request administrative review or to file a civil suit.
7. You did not receive a notice of the determination or decision.
8. You sent the request to another government agency in good faith within the time limit and the request did not reach us until after the time period had expired.
9. Unusual or unavoidable circumstances exist, including the circumstances described in 20 C.F.R. §404.911(a)(4), which show you that you could not have known of the need to file timely, or which prevented you from filing timely. 20 C.F.R. §404.911(a)(4) provides that SSA will consider:

Whether you had any physical, mental, educational or linguistic limitations (including any lack of facility with the English language) which prevented you from filing a timely request or from understanding or knowing about the need to file a timely request for review.

Although by the terms of the regulation itself these examples do not contain all the possibilities, try to develop an argument that your client's situation is similar to one or more of the examples. The Appeals Council is erratic in its application of the "good cause" regulation. Always request an extension when the situation warrants it.

One situation not mentioned in the examples in the regulation arises from time to time: a claimant thought that a representative sent in the Request for Review, which is included as an example of good cause in HALLEX I-3-1-1 E.3. It has long been Appeals Council policy to potentially find good cause in this circumstance.. An AC Meeting Note dated February 25, 2005 finds that a claimant's reliance on the representative may, depending on the facts, establish good cause. Here is the meeting note:

The Appeals Council has considered the issue of whether a claimant's reliance on a representative to file a request for hearing, request for review or to file a civil action can establish good cause for missing a deadline for such a request pursuant to 20 CFR 404.911 and 416.1411. Also see 404.982 and 416.1482.

The Appeals Council agrees, in appropriate circumstances, that such reliance may establish good cause. However, the proper exercise of discretionary judgment on this issue requires consideration of all relevant circumstances contributing to the delay, including the actions and/or inactions of the claimant as well as the actions and/or inactions of the representative. The Appeals Council observes that such reliance would neither per se establish good cause nor preclude a finding of good cause.

The Appeals Council's position is consistent with the regulatory language set forth in 20 CFR 404.911 and 416.1411. The good cause provisions in these regulations are specifically addressed to "you", i.e., the claimant, and direct consideration of circumstances that prevented the claimant from making the request for hearing, the request for review or commencing a civil action on time. 20 CFR 404.911(a) cites examples as to when good cause may be found to exist. The regulatory standard contemplates and requires consideration of the individual facts of a particular case before a good cause determination is made and is consistent with recognition of the non-adversarial, quasi-judicial nature of Social Security Administration's hearings and appeals process.

This position is consistent with the statement of policy presented in the Social Security Administration's Program Circulars of December 1996 and September 1997 and incorporated into POMS SI 04005.015.

As clarified, the Appeals Council will continue to apply this policy on all late-filed requests for review or late filed civil actions raising this issue. In requests for review of Administrative Law Judge dismissals in which the Administrative Law Judge found the claimant had not established good cause for the late filing, the Appeals Council will apply an abuse of discretion standard. In so doing, the Appeals Council will determine whether the dismissal order reflects the development and rationale required in HALLEX I-2-4-15B.

Perhaps as a warning to lawyers not to try to use this good cause example as a way to easily defeat the time limit, HALLEX II-3-1-1 E.3. Note states:

The AC must not infer good cause for late filing merely because a claimant has a representative, but must consider a claimant's good cause statement indicating reliance on a representative. If a representative has established a pattern of filing untimely appeals, or the claimants of a particular representative develop a pattern of submitting good cause statements for late filing citing reliance on the representative, the AC will consider whether circumstances warrant a referral to the Office of the General Counsel (OGC) as a possible violation of our rules. See HALLEX I-1-1-50 for instructions on making referrals to OGC.

Sometimes the reason for delay in requesting review is that an unrepresented claimant did not receive a copy of the ALJ decision within 65 days of the date of the decision. You may approach this problem in two different ways. Invoke the "good cause" regulation and request an extension under 20 C.F.R. §404.968(b); and

argue that the Request for Review was timely under 20 C.F.R. §404.968(a)(1). Theoretically the time limit begins to run from the date the claimant actually received the decision. But note that 20 C.F.R. §404.901 provides this definition: "*Date you receive notice* means 5 days after the date on the notice, unless you show us that you did not receive it within the 5-day period."

Even though failure to receive the decision is an example of good cause for missing a deadline in 20 C.F.R. §404.911(b)(7), as a rule, you're going to need more than the claimant's word for when the ALJ decision was received. The problem, as SSA sees it, is that the deadline for appeal is no deadline at all if it can be overcome simply by a claimant's statement that the ALJ decision was not timely received. Thus, unless the claimant's address on the ALJ decision is wrong or the claimant moved, generally you'll need help from someone at the hearing office or the local office in order to demonstrate that it is at least plausible that the claimant did not receive the ALJ decision within 65 days of the date on the decision. SSA employees are usually willing to check SSA's records to see if there is any indication that the claimant may not have timely received the ALJ decision. *Solberg v. Secretary of Dep't of Health & Human Services*, 583 F. Supp. 1095 (E.D. Wis. 1984), applied the presumption that a properly mailed letter is received. According to *Solberg*, this presumption must be overcome by some evidence greater than a claimant's own "self-serving" affidavit.

If the Appeals Council fails to find good cause to extend a filing deadline, the claimant's case may end since the general rule is that federal courts are without jurisdiction to review the Appeals Council's refusal to grant an extension for filing a Request for Review. *Ensey v. Richardson*, 469 F.2d 664 (9th Cir. 1972), adopted by SSA as SSR 73-45c. This rule does not apply in the 11th Circuit pursuant to *Bloodsworth v. Heckler*, 703 F.2d 1233 (11th Cir. 1983), which was adopted by SSA as Acquiescence Ruling 99-4(11). But in all other circuits, an allegation of a constitutional due process violation provides the only basis for federal court jurisdiction to review an Appeals Council dismissal of an untimely appeal.

§514   Extension to Submit Evidence and a Brief

When you file the Request for Review, you may ask for a reasonable length of time to submit additional evidence and a brief. In actual practice, the Appeals Council routinely grants a 25 day extension, for submission of evidence or arguments. HALLEX I-3-1-14 B.1. The Appeals Council calls this a "first extension." HALLEX I-3-1-14 A says that if you initially request more than 25 days to submit additional evidence and a brief, the Appeals Council whether you have provided good cause for requesting "a longer than usual timeframe to submit additional evidence or arguments." If you request longer than 25 days without providing good cause, "the AC will deny the request," though it will provide 25 days. HALLEX I-3-1-14 A. Note 2. Indeed, even if you don't request an extension, if you simply request a bar code so that you can file new evidence and a brief electronically, you're likely to receive a 25 day extension from the date on the letter sending you the bar code.

If you cannot meet the time limit set in the "first extension," the Appeals Council, when it receives a request for a "second extension," "will review the request to determine whether there is good cause for providing another" extension. HALLEX I-3-1-14 B.2. As a rule, if you explain the extenuating circumstances, you will likely receive a letter from the Appeals Council allowing an additional 30 days. HALLEX I-3-1-14 B.2. Most lawyers find the Appeals Council to be reasonable in exercising its discretion in granting a second request for an extension. The letter granting the second request for an extension, however, will also tell you that no further extensions will be granted. Indeed, it appears to be Appeals Council policy to not even respond to a request for an additional (third) extension.

On the other hand, if the request for the second extension is turned down, the letter is likely to tell you that the Appeals Council "will proceed with our action based on the record we have." As a rule, though, if your brief and any new evidence are in the file (and the analyst is aware that they are there) before the time the Appeals Council acts on your client's case, the Appeals Council will consider your submission. But you have virtually no recourse if the Appeals Council does not consider your untimely brief and new evidence. Thus, do whatever you can to avoid finding yourself in this position.

The Appeals Council's practice of granting extensions by form letter that gives you 25 or 30 days from the date of the letter, creates both an opportunity and a problem. It creates an opportunity for a longer extension than you request. If you request a 30-day extension and you explain the extenuating circumstances, the request is likely to be granted; and it might be granted in a form letter dated weeks after your original request and give you an additional 25 or 30 days from the date on the letter. The problem created by this Appeals Council procedure concerns calendaring in your office the date a brief is due at the Appeals Council. Do you wait for the letter from the Appeals Council setting a firm deadline before you submit your brief? Or do you

plan to submit your brief within the 30-day extension time you originally requested?

If you wait for the Appeals Council to respond to your request for an extension, the danger is that the Appeals Council may not respond at all before issuing a letter turning down your client's appeal. Although you are likely to get the Appeals Council to vacate the denial of review once you manage to get the Appeals Council's attention, this is a big hassle.

Thus, because the Appeals Council is not very good at responding to extension requests, to keep from further delaying your client's case, even though you have not heard from the Appeals Council, try to meet the due date you suggested in your letter requesting an extension. The first sentence of your brief should explain about the extension request and that you are meeting the time limit you suggested despite the fact that you did not hear from the Appeals Council.

§515   Communicating With the Appeals Council

If you ask for time to submit additional evidence and/or a brief in conjunction with sending the Request for Review, you will receive instructions. If you're dealing with an electronic file, the Appeals Council will send you a mailing address (that includes the branch number and suite number), an electronic fax number, and a bar code. Although you are allowed to submit briefs or new evidence by mail, the best method (and the preferred method according to Appeals Council instructions) for submitting your brief to the Appeals Council is electronically—by electronic fax using the bar code as your cover sheet or using the RQID number from the bar code for submitting to the Electronic Records Express (ERE). Either method submits your brief directly to your client's electronic folder.

Be careful with your electronic submissions to the Appeals Council. If you mistakenly submit to the electronic fax number without using the bar code as your cover sheet, your submission will go into electronic limbo. It stays in limbo until SSA runs a cleanup operation to rescue documents, which it does from time to time.

If you mistakenly use a hearing level bar code instead of the bar code from the Appeals Council, your submission will make it to your client's electronic folder, but it will not generate any notice to the Appeals Council that it has arrived and it could be overlooked by Appeals Council staff.

If you are dealing with a paper case, the Appeals Council will provide you with a mailing address and a regular fax number so that you may fax your brief.

Faxing is better than mailing. Follow the Appeals Council's instructions carefully about including the branch number and your client's SSN on your fax cover page. In fact, for a paper case, it is a good idea to put the branch number and your client's Social Security number on every page of your brief.

Mail is the last choice, to be used only when there are no other options. Specific routing information (branch number and suite number, if one is provided) must be put on the envelope. Always send everything to the Appeals Council by certified mail, return receipt requested.

The Appeals Council asks that briefs be submitted by only one method. That is, do not submit your brief by fax and then also mail it to the Appeals Council.

The Appeals Council's handling of paper documents (by regular fax or mail) is inefficient and subject to error, especially when backlogs are large. There is nothing more frustrating than timely submitting new evidence and a brief, and receiving weeks later a routine denial letter from which it is obvious that your submission was not "associated with the file." This problem can be corrected by contacting the Appeals Council, requesting that the denial be vacated and that a new decision be issued after consideration of your brief and new evidence. Be sure your letter asks for an extension for filing in federal court if the Appeals Council does not change its mind. *See* §551.

§515.1 Public Inquiries Staff

You can check the status of an appeal by contacting the public inquiries staff at 877-670-2722. If you have the branch's regular fax number it is tempting to send a fax directly to the branch, but it is hard to get anyone at a branch to talk with you about a case. Branches do not always respond to faxed requests for a call back. Branch telephone numbers often go directly to voicemail. Calls are not always returned. Even if you have an Appeals Council bar code, when you submit a letter to the Appeals Council electronically by using the ERE or electronic fax, you have to wonder if anyone at the Appeals Council reads it.

Telephoning the public inquiries staff gives you a real person to talk to who has access to the Appeals Council's case management system. Public inquiries staff can fax you a bar code so that you can submit new evidence to your client's electronic folder. Sometimes the public inquiries staff can resolve problems in a shorter time than it would take to actually get to speak with someone at the branch. In many circumstances, telephoning the public inquiries staff is the place to start to resolve a problem.

You can also fax the Public Inquiries Staff at 703-605-8021.

§515.2 Appeals Council Branch, Circuit Jurisdiction and Fax Numbers

The chart below, which is based on HALLEX I-3-0-7 last updated on 6/12/15, explains the jurisdictional breakdown of judicial circuits within the Office of Appellate Operations (OAO). The numerical breakdown under "Circuit Jurisdiction" depends on the last two digits of an individual's Social Security number.

The chart is organized by workload, and includes the jurisdictional breakdown for:
- Disability Processing Branches (DPBs) (processes disability claims);
- Retirement and Survivors Insurance and SSI (RSI) Branch (processes non-disability claims);
- Court Case Preparation and Review Branches (CCPRB) (processes civil actions); and
- Division of Quality Branches (DQB) (processes Appeals Council own motion reviews).

While you may use the fax numbers below to submit additional evidence to the Appeals Council, you should NOT use these numbers to submit a Request for Review to the Appeals Council. Rather, you may submit a Request for Review by fax to 703-605-7101 or 703-605-7201. You may also follow the instructions at www.socialsecurity.gov/appeals/reps/Appt_Rep_Guide_Req_AC_Review_Submit_Evidence.pdf.

The Appeals Council, which discourages telephone calls to the individual branches, no longer publishes these telephone numbers. Telephone numbers in the following chart are drawn from previous versions of HALLEX I-4-3-104, where earlier versions of this chart were located. The Appeals Council asks that telephone inquiries be directed to the OAO Congressional and Public Affairs Branch at 877-670-2722 or 703-605-8000.

DPBs (disability cases)

Branch	Circuit Jurisdiction (last two digits of SSN)	Branch Fax Number	Branch Telephone
1	9th (00-16)	703-605-7151	703-605-7150
2	9th (17-33)	703-605-7131	703-605-7180
3	9th (34-49)	703-605-7011	703-605-7210
4	9th (50-66)	703-605-7211	703-605-7240
5	9th (67-83)	703-605-7411	703-605-7270
6	9th (84-99)	703-605-7301	703-605-7300
7	2nd & 3rd (00-24)	703-605-7331	703-605-7330
8	2nd & 3rd (25-49)	703-605-7611	703-605-7450
9	2nd & 3rd (50-74)	703-605-7391	703-605-7390
10	2nd & 3rd (75-99)	703-605-7421	703-605-7420
23	5th & 7th (WI only) 10th (CO, NM, & OK only) (00-19)	410-597-0796	410-965-2703
24	5th & 7th (WI only) 10th (CO, NM, & OK only) (20-39)	410-594-2181	410-965-2704
25	5th & 7th (WI only) 10th (CO, NM, & OK only) (40-59)	410-594-2182	410-966-4913
26	5th & 7th (WI only) 10th (CO, NM, & OK only) (60-79)	410-597-0198	410-966-4914
27	5th & 7th (WI only) 10th (CO, NM, & OK only) (80-99)	410-597-0199	410-966-4931
28	4th & 7th (IL & IN only) 10th (KS, UT, & WY only) (00-19)	410-965-8639	410-966-8759
29	4th & 7th (IL & IN only) 10th (KS, UT, & WY only) (20-39)	410-965-7909	410-966-8766

DPBs (disability cases) Continued

Branch	Circuit Jurisdiction (last two digits of SSN)	Branch Fax Number	Branch Telephone
30	4th & 7th (IL & IN only) 10th (KS, UT, & WY only) (40-59)	410-965-7921	410-966-8783
31	4th & 7th (IL & IN only) 10th (KS, UT, & WY only) (60-79)	410-966-3457	410-966-8810
32	4th & 7th (IL & IN only) 10th (KS, UT, & WY only) (80-99)	410-966-3451	410-966-8823
33	11th (00-24)	410-965-4488	410-966-8826
34	11th (25-49)	410-965-9171	410-966-4500
35	11th (50-74)	410-965-4488	410-966-4710
36	11th (75-99)	410-966-3465	410-966-4717
38	1st, 8th & DC (00-24)	703-306-5111	703-306-5100
39	1st, 8th & DC (25-49)	703-306-5101	703-306-5110
40	1st, 8th & DC (50-74)	703-306-5121	703-306-5120
41	1st, 8th & DC (75-99)	703-306-5131	703-306-5130
42	6th (00-19)	703-306-5201	703-306-5140
43	6th (20-39)	703-306-5211	703-306-5200
44	6th (40-59)	703-306-5221	703-306-5210
45	6th (60-79)	703-306-5231	703-306-5220
46	6th (80-99)	703-306-5241	703-306-5230

RSI (non-disability cases)

Branch	Circuit Jurisdiction	Branch Fax Number
RSI	All circuits	703-605-7141

Court Case Preparation and Review Branches (civil actions)

Branch	Circuit Jurisdiction	Branch Fax Number
CCPRB – 1	7th & 9th Circuits	703-605-7441 703-605-7501
CCPRB - 2	1st, 3rd, 4th & 10th Circuits	703-605-7861 703-605-7631
CCPRB - 3	DC, Foreign Claims, 6th & 11th Circuits	703-605-7581 703-605-7241
CCPRB - 4	2nd, 5th & 8th Circuits	703-605-7621 703-605-7741
CCPRB – "V"	Overflow Workload	
Division of Quality (own motion reviews)		
Branch	Circuit Jurisdiction	Branch Fax Number
QRB – 1 through 9	NA	703-306-5090

§515.3 Appeals Council Ombudsman

When you cannot get a response from the Appeals Council branch and the public inquiries staff cannot answer your question, you may contact Teresa Jensen, the Appeals Council ombudsman. Contact Ms. Jensen by fax letter that explains the problem. Fax: 703-605-8691.

§515.4 Appeals Council Electronic Records Express Status Reports

The Electronic Records Express offers an Appeals Council status report that can be viewed online or downloaded. It does not provide very much information and, at least when it was first introduced in 2013, it did not provide any information at all about cases that are being handled by the five Court Case Preparation and Review Branches. Cases that have been to federal court tend to be the ones with the most problems.

§515.5 Appeals Council Email Address for Aged Court Remands

For court remands over six months old where action has not been taken, Appeals Council officials recommend writing to the Appeals Council at this dedicated email address: ODAR.OAO.Aged.Court.Remands@ssa.gov. In the email, include the following information:
- Case name (include full name of plaintiff). Do not include the plaintiff's Social Security number.
- Court that issued the remand order.
- Docket number.
- Date of remand order.
- PDF of remand order.
- Your contact information.

§516 Obtaining Evidence From the Appeals Council

If you had online access to your client's electronic folder while the claim was at the hearing level, your access should continue while your client's case is pending at the Appeals Council. If you began representation at the Appeals Council level and you have signed up for online access with SSA, you should be able to view your client's electronic folder online while the claim is at the Appeals Council. With access to your client's electronic folder, you will be able to download copies of exhibits and the hearing recording from your client's electronic folder. For an explanation how to sign up for online access

to your clients' electronic folders, *see* http://www.socialsecurity.gov/representation/eFolder.htm and §178.5 of this book.

If you do not have online access to your client's electronic folder or if your client's claim uses a paper file, you will have to ask that the Appeals Council mail you copies of requested exhibits. You may also ask the Appeals Council to send you a CD-ROM containing the recording of the hearing for use in preparation of your brief. *See* 20 C.F.R. §404.974. Whenever you ask for materials, the Appeals Council recommends that you put your request in bold font at the beginning of your letter. It is also a good idea to put such a request on the Request for Review itself.

The CD-ROM that you receive from the Appeals Council will be encrypted using the same encryption system that is used in hearing offices. *See* §201.6 for decrypting instructions.

The Appeals Council allows 25 to 45 days from the date on the letter transmitting requested materials for you to submit additional evidence and a brief.

Although 20 C.F.R. §404.974 says that you will be asked to pay for copies of "written evidence" and "a copy or summary of the transcript of oral evidence," in actual practice there is rarely a charge. When it is for "program purposes," i.e., a pending claim, the Appeals Council does not charge for one copy of exhibits or a CD-ROM containing the recording of the hearing. HALLEX I-3-1-21 A. When there is a charge, the Appeals Council waives charges of less than $50. If you request a transcript of the hearing, unless it is a transcript of a short hearing (which costs less than $50), you will be sent a CD-ROM along with a request that you pay for the transcript in advance at the rate of $2.50 per page. HALLEX I-3-1-21 C.2.a. Although most attorneys request transcripts from the Appeals Council only in extremely unusual circumstances, many attorneys hire transcription services to transcribe the recording of the hearing that they receive on CD-ROM or download from a client's electronic folder.

The recording of hearing testimony, whether you receive it on CD-ROM or download it from your client's electronic folder, uses FTR format or OGG format, neither of which are compatible with most CD players. For FTR format, the recording can be played on a computer after you have downloaded and installed the FTR player from www.fortherecord.com. For OGG format, you may download necessary files from www.vorbis.com. SSA says that if you have difficulty downloading the necessary files, you can request that they be sent to you on a CD-ROM by the Appeals Council.

If you want, you can request that SSA send you a copy of the hearing recording in compact disc audio

(CDA) format, which will play on most CD players, but some lawyers have complained about the quality of the hearing recording after it has been converted to CDA format. Thus, you're better off using the files in FTR or OGG format. The FTR player has an additional advantage. It provides the clock time from the hearing recording. If you want the Appeals Council to listen to a particular piece of crucial testimony, you can tell the Appeals Council precisely where that testimony is. For example, "at 10:06:30 a.m., the vocational expert testified that . . . ."

§520 Arguing Your Case to the Appeals Council

§521 Uses of the Hearing Recording

Whenever hearing testimony is important to your case—that is, in most cases—you must obtain a copy of the hearing recording. *See* §516. Only by using the hearing recording will you be able to quote hearing witnesses with full confidence in the accuracy of the quotation. Having your own copy of the recording also gives you a means of checking the accuracy of the transcript submitted to federal court, if the case goes that far. Such transcripts are often of poor quality. In addition, if the recording is lost or inaudible, the Appeals Council will remand the case for a new hearing. Unless you obtain a copy of the recording from the ERE (or, if you do not have ERE access, request a copy of the recording from the Appeals Council), any problems with the recording may not be discovered until after you file your client's case in federal court.

One court concluded: "It is impossible for the Appeals Court to conclude that a decision is supported by substantial evidence without even looking at the extent and content of the hearing testimony." *Gomez v. Sullivan*, 761 F. Supp. 746, 750 (D. Colo. 1991). But administrative appeals judges and appeals officers seldom listen to recordings, and the analysts who prepare summaries and recommendations to the AAJs do not routinely audit hearing recordings unless the claimant raises an issue about expert testimony at the hearing, or the ALJ decision's summary of expert witness testimony is obviously deficient, or there is the allegation of an unfair hearing. *See* HALLEX I-3-2-8. For this reason, the only way you can be sure that relevant hearing testimony is brought to the attention of the Council is to have the recording transcribed and submit all or part of the transcript as additional evidence to the Appeals Council.

§522 Oral Argument

Regulations provide for oral argument before the Appeals Council. A request for oral argument will be granted if the "case raises an important question of law or policy or that oral argument would help to reach a proper decision." Although the regulation provides for ten days advance notice, 20 C.F.R. §404.976(c), HALLEX I-3-8-12 A.4.b. says you will be given 20 days advance notice for appearance before the Appeals Council. As a practical matter, though, oral argument is seldom requested and rarely granted. In the early 1990s, a few oral arguments were held at various locations around the country with travel expenses for both the claimant and attorney paid for by the government, but this hasn't been done since then. Although nothing prevents a claimant's attorney from initiating a request for oral argument pursuant to 20 C.F.R. §404.976(c), HALLEX provides that the Appeals Council will notify a claimant and representative that they may request oral argument only after the Appeals Council assumes jurisdiction of a case. It will grant a request for oral argument when the requirements of the regulation, quoted above, are met and the Appeals Council doesn't feel that it can issue a fully favorable decision. HALLEX I-3-8-12.

§523 Standards for Appeals Council Review

The regulations, 20 C.F.R. §404.970(a)(1)—(4), provide that the Appeals Council will review a case if:
1. There appears to be an abuse of discretion by the administrative law judge;
2. There is an error of law;
3. The action, findings or conclusions of the administrative law judge are not supported by substantial evidence; or
4. There is a broad policy or procedural issue that may affect the general public interest.

These standards are more fully described below, §§523.1 to 523.3, and in Social Security Ruling 82-13, which initiated "own motion" review. *See* §541.

In addition, pursuant to 20 C.F.R. §404.970(b), if "new and material" evidence is submitted, the Appeals Council will review the case should it find that the

ALJ decision is contrary to the weight of the evidence currently of record. *See* §524.

§523.1   *Abuse of Discretion*

"If, in conjunction with a request for review, the Appeals Council receives an allegation of ALJ unfairness, prejudice, partiality, or bias, the Appeals Council will review the claimant's allegations and hearing decision under the abuse of discretion standard." SSR 13-1p. 20 C.F.R., §404.970(a)(1), the regulation that sets forth "cases the Appeals Council will review," see §523, states that the Appeals Council will review a case where "[t]here appears to be an abuse of discretion by the administrative law judge."

SSR 13-1p states that the Appeals Council:

> will find an abuse of discretion when an ALJ's action is erroneous and without any rational basis, or is clearly not justified under the particular circumstances of the case, such as where there has been an improper exercise, or a failure to exercise, administrative authority. For example, if the record shows that the ALJ failed to conduct a full and fair hearing by refusing to allow the claimant to testify or cross-examine witnesses, we will find that an abuse of discretion has occurred. An abuse of discretion may also occur where there is a failure to follow procedures required by law. An ALJ also abuses his or her discretion if the evidence in the record shows that the ALJ failed to recuse himself or herself from a case in which he or she was prejudiced or partial with respect to a particular claim or claimant, or had an interest in the matter pending for decision.

HALLEX I-3-3-2 A. provides these examples of abuse of discretion:
- Not permitting a claimant to submit evidence necessary to support his/her claim;
- Not postponing a scheduled hearing despite physician documentation of the claimant's unavailability for health reasons; and
- Not conducting a full and fair hearing, such as refusing to allow the claimant to testify or cross-examine witnesses.

SSR 82-13, which is referred to in HALLEX I-3-3-2, adds this:

> Although this concept cannot be defined comprehensively, examples of abuses of discretion include: failure to have the claimant submit evidence necessary to support his/her claim; failure to conduct a full and fair hearing; and failure to allow postponement of a scheduled hearing despite physician documentation of the claimant's unavailability for health reasons. An abuse of discretion may also occur where there is a failure to follow procedures required by law.

Although the Appeals Council may invoke its regulatory authority to review a case for abuse of discretion under 20 C.F.R. §404.970(a)(1), it approaches this as a very delicate matter. Instructions to analysts call for "a recommendation about whether the ALJ abused his or her discretion. However, the analyst must not include findings about the allegation of unfairness, prejudice, partiality, bias, misconduct, discrimination, or the equivalent. Instead, the analyst will limit conclusions regarding such issues to whether the record establishes an abuse of discretion by the ALJ." HALLEX I-3-2-25 B.3.a.

The Appeals Council's normal procedure when turning down a case is to acknowledge receipt of a claimant's arguments (without summarizing them), state that the Appeals Council considered the arguments and (without explaining) state that they do not provide a basis for changing the ALJ's decision. HALLEX I-3-5-15 B. In contrast to normal procedure, if bias is alleged, the specific allegations are supposed to be quoted in the Appeals Council's action or remand order followed by this sentence: "We considered your allegations solely as they relate to your case under the abuse of discretion standard in 20 CFR 404.970." HALLEX I-3-2-25 B.3.d.

Although the Appeals Council may base its decision or remand order on a finding of abuse of discretion, bias or misconduct will never be stated as the basis for an Appeals Council action. Instead, bias and misconduct are treated as personnel matters not relevant to evaluating the merits of a Request for Review. When an administrative appeals judge thinks that an ALJ may actually have engaged in "egregious conduct," SSR 13-1p provides for referral to the Division of Quality Service.

It may turn out that the Appeals Council is less reluctant to act on a claimant's allegations regarding an ALJ's conduct now that it need not label an ALJ as biased. Even so, the Appeals Council will almost certainly continue to be unpersuaded by purely statistical arguments based on a particular ALJ's low allowance rate. Indeed, SSR 13-1p states:

In considering allegations of unfairness, prejudice, partiality, or bias by the ALJ, the Appeals Council reviews information in the claimant's administrative record to determine whether to consider the alleged actions an abuse of discretion. The Appeals Council relies solely on information in the administrative record in determining this issue. The Appeals Council does not otherwise investigate the allegations or consider information or evidence that is not a part of the administrative record.

The same lack of success will likely hold for arguments that a hearing was not full or fair when these arguments are primarily based on outcome. On the other hand, ALJ misconduct that creates a hostile environment at the hearing may well persuade the Appeals Council to find an abuse of discretion. Before you raise the issue, consider whether the ALJ's conduct is the kind of misconduct that can be described with words such as these: coercive, critical, derogatory, impatient, inappropriate, intimidating, offensive, or sarcastic. On the other hand, garden variety discourtesy is not likely to be seen as involving an abuse of discretion. Bear in mind for arguments based on an ALJ's perceived hostile tone of voice that not every ear will hear the ALJ the same way.

If the Appeals Council finds abuse of discretion, one would think that remand to a different ALJ would be automatic. Not so, says HALLEX I-3-2-25 B.3.f. Note:

> Ordinarily, the AC will direct that a different ALJ handle the case on remand when it finds an abuse of discretion, regardless of whether the claimant specifically requested such a reassignment. However, this is not required. There may be circumstances in which an AAJ determines that it is unnecessary to direct the case to a different ALJ on remand.

§523.2   *Error of Law*

Error of law exists where there has been "misinterpretation or misapplication of, or failure to consider, pertinent provisions of law, regulations, and binding agency policies." SSR 82-13. "Binding agency policies" according to SSR 82-13 are "generally available as Social Security Rulings, but also may be available in some other form when they have been identified pursuant to 5 U.S.C. §552(a)(2) as statements of policy and interpretation which have been adopted as binding by the Commissioner of Social Security."

According to HALLEX I-3-3-3, Note 1, "While sub-regulatory issuances (including the Hearings, Appeals and Litigation Law manual) are not categorized as 'law' for this purpose, the Appeals Council will grant review under the 'error of law' standard if an administrative law judge (ALJ) does not adhere to sub-regulatory policy or procedure and the ALJ's non-compliance results in a due process violation."

The best cases for obtaining a remand or reversal by the Appeals Council are those involving an error of law by the ALJ. Review the ALJ's sequential disability analysis very carefully. *See* §504. Be sure that the ALJ's treatment of the issues in the sequential analysis accords with Social Security Rulings, particularly those SSRs published since 1981 based on "program policy statements." *See* Appendix 1 for a list of important Social Security Rulings. Pay special attention to the rulings published in July 1996, known as the "process unification rulings." Since they were published, these rulings have appeared in Appeals Council remand orders more than any other group of rulings.

§523.3   *Substantial Evidence*

"Substantial evidence" has the same definition here as it has in court: "such relevant evidence as a reasonable mind might accept as adequate to support a conclusion." 20 C.F.R. §404.901. *See also* SSR 82-13.

Here is what HALLEX I-3-3-4 says about substantial evidence:

A. General

An administrative law judge (ALJ) uses a preponderance of the evidence standard when making a decision. As defined in 20 CFR 404.901 and 416.1401, a preponderance of the evidence means that after considering the evidence as a whole, the existence of the fact to be proven is more likely than not. This is sometimes referred to as the "weight of the evidence" standard. *See* Hearings, Appeals and Litigation Law manual I-3-3-6 C NOTE.

However, when the Appeals Council (AC) reviews an ALJ's decision, it uses a substantial evidence standard rather than a preponderance of the evidence standard. As defined in 20 CFR 404.901 and 416.1401, substantial evidence means such relevant evidence as a reasonable mind might accept as adequate to support a conclusion. Substantial evidence requires less in support of a finding or conclusion than a preponderance of the evidence.

Under the standard set forth in 20 CFR 404.970 and 416.1470, if an ALJ's action, findings, or conclusions is supported by substantial evidence and there is no other basis for review present, the AC will deny the request for review or decline to take own motion review.

B. Applying the Substantial Evidence Standard of Review

1. Recommendation to the AC. When determining whether to recommend to the AC that an ALJ's decision is supported by substantial evidence, an Office of Appellate Operations analyst will consider the ALJ's action, findings, and conclusions, as well as any evidence the ALJ cited in the decision. Additionally, the analyst will evaluate the entire record, including the evidence the ALJ did not cite in the decision.

An analyst will recommend that the AC deny review or not take own motion review when the evidence shows that the ALJ's action, findings, and conclusions are supported by substantial evidence, and there is no other basis for granting review or taking own motion review.

NOTE 1:

If corrective action is needed but the record is otherwise complete, it may be appropriate for the AC to issue a corrective decision. When the AC issues a decision, it bases its decision on a preponderance of the evidence. *See* 20 CFR 404.979 and 416.1479.

NOTE 2:

When the AC is considering whether to take own motion review, it "will not ordinarily review a hearing decision where the end result would remain unchanged unless there is a compelling need to do so." *See* Social Security Ruling 82-13, Program For Ongoing Review of Hearing Decisions Pursuant To Section 304(g) of Public Law (P.L.) 96-265 Appeals Council's Review Authority.

2. AC Review. When evaluating whether an ALJ's action, findings, and conclusions are supported by substantial evidence, the AC will not substitute its judgment for that of the ALJ. If the ALJ's action, findings, and conclusions are supported by substantial evidence, and no other basis for granting review or taking own motion review is present, the AC will deny review or not take own motion review. It is irrelevant whether the ALJ could have made different findings based on the evidence of record or whether the AC agrees with the ALJ's findings. Because the AC uses a substantial evidence rule, an AC denial action or

refusal to take own motion review does not equate to AC "agreement" with the prior adjudication.

Despite how reasonable HALLEX I-3-3-4 appears, a case where the only allegation is a lack of substantial evidence usually gets short shrift at the Appeals Council. Reasonable minds may differ on what is "substantial." To claimants' representatives, the Appeals Council seems to uphold an ALJ denial if it can find *any evidence* to support it, whether it is substantial or not. For this reason, it is best not to rely solely on substantial evidence arguments.

In many cases, substantial evidence issues may be properly re-characterized as errors of law. For example, in cases involving pain, look first to see if the ALJ correctly followed SSR 96-7p and, if not, direct your argument at the ALJ's failure to follow the precepts of that Social Security Ruling. And then explain how following the ruling leads to a different result.

Many error of law arguments have substantial evidence issues embedded in them. Although it is an error of law not to provide *good* reasons for the weight given to a treating doctor opinion, 20 C.F.R. §404.1527(c)(2) and SSR 96-2p, the Appeals Council is likely to view this as a substantial evidence issue. Despite SSR 96-2p's provision that the "decision must contain specific reasons for the weight given to the treating source's medical opinion, supported by the evidence in the case record, and must be sufficiently specific to make clear to any subsequent reviewers the weight the adjudicator gave to the treating source's medical opinion and the reasons for that weight," if the ALJ decision provided at least some rationale, the Appeals Council will likely be deferential to it, even sometimes for quite tenuous and even mysterious reasoning. This Appeals Council proclivity is not a reason not to make this argument. It is a reason to keep looking for an error of law argument that is clear-cut.

The "substantial evidence" argument is usually a secondary argument, though a necessary one in order to address all issues. Use lack of substantial evidence as your primary argument only when 1) the evidence is absolutely overwhelmingly in your client's favor, or 2) you don't have a good "error of law" argument.

§524 Submitting New Evidence to Appeals Council

A regulation effective January 17, 2017, 20 C.F.R. § 404.970(a)(5), requires that evidence submitted to the Appeals Council be 1) new, 2) material, 3) relates to the period on or before the date of the hearing decision, 4) "there is a reasonable probability that the additional evidence would change the outcome of the decision," and 5) you also must:

> show good cause for not informing us about or submitting the evidence as described in § 404.935 because:

> (1) Our action misled you;

> (2) You had a physical, mental, educational, or linguistic limitation(s) that prevented you from informing us about or submitting the evidence earlier; or

> (3) Some other unusual, unexpected, or unavoidable circumstance beyond your control prevented you from informing us about or submitting the evidence earlier. Examples include, but are not limited to:

> (i) You were seriously ill, and your illness prevented you from contacting us in person, in writing, or through a friend, relative, or other person;

> (ii) There was a death or serious illness in your immediate family;

> (iii) Important records were destroyed or damaged by fire or other accidental cause;

> (iv) You actively and diligently sought evidence from a source and the evidence was not received or was received less than 5 business days prior to the hearing; or

> (v) You received a hearing level decision on the record and the Appeals Council reviewed your decision.

20 C.F.R. § 404.970(b)

Note that if you informed the ALJ at least 5 business days before the date of the hearing about evidence you have not yet received, you fulfilled the requirements of the five-day rule. If the ALJ refused to accept the evidence, you can submit it to the Appeals Council with an argument explaining how the evidence would change the outcome of the decision. Although most evidence won't meet this requirement, some evidence will.

According to 20 C.F.R. § 404.970(c), if you submit new evidence that does not meet the requirements set forth in 20 C.F.R. § 404.970(a)(5) and (b) or the

Appeals Council does not find you had good cause for missing the deadline to inform SSA about or submit evidence stated in 20 C.F.R. § 404.935, your client gets a consolation prize from SSA:

> the Appeals Council will send you a notice that explains why it did not accept the additional evidence and advises you of your right to file a new application. The notice will also advise you that if you file a new application within 6 months after the date of the Appeals Council's notice, your request for review will constitute a written statement indicating an intent to claim benefits under § 404.630. If you file a new application within 6 months of the Appeals Council's notice, we will use the date you requested Appeals Council review as the filing date for your new application.

This consolation prize will only rarely yield any additional months of back benefits in a Title II. That is, your client is likely to get the same amount of back benefits on the new claim by simply filing a new application when the Appeals Council denial is received. In Title II cases where the date last insured is after the date of the ALJ denial decision, if the Appeals Council denial comes more than 17 months after the date of the ALJ denial decision, filing a new application with the request for review as the filing date could give your client more months of back benefits than your client could get by simply filing a new application when the request for review is denied. The 17-month calculation is based on: 1) the earliest possible onset date SSA will find on a new application is the day after the ALJ denial decision because of res judicata; 2) there is a waiting period of five full months; and 3) a Title II application pays benefits for 12 months prior to the date of the application.

In SSI cases, on the other hand, the consolation prize is likely worth several thousand dollars to your client. The consolation prize is valuable enough that it very well may be worth the trouble to submit new evidence to the Appeals Council in all cases involving SSI claims. SSI claims otherwise do not pay benefits prior to the month after the date of the SSI application. Using the request for review as the date of application will give your client many more months of benefits than your client could get by filing a new SSI claim after the Appeals Council denial is received. But note this: While the consolation prize allows six months from the date of the Appeals Council denial to file a Title II claim, only 60 days are allowed to file an SSI claim. 20 C.F.R. § 416.1470(c).

§525   Effective Briefing

The Appeals Council is required to provide a reasonable opportunity for all parties to file briefs. 20 C.F.R. §404.975. No special form is required. Most attorneys send briefs in letter form.

Because arguments based on error of law are the best, make these arguments first. Set forth what the ALJ did and explain why the ALJ is wrong with appropriate citations to the regulations, rulings and HALLEX. Avoid extended quotations from regulations, etc., but quote selectively so that even someone unfamiliar with this area of law can understand your argument. Don't argue failure to follow case law except when there is no equivalent regulation, ruling or HALLEX provision. Examples of briefs written by the author in real cases appear at §527.

In cases where the ALJ completely misunderstood the medical evidence, consider this approach: Ask the claimant's doctor to write a critique of the ALJ decision, which you will submit as new medical evidence. submitted because the ALJ decision is misleading. Cf. 20 C.F.R. § 404.970(b)(1). In effect, the doctor writes your brief for you. This can be much more effective than one lawyer telling another lawyer how a third lawyer misunderstood some medical evidence. Tell the Appeals Council that if the letter is not acceptable under the regulations as new evidence, treat the doctor's letter as argument.

If your only argument is whether substantial evidence supports the ALJ decision, your real audience may be the federal court. Nevertheless, do everything you can to convince the Appeals Council that SSA will lose this case in federal court, something that the Appeals Council says it is concerned about even when it thinks the ALJ was right.

Practice Tip

Your client probably has a lot to say about the ALJ decision. Rather than spend an hour or more on the telephone going over the decision, ask your client to send you an annotated copy of the decision. That is, ask your client to make a copy of the decision and write comments in the margins with arrows pointing to specific decision language. Tell your client to pay special attention to erroneous factual statements.

Such annotated decisions can be extremely useful when you're writing your brief. Although much of what a client says about decisions may not address the peculiar substantial evidence and legal error issues for appeal, sometimes a client's comment will spark an inspiration that leads to a winning argument. When a decision has a lot of factual errors, asking your client is an efficient way to make sure you find them all. Some cases are remanded because of egregious factual errors.

§525.1   Be Brief

The optimum size for a brief to the Appeals Council is two to four pages. This is, indeed, a short brief, and it should be the goal for most briefs even though this goal might not be always achieved. No regulation restricts the length of your Appeals Council brief. Decision Review Board regulations (20 C.F.R. §§405.425(b) and 405.427(c)(1)), which set a maximum of 2,000 words (5 or 6 single spaced pages), never applied to the entire country and were rescinded by SSA in 2011. Nevertheless, you ought to view 2,000 words as the absolute maximum length for an Appeals Council brief.

Appeals Council observers tend to think that the best briefs are the short ones. Longer briefs run the risk of burying the best arguments and that you will lose your audience.

Although your brief doesn't need a lengthy explanation of the law, you must nonetheless tie your arguments as tightly as possible to regulations, rulings, and in the right circumstances, HALLEX as well. Analysts know the regulations and rulings, or can be relied on to look them up based on your citations. Show how the legal principles and SSA policies were violated by the ALJ decision. Focus your argument on the facts of the claimant's case.

§525.2   Be Careful

Appeals Council insiders and claimants' lawyers who read a lot of other lawyers' Appeals Council briefs often say brief writers are not careful enough. They see grand assertions that are not supported by the facts. They see a tone of outrage with nothing to support it. They see arguments that substantial evidence does not support an ALJ decision when the facts can be read as supporting two interpretations. They see arguments that a claimant's impairment meets a Listing without citation to medical evidence showing that each element of the Listing is met more than just on rare occasion.

§525.3   Emphasize Legal Error But Tell a Story

Legal arguments are best when coupled with an explanation that shows how the legal principles fit the facts of your client's case. Disability cases often involve compelling stories. A paragraph about your client's story may provide the glue that holds a brief together. After all, disability cases are about the difficulties real people have doing ordinary things. While legal principles provide the underpinnings of most successful arguments, the real-life facts may catch the analyst's attention and make a case appeal to the decision-maker.

But don't get carried away with describing the facts of your client's case. Subtle differences in your version of the facts versus the ALJ's version are unlikely to add to your argument. The Appeals Council will be inclined to accept the ALJ's version. Many ALJ decisions, though, do not give the reader a sense of what is really going on with the claimant. If the ALJ decision is deficient in describing the facts, it is up to you to explain your client's claim to the Appeals Council.

Every fact you put in the brief needs a reason for being there. Think about this: If you were going to explain this case to your mother in a few sentences, how would you do it? Often a short summary of the facts is all you need.

§525.4   Deal With Substantial Evidence Issue

If you have a good substantial evidence argument, be sure to present it. An argument that substantial evidence does not support the ALJ decision helps avoid a conclusion that the legal errors you point out are harmless. Sometimes the deficiencies in an ALJ decision are so great, it cannot withstand review under even the Appeals Council's deferential approach to reviewing substantial evidence arguments. *See* §523.3.

Briefly summarize the ALJ's conclusions that are not supported by substantial evidence; then show the lack of evidence supporting the ALJ's conclusions and the contrary evidence with appropriate citations to exhibit number and page number in the record. Quote from the medical evidence. Sometimes medical evidence summarized in a chart has a powerful visual impact.

§525.5   Focus Your Argument: Summarize, Explain and Conclude

Begin with a summary of your argument, then move on to the argument itself. End by telling the Appeals Council what you want it to do. Don't be shy about asking for outright reversal rather than remand in the appropriate case, but don't ask for reversal where remand is the only possible remedy.

§525.6   Write for Your Audience: The Analyst, the AAJ and the ALJ

Your first audience is the analyst. Some Appeals Council analysts are very knowledgeable about the Social Security disability program. Others might be new. You have a challenging job to write in such a way that you educate a new analyst but do not bore an experienced analyst. Often the administrative appeals judge or appeals officer will be persuaded to do what the analyst recommends. And because an administrative appeals judge or appeals officer might need to get through 5 or even 10 times the number of cases an analyst sees, the administrative appeals judge or appeals officer can be vulnerable to a recommendation that is wrong, but not obviously so.

Your brief thus has two audiences at the Appeals Council: first the analyst, then the decision maker—the administrative appeals judge or appeals officer. Insiders report that administrative appeals judges and appeals officers can and do reject analyst recommendations sometimes because of the claimant's attorney's brief. If you write four pages, it is reasonable to expect that the administrative appeals judge or the appeals officer will read all of it, and compare your arguments with the analyst's recommendation. If you write not 4 pages but 14 pages, maybe not.

There is another member of the audience that you ought not to forget: the ALJ. If you obtain a remand for a new hearing, it will probably be in front of the same ALJ who denied the claim. The ALJ will certainly read your brief. So write your brief in a manner that will not unnecessarily alienate the ALJ.

In drafting a remand order, the analyst faces the same problem of ALJ relations that you face when writing your brief. Here is the instruction given to analysts about this very problem from HALLEX I-3-7-40 B1:

> OAO staff must focus attention on the issues that the ALJ will need to address on remand and not on the ALJ who issued the action. As explained in Hearings, Appeals and Litigation Law (HALLEX) manual I-2-1-55 D, hearing office management will usually assign a remand order to the same ALJ for processing, unless otherwise directed. Therefore, it is critical that the AC not discuss issues in a way that could undermine an ALJ's authority in future dealings with the claimant or representative.

Focus your argument against the decision, not against the ALJ. Describing the ALJ as part of an evil conspiracy bent on denying benefits to your client won't accomplish anything helpful to your client. If possible, refer to "the ALJ decision," not to "the ALJ." Indeed, there is seldom a reason to mention the ALJ by name in your brief. If you can adopt a tone that evokes the image of a simple mistake of law and fact, do so.

At the same time, though, you have points to make in your brief. If your brief turns mushy because you're afraid of offending the ALJ, you may never have to face the possibility of the ALJ reading it because the Appeals Council may deny the appeal.

§525.7   Address All Issues

Even though there is no requirement to exhaust administrative remedies by raising all issues before the Social Security Administration, it is good practice to at least mention all the issues you might want to raise later in federal court. You might impress someone at the Appeals Council that the main arguments in your brief are just the tip of an iceberg of legal and factual errors.

Some district court judges and magistrate judges pay special attention to the lawyer's arguments presented to the Appeals Council. If you did not request relief from the agency on a particular error, a federal court judge may wonder why you expect the federal court to grant relief. It does not weaken your case in federal court to have presented all issues to the Appeals Council. It may strengthen your federal court claim if the judge concludes that the Appeals Council was stonewalling.

§525.8   Write Clearly and Concisely

For most people, writing is hard work. Most people don't turn out a polished final product on the first draft. Editing, rethinking, rewriting, throwing things out and starting over with new ideas are all part of the process. In the real world practices of most lawyers, it is hard to find the time to do this. But you have to do something to make your brief stand out from all the rest of the briefs received by the Appeals Council. Sending a polished work product is one of the best ways to do this.

Make your brief easy to read. Here are some suggestions of things to avoid:
- **SSA acronyms**: Don't use them without translation. For readability, use newspaper style, not lawyer style, to explain acronyms. E.g., date last insured (DLI). Then you may feel free to refer to DLI in the rest of the brief.
- **SSA jargon**: It takes only a little effort to avoid SSA jargon. Densely written, jargon filled paragraphs are not easy to read, even for SSA insiders.
- **Lawyer jargon**: Avoid lawyer jargon as much as possible, even those little words that lawyers love and everyone else thinks are just weird, e.g., hereinafter. Most such words are unnecessary and add absolutely nothing to your brief.

§525.9   Cite Exhibits With Page Numbers

If you want the Appeals Council to pay attention to something in the record, cite both the exhibit number and the page number. With electronic files, this has become considerably easier to do than with paper files. Many ALJ decisions and lawyers' offices use this format for citing exhibit number and page: Exhibit 23F-12.

For the decision, cite to page and even to paragraph.

§526   Remand Policy

Since 1987 SSA policy has provided that Appeals Council remands, including those resulting from federal court remand, are assigned to the ALJ who originally heard the case unless:
- The case has already been remanded to that ALJ once before; or
- The Appeals Council or the federal court directs that the case be assigned to a different ALJ.

See HALLEX 1-2-1-55 D.11.

As noted in §525.6, this policy obviously affects the way an attorney writes a brief to the Appeals Council. It is important to avoid alienating the ALJ who made the decision so that the claimant has a chance of winning on remand.

Few Appeals Council remand orders require that a different ALJ be assigned to a case for a new hearing. Usually the Appeals Council doesn't even respond to an attorney's request that a different ALJ be assigned. Thus, for the first remand hearing, your client will probably have to go before the same ALJ who denied the case previously.

§527   Sample Briefs

The following are real briefs from real cases. They have not been edited other than names have been changed and Social Security numbers have been removed. The Appeals Council issued fully favorable decisions in the cases in which the sample briefs were submitted in §§527.1, 527.2 and 527.3. The other two were remanded for additional hearings.

There are many different ways to write effective Appeals Council briefs. Some lawyers report success with briefs that look like miniature federal court briefs with fewer case citations. They say this is an efficient way to organize a brief and it creates the image that the case is ready to go to federal court if the Appeals Council turns down the appeal.

Many commentators recommend argument headings, a recommendation the author has not yet adopted despite agreeing it may be a good idea.

§527.1   Sample Brief: Disabled Adult Child Benefits

THOMAS E. BUSH, S.C.

REPRESENTING THE DISABLED:	310 WEST WISCONSIN AVENUE	ATTORNEY:
• SOCIAL SECURITY DISABILITY	SUITE 930E	THOMAS E. BUSH
• LONG TERM DISABILITY	MILWAUKEE, WISCONSIN 53203	LEGAL ASSISTANT:
		RACHEL KAPLAN

TELEPHONE (414) 765-9333

FAX (414) 765-0459

October 18, 2006

Appeals Council, SSA
Office of Disability Adjudication and Review
Attn: Branch 24, Suite I-Q-31
5107 Leesburg Pike
Falls Church, VA 22041-3255

Re: Albert Green   Fax: 410-594-2181, Attn: Branch 24
SSN:
WE: Michael T. Green
WE SSN:

Dear Appeals Council:

You allowed me until today to submit this three-page letter brief in the disabled adult child claim of Albert Green on his father's account.

The decision found that before age 22, Mr. Green did not meet SSA's de minimus requirement of having a severe impairment. Finding No.4. Yet the record reflects that Mr. Green, who is now 52 years old and has been found entitled to SSI benefits, has never lived outside his parents' home. He lived with his parents until they died. His parents supported him and helped him obtain and attend his long term part time job of crossing guard, a job that could not be sustained after his mother, the last to die, took ill. After a short period of time, Mr. Green's brother and sister took over the parents' roles of supervising him. It appears from the record that Mr. Green is incapable of living independently and never has been capable of living independently. He has had life-long problems with memory and exercising poor judgment.

It is true that there is not much evidence in the file from before Mr. Green's 22nd birthday. All there is that actually comes from this period is Mr. Green's high school transcript, which shows an IQ in the borderline range. Exhibit 6F, p. 13. In fact, the ALJ decision found that Mr. Green suffered from the medically determinable impairment of Borderline Intellectual Functioning Disorder before he turned 22. Finding 3. However, Mr. Green's brother, Michael C. Green, described the claimant's condition as life-long and having significant deficits in adaptive behavior.

Neuropsychological testing was done by Ralph Jones, Ph.D., who prepared a report dated November 20, 2005. Exhibit 12F. Dr. Jones found that Mr. Green "demonstrated cognitive impairment of the sort that typically occurs in early life diffuse brain injury. The birth difficulty noted at delivery (typically hypoxia due to respiratory distress) is consistent with Albert' general executive, conceptual deficit and memory difficulty." Exhibit 12F, p. 5. Dr. Jones concluded that "Albert suffered an early life diffuse brain injury, probably at birth, causing general intellectual power deficits, a dysexecutive impairment, and memory difficulties that have left him with life-long limited adaptive ability." Exhibit 12F, p. 7.

From this record, it appears that Albert Green has deficits in understanding, carrying out and remembering simple instructions, using judgment, responding appropriately to supervision, co-workers and usual work situations and dealing with changes in a routine work situation. It appears that these deficits date back long before age 22.

The ALJ decision failed to use the special technique described in 20 C.F.R. §404.1520a. That is, the ALJ decision found that Mr. Green had the medically determinable impairment of borderline intellectual functioning but did not proceed to rating the degree of functional limitations resulting from the impairment in accordance with 20 C.F.R. §404.1520a(c).

The ALJ decision did not discuss Dr. Jones's report, which stands for the proposition that neuropsychological testing reveals a pattern of limitations consistent with an early life brain injury. It is impossible to decide this case without discussing Dr. Jones's report. Otherwise, there is a failure to "reconcile any significant inconsistencies." SSR 86-8p. According to SSR 86-8p when there is a finding that an impairment is not severe, "the rationale must show that the impairment(s) would not have more than a minimal effect on the performance of basic work-related functions." Emphasis in original. The ALJ decision is conclusory in this regard, reciting regulations rather than explaining it.

It is true that Albert has repeatedly told people, including the ALJ, that there is little or nothing wrong with him. The ALJ states that Albert "stated that he does his own cooking and cleaning and is able to do some of the repairs around the house." Decision, p. 4. Michael Green, Albert's brother, disputed each of these points. Michael stated that his brother is unable to do any of these things without supervision and even then it is difficult to get Albert to finish tasks.

Albert, who is actually not at all credible when he describes his virtually unlimited capacity for doing things, is found "not entirely credible." Decision, p. 4. Michael's credibility is not addressed in the decision.

Please reverse the decision by finding Mr. Green disabled prior to age 22. In the alternative, please remand this case for further proceedings consistent with the law.

Sincerely,

Thomas E. Bush

cc: Albert Green

§527.2 Sample Brief: Date Last Insured Problem

THOMAS E. BUSH, S.C.

REPRESENTING THE DISABLED:	310 WEST WISCONSIN AVENUE	ATTORNEY:
• SOCIAL SECURITY DISABILITY	SUITE 930E	THOMAS E. BUSH
• LONG TERM DISABILITY	MILWAUKEE, WISCONSIN 53203	LEGAL ASSISTANT:
		RACHEL KAPLAN

TELEPHONE (414) 765-9333

FAX (414) 765-0459

September 2, 2008

Appeals Council
Office of Hearings and Appeals, SSA
Attn.: Branch 25, Suite 1-Q-31
5107 Leesburg Pike
Falls Church, VA 22041-3255

Re: Charles Adams   Fax: 410-594-2182, Attn: Branch 25
SSN:

Dear Appeals Council:

I was allowed until September 2, 2008 to send you this three-page letter brief in the case of Charles Adams.

Mr. Adams says that he is disabled because he is "constantly fatigued," tires quickly and has chest pain when he exerts himself. Exhibit B-2E. He testified that before his date last insured of December 31, 2004, three or four days out of seven he wouldn't get anything done because he was too fatigued. He often napped during the day, falling asleep on the couch.

State agency doctors found that before his date last insured, Mr. Adams was limited to sedentary work. Exhibits B-2F, B-6F, B-7F. David L. Groden, M.D., Mr. Adams's cardiologist who initially saw him for testing in May 2004 and then for regular treatment beginning in September 2005, completed a Cardiac Residual Functional Capacity Questionnaire in March 2008 in which he described Mr. Adams's capacity for working since 2004. Dr. Groden described several limitations that reduce Mr. Adams's residual functional capacity (RFC) below that necessary for a full range of sedentary work: Mr. Adams could not work full time; he would need unscheduled breaks twice daily for an hour each; he needed to elevate his legs above knee level about 75% of the time when he sat; and, because of bad days, Dr. Groden estimated that Mr. Adams would miss work more than four days per month. Exhibit B-11F.

Dr. Groden identified the following clinical findings as supporting his description of Mr. Adams's RFC: "Dyspnea with very light activity. Exertional chest pain. Echo: severe left ventricular dysfunction. Abnormal stress test with evidence of previous M[yocardial] I[nfarction]. Severe L[eft] V[entricular] enlargement. E[jection] F[raction] = 26%." Exhibit B-11F, p. 1. The connection between left ventricular dysfunction and fatigue is well known. "Left ventricular failure causes shortness of breath and fatigue." *The Merck Manual Online*, http://www.merck.com/mmpe/sec07/ch074/ch074a.html.

Since no medical expert testified at the hearing and the ALJ did not pay attention to the analysis by the state agency doctors, it is apparent that the ALJ decision rejected Dr. Groden's opinion based on the ALJ's own reading of the medical evidence. For example, the decision pointed out that when Mr. Adams returned to Dr. Groden in September 2005, he reported being bothered by exertional symptoms for just two months. Decision, p. 3, emphasis in original. Yet, this is a case in which the disabling symptom is fatigue. A myocardial perfusion study done in September 2005 found an ejection fraction of 24%. Dr. Groden noted that the September 2005 study was "essentially unchanged from the prior examination performed on 5/26/04."

The decision found that through his date last insured Mr. Adams had the capacity for "up to a wide range of low-stress light work." Decision p. 4 and Finding #5. In violation of SSR 96-8p, the ALJ decision included no function-by-function assessment of Mr. Adams's capacity for sitting, standing, walking, bending, lifting, etc. In violation of SSR 96-6p, the decision ignored the fact that the state agency doctors found Mr. Adams limited to sedentary work. The decision did not address the specific limitations set forth by Dr. Groden that reduced Mr. Adams's RFC below that necessary for sedentary work – the need for breaks, the need to elevate legs when sitting, missing work because of bad days.

Although the decision mentions 20 C.F.R. §404.1529, it does not perform the analysis required by that regulation. The decision makes no finding whether Mr. Adams's cardiac impairments could cause the fatigue he alleges, which is required by 20 C.F.R. §404.1529(b). The decision does not address the significant objective medical evidence, Mr. Adams's consistently low ejection fraction, let alone the "other evidence" required to be considered by 20 C.F.R. §404.1529(c)(3). The decision does not make the credibility finding required by 20 C.F.R. §404.1529(c)(4) and SSR 96-7p. The decision relies on statements such as that Mr. Adams was reportedly "asymptomatic" or "doing well" or "overall feeling pretty good," decision, p. 3, without placing such statements in context and without mentioning the fact that Mr. Adams's wife testified at the hearing that her husband "downplays" his symptoms.[1]

The decision found that Mr. Adams was capable of returning to his past relevant work, yet the decision did not compare Mr. Adams's residual functional capacity with the requirements of past relevant work in violation of 20 C.F.R. §404.1520(f).

This case may be one that could be decided in Mr. Adams's favor with the opinion of an Appeals Council medical expert who would need to address only this question: Is Dr. Groden's opinion in Exhibit B-11F entitled to controlling weight because it is well supported by medically acceptable clinical and laboratory diagnostic techniques? Dr. Groden cites the consistently low ejection fraction, so low that it would meet the cardiac listings were it not for the results of treadmill stress tests. In May 2004 Mr. Adams reached an exercise level of 12.5 METS. It is referred to as a "nondiagnostic treadmill EKG stress test based on an abnormal baseline EKG." There were occasional isolated premature ventricular contractions beginning about 4 minutes into exercise. Exhibit B-3F.

If the Appeals Council cannot issue a fully favorable decision as of the amended alleged onset date of March 1, 2004, this case must be remanded for a new hearing and a proper decision.

Sincerely,

Thomas E. Bush
cc: Charles Adams

---

[1] Also, careful reading of Dr. Groden's contemporaneous notes demonstrates qualifications on how well Mr. Adams is doing. Consider this paragraph from the November 9, 2005 note in Exhibit B-5F:

In summary, the patient is doing fairly well from a cardiac standpoint. He denies any angina and manifests no signs or symptoms of congestive heart failure. He remains New York Heart Association functional class II. Nonetheless, recent cardiac diagnostic testing has demonstrated severe ischemic cardiomyopathy with ejection fraction ranging between 11% and 21%. Furthermore, an EKG performed on September 26, 2005, revealed a bifascicular block with right bundle branch block and left posterior fascicular block and a QRS duration of 160 msec.

§527.3   Sample Brief: Closed Period ALJ Decision

THOMAS E. BUSH, S.C.

<table>
<tr><td>REPRESENTING THE DISABLED:</td><td>310 WEST WISCONSIN AVENUE</td><td>ATTORNEY:</td></tr>
<tr><td>• SOCIAL SECURITY DISABILITY</td><td>SUITE 930E</td><td>THOMAS E. BUSH</td></tr>
<tr><td>• LONG TERM DISABILITY</td><td>MILWAUKEE, WISCONSIN 53203</td><td>LEGAL ASSISTANT:</td></tr>
<tr><td></td><td></td><td>RACHEL KAPLAN</td></tr>
</table>

TELEPHONE (414) 765-9333

FAX (414) 765-0459

July 10, 2009

Appeals Council
Office of Hearings and Appeals, SSA
Attn.: Branch 24, Suite 1-Q-31
5107 Leesburg Pike
Falls Church, VA 22041-3255

Re: Eunice Smith   Fax: 410-594-2181, Attn: Branch 24
SSN:

Dear Appeals Council:

In a letter faxed to you on June 11, 2009, I asked to be allowed until July 10, 2009 to send you this letter consisting of six pages in the case of Eunice Smith. I also enclose the following additional evidence:

- Letter from James Brown, M.D., dated 6/9/09, 2 pages.
- Records from Advanced Healthcare dated 4/5/06 to 5/4/09, 24 pages.
- Neuropsychological consultation by David Jones, Ph.D., dated 3/20/09, 5 pages.

Eunice Smith, who suffered a traumatic brain injury in an auto accident on July 4, 2004, was found disabled by the ALJ decision for a closed period of disability from the date of the accident until November 1, 2006, when she was found to have improved. No objective evidence supports the ALJ decision's conclusion that there was medical improvement. Instead, Ms. Smith was found "not credible beginning on November 2, 2006." Decision p. 9.

As a result of the accident, Ms. Smith suffered a cognitive decline from her previous high level of functioning,[1] attention difficulties that increase when she attempts to do things over an extended period, a personality change, impulsivity, "disinhibited behavior," difficulty regulating emotions, difficulty making decisions and "spatial confusion," all of which appear to be organically related. See the enclosed neuropsychological evaluation. Although most of these organic deficits may be described as mild, Ms. Smith's psychological adjustment problems have been quite severe. As a result, she has a very low stress tolerance leading her psychiatrist, James Brown, M.D., to predict that she would decompensate when faced with competitive work stressors. See his enclosed letter and Exhibit 25F.

The difficulty that Ms. Smith has had with nausea, vomiting and diarrhea since her accident is probably stress related. Doctors were unable to find an organic explanation. Improvement in this one area of symptoms is what the ALJ decision points to as medical improvement. There was no improvement in medical signs or findings.

The crux of this case is Ms. Smith's poor stress tolerance. Yet, Ms. Smith's difficulty handling stress is mentioned only twice in the decision. It was mentioned once in connection with a discussion of the psychological consultative

---

[1] Her work history is illustrative. For many years she worked as a stock broker. Exhibit 2E, p. 3.

examination: "In this assessment, Dr. Polczinski opined that the claimant appeared to have resumed performing activities of daily living within the home setting on an independent basis and, while she reported difficulty handling stress as a residual of her brain injury, her other activities appeared quite good with at least high average intellectual abilities, very functional memory, ability to understand at least mildly complex directions, and attention and concentration at least adequate for simplified tasks." Decision, p. 5.

In fact, Dr. Polczinski's treatment of stress tolerance was more balanced than portrayed by the ALJ decision:

> It does appear that her primary difficulties at this time are the management of stress. She appears to become frequently overwhelmed in the face of what would appear to be a minor level of stress such as arguments between her daughters. This would appear to be related to some residual deficits associated with her brain injury. It would appear that the difficulties are frontal lobe in nature. It does appear that she has significant problem with the management of stress as a consequence. Likely, these difficulties could preclude her from her previous employment. However, it would suggest her abilities do appear to be quite good. Likely, her intellectual ability is at least in the high average range. Her memory appears to be very functional. Consequently, it would appear that she could understand at least mildly complexed (sic) directions presented to her. Her attention and concentration abilities appear to be adequate at least for simplified task. Her memory does appear to be adequate as well. She appears to have good social judgment and would be able to relate appropriately to co-workers and supervisors. *Her primary difficulty would be with the management of stress. A sudden and even minor level of stress could become problematic for her. This may adversely affect perseverance as well.*[2]

Exhibit 4F, p. 7, emphasis added. Stress was mentioned a second time in the decision as follows: "difficulties in this area including handling stress . . . would have caused additional restrictions best addressed through the nonexertional limitations detailed below." Decision, p. 6. Yet, an inability to handle even a minor level of stress is not included in the decision's description of residual functional capacity applicable after November 1, 2006. Only a few of the things Dr. Brown indicated that Ms. Smith found stressful were included.[3] Exhibit 25F, p. 5. Finding # 14, p. 9, provides:

> 14. After careful consideration of the entire record, the undersigned finds that, beginning on November 2, 2006, the claimant had the residual functional capacity to perform a full range of work at all exertional levels but with nonexertional limitations that would restrict her to work involving simple, routine, and repetitive tasks, in a work environment free of fast paced production requirements and involving only simple, work-related decisions with few if any work place changes.[4]

Ms. Smith has also suffered disabling headaches that since December 2007[5] have been accompanied by bruising under her eyes in the area of the reconstructive surgery she had following her accident. Although her doctors don't quite know what to make of this, because there are visible and quite dramatic changes in Ms. Smith's appearance during a headache, it appears to have an organic basis. See Exhibit 22F beginning at p. 24; also see the pictures at

---

[2] If Dr. Polczinski agrees that "a sudden and even minor level of stress could become problematic" for Ms. Smith, which is among the things that Ms. Smith's treating psychiatrist, James Brown, M.D., said in the enclosed letter and in Exhibit 25F, it is hard to see how Dr. Polczinski's opinion provides a "much more accurate assessment of her true abilities" as found by the ALJ decision. Decision, p. 10. Thus, the stated basis for rejecting the opinion of the treating doctor was not a "good reason" within the meaning of 20 C.F.R. §404.1527(c)(2).

[3] Among the things not included were working within a schedule, completing tasks, working with other people, working with the public, dealing with supervision, getting to work regularly, remaining at work for a full day, fear of failure at work, monotony of routine. Exhibit 25F, p. 5.

[4] This is a sort of one-size-fits-all RFC description that violates the precept of SSR 85-15 that stress is "highly individualized." At the hearing, after the vocational expert was asked a question using this RFC, questions to the VE about the things on Dr. Brown's list did not get very far:
   Atty: No, just a second. These jobs – let's take a look at I believe it's page five of this [Exhibit 25F], the list of things that she finds stressful. I would assume that you would say that the jobs that you identified are low stress, right? Or not. That wasn't part of the hypothetical question, what if it is?
   VE: I don't comment on stress. Stress is internal. I don't have a test for stress.
   Atty: So you don't know if these jobs are low stress, is that…
   VE: I don't comment on stress.

[5] Severe headaches appear as a problem in the medical records since May 2007. Exhibit 22F, p. 4.

Exhibits 12E, 13E, 14E. These headaches, which occur once a month or so, are accompanied by nausea and some vomiting. Ms. Smith testified that she spends the first few days of a headache in bed. Thus, the headaches are bad enough to prevent Ms. Smith from going to work at least a few days per month. As such, she would be unable to sustain employment, especially since the vocational expert testified at the hearing that employers would tolerate missing work only one day per month.

The ALJ decision's treatment of Ms. Smith's headaches was inaccurate. The ALJ decision stated:

> With regard to alleged headaches, the record contains relatively little evidence of the claimant seeking ongoing medical attention for this condition. It is noted, however, that she received a Botox injection on February 25, 2008 with instructions that it could be repeated after three months if successful (Exhibits 11F, 14F, 18F, 20F).

Decision, p. 9. In fact, most of the 71 pages of Exhibit 22F, an exhibit not cited at all in the decision, are devoted to headache treatment.

The decision also stated: "She testified that she does not take any medication for frequent headaches although they reportedly continuing to occur 1-2 times per month, last for days, and sometimes requiring her to spend the first few days in bed." Decision, p. 10.

Here is Ms. Smith's hearing testimony about medication for headaches:

> I actually don't take anything. The doctor was not able to identify any type…I tried several different medications and none of them worked. The only thing that is available is to actually to go to the hospital and to have – there's an IV therapy that is a variety of different medication that's injected into the IV at different times, but that's a fairly lengthy process and then that leaves me pretty wiped out for a couple of days after as well.[6]

The ALJ did not find credible Ms. Smith's testimony that nausea had returned in the six months before the hearing. "Similarly, little to no evidence was provided to show that she has sought additional treatment for nausea, despite her allegations that this condition has returned within the past few months and occurs daily." Decision, p. 10.

Here is the exchange at the hearing on these symptoms:

Judge: I understand that you were having pretty much constant nausea, diarrhea and all that, starting about a month or within the month after you got out of the hospital from the motor vehicle accident and it went on for like two and a half years, but then you started taking something called Amitriptyline, something like that, back in probably late October of 2006 and you said that you had success, the nausea was gone and now your stools were down to a more normal, bearable as you put it, level. Does that – It seems like the nausea was solved as of a while back.

Eunice: Yeah, but it has come back now and I was offered a stronger dosage of the medication which I could take, but it's also something that has a drowsy effect and it's also something that can cause constipation. So there would be a – I'd have to try to figure out how to make that workable.

Judge: When did it start coming back? I mean it looked like success according to the records and I didn't seen any more evidence that you'd been treated for nausea after that.

Eunice: I talked to him on the phone about it. Well, I also have nausea with the headache so sometimes it's hard to differentiate if it's that or the other. But I also do have many days where I will have a lot of diarrhea as well.

---

[6] Ms. Smith had IV therapy on December 7, 2007, Exhibit 22F, p. 25, and April 21, 2008, Exhibit 22F, p. 57. She had another IV infusion on March 12, 2009. See enclosed records from Advanced Healthcare.

Rather than a lack of credibility a much more logical explanation about the return of nausea and diarrhea is that they returned in response to added stress in Ms. Smith's life as a result of her husband filing for divorce and Ms. Smith's attempted suicide in September 2008.

The decision in this case finding medical improvement is legally erroneous and factually wrong. It is not supported by substantial evidence. The new evidence submitted with this brief relates back to before the date of the ALJ decision. The ALJ decision's findings and conclusions are contrary to the weight of the evidence currently of record. 20 C.F.R. §404.970(b). As such, remand is necessary so that a legally and factually sufficient decision can be issued.

But before you remand the case, please consider giving controlling weight to the enclosed opinion from Dr. Brown that Ms. Smith cannot withstand the stress of competitive work and issuing a fully favorable decision. Dr. Brown's opinion is as supported by medical signs and laboratory findings as any such opinion about stress tolerance can be. Ms. Smith has a documented brain injury with medically determinable residuals. See the enclosed neuropsychological evaluation by Dr. Jones. Dr. Brown's opinion is not contradicted by any substantial evidence in the record. The opinion of the consultative examiner, Dr. Polczinski, was that even minor stress could be problematic for Ms. Smith. Exhibit 4F, p. 7. The fact that Dr. Jones holds out hope of improvement through psychological counseling does not contradict Dr. Brown's opinion. As such, Dr. Brown's opinion should be given controlling weight. SSR 96-2p.

Sincerely,

Thomas E. Bush
Enclosures
cc: Eunice Smith

§527.4   Sample Brief: Multiple Errors

THOMAS E. BUSH, S.C.

REPRESENTING THE DISABLED:	310 WEST WISCONSIN AVENUE	ATTORNEY:
• SOCIAL SECURITY DISABILITY	SUITE 930E	THOMAS E. BUSH
• LONG TERM DISABILITY	MILWAUKEE, WISCONSIN 53203	LEGAL ASSISTANT:
		RACHEL KAPLAN

TELEPHONE (414) 765-9333

FAX (414) 765-0459

June 7, 2010

Appeals Council, SSA
Office of Disability Adjudication and Review
Branch 23, Suite 1-Q-31
5107 Leesburg Pike
Falls Church, VA 22041-3255

Re: Christine Lee
SSN:

Dear Appeals Council:

The Appeals Council's notice dated May 11, 2010 allowed me until June 7, 2010 to electronically file this three-page brief in the case of Christine Lee.

On June 10, 2003 Christine Lee was involved in a serious auto accident in which she was ejected from her vehicle. She suffered a neck fracture that was repaired with a cervical fusion and fractured her left scapula which healed on its own. Although her neck and scapula healed, her life never returned to normal. She has suffered from chronic pain. In recent years, she has been plagued by insomnia. When she completed her Function Report on August 28, 2007, Ms. Lee described the capacity to be up 2 ½ to 3 hours before needing to lie down. Exhibit 5E, p. 8.

The ALJ decision has seven serious errors: 1) The ALJ decision (page 5) found a severe mental impairment but assigned no mental limitations in the RFC assessment (Finding #4) in violation of 20 C.F.R. §404.1545(e). 2) Had proper weight been accorded to the medical source statement of Dr. Holcomb, Exhibit 30F, it should have been adopted in accordance with 20 C.F.R. §404.1527(d) and SSR 96-2p. 3) The decision failed to provide good reasons for rejecting Dr. Holcomb's medical source statement in violation of 20 C.F.R. §404.1527(d)(2). 4) The credibility determination[1] (page 6) does not meet the requirements of SSR 96-7p that specific reasons be provided for the finding on credibility. 5) The ALJ decision does not even mention the testimony of Pamela Lee, the claimant's mother, about the help the claimant needs with activities of daily living, frequent need to lie down, observations of manipulative limitations, and bad days.[2]

6) The decision (page 7) failed to resolve conflicts with the DOT and 7) accepted vocational expert testimony that conflicts with SSA policy. VE testimony included semiskilled jobs (SVP 3) in answer to hypothetical questions in violation of SSR 00-4p and 20 C.F.R. §404.1568.

Steven W. Holcomb, M.D., is Ms. Lee's primary physician whom she has seen about every three months since February 2007. Exhibits 6F and 23F. In September 2008, he agreed to take over the job of prescribing Ms. Lee's

---

[1] "After careful consideration of the evidence, the undersigned finds that the claimant's medically determinable impairments could reasonably be expected to cause the alleged symptoms; however, the claimant's statements concerning the intensity, persistence and limiting effects of these symptoms are not credible to the extent they are inconsistent with the above residual functional capacity assessment."

[2] In determining credibility, the ALJ also is required to consider statements from "other persons about the symptoms and how they affect the individual." SSR 96-7p. See also 20 C.F.R. §404.1529(c)(3).

pain medications. Exhibit 23F, p. 13. On January 14, 2010 Dr. Holcomb completed a Physical Medical Source Statement, Exhibit 30F, in which he described Ms. Lee as needing three or four breaks in an 8-hour workday from 30 to 60 minutes each time. Exhibit 30F, p. 2. He described significant manipulative limitations, Exhibit 30 F. p. 3, stated she was likely to be off task 25% of the time or more and predicted that if she were working a full time job she would miss work more than 4 days per month. He noted, "I am firmly convinced of her inability to work in any competitive environment." Exhibit 30F. p. 4.

The ALJ decision (page 5) stated that "Dr. Holcomb's opinion is not supported by the other[3] objective evidence or the claimant's reported level of daily activity." It is virtually impossible to make sense of this statement either as a legal or factual matter. In the face of this record, to say that that Dr. Holcomb's opinion is "not supported" by objective evidence is absurd. Under the regulations, to give Dr. Holcomb's opinion controlling weight, it must be "well-supported by medically acceptable clinical and laboratory diagnostic techniques," 20 C.F.R. §404.1527(d)(2), for which an argument could be made that it indeed is well supported. Otherwise, the issue is the degree to which Dr. Holcomb's opinion can reasonably be accepted as consistent with the objective medical evidence and other evidence. See 20 C.F.R. §404.1529(c)(3) and (c)(4). Dr. Holcomb's opinion is certainly consistent with the objective evidence.[4]

The statement that Dr. Holcomb's opinion is not supported by Ms. Lee's "reported level of daily activity" is simply false. Her hearing testimony, the hearing testimony of her mother, and the Function Report, Exhibit 5E, especially page 8, all describe the need to lie down several times during the day. Dr. Holcomb's opinion is fully consistent with this need. Exhibit 30F, p. 2.

The following illogical statement (decision, page 5) may or may not be part of the explanation for the weight given to Dr. Holcomb's opinion: "The evidence of record shows the claimant has continued to be seen for complaints of pain, but the more recent notes show she has progressed with care and improved in terms of her pain."[5] No citations to the record are provided for this proposition. The last note from Dr. Holcomb, which is dated July 9, 2009, concludes: "The patient remains disabled with the severity of her pain and her limitations to daily activities." Exhibit 23F, pp. 20 – 21. The same July 9, 2009 note also states: "The patient continues to have quite severe pain down her arms, significant neck and back pain." Exhibit 23F, p. 20.[6]

In short, the decision failed to provide "good reasons" within the meaning of 20 C.F.R. §404.1527(d)(2) for the weight given to Dr. Holcomb's opinion.

Each of the seven errors described at the beginning of this brief is sufficient to require that this case be remanded for another hearing and a new decision that comports with Social Security regulations and rulings. On the other hand, Dr. Holcomb's medical source statement could be adopted by the Appeals Council in conjunction with issuing a fully favorable decision in this case. We ask that the Appeals Council consider doing so.

Sincerely,

Thomas E. Bush
cc: Christine Lee

---

[3] What is "other objective evidence"? This is not a term that appears in Social Security regulations or rulings.

[4] In the context of this case involving residuals of a serious auto accident and cervical fusion, Dr. Holcomb specifically mentions decreased range of motion throughout axial skeleton, consistent pain behavior – worst with neck and thoracic, numbness and loss of coordination to arms, nerve pain radiating through arms, depression. Exhibit 30F, p. 1.

[5] Is this an argument that Ms. Lee might have been disabled in the past but is no longer disabled and therefore never was disabled?

[6] One can virtually always find ups and downs in medical records. For example, in Dr. Holcomb's April 9, 2009 note, Ms. Lee did appear to be doing better. Exhibit 23F, p. 18. The fact that there are such fluctuations shows the importance of a "longitudinal perspective," see 20 C.F.R. §404.1527(d)(2), when assessing how well a claimant is doing over the long term.

§527.5   Sample Brief: Proper Evaluation of Treating Doctor Opinions and New Evidence

THOMAS E. BUSH, S.C.

REPRESENTING THE DISABLED:	310 WEST WISCONSIN AVENUE	ATTORNEY:
• SOCIAL SECURITY DISABILITY	SUITE 930E	THOMAS E. BUSH
• LONG TERM DISABILITY	MILWAUKEE, WISCONSIN 53203	LEGAL ASSISTANT:
		RACHEL KAPLAN

TELEPHONE (414) 765-9333

FAX (414) 765-0459

August 17, 2007

Appeals Council, SSA
Office of Disability Adjudication and Review
ATTN: Branch 23, Suite 1-Q-31
5107 Leesburg Pike
Falls Church, VA 22041-3255

Re: Berkana Sarek   Fax: 410-597-0796, Attn: Branch 23
SSN:

Dear Appeals Council:

I was allowed until August 17, 2007 to send you this four-page brief in the case of Berkana Sarek. I also enclose letters from Martha Lynde, Ph.D., and Howard Williams M.D., dated August 10, 2007, and a 6-page critique of the ALJ decision written by Michael DeMille, a long-time friend of Ms. Sarek's.

Berkana Sarek suffers from fibromyalgia/ chronic fatigue syndrome and bipolar disorder. Her physical impairment prevents her from performing full time work of any sort, not even sedentary work, because of fatigue and pain. On her disability report, Exhibit B-1E, Ms. Sarek described herself as too tired to work. None of her descriptions of daily activities, either in hearing testimony or in anything submitted to SSA are remotely consistent with a capacity to do full time light work. See Exhibits B-1E, B-4E, B-5E, B-8E. Her friend, Michael DeMille, who testified at the hearing and completed Exhibits B-3E and B-6E and took the dramatic pictures of Ms. Sarek's terminally cluttered home in Exhibit B-10E, provides a description of Ms. Sarek's daily activities that certainly does not indicate a capacity for light work. Indeed, because of her impairments, Ms. Sarek was limited to part time sedentary work in 1998. She stopped working in February 2000. Exhibit B-7E, p. 8, B-6E.

Yet, the ALJ decision concludes that Ms. Sarek's activities of daily living are consistent with a capacity for full time light work, standing and walking for 6 hours out of 8 and occasionally lifting up to 20 lbs. Finding #5. For this proposition, the ALJ decision points to Ms. Sarek's ability "to go grocery shopping, do housecleaning[1] and have several social outings per month, attending events like dinners, movies or university lectures," go to the State Fair, art shows, take a vacation in November 2005, sell on E-Bay, baby-sitting a 12-year-old. Decision, p. 7. To the contrary, such activities do not demonstrate a capacity for sustained light work. It would be a stretch to say that such activities, taken out of context as was done in this ALJ decision, demonstrate a capacity for sedentary work.[2] But sustained light work? No way.

---

[1] See the photos taken by Mr. DeMille. Although at the hearing the ALJ stated that the photos would be B-10E and the photos are discussed on page 7 of the decision, the exhibit list shows the unofficial transcript of VE testimony, which was submitted after the hearing, as B-10E. If the exhibit file does not contain the 8-page exhibit consisting of a letter from Mr. DeMille and seven pages of photographs, please contact me and I will provide a copy.

[2] Ms. Sarek was born on September 15, 1955. Thus, she turned 50 years old on September 15, 2005, which was 15 days before her date last insured of September 30, 2005. Had she been found limited to sedentary work, the ALJ would have had to find her disabled as of her 50th birthday pursuant to Rule 201.14 of the Medical-Vocational Guidelines.

The ALJ decision's evaluation of Ms. Sarek's mental impairment is even worse than the evaluation of her physical. Over the past few years Ms. Sarek has been treated by Howard Williams, M.D., a psychiatrist, and two psychologists, Edward Robinson, Ph.D., and Martha Lynde, Ph.D.[3] All three doctors have opined that Ms. Sarek is incapable of working because of her mental impairment. Exhibits B-7F, B-21F, B-22F, B-25F. In the enclosed letter Dr. Williams points to the variability of Ms. Sarek's behavior: "The judge has simply elected to notice and cite the indications of good functioning." The enclosed letter from Dr. Lynde points out that the ALJ misinterpreted her notes, stating, "While Ms. Sarek has made progress in some areas of functioning, my notes reflect ongoing suicidal ideation, difficulty in concentration and focus, and personality characteristics that at this time are not compatible with an individual who can sustain employment."

Dr. Robinson's notes, which are difficult to read, contain many references to hypomania, pressure of speech, flight of ideas. There are some references to circumstantiality, visual hallucinations, extremely depressed, crying, intrusive thoughts and suicidal ideation. There are also several references to "doing OK," just as one would expect for a Bi-Polar Disorder. Exhibit B-18F.

Dr. Williams's notes, which were first provided to SSA at the hearing level, are cryptic and filled with abbreviations. Nevertheless, they are not inconsistent with Dr. Williams's conclusions, including the two conclusions by Dr. Williams that were criticized by the ALJ. Dr. Williams indicated that Ms. Sarek has had four or more episodes of decompensation. Decision p. 9. Although there are not three episodes of decompensation within one year as required by the Listings, Dr. Williams's notes show decompensation in May 2001 and March 2002 and perhaps April 2004 and May-June 2005. (One needs to pay close attention to medication changes when reviewing Dr. Williams's notes as is recommended by the mental Listings, §12.00 C4.) Exhibit B-20F. See also the enclosed notes about the hearing decision written by Mr. DeMille, p. 3, where he describes five episodes of decompensation, with the latest in 2004.

The ALJ also criticizes Dr. Williams for stating that Ms. Sarek suffered a decline in intellectual functioning. Although it is true that there is no IQ testing in the record, Dr. Williams could easily have inferred this conclusion from discussions with Ms. Sarek, who complains about cognitive problems, or with Mr. DeMille, who described Ms. Sarek's cognitive decline in Exhibit B-6E, p. 11 and also described it at the hearing.

An ALJ is required to give "good reasons" for not accepting the opinions of treating sources. 20 C.F.R. §404.1527(d)(2). The reasons stated by the ALJ in this case do not stand up to close analysis.[4]

The ALJ obviously had some questions about the opinions from Drs. Robinson, Williams and Lynde and he had questions about their treatment notes. Instead of denying the claim outright in such circumstance, the regulations provide that SSA "will seek additional evidence or clarification from your medical source when the report from your medical source contains a conflict or ambiguity that must be resolved, the report does not contain all the necessary information, or does not appear to be based on medically acceptable clinical and laboratory diagnostic techniques." 20 C.F.R. §404.1512(e)(1).

The ALJ decision's description of mental RFC is: "to reduce stress and her need to concentrate, the claimant can perform unskilled to marginally semiskilled work with only occasional contact with co-workers and supervisors and no contact with the public." Finding # 5. To say that she can perform marginally semiskilled work avoids the function-by-function RFC requirement of SSR 96-8p and it invites the vocational expert to include semiskilled jobs in answer to hypothetical questions about whether jobs exist in significant numbers in the economy without ever addressing the issue of transferable skills.[5] Indeed, the ALJ decision found transferability of skills to be not

---

[3] Martha Lynde recently received her Ph.D. She did not have the Ph.D. when she completed the Mental Impairment Questionnaire on January 17, 2007. Exhibit B-22F.

[4] The ALJ stated some additional reasons that are, in fact, legally wrong. On page 9 of the decision the ALJ suggested that he could not accept the opinions of Drs. Robinson, the psychologist, and Whit, Ms. Sarek's internist, that Ms. Sarek was unable to work because such statements are administrative findings, not opinions. This is a misinterpretation of SSR 96-5p. On page 10, the ALJ states that he will not give significant weight to the opinion of Ms. Lynde because she is not an acceptable medical source. This is a misinterpretation of SSR 06-3p.

[5] In fact, this came up at the hearing the other way around. The hypothetical question to the VE included a requirement that jobs be unskilled. But the VE was not able to come up with enough unskilled jobs to satisfy the requirement that jobs exist in significant numbers. She included semiskilled jobs on her own.

material. Finding # 9. The vocational expert never told us how many unskilled jobs were within the capacity described in the ALJ's hypothetical question. See decision, p. 11.

The testimony of the vocational expert, an unofficial transcript of which was submitted to the ALJ after the hearing, not only uses SVP 3 jobs, it also relies on the O*NET. The VE was unable to provide DOT numbers for the jobs she cited and the ALJ refused to require her to provide them after the hearing. One is forced to wonder, then, what part of the VE's testimony, in fact, was consistent with the DOT and what part diverged from the DOT. For the parts that are not consistent with the DOT, the ALJ is directed by SSR 00-4p to explain how the conflict was resolved. That was not done. See decision, p. 11.

This is a strong case on the facts with support for disability from four treating doctors. The primary evidence of no disability comes from a one-time psychological consultative evaluation. Exhibit B-8F. If Ms. Sarek's condition is as variable as Dr. Williams suggests, it isn't surprising that she could go to a consultative examination on a good day.

This would be an appropriate case for the Appeals Council to reverse and award benefits. Indeed, disability is supported by four treating doctors and based on the RFC given by the ALJ to the VE, the VE was unable to come up with unskilled jobs existing in significant numbers in the economy.

Otherwise, this case needs to be remanded for legal errors in the decision to be corrected and for the ALJ to recontact the doctors and then write a decision that is supported by the record.

Sincerely,

Thomas E. Bush
Enclosures
cc: Berkana Sarek

§530   Substantive Issues

§531   Reopening by the Appeals Council at the Claimant's Request (HALLEX I-3-9)

In conjunction with an appeal to the Appeals Council, a claimant may request that the Appeals Council reopen an ALJ decision or a decision of the Appeals Council itself. *See* §509. Reopening rules, however, are quite convoluted. *See* §§370 *ff.* Because HALLEX I-3-9 provides an excellent discussion, we reprint it here. Note, however, that different rules apply to DSI cases from SSA's Boston region. *See* 20 C.F.R. §405.601.

Chapter I-3-9. Post-Adjudicative Actions

Table of Contents

I-3-9-1.   Reopening and Revising Determinations and Decisions

Last Update: 7/27/15 (Transmittal I-3-121)

A. General

Under 20 CFR 404.987 and 416.1487, a determination or decision becomes final if the claimant does not request review within the time period for appeal or the Social Security Administration (SSA) does not notify the claimant of its intent to revise a determination or decision before it becomes final and binding. In most situations, the established time period for requesting review of a determination or decision is 60 days. See 20 CFR 404.909, 404.933, 404.968, 416.1409, 416.1433, and 416.1468. (If the claimant requests exceptions to an administrative law judge decision in a case remanded by a Federal court, see 20 CFR 404.984(b) and 416.1484(b), as well as Hearings, Appeals and Litigation Law (HALLEX) manual I-4-4-13). For more information about administrative finality at the hearing level, see generally HALLEX I-2-8-5.

However, under the same authority and under certain conditions, SSA may reopen and revise a determination or decision after it is final and binding, either on SSA's own initiative or at the request of a party to the determination or decision. Generally stated, under 20 CFR 404.988 and 416.1488, an adjudicator may reopen a determination or decision:

Within 12 months of the date of the notice of the initial determination, for any reason (see HALLEX I-3-9-30);

Within four years (title II) or two years (title XVI) of the date of the notice of the initial determination if SSA finds good cause (see HALLEX I-3-9-40); and

At any time if it was obtained by fraud or similar fault (see HALLEX I-3-10-7); and

At any time in title II cases for the reasons set forth in 20 CFR 404.988(c) (see HALLEX I-3-9-60).

NOTE 1:

While the regulations are written in permissive terms, as a general practice, if both the conditions and timeframes for reopening are met, the SSA component with jurisdiction will usually reopen a determination or decision.

NOTE 2:

For cases SSA adjudicates beyond the hearing level in Region 1, the time frame for reopening for good cause is six months from the date of the final hearing decision, and SSA will not find that "new and material evidence" under 20 CFR 404.989(a)(1) and 416.1489(a)(1) is a basis for good cause. See 20 CFR 405.601.

Information about computing the time period for reopening is found in HALLEX I-3-9-20.

B. Reopening by the Appeals Council (AC)

When a case is properly before the AC and the conditions for reopening exist, the AC has the authority to consider the issue of reopening and revising. See generally HALLEX I-3-9-5.

The claimant may expressly request reopening or may submit information that implies a request for reopening. See HALLEX I-3-9-10.

The AC may also consider reopening an otherwise final action on its own initiative. For example, if the AC is unable to review a protest case (see HALLEX I-3-6-54) using its own motion authority under 20 CFR 404.969 and 416.1469, it may consider whether the conditions for reopening a case exist under 20 CFR 404.987 and 416.1487.

Additionally, the AC may consider reopening and revising a prior favorable determination or decision when the AC reaches a conclusion on a subsequent application that conflicts with or adversely affects a claimant's entitlement, earnings record, insured status, etc. For example, the AC may find that the claimant does not have earnings from self-employment for deduction purposes, and that the earnings are not earnings for entitlement purposes. In this event, the AC must reopen and revise the prior award to disallow the claim or to reduce the amount of monthly benefits, whichever is appropriate.

When the AC declines to reopen a prior determination or decision, it is a threshold inquiry only, meaning the AC does not adjudicate the merits of the prior claim.

I-3-9-5. Appeals Council Jurisdiction to Reopen and Revise a Determination or Decision

Last Update: 7/27/15 (Transmittal I-3-121)

A. Determinations

The Appeals Council (AC) has primary jurisdiction to consider reopening and revising any initial determination, or reconsidered determination, if the case is properly before the AC on the basis of a request for review, a subsequent application, own motion review, or other appropriate jurisdiction. For a common example, see Hearings, Appeals and Litigation Law (HALLEX) manual I-1-10-30 C.

B. Administrative Law Judge (ALJ) Decisions

Unless the decision is pending in or was decided by a Federal court, the AC has primary jurisdiction to consider reopening and revising any ALJ decision if the AC has jurisdiction over a subsequent application (whether on request for review, on own motion, or other appropriate jurisdiction).

The AC also has authority to reopen and revise any final determination or decision in which an ALJ has primary jurisdiction, but will generally do so only if the particular circumstances allow the AC to act more expeditiously than an ALJ. See HALLEX I-2-9-5 for an ALJ's authority to reopen and revise an otherwise final determination or decision.

NOTE:

The regulations at 20 CFR 404.988 and 416.1488 address reopening final determinations or decisions. For information about vacating an ALJ dismissal, see 20 CFR 404.960 and 416.1460. See also HALLEX I-3-5-72 if the ALJ dismissed the request for hearing and additional evidence, legal argument, or contentions were submitted to the AC.

C. AC Decisions

The AC has primary jurisdiction to consider reopening and revising its own decisions (unless the decision is pending in Federal court).

I-3-9-6. Administrative Law Judge Requests Jurisdiction to Reopen and Revise Decision

Last Update: 7/27/15 (Transmittal I-3-121)

When an administrative law judge (ALJ) requests that the Appeals Council (AC) return jurisdiction to the ALJ in order to issue a more favorable action, the AC treats the request as a request for remand. For processing instructions, see Hearings, Appeals and Litigation Law (HALLEX) manual I-3-7-25.

NOTE:

Although the regulations limit reopening actions to "decisions," an ALJ may also request jurisdiction after dismissing a request for hearing in order to issue a more favorable action. For more information about this situation, see HALLEX I-3-7-25.

I-3-9-10. Claimant Requests Reopening (Express and Implied)

Last Update: 7/27/15 (Transmittal I-3-121)

A. General

A claimant may expressly request that the Appeals Council (AC) reopen and revise a final determination or decision. Additionally, a claimant may submit additional evidence or information that implies a request for reopening. For example, a claimant may allege an onset date of disability within a previously adjudicated period.

When a claimant does not specifically request AC review but submits a reopening request to the AC, the AC treats the reopening request as a request for review. If, after the AC has denied review, a claimant submits an express request for reopening or additional information that implies a request for reopening, the AC will treat the request as a request to reopen the administrative law judge (ALJ) decision. See processing instructions in Hearings, Appeals and Litigation Law (HALLEX) manual I-3-5-50 C.2.

NOTE:

Under 20 CFR 404.903(l) and 416.1403(a)(5), if the adjudicator at the initial, reconsideration, or hearing level concluded that the criteria for reopening were not met, the claimant has no right to request review of the reopening action. If the prior adjudicator did not address a reopening issue, the AC will evaluate whether a basis for granting review is present (see HALLEX I-3-3-1).

B. AC Action on Reopening Request

When a claimant expressly requests reopening, the AC will specifically address the request in its action document. If the claimant implied a request for reopening, the AC will use its best judgment in determining whether it will specifically address the issue in its action document.

1. AC Denies Request for Review

If the AC denies the request for review, the language the AC will use in its denial notice depends on the circumstances.

- If the AC denies the request to reopen, the analyst will use the language in the Document Generation System (DGS) Stored Paragraph 9 (all templates).
- If the AC refers the request for reopening to an ALJ for further consideration, the analyst will use the language in DGS Stored Paragraph 9A (all templates).
- If the ALJ already considered the request for reopening and denied the request, the analyst will use the language in DGS Stored Paragraph 9B (all templates).

2. AC Grants Review

If the AC remands the case, the language the AC will use in the remand order depends on the circumstances:

- If the AC reopens an ALJ decision, the analyst will use the language in DGS REM 47;
- If the AC affirms an ALJ's finding that a claimant is disabled but is remanding a case for further proceedings (e.g., the AC is remanding a partially favorable decision), the analyst will use the language in DGS REM 48;
- If the AC remands a case to an ALJ and is reopening a determination on a subsequent application, the analyst will use DGS REM 45x; or
- If the AC remands a case to an ALJ but is affirming a determination on a subsequent application, the analyst will use DGS REM 46x.

If the AC issues a decision, the analyst will use the language in the appropriate DGS decisional templates (depending on whether the decision is fully favorable, partially favorable, or unfavorable).

I-3-9-20. Computing the Time Periods for Reopening

Last Update: 7/27/15 (Transmittal I-3-121)

A. Compute From the Date of the Initial Determination Notice

In determining whether the conditions for reopening and revising a final determination or administrative law judge (ALJ) decision are met, the Appeals Council (AC) will compute the time between:

- The date of the notice of the initial determination on the application the AC is considering reopening; and
- The date of the claimant's request for reopening or the date the Social Security Administration takes action to reopen the determination or decision.

The date of the request for reopening will vary from case to case depending on the circumstances. To illustrate, in some cases:

- The date of the request for reopening is the filing date of the new application because the claimant raises the issue of reopening (express or implied) in the application. For example, reopening is an issue implied in the application if the claimant alleges an onset of disability during a prior adjudicated time period.
- The claimant may not have raised the issue of reopening before the AC level. In that circumstance, the AC computes reopening from the date of the request for reopening (or if on its own initiative, the date the AC first identified the issue).
- The AC may receive a referral from another component about a processing issue that would require the AC to reopen the case to correct the issue. In that circumstance, if the time to exercise own motion review has passed, the AC would compute reopening from the date it received the referral.

B. Reopening Multiple Prior Determinations or Decisions

Under limited circumstances, the AC may reopen multiple prior determinations or decisions. The AC will use the same criteria in subsection A above to compute the time period for reopening any earlier determination or decision.

NOTE:

When evaluating whether to reopen an even earlier determination or decision, the AC will not use the date from a prior determination or decision it reopens as the date of the "request for reopening" (sometimes referred to as "stacking applications" or "the domino effect").

For an illustrative example of reopening multiple applications, see Hearings, Appeals, and Litigation Law manual I-2-9-20 B.

C. Acquiescence Rulings (AR) That Expand the Time To Request Reopening

In the Fourth Circuit, AR 90-4(4): Culbertson v. Secretary of Health and Human Services provides an expanded timeframe in which certain claimants may request reopening on a prior determination. In short, if an adjudicator determines that mental incompetence prevented the claimant from understanding the procedures for requesting administrative review of a prior determination, and the claimant had no individual who was legally responsible for prosecuting the claim, he or she will not apply res judicata or administrative finality even if more than four years have elapsed in a title II claim or two years in a title XVI claim. Rather, the AC will reopen the prior determination and issue a revised determination.

NOTE:

If there is a question about the sufficiency of the prima facie case regarding the claimant's mental incompetence, the AC will see AR 90-4(4) and take appropriate action based on the facts of the case before it.

The Ninth Circuit also provides an expanded timeframe in which certain claimants may request reopening. AR 92-7(9): Gonzalez v. Sullivan applies only to claimants in the Ninth Circuit who received an adverse initial determination prior to July 1, 1991 and did not timely appeal that determination. For the purposes of this AR, the time limits for reopening and revising final agency determinations do not apply when the claimant meets the criteria outlined in the AR.

In addition to these ARs, see also Social Security Ruling (SSR) 91-5p, Mental Incapacity and Good Cause for Missing the Deadline to Request Review, when applicable (e.g., the claimant was unrepresented at the time of the prior administrative action), and SSR 95-1p, Policy Interpretation Ruling Title II and Title XVI: Finding Good Cause for Missing the Deadline to Request Administrative Review Due to Statements in the Notice of Initial or Reconsideration Determination Concerning the Right to Request Administrative Review and the Option to File a New Application, as applicable.

I-3-9-30. Reopening for Any Reason Within 12 Months

Last Update: 7/27/15 (Transmittal I-3-121)

The Appeals Council (AC) may reopen an initial, revised, or reconsidered determination or a decision or revised decision under title II or title XVI for any reason within 12 months from the date of the notice of the initial determination (see 20 CFR 404.988(a) and 416.1488(a)).

However, reopening within 12 months is not automatic. The AC can deny a request to reopen within 12 months if there is no reason to revise the prior determination or decision.

NOTE:

This does not mean the claimant has to submit a reason for revising the prior determination or decision. Rather, the AC will evaluate whether the record demonstrates a reason for revising the prior determination or decision.

I-3-9-40. Reopening for Good Cause

Last Update: 7/27/15 (Transmittal I-3-121)

A. Time Limits for Reopening

The Appeals Council (AC) may reopen a determination or decision, which is otherwise final, for good cause as follows:

- after the 12-month period for reopening for any reason, but within 4 years from the date of the notice of the initial determination in a claim under title II; or

- after the 12-month period for reopening for any reason, but within 2 years from the date of the notice of the initial determination in a claim under title XVI.

See generally 20 CFR 404.988(b), 404.989, 416.1488(b), and 416.1489. See also Hearings, Appeals and Litigation Law (HALLEX) manual I-3-9-20 C for Acquiescence Rulings that expand the time period for requesting review.

NOTE:

For cases the Social Security Administration (SSA) adjudicates beyond the hearing level in Region 1, the time frame for reopening for good cause is six months from the date of the final hearing decision, and the AC may not find that "new and material evidence" under 20 CFR 404.989(a)(1) and 416.1489(a)(1) is a basis for good cause. See 20 CFR 405.601.

B. Good Cause Defined

Good cause for reopening a determination or decision exists under the following circumstances:
- New and material evidence is furnished;
- A clerical error in the computation or recomputation of benefits was made for a claim under title II, or a clerical error was made for a claim under title XVI; or
- The evidence that was considered in making the determination or decision clearly shows on its face that an error was made.

NOTE:

As explained in subsection A above, in Region 1, the AC may not find that "new and material evidence" is a basis for good cause. See 20 CFR 405.601.

However, the good cause for reopening rules generally do not apply if the circumstances in Social Security Ruling (SSR) 91-5p, Mental Incapacity and Good Cause for Missing the Deadline to Request Review exist. Under SSR 91-5p:
- If a claimant presents evidence that mental incapacity prevented him or her from timely requesting review of an adverse determination, decision, dismissal, or review by a Federal district court, and
- The claimant had no one legally responsible for prosecuting the claim at the time of the prior administrative action (e.g., a parent of a claimant who is a minor, legal guardian, attorney, or other legal representative),
- Then, SSA will determine whether or not good cause exists for extending the time to request review. If the claimant satisfies the substantive criteria, the time limits in the reopening regulations do not apply. Regardless of how much time has passed since the prior administrative action, the claimant can establish good cause for extending the deadline to request review of that action.

C. New and Material Evidence

1. Definition

To satisfy the regulatory standard for reopening, evidence is "new and material" when the evidence:
- is not part of the claim(s) record as of the date of the administrative law judge (ALJ) decision or determination;
- is relevant, i.e., involves or is directly related to issues adjudicated in the prior decision or determination;
- relates to the period on or before the date of the decision or determination; and
- shows that the decision or determination is contrary to the weight of the evidence.

NOTE 1:

The weight of the evidence is defined as the balance or preponderance of evidence. See HALLEX I-3-3-6 C NOTE. In other words, the weight of the evidence means it is "more likely than not" that the totality of evidence, including the additional evidence, would change the ALJ's action, findings, or conclusion.

NOTE 2:

As explained in subsection A above, in Region 1, the AC may not find that "new and material evidence" is a basis for good cause. See 20 CFR 405.601.

For discussion relating to when the AC will consider additional evidence in association with a request for review, see HALLEX I-3-3-6.

EXAMPLES:

- New medical evidence shows that the claimant's impairment met the severity requirements of an impairment listed in Appendix 1, Subpart P, during the previously adjudicated period and that an allowance based on the prior application is warranted.

- New medical evidence shows that the original medical prognosis did not prove to be accurate and that an allowance based on a prior application is warranted; e.g., the prior adjudicator believed that the claimant's broken hip would be healed within 12 months, but later medical evidence shows that the broken hip had not healed sufficiently within 12 months to permit the claimant's return to substantial gainful activity.

2. Effect of New and Material Evidence

New and material evidence may not always warrant a different conclusion.

New and material evidence may produce a significant change in a factor of entitlement that warrants a revision of a prior unfavorable determination or decision, but does not change the ultimate unfavorable determination or decision.

3. New and Material Evidence Submitted After Expiration of Time to Reopen

If the claimant submits new and material evidence after the prescribed time for reopening has expired and the evidence warrants an allowance during the previously adjudicated period, the AC may establish the onset date as shown by the evidence. However, the claimant is only entitled to benefits or a period of disability based on the current application.

D. Clerical Error

A clerical error is a mathematical error or misapplication of benefit tables, or other similar issue, that resulted in an incorrect payment of a monthly benefit or an incorrect lump-sum death payment. It ordinarily occurs in the computation or recomputation of benefits.

NOTE:

Under title II, the AC may generally only reopen a determination or decision that is otherwise final within 4 years from the date of the notice of the initial determination. However, if a determination or decision was fully or partially unfavorable to the claimant due to a clerical error, the title II determination or decision may be reopened at any time. See 20 CFR 404.988(c)(8) and HALLEX I-3-9-60 A.8.

E. Error on the Face of the Evidence on Which the Determination or Decision Is Based

Error on the face of the evidence is an obvious error that clearly causes an incorrect determination or decision. The following are examples of error on the face of the evidence:

- The adjudicator relied on the wrong person's medical report or earnings record.
- In a title II only claim, onset of disability was established after the claimant last met the special earnings requirements.
- Benefits in a cessation case were terminated as of the month disability ceased, rather than being terminated as of the close of the second month following the month in which disability ceased.
- Evidence in the possession of SSA at the time the determination or decision was made clearly shows that the determination or decision was incorrect.

EXAMPLE:

While a claim was being processed, the claimant submitted a medical report to the field office that would have resulted in a different conclusion. However, the medical report was not associated with the claim file until after the determination or decision became final.

NOTE:

Under title II, the AC may generally only reopen a determination or decision that is otherwise final within 4 years from the date of the notice of the initial determination. However, if a determination or decision was fully or partially unfavorable to the claimant, due to an error that appears on the face of the evidence that was considered when the determination or decision was made, the AC can reopen at any time. See 20 CFR 404.988(c)(8) and HALLEX I-3-9-60 A.

F. Change in Legal Interpretation or Administrative Ruling

A change of legal interpretation or administrative ruling may be the result of a change in a regulation, a decision of the United States Supreme Court, a Federal court order in a class action case, or the issuance of an SSR or an Acquiescence Ruling.

A change of legal interpretation or administrative ruling is not "good cause" to reopen a determination or decision under the 2 or 4 year rules. Although a change of legal interpretation or administrative ruling may be a basis for reopening within 12 months of the date of the notice of the initial determination, reopening is appropriate only if the result would be more favorable to the claimant.

G. Effect of Change in Statutory Provision

If a statute has been amended, any reopening depends on the provisions of the amendment itself. The amendment will provide the effective date of the change and indicate its effect on any prior determinations or decisions.

I-3-9-50. Diligent Pursuit of an Investigation

Last Update: 7/27/15 (Transmittal I-3-121)

A. General

Under 20 CFR 404.991a and 416.1491, the Appeals Council (AC) may revise a determination or decision after the applicable time period specified in Hearings, Appeals, and Litigation Law (HALLEX) manual I-3-9-30 or I-3-9-40 expires if the Social Security Administration (SSA) begins an investigation into whether to revise the determination or decision before the time period expired. SSA may begin the investigation either based on a request by the claimant or on its own initiative. The investigation is the process of SSA gathering facts after reopening a determination or decision to determine if a revision of the determination or decision is appropriate.

B. Definition

Diligent pursuit means that in light of the facts and circumstances of a particular case, SSA undertakes the necessary action and carries out the action as promptly as circumstances permit.

Diligent pursuit is presumed to be met if SSA concludes the investigation and, if necessary, revises the determination or decision within 6 months from the date SSA begins the investigation.

C. Investigation Diligently Pursued to Its Conclusion

If SSA diligently pursued the investigation to its conclusion, the AC may revise the determination or decision. The revision may be favorable or unfavorable to the claimant.

D. Investigation Not Diligently Pursued to Its Conclusion

If SSA did not diligently pursue the investigation to its conclusion, the AC will only revise the determination or decision if a revision is favorable to the claimant. The AC will not revise the determination or decision if it will be unfavorable to the claimant.

I-3-9-60. Reopening at Any Time

Last Update: 7/27/15 (Transmittal I-3-121)

A. Title II Cases

As set forth in 20 CFR 404.988(c), the Appeals Council (AC) may reopen a determination or decision that is otherwise final at any time in the following circumstances:

- The determination or decision was obtained by fraud or similar fault (see Hearings, Appeals and Litigation Law (HALLEX) manual I-3-10-7);
- Another person files a claim on the same earnings record and allowance of that claim adversely affects the earlier claim;
- A person previously determined to be dead and on whose earnings record entitlement is based, is later found to be alive;

- The claim was denied because the claimant could not prove that the wage earner died and death is later established by a presumption of death under 20 CFR 404.721(b) or by location or identification of his or her body;
- The Railroad Retirement Board has awarded duplicate benefits on the same earnings record;
- The determination or decision denies the person on whose earnings record the claim is based gratuitous wage credits for military or naval service because another Federal agency (other than the Department of Veterans Affairs) has erroneously certified that it has awarded benefits based on the service;
- The determination or decision credits the earnings record of the person on which the claim is based with gratuitous wage credits and another Federal agency (other than the Department of Veterans Affairs) certifies that it has awarded benefits based on the same period of service for which the wage credits were granted;
- The claimant was denied for lack of insured status, but earnings for the appropriate period of time were later credited to the claimant's earnings record under the conditions described in 20 CFR 404.988(c)(7);
- The determination or decision is fully or partially unfavorable to a party, but only to correct a clerical error or an error that appears on the face of the evidence that was considered when the determination or decision was made;
- A claimant is found entitled to monthly benefits or to a lump-sum death payment based on the earnings of a deceased person, and it is later established that the claimant was convicted of a felony or an act in the nature of a felony for intentionally causing the deceased person's death;
- A claimant is found entitled to monthly benefits or to a lump-sum death payment based on the earnings of a deceased person, and it is later established that, if the claimant was subject to the juvenile justice system, the claimant was found by a court of competent jurisdiction to have intentionally caused the person's death by committing an act which, if committed by an adult, would have been considered a felony or an act in the nature of a felony;
- The determination or decision denies the person on whose earnings record the claim is based deemed wages for internment during World War II because of an erroneous finding that a benefit based upon the internment has been determined by an agency of the United States to be payable under another federal law or under a system established by that agency;
- The determination or decision awards the person on whose earnings record the claim is based deemed wages for internment during World War II and a benefit based upon the internment is determined by an agency of the United States to be payable under another federal law or under a system established by that agency;
- The determination or decision is incorrect because the claimant was convicted of a crime that affected his or her right to receive benefits or his or her entitlement to a period of disability; or
- The determination or decision is incorrect because the claimant's conviction of a crime that affected his or her right to receive benefits or his or her entitlement to a period of disability is overturned.

B. Title XVI Cases

As set forth in 20 CFR 416.1488(c), the AC may reopen a determination or decision that is otherwise final, at any time when such determination or decision was obtained by fraud or similar fault. See HALLEX I-3-10-7.

I-3-9-70. Protest Cases

Last Update: 7/27/15 (Transmittal I-3-121)

As noted in Hearings, Appeals and Litigation Law (HALLEX) manual I-3-6-10, if an effectuating component believes an Office of Disability Adjudication and Review (ODAR) decision is contrary to the law, regulations, or rulings, it will forward the decision to the Office of Appellate Operations (OAO) for further consideration. An effectuating component may also refer a decision if it receives additional evidence that shows further action is required in the case.

NOTE:

Program Operations Manual System DI 42010.025 permits effectuating components to reopen and revise prior unappealed initial or reconsidered determinations when effectuating ODAR decisions. If OAO receives a protest for an initial or reconsidered determination, it will return the protest to the effectuating component, citing the above reference and indicating that the effectuating component has jurisdiction to reopen and revise the prior determination.

When it is appropriate to act on the protest (see HALLEX I-3-6-10 D), the Appeals Council (AC) will use its own motion authority whenever possible. When using its own motion authority is not possible but the AC agrees action is appropriate, the AC will consider whether it can reopen the decision, using the procedures outlined in HALLEX I-3-9-80.

The AC will respond to the component that submitted the protest using the procedures in HALLEX I-3-6-10.

I-3-9-80.   Analyst Recommendation to the Appeals Council Regarding Reopening of a Prior Determination or Decision (For Revision or Remand)

Last Update: 7/27/15 (Transmittal I-3-121)

When the issue of reopening is before the Appeals Council (AC), as part of the substantive review of the case pending before the AC, the analyst will also review whether reopening and revising a prior determination or decision is appropriate. In doing so, the analyst will keep in mind the following:

• If a prior paper claim(s) file is part of the reopening question, the analyst will obtain the claim(s) file before evaluating the issue, whenever possible. See Hearings, Appeals and Litigation Law (HALLEX) manual I-3-1-23.

• If there are time restraints on the reopening issue present in the case, such as a date by which reopening must be initiated, the analyst must clearly note this in his or her analysis and immediately notify his or her branch chief.

• Unless the AC has already taken action (see HALLEX I-3-5-50), the AC treats a request for reopening as a request for review. See HALLEX I-3-9-10 A.

• If the reopening issue was before the prior adjudicator but was not addressed in the case pending before the AC, the AC will evaluate whether a basis for granting review is present (see HALLEX I-3-3-1). In some cases, the analyst may recommend further development to determine whether reopening and revision in the case is warranted. For example, if the administrative law judge (ALJ) had jurisdiction to reopen and revise the prior decision but did not consider the issue, and there is a question as to whether good cause exists that requires further development or proceedings, the analyst may recommend the AC remand the case to the ALJ for consideration of the issue.

I-3-9-84.   Notice of Proposed Revision of Prior Decision

Last Update: 4/1/16 (Transmittal I-3-137)

A. When Advance Notice Is Required

Under 20 CFR 404.992 and 416.1492, the Appeals Council (AC) must give the claimant notice that it intends to reopen and revise a prior determination or decision, unless the proposed revision is fully favorable to the claimant.

Additionally, when the AC proposes to revise a prior decision based on additional evidence, the AC must offer the claimant the opportunity for a hearing. If the claimant requests a hearing, the AC will remand the case to an administrative law judge (ALJ) to conduct a hearing on the issue. However, if the claimant waives the right to a hearing, the AC may proceed with its proposed action.

NOTE:

In a title XVI claim where the claimant is in payment status, it is irrelevant whether the AC is proposing a revision based on additional evidence. In accordance with the decision in *Goldberg v. Kelly*, 397 U.S. 254, 90 S.Ct. 1011, 25 L.Ed.2d 287 (1970), the AC will give notice of a proposed revision when the revision is not fully favorable and offer the claimant the right to request a hearing. *See* 20 CFR 416.1336.

B. Content of Advance Notice of Proposed RevisionWhen notice is required (see subsection A above), the notice will include the following information:

• The authority for the action (i.e., the regulatory basis for reopening);

• The nature and rationale of proposed revisions;

• The right to request a hearing (when applicable);

• The opportunity to submit additional evidence or a written statement, even if the claimant waives the right to a hearing; and

- A statement that the AC will proceed with its action if the claimant does not request a hearing (if applicable) or has nothing further to submit.

Additionally, if the claimant received a favorable decision that the AC proposes to reopen, the notice must also include the following, as applicable:

- If a favorable ALJ decision is being reopened and benefit payments have not been effectuated, the notice must include a closing paragraph that sets forth the section 8001 provisions. For more information on 8001 benefits, *see* Hearings, Appeals and Litigation Law (HALLEX) manual I-3-6-40.
- In a title XVI claim where the claimant is in payment status, the notice must include a statement advising the individual that if a hearing is requested within 10 days, payments will continue until a hearing decision is rendered. If no hearing is requested, payments will continue until the AC issues a decision. *See* 20 CFR 416.1336. (If the claimant requests a hearing, *see also* benefit continuation remand instructions in HALLEX I-3-7-40).

C. Proffering Evidence

Unless additional evidence on which the AC is relying to revise a prior decision was submitted by the claimant or an appointed representative, if any, or the proposed revision is based on evidence that was before the ALJ or the AC at the time the prior decision was made, the AC will proffer the additional evidence to the claimant and appointed representative, if any. For procedures on proffering evidence, *see* HALLEX I-3-2-16.

NOTE:

Although a protest or referral memorandum from another agency component (*see* HALLEX I-3-6-10) that objects to a prior decision is not considered new or material evidence, the AC will afford the claimant the right to examine and comment on the information if the revised decision based on the referral will be less than fully favorable.

I-3-9-90. Post-Appeals Council Action Correspondence

Last Update: 3/2/15 (Transmittal I-3-101)

The chart below provides general guidance concerning the disposition of correspondence or evidence received after the Appeals Council (AC) denies a request for review, issues a decision, or reviews a case on its own motion.

Situation	Receipt	Clearance Signature
Extension of time (EOT) with or without new evidence or contentions	Received but not associated prior to release of AC denial notice or AC decision	AC
Request for exhibits, recording, or both	Received but not associated prior to release of AC denial notice or AC decision	AC
Request for reopening, correspondence, or evidence	In response to denial notice or AC decision	AC
Correspondence, evidence, or legal argument received after civil action (CA) period (no specific request to reopen or EOT to file CA)	After original CA period or no right to CA	AC
Second request for review received	After CA period	Office of Appellate Operations Manager
Request for Review received after the AC has taken own motion (OM) review	After OM taken	AC

Situation	Receipt	Clearance Signature
Request for an EOT to file a CA	During original CA period	AC
	After original CA period	AC
Request for reopening (being denied) and EOT to file CA	During original CA period	AC
	After original CA period	AC

I-3-9-92.   Requests for Extensions of Time to File Civil Action

Last Update: 3/2/15 (Transmittal I-3-101)

A. General

Under section 205(g) of the Social Security Act, the Commissioner may extend the amount of time provided to file a civil action. Per agency regulations, the request for an extension of time (EOT) to file a civil action must be in writing and must provide good cause for why the deadline was not (or cannot be) met. See 20 CFR 404.982, 405.505, and 416.1482.

NOTE:

If a claimant or representative, if any, orally requests an EOT, Office of Appellate Operations (OAO) staff must inform the claimant or representative that the request must be submitted in writing and that a good cause reason for the request must be included in the writing. OAO staff will then prepare a form SSA-5002, Report of Contact, to document the conversation and associate the form with the claim(s) file.

A claimant or representative, if any, must specifically request an EOT. The submission of additional evidence or general correspondence to the Appeals Council (AC) within or after the 60-day period to file a civil action does not constitute an EOT request. Rather, the AC will handle the additional information using the procedures in Hearings, Appeals and Litigation Law (HALLEX) manual I-3-5-50.

As explained below, approving an EOT requires evaluating good cause. Therefore, an AC member must always review and sign actions on EOT requests. See generally HALLEX I-3-9-90.

EOT requests must be processed as soon as possible after receipt. Processing EOT requests in a timely manner saves resources for both the agency and the claimant, especially when the AC denies the request.

B. EOT Requests Submitted Before a Civil Action Is Filed

Generally, a Court Case Preparation and Review Branch (CCPRB) handles EOT requests to file a civil action, unless the claimant or appointed representative submits an EOT request with another request that requires action by a Disability Program Branch (DPB) or there is another action required by the DPB in association with the EOT request.

If the claimant or appointed representative, if any, does not provide a good cause reason for requesting an EOT, the AC will deny the request. In evaluating whether there is a good cause reason, the AC uses the good cause standards in 20 CFR 404.911, 405.20, and 416.1411.

NOTE:

Any delay in the AC's response to an EOT request is not a factor the AC considers in determining whether good cause exists for not filing a civil action within the stated time.

When an EOT is granted, the AC will generally provide up to 30 days from the date of the notice granting the EOT (or, if more appropriate, up to 30 days from the date of the civil action filing deadline) to file a civil action. However, the AC may grant more or less time depending on the circumstances of the individual case.

When the AC denies the request for an EOT, the AC will include in the notice a sufficient rationale explaining its finding that there is not a good cause reason to extend the time to file a civil action.

C. EOT Requests Filed After a Civil Action Is Filed

When an EOT is not submitted or received until after the claimant has filed a civil action, the EOT will be handled by a CCPRB using the instructions in subsection B above.

I-3-9-95.   Administrative Law Judge Requests Clarification of Remand Order

Last Update: 6/5/15 (Transmittal I-3-115)

A. General

An administrative law judge (ALJ) may seek clarification of an Appeals Council (AC) remand order only when the ALJ cannot carry out the directive(s) set forth in the order, or the directive(s) appears to have been rendered moot. ALJs may not seek clarification of AC remand orders under any other circumstances.

There are two types of clarification requests: expedited clarification requests and formal clarification requests. Expedited clarification requests are used when the sole reason for remand is a missing claims folder, missing recording, or both, and the folder, recording, or both are subsequently found. Formal clarification requests apply in all other circumstances.

NOTE:

The term "missing recording" also encompasses inaudible recordings. If a case is remanded solely because the hearing recording is inaudible, but the recording is later found to be completely audible, the expedited clarification process may be used.

For more information about the clarification process at the hearing level, see Hearings, Appeals and Litigation Law manual (HALLEX) I-2-1-85. If the AC remand order is pursuant to a Federal court order, the instructions in HALLEX I-4-3-60 apply.

B. Notification From ALJ of Request for Clarification

After an ALJ obtains the necessary concurrences (as described in HALLEX I-2-1-86 or I-2-1-87), the ALJ will:

- Prepare a written request to the AC confirming that the Chief Administrative Law Judge approved the request for clarification;
- If making a formal clarification request, notify the claimant and representative, if any, of the request and associate the correspondence with the claim(s) file;
- Send the approved clarification request to the AC via email to ODAR OAO; and
- Wait for a response from the AC.

NOTE:

If the claim(s) file is paper and the ALJ is requesting formal clarification, the ALJ will not send the claim(s) file until the AC requests the claim(s) file. If the claim(s) file is paper and the ALJ is requesting expedited clarification, the ALJ will send the claim(s) file to the AC when making the request.

The Executive Director's Office (EDO) in the Office of Appellate Operations (OAO) is responsible for evaluating all requests for clarification at the AC level. After the EDO has reviewed a request for clarification, the EDO will add a Remark in the Appeals Review Processing System (ARPS) and provide further instruction to the branch with jurisdiction. If it is unclear whether the EDO has evaluated a request for clarification, the branch will contact the EDO for further instructions by sending an email to ODAR OAO.

The EDO will respond to the ALJ's request for clarification as soon as possible after receiving the request. The EDO may either deny the request for clarification or take the necessary action to process the request.

C. EDO Actions

1. Denying a Request for Clarification

The EDO will deny a request for clarification if the request does not meet one of the criteria for clarification, i.e., the ALJ cannot carry out the directive(s) set forth in the order, or the directive(s) appears to have been rendered moot. When neither criterion is met, the EDO will send a memorandum to the ALJ, denying the request for clarification. The EDO will also send a copy of the memorandum to the claimant, the representative (if any), and the Chief Administrative Law Judge (Attention: Director, Division of Field Procedures). When a formal clarification is involved, the EDO will also send a copy to the Regional Chief Administrative Law Judge. If a paper claim(s) file was sent to the AC, the EDO will also return the claim(s) file to the ALJ.

NOTE:

The AC cannot accept a request for clarification once an ALJ has held a new hearing.

The EDO may also return a case if either of the following applies:

- The record does not show that the ALJ notified the claimant and representative, if any, of the request. However, the EDO will not return a case for this reason if the EDO has another reason for denying the request for clarification.
- The ALJ did not receive the necessary approvals to submit a clarification request.

In either case, the EDO may either reply directly to the ALJ with a copy to the Chief Administrative Law Judge, or refer the case to the Office of the Chief Administrative Law Judge (OCALJ) for further action.

2. Granting a Request for Clarification

If the EDO determines clarification is appropriate, the EDO will take the following actions.

a. Vacate the Remand Order

The EDO will prepare an order vacating the remand order for the signature of the Executive Director, or his or her designee, using the template in the Document Generation System. Once the vacate order is signed, the EDO will associate the order with the claim(s) file, and mail the vacate order to the claimant and representative, if any.

b. Notify the Hearing Office

Once the remand order is vacated, the EDO must immediately notify the hearing office (HO) with jurisdiction over the case. The EDO will generally notify the HO by replying to the original email requesting clarification. In the reply, the EDO will inform the HO that a vacate order has been issued and associated with the record. If the claim(s) file is paper, the EDO will attach a scanned copy of the vacate order to the email.

The EDO will also ask the HO to close the hearing level case in the Case Processing and Management System (CPMS) as soon as possible. If the hearing level case is not closed in CPMS within a reasonable period of time, the EDO will contact OCALJ for further assistance. Once the case is closed in CPMS, the EDO will reactivate the request for review in ARPS.

c. Notify the Branch Chief

The EDO will also notify the branch chief in the branch with jurisdiction over the claim(s) that the claim is reinstated. The EDO will document in the remarks section in ARPS that the case has been returned to the branch for processing. If a paper file is involved, the EDO will forward the claim(s) file to the branch chief.

D. Branch Actions

When a remand order is vacated, a claimant is given 20 days to provide further comment to the AC.

The branch chief will assign the case as soon as possible after the 20-day diary has expired, and the analyst will review the reinstated request for review in accordance with HALLEX I-3-1. As applicable, the analysis should include any information submitted by the claimant or representative in response to the vacate order. The analyst will recommend an action and prepare a new action document.

I-3-9-97. Death of Claimant Shortly After Appeals Council Action

Last Update: 7/27/15 (Transmittal I-3-121)

If a claimant dies shortly after the Appeals Council (AC) issues an unfavorable decision, the AC may consider reopening its decision. See the instructions in Hearings, Appeals, and Litigation Law manual I-3-8-35.

§532 Dealing With ALJ Dismissals

A request for hearing may be dismissed by an ALJ pursuant to 20 C.F.R. §404.957 under several circumstances: 1) the claimant requests to withdraw the request for hearing; 2) neither the claimant nor representative appears for the hearing without good cause; 3) the doctrine of *res judicata* applies; 4) the claimant has no right to a hearing; 5) a hearing was not requested timely; and 6) the claimant dies and there are no other parties who can be substituted for the claimant. Situations faced by a claimant's attorney that warrant discussion here involve *res judicata* and failure to appear.

Appealing a *res judicata* dismissal requires a full blown brief on the merits, possibly a brief of the length and magnitude of a federal court brief. None of the admonitions about short briefs to the Appeals Council applies when faced with a *res judicata* dismissal. New evidence, if relevant, must be submitted. The Appeals Council presents the claimant's last chance of obtaining Social Security disability benefits. Federal court review probably won't be possible. Indeed, because some ALJs are so quick to dismiss *res judicata* cases, often without first requesting that the claimant's attorney submit a brief, the Appeals Council may present the only level of review where the issues are briefed. Administrative Appeals Judges do seem to recognize the gravity of the claimant's predicament when faced with *res judicata* dismissal and take seriously their duty to carefully review the claimant's case. Many *res judicata* cases are rescued by the Appeals Council.

While *res judicata* cases usually involve painstaking analysis of the substantive evidence, there are two scenarios for which effective arguments can be made relatively briefly: 1) the ALJ has applied *res judicata* without having either the file for the prior final decision or determination, or any other basis for knowing whether newly submitted evidence was considered previously. HALLEX I-2-40J. And 2) as HALLEX I-2-4-40D explains, there has been a "change in the issues" in the form of a change to a relevant listing subsequent to the prior determination or decision.

Cases involving dismissal for failure to appear usually need careful review of whether procedural rules were followed by the ALJ in dismissing the case. Such cases also include the good cause issue: Why did the claimant fail to appear?

Dismissal is never the appropriate remedy if the claimant's representative, who continues to represent the claimant, appears for the hearing. HALLEX I-2-4-25 D.2. 20 C.F.R. §404.957(b) describes two situations where dismissal is appropriate when neither a claimant nor a representative appear for a hearing.

The situations differ based on whether there is evidence that the claimant or representative received the notice of hearing. If there is evidence that either the claimant or the representative received the notice of hearing "and the claimant does not have a physical, mental, educational, or linguistic limitation that may affect the ability to understand the Notice of Hearing," the case may be dismissed without first sending a notice asking why the claimant did not appear. HALLEX I-2-4-25 C.3.a. Otherwise a notice to show cause is required. HALLEX I-2-4-25 C.

If the claimant never received the notice of hearing, the procedures set forth in 20 C.F.R. §404.938 are supposed to guard against a precipitous dismissal. If either the claimant or representative fails to acknowledge the notice of hearing, a hearing office employee "will attempt to contact you for an explanation." If the claimant and representative fail to appear for the hearing and the "acknowledgment" of notice of hearing was not returned, HALLEX I-2-4-25 C.3.b. instructs the ALJ to determine if "the contact procedures required by 20 CFR 404.938 and 416.1438 were followed (as described in HALLEX I-2-3-20), and there is no indication of 'good cause' for failure to appear," the ALJ may dismiss the claim without first issuing a Request to Show Cause for Failure to Appear. This HALLEX section also provides: "An ALJ may not use a Request to Show Cause for Failure to Appear after the fact as an alternative to following proper notice procedures prior to the hearing. A Request to Show Cause for Failure to Appear is unnecessary if the ALJ followed all the contact procedures prior to the hearing."

The ALJ is instructed to find "good cause" for failure to appear if the claimant and representative allege that they were not properly notified of the scheduled hearing and there is no evidence to show that they received the hearing notice. HALLEX I-2-4-25 C.1.a. If no contact was attempted by the hearing office when the "acknowledgment of notice of hearing" was not returned, the ALJ may not dismiss the request for hearing for failure to appear. HALLEX 2-4-25 C. If correct procedures were not followed at the hearing office, the Appeals Council will remand the case. On the other hand, if the evidence shows that the claimant and representative received the hearing notice and they have not given any other reason for failing to appear at the scheduled hearing, good cause cannot be found, and the request for hearing may be properly dismissed. HALLEX I-2-4-25 C.3.a.

Nevertheless, if the evidence of record appears to support a fully favorable decision and thus the hearing may not be necessary, the ALJ is supposed to consider whether he or she can issue a fully favorable decision instead of dismissing the request for hearing. HALLEX I-2-4-25 C.1.a. Note. In an appropriate case, you may argue to the Appeals Council that the ALJ erred by failing to issue a fully favorable decision without a hearing even where there is no good cause for the claimant's failure to appear. Also, if the claimant waived a hearing but the ALJ scheduled a hearing anyway, the ALJ is supposed to issue a decision on the merits. Dismissal is not appropriate. HALLEX I-2-4-25 F.

If a claimant or representative requests the ALJ to change the time or place set for the hearing, the ALJ must consider whether the claimant or representative has good cause for requesting the change. If the ALJ finds that the person requesting the change does not have good cause, the ALJ must notify the person of his or her finding. Then, if neither the claimant nor the representative appears at the time and place set for the hearing, the ALJ may dismiss the request for hearing for failure to appear. HALLEX I-2-4-25 E.

§540 Appeals Council Action on Favorable Decisions

§541 Own Motion Review

The Appeals Council may review a favorable ALJ decision on its own motion. This review may be triggered by a protest memorandum from the effectuating component of SSA, by random selection or by "selective sampling" using statistical methods to identify cases that "exhibit problematic issues or fact patterns that increase the likelihood of error." 20 C.F.R. §404.969(b)(1).

The Appeals Council is supposed to give notice that it will be reviewing a case within 60 days of the date of the ALJ decision. 20 C.F.R. §404.969(a). Usually this notice takes the form of a short letter providing a very brief and conclusory explanation for the review, e.g., the ALJ decision is not supported by substantial evidence. The letter also will state that the Appeals Council will provide a more detailed explanation later. If the review was triggered by a protest from a component of SSA, the Appeals Council will send a copy of the protest memorandum.

At this point, if the hearing testimony is important to your client's case and you cannot get the hearing recording from the ERE yourself, request a copy of the hearing recording from the Appeals Council.

Later, the Appeals Council will send the claimant and attorney a draft version of its decision. The claimant's attorney will be allowed 30 days to comment but the Appeals Council will allow additional time, if necessary.

Congress has required that the Appeals Council issue its decision in own motion review cases within 110 days of the ALJ decision. If the Appeals Council fails to do so, SSA must commence payment of interim benefits. Delays in excess of 20 days caused by the claimant or representative won't be counted against SSA. If the claimant loses, such payments will not be treated as overpayments unless there is fraud involved. See 42 U.S.C. §§423(h) and 1383(a)(8) and 20 C.F.R. §404.969(d).

The stated standard for review initiated on the Appeals Council's own motion is the same as if a claimant initiates review, discussed at §523. However, in practice the Appeals Council uses a double standard for substantial evidence reviews. Where just about anything will be found to be substantial evidence in support of an ALJ denial decision, almost nothing will be found to constitute substantial evidence in support of an ALJ allowance decision. The Appeals Council will not conduct a searching analysis of substantial evidence, but will simply assert that the ALJ decision is not supported by substantial evidence and then move on to its own analysis of the evidence.

When you argue your client's case in a letter to the Appeals Council, argue both why the ALJ decision was supported by substantial evidence and why the Appeals Council's proposed decision is legally and factually wrong. Look for possible due process implications. Where appropriate, make the case turn on a credibility determination that has already been made by the ALJ. If a crucial credibility determination has not been made, make a solid argument that it is the sort of credibility determination that can only be made at a face-to-face hearing. This last consideration is important, since if you successfully argue that a credibility determination is necessary but your position is weak on the face-to-face issue, you may be stuck with an adverse credibility determination made directly by the Appeals Council.

Most of the federal circuit courts of appeal focus their review on the final decision of the Commissioner of Social Security, that is, the Appeals Council decision. Thus, most federal courts will not examine the question whether the Appeals Council was correct in concluding that an ALJ decision was not supported by substantial evidence. Instead, the federal court will look only at the issue of whether the Appeals Council decision is supported by substantial evidence or is otherwise contrary to law. See Bauzo v. Bowen, 803 F.2d 917, 921 (7th Cir. 1986), and the cases cited in that case from seven other circuits.

Nevertheless, Appeals Council reversal cases tend to be good cases for federal court review. They usually present good issues, such as the validity of the Appeals Council determining residual functional capacity based on bare medical findings, which was one of the issues on which *Bauzo* was remanded.

§542 Reopening by the Appeals Council

If the Appeals Council is unable to decide within the 60-day time limit provided by 20 C.F.R. §404.969(a) whether to take own motion review of an ALJ decision, the Appeals Council may nevertheless reopen the case if the requirements of 20 C.F.R. §§404.987 and 404.988 are met. *See* 20 C.F.R. §404.969(d). If the Appeals Council decides to reopen the decision, interim benefits may be paid as in other own motion review cases. *See* §541.

When SSA revised the own motion review regulation to make it explicit that the Appeals Council could conduct its own motion review after the 60 day time limit by using the reopening regulations, it rescinded Acquiescence Ruling 87-2(11) pertaining to *Butterworth v. Bowen*, 796 F.2d 1379, 1385-88 (11th Cir. 1986). 63 Fed. Reg. 36726 (July 7, 1998). *Butterworth* had held that the power of the Appeals Council to reopen a decision was restricted by the 60-day time limit provided by 20 C.F.R. §404.969.

Butterworth was the second Acquiescence Ruling withdrawn that dealt with the Appeals Council's reopening authority. The First Circuit Court of Appeals held that the reopening regulations should be interpreted to allow reopening only on motion of a claimant in *McCuin v. Secretary of Health & Human Services*, 817 F.2d 161, 174 (1st Cir. 1987), adopted as AR 88-5(1). This acquiescence ruling was withdrawn when SSA promulgated a revised 20 C.F.R. §404.987, which made it explicit that SSA could reopen on its own initiative.

Several appellate courts have examined the basis on which the Appeals Council took jurisdiction under the reopening regulations. They looked to see, for example, if "good cause" supported reopening pursuant to 20 C.F.R. §404.989. *Zimmermann v. Heckler*, 774 F.2d 615, 617 (4th Cir. 1985); *Cieutat v. Bowen*, 824 F.2d 348, 357 (5th Cir. 1987); *Fox v. Bowen*, 835 F.2d 1159, 1162-63 (6th Cir. 1987); *Munsinger v. Schweiker*, 709 F.2d 1212, 1215 (8th Cir. 1983); *Overend v. Sullivan*, 879 F.2d 673, 675 (9th Cir. 1989); *Descheenie on behalf of Descheenie v. Bowen*, 850 F.2d 624, 628 n.9 (10th Cir. 1988) and *Sheppard v. Sullivan*, 906 F.2d 756, 758-760 (1990). This approach contrasts with the refusal of some courts to look at the substantive basis of the Appeals Council's jurisdiction when exercising own motion review under 20 C.F.R. §404.969.

§550 After Receiving an Appeals Council Denial Decision

§551 When AC Fails to Consider Brief or New Evidence

When you receive an Action of Appeals Council on Request for Review that does not mention the brief or new evidence you sent (see HALLEX I-3-5-15 B.), it is likely that the brief or new evidence were not associated with the file before the Appeals Council denied the appeal.

It happens often enough that the Appeals Council fails to associate your brief or new evidence with the file before denying the Request for Review that the Appeals Council is used to receiving requests that it vacate its Action and consider your submission. According to HALLEX I-3-5-50 C.1.: "Occasionally, a claimant will submit additional evidence for AC review before the AC releases its denial notice, but the evidence is not associated with the file until after the AC releases its denial notice. In these instances, the AC must consider the claimant's request for review again."

Just for good measure always request an extension for filing in federal court. An extension is unnecessary, of course, if the Appeals Council actually considers the claimant's request for review again. The time for filing will run from the date of a new denial letter. But if after the time runs out for filing in federal court you get a letter from the Appeals Council saying it already considered your submission and it is not going to consider it again, your client could lose the right to file in federal court. Some lawyers might want to argue that in this circumstance the request for an extension to file in federal court is implicit. But the Appeals Council does not recognize an implicit request for an extension to file in federal court. "The submission of additional evidence or general correspondence to the AC within or after the 60-day period to file a civil action does not constitute" a request for an extension of time to file the action. HALLEX I-3-9-92 A.

The challenge, as with so many similar situations dealing with SSA, is getting the attention of the right people at the Appeals Council. If telephoning and faxing a letter to the branch inquiring if the Appeals Council had your submission does not work, fax a letter to Teresa Jensen, the Appeals Council ombudsman, at 703-605-8691.

§552 Extension to File in Federal Court

When a claimant (or lawyer) fails to file a federal court action within the 60-day time limit, if there is good cause for missing the deadline the Appeals Council may grant an extension of time to file the federal court action. 20 C.F.R. § 404.982. *See also* 42 U.S.C. § 405(g). Requesting an extension to file in federal court is similar to asking SSA to excuse the lateness of any other appeal. The same requirement to explain why the deadline was missed and the same "good cause" standard from 20 C.F.R. § 404.911 are used. See §513 and §158. HALLEX I-3-9-92 A. provides:

> Per agency regulations, the request for an extension of time (EOT) to file a civil action must be in writing and must provide good cause for why the deadline was not (or cannot) be met. . . . A claimant or representative, if any, must specifically request an EOT. The submission of additional evidence or general correspondence to the AC within or after the 60-day period to file a civil action does not constitute an EOT request.

There are two procedural differences between requesting an extension of time to file in federal court and requesting an extension to file an administrative appeal. When a claimant is late with an administrative appeal, you always provide a good cause statement (which functions as a request for an extension for filing the appeal) in conjunction with actually filing the appeal. Although you can file the federal court action at the same time you request an extension from the Appeals Council, most lawyers do not. Instead, they request an extension from the Appeals Council and wait until the extension is granted before filing the federal court action. Then they include in the complaint a statement that an extension was granted, which makes the federal court action timely filed. If an extension is not granted, it is not an issue that can be presented to the federal court (unless refusal to grant an extension can be characterized as a due process violation).

The other difference from an administrative appeal is that it is possible to request an extension to file in federal court *before* the time for filing has run out. Here is a common situation. Let's say you are approached by a potential client who has just received an Appeals Council denial letter. Let's also say neither a complete copy of the hearing exhibit file nor the recording of the hearing is available. Without seeing either or both of these, you won't be able to tell if this claimant has a viable case or not. It is essential for you to examine the medical records or listen to the hearing recording before committing to taking this case into federal court. Under these circumstances you can request records and the hearing recording from the Appeals Council and, in the same letter, request an extension to allow filing in federal court up to 30 days

after receipt of the records and recording from the Appeals Council. Your letter to the Appeals Council explains that it is essential to review the records and hearing recording in order to evaluate the claimant's appeal. In the past the Appeals Council has always found good cause for an extension to file in federal court in this circumstance.

It is unlikely that HALLEX I-3-9-92 changes the result in the hypothetical situation described above, though it appears to change the level of detail that must be provided in the explanation of good cause. In the past, the Appeals Council granted extensions in this circumstance with little or no explanation of good cause because good cause is implicit in the situation where a lawyer is approached by a new potential client after the Appeals Council denied review. It is obvious that a lawyer would need to review the file before agreeing to represent a new client. Under the current rule, you may assume that nothing is obvious; nothing is implicit. HALLEX I-3-9-92 B. provides that if "the claimant (or representative, if any) does not provide a good cause reason for requesting an [extension of time], the AC will deny the request."

How much explanation of good cause is necessary? You must answer all the obvious questions. In the situation described above, if you think that the Appeals Council may wonder why you cannot get the file from the claimant's former attorney, maybe you need to explain that, too. Because it is hard to tell how much explanation the Appeals Council may require, you must err on the side of providing too much explanation rather than too little.

While the Appeals Council will likely continue to find good cause in the situation described above, in other situations, even when the request for an extension is submitted within the time the case could otherwise be timely filed in federal court, there is cause for concern. Note that HALLEX I-3-9-92 B. Note provides: "Any delay in the AC's response to an [extension of time] request is not a factor the AC considers in determining whether good cause exists for not filing a civil action within the stated time period." In other words, SSA wants to discourage Appeals Council decision makers from making a more lenient decision when considering the fact that the slowness of the Appeals Council itself contributed to the loss of the claimant's right to timely file in federal court. When a dilatory Appeals Council turns down an extension request after the time for filing in federal court, it is no consolation that HALLEX I-3-9-92 A. provides: "EOT requests must be processed as soon as possible after receipt. Processing EOTs in a timely manner saves resources for both the agency and the claimant, especially when the AC denies the request."

What happens if a pro se claimant writes an outraged letter to the Appeals Council right after receiving a typical Appeals Council denial (that explains nothing) demanding a better explanation? Let's say that after the time has run for timely filing the case in federal court, the claimant receives an explanation, but the letter says nothing about extending the time for filing in federal court. Suppose this claimant then comes to you. You may be able to use 20 C.F.R. § 404.911(b)(5) to establish good cause. 20 C.F.R. § 404.911(b)(5) provides:

> (5) You asked us for additional information explaining our action within the time limit, and within 60 days of receiving the explanation you requested reconsideration or a hearing, or within 30 days of receiving the explanation you requested Appeal Council review or filed a civil suit.

Note that in this situation the regulation appears to require that you file the action within 30 days of the claimant receiving the explanation. The Appeals Council still must find good cause. Presumably it would do so under 20 C.F.R. § 404.911(b)(5).

§560 Appealing an ALJ Denial Decision After Federal Court Remand

If an ALJ issues another denial decision after a case has been remanded by the federal court, very different appeal procedures apply. First, an appeal to the Appeals Council is actually optional. If you want, you can skip the Appeals Council altogether and file the claimant's case in federal court after the ALJ decision becomes "final." If the Appeals Council does not review the ALJ decision on its own motion within 60 days of the date of the ALJ decision pursuant to 20 C.F.R. §404.984(c), the ALJ decision becomes final on the 61st day. You will then have 60 days to file the claimant's case in federal court. Thus, counting from the date of the ALJ decision, you will have from day 61 to day 120 to timely file the case in federal court. See 20 C.F.R. §404.984(d). (Skipping the Appeals Council in this circumstance is not something that lawyers do often and is not a procedure recommended by the author.)

Second, the time limit for this appeal is 30 days, not 60 days. 20 C.F.R. §404.984(b). Third, it is not appropriate to file a Request for Review of Hearing Decision, Form HA-520. Instead, you must submit "exceptions" to the Appeals Council in which you set forth in writing specific reasons for disagreeing with the ALJ decision. 20 C.F.R. §404.984(b)(1).

When an ALJ decision is sent out in court remand cases, hearing office clerical personnel are supposed to attach a special notice that gives the above information about the 30-day time limit, describes the requirement for filing exceptions, and explains the time limit for filing in federal court if no exceptions are filed. But sometimes such decisions come instead with the standard notice containing the 60-day time limit, etc. If this happens and a Request for Review is sent to the Appeals Council more than 30 days from the date of the ALJ decision, or if the Request for Review does not sufficiently state "exceptions," it has been the practice of the Appeals Council to excuse the error and call for written exceptions. Sometimes when the wrong notice is sent, it will be discovered immediately at the Appeals Council. The Appeals Council will then send a letter providing the correct information about appealing and allow 30 days from the date of the Appeals Council's letter to file exceptions.

Practice Tips

If you're like most lawyers who handle a lot of Social Security disability cases, you probably don't regularly read the appeal notices that come attached to the decisions you receive. Therefore, you need to set up a foolproof system to remind yourself that you must file exceptions in a court remand case within 30 days of the ALJ decision.

If you need more than 30 days to file exceptions, the Appeals Council will grant a timely request for a 30-day extension; however, according to 20 C.F.R. §404.984(b)(1), a request for an extension of more than 30 days "should include a statement of reasons as to why you need the additional time." If you need a copy of the hearing recording in order to prepare your exceptions (and you cannot get this yourself from the ERE), the Appeals Council will grant a request for a 30 day extension from the time you are sent a copy of the hearing recording.

The only differences between written exceptions and a regular Appeals Council brief are that: (1) the exceptions should include argument headings; and (2) you should fully set forth the arguments that you would use in federal court, rather than simply summarizing them.

In response to written exceptions, the Appeals Council may assume jurisdiction of the case, but it has no time limit for assuming jurisdiction in this circumstance. 20 C.F.R. §404.984(b)(3). If it assumes jurisdiction, the regulations state that "any issues related to your claim may be considered by the Appeals Council whether or not they were raised in the administrative proceedings following the court's remand order." 20 C.F.R. §404.984(a). The Appeals Council may issue its own final decision or remand the case again. 20 C.F.R. §404.984(b)(3).

The Appeals Council also may assume jurisdiction of the case even when no exceptions are filed as long as it does so within 60 days of the date of the ALJ decision. In such a case, the Appeals Council will send notice to the claimant and attorney and provide an opportunity to file briefs. 20 C.F.R. §404.984(c).

If you need to contact someone at the Appeals Council about your client's case, note that the appeal of an ALJ decision after court remand will not be handled by one of the regular Appeals Council branches. Instead, it will be handled by the "court case preparation and review branch" assigned to your circuit. See §515.2 or HALLEX I-3-0-7.

Chapter 6

Federal Court Review

§600   Considerations Prior to Filing

Claimants initiate over 15,000 civil actions per year challenging denials of Social Security and SSI benefits. Administrative Office of the U.S. Courts, Federal Judicial Caseload Statistics (Mar. 31, 2012). In recent years, the district courts granted the plaintiffs judicial relief about than half the time. Roughly speaking, the district courts held that plaintiffs were disabled about 3 to 5% of the time and remanded about 45 to 48% of cases for additional administrative action. See §156. Not only did plaintiffs obtain some judicial relief in about half of civil actions, in the vast majority of such cases, the Social Security Administration (SSA) was ordered to pay attorney fees under the Equal Access to Justice Act (EAJA), 28 U.S.C. § 2412(d). For a discussion of EAJA attorney fees, see §§760-769 of this book. Thus, litigation is important and beneficial to thousands of plaintiffs and their attorneys.

While plaintiffs obtain judicial relief in about half of the Social Security cases filed nationwide, many district courts deviate from the norm. A particular district court may affirm two-thirds of final SSA decisions denying benefits, while another district court may provide plaintiffs with relief in two-thirds of cases. Within a district court, individual judges may decide cases in markedly different ways. In federal court litigation, just as in other legal cases, it is important to know the judges.

If a case is remanded by a federal court for additional administrative action, the claimant is more likely to win at a remand hearing than those claimants having administrative law judge (ALJ) hearings for the first time. The overall percentage of favorable decisions issued by ALJs from 2001 through 2004 ranged from 61.0% to 61.7%. During the same period, after court remand, favorable ALJ decisions ranged from 66.5% to 69.0%.

There are those within the Social Security Administration who are embarrassed by claimants' success in federal court. Some SSA insiders worry that claimants' success in federal court demonstrates that one-half of ALJ denial decisions are defective, though this would be true only if the cases that went to federal court represented a random sample of ALJ decisions. Many within SSA say they are puzzled that claimants are so successful in federal court when SSA's own quality analysis of ALJ decisions shows that 90% of ALJ decisions are correct. See http://www.ssa.gov/performance/2005/FY2005_APP_Appendices.doc.

Although SSA is concerned, in its own way, with the quality of ALJ decisions, it has never placed great emphasis on reducing claimants' success in federal court. The number of cases that go to federal court represents too tiny a percentage of the three million applications that are filed every year or the more than 600,000 ALJ decisions issued every year. Although the Appeals Council remands or awards benefits in less than 20% of the approximately 160,000 cases that come before it every year, in raw numbers the Appeals Council remands or awards benefits in nearly five times the number of cases remanded or awarded benefits by the federal courts.

Claimants' lawyers tend not to view cases that go to federal court as a random sample of ALJ denial decisions. Instead, claimants' lawyers, especially the litigators, those who handle many federal court cases, know that they themselves pick the strongest cases to take to federal court, and because there is such a significant time investment involved in taking a case to federal court, they expect that other lawyers also carefully pick cases for federal district court appeals. Thus, the litigators wonder how it is that claimants lose about half the time in federal court. Those who specialize in federal court litigation do not lose anywhere near this much.

It is apparent from reading federal court decisions that many appealed cases were doomed to failure from the outset by the weakness of the plaintiffs' arguments. What is striking, though, is that claimants in many such cases appear to be more impaired than other claimants whose ALJ hearings we routinely win. Thus, it is apparent why their attorneys filed complaints. These cases illustrate why a decision to take a case to federal court should not be based *solely* on how impaired a claimant appears to be.

The majority of attorneys who find success in federal court do not pick cases to litigate based on their sympathy for a claimant. Instead, successful litigators look for strong facts and solid arguments involving clear legal principles. They look for violations of Social Security regulations and rulings and transgressions of circuit court case law. And the most successful litigators recognize it is never enough to say that an ALJ violated this or that legal rule. Successful litigators recognize that to obtain judicial relief, the error must be harmful.

While there are attorneys who have remarkable success in federal court, there are also claimants' lawyers who have never taken a case to federal court themselves and never refer the claimant to a lawyer who does. Avoidance of federal court litigation can be a mistake, a lost opportunity for the claimant and the attorney.

The main reason to litigate, of course, is to obtain benefits for your client. But there are other reasons too. Federal court work sharpens the skills you use to prove disability to the agency. There are few experiences as educational as reading a transcript of your own direct and cross-examination and noting all the questions you should have asked—or questions you should not have asked. Similarly, the judicial post mortem of your administrative advocacy may reveal regrettable concessions such as that the vocational expert is well qualified to render an opinion about the incidence of jobs or that the claimant's mental condition need not be considered even in combination with the claimant's other impairments. Additionally, both SSA's attorney and the court will provide a meaningful critique of your oral and written advocacy and your development of the factual record, including the medical evidence.

To litigate successfully, an attorney must develop a strong grasp of central legal principles and the ambiguity of many legal rules. Litigation thus provides continuing legal education in Social Security law.

Although not all ALJs are responsive to judicial review of their administrative denials of benefits, enough ALJs take seriously a court's discussion of errors in their decisions that, in a sense, a byproduct of litigation is continuing legal education for the ALJ as well.

Many experienced attorneys think that failure to pursue an erroneous denial into federal court encourages further erroneous denials by ALJs. Despite the fact that SSA gives no precedential value to district court decisions, these attorneys think that a successful history of federal court appeals is a deterrent to future ALJ denial decisions involving similar issues.

§601 Is There a Final Decision of the Commissioner?

A federal district court has jurisdiction to review a "final decision" of the Commissioner of Social Security. 42 U.S.C. § 405(g). To receive a final decision, a claimant must exhaust administrative remedies. This means that a claimant must pursue the claim through each administrative appeal level that the agency requires. A complaint challenging a final decision must be "commenced within sixty days after the mailing to him of notice of such decision or within such further time as the Commissioner of Social Security may allow." 42 U.S.C. § 405(g).

The "final decision" of the Commissioner is usually the ALJ decision, but an ALJ decision usually does not become a "final decision" until the Appeals Council refuses to review it. As a rule, rather than issuing another full-fledged decision, the Appeals Council will send the claimant and attorney a letter saying that it is denying the claimant's request for review and stating that the ALJ decision stands as the Commissioner's final decision. The letter from the Appeals Council

will give notice of the 60-day time limit for filing a complaint in federal district court and tell you that to serve the summons and complaint on the Commissioner of Social Security you must serve SSA's Office of General Counsel (OGC) that is responsible for handling litigation in the particular judicial district in which the complaint is filed. The letter will tell you how to find the address of that OGC office. The letter will state that the local United States Attorney and the Attorney General of the United States must also be served.

If a claimant fails to timely appeal each denial, there is no "final decision" for a federal court to review. Even in several circumstances where a claimant has the right to appeal an ALJ's action to the Appeals Council, federal court review may be unavailable. For example, if an ALJ, instead of issuing a decision, *dismisses* a claimant's request for hearing (because an appeal was untimely, the claimant failed to appear at the hearing, or a prior denial is *res judicata*), the claimant may request review by the Appeals Council; but, if the Appeals Council denies review, there is no "final decision" within the meaning of 42 U.S.C. § 405(g). When the Appeals Council denies review under such circumstances, its letter will not include information about filing the case in federal court. Without a "final decision," a claimant may not be able to appeal to federal court, at least not using 42 U.S.C. § 405(g) as the jurisdictional basis for the action.

Civil actions may be initiated in these otherwise non-reviewable cases by alleging a constitutional jurisdictional basis or invoking mandamus jurisdiction. Because federal courts are very sparing in acknowledging jurisdiction in these cases, this approach should be reserved for the most egregious violations of a claimant's rights. Nevertheless, such appeals probably have greater success than is reflected by reported cases. A truly egregious violation of a claimant's rights may prompt the agency to voluntarily provide a claimant with a new hearing.

§602 Standard of Review

In federal court there are only two types of challenges to a final decision of the Commissioner of Social Security: (1) the decision is not supported by substantial evidence; and (2) the Commissioner committed some legal error in the decision.

The substantial evidence standard is found in 42 U.S.C. § 405(g), which states: "The findings of the Commissioner as to any fact, if supported by substantial evidence, shall be conclusive." In *Richardson v. Perales*, 402 U.S. 389, 401 (1971), the Supreme Court explained that substantial evidence is "more than a mere scintilla. It means such relevant evidence as a reasonable mind might accept as adequate to support a conclusion." In *Universal Camera Corp. v. NLRB*, 340 U.S. 474, 488 (1951), the Supreme Court stated:

> The substantiality of evidence must take into account whatever in the record detracts from its weight. [A] reviewing court is not barred from setting aside a[n agency] decision when it cannot conscientiously find that the evidence supporting that decision is substantial, when viewed in the light that the record in its entirety furnishes, including the body of evidence opposed to the [agency's] view.

Federal courts will also review decisions of the Commissioner for errors of law. In *White v. Apfel*, 167 F.3d 369, 373 (7th Cir. 1999), a federal court described this type of review: "We need not defer, however, to conclusions of law, and if the Commissioner commits an error of law, we may reverse without regard to the volume of evidence in support of the factual findings."

§603   The Role of the Federal Courts

Substantial Evidence

A federal court does not decide factual issues in a disability case. It is the agency's job to make factual findings. Nor does a federal court decide if a finding of fact is correct. Instead, a court reviews the evidence simply to determine if there is *enough* evidence to support the agency's decision.

Suppose there is a mountain of evidence supporting disability and only a small molehill of evidence supporting a conclusion that a claimant is not disabled. It is a court's job to decide if the evidence is sufficient to support the conclusion that the claimant is not disabled even when the court, if it were allowed to exercise its own judgment, would come to a contrary conclusion.

How much evidence is enough? We know that the evidence must be more than a "scintilla." But is a small molehill of evidence supporting non-disability sufficient in the face of a mountain of evidence supporting disability? Most claimants' representatives would say "not usually." But most practitioners would also say that they have seen cases going both ways in the mountain versus molehill situation.

Substantial evidence must support every element of a finding that a claimant is not disabled. Sometimes no evidence whatsoever supports a crucial aspect of a finding of non-disability. In this circumstance, a molehill of uncontradicted evidence may demonstrate

that the agency's decision is not supported by substantial evidence.

The substantial evidence standard is one of those legal doctrines that is easier to apply than to describe. Because the doctrine is applied on a case-by-case basis, it is easiest to understand when looking at the facts of a particular case. Therefore, if you have not yet done so, read several substantial evidence decisions from your appellate court and your district court. Be sure to read decisions going both ways, for the claimant and against the claimant.

The substantial evidence standard is the same nationwide, but the way it is applied differs from judge to judge. Sometimes judges appear to bend over backwards to find substantial evidence supporting an ALJ denial decision. Other judges will look carefully at every conclusion by an ALJ and find a lack of substantial evidence sometimes where, at first glance, there appears to be a lot of evidence supporting the ALJ position.

It is important to recognize that issues of fact and law often become intertwined in disability cases. A court's finding that *substantial evidence* does not support an agency decision may contain an implicit finding that the fact-finder made a *legal error* when evaluating the evidence. A court may hold explicitly that substantial evidence does not support an agency finding because an improper legal standard has been applied. Or a court may find an absence of substantial evidence when the real error in the ALJ decision is failure to explain the basis for the decision.

To understand the law in your circuit, do not spend too much time on substantial evidence cases. Such cases are useful mostly when researching issues involving a specific impairment. For the broad picture of the state of the law in your circuit, focus on the cases that turn on legal error.

Errors of Law

To identify an error of law, the federal courts first must determine what the law is. Courts begin by looking at what the Social Security Administration says the law is. A court must consider SSA's position with deference. For this reason, it is difficult to show that SSA's position is invalid. Therefore, most findings of legal error are based on the agency fact-finder's failure to follow the agency's own rules. This approach simplifies district court litigation since you generally do not need to prove that SSA policy is wrong, but only that the agency fact-finder did not follow it.

Sometimes the federal courts, with a little help from obfuscation by SSA's attorneys, misinterpret SSA policy. Sometimes federal courts make mistakes so that the challenge you must face is how to deal with an erroneous precedential decision from your circuit or district court. In this situation, a later, clearer statement of SSA's position in, for example, a Social Security Ruling makes your job much easier. The interpretation in a later Social Security Ruling ought to control the outcome of your client's case. Social Security Rulings are binding authority. 20 C.F.R. § 402.35.

Federal courts occasionally find that SSA failed to follow general principles of law. This group of cases is important and has been responsible for development of Social Security law. Several court-fashioned rules based on broad legal principles were later adopted, to one degree or another, by SSA as official policy: the shift of the burden of proof to the Commissioner at step 5 of the sequential evaluation process; the "treating doctor rule" which requires adoption of the treating doctor's opinion unless the ALJ states good reasons not to; and the requirement that the ALJ assess credibility in pain cases. If the case law in your circuit imposes more stringent requirements than the rules adopted by SSA, argue that the case law controls. On the other hand, where case law in your circuit on a particular issue is less favorable to your client, you can argue that SSA policy controls.

Certain appellate cases hold that SSA erroneously interpreted the Social Security Act or its regulations. These decisions conflict with SSA policy. Although this is the smallest category of decisions by federal courts, these cases deserve special attention. Some, but not all, significant court decisions contrary to SSA policy are later published by SSA as "acquiescence rulings." That is, SSA agrees to follow the circuit court decision, but only within the circuit that issued the decision. See Appendix 1, *infra*, Guide to Important Social Security Rulings and Acquiescence Rulings.

§604   *Analyzing the Case*

Is the claimant disabled?

Before you file a case in federal court, analyze it the same way you analyze a case for an ALJ hearing. You need a theory of disability based on the five-step sequential evaluation process. A solid theory plus a little intuition about what limitations will be accepted by an ALJ are the essential ingredients of a successful ALJ hearing practice. This sort of analysis is necessary because a favorable result in federal court likely means that the plaintiff will receive a new hearing. At any new hearing, you will need to show that the claimant is disabled.

But after you have concluded that the claimant would have a good case before an ALJ, put aside this conclusion. While it is tempting to base the decision

whether to take a case to federal court solely on your belief that your client is disabled, this is the recipe for losing in federal court. Your prospects for success are based on other factors, including the following:

What evidence supports the ALJ decision?

Look carefully at the evidence cited by the ALJ as supporting the decision. Does it really say what the ALJ says it says? Does the decision make sense? How much evidence is there contrary to the ALJ's position? Does the ALJ adequately explain why evidence demonstrating disability was rejected?

Look at evidence supporting each element of the ALJ decision. For example, look at the evidence supporting every aspect of the residual functional capacity finding. Look at the evidence supporting the vocational findings at step 5. Attorneys who specialize in federal court litigation try to find ways to characterize crucial elements of the claimant's proof as uncontradicted.

What are the legal errors in the ALJ decision?

When you review the ALJ decision, you may find some substantial evidence arguments. Indeed, such arguments are present in most cases. But lawyers who litigate many federal court cases rarely file a case in which the primary issue involves reviewing the evidence to see if it is substantial. Instead, they look for legal error. They look for instances where the ALJ decision failed to follow a Social Security Ruling or regulation. They look for transgressions of appellate case law. They often frame a substantial evidence argument as a legal argument involving, for instance, the ALJ's failure to properly evaluate a treating doctor's opinion. The 1996 "process unification" Social Security Rulings—SSRs 96-1p through 96-9p—are a treasury of legal arguments because they set forth a number of things that an ALJ "must" do in evaluating a case and writing a decision. An argument that the ALJ failed to do one of these things is usually stronger than a substantial evidence argument.

Is the legal error harmless?

Not every technical violation of a Social Security Ruling will result in a remand by the federal court. You need to explain how the ALJ would have made a different decision if the ALJ had not made a legal error.

Does the case have compelling facts?

Compelling facts and a sympathetic claimant are not essential. But they help. When your brief tells a compelling story, it adds weight to your legal arguments.

§610   Initiating the Civil Action: Procedure

§611   Filing and Service of Summons and Complaint

From the commencement of a federal court action to a final judgment, including any remand for further administrative proceedings, a federal court action can take more than a year.

Federal court action in most districts is commenced with filing and service of a summons and complaint. (At least one district court has decided that service of a summons is unnecessary—the Eastern District of Wisconsin.)

The Action of Appeals Council on Request for Review, the letter that a claimant receives from the Appeals Council denying the appeal, states the time limit for filing in federal court (60 days from receipt of the letter with a presumption that the letter is received within five days of the date on the letter) and provides instructions for finding the address for service of the summons and complaint on the Commissioner of Social Security by serving SSA's Office of General Counsel that is responsible for processing and handling litigation in the particular judicial district in which the complaint is filed. (The Commissioner is the named defendant in federal court review of a disability case as a result of the Social Security Independence and Program Improvement Act of 1994, which took effect March 31, 1995. Previously, the Secretary of Health and Human Services was the named defendant in these cases.)

Simple notice pleading is all that is required. The sample complaint at §612 may be used for most cases. Note that the language appearing in brackets on the sample complaint applies to SSI claims. Whenever there is SSI involved, the jurisdictional basis is founded on both 42 U.S.C. §§ 405(g) and 1383(c)(3).

Rule 5.2(a)(1) of the Federal Rules of Civil Procedure requires that only the last four digits of a Social Security number be included in any filing with the court. However, some districts have local rules requiring that the full SSN appear in the complaint. Check local rules.

Practice Tip

Although the sample complaint will work for most circumstances, before you use this form, just like any other form, consider whether there is any reason to write a special complaint specifically explaining the Commissioner's errors in your client's case. Reasons may include:

1. Your client's case is being filed *in forma pauperis*. Courts have been known to require an explanation why the case is not frivolous pursuant to 28 U.S.C. § 1915(e)(2) beyond that provided in paragraphs 6 and 7 of the sample complaint.

2. Your client's case is procedurally or factually unusual, e.g., there is a reopening issue, a dismissal is involved, or mandamus relief is sought.

3. You hope to get the attention of an agency attorney who might choose to offer settlement prior to answering the complaint.

4. You want to ask only that the court find your client entitled to benefits. That is, you may want to appeal if the court remands the case for another hearing.

5. New evidence submitted to the Appeals Council is at issue.

6. A remand under sentence six of 42 U.S.C. § 405(g) (when new evidence is submitted to the court) is desired at least as an alternative remedy.

7. The claimant is incompetent or a minor.

Service may be effected on the Commissioner by sending a copy of the summons and complaint by registered or certified mail to SSA's Office of General Counsel (OGC), which is responsible for processing and handling litigation in the particular judicial district in which the complaint is filed. *See* 20 C.F.R. § 423.1(a) and Rule 4(i)(2) of the Federal Rules of Civil Procedure (Fed. R. Civ. P.). Addresses are published from time to time in the Federal Register. The list in §611.1 is from 79 Fed. Reg. 4519 (2014). Before you use it, though, check the Federal Register online to see if there have been any changes. It is important to consult a current list even if you know the address of the OGC office that otherwise serves the region in which the court sits. OGC distribution of litigation responsibilities does not follow standard SSA regional geographic jurisdiction.

Also serve the United States Attorney for the district in which the claimant resides either by personal service or registered or certified mail addressed to the civil process clerk, Fed. R. Civ. P. 4(i)(1)(A), and serve the Attorney General of the United States, 950 Pennsylvania Avenue, N.W., Washington, D.C. 20530-0001 by registered or certified mail, Fed. R. Civ. P. 4(i)(1)(B).

§611.1 Addresses for Service of Process on Commissioner

Jurisdictional Responsibilities of OGC Offices:

Alabama
U.S. District Court—Middle District of Alabama: Office of the Regional Chief Counsel, Atlanta (Region IV).
U.S. District Court—Northern District of Alabama: Office of the Regional Chief Counsel, Atlanta (Region IV).
U.S. District Court—Southern District of Alabama: Office of Program Law, Baltimore.

Alaska
U.S. District Court—Alaska: Office of the Regional Chief Counsel, Seattle (Region X).

Arizona
U.S. District Court—Arizona: Office of the Regional Chief Counsel, Seattle (Region X).

Arkansas
U.S. District Court—Eastern District of Arkansas: Office of the Regional Chief Counsel, Dallas (Region VI).
U.S. District Court—Western District of Arkansas: Office of the Regional Chief Counsel, Dallas (Region VI).

California
U.S. District Court—Central District of California: Office of the Regional Chief Counsel, San Francisco (Region IX).
U.S. District Court—Eastern District of California: Office of the Regional Chief Counsel, San Francisco (Region IX).
U.S. District Court—Northern District of California: Office of the Regional Chief Counsel, San Francisco (Region IX).
U.S. District Court—Southern District of California: Office of the Regional Chief Counsel, San Francisco (Region IX).

Colorado
U.S. District Court—Colorado: Office of the Regional Chief Counsel, Denver (Region VIII).

Connecticut
U.S. District Court—Connecticut: Office of the Regional Chief Counsel, New York (Region II).

Delaware
U.S. District Court—Delaware: Office of the Regional Chief Counsel, Philadelphia (Region III).

District of Columbia
U.S. District Court—District of Columbia: Office of the Regional Chief Counsel, Philadelphia (Region III).

Florida
U.S. District Court—Middle District of Florida: Office of the Regional Chief Counsel, Atlanta (Region IV).
U.S. District Court—Northern District of Florida: Office of the Regional Chief Counsel, Atlanta (Region IV).
U.S. District Court—Southern District of Florida: Office of the Regional Chief Counsel, Atlanta (Region IV).

Georgia
U.S. District Court—Middle District of Georgia: Office of the Regional Chief Counsel, Atlanta (Region IV).
U.S. District Court—Northern District of Georgia: Office of the Regional Chief Counsel, Atlanta (Region IV).
U.S. District Court—Southern District of Georgia: Office of the Regional Chief Counsel, Atlanta (Region IV).

Guam
U.S. District Court—Guam: Office of the Regional Chief Counsel, San Francisco (Region IX).

Hawaii
U.S. District Court—Hawaii: Office of the Regional Chief Counsel, San Francisco (Region IX).

Idaho
U.S. District Court—Idaho: Office of the Regional Chief Counsel, Seattle (Region X).

Illinois
U.S. District Court—Central District of Illinois: Office of the Regional Chief Counsel, Chicago (Region V).
U.S. District Court—Northern District of Illinois: Office of the Regional Chief Counsel, Chicago (Region V).
U.S. District Court—Southern District of Illinois: Office of the Regional Chief Counsel, Chicago (Region V).

Indiana
U.S. District Court—Northern District of Indiana: Office of the Regional Chief Counsel, Chicago (Region V).
U.S. District Court—Southern District of Indiana: Office of the Regional Chief Counsel, Chicago (Region V).

Iowa
U.S. District Court—Northern District of Iowa: Office of the Regional Chief Counsel, Dallas (Region VI).
U.S. District Court—Southern District of Iowa: Office of the Regional Chief Counsel, Dallas (Region VI).

Kansas
U.S. District Court—Kansas: Office of the Regional Chief Counsel, Denver (Region VIII).

Kentucky
U.S. District Court—Eastern District of Kentucky: Office of the Regional Chief Counsel, Denver (Region VIII).
U.S. District Court—Western District of Kentucky: Office of the Regional Chief Counsel, Chicago (Region V).

Louisiana
U.S. District Court—Eastern District of Louisiana: Office of the Regional Chief Counsel, Dallas (Region VI).
U.S. District Court—Middle District of Louisiana: Office of the Regional Chief Counsel, Dallas (Region VI).
U.S. District Court—Western District of Louisiana: Office of the Regional Chief Counsel, Dallas (Region VI).

Maine
U.S. District Court—Maine: Office of the Regional Chief Counsel, Boston (Region I).

Maryland
U.S. District Court—Maryland: Office of Program Law, Baltimore.

Massachusetts
U.S. District Court—Massachusetts: Office of the Regional Chief Counsel, Boston (Region I).

Michigan

U.S. District Court—Eastern District of Michigan: Office of the Regional Chief Counsel, Boston (Region I).

U.S. District Court—Western District of Michigan: Office of the Regional Chief Counsel, Boston (Region I).

Minnesota

U.S. District Court—Minnesota: Office of the Regional Chief Counsel, Dallas (Region VI).

Mississippi

U.S. District Court—Northern District of Mississippi: Office of the Regional Chief Counsel, Dallas (Region VI).

U.S. District Court—Southern District of Mississippi: Office of the Regional Chief Counsel, Dallas (Region VI).

Missouri

U.S. District Court—Eastern District of Missouri: Office of the Regional Chief Counsel, Kansas City (Region VII).

U.S. District Court—Western District of Missouri: Office of the Regional Chief Counsel, Kansas City (Region VII).

Montana

U.S. District Court—Montana: Office of the Regional Chief Counsel, Seattle (Region X).

Nebraska

U.S. District Court—Nebraska: Office of the Regional Chief Counsel, Dallas (Region VI).

Nevada

U.S. District Court—Nevada: Office of the Regional Chief Counsel, San Francisco (Region IX).

New Hampshire

U.S. District Court—New Hampshire: Office of the Regional Chief Counsel, Boston (Region I).

New Jersey

U.S. District Court—New Jersey: Office of the Regional Chief Counsel, Philadelphia (Region III).

New Mexico

U.S. District Court—New Mexico: Office of the Regional Chief Counsel, Denver (Region VIII).

New York

U.S. District Court—Eastern District of New York: Office of the Regional Chief Counsel, New York (Region II).

U.S. District Court—Northern District of New York: Office of the Regional Chief Counsel, New York (Region II).

U.S. District Court—Southern District of New York: Office of the Regional Chief Counsel, New York (Region II).

U.S. District Court—Western District of New York: Office of the Regional Chief Counsel, New York (Region II).

North Carolina

U.S. District Court—Eastern District of North Carolina: Office of Program Law, Baltimore.

U.S. District Court—Middle District of North Carolina: Office of the Regional Chief Counsel, Philadelphia (Region III).

U.S. District Court—Western District of North Carolina: Office of Program Law, Baltimore.

North Dakota

U.S. District Court—North Dakota: Office of the Regional Chief Counsel, Dallas (Region VI).

Northern Mariana Islands

U.S. District Court—Northern Mariana Islands: Office of the Regional Chief Counsel, San Francisco (Region IX).

Ohio

U.S. District Court—Northern District of Ohio: Office of the Regional Chief Counsel, Chicago (Region V).

U.S. District Court—Southern District of Ohio: Office of the Regional Chief Counsel, Chicago (Region V).

Oklahoma

U.S. District Court—Eastern District of Oklahoma: Office of the Regional Chief Counsel, Denver (Region VIII).

U.S. District Court—Northern District of Oklahoma: Office of the Regional Chief Counsel, Denver (Region VIII).

U.S. District Court—Western District of Oklahoma: Office of the Regional Chief Counsel, Denver (Region VIII).

Oregon

U.S. District Court—Oregon: Office of the Regional Chief Counsel, Seattle (Region X).

Pennsylvania

U.S. District Court—Eastern District of Pennsylvania: Office of the Regional Chief Counsel, Philadelphia (Region III).

U.S. District Court—Middle District of Pennsylvania: Office of the Regional Chief Counsel, Philadelphia (Region III).

U.S. District Court—Western District of Pennsylvania: Office of the Regional Chief Counsel, Philadelphia (Region III).

Puerto Rico

U.S. District Court—Puerto Rico: Office of the Regional Chief Counsel, New York (Region II).

Rhode Island

U.S. District Court—Rhode Island: Office of the Regional Chief Counsel, Boston (Region I).

South Carolina

U.S. District Court—South Carolina: Office of the Regional Chief Counsel, Philadelphia (Region III).

South Dakota

U.S. District Court—South Dakota: Office of the Regional Chief Counsel, Dallas (Region VI).

Tennessee

U.S. District Court—Eastern District of Tennessee: Office of the Regional Chief Counsel, Kansas City (Region VII).

U.S. District Court—Middle District of Tennessee: Office of the Regional Chief Counsel, Kansas City (Region VII).

U.S. District Court—Western District of Tennessee: Office of the Regional Chief Counsel, Kansas City (Region VII).

Texas

U.S. District Court—Eastern District of Texas: Office of the Regional Chief Counsel, Dallas (Region VI).

U.S. District Court—Northern District of Texas: Office of the Regional Chief Counsel, Dallas (Region VI).
U.S. District Court—Southern District of Texas: Office of the Regional Chief Counsel, Dallas (Region VI).
U.S. District Court—Western District of Texas: Office of the Regional Chief Counsel, Dallas (Region VI).
Utah
U.S. District Court—Utah: Office of the Regional Chief Counsel, Denver (Region VIII).
Vermont
U.S. District Court—Vermont: Office of the Regional Chief Counsel, New York (Region II).
Virgin Islands
U.S. District Court—Virgin Islands: Office of the Regional Chief Counsel, New York (Region II).
Virginia
U.S. District Court—Eastern District of Virginia: Office of the Regional Chief Counsel, Philadelphia (Region III).
U.S. District Court—Western District of Virginia: Office of the Regional Chief Counsel, Philadelphia (Region III).
Washington
U.S. District Court—Eastern District of Washington: Office of the Regional Chief Counsel, Seattle (Region X).
U.S. District Court—Western District of Washington: Office of the Regional Chief Counsel, Seattle (Region X).
West Virginia
U.S. District Court—Northern District of West Virginia: Office of the Regional Chief Counsel, Philadelphia (Region III).
U.S. District Court—Southern District of West Virginia: Office of the Regional Chief Counsel, Philadelphia (Region III).
Wisconsin
U.S. District Court—Eastern District of Wisconsin: Office of the Regional Chief Counsel, Chicago (Region V).
U.S. District Court—Western District of Wisconsin: Office of the Regional Chief Counsel, Chicago (Region V).
Wyoming
U.S. District Court—Wyoming: Office of the Regional Chief Counsel
Denver (Region VIII).

Addresses of OGC Offices
Office of Program Law
Office of the General Counsel
Social Security Administration
6401 Security Boulevard
Altmeyer Building, Room 617
Baltimore, MD 21235-6401

Office of the Regional Chief Counsel, Region I
Social Security Administration
JFK Federal Building, Room 625
15 New Sudbury Street,
Boston, MA 02203-0002

Office of the Regional Chief Counsel, Region II
Social Security Administration
26 Federal Plaza, Room 3904
New York, NY 10278-0004

Office of the Regional Chief Counsel, Region III
Social Security Administration
300 Spring Garden Street, 6th Floor
Philadelphia, PA 19123-2932

Office of the Regional Chief Counsel, Region IV
Social Security Administration
Sam Nunn Atlanta Federal Center
61 Forsyth Street, SW., Suite 20T45
Atlanta, GA 30303-8910

Office of the Regional Chief Counsel, Region V
Social Security Administration
200 W. Adams Street, 30th Floor
Chicago, IL 60606-5208

Office of the Regional Chief Counsel, Region VI
Social Security Administration
1301 Young Street, Suite A-702
Dallas, TX 75202-5433

Office of the Regional Chief Counsel, Region VII
Social Security Administration
Richard Bolling Federal Building,
601 East 12th Street, Room 965
Kansas City, MO 64106-2898

Office of the Regional Chief Counsel, Region VIII
Social Security Administration
1961 Stout Street, Suite 4169
Denver, CO 80294-4003

Office of the Regional Chief Counsel, Region IX
Social Security Administration
160 Spear Street, Suite 800
San Francisco, CA 94105-1545

Office of the Regional Chief Counsel, Region X
Social Security Administration
701 Fifth Avenue, Suite 2900 M/S 221A
Seattle, WA 98104-7075

§612   Sample: Complaint

UNITED STATES DISTRICT COURT
_____ DISTRICT OF _____|

Client's Name,

Plaintiff,

v.   Case No. _____

Commissioner of Social Security,

Defendant.

<u>COMPLAINT</u>

Plaintiff, by attorney, _____, alleges as follows:

1.   The jurisdiction of this Court is invoked pursuant to 42 U.S.C. § 405(g) [and 42 U.S.C. § 1383(c)(3)] to review a decision of the Commissioner of Social Security denying Plaintiff's application for Social Security Disability [and Supplemental Security Income Disability] benefits for lack of disability.

2.   This action is an appeal from a final administrative decision denying Plaintiff's claim and commenced within the appropriate time period set forth in the Action of Appeals Council on Request for Review dated _____.

3.   The last four digits of plaintiff's Social Security number (SSN) are _____. Plaintiff's full SSN is omitted from this complaint in compliance with Rule 5.2(a)(1) of the Federal Rules of Civil Procedure.

4.   Plaintiff resides in [City and State], County of _____, within the jurisdiction of this court.

5.   The defendant is the Commissioner of Social Security of the United States of America.

6.   Plaintiff is disabled.

7.   The conclusions and findings of fact of the defendant are not supported by substantial evidence and are contrary to law and regulation.

WHEREFORE, plaintiff prays that this Court:

1) reverse the decision of the defendant; and

2) find that plaintiff is entitled to disability benefits under the provisions of the Social Security Act; or

3) remand the case for a further hearing; and

4) award attorney's fees under the Equal Access to Justice Act, 28 U.S.C. § 2412(d), on the grounds that the Commissioner's action in this case was not substantially justified; and

5) order such other and further relief as the Court deems just and proper.

Dated _____   s/ [Attorney's Name]
                                       [Attorney's Name]
                                       Bar Number: _____
                                       Attorney for Plaintiff

P.O. Address: _____
Telephone: _____
Fax: _____
E-mail: _____

§613   Filing **In Forma Pauperis**

Because of the very limited resources of most Social Security disability and SSI claimants, many disability cases are filed *in forma pauperis* pursuant to 28 U.S.C. § 1915. Many district courts have forms to be completed by the plaintiff online and insist that you use the district court's form for filing *in forma pauperis*. Check with the clerk of court. In those districts where the court does not insist that you use the court's form, you may use the sample application and affidavit that appears in §613.1. Eligibility to receive welfare benefits establishes inability to afford to pay the filing fee, for it demonstrates that a government agency has evaluated the claimant's income and assets and found them negligible. For those claimants who are not receiving welfare benefits, you may need to file a more detailed financial statement than that set forth in the sample. Also, some districts require a more detailed statement than that in the sample even for claimants who are receiving welfare benefits. *Cf.* Fed. R. App. P. Form 4. Check local practice with a phone call to the clerk's office.

Some courts require an explanation why the case is not frivolous pursuant to 28 U.S.C. § 1915(e)(2) beyond that provided in paragraphs 6 and 7 of the sample complaint. If your client's case is being filed in such a jurisdiction, you will need to add more specific allegations to the complaint to show that it is not frivolous or add the specific allegations to the plaintiff's affidavit.

§613.1 Sample: Application and Affidavit for Leave to Proceed In Forma Pauperis

UNITED STATES DISTRICT COURT
_____ DISTRICT OF _____|

(Client's Name)

Plaintiff,

APPLICATION AND AFFIDAVIT FOR LEAVE TO PROCEED <u>IN FORMA PAUPERIS</u>

v.

Civil Action No. _____

Commissioner of Social Security,
           Defendant.

STATE OF _____)
) SS.
_____ COUNTY   )

(Plaintiff's Name), being first duly sworn, on oath states:

1. I am an adult citizen of the State of _____ and reside at _____ _____ with (*identify family members*).

2. I have commenced an action in this court to review a decision of the Commissioner of Social Security denying my request for Social Security disability benefits and Supplemental Security Income disability benefits for lack of disability.

3. I believe I am entitled to win this lawsuit as shown by the complaint filed with this Affidavit [and because _____].

4. I am not presently employed and my only source of support for myself and (*identify family members*) is public assistance in the form of [Temporary Assistance to Needy Families, general assistance, etc.] in the amount of $___ per month; I am without savings of any kind; I do not own an automobile or any real estate, stocks, bonds, notes or other valuable property (excluding ordinary household furnishings and clothing); and because of my poverty I am unable to pay the fees and costs of this action or to give security therefor, and still be able to provide myself and my family with the necessities of life.

WHEREFORE, I ask the Court that I may be authorized to prosecute this action *in forma pauperis*, without prepayment of costs or security therefor, and without having to pay for service of legal papers, pursuant to 28 U.S.C. § 1915.

(*Plaintiff's Name*)

Subscribed and sworn to before
me this _____ day of _____

_____
Notary Public, State of _____
My commission: _____

§613.2 Sample: Order Granting Leave to Proceed *In Forma Pauperis*

UNITED STATES DISTRICT COURT
_____ DISTRICT OF_____ ⌡

Client's Name

             Plaintiff,

    v.   Civil Action No. _____

Commissioner of Social Security,

             Defendant.

ORDER GRANTING LEAVE TO
PROCEED *IN FORMA PAUPERIS*

In reliance on the presentations set forth in the attached application and affidavit,

IT IS ORDERED that the Plaintiff in the above-entitled proceeding be, and hereby is, permitted to prosecute said proceedings to conclusion without prepayment of costs or giving security therefor, and without paying U.S. Marshal service fees, pursuant to 28 U.S.C. § 1915.

Dated at _____, _____, this _____ day of _____, 19_.

BY THE COURT:

_____
United States District Judge/Magistrate Judge

§614 Filing Checklist

As a rule prepare the following for filing. Check local practice with the office of the clerk of the district court. (Many courts have home pages on the Internet that describe local practice for disability appeals. Many court home pages provide forms for download.)

1. Check for the filing fee (currently $400) or Application and Affidavit for Leave to Proceed *In Forma Pauperis* and proposed order; (*see* samples, §§614 and 615);

2. Summons (a special federal court form must be obtained from the clerk);

3. Complaint (*see* the sample complaint, §612);

4. Civil cover sheet (a special form must be obtained from the district court's website or from the clerk); and

5. Any additional form required by local rules.

All districts use the CM/ECF electronic filing system. Most districts allow complaints, etc., to be filed electronically and allow the filing fee be paid online.

§615 Proof of Service

According to Fed. R. Civ. P. 4(l)(1) an affidavit is required for proof of service to the court. Pursuant to 28 U.S.C. § 1746, an unsworn declaration under penalty of perjury may be used, which avoids the need for the document to be notarized.

File proof of service as soon as you send the initiating documents by certified mail to the Commissioner, United States Attorney for the district in which you file the case, and the U.S. Attorney General. You don't have to wait for the green cards to be returned. Indeed, it is most efficient to prepare and file the proof of service document immediately.

Then, as you receive the green cards from the three people served, file them with the court.

§615.1 *Sample: Proof of Service*

UNITED STATES DISTRICT COURT
_____DISTRICT OF_____
_____DIVISION

PLAINTIFF NAME ,

Plaintiff,

v.   Case No.

COMMISSIONER NAME ,
[Acting] Commissioner of Social Security,
Defendant.

PROOF OF SERVICE

ATTORNEY NAME certifies under penalty of perjury under the laws of the United States of America that the following is true and correct:

1. I am the attorney for plaintiff, PLAINTIFF NAME, in the above-entitled action.
2. On DATE, under my supervision copies of the [summons and] complaint in the above-entitled action were mailed with proper postage by certified mail, return receipt requested, to the following:

COMMISSIONER NAME
[Acting] Commissioner of Social Security
c/o Office of the Regional Chief Counsel
ADDRESS

Attorney General of the United States
950 Pennsylvania Avenue, N.W.
Washington, DC 20530

Civil Process Clerk
Office of the United States Attorney
ADDRESS

TODAY'S DATE   s/ ATTORNEY NAME
                                         ATTORNEY NAME
                                         State Bar No.: _____
                                         Attorney for Plaintiff

P.O. Address:
FIRM NAME
FIRM ADDRESS

Telephone: FIRM TELEPHONE
Fax: FIRM FAX
Email: ATTORNEY EMAIL

CERTIFICATE OF ELECTRONIC SERVICE

I certify that on DATE, I electronically filed the above with the Clerk of Court using the ECF system, which will send notification to:

[Assistant] U.S. Attorney
ADDRESS
EMAIL

s/ ATTORNEY NAME
ATTORNEY NAME
State Bar No.: _____
Attorney for Plaintiff

§616 Service Checklist

1. Be sure the U.S. Attorney for the district in which the case is filed is served by personal service or by certified mail, return receipt requested, addressed to the civil process clerk at the Office of the U.S. Attorney. Fed. R. Civ. P. 4(i)(1)(A).

2. By certified mail, return receipt requested, serve the Attorney General of the United States, 950 Pennsylvania Avenue, N.W., Washington, D.C. 20530-0001. Fed. R. Civ. P. 4(i)(1)(B).

3. By certified mail, return receipt requested, serve the Commissioner of Social Security by sending a copy of the summons and complaint by registered or certified mail to SSA's Office of General Counsel, which is responsible for processing and handling litigation in the particular judicial district in which the complaint is filed. *See* 20 C.F.R. § 423.1 and Rule 4(i)(2) of the Federal Rules of Civil Procedure (Fed. R. Civ. P.). Find the address for service at §611.1 or on the Internet at www.socialsecurity.gov.

4. File Proof of Service as soon as you mail the summonses and complaints to the three people who must be served.

5. When you receive the green return receipt cards in the mail, file copies of the green cards with the court.

§617 Calendar Tips

1. When you file the action and serve the summonses and complaints, make a calendar notation to expect to receive the answer and administrative transcript about 65 days later.

2. Have your secretary pin the certified mail slip to a bulletin board, to be removed only when the return receipt arrives. An old slip still on the bulletin board flags a problem.

3. If you don't receive a return receipt in a reasonable time, send another copy. You are allowed 120 days to effectuate service. Fed. R. Civ. P. 4(m). Also, as long as you effect service on either the U.S. Attorney or the Attorney General of the United States, the court will allow a "reasonable time" for "curing the failure to serve multiple officers" of the government. Fed. R. Civ. P. 4(i) (3).

4. If you do not receive the answer and administrative transcript in about 65 days, call the clerk of court to determine whether an answer and administrative record were filed. It they have not been filed, contact the U.S. Attorney's office directly.

§620 Post-Filing Procedure

§621 Answer

The Commissioner is allowed 60 days to answer the complaint. Along with the answer will be filed a transcript of the administrative proceedings containing all of the hearing exhibits, the ALJ decision, a transcript of the ALJ hearing, any new exhibits added by the Appeals Council, and the Appeals Council's action or decision. When you receive this package, make sure it's complete, all copies are legible, and there are not material omissions in the hearing transcript due to inaudibility of the audiotape of the hearing. If there is a defect in the transcript of administrative proceedings, bring an appropriate motion as soon as possible.

Practice varies from district to district. In many districts, you may be given the opportunity to consent to magistrate judge jurisdiction to issue a final decision pursuant to 28 U.S.C. § 636(c). In many districts if either party refuses to consent, the case is assigned to the magistrate judge anyway to issue a report and recommendation to the federal district court judge.

The review conducted by the federal court is usually a review only of the documentary record. As a rule, new evidence is considered only rarely and evidentiary hearings are seldom held. No jury is ever empanelled. 42 U.S.C. § 405(g) empowers the court to enter judgment only "upon the pleadings and transcript of record." Evidentiary hearings on limited issues occur only infrequently when new evidence is presented under sentence six of 42 U.S.C. § 405(g).

§622 Motion for Summary Judgment Under Sentence Four of 42 U.S.C. § 405(g)

When you have a complete and workable administrative record, prepare a motion for summary judgment with supporting brief pursuant to Rule 56 of the Federal Rules of Civil Procedure. Strictly speaking, while courts usually refer to the motion filed in a disability case as a motion for summary judgment, the procedure is akin to a motion for judgment on the pleadings under Fed. R. Civ. P. 12(d) because the administrative record is part of the Commissioner's answer. In most cases, claimants seek relief under sentence four of 42 U.S.C. § 405(g) which provides that "[t]he court shall have power to enter, upon the pleadings and transcript of the record, a judgment affirming, modifying, or reversing the decision of the Commissioner of Social Security, with or without remanding the cause for a rehearing."

In some districts, oral argument is regularly scheduled. In others, oral argument is granted by a court only in unusual circumstances.

§623 Motion for Remand for Consideration of New Evidence

Although arguably a motion for remand isn't necessary, (see sentence six of 42 U.S.C. § 405(g) which says that the court "may at any time order additional evidence to be taken before the commissioner"), it is usually the prudent thing to do. In the motion or supporting brief, explain why the requirements for a sentence-six remand are met. You must show that the evidence is (1) new, (2) material and (3) that there is "good cause for the failure to incorporate such evidence into the record in a prior proceeding." Sometimes an affidavit similar to that contemplated by Fed. R. Civ. P. 56 may be necessary to address the "good cause" issue.

§624 Effective Briefing

Deadlines for briefing may be established by local rule or the court may issue a briefing schedule. Check local practice with the office of the clerk of the district court or with a clerk for a judge or magistrate judge.

Experienced clerks who work for judges or magistrate judges are goldmines of procedural information. But beware: this clerk may be the person who writes the first draft of the decision in your client's case. Since federal court review of a disability case is an adversarial proceeding, any discussion of the merits of your client's case with such a clerk is forbidden. Nevertheless, by listening carefully to what the clerk tells you about procedure, you may learn about the audience for whom you are writing the brief in your client's case.

The issues raised in a Social Security case frequently involve complex and technical factual and legal questions. A clear explanation in plain language will make the court's job easier and will be appreciated.

Most briefs begin with a summary of the procedural history of the claim and statement of facts. A compelling statement of facts with specific detailed references to the transcript can be decisive. The factual summaries in the ALJ decisions are frequently organized exhibit by exhibit, yielding only a vaguely chronological presentation of the facts. It is more effective to organize facts chronologically or topically, depending on the case. It also helps to define unfamiliar medical terms by citation to a standard medical dictionary. Without exception, each factual assertion should be supported by a specific citation to the administrative record.

Whether you write the statement of facts first or outline your argument first is a matter of personal preference. Many attorneys work back and forth, drafting a preliminary outline of the argument before beginning the factual statement. Preparing a detailed factual statement often yields additional ideas for legal arguments based on the facts. No matter how you prepare it, the factual statement should be fair and complete and should dovetail with the legal argument.

Present legal arguments succinctly. An argument that substantial evidence does not support the factual findings of the Commissioner, once you understand the legal principles, can be written with very little reference to case law. Once you have written a draft of your argument, add citations to cases for the general legal principles involved and search for cases to cite that involve similar facts. Do not worry if you cannot find any cases on point. Virtually by definition an argument involving a lack of substantial evidence is an original argument—every case is different.

Use a similar method when writing arguments based upon errors of law. Write a draft of your argument following Social Security regulations and rulings. They are a more discrete and manageable body of law than case law. Then research and add case citations and appropriate quotations for crucial points. Citations of precedential appellate court decisions are particularly helpful. String cites for general legal principles are unnecessary. You may assume that the judge is familiar with the general analytical framework for evaluating disability claims.

§625 Research Tips

Many attorneys who handle a lot of Social Security cases in federal court use on-line research products available from Westlaw or Lexis-Nexis. Some attorneys use products available on CD-ROM—either West's Social Security Library or Social Security Excellence—to do legal research.

Lawyers who specialize in federal court representation have their own brief banks, usually a computerized collection of briefs, that they draw upon for arguments for issues that come up over and over. For newer attorneys, *Bohr's Social Security Issues Annotated* by Sarah H. Bohr provides, in effect, a brief bank. You can install the disks that come with *Bohr's* on your computer to make your own electronic brief bank. The *Social Security Advisory Service* by Peter S. Young, Robert C. Dawes and J. Kevin Morton is useful. See Appendix 2 for ordering information. NOSSCR also has research materials and copies of briefs on various issues available for sale.

§630 Practice Before U.S. Magistrate Judges

§631 Whether to Consent to Magistrate Judge Jurisdiction

A U.S. Magistrate Judge may issue a final decision pursuant to 28 U.S.C. § 1291 if both parties have consented to the magistrate judge's jurisdiction over the case. 28 U.S.C. § 636(c); Fed. R. Civ. P. 73. If consent is given, the magistrate judge's disposition of the case is equal in all respects to disposition of a case by a U.S. District Judge. When both parties consent to magistrate judge jurisdiction, appeal from a magistrate judge's disposition is to an appellate court.

If either party refuses to consent, a federal district judge may, nevertheless, refer the case to a magistrate judge for a recommended decision. 28 U.S.C. § 636(b); Fed. R. Civ. P. 72. The federal district judge will later issue the final decision of the court.

Lawyers who specialize in federal court representation of claimants make their decisions whether or not to consent to magistrate judge jurisdiction based on experience and knowledge of the particular judges involved. If you're new to federal court representation, ask a more experienced attorney whether or not to consent. You can also search reported cases for decisions by the magistrate judge and base your decision on reading several of the magistrate judge's decisions. If you can't decide, don't consent.

Unless the district judge is known to be substantially less sympathetic to claimants than the magistrate judge (in which case you would want the magistrate judge to issue a final decision), refusal to consent to exercise of jurisdiction by a magistrate judge generally has the beneficial effect of allowing the plaintiff an additional level of review. If the magistrate judge's recommendation is adverse to the plaintiff, it is easier to present your objections to the district judge than to take an appeal to the circuit court of appeals. And if you lose before the district judge, you can still take the case to the court of appeals.

§632 Specific Objections Required to Magistrate Judge Recommendation

Objections to a magistrate judge's recommendation must be filed and served within ten days after service of the recommendation. Objections must be specific. An objection that says, for example, "The plaintiff objects to the magistrate judge's recommendation for all the reasons stated in the plaintiff's brief supporting the motion for summary judgment in this case" is insufficient. Objections must specifically address the magistrate judge's conclusions. *See Howard v. Secretary of HHS*, 932 F.2d 505, 509 (6th Cir. 1991).

Failure to timely object to the magistrate judge's report and recommendation on specific issues may foreclose appeal on those issues, pursuant to rules of the individual appellate courts adopted in most circuits. *See, e.g., Howard v. Secretary of HHS*, 932 F.2d 505, 508 (6th Cir. 1991); *Thomas v. Arn*, 474 U.S. 140 (1985). Consider what can happen to your client's appeal rights if a magistrate judge recommends giving half a loaf and you make no objection. Let's say that a magistrate judge recommends remanding a case for rehearing on only one issue out of four issues briefed by the plaintiff. If the district judge refuses to accept the magistrate judge's recommendation and, instead, decides the case against the plaintiff, the plaintiff will be able appeal on only one issue. Without an objection from the plaintiff's attorney on the other three issues on which the magistrate judge recommended a decision against the plaintiff, appeal may be foreclosed. Thus, whenever a magistrate judge recommendation goes against your client on a particular issue, you need to consider filing objections even when you do not disagree with the magistrate judge's ultimate recommendation to remand the case for rehearing.

A party may respond to another party's objections within ten days of service of the objections. The time for filing objections may be extended by the court on motion of a party. The U.S. District Judge is required to make a *de novo* determination of any portion of the magistrate judge's recommendation to which specific written objections have been made. The district judge may accept, reject, or modify the magistrate judge's recommended decision, or recommit the matter to the magistrate judge with instructions. Fed. R. Civ. P. 72.

§633 Time Limit for Objections to Magistrate Judge Recommendation

When you receive a report and recommendation, immediately calculate a due date for objections. To calculate a due date, you must understand two Federal Rules of Civil Procedure and the notice accompanying the report and recommendation.

Rule 72(b) requires you to "serve" and "file" specific objections within 10 days of "service." Fed. R. Civ. P. 72(b). A time limit of less than 11 days is calculated without counting weekends and holidays. Fed. R. Civ. P. 6(a). Therefore, Rule 72(b)'s 10-day time limit is calculated by counting only working days. When a time limit runs from "service," if service is by mail or electronic filing three days are added "after the period would otherwise expire under Rule 6(a)," which is the rule that said not to count weekends and holidays. Fed. R. Civ. P. 6(d). Therefore, three days are added to the end of the 10-day period (calculated not counting weekends and holidays). When adding these three days, though, you count weekends and holidays. But if the count ends on a weekend or holiday, the deadline is extended to the next working day.

To make sure this is clear, let's run through an example. Say the Report and Recommendation is issued and you receive it electronically on the same day, the 1st of the month, a Wednesday. Assuming that there are no intervening holidays, the ten working day period expires in two weeks on Wednesday, the 15th of the month. To this calculation you get to add three days—Thursday, Friday and Saturday. But since this calculation ends on a weekend, the deadline rolls over to the next working day, Monday, the 20th of the month.

A notice accompanying a Report and Recommendation may give a precise due date and may or may not reference Rule 72(b). If the precise due date given in the notice is later than the due date under Rule 72(b), then you may rely on the later due date. If the precise due date given in the notice is sooner than the due date under Rule 72(b), a claimant should use the earlier due date but in no case should file objections later than the due date under Rule 72(b). If necessary, you can argue that a court cannot shorten the time period of Rule 72(b).

There is authority that Rule 72(b)'s ten-day time limit to submit objections is not jurisdictional. E.g., *Kruger v. Apfel*, 214 F.3d 784, 786-87 (7th Cir. 2002). If the ten-day time limit is not jurisdictional, then, in theory, the time for filing objections may be extended by the court on motion of a party. Understand, however, that rarely does a litigant request an extension to file objections to a Report and Recommendation and that a court may deny any such request without explanation. Request an extension of time to file objections only if you are positive that the ten-day time limit is not jurisdictional in the relevant circuit and if there are very special reasons for doing so, such as that you were recently retained to represent your client.

§640 Remedies: Reversal With and Without Remanding for Rehearing

Under sentence four of 42 U.S.C. § 405(g), a federal court can affirm, modify, or reverse a decision of the Commissioner with or without remanding the case for a rehearing. Under sentence six of 42 U.S.C. § 405(g), the court can only remand the case for further action by the Commissioner or for additional evidence to be taken before the Commissioner.

§641 Reversal Without Remanding for a Rehearing

Sentence four of 42 U.S.C. § 405(g) gives a court the power to modify or reverse the Commissioner's decision without remanding the case for a new hearing. The following circumstances may cause a court to reverse a final decision without remanding a case for further hearing:

- The administrative record is fully developed;
- The plaintiff has carried the burden of proving inability to return to past relevant work;
- Evidence in the record as a whole indicates that the claimant is disabled; and
- Further administrative proceedings would merely delay the receipt of benefits.

See McQueen v. Apfel, 168 F.3d 152, 156 (5th Cir. 1999); *Wilder v. Apfel*, 153 F.3d 799 (7th Cir. 1998); *Burress v. Apfel*, 141 F.3d 875 (8th Cir. 1998).

If your argument is that the plaintiff's impairments meet the Listings, reversal without a remand for a rehearing is the appropriate remedy. *See, e.g., Lester v. Chater*, 81 F.3d 821, 834 (9th Cir. 1995); *Guzman v. Bowen*, 801 F.2d 273, 275 (7th Cir. 1986).

§642 Voluntary Remand and Remand Instead of Default Judgment

Under the first part of sentence six of 42 U.S.C. § 405(g) a court "may, on motion of the Commissioner made for good cause shown before he files his answer, remand the case to the Commissioner for further action by the Commissioner."

Thus, the government may voluntarily move to remand the case before filing an answer. This provision has been used by SSA when it has second thoughts about defending a case in court.

Congress intended this clause to apply to those circumstances where SSA lost the administrative record or where the hearing recording cannot be adequately transcribed—circumstances which in other sorts of cases would prompt motions for default judgment. However, when a record is lost, judgment against the United States by default may not be obtained unless "the claimant establishes a claim or right to relief by evidence satisfactory to the court." Fed. R. Civ. P. 55(e). Rule 55(e) and 42 U.S.C. § 405(g) by which the court has power to enter judgment "upon the pleadings and transcript of the record" operate to make it the general rule that the transcript must first be filed before a default judgment against the government can be obtained in a Social Security disability case. *Poe v. Mathews*, 472 F.2d 137 (6th Cir. 1978). Some district courts have entered default judgments anyway, arguing that Congress could not have intended a result that renders Rule 55(e) a nullity. *Stanley v. Heckler*, 604 F. Supp. 1102, 1104 (D. Mont. 1985), and *Byrd v. Heckler*, 576 F. Supp. 547 (Wash. D.C. 1983).

On remand, courts rarely order time limits [*Engelhart v. Schweiker*, 558 F. Supp. 112 (D.S.D. 1983)] and interim benefits paid. For examples of cases in which courts ordered interim benefits paid when remand was due to the Commissioner's loss of or inability to transcribe the hearing tape, *see La Bonne v. Heckler*, 574 F. Supp. 1016 (D. Minn. 1983) *and Gomaz v. Heckler*, 591 F. Supp. 1122 (E.D. Wis. 1984).

§643 Remand to Evaluate New Evidence

The second part of sentence six of 42 U.S.C. § 405(g) permits a court at any time to order that additional evidence be taken before the Commissioner "but only upon a showing that there is new evidence which is material and that there is good cause for the failure to incorporate such evidence into the record in a prior proceeding." This provision should be invoked, at least as an alternative to other remedies, when, after the case has been filed in federal court, you come

into possession of additional evidence related to the claimant's condition on or before the date of the ALJ decision.

If the additional evidence surfaces before you file in federal court, you must decide whether to submit it to the Appeals Council with a request to reconsider its action and to extend the time limit for filing in federal court (*see* §552) or submit the evidence only to the federal court. Because courts tend to be suspicious and stingy in applying the good cause requirement for a sentence-six remand, submitting additional evidence to the Appeals Council may be best. The Appeals Council may reconsider its action. If not, it will include the additional evidence in the administrative record though circuit law differs on how such evidence that was never seen by the ALJ is evaluated by a court. See §652.

If you try to submit new evidence to the federal court, especially if you represented the claimant before the agency, you will have to do a whole lot of explaining why you failed to provide this important evidence to the agency. "Where the reasons for pursuing additional evidence are apparent while the case is still subject to administrative review, and there is no impediment to obtaining the evidence, no good cause has been demonstrated for failing to bring the evidence to the Secretary's attention." *Anderson v. Bowen*, 868 F.2d 921, 928 (7th Cir. 1989). For a case in which good cause was found, *see Sears v. Bowen*, 840 F.2d 394, 399-400 (7th Cir. 1988).

Different appellate courts and different appellate panels within the same circuit apply different interpretations of the good cause, newness, and materiality requirements for a clause-two, sentence six remand. There is no substitute for reviewing each and every sentence-six case from your circuit and for being familiar with inter- and intra-circuit conflicts. Many sentence-six cases are analytically unsound.

§644 Sentence-Four Reversals With Remanding for a Rehearing

Where there is an error of law or when substantial evidence does not support the Commissioner's decision, under sentence four of 42 U.S.C. § 405(g) a court may reverse the agency's final decision with a remand for a rehearing. Sentence four provides that a court shall have the power to enter "a judgment affirming, modifying, or reversing the decision of the Commissioner, with or without remanding the cause for a rehearing." Federal courts remand cases for rehearings much more often than they reverse and award benefits under this provision of the statute, even where there is no possibility that SSA can deny the claimant if SSA follows the court's decision on remand.

§645 Appealability of Remand Orders

Cases reversed and remanded to the agency pursuant to the *fourth* sentence of 42 U.S.C. § 405(g) are immediately appealable by either party, since immediate entry of final judgment is required at the time of a fourth sentence remand. A claimant may appeal a remand order because the claimant wants the court to reverse the decision of the Commissioner and award benefits instead of remanding the case. *Forney v. Apfel*, 118 S. Ct. 1984 (1998).

In cases remanded under the *sixth* sentence of 42 U.S.C. § 405(g), final judgment is not entered until the post-remand proceedings are completed. *Melkonyan v. Sullivan*, 501 U.S. 89, 98 (1991). Sixth sentence remands are those ordered because of the Commissioner's motion before answer or where there is new evidence, described in §§642 and 643. The agency may but a claimant may not appeal a sentence-six remand order.

§646 Procedure at SSA on Remand

Cases remanded by a federal court to the Appeals Council and then remanded by the Appeals Council for a new hearing are usually assigned to the same ALJ who issued the original decision— unless the claimant has received two unfavorable decisions from that ALJ or unless the court's remand order or the Appeals Council's remand order specifies that the case be heard by a different ALJ. *See* HALLEX I-2-1-55 D.11 and §526 of this book. *See also* HALLEX I-4-6-30 B.10. If you do not want to take your client's case back before the same ALJ who denied benefits previously, you may request that the federal court order that a different ALJ hear the case on remand. This request may or may not be granted, within the discretion of the court. *Compare Travis v. Sullivan*, 985 F.2d 919, 924 (7th Cir. 1993) ("we believe that the district court exceeded its authority in ordering a new ALJ to take over the case on remand"), *with Rohan v. Chater*, 98 F.3d 966, 971 (7th Cir. 1996) ("We recommend that the Commissioner assign this case to a different ALJ for all further proceedings."). When a federal court recommends but does not order a new ALJ to be assigned on remand, the Appeals Council almost always orders that a different ALJ hear the case on remand.

In some cases the ALJ on remand may undertake a *de novo* review of the record, the same way a case would be evaluated if the claimant were having a first hearing before an ALJ. In other cases the range of issues may be limited by federal court orders—often referred to as the law of the case—or Appeals Council remand orders. For example, a federal court order may state that a claimant cannot perform past relevant work and limit the issue on remand to whether the Commissioner can demonstrate that the claimant can perform other jobs existing in significant numbers in the national economy. Remand orders often impose several requirements, including taking vocational or medical testimony or recontacting a treating source.

20 C.F.R. § 404.983 provides that after remand by the federal court, the Appeals Council may (1) issue a decision, (2) remand the case to an ALJ with instructions to issue a decision, or (3) remand the case to an ALJ to take action and return the case to the Appeals Council with a recommended decision. The option of ordering that an ALJ issue a recommended decision, the standard procedure after court remand in the 1980s, is currently seldom exercised by the Appeals Council. When this option is selected, the procedure set forth in 20 C.F.R. § 404.977 is followed. A claimant is allowed 20 days from the date of a recommended decision to file objections.

As a rule, the Appeals Council will remand a case to an ALJ to issue a final decision. 20 C.F.R. § 404.984(b) states that if a claimant disagrees with an ALJ decision after federal court remand, the claimant must, within 30 days, submit "a written statement to the Appeals Council setting forth reasons for disagreeing with the decision of the administrative law judge." See §560 on preparing exceptions. Then, the Appeals Council may assume jurisdiction and issue a new decision or it may simply issue a notice explaining why no change in the decision of the ALJ is warranted.

The regulation does not require that exceptions be filed. If no exceptions are filed and the Appeals Council does not assume jurisdiction on its own within 60 days of the date of the ALJ decision, the ALJ decision becomes the final decision of the Commissioner. 20 C.F.R. § 404.984(d). It is not clear whether failure to file exceptions with the Appeals Council after an unfavorable ALJ decision on remand has an effect on the jurisdiction of the federal court in any action after remand. Because these rules were written at a time when the federal courts retained jurisdiction of cases they remanded, which is no longer the case except for remands under sentence six of 42 U.S.C. § 405(g), prudence dictates filing exceptions with the Appeals Council. Because many circuits require that arguments to be used in court be first raised with SSA, it is important to raise all issues with the Appeals Council.

§647 Court Procedure Following Sixth Sentence Remand

If your client's case is one of the relatively few cases remanded pursuant to sentence six of 42 U.S.C. § 405(g), the Commissioner, following completion of remand proceedings, must file with the court a supplementary transcript containing the new decision. If the decision on remand is favorable to the claimant, a final judgment is supposed to be entered by the court after the Commissioner files the supplemental transcript. However, because the Commissioner is notoriously slow, it may be expeditious for a plaintiff to waive filing the official supplemental transcript. Instead, the plaintiff can file a copy of the final decision as a substitute for the official transcript. At this time plaintiff's attorney may bring motions for award of attorney's fees to be paid out of the claimant's past-due benefits pursuant to 42 U.S.C. § 406(b) (*see* §§750-757), and/or to be paid by the government pursuant to the Equal Access to Justice Act, 28 U.S.C. § 2412(d) (*see* §§760-794). If the decision on remand is unfavorable to the claimant, the claimant may file a motion for summary judgment challenging the agency's new final decision.

§648 Court Procedure Following Fourth Sentence Remand

If the plaintiff's case is remanded pursuant to sentence four of 42 U.S.C. § 405(g) and if the plaintiff is unsuccessful on remand, what is the proper procedure for taking the case back to court? According to *Shalala v. Schaefer*, 509 U.S. 292, 299 (1993), quoting *Sullivan v. Finkelstein*, 496 U.S. 617, 624-625 (1990), "Under § 405(g), 'each final decision of the Secretary [is] reviewable by a separate piece of litigation[.]'" Thus, the plaintiff must file a new complaint. Check with your district court to see if any local procedures have been established that may affect how such a new civil action is handled by that court. For example:

- Will the plaintiff have to pay an additional filing fee? One court, the United States District Court for the Western District of Virginia, issued a standing order waiving payment of an additional filing fee for fourth sentence remand cases where the plaintiff is unsuccessful on remand. Reprinted in *Social Security Forum*, Vol. 15, No. 8, August 1993, p. 5.
- If the plaintiff was allowed to file *in forma pauperis* in the first action, will *in forma pauperis* filing be allowed again without submitting a new formal motion and order?
- Will the case be assigned to the same judge?

§650 Substantive Issues

§651 The Law of the Case

Often a remand order accompanying a court's judgment reversing a final agency decision will specify what the agency must do next. An ALJ may be required to obtain the testimony of a vocational or medical expert or obtain medical evidence of functional limitations from a treating or consulting medical source. The remand order may direct the ALJ to properly evaluate a claim under step 5 of the sequential evaluation process. The directions of the court or the Appeals Council issuing the remand order are binding on the ALJ.

Failure to follow a remand order constitutes reversible error. For example, if a court remands a case because the ALJ improperly applied the grids with directions that SSA properly evaluate the case under step 5, it is contrary to the law of the case for the ALJ then to deny a claim at *step 4* by finding that the claimant could perform past work. *See Key v. Sullivan*, 925 F.2d 1056 (7th Cir. 1991); *but see Steahr v. Apfel*, 151 F.3d 1124 (8th Cir. 1998), which is factually similar to *Key* but the court decided that the law of the case doctrine did not apply. See especially the thoughtful dissent by Circuit Judge Heaney. *See also Brachtel v. Apfel*, 132 F.3d 417 (8th Cir. 1997); *Angevine v. Sullivan*, 881 F.2d 519 (7th Cir. 1989). Be sure to raise to the ALJ and the Appeals Council the meaning of any remand order.

§652 Treatment of Evidence Submitted to Appeals Council

After an ALJ renders a decision, a claimant may submit additional evidence to the Appeals Council in conjunction with a request for review. 20 C.F.R. § 404.970(b). The regulation imposes no "good cause" requirement for failure to submit the evidence to the ALJ. Under the regulations, the Appeals Council is supposed to grant a claimant's request for review based on the additional evidence if the additional evidence is "new," if the additional evidence is "material," and, based on the entire record including the new and material evidence, the ALJ decision is "contrary to the weight of the evidence currently of record." 20 C.F.R. § 404.970(b). Lawyers for claimants instinctively want the federal courts to address the Appeals Council's failure to do an adequate job of assessing the new evidence and weighing all the evidence in the case. When the Appeals Council fails even to address the new evidence, a claimant's lawyer usually asks the federal courts to remand the case to assess the new evidence.

SSA says that the Appeals Council's denial of review is never subject to judicial review even if the Appeals Council made errors when reviewing the additional evidence or failed to address the new evidence at all. Because judicial review is limited to the Commissioner's "final decision," *see* 42 U.S.C. § 405(g), and because the ALJ decision is the Commissioner's "final decision" when the Appeals Council denies review, *see* 20 C.F.R. § 422.210(a), SSA argues that the Appeals Council's denial of review cannot be reviewed by a federal court no matter what sort of error the Appeals Council made in conjunction with the additional evidence. Not all courts have agreed with SSA that they cannot review the Appeals Council's denial of review. And courts have struggled with how to treat evidence submitted to the Appeals Council:

- Can the additional evidence submitted to the Appeals Council be used to show that substantial evidence does not support the ALJ decision?
- May the additional evidence submitted to the Appeals Council be considered under sentence six of 42 U.S.C. § 405(g)? If so, is that additional evidence relevant only under sentence six, i.e., is it improper to consider the additional evidence except under sentence six?
- Is the Appeals Council's denial of review after considering the additional evidence subject to judicial review? If so, is it reviewable for factual and/or legal error? If the Appeals Council's denial of review may be reviewed by a federal court, is it reviewed under the substantial evidence standard or for an abuse of discretion?
- If the Commissioner does not include additional evidence timely submitted to the Appeals Council in the administrative record, can a court review whether the additional evidence should have been included in the administrative record?

It is essential to understand how the relevant circuit precedents answer—and do not answer—these questions. It is also essential to note conflicts within circuit law.

First Circuit: *Mills v. Apfel*, 244 F.3d 1 (1st Cir. 2001).

Second Circuit: *Perez v. Chater*, 77 F.3d 41 (2d Cir. 1996).

Third Circuit: *Matthews v. Apfel*, 239 F.3d 589 (3d Cir. 2001) (cited in *Reefer v. Barnhart*, 326 F.3d 376 (3d Cir. 2003)).

Fourth Circuit: *Meyer v. Astrue*, 662 F.3d 700 (4th Cir. 2011); *Wilkins v. Secretary, Dep't of Health and Human Servs.*, 953 F.2d 93 (4th Cir. 1991) (en banc).

Fifth Circuit: *Higginbotham v. Barnhart*, 405 F.3d 332 (5th Cir. 2005).

Sixth Circuit: *Cotton v. Sullivan*, 2 F.3d 692 (6th Cir. 1993) (cited in *Cline v. Commissioner of Social Security*, 96 F.3d 146 (6th Cir. 1996)).

Seventh Circuit: *Farrell v. Astrue*, 692 F.2d 767 (7th Cir. 2012); *Keys v. Barnhart,* 347 F.3d 990 (7th Cir. 2003); *Perkins v. Chater*, 107 F.3d 1290 (7th Cir. 1997); *Eads v. Secretary of Dep't of Health and Human Servs.*, 983 F.2d 815 (7th Cir. 1993); *Scivally v. Sullivan,* 966 F.2d 1070 (7th Cir. 1992); *Damato v. Sullivan,* 945 F.2d 982, 989 (7th Cir. 1991); *Nelson v. Bowen*, 855 F.2d 503 (7th Cir. 1988).

Eighth Circuit: *Bergmann v. Apfel*, 207 F.3d 1065 (8th Cir. 2000); *Riley v. Shalala*, 18 F.3d 619, 622 (8th Cir. 1994); *Nelson v. Sullivan*, 966 F.2d 363, 366 (8th Cir. 1992); *Browning v. Sullivan*, 958 F.2d 817 (8th Cir. 1992); but *see Sullins v. Shalala*, 25 F.3d 601 (8th Cir. 1994).

Ninth Circuit: *Brewes v. Commissioner*, 682 F.3d 1157 (9th Cir. 2012); *Harman v. Apfel*, 211 F.3d 1172 (9th Cir. 2000); *Ramirez v. Shalala*, 8 F.3d 1449, 1452 (9th Cir. 1993); but *see Mayes v. Massanari*, 276 F.3d 453 (9th Cir. 2001).

Tenth Circuit: *Krauser v. Astrue*, 638 F.3d 1324 (10th Cir. 2011); *Chambers v. Barnhart*, 389 F.3d 1139 (10th Cir. 2004); *O'Dell v. Shalala*, 44 F.3d 855 (10th Cir. 1994) (cited in *Threet v. Barnhart*, 353 F.3d 1185 (10th Cir. 2003); *Angel v. Barnhart*, 329 F.3d 1208 (10th Cir. 2003)).

Eleventh *Circuit: Falge v. Apfel*, 150 F.3d 1320 (11th Cir. 1998) (cited in *Vega v. Commissioner of Social Security*, 265 F.3d 1214 (11th Cir. 2001)).

§653 Post Hoc *Rationalizations*

You will find in many cases that the Commissioner's brief, which is filed in response to your arguments, offers the court a rationale for upholding the ALJ decision that does not appear in the ALJ decision itself. Such post hoc rationalizations are improper. The leading cases are to two U.S. Supreme Court decisions in the same case. *SEC v. Chenery Corp.*, 318 U.S. 80, 88 (1943); and *SEC v. Chenery Corp.*, 332 U.S. 194, 196 (1947). In the second case, the Court summarized its position:

> When the case was first here, we emphasized a simple but fundamental rule of administrative law. That rule is to the effect that a reviewing court, in dealing with a determination or judgment which an administrative agency alone is authorized to make, must judge the propriety of such action solely by the grounds invoked by the agency. If those grounds are inadequate or improper, the court is powerless to affirm the administrative action by substituting what it considers to be a more adequate or proper basis. To do so would propel the court into the domain which Congress has set aside exclusively for the administrative agency.

We also emphasized in our prior decision an important corollary of the foregoing rule. If the administrative action is to be tested by the basis on which it purports to rest, that basis must be set forth with such clarity as to be understandable. It will not do for a court to be compelled to guess at the theory underlying the agency's action; nor can a court be expected to chisel that which must be precise from what the agency has left vague and indecisive. In other words, "We must know what a decision means before the duty becomes ours to say whether it is right or wrong."

SEC v. Chenery Corp., 332 U.S. 194, 196-197 (1947), citations omitted.

Your job in the reply brief is to identify such post hoc rationalizations and explain why they are improper. All circuits have cases that may help your argument:

First Circuit: *Maine Gen. Med. Ctr. v. Shalala*, 205 F.3d 493, 501 (1st Cir. 2000).

Second Circuit: *Melville v. Apfel*, 198 F.3d 45, 52 (2d Cir. 1999); *Snell v. Apfel*, 177 F.3d 128, 134 (2d Cir. 1999).

Third Circuit: *Fargnoli v. Massanari*, 247 F.3d 34, 44 n.7 (3d Cir. 2001); *Sykes v. Apfel*, 228 F.3d 259, 271 (3d Cir. 2000); *Cotter v. Harris*, 642 F.2d 700, 707 n.7 (3d Cir. 1981).

Fourth Circuit: *Cunningham v. Harris*, 658 F.2d 239, 244 n.3 (4th Cir. 1981); *Combs v. Weinberger*, 501 F.2d 1361, 1363 n.2 (4th Cir. 1974).

Fifth Circuit: *Newton v. Apfel*, 209 F.3d 448, 455 (5th Cir. 2000); *Scott v. Shalala*, 30 F.3d 33, 35 (5th Cir. 1994).

Sixth Circuit: *Albertson's Inc. v. NLRB*, 301 F.3d 441, 453 (6th Cir. 2002).

Seventh Circuit: *Golembiewski v. Barnhart*, 322 F.3d 912, 916 (7th Cir. 2003); *Steele v. Barnhart*, 290 F.3d 936, 941 (7th Cir. 2002); *O'Connor v. Sullivan*, 938 F.2d 70, 73 (7th Cir. 1991).

Eighth Circuit: *Banks v. Massanari*, 258 F.3d 820, 824 (8th Cir. 2001).

Ninth Circuit: *Connett v. Barnhart*, 340 F.3d 871, 974 (9th Cir. 2003); *Pinto v. Massanari*, 249 F.3d 840, 847-48 (9th Cir. 2001).

Tenth Circuit: *Allen v. Barnhart*, 357 F.3d 1140, 1145 (10th Cir. 2004); *Reyes v. Bowen*, 845 F.2d 242, 244 (10th Cir. 1988).

Eleventh Circuit: *Owens v. Heckler*, 748 F.2d 1511, 1516 (11th Cir. 1984).

D.C. Circuit: *Butler v. Barnhart*, 353 F.3d 992, 1002 & n.5 (D.C. Cir. 2004); *Brown v. Bowen*, 794 F.2d 703, 708 n.7 (D.C. Cir. 1986).

§660 If You Lose

§661 Rule 59(e) Motion

Rule 59(e) of the Federal Rules of Civil Procedure allows a party to file a motion to alter or amend judgment within 10 days of entry of judgment. Such a motion is appropriate when a court has patently misunderstood a party, made a decision outside the adversarial issues presented by the parties, or has made an error "not of reasoning but of apprehension." *Refrigeration Sales Co. v. Mitchell-Jackson, Inc.*, 605 F. Supp. 6, 7 (N.D. Ill. 1983), aff'd, 770 F.2d 98 (7th Cir. 1985). A Rule 59(e) motion may also be based on an intervening change in controlling law, new evidence, need to correct a clear error of law or fact, and to prevent manifest injustice. *Hester Industries v. Tyson Foods*, 985 F. Supp. 83, 84 (N.D.N.Y. 1997). Although you cannot use a Rule 59(e) motion simply to reargue the case, many cases present issues that may be addressed with such a motion. Refer to appellate case law within your circuit for the precise standard for a Rule 59(e) motion. There are circuit variations. The cases cited here are simply examples.

When you file a Rule 59(e) motion, the time for appeal is stayed. However, you may file only one Rule 59(e) motion. An additional post-decision motion, or a motion where Rule 59(e) is inapplicable, must be brought under Fed. R. Civ. P. 60(b), which pertains to relief from judgment for a host of reasons including "mistake" and others not general applicable to disability appeals plus "any other reason justifying relief from the operation of the judgment." A Rule 60(b) motion, which may be brought up to one year after judgment is entered, does not stay the time for appeal, although you may request that the court order such a stay in conjunction with this motion.

§662 Appeal to Court of Appeals

As with any other civil action in federal court, you have the right to appeal an adverse district court judgment to the Court of Appeals. However, it is very important, not just in your case but for the development of disability law in general, that great care be exercised in choosing cases for review by the circuit court.

SSA wins nineteen out of twenty cases there. There is great potential for making bad law in many cases. Before you take any case to the court of appeals, consult with other knowledgeable lawyers about the prospects for success of a particular case.

Chapter 7

Attorney's Fees

---

§700 The Fee Agreement Process for Approval of Attorney Fees

Attorney fees in Social Security disability and SSI cases are regulated. 42 U.S.C. §§ 406(a) and 1383(d)(2). The Social Security Administration (SSA) must approve your fee for work done before the agency unless one of the very limited exceptions to this rule applies. *See* §746. If you accept an unauthorized fee, you could be punished by a fine not exceeding $500.00 or by imprisonment not exceeding one year, or both. 42 U.S.C. § 406(a)(5). You could also lose your right to practice before the Social Security Administration. 20 C.F.R. §§ 404.1740(c)(2) and 404.1745(b) & (c).

Two Fee Approval Systems

Two alternative systems with entirely different procedures, rules and time limits govern fee approval. One system, the fee petition process, described in §§720-739, is slow, burdensome, generally stingy and leaves inordinate discretion in the hands of decision makers. The other system, the fee agreement process, which provides for streamlined approval and payment of attorney fees, works better in the majority of cases.

Fee Petition Process Problems

The primary problem with the fee petition system is the typically long delay before payment. When the fee petition process is used, it is not unusual for it to take six months or more from the date of the favorable decision for a fee petition to be approved and another three months for payment to be made. In most hearing offices fee petitions are not handled expeditiously. Cynics say this is a deliberate effort by decision makers to discourage use of fee petitions and encourage use of the fee agreement process, a system that requires very little decision maker time. Those more charitable are not surprised that decision makers, who dislike the fee petition process almost as much as attorneys do and who have been busy with a large backlog of claims in recent years, give fee petition approval low priority.

The fee petition process is not only slow, it is also stingy. Attorneys seldom feel that they are paid the full value of their services under a system that steadfastly refuses to consider the contingent nature of fees and only rarely rewards outstanding work. For example, if you win tens of thousands of dollars for your client because of a brilliant inspiration that took very little time, you're likely to be granted a fee commensurate with the small amount of time spent on the case rather than a fee commensurate with your brilliant inspiration. An arbitrary hourly rate cap, a factor not listed for consideration in the regulations, is silently applied.

Fee Agreement Process

The fee agreement process, designed to address the limitations of the fee petition system, is faster; and, although it contains traps for those who do not carefully follow its complicated rules, it is a vast improvement. Nevertheless, one cannot expect too much from the fee agreement process. When the fee agreement process began, many attorneys thought that at last SSA had recognized the contingent nature of fees. These attorneys also thought that by using the fee agreement process, they could represent almost all claimants without having to worry about the adequacy of fees in any single case. They thought that average fees would be adequate. But attorneys have discovered that it remains necessary to avoid using the fee agreement process in too many cases with small or non-existent back benefits because the good-paying cases may not sufficiently bring up the overall average.

Fee Agreement Process Problem—Appeals Beyond ALJ Hearing

Attorneys have found that the fee agreement process pays smaller fees than the fee petition process in time-consuming cases such as those involving appeals beyond the ALJ hearing level. Indeed, the more hours an attorney spends on a case, the lower the average hourly fee because under the fee agreement process, fees are limited to a maximum of $6,000. As we shall see, however, there is a way to seek higher fees in cases involving appeals beyond the ALJ hearing level by using a two-tiered fee agreement. *See* §703 and the two-tiered fee agreement in §178.3.1.

Fee Agreement Process Problem—Subsequent Applications

In a case where a second application is paid while the first is on appeal to federal court (or in those rare cases where SSA allows a second application to be filed while a case is on appeal to the Appeals Council), SSA will treat the two applications as one case for purposes of applying the fee agreement cap. The attorney may spend an average amount of time on the case involving the second application and receive a $6,000 fee. After winning on the first application, the one that took years of work, the attorney will be dismayed to discover that it is SSA's position that no additional fee is due under the fee agreement process. Because the attorney accepted the fee from the case involving the second application, SSA says the attorney elected to treat the entire case as coming under the fee agreement process. The attorney has already received a maximum fee. *See* §716.1. However, if the case went to federal court, the court can approve an additional fee under 42 U.S.C. § 406(b). *See* §§750 *ff.*

Fee Agreement Process Problem—Partially Favorable Decisions

The fee agreement process discourages appeals, especially appeals of partially favorable decisions. *See* §716. It discourages taking hard cases at a time when SSA says that its goal is to have ALJs hear only hard cases—with easier cases being paid at a lower level of review.

Fee Agreement Process Problem—The Cap

Part of the problem is that the fee agreement process places a cap on attorney fees, which is currently $6,000. The Social Security Act provides that the Commissioner of Social Security "from time to time" may increase the cap by no more than the annual COLA percentage increase. 42 U.S.C. § 406(a)(2)(A). The cap has been raised only twice since 1991 when the fee agreement process was instituted. The Commissioner raised the cap to $5,300 applicable to favorable decisions issued on or after February 1, 2002. 67 Fed. Reg. 2,477 (2002). The cap was raised to $6,000 applicable to favorable decisions issued on or after June 22, 2009. 74 Fed. Reg. 6080 (2009). *See also* HALLEX I-1-2-12 A.3.

Many observers question whether a cap is appropriate at all in a hard-fought case or where lawyer creativity increases back benefits by, for example, reopening an earlier application. There are those who argue that without a cap on fees, the lawyer's interests and the client's interests would be congruent—both would want to maximize the recovery in each case. With a cap on fees, if the lawyer has already received a maximum fee, what is the lawyer's interest in appealing a partially favorable decision? It is a good thing that most lawyers are motivated not only by law office economics but also by professional responsibility to the client, lawyer ethics and a desire to do the right thing. Otherwise, very few appeals of a partially favorable decision would be taken.

No Fee Agreement Process Regulations

Another part of the problem with the fee agreement process is that the Commissioner never published regulations required by 42 U.S.C. § 406(a)(3) for dealing with appeals. Instead, decision makers rely on the HALLEX and the POMS and, for fee issues not covered, they appear to make up the rules as they go along based on principles that often ignore the realities of modern-day law practice. *See* §709.

Fee Agreement Process Exceptions

You will need to pay special attention to SSA's set of exceptions, circumstances where the fee agreement process does not apply, that appear only in the HALLEX and POMS. The most common exceptions involve multiple representatives:

- Where the claimant had a prior representative;
- Where the claimant appoints multiple representatives from the same firm and all do not sign a common fee agreement; and
- Where the claimant appoints multiple representatives and all are not members of a single law firm.

SSA says that these exceptions themselves will not apply if the extra representative waives his or her fee.

There are also exceptions for when a representative dies before a favorable decision is issued and when a state court declares the claimant legally incompetent and the claimant's legal guardian does not sign the fee agreement. In addition, if a federal court issues a decision awarding benefits, SSA says that the representative's fee for work before the agency will not be paid under the fee agreement process. Whenever an exception applies, it will be necessary for you to file a fee petition to obtain your fee. *See* §705.

When to Use the Fee Petition System

In most cases where past-due benefits accumulate, the fee agreement process is the better fee approval system. Because it is the best way to obtain a minimum fee, the fee petition process is recommended for cases where you can predict in advance that past-due benefits will be minimal (such as where a claimant is recently disabled or offsets apply) or non-existent (such as benefit termination, overpayment or other post-entitlement cases). The fee petition process is otherwise simply too much trouble for too little reward.

Of course, if you could predict in advance which case would become a protracted one, one that you would fight for years, you would choose the fee petition process for that case. Although such predictions are usually impossible, it is possible to make a contract with your client that applies the fee agreement process, for example, through the first ALJ hearing; but after that, the fee petition process applies. *See* §703 and the two-tiered fee agreement at §178.3.1.

§701 Conditions for Fee Agreement Process

The fee agreement process for obtaining approval of a fee provides for virtually automatic payment of your fee if:

1. You agree to limit your fee to the lesser of 25 percent of total past-due benefits (including combined past-due benefits in concurrent claims) or $6,000 (or such higher limit as the Commissioner of Social Security may set under 42 U.S.C. § 406(a)(2)(A));
2. The fee agreement is signed by both the claimant and the attorney;

3.   SSA receives your fee agreement before a favorable decision is issued;
4.   No exception to the fee agreement process applies;
5.   A favorable decision is issued;
6.   The claim results in past-due benefits; and
7.   There is no objection from the claimant, an auxiliary beneficiary or the decision maker.

§702 The Lesser of 25% of Past-Due Benefits or $6,000

To qualify for the fee agreement process, the fee stated in the agreement must be limited to the lesser of 25 percent of past-due benefits or $6,000. This crucial limitation is based on 42 U.S.C. § 406(a)(2)(A)(ii), which provides that the fee agreement process will apply if:
The fee specified in the agreement does not exceed the lesser of—
(I) 25 percent of the total amount of such past-due benefits (as determined before any applicable reduction under section 1320a-6(a) of this title [pertaining to the SSI windfall offset]), or
(II) $4,000 ....
The $4,000 cap set by the statute was raised to $5,300 by action of the Commissioner of Social Security under the authority of 42 U.S.C. § 406(a)(2)(A) effective February 1, 2002. 67 Fed. Reg. 2,477 (2002). The cap was raised to $6,000 effective June 22, 2009. 74 Fed. Reg. 6080 (2009). *See also* HALLEX I-1-2-12 A.3.

Although another increase in the cap is not expected soon, you may, if you wish, include reference in your fee agreement to the Commissioner's authority to raise the cap by no more than the COLA applicable to Title II benefits pursuant to 42 U.S.C. § 406(a)(2)(A): "The Commissioner of Social Security may from time to time increase the dollar amount under clause (ii)(II) to the extent that the rate of increase in such amount, as determined over the period since January 1, 1991, does not at any time exceed the rate of increase in primary insurance amounts under section 415(i) of this title since such date." *See* HALLEX I-1-2-12 A.3. Note 1. The fee agreement that appears at §178.3.1 qualifies.

§703 Possible Additional Fee Agreement Provisions

Allowed: Representative May Seek Administrative Review
Many attorneys would like SSA to approve a fee agreement that allows for automatic payment of a fee up to $6,000 with the right to file a fee petition to ask for

more money in unusual cases. Although SSA explicitly says that such an agreement will not be approved, HALLEX I-1-2-12 C.3.a., the statute itself provides the attorney with the right to appeal the amount of the fee calculated under the formula stated in the statute, 42 U.S.C. § 406(a)(3)(A)(ii), and SSA says that reference to the attorney's appeal rights may be included in a fee agreement. HALLEX I-1-2-12 C.2.

SSA will approve a fee agreement, which provides that the representative may seek administrative review "of the amount of the fee if the past-due benefits do not exceed a certain amount." HALLEX I-1-2-12 C.2. For example, a fee agreement will be approved containing this provision: "If SSA favorably decides the claim, the representative's fee will be 25 percent of the past-due benefits or $6,000, whichever is less, except if the past-due benefits do not exceed $1,250, the representative may seek administrative review of the amount that would otherwise be the maximum fee." This merely indicates the representative's intent to request administrative review if a desired fee is not realized.

Not Allowed: Representative May Petition for a Greater Fee
Although a fee agreement can include reference to seeking administrative review, a fee agreement will not be approved if it contains language such as this: "If 25 percent of the past-due benefits exceeds $6,000, the representative will receive a fee of $6,000 and retains the right to petition for an additional fee." HALLEX I-1-2-12 C.3.a. Note includes this explanation: "Do not confuse 'petition' with 'request administrative review.' Whereas a representative retains the right to request administrative review under the fee agreement process, he/she may not substitute the fee petition process for the fee agreement process after SSA issues a favorable decision."

Not Allowed: Minimum Fee Clause
SSA takes the position that compliance of the fee agreement with the statute must be apparent from the face of the agreement at the time the fee agreement is approved. For this reason, SSA will not accept a fee agreement that calls for a minimum fee. HALLEX I-1-2-12 C.3.a. In other words, SSA will reject a fee agreement that says that "the fee will be 25 percent of past-due benefits or $6,000, whichever is less, except that if 25 percent of past-due benefits does not exceed $1,500, the representative's fee will be $1,500." HALLEX I-1-2-12 A.3. Note 3. Attorneys have argued that such an agreement could be approved subject to 25 percent of past-due benefits being over $1,500. But SSA has rejected this argument.

Allowed: Lesser Fee and Fee if Claim Denied

On the other hand, a fee agreement calling for a lesser fee than that permitted by the statutory limitation will be approved. A fee agreement that comports with the statute but also provides for a fee if the claim is denied will be approved since the question whether the fee agreement complies with the statute will be addressed only when a favorable decision is issued. The language pertaining to what happens if the claim is denied is therefore irrelevant to its compliance with the statutory requirement.

Allowed: Third-Party Payment, Share Fee With Referring Attorney, Interest, Taxes

SSA will approve a fee agreement stating that a third party will pay the representative a fee equal to the lesser of 25 percent of past-due benefits or $6,000, and the claimant will have no liability for paying the fee. A fee agreement will be approved that states that the representative will share the authorized fee with another person who referred the case. SSA also says that it will approve a fee agreement that charges interest on the unpaid balance of the authorized fee. HALLEX I-1-2-12 C.2 and POMS GN 03940.003C.2.

SSA allows provisions in fee agreements regarding payment of expenses or state sales tax. HALLEX I-1-2-12 C.2.

Allowed: Two-Tiered Fee Agreement

SSA will approve a two-tiered fee agreement; that is, a contract that makes the fee agreement process apply through a certain level of administrative review and the fee petition process applies after that. When the second tier is applicable, that is, when it will be necessary to file a fee petition, SSA decision makers must disapprove the fee agreement. HALLEX I-1-2-15 provides an example below of when a two-tiered fee agreement will be approved and when it will be disapproved:

The claimant and representative submit a fee agreement that provides the following:

1. If SSA favorably decides the claim(s) at or below the first Administrative Law Judge (ALJ) hearing decision, the fee shall be the lesser of 25 percent of past-due benefits or $6,000.
2. If the claim progresses beyond that level of the administrative review process, the representative will request a fee through the fee petition process.

If the applicable clause is the first clause, the requirement of § 206(a)(2)(A)(ii) of the Social Security Act is satisfied (i.e., the fee requested did not exceed the lesser of 25 percent of past-due benefits or $6,000), and the ALJ will approve the agreement if it meets all other conditions for approval and no exceptions apply.

If the second clause applies (*e.g.*, the ALJ issues the first favorable decision following a remand by the Appeals Council (AC)), § 206(a)(2)(A)(ii) of the Social Security Act would not be satisfied and the ALJ will disapprove the fee agreement because the fee specified was not limited to the lesser of 25 percent of past-due benefits or $6,000.

If the representative's involvement begins after the initial hearing decision and the representative and claimant enter into an agreement that applies to administrative decisions made through the initial hearing decision, the SSA decision maker cannot approve the fee agreement.

Practice Tip

Note that if you become involved in a claimant's case after an ALJ denial decision has been issued and your contract contains the language of the HALLEX sample two-tiered fee agreement, it is pointless to file this agreement with SSA. There are no circumstances under which the fee agreement process can be invoked since the sample contract makes the fee agreement process applicable only through the first ALJ decision, which was issued before you got involved in the case.

The sample contract provided in this book, §178.3.1, on the other hand, is designed to make the fee agreement process apply through the first ALJ decision after the date of the agreement, no matter when you become involved.

§704   Timely Submission of the Fee Agreement to SSA

The statute requires that the fee agreement be presented to SSA before SSA issues a favorable determination regarding the claim. 42 U.S.C. § 406(a)(2)(A)(i). You can turn in the fee agreement on the day of the hearing or at any time up to the day before the favorable decision is issued. But it is better to submit it early. The best time to submit the fee agreement is when you send an Appointment of Representative form to SSA. *See* §§182 and 183 for form transmittal letters.

Indeed, SSA takes the position that for the fee agreement process to apply, you must submit the fee agreement before the first favorable decision is issued after you enter the case. For example, say you enter the case at the reconsideration stage but fail to submit a fee agreement. If a partially favorable determination is issued on reconsideration, SSA says your fee agreement will not be approved if you submit it when you later appeal the claimant's case to the ALJ hearing level. HALLEX I-1-2-14 A. and POMS GN 03940.004C.1.

Before electronic Social Security files became the norm, it was a common occurrence that a paper contract did not get associated with the paper Social Security file before a favorable decision was issued. This problem can be solved by persistence and proof that the contract was timely submitted. Once SSA figures out that a contract had, in fact, been timely submitted, it is supposed to approve the fee agreement and pay the fee under the fee agreement process. *See*, for example, HALLEX I-1-2-21 C.3.

With electronic files, no matter which component of SSA receives your contract, all components have access to it in the electronic folder. Problems still occur, though, when the contract does not make it to the electronic folder. A contract and Appointment of Representative form are usually the first documents submitted by a representative, and these initial documents are usually submitted on paper. Thus, someone at SSA must scan and insert these documents into the electronic folder. Although it doesn't happen often that a contract does not make it to the electronic folder, it is nevertheless good practice to be able to prove that your contract was submitted to SSA. Some lawyers submit the contract and Appointment of Representative form by certified mail. Others hand deliver them to a local office or a hearing office and obtain a received stamp on a copy. Others fax the contract and Appointment of Representative form which produces a fax confirmation.

Always submit such things with a cover letter. State in your cover letter that you are sending the fee agreement so that the "fee agreement process" will apply to your fee in the case. *See* sample cover letters at §§182, 183, 192, 193. In later letters to SSA, mention that you submitted a fee agreement. Because the Appointment of Representative form, SSA-1696, *see* §178.2.1, is always treated by SSA as an important document, some attorneys attach the fee agreement and state on the Appointment of Representative form: FEE AGREEMENT ATTACHED.

Because SSA says it will accept a fee agreement that is combined with the Appointment of Representative document, HALLEX I-1-2-11, some lawyers submit only one document. A lawyer who does this is able to argue that if SSA recognizes the lawyer as the claimant's representative, i.e., SSA must have received the appointment form, SSA must have also received the contract.

If an ALJ denial decision is issued before you have sent the fee agreement to SSA, you may send a fee agreement to the Appeals Council. Be sure to send it by fax or by certified mail, return receipt requested, so that you can prove when the Appeals Council received it.

If you filed your fee agreement with the hearing office in a case where an ALJ issues a denial decision, it is unnecessary to file the fee agreement again with the Appeals Council. If the Appeals Council reverses the ALJ and issues a favorable decision, the Appeals Council should also approve your fee agreement. Once a fee agreement is submitted to SSA, unless it expires by its own terms, it remains in effect throughout the administrative appeal process of a claim, and during the administrative proceedings following a court remand. HALLEX I-1-2-11.

§705   *Exceptions to the Fee Agreement Process*

According to HALLEX I-1-2-12 B, a fee agreement will not be approved in the following situations, thus making a fee petition necessary to obtain your fee:

1. The claimant appointed more than one representative associated in a firm, partnership or legal corporation and all representatives did not sign a single fee agreement.

NOTE: This exception does not apply if the representative(s) who did not sign the fee agreement waived charging and collecting a fee.

2. The claimant appointed representatives who are not members of a single firm, partnership or legal corporation.

NOTE: This exception does not apply if the claimant and the appointed representative(s) from a single firm, partnership or legal corporation signed the fee agreement and any other appointed representative(s) waived charging and collecting a fee.

Example:

The claimant appointed attorneys Brown and Smith of the law firm Brown and Smith PC as her representatives. Subsequently, the claimant also appoints attorney Jones of the law firm Black and Jones PC. The claimant and attorneys Brown and Smith enter into a fee agreement that they submitted to SSA. Attorney Jones waived charging and collecting a fee. The decision maker in this situation would approve the fee agreement. However, if attorneys Brown and Jones had submitted the fee agreement and attorney Smith had waived charging and collecting a fee, the decision maker would have to disapprove the fee agreement because the representatives who signed the fee agreement were not members of a single firm, partnership or legal corporation.

3. The claimant discharged a representative or a representative withdrew from the case before SSA favorably decided the claim.

NOTE: If the claimant appointed another representative after discharging the former representative or after the former representative withdrew, this exception does not apply if the former representative waived charging and collecting a fee.

4. The representative died before SSA issued the favorable decision.

When the representative dies before SSA issues a favorable decision and the claimant or representative submitted an otherwise valid fee agreement, the decision maker will:

• disapprove the fee agreement, and

• notify the parties, including the deceased's estate, that the agreement is excepted from the fee agreement process, but that the estate of the deceased representative may request SSA's authorization to charge and collect a fee by filing a fee petition.

5. A State court declared the claimant legally incompetent and the claimant's legal guardian did not sign the fee agreement.

NOTE: If SSA determined that the claimant is mentally incapable of managing his or her funds or is in the process of evaluating the claimant's mental capability, the effectuating component will defer sending notice regarding the amount of the fee under the fee agreement until SSA has selected a representative payee.

None of the above exceptions appear in the statute.

Here is an exception that SSA says appears in the statute, although SSA's interpretation might not have occurred to you. SSA says that the fee agreement process applies only when the Social Security Administration, not a federal court, issues the favorable decision. That is, in those rare instances where a federal court issues a favorable decision that orders SSA to pay the claimant, SSA says that the fee agreement process cannot apply to the part of your fee for representation before the agency. Thus, to be paid for your work before the agency, after the federal court sets the fee for court representation,

SSA says you must send a fee petition to the Attorney Fee Branch at the Appeals Council. *See Social Security Forum*, Volume 23, No. 3, March 2001, p. 50.

§706   *Approval of Fee Agreement*

If your fee agreement contains the magic language, is signed by both you and your client, is submitted before the favorable decision is issued, and no exceptions apply, it must be approved by the decision maker when a favorable decision is issued. This is not a discretionary task. The statute provides if the criteria are met, the Commissioner shall approve the agreement at the time of the favorable determination. 42 U.S.C. § 406(a)(2)(A).

SSA has said that you do not have to submit an original fee agreement. A photocopy or fax is good enough. A representative may use a stamped signature; but a fee agreement stamped only with a firm name is not acceptable. Although the contract can be with the law firm, if someone other than the appointed representative is the only person who signed the fee agreement on behalf of the firm, the decision maker must disapprove the fee agreement. But if all appointed representatives sign the fee agreement, it doesn't matter if there are additional signatures on the fee agreement as long as everyone who signed is a member of the same firm. HALLEX I-1-2-12 A.2.

There is no requirement that a representative's signature be legible; but if the signature raises a question about the representative's identity, the decision maker is instructed to contact the representative. HALLEX I-1-2-12 A.2.

The HALLEX states that, with a favorable decision, SSA will mail "the determination on the fee agreement in a written notice separate from the decision on the claim" to the claimant and representative. HALLEX I-1-2-17 A. If the decision maker has disapproved the fee agreement, notice will be given informing the claimant and the attorney of the right to request administrative review. HALLEX I-1-2-17 A.2. Review at this point is limited to the issue of whether or not the fee agreement ought to have been approved. *See* §707. This administrative review is not to be confused with the review available to the claimant, affected auxiliaries, the decision maker and the attorney on the amount of the fee. *See* §§712, *et seq*. Thus, the opportunity for administrative review is presented twice in the fee agreement process.

If the decision maker fails to address the issue of whether or not the fee agreement is approved, bring this immediately to the attention of the decision maker. A sample letter for this purpose appears at §406. HALLEX I-1-2-21 C.3 states that if the ALJ did not make a fee agreement determination, "the ALJ must review the fee agreement, make his/her determination, and send a copy to the claimant, the representative, and the P[rocessing] C[enter]. . . ." Indeed, if a fee agreement is found in the file at the time benefits are being paid, the payment center has instructions to contact the decision maker to obtain an order approving or disapproving the fee agreement. POMS GN 03940.025C.3. HALLEX I-1-2-21 C.3 Note.

§707 Administrative Review if the Decision Maker Disapproves the Fee Agreement

If the decision maker disapproves a fee agreement, the notice that comes with the favorable decision will advise the parties of the right to request administrative review. The claimant or representative must file a request for administrative review within 15 days of receiving the notice. HALLEX I-1-2-17 A.2. Absent evidence to the contrary, SSA assumes receipt of the notice within five days of the date of the notice. HALLEX I-1-2-41 C.

The notice will state the address of where to send the appeal. For the appeal of an ALJ order, this administrative review will go to the Regional Chief Administrative Law Judge (RCALJ) unless it was the RCALJ who made the decision, in which case it will go to the Chief ALJ or deputy. If the Appeals Council made the decision, administrative review will go to the Deputy Chair of the Appeals Council. HALLEX I-1-2-42 B.

After receiving a timely request for administrative review, the reviewing official must notify the parties, including the decision maker who disapproved the fee agreement, that they will be allowed 15 days to comment. HALLEX I-1-2-42 C. Only after the comment period has lapsed will a notice be issued concerning the final determination on the fee agreement. The notice will indicate that the determination is not subject to further review. HALLEX I-1-2-42 E.

Administrative review can be useful for testing contracts at the limit of that which is allowed under the statute. Once a contract passes muster on administrative review, it is helpful to submit a copy of the administrative review order along with similar contracts filed in other cases.

§708 Changing the Terms of a Fee Agreement

When SSA raised the fee cap to $6,000, which was effective June 22, 2009, SSA decision makers were instructed to accept a revised fee agreement with the $6,000 cap as long as it was submitted before a favorable decision was issued. HALLEX I-1-2-12 C.1 provides, "The decision maker will act on the most recently

negotiated and signed fee agreement SSA received before the date of the favorable decision." Also, HALLEX I-1-2-11 states that a contract "may be amended, before the date of the favorable decision, to comply with the requirements of the fee agreement process."

In other circumstances, there may be times where you and your client want to abandon a fee agreement that has been filed with SSA and, instead, use the fee petition process for approval of the fee. For example, in those rare cases involving multiple remands by the Appeals Council and multiple hearings, a $6,000 fee may be only a small fraction of the claimant's back benefits and may not adequately compensate the attorney for the time involved in the case. How do you withdraw a fee agreement?

First, be sure your state bar rules allow changing the terms of a fee agreement in the middle of a case.

Second, be sure you address this question before a favorable decision is issued. After a favorable decision is issued, SSA will not allow you to change the terms of your agreement with your client, even if you have your client's full approval. Thus, your only recourse at that point will be to appeal the amount of your fee, not a wholly satisfactory alternative since you will have to explain why the fee amount determined under the fee agreement process is not reasonable and you will have no opportunity for further appeal. *See* §715.

Third, SSA's instructions say nothing about changing from the fee agreement process to the fee petition process during the pendency of an administrative action, that is, before a favorable decision is issued. Nevertheless, because HALLEX I-1-2-12 provides that the "decision maker will act on the most recently negotiated and signed fee agreement SSA received before the date of the favorable decision," instead of trying to withdraw a fee agreement, submit a new contract that does not meet the requirements of the fee agreement process. The decision maker will have to issue an order disapproving the fee agreement. The following procedure should work:

1. Make a new fee agreement (e.g., a straight 25 percent contingent fee) with your client;
2. Include in the new fee agreement a statement that you and your client have agreed that the earlier agreement is null and void and that when you file a fee petition, you will include all time spent working on the client's case; and
3. Send a copy of the new agreement to SSA with a letter explaining that the new agreement supersedes the old one and that you intend to file a fee petition in this client's case once a favorable decision is issued.

The extra language for a superseding fee agreement, described in #2 above, is to avoid any argument by SSA that your new fee agreement applies only to hours worked after the date of the new agreement, thus treating all time spent on the case previously as time spent on a lost cause.

A few ALJs have treated superseding contracts as null and void on the grounds that there was no consideration, that is, nothing of value was given to the claimant in exchange for signing a new contract. Thus, the earlier contract would be approved under the fee agreement process. The solution to this problem is simple: 1) give consideration; and 2) explain the consideration in the new contract. For example, assuming your state bar rules allow it, you could relieve the claimant of the obligation to pay expenses under the new contract. Also, assuming that your original contract does not commit you to represent the claimant on an appeal, a new contract can be negotiated at the critical juncture where you agree to appeal the claimant's case.

Practice Tip

A two-tiered contract, such as the one in this book, §178.3.1, automatically switches the case to the fee petition process after receiving an ALJ denial decision. What if after getting the ALJ denial decision, you and your client want to switch back to the fee agreement process? If you and your client sign, date and submit to SSA a new contract using the language of the two-tiered fee agreement in this book, you have effectively switched back to the fee agreement process until the next ALJ decision is issued. HALLEX I-1-2-11 specifically provides for amending a contract "to comply with the requirements of the fee agreement process." Since the new contract limits your fee, no one can complain that there is no consideration. If you receive another ALJ denial decision, the new contract automatically switches to the fee petition process.

§709 Law Firms, Paralegals and Multiple Representatives

Those most charitable to SSA say that SSA simply does not understand how lawyers work in law firms. Others view the impediments to efficient representation created by SSA as examples of anti-lawyer bias within SSA. Whichever way you view it, you need to be aware of SSA's rules so that you may avoid pitfalls. At the same time, however, note that these law firm-unfriendly rules are not always followed for reasons such as "system limitations," *e.g.*, SSA's computer system is not good at keeping track of multiple representatives, or the fact that many administrative law judges once worked in law firms. This presents a peculiar predicament for office

management: Do you ignore some of the rules discussed below?

Law firms, which are legal entities, regard clients to be clients of the firm, not of the individual lawyers. Contracts are made between the client and the firm. Fees received are property of the firm. In disability cases, for a variety of different reasons, law firms often want to appoint multiple representatives for a claimant. Some firms want the flexibility to have one of several lawyers attend the hearing, depending on the work load. Some firms, desiring to protect themselves against potential problems created by an associate leaving the firm, appoint an owner of the firm and an associate. Some firms want to appoint a paralegal and an attorney as the representatives and send the paralegal to the hearing.

All Appointed Representatives Must Sign a Single Fee Agreement

Although SSA has agreed that a contract may be between the client and the firm, in practice it treats the case as if the contract were between the claimant and each individual appointed representative. For a contract to be approved under the fee agreement process, the contract must be signed by all of the claimant's appointed representatives. If it turns out that there is someone from the firm appointed as a representative who did not sign the contract, the contract must be disapproved unless the representative who did not sign the contract waives charging and collecting a fee. HALLEX I-1-2-3 B and I-1-2-12 B.1.

Some law firms have had representatives who were appointed after the date on the fee agreement simply sign the original fee agreement and resubmit it to SSA. This is insufficient under standard contract law, especially for ALJs who view the contract as between the claimant and each appointed representative. ALJs have been known to treat such a contract as invalid unless the claimant signs (or at least initials) and dates the contract again.

Reduction of Fee if Co-Representative From Same Firm Waives Fee

Although this doesn't always happen in practice, when it comes time to pay the fee, SSA's rules require the payment center to divide the fee by the number of appointed representatives and pay each representative separately. If one representative from the same firm as the other representatives waives charging and collecting a fee, that representative's share is supposed to be paid to the claimant, thus reducing the total fee paid in the case. *See* §709.1 and §709.2, HALLEX I-1-2-18 and POMS GN 03940.009A. In other words, fee reduction occurs only in very limited circumstances. When a co-representative from outside the firm waives charging and collecting a fee, there is no fee reduction. See EM-13024, §709.2.

Successive Representatives

When a claimant fires a representative or a representative withdraws from a case and a new representative is appointed, no fee agreement will be approved unless the previous representative waives charging and collecting a fee. Under these circumstances, SSA says it will not proportionately reduce the fee if the representatives are not from the same firm. But SSA will send half of the fee back to the claimant "if the former and successor representative are affiliated or other circumstances indicate that the successor representative could obtain fees for the work of a former representative." *See* the answer to question 6, §709.1, from *Social Security Forum*, Vol. 25, No. 7, July 2003, p. 16. See also EM-13024, §709.2.

Paralegal Representatives

If both an attorney and a paralegal sign Appointment of Representative forms and a fee agreement, when it comes time to pay the fee, SSA is supposed to pay one-half of the authorized fee to the attorney and, unless the paralegal has been qualified as eligible for direct payment of fees, send the other half to the claimant. SSA will send the paralegal and the claimant a letter saying that since the paralegal is not an attorney, it will be necessary for the paralegal to collect the paralegal's share of the fee from the claimant. POMS GN 03920.050A.2.b.

When Non-Appointed Representative Appears at Hearing

If a paralegal or another attorney appears at a hearing without being an appointed representative, the ALJ is instructed to assume that he or she is acting as a "co-representative" "because the representative may not delegate to an unappointed assistant the authority to undertake tasks that require making significant decisions regarding the case, such as appearing as the claimant's advocate in a hearing before an ALJ." The ALJ is supposed to ask the claimant to officially appoint the person who appears at the hearing as a co-representative. POMS GN 03940.003 C.3.b. If this "co-representative" did not sign the fee agreement, the ALJ is supposed to disapprove the fee agreement. If the "co-representative" signed the fee agreement, it will be approved. HALLEX I-1-2-12 C.3.b. If the co-representative is a paralegal who has not been qualified for direct payment of fees, the paralegal's share of the fee must be collected directly from the claimant.

Creating an Association With the Firm for Outside Lawyer

Sometimes, because of schedule conflicts, a law firm will make arrangements for a lawyer from outside the firm to handle a hearing for a client. This is done so that the client will get an earlier hearing than would otherwise be possible. If a lawyer from outside the firm appears at the hearing, he or she must waive a fee in order for the fee agreement to be approved. Although the waiver does not reduce the fee pursuant to EM-13024, §709.2, if the lawyer is paid for handling the hearing. SSA may view the lawyer as receiving an unauthorized fee and submitting a fraudulent waiver to SSA.

There are two ways to deal with this situation within SSA's rules. First, everyone could be paid using the fee petition process. Second, although it is cumbersome, it is possible to satisfy SSA that the outside lawyer is associated with the firm. To accomplish this, the outside lawyer must complete an SSA-1699, see §178.4.1, that includes the firm name, address, EIN, etc. (SSA allows a lawyer to have multiple SSA-1699s on file showing associations with multiple firms.) The outside lawyer must submit an SSA-1695, see §178.4.2, that includes the firm's EIN; and a new fee agreement must be submitted that is signed by all representatives, including the lawyer from outside the firm (who is now treated by SSA as associated with the firm). The fee agreement will be approved. No SSA rules are violated when the outside lawyer is paid by the firm.

Qualified Non-Attorney Representatives

Beginning in 2005, under the Social Security Protection Act of 2003, SSA conducted a demonstration project in which qualified non-attorneys had the option of having fees withheld by SSA and paid directly to the non-attorney representatives. This program was made permanent in 2010. Pub. L. No. 111-142. To qualify, non-attorneys must: 1) hold a bachelor's degree or equivalent experience; 2) pass an examination written and administered by SSA; 3) secure professional liability insurance or the equivalent; 4) undergo a criminal background check; and 5) complete continuing education courses.

§709.1   *SSA Answers to NOSSCR: Fee Agreements and Multiple Representatives*

The following document contains answers to questions submitted to SSA by NOSSCR. These answers were originally published in the *Social Security Forum*, Vol. 25, No. 7, July 2003, pp. 13-16 with a cover letter from William C. Taylor, Acting Deputy Associate Commissioner for Field Operations, dated May 27,

2003. At the time it was issued, this document was circulated within SSA payment centers. It is reprinted here with permission of NOSSCR to make it more easily accessible because it continues to be a clear summary of SSA policy on multiple representatives, except that some non-attorney representatives became eligible for fee withholding as of February 28, 2005. There are also a few out-of-date citations that are identified in brackets in the text.

Fee Agreements and Multiple Representatives

1. If an attorney is the claimant's appointed representative, can a paralegal from the same office represent the claimant at the hearing?

Yes, if the claimant appoints the paralegal as his/her representative, in writing, and the paralegal meets the requirements set forth in SSA's regulations. Assuming that the paralegal is not an attorney, he/she must be:

- Generally known to have a good character and reputation;

- Capable of giving valuable help to the claimant in connection with the claim;

- Not disqualified or suspended from acting as a representative in dealings with SSA; and

- Not prohibited by any law from acting as a representative. (20 CFR §§ 404.1705(b) and 416.1505(b).)

SSA considers the types of tasks an advocate for the claimant must perform at an oral hearing before an Administrative Law Judge or other agency official to constitute the essence of representation. Accordingly, SSA requires that an individual appearing at an oral hearing as the claimant's sole advocate be appointed by the claimant. (Hearings, Appeals, and Litigation Law manual (HALLEX) 1-1-2-12 C.3.b.; Program Operations Manual System (POMS) GN 03910.025 3.)

To appoint the paralegal, the claimant must sign Form SSA-1696-U4 (Appointment of Representative) or an equivalent written notice of appointment, naming the paralegal as his/her representative. A nonattorney representative must also sign the notice accepting the appointment, as required by regulation. (20 CFR §§ 404.1707 and 416.1507; POMS GN 03910.040B.l.)

Unless the claimant discharges the attorney, or the attorney withdraws from the case, SSA will consider the attorney and the paralegal to be co-representatives. SSA will make contacts with, and send requests for development or copies of notices to, only the principal representative. Therefore, the claimant should indicate on Form SSA-1696, or otherwise state for the record, who the principal representative is. Form SSA-1696 has a specific item requesting this information. (POMS GN 03910.040D.)

If the claimant intends that his/her appointment of a representative supersede a previous appointment in the same claim or if a representative withdraws from the claim, SSA must receive a written statement to that effect. Otherwise, SSA will continue to recognize both appointed representatives until their services end and their authority to represent the claimant expires. For how SSA treats fees in such situations, please refer to responses to questions 4, 5, and 6 below.

2. My office has several attorneys. When a client comes to our office, we do not know who will be at the hearing.

   a. How can we be sure our appointment of representative will be acknowledged and our fee agreement will be approved?

The claimant must appoint an individual (or individuals) as his or her representative(s). SSA does not recognize entities (firms, partnerships, corporations, or other businesses) as representatives. (20 CFR §§ 404.1703, 404.1707, 416.1503, and 416.1507; HALLEX 1-1-1-10.)

When SSA receives a notice of appointment (see response to question 1) appointing someone in your office as a claimant's representative, that person should receive the representative's copy of Form SSA-1696, or the original of Form SSA-LI697-U3 (Notice to Representative of Claimant Before the Social Security Administration). (HALLEX 1-1-1-11; POMS GN 03910.040H.) If the representative or the claimant submitted the signed notice of appointment and did not receive such acknowledgment, contact the SSA office to which the notice was submitted in order to ensure that the appointment is properly reflected on SSA's records.

SSA will approve a fee agreement, and will authorize the fee amount specified in the approved agreement, if the fee agreement meets the statutory requirements set forth in sections 206(a)(2)(A) and 1631(d)(2)(A) of the Social Security Act and no exceptions to the fee agreement process apply. (HALLEX 1-1-2-12.) One exception relevant to the question is as follows: if the claimant appoints more than one representative in a firm, partnership, or legal corporation, SSA will disapprove the fee agreement if all the appointed representatives did not sign the same fee agreement, unless the representative(s) who did not sign waived charging and collecting a fee in the case. (HALLEX 1-1-2-12 B.l.) SSA instituted this requirement to ensure that claimants are not obligated to pay higher fees than are contemplated in the statutory provisions for representation work in a single matter before the agency.

b. Who should sign the fee agreement and the appointment of representative form?

The person or persons who will actually represent the claimant should sign the documents. SSA cannot prescribe how attorneys should manage their practices. However, since SSA recognizes the individual, not the business, as the claimant's representative, SSA's rules and instructions regarding representation, authorization of fees, and direct payment of fees contemplate that the claimant will be represented by, and owe fees for services to, one or a small number of representatives. The claimant should only appoint the individual or individuals who will actually perform representation duties on his or her behalf, not other individuals in the firm.

3. I am a solo practitioner with a working relationship with another attorney in another office. If one of us represents a claimant but is unavailable to attend the hearing, the other one will represent the claimant at the hearing. Who should sign the appointment of representation form and the fee agreement?

As stated in the previous response, SSA cannot prescribe how attorneys should manage their practices. In the situation described in the question, both attorneys provide representation services; therefore, SSA would require that both be appointed. In general, if the claimant appoints two representatives from different firms, partnerships, or legal corporations, any fee agreement is excepted from the fee agreement process. However, if the claimant and one representative entered into a fee agreement and the other representative submits a statement waiving a fee before the decision maker acts on the fee agreement, the decision maker will approve the fee agreement if it meets the statutory requirements and is not otherwise excepted. (HALLEX 1-1-2-12 B.2.) A waiver is a clear and unequivocal statement, in writing, that the representative waives the fee. Completion of section III (Waiver of Fee) of Form SSA-1696, or the "Waiver of Fee" section of Form SSAL1697 satisfies this requirement. Such a waiver would affect how much SSA can authorize under the fee agreement process (see questions 4 and 5). If you have such an arrangement with another attorney, both attorneys may wish to consider requesting fees under the fee petition process.

4. How is the fee authorized if the claimant has more than one appointed representative?

In the fee agreement process, assuming that the fee agreement meets the statutory requirements and is not excepted (see response to question 2a), the decision maker will approve the fee agreement. SSA will then authorize to each appointed co-representative an equal share of the total fee amount calculated under the terms of the approved agreement. Because SSA does not consider individual services in authorizing fees under the fee agreement process, the agency considers each co-representative entitled to an equal share of the total amount authorized for all the representation work in the case. For example, if the claimant appointed two representatives from a firm, partnership, or legal corporation, SSA would authorize half the total amount calculated under the terms of the fee agreement to each. (POMS GN 03940.001J.1 [this POMS section no longer exists, see POMS GN 03940.009A]; HALLEX I-1-2-18). See question 5 for an exception to this rule.

In the fee petition process, each appointed representative must file a fee petition providing the information about his or her services in the case requested on Form SSA-1560-U4 (Petition to Obtain Approval of a Fee for Representing a Claimant Before the Social Security Administration). (HALLEX 1-1-2-53 A.) SSA evaluates each representative's services separately and authorizes separate fees to each. One representative's services may not be included in another representative's fee petition. An SSA fee authorizer evaluates the information on the fee petition and authorizes a reasonable fee for services. In doing so, SSA considers the purpose of the program (title II, title XVI, or both), together with:

- The extent and type of services the representative performed;

- The complexity of the case;

- The level of skill and competence required of the representative in performing the services;

- The amount of time the representative spent on the case;

- The results the representative achieved;

- The level of review to which the claim was taken and the level of review at which the representative became the claimant's representative; and

- The amount of fee the representative requests for his or her services, including any amount authorized or requested before, but not including the amount of any expenses he or she incurred. (HALLEX 1-1-2-57 A.)

There is no statutory limit on the amount SSA may authorize to one or more than one representative(s) under the fee petition process. However, SSA procedures limit to $7,000 [currently $10,000] the amount the decision maker with initial jurisdiction over the fee petition may authorize. If the decision maker with initial jurisdiction recommends a higher fee than is within his/her discretionary authority, a reviewing official must review the recommendation and authorize the fee. (HALLEX 1-1-2-6.)

5. What happens if the claimant has more than one representative, and one or more co-representative(s) did not sign the fee agreement but waives charging the fee?

This provides an exception to the general procedure stated in the first paragraph of the response to question 4. If the decision maker finds that an appointed co-representative waived charging and collecting a fee, the decision maker will approve a fee agreement not signed by that co-representative if the fee agreement is otherwise acceptable. (HALLEX 1-1-2-12 B.1. NOTE and 1-1-2-12 B.2. NOTE.) However, in such cases, SSA will reduce the total amount of fees authorized under the approved fee agreement as follows. SSA will calculate the total fee amount under the terms of the approved agreement, divide that amount by the number of appointed representatives (including any representative(s) who waived a fee), and authorize equal shares to each appointed representative who did not waive a fee. SSA will not authorize to any other representative any share calculated for a representative who waived a fee. (POMS GN 03940.001J.1 [this POMS section no longer exists, see POMS GN 03940.009A]; HALLEX 1-1-2-18.) Waiver of a fee does not constitute a transfer or assignment of the right to charge and collect a fee based on those services to another person. (HALLEX I-1-2-10 A.)

SSA has instituted this procedure in the fee agreement process in order to prevent situations in which representatives undertake to "waive" fees in an attempt to transfer or assign the right to charge and collect the fee from one representative to another. For example, the paralegal representative whose situation was discussed in the response to question 1 cannot "waive" a fee and thereby transfer the right to his or her share of the total fee amount to the attorney co-representative. Such a situation is not a true waiver, but potential collection of fees by the attorney for representation services performed by the paralegal. Because SSA deems half the total amount calculated under the approved fee agreement to represent compensation for work done by the paralegal, if the paralegal waives his or her right to that money, it reverts to the claimant.

6. What happens if the claimant fires one representative and appoints another representative, so that there are two successive representatives?

Assuming that this question is directed to the fee agreement process, it could refer to more than one scenario, depending on whether one or both representatives entered into a fee agreement with the claimant. In general, the decision maker would disapprove any fee agreement filed by either representative. (HALLEX 1-1-2-12 B.3.) However, if the former representative waived charging and collecting a fee and the decision maker considers the fee agreement filed by the successor representative, the decision maker will approve the successor representative's fee agreement if the agreement meets the statutory requirements, the former representative's waiver is clearly and unequivocally documented in the file at the time of the decision, and the fee agreement is not otherwise excepted. (HALLEX 1-1-2-12 B.3. NOTE.)

If a decision maker approves a fee agreement in this type of situation, we will generally not apply the reduction to the total fee amount described in the responses to questions 4 and 5 if the representatives are not affiliated in the same business entity. If a former representative left the case before SSA reached a favorable decision and clearly waived any interest in a fee, and a successor representative not affiliated with the former representative obtained a favorable result, we will generally assume that the situations do not constitute co-representation as discussed above in the responses to questions 4 and 5, and that there is no collection of fees by the successor representative for any work other than his or her own.

We will continue to apply the procedure described in the response to question 5 if the former and successor representatives are affiliated or other circumstances indicate that the successor representative could obtain fees for the work of the former representative. For example, in the situation described in question 1, we would consider the attorney and the paralegal co-representatives for purposes of determining how much to authorize under an approved fee agreement, regardless of whether one representative left the case and waived a fee.

7. If the claimant has more than one co-representative, will SSA withhold past-due benefits for direct payment of an authorized fee?

Yes, if at least one of the representatives is an attorney. By law, SSA will pay a fee authorized to an attorney representative from a claimant's past-due benefits, not in excess of 25 percent of such benefits. Therefore, if the claimant is represented by an attorney representative, SSA initially withholds 25 percent of the past-due benefits resulting from a favorable determination or decision for payment of fees. (POMS GN 03920.035.) There is no provision for direct payment of fees to non-attorney representatives. [As of February 28, 2005, some non-attorney representatives are eligible for direct payment, which is addressed in the current POMS GN 03920.035.]

Once SSA authorizes fees to each co-representative under either the fee agreement or fee petition process, SSA pays to each attorney representative to whom fees were authorized either the equal share calculated under a fee agreement (see responses to questions 4 and 5) or the amount authorized for services under the fee petition process (see response to question 4), up to a total amount for all fee payments of 25 percent of past-due benefits. SSA will not directly pay any amount it authorizes to a non-attorney representative. If the total amount authorized to all attorney representatives exceeds 25 percent of past-due benefits (which may happen either in the fee petition process or on administrative review in the fee agreement process), SSA will pay to each attorney representative a share of the total amount withheld in the same proportion that the attorney's authorized fee bears to the total authorized fees. (POMS GN 03920.050.) After fees authorized to attorneys are paid, SSA releases any excess funds it withheld to the claimant.

§709.2 EM-13024 Distributing Fees When All Appointed Representatives Who Are Not Members of the Same Entity as Those With an Approved Fee Agreement Waive Their Fees

Effective Dates: 07/16/2013 - Present

Identification Number:	**EM-13024**
Intended Audience:	All RCs/ARCs/ADs/FOs/TSCs/PSCs/OCO/OCO-CSTs/ODAR
Originating Office:	ORDP OISP
Title:	**Distributing Fees When All Appointed Representatives Who Are Not Members of the Same Entity as Those with an Approved Fee Agreement Waive Their Fees—POMS Instructions Will Follow Shortly**
Type:	EM - Emergency Messages
Program:	**Title II (RSI); Title XVI (SSI)**
Link To Reference:	See References at the end of this EM.

Retention Date: July 15, 2017

Purpose

We are modifying our appointed representative fee distribution procedure in one fee situation. This emergency message (EM) provides instructions on how technicians should distribute an authorized fee when there are appointed representatives from multiple entities; there is an approved fee agreement from one or more representatives in a single entity; and all other appointed representatives waive charging and collecting a fee.

The new policy does not change the existing instructions that decision makers follow when they approve or disapprove a fee agreement (GN 03940.003B).

A. Background

Currently, to determine the individual fees in a multiple representative situation, we divide the total fee amount under the approved fee agreement by the total number of representatives, including those representatives who waive their fees. We then allow an equal share of the fee to each representative who did not waive a fee and allocate the remaining "waived share(s)" to the claimant. (GN 03940.009A). We are modifying this procedure, as explained in this EM.

B. New fee distribution procedure

1. Apply the new fee distribution procedure when the situation meets all of the following conditions:
   - The claimant appoints representatives from more than one entity;
   - We have an approved fee agreement from a representative or multiple representatives in a single entity;
   - All other representatives waive charging and collecting a fee, either from any source (i.e., worked pro bono) OR from the claimant and

any auxiliary beneficiary or eligible spouse because a third-party entity or government agency pays the fee from its funds, as described in GN 03920.010; AND
   - The decision maker approves the fee agreement because it meets all of our requirements. See GN 03940.002 and GN 03940.003.

2. Under the new procedure, distribute the authorized fees based upon an approved fee agreement in the following manner:
   a. Divide the total authorized fee amount by the number of appointed representatives who are members of the same entity as those representatives who signed onto the fee agreement, including those representatives from the same entity who waived charging and collecting a fee.

NOTE: Do not consider the appointed representatives from any other entity when dividing the total authorized fee amount.

   b. Allocate the apportioned amount to each appointed representative signing onto the fee agreement, but only directly pay the apportioned amount to those who qualify.

NOTE: In a situation where appointed representatives from the same entity waive their fees, allocate to the claimant any remaining portion of the authorized fee.

If the representative meets all of the conditions, follow this new procedure regardless of whether the representatives who waived their fees:
   - withdrew from the case,
   - had their appointments revoked, or
   - remain appointed.

If all of the conditions for applying this policy are not met, follow the current procedures for allocating the authorized fee in GN 03940.009A.

C. Examples of fee distribution
Following are examples of fee distribution:

Example 1: The claimant appointed two representatives from Firm A and one representative from Firm B. The representative from Firm B waived his or her fee. The two representatives from Firm A have an approved fee agreement that each of them signed, and SSA determines a fee of $6,000. The representatives from Firm A will receive $3,000 each.

Example 2: The claimant appointed two representatives from Firm A, one representative from Firm B, and one representative who is a sole practitioner. The representative from Firm B waived his or her fee from any source. The sole practitioner waived charging and collecting a fee from the claimant or any auxiliary beneficiaries because a third party entity will be paying his or her fee. The two representatives from Firm A have an approved fee agreement that each of them signed, and SSA determines a fee of $6,000. The representatives from Firm A will receive $3,000 each.

Example 3: The claimant appointed two representatives from Firm A and one representative from Firm B. One of the representatives from Firm A signed a fee agreement. The second representative from Firm A and the representative from Firm B both waived charging and collecting a fee from any source. At the time of a favorable decision, the decision maker approved the fee agreement; subsequently, SSA determines a fee of $6,000. The Firm A representative who had an approved fee agreement will receive $3,000, but the "waived share" of $3,000 for the second representative from Firm A should go to the claimant.

Direct all program-related and technical questions to your RO or PSC OA support staff, who may refer questions or problems to their Central Office contacts.

References:
GN 03920.020 Waiver of Fee or of Direct Payment of Representative's Fee
GN 03940.003 Fee Agreement Evaluation
GN 03940.009 Payment of Representative's Fee

§709.3 When an Associate Leaves the Firm

Most potential problems that arise when an associate leaves a firm can be ameliorated by an understanding between the associate and the firm about what happens to cases, fees, etc., when the associate leaves.

The potential problem that strikes fear in the hearts of law firm principals everywhere is that when an associate leaves, a fee agreement will not be approved because the associate is no longer a member of the firm. If the associate waives the fee, the fear has been that the associate's share of the fee will go back to the claimant. If the associate does not waive the fee, the fee agreement will be disapproved--making a fee petition necessary.

Many law firms have dealt with this problem by having the associate sign a document that says something like this:

> During the course of employment as a salaried associate with ABC Law Firm, I represented clients in their claims for Social Security and Supplemental Security Income (SSI) benefits. All of the claimants I represented were clients of ABC Law Firm. Any attorneys fees received from successful representation on those cases belong to ABC Law Firm. To date, some of those cases remain pending at the Office of Disability Adjudication and Review (ODAR), or in the future, may return to ODAR as the result of Appeals Council remand orders. I assign all rights, entitlement and interest in all attorney fees due in any of these cases now pending before the Social Security Administration to ABC Law Firm. All attorney fees in those cases belong to ABC Law Firm, not to me personally. I waive any personal right to collect a fee in these cases.

SSA has never addressed how to deal with questions that arise when an associate leaves a law firm. No POMS or HALLEX addresses the subject. Although SSA officials have initially insisted that EM-13024 cannot be read to apply when an associate leaves a firm, it would flout the logic of EM-13024 to say that a fee agreement must be disapproved because all representatives are not members of a single firm and then send the associate's share of the fee to the claimant because a member of the firm waived a fee.

The cumbersome way SSA deals with an attorney's address change, see §178.7, allows a law firm and associate some flexibility to choose where post-favorable decision notices and attorney fee payments are mailed. Even if the associate submits a new SSA-1699 with the name and address of the new firm, unless the associate submits an SSA-1695 for each individual case, notices and fees for those cases will still be mailed to the associate's former address, the address of the law firm.

§710 Payment of the Fee Under the Fee Agreement Process

Payment of the fee is usually virtually automatic under the fee agreement process. The fee is paid around the time that the Notice of Award is issued. Even though all parties and the ALJ will get notice of the amount of the fee and have the right to object, rare objections are dealt with after the fee is paid. Nevertheless, although payment of the fee is smoothly accomplished in the vast majority of cases, you will find that there will always be a few problem cases.

There are two places where the process can go awry: 1) issuance of the Notice of Award, and 2) issuance of payment. It is necessary for you to establish a system in your office to make sure you can identify cases that have run off track. As long as you don't ignore it, all you need is a simple calendaring system that reminds you to check the status of your client's case 45 days after the date of the favorable decision and every 30 days after that.

Title II Benefits

Shortly after the date of a favorable ALJ decision, sometimes within only a few days, you and your client should receive the Title II Notice of Award containing a summary of benefits to be paid to the claimant and fee authorization information, including the notice of right to object to the fee within 15 days. The Title II processing center (usually the Office of Central Operations (OCO) in Baltimore, except for beneficiaries over age 54 whose payments are processed by regional program service centers) is supposed to process the fee for payment at the same time the Notice of Award is issued. Indeed, often the fee is received before the Notice of Award even for those attorneys who have not elected to have direct deposit of fees.

When you don't receive a correct Notice of Award or any notice within 45 days after the favorable decision, SSA recommends that you contact the representative call center, 877-626-6363, at OCO or the appropriate regional program service center. *See* §441 for help in figuring out where the case is being processed.

If you have received the notice but you have not received payment of your fee, contact the processing unit or module (usually referred to as the "mod") at OCO or a regional program service center after waiting for payment for 45 days from the date of the Notice of Award. For claimants under age 54, SSA provides a toll-free fax number for OCO, 877-385-0643, and telephone numbers for individual mods. *See* http://www.socialsecurity.gov/representation/ pct_contact_info_under54.htm. Although we provide this information at §444, it is a good idea to always check SSA's website to see if a number has changed.

Although speaking with someone at an OCO mod usually gets results, they do not always answer the telephone and they do not always return phone calls in response to a recorded message you leave. There are the inefficiencies of telephone tag to consider. For these reasons, in the author's office, unless the problem is one that can *only* be resolved by talking with someone at an OCO mod, the first contact is usually by fax to the toll-free fax number. We calendar follow up for 30 days later.

Note that although we provide fax numbers for individual mods at §444 (which SSA does not provide on its website), unless you have been given instructions to fax to a specific individual's attention, it works best to use the toll-free fax number.

If you want to try to speak with someone, try telephoning the OCO mod manager or deputy early in the morning. If no one picks up, leave a message. If you actually get to speak with someone, be sure to ask for his or her name, position and direct telephone number. Also ask for advice about when to follow up. Do not assume that speaking with someone once at the OCO mod will *always* resolve the problem (although it usually does). Plan on regular follow up.

If after several months of telephoning and faxing, the problem is not resolved, consider telephoning the office of the division director for the appropriate mod. *See* §444 for telephone numbers for the offices of the four division directors.

For claimants over age 54, telephone the regional program service center using phone numbers provided by SSA at http://www.socialsecurity.gov/representation/ pct_contact_info_54older.htm. Unlike OCO, the telephone numbers provided by SSA are usually answered. Thus, there appear to be fewer follow-up problems. When problems arise, fax a letter describing the problem to the operations manager or to the operations analysis staff at the fax number for the appropriate payment center that appears in §446. With all follow-up letters, be sure to include copies of previous correspondence and details about your efforts to call.

Practice Tips

• Use SSA's website. It provides payment center telephone numbers that are linked from the Attorneys & Appointed Representatives Home page at http://www. socialsecurity.gov/representation/index.htm.

• When the problem with payment of your fee is coupled with a problem with payment of benefits to your client, telephone the OCO representative call center at 877-626-6363. Once you get past the third degree about your knowledge of your client's case to prove you are who you say you are, this call center will address payment problems for both you and your client. They won't let you discuss more than one claimant per call, though. And they won't deal with a case in which the *only* problem involves attorney fees.

• If there is a delay in sending the Notice of Award, telephone the OCO representative call center at 877-626-6363.

• If the delay in paying back benefits and attorney fees is because your client needs a representative payee, it is easier to help your client arrange for a representative payee than it is to argue with payment center staff about why attorney fees should be held up because of this.

• When the problem involves only attorney fees, first try faxing a letter to OCO about fee payment problems using the toll-free fax number: 877-385-0643.

• When the problem involves only attorney fees, if there is no response to your fax after 30 days, you may either fax a follow-up letter or try telephoning the processing unit using phone numbers provided on SSA's website, which also appear at §§444 and 446. Group your cases by payment center and mod. Unlike the OCO representative call center that will deal with only one case per call, if you get through to someone, he or she will usually address all cases on your list of problems that are handled by that mod.

• When you speak with someone at a payment center, that person may instruct you to fax something to the payment center. If they do not, consider whether it is appropriate to volunteer to fax a letter summarizing your telephone call. Ask for a fax number. If you forget or they won't give you a fax number, consider faxing a letter anyway as a way of putting the substance of your call in writing. *See* §§444 and 446 for fax numbers. You may be glad later that you have this documentation if the problem is not resolved.

• Try to head off delays caused when SSA does not have enough information to calculate the worker's compensation offset or to determine that it is inapplicable. Submit information about worker's compensation decisions, settlements and payments to the claimant's electronic file when the case is at the hearing level. Otherwise, gather worker's compensation information and telephone the processing center for instructions on how to submit it.

• Never mail a letter to Baltimore or one of the regional program service centers. Fax letters and necessary documents. *See* §§444 and 446 for fax numbers.

• Don't fax a list of problem cases. Discuss only one case in each letter. Faxed letters are scanned, placed in your client's paperless file and electronically routed for problem resolution. This cannot be done when your letter contains a list of cases.

• If your case has at any time been to federal court and if your client is under age 54, the claim is probably assigned to the Special Appeals and Examining Section (SAES), also known as "court case staff," in Baltimore. Processing court cases involves much manual work by court case staff. A full 25 percent attorney fee is supposed to be held until both an administrative and federal court fee is paid or waived. When you're not going to file fee petitions for the full 25 percent, be sure to tell SAES that you're waiving any additional fee and ask that excess withholding be released to your client. SAES telephone number: 410-966-8411; fax: 410-966-1998.

• If SAES is unresponsive, ask the Division Director of Division I to address problems. *See* §444 for Division I Director telephone numbers.

• If anyone should ever telephone you from Baltimore or a regional program service center, don't let your shock at being phoned keep you from asking for the name, position, phone and fax numbers of the person calling. Keep good notes about what you are told. Ask for a suggestion about when to follow up.

• When you have an unusual fee payment problem, consider trying to enlist the aid of a supervisor at a local office.

• Your own congressman or senator is a good resource for help with truly unusual situations.

• When you have not received your fee after a reasonable time, if the case is being processed in Baltimore, either telephone the mod or fax this letter to the OCO toll-free fax number:

I have received a letter indicating that I would be sent a fee of $_____. That letter is dated _____ [date], _____ [number of days] days ago. I have not yet received my fee. Please look into this matter and send me the check as soon as possible. Thanks.

• When you're simply requesting payment of a fee that has been approved in a Notice of Award that gives the appropriate information about the need to object to the fee within 15 days, you don't need to send the processing unit a copy of the Notice of Award. However, when you're writing about a less common situation, it is a good idea to send along a copy of the award letter and any other documents that help explain the problem.

• If the Notice of Award erroneously directs you to file a fee petition, telephoning the processing unit may work best.

• Usually a Notice of Award telling you to file a fee petition is simply a keying error in the notice that does not affect payment. However, if you know of any reason that the decision maker should not have approved your fee agreement in the first place, e.g., there was an attorney involved in the case before you who did not waive charging and collecting a fee, it may be that this was discovered at the payment center. Thus, it is possible that the Notice of Award was intended to notify you that the fee agreement was approved incorrectly. *See* POMS GN 03940.001F, GN 03940.020G and GN 03940.025C.4. If this is the situation, you'll save time by filing a fee petition promptly.

     •   If the Notice of Award underpays your client, your fee will also be underpaid. If SSA fixes the problem later without your involvement, your fee will not be increased. SSA's rules provide that increases or decreases in past-due benefits, after a representative's fee has been authorized, will not affect the amount of the representative's fee. Limited exceptions to this rule apply if there was an "input coding error" (POMS GN 03920.040A) or SSA "inadvertently" authorized a fee using unverified worker's compensation or public disability offset amounts to compute the past-due benefits. POMS GN 03920.040B. If you successfully appeal the Notice of Award, the revised award letter will increase your fee. POMS GN 03920.040B. If there is a request for administrative review of the amount of the fee, SSA uses the most recently calculated past-due benefit amount when it notifies the parties of the amount of the fee after administrative review. POMS GN 03920.040B and HALLEX I-1-2-47 C.2. Note.

     •   As a rule, when 25% of back benefits is more than $6,000, SSA withholds only $6,000. Sometimes, however, the Notice of Award states that SSA is withholding more than $6,000 for attorney fees, a fact that can be corroborated by adding up the numbers provided in the Notice of Award. When this happens, send a fax to the payment center asking SSA to release the excess withholding to your client. Since the only way you can find out if your client has received the excess withholding is from your client, you need to alert your client to the fact that the payment for excess withholding should be coming and if it doesn't come soon, your client needs to contact you so that you can follow up.

     •   If you receive payment for a fee but do not receive a Notice of Award shortly after that, ask your client for a copy of the Notice of Award. If that doesn't work, send the processing unit this letter:

> I received payment for attorney fees in the case of _____ in the amount of $_____. I assume that this amount is correctly paid; however, I never received my copy of the Notice of Award in this case. Please send me a copy.

Auxiliary Benefits

When you get the favorable decision, remind your client to file for auxiliary benefits for children and spouse. Note that sample letters at §§403, 404, and 404.1 include this reminder. It is often necessary, though, to discuss filing for auxiliary benefits in a telephone conversation with your client.

POMS states that SSA will not delay action on payment of the fee from the primary claimant's award while processing the auxiliary claims, that is, claims for the claimant's children and spouse. POMS GN 03940.035B. Payment of attorney fees on the auxiliary claims is supposed to follow the same procedures as payment of the fee from the primary claimant's back benefits: The check for the fee should be processed around the same time the 15-day notice on the auxiliary claim is issued. Payment of fees from auxiliary benefits is the place where the fee agreement process most often goes wrong.

Practice Tips

     •   Because auxiliary benefits are often processed and entered into SSA's computer by the local offices, when there are auxiliaries involved, send the local office a letter after you get the favorable decision and the order approving your fee agreement. Remind local office personnel that attorney fees should be withheld and paid from auxiliary benefits and that you should be sent copies of all auxiliary award letters.

     •   SSA often fails to send the attorney a copy of auxiliary award letters, and all too frequently SSA fails to withhold attorney fees on auxiliary benefits. Keep a close watch on this potential problem by tracking cases where there are possible payments to auxiliaries. In the author's office, Title II cases involving children are flagged on the computer, and we keep children's names and dates of birth on the computer. Contact the local office or the processing unit at the appropriate payment center about auxiliary payment status if you have heard nothing one to two months after the primary beneficiary is paid. Even though auxiliary benefits are processed at the local offices, it is the payment center that will correct any problem with withholding and payment of attorney fees from auxiliary benefits.

SSI Benefits

In order to calculate the SSI fee, the amount of the SSI windfall offset is deducted from the total amount of back SSI benefits, but the amount of any welfare recoupment under an interim assistance agreement is not to be deducted from SSI back benefits prior to calculating the amount of attorney fees. POMS GN 03940.007B.1. 42 U.S.C. § 1383(d)(2)(A)(i).

When you receive the favorable decision, it is a good idea to notify the local office that the fee agreement process applies and that you will be expecting direct payment of your fee. *See* §405, for a sample letter.

In a case involving only SSI benefits, the notice stating the amount of your fee, which gives you, the claimant and the ALJ 15 days to object, ought to be issued at the time the SSI benefit notice is sent to the claimant and to you. Payment for attorney fees should be made around the same time. If you do not receive the notice about your fee and prompt payment, contact the local office soon after receiving the benefit notice.

If you have waived withholding and direct payment, you still need the notice about your fee to tell you how much your fee is out of SSI back benefits. Until you receive the SSI fee notice, any fee your client pays you out of back SSI benefits must remain in your trust account.

Knowing when to contact the local office about the SSI fee in a concurrent case is more difficult. Before determining and paying the SSI portion of the fee, the local office is supposed to wait until all Title II attorney fees are determined (that is, fees out of the claimant's own back benefits plus fees out of the back benefits of any auxiliaries) and the SSI windfall offset, if any, is calculated. The SSI component must wait until 1) the amount of the Title II portion of the fee is determined (so that SSA can be sure that the SSI portion of the fee won't cause the total fee to exceed $6,000); and 2) the amount of the SSI windfall offset is calculated (because where there is an offset, it reduces the amount of the SSI fee).

(Note that an objection to the fee submitted when the Title II portion of the fee is calculated is not supposed to delay calculation of the fee out of the SSI portion. Indeed, so that the decision maker is able to evaluate the entire fee, it is essential that the fee out of the SSI portion of the case be calculated when there is an objection to the fee. HALLEX I-1-2-44 F.2.)

If attorney fees for the claimant and auxiliaries are calculated and paid and the SSI offset is calculated but an SSI 15-day letter still is not forthcoming, it is time to write to the local office requesting that it calculate and pay attorney fees out of the SSI part of the case. Provide the local office with information from the Title II part of the case to demonstrate that it's okay to issue the SSI attorney fee letter and pay SSI attorney fees. Providing this information to the local office is one way to encourage speedy issuance of an SSI attorney fee letter. If writing doesn't work, telephone the SSI claims representative. If that doesn't work, call an SSI supervisor or speak with the local office manager. Developing a good working relationship with local office personnel is important.

Practice Tips

• If the case involves only SSI, you should get the notice setting the amount of your fee around the time you get the notice about the claimant's back benefits. Sometimes they come in the same envelope. If you do not promptly get this notice, send the following letter to the local office:

This office represented _____ in an SSI case in which we received approval of a fee agreement. We have not yet received a letter from you authorizing the fee, nor have we received payment. According to our calculations based on the information we have received from you that our client's back SSI benefits totaled $_____, the fee should be $_____.

Please issue payment and the SSI attorney fee notice as soon as possible.

• In a concurrent case, if there are no auxiliaries to be paid, send the following letter to the local office:

This office represented _____ in a claim for concurrent benefits in which we received approval of a fee agreement. We have not received a letter from you authorizing the fee out of the SSI portion of the case, nor have we received payment for the SSI part of the attorney fees.

We received a letter dated _____, authorizing $_____ as our fee out of our client's back T2 benefits.

Please calculate and pay the SSI part of the attorney fee and issue the SSI attorney fee notice as soon as possible.

• Watch out for SSI attorney fee over-payments created because someone at the local office did not wait for attorney fees to be paid from auxiliary benefits before paying the SSI part of the fee. If you receive more than the maximum fee, contact the local office for instructions—whether you should pay the excess to your client or return it to SSA.

§711　　Notice and Right to Object

When the fee agreement process applies, SSA sends a notice required by 42 U.S.C. § 406(a)(2)(C) to the claimant, auxiliaries and the representative that shows:

• The past-due benefits amount;
• The amount of past-due benefits payable to the claimant, any auxiliary beneficiary(ies), and/or an eligible spouse;
• The amount of the fee resulting from the fee agreement; and
• The right to request administrative review of the amount of the fee within 15 days of receiving the notice. POMS GN 03940.008B.

The notice will require that requests to review the amount of the fee be sent to the Attorney Fee Branch at the Appeals Council. The Attorney Fee Branch will forward the appeal to the appropriate reviewing official.

§712 Procedure on Administrative Review of the Fee

If the claimant, an auxiliary, the attorney or decision maker timely objects to the fee (or establishes good cause for late filing—*see* POMS GN 03960.025), the reviewing official will send a notice to all other parties asking for comments within 15 days. If the issue is whether the amount of the fee is reasonable (an issue that could be raised by the claimant, an auxiliary or you), the reviewing official may need to evaluate your services and the time you spent working on the case. HALLEX I-1-2-47 B. Therefore, be prepared to send to the reviewing official an itemization of the time you spent working on the case. This information is similar to that which appears on a fee petition and, in fact, a note at HALLEX I-1-2-47 B.1 states that a fee petition may be used to gather this information. However, don't send a fee petition until it is requested because many objections can be resolved without evaluating your services. If you send an itemization of your time working on the case, be sure to send a copy to the other parties and indicate clearly to the reviewing official that you have done so. HALLEX I-1-2-47 B.1.

If the favorable decision was issued by an ALJ, that ALJ will review the fee unless the ALJ made the objection. (Note that the $10,000 limit on the ALJ's fee approval authority, which applies to fee petitions, does not apply to requests for administrative review of the amount of a fee determined under the fee agreement process. *See* HALLEX I-1-2-44 C.1. and HALLEX Transmittal No. I-1-44, available on the Internet at http://www.ssa.gov/OP_Home/hallex/ TS/tsi-1-44. html.) If the Appeals Council issued the favorable decision, the Deputy Chair of the Appeals Council will review the fee unless an administrative appeals judge makes the objection to the fee. HALLEX I-1-2-44 C.2.

When an ALJ objects to the fee, the Regional Chief ALJ (RCALJ) conducts the fee review, unless the Deputy Chair requested review of the fee, in which case the Chair of the Appeals Council will conduct the review of the fee. HALLEX I-1-2-44 C.2.

§713 Objection by the Decision Maker

A decision maker has the right to request administrative review of the fee only when there is evidence that the representative did not adequately represent the claimant's interest or that the fee is clearly excessive in light of the services provided. HALLEX I-1-2-46 B.2.

The decision maker, like everyone else, has only 15 days to request review. But the decision maker does not automatically receive a copy of the Notice of Award. POMS GN 03940.008C. Instead, hearing offices and the Appeals Council flag cases at the request of the decision maker so that the decision maker will receive a copy of the Notice of Award or an email from the payment center that says how much the attorney will receive. The decision maker can then decide whether or not to request administrative review. HALLEX I-1-2-21 C.

Because of the high standard that must be met by the decision maker, as well as the short time limit, decision makers do not request review often. However, ALJs may target claimants' attorneys with a reputation for providing inadequate services, and can and do file fee objections in appropriate cases.

These rules are based on the statute, 42 U.S.C. § 406(a)(3)(A), which explicitly provides: "The adjudicator may request the Commissioner to reduce the maximum fee only on the basis of evidence of the failure of the person representing the claimant to represent adequately the claimant's interest or on the basis of evidence that the fee is clearly excessive for services rendered."

The following examples of circumstances that meet the statutory standard for objection to the fee by the decision maker are provided in HALLEX I-1-2-46 B.2:

1. The representative delayed the claim(s) by procedural missteps or by repeatedly requesting extensions of time to submit readily available information or evidence.

2. The ALJ was ready to issue a favorable decision when SSA received a claimant's Appointment of Representative form and a fee agreement. The $3,700 fee which resulted under the approved agreement is clearly excessive for the time it took the representative to interview the claimant, complete an Appointment of Representative form and a fee agreement, and submit them.

If the reviewing official does not find evidence showing inadequate representation or a clearly excessive fee and no clear clerical error in the amount of the fee, the reviewing official is supposed to send a letter telling the decision maker that evidence of inadequate representation or a clearly excessive fee was not found, that SSA will not review the determination, and the determination of the amount the representative may charge in the case is final. HALLEX I-1-2-46 B.2.b.

§714   *Objection by the Claimant or Auxiliary*

According to HALLEX I-1-2-44 A.1, the claimant or an affected auxiliary has a right to request administrative review of the amount of the fee approved under the fee agreement process. However, note that SSA will not modify a fee solely because an auxiliary objects to sharing in the payment of the fee. *See* SSR 68-61c, which adopted, as a Social Security ruling, *Hopkins v. Cohen*, 390 U.S. 530 (1968).

HALLEX I-1-2-47 A.4 states a list of factors to assess whether the fee determined under the fee agreement process "is reasonable and to decide whether to affirm or modify a fee and, if so, to what extent":

• The expectation of the parties when they entered into the fee agreement, as expressed in the written agreement filed with SSA.

• For Title XVI cases, the purpose of the supplemental security income program (*i.e.*, to assure a minimum level of income for recipients who otherwise do not have sufficient income and resources to maintain a standard of living at the established Federal minimum income level).

• For Title II cases, the purpose of the program (*i.e.*, to provide a measure of economic security for program beneficiaries).

• The type and extent of services provided.

• The results the representative achieved or did not achieve.

• The amount the representative requested for his or her services, including any amount authorized or requested before, but not including the amount of any expenses incurred.

• The administrative review level at which the claimant retained the representative and the level to which the representative took the claim.

• The complexity of the case based on the work or documentation needed to resolve the issues.

• The level of skill and competence required of the representative in providing the services.

• The amount of time the representative spent on the case.

§715   *Objection by Attorney*

Although HALLEX I-1-2-44 A.1. says that a representative has a "right to request administrative review of the amount of the fee approved under the fee agreement process" and the statute allows for attorney appeals, 42 U.S.C. § 406(a)(3)(A)(ii), such appeals ought to be reserved for unusual situations. Many ALJs and claimants do not look kindly upon fee appeals by attorneys. Caution is appropriate because, in response to fee appeals by attorneys, ALJs have been known to reduce fees to less than the amount that was paid under the fee agreement process. When the attorney appeals, the HALLEX does not require a determination that the fee approved under the fee agreement is "clearly excessive for services rendered" or *prima facie* evidence showing inadequate representation before the fee may be reduced. (Compare the higher standard for when the decision maker objects to the fee. *See* §713.) Instead, SSA takes the position that the reviewing official's job is simply (1) to decide if the fee determined under the fee agreement is reasonable and (2), if not, to determine a reasonable fee. HALLEX I-1-2-47 C. If the ALJ determines that a reasonable fee is less than what you already received, you'll have to give some money back to the claimant. There is no right to further administrative appeal (although, some attorneys think under certain circumstances SSA may be vulnerable to a mandamus action in federal court, since SSA never promulgated the regulations that Congress required more than a decade ago when it established the fee agreement process).

If you are going to request administrative review of the amount of your fee, make sure you have a case that warrants a higher fee. In the author's opinion, such a case is one in which the claimant receives a very large back benefit award, one where 25% of past-due benefits significantly exceeds $6,000. It is a case where the attorney put in an inordinate number of hours, so many hours, in fact, that a $6,000 fee looks unreasonably small. And it is a case in which the client agrees to the higher fee.

Plan ahead. Consider whether you want to address the possibility of appeal in the contract with your client. *See* §703. Note that the sample contract at §178.3.1 acknowledges the possibility of an appeal by the attorney and limits the amount requested on appeal to 25% of past-due benefits. With such a clause in the fee agreement, you can argue that not only was the possibility of a fee appeal within the "expectation of the parties when they entered into the fee agreement," *cf.* HALLEX I-1-2-47 A.4., but also the amount of the fee to be requested on appeal was expressly stated. With such a clause in your contract, however, you cannot appeal when 25% of past-due benefits yields a ridiculously small fee.

Where a client agrees to join in a fee appeal, this factor ought to weigh heavily in favor of the increase sought. Nevertheless, SSA does not address this possibility. The statute itself assumes that claimants will want to appeal only to "reduce the maximum fee," 42 U.S.C. § 406(a)(3)(A)(i), just as it assumes that the attorney will want to appeal only to "increase the maximum fee," 42 U.S.C. § 406(a)(3)(A)(ii), assumptions not wholly consistent with real life experience.

In any case, the attorney must overcome the presumption in the minds of many ALJs that the fee amount determined under the fee agreement is reasonable for the services rendered. To do so, it is necessary to submit, in effect, the equivalent of a fee petition, showing all time spent on the case and explaining all actions taken. Even though you may submit a fee petition as part of your appeal, remember that appealing a fee agreement is very different from submitting a fee petition in a case where the fee agreement process does not apply. For one thing, you won't be able to appeal the decision. 42 U.S.C. § 406(a)(C)(3). For another, you will need to submit an argument explaining why the fee calculated under the fee agreement does not provide reasonable compensation. (If you make a mistake and simply send a fee petition instead of requesting administrative review of the amount of the fee, SSA's instructions are to treat receipt of a fee petition within 15 days of the date of a Notice of Award as a timely request for administrative review. HALLEX I-1-2-44 A. and POMS GN 03960.010B.1.d.)

If the real reason the fee is surprisingly low is that SSA made a mistake in calculating the claimant's past-due benefits, request reconsideration of the Notice of Award rather than appealing the fee. If SSA recalculates past-due benefits in conjunction with such an appeal, SSA will also recalculate the attorney fee. On the other hand, if there is no request for reconsideration of the Notice of Award but SSA adjusts the amount of past-due benefits after notifying the parties of the amount of the fee, SSA applies its rules of administrative finality. It will not adjust the fee either up or down. A limited exception to this rule applies where SSA used unverified worker's compensation or public disability benefit offset amounts in calculating the representative's fee in the first place. POMS GN 03920.040B.

Rather than appealing a fee under the fee agreement process, it is better to anticipate when your fee may be insufficient and take appropriate action before the date of the favorable decision. For example, consider using the fee petition process to obtain your fee (in cases likely to produce low-back benefits), *see* §720 *ff.*; consider using a two-tiered fee agreement, *see* §178.3.1; or consider submitting a superseding fee contract to change the terms of a fee agreement. *See* §708.

Some ALJs have taken the position that if you appeal the amount of your fee, you must hold in your trust account any money paid under the fee agreement process. This is wrong. No such requirement appears in any official SSA publication. In fact, an informal opinion prepared for NOSSCR dated January 17, 2001 states that the attorney may accept the fee.

Although it is possible for SSA to find good cause for late filing of a request for administrative review of the amount of the fee (*see* POMS GN 03960.025), SSA says that it will not pay directly any fee increased when the request for administrative review is untimely. POMS GN 03960.025A.3.

§716 *Problems With Partially Favorable Decisions*

Let's say you've spent many hours on a hard-fought case and you get a partially favorable decision from an ALJ in a case in which you have filed a standard fee agreement with a fee cap of $6,000, not a two-tiered fee agreement. Let's also say that your fee on the partially favorable decision is $6,000, according to a Notice of Award received a few weeks after the partially favorable decision. You appeal the partially favorable decision. You research and write an excellent (and time consuming) brief; and the Appeals Council finds your client disabled as of the originally alleged onset date. A second Notice of Award says that your client will get many thousands of dollars of additional back benefits, but the award letter does not mention your fee. Considering how hard you worked, how many hours you spent and how creative your legal arguments were, both you and your client think you deserve an additional fee. How and when do you appeal your fee?

According to SSA, your time to appeal ran out 15 days after you got the first Notice of Award, the one saying your fee was $6,000. Although SSA may find good cause for late filing of a request for administrative review, especially if you send it within 15 days of receipt of the second Notice of Award, it won't pay your fee directly to you if your client refuses to pay you. POMS GN 03960.025A.3. Thus, if you are ever in this situation, be sure to send a letter to SSA within 15 days of receipt of the first award letter that says the following: "If additional benefits are payable as a result of our appealing the ALJ's partially favorable decision, I intend to seek approval to charge a fee greater than $6,000. At the conclusion of the case, I will identify the amount I want to charge, the amount authorized before, the services performed for the claimant . . . and the time spent on each type of service."

See Social Security Forum, September 1998, pp. 9-10.

If your fee was anything less than $6,000 on the partially favorable ALJ decision, after you win at the Appeals Council, you will get a notice setting an additional fee (up to a grand total of $6,000). You may appeal the fee stated in that notice within 15 days of receipt of the notice.

If your fee agreement, which was approved when the partially favorable decision was issued, was acted upon before June 22, 2009 (or, if approved later, the fee agreement did not incorporate the $6,000 fee cap), your fee for the entire case is limited to $5,300. SSA's position is that once a fee agreement has been approved, it remains in effect throughout the rest of the case. The fee cap that applied when the fee agreement was approved remains in effect.

What happens if your fee agreement calls for a two-tiered arrangement in which the fee agreement process applies through the first ALJ hearing and the fee petition process applies beginning at the Appeals Council level? When does the second tier, the one that calls for a fee petition to be submitted, become operative? SSA's position is that the second tier never becomes operative. SSA says that once an order is issued approving a fee agreement, it remains in effect unless it is vacated. HALLEX I-1-2-14.

It is SSA's position that once a partially favorable decision and an order approving a fee under the fee agreement process is issued, unless that order is vacated, the fee agreement process applies to the rest of the claimant's case. Thus, if the Appeals Council issues a fully favorable decision, the fee agreement process applies to your fee even when you have a two-tiered fee agreement. On the other hand, if the Appeals Council vacates the partially favorable ALJ decision and remands the case, the Appeals Council's action nullifies the favorable decision and thereby vacates the ALJ's order approving the fee agreement. Therefore, if a favorable decision is issued on remand, the second tier of the fee agreement applies. You may proceed under the fee petition process. *See Social Security Forum*, November 1998, p.15. Note, however, that if the Appeals Council remands a partially favorable decision without vacating the entire decision, SSA's position is that the fee agreement process applies on remand because the ALJ's order approving the fee agreement remains in effect. HALLEX I-1-2-14.

SSA imposes no requirement that you place your fee in a trust when you receive it if you are in the process of appealing the partially favorable decision, whether you have a two-tiered fee agreement or not. If the partially favorable decision is vacated and remanded by the Appeals Council and you end up losing the case,

you will have to give back whatever fee you collected initially. HALLEX I-1-2-14. If on remand to the ALJ your client gets a fully favorable decision, you will need to file a fee petition to obtain your fee if it was a two-tiered fee agreement that was initially approved. HALLEX I-1-2-14.

§716.1 Problems With Subsequent Applications

In a case where a subsequent application is paid while the earlier application is on appeal, SSA will treat the two applications as one claim for purposes of applying the fee agreement cap. "[F]or purposes of determining a fee for representation, SSA considers the two applications to be parts of a single claim process. Accordingly, SSA will apply the fee agreement rules as if there were a single application or claim." POMS GN 03940.038A.

Anticipating that some attorneys may seek a way around this rule, SSA says that any fee agreement must be disapproved if it includes a provision that the "representative is unwilling to accept the statutory cap if the claimant files a subsequent application." HALLEX I-1-2-16 C.2.e.

When a maximum $6,000 fee is awarded on the subsequent application while the first one is pending in federal court or at the Appeals Council after remand by the federal court, SSA says that the time to request administrative review is when the subsequent application is effectuated and you receive the notice that your fee is $6,000. Thus, the best practice is to follow the same procedure that is followed when appealing a partially favorable decision. That is, send a letter within 15 days saying you may want to request administrative review of the amount of the fee if you are successful in the claimant's earlier application. *See* §716.

If you fail to reserve your right to request administrative review at this point, SSA says it will find good cause for late filing of a request for administrative review as long as administrative review is requested within 15 days of receiving the notice SSA issues when implementing the decision on the prior application. HALLEX I-1-2-16 C.2.d. However, because you did not appeal timely, SSA won't pay any additional fee directly to you if your client refuses to pay you. POMS GN 03960.025A.3.

In addition to applying the statutory cap in a claim involving two applications, SSA will also apply the multiple representative exception to the fee agreement process in deciding whether to approve a fee agreement. For example, if you represent the claimant in the prior application and an attorney from another firm represents the claimant in the subsequent application, neither of you can have a fee agreement approved. You have run afoul of an exception to the fee agreement process, which provides that all appointed representatives must be members of a single firm, partnership or legal corporation, unless the representative from outside the firm waives his or her fee. HALLEX I-1-2-12 B.2. *See* §705.

You can also run into problems with the multiple representative exception to the fee agreement process, even if all representatives involved are from the same firm, if all representatives do not sign the fee agreement. HALLEX I-1-2-12 B.1. Thus, if you want the fee agreement process to apply, make sure that the same representatives represent the claimant in both applications and the same representatives sign both fee agreements. In fact, you can use one fee agreement with both applications. SSA says that in the subsequent application it will accept a photocopy of the fee agreement filed in the prior application. HALLEX I-1-2-16 C.3.a. The copy of the fee agreement should be "annotated by the claimant or representative to indicate that the fee agreement applies in the subsequent application." POMS GN 03940.038D.2.c.

But what if you use a two-tiered fee agreement? That is, a fee agreement providing that if the claimant wins at or below the ALJ hearing level, the fee agreement process applies to the case, but if the claimant wins later, a fee petition will be submitted. SSA says that if the claimant is awarded benefits on the subsequent application at the initial or reconsideration stages, the first tier—the fee agreement process tier—applies. When assessing whether a two-tiered fee agreement applies, SSA looks at the particular application rather than the entire claim. If the claimant is awarded benefits at the initial or reconsideration stages in the subsequent application, SSA says that the first tier applies in any two-tiered fee agreement filed in conjunction with that application. The "decision maker will not consider the level at which the prior application is pending in deciding whether to approve or disapprove the agreement." POMS GN 03940.038C.4. Once the fee agreement is approved in the subsequent application, it will govern the fee in the entire claim (unless approval of the fee agreement is rescinded for some other reason).

Although SSA directs that information be gathered regarding representatives and the fee agreement in the prior application, SSA recognizes it is entirely possible that the decision maker who evaluates the fee agreement in the subsequent claim will not have a copy of the fee agreement and Appointment of Representative form from the prior claim. Thus, a decision maker could be unaware that, for example, a multiple representative exception to the fee agreement process applies, which would require disapproval of the fee agreement. Therefore, when the decision maker in the prior application later issues a favorable decision, that decision maker has instructions to consider whether the fee agreement was correctly evaluated in the subsequent application. POMS GN 03940.038C.5. HALLEX I-1-2-16 C.5.

If an ALJ or the Appeals Council issues a favorable decision on a prior application and reopens the determination in the subsequent application, "any approval of a fee agreement based on that favorable determination is vacated." Then, the decision maker is instructed to "approve or disapprove the **latest-dated** fee agreement filed in connection with either application." HALLEX I-1-2-16 D.1, emphasis in original.

If the decision maker does not reopen the determination in the subsequent application, the "decision maker will review any fee agreement approval issued in conjunction with the subsequent application to determine whether it is still correct, considering information regarding representation in both the prior and subsequent application files." HALLEX I-1-2-16 D.2. When a fee agreement has been correctly approved in the subsequent application, it applies to the entire claim. Thus, the decision-maker is instructed to take no other action.

If, in conjunction with issuing a favorable decision, the decision-maker discovers that the fee agreement in the subsequent application should not have been approved (*e.g.*, because different representatives were involved in the two applications), the decision-maker is supposed to rescind the approval and "disapprove any fee agreement filed in connection with the subsequent application, and if applicable, disapprove any fee agreement filed in connection with the prior application." HALLEX I-1-2-16 D.2.b. Thus, it will be necessary for both representatives to file fee petitions.

However, if the decision maker in the prior application does not issue a favorable decision and does not reopen the subsequent application, the "decision maker will not act on a fee agreement or review any action the decision maker in the subsequent application took on a fee agreement." HALLEX I-1-2-16 C.5.

These rules are so complicated that SSA decision makers are likely to make errors. It may be necessary for you to request administrative review of a decision maker's action on your fee agreement. Remember that you must do so within 15 days of receipt of the decision maker's approval or disapproval of your fee agreement.

In addition, it may be necessary for you to request administrative review of the amount of the fee paid under the fee agreement process, or you may have to file a fee petition in a claim involving two applications for benefits. Detailed time records are essential both for administrative review of the amount of a fee and for filing a fee petition.

HALLEX I-1-2-16 G provides the following examples to illustrate the application of SSA policy on subsequent applications:

1. Fee Agreement Approved in Subsequent Application—Same Representative Filed the Same Fee Agreement in Prior Application—Determination in Subsequent Application Not Reopened

• In filing her subsequent application in February 2002, the claimant indicates that she is represented by attorney Kirk of the firm of Kirk, Spock and McCoy, P.C., in a request for review pending before the AC (Appeals Council). The claimant and Mr. Kirk entered into a fee agreement on February 1, 2002, providing that:

• The fee will not exceed the lesser of 25 percent of past-due benefits or $5,300, if SSA favorably decides the claim(s) at or before the level of the first ALJ hearing decision in the case; and

• The fee will equal 25 percent of past-due benefits if the claim progresses beyond that level of the administrative appeals process.

• The FO (Field Office) adjudicator determines that the claimant also wishes Mr. Kirk to represent her in her subsequent application, and obtains copies of the appointment and fee agreement, annotated to indicate that Mr. Kirk also represents the claimant in the subsequent application.

• When making a favorable initial determination on the subsequent application, the FO adjudicator approves the fee agreement between the claimant and Mr. Kirk. (At the initial determination level, the first "tier" in the fee agreement applied.)

The PC (Payment Center) calculates that the past-due benefits resulting from the favorable decision in the subsequent application were $12,000. Based on the approved fee agreement, the PC releases a notice authorizing a fee of $3,000 to Mr. Kirk, and directly pays him that amount less the applicable user fee.

• In the prior application pending at the AC, the claimant also had appointed Mr. Kirk, and had entered into a fee agreement on April 2, 2000, with the same terms as those in the agreement approved in the subsequent application, except that the fee cap was then $4,000.

• The AC issues a favorable decision in the prior application, affirming the findings in the determination on the subsequent application and further finding an earlier date of onset.

• The "A" Member AAJ (Administrative Appeals Judge) reviews the appointments of representatives and the fee agreement approval in the subsequent application.

• Because the fee agreement with Mr. Kirk has already been approved, and there is no other appointed representative in the claim, the AAJ takes no action on the fee agreement.

NOTE: The AAJ does not evaluate the fee agreement under the second "tier" because SSA reached a favorable determination under the first. Refer to I-1-2-16(D.5.).

• The PC calculates that the additional past-due benefits resulting from the AC's favorable decision are $20,000. Based on the fee agreement approved in the subsequent application, the PC sends notice authorizing an additional fee of $2,300 ($5,300 less the $3,000 previously authorized), and directly pays Mr. Kirk that amount (less the applicable user fee).

• If any party requests administrative review of the amount of the fee based on the notice released in the prior application, the Attorney Fee Officer, as the reviewing official, will consider the amount of fees authorized in both the prior and subsequent applications in determining an overall fee for services throughout the entire claims process.

2. Fee Agreement Approved in Subsequent Application—Different Representative Was Appointed in Prior Application—Determination in Subsequent Application Not Reopened

• In the subsequent application, the claimant appoints attorney Kirk of the firm of Kirk, Spock and McCoy, P.C. The claimant and Mr. Kirk entered into a fee agreement on February 1, 2002, specifying a fee not to exceed the lesser of 25 percent of past-due benefits or $5,300.

• The FO approves the fee agreement between the claimant and Mr. Kirk when making favorable determination on the subsequent application.

• The PC calculates that the title II past-due benefits resulting from the favorable determination in the subsequent application are $18,000. Based on the approved fee agreement, the PC releases a notice authorizing a fee of $4,500 to Mr. Kirk, and directly pays him that amount less the applicable user fee.

• In the prior application on review at the AC, the claimant had appointed Mr. Kirk, and had also appointed attorney Spock of the same firm. The claimant and Messrs. Kirk and Spock had entered into a fee agreement on April 1, 1999, providing that:

• The fee will not exceed the lesser of 25 percent of past-due benefits or $4,000 if SSA favorably decides the claim(s) at or before the level of the first ALJ hearing decision in the case; and

• The fee will be equal to 25 percent of past-due benefits if the claim progresses beyond that level of the administrative appeals process.

• Neither the previous appointment nor the previous fee agreement had been made available to the decision maker in the FO.

• The AC issues a favorable decision in the prior application, affirming the findings in the determination on the subsequent application and further finding an earlier date of onset.

• The "A" Member AAJ reviews the appointments of representatives in both the prior and subsequent applications and the fee agreement approval in the subsequent application. The AAJ notes that an exception applies because the claimant appointed an attorney (Mr. Spock) who did not sign the fee agreement in the subsequent application. Therefore, the fee agreement approval must be rescinded and the agreement disapproved.

The AAJ:

• Issues an order to Messr. Kirk rescinding the fee agreement approval the FO issued (in connection with the subsequent application and the fee agreement dated February 1, 2002) and disapproving that fee agreement. The basis for the disapproval is that an exception applies: The claimant appointed more than one representative from a law firm; all representatives did not sign a single fee agreement; and the representative who did not sign the fee

agreement, did not waive charging and collecting a fee.

• Issues an order to Messrs. Kirk and Spock disapproving the fee agreement submitted in connection with the prior application. Because the second "tier" of the agreement provides for a fee that exceeds the statutory limits at the level of the AC review, the first basis for the disapproval is that it specifies a fee that is not limited to the lesser of 25 percent of past-due benefits or $5,300. The second basis is that an exception applies: The claimant appointed more than one representative from a law firm; all representatives did not sign a single fee agreement; and the representative who did not sign the fee agreement, did not waive charging and collecting a fee.

• The AAJ's orders notify Messrs. Kirk and Spock that they must send their fee petitions to the AFB in order to charge and collect fees.

• The PC notifies Mr. Kirk that the fee based on the incorrectly approved fee agreement is no longer the authorized fee. However, Mr. Kirk's fee petition may include services performed in connection with both applications.

• The PC calculates that the additional Title II past-due benefits resulting from the AC's favorable decision are $30,000. The PC recalculates the past-due benefits under the rules for "Partially Favorable Decisions— Decision More Favorable on Appeal" in POMS GN 03920.030B and withholds the appropriate amount.

• After Mr. Kirk and Mr. Spock file fee petitions, OHA's AFB authorizes reasonable fees based on the attorneys' services.

• Based on the authorizations, the PC determines (1) whether Mr. Kirk is owed any additional direct payment from withheld Title II past-due benefits, considering the previous authorization to him of $4,500, or whether he owes money back (*i.e.*, if the authorization on the fee petition was for less than $4,500); and (2) how much, if any, to pay to Mr. Spock from withheld Title II past-due benefits.

§717 *Avoid Excessive Fees*

Although the fee agreement process pays poorly in hard cases, it sometimes provides windfalls in easy cases. SSA has never done a good job of setting attorney fees. For this reason, although there is a statutorily created system for reviewing excessive fees, it is up to the attorney to see to it that he or she does not accept an excessive fee. To do so would violate Rule 1.5 of the ABA Model Rules of Professional Conduct (or the comparable rule adopted by all states).

The statute provides for the maximum fee payable under the fee agreement process. An attorney may and sometimes should accept less. You may simply refund to your client whatever part of the fee you feel is excessive.

§718   Erroneous Fee Payments

A bizarre by-product of the fee agreement process is the number of erroneous fee payments sent to attorneys by SSA. You will avoid future problems by developing a good system in your office for identifying duplicate payments and dealing with them at the time they are received. Keep good records about the fees to which you are entitled. Keep such records forever. Ask yourself this: If, as has been known to happen, SSA identifies what it thinks is an excess payment and demands its return years after you received the payment, will you have retained enough records to determine if SSA is correct?

Usually excess payments of attorney fees should be returned to SSA, not to the claimant. Such payments most often represent a duplicate fee payment or some other error at the processing center that may not affect the amount to which the claimant is entitled. If you forward such an erroneous payment to a claimant, when SSA catches its error, it is likely to insist that you are responsible for paying the money back to SSA. Thus, it is best to return the check to a local Social Security office and get a receipt. *See* "SSA Instructions for Duplicate or Excess Payments," in *Social Security Forum*, Vol. 22, No. 2, February 2000, p. 25.

Sometimes even when you waive direct payment of the attorney fee, SSA will send you a check anyway. Of course, SSA will have deducted the user fee. SSA says that it is not necessary for you to return such a check to SSA so that it can send the full amount of the fee to the claimant as you originally requested. Instead, SSA says that if it received the waiver of direct payment before the date the decision maker approved the fee agreement in a fee agreement case or on or before the date SSA received the fee petition in a fee petition case, it will refund the amount of the user fee to the claimant. Since the user fee should not have been deducted from your fee, you may collect the amount of the user fee from the claimant. POMS GN 03920.051. Note that SSA says that it will try to honor any waiver of direct payment that is received before payment is made; however, if it fails to do so in circumstances where the waiver of

direct payment was received after the decision maker approved the fee agreement, SSA will not correct its error by sending the user fee to the claimant. POMS GN 03920.051B.2. *See also* §748.

§719   If You Are Fired or Withdraw

If your client fires you or you withdraw from representing your client before the case is finished, the fee agreement process cannot be used for obtaining a fee for your work on the case so far. POMS GN 03940.003B.3. If you want to obtain a fee, it will be necessary to use the fee petition process. POMS GN 03940.001A. However, SSA makes even that difficult. First, unless you have written authorization from your former client, SSA will not provide you with a copy of the favorable ALJ decision or award letter. POMS GN 03940.008C, Note. Second, SSA will not make direct payment of a fee from money withheld from a claimant's past-due benefits to a representative who has withdrawn or been discharged from representing a claimant. POMS GN 03920.017A., Note, GN 03930.035B., Note.

If you do not waive your fee when your representation ends, a subsequent attorney cannot use the fee agreement process to obtain a fee in the claimant's case. In exchange for payment from the new attorney, some attorneys have been known to offer to waive the fee so that the new attorney can use the fee agreement process. However, accepting a fee under such circumstances is a fee violation. 20 C.F.R. § 404.1740(c)(2) and *cf.* POMS GN 03920.020F. Indeed, simply making arrangements for payment of such a fee may be a fee violation. 20 C.F.R. § 404.1740(c)(2).

Practice Tips

•   If your client moves away before any significant work is done on the client's case, help your client find a new attorney near the client's new home and waive your fee.

•   If your work is almost finished on the case when your client moves, consider whether it is feasible to continue representing your client. Note that no SSA rule prohibits a claimant from returning for a hearing near your office, although SSA will not pay travel expenses. 20 C.F.R. § 404.999c(d)(4). If you travel to a hearing near your client's new home, SSA will pay your travel expenses up to a maximum amount based on mileage from the farthest point within the geographic area served by the hearing office. 20 C.F.R. § 404.999c(d)(3).

• Find a co-counsel near your client's new home willing to file a fee petition. It will be necessary for both of you to file fee petitions to obtain your fees. However, be prepared for this: Because of the stinginess of some ALJs when evaluating fee petitions, the total fee received by both of you may be less than what one of you would have received under the fee agreement process.

§720 The Fee Petition Process

The fee petition process is the default method for obtaining approval of fees from SSA. If, for one reason or another, you do not (or cannot) use the fee agreement process for obtaining approval of your fee, you must use the fee petition process. This cumbersome system *must* be used whenever one of the exceptions to the fee agreement process applies. *See* §705. It must be used whenever your client's case does not accumulate back benefits. Thus, any fee must be approved using the fee petition process in all post-entitlement cases such as those involving continuing disability reviews or over payments.

You may find it to your advantage to plan from the beginning of the case to use the fee petition process when you can predict in advance that an exception to the fee agreement process will apply or that no back benefits (or very small back benefits) will be awarded in an initial claim for disability benefits. If you use the fee petition process, your contract with your client can use virtually any method of calculating attorney fees. *See* §723.

There are also circumstances where a fee agreement was first approved and then later disapproved so that you must use the fee petition process to obtain approval of a fee that you already received. *See*, for example, §716.1.

If you use the two-tiered fee agreement recommended by this book (see §178.3.1), when the first ALJ hearing decision is favorable, your fee will be limited to the lesser of 25 percent of past due benefits or $6,000 and paid under the fee agreement process. If you lose at the first ALJ hearing but win the case later, the second tier, which does not limit your fee to $6,000, will come under the fee petition process. When the second tier applies, to keep SSA from erroneously paying your fee under the fee agreement process, the decision maker who issues the favorable decision must *disapprove* the fee agreement (because the fee agreement is not limited to $6,000). *See* §727.

§721 The Myth of the 25% Limit on Attorney Fees

There is a myth that attorney fees are limited to 25% of past-due benefits for representing claimants before

SSA in Social Security disability cases. Although there is such a limit for federal court representation, no percentage limit is imposed by statute, rule or regulation for representing a claimant before the Social Security Administration. "There is no maximum fee amount that can be authorized in the fee petition process." HALLEX I-1-2-57.

Under 42 U.S.C. § 406(a) there is no percentage limitation on the amount of a "reasonable fee" that the Commissioner may set in an individual case; however, there is a limit of 25% of past-due benefits that may be paid directly by the Social Security Administration. 42 U.S.C. § 406(a)(4)(A). If you are authorized a fee greater than 25%, the fee authorization will indicate that you will have to look to the claimant for payment of any fee in excess of the 25% withheld and sent directly to you.

In *Horenstein v. Secretary of Health & Human Servs.*, 35 F.3d 261, 262 (6th Cir. 1994), the Sixth Circuit Court of Appeals held that the statute did not cap attorney fees at 25% for work before the agency. "Congress made distinct and explicit provisions for a 'reasonable fee' for work done before the Secretary under section 406(a)(1) and that there is no requirement that such an award be made from past-due benefits." In *Buchanan v. Apfel*, 249 F.3d 485, 492 (6th Cir. 2001), the court held that the determination of a "reasonable fee" was governed by 20 C.F.R. § 404.1725(b) for Social Security disability benefits, and § 416.1525(b) for SSI benefits. In *Buchanan*, where it was alleged that ALJs applied a 25% fee cap rather than following the regulations, the court found that there was *mandamus* jurisdiction to compel SSA to follow its regulations.

§722 Summary of Fee Petition Process Rules

• No fee may be "received" by an attorney without first obtaining a fee authorization (though a fee may be paid in advance into the attorney's trust account—see §724).
• Upon petition, SSA is required to set a fee for the attorney, whether the attorney wins or loses, unless the attorney's agreement with the claimant does not allow for a fee under such circumstances.
• If the attorney is successful, SSA must approve a fee that will reasonably compensate the attorney for services rendered.
• If there are past-due benefits, SSA must certify part of them for the attorney fee and pay that amount directly to the attorney, up to 25% of the award.
• If the attorney is successful, but there are no past-due benefits, SSA must still, on petition by the attorney, determine a fee that the attorney may

collect directly from the client if the agreement with the client allows it.

- If the fee approved is larger than 25% of the amount of past-due benefits, SSA should certify one-fourth of the past due benefits directly to the attorney and authorize collection of the remainder directly from the client.
- The attorney may not legally collect a fee larger than, or in addition to, the fee set by SSA.

§723 Possible Fee Arrangements

The regulations concerning the fee petition process make no mention of fee contracts with your client. Fee contracts are not listed as a factor for consideration in determining a reasonable fee, although the amount of fee requested is considered. 20 C.F.R. § 404.1725(b)(vii). See §725. Nevertheless, the fee petition, form SSA-1560, §733, asks if you have a fee agreement with your client; and if the answer is "yes," it asks that you attach a copy. Indeed, good law practice requires that the attorney and client have an understanding about fees. Rule 1.5(b) of the Model Rules of Professional Conduct of the ABA states that the fee agreement shall be "preferably in writing."

Fee contracts with your clients may be contingent or noncontingent. Most Social Security claimants prefer contingency fees because they do not have the money to pay attorneys if they lose their cases. Where a claimant does have the money to pay an attorney, however, a lawyer normally has an obligation to offer a prospective client an alternative fee arrangement before accepting a matter on a contingent fee basis. See Informal Opinion 86-1521 from the Standing Committee on Ethical and Professional Responsibility of the American Bar Association.

The fee may be calculated on any basis agreeable to the parties. It may be a fixed amount, e.g., $3,000, the fee arrangement most often seen in post-entitlement cases such as overpayment or continuing disability review cases. In cases where past-due benefits accumulate, the fee arrangement may be any percentage of past-due benefits; it may also be a combination of methods, such as 25% of past-due benefits with a minimum fixed amount or hourly rate.

§724 Fees May Be Paid in Advance

An attorney may place a fee into a trust account before SSA approves the fee. This is not considered to be a violation of SSA's Rules of Conduct for representatives. POMS GN 03970.010E.2, Note. For

example, when you take a case on a noncontingency basis, you may ask your client to pay into your trust account all or part of the fee. If you do so, you must disclose to SSA that you are holding funds in your trust account when you submit your fee petition. See Social Security Ruling 82-39.

Sometimes SSA will erroneously apply fee agreement procedures to a case that you know is supposed to be treated as a fee petition case. When SSA erroneously sends you a fee under such circumstances, this fee should be deposited in your trust account pending submission of a fee petition and receipt of a fee authorization. Be sure to disclose on your fee petition that you are holding funds in trust.

In a fee agreement case, you are also supposed to notify SSA when you are holding money in trust. In a concurrent case, SSA says that "funds in a trust or escrow account will not reduce the amount of direct payment a representative receives from a claimant's Title II past-due benefits, unless the Title II fee is the maximum fee allowed. SSA will not reduce the direct payment amount because SSA may authorize an additional fee amount for the Title XVI portion of the claim." POMS GN 03920.025C.2.b. Once the SSI part of the fee is authorized, SSA will deduct the amount in trust from the SSI part of the fee.

You may not withdraw the fee from the trust account until you receive authorization from SSA for your fee. If SSA authorizes less than the amount held in your trust account, you must promptly pay the excess to the claimant.

§725 SSA's Rules for Evaluating a Fee Request

The regulation for evaluating a request to approve a fee, 20 C.F.R. § 404.1725(b), provides the following:

(b) Evaluating a request for approval of a fee
(1) When we evaluate a representative's request for approval of a fee, we consider the purpose of the Social Security program, which is to provide a measure of economic security for the beneficiaries of the program, together with—
  (i) The extent and type of services the representative performed;
  (ii) The complexity of the case;
  (iii) The level of skill and competence required of the representative in giving the services;
  (iv) The amount of time the representative spent on the case;
  (v) The results the representative achieved;
  (vi) The level of review to which the claim was taken and the level of the review at which the

representative became your representative; and

(vii) The amount of fee the representative requests for his or her services, including any amount authorized or requested before, but not including the amount of any expenses he or she incurred.

(2) Although we consider the amount of benefits, if any, that are payable, we do not base the amount of fee we authorize on the amount of the benefit alone, but on a consideration of all the factors listed in this section. The benefits payable in any claim are determined by specific provisions of law and are unrelated to the efforts of the representative. We may authorize a fee even if no benefits are payable.

See also 725.1 HALLEX I-1-2-57 and POMS GN 03930.105, for examples of use of SSA's criteria for evaluating a fee petition.

§725.1 HALLEX I-1-2-57—
Evaluating Fee Petitions

There is no maximum fee amount that can be authorized in the fee petition process. A fee authorizer evaluating a petition must consider the following criteria for evaluating fee petitions and determining a representative's reasonable fee.

A. Criteria for Evaluating Fee Petitions

When evaluating the fee petition to determine a reasonable fee for representation, the fee authorizer must consider the factors listed below.

1. Purpose of the Program

The fee authorizer must consider the purpose of the program. For title II, this purpose is to provide the measure of economic security for program beneficiaries. For title XVI, the purpose is to assure a minimum level of income for supplemental security income recipients who otherwise do not have sufficient income and resources to maintain a standard of living at the established federal minimum income level.

2. Services Provided

Depending on the circumstances in the case, the fee authorizer also will consider whether the representative:

• Researched relevant law or rulings.
• Searched old records to obtain the evidence.
• Arranged a medical examination.

• Submitted medical or lay evidence of disability or other factors of entitlement.
• Contacted the Social Security Administration (SSA) as needed about the status of the claim.
• Participated at the hearing.
• Promoted timely decision making or acted in a way that delayed the issuance of the decision without justification.

NOTE:

Recognize that SSA does not set a standard value for each type of service because of the variety of activities in which a representative may engage and because the same activity may be more demanding in one situation than another. Even routine services are necessary and have value.

Examples:

1. A representative submitted a copy of a hospital report that served as the primary basis for the Administrative Law Judge (ALJ) finding the claimant disabled.
2. A representative submitted a copy of medical evidence she had used successfully in a recent workers' compensation claim to support the claim for a period of disability and disability insurance benefits. The representative provided SSA with readily available evidence we may not have had. However, the submission of new medical evidence relating to the period before insured status expired would have been a far more valuable service.

3. Complexity of the Case

Evaluate the complexity of the case based on the work or documentation needed to resolve the issues. Do not underestimate complexity because of the representative's knowledge or experience as a representative.

Example: A representative contacted numerous sources for information used to establish the claimant's date of birth, a task of some complexity.

4. Level of Skill and Competence Required in Providing the Services

Consider the issues involved and the probing the representative did to resolve them. Do not base the assessment on what the fee authorizer would have done following existing instructions or on what the representative could have done theoretically, given his/her expertise.

Example: One representative submitted a copy of the evidence he used in the claimant's workers' compensation claim. A representative in another case scheduled a medical examination and submitted the results for evaluation, along with other new evidence showing the claimant's condition. The representative's actions in the second case demonstrate greater skill and competence.

5. Amount of Time Spent on the Case

Credit the time allegedly spent on services (e.g., one hour to arrange a medical appointment), unless the time seems exaggerated or inordinate (e.g., 20 hours to research when the fee authorizer knows the representative regularly handles social security claims).

Refer to B. below for time to exclude.

6. Results the Representative Achieved

Consider the results achieved along with all the other factors.

Do not permit this factor to completely override the others. If SSA made a favorable determination on one claim and an unfavorable determination on another claim, the fee authorizer should not disregard the other factors and authorize the fee amount the representative requests in the first, but authorize no fee in the second, simply because of the outcome.

EXCEPTION:

If the representative and claimant have entered into a contingency contract, providing that there will be no fee if the claim is not favorably decided, SSA will honor that provision. In such a case, SSA will not authorize any fee for services if the representative petitions.

Do not authorize the fee primarily on the basis of the amount of benefits awarded (or lack thereof); the benefit amount payable is unrelated to the extent or caliber of services the representative provided.

Example: An assessment of his client's description of symptoms prompted the representative to develop evidence of a medical condition the field office and Disability Determination Services had overlooked. This established the claimant's entitlement to disability insurance benefits. When evaluating, you credit the favorable results the representative achieved. You also credit the representative's demonstrated skill and competence in a case complicated by the claimant

stressing the symptoms of a medical condition that alone was not disabling, and SSA not recognizing the significance of his other symptoms.

7. Level(s) in the Administrative Process

Consider the level(s) in the administrative process at which the representation began.

Example: If the claimant appointed the representative after receiving notice of the reconsideration determination and the ALJ favorably decided the claim, assume the representative interviewed the claimant about what had happened thus far, researched the law and eligibility factors, and determined whether new evidence was available.

8. Amount of Fee Requested

Consider the amount the representative requested and apply all of the factors listed above in conjunction with the excluded items identified in B. below. After considering these factors, if the fee the representative requested is reasonable for the services he/she provided, authorize a fee in the amount requested. The fee authorizer may authorize a fee in a lesser amount than that requested, providing it is reasonable.

B. Excluded Activities

In evaluating the amount of time a representative spent on the case, the fee authorizer must exclude any time claimed for:

• preparing the fee petition or any other activities related to charging or collecting a fee, such as status inquiries; and
• services the representative did not provide before SSA. (See I-1-2-5 and I-1-2-71 B.)

C. Expenses

The representative's expenses are not considered part of the fee for services. The representative must look to the claimant for reimbursement of any expenses.

D. Concurrent Titles II and XVI Cases

Pursuant to Social Security Ruling SSR 83-27 (C.E. 1983, p. 77), SSA determines a reasonable fee for the services provided in connection with both the titles II and XVI programs when all the circumstances below apply.

The concurrent titles II and XVI claims, or post-entitlement or post-eligibility actions, involved a common substantive issue (e.g., disability).

Although some services may have been unique to the title II or XVI claim or post-entitlement action, most of the representative's services focused on resolving the common issue. The representative did not perform two sets of services different in most respects.

The services the representative provided led to favorable determinations or decisions in both cases.

If the representative is eligible for direct fee payment under SSR 83-27, SSA will certify the fee amount for direct payment from title II past-due benefits withheld unless a portion of the fee amount is attributable to services provided exclusively in connection with the title XVI program.

When evaluating the fee petition to determine a reasonable fee for representation in concurrent titles II and XVI cases that involved a common substantive issue, consider the circumstances above, as well as:

- The purposes of the programs, in A.1. above; and
- The factors listed in A.2. through A.8. above.

If all the criteria and factors are met and SSA is withholding for possible direct payment of a representative's fee, decide whether any services were so unique to the supplemental security income program that you must designate a portion of the fee amount as attributable to title XVI exclusively.

E. Documenting the Fee Rationale

Complete the Form SSA-1178 (Evaluation of Fee Petition for Representation) (refer to POMS GN 03930.150B.) to document the rationale for setting the fee. Use this form to show the amount of the fee you find reasonable, and to explain and document your rationale. The rationale must reflect how you set the fee using the factors in A.1. through A.8. above.

If the amount of the fee you believe is reasonable is $10,000 or less, file the SSA-1178 in the hearing office or Appeals Council file when the SSA-1560A-U5 is distributed. (See I-1-2-58 for procedures on processing the SSA-1560A-U5.)

If the amount of the fee you believe is reasonable exceeds $10,000, send the recommendation you prepared on the SSA-1178 to the authorizing official with the SSA-1560A-U5. Refer to I-1-2-57 E, Authority to Approve Fee Petition.

§726   SSA's Rules Are Insufficient to Determine a Fee

A comparison of the rules SSA uses for evaluating the reasonableness of attorney fees with the ABA Model Rules of Professional Conduct (*see* §752, as well as the older Model Code of Professional Responsibility), demonstrates several peculiarities of SSA's approach.

First, SSA's rules do not take into account the contingent nature of a fee agreement, except to note that if a claim with a contingent fee agreement is unsuccessful, SSA will honor that provision. HALLEX I-1-2-57 A.6. Rule 1.5(a)(8) of the Model Rules of Professional Conduct, on the other hand, identifies the contingency of fees as a factor to be considered in evaluating the reasonableness of a fee.

Second, SSA's rules do not consider the experience, reputation and ability of the lawyer performing the services. The Model Rules of Professional Conduct identify these as proper factors for consideration as well. Rule 1.5(a)(7).

Third, SSA's rules do not expressly consider the prevailing market rate. The Model Rules of Professional Conduct, on the other hand, state that a factor for consideration is "the fee customarily charged in the locality for similar legal services" (Rule 1.5(a)(3)), as well as the amount involved in the case (Rule 1.5(a)(4)).

Fourth, SSA's rules do not relate the factors to be considered and the dollar amount of a fee. Under 20 C.F.R. § 404.1725(b)(2), SSA considers the amount of benefits awarded, but rejects a percentage approach to the calculation of attorney fees because the "benefits payable in any claim are determined by specific provisions of law and are unrelated to the efforts of the representative."

In short, SSA's rules do not provide decision makers with sufficient guidance for determining a fee. Nothing in SSA's rules tells how to weigh the listed factors, or how to translate those factors into a dollar amount of a fee. In practice, SSA decision makers place most emphasis on the amount of time the representative spent on the case, a factor identified at 20 C.F.R. § 404.1725(b)(iv), and then use an hourly rate plucked out of thin air as a yardstick to measure a fee request. Such hourly rates are not among SSA's factors to be considered. For this reason, authorized fees vary greatly from decision maker to decision maker.

§727   Two-Tiered Fee Agreement and the Fee Petition Process

The fee agreement process and the fee petition process are mutually exclusive. HALLEX I-1-2-1 A. Once the fee agreement process applies to a case, there is nothing you can do to voluntarily switch to the fee petition process. For example, an appeal of the amount of the fee determined under the fee agreement process is conducted under fee agreement process appeal rules, which are different from fee petition process appeal rules. Compare §§711 – 715 and §739.

The one situation where SSA has allowed the fee agreement process and the fee petition process to coexist is the two-tiered fee agreement. SSA will approve a contract that limits the fee to the lesser of 25 percent of past due benefits or $6,000 and thereby makes the fee agreement process apply if a favorable decision is issued at or below a certain level of administrative review, such as the ALJ hearing level, and the contract is not limited to $6,000 (thereby making the fee petition process apply) if the favorable decision is issued after that. Thus, if a (fully or partially) favorable decision is issued at or below the ALJ hearing level, the contract will be approved so that the fee agreement process applies to payment of the fee.

When a favorable decision is issued later, that is, when the second tier applies, the fee agreement is supposed to be disapproved by the decision maker (because the fee is not limited to $6,000). HALLEX I-1-2-15. The order disapproving the fee agreement takes the contract out of the fee agreement process so that it is appropriate to file a fee petition to obtain the fee.

ALJs have become so used to approving fee agreements that they make a lot of mistakes by approving two-tiered fee agreements that ought to be disapproved because the fee petition tier applies. When this happens, you need to contact the decision maker immediately to request that the order approving the fee agreement be rescinded and an order disapproving the fee agreement be issued. If a corrective order is not forthcoming, it is necessary to request administrative review of the order approving of the fee agreement to ask that the fee agreement be disapproved. HALLEX I-1-2-43 E.3. You have 15 days from the day you received the order approving the fee agreement to request administrative review. HALLEX I-1-2-42 A.

If you do not request administrative review of approval of the fee agreement, although it is possible that the payment center might catch the error and refer the matter to the Regional Chief ALJ per HALLEX I-1-2-49 A.1, you are likely to be paid under the fee agreement process. When you receive the fee check, you will have

a dilemma. The fee agreement was approved in error. Issuance of the check compounds the error. It would be prudent to deposit the check in your trust account and request administrative review of approval of the fee agreement at that point despite its untimeliness. If administrative review is denied as being untimely, you may move the fee from your trust account to your office account. If administrative review is granted and the fee agreement is disapproved, you'll need to file a fee petition to obtain approval of your fee.

§730   Submitting a Fee Petition and Obtaining a Fee Authorization From SSA

As a rule, these days, fee petitions are filed in cases requiring more than one ALJ hearing when the second tier of a two-tiered fee agreement applies (see the discussion at §178.3 and sample agreement at §178.3.1), or when an exception applies to the fee agreement process that makes impossible approval of a fee agreement that otherwise meets the requirements of the fee agreement process. *See* §705. Both circumstances require the decision maker to disapprove the fee agreement. Disapproval of the fee agreement, of course, doesn't mean that you are not entitled to a fee. It merely means that you must file a fee petition in order to obtain approval of your fee from SSA.

When you receive a correct order disapproving your fee agreement, send the ALJ a "notice of intent to file a fee petition." *See* sample at §407. If the case involves SSI, send the local office a letter explaining that you will file a fee petition with the ALJ when all benefits are computed. Ask that attorney fees be withheld from back SSI benefits and that you be notified how much your 25 percent fee should be out of your client's back SSI benefits. Tell the local office that you will provide a copy of the fee authorization when you receive it.

§731   Keep Good Time Records

The most important factor SSA uses to evaluate a fee petition is the amount of time actually spent working on the case. Accordingly, it is extremely important to keep good time records. Good records are prepared when you do the work. They provide detailed descriptions of work performed so that the decision maker can see the reasons for each task and the amount of time spent.

SSA does not require that time be kept using a particular system, i.e., in quarter hours or tenths of an hour. In fact, SSA shows a sample time record using the quarter hour system. POMS GN 03930.020C.3. Nevertheless, the quarter hour system is viewed by many SSA decision makers as one that leads to over estimating time spent on a case. Many decision makers seem to regard any hint of padding time records as a reason to reduce a requested fee.

Despite the fact that SSA's sample time record offers little explanation of work done, POMS GN 03930.020C.3, the more explanation you provide in your time records, the better. If you wrote a detailed letter to the claimant's doctor, note the issues raised in the letter. If legal research was required, explain the issue and its importance to the case. If you have a conference with a lay witness, identify the witness and what you discussed.

Try to account, completely and without exaggeration, for all time spent on a claimant's case. Because every time-keeping system is fallible, it is worthwhile to compare your time records to the file when you prepare a fee petition. Make sure there are time records for each letter sent and letter received and for each collection of medical records reviewed. It is entirely proper to recreate time spent on a case as long as you can do it honestly.

If you delegate tasks in your office to a paralegal or to another attorney, you may include the time of this unappointed assistant in your fee petition. However, if the person to whom you delegate tasks is also appointed as a representative, according to SSA you may not include this person's time in your fee petition. Instead, SSA says that each appointed "representative who wants to charge and collect a fee for his/her services must file a fee petition and request a fee for the services he/she performed." HALLEX I-1-2-53 A. It is hard to understand the public policy basis for such a rule, which results in nothing other than making a cumbersome fee petition process even more difficult. Oftentimes, though, this rule is not strictly enforced by decision makers.

Because the substantial time spent to prepare the fee petition will not be considered, HALLEX I-1-2-57 B, it is best to leave it out. For cases that have gone to federal court, do not include any federal court time in your fee petition. Whether to include time spent after the Appeals Council denies review but before filing in federal court depends on the purpose of the time spent. *See* HALLEX I-1-2-71 B.1 & 2.

§732   *How to Submit a Fee Petition*

Once all work on the claimant's case has been completed and you have sufficient information to calculate your fee, you may petition for approval of your fee. According to POMS GN 03930.020C.3, SSA requires the following information in a fee petition:

- The dates services began and ended;
- The services provided (e.g., preparation of correspondence, research, travel and attendance at the hearing);
- The dates and amount of time spent on each type of service;
- The amount of the fee requested;
- The amount of the fee requested or charged for services provided in the same matter before any State or Federal court;
- The amount of money, if any, the representative received toward payment of the fee and has held in a trust or escrow account;
- The amounts, and a list, of any expenses the representative incurred for which the representative has been paid or expects to be paid; and
- A statement affirming that the representative sent a copy of the petition and any attachments to the claimant.

Although SSA does not require that you use the official form, so that you're sure to provide all information SSA requires and so that SSA clerks recognize your petition for what it is, it is best to use the official form. Complete the Petition to Obtain Approval of a Fee for Representing a Claimant Before the Social Security Administration, SSA-1560, an electronic version of which can be obtained on the Internet at http://www.ssa.gov/online/ssa-1560.pdf and is reproduced at §733. This form includes a file copy, claimant copy, representative copy and ODAR copy. The file and ODAR copies are sent to SSA. Retain the representative copy for your records. You must send the claimant's copy to the claimant and state in your cover letter that you have done so. Be sure to provide all of the information requested on the form. HALLEX I-1-2-56 A.2. Include the dollar amount of the requested fee. If you insert a percentage of back benefits instead of a dollar amount, the fee petition may be returned to you.

The fee petition has a place for your client's signature indicating approval of your fee. Although the client's signature is optional, it is a good idea. With your client's signature on the fee petition, the petition can be processed without SSA waiting 30 days to see if the client has any comments on the requested fee. HALLEX I-1-2-56 B. In addition, although the claimant's agreement to a fee is not a factor listed by SSA in C.F.R. § 404.1725(b) to be considered when evaluating a request for approval, most ALJs nonetheless consider it.

§733   Form: Petition to Obtain Approval of a Fee for Representing a Claimant Before the Social Security Administration

SOCIAL SECURITY ADMINISTRATION   **TOE 850**   Form Approved
OMB No. 0960-0104

PETITION TO OBTAIN APPROVAL OF A FEE FOR REPRESENTING A CLAIMANT BEFORE THE SOCIAL SECURITY ADMINISTRATION	**IMPORTANT INFORMATION ON REVERSE SIDE**

I request approval to charge a fee of: Fee$ _____ (Show the dollar amount)

for services performed as the representative of:

My Services Began: ____ / ____ / _____   Type(s) of claim(s)
                    Month   Day   Year

My Services Ended: ____ / ____ / _____

Enter the name and the Social Security number of the person on whose Social Security record the claim is based.

__ __ __ / __ __ / __ __ __ __

1. Itemize on a separate page or pages the services you rendered before the Social Security Administration (SSA). List each meeting, conference, item of correspondence, telephone call, and other activity in which you engaged, such as research, preparation of a brief, attendance at a hearing, travel, etc., related to your services as representative in this case. Attach to this petition the list showing the dates, the descriptions of each service, the actual time spent in each, and the total hours.

2. Have you and your client entered into a fee agreement for services before SSA?   ☐ YES   ☐ NO

   If "yes," please specify the amount on which you agreed, and attach a copy of the agreement
   to this petition. $ _____   and   ☐ See attached

3. (a) Have you received, or do you expect to receive, any payment toward your fee from any source other than from funds which SSA may be withholding for fee payment?   ☐ YES   ☐ NO

   (b) Do you currently hold in a trust or escrow account any amount of money you received toward payment of your fee?   ☐ YES   ☐ NO

   If "yes" to either or both of the above, please specify the source(s) and the amount(s).

   Source: _____ $ _____

   Source: _____ $ _____

   Note: If you receive payment(s) after submitting this petition, but before the SSA approves a fee, you have an affirmative duty to notify the SSA office to which you are sending this petition.

4. Have you received, or do you expect to receive, reimbursement for expenses you incurred?   ☐ YES   ☐ NO
   If "yes," please itemize your expenses and the amounts on a separate page.

5. Did you render any services relating to this matter before any State or Federal court?   ☐ YES   ☐ NO

   If "yes," what fee did you or will you charge for services in connection with the court proceedings?
   Please attach a copy of the court order if the court has approved a fee. $ _____

6. Have you been disbarred or suspended from a court or bar to which you were previously admitted to practice as an attorney?
                                                                              ☐ YES   ☐ NO

7. Have you been disqualified from participating in or appearing before a Federal program or agency?   ☐ YES   ☐ NO

I declare under penalty of perjury that I have examined all the information on this form, and on any accompanying statements or forms, and it is true and correct to the best of my knowledge.

Signature of Representative	Date	Address (include Zip Code)

Firm with which associated, if any	Telephone No. and Area Code

[Note: The following is optional. However, SSA can consider your fee petition more promptly if your client knows and already agrees with the amount you are requesting.]

I understand that I do not have to sign this petition or request. It is my right to disagree with the amount of the fee requested or any information given, and to ask more questions about the information given in this request (as explained on the reverse side of this form). I have marked my choice below.

☐ I agree with the $ _____ fee which my representative is asking to charge and collect. By signing this request, I am not giving up my right to disagree later with the total fee amount the Social Security Administration authorizes my representative to charge and collect.

OR

☐ I do not agree with the requested fee or other information given here, or I need more time. I understand I must call, visit, or write to SSA within 20 days if I have questions or if I disagree with the fee requested or any information shown (as explained on the reverse sides of this form).

Signature of Claimant	Date

Address (include Zip Code)	Telephone No. and Area Code

Form **SSA-1560-U4** (03-2014) EF (03-2014)   **FILE COPY**
Destroy Prior Editions

INSTRUCTIONS FOR USING THIS PETITION

Any attorney or other representative who wants to charge or collect a fee for services, rendered in connection with a claim before the Social Security Administration (SSA), is required by law to first obtain SSA's approval of the fee [sections 206(a) and 1631(d)(2) of the Social Security Act (42 U.S.C. 406(a) and 1383(d)(2)) and sections 404.1720 and 416.1520 of Social Security Administration Regulations Numbers 4 and 16, respectively.] The only exceptions are 1) when a third party entity, (i.e. a business, firm, or government agency) will pay the fee and any expenses from its own funds and the claimant and any auxiliary beneficiaries incur no liability, directly or indirectly, for the cost(s); (2) when a court has awarded a fee for services provided in connection with proceedings before us to a legal guardian, committee, or similar court-appointed office; or (3) when representational services were provided before the court. A representative who has provided services in a claim before both the Social Security Administration and a court of law may seek a fee from either or both, but neither tribunal has the authority to set a fee for the other [42 U.S.C. 406(a) and (b)].

When to File a Fee Petition

The representative should request fee approval only after completing all services (for the claimant and any auxiliaries). The representative has the option to petition either before or after SSA effectuates the determination(s). In order to receive direct payment of all or any part of an authorized fee from past-due benefits, the attorney representative or non-attorney representative whom SSA has found eligible to receive direct payment should file a request for fee approval, or written notice of intent to file a request **within 60 days** of the date of the notice of the favorable determination is mailed. When there are multiple claims on one account and the attorney or non-attorney will not file the petition within 60 days after the mailing date of the first notice of favorable determination, he or she should file a written notice of intent to file a request for fee approval within the 60-day period.

Where to File the Petition

The representative must first give the "Claimant's Copy" of the SSA-1560-U4 petition to the claimant for whom he or she rendered services, with a copy of each attachment. The representative may then file the original and third carbon copy, the "OHA Copy," of the SSA-1560-U4, and the attachment(s), with the appropriate SSA office:

- If a court or the Appeals Council issued the decision, send the petition to the Office of Hearings and Appeals. Attention: Attorney Fee Branch, 5107 Leesburg Pike, Falls Church, VA 22041-3255.
- If an Administrative Law Judge issued the decision, send the petition to him or her using the hearing office address.
- In all other cases, send the petition to the reviewing office address which appears at the top right of the notice of award or notice of disapproved claim.

Evaluation of a Petition for a Fee

If the claimant has not agreed to and signed the fee petition, SSA does not begin evaluating the request for 30 days. SSA must decide what is a reasonable fee for the services rendered to the claimant, keeping in mind the purpose of the social security or supplemental security income program. When evaluating a request for fee approval, SSA will consider the (1) extent and type of services the representative performed; (2) complexity of the case; (3) level of skill and competence required of the representative in giving the services; (4) amount of time he or she spent on the case; (5) results achieved; (6) levels of review to which the representative took the claim and at which he or she became the representative; and (7) amount of fee requested for services rendered, including any amount authorized or requested before but excluding any amount of expenses incurred. SSA also considers the amount of benefits payable, if any, but authorizes the fee amount based on consideration of all the factors given here. The amount of benefits payable in a claim is determined by specific provisions of law unrelated to the representative's efforts. Also, the amount of past-due benefits may depend on the length of time that has elapsed since the claimant's effective date of entitlement.

Disagreement

SSA notifies both the representative and the claimant of the amount which it authorizes the representative to charge. If either or both disagree, SSA will further review the fee authorization when the claimant or representative sends a letter, explaining the reason(s) for disagreement, to the appropriate office **within 30 days** after the date of the notice of authorization to charge and receive a fee.

Collection of the Fee

Basic liability for payment of a representative's approved fee rests with the client. However, SSA will assist in fee collection when the representative is an attorney or a non-attorney whom SSA has found eligible to receive direct payment, and SSA awards the claimant benefits under Title II or Title XVI of the Social Security Act. In these cases, SSA generally withholds 25 percent of the claimant's past-due benefits. Once the fee is approved, SSA pays the attorney or the eligible non-attorney from the claimant's withheld funds. **This does not mean that SSA will approve as a reasonable fee 25 percent of the past-due benefits.** The amount payable to the attorney or eligible non-attorney from the withheld benefits is subject to the assessment required by section 206(d) and 1631(d)(2)(C) of the Social Security Act, and it is also subject to offset by any fee payment(s) the attorney or eligible non-attorney has received or expects to receive from an escrow or trust account. If the approved fee is more than the amount of the withheld benefits, collection of the difference is a matter between the attorney or eligible non-attorney and the client. SSA will not pay a fee from withheld past-due benefits when the authorized fee is for an attorney or non-attorney who was discharged by the client or who withdrew from representing the client.

Penalty for Charging or Collecting an Unauthorized Fee

Any individual who charges or collects an unauthorized fee for services provided in any claim, including services before a court which has rendered a favorable determination, may be subject to prosecution under 42 U.S.C. 406 and 1383 which provide that such individual, upon conviction thereof, shall for each offense be punished by a fine not exceeding $500, by imprisonment not exceeding one year, or both.

Privacy Act

Sections 206 and 1631(d) of the Social Security Act, as amended, authorize us to collect this information. We will use the information you provide to determine a fair value for services you rendered to the claimant named on the form. Furnishing us this information is voluntary. However, failing to provide us with all or part of the information may affect the amount you are requesting. We rarely use the information you supply for any purpose other than determining a fair value for services. However, we may use the information for the administration of our programs including sharing information:

1. To comply with Federal laws requiring the release of information from our records (e.g., to the Government Accountability Office and Department of Veterans Affairs); and,
2. To facilitate statistical research, audit, or investigative activities necessary to assure the integrity and improvement of our programs (e.g., to the Bureau of the Census and to private entities under contract with us).

A complete list of when we may share your information with others, called routine uses, is available in our Privacy Act System of Records Notice 60-0003, entitled Attorney Fee File. Additional information about this and other system of records notices and our programs are available from our Internet website at www.socialsecurity.gov or at your local Social Security office.

We may share the information you provide to other health agencies through computer matching programs. Matching programs compare our records with records kept by other Federal, State, or local government agencies. We use the information from these programs to establish or verify a person's eligibility for federally funded or administered benefit programs and for repayment of incorrect payments or delinquent debts under these programs.

Paperwork Reduction Act Statement - This information collection meets the requirements of 44 U.S.C. § 3507, as amended by section 2 of the Paperwork Reduction Act of 1995. You do not need to answer these questions unless we display a valid Office of Management and Budget control number. We estimate that it will take about 30 minutes to read the instructions, gather the facts, and answer the questions. *Send **only** comments relating to our time estimate above to*: *SSA, 6401 Security Blvd, Baltimore, MD 21235-6401.*

Form **SSA-1560-U4** (03-2014) EF (03-2014)

SOCIAL SECURITY ADMINISTRATION   **TOE 850**   Form Approved
                                                                                 OMB No. 0960-0104

PETITION TO OBTAIN APPROVAL OF A FEE FOR REPRESENTING A CLAIMANT BEFORE THE SOCIAL SECURITY ADMINISTRATION

IMPORTANT INFORMATION ON REVERSE SIDE

I request approval to charge a fee of: Fee $ (Show the dollar amount)

for services performed as the representative of:

My Services Began: ____ / ____ / _____   Type(s) of claim(s)
                    Month Day   Year

My Services Ended: ____ / ____ / _____

Enter the name and the Social Security number of the person on whose Social Security record the claim is based.

___ ___ ___ / ___ ___ / ___ ___ ___ ___

---

1. Itemize on a separate page or pages the services you rendered before the Social Security Administration (SSA). List each meeting, conference, item of correspondence, telephone call, and other activity in which you engaged, such as research, preparation of a brief, attendance at a hearing, travel, etc., related to your services as representative in this case. Attach to this petition the list showing the dates, the descriptions of each service, the actual time spent in each, and the total hours.

2. Have you and your client entered into a fee agreement for services before SSA?   ☐ YES   ☐ NO

If "yes," please specify the amount on which you agreed, and attach a copy of the agreement
to this petition. $ _____   and ☐ See attached

3. (a) Have you received, or do you expect to receive, any payment toward your fee from any source
        other than from funds which SSA may be withholding for fee payment?   ☐ YES   ☐ NO

   (b) Do you currently hold in a trust or escrow account any amount of money you received toward
       payment of your fee?   ☐ YES   ☐ NO

   If "yes" to either or both of the above, please specify the source(s) and the amount(s).

   Source: _____ $ _____

   Source: _____ $ _____

   Note: If you receive payment(s) after submitting this petition, but before the SSA approves a fee, you have an affirmative duty to notify the
   SSA office to which you are sending this petition.

4. Have you received, or do you expect to receive, reimbursement for expenses you incurred?   ☐ YES   ☐ NO
   If "yes," please itemize your expenses and the amounts on a separate page.

5. Did you render any services relating to this matter before any State or Federal court?   ☐ YES   ☐ NO

   If "yes," what fee did you or will you charge for services in connection with the court proceedings?
   Please attach a copy of the court order if the court has approved a fee. $ _____

6. Have you been disbarred or suspended from a court or bar to which you were previously admitted to practice as an attorney?

                                                                                               ☐ YES   ☐ NO

7. Have you been disqualified from participating in or appearing before a Federal program or agency?

                                                                                               ☐ YES   ☐ NO

I declare under penalty of perjury that I have examined all the information on this form, and on any accompanying statements or forms, and it is true and correct to the best of my knowledge.

Signature of Representative	Date	Address (include Zip Code)
Firm with which associated, if any		Telephone No. and Area Code

[Note: The following is optional. However, SSA can consider your fee petition more promptly if your client knows and already agrees with the amount you are requesting.]

I understand that I do not have to sign this petition or request. It is my right to disagree with the amount of the fee requested or any information given, and to ask more questions about the information given in this request (as explained on the reverse side of this form). I have marked my choice below.

☐   I agree with the $ _____ fee which my representative is asking to charge and collect. By signing this request, I am not giving up my
    right to disagree later with the total fee amount the Social Security Administration authorizes my representative to charge and collect.

OR

☐   I do not agree with the requested fee or other information given here, or I need more time. I understand I must call, visit, or write to SSA
    within 20 days if I have questions or if I disagree with the fee requested or any information shown (as explained on the reverse sides of this
    form).

Signature of Claimant	Date
Address (include Zip Code)	Telephone No. and Area Code

Form **SSA-1560-U4** (03-2014) EF (03-2014)   **CLAIMANT'S COPY**
Destroy Prior Editions

WHAT YOU SHOULD KNOW

This is a copy of a petition, or request, your representative made to the Social Security Administration (SSA) for approval to charge a fee for services performed in connection with your claim.

If You Have Questions or Disagree Now

If you have questions or if you disagree with the fee requested or any information shown, contact SSA **within 20 days** from the date of this request. You may call or visit your local Social Security office or you may write to the office which last took action in your case.

- Write to the SSA office address which appears at the top right on your notice of award or notice of disapproved claim, unless you know that your claim went to the Appeals Council or an Administrative Law Judge of the Office of Hearings and Appeals.
- If an Administrative Law Judge made the last decision in your case, write to him or her using the hearing office address.
- If the Appeals Council or a court made the last decision in your case, write to the Office of Hearings and Appeals, Attention: Attorney Fee Branch, 5107 Leesburg Pike, Falls Church, VA 22041-3255.

If you decide to call, visit, or write, act quickly so that your questions reach the correct office **within 20 days**.

For Your Protection

Until you receive notice that SSA has approved a fee, you should not pay your representative unless the payment is held in an escrow or trust account. If you are charged or pay any money after you receive your copy of this petition but before you receive notice of the fee amount your representative may charge, report this to SSA immediately.

What Happens Next

No matter what you may have agreed to in writing, SSA decides how much your representative may charge you for his or her services. SSA must decide what is a reasonable fee for the work your representative did, keeping in mind the purpose of the social security or supplemental security income program. **SSA does not automatically approve 25 percent of any past-due benefits as a reasonable fee.** SSA must consider the (1) extent and type of services the representative performed; (2) complexity of your case; (3) level of skill and competence required of your representative in giving the services; (4) amount of time he or she spent on your case; (5) results achieved; (6) levels of review to which your representative took your claim and at which he or she became your representative; and (7) amount of fee he or she requests, including any amount requested or authorized before but excluding any amount of expenses incurred. SSA also considers the amount of benefits payable, if any, but approves a fee amount based on all the factors given here. This is because the amount of benefits payable to you is determined by the law and regulations, not by your representative's efforts. Also, the amount of past-due benefits may depend on the length of time that has gone by since your effective date of entitlement.

What Happens Later

SSA will send you a written notice showing the fee amount your representative may charge you based on this request. If you disagree with the amount approved, you must write to say you disagree and to give your reasons, sending your letter to the SSA office address shown on the "Authorization to Charge and Receive a Fee" **within 30 days** of the date on that notice. **You may disagree with the fee approved, even if you do not disagree now with the fee amount your representative is requesting.**

The law and regulations say that part of any past-due social security or supplemental security income benefits payable to you, under Title II or Title XVI of the Social Security Act must be used toward the payment of your representative's fee if he or she is an attorney or a non-attorney whom SSA has found eligible to receive direct payment. The amount SSA may pay your attorney or eligible non-attorney directly is the **smallest** of the following:

- twenty-five percent (25%), or one-fourth, of the total past-due benefits payable to you as a result of the claim;
- the fee amount approved; or
- the amount which you and your attorney or eligible non-attorney agreed upon as the fee for his or her services (shown on the reverse in item 2 of this petition).

SSA will not pay a fee to an attorney or non-attorney representative if you discharged the representative or he or she withdrew from representing you.

Privacy Act

Sections 206 and 1631(d) of the Social Security Act, as amended, authorize us to collect this information. We will use the information you provide to determine a fair value for services you rendered to the claimant named on the form. Furnishing us this information is voluntary. However, failing to provide us with all or part of the information may affect the amount you are requesting. We rarely use the information you supply for any purpose other than determining a fair value for services. However, we may use the information for the administration of our programs including sharing information:

1. To comply with Federal laws requiring the release of information from our records (e.g., to the Government Accountability Office and Department of Veterans Affairs); and,
2. To facilitate statistical research, audit, or investigative activities necessary to assure the integrity and improvement of our programs (e.g., to the Bureau of the Census and to private entities under contract with us).

A complete list of when we may share your information with others, called routine uses, is available in our Privacy Act System of Records Notice 60-0003, entitled Attorney Fee File. Additional information about this and other system of records notices and our programs are available from our Internet website at www.socialsecurity.gov or at your local Social Security office.

We may share the information you provide to other health agencies through computer matching programs. Matching programs compare our records with records kept by other Federal, State, or local government agencies. We use the information from these programs to establish or verify a person's eligibility for federally funded or administered benefit programs and for repayment of incorrect payments or delinquent debts under these programs.

Paperwork Reduction Act Statement - This information collection meets the requirements of 44 U.S.C. § 3507, as amended by section 2 of the Paperwork Reduction Act of 1995. You do not need to answer these questions unless we display a valid Office of Management and Budget control number. We estimate that it will take about 30 minutes to read the instructions, gather the facts, and answer the questions. *Send **only** comments relating to our time estimate above to: SSA, 6401 Security Blvd, Baltimore, MD 21235-6401.*

Form **SSA-1560-U4** (03-2014) EF (03-2014)

SOCIAL SECURITY ADMINISTRATION | TOE 850 | Form Approved OMB No. 0960-0104

PETITION TO OBTAIN APPROVAL OF A FEE FOR REPRESENTING A CLAIMANT BEFORE THE SOCIAL SECURITY ADMINISTRATION

IMPORTANT INFORMATION ON REVERSE SIDE

I request approval to charge a fee of:

Fee$ _____ (Show the dollar amount)

for services performed as the representative of:

My Services Began: ____ / ____ / _____
Month   Day   Year

Type(s) of claim(s)

My Services Ended: ____ / ____ / _____

Enter the name and the Social Security number of the person on whose Social Security record the claim is based.

__ __ __ / __ __ / __ __ __ __

1. Itemize on a separate page or pages the services you rendered before the Social Security Administration (SSA). List each meeting, conference, item of correspondence, telephone call, and other activity in which you engaged, such as research, preparation of a brief, attendance at a hearing, travel, etc., related to your services as representative in this case. Attach to this petition the list showing the dates, the descriptions of each service, the actual time spent in each, and the total hours.

2. Have you and your client entered into a fee agreement for services before SSA? ☐ YES ☐ NO
If "yes," please specify the amount on which you agreed, and attach a copy of the agreement to this petition. $ _____ and ☐ See attached

3. (a) Have you received, or do you expect to receive, any payment toward your fee from any source other than from funds which SSA may be withholding for fee payment? ☐ YES ☐ NO
(b) Do you currently hold in a trust or escrow account any amount of money you received toward payment of your fee? ☐ YES ☐ NO
If "yes" to either or both of the above, please specify the source(s) and the amount(s).
Source: _____ $ _____
Source: _____ $ _____
Note: If you receive payment(s) after submitting this petition, but before the SSA approves a fee, you have an affirmative duty to notify the SSA office to which you are sending this petition.

4. Have you received, or do you expect to receive, reimbursement for expenses you incurred? ☐ YES ☐ NO
If "yes," please itemize your expenses and the amounts on a separate page.

5. Did you render any services relating to this matter before any State or Federal court? ☐ YES ☐ NO
If "yes," what fee did you or will you charge for services in connection with the court proceedings? Please attach a copy of the court order if the court has approved a fee. $ _____

6. Have you been disbarred or suspended from a court or bar to which you were previously admitted to practice as an attorney? ☐ YES ☐ NO

7. Have you been disqualified from participating in or appearing before a Federal program or agency? ☐ YES ☐ NO

I declare under penalty of perjury that I have examined all the information on this form, and on any accompanying statements or forms, and it is true and correct to the best of my knowledge.

Signature of Representative | Date | Address (include Zip Code)

Firm with which associated, if any | Telephone No. and Area Code

[Note: The following is optional. However, SSA can consider your fee petition more promptly if your client knows and already agrees with the amount you are requesting.]

I understand that I do not have to sign this petition or request. It is my right to disagree with the amount of the fee requested or any information given, and to ask more questions about the information given in this request (as explained on the reverse side of this form). I have marked my choice below.

☐ I agree with the $ _____ fee which my representative is asking to charge and collect. By signing this request, I am not giving up my right to disagree later with the total fee amount the Social Security Administration authorizes my representative to charge and collect.

OR

☐ I do not agree with the requested fee or other information given here, or I need more time. I understand I must call, visit, or write to SSA within 20 days if I have questions or if I disagree with the fee requested or any information shown (as explained on the reverse sides of this form).

Signature of Claimant | Date

Address (include Zip Code) | Telephone No. and Area Code

Form **SSA-1560-U4** (03-2014) EF (03-2014)
Destroy Prior Editions   **REPRESENTATIVE'S COPY**

INSTRUCTIONS FOR USING THIS PETITION

Any attorney or other representative who wants to charge or collect a fee for services, rendered in connection with a claim before the Social Security Administration (SSA), is required by law to first obtain SSA's approval of the fee [sections 206(a) and 1631(d)(2) of the Social Security Act (42 U.S.C. 406(a) and 1383(d)(2)) and sections 404.1720 and 416.1520 of Social Security Administration Regulations Numbers 4 and 16, respectively.] The only exceptions are 1) when a third party entity, (i.e. a business, firm, or government agency) will pay the fee and any expenses from its own funds and the claimant and any auxiliary beneficiaries incur no liability, directly or indirectly, for the cost(s); (2) when a court has awarded a fee for services provided in connection with proceedings before us to a legal guardian, committee, or similar court-appointed office; or (3) when representational services were provided before the court. A representative who has provided services in a claim before both the Social Security Administration and a court of law may seek a fee from either or both, but neither tribunal has the authority to set a fee for the other [42 U.S.C. 406(a) and (b)].

When to File a Fee Petition

The representative should request fee approval only after completing all services (for the claimant and any auxiliaries). The representative has the option to petition either before or after SSA effectuates the determination(s). In order to receive direct payment of all or any part of an authorized fee from past-due benefits, the attorney representative or non-attorney representative whom SSA has found eligible to receive direct payment should file a request for fee approval, or written notice of intent to file a request **within 60 days** of the date of the notice of the favorable determination is mailed. When there are multiple claims on one account and the attorney or non-attorney will not file the petition within 60 days after the mailing date of the first notice of favorable determination, he or she should file a written notice of intent to file a request for fee approval within the 60-day period.

Where to File the Petition

The representative must first give the "Claimant's Copy" of the SSA-1560-U4 petition to the claimant for whom he or she rendered services, with a copy of each attachment. The representative may then file the original and third carbon copy, the "OHA Copy," of the SSA-1560-U4, and the attachment(s), with the appropriate SSA office:

- If a court or the Appeals Council issued the decision, send the petition to the Office of Hearings and Appeals. Attention: Attorney Fee Branch, 5107 Leesburg Pike, Falls Church, VA 22041-3255.
- If an Administrative Law Judge issued the decision, send the petition to him or her using the hearing office address.
- In all other cases, send the petition to the reviewing office address which appears at the top right of the notice of award or notice of disapproved claim.

Evaluation of a Petition for a Fee

If the claimant has not agreed to and signed the fee petition, SSA does not begin evaluating the request for 30 days. SSA must decide what is a reasonable fee for the services rendered to the claimant, keeping in mind the purpose of the social security or supplemental security income program. When evaluating a request for fee approval, SSA will consider the (1) extent and type of services the representative performed; (2) complexity of the case; (3) level of skill and competence required of the representative in giving the services; (4) amount of time he or she spent on the case; (5) results achieved; (6) levels of review to which the representative took the claim and at which he or she became the representative; and (7) amount of fee requested for services rendered, including any amount authorized or requested before but excluding any amount of expenses incurred. SSA also considers the amount of benefits payable, if any, but authorizes the fee amount based on consideration of all the factors given here. The amount of benefits payable in a claim is determined by specific provisions of law unrelated to the representative's efforts. Also, the amount of past-due benefits may depend on the length of time that has elapsed since the claimant's effective date of entitlement.

Disagreement

SSA notifies both the representative and the claimant of the amount which it authorizes the representative to charge. If either or both disagree, SSA will further review the fee authorization when the claimant or representative sends a letter, explaining the reason(s) for disagreement, to the appropriate office **within 30 days** after the date of the notice of authorization to charge and receive a fee.

Collection of the Fee

Basic liability for payment of a representative's approved fee rests with the client. However, SSA will assist in fee collection when the representative is an attorney or a non-attorney whom SSA has found eligible to receive direct payment, and SSA awards the claimant benefits under Title II or Title XVI of the Social Security Act. In these cases, SSA generally withholds 25 percent of the claimant's past-due benefits. Once the fee is approved, SSA pays the attorney or the eligible non-attorney from the claimant's withheld funds. **This does not mean that SSA will approve as a reasonable fee 25 percent of the past-due benefits.** The amount payable to the attorney or eligible non-attorney from the withheld benefits is subject to the assessment required by section 206(d) and 1631(d)(2)(C) of the Social Security Act, and it is also subject to offset by any fee payment(s) the attorney or eligible non-attorney has received or expects to receive from an escrow or trust account. If the approved fee is more than the amount of the withheld benefits, collection of the difference is a matter between the attorney or eligible non-attorney and the client. SSA will not pay a fee from withheld past-due benefits when the authorized fee is for an attorney or non-attorney who was discharged by the client or who withdrew from representing the client.

Penalty for Charging or Collecting an Unauthorized Fee

Any individual who charges or collects an unauthorized fee for services provided in any claim, including services before a court which has rendered a favorable determination, may be subject to prosecution under 42 U.S.C. 406 and 1383 which provide that such individual, upon conviction thereof, shall for each offense be punished by a fine not exceeding $500, by imprisonment not exceeding one year, or both.

Privacy Act

Sections 206 and 1631(d) of the Social Security Act, as amended, authorize us to collect this information. We will use the information you provide to determine a fair value for services you rendered to the claimant named on the form. Furnishing us this information is voluntary. However, failing to provide us with all or part of the information may affect the amount you are requesting. We rarely use the information you supply for any purpose other than determining a fair value for services. However, we may use the information for the administration of our programs including sharing information:

1. To comply with Federal laws requiring the release of information from our records (e.g., to the Government Accountability Office and Department of Veterans Affairs); and,
2. To facilitate statistical research, audit, or investigative activities necessary to assure the integrity and improvement of our programs (e.g., to the Bureau of the Census and to private entities under contract with us).

A complete list of when we may share your information with others, called routine uses, is available in our Privacy Act System of Records Notice 60-0003, entitled Attorney Fee File. Additional information about this and other system of records notices and our programs are available from our Internet website at www.socialsecurity.gov or at your local Social Security office.

We may share the information you provide to other health agencies through computer matching programs. Matching programs compare our records with records kept by other Federal, State, or local government agencies. We use the information from these programs to establish or verify a person's eligibility for federally funded or administered benefit programs and for repayment of incorrect payments or delinquent debts under these programs.

Paperwork Reduction Act Statement - This information collection meets the requirements of 44 U.S.C. § 3507, as amended by section 2 of the Paperwork Reduction Act of 1995. You do not need to answer these questions unless we display a valid Office of Management and Budget control number. We estimate that it will take about 30 minutes to read the instructions, gather the facts, and answer the questions. *Send **only** comments relating to our time estimate above to:* SSA, 6401 Security Blvd, Baltimore, MD 21235-6401.

Form **SSA-1560-U4** (03-2014) EF (03-2014)

SOCIAL SECURITY ADMINISTRATION	TOE 850	Form Approved OMB No. 0960-0104

PETITION TO OBTAIN APPROVAL OF A FEE FOR REPRESENTING A CLAIMANT BEFORE THE SOCIAL SECURITY ADMINISTRATION

IMPORTANT INFORMATION ON REVERSE SIDE

I request approval to charge a fee of:

Fee$ _____ (Show the dollar amount)

for services performed as the representative of:

My Services Began: ____ / ____ / _____
               Month   Day   Year

Type(s) of claim(s)

My Services Ended: ____ / ____ / _____

Enter the name and the Social Security number of the person on whose Social Security record the claim is based.

___ ___ ___ / ___ ___ / ___ ___ ___ ___

1. Itemize on a separate page or pages the services you rendered before the Social Security Administration (SSA). List each meeting, conference, item of correspondence, telephone call, and other activity in which you engaged, such as research, preparation of a brief, attendance at a hearing, travel, etc., related to your services as representative in this case. Attach to this petition the list showing the dates, the descriptions of each service, the actual time spent in each, and the total hours.

2. Have you and your client entered into a fee agreement for services before SSA? ☐ YES ☐ NO

   If "yes," please specify the amount on which you agreed, and attach a copy of the agreement to this petition. $ _____ and ☐ See attached

3. (a) Have you received, or do you expect to receive, any payment toward your fee from any source other than from funds which SSA may be withholding for fee payment? ☐ YES ☐ NO

   (b) Do you currently hold in a trust or escrow account any amount of money you received toward payment of your fee? ☐ YES ☐ NO

   If "yes" to either or both of the above, please specify the source(s) and the amount(s).

   Source: _____ $ _____

   Source: _____ $ _____

   Note: If you receive payment(s) after submitting this petition, but before the SSA approves a fee, you have an affirmative duty to notify the SSA office to which you are sending this petition.

4. Have you received, or do you expect to receive, reimbursement for expenses you incurred? ☐ YES ☐ NO
   If "yes," please itemize your expenses and the amounts on a separate page.

5. Did you render any services relating to this matter before any State or Federal court? ☐ YES ☐ NO

   If "yes," what fee did you or will you charge for services in connection with the court proceedings? Please attach a copy of the court order if the court has approved a fee. $ _____

6. Have you been disbarred or suspended from a court or bar to which you were previously admitted to practice as an attorney? ☐ YES ☐ NO

7. Have you been disqualified from participating in or appearing before a Federal program or agency? ☐ YES ☐ NO

I declare under penalty of perjury that I have examined all the information on this form, and on any accompanying statements or forms, and it is true and correct to the best of my knowledge.

Signature of Representative	Date	Address (include Zip Code)
Firm with which associated, if any		Telephone No. and Area Code

[Note: The following is optional. However, SSA can consider your fee petition more promptly if your client knows and already agrees with the amount you are requesting.]

I understand that I do not have to sign this petition or request. It is my right to disagree with the amount of the fee requested or any information given, and to ask more questions about the information given in this request (as explained on the reverse side of this form). I have marked my choice below.

☐   I agree with the $ _____ fee which my representative is asking to charge and collect. By signing this request, I am not giving up my right to disagree later with the total fee amount the Social Security Administration authorizes my representative to charge and collect.

OR

☐   I do not agree with the requested fee or other information given here, or I need more time. I understand I must call, visit, or write to SSA within 20 days if I have questions or if I disagree with the fee requested or any information shown (as explained on the reverse sides of this form).

Signature of Claimant	Date
Address (include Zip Code)	Telephone No. and Area Code

Form **SSA-1560-U4** (03-2014) EF (03-2014)
Destroy Prior Editions

OHA COPY

INSTRUCTIONS FOR USING THIS PETITION

Any attorney or other representative who wants to charge or collect a fee for services, rendered in connection with a claim before the Social Security Administration (SSA), is required by law to first obtain SSA's approval of the fee [sections 206(a) and 1631(d)(2) of the Social Security Act (42 U.S.C. 406(a) and 1383(d)(2)) and sections 404.1720 and 416.1520 of Social Security Administration Regulations Numbers 4 and 16, respectively.] The only exceptions are 1) when a third party entity, (i.e. a business, firm, or government agency) will pay the fee and any expenses from its own funds and the claimant and any auxiliary beneficiaries incur no liability, directly or indirectly, for the cost(s); (2) when a court has awarded a fee for services provided in connection with proceedings before us to a legal guardian, committee, or similar court-appointed office; or (3) when representational services were provided before the court. A representative who has provided services in a claim before both the Social Security Administration and a court of law may seek a fee from either or both, but neither tribunal has the authority to set a fee for the other [42 U.S.C. 406(a) and (b)].

When to File a Fee Petition

The representative should request fee approval only after completing all services (for the claimant and any auxiliaries). The representative has the option to petition either before or after SSA effectuates the determination(s). In order to receive direct payment of all or any part of an authorized fee from past-due benefits, the attorney representative or non-attorney representative whom SSA has found eligible to receive direct payment should file a request for fee approval, or written notice of intent to file a request **within 60 days** of the date of the notice of the favorable determination is mailed. When there are multiple claims on one account and the attorney or non-attorney will not file the petition within 60 days after the mailing date of the first notice of favorable determination, he or she should file a written notice of intent to file a request for fee approval within the 60-day period.

Where to File the Petition

The representative must first give the "Claimant's Copy" of the SSA-1560-U4 petition to the claimant for whom he or she rendered services, with a copy of each attachment. The representative may then file the original and third carbon copy, the "OHA Copy," of the SSA-1560-U4, and the attachment(s), with the appropriate SSA office:

- If a court or the Appeals Council issued the decision, send the petition to the Office of Hearings and Appeals. Attention: Attorney Fee Branch, 5107 Leesburg Pike, Falls Church, VA 22041-3255.
- If an Administrative Law Judge issued the decision, send the petition to him or her using the hearing office address.
- In all other cases, send the petition to the reviewing office address which appears at the top right of the notice of award or notice of disapproved claim.

Evaluation of a Petition for a Fee

If the claimant has not agreed to and signed the fee petition, SSA does not begin evaluating the request for 30 days. SSA must decide what is a reasonable fee for the services rendered to the claimant, keeping in mind the purpose of the social security or supplemental security income program. When evaluating a request for fee approval, SSA will consider the (1) extent and type of services the representative performed; (2) complexity of the case; (3) level of skill and competence required of the representative in giving the services; (4) amount of time he or she spent on the case; (5) results achieved; (6) levels of review to which the representative took the claim and at which he or she became the representative; and (7) amount of fee requested for services rendered, including any amount authorized or requested before but excluding any amount of expenses incurred. SSA also considers the amount of benefits payable, if any, but authorizes the fee amount based on consideration of all the factors given here. The amount of benefits payable in a claim is determined by specific provisions of law unrelated to the representative's efforts. Also, the amount of past-due benefits may depend on the length of time that has elapsed since the claimant's effective date of entitlement.

Disagreement

SSA notifies both the representative and the claimant of the amount which it authorizes the representative to charge. If either or both disagree, SSA will further review the fee authorization when the claimant or representative sends a letter, explaining the reason(s) for disagreement, to the appropriate office **within 30 days** after the date of the notice of authorization to charge and receive a fee.

Collection of the Fee

Basic liability for payment of a representative's approved fee rests with the client. However, SSA will assist in fee collection when the representative is an attorney or a non-attorney whom SSA has found eligible to receive direct payment, and SSA awards the claimant benefits under Title II or Title XVI of the Social Security Act. In these cases, SSA generally withholds 25 percent of the claimant's past-due benefits. Once the fee is approved, SSA pays the attorney or the eligible non-attorney from the claimant's withheld funds. **This does not mean that SSA will approve as a reasonable fee 25 percent of the past-due benefits.** The amount payable to the attorney or eligible non-attorney from the withheld benefits is subject to the assessment required by section 206(d) and 1631(d)(2)(C) of the Social Security Act, and it is also subject to offset by any fee payment(s) the attorney or eligible non-attorney has received or expects to receive from an escrow or trust account. If the approved fee is more than the amount of the withheld benefits, collection of the difference is a matter between the attorney or eligible non-attorney and the client. SSA will not pay a fee from withheld past-due benefits when the authorized fee is for an attorney or non-attorney who was discharged by the client or who withdrew from representing the client.

Penalty for Charging or Collecting an Unauthorized Fee

Any individual who charges or collects an unauthorized fee for services provided in any claim, including services before a court which has rendered a favorable determination, may be subject to prosecution under 42 U.S.C. 406 and 1383 which provide that such individual, upon conviction thereof, shall for each offense be punished by a fine not exceeding $500, by imprisonment not exceeding one year, or both.

Privacy Act

Sections 206 and 1631(d) of the Social Security Act, as amended, authorize us to collect this information. We will use the information you provide to determine a fair value for services you rendered to the claimant named on the form. Furnishing us this information is voluntary. However, failing to provide us with all or part of the information may affect the amount you are requesting. We rarely use the information you supply for any purpose other than determining a fair value for services. However, we may use the information for the administration of our programs including sharing information:

1. To comply with Federal laws requiring the release of information from our records (e.g., to the Government Accountability Office and Department of Veterans Affairs); and,
2. To facilitate statistical research, audit, or investigative activities necessary to assure the integrity and improvement of our programs (e.g., to the Bureau of the Census and to private entities under contract with us).

A complete list of when we may share your information with others, called routine uses, is available in our Privacy Act System of Records Notice 60-0003, entitled Attorney Fee File. Additional information about this and other system of records notices and our programs are available from our Internet website at www.socialsecurity.gov or at your local Social Security office.

We may share the information you provide to other health agencies through computer matching programs. Matching programs compare our records with records kept by other Federal, State, or local government agencies. We use the information from these programs to establish or verify a person's eligibility for federally funded or administered benefit programs and for repayment of incorrect payments or delinquent debts under these programs.

Paperwork Reduction Act Statement - This information collection meets the requirements of 44 U.S.C. § 3507, as amended by section 2 of the Paperwork Reduction Act of 1995. You do not need to answer these questions unless we display a valid Office of Management and Budget control number. We estimate that it will take about 30 minutes to read the instructions, gather the facts, and answer the questions. *Send **only** comments relating to our time estimate above to*: *SSA, 6401 Security Blvd, Baltimore, MD 21235-6401.*

Form **SSA-1560-U4** (03-2014) EF (03-2014)

§734   *Where to Send a Fee Petition*

If you are requesting a fee in a case you lost, as a rule, send the fee petition to the component of SSA that took the last unfavorable action on your client's appeal. If there has been a favorable decision, send the fee petition to the component of SSA, usually the ALJ or Appeals Council, which issued the favorable decision. If the ALJ issued a partially favorable decision that was appealed to the Appeals Council, which denied review, send the fee petition to the Attorney Fee Branch at the Appeals Council. HALLEX I-1-2-53 C. If a court issued the favorable decision, a petition to be paid for administrative work must be sent to the Attorney Fee Branch at the Appeals Council. POMS GN 03930.020C.9.

SSA has not made any provisions for filing a fee petition on the ERE. Nevertheless, it is possible to place a fee petition in your client's electronic folder, even though no one at SSA will receive an electronic notice that anything was filed. There is no ERE filing category available to representatives called "fee petition," but if you identify it as a "Fee Agreement," one of the available categories, it will end up in the correct B section of the electronic folder. Putting the fee petition in the electronic folder helps keep it from getting lost. But no one at SSA is going to know it is there until you tell them. Fax a letter notifying the ALJ that you put the fee petition on the ERE. In your letter, inquire whether the ALJ also wants you to submit a paper copy. Then follow up with the ALJ's assistant.

If your client received a favorable initial or reconsideration determination, as a rule you must send your fee petition to the address on the award letter. POMS GN 03930.020C.9. Send it by certified mail, return receipt requested. For regular Title II and concurrent claims approved at the initial or reconsideration stage where the claimant is under age 54, the fee petition will be authorized at the Office of Central Operations in Baltimore. Fee petitions for all claimants over age 54 are processed at the regional program service centers. POMS GN 03930.015 A. Although fee petitions for all SSI-only claims are also processed at regional program service centers, SSA directs that such fee petitions be sent to the claimant's local office. POMS GN 03930.020C.9.

Widows cases are processed at regional payment centers. Disabled adult child claims are processed at the payment center that has jurisdiction over the parent's claim—usually the regional program service center except in cases where the parent is under age 54 and receiving disability benefits. These are processed at the Office of Central Operations in Baltimore. POMS GN 03930.015 A.2.

You may speed receipt of your fee petition by using the Fee Petition Transmittal Flag that appears at §734.1. You may simply photocopy the form from this book and attach it as a cover sheet to your fee petition.

Begin sending monthly follow-up letters about 45 days after mailing. Be prepared to wait a long time, and be prepared for two frustrating possibilities. First, your fee petition may be lost and you will have to resubmit it. Second, the fee actually approved may be unrealistically low.

§734.1   Form: Fee Petition Transmittal Flag

TO: OFFICE OF CENTRAL OPERATIONS
       1500 WOODLAWN DRIVE
       BALTIMORE, MD 21241

FROM: _____

         _____

         _____

FOR INTERNAL USE ONLY

TOEL 1 – ATFEE
TOEL 2 – PET

TO LOC – CA PROC

CLAIMANT: _____   SSN: __ __ __ - __ __ - __ __ __ __

FEE PETITION TRANSMITTAL FLAG

This transmittal flag is to be used **only** for fee petitions being sent for review and fee authorization to the Office of Central Operations (Formerly ODIO). OCO is responsible for authorization of attorney fees under the fee petition process when:
- ✓ Services were provided at the initial or reconsideration level; and
- ✓ The primary beneficiary is under age 55; and
- ✓ Services were under Title II only; or
- ✓ Services were under Concurrent Title II / Title XVI .
   (OCO does not authorize fees relative to Title XVI only services.)

Attached is a fee petition submitted for your review and fee authorization.

My services were provided this claimant in connection with:

❑   A CLAIM FOR SOCIAL SECURITY DISABILITY BENEFITS

❑   A CONTINUING DISABILITY REVIEW (CDR)

❑   OTHER _____

NOTE: All Title XVI only fee petitions should be sent to the Program Service Center with jurisdiction for the social security number.

Transmittal Flag for SSA-1560-U4 (OCO, 5/98)

§735   When to Submit a Fee Petition

You must wait until all of your work is completed on the case before filing the fee petition. For example, if your client receives a partially favorable decision, which you appeal, you are not supposed to file a fee petition until all work on the appeal is finished. HALLEX I-1-2-53 B. If you are still providing services to the claimant for which you intend to charge a fee, SSA is supposed to return your fee petition to you. HALLEX I-1-2-56 A.3.

If your fee is calculated on an hourly basis, you may submit your fee petition promptly after you receive the decision and after you have seen to it that your client is paid back benefits—that is, when your work is done on the case. But, if your fee is calculated on the basis of a percentage of past-due benefits, you must wait until an award letter is issued showing the total amount of benefits awarded. Especially in concurrent cases involving both Social Security disability and SSI benefits, it may take more than two months from the date of the favorable decision for all benefits to be calculated.

Although there is no time limit for filing a fee petition, direct payment of attorney fees requires that a petition or written notice of intent to submit a fee petition be filed within 60 days of the date of the favorable decision. 20 C.F.R. § 404.1730(c)(1), HALLEX I-1-2-53 B.2, POMS GN 03930.020.C.7.b. As soon as a favorable decision is received, notify the ALJ by letter that you intend to file a fee petition as soon as all past-due benefits are calculated. *See* sample letter §407.

Sometimes your client is paid but no award letter is forthcoming. If this happens, contact the payment center to request that the Notice of Award be issued. *See* §§444 and 446 for telephone and fax numbers and the discussion at §§441 and 710. If contacting the payment center does not work, ask the ALJ to request a copy of an SSA document known as a Form SSA-1129, Attorney Fee Case—Past Due Benefit Summary. This form, which is not prepared unless requested by an ALJ, will show you SSA's calculation of the amount of withheld fees. POMS GN 03920.045A.

If SSA releases the money withheld for direct payment of attorney fees to the claimant because you failed to file a timely fee petition or give notice of your intent to do so, you still must submit a fee petition and SSA will act on it. However, you will have to collect your fee directly from your client. POMS GN 03930.020C.7.b.

Some attorneys prefer to collect their fees from their clients, since fees can be paid by the client a month or more earlier than checks issued in response to a fee authorization. The "user fee" is also avoided when the client pays the fee directly to the attorney. Although you can hold the fee in your trust account, the fee must be authorized before it is actually received by the attorney. SSR 82-39. If you decide to collect your fee from your client, be sure to check the correct box indicating that you are "charging a fee but waiving direct payment" located at the bottom of the Appointment of Representative Form to accomplish release of fees most expeditiously. *See* §178.2.1. Although SSA says that it will try to honor a waiver of direct payment of a fee if it receives it at any time before the fee is actually paid, SSA will refund an erroneously withheld user fee only if it receives the waiver no later than the date SSA receives the fee petition. POMS GN 03920.051B.

§736   Wait for Payment of Auxiliary Benefits

When benefits are to be paid not only to the claimant, but also to other members of the claimant's family, many months may pass before all benefits are paid. A petition for a fee based upon a percentage of all past-due benefits paid on the claimant's account must wait until the auxiliary benefits are paid. According to SSA, "Multiple authorizations based on multiple fee petitions for the same services are not appropriate, even if additional past-due benefits are available." HALLEX I-1-2-53 B. For example, if $2,000 is approved for attorney fees from the claimant's past-due benefits, SSA won't allow a second fee petition for an additional $1,000 later withheld out of the claimant's children's benefits unless you can show additional work on the case related to obtaining the auxiliary benefits.

If you mistakenly submit a fee petition that neglects family benefits, you may be able to withdraw it and petition for a higher fee if you catch the mistake before your fee is authorized. If your fee has already been authorized and you are still within the 30-day time limit for a fee appeal, you may attempt to correct your error by an administrative appeal of your fee. If the 30-day time limit to appeal a fee authorization has run, you may be out of luck. You will need an exceptionally creative argument why SSA should increase your fee.

§737   Submit a Written Argument for Approval of Fee

By the time your fee petition goes to an ALJ, the ALJ may not remember what you did in the case to help the ALJ conclude that your client was disabled.

Thus, it is helpful to send a short letter with your fee petition explaining how your efforts helped win your client's case. Describe why your fee should be approved, emphasizing the factors set forth in 20

C.F.R. § 404.1725(b). Consider adding comments to demonstrate how your requested fee is reasonable under the ABA's Model Rules of Professional Conduct, Rule 1.5, or the equivalent that has been adopted in your state. Discuss prevailing hourly rates in your community and consider quoting Justice Brennan's concurrence and dissent in *Hensley v. Eckerhart*, 461 U.S. 424, 448 (1983), a case involving court-awarded attorney's fees under the Civil Rights Attorney's Fees Awards Act:

> Most attorneys paid an hourly rate expect to be paid promptly and without regard to success or failure. Customary rates reflect those expectations. Attorneys who take cases on contingency, thus deferring payment of their fees until the case has ended and taking upon themselves the risk that they will receive no payment at all, generally receive far more in winning cases than they would if they charged an hourly rate. The difference, however, reflects the time-value of money and the risk of non-recovery usually borne by clients in cases where lawyers are paid an hourly rate.

If your client supports your fee and has signed the fee petition indicating approval, this is worth mentioning in your cover letter. When your client strongly supports your fee, a letter from the client explaining how pleased your client was with your services might encourage the ALJ to approve a higher than usual fee.

Some lawyers submit full-scale briefs to the ALJ detailing what they did in the case. A sample brief based on one written by Attorney Michael Williamson of Nashville, Tennessee appears at §737.1.

§737.1 Sample Fee Petition Brief

Judge Full Name
Administrative Law Judge
Office of Disability Adjudication & Review
Street Address
City State Zip

Re:
SSN:
DOB:

SUBMISSION OF ATTORNEY FEE PETITION

Dear Judge Last Name:

I.　Submission of Fee Petition seeking approval of an attorney fee of $_____ for my representation of X before SSA.

I write to submit my Fee Petition seeking approval of an attorney fee of $_____ . I include the following:

1.　Appointment of Representative (Form SSA-1696-U4) executed on _____ ;
2.　Attorney fee agreement executed on _____ and which expired by its own terms by virtue of the fact that X's claim was denied at hearing level and thus had to be appealed to the Appeals Council;
3.　Fee Petition;
4.　Itemizations of time and also expenses advanced (regarding which X has already made reimbursement); and
5.　DIB Award Notice dated _____ (25% of past-due DIB withheld for attorney fee = $_____)

II.　Pursuant to the eight "Criteria for Evaluating Fee Petitions" set forth in 20 CFR § 404.1725(b) and discussed/explained in detail in HALLEX I-1-2-57, the requested fee of $_____ should be found to be reasonable and, accordingly, approved [or recommended to be approved by the RCALJ].

1. Consideration of the fee petition pursuant to Criteria No. 1 of HALLEX I-1-2-57, the "Purpose of the Program."

HALLEX I-1-2-57 A. 1. provides that the fee authorizer must consider the "purpose of the program," and states that in Title II cases, the purpose of the program is "to provide the measure of economic security for program beneficiaries." My representation, and the requested fee, are consistent with this purpose. X has received substantial past-due benefits totaling over $_____ and s/he receives continuing DIB. X has been "provided with a measure of economic security," and thus the purpose of the program has been well served.

2. Consideration of the fee petition pursuant to Criteria No. 2, the "Services Provided."

HALLEX I-1-2-57 A. 2. states:

Depending on the circumstances in the case, the fee authorizer also will consider whether the representative:

- Researched relevant law or rulings.
- Searched old records to obtain the evidence.
- Arranged a medical examination.
- Submitted medical or lay evidence of disability or other factors of entitlement.
- Contacted the Social Security Administration (SSA) as needed about the status of the claim.
- Participated at the hearing.
- Promoted timely decision making or acted in a way that delayed the issuance of the decision without justification.

I performed each and every one of these services for X. I researched the relevant law and rulings and submitted relevant authority; I obtained and submitted all of her treatment records; and I thoroughly studied all of these records to identify all evidence that supported X's claim.

Regarding the arranging of medical examinations, I advanced the cost of obtaining testimony at the hearing of X's treating psychologist, and I facilitated this psychologist's preparation for his hearing testimony by providing copies of X's voluminous records and discussing X's very complex history.

Regarding contact with SSA as needed about the status of her claim, my time itemization documents frequent and timely contact with SSA, ODAR and the Appeals Councils to facilitate the consideration of X's claim.
Regarding participation at hearings, I represented X at two ALJ hearings.

Regarding the evaluation of the "services provided" by the representative, HALLEX I-1-2-57A.2 sets forth two examples:

Examples:
1. A representative submitted a copy of a hospital report that served as the primary basis for the Administrative Law Judge (ALJ) finding the claimant disabled.

2. A representative submitted a copy of medical evidence she had used successfully in a recent workers' compensation claim to support the claim for a period of disability and disability insurance benefits. The representative provided SSA with readily available evidence we may not have had. However, the submission of new medical evidence relating to the period before insured status expired would have been a far more valuable service.

I did submit "new medical evidence relating to the period before" X's DLI. The submission of such evidence is characterized in Example 2 as "a far more valuable service." Furthermore, I played an instrumental role in the development and presentation of the evidence which ultimately established that her impairments were disabling prior to her DLI.

3. Consideration of the fee petition pursuant to Criteria No. 3, the "Complexity of the Case."

HALLEX I-1-2-57 A. 3. provides that the complexity of the case is evaluated "based on the work or documentation needed to resolve the issues." The following "Example" is given:

> **Example:** A representative contacted numerous sources for information used to establish the claimant's date of birth, a task of some complexity.

When one looks at the "work or documentation needed (and performed) to resolve the issues" in X' case, one sees dozens of hours of highly skilled and very thorough development and presentation of the evidence and the needed documentation. Obviously, I "contacted numerous sources for information used to establish" the nature and severity of X's disabling conditions. Evaluating the complexity of X' case "based on the work or documentation needed to resolve the issues" establishes that her case was very complicated by virtue of her long history of physical and mental impairments, the remote onset date that had to be established, the tortured procedural history (including res judicata dismissals) of her claims, etc. I respectfully submit that I skillfully and successfully investigated and documented X's psychological conditions, and addressed each and every other issue in the case.

4. Consideration of the fee petition pursuant to Criteria No. 4, the "Level of Skill and Competence Required in Providing Services."

HALLEX I-1-2-57 A. 4 provides that the fee authorizer should "consider the issues involved and the probing the representative did to resolve them." The "Example" given reads as follows:

> **Example:** One representative submitted a copy of the evidence he used in the claimant's workers' compensation claim.
> A representative in another case scheduled a medical examination and submitted the results for evaluation, along with

this new evidence showing the claimant's condition. The representative's actions in the second case demonstrate greater skill and competence.

The issues in this case, especially those pertaining to the X's multiple physical and mental conditions, etc. were very complicated, and the "probing (I) did to resolve them" had to be, and was, very extensive. The Example establishes that when a representative schedules medical examinations and submits the results along with other new evidence showing the claimant's condition, the representative has demonstrated "greater skill and competence" than someone who just submits a copy of evidence used in a workers' compensation claim. The great lengths I went to develop the evidence and my successful presentation of this evidence demonstrates great skill and competence.

5. Consideration of the fee petition pursuant to Criteria No. 5, the "Amount of Time Spent."

I respectfully submit that all of my itemized time,   hours, should be credited, and that none of my time can in any way be characterized as "exaggerated or inordinate."

6. Consideration of the fee petition pursuant to Criteria No. 6, the "Results the Representative Achieved."

The "Example" given in HALLEX I-1-2-57 A. 6. reads as follows:

> **Example:** An assessment of his client's description of symptoms prompted the representative to develop evidence of a medical condition the field office and Disability Determination Services had overlooked. This established the claimant's entitlement to disability insurance benefits. When evaluating, you credit the favorable results the representative achieved. You also credit the representative's demonstrated skill and competence in a case complicated by the claimant stressing the symptoms of a medical condition that alone was not disabling, and SSA not recognizing the significance of his other symptoms.

Pursuant to the above "Example," I should receive a good deal of credit for the favorable results I achieved on X' behalf because of the very extensive role I played in the thorough development and presentation of her impairments, especially her mental impairments, and the work that I did to overcome all of the prior Unfavorable ALJ decisions and the application of *res judicata*.

7. Consideration of the fee petition pursuant to Criteria No. 7, the "Level(s) in the Administrative Process."

The "Example" given in HALLEX I-1-2-57 A. 7. reads as follows:

> **Example:** If the claimant appointed the representative after receiving notice of the reconsideration determination and the ALJ favorably decided the claim, assume the representative interviewed the claimant about what had happened thus far, researched the law and eligibility factors, and determined whether this new evidence was available.

This "Example" is applicable to X's case. She came to me to when her DIB claim was at the hearing level. I interviewed her on multiple occasions, researched the law and eligibility factors, and determined that there was evidence available which had not been submitted, and that *res judicata* had improperly been applied to the denial of her first DIB claim. The new evidence I submitted proved critically important in establishing disability. My work in this regard ultimately resulted in the Fully Favorable Decision.

8. Consideration of the fee petition pursuant to Criteria No. 8, the "Amount of Fee Requested."

I am requesting a fee of $_____, and respectfully submit that this fee is very reasonable based upon consideration of the above-noted criteria or factors.

III. Consideration of the fee petition pursuant to the "Evaluation Considerations" set forth in HALLEX I-1-2-58 B. 2.

HALLEX I-1-2-58 B. 2. reads, in relevant part, as follows:

2.   Evaluation Considerations
•   Positive aspects Summarize those services that advanced the development of the claim, or contributed significantly to a favorable determination. If the authorized fee is greater than that requested, explain why it is reasonable.
•   Neutral or negative aspects
Summarize those services:
 -- that were not provided in proceedings before SSA;
 -- that negatively affected the development of the claim;
 -- the value of which is compromised because the time spent is unreasonable; and/or
 -- that although neutral, do not support a fee in the amount requested.

The services that I provided that "advanced the development" of X's claim and "contributed significantly to the favorable determination" include the following:

•   Extensive contact with both X and her father;
•   Representation of X at two administrative law judge hearings;
•   Representation of X before the Appeals Council;
•   Obtaining and submitting all extant medical records;
•   Obtaining testimony of the treating physician at the hearing;
•   Advancing $_____ in expenses to obtain and submit medical and other evidence, etc.;
•   Submission to both the ALJ and the Appeals Council of extensive written argument.

All of these "positive aspects" of my representation indicate that the requested fee of $_____ is reasonable.

I would respectfully submit that there were no "negative aspects" to my services. None of my time spent representing X was "unreasonable"; none of my services "negatively affected the development of the claim," but quite to the contrary; and I did not fail to provide services which were necessary. In short, there are no "neutral or negative aspects" to my representation which would indicate that the requested fee is not reasonable.

IV.   Thank you for your consideration of my fee petition.

I respectfully submit that I have earned the requested fee. I hope that you will agree that the requested fee is very reasonable, and accordingly recommend the authorization of a fee of $_____

I appreciate your consideration of my fee petition.

Sincerely,

§738   Obtaining Fees in Excess of $10,000

The administrative law judge can approve fees up to $10,000. Chief Judge Bulletin (CJB) 10-01, effective January 21, 2010 amended HALLEX I-1-2-52 C. NOSSCR Social Security Forum Vol. 32, No. 3, March 2010, p. 12. POMS GN 03930.015 D. If you petition for more, the ALJ must 1) approve a fee of $10,000 or less or 2) send the petition to the regional chief administrative law judge for approval. If the ALJ thinks you are entitled to more than $10,000, the ALJ must write a memorandum to the regional office recommending the amount the ALJ believes should be approved.

At that point, the administrative law judge may become your advocate. For example, if you have requested a $12,000 fee, the ALJ can allow $10,000 or less, or the ALJ can recommend any amount between $10,000 and $12,000. The ALJ can write a curt one-sentence memorandum to the regional office saying that a fee of $10,025 will adequately compensate you, or the ALJ can write a detailed statement setting out why you should receive the full $12,000. The regional office does not have to follow this recommendation, but it does give the recommendation considerable weight. So give the administrative law judge what he or she needs to help you. Detailed records are essential, and a statement from you describing any special work or particular difficulty you encountered makes the ALJ's job easier. In short, without so labeling it, you can write the ALJ's memorandum to the regional office for the ALJ.

§739   Appealing a Fee Authorization

If you are dissatisfied with an authorized fee, you may request administrative review. The fee authorization itself directs where to send your appeal. Appeal of a fee authorization issued by an ALJ, for example, goes to the regional chief administrative law judge whose name and address appear on the fee authorization.

You are allowed 30 days from the date of the authorization to appeal. Note that this time runs from the date of the authorization, *not the date of receipt*. If your fee appeal is late, it will not be processed unless you can show good cause for a late filing. *See* 20 C.F.R. § 404.1720(d)(2) and HALLEX I-1-2-61 B.

You are required to send a copy of your fee appeal letter to your client. 20 C.F.R. § 404.1720(d)(1). Be sure to indicate in your appeal letter that you have sent your client a copy of the appeal letter and enclosures. As part of your appeal papers, send copies of the fee authorization, your fee petition, and the letter you wrote to the ALJ explaining why the ALJ should approve your requested fee, in addition to a letter explaining why your requested fee was reasonable and why reducing your fee was not reasonable. Be sure to point out any factual errors made by the ALJ and any errors applying the law.

According to HALLEX I-1-2-61 C. the reviewing official will not modify an initial fee determination "solely because one of the parties protested" or "merely to substitute the judgment of the reviewer for the judgment of the original authorizer." Instead, the purpose of administrative review is to decide whether the protested fee was based on "complete and accurate knowledge of the facts" and proper application of the Act and regulations. If new and material information is submitted, the reviewing official "ordinarily modifies" the fee. HALLEX I-1-2-61 C.

There is no right to a hearing or further administrative or judicial appeals on the issue of attorney fees. Generally, courts have not found a constitutional right to federal court review of attorney fees. *See*, for example, SSR 82-19c.

§740   Fee Issues Applicable to Both the Fee Agreement Process and the Fee Petition Process

§741   How to Calculate Past-Due Benefits

The most common fee charged in Social Security disability cases is 25% of past-due benefits with or without a $6,000 cap. 20 C.F.R. § 404.1703 defines "past-due benefits" as follows:

> "Past-due benefits" means the total amount of benefits payable under Title II of the Act to all beneficiaries that has accumulated because of a favorable administrative or judicial determination or decision, up to but not including the month the determination or decision is made.

Despite the fact that this regulation was published in 1980 and remains on the books, it is not followed by SSA except in cases involving a favorable decision, that is a decision in which benefits are awarded, by a federal court. POMS GN 03920.060B. SSA's Office of General Counsel concluded that this attempted change in the prior regulation did not comply with applicable notice requirements. Thus, SSA follows the regulation that was in effect prior to 1980, which defines "past-due benefits" paid pursuant to an administrative decision as those benefits paid through the month before the month the favorable decision is "effectuated," that is, when benefits are calculated and the directions for payment are issued. HALLEX I-1-2-7 A.1 and POMS GN 03920.030B.1. This interpretation usually increases the basis for calculating the attorney's fee, since the effectuation of a decision may occur a month or more after the disability finding.

Past due benefits withheld for direct payment to a wage earner's attorney include benefits paid to auxiliaries who are not separately represented by someone else. POMS 03920.035B.

In SSI cases (including the SSI portion of concurrent cases), attorney fees are calculated by SSA based on benefits paid through the month of effectuation. HALLEX I-1-2-7 A.2 and POMS GN 03920.031B.

When calculating past-due benefits for attorney fee withholding and payment, SSA does not adjust the amount of benefits because of an overpayment arising during a period of time not adjudicated by the favorable decision. Thus, such an overpayment will not affect your fee, but this overpayment will be deducted from the benefits paid to the claimant. POMS GN 03920.030B.5. On the other hand, continuing benefits (paid when the claimant elects to continue benefits while appealing) or interim benefits (paid when the Appeals Council is reviewing a favorable ALJ decision) are not included in the calculation of past-due benefits. POMS GN 03920.030C.

The POMS provides that fees are subject to SSA's regular rounding procedures set forth in POMS RS 00601.020B. SSA will round to the nearest cent if the fee ends up with a fraction of a penny. POMS GN 03920.017F. However, when multiple representatives are paid, SSA does not change the total fee. It pays odd cents to one or more of the representatives. POMS GN 03920.017F.

§742 Payment of Attorney Fees in SSI Cases

The rules governing attorney fees in SSI cases, 20 C.F.R. §§ 416.1500-416.1599, are the same as those for the Social Security disability program without exception. Until February 28, 2005, the Social Security Administration assumed no responsibility for payment of fees out of SSI back benefits, so that no portion of SSI benefits was withheld for direct payment to attorneys. Beginning on February 28, 2005, SSA withholds and pays attorney fees from SSI back benefits. The user fee will apply.

§743 Calculating a Percentage Fee in an SSI Offset Case

In concurrent cases involving both Title II and SSI benefits, the greatest part of past-due benefits actually received by your client is commonly from SSI benefits. A large part of this payment, which, in fact, represents an overpayment, will ultimately be deducted from the claimant's past due Social Security disability benefits as an "SSI windfall offset." *See* §411.

Social Security disability attorney fees are withheld out of the *gross* amount of past-due Social Security disability benefits, that is, the amount before reduction for the SSI offset. SSI attorney fees are withheld and paid by SSA from the net amount of SSI benefits due, that is, after the SSI offset is deducted from the total amount of SSI back benefits.

Your fee, if calculated as one-quarter of the SSI benefits plus one-quarter of the unreduced Social Security disability benefits, will exceed 25% of the total back benefits paid by both programs once the offset is applied. To check SSA's calculation of your fee out of SSI back benefits, it will be necessary to calculate the amount of SSI back benefits to which the claimant is actually entitled. Your fee should be 25% of this amount. *See* §431 for a worksheet and §434 for a shortcut calculation.

§744 Other Offsets

SSA offsets worker's compensation benefits in some but not all states. Some, but not all, public disability benefits are offset also. *See* §§438-439. Attorney fee withholding is calculated *after* these offsets are deducted. Thus, 25 percent of past-due benefits are based on the *net* rather than the gross Social Security disability benefits. Sometimes the amount withheld for direct payment of attorney fees is miniscule.

The best way to deal with this problem is to anticipate it and come to an agreement with your client concerning calculation of attorney fees. You may calculate attorney fees based on the unreduced back benefits or any other reasonable basis, but such an agreement must be approved through the fee petition rather than the fee agreement process. A clearly written fee agreement is essential to good client relations.

If you failed to anticipate a problem with offsets in a case in which you were already planning to use the fee petition process, nothing prevents you from negotiating a new agreement with your client so that you will get a fair fee. If you have already brought this claimant's case under the fee agreement process, your only option is to appeal an inadequate fee yourself. *See* §715. But, before you do this, obtain your client's approval.

§745 Obtaining Reimbursement for Expenses

You are entitled to reimbursement for legitimate out-of-pocket expenses according to the terms of your agreement with your client. The fee petition asks that you itemize expenses. However, SSA will not send you a check to pay these expenses. You must collect these from your client.

Many attorneys send an itemized statement of expenses to each client as soon as a favorable decision is received, with a request that expenses be paid from past-due benefits when the client's lump-sum check arrives.

§746   Fee Approval Regulations Do Not Apply in All Circumstances

There are only three circumstances in which SSA has acknowledged that the fee approval regulations do not apply—two appear in the regulations and the other in an informal letter. If you are paid for representing a claimant by an "entity"—any business, firm or other association, for-profit or nonprofit organization—or government agency, you will not be required to have your fee approved as long as: 1) the claimant and auxiliaries are free of any liability for fees or expenses; and 2) you submit a written statement in the form and manner required by SSA waiving the right to charge and collect a fee and any expenses from the claimant and auxiliaries. 20 C.F.R. § 404.1720(e)(1). Waiver of reimbursement for expenses is required. Note that the current Appointment of Representative form, §178.2.1, includes a checkbox to indicate that you are "waiving fees and expenses from the claimant and any auxiliary beneficiaries." Be sure to check this box if your fee will be paid by an "entity."

"Entity" is defined in 20 C.F.R. § 404.1703 as "any business, firm, or other association," including for-profit organizations and not-for-profit organizations. Profit making entities are likely to be long term disability insurance (LTD) carriers, which often pay representatives to assist with an insured's Social Security disability claim. If all of the requirements of the regulation are met, you do not have to seek approval of your fee from SSA if you are paid by such an entity. *See also* POMS GN 03920.010B.

The regulations also provide that if you represent a claimant before SSA and a court authorizes your fee as a legal guardian or court-appointed representative, you do not need to seek approval of your fee from SSA. 20 C.F.R. § 404.1720(e)(2).

If a claimant doesn't appoint you as a representative and you do not perform what SSA regards to be "services" in connection with a claim, you may charge a fee without first getting it approved by SSA. The only example of this appears in an SSA opinion letter which was sent to NOSSCR. SSA approved the practice of some attorneys who charge a fee for evaluating a case but ultimately decide not to represent the claimant.

Such attorneys request money from the claimant at the initial interview. If the attorney accepts the case for representation, the money is put into a trust account to be used for payment of expenses in the claimant's case. If the attorney evaluates the case and decides to decline representation, the payment is accepted for case evaluation, something which SSA has said is not "services." Contact NOSSCR for a copy of the SSA opinion letter.

Do the fee-setting regulations apply if an attorney provides "services" in connection with a pending claim but the attorney is not officially appointed as a "representative" pursuant to 20 C.F.R. § 404.1707? For example, can you counsel a claimant in an overpayment case and avoid the operation of the fee-setting regulations by never being appointed as the representative? Some attorneys have been known to argue that unless they are appointed as a representative, the fee-setting regulations do not apply. They point out that only appointed representatives are required to file fee petitions under 20 C.F.R. § 404.1720(b).

Nevertheless, SSA's policy is that an SSA fee authorization is required "irrespective of whether" the attorney "was ever recognized by SSA as a claimant's representative, or the individual did not deal directly with or actually contact SSA." POMS GN 03920.005B. Thus, SSA may argue that the ambiguous language of 20 C.F.R. § 404.1740(c) is broad enough to impose penalties on an attorney who charges a fee that is not approved. This controversy illustrates yet another example of the poor quality draftsmanship in the attorney fee regulations. Cf. §726. Because penalties are involved, caution is appropriate. For an exceptionally broad interpretation of services, *see* SSR 65-33c, which adopted as a Social Security ruling the court's decision in *United States v. Lewis*, 235 F. Supp. 220 (E.D. Tenn 1964), a criminal case in which defendant Lewis, an accountant, assisted with preparation of fraudulent self-employment tax returns in order to establish eligibility for Social Security benefits. This was found to constitute services in connection with a claim for Social Security benefits.

§747   Coping With SSA's Failure to Withhold Attorney Fees

Occasionally SSA fails to withhold attorney fees for direct payment to the attorney. If this happens, the first thing you need to do is try to collect from your client. If your client pays, there will be no user fee. If your client refuses to pay you (or cannot pay you because all back benefits have been spent), you may request payment from SSA. It is SSA's policy to pay such fees, and create an overpayment on the client's account to carry out the Commissioner's statutory duties under 42 U.S.C. § 406(a) by paying your fee. POMS GN 03920.055.

Withheld benefits in excess of an authorized fee may be released to the claimant while a fee appeal is pending. If you are authorized a higher fee and your client does not pay you, SSA is supposed to follow the same procedure. POMS GN 03950.050. But if your request for administrative review of the amount of the fee was untimely, even if SSA found good cause for the delay in appealing, SSA will refuse to pay the fee. POMS GN 03920.055C, Note and GN 03960.025A.3. You must collect the additional fee from your client.

When you want SSA to pay you and create an overpayment on your client's account, if your client is over age 54, telephone the regional program service center for faxing instructions. If your client is under age 54, you may fax a letter to the OCO toll-free fax number (877-385-0643) describing the situation, including your efforts to obtain payment from your client. Include a copy of the letter from SSA that tells you that you must try to collect the fee from your client. A bold reference line may help your letter be routed to the proper person. Put this address on your letter:

    SSA
    Office of Central Operations
    Attention: Claims Authorizer, MOD ____
    Security West Building
    1500 Woodlawn Drive
    Baltimore, MD 21241

Re: Request to create overpayment and pay attorney fees

§748   The User Fee

For attorneys' fees paid directly to the attorney pursuant to any favorable decision, SSA is supposed to deduct a user fee to pay SSA's administrative costs for "determining and certifying fees to attorneys from the past-due benefits of claimants," calculated at the rate of 6.3% of the amount of the fee. 42 U.S.C. § 406(d)(2)(B)(ii). For fees paid by SSA on or after September 1, 2004, the user fee was capped at $75, with COLA adjustments to be applied on December 1 in subsequent years beginning in 2006. Effective December 1, 2013, for example, the user fee cap is $89. 42 U.S.C. § 406(d)(2)(A).

The cap applies on a "per case" basis. Concurrent cases are treated as one case. POMS GN 03920.019C. Where multiple representatives are paid, the cumulative user fee is not supposed to exceed the amount of the user fee cap. POMS GN 03920.019E.

The Act itself includes a "prohibition on claimant reimbursement." An attorney may not "directly or indirectly, request or otherwise obtain reimbursement for such assessment from the claimant whose claim gave rise to the assessment." 42 U.S.C. § 406(d)(4).

When calculating the user fee, it is SSA's practice to round to the nearest penny. POMS GN 03920.017F. The user fee is calculated only on the amount paid directly. For example, if the full fee is $1,500 but the attorney notifies SSA that $500 is held in a trust account, the attorney is sent a check for $1,000 minus the user fee based on $1,000, not the full $1,500 fee. POMS GN 03920.019C.

Since so many fees arrive before the award letter, it is useful to calculate the full attorney fee so that you can determine if the award letter, when it arrives, corresponds with the attorney fee received. For larger attorney fees, simply adding the amount of the user fee cap to the amount received yields the full attorney fee. For fees of less than the user fee cap / .063 (e.g., $88 / .063 = $1,396.83), to determine the full fee based on the amount of the attorney fee check, use this formula: amount received / .937. The formula for determining the user fee, based on the amount of a check received, is (amount received / .937) x .063. For both formulas, though, you need to make an allowance for SSA's unusual "rounding up" procedure.

If you waive direct payment of the fee, SSA is supposed to send the entire attorney fee—without deduction of the user fee—to your client with directions for the client to send the attorney fee to you. What happens when SSA sends you the attorney fee anyway—after deducting the user fee? When SSA makes this mistake, its policy is to correct its error by sending the user fee to the claimant who can then send it to you. But for SSA to make this correction, you must meet SSA's special deadline for waiving direct payment.

If you waive direct payment on or before the date the fee agreement is approved in a fee agreement case or on or before the date SSA receives your fee petition in a fee petition case, SSA will refund the user fee to the claimant if it makes a mistake by sending you the attorney fee check (minus the user fee) anyway. You can then collect the amount of the user fee from the claimant so that you will end up with a full fee, unreduced by the user fee. SSA says it will try to honor any waiver of direct payment that it receives before payment is actually made, but if it makes a mistake in circumstances where you do not meet SSA's special deadline for waiving direct payment, it will not refund the user fee. POMS GN 03920.051.

Practice Tip

Although there may be other reasons to do so, do not waive direct payment of the attorney fee if your only motivation is to avoid the user fee. By the time many claimants win their Social Security disability cases, their debts may exceed the amounts of their back benefits; and sometimes claimants' lawyers are not be among the first creditors paid. Thus, waiving direct payment could result in the claimant paying no fee at all, since sometimes it can be very difficult to collect a fee from a claimant. After the user fee was capped, the risk of receiving no fee at all far exceeds the cost of paying the user fee.

§749   How to Return a Check to SSA

When you receive an incorrect payment from SSA, put the money into your trust account and write to SSA. Address your letter to the local office if the overpayment involves SSI. If the overpayment involves Title II benefits, address your letter to either the local office or the program service center. Explain why you believe you were overpaid; explain that you are holding the money in trust; and state that if SSA agrees you were overpaid, you await SSA's instructions for returning the money.

Resist any temptation to mail a refund check to your client. Although the money probably does belong to your client, it is hard to tell with certainty. The money might not actually belong to your client. And even if it is your client's money, if you send the money to your client, SSA's records will look like you were overpaid. Even if you send SSA a copy of your letter that sends a check to your client, no one at SSA may actually take the time to figure out that SSA made a mistake. No one will correct SSA's computer records. In the past SSA has been known to develop and run computer programs designed to identify over payments. SSA has been known to send letters to lawyers years after payments were made threatening dire consequences unless you return the money to SSA immediately.

You want SSA to recognize that it made a mistake and correct its records. It will not necessarily do this simply in response to a check that you mail in. Many lawyers who have practiced in this area for years tell stories about returning money to SSA before SSA has recognized its error. They say they received the incorrect payment from SSA again, sometimes more than once. One lawyer reported receiving the same erroneous payment four times. This is despite sending cover letters with each check explaining SSA's mistaken overpayment. Apparently no one at SSA reads cover letters enclosing checks. And if they do, they do not make the necessary computer entries to correct SSA's records.

Usually a letter gets attention if it says you have been overpaid and you are waiting for instructions for returning money to SSA. Even so, it may be necessary to follow up after a few months to make sure your letter was not lost.

When you get instructions, they usually tell you to send a check with your client's SSN on it to the local office. If so, consider hand delivering the check and requesting a receipt on the spot. It is prudent to save this receipt forever, but assuming all the correct entries were made in SSA's computer system, you're unlikely to need it.

§750   Attorney Fees in Federal Court

To collect a fee for work in federal court, you need to have a contract with your client that deals with federal court fee issues. Although some attorneys use one contract that covers both administrative and federal court representation in a case, this book recommends using two separate contracts. Since the vast majority of cases do not go to federal court, including provisions about federal court litigation in a contract that will in all likelihood apply only to agency-level representation unnecessarily complicates the contract and may create the impression that you have already agreed to take the claimant's case to federal court if the case is lost before the agency. Indeed, both the courts and SSA treat federal court fees and fees for representation before the agency as separate matters involving entirely different rules for approval of fees. Thus, this book provides two contracts: a contract for administrative representation, §178.3.1, and a separate contract for federal court representation, §758, which applies in addition to the contract for representation before the Social Security Administration. The federal court contract has the following provisions:

- Twenty-five percent maximum fee, including the fee for administrative work;
- Right to retain associate or outside counsel —with no additional cost to the claimant;
- Notice that the fee may amount to several hundred dollars per hour;
- Assignment of EAJA fee to the attorney, which allows the government to pay the fee directly to the attorney and may have beneficial tax implications for the claimant;
- Right to endorse and deposit an EAJA check that is sent to the attorney in the name of the claimant;
- Right to maximize the total fee obtained by the attorney; and
- No commitment to take the case to the court of appeals.

For all fees authorized by a federal court after January 1, 2007 out of a claimant's back benefits, in order for you to receive direct payment of the fee, you must have registered for direct payment by submitting Form SSA-1699 and you must have submitted Form SSA-1695 to the claimant's local office before SSA receives the court's order authorizing payment of the fee. POMS GN 03920.017B.5. *See* §178.4. POMS GN 03920.060E provides for notice to the attorney of these requirements at the time SSA is effectuating the claim and paying the claimant's back benefits.

§751   A 25-Percent Limit on Attorney Fees in Federal Court

42 U.S.C. § 406(b)(1)(A) provides:

> Whenever a court renders a judgment favorable to a claimant under this subchapter who was represented before the court by an attorney, the court may determine and allow as part of its judgment a reasonable fee for such representation, not in excess of 25 percent of the total of the past-due benefits to which the claimant is entitled by reason of such judgment, and the Commissioner of Social Security may, notwithstanding the provisions of section 405(i) of this title, but subject to subsection (d) of this section, certify the amount of such fee for payment to such attorney out of, and not in addition to, the amount of such past-due benefits. In case of any such judgment, no other fee may be payable or certified for payment for such representation except as provided in this paragraph.

This section of the Social Security Act establishes a limit on attorney fees of 25% of past-due benefits for federal court representation. However, the federal court 25% fee "is in addition to the fee, if any, the Social Security Administration (SSA) authorizes for proceedings at the administrative level." HALLEX I-1-2-71 A. (Note that the sample contract at §758 limits the fee to 25% for both administrative and federal court work, which generally provides an adequate fee. If you want to seek a 25% fee from each forum, which may be considered in unusual cases involving limited back benefits, you will need to change the sample contract.)

Section 406(b) also requires that Social Security disability cases be taken to federal court on a contingent fee basis not in excess of a maximum 25 percent fee. Section "406(b) governs the total fee a claimant's attorney may receive for court representation; any endeavor by the claimant's attorney to gain more than that fee, or to charge the claimant a noncontingent fee, is a criminal offense." *Gisbrecht v. Barnhart*, 122 S. Ct. 1817, 1827-1828 (2002).

42 U.S.C. § 406(b)(1) provides the basis for SSA withholding attorney fees and paying the attorney directly pursuant to a federal court's order. *See* 20 C.F.R. §§ 404.1728(b) and 404.1730.

Although this may not occur to you if you look only at the regulation, SSA applies different rules when calculating past-due benefits based on an administrative decision compared to a federal court decision. The regulation provides that past-due benefits "means the total amount of benefits under title II of the Act that has accumulated to all beneficiaries because of a favorable administrative or judicial determination or decision, up to but not including the month the determination or decision is made." 20 C.F.R. § 404.1703. For cases in which the favorable decision is made by the agency, this regulation is interpreted to include the payment determination. Thus, past-due benefits accumulate up to the month before an SSA decision is effectuated, which is often a month or more after an ALJ decision. POMS GN 03920.030B. *Cf.* POMS GN 03920.060B.

Although past-due benefits include an extra month or so of back benefits for an ALJ decision when compared to a case in which the federal court finds the claimant disabled and directs SSA to pay benefits, when SSA tries to apply this rule to court remand cases, the difference can be a year or more in back benefits if one uses the month before the court remanded the case to stop the accumulation of past-due benefits.

42 U.S.C. § 406(b)(2) provides criminal penalties for a lawyer who "charges, demands, receives, or collects" a fee in excess of that allowed by the federal court.

§752   To Set a Fee, Federal Courts Look First to the Contingent Fee Contract, Then Test It for Reasonableness

To set a fee in a Social Security case, *Gisbrecht v. Barnhart*, 122 S. Ct. 1817, 1828 (2002), requires the federal courts to look first to the contingent fee contract, then test it for reasonableness. *Gisbrecht* rejected the lodestar approach used by many federal courts, which called for a court to first determine a reasonable hourly rate.

Gisbrecht provides only a few examples of how to test the contingent fee contract for reasonableness. *Gisbrecht*, 122 S. Ct. at 1828, said that a court should look at:
- The character of the representation;
- Whether representation was substandard;
- Whether the attorney was responsible for delay;
- The results the representative achieved;
- Whether benefits are large in comparison to the time spent on the case;

- Whether the attorney is receiving a windfall.

The burden of showing that the fee is reasonable is on the attorney. "Within the 25 percent boundary . . . the attorney for the successful claimant must show that the fee sought is reasonable for the services rendered." *Gisbrecht v. Barnhart*, 122 S. Ct. 1817, 1828 (2002). To meet this burden, some attorneys include in their memoranda only the factors identified in *Gisbrecht*. Others take a more expansive approach. These attorneys recognize that it is likely a federal court, while taking the fee contract as the starting place, will consider other factors that are brought to its attention, especially if the other factors are things courts have looked at in the past to evaluate the reasonableness of a fee, such as those contained in Rule 1.5 of the ABA's Model Rules of Professional Conduct:

1. The time and labor required, the novelty and difficulty of the questions involved, and the skill requisite to perform the legal service properly;
2. The likelihood, if apparent to the client, that the acceptance of the particular employment will preclude other employment by the lawyer;
3. The fee customarily charged in the locality for similar legal services;
4. The amount at issue and the results obtained;
5. The time limitations imposed by the client or by the circumstances;
6. The nature and length of the professional relationship with the client;
7. The experience, reputation, and ability of the lawyer or lawyers performing the services; and
8. Whether the fee is fixed or contingent.

One of the leading cases on attorney fees in federal court, *Johnson v. Georgia Highway Express, Inc.*, 488 F.2d 714 (5th Cir. 1974), involved an award of attorney fees under the Civil Rights Act of 1964. The factors set forth in *Johnson* are essentially the same as those set forth in the ABA Model Rules of Professional Conduct.

§753 Attorney Fees in SSI Cases Are Regulated

Attorney fees in SSI cases are treated the same as attorney fees in Social Security disability cases. Effective as of February 28, 2005 for five years and later made permanent, Congress amended a section of Title XVI of the Social Security Act, which deals with SSI, 42 U.S.C. § 1383(d)(2). This change made applicable to SSI attorney fees all of 42 U.S.C. § 406, pertaining to Social Security disability attorney fees both before the agency, § 406(a), and in federal court, § 406(b). Previously only part of § 406(a) was applicable to SSI attorney fees, leaving SSI attorney fees in federal court unregulated.

In the past, the U.S. Supreme Court held that a federal court did not have the authority to order SSA to withhold and pay attorney fees from SSI benefits. *Bowen v. Galbreath*, 485 U.S. 74 (1988). This case is now inapplicable. If SSA fails to withhold attorney fees from SSI back benefits, a court has the power to order SSA to pay the fee if the attorney cannot collect from the claimant.

§754 Coping With SSA's Failure to Withhold and Pay Court-Approved Attorney Fees

When SSA fails to withhold and pay court-approved attorney fees, even without any court order, SSA should create an overpayment on your client's account and pay you following the same procedures it follows when there is no federal court involvement in a case. *See* POMS GN 03920.055C. *See also* §747. However, in this situation POMS is non-committal. POMS, which applies to federal court approved attorney fees from both Social Security disability and SSI benefits, directs SSA personnel to "contact the Office of the General Counsel for further instructions." POMS GN 03920.060B.5.

When SSA fails to withhold and pay attorney fees approved by a federal court, you need to follow the same procedures you would follow if the case never went to federal court. *See* §747. That is, once you determine that your client cannot or will not pay you, ask SSA to create an overpayment on your client's account and pay you directly. At the same time, contact the attorney from SSA's Office of General Counsel who was involved in your client's case in federal court to ask for assistance. Allow a reasonable time for SSA's bureaucracy to create an overpayment on your client's account and pay you. If your fee is not forthcoming after a reasonable time, bring a motion in federal court.

§755 Fees for Representation Before Both the Federal Court and SSA

Although you might wish to ask the federal court to approve a 25% fee as payment for all of your work on this case from the administrative level to federal court, you may not. And although you might want to ask SSA to approve your fee for representation both before the agency and in federal court, you cannot do that either. Both SSA and the courts treat administrative representation and federal court representation in the same claim as two separate matters requiring separate fee requests: a fee agreement or fee petition for administrative work under 42 U.S.C. § 406(a) and a 42 U.S.C. § 406(b) motion for court work.

When evaluating your fee, the federal court is not supposed to consider the time you spent on the claimant's case when it was before the agency. Such fees are authorized under 42 U.S.C. § 406(a), which requires the fee to be set by the agency. Fees for representation in federal court, on the other hand, are authorized by the court under 42 U.S.C. § 406(b). Thus, when SSA considers your fee petition, it will not consider the time you spent representing the plaintiff in federal court. HALLEX I-1-2-57 B. Indeed, SSA has even told decision makers to look carefully at attorney-time spent after the Appeals Council denies review but before the case is filed in federal court. SSA usually treats this as services before the court. HALLEX I-1-2-71 B.

SSA takes the position that it can authorize a Title II fee greater than 25 percent of past-due benefits and that for a claim that has been taken to federal court, a combined fee, in fact, may exceed 25 percent of past-due benefits. *See* the explanation of SSA policy in acquiescence ruling, AR 87-1(6). (Although this acquiescence ruling, which previously established a different procedure for the Sixth Circuit, became obsolete when the case to which AR 87-1(6) acquiesced, *Webb v. Richardson*, 472 F.2d 529 (6th Cir. 1972), was overruled by *Horenstein v. Secretary of Health & Human Servs.*, 35 F.3d 261 (6th Cir. 1994), it contains a good exposition of current SSA policy in the section of the ruling that explains how *Webb* differs from SSA policy.)

Nevertheless, if you are seeking a 25 percent fee, that is, a grand total 25 percent fee from both forums, depending on the facts and how much time you spent on the claimant's case in each forum, it might be possible to file one request, either with the court or SSA, asking for approval of the entire fee. Although you may not include in your request time spent in the other forum, you may certainly point out that if your full requested fee is approved, you will not request approval of a fee by the other forum.

The procedure to be followed, according to SSA, depends on whether SSA or a federal court issued the decision granting benefits. If you represent a Social Security disability claimant in federal court in a case where the court reverses the Commissioner and awards benefits, petition for your fee by motion to the federal court pursuant to 42 U.S.C. § 406(b)(1). In such a case, SSA says that the fee agreement process does not apply. *See* §705. Therefore, a fee petition, which must be sent to the Attorney Fee Branch at the Appeals Council, will be necessary. *Cf.* HALLEX I-1-2-33 B.

But if SSA issued the decision awarding benefits, a fee agreement may be approved for the part of the fee for representation before the agency. Otherwise, you will need to file a fee petition with the SSA decision maker who issued the favorable decision following federal court remand; and you will also need to file a motion for your fee to be approved by the federal court.

When SSA issues the decision awarding benefits, SSA sometimes objects to the amount of the fee requested to be approved by the federal court on the grounds that the definition of past-due benefits includes only those benefits that accumulate up to the month before the court remanded the case. 20 C.F.R. § 404.1703.

At first reading, 42 U.S.C. § 406(b) appears to present a problem for timely requesting the court to authorize a fee out of a claimant's back benefits when the court remands the case for further proceedings under sentence four of 42 U.S.C. § 405(g); but most courts that have addressed this have not found it to be a problem. The statute says that the court "may determine and allow *as part of its judgment* a reasonable fee." 42 U.S.C. § 406(b) (emphasis added). When a case is remanded for a new hearing under sentence four of 42 U.S.C. § 405(g), judgment is entered. It may be more than a year later before a favorable decision is issued by an ALJ. Since there are time limits and other rules for amending judgment, how can a court determine the fee "as part of its judgment"?

Although the Commissioner has not been known to oppose payment of fees using this argument on their own motion courts have occasionally raised the question of how the fee can be allowed as part of the judgment entered a year or more earlier. Indeed, this problem could arise even when a court awards benefits because it sometimes takes SSA several months to calculate back benefits and notify the parties how much has been withheld for direct payment of attorney fees. This was the issue addressed in *Smith v. Bowen*, 815 F.2d 1152 (7th Cir. 1987). In that case the court concluded, "Reading the statute as a whole, we do not believe Congress meant that the only time at which fees could be awarded is the time of the judgment. By authorizing the attorney to be paid directly out of the claimant's past-due benefits, Congress intended to make it easier, not harder for attorneys to collect their fees." 815 F.2d at 1155. The court held that a petition for approval of fees must be brought within a reasonable time. It also noted that time limits could be set by local rule.

In *McGraw v. Barnhart*, 450 F.3d 493, 505 (10th Cir. 2006), the Tenth Circuit adopted the "reasonable time" rule and stated that fees under 42 U.S.C. § 406(b) could be sought under the authority of Fed. R. Civ. P. 60(b)(6), which provides for relief from judgment or order for "any other reason justifying relief from the operation of the judgment." In *Pierce v. Barnhart*,

440 F.3d 657, 663-64 (5th Cir. 2006) and *Bergen v. Comm'r of Soc. Sec.*, 454 F.3d 1273, 1277-1278 (11th Cir. 2006), the courts held that Fed. R. Civ. P. 54(d)(2)(B), which provides a 14-day time limit for motions for attorney fees, applied to motions under 42 U.S.C. § 406(b). The *Bergen* court specifically rejected the Seventh Circuit's "reasonable time" rule stated in *Smith* because the current version of Fed. R. Civ. P. 54(d)(2)(B) was not in effect in 1987 when the court issued its decision. The *Bergen* court recommended when judgment is entered that plaintiff's attorney move the court to extend the 14-day time limit provided by Fed. R. Civ. P. 54(d)(2)(B), and ask that the court include in the judgment a statement that attorney fees may be applied for within a specified time after the determination of plaintiff's past-due benefits. 454 F.3d 1273, 1278, n.2.

Practice Tip

Check your local rules for time limits to bring a motion for attorney fees under 42 U.S.C. § 406(b). Consider whether you need to bring a motion when the court enters judgment under sentence four of 42 U.S.C. § 405(g) in order to protect your right to request attorney fees after SSA calculates the claimant's past-due benefits.

§756 Maximizing Your Fee and Minimizing Bureaucratic Hassle

Unless the fee agreement process applies to your fee for work before the agency, for cases that have been to federal court, SSA requires that you file a fee petition to obtain your fee for administrative work. It is not unusual for a fee petition to take six months to one year to be approved. You also have to file a motion with the federal court, in effect, another fee petition, to approve your fee for federal court work. Because preparing fee petitions is not an enjoyable task, it is worthwhile to think about whether you can accomplish your goal of obtaining a reasonable fee by filing a request for approval of the entire fee by only one forum.

If the fee agreement process applies to your fee for representation before SSA, a shortcut is automatic. You can then ask the federal court to approve the rest of a 25% fee. Unless a very large fee is at stake and you spent an exceptional amount of time representing your client before SSA, it may be most expeditious simply to allow the fee agreement process to run its course (i.e., do not appeal the amount of the fee under the fee agreement process) in order to obtain a $6,000 fee for

representing the claimant before SSA, *see* §§700 *ff.* and ask the court to approve the remaining portion of a 25 percent fee. On the other hand, when a large fee is at stake and you have spent enough time working on the claimant's case before the agency to justify a higher fee, you may want to request administrative review of the fee determined under the fee agreement process. *See* §715.

Most of the time, though, after a case has been to federal court, the fee agreement process will not apply because you used a two-tiered fee agreement or for some other reason; and ordinarily you do not want the $6,000 cap for administrative fees to apply to a case in which benefits have built up over many years. In these instances, the *fee petition process* applies to your work before SSA. Here are some suggestions for obtaining your fee as quickly as possible:

1. Ask for the full fee from whichever forum awarded benefits. Include in your request a statement that if the full fee is approved, you will not ask for any additional fee from the other forum. If SSA awarded benefits, answer question 5 on the fee petition this way: "No fee will be requested from the federal court out of the claimant's past-due benefits if this fee petition is approved." *See* the fee petition at §733. If the federal court awarded benefits, you may adapt to this situation the sample motion for approval of attorney fees pursuant to 42 U.S.C. § 406(b) at §757. A supporting attorney's affidavit may be adapted from the affidavit appearing in §787.

2. If most of the compensable time was spent in the forum that did *not* award benefits, consider seeking fees from the forum where most of the work was done for your full fee, and waiving your fee from the other forum. Caution is appropriate, though. You need to know the likelihood that the judge will approve your full fee.

3. If you were paid EAJA fees at the time your client's case was remanded for a new hearing pursuant to the fourth sentence of 42 U.S.C. § 405(g), after the client is found disabled by SSA, it is usually worthwhile to spend the time necessary to try to obtain approval of the maximum possible fee from SSA. That is, make sure your time itemization includes sufficient detail to show *what* you worked on and *why* you spent so much time on the claimant's case; and write a cover letter to the ALJ explaining why your requested fee is reasonable under the circumstances. If you can get a full 25 percent fee authorized by SSA, you will have maximized your fee in the claimant's case. Your total fee for the case will be the 25 percent fee authorized by SSA *plus* the EAJA fee. Because the § 406(a) fee is not offset by the EAJA award, you keep both the full § 406(a) fee and the EAJA award. In other words, the total fee you receive will be

more than 25% of the past-due benefits, but the amount the claimant pays will not exceed that amount.

If SSA does not approve the full 25 percent fee, figure out what remains of the 25 percent of back benefits withheld by SSA. If SSA is holding less than the amount of the EAJA attorney fee award, write SSA to tell it to release the withheld money to your client. If there is more than the EAJA fee still being held by SSA, you can ask the federal court to approve that amount as your fee; but you're going to have to refund to your client the amount of the EAJA fee. This is because you are not entitled to double payment for the same work. *See* §768.

This is easiest to understand with examples. Let's say you received a $3,000 EAJA fee when the case was remanded. And let's say the claimant's back benefits total $24,000. SSA withheld $6,000 for payment of the attorney fee once it is approved. If SSA approves $6,000 as your fee for administrative work, your total fee for the case is $9,000, $6,000 approved by SSA plus the $3,000 EAJA fee approved by the court. You have obtained the maximum possible fee for the claimant's case.

If, on the other hand, the ALJ approved $5,000 (and the Regional Chief Administrative Law Judge (RCALJ) refused to raise the fee on appeal), it is pointless to do anything other than ask that the $1,000 SSA is still holding to pay an approved fee be released to the claimant. The law provides that if you receive EAJA fees and fees approved by a federal court under 42 U.S.C. § 406(b), you must refund to the claimant the smaller amount. *See* §768. If the federal court were to approve a fee of $1,000 out of the claimant's back benefits, you would have to refund that $1,000 to the claimant. Your total fee for this case is $8,000, $5,000 for administrative work and the $3,000 EAJA fee for your work in federal court.

Let's take another example. Let's say the back benefits and the EAJA award are the same as the above example but the ALJ approved only $2,000 as your fee for administrative work (and the RCALJ refused to increase the fee on appeal). SSA is still holding $4,000 to pay attorney fees for federal court work out of the claimant's back benefits. If the federal court approves $4,000 as your 42 U.S.C. § 406(b) fee for federal court work, this will result in a net gain of $1,000 to you because you must refund the smaller, $3,000 EAJA fee to the claimant. *See* §768. (In fact, most attorneys explain this calculation to the federal court and ask that the federal court 1) approve the $4,000 fee and 2) direct SSA to release $3,000 to the claimant as reimbursement for the EAJA fee previously awarded to the attorney.) If the federal court approves the additional fee, your total fee for the case is $6,000, $2,000 for work before the agency and $4,000 for work in federal court awarded under 42 U.S.C. § 406(b).

4. In a case remanded to SSA under the sixth sentence of 42 U.S.C. § 405(g), consider petitioning SSA for your full contingent fee out of your client's back benefits, and asking the federal court for additional fees under the Equal Access to Justice Act. *See* §§766, 768, 774 and 788.

§757   Sample: Motion for Authorization of Attorney Fees

UNITED STATES DISTRICT COURT

_____ DISTRICT OF _____

_____, Plaintiff, v. Commissioner of Social Security, Defendant.	)) MOTION FOR AUTHORIZATION) OF ATTORNEY FEES) PURSUANT TO) 42 U.S.C. § 406(b)))) Case No. _____))

Petitioner, _____, attorney for Plaintiff, _____, hereby moves this Honorable Court, pursuant to §206(b)(1) of the Social Security Act, 42 U.S.C. § 406(b)(1), for an award of an attorney fee in the amount of $_____. In support of this motion Petitioner states as follows:

1. Petitioner represented Plaintiff in a civil action before this court for judicial review of the Commissioner's unfavorable decision. The Court reversed and remanded the case for further proceedings on _____. Thus, the Court has jurisdiction over this fee petition pursuant to 42 U.S.C. § 406(b).

2. After remand by this Court, an administrative law judge (ALJ) issued a favorable decision on _____, finding the plaintiff disabled as of _____. On _____, the Social Security Administration issued a Notice of Award finding that the plaintiff was due $_____ in total past-due benefits. Of this amount, $_____ represents 25% of the award and was withheld for the direct payment of an attorney fee by the Social Security Administration. See Notice of Award attached as Exhibit A.

3. Section 206(b)(1) of the Social Security Act permits the court to award a reasonable fee for work before the court not to exceed 25% of past-due benefits to which the claimant is entitled by reason of a judgment rendered in favor of the claimant. 42 U.S.C. § 406(b)(1). Pursuant to _Smith v. Bowen_, 815 F.2d 1152, 1156 (7th Cir. 1987), this petition is brought within a reasonable time after calculation by SSA of past due benefits and issuance of the Notice of Award.

4. Plaintiff requests that $_____ be awarded to counsel in accordance with the fee contract signed by the Plaintiff. Plaintiff's attorney has requested that the Social Security Administration approve $_____ as his fee for work before the agency. Thus, plaintiff's attorney is requesting a full 25% fee for work before the agency and federal court, which is in accordance with the fee contract. See Fee Contract attached as Exhibit B.

5. The 406(b) fee request in this petition is reasonable. In _Hensley v. Eckerhart_, 461 U.S. 424, 435 (1983), the Supreme Court held that attorneys should recover a "fully compensatory fee" when the client receives "excellent results." The Supreme Court considers contingency representation an important factor in awarding an enhanced fee:

> Attorneys who take cases on contingency, thus deferring payment of their fees until the case has ended and taking upon themselves the risk that they will receive no payment at all, generally receive far more in winning cases than they would if they charged an hourly rate. The difference, however, reflects the time-value of money and the risk of non-recovery usually borne by clients in cases where lawyers are paid an hourly rate.

_Id._ at 448-449 (Brennan, J., concurring).

6. In *Gisbrecht v. Barnhart*, 535 U.S. 789, 805 (2002), Justice Ginsberg looked at the legislative history of the Social Security Act and how Congress intended to protect claimants from "inordinately large fees" and she determined that:

> [N]othing in the text or history of § 406(b) reveals a "design to prohibit or discourage attorneys and claimants from entering into contingent fee agreements." Given the prevalence of contingent-fee agreements between attorneys and Social Security claimants, it is unlikely that Congress, simply by prescribing "reasonable fees," meant to outlaw, rather than to contain, such agreements.

Gisbrecht v. Barnhart, 535 U.S. 789, 805 (2002).

7. The fee requested is also in line with the Seventh Circuit's holding in *McGuire, et al. v. Sullivan*, 873 F. 2d 974 (7th Cir. 1989). Precluding counsel from receiving full contingency fees for work performed on cases actually won would be a disincentive and effectively eliminate access to experienced counsel for claimants intending to appeal the Commissioner's final determination denying benefits. The court in *McGuire*, a pre-*Gisbrecht* Seventh Circuit decision approving contingent representation, determined that where there is a contingent fee contract between the claimant and attorney, the contract, not the hourly rate for services rendered, is the proper starting point in considering the reasonableness of a fee:

> We recognize that other courts have determined that the lodestar rate is the proper starting place in analyzing social security fee request and therefore have emphasized the reasonableness of the hourly rate of compensation from the award over the contingency agreed to by the parties. Nevertheless we follow the *McKittrick* court's reasoning that simply determining a reasonable hourly rate is inappropriate when an attorney is working pursuant to a reasonable contingency contract. A court may award a fee up to that provided in the contract so long as the court has reviewed its reasonableness. *McKittrick*, 378 F.2d at 875-76. Therefore, in reviewing social security fee applications where there is a contingency contract in effect, whether or not the proper starting place is a lodestar hourly rate, the contingency amount agreed to by the client should also be considered and a reasonable amount determined so long as it is no more than twenty-five percent.

Id. at 980.

8. Counsel's office began representation of Plaintiff before the agency in _____. At the U.S. District Court where several separate issues were presented to the Court for review, the court reversed the Commissioner's decision and remanded for further administrative proceedings. Plaintiff eventually prevailed upon remand due to Petitioner's efforts, who ultimately persuaded an ALJ to award benefits. See Petitioner's professional qualifications attached as Exhibit C.

9. Plaintiff's past-due benefits amount to $_____. Therefore, the contingent fee that Plaintiff will pay for the court work amounts to approximately ___ percent of the total award. Further, EAJA fees were awarded in this case in the amount of $_____. Whenever EAJA fees and fees under § 406(b) are awarded in the same case, the smaller fee is to be refunded to plaintiff pursuant to section 206 of Pub. L. 96-481, as amended by Pub. L. 99-80, §3, Aug. 5, 1985, 99 Stat. 186, thus reducing plaintiff's out of pocket fee for federal court work to $_____ or approximately _____% of the total past due benefits.

10. Plaintiff, _____, approves the fee out of his back benefits and understands that he will receive a refund of the EAJA fee. See letter from plaintiff attached as Exhibit D.

11. Given the contingent nature of the representation, the express contract between Plaintiff and his attorney, Plaintiff's agreement with this fee, and the absence of any reasons why the award from the overall past-due benefits as outlined above would be unjust, counsel seeks a fee authorization in the amount of $_____ pursuant to §206(b)(1) of the Social Security Act. See Time Log attached as Exhibit E.

Dated at _____, this ____ day of _____, 20__.

Respectfully submitted,

_____

Attorney for Plaintiff

P.O. Address:

§758   Form: Federal Court Fee Contract

[Author's Note: This contract voluntarily includes a cumulative cap of 25% of past-due benefits of 42 U.S.C. § 406(a) and 42 U.S.C. § 406(b) fees taken together, which may not be appropriate for all practices. For example, if you do not represent the claimant during the administrative proceedings on court remand, the § 406(a) fee the claimant's representative on remand receives will diminish the amount of a § 406(b) fee you can receive. Circuit law may require a cumulative cap. *Compare Morris v. Soc. Sec. Admin.*, 689 F.2d 495, 497-98 (4th Cir.1982) (recognizing a cumulative cap); *Dawson v. Finch*, 425 F.2d 1192, 1195 (5th Cir. 1970) (same) with *Clark v. Astrue*, 529 F.3d 1211, 1218 (9th Cir. 2008) (finding no cumulative cap); *Wrenn ex rel. Wrenn v. Astrue*, 525 F.3d 931, 936 (10th Cir. 2008) (same); *Horenstein v. Sec'y of Health & Human Servs.*, 35 F.3d 261, 262 (6th Cir.1994) (en banc).]

PLEASE READ CAREFULLY

FEE CONTRACT—FEDERAL COURT
SSI/SOCIAL SECURITY DISABILITY

I hereby employ _____ to represent me in federal court review of my SSI/SOCIAL SECURITY DISABILITY case. I agree that my attorney shall charge and receive as the fee an amount equal to twenty-five percent (25%) of the past-due benefits that are awarded to *my family* and me in the event my case is won.

My attorney may retain associate or outside counsel. If associate or outside counsel is retained, that will not increase the amount of my fee.

In addition to the fee, I agree to pay my attorney's reasonable out-of-pocket expenses that are incurred in representing me. Such expenses may include federal court filing fees, computerized legal research services, long distance telephone calls, long distance fax transmissions, medical reports, expert witness fees, transcript preparation charges, photocopying, postage, and travel. I will receive an itemized bill for these expenses. I understand that I will have to pay these expenses whether I win or lose my case; however, the fee that I must pay is based on winning my case. I will not be charged a fee if I do not receive past-due benefits.

My attorney has explained to me that it is the law that the attorney fee must be approved by the federal court for representation in federal court and by the Social Security Administration for representation before the Social Security Administration. I understand that the total fee could amount to many thousands of dollars or many hundreds of dollars per hour on an hourly basis; I understand that my attorney is accepting my case because of the possibility of obtaining substantial fees. I agree to cooperate in any way that I can so that my attorney's full fee is authorized. I understand that my attorney may seek the maximum fee this contract allows under the law. My attorney does not promise to minimize either the attorney fee he or she receives or that I pay under this contract.

I understand that sometimes a court will order the government to pay attorney fees pursuant to the Equal Access to Justice Act (EAJA). If this happens, *I hereby promise to pay and I assign any court-awarded EAJA attorney fees to my attorney.* I agree that any such payment belongs to my attorney to the extent that the law allows; and I authorize my attorney to settle the amount of any EAJA fee using his or her professional judgment. If my attorney receives an EAJA check made payable to me, I hereby explicitly give authority to my attorney to endorse the check with my name and deposit it in my attorney's general office account. I agree that any EAJA fee should be delivered to my attorney. If the government collects a debt that I owe from any EAJA fee, I understand that I still must pay the fee to my attorney.

It is possible that I will not pay any attorney fee out of my past-due benefits for my attorney's work on my behalf in court, but rather my attorney will receive the EAJA award as his or her sole compensation for representing me in court. However, my attorney has the right under this contract to ask the court to award as much as 25% of my past-due benefits for representing me in court. If the court awards an attorney fee out of my past-due benefits and also awards an EAJA fee for that same work, I will be refunded or credited with the amount of the smaller fee.

In no case will the fee that comes out of the back benefits paid on my account be greater than 25% of back benefits (including the fee paid for work on my case before the Social Security Administration).

I understand that the Social Security Administration is supposed to hold out 25% of the past-due benefits and pay the approved fee to my attorney. If for any reason SSA fails to withhold money from my past-due benefits for direct payment of the fee to my attorney, I promise to pay my attorney from the past-due benefits I receive.

My attorney has not promised that I will win my case. I recognize that I may lose my case. My attorney has informed me that a court may take many months and as much as several years to decide my case.

This agreement terminates at the option of my attorney if we lose in the federal district court. My attorney will mail me at my last known address a copy court's final decision in my case.

This contract is in addition to any other fee agreement I have signed or will sign with my attorney for representation before the Social Security Administration.

_____
Signature

_____
Date

_____
Social Security Number

ACCEPTED AND APPROVED FOR THE LAW FIRM:

_____
Signature

_____
Date

§760   Equal Access to Justice Act (EAJA)

§761   Legislative History of the EAJA

The Equal Access to Justice Act, 28 U.S.C. § 2412(d), provides for awards of attorney fees against the federal government under certain circumstances. The EAJA was passed originally in 1980 as Public Law 96-841 to be in effect from October 1, 1981 to October 1, 1984, on which date it expired. In 1985 Congress, in Public Law 99-80, repealed the section of the EAJA that had caused it to expire and made a few amendments to its substance. The EAJA now contains no expiration date.

In 1996, Congress amended the EAJA again. Public Law 104-121, raised the EAJA hourly rate from $75, applicable since 1981, to $125 for cases filed on or after March 29, 1996.

§762   Prerequisites for Awarding Attorney Fees

For a Social Security disability or SSI claimant to obtain an award of attorney fees against the federal government pursuant to the EAJA, 28 U.S.C. § 2412(d), the federal court must find that:

1. Claimant was a prevailing party;
2. Claimant had a net worth not exceeding two million dollars at the time the action was filed;
3. Position of the United States in the litigation or in the action (or failure to act) of the agency on which the civil action is based was not substantially justified and that there are no special circumstances that make an award under the EAJA unjust; and
4. Application for fees was made within 30 days of final judgment, defined as the date a judgment is no longer appealable, i.e., 90 days from the date of entry of judgment in most circumstances.

In addition, the court must find an appropriate hourly rate and determine whether the time spent by the attorney on the case is adequately explained and is reasonable.

The government has litigated all these issues. Some hapless attorneys have had EAJA fees denied because not all of the i's were dotted or t's crossed in their applications. A successful EAJA motion requires careful preparation.

Practice Tip

After you win your client's case in federal court but well before an EAJA motion is due, e-mail a summary of your time spent on the case with the applicable hourly rate to the government's attorneys along with an offer to settle the EAJA claim. Send the settlement request both to the Assistant United States Attorney, who signed the pleadings, and to the attorney from SSA's Office of General Counsel (OGC), who wrote the briefs in the case and likely has EAJA settlement authority. In your cover letter, explain that you will be filing an EAJA motion by a certain date; and you'd like to know before that date if the government will stipulate to paying EAJA fees.

§763   Prevailing Party

The EAJA provides that "a court shall award to a prevailing party . . . fees and other expenses. . ." When an EAJA fee is awarded to your client, unless you have an assignment of the fee signed by your client, the check for the fee will be mailed in your client's name to your office. For this reason, most lawyers ask their clients to sign an assignment. See sample at §782. Such assignments have usually been honored by SSA and the courts so that checks were paid in the attorney's name. Just to cover all bases, many lawyers include language in their federal court contracts that says if the lawyer receives the check in the name of the client, the lawyer has the client's authorization to endorse the check. See sample language in the federal court contract in this book, §758.

When your client owes a debt to the government, the government says it can deduct that debt from the EAJA fee, a position upheld by the U.S. Supreme Court in Astrue v. Ratliff, 560 U.S. ___, 130 S.Ct. 2521 (2010). SSA says that after Ratliff when no debt is owed to the government by plaintiff, an assignment of the EAJA fee will be honored. The check will be mailed to the attorney in the attorney's name. When the plaintiff owes a debt, the debt will be deducted and even if there is an assignment of the fee to the attorney, the check for any balance will be made payable to the plaintiff and sent to the attorney. See NOSSCR Social Security Forum, Vol. 32, No. 7, July 2010, p. 13. To find out if your client owes a debt to the government, have your client telephone the U.S. Treasury Department at 800-304-3107.

Whenever a court either reverses the decision of the Commissioner and awards benefits or reverses and remands the case for further proceedings before SSA pursuant to sentence four of 42 U.S.C. § 405(g), the plaintiff is a prevailing party. Sentence four provides that the court has the power to enter a "judgment affirming, modifying, or reversing the decision of the Commissioner with or without remanding the cause for a rehearing." A plaintiff who obtains a sentence-four judgment reversing the Commissioner and remanding the case for a new hearing is a "prevailing party" for the purposes of the EAJA because the plaintiff succeeded on a significant issue that achieved some of the benefit sought in bringing the suit. *Shalala v. Schaefer*, 509 U.S. 292, 302 (1993).

A plaintiff whose case is remanded for additional proceedings before SSA pursuant to sentence six, on the other hand, does not become a prevailing party until the case is won on remand. Sentence six of 42 U.S.C. § 405(g) provides for remand in just two situations: 1) where new and material evidence is presented to the court and there is good cause for the failure to incorporate that evidence into the record of the prior proceeding; or 2) where the Commissioner requests remand before answering the complaint. *See* §§623 and 642-643.

§764   Meaning of "Substantially Justified"

While the claimant must allege that the position of the United States, either at the agency level or in federal court, was not substantially justified, the burden is on the government to prove substantial justification. *See* 28 U.S.C. §§ 2412(d)(1)(B) and 2412(d)(2)(D).

In *Pierce v. Underwood*, 487 U.S. 552 (1988), the appeal of an action against HUD, the United States Supreme Court addressed the meaning of the words "substantially justified" in the EAJA. The Court noted that the word "substantial" could have two quite different connotations. Of the two possibilities, the Supreme Court said that the word "substantially" means essentially the same thing as the word "substantial" as that term is used in assessing whether or not "substantial evidence" supports agency action in judicial review under the Administrative Procedure Act, in other words, "such relevant evidence as a reasonable mind might accept as adequate to support a conclusion." *Pierce v. Underwood*, 487 U.S. at 565.

The Supreme Court went on to say that "substantially justified" as that term is used in the EAJA meant, "'justified in substance or in the main'—that is justified to a degree that could satisfy a reasonable person. That is no different from the 'reasonable basis both in law and fact' formulation adopted by the Ninth Circuit and the vast majority of other courts of appeals that have addressed this issue." *Pierce v. Underwood*, 487 U.S. at 565.

Abstract discussion of how to determine whether the Commissioner's position was "substantially justified" is no substitute for reading decisions that apply this principle to claimants' cases. Consider developing an analysis similar to that used in *Russell v. Sullivan*, 930 F.2d 1443 (9th Cir. 1991), in which no substantial justification was found for the ALJ's failure to include

in a hypothetical question to a vocational expert Russell's inability to sit for prolonged periods, a fact confirmed by the treating physician's uncontroverted opinion. In support of its decision, the Ninth Circuit cited several cases with similar fact situations where EAJA fees were awarded.

In many federal court cases, a pivotal issue is the failure of the ALJ to follow a clear directive in a Social Security ruling or regulation. How can violating a Social Security ruling or regulation ever be substantially justified?

Determining substantial justification is a fact-specific inquiry.

Practice Tip

There are three approaches to briefing the issue of substantial justification in an EAJA application. First, because the agency has the burden of proof on this issue, a plaintiff may merely allege in the motion that the agency's position was not substantially justified. Full argument may be provided in a reply brief if the agency argues that its position was substantially justified. Second, a plaintiff may simply sketch out the argument that the agency's position was not substantially justified with additional argument to be provided in reply. Third, a plaintiff may fully brief the issue in the initial brief. Different approaches may be appropriate for different cases; but as a rule, the first or second approach is best. If you fully brief the issue, you are not taking strategic advantage of the fact that the burden of proof is on the government.

Further, if you spend considerable time fully briefing the issue, you may learn that the government not only concedes its position is not substantially justified, but also proposes that the court not award attorney fees for the time you spent addressing substantial justification. The government may persuade a court that you should not be paid for litigating an uncontested issue. On the other hand, if you learn while attempting to negotiate a settlement on EAJA fees that the government intends to argue that its position was substantially justified, an initial full brief on the issue may take some punch out of the government's argument.

§765   Calculation of Attorney Fees and Expenses Paid Under EAJA

The EAJA, which took effect on October 1, 1981, provided that attorney fees would be based on prevailing market rates but "shall not be awarded in excess of $75 per hour unless the court determines that an increase in the cost of living or a special factor, such as the limited availability of qualified attorneys for the proceedings involved, justifies a higher fee." 28 U.S.C. § 2412(d)(2)(A). In 1996, Public Law 104-121 raised the maximum EAJA hourly rate to $125 for cases filed on or after March 29, 1996. Increases in the cost of living under the amended EAJA are calculated from March 1996 to raise this maximum hourly rate.

Cost of living increases were routinely awarded using the consumer price index for all urban consumers known as the CPI-U, available from the Bureau of Labor Statistics of the U.S. Department of Labor, to calculate the increase in the cost of living applicable to the $75 per hour limit. After the statute was amended, some courts, taking the position that prevailing market rates were less than the $125 per hour maximum anyway, awarded fees at what they determined to be the lesser prevailing hourly rate. Thus, it is essential to show the court the prevailing market rate in your area. This can be done by affidavits from other attorneys or studies done by bar associations, *etc.*

In *Pierce v. Underwood,* 487 U.S. 552, 573 (1988), the Supreme Court severely limited the possibility that a "special factor" could apply in a disability case that would justify a fee higher than that set by the statute plus cost of living increases. None of the factors normally considered by courts in evaluating the reasonableness of attorney fees, discussed in §752, including the contingent nature of fees, was considered by the Court to be "special." All of those factors were determined to be "too generally applicable to be regarded as a 'special' reason for exceeding the statutory cap." The Court stated:

> [T]he "special factor" formulation suggests Congress thought that $75 an hour was generally quite enough public reimbursement for lawyers' fees, whatever the local or national market might be. If that is to be so, the exception for "limited availability of qualified attorneys for the proceedings involved" must refer to attorneys "qualified for the proceedings" in some specialized sense, rather than just in their general legal competence. We think it refers to attorneys having some distinctive knowledge or specialized skill needful for the litigation in question—as opposed to an extraordinary level of the general lawyerly knowledge and ability useful in all litigation. Examples of the former would be an identifiable practice specialty such as patent law, or knowledge of foreign law or language. Where such qualifications are necessary and can be obtained only at rates in excess of the $75 cap, reimbursement above that limit is allowed.

487 U.S. at 572.

Courts award increases in the hourly rate over the statutory maximum only sparingly, for reasons other than inflation. *See Pierce v. Underwood,* 487 U.S. 552, 571-73 (1988) (discussing "special factors").

Courts have rejected arguments that expertise in Social Security/SSI law or Social Security/SSI litigation involving individual civil actions (in contrast to class actions) may constitute a "special factor" warranting an enhancement of the EAJA's statutory rate. *See Hyatt v. Barnhart,* 315 F.3d 239, 249-50 (4th Cir. 2002) (holding that expertise in Social Security law and class actions did not constitute a special factor); *Raines v. Shalala,* 44 F.3d 1355, 1359-62 (7th Cir. 1995) (expertise in Social Security law was not a special factor justifying enhancing the EAJA's statutory rate); *Stockton v. Shalala,* 36 F.3d 49, 50 (8th Cir.1994) (reversing enhancement for attorney's expertise in an ordinary Social Security disability case); *Harris v. Railroad Ret. Bd.,* 990 F.2d 519, 521 (10th Cir. 1993) (holding that a Social Security specialist's expertise is not necessarily a special factor); *Begley v. Secretary of Health & Human Servs.,* 966 F.2d 196, 200 (6th Cir.1992) (vacating and remanding an award to counsel in a Social Security class action case for consideration of "special factors" because "[t]he district court failed to exercise its discretion to decide the[] issues"); *Chynoweth v. Sullivan,* 920 F.2d 648, 650 (10th Cir. 1990) (refusing to enhance the EAJA's statutory rate for expertise in Social Security law); *Pirus v. Bowen,* 869 F.2d 536, 542 (9th Cir. 1989) (holding that practice specialty in Social Security disability law, and experience with class action challenges under that law, can be a specialty that falls within the parameters of *Underwood*).

In 1987 the Labor Department began publishing a revision of the consumer price index for all urban consumers focusing on "legal service fees" inflation, which has been substantially greater than the consumer price index for all items. The "legal services" index was accepted by several district courts, but the government successfully appealed this issue. *See Sullivan v. Sullivan,* 958 F.2d 574 (4th Cir. 1992), *Dewalt v. Sullivan,* 963 F.2d 27 (3d Cir. 1992), and *Harris v. Sullivan,* 968 F.2d 263 (2d Cir. 1992).

When courts award an hourly rate greater than the statutory maximum because of inflation, they generally use the consumer price index for all urban consumers, the "CPI-U, all items," in calculating the maximum hourly rate for awards under EAJA. Because courts differ in accepting the national, regional and local CPI-U, you will need to check to see which index is used by your district court. If you can discern no preference, choose the CPI-U with the highest inflation rate. You can obtain the CPI-U from the Bureau of Labor Statistics. *See* http://www.bls.gov/

For a case filed on or after March 29, 1996, to calculate the cost of living increase since March 1996, divide the current CPI-U by the CPI-U for March 1996. Then multiply the result by $125. The Ninth Circuit provides a useful calculation of annual EAJA rates using national CPI data. *See* http://www.ca9.uscourts.gov/ (search for "EAJA") (2001 ($142.18), 2002 ($144.43), 2003 ($147.72), 2004 ($151.65), 2005 ($156.79), 2006 ($161.85), 2007 ($166.46), 2008 ($172.85)).

The government has had some success in arguing that cost of living increases applied to the statutory maximum hourly rate should be calculated as of the year the work was done rather than at the time the EAJA award is granted—which often can be a year or more later. Compare *United States v. Aisenberg*, 358 F.3d 1327, 1345-46 & n.28 (11th Cir. 2004) (using historic rates); *Sorenson v. Mink*, 239 F.3d 1140, 1148-49 (9th Cir. 2001) (same); *Kerin v. U.S. Postal Serv.*, 218 F.3d 185, 194 (2d Cir. 2000) (same); *Masonry Masters, Inc. v. Nelson*, 105 F.3d 708, 710-714 (D.C. Cir. 1997) (same); *Marcus v. Shalala*, 17 F.3d 1033, 1038-40 (7th Cir. 1994) (same); *Perales v. Casillas*, 950 F.2d 1066 (5th Cir.1992) (same) with *Garcia v. Schweiker*, 829 F.2d 396, 402 (3d Cir.1987) ("By calculating the total fee amount by using the closest available Consumer Price Index to the date on which the plaintiff became a prevailing party, as Community Legal Services does here, attorneys will receive, in today's dollars, the purchasing power to which they are entitled"). Check your circuit and local case law.

Clearly for past years there is one annual rate, not twelve monthly rates for each year. For the most recent year, you should pick a relevant month to use for the interim hourly rate. While you could calculate an hourly rate for each month in the most recent year, such a calculation would be cumbersome. You should be able to convince a court to use, for example, the rate for the first six months of the year or for the most recent month.

The EAJA provides for payment of expenses, which include "the expenses of expert witnesses, the reasonable cost of any study, analysis, engineering report, test, or project *which is found by the court to be necessary for the preparation of the party's case*." 28 U.S.C. § 2412(d)(2)(A) (emphasis added). In the usual Social Security disability case, the specific examples of expenses from 28 U.S.C. § 2412(d)(2)(A) are rarely encountered, though expenses for expert witnesses and the purchase of medical records for use at the remand hearing are awarded in those relatively rare circumstances when the case is remanded under the sixth sentence of 42 U.S.C. § 405(g). *See* §766. Courts generally interpret 28 U.S.C. § 2412(d)(2)(A) by emphasizing the words italicized above so that expenses may be awarded for anything that is necessary for the preparation of the claimant's case. The

examples, therefore, are not exclusive. *See*, for example, *Aston v. Secretary of Health & Human Services*, 808 F.2d 9, 12 (2d Cir. 1986).

In a case remanded under the fourth sentence of 42 U.S.C. § 405(g), attorneys typically include in EAJA petitions virtually any charge that could be submitted for payment by a private client: paralegal hourly charges, law student hourly charges, on-line legal research, attorney travel, postage, long distance telephone charges, copying expenses, etc. *See, for example, Jean v. Nelson*, 863 F.2d 759, 778 (11th Cir. 1988), *aff'd on other grounds, Commissioner, INS v. Jean*, 496 U.S. 154 (1990).

For paralegals and law students, it is necessary to establish the market rate for their charges. *See Richlin Sec. Serv. Co. v. Chertoff*, 128 S. Ct. 2007 (2008) (discussing the market rate for paralegal services). If you routinely charge private clients a certain hourly rate for such services, an affidavit to this effect should suffice. Otherwise, it will be necessary to obtain affidavits from other attorneys about what they charge clients for paralegal and law student services. Lawyers, who have previously received EAJA fees for paralegal or law student services, often cite court decisions in their earlier cases.

Payment of "costs" under 28 U.S.C. §§ 2412(a)(1) and 1920, typically the $350 filing fee, is not technically part of the EAJA. Although you can include such costs in your EAJA motion and courts generally order them paid when they issue EAJA orders, the government pays such costs separately—out of funds other than those appropriated for payment of EAJA awards. It is more expeditious to obtain reimbursement of such "costs" by filing a Bill of Costs rather than including them in an EAJA motion. *See* §793.

§766 EAJA Fees for Time Spent Representing Claimant on Remand

The EAJA has two sides: a civil-action side, 28 U.S.C. § 2412(d), and an administrative side, 5 U.S.C. § 504. *See, especially, Sullivan v. Hudson*, 490 U.S. 877, 890-92 (1989). A representative for a claimant for Social Security benefits or SSI cannot receive an EAJA fee under the administrative side because such a fee is restricted to an "adversary adjudication" and an administrative proceeding for Social Security disability benefits is not an "adversary adjudication." *Id.* But that does not foreclose in all cases the receipt of an EAJA fee for representation of a claimant before the agency.

In *Sullivan v. Hudson*, 490 U.S. 877, 892 (1989), the Supreme Court held that where a district court "retains continuing jurisdiction over the case pending a decision from the Secretary which will determine the claimant's entitlement to benefits, the proceedings on remand are an integral part of the civil action" for which EAJA fees are available. In *Shalala v. Schaefer*, 509 U.S. 292, 298-303 (1993), the Court restricted the holding of *Hudson* to apply only to those rare cases that are remanded pursuant to sentence six of 42 U.S.C. § 405(g), that is, cases remanded because there is new evidence or cases remanded on motion of the Commissioner before answer. *See* §§642-643. In other words, you can obtain an EAJA fee under 28 U.S.C. § 2412(d) for work before the agency so long as that work is performed during a sentence-six remand.

Note that in those rare cases when a remand is ordered pursuant to sentence six, the EAJA award may include the costs and expenses incurred during the administrative proceedings on remand, *e.g.*, reimbursement for medical records and experts. 28 U.S.C. § 2412(a). *See* §765. "[N]o expert witness shall be compensated at a rate in excess of the highest rate of compensation for expert witnesses paid by the United States." 28 U.S.C. § 2412(d)(2)(A).

§767 Time on EAJA Motion and Appeal of EAJA Denial

Time spent preparing an EAJA application and litigating EAJA-related issues is compensable. There is no requirement that the court delve into the issue of whether the government was substantially justified in opposing the EAJA award. If the government's position in the underlying litigation was not substantially justified, either at the agency level or in its litigation position, then an EAJA award is appropriate and time for bringing the EAJA motion is compensable. *Commissioner, INS v. Jean,* 496 U.S. 154 (1990). Nevertheless, there is an exception to this rule explained in footnote 10 of *Jean*:

> Because *Hensley v. Eckerhart*, 461 U.S. 424, 437 (1983), requires the district court to consider the relationship between the amount of the fee awarded and the results obtained, fees for fee litigation should be excluded to the extent that the applicant ultimately fails to prevail in such litigation. For example, if the Government's challenge to a requested rate for paralegal time resulted in the court's recalculating and reducing the award for paralegal time from the requested amount, then the applicant should not receive fees for the time spent defending the higher rate.

Jean, 496 U.S. at 163, n.10. In other words, a court may deny EAJA fees for any EAJA-related issue that the plaintiff loses.

Foresight helps obtain an EAJA award for EAJA litigation. For example, if you merely allege in your

EAJA application that the agency's position was not substantially justified, if the agency then contends that its position was substantially justified, you will reply to this contention and, citing *Jean*, file a supplemental fee request. You may add a comment that, by not briefing the issue of substantial justification initially, you may have minimized unnecessary fees for fee-related issues.

Practice Tip

Although keeping detailed time records is a good idea for all phases of federal court litigation, when you are litigating fees, it is prudent to provide an even more detailed description of the time expended on an issue-by-issue basis. For example, if your time records contain multiple entries that say something like: "Research on attorney fee issues," and the court rejects your position on one attorney fee issue out of six, when the court reduces your time for work on the losing issue, it may make a greater reduction than would otherwise be required if you had provided the court with sufficient detail for it to figure out how much time was actually spent on the losing issue.

§768 Applications for Fees Under EAJA and 42 U.S.C. § 406

Section 206 of Pub. L. 96-481, as amended by Pub. L. 99-80, § 3, Aug. 5, 1985, 99 Stat. 186, provides:

> (b) Section 206(b) of the Social Security Act (42 U.S.C. § 406(b)(1)) [section 406(b) of Title 42, The Public Health and Welfare] shall not prevent an award of fees and other expenses under section 2412(d) of Title 28, United States Code [subsection (d) of this section]. Section 206(b)(2) of the Social Security Act [section 406(b)(2) of Title 42] shall not apply with respect to any such award but only if, where the claimant's attorney receives fees for the same work under both section 206(b) of that Act [section 406(b) of Title 42] and section 2412(d) of Title 28, United States Code [subsection (d) of this section], the claimant's attorney refunds to the claimant the amount of the smaller fee.

The purposes of this statute (which has never been codified as part of the United States Code are twofold. First, the statute removes any barrier to an award of EAJA attorney fees in Social Security disability cases that may be implied by 42 U.S.C. § 406(b)(1)(A)—which provides that no fee other than that provided under the Social Security Act shall be awarded in a Social Security disability case. Secondly, it makes the criminal penalties for accepting a fee, other than that awarded by the court under the Social Security Act, inapplicable so long as the attorney refunds the smaller of the fees awarded under 42 U.S.C. § 406(b) or the EAJA to the claimant.

In short, you *may not* keep both EAJA fees and court-ordered fees awarded under 42 U.S.C. § 406(b)(1) for the same work. The criminal penalties found in 42 U.S.C. § 406(b)(2) for accepting unauthorized fees apply if you do. Courts "must entertain dual fee applications under the Social Security Act and the EAJA in appropriate cases." *Wells v. Bowen*, 855 F.2d 37, 42 (2d Cir. 1988). *See also, Coup v. Heckler*, 834 F.2d 313 (3d Cir. 1987).

You *may* request and keep a fee payable from past-due benefits for *administrative representation*, plus any additional EAJA fees awarded for *federal court representation* in the same case because both the federal courts and SSA treat the matter as two separate cases. The fee for administrative representation is granted pursuant to 42 U.S.C. § 406(a). *See* §787 for a sample attorney's supporting affidavit for use with a motion to award attorney fees under both the EAJA and 42 U.S.C. § 406(b).

The *spirit* of the law is to avoid attorneys being paid twice for the same work. However, the letter of the law does not apply to EAJA fees obtained for remand time pursuant to *Sullivan v. Hudson*, 490 U.S. 877 (1989), and fees approved for the same time by the agency under 42 U.S.C. § 406(a). Nevertheless, the best practice for attorneys is to avoid accepting two fees for the same work unless it is with the express approval of both the court and the claimant.

§769 Attorney's Duty to Bring EAJA Applications in Appropriate Cases

One of the goals of the EAJA is to ensure that qualified attorneys will represent individuals in litigation against the government. The EAJA accomplishes this goal in the context of a Social Security disability case by making an additional source of attorney fees available. This provides an added incentive to take a case to federal court. For example, because of the extensive time commitment involved in federal court representation, cases with small past-due benefits are not attractive to attorneys in private practice. Attorneys are expected to invoke this incentive system by obtaining EAJA fees for federal court representation *and* obtaining an appropriate fee out of past-due benefits for

representation before SSA (which may be the entire 25 percent of past-due benefits).

The EAJA has an additional purpose, which is to reimburse claimants for all or part of the cost of litigation against the federal government. This purpose will not be fulfilled if, in cases with high past-due benefits, attorneys seek only the court-approved fees under 42 U.S.C. § 406(b). Attorneys owe it to their clients to bring EAJA motions so that the clients can get back some of the money they spent for attorney fees out of their awarded benefits. Indeed, several district courts have indicated that in appropriate cases where applications for fees under the EAJA are *not* filed, they will reduce any requested fee under 42 U.S.C. § 406(b) accordingly. *See, Shepherd v. Apfel*, 981 F. Supp. 1188, 1194-1195 (S.D. Iowa 1997); *Knagge v. Sullivan*, 735 F. Supp. 411, 415 (M.D. Fla. 1990); *Dowdy v. Bowen*, 636 F. Supp. 591, 594 (W.D. Mo. 1986); and *Taylor v. Heckler*, 608 F. Supp. 1255, 1260 (D.N.J. 1985).

§770 EAJA Time Limit

An EAJA motion must be filed within 30 days of the date that a judgment is no longer appealable. *See*, 28 U.S.C. §§ 2412(d)(a)(B) and 2412(d)(2)(G). As a general rule, because the government has 60 days to appeal a final decision of the district court, the EAJA motion must be filed during the window of opportunity between 60 and 90 days from the date of entry of judgment. Exceptions to this rule may arise when the court's decision is based on a recommendation of a U.S. Magistrate Judge to which neither party objects (*see* §772) or on a stipulation or settlement (*see* §773). Beware. The government tends to have more success challenging the timeliness of EAJA motions than it does challenging their merit.

As a rule, nothing bad happens if you file an EAJA motion early. Thus, if there is any question about determining the EAJA filing window, it is best to file according to the theory that yields the earliest possible deadline. The fear of early filing is generated by the largely theoretical possibility that after it is no longer possible to timely file the EAJA motion, a court will throw out a premature EAJA filing. If the government should object to a premature EAJA filing, you may ask the court to hold the EAJA motion in abeyance until the government can no longer appeal the case, and treat the motion as timely filed. Some lawyers file the EAJA motion a second time, just to be sure. "File early and file often," is the mantra of the Lorain, Ohio attorney known as Dr. EAJA, Kirk Roose.

The EAJA's time limit is not jurisdictional, but rather a statute of limitations. *See Scarborough v. Principi*, 541

U.S. 401 (2004). Hence, that time limit can be waived by the agency and it is subject to equitable tolling.

§771   Court Reversal With or Without Remand for Rehearing Pursuant to Sentence Four of 42 U.S.C. § 405(g)

When a court reverses the Commissioner and remands the case pursuant to the fourth sentence of 42 U.S.C. § 405(g), the plaintiff is a prevailing party for purposes of the EAJA. This was always the rule if the court remanded a case for benefits to be paid. After *Shalala v. Schaefer*, 509 U.S. 292, 302-303 (1993), the rule was extended to apply to all cases remanded under the fourth sentence of 42 U.S.C. § 405(g), including those remanded for a new hearing.

Usually when the court reverses the Commissioner and remands the case for payment of benefits or for a new hearing, the EAJA motion must be filed between 60 and 90 days from the date of entry of judgment. Exceptions to this rule may apply when the court's decision is based on the recommendation of a U.S. Magistrate Judge *and* there is no objection by either party, *see* §772, or when the court's decision is based on stipulation or settlement of the parties. *See* §773.

When a court reverses the Commissioner's final decision and orders benefits paid rather than remanding the case for a new hearing, it is usually because the action of the Social Security Administration in denying benefits was exceptionally egregious. Thus, in such court reversal cases, there is seldom a problem demonstrating that the position of the government was not substantially justified within the meaning of the EAJA. Indeed, an award of EAJA fees is so common in such cases that failure of a claimant's attorney to file an EAJA motion to obtain reimbursement for at least a portion of the client's attorney fees probably constitutes malpractice. *See* §769.

§772   Court Reversal With or Without Remanding for Rehearing Based on U.S. Magistrate Judge Recommendation

When the judgment of the district court reversing the Commissioner, with or without remanding the case for a rehearing, follows a report and recommendation of a U.S. Magistrate Judge pursuant to 28 U.S.C. § 636(b)(1) to which neither the plaintiff nor the government objects, a complication may be added to the calculation of the date the EAJA motion is due. The parties are allowed 10 days after service to object to a magistrate judge's recommendation pursuant to 28 U.S.C. § 636(b)

(1)(C). *See* §633. If neither party objects and the court enters judgment, have both parties waived their right to appeal? If so, does the 30-day period begin to run immediately from the date of entry of judgment?

The answer to this question differs from circuit to circuit. The answer depends not on the language of 28 U.S.C. § 636, but rather, on circuit law concerning waiver of appeal when a party fails to object to a magistrate judge's report and recommendation. In *Thomas v. Arn*, 474 U.S. 140 (1985), the Supreme Court held that a court of appeals may adopt such a rule conditioning appeal.

Nevertheless, the impact is unclear of such a circuit rule on determining whether a judgment can be appealed. The Supreme Court has noted before that the applicable Sixth Circuit rule was not "jurisdictional" because the Sixth Circuit excused the procedural default in *Thomas v. Arn*, 474 U.S. 140, 146 (1985). Using this rationale, could not the government appeal within 60 days of the date of entry of judgment, asking the court of appeals to excuse its failure to timely object to the magistrate judge's recommendation? If so, the judgment does not become final until 60 days after entry.

Check the case law in your circuit on this issue. When in doubt, file your EAJA motion sooner rather than later.

§773   Stipulated Reversal With or Without Remanding for Rehearing

As occasionally occurs, let us say that you stipulate or settle with the government that judgment is to be entered for your client and the case is to be sent back to SSA either for payment of benefits or rehearing pursuant to sentence four of 42 U.S.C. § 405(g). Is the judgment final and not appealable because it is based on the stipulation or settlement? If so, the EAJA motion is due within 30 days of entry of judgment. There is conflicting circuit law regarding whether a party may appeal a district court's adoption of the settlement of the parties.

Whenever a stipulation or settlement, in effect, results in judgment for the plaintiff under sentence four of 42 U.S.C. § 405(g), the best practice is to assume that it is not appealable and file the EAJA motion within 30 days of entry of judgment. However, in most instances, a plaintiff may successfully argue that the EAJA's 30-day time limit runs after the appeal period of Federal Rule of Appellate Procedure 4 even in a case in which a stipulation or settlement disposed of the merits.

Practice Tips

If the government alleges that your EAJA motion was untimely following a stipulated remand of the case, recall that the time limit runs from the date of entry of judgment, not from the date of the court's order. Many times, especially with stipulated remands but in other cases as well, the clerk's office fails to enter judgment under Rule 58 of the Federal Rules of Civil Procedure. To find out if judgment was entered, telephone the office of the clerk of court or check the PACER docket online. If judgment was not entered, it is a simple matter to request that a Rule 58 judgment be entered. Entry of judgment starts the EAJA clock running. If no Rule 58 judgment is entered, the order disposing of the matter functions as a judgment after 150 days. *See* Fed. R. Civ. P. 58. The absence of a separate judgment therefore does not extend forever the time within which to file an EAJA motion.

You can, of course, avoid all these potential problems by addressing EAJA fees when you are negotiating settlement of your client's disability case. Come to an agreement on both issues at the same time. However, do not allow the lack of a settlement of EAJA fee interfere with a settlement of the merits. The EAJA fee can always be litigated after the merits disposition.

§774 Remands Under Sixth Sentence of 42 U.S.C. § 405(g)

In *Melkonyan v. Sullivan*, 501 U.S. 89 (1991), the Supreme Court explained the time limit for filing EAJA motions in those cases remanded pursuant to sentence six of 42 U.S.C. § 405(g). A "sentence six remand" is a remand made where new evidence exists and there was good cause not to include such new evidence in the administrative proceeding, or a remand made on motion of the Commissioner prior to answer. The rule in such cases is that "the filing period does not begin until after the postremand proceedings are completed, the Secretary returns to court, the court enters a final judgment, and the appeal period runs." 501 U.S. at 102.

§775 Circuit Court of Appeals Cases

When a claimant wins a case at a circuit court of appeals, what is the time limit for filing an EAJA motion? The answer to this question is not at all settled. There are three theories:

• After the appellate court sends the case back to the district court, the EAJA 30-day time limit begins to run immediately when the district court enters a Rule 58 judgment; *see O'Connor v. Shalala*, 23 F.3d 1232 (7th Cir. 1994)

• EAJA 30-day window for filing begins to run only after the time allowed for filing a petition for a writ of *certiorari* to the U. S. Supreme Court has passed (petition for a writ of *cert.* must be filed within 90 days from date of a court of appeals decision. 28 U.S.C. § 2101(c))

• EAJA time limit begins to run immediately when the appellate court issues its decision—check the law of your circuit and, if there is any question, file your EAJA application under the earliest possible theory

An EAJA motion following a successful appellate disposition of a claimant's case is normally filed in the district court. However, circuit law may permit, but not require, filing in the appellate court. *See Orn v. Astrue*, 511 F.3d 1217 (9th Cir. 2008) (allowing filing directly with the appellate court).

§780 EAJA Sample Pleadings

The following are sample motions and affidavits for obtaining an order for the government to pay attorney fees under the Equal Access to Justice Act, 28 U.S.C. § 2412(d). These are samples only. They will inevitably need to be adapted to your fact situation and law in your circuit and district court. For example, some courts require that cost of living increases be applied as of the year when the work was done rather than the year when the EAJA motion is submitted. *See* the attorney affidavit in §783 and compare to the similar affidavits in §§787 and 788.

When a court either reverses the decision of the Commissioner and awards benefits or remands the case for further proceedings pursuant to sentence four of 42 U.S.C. § 405(g), since the plaintiff is a prevailing party in both circumstances, you may use the same motion to apply for EAJA fees. A sample motion appears in §781; a supporting affidavit of plaintiff appears at §782; an affidavit from plaintiff's attorney appears at §783; and a simple supporting memorandum appears at §784. These may be adapted to your own circumstances.

There is no consensus among courts about procedure for requesting entry of judgment and EAJA attorney fees in cases involving sixth sentence remands. Strictly interpreted, here is the procedure:

1. Wait for the Commissioner to file a supplemental transcript
2. Move for judgment (*see* sample, §785)
3. Wait for judgment to be entered and the appeal period to run
4. Within 30 days file an EAJA motion (*see* sample, §786)

Because the government is notoriously slow in filing the supplemental transcript, it may be necessary to file a motion to compel the Commissioner to file the supplemental transcript. Another alternative is to file a copy of SSA's final decision attached to an affidavit supporting a motion for judgment and award of EAJA attorney fees, combining steps 2 and 4 above. *See, e.g., Andino v. Heckler*, 609 F. Supp. 293 (E.D. Wis. 1985).

We have included three sample attorney's affidavits, one designed for a fourth sentence remand with or without requiring a new hearing, §783, one designed for a sixth sentence remand situation, §788, and the third for use in a case in which the court reverses the decision of the Commissioner and awards benefits, §787. At the same time the affidavits at §§787 and 788 illustrate the interplay between EAJA fees and fees awarded out of a claimant's past due benefits under 42 U.S.C. § 406(b). The affidavit in §787 asks that the § 406(b) fee, the greater fee, be awarded to plaintiff's attorney and the EAJA fee, the smaller fee, be paid to plaintiff as reimbursement for part of plaintiff's attorney fees. The affidavit in §788 is an example of fee maximization: The attorney is requesting a 25 percent fee approved by SSA for administrative work and an EAJA award for federal court work.

Practice Tip

When you file your EAJA motion, be sure you have established that your client's net worth was less than two million dollars at the time the EAJA action was begun. *See Sosebee v. Astrue*, 494 F.3d 583 (7th Cir. 2007) (discussing when proof of net worth must be provided). If the case was filed *in forma pauperis*, you need only draw the court's attention to the fact that the court has already determined this. If the case was not filed *in forma pauperis*, prepare an affidavit for the plaintiff to sign. A sample is provided in §782. Note that the sample affidavit also assigns the EAJA fee to the attorney. This is done to avoid the delay involved in getting your client to sign the check for the EAJA fee. Use such an assignment to request that the federal court direct that the EAJA fee be paid to you.

§781   Sample: EAJA Motion for Award of Attorney Fees (Fourth Sentence Remand)

UNITED STATES DISTRICT COURT
_____DISTRICT OF _____

_____,	)	
Plaintiff,	)	MOTION FOR AWARD
	)	OF ATTORNEY FEES
v.	)	PURSUANT TO THE
Commissioner of Social Security,	)	EQUAL ACCESS TO JUSTICE ACT,
Defendant.	)	28 U.S.C. § 2412(d)
	)	
	)	Case No. _____
	)	

Plaintiff, by Attorney _____, hereby moves the Court to award attorney fees to be paid by the defendant pursuant to the Equal Access to Justice Act, 28 U.S.C. § 2412(d). Plaintiff asks for an award of attorney's fees in the amount of $_____ to be paid directly to plaintiff's attorney calculated at the rate of $_____ per hour for _____ hours of work on this case in federal court. Time spent on this case is itemized in plaintiff's attorney's attached affidavit.

This motion is brought within the time limit stated in 28 U.S.C. § 2412(d)(1)(B), which requires that this motion be brought within 30 days of "final judgment." "Final judgment" is defined as "a judgment which is final and not appealable" in 28 U.S.C. § 2412(d)(2)(G). A judgment against the United States becomes final and not appealable when the 60-day time limit for appeal runs. Thus, this motion is brought within 30 days of the last day this judgment could have been appealed, i.e., within 90 days of the date judgment was entered.

Plaintiff is entitled to receive attorney fees pursuant to the Equal Access to Justice Act because plaintiff is the prevailing party in this action under Shalala v. Schaefer, 509 U.S. 292, 302-303 (1993), is an individual whose net worth did not exceed two million dollars at the time the action was filed as is demonstrated by plaintiff's attached affidavit, and the position of the United States in this litigation was not substantially justified. Although the burden of proof on the issue of substantial justification is on the government, plaintiff's supporting memorandum briefly addresses this issue.

There are no special circumstances in this case that make an award under the EAJA unjust.

This motion is supported by an affidavit of plaintiff, an affidavit of plaintiff's attorney, and a memorandum.

Dated at _____,
this ____ day of _____, 20__.

Respectfully submitted,

_____
Attorney for Plaintiff

P.O. Address:

§782   Sample: Plaintiff's Affidavit and Assignment of EAJA Fee

UNITED STATES DISTRICT COURT
_____ DISTRICT OF _____

_____

_____,   )
_____,   )
Plaintiff,   )   PLAINTIFF'S AFFIDAVIT
)   AND ASSIGNMENT
v.   )   OF EAJA FEE
)
Commissioner of Social Security,   )
Defendant.   )
)   Civil Action No.

_____

STATE OF _____)
) SS.
_____ COUNTY)

Plaintiff's Name, being first duly sworn, on oath states:

1.   I am the plaintiff in the above-captioned action.

2.   At the time this action was begun my net worth was less than two million dollars.

3.   I hereby assign any entitlement that I may have to a fee under the Equal Access to Justice Act (EAJA), 28 U.S.C. § 2412(d), to my attorney, _____. I acknowledge that the fee compensates my attorney for representing me before the United States District Court. Therefore, I ask that the EAJA award be made payable to _____ and not to me as Plaintiff.

4.   WHEREFOR, I assign any right or interest I may have in the award of an EAJA fee and understand that the EAJA award shall be paid to my attorney, _____, to compensate counsel for the work performed on this case in the U.S. District Court.

                                          _____
                                          Plaintiff

Subscribed and sworn to before me
this ___ day of _____, 20___.

_____
Notary Public, State of _____
My commission expires:_____

§783   Sample: Plaintiff's Attorney's Affidavit (Fourth Sentence Remand)

UNITED STATES DISTRICT COURT
_____DISTRICT OF _____

_____,	)	PLAINTIFF'S ATTORNEY'S
Plaintiff,	)	AFFIDAVIT IN SUPPORT
	)	OF MOTION FOR AWARD OF
v.	)	ATTORNEY'S FEES PURSUANT
	)	TO THE EQUAL ACCESS
Commissioner of Social Security,	)	TO JUSTICE ACT,
Defendant.	)	28 U.S.C. § 2412(d)
	)	
	)	Case No._____

STATE OF _____)
) ss.
_____ COUNTY)

_____, being first duly sworn, states:

1.   I am an attorney licensed to practice law in the State of _____, admitted to practice before the United States District Court for the _____ District of _____, and I am the attorney for plaintiff in this action.

2.   As a result of this Court's reversal of the Commissioner's final decision and remand of this case, plaintiff is a prevailing party under Shalala v. Schaefer, 509 U.S. 292, 302-303 (1993).

3.   My experience in this area of law practice is summarized on the attached resume.

4.   My regular non-contingent hourly rate is $_____. In Social Security cases I usually agree to represent clients on a contingent fee basis of 25 percent of past-due benefits. When I win a contingent case, I expect to receive more than my regular hourly rate in order to compensate me for the risk of non-recovery involved in taking a case on a contingent fee basis.

5.   My time working on this case in federal court is itemized on the attached printout which shows that in [year] I spent ____ hours on this case, in [year] I spent ____ hours on this case, in [year] I spent ____ hours on this case, totaling _____ hours.

6.   All of the time spent on this case was necessary in order to provide effective representation to my client. [The following paragraph is a sample showing calculation of cost of living increases for 2006, 2007 and 2008; but beware, not all courts require that the cost of living be calculated and applied to attorney fees annually.]

7.   For civil actions commenced on and after March 29, 1996, $125.00 per hour is the EAJA's statutory rate. 28 U.S.C. § 2412(d)(2)(A). See Pub. L. 104-121, § 232(b)(1); 110 Stat. 847, 863-64 (1996). The hourly rate for 2006 is $161.85; the hourly rate for 2007 is $166.46; and the hourly rate for 2008 is $172.85. In March 1996, the CPI-All Items Index was 155.7. Available at http://www.bls.gov. The increase in the cost of living for 2006 is 1.29 (201.6/155.7). Therefore, the hourly rate for 2006 is $161.85 ($125.00 x 1.29). The increase in the cost of living for 2007 is 1.33 (207.342/155.7). Therefore, the hourly rate for 2007 is $166.46 ($125.00 x 1.33). The increase in the cost of living for 2008 is 1.38 (215.303/155.7). Therefore, the hourly rate for 2008 is $172.85 ($125.00 x 1.364). These hourly rates are below the market rate for the same kind and quality of legal services as performed in this case. To minimize attorney fees for the fee litigation, Plaintiff does not present extended argument about the hourly rates requested. If the Commissioner disagrees with the hourly rates, Plaintiff will present additional argument about the rates in a reply brief and request reasonable attorney fees for that additional argument.
        Plaintiff thus requests the following fees:

        Attorney   Hours   Hourly Rate (Year) Total
        [Insert tabular presentation of fees requested.]

8.   I ask that the Court order attorney's fees paid by the government pursuant to the Equal Access to Justice Act, 28 U.S.C. § 2412(d), in the amount of $_____.

                                        _____
                                        Attorney for Plaintiff

Subscribed and sworn to before me
this ____ day of _____, 20__.

_____
Notary Public, State of _____
My commission expires:_____

§784   *Sample: Memorandum Supporting EAJA Motion*

UNITED STATES DISTRICT COURT

_____ DISTRICT OF _____

	)	
_____,	)	MEMORANDUM SUPPORTING
Plaintiff,	)	MOTION FOR ATTORNEY FEES
	)	PURSUANT TO THE
v.	)	EQUAL ACCESS TO JUSTICE
	)	ACT, 28 U.S.C. § 2412(d)
Commissioner of Social Security,	)	
Defendant.	)	
	)	Case No. _____

In order to be entitled to an award of attorney fees pursuant to the Equal Access to Justice Act, 28 U.S.C. § 2412, the Court must find that the position of the government was not "substantially justified," that the plaintiff is the prevailing party, and that no "special circumstances" make an award of fees unjust. 28 U.S.C. § 2412(d)(1)(A).

Shalala v. Schaefer, 509 U.S. 292, 302-303 (1993), made it clear that a plaintiff who obtains judgment and remand pursuant to sentence four of 42 U.S.C. § 405(g) is a prevailing party because the plaintiff has achieved "some of the benefit . . . sought in bringing suit."

Pursuant to the Equal Access to Justice Act, the burden of proof is on the defendant to demonstrate to the Court that the Commissioner's position in this civil action was substantially justified. Marcus v. Shalala, 17 F.3d 1033, 1036 (7th Cir. 1994). "Whether or not the position of the United States was substantially justified shall be determined on the basis of the record (including the record with respect to the action or failure to act by the agency upon which the civil action is based) which is made in the civil action for which fees and other expenses are sought." 28 U.S.C. § 2412(d)(1)(B) as amended. See also, § 2412(d)(2)(D) as amended.

The government's position is substantially justified if it is "justified to a degree that could satisfy a reasonable person." Pierce v. Underwood, 487 U.S. 552, 565 (1988). "A position can be substantially justified even though it is not correct . . . .." Underwood, 487 U.S. at 566 n.2.

It will be left to the government to meet its burden of showing that its position in this case, both at the agency level and in court, was substantially justified. However, a few comments are in order.

[Insert comments re: no substantial justification.]

There is no substantial justification for the ALJ decision in this case. There are no special circumstances that render payment of attorney fees under the EAJA unjust. Accordingly, the Court should order payment of attorney fees.

Dated at _____ this ____ day of _____, 200__.

Respectfully submitted,

_____

Attorney for Plaintiff

P. O. Address:

§785   Sample: Motion for Judgment (Sixth Sentence Remand)

UNITED STATES DISTRICT COURT
_____ DISTRICT OF _____

_____,	)	
	)	
Plaintiff,	)	
	)	MOTION FOR JUDGMENT
v.	)	
	)	
Commissioner of Social Security,	)	
Defendant.	)	
	)	Case No.

Plaintiff, by his/her attorney, _____, hereby moves the court pursuant to 42 U.S.C. § 405(g) to enter judgment for plaintiff in the above-captioned matter by affirming the final decision of the Commissioner dated _____, a copy of which is attached to this motion. Plaintiff waives filing of a supplemental transcript by the Commissioner.

Plaintiff brings this motion for judgment as a prerequisite to filing a motion for award of attorney fees pursuant to the Equal Access to Justice Act.

Dated at _____,
this ____ day of _____, 20__.

Respectfully submitted,

_____
Attorney for Plaintiff

P.O. Address:

§786   *Sample: EAJA Motion for Award of Attorney Fees (Sixth Sentence Remand)*

UNITED STATES DISTRICT COURT

_____ DISTRICT OF _____

	)	
_____,	)	
Plaintiff,	)	MOTION FOR AWARD
	)	OF ATTORNEY FEES
v.	)	PURSUANT TO THE
	)	EQUAL ACCESS TO JUSTICE
Commissioner of Social Security,	)	ACT, 28 U.S.C. § 2412(d)
Defendant.	)	
	)	Case No.

Plaintiff, by Attorney _____, hereby moves the Court to award attorney fees to be paid by the defendant pursuant to the Equal Access to Justice Act, 28 U.S.C. § 2412(d). Plaintiff asks for an award of attorney's fees in the amount of $_____ to be paid directly to plaintiff's attorney calculated at the rate of $_____ per hour for _____ hours of work on this case in federal court and on remand before the Social Security Administration. Time spent on this case is itemized in plaintiff's attorney's attached affidavit. Request for payment of EAJA fees for attorney time representing plaintiff before the Social Security Administration on remand is made pursuant to Sullivan v. Hudson, 490 U.S. 877 (1989), as clarified by Melkonyan v. Sullivan, 501 U.S. 89 (1991).

This motion is brought within the time limit stated in 28 U.S.C. § 2412(d)(1)(B), which requires that this motion be brought within 30 days of "final judgment." "Final judgment" is defined as "a judgment which is final and not appealable" in 28 U.S.C. § 2412(d)(2)(G). A judgment against the United States becomes final and not appealable when the 60-day time limit for appeal runs. Thus, this motion is brought within 30 days of the last day this judgment could have been appealed, i.e., within 90 days of the date judgment was entered.

Plaintiff is entitled to receive attorney fees pursuant to the Equal Access to Justice Act because plaintiff is the prevailing party in this action, is an individual whose net worth did not exceed two million dollars at the time the action was filed as is demonstrated by plaintiff's attached affidavit, and the position of the United States in this case, either at the agency or in this litigation, was not substantially justified. Although the agency has the burden of proof on the issue of substantial justification, plaintiff's supporting memorandum briefly addresses this issue.

There are no special circumstances in this case that make an award under the EAJA unjust.

This motion is supported by an affidavit of plaintiff, an affidavit of plaintiff's attorney, and a memorandum.

Dated at _____,
this ____ day of _____, 20__.

Respectfully submitted,

_____

Attorney for Plaintiff

P.O. Address:

§787   Sample: Plaintiff's Attorney's Affidavit (Court Reversal Case Also Asking for Approval of 42 U.S.C. § 406(b) Fees)

UNITED STATES DISTRICT COURT
_____ DISTRICT OF _____

_____, Plaintiff, v. Commissioner of Social Security, Defendant.	)) PLAINTIFF'S ATTORNEY'S) AFFIDAVIT IN SUPPORT) OF MOTION FOR AWARD OF) ATTORNEY'S FEES PURSUANT) TO 42 U.S.C. § 406(b)AND) THE EQUAL ACCESS TO) JUSTICE ACT,) 28 U.S.C. § 2412(d))) Case No. _____

STATE OF _____   )
) ss.
_____ COUNTY   )

_____, being first duly sworn, states:

1.   I am an attorney licensed to practice law in the State of _____, admitted to practice before the United States District Court for the _____ District of _____, and I am the attorney for plaintiff in this action.

2.   As a result of this court's judgment in this case dated _____ finding plaintiff disabled, Social Security disability benefits have been paid.

3.   Plaintiff and I have an attorney fee contract for a contingent 25% of past-due benefits, which fees must be approved by this court pursuant to 42 U.S.C. § 406(b). A copy of our fee contract dated _____ is attached.

4.   Plaintiff has received a check for $_____ in past due Social Security disability benefits. According to the Notice of Award dated _____, a copy of which is attached, $_____ has been withheld by the Social Security Administration (SSA) for direct payment of attorney fees. This amount constitutes 25% of plaintiff's past-due benefits, which is the amount of the fee to which plaintiff has agreed.

5.   I am also requesting that the court award attorney fees pursuant to the Equal Access to Justice Act (EAJA), 28 U.S.C. § 2412(d). Approval of a fee pursuant to 42 U.S.C. § 406(b) and the EAJA present somewhat different issues. The EAJA, for example, contains a limit on the hourly rate of attorney fees while 42 U.S.C. § 406(b) does not. It is not inconsistent for a court to award a reasonable contingent fee of 25% of past due benefits as the attorney fee pursuant to 42 U.S.C. § 406(b) and for the court to determine that the federal government must reimburse plaintiff for part of these fees by calculating a fee at an hourly rate pursuant to the EAJA. When fees are awarded pursuant to 42 U.S.C. § 406(b) and the EAJA, an attorney is not allowed to keep both fees. The 1985 amendment to the EAJA provided that if fees are awarded to an attorney under both statutes, the attorney must refund to the plaintiff the amount of the smaller fee. See section 3 of Public Law 99-80. If I were awarded attorney fees for both statutes, I would follow this provision; however, because the requested EAJA fees are less than the fees requested pursuant to 42 U.S.C. § 406(b), I ask that the court order the EAJA attorney fees paid directly to plaintiff as reimbursement for a portion of the attorney fees awarded pursuant to 42 U.S.C. § 406(b).

6.   I have the following experience in this area of law practice: [set forth experience].

7.   My regular non-contingent hourly rate is $_____. In Social Security cases, I, like most attorneys who handle such cases, usually agree to represent clients on a contingent fee basis of 25% of past-due benefits. When I win a contingent fee case, I expect to receive more than my regular non-contingent hourly rate in order to compensate me for the risk on non-recovery involved in taking a case on a contingent fee basis. I have received fees comparable to the fee requested pursuant to 42 U.S.C. § 406(b) in other Social Security cases, both in court and before SSA.

8.   The fees customarily charged in this locality for similar legal services range from $_____ per hour to $_____ per hour according to [cite studies or attach affidavits from other attorneys]. Percentage fees in contingent cases range from _____ percent in worker's compensation cases to _____ percent in personal injury cases.

9.   This case presented the following issues, which I briefed: [state issues] [if issues are novel and difficult, explain].

10.   [If any of the other factors set forth in Rule 1.5 of the ABA's Model Rules of Professional Conduct are relevant to this case, set them forth here.]

11.   I spent a total of _____ hours representing plaintiff before the Social Security Administration. Those hours are not included in the itemized time below, which time is limited to time spent representing plaintiff in federal court. If the court approves my full 25% contingent fee, I will not request SSA to approve any additional fee.

12.   The following is an itemization of my time working on this case in federal court:
[itemize time]

13.   All of the time spent on this case was necessary in order to provide good representation to my client.

14.   The hours I spent representing plaintiff before this court if compensable at $125 per hour, the maximum allowed under the EAJA (without the court considering some special factor), would total $_____. However, there has been an increase in the cost of living since the amendment to the EAJA took effect on March 29, 1996. Cost of living increase is specifically mentioned in the EAJA as a factor justifying a fee greater than $125 per hour. 28 U.S.C. § 2412(d)(2)(A)(ii). According to the Consumer Price Index for this region as reported by the Bureau of Labor Statistics, there has been a _____ percent increase in the cost of living from March 29, 1996 to date. See the attached information from the Bureau of Labor Statistics. Applying this cost of living increase to $125 per hour yields an hourly rate of $_____. If attorney fees are calculated at this rate for _____ hours, they total $_____.

15.   I ask that the court order attorney fees paid by the government to plaintiff pursuant to the Equal Access to Justice Act in the amount of $_____. This amount is intended to reimburse plaintiff for part of plaintiff's attorney fees awarded pursuant to 42 U.S.C. § 406(b).

16.   Pursuant to 42 U.S.C. § 406(b), I ask that the court authorize as my fee for representing plaintiff the sum of $_____, which amount constitutes 25% of plaintiff's past-due benefits.

_____
Attorney for Plaintiff

Subscribed and sworn to before me
this ___ day of _____, 20__.

_____
Notary Public, State of _____
My commission expires:_____

P.O. ADDRESS:

§788   Sample: Plaintiff's Attorney's Affidavit (Sixth Sentence Remand)

UNITED STATES DISTRICT COURT
_____ DISTRICT OF _____

_____, Plaintiff, v. Commissioner of Social Security, Defendant.	)) PLAINTIFF'S ATTORNEY'S) AFFIDAVIT IN SUPPORT OF) MOTION FOR AWARD OF) ATTORNEY'S FEES PURSUANT) TO THE EQUAL ACCESS) TO JUSTICE ACT,) 28 U.S.C. § 2412(d))) Case No. _____

STATE OF _____   )
) ss.
_____ COUNTY   )

_____, being first duly sworn, states:

1.   I am an attorney licensed to practice law in the State of _____, admitted to practice before the United States District Court for the _____ District of _____, and I am the attorney for plaintiff in this action.

2.   As a result of this court's remand of this case and the subsequent decision dated _____, plaintiff was found disabled by the Social Security Administration (SSA). A copy of this decision appears at pp. _____ in the supplemental administrative record.

3.   A copy of the Notice of Award dated _____ is attached. I am petitioning SSA for a fee of $_____ (which amount constitutes 25% of plaintiff's past-due benefits and is the amount of the fee to which plaintiff has agreed) for my work before the agency, which involved hearing representation and representing plaintiff before the Appeals Council. I am asking for a fee for my federal court representation based on the Equal Access to Justice Act (EAJA). If granted, such a fee will not come out of plaintiff's past-due benefits or affect my fee for work before the agency in any way. However, _____ hours of my work are attributable to work before SSA on remand. If I am awarded EAJA fees for these hours, I will pay the fees attributable to these hours to plaintiff so that I am not paid twice for this same work. Because I do not know how much SSA will award as my fee or if this court will award fees under the EAJA, I ask to reserve my right to move this court to approve a fee pursuant to 42 U.S.C. § 406(b) in the event that my total fee for representation before the agency and in federal court is less than 25% of plaintiff's past-due benefits.

4.   I have the following experience in this area of law practice: [set forth experience].

5.   My regular non-contingent hourly rate is $_____. In Social Security cases, I, like most attorneys who handle such cases, usually agree to represent clients on a contingent fee basis of 25% of past-due benefits. When I win a contingent fee case, I expect to receive more than my regular non-contingent hourly rate in order to compensate me for the risk of non-recovery involved in taking a case on a contingent fee basis.

6.   The fees customarily charged in this locality for similar legal services range from $_____ per hour to $_____ per hour according to [cite studies or attach affidavits from other attorneys]. Percentage fees in contingent cases range from _____ percent in worker's compensation cases to _____ percent in personal injury cases.

7.   This case presented the following issues, which I briefed: [state issues] [if issues are novel and difficult, explain].

8.   [If any of the other factors found in Rule 1.5 of the ABA's Model Rules of Professional Conduct are relevant to this case, set them forth here.]

9.   The following is an itemization of my time working on this case in federal court:
[itemize time]

10.   All of the time spent on this case was necessary in order to provide good representation to my client.

11.   The hours I spent representing plaintiff before this court if compensable at $125 per hour, the maximum allowed under the EAJA (without the court considering some special factor), would total $_____. However, there has been an increase in the cost of living since the amendment to the EAJA took effect on March 29, 1996. Cost of living increase is specifically mentioned in the EAJA as a factor justifying a fee greater than $125 per hour. 28 U.S.C. § 2412(d)(2)(A)(ii). According to the Consumer Price Index for this region as reported by the Bureau of Labor Statistics, there has been a _____ percent increase in the cost of living from March 29, 1996 to date. See the attached information from the Bureau of Labor Statistics. Applying this cost of living increase to $125 per hour yields an hourly rate of $_____. If attorney fees are calculated at this rate for _____ hours, they total $_____, which amount includes $_____ for _____ hours of attorney time before the Social Security Administration on remand.

12.   I ask that the court order attorney fees paid by the government pursuant to the Equal Access to Justice Act in the amount of $_____, of which $_____ will be paid to plaintiff for reimbursement of a portion of plaintiff's attorney fees.

                                         _____
                                         Attorney for Plaintiff

Subscribed and sworn to before me
this ___ day of _____, 20___.

_____
Notary Public, State of _____
My commission expires:

P.O. ADDRESS:

§790　Payment of EAJA Fees

The U.S. Attorney's Office is in charge of sending a court's EAJA order to EAJA payment staff at SSA's Office of Regional Counsel. The EAJA payment staff reads the EAJA order, determines how much to pay and to whom, and inputs the information into SSA's computer. It then forwards the file to SSA's Office of Finance, which, in turn, processes the case to be paid by the U.S. Treasury.

Attorneys who handle a lot of cases in which EAJA fees are awarded report that it speeds processing and payment to send a copy of the court's order directly to the EAJA payment staff at the Office of Regional Counsel. It is most expeditious to fax the court's order to the fax numbers listed for the payment staff that appears on the list at §792.1.

SSA generally honors assignments of EAJA fees signed by the plaintiff so that the EAJA check is made payable to the attorney. But, pointing to the language of the EAJA itself, which provides for an award of attorney fees to a "prevailing party," 28 U.S.C. § 2412(d)(1)(A), SSA says the EAJA fee is the property of the plaintiff, not the attorney. Because 31 C.F.R. § 285.5(e)(6) provides that "[a]n assigned payment will also be subject to offset to collect delinquent debts owed by the assignor," SSA takes the position that an assignment of an EAJA fee to you does not interfere with its duty to comply with the federal mandate to collect by "administrative offset" debts owed to the government by the plaintiff. Therefore, SSA will deduct from EAJA payments the plaintiff's debts such as money owed for student loans, VA loans, small business loans, *etc.*, and, when a state government elects to participate, child support. 31 U.S.C. § 3716. SSA does not give advance notice of this. Thus, you may discover when you receive the EAJA check, even if it comes in your name, that your client's debts to the government have been deducted from your EAJA fee.

At the time of this writing, there is a split in the circuits regarding the offset of federal debts by the EAJA. *Compare Stephens v. Astrue*, 565 F.3d 131, 139 (4th Cir. 2009) (concluding that EAJA fees are payable to the party, not the attorney); *Reeves v. Astrue*, 526 F.3d 732, 738 (11th Cir. 2008) (same) *cert. denied*, 129 S. Ct. 724 (2008); *Manning v. Astrue*, 510 F.3d 1246, 1252-55 (10th Cir. 2007) (same), *cert. denied*, 129 S. Ct. 486 (2008); *with Marre v. United States*, 117 F.3d 297, 304 (5th Cir.1997) (concluding, in a context other than Social Security benefits, that attorney's fees under a statute similar to the EAJA were payable directly to attorney);

Ratliff v. Astrue, 540 F.3d 800, 802 (8th Cir. 2008), *cert. granted*, 78 U.S.L.W. 3011 (U.S. Sept. 30, 2009) (No. 08-1322) (EAJA fees are payable to the attorney).

Practice Tips

Say you have an assignment of EAJA fees signed by the plaintiff, which you submitted to the court as part of your request that the court order EAJA fees paid directly to you. Instead, as sometimes happens, the court issues an order that fails to specify the payee of the EAJA fees. Without any information other than that appearing in the court's order, the EAJA payment staff will process these fees for payment to the plaintiff (care of your office). But if you fax a copy of the court's order along with a copy of the assignment to the EAJA payment staff, the EAJA payment staff may process the EAJA fees for payment directly to you.

§791　Payment by Mandatory Direct Deposit

In 1997 SSA announced a program to have EAJA fees paid by direct deposit to the attorney's bank account in accordance with a directive from Congress that, as much as possible, the government pay its bills by direct deposit. To accomplish this, SSA asked attorneys to complete a form called Attorneys and Legal Organizations ACH Vendor/Miscellaneous Payment Enrollment Form, a copy of which is reproduced at §794.

Although many EAJA checks are still issued to attorneys, and, of course, EAJA fees that are payable to the plaintiff are still paid by a check mailed to the attorney's office, those attorneys who have signed up report that direct deposit payments do seem to arrive a bit more quickly than checks; but they complain that often they do not know that the money arrived until they get their bank statement. Signing up to receive e-mail notification that an EAJA payment has been deposited to your checking account may solve this problem. You may enroll at http://www.ipp.gov.

If you complete the form to sign up for direct deposit, be sure to include your Taxpayer ID No. and the necessary financial institution information. According to an information sheet from SSA, you may sign this form as the "authorized official" or you may have someone from your bank sign the form.

Send the form to SSA, Office of Finance, Attention: Direct Deposit, Post Office Box 47, Baltimore, MD

21235. If you prefer you may fax the form to the Office of Finance at 410-965-9248.

§792   Dealing With Payment Delays

If you have not received payment of EAJA fees in about 30 days from the date of the order awarding fees, you may check on the status of payment by telephoning the EAJA contacts at the Office of Regional Counsel, who will be able to tell you if the order has been processed and forwarded to the Office of Finance. A list of contacts appears at §792.1. Find the appropriate contact by locating your district court on the list. Take a good look at this list. Do not assume that because you know the SSA region for your state, that the court will be assigned to that region. Several courts are assigned to unexpected regions. For example, the three district courts in Tennessee are assigned to three different regions. Note also that Baltimore, in effect, functions as the eleventh region with five district courts assigned to it.

You can check the status of payment at the Office of Finance by telephoning (410) 965-0607.

§792.1   EAJA Fee Payment Contacts

REGION I

Connecticut, Massachusetts, Maine, New Hampshire, Puerto Rico,
Rhode Island, Vermont, M.D. North Carolina, S.D. Georgia, S.D.
Mississippi, W.D. North Carolina

Lead:	Lisa M. Green (617) 565-1833
Backup:	Camille Spert (617) 565-4286
FAX:	617-565-4447

REGION II

New Jersey, Virgin Islands, E.D. New York, N.D. New York, S.D.
New York, W.D. New York

Lead:	Darleen MacIntosh (212) 264-3650, x221
Backup:	Dennis Canning (212) 264-3650, x231
FAX:	212-264-6372

REGION III

Delaware, E.D. Pennsylvania, M.D. Pennsylvania, N.D. West Virginia,
S.D. West Virginia, W.D. Pennsylvania, W.D. Virginia

Lead:	Joann Hilinski (215) 597-1256
Backup:	Jody Sharp (215) 597-3627
FAX:	215-597-4136

REGION IV

E.D. Kentucky, M.D. Florida, M.D. Georgia, N.D. Alabama, N.D. Georgia,
W.D. Kentucky

Lead:	Jozette Cooper (404) 562-0289
Backup:	Arthurice "Thedy" Brundidge (404) 562-1003
FAX:	404-562-1061

REGION V

C.D. Illinois, D. Minnesota, E.D. Michigan, E.D. Tennessee, E.D.
Wisconsin, N.D. Illinois, N.D. Indiana, N.D. Ohio, S.D. Illinois,
S.D. Indiana, S.D. Ohio, W.D. Michigan, W.D. Wisconsin

Lead:	Steven Frank (312) 353-8379
Backup:	Doretha McCraney (312) 353-9232
FAX:	312-353-5876

REGION VI

D. New Mexico, E.D. Arkansas, E.D. Louisiana, E.D. Oklahoma, E.D.
Texas, M.D. Louisiana, N.D. Oklahoma, N.D. Texas, S.D. Texas, W.D.
Arkansas, W.D. Louisiana, W.D. Oklahoma, W.D. Texas

Lead:	Linda B. Williams (214) 767-4240
Backup:	Artie Blanks (214) 767-9210
FAX:	214-767-9228

REGION VII

D. Kansas, D. Nebraska, E.D. Missouri, M.D. Alabama, N.D. Florida,
N.D. Iowa, N.D. Mississippi, S.D. Florida, S.D. Iowa, W.D. Missouri,
W.D. Tennessee

W.D. Missouri:	Leon Jones
	(816) 936-5786
	Fax: (816) 936-5963

S.D. Florida, N.D. Florida,
W.D. Tennessee, N.D. Mississippi,
D. Kansas: Joyce Boehm
                                       (816) 936-5769
                                       Fax: (816) 936-5963

S.D. Iowa, N.D. Iowa, M.D. Alabama
E.D. Missouri, D. Nebraska: Rhonda Echols
                                       (816) 936-5789
                                       Fax: (816) 936-5757

BACKUP FOR ALL DISTRICTS: Rhonda Wheeler
                                       816-936-5779
                                       Fax: (816) 936-5963

REGION VIII

D. Colorado, D. Montana, D. North Dakota, D. South Carolina,
D. South Dakota, D. Utah, D. Wyoming, S.D. Alabama
Lead: Roy Matheson (303) 844-0460
Backup: Denise Sanchez (303) 844-0016
FAX: 303-844-0770

REGION IX

American Samoa, D. Arizona, C.D. California, Canal Zone, D. Hawaii,
D. Nevada, E.D. California, Guam, Northern Marianas, N.D. California,
S.D. California
Lead: Thomas Yip (415) 977-8973
                Bill Brilhante (415) 977-8934
Backup: Karen Bell (415) 977-8938
FAX: 415-744-0134

REGION X

D. Alaska, D. Idaho, D. Oregon, E.D. Washington, W.D. Washington
Lead: Rebecca Halvorsen (206) 615-2271
Backup: Christine Hendon (206) 615-2539
FAX: 206-615-2531

BALTIMORE

D. District of Columbia, D. Maryland, E.D. North Carolina, E.D.
Virginia, M.D. Tennessee
Lead: Sandy Harrison (410) 965-3458
FAX: 410-965-3107

§793   Payment of Costs and Expenses

The EAJA, 28 U.S.C. §§ 2412(d)(1)(A), provides for payment of "fees and other expenses, *in addition to any costs* awarded pursuant to" 28 U.S.C. §§ 2412(a), which is not part of the EAJA. Thus, *expenses*, which include "the expenses of expert witnesses, the reasonable cost of any study, analysis, engineering report, test, or project which is found by the court to be necessary for the preparation of the party's case," within the meaning of 28 U.S.C. §§ 2412(d)(2)(A), will be paid under the EAJA. *See* §765. But the government pays costs from a different source. The U.S. Attorney's Office is responsible for processing costs for payment.

If the court's order directs the government to pay "costs" or anything specifically included in the definition of costs, such as the filing fee, the EAJA fees section will not process such costs as part of the EAJA award. *See* 28 U.S.C. §§ 2412(a)(1) and 1920. Although you will eventually be paid such "costs," it probably will be only after you have followed up with the U.S. Attorney's Office when you notice, for example, that the $350 filing fee has been deducted from the EAJA money you received.

Practice Tip

Costs, which in the typical Social Security case include only the $350 filing fee, are paid faster and more reliably if you do not include them in the EAJA motion in the first place. Instead, follow your court's procedure for taxing costs at the conclusion of a case by submitting a Bill of Costs on a form that you can obtain from the clerk of court. The government never opposes payment of legitimate costs. If you follow the rules for taxing costs, a plaintiff who prevails in the underlying action is entitled to reimbursement of costs pursuant to 28 U.S.C. §§ 2412(a)(1) and 1920 without regard to whether the plaintiff wins or loses the EAJA motion. The only time you should include costs in your EAJA motion is if you miss the deadline for taxing costs according to the procedure set by the district court.

§794 *Form: Attorneys and Legal Organizations ACH Vendor/Miscellaneous Payment Enrollment Form*

**ATTORNEYS AND LEGAL ORGANIZATIONS
ACH VENDOR/MISCELLANEOUS PAYMENT
ENROLLMENT FORM**

This form is used for Automated Clearing House (ACH) payments with an addendum record that contains payment-related information processed through the Vendor Express Program. Recipients of these payments should bring this information to the attention of their financial institution when presenting this form for completion.

PRIVACY ACT STATEMENT

The following information is provided to comply with the Privacy Act of 1974 (P.L. 93-579). All information collected on this form is required under the provisions of 31 U.S.C. 3322 and 31 CFR 210. This information will be used by the Treasury Department to transmit payment data, by electronic means to vendor's financial institution. Failure to provide requested information may delay or prevent the receipt of payment through the Automated Clearing House Payment System.

AGENCY INFORMATION

FEDERAL PROGRAM AGENCY:
SOCIAL SECURITY ADMINISTRATION

AGENCY IDENTIFIER: SSA AGENCY LOCATION CODE (ALC): 28040001 ACH FORMAT: ■ CCD+ □ CTX □ CTP

ADDRESS:
SOCIAL SECURITY ADMINISTRATION
P.O. BOX 47, BALTIMORE, MARYLAND 21235

CONTACT PERSON NAME: CHRISTINA LILLY, OFFICE OF FINANCE, SSA TELEPHONE NUMBER: (410) 965-6119

ADDITIONAL INFORMATION:
FAX NUMBER-(410) 965-9248

PAYEE/COMPANY INFORMATION

NAME: SSN NO. OR TAXPAYER ID NO.:

ADDRESS:

CONTACT PERSON NAME: TELEPHONE NUMBER: ( )

FINANCIAL INSTITUTION INFORMATION

NAME:

ADDRESS:

ACH COORDINATOR NAME (BANK REP.): TELEPHONE NUMBER: ( )

NINE-DIGIT ROUTING TRANSIT NUMBER:

DEPOSITOR ACCOUNT TITLE:

DEPOSITOR ACCOUNT NUMBER:

TYPE OF ACCOUNT: □ CHECKING □ SAVINGS

SIGNATURE AND TITLE OF AUTHORIZED OFFICIAL: (COULD BE THE SAME AS ACH COORDINATOR) TELEPHONE NUMBER: ( )

3881-182 AGENCY COPY

(This page intentionally left blank.)

Appendices

Appendix 1: Guide to Important Social Security Rulings and Acquiescence Rulings

This index consists of two parts. The first part is organized following the sequential evaluation process. The second part deals with other issues arranged alphabetically. All current rulings and Acquiescence Rulings dealing with disability issues are included.

Note that an Acquiescence Ruling, identified AR, applies only in the circuit in which the court decision was made. The circuit number appears in parentheses following the number of the Acquiescence Ruling.

Part 1: The Sequential Evaluation Process

General:
- SSR 82-53 Basic Disability Evaluation Guides
- SSR 86-8   The Sequential Evaluation Process

Note: In both of the above rulings, discussion of determination of disability for SSI children no longer applies and discussion of widow(er)s' entitlement to Title II benefits has been superseded by SSR 91-3p.

Age 65 or Older:
- SSR 03-3p Evaluation of Disability and Blindness in Initial Claims for Individuals Age 65 or Older

Young Adults:
- SSR 11-2p Documenting and Evaluating Disability in Young Adults

Onset and Duration:
- SSR 82-52 Duration of the Impairment
- SSR 83-20 Onset of Disability

Step 1: Is the Claimant Engaged in Substantial Gainful Activity?

- SSR 76-4a Rebuttal of Presumption of Ability to Engage in Substantial Gainful Activity
- SSR 83-33 Determining Whether Work Is Substantial Gainful Activity-Employees
- SSR 83-34 Determining Whether Work Is Substantial Gainful Activity-Self Employed Persons
- SSR 83-35 Averaging of Earnings in Determining Whether Work Is Substantial Gainful Activity
- SSR 84-24 Determination of Substantial Gainful Activity for Persons Working in Special Circumstance—Work Therapy Programs in Military Service—Work Activity in Certain Government Sponsored Programs
- SSR 84-26 Deducting Impairment Related Work Expenses From Earnings in Determinations as to Substantial Gainful Activity Under Titles II and XVI and as to Countable Earned Income Under Title XVI
- SSR 94-1c *Dotson v. Shalala*, 1 F.3d 571 (7th Cir. 1993)—Illegal Activity as Substantial Gainful Activity
- SSR 05-02 Determination of Substantial Gainful Activity if Substantial Work Activity Is Discontinued or Reduced—Unsuccessful Work Attempt
- SSR 12-1p Title II: Determining Whether Work Performed in Self-Employment by Persons Who Are Blind Is Substantial Gainful Activity and Treatment of Income Resulting From the Randolph-Sheppard Act and Similar Programs

Step 2: Is the Claimant's Impairment "Severe"?

- SSR 85-28 Medical Impairments That Are Not Severe
- SSR 88-3c *Bowen v. Yuckert*, 482 U.S. 137 (1987)—Validity of the Severity of Impairment Regulation
- SSR 96-3p Considering Allegations of Pain and Other Symptoms in Determining Whether a Medically Determinable Impairment Is Severe

- SSR 96-4p Symptoms, Medically Determinable Physical and Mental Impairments, and Exertional and Non-Exertional Limitations

Step 3: Does the Claimant's Impairment(s) Meet or Equal an Impairment in the Listing of Impairments?

Medical Equivalence:
- SSR 90-5c *Adams v. Bowen*, 872 F.2d 926 (9th Cir. 1989), *cert. denied*, 110 S.Ct. 151 (1989)—Sections 216(i)(1)(B) and 223(c)(1) and (d)(1)(B) of the Social Security Act—Interpreting the Statutory Blindness Provision
- SSR 96-6p Consideration of Administrative Findings of Fact by State Agency Medical and Psychological Consultants and Other Program Physicians and Psychologists at the Administrative Law Judge and Appeals Council Levels of Administrative Review; Medical Equivalence

Specific Impairments (Most of the following discuss RFC as well as the requirements for meeting the Listings):
- SSR 82-57 Loss of Speech
- SSR 90-5c Blindness—*Adams v. Bowen*, 872 F.2d 926 (9th Cir. 1989) *cert. denied*, 493 U.S. 851 (1989)
- SSR 02-1p Evaluation of Obesity
- SSR 03-1p Development and Evaluation of Disability Claims Involving Post Polio Sequelae
- SSR 03-2p Evaluating Cases Involving Reflex Sympathetic Dystrophy Syndrome/Complex Regional Pain Syndrome
- AR 03-1(7) *Blakes v. Barnhart*, 331 F.3d 565 (7th Cir. 2003)—Court Cases Involving Sections 12.05 and 112.05 of the Listing of Impairments That Are Remanded for Further Proceedings
- SSR 06-1p Evaluating Cases Involving Tremolite Asbestos-Related Impairments
- SSR 07-1p Evaluating Visual Field Loss Using Automated Static Threshold Perimetry
- SSR 12-2p Evaluation of Fibromyalgia
- SSR 14-1p Evaluating Cases Involving Chronic Fatigue Syndrome (CFS)
- SSR 14-2p Evaluating Diabetes Mellitus
- SSR 14-3p Evaluating Endocrine Disorders Other Than Diabetes Mellitus
- SSR 15-1p Evaluating Cases Involving Interstitial Cystitis
- SSR 16-4p Using Genetic Test Results to Evaluate Disability
- AR 15-1(4) *Radford v. Colvin*, 734 F.3d 288 (4th Cir.2013): Standard for Meeting Section 1.04A of the Listing of Impairments—Disorders of the Spine with Evidence of Nerve Root Compression

Between Steps 3 and 4 – What is the Claimant's RFC?

Determining Residual Functional Capacity:
- SSR 85-16 Residual Functional Capacity for Mental Impairments
- SSR 96-8p Assessing Residual Functional Capacity in Initial Claims
- SSR 16-3p Evaluation of Symptoms in Disability Claims

Step 4: Is the Claimant Capable of Past Relevant Work?

Past Relevant Work:
- SSR 82-40 The Vocational Relevance of Past Work Performed in a Foreign Country
- SSR 82-61 Past Relevant Work—The Particular Job or the Occupation as Generally Performed
- SSR 82-62 A Disability Claimant's Capacity to Do Past Relevant Work, In General
- SSR 05-01c *Barnhart v. Thomas*, 540 U.S. 20 (2003)—Whether Past Relevant Work Must Exist in Significant Numbers in the Economy

***Step 5: Does the Claimant's Impairment Prevent Performance of
                   Any Other Work?***

Use of Medical-Vocational Guidelines:
·   SSR 83-5a Medical-Vocational Guidelines—Conclusiveness of Rules
·   SSR 83-10 Determining Capability to Do Other Work—The Medical-Vocational Rules of Appendix 2
·   SSR 83-11 Capability to Do Other Work—The Exertionally Based Medical-Vocational Rules Met
·   SSR 83-12 Capability to Do Other Work—The Medical-Vocational Rules as a Framework for Evaluating
                  Exertional Limitations Within a Range of Work or Between Ranges of Work
·   SSR 83-14 Capability to Do Other Work—The Medical-Vocational Rules as a Framework for Evaluating a
                  Combination of Exertional and Non-Exertional Impairments
·   SSR 83-46c *Heckler v. Campbell*, 461 U.S. 458 (1983)—Validity of Medical-Vocational Guidelines
·   SSR 85-15 Capability to Do Other Work—The Medical-Vocational Rules as a Framework for Evaluating
                  Solely Non-Exertional Impairments
·   AR 86-3(5) *Martinez v. Heckler*, 735 F.2d 795 (5th Cir. 1984)—Individuals Who Are Illiterate and Unable to
                  Communicate in English
·   AR 01-1(3) *Sykes v. Apfel*, 228 F.3d 259 (3d Cir. 2000)—Using the Grid Rules as a Framework for Decision-
                  Making When an Individual's Occupational Base Is Eroded by a Non-Exertional Limitation
·   AR 14-1(8) Brock v. Astrue, 674 F.3d 1062 (8th Cir. 2012): Requiring Vocational Specialist (VS) or
                  Vocational Expert (VE) Evidence When an Individual has a Severe Mental Impairment(s)

Use of Vocational Expert:
·   SSR 00-4p Use of Vocational Expert and Vocational Specialist Evidence, and Other Reliable Occupational
                  Information in Disability Decisions

RFC for Less Than a Full Range of Sedentary Work:
·   SSR 96-9p Determining Capability to Do Other Work—Implications of a Residual Functional Capacity for
                  Less Than a Full Range of Sedentary Work

Transferability of Work Skills:
·   SSR 82-41 Work Skills and Their Transferability as Intended by the Expanded Vocational Factors
                  Regulations Effective February 26, 1979

The "Worn Out Worker" and the Aged Non-Worker With Limited Education:
·   SSR 82-63 Medical-Vocational Profiles Showing an Inability to Make an Adjustment to Other Work

Failure to Follow Prescribed Treatment:
·   SSR 82-59 Failure to Follow Prescribed Treatment

Part 2: Other Issues

ALJ Bias:
·   SSR 13-1p Agency Processes for Addressing Allegations of Unfairness, Prejudice, Partiality, Bias,
                  Misconduct, or Discrimination by Administrative Law Judges (ALJs)

Americans With Disabilities Act:
·   SSR 00-1c *Cleveland v. Policy Management Systems Corporation*, 526 U.S. 795, 119 S.Ct. 1597 (1999)—
                  Claims Filed Under Both the Social Security Act and the Americans With Disabilities Act

Appeals Council Review:
·   SSR 82-13 Program for Ongoing Review of Hearing Decisions Pursuant to Section 304(g) of Public Law
                  (P.L.) 96-265—Appeals Council's Review Authority

- SSR 95-2c *Harper v. Secretary*, 978 F.2d 260 (6th Cir. 1992)—Authority of Appeals Council to Dismiss a Request for Hearing for a Reason for Which the Administrative Law Judge Could Have Dismissed the Request—*Res Judicata*
- SSR 11-1p Procedures for Handling Requests to File Subsequent Applications for Disability Benefits

Attorneys Fees:
- SSR 65-33c *United States v. Lewis and Hicks*, 235 F. Supp. 220 (E.D. Tenn. 1964)—Representation of Claimant—Fees for Services—Violation
- SSR 66-19c *Watson and Plank v. Celebrezze*, 246 F. Supp. 764 (E.D. Tenn. 1967)—Judicial Review—Attorney's Fees Fixed by Administration
- SSR 67-54c *Gardner v. Menendez*, 373 F.2d 488 (1st Cir. 1965)—Representation of Claimant—Fixing Amount of Attorney's Fees—Administrative and Court Proceedings
- SSR 68-47c *Randolph v. U.S.A.*—Representation of Claimant—Attorney's Fees—Authority to Regulate and Approve Amount
- SSR 68-61c *Hopkins v. Cohen*, 390 U.S. 530 (1968)—Past-Due Benefits for Calculation of Attorney Fees Include Amount of Benefits Paid to Auxiliaries
- SSR 72-14c *Schneider v. Richardson*, 441 F.2d 1320 (6th Cir. 1971)—Representation of Claimant—Determination of Attorney's Fees—Administrative Proceedings
- SSR 72-31c *Whitehead v. Richardson*, 466 F.2d 126 (6th Cir. 1971)—Representation of Claimant—Favorable Award of Benefits to Claimant—Determination of Attorney's Fees
- SSR 80-20c *Whitt v. Califano*, 601 F.2d 160 (4th Cir. 1979)—Black Lung Benefits—Representation of Claimant—Fixing Amount of Attorney's Fees—Administrative and Court Proceedings
- SSR 82-19c *Rahman v. Harris*, 490 F. Supp. 376 (E.D. Mich. 1980), CCH Unemp. Ins. Rep §17,212—Judicial Review—Attorney's Fees Fixed by Administrative Review—Constitutionality
- SSR 82-39 Use of Trust or Escrow Accounts in Collection of Attorney's Fees
- SSR 90-3c *Weisbrod v. Sullivan*, 875 F.2d 526 (5th Cir. 1989)—Validity of Regulation for Determining Attorney Fees
- SSR 94-3c *Shalala v. Schaefer*, 509 U.S. 292 (1993)—Timely Filing for Attorney's Fees Under the Equal Access to Justice Act

Childhood Disability Claims:
- SSR 98-1p Determining Medical Equivalence in Childhood Disability Claims When a Child Has Marked Limitation in Cognition and Speech
- SSR 05-3p Title XVI: Determining Continuing Disability at Step 2 of the Medical Improvement Review Standard Sequential Evaluation Process for Children Under Age 18—Functional Equivalence
- SSR 09-1p Title XVI: Determining Childhood Disability Under the Functional Equivalence Rule—The "Whole Child" Approach
- SSR 09-2p Title XVI: Determining Childhood Disability—Documenting a Child's Impairment-Related Limitations
- SSR 09-3p Title XVI: Determining Childhood Disability—The Functional Equivalence Domain of "Acquiring and Using Information"
- SSR 09-4p Title XVI: Determining Childhood Disability—The Functional Equivalence Domain of "Attending and Completing Tasks"
- SSR 09-5p Title XVI: Determining Childhood Disability—The Functional Equivalence Domain of "Interacting and Relating with Others"
- SSR 09-6p Title XVI: Determining Childhood Disability—The Functional Equivalence Domain of "Moving About and Manipulating Objects"
- SSR 09-7p Title XVI: Determining Childhood Disability—The Functional Equivalence Domain of "Caring for Yourself"
- SSR 09-8p Title XVI: Determining Childhood Disability—The Functional Equivalence Domain of "Health and Physical Well-Being"

Child Relationship:
· SSR 06-02p Adjudicating Child Relationship Under Section 216(h)(2) of the Social Security Act When DNA Test Shows Sibling Relationship Between Claimant and a Child of the Worker Who Is Entitled Under Section 216(h)(3) of the Social Security Act

Cross-Examination:
· AR 91-1(5) *Lidy v. Sullivan*, 911 F.2d 1075 (5th Cir. 1990)—Claimant Has an Absolute Right to Subpoena and Cross-Examine an Examining Physician

Drug Addiction and Alcoholism:
· SSR 13-2p Evaluating Cases Involving Drug Addiction and Alcoholism (DAA)

Federal Court Decisions:
· SSR 96-1p Application by the Social Security Administration of Federal Circuit Court and District Court Decisions

Federal Court Review:
SSR 73-45c *Ensey v. Richardson*, 469 F.2d 664 (9th Cir. 1972)—Administrative Appeals Rights—Request for Hearing—Time Limitation
· AR 99-4(11) *Bloodsworth v. Heckler*, 703 F.2d 1233 (11th Cir. 1983)—Appeals Council Dismissal of an Untimely Request for Review Is a Final Decision Conferring Federal Court Jurisdiction
· AR 16-1(7) Boley v. Colvin, 761 F.3d 803 (7th Cir. 2014): Judicial Review of an Administrative Law Judge's Order Finding No Good Cause for a Late Hearing Request and Dismissing the Request as Untimely

Felony Conviction:
· SSR 83-21 Person Convicted of Felony
  Note: The part of this ruling that deals with suspension of Social Security benefits for imprisoned felons is outdated. Currently a Title II beneficiary who is incarcerated for 30 days or more following conviction of any crime, including a misdemeanor, will have his or her benefits suspended.

Fraud or Similar Fault
· SSR 16-1p Fraud and Similar Fault Redeterminations Under Sections 205(u) and 1631(e)(7) of the Social Security Act
· SSR 16-2p Evaluation of Claims Involving the Issue of "Similar Fault" in the Providing of Evidence

Freedom of Information Act/(FOIA)/Privacy Act:
· SSR 92-1p Request Under the Privacy Act or the Freedom of Information Act for Access to Records and for Disclosure of Material Maintained by the Office of Hearings and Appeals

Fugitive Felons:
· AR 06-1(2) *Fowlkes v. Adamec*, 432 F.3d 90 (2d Cir. 2005)—Determining Whether an Individual Is a Fugitive Felon Under the Social Security Act—Titles II and XVI of the Act

Hearing Procedure:
· SSR 97-2p Prehearing Case Review by Disability Determination Services

Medical Opinions: SSA plans to rescind these rulings effective 3/27/17
· SSR 96-2p Giving Controlling Weight to Treating Source Medical Opinions
· SSR 96-5p Medical Source Opinions on Issues Reserved to the Commissioner
· SSR 96-6p Consideration of Administrative Findings of Fact by State Agency Medical and Psychological Consultants and Other Program Physicians and Psychologists at the Administrative Law Judge and Appeals Council Levels of Administrative Review; Medical Equivalence
· SSR 06-3p Considering Opinions and Other Evidence From Sources Who Are Not "Acceptable Medical Sources" in Disability Claims; Considering Decisions on Disability by Other Governmental and Nongovernmental Agencies

Overpayments:
- AR 92-5(9) *Quinlan v. Sullivan*, 916 F.2d 524 (9th Cir. 1990)—A Finding That Recovery of an Overpayment Is "Against Equity and Good Conscience" Is Not Limited to the Specific Circumstances Set Forth in the Regulations

Reopening:
- SSR 61-60 Computing Time Period for Reopening Determination
- SSR 67-22 Finality of Decision—Reopening on Basis of New and Material Evidence—Good Cause
- SSR 85-6c *Munsinger v. Schweiker*, 709 F.2d 1212 (8th Cir. 1983)—Disability—Reduction of Benefits Due to Receipt of a Lump-Sum Workers' Compensation Settlement—Finality of Decision—Reopening for Error of Law
- SSR 88-1c *Monger v. Bowen*, 817 F.2d 15 (4th Cir. 1987)—Judicial Review—Appeal From Administration's Refusal to Reopen Prior Final Decision
- SSR 91-5p Mental Incapacity and Good Cause for Missing the Deadline to Request Review
- SSR 95-1p Finding Good Cause for Missing the Deadline to Request Administrative Review Due to Statements in the Notice of Initial or Reconsideration Determination Concerning the Right to Request Administrative Review and the Option to File a New Application
- AR 90-4(4) *Culbertson v. Secretary*, 859 F.2d 319 (4th Cir. 1988); *Young v. Bowen*, 858 F.2d 951 (4th Cir. 1988)—Waiver of Administrative Finality in Proceedings Involving Unrepresented Claimants Who Lack the Mental Competence to Request Administrative Review
- AR 92-7(9) *Gonzalez v. Sullivan*, 914 F.2d 1197 (9th Cir. 1990)—When Denial Determination Fails to Give Adequate Notice of Implications of Failure to Appeal, Administrative Finality Doctrine Will Not Apply
- SSR 17-1p Reopening Based on Error on the Face of the Evidence – Effect of a Decision by the Supreme Court of the United States Finding a Law That We Applied To Be Unconstitutional.

Res Judicata:
- SSR 63-41 Section 205(b); 221(d)—Right to Hearing
- SSR 68-12a 205(a), 216(i) and 223—Finality of Decision—New and Material Evidence of Disability—*Res Judicata*
- SSR 71-32c *Easley v. Finch*, 431 F.2d 1351 (4th Cir. 1970)—Sections 205(g) and 221(d)—Judicial Review—*Res Judicata*
- SSR 86-16a Finality of Decision—New and Material Evidence of Paternity—*Res Judicata*
- AR 97-4(9) *Chavez v. Bowen*, 844 F.2d 691 (9th Cir. 1988)—Effect of a Prior Final Decision That a Claimant Is Not Disabled, and of Findings Contained Therein, on Adjudication of a Subsequent Disability Claim Arising Under the Same Title of the Social Security Act
- AR 98-3(6) *Dennard v. Secretary of Health and Human Services*, 907 F.2d 598 (6th Cir. 1990)—Effect of a Prior Finding of the Demands of Past Work on Adjudication of a Subsequent Disability Claim Arising Under the Same Title of the Social Security Act
- AR 98-4(6) *Drummond v. Commissioner of Social Security*, 126 F.3d 837 (6th Cir. 1997)—Effect of Prior Findings on Adjudication of a Subsequent Disability Claim Arising Under the Same Title of the Social Security Act
- AR 00-1(4) *Albright v. Commissioner of the Social Security Administration*, 174 F.3d 473 (4th Cir. 1999)—Effect of Prior Disability Findings on Adjudication of a Subsequent Disability Claim

Termination of Benefits:
- SSR 82-66 Establishing the Cessation Date in a Continuing Disability Case
- AR 86-4(3) *Paskel v. Heckler*, 768 F.2d 540 (3d Cir. 1985)—Necessity of a Determination Under Sections 225(b) and/or 1631(a)(6) of the Social Security Act for a Disability Benefits Recipient Engaged in an Approved Vocational Rehabilitation Program Prior to Cessation of His or Her Benefits Based on Medical Recovery
- AR 86-5(9) *Leschniok v. Heckler*, 713 F.2d 520 (9th Cir. 1983)—Necessity of a Determination Under Sections 225(b) and/or 1631(a)(6) of the Social Security Act for a Disability Benefits Recipient

Engaged in an Approved Vocational Rehabilitation Program Prior to Cessation of His or Her Benefits Based on Medical Recovery

· SSR 13-3p Title II: Appeal of an Initial Medical Disability Cessation Determination or Decision

Waiver of Hearing:
· SSR 79-19 Waiver of Personal Appearance at a Hearing

Widow's Disability Evaluation:
· SSR 91-3p Determining Entitlement to Disability Benefits for Months Prior to January 1991 for Widows, Widowers and Surviving Divorced Spouses Claims

Workers' Compensation Offset:
· SSR 97-3 Reduction of Disability Insurance Benefits Due to Receipt of State Workers' Compensation—Validity of an Amended Stipulation on a Prior Workers' Compensation Settlement and Award—Minnesota

(Revised as of 3/15/17)

Appendix 2: Sources of Information

By Eric Schnaufer and Thomas E. Bush

Government Printing Office and Bookstores

Government Printing Office (GPO). Many useful reference materials, only some of which are mentioned below, may be obtained from the GPO. The GPO's Internet site, http://www.gpo.gov/, includes ordering information and a catalogue of products in a searchable database. GPO Telephone: (866) 512-1800. Fax: (202) 512-2104. Internet: http://bookstore.gpo.gov/.

Bookstores. Prices, availability, and current editions of many of the books listed below may be found on the Internet. *See* Amazon.com, http://www.amazon.com/, and Reiter's Scientific and Professional Books, http://www.reiters.com/.

General Commercial Legal Products

There are two main types of commercial electronic Social Security law products: CD-ROM and Internet-only products, the costs of which are comparable. It is necessary to subscribe to one of the CD-ROM or Internet-only products because free legal authority available on the Internet is inadequate.

CD-ROM: Thomson Reuters's Social Security Library

Thomson Reuters markets one CD-ROM product: Social Security Library. The Library includes, among other resources, Social Security case law, the Social Security Act, regulations, Social Security Rulings, the Hearings, Appeals and Litigation Law Manual (HALLEX), and the *Dictionary of Occupational Titles.*

A subscription to the Library includes CD-ROMs issued every three months. The Library includes, as part of its subscription price, unlimited Internet access to the most recent Social Security authority, including new case law, statutes, regulations, and rulings. Some subscribers to the Library don't take full advantage of the Internet access included in the subscription price.

The Library has as an extra-cost option the *Program Operations Manual System* (*POMS*) with internal hyperlinks, but this option is unnecessary given that the *POMS* is available at no cost from Social Security Online. *See* https://secure.ssa.gov/poms.nsf/home!readform.

Premise software is used to access the Library. To order, contact Thomson Reuters. Telephone: (888) 728-7677. Internet: http://legalsolutions.thomsonreuters.com/law-products/.

Internet-Only: Thomson Reuters and LexisNexis

Thomson Reuters and LexisNexis have competing Internet-only products. With these products, legal authority is available only via the Internet. Both the Thomson Reuters and Lexis Nexis products include the same core legal authority such as case law, the Social Security Act, regulations, rulings, and the HALLEX. Thomson Reuters has two Internet-only products: Social Security Gold and Social Security Platinum, the latter having additional secondary sources. Lexis-Nexis includes NOSSCR's Social Security Practice Guide (*see* below) in its Internet-only Social Security Disability Premium.

To order, contact Thomson Reuters. Telephone: (888) 728-7677. Internet: http://legalsolutions.thomsonreuters.com/law-products/. LexisNexis. Telephone: (877) 394-8826. Internet: www.lexisnexis.com/.

Legal Information

Statute. The Social Security Act is best used in electronic format. The commercial products mentioned above include the Social Security Act. Social Security Online has a relatively current version of the Social Security Act. *See* http://www.socialsecurity.gov/OP_Home/ssact/. For recent amendments to the Social Security Act, it is necessary to visit Library of Congress. *See* https://www.congress.gov/. A useful printed version of the Social Security Act is included in Thomson Reuters's annual Federal Social Security Laws: Selected Statutes and Regulations, which costs about $303.00. A new edition ships in about April of each year. Contact Thomson Reuters's Telephone: (888) 728-7677. Internet: http://legalsolutions.thomsonreuters.com/law-products/.

Regulations. Title 20 of the Code of Federal Regulations (C.F.R.) covers most Social Security matters. Many disability-related regulations for Title II claims are found at 20 C.F.R. §§ 404.1501-.1599. The corresponding Title XVI (supplemental security income) regulations are found at 20 C.F.R. §§ 416.901-.998. These regulations are published in a single volume, 20 C.F.R. Parts 400 to 499. The annual printed version of this volume is revised as of April 1st and is available from the GPO in the summer of each year. The 20 C.F.R. for 2015 costs $70.00. (According to *The Bluebook: A Uniform System of Citation* (20th ed. 2015), regulations should be cited to the most recent edition of the printed C.F.R. For ordering information, *see* http://www.legalbluebook.com/.)

The C.F.R. is available online at http://www.gpo.gov/fdsys/browse/collectionCfr.action?collectionCode=CFR in text and Adobe's PDF format, which is identical to the annual printed C.F.R. Social Security Online may or may not have the current annual C.F.R. *See* http://www.socialsecurity.gov/OP_Home/cfr20/cfrdoc.htm. Unfortunately, the Social Security Online version of 20 C.F.R. may not correspond precisely to the most recent, official annual printed C.F.R. A representative needs to check the accuracy of the Social Security Online version of 20 C.F.R.

Recent proposed and final regulations not in the current C.F.R. are published in the daily Federal Register. *See* https://www.federalregister.gov/.

As an alternative to the annual C.F.R. used in conjunction with more recent regulations announced in the Federal Register, there is a version of the C.F.R. reflecting all regulatory changes until a very recent date. *See* http://www.ecfr.gov/cgi-bin/ECFR?page=browse/.

Thomson West's *Federal Social Security Laws* is revised annually according to a different time schedule than the official 20 C.F.R. and thus may contain slightly different regulations than the corresponding year's C.F.R. It costs $303.00. Contact Thomson Reuters. Telephone: (888) 728-7677. Internet: http://legalsolutions.thomsonreuters.com/law-products/.

Rulings. A Social Security Ruling (SSR) is an interpretive rule issued by the Commissioner of Social Security that sets forth and explains SSA policy. SSRs are binding on all agency adjudicators. 20 C.F.R. § 402.35(b). In litigation, an SSR is generally controlling authority. *E.g., Barnhart v. Walton*, 535 U.S. 212, 219 (2002); *Heckler v. Edwards*, 465 U.S. 870, 873, n.3 (1984). There are cases in every Circuit enforcing SSRs. Many Supreme Court decisions address the legal status of subregulatory legal authority. *E.g., Washington State Dep't of Soc. and Health Servs. v. Guardianship of Estate of Keffeler*, 537 U.S. 371 (2003).

In an Acquiescence Ruling (AR), SSA agrees to follow in a particular federal judicial circuit a precedential appellate decision from that circuit that is contrary to agency policy. *See* 20 C.F.R. §§ 404.985 and 416.1485.

Neither the GPO nor SSA sells printed versions of rulings. SSRs and ARs can be accessed from Social Security Online at http://www.socialsecurity.gov/OP_Home/rulings/rulings.html. New SSRs and ARs are published in the Federal Register at http://www.gpo.gov/fdsys/browse/collection.action?collectionCode=FR. The author of this book has links to important SSRs at his website. *See* http://www.tebush.com/teb/SSRs_files/SSRs.htm. The most comprehensive discussion of SSRs appears in David Traver's treatise discussed below.

HALLEX. The manual of the Office of Hearings and Appeals—*Hearings, Appeals and Litigation Law Manual* (*HALLEX*)—is the main source of information about procedures before ALJs and the Appeals Council. The HALLEX is binding on ALJs and the Appeals Council. *See* SSR 13-2p. Social Security Online has the official *HALLEX* at http://www.socialsecurity.gov/OP_Home/hallex/hallex.html. The relevance of the *HALLEX* has been the subject of litigation. *Compare Bunnell v. Barnhart*, 336 F.3d 1112 (9th Cir. 2003) *with Clark v. Astrue*, 29 F.3d 1211, 1216 (9th Cir. 2008) *and Newton v. Apfel*, 209 F.3d 448 (5th Cir. 2000). The Appeals Council routinely enforces *HALLEX* provisions. The most efficient way to search the *HALLEX* is to use NOSSCR's Web Links. *See* http://nosscr.org/helping-you/web-links.

Program Operations Manual System (POMS). The POMS is binding on Agency adjudicators, including ALJs. *See* SSR 13-2p. The public version of the *POMS* is available for free on the Internet. *See* https://secure.ssa.gov/apps10/poms.nsf/Home?readform. A more extensive version is available to SSA employees through SSA's computer system. The most efficient way to search the POMS is to use NOSSCR's Web Links. *See* http://nosscr.org/research-advocates.

Social Security Handbook. The *Handbook* is not an official source of law, but is a useful, succinctly written survey not only of disability insurance benefits but also of retirement and survivor's benefits, health insurance benefits, supplemental security income, and black lung benefits. The *Handbook*'s primary weakness is that it does not give citations to provisions of the Social Security Act or regulations. The *Handbook* is at Social Security Online at https://socialsecurity.gov/OP_Home/handbook/handbook.html.

Congressional Committee Reports. Various committees of the House and the Senate conduct periodic hearings and issue reports regarding the Social Security program. These reports may alert the practitioner to developments that might affect a law practice, and may help in understanding congressional intent underlying Social Security legislation. Information regarding the availability of a specific report may be obtained from local offices of Senators or Congresspersons, or through the GPO. Some reports are published in the United States Code Congressional and Administrative News, often available in law libraries, or available from the Library of Congress at https://www.congress.gov/. The Web site of the Subcommittee on Social Security of the Committee on Ways and Means is particularly useful. *See* http://waysandmeans.house.gov/.

Medical Information

Dorland's Illustrated Medical Dictionary. *Dorland's Illustrated Medical Dictionary* (32nd ed. 2011) is the standard, widely available reference, costing about $30.00 for the hardback. It is the medical dictionary with which ALJs are most familiar. *See* http://www.dorlands.com/. There are many other medical dictionaries including *Stedman's Medical Dictionary* (28th ed. 2006), costing about $45.00. *See* https://www.lww.com/stedmans. Practitioners may find that several dictionaries are needed to understand medical terms. Medical dictionaries are available in both printed and electronic versions.

Physicians' Desk Reference. The *Physicians' Desk Reference* (70th ed. 2015) (*PDR*) is the most recent edition of an essential annual reference guide to Food and Drug Administration information about prescription drugs. The hardback 2016 edition, published in November 2015, costs $80.00.

Diagnostic and Statistical Manual of Mental Disorders. The American Psychiatric Association's *Diagnostic and Statistical Manual of Mental Disorders-5* (5th ed. 2013) is needed to understand current medical records and to represent claimants. The *DSM-IV-TR* is $121.00 in paperback. An online version is also available. (The *DSM-IV-TR* supersedes the *Diagnostic and Statistical Manual of Mental Disorders* (4th ed. 1994).) Internet: http://www.appi.org/; http://www.psychiatryonline.com/. Three earlier editions of the manual are needed to understand the meaning and genesis of mental impairment regulations and older medical records. *See* Amer. Psychiatric Ass'n, *Diagnostic and Statistical Manual of Mental Disorders* (4th ed. Text Revision 2000); Amer. Psychiatric Ass'n, *Diagnostic and Statistical Manual of Mental Disorders* (3d ed. rev. 1987); Amer. Psychiatric Ass'n, *Diagnostic and Statistical Manual of Mental Disorders* (3d ed. 1980).

Harrison's. *Harrison's Principles of Internal Medicine* (18th ed. 2011) is an authoritative medical textbook. The hardcover version is about $225.00. *Harrison's* is also available online. Internet: http://accessmedicine.mhmedical.com.

Current Medical Diagnosis. *Current Medical Diagnosis and Treatment 2015* (2014) costs about $35.00 in paperback and sometimes has descriptions of diseases that are more understandable than *Harrison's*.

Clinician's Handbook. *The Clinician's Handbook: Integrated Diagnostics, Assessment, and Intervention in Adult and Adolescent Psychopathology* (5th ed. 2006), by Robert G. Meyer & Christopher M. Weaver, provides correlates for the MMPI-2, IPAT's Cattell Sixteen Personality Factor Questions (16PF) Test, the Wechsler Adult Intelligence Scale-Revised, the Millon Clinical Multiaxial Inventory, the Rorschach Ink Blot Technique, and the Thematic Apperception Tests and drawing tests. It is an immense help for representatives who need to understand psychometric testing; it costs about $68.00.

Heart Disease. The standard cardiac text is *Braunwald's Heart Disease: A Textbook of Cardiovascular Medicine* (10th ed. 2014), which costs about $225.00 in hardcover.

Primer on the Rheumatic Diseases. The (13th Corrected ed. 2008) by the Arthritis Foundation provides easy to understand information about rheumatic diseases at the price of about $65.00. Internet: http://www.afstore.org/.

Guides to the Evaluation of Permanent Impairment. The American Medical Association's *Guides to the Evaluation of Permanent Impairment* (6th ed. 2007) is a system for rating impairments as percentages of impairment of the whole person, most useful in worker's compensation cases in some states. *Guides* includes diagrams of range of motion and charts and tables concerning degree of impairment of various body systems. The price is about $140.00 and it may be ordered through bookstores.

The Merck Manual. *The Merck Manual of Diagnosis and Therapy* (19th ed. 2011) is a standard medical reference. The hardcover is about $60.00. Almost the same reference is available on the Internet at no cost. Internet: http://www. merckmanuals.com.

Medical Acronyms and Abbreviations. *Jablonski's Dictionary of Medical Acronyms and Abbreviations with CD-ROM* (6th ed. 2008) is worth its price of about $33.00.

Internet. The Internet is a central source for medical information for professionals and the lay public. You may mine the main Internet repositories: National Library of Medicine Gateway, http://gateway.nlm.nih.gov/gw/Cmd; PubMed, http://www.ncbi.nlm.nih.gov/pubmed; MedlinePlus, http://www.nlm.nih.gov/medlineplus; PMC, http://www.ncbi. nlm.nih.gov/pmc/; and Medscape, http://www.medscape.com.

Vocational Information

Dictionary of Occupational Titles. The Department of Labor's *Dictionary of Occupational Titles* (4th ed. rev. 1991) (DOT) is the standard vocational reference source for SSA and practitioners. Most of the jobs in the national economy are described in the DOT. The DOT, discussed in detail in §346 of this book, provides information about a claimant's past work and possible other work. *See also* SSR 00-4p. Although the DOT is out of print, it is available in electronic form from several sources, including West's Social Security Library and Social Security Excellence. A not-very-useful version is on the Internet at http://www.oalj.dol.gov/libdot.htm.

Selected Characteristics. The Department of Labor's *Selected Characteristics of Occupations Defined in the Revised Dictionary of Occupational Titles* (1991) is a companion to the *DOT* that includes vital information about the characteristics of occupations. Current commercial electronic products often usefully merge the data from the *DOT* and *Selected Characteristics*.

Occupational Outlook Handbook. The biannual *Occupational Outlook Handbook* (2014-15 ed.) (*OOH*), from the Department of Labor, has useful information such as how some jobs are actually performed. The *OOH* is on the Internet at http://www.bls.gov/ooh/.

Enhanced Guide. Now out of print, *The Enhanced Guide for Occupational Exploration* (2d ed. 1995) uses United States Department of Labor data to describe thousands of occupations and is a useful supplement to the *DOT*. There is also the *Enhanced Occupational Outlook Handbook* (7th ed. 2009), integrating O*NET data. The paperback is $39.95. Contact Jist Works. Telephone: (800) 328-1452. Internet: http://jist.emcp.com/.

The Revised Handbook. *Revised Handbook for Analyzing Jobs* (1991) from the Department of Labor is a companion to the 1991 edition of the *DOT* and explains in detail the methodology used to compile job data and write the *DOT* job definitions. The *Revised Handbook* has been reprinted by Elliott & Fitzpatrick and costs $18.95. Contact Elliott & Fitzpatrick, 1135 Cedar Shoals Drive, Athens, GA 30605. Telephone (800) 843-4977. Internet: http://www. elliottfitzpatrick.com/.

Job Browser Pro. Job Browser Pro is perhaps the most common source for job-incidence data at the hearing level. A representative should have the same source as a vocational expert. Contact SkillTRAN. *See* http://www.skilltran. com/.

Occupational Employment Quarterly. U.S. Publishing's *Occupational Employment Quarterly* is commonly used by vocational experts for job-incidence data. U.S. Publishing also publishes the *Specific Occupation Selector Manual* (5th ed.), which costs $97.00 and which is essential for intelligent use of the *Occupational Employment Quarterly*. *See* §348.8 of this book for a discussion of using the *Manual* and the *Occupational Employment Quarterly*. Contact U.S. Publishing, P.O. Box 7722, Overland Park, KS 66207. Telephone: (800) 676-6643. Internet: http://www.uspublishing.net/.

O*NET. The Department of Labor has replaced the DOT with the O*NET; but according to SSA, the O*NET is not to be used in Social Security disability proceedings. Internet: http://www.onetcenter.org/.

Other Information

Social Security Disability Advocate's Handbook. David Traver's *Social Security Disability Advocate's Handbook* discusses vocational matters and SSRs in more detail than elsewhere. It costs $204.00. Contact James Publishing. Telephone: (866) 725-2637. Fax: (714) 556-4133. Internet: http://www.jamespublishing.com/.

Social Security Law and Practice. West's *Social Security Law and Practice* is a multi-volume practice guide that is updated regularly. The price is about $5,340.00. Contact Thomson Reuters. Telephone: (888) 728-7677. Internet: http://legalsolutions.thomsonreuters.com/law-products/.

NOSSCR Social Security Forum. The National Organization of Social Security Claimants' Representatives (NOSSCR) publishes the monthly *Social Security Forum*. The *Forum* has timely information about the disability program and other aspects of Social Security practice. NOSSCR members, who may contribute to the *Forum*, receive the *Forum* as part of their membership. Everyone who practices in this area of law ought to consider joining. The *Forum* is also available by subscription. To become a NOSSCR member or subscribe to the *Forum*, contact NOSSCR, 560 Sylvan Ave, Suite 2200, Englewood Cliffs, NJ 07632. Telephone: (201) 567-4228. Fax: (201) 567-1542. Internet: http://www.nosscr.org/.

Social Security Practice Guide. *Social Security Practice Guide* by NOSSCR is a multi-volume compendium of articles on virtually every aspect of representing disability claimants, including extensive discussion of medical issues written by doctors. Different versions are about $2,000 per year. Contact LexisNexis. Telephone: (877) 394-8826. Internet: http://www.lexisnexis.com.

Bohr's Social Security Issues Annotated. *Bohr's Social Security Issues Annotated* (2014), by Sarah H. Bohr and Kimberly V. Cheiken, is a compendium of case law developments. It costs $239.00 and is updated annually. Contact James Publishing. Telephone: (866) 725-2637. Fax: (714) 556-4133. Internet: http://www.jamespublishing.com/.

SSA Brochures. SSA publishes in understandable language pamphlets and brochures describing its various programs. These documents may be obtained from any Social Security office and from Social Security Online at http:// https://www.ssa.gov/pubs/.

Federal Court Rules. Thomson Reuters's *Federal Civil Judicial Procedure and Rules* (2014) includes the Federal Rules of Civil Procedure, 28 U.S.C., the Federal Rules of Evidence, and other important law. The price is about $152.00. Litigators should subscribe to this annual paperback. Contact Thomson Reuters. Telephone: (888) 728-7677. Internet: http://legalsolutions.thomsonreuters.com/law-products.

Other Internet Resources

The best starting point for researching Social Security legal authority is NOSSCR's Research for Social Security Advocates: http://www.nosscr.org/research-advocates. That web page has preset Google searches for Social Security authority on SSA Online. It should be the starting point for your ordinary searches of the Social Security Act, the regulations, SSRs, ARs, the HALLEX, and the POMS.

There are three main sites for the Supreme Court. *See* http://www.supremecourtus.gov/; https://www.law.cornell.edu/supremecourt/text/home; and http://scholar.google.com/.

There are several Internet sites with appellate case law for each circuit at no charge. Locate the links at http://findlaw.com/casecode/; http://www.uscourts.gov/court-locator; http://scholar.google.com/; https://www.zotero.org/groups/social_security; and http://www.schnaufer.com/case.htm.

District court decisions are found primarily in commercial databases such as Westlaw and Lexis. Google Scholar also has some PACER district court decisions, as does Federal Digital System. *See* http://www.gpo.gov/fdsys/search/home.action.

The Government Accountability Office (GAO), http://www.gao.gov/, publishes recent GAO reports and testimony about Social Security and SSI.

The Subcommittee on Social Security of the Committee on Ways and Means publishes important testimony about current issues in Social Security law and the administration of SSA. *See* http://waysandmeans.house.gov/.

Do not forget to visit Social Security Online, http://www.socialsecurity.gov/, for official SSA pronouncements.

The Social Security Advisory Board also has reports that might become the basis for reform of the disability programs. *See* http://www.ssab.gov/.

There are several major law-on-the-Internet sites. Google Scholar is the most useful, followed by OpenJurist. *See* http://openjurist.org/.

There are several Internet sites specifically for Social Security claimants' attorneys or representatives. See http://socsecnews.blogspot.com/ (Charles Hall); https://www.zotero.org/groups/social_security and http://www.law.cornell.edu/socsec/ (Prof. Peter Martin at Cornell); and http://www.schnaufer.com/ (Eric Schnaufer).

Appendix 3:   Dictionary of Occupational Titles

U.S. Department of Labor

Employment and Training Administration

1991

Appendix 1

APPENDIX C

COMPONENTS OF THE DEFINITION TRAILER

The following descriptions of the components of the Definition Trailer are in inverse order to their placement in the trailer.

I. DATE OF LAST UPDATE (DLU)

Listed as the final element in the trailer following the definition, the Date of Last Update indicates the last year in which material was gathered for that occupation. A DLU of ''77'' would indicate that the occupation has not been studied by an analyst since publication of the fourth edition DOT in 1977.

II. SPECIFIC VOCATIONAL PREPARATION (SVP)

Specific Vocational Preparation is defined as the amount of lapsed time required by a typical worker to learn the techniques, acquire the information, and develop the facility needed for average performance in a specific job-worker situation.

This training may be acquired in a school, work, military, institutional, or vocational environment. It does not include the orientation time required of a fully qualified worker to become accustomed to the special conditions of any new job. Specific vocational training includes: vocational education, apprenticeship training, in-plant training, on-the-job training, and essential experience in other jobs.

Specific vocational training includes training given in any of the following circumstances:

a. Vocational education (high school; commercial or shop training; technical school; art school; and that part of college training which is organized around a specific vocational objective);

b. Apprenticeship training (for apprenticeable jobs only);

c. In-plant training (organized classroom study provided by an employer);

d. On-the-job training (serving as learner or trainee on the job under the instruction of a qualified worker);

e. Essential experience in other jobs (serving in less responsible jobs which lead to the higher grade job or serving in other jobs which qualify).

The following is an explanation of the various levels of specific vocational preparation:

Level	Time
1	Short demonstration only
2	Anything beyond short demonstration up to and including 1 month
3	Over 1 month up to and including 3 months
4	Over 3 months up to and including 6 months
5	Over 6 months up to and including 1 year
6	Over 1 year up to and including 2 years
7	Over 2 years up to and including 4 years
8	Over 4 years up to and including 10 years
9	Over 10 years

Note: The levels of this scale are mutually exclusive and do not overlap.

III. GENERAL EDUCATIONAL DEVELOPMENT (GED)

General Educational Development embraces those aspects of education (formal and informal) which are required of the worker for satisfactory job performance. This is edu-

Scale of General Education Development (GED)

LEVEL	REASONING DEVELOPMENT	MATHEMATICAL DEVELOPMENT	LANGUAGE DEVELOPMENT
6	Apply principles of logical or scientific thinking to a wide range of intellectual and practical problems. Deal with nonverbal symbolism (formulas, scientific equations, graphs, musical notes, etc.) in its most difficult phases. Deal with a variety of abstract and concrete variables. Apprehend the most abstruse classes of concepts.	Advanced calculus: Work with limits, continuity, real number systems, mean value theorems, and implicit functions theorems. Modern Algebra: Apply fundamental concepts of theories of groups, rings, and fields. Work with differential equations, linear algebra, infinite series, advanced operations methods, and functions of real and complex variables. Statistics: Work with mathematical statistics, mathematical probability and applications, experimental design, statistical inference, and econometrics.	Reading: Read literature, book and play reviews, scientific and technical journals, abstracts, financial reports, and legal documents. Writing: Write novels, plays, editorials, journals, speeches, manuals, critiques, poetry, and songs. Speaking: Conversant in the theory, principles, and methods of effective and persuasive speaking, voice and diction, phonetics, and discussion and debate.
5	Apply principles of logical or scientific thinking to define problems, collect data, establish facts, and draw valid conclusions. Interpret an extensive variety of technical instructions in mathematical or diagrammatic form. Deal with several abstract and concrete variables.	Algebra: Work with exponents and logarithms, linear equations, quadratic equations, mathematical induction and binomial theorem, and permutations. Calculus: Apply concepts of analytic geometry, differentiations and integration of algebraic functions with applications. Statistics: Apply mathematical operations to frequency distributions, reliability and validity of tests, normal curve, analysis of variance, correlation techniques, chi-square application and sampling theory, and factor analysis.	Same as Level 6.
4	Apply principles of rational systems to solve practical problems and deal with a variety of concrete variables in situations where only limited standardization exists. Interpret a variety of instructions furnished in written, oral diagrammatic, or schedule form.	Algebra: Deal with system of real numbers; linear, quadratic, rational, exponential, logarithmic, angle and circular functions, and inverse functions; related algebraic solution of equations and inequalities; limits and continuity, and probability and statistical inference. Geometry: Deductive axiomatic geometry, plane and solid; and rectangular coordinates. Shop Math: Practical application of fractions, percentages, ratio and proportion, mensuration, logarithms, slide rule, practical algebra, geometric construction, and essentials of trigonometry.	Reading: Read novels, poems, newspapers, periodicals, journals, manuals, dictionaries, thesauruses, and encyclopedias. Writing: Prepare business letters, expositions, summaries, and reports, using prescribed format and conforming to all rules of punctuation, grammar, diction, and style. Speaking: Participate in panel discussions, dramatizations, and debates. Speak extemporaneously on a variety of subjects.

LEVEL	REASONING DEVELOPMENT	MATHEMATICAL DEVELOPMENT	LANGUAGE DEVELOPMENT
3	Apply commonsense understanding to carry out instructions furnished in written, oral, or diagrammatic form. Deal with problems involving several concrete variables in or from standardized situations.	Compute discount, interest, profit and loss; commission, markup, and selling price; ratio and proportion, and percentage. Calculate surfaces, volumes, weights, and measures. Algebra: Calculate variables and formulas; monomials and polynomials; ratio and proportion variables; and square roots and radicals. Geometry: Calculate plane and solid figures; circumference, area, and volume. Understand kinds of angles, and properties of pairs of angles.	Reading: Read a variety of novels, magazines, atlases, and encyclopedias. Read safety rules, instructions in the use and maintenance of shop tools and equipment, and methods and procedures in mechanical drawing and layout work. Writing: Write reports and essays with proper format, punctuation, spelling, and grammar, using all parts of speech. Speaking: Speak before an audience with poise, voice control, and confidence, using correct English and well-modulated voice.
2	Apply commonsense understanding to carry out detailed but uninvolved written or oral instructions. Deal with problems involving a few concrete variables in or from standardized situations.	Add, subtract, multiply, and divide all units of measure. Perform the four operations with like common and decimal fractions. Compute ratio, rate, and percent. Draw and interpret bar graphs. Perform arithmetic operations involving all American monetary units.	Reading: Passive vocabulary of 5,000–6,000 words. Read at rate of 190–215 words per minute. Read adventure stories and comic books, looking up unfamiliar words in dictionary for meaning, spelling, and pronunciation. Read instructions for assembling model cars and airplanes. Writing: Write compound and complex sentences, using cursive style, proper end punctuation, and employing adjectives and adverbs. Speaking: Speak clearly and distinctly with appropiate pauses and emphasis, correct pronunciation, variations in word order, using present, perfect, and future tenses.
1	Apply commonsense understanding to carry out simple one- or two-step instructions. Deal with standardized situations with occasional or no variables in or from these situations encountered on the job.	Add and subtract two digit numbers. Multiply and divide 10's and 100's by 2, 3, 4, 5. Perform the four basic arithmetic operations with coins as part of a dollar. Perform operations with units such as cup, pint, and quart; inch, foot, and yard; and ounce and pound.	Reading: Recognize meaning of 2,500 (two- or three-syllable) words. Read at rate of 95–120 words per minute. Compare similarities and differences between words and between series of numbers. Writing: Print simple sentences containing subject, verb, and object, and series of numbers, names, and addresses. Speaking: Speak simple sentences, using normal word order, and present and past tenses.

COMPONENTS OF THE DEFINITION TRAILER

cation of a general nature which does not have a recognized, fairly specific occupational objective. Ordinarily, such education is obtained in elementary school, high school, or college. However, it may be obtained from experience and self-study.

The GED Scale is composed of three divisions: Reasoning Development, Mathematical Development, and Language Development. The description of the various levels of language and mathematical development are based on the curricula taught in schools throughout the United States. An analysis of mathematics courses in school curricula reveals distinct levels of progression in the primary and secondary grades and in college. These levels of progression facilitated the selection and assignment of six levels of GED for the mathematical development scale.

However, though language courses follow a similar pattern of progression in primary and secondary school, particularly in learning and applying the principles of grammar, this pattern changes at the college level. The diversity of language courses offered at the college level precludes the establishment of distinct levels of language progression for these four years. Consequently, language development is limited to five defined levels of GED inasmuch as levels 5 and 6 share a common definition, even though they are distinct levels.

IV. PHYSICAL DEMANDS - STRENGTH RATING (Strength)

The Physical Demands Strength Rating reflects the estimated overall strength requirement of the job, expressed in terms of the letter corresponding to the particular strength rating. It represents the strength requirements which are considered to be important for average, successful work performance.

The strength rating is expressed by one of five terms: Sedentary, Light, Medium, Heavy, and Very Heavy. In order to determine the overall rating, an evaluation is made of the worker's involvement in the following activities:

a. Standing, Walking, Sitting

   Standing - Remaining on one's feet in an upright position at a work station without moving about.

   Walking - Moving about on foot.

   Sitting - Remaining in a seated position.

b. Lifting, Carrying, Pushing, Pulling

   Lifting - Raising or lowering an object from one level to another (includes upward pulling).

   Carrying - Transporting an object, usually holding it in the hands or arms, or on the shoulder.

   Pushing - Exerting force upon an object so that the object moves away from the force (includes slapping, striking, kicking, and treadle actions).

   Pulling - Exerting force upon an object so that the object moves toward the force (includes jerking).

Lifting, pushing, and pulling are evaluated in terms of both intensity and duration. Consideration is given to the weight handled, position of the worker's body, and the aid given by helpers or mechanical equipment. Carrying most often is evaluated in terms of duration, weight carried, and distance carried.

Estimating the Strength factor rating for an occupation requires the exercise of care on the part of occupational analysts in evaluating the force and physical effort a worker must exert. For instance, if the worker is in a crouching position, it may be much more difficult to push an object than if pushed at waist height. Also, if the worker is required to lift and carry continuously or push and pull objects over long distances,

COMPONENTS OF THE DEFINITION TRAILER

the worker may exert as much physical effort as is required to similarly move objects twice as heavy, but less frequently and/or over shorter distances.

c.   Controls

Controls entail the use of one or both arms or hands (hand/arm) and/or one or both feet or legs (foot/leg) to move controls on machinery or equipment. Controls include but are not limited to buttons, knobs, pedals, levers, and cranks.

Following are descriptions of the five terms in which the Strength Factor is expressed:

S-Sedentary Work - Exerting up to 10 pounds of force occasionally (Occasionally: activity or condition exists up to 1/3 of the time) and/or a negligible amount of force frequently (Frequently: activity or condition exists from 1/3 to 2/3 of the time) to lift, carry, push, pull, or otherwise move objects, including the human body. Sedentary work involves sitting most of the time, but may involve walking or standing for brief periods of time. Jobs are sedentary if walking and standing are required only occasionally and all other sedentary criteria are met.

L-Light Work - Exerting up to 20 pounds of force occasionally, and/or up to 10 pounds of force frequently, and/or a negligible amount of force constantly (Constantly: activity or condition exists 2/3 or more of the time) to move objects. Physical demand requirements are in excess of those for Sedentary Work. Even though the weight lifted may be only a negligible amount, a job should be rated Light Work: (1) when it requires walking or standing to a significant degree; or (2) when it requires sitting most of the time but entails pushing and/or pulling of arm or leg controls; and/or (3) when the job requires working at a production rate pace entailing the constant pushing and/or pulling of materials even though the weight of those materials is negligible. NOTE: The constant stress and strain of maintaining a production rate pace, especially in an industrial setting, can be and is physically demanding of a worker even though the amount of force exerted is negligible.

M-Medium Work - Exerting 20 to 50 pounds of force occasionally, and/or 10 to 25 pounds of force frequently, and/or greater than negligible up to 10 pounds of force constantly to move objects. Physical Demand requirements are in excess of those for Light Work.

H-Heavy Work - Exerting 50 to 100 pounds of force occasionally, and/or 25 to 50 pounds of force frequently, and/or 10 to 20 pounds of force constantly to move objects. Physical Demand requirements are in excess of those for Medium Work.

V-Very Heavy Work - Exerting in excess of 100 pounds of force occasionally, and/or in excess of 50 pounds of force frequently, and/or in excess of 20 pounds of force constantly to move objects. Physical Demand requirements are in excess of those for Heavy Work.

V. GUIDE FOR OCCUPATIONAL EXPLORATION (GOE)

Many youths and other jobseekers are unprepared for an effective job search because of a lack of knowledge about the kinds of jobs to look for. They have difficulty relating their interest, skills, and potentials to appropriate occupations. To be effective, vocational counselors must have sufficient information to match an individual's interest, temperaments, potential ability and other personal traits to specific career fields and work requirements.

The *Guide for Occupational Exploration* was designed by the US Employment Service to provide career counselors and other DOT users with additional information about the interests, aptitudes, entry level preparation and other traits required for successful performance in various occupations. The GOE is also useful in self-assessment and counselor-assisted settings to help people understand themselves realistically in regard to their ability to meet job requirements. Descriptive information provided for

COMPONENTS OF THE DEFINITION TRAILER

each work group assists the individual in evaluating his or her own interests and relating them to pertinent fields of work.

The GOE code assigned to a definition provides a link between the occupation defined and the GOE arrangement of occupations with similar interests, aptitudes, adaptability requirements, and other descriptors.

The GOE coding structure classifies jobs at three levels of consideration. The first level divides occupations according to twelve interest areas corresponding to interest factors identified through research conducted by the former Division of Testing in the US Employment Service. The interest factors, identified by a two-digit code, are defined in terms of broad interest requirements of occupations as well as vocational interests of individuals. The twelve interest areas are defined as follows:

01 Artistic	05 Mechanical	09 Accommodating
02 Scientific	06 Industrial	10 Humanitarian
03 Plants-Animals	07 Business Detail	11 Leading-Influencing
04 Protective	08 Selling	12 Physical Performing

The interest areas are then subdivided into work groups (the second set of two digits within the six-digit GOE code). Each work group contains occupations requiring similar worker traits and capabilities in related work settings. The GOE contains descriptive information for each work group and identifies each occupation in the group with a four-digit code and title. In many interest areas, occupations that require the most education, training, and experience are in the first group, while those requiring less formal education or experience are listed in the last group.

Work groups are then subdivided into subgroups (the third two-digit set in the GOE code) of occupations with even more homogeneous interests, aptitudes, and adaptability requirements. Each subgroup is identified by its unique six-digit code and title. Individual occupations are listed alphabetically within subgroups. Some subgroups contain occupations from more than one industry, listed within alphabetized industries.

Appendix 4:   Vocational Expert Self-Study Guide, Part 4, The Hearing

Social Security Administration
OHA Training Series

Vocational Experts

Testifying at Disability Hearings: A Self Study Guide

January, 1984
SSA Pub. No. 70-009

Social Security Administration
OHA Training Series

Vocational Experts

Testifying at Disability Hearings: A Self Study Guide

January 1984
SSA Pub. No. 70-009

Reprinted from the Social Security Administration OHA Training Series.

The Hearing

Preliminary Questions

In introducing the VE at the hearing, the ALJ will pose certain standard procedural questions that will establish for the record the VE's competence in vocational matters relevant to SSA disability claims, his or her professional qualifications, independence, and impartiality as a witness under contract with OHA. As a matter of procedure, a written resume of the VE's experience and background is entered as an exhibit in the hearing record. The VE will normally be asked to testify whether the resume entered into the hearing record is an accurate and up-to-date reflection of his or her experience and background.

Notwithstanding the fact that the resume is used to establish the VE's credentials for the record, it is also essential to establish that the VE is familiar with the SSA regulations that are applicable when vocational factors are being considered. In addition, the VE will be expected to be familiar with various source documents concerning job information listed in the SSA regulations, sections 404.1509(c) and 416.909(c).

During the Hearing:

- Impartiality is maintained
- You provide detailed reasoning to support your opinions
- You provide the facts upon which your conclusions are based

---

Testimony Concerning Past Relevant Work (PRW)

1. Physical Demands of all PRW

The VE should be prepared to testify concerning the exertional level of the claimant's past relevant work, usually the work he or she has performed in the last 15 years. (See Glossary)

Physical demands should be stated in terms of sedentary, light, medium, heavy, or very heavy as those terms are defined in the regulations and the Dictionary of Occupational Titles. The explanation should be based on the extent to which the claimant was required in the actual performance of the work to lift, carry, push, pull, sit, stand and walk (the primary "exertional" demands). The VE should also consider the extent to which the following were required: climbing, balancing, stooping, kneeling, crouching, crawling, reaching, handling, fingering, feeling, talking, hearing, and seeing. Also included in his or her consideration should be any untoward environmental or similar aspects of the job (indoors, outdoors, extremes of heat or cold, wetness, noise and vibration, and exposure to fumes, odors, or toxic conditions).

2. Skill Level of PRW

If the claimant's past relevant work was at either a skilled and/or semi-skilled level, then he or she will have acquired certain skills. The VE should be prepared to testify concerning these acquired skills and whether they were performed in a skilled or semi-skilled job. Refer to the section on skill level.

VE Testimony Should Include:

- Prior skill level
- Prior physical demand level
- Identification of any transferable skills
- Citation of specific occupations
- Citation of specific number of jobs in the area

---

3. Improper Testimony

The Vocational Expert is expected to testify only on vocational issues and only on those vocational issues which are relevant to the requirements of the statute, regulations and rulings. Thus, the VE is not to:

a. Provide his or her own evaluation of the medical evidence. This is to be provided by the ALJ in the form of one or more hypothetical questions with similar rights extended to the claimant.

b. State whether the claimant is a proper candidate for vocational rehabilitation.

c. State whether a claimant can compete with unimpaired individuals for available employment.

d. State whether job vacancies exist or whether the claimant would be hired for existing jobs.

e. State whether a claimant can perform in a specific occupation with the same degree of efficiency or productivity as individuals with less than severe or no impairments.

f. State whether the claimant is or is not "disabled."

Hypothetical Questioning

The examination of the VE concerning the possible types of work a claimant can do is accomplished by the use of hypothetical questions. This type of questioning asks the expert to assume the presence of varying medical-vocational profiles and to suggest any occupations which persons with such profiles could be expected to perform. These hypotheticals will be phrased in nonmedical terminology which describes restrictions on reaching, walking, lifting, thinking, seeing, etc. If the limitations to be considered in a question have not been made explicit, it is imperative that the expert request clarification in order to provide an answer. Failure to do so leaves an unanswered question in the record as to the basis for the testimony and, therefore, as to its validity. This type of questioning has proven to be effective because it places the burden of interpreting medical evidence where it properly belongs—with the ALJ.

1. Ability to Perform Past Relevant Work

The test for disability under the Social Security Act is an inability to perform not only previous work, but also any other work. Thus, the hypothetical questioning generally begins with questions regarding an individual's ability to do past work. This calls for the expert to make a rather straightforward comparison of the limitations furnished in the question with the physical and mental demands of past jobs as they were performed by the claimant. It is a matter of published Social Security Administration policy that factors such as a change of residence from where the job was performed (including a move to the U.S. from a foreign country), a lack of job openings or employers' hiring practices are not to be considered (see SSR 82-40, p.92 in Appendix). The primary departure from this straightforward comparison of what a person can still do with what his or her past job(s) actually required occurs when the particular job which the claimant performed involved functional demands significantly in excess of those generally required for the job by other employers. In such an instance, the expert may also be asked to describe the functional demands and job duties of the occupation as generally required by employers throughout the national economy (see SSR 82-61, page 94 in Appendix).

2. Work Adjustment to Unskilled Jobs

UNDER THE SOCIAL SECURITY REGULATIONS, THE DECISION ON WHETHER A PERSON CAN PERFORM OTHER WORK IS A TWO-STEP PROCESS, THE FIRST IS TO DETERMINE THE PERSON'S OCCUPATIONAL BASE, I.E., THE OCCUPATIONS THAT HE OR SHE HAS THE REMAINING PHYSICAL AND MENTAL CAPACITY TO PERFORM. THE SECOND IS TO DECIDE, GIVEN THE INDIVIDUAL'S AGE, EDUCATION, AND WORK EXPERIENCE, WHETHER HE OR SHE CAN BE EXPECTED TO MAKE A WORK ADJUSTMENT TO JOBS IN THE OCCUPATIONAL BASE.

Regulations which became effective in February 1979 contain medical-vocational guidelines or rules which, in certain instances, take administrative notice both of the size of the occupational base and also the question of work adjustment. Under these rules, the occupational base for a person who can perform a full range of sedentary work consists of approximately 200 unskilled occupations. For a person who can perform a full range of light work, there are an additional 1400 unskilled occupations giving a total of 1600 occupations in the base. Finally, a person who can perform medium work has an occupational base which includes an additional 900 occupations, giving a total of approximately 2500 occupations in that base. (A list of the 200 sedentary and 1400 light occupations is found on page 134 of the Appendix.) For persons with transferable skills, the size of the occupational base is increased by the inclusion of the skilled and semi-skilled jobs which he or she can perform.

For impaired persons whose remaining physical and mental abilities coincide with the ability to perform at the unskilled sedentary, light, or medium exertional levels, the rules take administrative notice of vocational factors such as age, education, and work experience and their effect on the ability to make a work adjustment. In some situations, vocational factors may be so adverse that a person who can no longer perform his or her past work, but who is capable of performing a full range of medium work (with an occupational base of 2500) will be found disabled, i.e., unable to make a work adjustment. For example, Rule 203.01 in Table No. 3, Appendix 2, Subpart P of Regulations No. 4 provides that a person between the ages of 60 to 64, with a 6th grade education or less, who has unskilled or no past work experience and who is limited to medium work would be found disabled. At the other extreme, Rule 201.23 in Table No. 1 indicates that the vocational advantage of being a younger individual can overcome the combined adversities of illiteracy, lack of any work experience, and impairments that preclude all but sedentary work.

The medical-vocational guidelines were published in an effort to bring more consistency to SSA's disability program. In this vein, although the rules cannot be used to direct decisions where they do not directly apply (for people who can do more than sedentary but less than light work or people with nonexertional impairments), they are still to be used as a framework for decisionmaking. For this reason, it is essential that VEs have a basic understanding of the principles of the rules. Thus, a VE may be called to testify in a case in which the claimant, if limited to sedentary work, would be found "disabled" by direction of a rule, but if limited to light work, a different rule would direct "not disabled". The medical evidence in that case may show that the claimant can perform a full range of sedentary work but a limited range of light work. The VE then will be asked, using the weight to be attributed to the claimant's age, education and work experience by the regulations and his or her own expertise, to offer an opinion as to the existence of a number of light, unskilled jobs existing in the national economy which the individual, taking into account his or her physical and/or mental limitations, can perform.

Transferability of Skills

Under the regulations of the Social Security Administration, transferability of skills means applying work skills which a person has demonstrated in vocationally relevant past jobs to meet the requirements of other skilled or semi-skilled jobs. Since the administrative notice provisions of the medical-vocational rules do not cover skilled or semi-skilled jobs, VEs will frequently be called to testify when transferability is at issue. The following discussion of transferability is drawn from Social Security Ruling 82-41, the complete text of which begins on page 79 of the Appendix.

Transferring Skills: When?

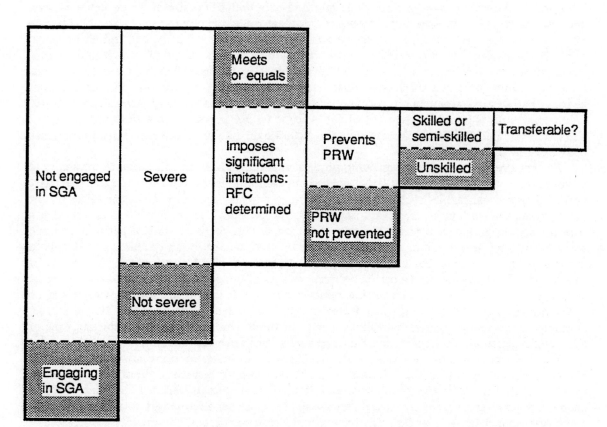

1. How Transferability is Determined in General

Transferability is most probable and meaningful among jobs in which:

(1) the same or a lesser degree of skill is required (from a skilled to a semi-skilled or another skilled job, or from one semi-skilled to another semi-skilled job), because people are not expected to do more complex jobs than they have actually performed, (2) the same or similar tools and machines are used; and (3) the same or similar raw materials, products, processes or services are involved. A complete similarity of all these factors is not necessary. There are degrees of transferability ranging from very close similarities to remote and incidental similarities among jobs.

Generally, the greater the degree of acquired work skills, the less difficulty an individual will experience in transferring skills to other jobs except when the skills are such that they are not readily usable in other industries, jobs and work settings. Reduced residual functional capacity (RFC) and advancing age are important factors associated with transferability because the lower the RFC, the fewer jobs will be within an individual's physical or mental capacity to perform, and advancing age decreases the possibility of making a successful vocational adjustment.

2. Medical Factors and Transferability

All functional limitations included in the RFC (exertional and nonexertional) must be considered in determining transferability. For example, exertional limitations may prevent a claimant from operating the machinery or using the tools associated with the primary work activities of his or her PRW. Similarly, environmental, manipulative, postural, or mental limitations may prevent a claimant from performing semi-skilled or skilled work activities essential to a job. Examples are watchmakers with hand tremors, house painters with severe allergic reactions to paint fumes, craftsmen who have lost eye-hand coordination, construction machine operators whose back impairments will not permit jolting, and business executives who suffer brain damage which notably lowers their IQs. These factors as well as the general capacity to perform a broad category of work (sedentary, light or medium) must be considered in assessing whether or not a claimant has transferable work skills.

3. Age and Transferability

To find that an individual who is age 55 or over and is limited to sedentary work exertion has skills transferable to sedentary occupations, there must be very little, if any, vocational adjustment required in terms of tools, work processes, work settings or the industry. The same is true for individuals who are age 60 and older and are limited to light work exertion. Individuals with these adverse vocational profiles cannot be expected to make a vocational adjustment to substantial changes in work simply because skilled or semi-skilled jobs can be identified which have some degree of skill similarity with their PRW. In order to establish transferability of skills for such individuals, the semiskilled or skilled job duties of their past work must be so closely related to other jobs which they can perform that they could be expected to perform these other identified jobs at a high degree of proficiency with a minimal amount of job orientation.

4. Unusual Skills

Generally, where job skills are unique to a specific work process in a particular industry or work setting, e.g., carpenter in the construction industry, skills will not be found to be transferable without the need for more than a minimal vocational adjustment by way of tools, work processes, work settings, or industry. On the other hand, where job skills have universal applicability across industry lines, e.g., clerical, professional, administrative, or managerial types of jobs, transferability of skills to industries differing from past work experience can usually be accomplished with very little, if any, vocational adjustment where jobs with similar skills can be identified as being within an individual's RFC.

The regulations also provide that when skills are so specialized or have been acquired in such an isolated vocational setting (like many jobs in mining, agriculture or fishing) that they are not readily usable in other industries, jobs, and work settings, they will be considered not transferable. Some examples are placer miners, bee-keepers, or spear fishermen.

5. Transferability from Semi-Skilled Work

At the lower level of semi-skilled work (just above unskilled) are jobs like those of a chauffeur and some sewing machine operators. Transferability of skills is not usually found from this rather simple type of work.

Slightly more complex, at a higher level of semi-skilled work, are jobs like that of a nurse aide, who may also serve food to people. A nurse aide ordinarily performs other tasks which do not provide a special advantage over unskilled workers, such as dusting and cleaning rooms, changing bed linens, and bathing, dressing and undressing patients. The only duties which suggest transferable skills are those related to "nurse" rather than "aide"—Taking and recording the rates of temperature, pulse and respiration; and recording food and liquid intake and output. However, These occasional or incidental parts of the overall nurse aide job, which are a small part of a higher skilled job (nurse), would not ordinarily give a meaningful vocational advantage over unskilled work. The extent of such duties, however, may vary with individual nurse aides.

On the other hand, a semi-skilled general office clerk (administrative clerk), doing light work, ordinarily is equally proficient in, and spends considerable time doing typing, filing, tabulating and posting data in record books, preparing invoices and statements, operating adding and calculating machines, etc. These clerical skills may be readily transferable to such semi-skilled sedentary occupations as typist, clerk-typist and insurance auditing control clerk.

6. Transferability from Skilled Work

At the lower level of skilled work are jobs like bulldozer operator, firebricklayer, and hosiery knitting machine operator. At the upper end of skilled work are jobs like architect, aircraft stress analyst, air-conditioning mechanic, and various professional and executive or managerial occupations. People with highly skilled work backgrounds have a much greater potential for transferability of their skills because potential jobs in which they can use their skills encompass occupations at the same and lower skill levels, through semi-skilled occupations. Usually the higher the skill level, the more the potential for transferring skills increases.

In testifying on transferability of skills, VEs should rely first and foremost on their own personal knowledge obtained through training and experience. In addition, the DOT and ancillary texts can be of great value. For example, the *Selected Characteristics of Occupations Defined in the Dictionary of Occupational Titles* (1981) groups all occupations into one of 12 interest groups and a further breakdown into 66 work-groups. The work-groups are selected on the basis of similar adaptabilities and capabilities.

These work-groups are broken down further into specific occupations showing the industry in which they are found, the strength factor, environmental conditions, math and reading skill requirements and Specific Vocational Preparation (SVP). Thus, after identifying the work-group of the claimant's prior occupation, the VE can then ascertain which occupations in the same or related work-group, if any, are compatible with the hypothesized medical restrictions and involve use of the same or similar tools and machines, raw materials, products, processes or services as the prior occupation.

The 6-digit GOE subgroup (within the 4-digit GOE work group) which contains the claimant's prior occupation is the place to begin research. If related occupations are not found here or in other subgroups of the pertinent work-group, reference should be made to other work-groups which have a connection with the prior occupations, since insufficient research could lead to an improper conclusion that transferability of skills does not exist.

Incidence of Jobs

Under Social Security regulations a person is considered disabled if he or she is unable to perform any substantial gainful activity, i.e., any work which exists in the national economy. Work "exists in the national economy" when it exists in significant numbers either in the region where the claimant lives or in several other regions of the country. Therefore, if the VE should identify one or more occupations or job titles as suitable for the claimant, it is necessary to furnish for each occupation the approximate number of jobs existing in the claimant's region and/or several regions of the country. For this, the VE should rely upon his or her own placement experience, knowledge gained from doing job analyses for employers or conducting personal job surveys for industry and commerce. The VE may also refer to local, state and regional industrial directories and other resource material.

The "significant numbers" test is not further quantified in the regulations; it is up to the ALJ to decide whether, in each occupation suggested, the number of jobs a person can perform is significant. Therefore the expert should avoid characterizing the number of jobs as "significant", "large", "substantial", etc. The more specific the VE can be as to numbers of jobs and their locations, the more objective and useful the testimony will be.

Testifying on Number of Jobs Within Occupations

1. ALJ asks whether there are occupations within the claimant's RFC
2. VE responds, "There are two occupations to consider: an optical equipment inspector and an optical instrument assembler. There are 200 inspector jobs and 600 assembler jobs in the area."
3. The ALJ decides whether the 800 total jobs are significant.

Note that the test for disability deals with *work* which exists rather than *job openings* which exist. The regulations indicate that the following are *not* factors in determining the existence of work:

   a. Inability to get work
   b. Lack of work in the local area
   c. Hiring practices of employers
   d. Technological changes in the industry in which the claimant has worked
   e. Cyclical economic conditions
   f. No job openings
   g. The claimant would not actually be hired
   h. The claimant does not wish to do a particular type of job

Examples of Testimony

1. The following is an example of appropriate VE questioning and testimony.

In this case, the VE was called to provide testimony on the skill level of past work and transferability of skills.

ALJ: How would you classify Mrs. Smith's past relevant work as a licensed practical nurse in terms of skill levels and physical demands?

VE: This work is skilled. The skills acquired in this occupation are applying technical knowledge and special medical skills to care for or treat sick or handicapped persons; instruction, planning and directing work of others and keeping accurate records of patient's medical status, treatment, etc. The physical demand level is medium requiring lifting 50 lbs. maximum with frequent lifting or carrying objects weighing 25 lbs. She was required to engage in extensive reaching, handling, feeling, talking, hearing and seeing.

ALJ: The claimant has testified today that she can sit for up to 3 hours, can stand and/or walk for no more than 30 minutes before experiencing severe pain, can lift no more than 5 pounds and must lie down for at least 2 hours in any 8 hour period to relieve the pain. If I accept that assessment of her restrictions, could the claimant, considering her age, 53, education, 10th grade, and work experience, engage either in her past work or, if not, could she transfer her skills to perform other skilled or semi-skilled work?

VE: Assuming those limitations, she could engage in neither her past occupations nor any other occupations. I base this answer primarily on her need to lie down for at least 2 hours in any 8 hour period.

ALJ: If I should find from the evidence that the claimant can sit for up to 3 hours at a time, stand and/or walk for no more than 30 minutes at a time, lift 7 pound objects and carry them at least 100 feet, and requires glasses for reading and close work, can she engage in her past work or, if not, could she transfer her skills to perform other skilled or semi-skilled work?

VE: She cannot engage in her past occupation. With the restrictions posed, she can engage in only sedentary work. Considering the skills acquired in her past work she is capable only of sedentary occupations in the medical service field and some in the clerical field. There are two occupations in the medical service field which are both sedentary and for which she has the necessary skills. These are hospital-admitting clerk and outpatient-admitting clerk. These occupations can also be found in the larger nursing homes or similar facilities. Her skills requiring medical knowledge, keeping records and dealing with emergency situations would be transferable to these occupations, they are found in work settings similar to those of her former work and involve similar services. There is another sedentary occupation, similar to the other two, but not classified as a medical service occupation, which she would be well-suited for, rehabilitation clerk. The hospital admitting clerk is a skilled occupation, the others are semi-skilled.

ALJ: Approximately how many jobs in each of these occupations exist in the Milwaukee area? How many nationally?

VE: In the Milwaukee area there are approximately 200 hospital-admitting clerks and outpatient-admitting clerks; and about 40-50 rehabilitation clerks. Nationally there are approximately 10,000 admitting clerks.

2. The following exchange illustrates what happens when the ALJ fails to use hypothetical questions and the VE fails to seek clarification.

ALJ: You've been present throughout. Right?

VE: Yes, sir, that's correct.

ALJ: You have examined the evidence. Right?

VE: Yes sir, that's correct.

ALJ: On the basis of those portions of documentary evidence which have significance to you, do you have an opinion whether there are' any jobs existing in the greater L.A. area in significant numbers that you you believe the claimant could perform?

VE: Yes, I do, your honor. My opinion is based upon the reports of Drs. Warren and Morris. Based on these reports, there appears to be no reason why this woman couldn't engage in at least sedentary entry level work: Sticker—40,000 jobs. inspector/checker—5,000; 9,500 glass selector jobs, and bench assembly—74,000 jobs.

ALJ: Based on testimony and observation of the claimant, do you have an opinion?

VE: Yes, my opinion is the same as previously stated.

In this example, the VE was led to evaluate both the medical evidence and the claimant's testimony and appearance at the hearing. Both of these are functions which the ALJ should perform.

Appendix 5: Unskilled Sedentary Occupations

(For definitions of the classifications, *see* page A-43.)

DOT Code	Occupational Title	Industry	SVP	Reasoning	Math	Language	Reaching	Handling	Fingering	Near Acuity	Depth Perception	Rep. or Short Cycle	General Learning	Verbal Aptitude	Numerical Aptitude	Spatial Aptitude	Form Perception	Clerical Aptitude	Motor Coordination	Finger Dexterity	Manual Dexterity	Census Code
017.684-010	Taper, Printed Circuit Layout	Electronic Components	2	2	2	2	F	F	F	F	F	N	4	4	4	3	4	3	4	2	3	896
205.367-014	Charge-Account Clerk	Clerical and Kindred	2	3	2	3	F	F	F	O		N	3	3	4	5	4	3	4	4	4	531
205.367-030	Election Clerk	Government Services	2	3	2	2	O	O	O	O		N	3	3	4	5	4	3	4	4	4	586
209.567-014	Order Clerk, Food and Beverage	Hotel and Restaurant	2	3	1	2	F	F	F	F		N	3	3	4	5	4	3	4	4	4	535
209.587-010	Addresser	Clerical and Kindred	2	2	1	2	F	F	F	C		Y	4	4	4	4	4	3	4	4	3	582
214.587-010	Telegraph Service Rater	Telephone and Telegraph	2	2	2	2	F	F	F	F		Y	3	4	3	5	4	3	3	4	4	511
219.587-010	Parimutuel – Ticket Checker	Amusement and Recreation	2	3	3	3	C	C	C	C		N	3	3	4	4	3	3	3	4	3	512
221.587-042	Weave-Defect-Charting Clerk	Textile	2	2	1	2	C	C	C	F		Y	4	4	4	4	4	3	4	4	4	560
237.367-014	Call Out Operator	Business Services	2	3	2	3	O	O	O	F		Y	3	3	4	4	5	3	3	3	4	523
237.367-046	Telephone Quotation Clerk	Financial Services	2	3	2	3	F	F	F	F		Y	3	3	3	4	3	3	4	4	4	540
239.687-014	Tube Operator	Clerical and Kindred	2	2	1	2	F	F	O	O		Y	3	3	4	4	4	3	3	4	3	551
249.587-014	Cutter-and-Paster, Press Clippings	Business Services	2	2	1	1	F	F	O	O		Y	4	4	4	4	4	4	3	4	4	586
249.587-018	Document Preparer, Microfilming	Business Services	2	3	1	2	F	F	F	F		N	3	4	4	3	4	3	4	4	4	586
349.665-010	Scoreboard Operator	Amusement and Recreation	2	3	2	3	F	F	F			Y	3	3	4	4	3	4	3	5	4	272
379.367-010	Surveillance-System Monitor	Government Services	2	3	1	3	F		F	F	F	Y	3	3	4	4	4	4	4	4	4	395
521.687-010	Almond Blancher, Hand	Canning and Preserving	1	1	1	1	F	F	F	F		Y	4	4	4	4	4	5	4	3	3	895
521.687-086	Nut Sorter	Canning and Preserving	2	1	1	1	F	F	F	F	F	Y	4	4	5	5	4	5	3	3	4	874
529.665-014	Washroom Operator	Sugar & Confectionery Products	2	2	1	2	F	F				Y	4	4	5	4	4	5	3	4	3	886
529.666-014	Cigarette Making Machine Catcher	Tobacco	2	2	1	2	C	C	F	F		Y	4	4	4	4	3	4	3	4	3	874
529.685-058	Cigar Head Piercer	Tobacco	2	2	1	1	F	F	F	F	F	Y	4	4	4	4	4	5	4	4	4	896
529.687-138	Leaf Tier	Tobacco	1	1	1	1	F	F	F			Y	4	4	5	4	4	5	4	4	4	962

DOT Code	Occupational Title	Industry	SVP	Reasoning	Math	Language	Reaching	Handling	Fingering	Near Acuity	Depth Perception	Rep. or Short Cycle	General Learning	Verbal Aptitude	Numerical Aptitude	Spatial Aptitude	Form Perception	Clerical Aptitude	Motor Coordination	Finger Dexterity	Manual Dexterity	Census Code
539.485-010	Weight Tester	Paper and Pulp	2	3	3	3	F	F	O	F		Y	3	4	3	5	4	3	4	4	4	874
559.687-014	Ampoule Sealer	Pharmaceuticals	2	2	1	1	F	F	F	F	O	Y	4	4	5	4	4	5	3	3	4	964
559.687-034	Egg Processor	Pharmaceuticals	2	2	1	1	F	F	F	F	F	Y	4	4	5	4	4	4	3	3	3	896
574.685-010	Coater, Brake Linings	Misc. Nonmetal Mineral Products	2	2	1	2	C	C		C		Y	4	4	4	4	4	4	4	4	3	881
579.684-022	Mica-Plate Layer, Hand	Mining and Quarrying	2	2	1	1	F	F	F			Y	4	4	4	4	3	4	3	4	3	896
585.665-010	Napper Tender	Knitting	2	2	1	1	C	C	C	F	O	Y	4	4	5	4	4	4	4	4	3	896
585.685-062	Label Pinker	Narrow Fabrics	2	2	1	1	F	F	F	F	O	Y	4	4	5	4	4	4	3	4	3	840
615.685-014	Clearance Cutter	Clock, Watch, & Allied Products	2	2	1	1	F	F	O			Y	4	4	5	4	4	5	3	4	4	795
652.685-038	Ink Printer	Jewelry, Silverware, Plated Ware	2	2	1	2	F	F	F	O		Y	4	4	5	4	4	5	3	4	3	826
654.687-014	Pager	Machinery Manufacturing	2	2	1	1	F	F	F			Y	4	4	4	4	3	5	3	3	3	896
669.687-014	Dowel Inspector	Woodworking	2	1	1	1	F	F	O	F		Y	4	5	5	4	3	5	4	3	4	874
673.685-042	Convex-Grinder Operator	Button and Misc. Notions	2	2	1	1	F	F	F	F		Y	4	4	5	4	4	5	3	3	3	865
681.685-030	Carding-machine Operator	Textile products, NEC	2	1	1	1	F	F	O		F	Y	4	4	4	4	4	5	4	4	4	842
683.687-018	Hander-In	Narrow Fabrics	2	2	1	1	F	F	F	F		Y	4	4	4	4	4	5	4	3	4	895
685.687-014	Cuff Folder	Knitting	2	1	1	1	F	F	F	F		Y	4	4	5	5	4	5	4	3	4	895
685.687-026	Topper	Knitting	2	1	1	1	F	F	F	F		Y	4	4	5	4	4	5	3	3	3	896
689.585-018	Stringing-Machine Tender	Textile Products, NEC	2	2	1	2	F	F	F	F		Y	4	4	4	4	4	4	3	4	3	896
690.685-194	Grinding-Machine Operator, Automatic	Button and Misc. Notions	2	2	1	2	F	F		F	F	Y	4	4	5	3	3	5	4	4	4	865
690.685-258	Laminator I	Leather Products	2	2	1	1	C	C	F	F	F	Y	4	4	4	4	3	4	3	4	4	872
690.686-046	Plastic-design Applier	Boot and Shoe	1	1	1	1	C	C				Y	4	4	5	4	4	4	4	4	3	963
690.686-066	Toggle-Press Folder-and-Feeder - Automatic	Boot and Shoe	2	1	1	1	C	C			F	Y	4	4	4	4	4	4	3	4	3	963
692.685-130	Pinking-Machine Operator	Button and Misc. Notions	2	2	1	2	F	F	O	F	F	Y	4	4	4	4	4	4	4	4	3	871

DOT Code	Occupational Title	Industry	SVP	Reasoning	Math	Language	Reaching	Handling	Fingering	Near Acuity	Depth Perception	Rep. or Short Cycle	General Learning	Verbal Aptitude	Numerical Aptitude	Spatial Aptitude	Form Perception	Clerical Aptitude	Motor Coordination	Finger Dexterity	Manual Dexterity	Census Code
692.685-206	Stop Attacher	Button and Misc. Notions	2	2	1	2	F	F	F	F	O	Y	4	4	4	3	3	4	3	4	3	896
692.685-254	Window-Shade Ring Sewer	Furniture and Fixtures	2	2	1	1	F	F	F	F		Y	4	4	4	4	3	4	4	4	4	832
692.685-266	Zipper trimmer, Machine	Button and Misc. Notions	2	2	1	1	F	F	F	F		Y	4	4	4	3	3	4	3	4	3	871
694.686-010	Clip loading Machine Feeder	Ordnance and Accessories	2	1	1	1	C	C	C			Y	4	4	4	4	3	4	4	4	3	963
700.687-018	Brimer	Fabricated Metal Products, NEC	2	1	1	1	F	F	O	F		Y	4	4	4	4	4	5	3	4	3	896
700.687-026	Charger II	Jewelry, Silverware, Plated Ware	2	2	1	1	F	F	F			Y	4	4	5	4	4	5	4	3	3	896
700.687-062	Preparer	Jewelry, Silverware, Plated Ware	2	2	1	1	F	F	O	F		Y	4	4	5	4	4	5	4	4	4	896
706.684-030	Atomizer Assembler	Misc. Fabricated Products EC	2	2	1	1	F	F	F	F	O	Y	4	4	4	3	4	4	3	3	4	896
712.687-018	Gauger	Protective and Medical Devices	2	2	1	2	F	F	F	F		Y	4	4	4	4	4	5	3	4	3	874
712.687-034	Suture Winder, Hand	Protective and Medical Devices	2	2	1	1	F	F	F	F		Y	4	5	4	4	4	5	3	3	4	895
713.684-034	Polisher, Implant	Optical Goods	2	2	1	1	F	F	F	F	O	Y	4	4	4	4	3	4	4	3	3	865
713.684-038	Polisher, eyeglass frames	Optical Goods	2	2	1	1	F	F	F	F		Y	4	4	5	4	3	5	4	3	4	800
713.687-018	Final Assembler	Optical Goods	2	1	1	1	F	F	F	F		Y	4	4	5	4	4	5	3	3	3	896
713.687-026	Lens Inserter	Optical Goods	2	1	1	1	F	F	F	F		Y	4	4	4	4	4	4	4	3	4	896
715.684-010	Adjuster, Alarm Mechanism	Clock, Watch, & Allied Products	2	2	1	2	F	F	F	F		Y	4	4	4	3	4	4	4	3	3	896
715.684-026	Bench Hand	Clock, Watch, & Allied Products	2	1	1	1	C	C	C	C		Y	4	4	5	3	3	5	3	2	3	896
715.684-082	Dial Screw Assembler	Clock, Watch, & Allied Products	2	2	1	2	C	C	C	C		Y	4	4	4	3	3	4	3	2	3	896
715.684-138	Lacquerer	Clock, Watch, & Allied Products	2	1	1	1	F	F	O	F		Y	4	4	5	4	3	5	4	4	3	881

DOT Code	Occupational Title	Industry	SVP	Reasoning	Math	Language	Reaching	Handling	Fingering	Near Acuity	Depth Perception	Rep. or Short Cycle	General Learning	Verbal Aptitude	Numerical Aptitude	Spatial Aptitude	Form Perception	Clerical Aptitude	Motor Coordination	Finger Dexterity	Manual Dexterity	Census Code
715.684-148	Oiler	Clock, Watch, & Allied Products	2	2	1	1	C	C	C	F	O	Y	4	4	5	4	3	5	3	3	3	896
715.684-178	Set-Staff Fitter	Clock, Watch, & Allied Products	2	2	1	1	C	C	C	C	O	Y	4	4	5	4	3	5	3	3	3	896
715.685-050	Press Operator, Pierce and Shave	Clock, Watch, & Allied Products	2	2	1	1	C	C	F	F	O	Y	4	4	4	3	3	4	3	4	3	795
715.685-038	Mainspring Winder and Oiler	Clock, Watch, & Allied Products	2	2	1	1	C	C	O	F	O	Y	4	4	5	4	4	5	4	4	3	896
715.687-010	Band Attacher	Clock, Watch, & Allied Products	2	1	1	1	C	C	C	F	O	Y	4	4	5	4	4	5	4	3	3	896
715.687-018	Crystal Attacher	Clock, Watch, & Allied Products	2	1	1	1	C	C	C	O	O	Y	4	4	5	4	3	5	3	3	3	896
715.687-022	Dial Brusher	Clock, Watch, & Allied Products	2	1	1	1	C	C	C	F	F	Y	4	4	5	4	4	5	3	3	3	896
715.687-026	Dipper, Clock and Watch Hands	Clock, Watch, & Allied Products	2	2	1	2	C	C	F			Y	4	4	5	5	4	5	4	4	4	881
715.687-078	Mainspring Former, Arbor End	Clock, Watch, & Allied Products	2	2	1	1	C	C	F	F		Y	4	4	5	4	4	5	4	3	4	896
715.687-082	Mainspring Former, Brace End	Clock, Watch, & Allied Products	2	2	1	1	C	F	F	F		Y	4	4	5	4	4	5	4	3	3	896
715.687-086	Masker	Clock, Watch, & Allied Products	2	1	1	1	F	F	F	F		Y	4	4	5	4	4	5	4	4	4	881
715.687-090	Motor Polarizer	Clock, Watch, & Allied Products	2	1	1	1	F	F	O			Y	4	4	4	4	4	4	3	4	4	895
715.687-094	Mounter, Clock and Watch Hands	Clock, Watch, & Allied Products	2	1	1	1	C	C	C	C	F	Y	4	4	4	4	4	4	4	3	3	896
715.687-098	Painter, Clock and Watch Hands	Clock, Watch, & Allied Products	2	1	1	1	C	C	C	C	F	Y	4	4	5	4	4	5	3	3	4	881
715.687-114	Rotor Assembler	Clock, Watch, & Allied Products	2	2	2	1	C	C	C	F	O	Y	4	4	5	4	4	5	4	3	3	896
716.687-030	Lens-Block Gauger	Optical Goods	2	2	2	2	F	F	F	F	F	Y	4	4	5	4	4	4	4	4	4	874

DOT Code	Occupational Title	Industry	SVP	Reasoning	Math	Language	Reaching	Handling	Fingering	Near Acuity	Depth Perception	Rep. or Short Cycle	General Learning	Verbal Aptitude	Numerical Aptitude	Spatial Aptitude	Form Perception	Clerical Aptitude	Motor Coordination	Finger Dexterity	Manual Dexterity	Census Code
723.687-010	Patcher	Household Appliances	2	2	1	1	F	F	F	F		Y	4	4	5	4	4	5	4	3	3	896
725.684-018	Stem Mounter	Lighting Fixtures	2	2	1	1	C	C	C	C		Y	4	4	4	3	3	5	3	3	3	772
725.687-022	Getterer	Lighting Fixtures	2	1	1	1	F	F	F	F		Y	4	4	4	4	4	5	3	3	3	896
726.684-050	Film Touch-Up Inspector	Electronic Components	2	2	1	1	C	C	C	C	C	Y	4	4	4	4	3	4	3	3	4	874
726.684-110	Touch-Up Screener, Printed Circuit Board Assembly	Electronic Components	2	2	1	2	F	F	F	C		Y	4	4	4	4	3	3	3	3	3	874
726.685-066	Bonder, Semiconductor	Electronic Components	2	2	1	2	O	C	C	C	C	Y	4	4	4	4	4	4	3	3	4	822
726.687-030	Loader, Semiconductor Dies	Electronic Components	2	2	1	2	C	C	C	C	C	Y	4	4	5	4	4	4	4	3	4	896
726.687-046	Wafer Breaker, Semiconductors	Electronic Components	2	2	1	2	C	C	C	C	C	Y	4	4	5	4	4	4	4	3	3	896
729.684-018	Dial Marker	Electrical Equipment	2	2	2	2	F	F	F	F	F	N	3	4	3	4	2	5	3	2	3	881
731.685-014	Stuffer	Toys, Games, Sports Equipment	2	2	1	1	F	F	O	O		Y	4	4	4	4	4	4	4	4	3	880
731.687-014	Finisher	Misc. Fabricated Products NEC	2	2	1	1	F	F	F	F	F	Y	3	4	4	3	4	5	3	3	3	896
732.587-010	Golf-Ball Trimmer	Toys, Games, Sports Equipment	2	2	1	1	F	F	F	F	F	Y	4	4	4	3	4	4	3	3	4	896
732.684-062	Fishing-Reel Assembler	Toys, Games, Sports Equipment	2	2	1	1	F	F	F		F	Y	4	4	4	4	4	4	3	3	3	896
733.684-026	Smoother	Pen, Pencil, Marking Device Mfg.	2	2	1	1	C	C	C	F	F	Y	4	4	4	4	4	4	3	3	3	800
734.687-010	Feather Shaper	Button and Misc. Notions	2	2	1	2	F	F	F	F		Y	4	4	4	4	3	4	4	3	3	896
734.687-010	Acetone-Button Paster	Button and Misc. Notions	2	1	1	1	C	C	C	C	C	Y	4	4	5	4	4	5	3	2	3	896
734.687-018	Assembler	Button and Misc. Notions	2	1	1	1	C	C	C	C	C	Y	4	4	5	4	4	5	3	3	3	896

DOT Code	Occupational Title	Industry	SVP	Reasoning	Math	Language	Reaching	Handling	Fingering	Near Acuity	Depth Perception	Rep. or Short Cycle	General Learning	Verbal Aptitude	Numerical Aptitude	Spatial Aptitude	Form Perception	Clerical Aptitude	Motor Coordination	Finger Dexterity	Manual Dexterity	Census Code
734.687-034	Buckle Wire Inserter	Button and Misc. Notions	1	1	1	1	C	C	C	C		Y	4	4	5	4	4	5	3	3	3	896
734.687-042	Button Reclaimer	Knitting	2	1	1	1	F	F	F	F		Y	4	4	5	4	4	5	4	4	4	874
734.687-074	Hot-Stone Setter	Button and Misc. Notions	2	1	1	1	F	F	F	F	F	Y	4	4	5	4	4	5	4	3	4	896
734.687-086	Slide Fastener Chain Assembler	Button and Misc. Notions	2	2	1	1	F	F	F	F	F	Y	4	4	4	4	3	5	4	3	3	896
734.687-090	Sticker	Button and Misc. Notions	1	1	1	1	C	C	C	C		Y	4	4	5	4	4	5	3	3	3	896
734.687-094	Zipper Trimmer, Hand	Button and Misc. Notions	2	2	2	2	F	F	F	F	F	Y	4	4	4	3	3	4	2	4	4	874
734.687-126	Splitter, Hand	Button and Misc. Notions	2	1	1	1	F	F	F	F	F	Y	4	4	5	4	3	5	3	3	3	871
735.687-018	Painter	Jewelry, Silverware, Plated Ware	2	2	1	2	F	F	F	F	F	Y	4	4	4	4	3	4	3	3	3	881
735.687-022	Pin-or-Clip Fastener	Jewelry, Silverware, Plated Ware	2	2	1	1	F	F	F	F	F	Y	4	4	4	4	4	5	3	3	4	896
735.687-034	Stone Setter	Jewelry, Silverware, Plated Ware	2	2	1	1	F	F	F	F	F	Y	4	4	4	4	3	5	3	3	3	896
737.587-010	Bandoleer Straightener – Stamper	Ordnance and Accessories	2	1	1	1	C	F	F	F		Y	4	4	4	5	3	4	4	3	4	895
737.687-026	Check Weigher	Ordnance and Accessories	2	1	1	1	C	C	F	C		Y	4	4	4	4	4	4	3	3	3	874
737.687-126	Shadowgraph-Scale Operator	Ordnance and Accessories	2	2	1	2	F	F	F	F	F	Y	4	4	4	4	4	4	3	3	3	874
739.684-094	Lamp-shade Assembler	Misc. Fabricated Products NEC	2	2	1	1	F	F	F	F	F	Y	4	4	4	4	3	5	3	3	4	896
739.684-162	Umbrella Tipper, Hand	Misc. Fabricated	2	2	1	1	F	F	F	F	F	Y	4	4	4	4	4	4	3	3	3	835
739.685-046	Tapper, Bit	Misc. Fabricated Products NEC	2	2	1	1	F	F	F			Y	4	4	5	4	4	5	3	4	3	822
739.685-050	Tapper, Shank	Misc. Fabricated Products NEC	2	2	1	1	F	F		F	F	Y	4	4	5	3	4	5	4	4	3	896

DOT Code	Occupational Title	Industry	SVP	Reasoning	Math	Language	Reaching	Handling	Fingering	Near Acuity	Depth Perception	Rep. or Short Cycle	General Learning	Verbal Aptitude	Numerical Aptitude	Spatial Aptitude	Form Perception	Clerical Aptitude	Motor Coordination	Finger Dexterity	Manual Dexterity	Census Code
739.685-054	Umbrella Tipper, Machine	Misc. Fabricated Products NEC	2	1	1	1	F	F	F	F		Y	4	4	5	4	4	5	3	3	3	896
739.687-066	Compact Assembler	Jewelry, Silverware, Plated Ware	2	2	1	1	F	F	F	F	F	Y	4	4	5	4	4	5	4	4	3	896
739.687-086	Eye-Dropper Assembler	Glass Products	2	2	1	1	C	C	C		F	Y	4	4	4	4	4	5	4	3	4	896
739.687-182	Table Worker	Misc. Fabricated Products NC	2	1	1	1	F	F	F	F	F	Y	4	4	5	4	4	5	4	4	4	874
740.687-010	Button Spindler	Button and Misc. Notions	2	1	1	1	F	F	F	F	F	Y	4	4	5	5	5	5	3	3	3	881
754.684-018	Bit Shaver	Misc. Fabricated Products EC	2	2	1	1	F	F	F	F	F	Y	4	4	4	4	3	5	3	3	3	865
770.687-026	Jewel Stringer	Clock, Watch, & Allied Products	2	2	1	1	C	C	C	C		Y	4	4	5	4	3	5	3	2	3	895
774.687-014	Lacer	Misc. Nonmetal Mineral Products	2	2	1	1	F	F	F	F	F	Y	4	4	5	4	3	5	4	2	3	896
775.687-022	Gold Burnisher	Pottery and Porcelain Ware	2	2	1	1	F	F	F	F	F	Y	4	4	4	4	3	4	3	3	3	865
779.684-034	Level-Vial Sealer	Cutlery, Handtools, Hardware	2	2	1	1	F	F	F	F	F	Y	4	4	4	4	2	4	3	3	3	896
779.687-018	Glass-Bulb Silverer	Glass Products	2	1	1	1	C	C	C	F		Y	4	4	5	4	4	5	4	3	4	881
779.687-038	Waxer	Glass Products	2	1	1	1	C	C				Y	4	5	5	5	4	5	4	4	3	895
782.687-030	Puller - Through	Glove and Mitten	1	1	1	1	F	F	F	F	F	Y	4	4	4	4	4	5	3	3	3	895
782.687-046	Sack Repairer	Any Industry	2	2	1	1	F	F	F	F	F	Y	4	4	4	5	4	5	3	3	3	832
784.684-030	Foundation Maker	Hat and Cap	2	2	1	2	F	F	F	F	F	Y	4	4	5	4	3	5	3	3	3	896
784.687-026	Endband Cutter, Hand	Hat and Cap	2	2	1	1	F	F	F	F	F	Y	4	4	4	3	3	4	4	4	3	871
788.687-022	Buckler and Lacer	Boot and Shoe	2	1	1	1	C	C	C			Y	4	5	5	4	4	5	3	3	3	895
788.687-114	Shank Taper	Boot and Shoe	2	1	1	1	C	C				Y	4	5	5	5	4	5	4	4	3	895
788.687-158	Vamp-Strap Ironer	Boot and Shoe	2	1	1	1	F	F	O	F	F	Y	4	4	5	4	4	5	4	4	3	896
788.687-166	White-Shoe Ragger	Boot and Shoe	2	1	1	1	C	C				Y	4	4	5	4	4	5	4	4	4	881

DOT Code	Occupational Title	Industry	SVP	Reasoning	Math	Language	Reaching	Handling	Fingering	Near Acuity	Depth Perception	Rep. or Short Cycle	General Learning	Verbal Aptitude	Numerical Aptitude	Spatial Aptitude	Form Perception	Clerical Aptitude	Motor Coordination	Finger Dexterity	Manual Dexterity	Census Code
789.687-022	Buffing Turner-and-Counter	Textile Products, NEC	2	1	1	1	F	C	C	F	F	Y	4	4	4	4	4	4	4	3	4	896
789.687-174	Thread Separator	Textile Products, NEC	2	1	1	1	F	F	F	F		Y	4	5	5	4	4	5	4	3	4	895
919.663-022	Escort-Vehicle Driver	Motor Vehicle Transportation	2	2	1	2	F	F	F	F	F	Y	4	4	4	4	4	4	3	4	3	913
920.687-030	Bander, Hand	Tobacco	2	2	1	1	C	C	C	C		Y	4	4	5	4	4	5	4	4	4	964
976.684-018	Mounter, Hand	Photofinishing	2	2	1	1	F	F	O	F	F	Y	4	4	4	4	4	4	3	3	3	871
979.687-026	Type-Copy Examiner	Machinery Manufacturing	2	2	1	2	F	F	F	F		Y	4	4	4	4	2	3	4	4	4	874

Appendix 5: Definitions

Specific Vocational Preparation
1   Short demonstration only
2   Anything beyond short demonstration up to and including one month

Reasoning, Math, Language
See Appendix 3

Physical Demands

C   Constantly -- more than 66% of the time
F   Frequently -- from 33 to 66% of the time
O   Occasionally -- up to 33% of the time

Repetitive or Short Cycle Work
Involves performing a few routine and uninvolved tasks over and over again according to set procedures, sequence, or pace with little opportunity for diversion or interruption. Interaction with people is included when it is routine, continual, or prescribed.

Aptitudes
1   Top 10% of population
2   67 - 89% of population
3   34 - 66% of population
4   10 - 33% of population
5   Below 10% of population

The disk that comes with this book includes a Microsoft Excel spreadsheet containing all of the data on this chart. Using the spreadsheet, you can sort the chart based on any criteria.

Phrasing Hypothetical Questions to Vocational Experts Training Guide

Manipulative Limitations

Mental Impairment Limitations

SSR 00-4p

Hypothetical Question to VEs

PHRASING HYPOTHETICAL QUESTIONS TO VES

TABLE OF CONTENTS

PHRASING HYPOTHETICAL QUESTIONS TO VES

INTRODUCTION

This workbook contains much of the information in the broadcast you are viewing on Phrasing Hypothetical Questions to Vocational Experts (VEs). We included biographies of our faculty, answers to the questions posed during the broadcast, and forms used in the disability adjudicatory process in the Appendix as reference materials.

The use of a Vocational Expert (VE) at steps 4 and 5 of the sequential evaluation may be necessary to determine whether the claimant can perform any past relevant work or whether other work exists in the national economy that the claimant can perform.

At step 5, we know that use of a VE may be appropriate when a claimant has only exertional limitations and the residual functional capacity (RFC) falls between ranges of exertional levels, i.e., stand/walk four hours a day which is more than sedentary but less than a full range of light, and the appropriate GRID tables would direct different conclusions. VE input may also be appropriate if a claimant has a combination of exertional and nonexertional limitations. Another situation when it would be appropriate to use a VE is if a claimant has solely nonexertional limitations, such as individuals with mental impairments. Part of the process of determining whether an individual can perform past relevant work or other work in the national economy involves posing a hypothetical question or a series of hypothetical questions to the VE.

MANIPULATIVE LIMITATIONS

Many impairments that are frequently seen in our cases result in limitations on the use of the hands and arms. The problem in determining these limitations is often with terminology and the failure to use terms that everyone understands. Phrases like … no more than "occasional repetitive handling" seem inconsistent and confusing if the terms aren't understood.

1. Is this an appropriate question to the VE? Assume that the individual has a rotator cuff injury. The Administrative Law Judge asks the VE to assume the claimant has a limited ability to use his arms for handling.

To pose clear and accurate hypothetical questions involving manipulative limitations to the VE, **defining** and **quantifying** those limitations would be helpful.

SSR 85-15 provides definitions of terms used to describe use of the upper extremities in work related activities. **Reaching** is defined as extending the hands and arms in any direction. **Handling** is defined as seizing, holding, grasping, turning or otherwise working primarily with the whole hand or hands. **Fingering** involves picking, pinching, or otherwise working primarily with the fingers. **Feeling** is defined as the use of the fingertips to feel the size shape, temperature, or texture of an object.

SSR 83-10 provides us with the definitions of the frequency of certain activities and these definitions are taken from the DOT. **Occasionally** is defined as occurring from very little up to one-third of the time, or approximately 2 hours in an 8-hour workday. **Frequent** is defined as occurring from one-third to two thirds of the time or approximately 6 hours in an 8-hour workday. Other terms that are used in the DOT but not specifically addressed in the regulations or rulings include **Constant** and **Never.**

2. Is this an appropriate hypothetical question? The Administrative Law Judge asks the VE to assume that because of diabetic neuropathy the claimant cannot perform work involving fine manipulation with the fingers.

Some of the problem areas with manipulative impairments are: Limitations on "fine manipulation" and limitations of repetitive use of the fingers or hands. Use of established terms that quantify the limitation, such as **occasionally** or frequently, may be helpful in avoiding these problem areas.

MENTAL IMPAIRMENTS AND HYPOTHETICAL QUESTIONS TO VES

The RFC portion of the hypothetical question posted to the vocational expert **must** be identical to the RFC finding in the decision. By writing out your RFC posed to the vocational expert, you can ensure that the decision contains the proper language. Some judges draft hypothetical questions before the hearing and make changes where necessary. Remember if a judge finds a "severe" mental impairment, the RFC portion of the VE hypothetical and the findings must include at least one mental limitation.

3. Assume that an individual has major depressive disorder. The claimant reports that he cannot tolerate stress. The ALJ instructs the vocational expert to assume an individual is "limited to low stress work." Is this a good hypothetical?

The major problem in this phrasing of the stress limitation is the failure to state the limitation in terms of specific, work-related functional abilities.

The judge needs to determine and state in functional terms the actual limitations of ability to perform work-related activities imposed by the claimant's mental impairment(s). The judge may do this in several ways. The judge may ask the claimant to identify the situations he or she finds stressful and the results of being exposed to such situations. If the claimant reports any such situations, the judge must of course determine if the record supports the specific limitations. The documentary evidence may also clearly outline the functional limitations imposed by the claimant's mental impairments. The judge should also carefully elicit testimony and consider the information about the claimant's daily activities.

Some examples of situations that have been found to be stressful include the following:

*   working with co-workers;

*   working with the public other than co-workers;

*   working with supervisors or co-workers if interpersonal interaction or discussion is required;

*   working at a production rate pace;

*   working at unprotected heights;

*   driving tractor-trailers that transport flammable liquids;

- making decisions; and

- using judgment.

If the claimant testified that he or she cannot work with the general public other than co-workers because such activity would be too stressful, and the record supports such functional limitation, the hypothetical question posed to the VE should reflect this specific limitation rather than a general restriction to low stress work. A proper hypothetical would be:

> Dr. VE, I want you to assume an individual has the same age, education, and work experience as the claimant. Further assume that this individual has no physical impairments or physical limitations, but has a severe mental impairment, depression. As a result, the individual is limited to occupations that do not require working in contact with the public other than co-workers. Are there any occupations such an individual could perform?

4. This is the best way to describe the limitation in a hypothetical? (True or False).

Let's consider another example. Assume that an individual has major depressive disorder. The DDS found that this mental impairment caused a moderate limitation of the individual's ability to maintain concentration, persistence, or pace, but no restriction of activities of daily living or maintenance of social functioning. The ALJ arrives at the same conclusions as the DDS and instructs the vocational expert to assume an individual has a "moderate limitation in ability to maintain concentration, persistence, or pace."

5. Is this the best way to describe the limitation in a hypothetical? (Yes or No)

The use of the term "moderate" is problematic because the definition used in the regulations is too broad. Several examples of proper phrasing of a limitation on the capacity to concentrate include the following:

- unable to perform any work activities on average for 2 minutes at a time, once per hour;

- unable to work in close proximity to others because the claimant is too easily distracted; and

- must be reminded of tasks 10 times each day on average by supervisor.

PHRASING HYPOTHETICAL QUESTIONS TO VES

We still must be sure the limitations imposed by symptoms are clearly defined in the VE hypothetical and RFC finding, even though they may be difficult to state in specific, work-related terms. Some of the descriptors frequently seen that are often problematic include the following:

- Moderate

- Fair

- Low

- Often

- Mild

- Excessive

- Repetitive

- Reasonable

- Unreasonable

Here's another example: Assume that an individual has major depressive disorder. The DDS found that this mental impairment caused a moderate limitation of the individual's ability to maintain concentration, persistence, or pace for the "B" Criteria of the Listings as outlined on the Psychiatric Review Technique Form. The DDS also found that the claimant's mental impairment caused no restriction of activities of daily living or maintenance of social functioning. The claimant also reports concentration difficulties. The ALJ arrives at the same conclusions as the DDS and instructs the vocational expert to assume an individual has a "moderate limitation in ability to maintain concentration, persistence, or pace."

6. This is the best way to describe the limitation in a hypothetical? Keypad Question: Is this good phrasing for a hypothetical? (True or False)

Mental RFC Assessment Form used by the DDS: Form SSA-4734-F4-SUP

Remember that the first two pages are summary conclusions and that the third page of this form is the RFC determination of the DDS. The introduction on the first page of the

PHRASING HYPOTHETICAL QUESTIONS TO VES

form describes these summary conclusions as follows. You may wish to follow along in the Appendix of your workbook.

> "This section is for recording summary conclusions derived from the evidence in file. Each mental activity is to be evaluated within the context of the individual's capacity to sustain that activity over a normal workday and workweek, on an ongoing basis. Detailed explanation of the degree of limitation in each category, as well as any other assessment information you deem appropriate, is to be recorded in Section III (Functional Capacity Assessment)."

Let's look at a specific example. Look at item number 11 on page 2 of the form: "The ability to complete a normal workday and workweek without interruptions from psychologically based symptoms and to perform at a consistent pace without an unreasonable number and length of rest periods." It would appear on its face that such claimant should have been found disabled if the DDS found the claimant's capacity in this area is "moderately limited." But when the DDS states the claimant has moderate difficulty with this activity, the DDS usually means the claimant has significant difficulty in performing certain types of occupations or certain specific work activities. For example, and only as an example, the DDS may conclude the claimant is unable to work with the general public other than co-workers. If the form is properly completed, the actual limitations should be outlined on page 3 of the form, although sometimes there is not as much detail as we might like to see. If the "moderate" block were checked for this entry, how would you determine the actual limitation or capacity associated with this factor?

Mental MSS Form used by Hearing Offices (Form HA-1152)

Once again, it is essential to understand the entries on this form, like the first two pages of the Mental RFC Assessment Form used by the DDS, are medical conclusions, not statements of functional abilities. A "moderate" capacity to "understand and remember short, simple instructions" means different things to different people. As we stated previously, the actual capacity in this area must be stated in terms of specific, work-related functional abilities.

The claimant's actual functional limitation or capacity in this area must be clearly stated so everyone who considers the hypothetical, such as the VE, the claimant, claimant's representative, the Administrative Appeals Judge, United States District Judge, and so on, has the same understanding.

PHRASING HYPOTHETICAL QUESTIONS TO VES

"B" Criteria from the PRTF (SSA-2506)

The "B" criteria on the PRTF are gross measures of impairment severity; they are not stated in terms of specific, work-related functional abilities that are sufficient to make a decision at step 4 or 5. Attempts by claimants' representatives to ask the VE questions may include an inadequate RFC.

Advise the representative that the DDS Mental RFC Assessment Form includes summary conclusions about functioning, not vocationally relevant functional capacities.

SSR 96-8p reminds us that, by regulation, "...the limitations in the paragraph B and paragraph C criteria are not an RFC assessment but are used to rate the severity of mental impairments at steps 2 and 3 of the sequential evaluation process. The mental RFC assessment used at steps 4 and 5 of the sequential evaluation process requires a more detailed assessment by itemizing various functions contained in the broad categories found in paragraphs B and C...."

It is up to the judge and counsel to phrase VE hypotheticals in terms of specific, work-related functional abilities.

PHRASING HYPOTHETICAL QUESTIONS TO VES

ISSUES CONCERNING SOCIAL SECURITY RULING 00-4P

Social Security Ruling 00-4p is a policy interpretation ruling regarding the use of vocational expert and vocational specialist evidence and other reliable occupational information in disability decisions that became effective on December 4, 2000.

SSA issued SSR 00-4p to clarify our standards on identifying and resolving conflicts or apparent conflicts between evidence provided by a vocational expert and the information published by the Department of Labor in the Dictionary of Occupational Titles, or DOT. This also includes its companion publication, the Selected Characteristics of Occupations Defined in the Revised Dictionary of Occupational Titles, or SCO.

In SSR 00-4p, SSA explained that although we rely primarily on the DOT and SCO for information about the requirements of work in the national economy at steps 4 and 5, we may use VE testimony to resolve complex issues. This policy was affirmed in the recent amendments to 20 CFR 404.1560 and 416.960 of the regulations that were effective September 25, 2003. The SSR states that occupational evidence provided by the VE should generally be consistent with occupational information in the DOT. When a conflict or apparent conflict between the VE evidence and the DOT is identified, the ALJ must obtain a reasonable explanation for the conflict before relying on the VE evidence to support a decision about whether the claimant is disabled.

SSR 00-4p states the Commissioner's policy that an ALJ has an affirmative duty to ask the VE on the record whether his or her testimony conflicts with the information in the DOT. SSR 00-4p states that ""When a VE or VS provides evidence about the requirements of a job or occupation, the adjudicator has an affirmative responsibility to ask about any possible conflict between the VE or VS evidence and the information provided in the DOT."

If a conflict is identified, then the ALJ must obtain a reasonable explanation for the conflict and explain the resolution of the conflict in the written decision. Here is a question that was raised during the broadcast.

Let's assume that:

- The ALJ poses a hypothetical question involving a younger individual with a high school education and unskilled past work experience.

- The individual can perform the full range of <u>sedentary</u> work activity as defined in the regulations with the <u>exception</u> that she must be allowed the opportunity every

PHRASING HYPOTHETICAL QUESTIONS TO VES

hour to get up and stand or walk for approximately 5 minutes in her work area (sit/stand option).

- The VE replies that such an individual can perform numerous occupations and provides the following examples: addresser (DOT code 209.587-010) and dowel inspector (DOT code 669.687-014). He also provides the number of these jobs in the national economy.

- The ALJ asks the VE if there are any conflicts between his testimony and the DOT.

- The VE says that these jobs are described in the DOT as sedentary. However, he says the DOT does not include information about an option for changing positions, or a sit/stand option.

- The VE also says that in his experience placing employees in these jobs and performing job surveys, about one-half of employers allow the job to be performed with this limitation.

- The VE also states that he already reduced the numbers by 50 percent in providing his earlier answer.

- The ALJ finds the claimant not disabled at Step 5, relying on jobs named by the VE, and using the medical-vocational guidelines, or Grids, as a framework for decision making.

- The hearing decision summarizes the VE testimony and provides rationale for how the conflict was resolved.

- In filing a request for review with the Appeals Council, the claimant's representative argues that the ALJ should not have relied on the VE evidence because it conflicts with the DOT which lists the jobs as requiring sedentary exertion.

7. True or False, the Appeals Council will agree with the representative on this issue?

SSR 00-4p makes it clear that the ALJ cannot rely on evidence provided by the VE if that evidence is based on underlying assumptions or definitions that are inconsistent with SSA's regulatory policies or definitions. Examples of this include the VE using a different definition for exertional levels; for skill levels; or for transferability of skills.

Here is a multiple choice question from the broadcast. Specific vocational preparation (SVP) is defined in the DOT as the amount of lapsed time required by a typical worker

PHRASING HYPOTHETICAL QUESTIONS TO VES

to learn the techniques, acquire the information, and develop the facility needed for average performance in a specific job-worker situation. SVP levels range from 1 to 9, with 1 being the shortest period of time. Look at the following SVP levels and the time involved with learning the average job:

- SVP level 1 is a short demonstration only

- SVP level 2 is anything beyond short demonstration up to and including 1 month

- SVP level 3 is over 1 month up to and including 3 months

- SVP level 4 is over 3 months up to and including 6 months.

8. Which of the above is consistent with SSA's definition of "unskilled" work?

    A. SVP level of 1 only,
    B. SVP levels of 1 and 2,
    C. SVP levels 1 through 3, or
    D. All of the SVP levels shown.

Here is a situation involving SSR 00-4p that appears at the Appeals Council frequently. What if in response to an ALJ's question about possible conflicts with the DOT the VE testifies that there are no conflicts?   But based on the ALJ's own experience with evidence provided by VEs in other cases or the ALJ's own experience using the DOT, the ALJ suspects that there may be a conflict. Should the ALJ rely on the VE's answer about conflicts without further inquiry? To illustrate, let's look at a true/false question.

Let's assume for purposes of this question that:

- The ALJ poses a hypothetical question involving a younger individual with a high school education and unskilled past work experience.

- The individual can perform the full range of sedentary work activity as defined in the regulations except that the claimant has bilateral upper extremity limitations and can only <u>occasionally</u> reach and <u>occasionally</u> handle objects.

- The VE replies that such an individual can perform numerous occupations and provides the following examples: addresser and dowel inspector. He also provides the number of these jobs in the national economy.

- In response to the ALJ's question as to whether there are any conflicts between his testimony and the information shown in the DOT, the VE replies "No."

PHRASING HYPOTHETICAL QUESTIONS TO VES

- The ALJ strongly suspects that the testimony may not be accurate. He seems to remember that other VEs have testified that these jobs require using the hands and arms most of the day. But presented with the VE testimony, neither he nor the claimant's representative questions the VE further regarding conflicts.

- The ALJ finds the claimant not disabled at Step 5, relying on jobs named by the VE, and using the Grids as a framework for decision making.

- In filing a request for review with the Appeals Council, the claimant's representative argues that the VE evidence conflicts with the DOT, which shows that both jobs require <u>frequent</u> reaching and handling.

9. True or false, the Appeals Council will agree with the representative on this issue?

The best way to avoid a remand is to be alert to possible conflicts even when the VE says the testimony is consistent. If an ALJ suspects that there is a conflict, even if the VE says there is not, then the ALJ should attempt to resolve the issue at the hearing. Of course an ALJ may decide to check the DOT and SCO after the hearing and discover at that point that there is an apparent conflict. In that situation, the ALJ should consider issuing interrogatories or holding a supplemental hearing to obtain a reasonable explanation for the apparent conflict.

Here is a recap as to what Social Security Ruling 00-4p requires.

The SSR places an affirmative duty on the ALJ to inquire about the consistency of VE evidence and occupational information in the DOT, including its companion publication the SCO.

- The ALJ must ask the VE, on the record, if the evidence he or she has provided conflicts with the DOT. **Reminder**: Always ask the question -even if you don't think there are any conflicts.

- If following this questioning of the VE, the VE evidence appears to conflict with the DOT, the ALJ must obtain a reasonable explanation for the apparent conflict. **Reminder**: Ask the VE the basis for the information he or she has provided that conflicts with the DOT. Also, remain alert to situations when the VE does not recognize the conflict, but you know from your own experience with prior VE testimony or using the DOT, that a conflict is likely.

- The ALJ must resolve such conflicts before relying on VE evidence to support a decision of disabled or not disabled. **Reminder**: Determine whether the VE's explanation is reasonable.

PHRASING HYPOTHETICAL QUESTIONS TO VES

- Finally, the ALJ must explain the resolution of the conflict in the decision. **Reminder**: Put it all in writing!

Remember also that the ALJ may not rely on VE evidence that is inconsistent with SSA's regulatory policies or definitions.

PHRASING HYPOTHETICAL QUESTIONS TO VES

APPENDIX: FACULTY BIOGRAPHIES

Frank Cristaudo

Under the executive leadership of the Deputy Commissioner of Office of Disability and Adjudication and Review, as Chief Administrative Law Judge, Judge Cristaudo is responsible for the administration of the national hearing operations of the Social Security Administration. With almost 1,100 federal Administrative Law Judges and more than 5,000 support staff in the Office of the Chief Administrative Law Judge, 10 regional offices, and over 140 hearing offices throughout the country, Social Security's hearing operation is one of the largest administrative judicial systems in the world.

Prior to his appointment as Chief Administrative Law Judge in 2006, Judge Cristaudo served as the Acting Deputy Chief Administrative Law Judge, Regional Chief Administrative Law Judge for the Philadelphia Region, Hearing Office Chief Administrative Law Judge in the Voorhees, New Jersey, Hearing Office, and as an Administrative Law Judge in the Voorhees and Savannah, Georgia, Hearing Offices.

He lectures and writes frequently on Social Security, leadership, and management topics, and is the author of **"The Vocational Expert Manual: The Use, Questioning, and Testimony of Vocational Experts"**, and **"27 Practices for Effective Leadership in Public Service"**.

Prior to his appointment as an Administrative Law Judge in 1990, he started his own general law practice and practiced law for twelve years with a specialty in Social Security Law. He also served as a Municipal Court Judge, Township Attorney, and instructor at LaSalle University and Rowan University. While engaged in the private practice of law, he argued a number of Social Security cases before the Court of Appeals for the Third Circuit, including **Wallace v. Sec. HHS,** 722 F.2d 1150 (3rd Cir. 1983), and **Woody v. Sec. HHS,** 859 F.2d 1156 (3rd Cir. 1988).

Before entering the practice of law, he was employed by the Social Security Administration at headquarters in Woodlawn, Maryland, as a Social Insurance Claims Examiner (Disability); Computer Specialist (Systems); and Methods and Procedures Analyst (Medicare). Judge Cristaudo has a B.A. from McDaniel College and a J.D. (cum laude) from Widener University School of Law.

PHRASING HYPOTHETICAL QUESTIONS TO VES

Dianne Egan Bobowski

Dianne Egan Bobowski was appointed an Administrative Appeals Judge in 1996. Judge Bobowski received her Bachelor of Arts degree from the University of New Orleans, a degree of Juris Doctor from George Mason University School of Law, and is a member of the Virginia State Bar. She started her career with SSA as a claims representative in the New Orleans, LA District Office in 1976. In 1983 she moved to Virginia to work for the Office of Hearings and Appeals, where she has worked as an analyst, attorney advisor, and policy staff director before her appointment to the Appeals Council.

Judge Bobowski is the founding chairperson of ODAR's Hispanic Affairs Advisory Council (HAAC) and a member of the Limited English Proficient (LEP) Agency workgroup. She also is a member of the Agency's Disability Training and Steering Committee.

Mary Kunz

Mary Kunz was appointed as an Administrative Law Judge in 2001. Judge Kunz received her Bachelor of Arts Degree from the University of Minnesota and Juris Doctor degree from William Mitchell College of Law in St. Paul Minnesota. She also received a Masters degree from St. Cloud State University.

In addition to being an attorney for ODAR, she also worked as an Appeals Officer for the Appeals Council. She also was the Regional Attorney in the Philadelphia Region prior to her selection as an administrative law judge. She has served as one of the primary trainers for new decision writers for many years and is known nationwide for her technical expertise in the area of Social Security disability law.

PHRASING HYPOTHETICAL QUESTIONS TO VES

APPENDIX: ANSWERS TO QUESTIONS

1. Is this an appropriate question to the VE?

   The answer is no. As we have seen with mental impairments, the term "limited" doesn't quantify the degree of limitation.

2. Is this an appropriate hypothetical question?

   The answer is No. As we will see, the term "fine manipulation" is not defined in the regulations, rulings, or the DOT. As a result, it is not clear what is meant by the use of that term.

3. Is this a good hypothetical?

   No, the major problem in this phrasing of the stress limitation is the failure to state the limitation in terms of specific, work-related functional abilities. A restriction to low stress work is problematic as it does not state in terms of specific, work-related functional abilities what it is the claimant can or cannot do.

4. This is the best way to describe the limitation in a hypothetical? (True or False). The answer is false. The use of the term "moderate" is problematic because the definition used in the regulations is too broad.

5. Is this best way to describe the limitation in a hypothetical? (Yes or No)

6. This is the best way to describe the limitation in a hypothetical? Is this good phrasing for a hypothetical? (True or False) The answer is basically true, but with an explanation. Some of you may wonder why I think that "occasional" is OK when terms such as "moderate" and "often" are not. The reason is that the word "occasional" is a term that's defined in the Dictionary of Occupational Titles—the DOT—and related publications, and in our rulings.

7. True or False, the Appeals Council will agree with the representative on this issue? The answer is FALSE. The Council will not agree with the claimant's representative because the ALJ is allowed to rely on the VE's testimony since the VE provided a reasonable explanation and the ALJ explained the resolution of the apparent conflict in the decision.

8. Which of the above is consistent with SSA's definition of "unskilled" work?

   A. SVP level of 1 only,
   B. SVP levels of 1 and 2,

PHRASING HYPOTHETICAL QUESTIONS TO VES

    C. SVP levels 1 through 3, or
    D. All of the SVP levels shown.

    The answer is <u>B</u>. As explained in SSR 00-4p, using the skill level definitions in 20 CFR 404.1568 and 416.968, unskilled work corresponds to SVP levels 1 and 2.

9. True or false, the Appeals Council will agree with the representative on this issue?

    The answer is <u>TRUE.</u> Judge Bobowski would agree with the representative. Despite the VE's testimony that there were no conflicts between the evidence he provided and the information shown in the DOT, there is an apparent conflict. The claimant's limitations in reaching and handling do not match the SCO's information on these nonexertional factors. Although SSR 00-4p does not require an ALJ to ensure the accuracy of VE testimony, the unidentified conflict and the incorrect VE testimony raise questions about the reliability of the VE evidence and whether the ALJ's decision is supported by substantial evidence.

PHRASING HYPOTHETICAL QUESTIONS TO VES

APPENDIX: AGENCY FORMS

This section of the Appendix contains copies of the two forms referenced during Judge Cristaudo's presentation.

- Mental RFC Assessment Form used by the DDS: Form SSA-4734-F4-SUP SA-4734

- ODAR Mental Medical Source Statement HA-1152

- Psychiatric Review Technique Form (PRTF) Form SSA-2506

PHRASING HYPOTHETICAL QUESTIONS TO VES

MENTAL RESIDUAL FUNCTIONAL CAPACITY ASSESSMENT

NAME	SOCIAL SECURITY NUMBER

CATEGORIES *(From IB of the PRTF)*	ASSESSMENT IS FOR:
	☐ Current Evaluation ☐ 12 Months After Onset: _____ *(Date)*
	☐ Date Last Insured: _____ *(Date)*
	☐ Other: _____ *(Date)* to _____ *(Date)*

I. SUMMARY CONCLUSIONS

This section is for recording summary conclusions derived from the evidence in file. Each mental activity is to be evaluated within the context of the individual's capacity to sustain that activity over a normal workday and workweek, on an ongoing basis. Detailed explanation of the degree of limitation for each category (A through D), as well as any other assessment information you deem appropriate, is to be recorded in Section III (Functional Capacity Assessment).

If rating category 5 is checked for any of the following items, you MUST specify in Section II the evidence that is needed to make the assessment. If you conclude that the record is so inadequately documented that no accurate functional capacity assessment can be made, indicate in Section II what development is necessary, but DO NOT COMPLETE SECTION III.

	Not Significantly Limited	Moderately Limited	Markedly Limited	No Evidence of Limitation in this Category	Not Ratable on Available Evidence
A. UNDERSTANDING AND MEMORY					
1. The ability to remember locations and work-like procedures.	1. ☐	2. ☐	3. ☐	4. ☐	5. ☐
2. The ability to understand and remember very short and simple instructions.	1. ☐	2. ☐	3. ☐	4. ☐	5. ☐
3. The ability to understand and remember detailed instructions.	1. ☐	2. ☐	3. ☐	4. ☐	5. ☐
B. SUSTAINED CONCENTRATION AND PERSISTENCE					
4. The ability to carry out very short and simple instructions.	1. ☐	2. ☐	3. ☐	4. ☐	5. ☐
5. The ability to carry out detailed instructions.	1. ☐	2. ☐	3. ☐	4. ☐	5. ☐
6. The ability to maintain attention and concentration for extended periods.	1. ☐	2. ☐	3. ☐	4. ☐	5. ☐
7. The ability to perform activities within a schedule, maintain regular attendance, and be punctual within customary tolerances.	1. ☐	2. ☐	3. ☐	4. ☐	5. ☐
8. The ability to sustain an ordinary routine without special supervision.	1. ☐	2. ☐	3. ☐	4. ☐	5. ☐
9. The ability to work in coordination with or proximity to others without being distracted by them.	1. ☐	2. ☐	3. ☐	4. ☐	5. ☐
10. The ability to make simple work-related decisions.	1. ☐	2. ☐	3. ☐	4. ☐	5. ☐

Form **SSA-4734-F4-SUP** (8-85)   1

PHRASING HYPOTHETICAL QUESTIONS TO VES

	Not Significantly Limited	Moderately Limited	Markedly Limited	No Evidence of Limitation in this Category	Not Ratable on Available Evidence
Continued—SUSTAINED CONCENTRATION AND PERSISTENCE					
11. The ability to complete a normal work-day and workweek without interruptions from psychologically based symptoms and to perform at a consistent pace without an unreasonable number and length of rest periods.	1. ☐	2. ☐	3. ☐	4. ☐	5. ☐
C. SOCIAL INTERACTION					
12. The ability to interact appropriately with the general public.	1. ☐	2. ☐	3. ☐	4. ☐	5. ☐
13. The ability to ask simple questions or request assistance.	1. ☐	2. ☐	3. ☐	4. ☐	5. ☐
14. The ability to accept instructions and respond appropriately to criticism from supervisors.	1. ☐	2. ☐	3. ☐	4. ☐	5. ☐
15. The ability to get along with coworkers or peers without distracting them or exhibiting behavioral extremes.	1. ☐	2. ☐	3. ☐	4. ☐	5. ☐
16. The ability to maintain socially appropriate behavior and to adhere to basic standards of neatness and cleanliness.	1. ☐	2. ☐	3. ☐	4. ☐	5. ☐
D. ADAPTATION					
17. The ability to respond appropriately to changes in the work setting.	1. ☐	2. ☐	3. ☐	4. ☐	5. ☐
18. The ability to be aware of normal hazards and take appropriate precautions.	1. ☐	2. ☐	3. ☐	4. ☐	5. ☐
19. The ability to travel in unfamiliar places or use public transportation.	1. ☐	2. ☐	3. ☐	4. ☐	5. ☐
20. The ability to set realistic goals or make plans independently of others.	1. ☐	2. ☐	3. ☐	4. ☐	5. ☐

II. **REMARKS:** If you checked box 5 for any of the preceding items or if any other documentation deficiencies were identified, you MUST specify what additional documentation is needed. Cite the item number(s), as well as any other specific deficiency, and indicate the development to be undertaken.

☐ Continued on Page 3

Form **SSA-4734-F4-SUP** (8-85)   2

PHRASING HYPOTHETICAL QUESTIONS TO VES

☐ Continued on Page 4

III. FUNCTIONAL CAPACITY ASSESSMENT

Record in this section the elaborations on the preceding capacities. Complete this section ONLY after the SUMMARY CONCLUSIONS section has been completed. Explain your summary conclusions in narrative form. Include any information which clarifies limitation or function. Be especially careful to explain conclusions that differ from those of treating medical sources or from the individual's allegations.

☐ Continued on Page 4

MEDICAL CONSULTANT'S SIGNATURE	DATE

Form **SSA-4734-F4-SUP** (8-85)   3

PHRASING HYPOTHETICAL QUESTIONS TO VES

MEDICAL SOURCE STATEMENT OF
ABILITY TO DO WORK-RELATED ACTIVITIES (MENTAL)
===
NAME OF INDIVIDUAL   SOCIAL SECURITY NUMBER

Please assist us in determining this individual's ability to do work-related activities on a sustained basis. "Sustained basis" means the ability to perform work-related activities eight hours a day for five days a week, or an equivalent work schedule. (SSR 96-8p). Please give us your professional opinion of <u>what the individual can still do despite his/her impairment(s)</u>. The opinion should be based on your findings with respect to medical history, clinical and laboratory findings, diagnosis, prescribed treatment and response, and prognosis.

For each activity shown below:

(1)   Respond to the questions about the individual's ability to perform the activity. When doing so, use the following definitions for the rating terms:
- <u>None</u>   --Absent or minimal limitations. If limitations are present they are transient and/or expectable reactions to psychological stresses.
- <u>Slight</u>   --There is some mild limitations in this area, but the individual can generally function well.
- <u>Moderate</u>--There is moderate limitation in this area but the individual is still able to function satisfactorily.
- <u>Marked</u>   --There is serious limitation in this area. The ability to function is severely limited but not precluded.
- <u>Extreme</u>   --There is major limitation in this area. There is no useful ability to function in this area.

(2)   Identify the factors (e.g., the particular medical signs, laboratory findings, or other factors described above) that support your assessment.

IT IS VERY IMPORTANT TO DESCRIBE THE FACTORS THAT SUPPORT YOUR ASSESSMENT.

WE ARE REQUIRED TO CONSIDER THE EXTENT TO WHICH YOUR ASSESSMENT IS SUPPORTED.

(1)   Is ability to understand, remember, and carry out instructions affected by the impairment?   ☐ No   ☐ Yes
If "no," go to question #2. If "yes," please check the appropriate block to describe the individual's restriction for the following work-related mental activities.

	None	Slight	Moderate	Marked	Extreme
Understand and remember short, simple instructions.	☐	☐	☐	☐	☐
Carry out short, simple instructions.	☐	☐	☐	☐	☐
Understand and remember detailed instructions.	☐	☐	☐	☐	☐
Carry out detailed instructions.	☐	☐	☐	☐	☐
The ability to make judgements on simple work-related decisions.	☐	☐	☐	☐	☐

What medical/clinical finding(s) support this assessment?

FORM HA-1152 (4/00)

PHRASING HYPOTHETICAL QUESTIONS TO VES

(2)   Is ability to respond appropriately to supervision, co-workers, and work pressures in a work setting affected by the impairment?   ☐ No   ☐ Yes
If "no," go to question #3. If "yes," please check the appropriate block to describe the individual's restriction for the following work-related mental activities.

	None	Slight	Moderate	Marked	Extreme
Interact appropriately with the public.	☐	☐	☐	☐	☐
Interact appropriately with supervisor(s).	☐	☐	☐	☐	☐
Interact appropriately with co-workers.	☐	☐	☐	☐	☐
Respond appropriately to work pressures in a usual work setting.	☐	☐	☐	☐	☐
Respond appropriately to changes in a routine work setting.	☐	☐	☐	☐	☐

What supports this assessment?

(3)   Are any other capabilities affected by the impairment?   ☐ No   ☐ Yes
If "yes," please identify the capability and describe how it is affected.

Capability   Effect
_____   _____
_____   _____
_____   _____

What medical/clinical findings support this assessment?

(4)   If the claimant's impairment(s) include alcohol and/or substance abuse, do these impairments contribute to any of the claimant's limitations as set forth above? If so, please list the specific limitations caused.

(5)   If you have concluded that the medical record indicates that the claimant's alcohol and/or substance use/abuse contributes to any limitations as set forth above, please identify and explain what changes you would make to your answers if the claimant was totally abstinent from alcohol and/or substance use/abuse.

(6)   Can the individual manage benefits in his/her own best interest?   ☐ No   ☐ Yes

_____   _____   _____
Physician's/Psychologist's Signature   Medical Specialty   Date

FORM HA-1152 (4/00)

PHRASING HYPOTHETICAL QUESTIONS TO VES

Psychiatric Review Technique Form "B" Criteria

RATING OF FUNCTIONAL LIMITATIONS
A. "B" Criteria of the Listings
Indicate to what degree the following functional limitations (which are found in paragraph B of listings 12.02-12.04, 12.06-12.08 and 12.10 and paragraph D of 12.05) exist as a result of the individual's mental disorder(s). NOTE: Item 4 below is more than a measure of frequency and duration. See 12.00C4 and also read carefully the instructions for this section.
Specify the listing(s) (i.e., 12.02 through 12.10) under which the items below are being rated _____
FUNCTIONAL LIMITATION DEGREE OF LIMITATION
Insufficient
1. Restriction of Activities None Mild Moderate Marked* Extreme* Evidence of Daily Living
Insufficient

2. Difficulties in Maintaining None Mild Moderate Marked* Extreme* Evidence Social Functioning
Insufficient

3. Difficulties in Maintaining None Mild Moderate Marked* Extreme* Evidence Concentration, Persistence,
or Pace One Four* or Insufficient

4. Repeated Episodes of None Two Three* More Evidence Decompensation, Each of Extended Duration
*Degree of limitation that satisfies the functional criterion.

Appendix 7: Social Security Administration Telephone Numbers and Addresses

Toll Free: (800) 772-1213
FOIA Requests: Freedom of Information Officer, SSA
                                                3-A-6 Operations Building
                                                6401 Security Blvd.
                                                Baltimore, MD 21235

Online FOIA Request: http://www.socialsecurity.gov/foia/

Appeals Council

Address: Appeals Council
                                                Office of Disability Adjudication & Review, SSA
                                                5107 Leesburg Pike
                                                Falls Church, VA 22041-3255

Fax: (703) 605-7101, (703) 605-7201

AC Public Inquiries Staff: Telephone: (877) 670-2722 or (703) 605-8000
                                                Fax: (703) 605-8021
Attorney's Fees   Office of Disability Adjudication & Review, SSA
(for cases authorized at   Attorney Fee Staff
Appeals Council level)   5107 Leesburg Pike
                                                Falls Church, VA 22041-3255
                                                Telephone: (703) 605-7900
                                                Fax: (703) 605-7901

Chief Administrative   Office of the Chief ALJ
Law Judge   Office of Disability Adjudication & Review, SSA
                                                5107 Leesburg Pike, Suite 1500
                                                Falls Church, VA 22041-3255
                                                Telephone: (703) 605-8500
                                                Fax: (703) 605-8501

Appeals Council Ombudsman
Terry Jensen   Fax: (703) 605-8691

SECOND AND THIRD FOLLOW-UP LETTER ADDRESSES AND FAX NUMBERS—SSI FEE AGREEMENTS ONLY

REGIONAL OFFICE ADDRESSES & FAX NUMBERS

Region I—BOSTON

States: Connecticut, Maine, Massachusetts, New Hampshire, Rhode Island, Vermont

Office of the Regional Commissioner
JFK Federal Building
Room 1900
Boston, MA 02203
Attorney Fee Specialist—Fax number (617) 565-9359
Executive Officer—Fax number (617) 565-2143

Region II—NEW YORK

States: New Jersey, New York, Puerto Rico, Virgin Island

Social Security Administration
NYPOC
Attn: Attorney Fee Specialist
26 Federal Plaza, Room 4032B
New York, NY 10278
Attorney Fee Specialist—Fax number (212) 264-2071

Social Security Administration
Attn: Executive Officer
26 Federal Plaza, Room 40-102
New York, NY 10278
Executive Officer—Fax number (212) 264-6847

Region III—PHILADELPHIA

States: Delaware, District of Columbia, Maryland, Pennsylvania, Virginia, West Virginia

Office of the Regional Commissioner
P.O. Box 8788
Philadelphia, PA 19104
Attorney Fee Specialist—Fax number (215) 597-5206
Executive Officer—Fax number (215) 597-2827

Region IV—ATLANTA

States: Alabama, Florida, Georgia, Kentucky, Mississippi, North Carolina, South Carolina, Tennessee

Office of the Regional Commissioner
61 Forsyth Street, SW
Suite 23T64
Atlanta, GA 30303-8907
Attorney Fee Specialist—Fax number (404) 562-1325
Executive Officer—Fax number (404) 562-5608

Region V—CHICAGO

States: Illinois, Indiana, Michigan, Minnesota, Ohio, Wisconsin

Office of the Regional Commissioner
Attn: Attorney Fee Specialist / Executive Officer
10th Floor
Social Security Administration
P.O. Box 8280
Chicago, IL 60680-8280
Attorney Fee Specialist—Fax number (312) 575-4221
Executive Officer—Fax number (312) 575-4016

Region VI—DALLAS
States: Arkansas, Louisiana, New Mexico, Oklahoma, Texas

Office of the Regional Commissioner
1301 Young Street
Suite 500
Dallas, TX 75202-5433
Attorney Fee Specialist—Fax number (214) 767-8267
Executive Officer—Fax number (214) 767-4259

Region VII—KANSAS CITY

States: Iowa, Kansas, Missouri, Nebraska

Office of the Regional Commissioner
Federal Building
Room 436
601 East 12th Street
Kansas City, MO 64106
Attorney Fee Specialist—Fax number (816) 936-5951
Executive Officer—Fax number (816) 936-5972

Region VIII—DENVER

States: Colorado, Montana, North Dakota, South Dakota, Utah, Wyoming

Office of the Regional Commissioner
Federal Building
Room 325
1961 Stout Street
Denver, CO 80294
Attorney Fee Specialist—Fax number (303) 844-3281
Executive Officer—Fax number (303) 844-6767

Region IX—SAN FRANCISCO

States: Arizona, California, Hawaii, Nevada, American Samoa, Guam

Office of the Regional Commissioner
Frank Hagel Federal Building
1221 Nevin Avenue
Richmond, CA 94801
Attorney Fee Specialist—Fax number (510) 970-8101
Executive Officer—Fax number (510) 970-8216

Region X—SEATTLE

States: Alaska, Idaho, Oregon, Washington

Office of the Regional Commissioner
701 Fifth Avenue
Suite 2900, M/S 303A
Seattle, WA 98104-7075
Attorney Fee Specialist—Fax number (206) 615-2643
Executive Officer—Fax number (206) 615-2193

Appendix 8: **Vocational Expert Handbook**

SOCIAL SECURITY ADMINISTRATION
OFFICE OF DISABILITY ADJUDICATION AND REVIEW
OFFICE OF THE CHIEF ADMINISTRATIVE LAW JUDGE

VOCATIONAL EXPERT HANDBOOK

June 2011

VOCATIONAL EXPERT HANDBOOK
Office of Disability Adjudication and Review
Office of the Chief Administrative Law Judge

Preface

Thank you for becoming a vocational expert for our Office of Disability Adjudication and Review (ODAR). This handbook provides the basic information you will need when you participate in administrative law judge (ALJ) hearings. The handbook explains Social Security's disability programs, the appeals process we use, your role and responsibilities, and technical information you must know.

We hope that you will find this handbook interesting and useful. If you have any comments or questions about it, please write or call:

Social Security Office of Disability Adjudication and Review
Office of the Chief Administrative Law Judge
5107 Leesburg Pike, Suite 1500
Falls Church, VA 22041
(703) 605-8500

Table of Contents

In General-Disability Overview, Vocational Experts, and the Social Security Appeals Process

What are Social Security's Disability Programs?

The Social Security Administration (SSA) administers several programs that pay disability benefits to individuals. Disability benefits may be paid to people who work in "covered" employment or self-employment and who pay sufficient Social Security taxes[1] to become "insured" for disability benefits. There are also disability benefits that may be paid to the disabled adult children of insured workers who retire, die, or are themselves disabled, and disability benefits that may be paid to certain disabled widows and widowers of insured workers. We often refer to these as "Title II" disability benefits in reference to the title of the Social Security Act[2] (the Act) that provides for these benefits.

We administer another disability program under Title XVI of the Act. Title XVI provides payments of Supplemental Security Income (SSI) to individuals who are age 65 or older, or blind, or disabled, and who have limited income and resources. SSI payments are funded from general tax revenues and not from Social Security taxes, because eligibility for Title XVI programs is not based on payment of Social Security taxes.

Where Do You Fit In?

We use Vocational Experts (VEs) to provide evidence at hearings before an administrative law judge (ALJ). At this level of our *administrative review process* people ask for a *de novo* hearing before an ALJ regarding a prior determination on their claim for benefits under the Social Security disability program.

The administrative review process is our term for a multi-step process of application (or other initial determination) and appeals.

In general, there are four levels in the SSA administrative review process:

---

[1] Federal Insurance Contributions Act (FICA) or Self-Employment Contributions Act (SECA) taxes.
[2] The Social Security Act, 42 U.S.C. 301 et seq., is the federal law governing Social Security Benefits.

1

- Initial determination

- Reconsideration

- ALJ hearing

- Appeals Council review

After they complete the administrative review process, claimants who are still dissatisfied with our final decision generally have the right to appeal to federal district court.

At the initial and reconsideration levels, state agencies (often called "Disability Determination Services" or *DDSs*) make disability determinations for us. Although DDSs are state agencies, we fully fund their operations, and they make disability determinations using our rules. DDSs obtain medical, vocational, and other evidence they need to make these determinations, including arranging for independent medical examinations, which we call "consultative examinations" (CEs), when they need them. In general, the determination at the DDS is made by a team consisting of a medical professional (called a *medical consultant* or *psychological consultant*) and a lay *disability examiner*.[3] While DDS adjudicators routinely contact claimants to collect information, they usually do not meet with claimants. The DDS disability determination is based on a weighing of documentary evidence in the claimant's case file.

Most people who qualify for disability benefits are found disabled by the DDS at the initial and reconsideration levels. Nevertheless, people whose claims are denied or who are otherwise dissatisfied with their determinations[4] may appeal their claims to the ALJ hearing level, the level at which you will be asked to provide evidence.

At certain times, we also review whether people who are already receiving disability benefits continue to be disabled. When such people are dissatisfied with our determination about whether they are still disabled, they too can appeal. The process is somewhat different from the initial claims process, but like the initial process, it has an ALJ hearing level, and you may be

---

[3] Depending on where you work, you may encounter variations to the foregoing procedures. For example, in some states there is no reconsideration level, and in some, a special kind of disability examiner called a "single decisionmaker" may make the initial determination alone in some cases without getting input from a medical or psychological consultant. This is because we are testing variations to our usual processes in some states.

[4] For example, some people are found disabled at the DDS level, but not for the entire period they claimed.

asked to provide evidence for such a hearing. We provide more information about this step beginning on page 20.

What is a "VE"?

A VE is a vocational professional who provides impartial expert opinion evidence that an ALJ considers when making a decision about disability. As a VE, you will usually testify in person at a hearing, although you may be asked to testify by video teleconferencing (VTC) technology or by telephone, and sometimes you may provide opinions in writing by answering written questions called *interrogatories* (which we explain on page 39).

What is an ALJ?

An ALJ is the official who presides at our administrative hearings. Our ALJs perform a number of duties, including administering oaths, examining witnesses, receiving evidence, making findings of fact, and deciding whether an individual is or is not disabled. Our ALJs are SSA employees and hold hearings on behalf of the Commissioner of Social Security.

What is "Disability" for Social Security Programs?

The Act provides two definitions of disability. One definition applies to all Title II claims and to claims of individuals age 18 and older under Title XVI (SSI). There is a separate definition for children (individuals who have not attained age 18) under the SSI program.[5]

The general definition of disability under Title II and for adults under Title XVI is:

> [The] inability to engage in any substantial gainful activity by reason of any medically determinable physical or mental impairment which can be expected to result in death or which has lasted or can be expected to last for a continuous period of not less than 12 months.

Under title II of the Act, a person may also be disabled based on blindness, which is defined as:

> [C]entral visual acuity of 20/200 or less in the better eye with the use of a correcting lens. An eye which is accompanied by a limitation in

---

[5] The definition is not based on work, so you will not be asked to testify in cases in which the only issue is whether a child is disabled for SSI purposes; therefore, we will not discuss SSI childhood disability further in this handbook.

the fields of vision such that the widest diameter of the visual field subtends an angle no greater than 20 degrees shall be considered . . . as having a central visual acuity of 20/200 or less.

The SSI program contains an identical definition of the term "blindness" for purposes of determining whether an individual is eligible for benefits based on blindness under the SSI program.

There is more detail to the definition of disability for adults in the Act— including provisions that require the ALJ to determine the claimant's ability:

- To do previous work, and
- To make an adjustment to other work considering the effects of his or her medical condition(s) and the *vocational factors* of age, education, and work experience.

We have detailed regulations and other rules defining all the terms in the Act and explaining our requirements for determining disability. We describe these rules in more detail beginning on page 12.

What Happens at the ALJ Hearing?[6]

In the vast majority of cases at the hearing level, ALJs hold hearings at which claimants, and sometimes other people,[7] appear and testify. This is generally the first time in the administrative review process that the claimant has a chance to see and talk to the person who will make the disability decision. However, a claimant may ask the ALJ to make a decision without an in-person hearing, based only on the documents in his or her case record. You may be asked to provide evidence in both kinds of cases, either by testifying at a hearing or by submitting written opinions in response to interrogatories.

At the hearing, the ALJ will have all of the documentary information that the DDS considered at the initial and reconsideration levels. The claimant generally also has submitted more evidence in connection with his or her appeal. Although ALJ hearings are more informal than court proceedings, the ALJ will swear in the claimant and any other witnesses, including you. Most claimants are represented by an attorney or other representative, but there is no requirement that the claimant have a representative. The hearing is non-adversarial; that is, there is no representative for SSA who argues in favor of the DDS determination. The ALJ is responsible for

---

[6] See page 9 of this handbook for additional information about prehearing review and preliminary questions the ALJ will ask you to establish your expertise and impartiality.
[7] Such as family members and medical and vocational expert witnesses.

assisting the claimant and following the Act, regulations, and other rules, and is an impartial decisionmaker.

The ALJ will ask you questions before you testify to establish your independence and impartiality, and your qualifications and competence to testify in vocational matters. If the ALJ does not already have it, you should provide him or her with a written résumé or curriculum vitae summarizing your experience and background, which the ALJ will enter into the case record as evidence. The ALJ will also ask you whether the résumé or curriculum vitae is accurate and up to date, and will likely ask you whether you are familiar with applicable SSA regulations and other rules. The ALJ will also ask the claimant and his or her representative, if any, whether they object to your testifying.

In many cases, all of the participants in the hearing will be present in the same room for the hearing. However, increasingly, we have been using VTC technology to improve our capacity to hold timely hearings. You may be asked to testify by VTC or by telephone. Regardless of how the testimony is given, the ALJ will question the claimant, you, and any other witnesses. The claimant and his or her representative will also have an opportunity to question you and other witnesses and to make arguments to the ALJ. The ALJ has the authority to determine the propriety of any questions asked. The hearing will be recorded.

You may be present throughout the entire hearing or the ALJ may decide that you should come into the hearing at a specific time. If you are not present throughout the hearing, the ALJ may summarize the relevant vocational testimony.

After the hearing, the ALJ will generally consider all the evidence and issue a written decision. Sometimes the ALJ will get more information after the hearing that necessitates additional questions of the vocational expert. The ALJ may then ask you to answer written questions called *interrogatories*.[8] These may be the ALJ's own questions or questions submitted by the claimant or his or her representative. The ALJ may also decide to hold another hearing called a *supplemental hearing*.

---

[8] Interrogatories are explained on page 39.

What is the Appeals Council?

The Appeals Council is the last level of appeal within SSA. There are no local Appeals Council offices throughout the country. The Appeals Council's headquarters is in Falls Church, Virginia; it also has offices in Baltimore, Maryland.

If the claimant is dissatisfied with the ALJ's decision, he or she may request Appeals Council review. The Appeals Council may grant, deny, or dismiss the request for review. If the Appeals Council denies the request to review the ALJ's decision, the ALJ's decision will become SSA's final decision. If the Appeals Council grants the request for review, it may make its own decision reversing, modifying, or affirming the ALJ's decision. In that case, the Appeals Council's decision becomes SSA's final decision.

In most cases, when the Appeals Council grants a request for review, it does not make its own decision. Instead, the Appeals Council *remands* (returns) the case to the ALJ for additional action, including possibly a new hearing and decision. You may be asked to testify at an ALJ hearing that results from an Appeals Council remand.

What are Federal Court Appeals?

If the claimant is dissatisfied with SSA's final decision in the administrative review process, he or she may file a civil action in a United States District Court. The district court may uphold, modify, or reverse SSA's final decision. In some cases, the district court will remand the case to SSA for further proceedings, which may include a new ALJ hearing and decision. You may be asked to testify at an ALJ hearing that results from a district court remand.

The claimant can continue to appeal his or her case in the federal courts to a United States Court of Appeals (a "circuit court") and eventually to the Supreme Court of the United States, although this is extremely rare. At each of these levels, it is possible that the court will remand the case to SSA for a new hearing at which you may be asked to testify.

Role of the VE

Responsibilities of the VE

ALJs use VEs in many cases in which they must determine whether a claimant can do his or her previous work or other work. A VE provides both factual and expert opinion evidence based on knowledge of:

- The skill level and physical and mental demands of occupations.

- The characteristics of work settings.

- The existence and incidence of jobs within occupations.

- Transferrable skills analysis and SSA regulatory requirements for *transferability* of work skills.

You should have:

- Up-to-date knowledge of, and experience with, industrial and occupational trends and local labor market conditions.

- An understanding of how we determine whether a claimant is disabled, especially at steps 4 and 5 of the *sequential evaluation process* we describe beginning on page 13.

- Current and extensive experience in counseling and job placement of people with disabilities.

- Knowledge of, and experience using, vocational reference sources, including:

  → The *Dictionary of Occupational Titles* (*DOT*) and the *Selected Characteristics of Occupations Defined in the Revised Dictionary of Occupational Titles* (*SCO*);[9]

  → *County Business Patterns* published by the Bureau of Census;

  → The *Occupational Outlook Handbook* published by the Bureau of Labor Statistics; and

---

[9] For simplicity, we refer only to the *DOT* in the remainder of this handbook. It should be understood that when we refer to the *DOT*, we mean the *SCO* as well whenever appropriate.

→ Any occupational surveys of occupations prepared for SSA by various state employment agencies.

We have rules for determining whether a claimant can make an adjustment to work other than work that he or she previously performed. ALJs frequently ask for VE testimony in these cases. We provide more details regarding these issues later in this handbook.

At the Hearing

You will provide evidence by answering questions posed by the ALJ and the claimant or the claimant's representative. Questions will typically be framed based on hypothetical findings of age, education, work experience, and functional limitations. You *may* answer questions about issues that could be decisive in a case, such as whether a claimant could still do his or her previous work given hypothetical findings about functional limitations an ALJ will provide you. You should never comment on medical matters, such as what you believe the medical evidence indicates about the claimant's diagnosis or the functional limitations caused by the claimant's impairment(s) (SSA's term for medical conditions), or whether you believe the claimant is disabled.

You will rarely have the opportunity to question the claimant directly during the hearing. If you have any questions—e.g., about an aspect of a claimant's testimony—or you need more information, you should inform the ALJ. The ALJ will decide whether the information is pertinent and how it should be elicited; the ALJ may ask the question himself or herself or allow you to ask the question.

The ALJ will not rely on your testimony alone to make his or her ultimate decision about disability or any of vocational findings that go into the decision. The ALJ will consider your testimony together with the other evidence in the case record, including the claimant's testimony at the hearing and any other testimony. Your testimony may also help the ALJ determine whether he or she needs more evidence in order to make a decision.

Conduct of the VE

You are giving sworn testimony and should conduct yourself as if you are testifying in a civil or criminal court. Give complete answers to the questions you are asked, and do not volunteer information. Whenever possible, you should phrase your answers in lay terms. To ensure impartiality, you must avoid any substantive contact with the ALJ before or after the hearing, and avoid face-to-face or telephone contact with the claimant or his or her representative, both before and after the hearing. You must disqualify yourself if you believe that you cannot be completely impartial, have prior knowledge of the case, or have had prior contact with the claimant. However, the ALJ will not disqualify you merely because you testified in a previous case regarding the same claimant.

Pre-Hearing Preparation

The ALJ will generally provide you with relevant portions of the case file before the hearing. (You must fully understand the importance of proper handling of this information; please read the next section "Protecting Personally Identifiable Information (PII)" carefully.) This will give you a chance to become familiar with the vocational evidence in the claim. It will also prepare you to answer the kinds of questions—such as questions about the requirements of the claimant's previous work and the existence of other work in the national economy—you can expect to get at the hearing. If after reviewing this information you believe that you need more information to provide adequate testimony, you should prepare a written list of your questions and refer them to the ALJ.

Generally, the period under consideration for establishment of disability in initial claims begins with the date the claimant alleges that he or she became disabled (commonly referred to as the *alleged onset date*, or AOD) and goes through the date of the ALJ's decision. However, there are situations requiring evaluation of the claimant's medical condition at an earlier time[10] or that start at a later time. The ALJ will advise you of the period under consideration.

Protecting Personally Identifiable Information (PII)

The Social Security Administration defines PII as any information which can be used to distinguish or trace an individual's identity (such as his or her name, Social Security number, biometric records, etc.) alone, or when combined with other personal or identifying information which is linked or linkable to a specific individual (such as date and place of birth, mother's maiden name, etc.). SSA is mandated to safeguard and protect the PII entrusted to the agency and to immediately report breaches to the Department of Homeland Security.

---

[10] For example, as we note in the next section, a worker's insured status under Title II can expire. In this situation, the worker can still qualify for disability benefits, but must show that he or she was disabled on or before this *date last insured*.

The claimant information the ALJ provides to you, which may be in paper or electronic form, must be protected against loss, theft, or inadvertent disclosure. Failure to take the proper steps to protect this information, or to immediately report to SSA when you suspect PII is compromised, could adversely affect your standing and may result in reduced requests for your services. To maintain good standing with SSA, follow these instructions to reduce the risk of PII loss, theft or inadvertent disclosure:

- Ensure your employees are fully aware of these procedures and the importance of protecting PII.
- If you are expecting to receive claimant information from SSA, and you have not received it within the expected time frame, immediately notify your SSA contact or alternate contact.
- Secure all SSA claimant information in a locked container, such as a locked filing cabinet, or while in transit, in a locked briefcase.
- Once you arrive at your destination, always move PII to the most secure location. Do not leave PII locked in a car trunk overnight.
- When viewing a claimant's file, prevent others in the area from viewing the file's contents.
- Ensure PII is appropriately returned or, upon receiving SSA's approval, destroyed when no longer needed.

In the event of a loss, theft, or disclosure you must immediately notify your primary SSA contact or alternate contact. Report the following information, as completely and accurately as possible:

- Your contact information
- A description of the loss, theft, or disclosure, including the approximate time and location of the incident
- A description of safeguards used, as applicable
- Whether you have contacted, or been contacted, by any external organizations (i.e., other agencies, law enforcement, press, etc.), and whether you have filed any other reports
- Any other pertinent information

If you are unable to reach your SSA contacts, call SSA's National Network Service Center (NNSC) toll free at 1-877-697-4889. Provide them with the information outlined above. Record the Change, Asset, and Problem Reporting System (CAPRS) number which the NNSC will assign to you. Limit disclosure of the information and details about the incident to only those with a need to know. The security/PII loss incident reporting process will ensure that SSA's reporting requirements are met and that security/PII loss incident information is only shared appropriately.

Delay in reporting may adversely affect SSA's ability to investigate and resolve the incident and may contribute to a determination of reduced requests for your services.

Determining Disability

You may be asked to give evidence in any kind of disability case under the programs we administer, except childhood disability cases under Title XVI. Most often, you will be giving evidence in cases of insured workers (see page 1) under Title II and adults claiming SSI disability benefits under Title XVI, or "concurrent" claims for both benefits. Less often, you may testify at hearings concerning the other kinds of disability cases described below.

Detailed Definitions of Disability

The Social Security Act defines disability in all Title II claims and in adult Title XVI claims as the inability to engage in any substantial gainful activity by reason of any medically determinable physical or mental impairment(s) which can be expected to result in death, or which has lasted or can be expected to last for a continuous period of not less than 12 months.[11] The latter part of the definition is the "duration requirement."

"Inability to engage in any substantial gainful activity" means that a claimant's impairment(s) must not only prevent him or her from performing previous work, but from making an adjustment to any other kind of substantial gainful work that exists in significant numbers in the national economy, considering his or her age, education, and previous work experience. The law specifies that it is irrelevant whether:

- The work exists in the immediate area where the claimant lives,

- A specific job vacancy exists, or

- The claimant would be hired if he or she applied for work.

In other words, the question is not whether the claimant can *get* a job, only whether he or she can *do* it.

---

[11] As we have already noted, there is also a statutory definition of blindness under Titles II and XVI, but under Title II, blindness is a kind of "disability," while under Title XVI it is a category separate from "disability." There is also a separate definition of disability under Title II for people who are at least 55 years old and blind. These technical, legal distinctions do not affect your work as a vocational expert. We provided the statutory definition of blindness on page 3 of this handbook.

Determining Initial Disability for All Title II and Adult Title XVI Cases

The Sequential Evaluation Process

We have extensive regulations and other rules that interpret the provisions of the Act described above and instruct our ALJs and other adjudicators on how to determine whether a claimant is disabled or still disabled. The rules interpreting the basic definition of disability for adults provide a five-step *sequential evaluation process* that we use to determine whether a claimant is disabled. We use different sequential processes to determine whether beneficiaries continue to be disabled (*Continuing Disability Review*, or CDR, and redeterminations of the disability of individuals who qualified for SSI as children when they reach age 18).

The sequential evaluation process requires the adjudicator to follow the steps in order, and at each step, either make a decision, in which case the evaluation stops, or decide that a decision cannot be made at that step. When the ALJ determines that a decision cannot be made at a given step, he or she goes on to the next step(s) until a decision can be made. 20 CFR 404.1520 and 416.920.[12]

Note that for each of the first four steps described below, we explain that the ALJ may stop and make a decision. However, with some exceptions,[13] ALJs generally do not make their decisions at the hearing. ALJs generally issue a written decision some time after the hearing. ALJs generally ask for information relevant to all of the steps of the sequential evaluation process at the hearing. The description below explains the steps that an ALJ follows when making disability decisions.

---

[12] "20 CFR" is a reference to Title 20 of the *Code of Federal Regulations* (CFR). The CFR is a compilation of all federal regulations, and Title 20 contains SSA's regulations. Regulation section numbers that start with the number "404" are Title II regulations; those that start with the number "416" are for Title XVI. See the List of References at the end of this handbook for more information about our regulations and other rules.

[13] The most common exception is under a rule we have that allows an ALJ to announce at the hearing that he or she has found that the claimant is disabled. ALJs cannot announce denial decisions at the hearing.

STEP 1:   Is the claimant engaging in substantial gainful activity?[14]

Substantial gainful activity (SGA) is work that: (a) involves doing significant physical or mental activities; and (b) is usually done for pay or profit, whether or not a profit is realized. Generally, we do not consider activities like self-care, household tasks, hobbies, therapy, school attendance, club activities, or social programs to be substantial gainful activity.

SGA is most often measured by gross monthly earnings. When countable monthly earnings are above a prescribed amount, which increases each year, the claimant is generally considered to be engaging in SGA. Self-employed individuals are engaging in SGA when they perform significant services in a business, work comparable to unimpaired individuals, or work which is worth the prescribed monthly SGA amount. Since the basic definition of disability is "inability to engage in any substantial gainful activity," we find that a claimant who is actually doing SGA is "not disabled" regardless of the severity of his or her impairment(s).

STEP 2:   Does the claimant have a "severe" impairment?

The ALJ will generally consider two issues at this step: whether the claimant has a "medically determinable impairment" and, if so, whether it is "severe."[15] The Act requires that the claimant show the existence of an impairment by medically acceptable clinical and laboratory diagnostic techniques, which we often refer to as "objective" medical evidence.

The word "severe" is a term of art in SSA's rules. An impairment or a combination of impairments is "severe" if it significantly limits a claimant's ability to do one or more basic work activities needed to do most jobs. Under SSA's rules, abilities and aptitudes necessary to do most jobs include physical functions, such as walking, standing, sitting, lifting, pushing, pulling, reaching, carrying, handling, seeing, hearing, and speaking. They also include mental functions, such as understanding, carrying out and remembering simple instructions; using judgment; responding appropriately to supervision, co-workers, and usual work situations; and dealing with changes in a routine work setting. 20 CFR 404.1521 and 416.921.

Even though the rules defining a "severe" impairment refer to basic work-related activities, you should not expect to provide any testimony about this

---

[14] 20 CFR 404.1574, 404.1575, 416.974, and 416.975 provide evaluation guides for determining whether work is SGA.

[15] There is no requirement to establish a medically determinable impairment that results in blindness under Title XVI.

step of the process. The ALJ will determine whether the claimant has any medically determinable impairments, whether they result in limitations, and whether any limitations affect the claimant's ability to do basic work-related activities, and should not need any information from you for these issues.

If the claimant does not have a medically determinable impairment, or if the medically determinable impairment(s) is not "severe," the claimant is not disabled and the analysis stops. If the claimant has at least one "severe" medically determinable impairment or a number of non-severe impairments that are severe when considered in combination, the ALJ goes to the next step.

> **STEP 3**:   Does the claimant have an impairment(s) that meets or medically equals a listed impairment in the Listing of Impairments?

The ALJ will find that the claimant is disabled when the objective medical and other findings associated with the claimant's medically determinable impairment(s) satisfies all of the criteria for an impairment described in the Listing of Impairments set out in Appendix 1, Subpart P of Part 404 of our regulations (the listings)[16] and meets the "duration requirement." Disability may also be established when the claimant has an impairment or a combination of impairments with findings that do not meet the specific requirements of a listed impairment, but are medically equivalent in severity to the findings of a listed impairment and meet the duration requirement.

The Listings describe, for each "body system," medically determinable impairments and associated findings that we consider severe enough to prevent an adult from doing "any gainful activity" regardless of his or her age, education, or work experience. Note that this is a stricter standard from the standard in the basic definition of disability for adults, "any *substantial* gainful activity." The listings describe a higher level of severity because they do not consider the vocational factors of previous work experience, age, and education that are considered at the last step of the sequential evaluation process.

You will not be asked to testify about anything related to the listings.

---

[16] We print the listings only in Part 404 (the Title II regulations) to save space in the CFR. They also apply to Title XVI.

Residual Functional Capacity (RFC)

If the claimant is not engaging in SGA and has at least one severe impairment that does not meet or medically equal a listing, the ALJ must assess the claimant's RFC before going on to step 4. The RFC assessment is a description of the physical and mental work functions the claimant can still perform in a work setting on a sustained basis despite his or her impairment(s).

RFC is the *most* that the claimant can still do despite the limitations caused by his or her impairment(s), including any related physical or mental symptoms, such as pain, fatigue, shortness of breath, weakness, or nervousness. However, at the hearing the ALJ may describe the claimant's functioning in terms of limitations and restrictions as well.

Note that the ALJ must consider limitations from *all* of the claimant's impairments, including limitations from any medically determinable impairment that is not "severe." As you saw under step 2, our definition of "severe" is based on work functioning. Therefore, an impairment that is not "severe" might still cause some slight or minimal limitations in functioning, and those limitations might affect the claimant's ability to do some jobs or job functions.

You should not be asked your opinion about the claimant's RFC, functional abilities, limitations, or restrictions. If you are asked (by an ALJ, a claimant, or a representative) you should not respond. Instead, as we explain below, the ALJ will pose one or more questions to you (called *hypotheticals,* see page 34) that will include various possible RFC findings that he or she might make.

There are two important additional agency policies about RFC you should know:

- First, RFC is generally what an individual can still do on a "regular and continuing basis," 8 hours a day, for 5 days a week, or an equivalent work schedule; that is, in a work setting.[17]

- Second, RFC considers only the effects of the claimant's medically determinable impairment(s). By rule, the ALJ cannot consider the

_____

[17] In some cases, the ALJ may ask you a hypothetical that is not consistent with full-time work. There are two main situations in which this will happen: 1. The ALJ is posing a hypothetical RFC that assumes that he or she has accepted a claimant's alleged limitations, and those allegations are inconsistent with full-time employment. 2. The ALJ is trying to determine whether the claimant is capable of doing previous work that was part-time work.

claimant's age, sex, body habitus,[18] or overall conditioning when determining RFC, but only limitations that result from documented medically determinable impairments.

See Social Security Ruling (SSR) 96-8p.[19]

The ALJ evaluates the claimant's ability to meet the physical, mental, sensory and other requirements of work. The ALJ considers physical abilities, including: exertional activities (e.g., sitting, standing, walking, lifting, carrying, pushing, and pulling); postural activities (e.g., stooping, climbing); manipulative activities (e.g., reaching, handling); vision; the physical aspects of communication (hearing, speaking); and environmental factors (e.g., tolerance of temperature extremes or dusty environments). The ALJ will also consider mental functions (e.g., understanding and remembering instructions of various complexities, concentrating, getting along with coworkers and the public, responding appropriately to supervision, and responding to changes in the workplace).

As suggested in the preceding paragraph, our rules recognize the same seven *exertional* (strength) limitations as in the *DOT*. All other physical limitations (including postural, manipulative, communicative, visual, and environmental) and mental limitations are *nonexertional*. Our rules also use the same strength ratings to categorize work as in the *DOT*; i.e., sedentary, light, medium, heavy, and very heavy.

STEP 4:   Can the claimant do past relevant work?

After assessing RFC, the ALJ will decide whether the claimant is able to do any *past relevant work* (PRW), either as the claimant actually performed it or as the work is generally performed in the national economy. The term "PRW" is generally defined as the work the claimant performed at the SGA level within the last 15 years (or before certain ending dates specified in our rules) and includes only jobs that lasted long enough for the claimant to learn to do them.

The ALJ will make this determination by comparing the claimant's RFC with the requirements of these jobs. For this step of the sequential evaluation process, the ALJ may call on you to provide information about such issues as:

---

[18] Note, however, that SSA may consider obesity to be a medically determinable impairment.

[19] A Social Security Ruling is a type of sub-regulatory rule that ALJs and our other adjudicators must follow. See the List of References at the end of this handbook for the title of this SSR and a list of important SSRs that you must know about.

- What a claimant's jobs were in the 15 years before the hearing or another date that the ALJ specifies,

- Whether they lasted long enough for the claimant to learn how to do them,

- The physical and mental demands of a job as the claimant says he or she *actually* performed it, and

- The physical and mental requirements of the job as it is usually performed in the national economy, if it is performed in the national economy.[20]

If there is PRW that the claimant can still do, the claimant is not disabled and the analysis stops. If the claimant cannot do any PRW, or does not have any PRW, the ALJ will continue to the last step.

STEP 5:   Can the claimant do other work?

If the ALJ finds that the claimant can no longer do any PRW, or the claimant does not have any PRW, the ALJ must finally consider whether the claimant can make an adjustment to other work which exists in significant numbers in the national economy. In making his finding on this issue, the ALJ must consider the claimant's RFC, age, education, and past relevant work experience. To do this, the ALJ must refer to the *Medical-Vocational Guidelines,* in Appendix 2 of Subpart P of Part 404 of our regulations[21] (often called the *grid rules* or the *grids*).[22] Appendix 2 includes three tables with rules that provide a matrix of various combinations of RFC, age, education, and past relevant work experience. When the facts of a claimant's case match a grid rule exactly, the rule directs a conclusion of either "disabled" or "not disabled." If the claimant's characteristics do not match a grid rule, the ALJ must use the rules in Appendix 2 as a *framework* for decision making. You will often be asked to testify in the latter type of case. We provide more

---

[20] Work a claimant performed outside of the United States can be PRW, but in that case we consider only how the claimant actually performed it, not how it is usually performed in another country. See SSR 82-40. Also **note** that PRW does not have to exist in significant numbers, so you will not have to be prepared to testify about numbers of jobs with regard to a claimant's PRW. The issue of significant numbers arises only at step 5.

[21] In some cases, an ALJ can find that a claimant is disabled under special rules that do not involve the grid rules we discuss in the rest of this paragraph and in more detail later in this handbook. You do not need to know about these rules. In the unlikely event that an ALJ needs your testimony to determine whether one of the special medical-vocational profiles applies in a case, he or she will give you instructions.

[22] We print the grid rules only in Part 404 (the Title II regulations) to save space in the CFR. They also apply to Title XVI.

information about the grid rules, the vocational factors, the other terms related to step 5, and questions you should be prepared to answer beginning on page 23 of this handbook.

At this last step of the sequential evaluation process, the ALJ must decide whether the claimant is disabled. If the claimant can make an adjustment to other work that exists in significant numbers in the national economy, he or she is not disabled. If not, the claimant is disabled.

NOTE: There is a provision in the Act that the ALJ cannot find a claimant disabled if the claimant has drug addiction or alcoholism, or "DAA" and the DAA is a contributing factor that is "material" to the finding that the claimant is disabled. In other words, if the ALJ determines that a claimant is disabled and that he or she has DAA, the ALJ must also determine whether the claimant would still be disabled if he or she stopped using drugs or alcohol. In this case, the ALJ will go through the sequential evaluation process again and make findings based on an assumption that the claimant has stopped substance use. This means that the ALJ may pose more questions to you about a claimant's ability to do previous work or other work based on a hypothetical RFC assessment that assumes that the claimant's DAA has stopped.

Determining Continuing Disability

In addition to adjudicating appeals involving a claimant's initial entitlement to disability benefits, ALJs also adjudicate claims involving appeals of determinations that individuals who were previously awarded disability benefits are no longer "disabled." There are two basic types of cases in this category.

- From time to time, we review the continuing disability of both adults and children under Titles II and XVI.[23] We refer to these cases as *continuing disability reviews* (CDRs), or "cessation" cases.

- Title XVI also requires that we redetermine the eligibility of individuals who qualified for SSI as children when they reach age 18, using the adult rules for initial disability claims. We refer to these cases as *age-18 redetermination* cases.

In these type of cases, the DDS will have already determined that the individual's disability ended on a specific date. The ALJ then considers whether the individual's disability ended on that date, at a later date, or not at all. In some—but not all—cases, the ALJ will consider whether the individual has become disabled again even if the disability did end in the past. The ALJ will give you instructions, and you will be asked questions, appropriate to the issues of the specific case.

As we have already noted, we use different sequential evaluation processes to evaluate whether an individual continues to be disabled than in initial claims for disability benefits. This is because there are different standards in the Act for determining, with a CDR, whether disability has ended. 20 CFR 404.1594 and 416.994.[24] The primary difference is that there generally must be evidence showing medical improvement in the individual's condition from the more recent of the date he or she was first found disabled or the last time we found that the disability continued. There are few differences between the opinions you will be asked to give in these cases and the opinions you are asked to give in cases involving initial applications for benefits.

---

[23] We review cases at frequencies ranging from as little as 6 months up to about 7 years depending on the probability that the individual's impairment(s) will improve to the point of nondisability. We do not send all individuals' cases to the DDS for a medical review. In many cases, we determine through a questionnaire we call a "mailer" that the individual's disability continues.

[24] The CDR sequential evaluation processes in Title II and Title XVI are slightly different from each other, but the differences do not affect your work as a VE.

CDRs and Medical Improvement

The Act provides that we generally cannot find that an individual's disability has ended unless we have evidence showing that:

- The impairment(s) upon which we last found him or her to be disabled or still disabled has medically improved, [25]

- The medical improvement is "related to the ability to work," in the case of adults, [26] *and*

- The individual is not disabled under the basic definition of disability.

To determine whether medical improvement has occurred, the ALJ will look only at the impairment(s) the individual had at the time of our most recent favorable disability decision; that is, either our initial decision that the individual was disabled or, if more recent, our last determination that the individual was still disabled. We call this the *comparison point decision* (CPD). The ALJ will compare the medical severity of the CPD impairment(s) at the time of the DDS's cessation determination to the severity of those impairments at the time of the CPD. Medical improvement is any decrease in the medical severity of those CPD impairments as shown by the signs, symptoms, and laboratory findings.

We have complex rules defining what the term "related to the ability to work" means. Even if there has been medical improvement related to the ability to work, the ALJ will find that disability continues if the individual has an impairment(s)—including any new impairment(s) that was not present at the time of the CPD— or a combination of impairments that meets the basic definition of disability; that is, if he or she is unable to engage in SGA. Suffice it to say that an ALJ may ask for your opinions about the same issues on which you will be testifying in hearings on initial claims.

Note: There is one important policy of which you should be aware. As we have explained, PRW is generally work that was performed in the past 15 years. However, we have a special rule for CDRs. We do not count work a person is doing or has done during a current period of entitlement based on disability as PRW when an ALJ determines whether the individual's disability has ended and must determine:

---

[25] There are certain specific and very limited exceptions to the requirement for showing medical improvement. See 20 CFR 404.1594(d) and (e), 416.994(b)(3) and (4), and 416.994a(e) and (f).
[26] There is no corresponding provision for children under SSI.

Vocational Expert Handbook

- Whether the individual has regained the ability to do any PRW, or

- Whether the individual has regained the ability to do other work.

See 20 CFR 404.1594(i) and 416.994(b)(8).

Age-18 Redeterminations

Title XVI of the Act requires that we "redetermine" the eligibility of individuals who were eligible for an SSI payment as a child when they reach age 18. The Act specifies that we must use the rules we use when we determine initial disability in adults, and not the medical improvement review standard we use in CDRs. Under our regulations, we use the adult sequential evaluation process we use to evaluate disability in initial adult claims, except that we do not use step 1 (Is the claimant engaging in SGA?). 20 CFR 416.987. Any testimony you give in these cases will be the same kind of testimony you give in initial adult claims.

The Medical-Vocational Guidelines in Appendix 2 to Subpart P of Part 404 (the "Grid Rules")

Our rules for determining disability at step 5 are very complex, and it would be impossible to explain them all in this handbook. Most of your testimony will be in cases involving determinations at step 5, so it is important that you read Appendix 2 (the *Medical-Vocational Guidelines*, or "grid rules"), the other regulations about how we make determinations at step 5, and the SSRs we list at the end of this handbook, to gain an understanding of what the ALJ will consider and ask you to testify about.

We begin with an overview of the grid rules and how the ALJ will make decisions using them. We follow with definitions of the vocational factors and other terms we use at this step and under the grid rules.

The most important thing to remember is that the ALJ cannot rely on your testimony if it is inconsistent with or contradicts our rules, so you must be aware of our various definitions and of how the grid rules work.

Introduction to the Grid Rules

In legal terms, the claimant generally has the "burden" of proving his or her disability claim. However, our rules provide that we have a limited burden of providing evidence that work exists in the national economy that the claimant can do when we find that a claimant is not disabled at step 5 of the sequential evaluation process. Proper application of the grid rules can satisfy this burden of production. The grid rules provide necessary supporting evidence of the existence of work in the national economy. They also help to ensure consistent decision making at step 5. Nevertheless, VEs are also an important source of information about the existence of work and claimants' abilities to adjust to other work. ALJs frequently use VEs to help them make their decisions at step 5.

The grid rules take *administrative notice* of the existence of unskilled jobs in the national economy so that the ALJ does not need to obtain other evidence of the existence of such work in every case that he or she denies at step 5. The regulations establish that there are approximately 200 unskilled sedentary occupations, 1,400 light unskilled occupations (or a total of 1,600 sedentary and light occupations), and 900 medium unskilled occupations (or a total of 2,500 sedentary, light, and medium occupations), with each occupation representing numerous jobs in the national economy. This information was established by various vocational resources SSA consulted when the rules were issued and at various times since; since the information has already been established in our regulations, we can take "administrative notice" of it without having to prove it again in every case.

Appendix 2 provides both a series of general and specific narrative guidelines for considering the effects of RFC, age, education, and work experience in determining whether an individual can make an adjustment to other work, and three "tables" that contain the specific rules. Each table addresses a different "maximum sustained work capability" or RFC; sedentary unskilled occupations (Table No. 1), light unskilled occupations (Table No. 2), and medium unskilled occupations (Table No. 3). Within each table are rules for people with the defined exertional RFC for the table and different combinations of age, education, and previous work experience.[27] When all of the facts of an individual's case match with all of the criteria of a particular rule, the rule directs a conclusion as to whether the individual is or is not disabled.

In order to do the *full range* of unskilled work in each of the exertional categories in the three tables,[28] the individual must have the capability to do all or substantially all occupations existing at an exertional level as required of the work as defined in our regulations and SSRs. Additionally, he or she must not have any nonexertional limitations (physical or mental) that would significantly reduce the number of occupations in one of the tables. When an individual has an exertional or nonexertional limitation(s) that significantly affects the ability to do the full range of work that is administratively noticed in a table, the rules in the table do *not* direct the decision as to whether the person is or is not disabled. In those cases, the ALJ must use the rules as a *framework* for decision making. The ALJ may obtain VE evidence to help determine whether there are jobs that exist in significant numbers in the national economy that the claimant can do. However, an ALJ may not rely on evidence provided by a VE if that evidence is based on underlying assumptions or definitions that are inconsistent with our regulatory policies or definitions.

To illustrate how the grid rules work, we provide an excerpt from Table No. 2, which we use in cases in which the claimant has the RFC for "light" work.

---

[27] Note that the tables do not cover every possible combination of factors.
[28] That is all or almost all of the 200 sedentary unskilled occupations, 1,600 sedentary and light unskilled occupations, or 2,500 of the sedentary, light, and medium unskilled occupations.

Table No. 2—Residual Functional Capacity: Maximum Sustained Work Capability Limited to Light Work as a Result of Severe Medically Determinable Impairment(s)

Rule	Age	Education	Previous work experience	Decision
202.01	Advanced age	Limited or less	Unskilled or none	Disabled.
202.02	.......do.........	......do....................	Skilled or semiskilled—skills not transferable	Do.*
202.03	......do.........	......do....................	Skilled or semiskilled—skills transferable[1]	Not disabled.
202.04	......do.........	High school graduate or more—does not provide for direct entry into skilled work[2]	Unskilled or none	Disabled.
202.05	......do.........	High school graduate or more—provides for direct entry into skilled work[2]	......do....................	Not disabled.
202.06	......do.........	High school graduate or more—does not provide for direct entry into skilled work[2]	Skilled or semiskilled—skills not transferable	Disabled.
202.07	......do.........	......do....................	Skilled or semiskilled—skills transferable[2]	Not disabled.
202.08	......do.........	High school graduate or more—provides for direct entry into skilled work[2]	Skilled or semiskilled—skills not transferable	Do.
202.09	Closely approaching advanced age	Illiterate or unable to communicate in English	Unskilled or none	Disabled.
202.10	......do.........	Limited or less—at least literate and able to communicate in English	......do....................	Not disabled.
202.11	......do.........	Limited or less	Skilled or semiskilled—skills not transferable	Do.
202.12	......do.........	......do....................	Skilled or semiskilled—skills transferable	Do.
202.13	......do.........	High school graduate or more	Unskilled or none	Do.
202.14	......do.........	......do....................	Skilled or semiskilled—skills not transferable	Do.
202.15	......do.........	......do....................	Skilled or semiskilled—skills transferable	Do.
202.16	Younger individual	Illiterate or unable to communicate in English	Unskilled or none	Do.
202.17	......do.........	Limited or less—at least literate and able to communicate in English	......do	Do.
202.18	......do.........	Limited or less	Skilled or semiskilled—	Do.

---

*"Do." is an abbreviation for "Ditto."

			skills not transferable	
202.19	......do..........	......do...	Skilled or semiskilled—skills transferable	Do.
202.20	......do.......	High school graduate or more	Unskilled or none	Do.
202.21	......do..........	......do.. ..	Skilled or semiskilled—skills not transferable	Do.
202.22	......do..........	......do...	Skilled or semiskilled—skills transferable	Do.

As you can see in the table excerpt, the older a claimant is, the issue of work adjustment becomes more significant. For example, under rules 202.13-202.15, we would not find a 54-year-old[29] high school graduate who can do the full range of light work disabled, regardless of his or her work experience. At age 55,[30] we would find the same person disabled, unless he or she has skills that are transferable to skilled or semiskilled work that is within his or her RFC. Education, including literacy and the ability to communicate in English, can also have an effect on the disability decision; see rule 202.09.

In many cases, the rules do not direct a decision. For example, under our definition of "sedentary" work, a claimant must be able to sit for at least 6 hours in an 8-hour workday on a sustained basis in order to do the full range of sedentary work. In order to do the full range of light work, a claimant must be able to stand and walk for a total of 6 hours in an 8-hour workday on a sustained basis. Some claimants cannot sit for 6 hours or stand and walk for 6 hours, but can sit for up to 4 hours and stand and walk the rest of the time. Such individuals may be able to do *some* sedentary occupations, and *some* light occupations, but not *all* of the sedentary or light occupations of which we take administrative notice. Therefore, they cannot do the "full range" of sedentary or light unskilled work, and the ALJ cannot use a grid rule to "direct" the decision.

In such cases, an ALJ may ask you to testify about the existence of occupations that a claimant with this RFC could do and about the claimant's ability to make an adjustment to other work considering the claimant's age, education, and any past relevant work experience. You will also have to be prepared to provide estimates of the number of jobs within each occupation both locally and nationally, whether the occupations are described in the *DOT,* and if they are, whether your description of the occupation is consistent with the *DOT's* description. Your testimony must also be consistent with our regulatory definitions and requirements, including the grid rules. For example, as we illustrated above, under the grid rules a 55-

---

[29] That is, "closely approaching advanced age." See definitions in section 2 below.
[30] That is, "advanced age."

year-old high school graduate who can do the *full* range of light and sedentary work is disabled unless he or she has transferable skills. Therefore, you should not testify that there are sedentary or light occupations that a hypothetical 55-year-old high school graduate who is limited to *less than* the full range of light work can do.[31]

VEs can also be especially helpful in cases in which claimants have only nonexertional limitations or both nonexertional and exertional limitations. For example, claimants with mental impairments and no physical limitations generally have the *exertional* capability to do work at every exertional level, including heavy and very heavy work, but may not be able to do every job that we take administrative notice of because of limitations from their mental disorders; e.g., they may not be able to do jobs that require frequent interaction with the public. In such cases, the ALJ may ask you for information about the effect of the impairment on the individual's *occupational base*, a term we use to describe the number of occupations that an individual is capable of performing. See, e.g., SSRs 83-10 and 85-15.

In the following sections, we provide brief definitions and guidance about the three vocational factors, the exertional levels of work, and our concepts of work "skills" and transferability. You should not rely on the descriptions in this handbook. It is essential that you become thoroughly familiar with the important policy statements we list at the end of this handbook. The information below is simply to give you a brief introduction to our terms and related rules, and the kinds of questions you can expect to be asked at an ALJ hearing.

Vocational Factors

Under our rules for step 5, there are three *vocational factors* the ALJ must consider: *age*, *education*, and *work experience*.[32]

---

[31] This is only a simple illustration of how you have to be aware that the grid rules might not match up with your experience in placing people in jobs. In a case like this, an ALJ would not need your testimony because the "framework" of the rules would establish that the claimant is disabled: the claimant would be disabled under the grid rules even if the ALJ found that he or she could do *more* than he or she could actually do. You should also know that an ALJ cannot use your testimony to rebut the conclusions in the grid rules. In the example in the text above, the ALJ cannot make a decision contrary to the mandate of the grid rules even if you are able to name occupations that the claimant can do.

[32] The vocational factors apply only at step 5. Even though we consider a claimant's previous work (PRW) at step 4, it is a different sort of inquiry, based solely on the claimant's RFC. We use the vocational factors at step 5 together with RFC to determine whether a claimant can make an adjustment to other work; i.e., work he or she has not done before.

a. Age

Age refers to a claimant's chronological age. We consider advancing age to be an increasingly limiting factor in the person's ability to make an adjustment to other work.

Our regulations use three broad age categories, although there are subcategories in two of them that apply in some cases.[33]

- Younger Person: Claimants under age 50. We also have a rule for some claimants who are age 45-49 and who are illiterate in English or unable to communicate in English.

- Person Closely Approaching Advanced Age: Claimants age 50-54.

- Person of Advanced Age. Claimants age 55 or older. We also have separate rules for some claimants in this category who are *closely approaching retirement age* (age 60 or older).

20 CFR 404.1563 and 416.963.

b. Education

Education primarily means formal schooling or other training that contributes to a claimant's ability to meet vocational requirements (for example, reasoning ability, communication skills, and arithmetical ability). Our rules provide that lack of formal schooling does not necessarily mean that the claimant is uneducated or lacks abilities achieved in formal education, although the ALJ will use the claimant's formal education level if there is no evidence to contradict it.

Our rules recognize that the importance of a claimant's education may depend on how much time has passed between the completion of formal education and the alleged onset of disability. The ALJ may also consider what the claimant has done with his or her education in a work, or other, setting (e.g., in hobbies). The rules provide the ALJ with the authority to determine that a given claimant's education is higher or lower than the actual grade he or she attained depending on a variety of factors, but such a finding is unusual.

---

[33] However, our regulations provide that we do not apply the age categories mechanically in a borderline situation. 20 CFR 404.1563(b) and 416.963(b). It is the ALJ's responsibility to determine when to use an age category that is different from the claimant's chronological age.

The term "education" also includes how well the claimant is able to communicate in English since this ability is often acquired or improved by education.

Our regulations define five educational categories: [34]

- Illiterate: The claimant cannot read or write a simple message in English, such as instructions or inventory lists, even if the claimant can sign his or her name.

- Inability to communicate in English: The claimant does not speak and understand English.

- Marginal Education: Generally, formal schooling at the 6th grade level or below. Marginal education means ability in reasoning, arithmetic, and language skills which are needed to do simple, unskilled types of jobs.

- Limited Education: Generally, formal schooling at the 7th through 11th grade level. Limited education means ability in reasoning, arithmetic, and language skills, but not enough to allow a person to do most of the more complex job duties needed in semi-skilled or skilled jobs.

- High School Education or Above: Generally, high school graduate or above. The term includes high school equivalency diplomas. We generally consider that someone with these educational abilities can do semi-skilled through skilled work.

20 CFR 404.1564 and 416.964.

c. **Work Experience**

Work experience means the claimant's PRW.

The ALJ will often ask you the following questions about a claimant's work experience:

- The *exertional level* of the occupation (in terms of "sedentary," "light," "medium," "heavy," and "very heavy"),

---

[34] However, note that the grid rules treat illiteracy and inability to communicate in English as a single category.

- The *specific exertional and nonexertional physical and mental requirements* of the occupation,

- The *skill level* of the occupation, and

- If the occupation was semiskilled or skilled, the *skills* the claimant used in the occupation and whether any of those skills are *transferable* to other occupations that are within the claimant's RFC.[35]

The ALJ may ask you these questions from the perspective of the job duties as described by the claimant, as described in the *DOT,* and based on your professional experience.

Exertional Categories

As we have already noted, we use the same terms as the DOT to categorize occupations according to their strength demands. We define these terms in our regulations and rulings, and you must be familiar with our definitions. **The ALJ cannot accept any testimony you give that is inconsistent or conflicts with SSA's definitions.**

We have a number of instructions that define the exertional categories. The following is only a brief summary of key features of our definitions. It is essential that you read and become familiar with the definitions in the policy documents we list at the end of this handbook.

- Sedentary Work: Sedentary occupations generally require sitting for up to a total of about 6 hours in an 8-hour workday. Although sedentary jobs involve sitting, a certain amount of walking and standing is often necessary to carry out job duties. Periods of standing or walking should generally total no more than about 2 hours out of an 8-hour workday. Sedentary work involves lifting no more than 10 pounds at a time and occasionally lifting or carrying articles like docket files, ledgers, and small tools.[36] Most unskilled sedentary jobs require good use of both hands and the fingers (bilateral manual dexterity) and sufficient vision to work with small objects.

---

[35] We define the terms in this list in the sections that follow.
[36] *Occasionally* means occurring from very little up to one-third of the workday, or up to about 2 hours out of an 8-hour workday.

- Light Work: Light work involves lifting no more than 20 pounds at a time, with frequent lifting or carrying of objects weighing up to 10 pounds.[37] Even though the weight the claimant may lift may be very little, a job is in the "light" category when it requires a good deal of walking or standing, or when it involves sitting most of the time with some pushing and pulling of arm or leg controls. Since frequent lifting or carrying requires an individual to be on his or her feet up to two-thirds of a workday, the full range of light work requires standing or walking, off and on, for a total of approximately 6 hours of an 8-hour workday. Sitting may occur intermittently during the remaining time. We consider that, if a claimant can do the full range of light work, he or she can also do the full range of sedentary work, unless there is some other limiting factor, such as loss of fine dexterity or inability to sit for long periods of time. While light occupations require use of the arms and hands to grasp and to hold and turn objects, they generally do not require use of the fingers for fine activities to the extent required in much sedentary work.

- Medium Work: Medium work involves lifting no more than 50 pounds at a time with frequent lifting or carrying of objects weighing up to 25 pounds. A full range of medium work requires standing or walking for a total of approximately 6 hours in an 8-hour work day. Medium work generally requires use of the arms and hands only to grasp, hold, or turn objects. It also often requires both considerable lifting and frequent bending or stooping.

- Heavy Work: Heavy work involves lifting no more than 100 pounds at a time with frequent lifting or carrying of objects weighing up to 50 pounds.

- Very Heavy: Very heavy work involves lifting objects weighing more than 100 pounds at a time with frequent lifting and carrying of objects weighing 50 pounds or more.

Skill Levels

Our rules classify work as *skilled, semiskilled,* and *unskilled.* A *skill* is knowledge of a work activity that requires the exercise of significant judgment beyond the carrying out of simple job duties. Skills are practical and familiar knowledge of the principles and processes of an art, science, or

---

[37] *Frequent* means occurring from one-third to two-thirds of the workday, or about 2-6 hours out of an 8-hour workday.

trade, combined with the ability to apply them in practice in a proper and approved manner. This includes activities like making precise measurements, reading blueprints, and setting up and operating complex machinery. A skill gives a person a special advantage over unskilled workers in the labor market. Skills are generally acquired through the performance of an occupation which is above the unskilled level; *a claimant cannot gain skills from performing unskilled work.*[38]

We distinguish "skills" from worker "traits." Traits are inherent qualities that a worker brings to the job, such as good eyesight or good eye-hand coordination. When an ALJ asks you whether a claimant has a "skill," you must be careful not to confuse the two terms. For example, the *traits* of coordination and dexterity may be contrasted with a *skill* in the use of the hands or feet for the rapid performance of repetitive work tasks. It is the acquired capacity to perform the work activities with facility that gives rise to potentially transferable skills.

You must be prepared to classify the claimant's past relevant work and any jobs that you identify in response to hypothetical questions (see page 34) as "skilled," "semiskilled," or "unskilled," as defined in our regulations and SSRs. These descriptions of the skill levels are based on the *DOT*'s specific vocational preparation (SVP) ratings for each described occupation. Unskilled work corresponds to an SVP of 1-2; semiskilled work to an SVP of 3-4; and skilled work to an SVP of 5-9. In general, we use the following definitions:

- Unskilled Work: Unskilled work is work which needs little or no judgment to do simple duties that can be learned on the job in a short period of time, usually 30 days or less. For example, unskilled occupations include work where the primary work duties are handling, feeding, and off-bearing, or machine tending in which a person can usually learn to do the job in 30 days or less, and little specific vocational preparation and judgment are needed. **A person does not gain work skills by doing unskilled jobs**.

- Semiskilled Work: Semiskilled occupations are more complex than unskilled ones and simpler than the more highly skilled types of occupations. They contain more variables and require more judgment than unskilled occupations. Even though semiskilled occupations typically require more than 30 days to learn, the

---

[38] Our rules also provide for the possibility that a claimant may have gained skills from education that provides for direct entry into skilled work, although this is a rare occurrence in our cases.

content of work activities in some semiskilled occupations may be little more than unskilled. Therefore, close attention must be paid to the actual complexities of the job in dealing with data, people, or objects and to the judgments required to do the work. Semiskilled occupations may require alertness and close attention to machine processes; inspecting, testing or looking for irregularities; tending or guarding equipment, property, materials, or persons against loss, damage or injury; or other types of activities which are similarly less complex than skilled work, but more complex than unskilled work. An occupation may be classified as semiskilled when coordination and dexterity are necessary, as when hands or feet must be moved quickly to do repetitive tasks.

- Skilled Work: Skilled occupations are more complex and varied than unskilled and semiskilled occupations. They require more training time and often a higher educational attainment. Abstract thinking in specialized fields may be required. For example, skilled work may require: judgment to determine the machine and manual operations to be performed in order to obtain the proper form, quality or quantity of material to be produced; laying out work, estimating quality, determining the suitability and necessary quantities of materials, making precise measurements, reading blueprints or other specifications, or making necessary computations or mechanical adjustments to control or regulate the work; or dealing with people, facts, figures, or abstract ideas at a high level of complexity.

Transferability of Skills

As you become more familiar with the grid rules, you will see that in many cases the skill level of a claimant's PRW does not affect the decision; i.e., the decision will be the same regardless of whether the claimant's PRW was unskilled or involved skills and whether the claimant has skills he or she can use in other work. However, as we have already noted, there are some situations in which a determination regarding transferability of skills can be decisive. In simple terms, *transferable skills* are skills that a claimant has from PRW that he or she can no longer perform but can use in other skilled or semiskilled work that is within his or her RFC.

Under our rules, transferability depends largely on the similarity of occupationally significant work activities among different jobs. Transferability is found most probable and meaningful among jobs in which:

- The same or a lesser degree of skill is required (from a skilled to a semiskilled or another skilled job, or from one semiskilled to another semiskilled job), because the claimant is not expected to perform more complex jobs than he or she performed in the past;

- The same or similar tools and machines are used; and

- The same or similar raw materials, products, processes or services are involved.

20 CFR 404.1568 and 416.968 and SSR 82-41.

Generally, the greater the degree of acquired work skills, the less difficulty the claimant will have in transferring skills to other jobs, except when the skills are such that they are not readily usable in any other industries, jobs, and work settings. Reduced RFC and advancing age are important factors associated with transferability because reduced RFC limits the number of occupations an individual can do, and advancing age decreases the possibility of making a successful vocational adjustment. In this regard, we have strict rules regarding transferability for some claimants who are at least 55 years old and even stricter rules for some claimants beginning at age 60.

When you are reviewing the evidence for the case before the hearing or in connection with interrogatories, you should note whether the claimant has any skilled or semiskilled PRW. If so, you should also be prepared to describe the skills. The ALJ may also pose hypothetical questions to you that assume one or more different RFC assessments, and you should be prepared to cite occupations to which the skills may be transferred or to explain why there are no transferable skills. If the claimant is age 55-59 or age 60 and older, you must also be prepared to testify about whether there is transferability under the rules for claimants of those ages.

Hypothetical Questions

In addition to questions requesting factual information—such as how the *DOT* describes the duties of a particular occupation—ALJs will often ask you hypothetical questions (often referred to as "hypotheticals"). As we explained earlier, ALJs do not know what their decisions will be when they enter the hearing. Therefore, in many cases, the ALJ will not have determined what the claimant's RFC is when he or she asks you for opinions about work.

Because of this, the ALJ will phrase some of his or her questions to you in hypothetical terms, posing potential findings in terms like this: "Assume an individual of the claimant's age, education level, and past work experience. If that person can sit for so many hours, stand for so many hours, lift so many pounds, and has the following mental limitations..."[39] The ALJ may ask you more than one such hypothetical question. Often, ALJs provide a hypothetical that assumes that they agree with all of a claimant's allegations and at least one other that assumes that they disagree to some extent or in certain particulars; for example, that the claimant has limitations in lifting weights, but not to the extent he or she alleges.

The first hypothetical may be about step 4 of the sequential evaluation process; that is, whether a person with hypothetical physical and mental limitations the ALJ specifies could do the claimant's PRW. More often, the ALJ will ask hypotheticals that will help him or her determine at step 5 whether the claimant can make an adjustment to other work that exists in the national economy, considering the claimant's age, education, work experience, and RFC. The ALJ will specify what facts you are to assume.

If you respond to a hypothetical that there are occupations the hypothetical individual can perform given the facts assumed, the ALJ will then ask you to give examples of those occupations. You should be prepared to provide:

- At least three examples (if possible), with an explanation of why you believe that the individual would be able to do the jobs given the hypothetical facts.

- Information about the numbers of jobs in each occupation both locally (e.g., by state or region) and nationally. Remember that it does not matter whether work exists in the immediate area in which the claimant resides, whether he or she would actually be hired, or if a specific vacancy exists, only how many of the jobs exist.

- The *DOT* numbers for the occupations if they are listed in the *DOT*, and whether there are any inconsistencies or apparent inconsistencies between the description of an occupation in the *DOT* and your testimony. See section 7 below for more information about this subject.

---

[39] The ALJ may even refer to a hypothetical claimant.

You **must** not give your opinion about:

- The claimant's diagnosis, prognosis, physical and mental limitations or restrictions, or any other medical issue.

- Whether the number of jobs within a given occupation is "significant."

- The claimant's residual functional capacity.

- Whether the claimant is disabled.

The ALJ will decide these issues. If you are asked your opinion about any of these issues, you should not answer.

The ALJ will also give the claimant and his or her representative a chance to ask you questions. They may ask you hypotheticals as well.

If you believe that any hypothetical question is incomplete (e.g., a hypothetical does not adequately describe the functional abilities of a hypothetical person for you to determine whether there is work they could do), you should ask the ALJ for clarification before you answer.

SSR 00-4p: Your Testimony, the *DOT*, and SSA's Rules

There is one more very important policy you must know about, set out in SSR 00-4p. Generally, occupational evidence you provide should be consistent with the DOT. SSR 00-4p provides that the ALJ must ask you about any possible conflict between the information you provide and the information in the DOT. If there is an inconsistency or conflict—or even an apparent inconsistency or conflict—between your testimony and a description in the *DOT,* the ALJ must ask you for a reasonable explanation for the difference (or apparent difference) between your testimony and the description in the *DOT.*

It is important that you identify these conflicts, if any to the ALJ. The ALJ is required to elicit an explanation from you for any apparent inconsistency between occupational information you provide and the information in the DOT. Neither VE testimony nor DOT information automatically "trumps" when there is a conflict. However, the ALJ cannot rely on such testimony without eliciting your explanation and documenting whether it provides a reasonable basis for relying on your testimony rather than the conflicting DOT information. SSR 00-4p provides examples of common reasons for conflicts between VE testimony and the DOT, including, but not limited to:

- Your testimony may include information that is not listed in the *DOT*. The *DOT* contains information about most, but not all, occupations. The *DOT's* occupational definitions are the result of comprehensive studies of how similar jobs are performed in different workplaces. The term "occupation," as used in the *DOT*, refers to the collective description of those jobs. Each occupation represents numerous jobs. Information about a particular job's requirements or about occupations not listed in the DOT may be available in other reliable publications, information obtained directly from employers, or from your experience in job placement or career counseling.

- The *DOT* lists maximum requirements of occupations as generally performed, not the range of requirements of a particular job as it is performed in specific settings. You may be able to provide more specific information about how jobs or occupations are performed than in the *DOT*.

You must also be alert to other appearances of conflict. For example, descriptions of jobs in the *DOT* may refer to job materials or processes that have been replaced by more modern materials or processes. If you name an occupation that currently exists, but that is performed differently from the way the *DOT* describes it, you should explain that there is a difference between the way the job is performed now (an apparent conflict) and explain it.

It is also important to remember a principle we have stated earlier in this handbook: The ALJ cannot accept an explanation from you that conflicts with our policies. For example:

- You may reasonably classify the exertional demands of an occupation you name differently than in the DOT based on other reliable occupational information, including your own experience; e.g., describing a particular occupation as "light" when the *DOT* classifies it as "medium." However, you may not redefine our terms for the exertional levels. For example, if all available evidence (including your testimony) establishes that the exertional demands of an occupation meet our regulatory definition of "medium" work (20 CFR 404.1567 and 416.967), the ALJ would not be able to rely on your testimony that the occupation is "light" work.

- Similarly, our definitions of skill levels are controlling. Again, there may be a good reason for classifying an occupation's skill level differently than in the *DOT,* but an ALJ would not accept your testimony if you said that unskilled work involves complex duties that take many months to learn, because that is inconsistent with our regulatory definition of unskilled work in 20 CFR 404.1568 and 416.968.

Interrogatories

As we have already noted, we may ask you to respond in writing to specific written questions referred to as *interrogatories*. You may receive interrogatories from the ALJ, but you may also receive interrogatories from hearing office staff before a case is assigned to an ALJ for a hearing.

After the case is assigned to an ALJ, you may receive interrogatories from the ALJ before or after the hearing. You may receive a copy of evidence—especially new evidence—pertinent to the interrogatories or a summary of case information. If you provide responses to interrogatories before a hearing, the ALJ may or may not ask you to also appear and testify at a hearing.

An ALJ may also send you interrogatories that were posed by the claimant or the claimant's representative. The ALJ must approve any interrogatories proposed by a claimant or representative. You should never answer interrogatories submitted directly to you from the claimant or his or her representative, and you should send your responses to interrogatories only to the ALJ. The ALJ and his or her staff will ensure that the claimant and his or her representative receive a copy.

Usually, the interrogatories will be in the form of a questionnaire. You may type or legibly write your responses directly on the questionnaire if space permits. If you need more space to answer a question, attach separate sheets of paper with your responses. You should answer all questions completely. It is especially important that you explain and support your responses with references to specific evidence in the case record you received from the hearing office. Identify the reports in which the information is contained. All correspondence between you and the ALJ will become part of the official case record.

If you have a question about any of the interrogatories, you should request clarification from the ALJ (or the Hearing Office Chief Administrative Law Judge if the case is not yet assigned to a particular ALJ) in writing. If you cannot answer a particular question or cannot answer it completely because of conflicts in the evidence or because the evidence is incomplete, you should respond by explaining why you cannot answer the question. If possible, you should also provide an opinion and recommendation to the ALJ about what evidence he or she could obtain to resolve the conflict or complete the record.

If the interrogatories relate to new evidence the ALJ received after you testified or responded to other interrogatories, you should state whether the new evidence changes any of your prior responses and why.

Note that in all cases, the ALJ will submit the questions and your responses for review to the claimant's representative (if the claimant has a representative) with a copy to the claimant (or just to the claimant if unrepresented). The claimant has the right to request a supplemental hearing or to produce other information, to rebut any of your responses.

List of References

Social Security's regulations are compiled in Title 20 of the *Code of Federal Regulations*. Social Security Rulings (SSRs) are published by the Commissioner to explain and give detail to principles set out in the Social Security Act and regulations. The following is a list of regulation sections and SSRs that you should be familiar with. Acquaintance with the regulations and SSRs is essential to a complete understanding of the role of vocational evidence in Social Security disability adjudication. However, we do not intend this list to be a complete reference to all Social Security policy related to disability benefits. The ALJ will tell you if there are other policy statements with which you must be familiar in a given case.

You can find the full text of the Act, regulations, SSRs, and other instructions online at http://www.socialsecurity.gov/regulations/. You can also find a link to these sources and other resources at: http://www.socialsecurity.gov/disability/.

- To go directly to the regulations that start with the number "404" (Part 404), go to this page: http://www.socialsecurity.gov/OP_Home/cfr20/404/404-0000.htm.

- The table of contents for the Part 416 regulations is on this page: http://www.socialsecurity.gov/OP_Home/cfr20/416/416-0000.htm.

- To find the SSRs by year, go to this page: http://www.socialsecurity.gov/OP_Home/rulings/rulfind1.html. The first number in an SSR citation is the year of publication. For example, SSR 96-8p was published in 1996.

The grid rules are found at 20 CFR Part 404, Subpart P, Appendix 2: http://www.socialsecurity.gov/OP_Home/cfr20/404/404-ap11.htm.

Regulation sections

20 CFR 404.1520, *Evaluation of disability in general*

20 CFR 416.920, *Evaluation of disability of adults, in general*

20 CFR 404.1545 and 416.945, *Your residual functional capacity*

20 CFR 404.1560 and 416.960, *When we will consider your vocational background*

20 CFR 404.1563 and 416.963, *Your age as a vocational factor*

20 CFR 404.1564 and 416.964, *Your education as a vocational factor*

20 CFR 404.1565 and 416.965, *Your work experience as a vocational factor*

20 CFR 404.1566 and 416.966, *Work which exists in the national economy*

20 CFR 404.1567 and 416.967, *Physical exertion requirements*

20 CFR 404.1568 and 416.968, *Skill requirements*

20 CFR 404.1569, *Listing of Medical-Vocational Guidelines in appendix 2,* and 416.969, *Listing of Medical-Vocational Guidelines in appendix 2 of subpart P of part 404 of this chapter*

20 CFR 404.1569a and 416.969a, *Exertional and nonexertional limitations*

Social Security Rulings

SSR 82-40
    Titles II and XVI: The Vocational Relevance of Past Work Performed in a Foreign Country

SSR 82-41
    Titles II and XVI: Work Skills and Their Transferability as Intended by the Expanded Vocational Factors Regulations effective February 26, 1979

SSR 82-61
    Titles II and XVI: Past Relevant Work — The Particular Job or the Occupation as Generally Performed

SSR 82-62
    Titles II and XVI: A Disability Claimant's Capacity to Do Past Relevant Work, In General

SSR 83-5a
    Sections 205, 216(i), 223(d), and 1614(a)(3) (42 U.S.C. 405, 416(i), 423(d), and 1382c(a)(3)) Disability — Medical-Vocational Guidelines — Conclusiveness of Rules

SSR 83-10
> Titles II and XVI: Determining Capability To Do Other Work — The Medical-Vocational Rules of Appendix 2

SSR 83-11
> Titles II and XVI: Capability to Do Other Work — The Exertionally Based Medical-Vocational Rules Met

SSR 83-12
> Titles II and XVI: Capability To Do Other Work — The Medical-Vocational Rules as a Framework for Evaluating Exertional Limitations Within a Range of Work or Between Ranges of Work

Note: SSR 83-13 was replaced by SSR 85-15 in 1985

SSR 83-14
> Titles II and XVI: Capability to Do Other Work — The Medical-Vocational Rules as a Framework for Evaluating a Combination of Exertional and Nonexertional Impairments

SSR 85-15
> Titles II and XVI: Capability To Do Other Work — The Medical-Vocational Rules as a Framework for Evaluating Solely Nonexertional Impairments

SSR 86-8
> Titles II and XVI: The Sequential Evaluation Process

SSR 96-8p
> Policy Interpretation Ruling Titles II and XVI: Assessing Residual Functional Capacity in Initial Claims

SSR 96-9p
> Policy Interpretation Ruling Titles II and XVI: Determining Capability to Do Other Work — Implications of a Residual Functional Capacity for Less Than a Full Range of Sedentary Work

SSR 00-4p
> Titles II and XVI: Use of Vocational Expert and Vocational Specialist Evidence, and Other Reliable Occupational Information in Disability Decisions

a. <u>Age</u>

Age refers to a claimant's chronological age. We consider advancing age to be an increasingly limiting factor in the person's ability to make an adjustment to other work.

Our regulations use three broad age categories, although there are subcategories in two of them that apply in some cases.[33]

- <u>Younger Person</u>: Claimants under age 50. We also have a rule for some claimants who are age 45-49 and who are illiterate in English or unable to communicate in English.

- <u>Person Closely Approaching Advanced Age</u>: Claimants age 50-54.

- <u>Person of Advanced Age</u>. Claimants age 55 or older. We also have separate rules for some claimants in this category who are *closely approaching retirement age* (age 60 or older).

20 CFR 404.1563 and 416.963.

b. <u>Education</u>

Education primarily means formal schooling or other training that contributes to a claimant's ability to meet vocational requirements (for example, reasoning ability, communication skills, and arithmetical ability). Our rules provide that lack of formal schooling does not necessarily mean that the claimant is uneducated or lacks abilities achieved in formal education, although the ALJ will use the claimant's formal education level if there is no evidence to contradict it.

Our rules recognize that the importance of a claimant's education may depend on how much time has passed between the completion of formal education and the alleged onset of disability. The ALJ may also consider what the claimant has done with his or her education in a work, or other setting (e.g., in hobbies). The rules provide the ALJ with the authority to determine that a given claimant's education is higher or lower than the actual grade he or she attained depending on a variety of factors, but such a finding is unusual.

---

[33] However, our regulations provide that we do not apply the age categories mechanically in a borderline situation. 20 CFR 404.1563(b) and 416.963(b). It is the ALJ's responsibility to determine when to use an age category that is different from the claimant's chronological age.

Appendix 9: **Medical Expert Handbook,** *pp. 8-36*

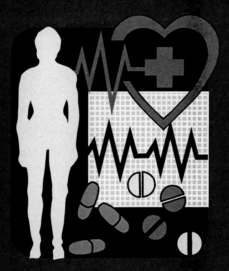

SOCIAL SECURITY ADMINISTRATION
OFFICE OF DISABILITY ADJUDICATION AND REVIEW
OFFICE OF THE CHIEF ADMINISTRATIVE LAW JUDGE

MEDICAL EXPERT HANDBOOK

June 2011

Role of the ME

Responsibilities of the ME

The ALJ's primary reason for seeking the advice of an ME is to gain a better understanding of the medical evidence in the case. An ME provides both factual information and expert opinion based on his or her medical or psychological knowledge and knowledge of SSA's rules. For example, you should be familiar with:

- What a *medically determinable impairment* is, and SSA's definitions of *symptoms, signs,* and *laboratory findings.*

- SSA's requirement to consider the combined effects of impairments.

- SSA's Listing of Impairments (commonly referred to as the "listings").[12]

- SSA's definitions of "meeting" and "medically equaling" specific listings.

- The concept of *residual functional capacity* (RFC) for all cases except SSI child cases, including the types of evidence and the kinds of physical and mental work-related limitations SSA considers in assessing RFC.

- In cases involving SSI claimants under age 18, the area(s) of pediatric medicine appropriate to the claim, typical child development and functioning, and SSA's policy of "functionally equaling the listings."

- SSA's concept of "duration" of disability.

You will provide evidence by answering questions posed by the ALJ, the claimant, and the claimant's representative. You *may* answer questions about medical issues that could be decisive in a case, such as whether a claimant's impairment(s) meets or medically equals a specific listing.[13] You *may* also answer questions which ask for your medical opinion about the nature and severity of a claimant's impairment(s), including symptoms,

---

[12] The listings are part of SSA's regulations, but we also publish them separately. See the List of References at the end of this handbook for citations.

[13] We explain the concepts of "meeting" and medically equaling a listing later in this handbook.

diagnosis and prognosis, what the claimant can still do despite impairment(s), and the claimant's physical or mental restrictions.[14] You should *never* comment on non-medical matters, such as whether you believe a claimant can do his or her previous work, or offer an opinion about whether a claimant is "disabled" even if you are asked.

You will rarely have the opportunity to question the claimant directly during the hearing. If you have any questions—e.g., about an aspect of a claimant's testimony—or if you need more information, you should inform the ALJ. The ALJ will decide whether the information is pertinent and how it should be elicited; the ALJ may ask the question himself or herself or allow you to ask the question. You should never conduct any type of physical or mental status examination of the claimant during the hearing, and should refuse to perform such an examination if asked.

The ALJ will not rely on your testimony alone to make his or her decision about disability or to make medical findings that go into that decision. The ALJ will consider your testimony, along with the other evidence in the case record, including the claimant's testimony at the hearing and any other testimony. Your testimony may also help the ALJ determine whether he or she needs more evidence in order to make a decision.

Conduct of the ME

You should conduct yourself as if you are testifying in a civil or criminal court. Give complete answers to the questions you are asked. Whenever possible, you should phrase your answers in lay terms. To ensure impartiality, you must avoid any substantive contact with the ALJ before or after the hearing, and avoid face-to-face or telephone contact with the claimant or his or her representative, both before and after the hearing. You must disqualify yourself if you believe that you cannot be completely impartial, have prior knowledge of the case, or have had prior contact with the claimant. However, the ALJ will not disqualify you merely because you testified in a previous case regarding the same claimant.

Pre-Hearing Preparation

The ALJ will generally provide you with relevant portions of the case file before the hearing. (You must fully understand the importance of proper handling of this information; please read the next section "Protecting Personally Identifiable Information (PII)" carefully.) This will give you a

---

[14] See 20 C.F.R. §§ 404.1527(a)(2) and 416.927(a)(2).

chance to become familiar with the medical aspects of the claim. It will also prepare you to answer the kinds of medical questions, such as questions about the nature and duration of the claimant's impairment(s), treatment and side effects, and the evidence about the claimant's functional limitations, you can expect to get at the hearing. If after reviewing this information you believe that you need more information to provide adequate testimony about the claimant's medical history, current treatment, prognosis, and the other issues we discuss in the following sections of this handbook, you should prepare a written list of your questions and refer them to the ALJ.

Generally, the period under consideration for establishment of disability in initial claims begins with the date the claimant alleges that he or she became disabled (commonly referred to as the *alleged onset date*, or AOD) and goes through the date of the ALJ's decision. However, there are situations requiring evaluation of the claimant's medical condition at an earlier time[15] or that start at a later time. The ALJ will advise you of the period under consideration.

Protecting Personally Identifiable Information (PII)

The Social Security Administration defines PII as any information which can be used to distinguish or trace an individual's identity (such as his or her name, Social Security number, biometric records, etc.) alone, or when combined with other personal or identifying information which is linked or linkable to a specific individual (such as date and place of birth, mother's maiden name, etc.). SSA is mandated to safeguard and protect the PII entrusted to the agency and to immediately report breaches to the Department of Homeland Security.

The claimant information the ALJ provides to you, which may be in paper or electronic form, must be protected against loss, theft, or inadvertent disclosure. Failure to take the proper steps to protect this information, or to immediately report to SSA when you suspect PII is compromised, could adversely affect your standing and may result in reduced requests for your services. To maintain good standing with SSA, follow these instructions to reduce the risk of PII loss, theft or inadvertent disclosure:

- Ensure your employees are fully aware of these procedures and the importance of protecting PII.

---

[15] For example, as we noted earlier in this handbook, under Title II a worker's insured status can expire. In this situation, the worker can still qualify for disability benefits, but must show that he or she was disabled on or before this *date last insured.*

- If you are expecting to receive claimant information from SSA, and you have not received it within the expected time frame, immediately notify your SSA contact or alternate contact.
- Secure all SSA claimant information in a locked container, such as a locked filing cabinet, or while in transit, in a locked briefcase.
- Once you arrive at your destination, always move PII to the most secure location. Do not leave PII locked in a car trunk overnight.
- When viewing a claimant's file, prevent others in the area from viewing the file's contents.
- Ensure PII is appropriately returned or, upon receiving SSA's approval, destroyed when no longer needed.

In the event of a loss, theft, or disclosure, you must immediately notify your primary SSA contact or alternate contact. Report the following information, as completely and accurately as possible:

- Your contact information
- A description of the loss, theft, or disclosure, including the approximate time and location of the incident
- A description of safeguards used, as applicable
- Whether you have contacted, or been contacted, by any external organizations (i.e., other agencies, law enforcement, press, etc.), and whether you have filed any other reports
- Any other pertinent information

If you are unable to reach your SSA contacts, call SSA's National Network Service Center (NNSC) toll free at 1-877-697-4889. Provide them with the information outlined above. Record the Change, Asset, and Problem Reporting System (CAPRS) number which the NNSC will assign to you. Limit disclosure of the information and details about the incident to only those with a need to know. The security/PII loss incident reporting process will ensure that SSA's reporting requirements are met and that security/PII loss incident information is only shared appropriately.

Delay in reporting may adversely affect SSA's ability to investigate and resolve the incident and may contribute to a determination of reduced requests for your services.

Determining Disability

You may be asked to give evidence in any kind of disability case under the programs we administer. Most often, you will be giving evidence in cases of insured workers under Title II and adults claiming SSI disability benefits under Title XVI, or "concurrent" claims for both benefits. Less often, you may testify at hearings concerning the other kinds of disability cases described below.

Detailed Definitions of Disability

The Social Security Act defines disability in all Title II claims and in adult Title XVI claims as the inability to engage in any substantial gainful activity by reason of any medically determinable physical or mental impairment(s) which can be expected to result in death, or which has lasted or can be expected to last for a continuous period of not less than 12 months.[16] The latter part of the definition is the "duration requirement."

For Social Security purposes, a physical or mental impairment is a physical or mental medical condition. A *medically determinable impairment* is an impairment that results from anatomical, physiological, or psychological abnormalities which can be shown by medically acceptable clinical and laboratory diagnostic techniques. Note that, while SSA considers a claimant's symptoms, the law specifies that there must be "objective" medical evidence to establish the existence of the impairment as well.

"Inability to engage in any substantial gainful activity" means that a claimant's impairment(s) must not only prevent him or her from performing previous work, but also from making an adjustment to any other kind of substantial gainful work that exists in significant numbers in the national economy, considering his or her age, education, and previous work experience. The law specifies that it is irrelevant whether the work exists in the immediate area where the claimant lives, whether a specific job vacancy exists, or whether the claimant would be hired if he or she applied for work. In other words, the question is not whether the claimant can *get* a job, only whether he or she can *do* it.

---

[16] As we have already noted, there is also a statutory definition of blindness under Titles II and XVI, but under Title II, blindness is a kind of "disability," while under Title XVI it is a category separate from "disability." There is also a separate definition of disability under Title II for people who are at least 55 years old and blind. These technical, legal distinctions do not affect your work as a medical expert. We provided the statutory definition of blindness on page 3 of this handbook.

Title XVI of the Act defines disability for children as a "medically determinable physical or mental impairment, which results in marked and severe functional limitations, and which can be expected to result in death or which has lasted or can be expected to last for a continuous period of not less than 12 months." The Act also states that the child must not be engaging in SGA. An impairment(s) causes marked and severe functional limitations if it meets or medically equals a specific listing, or if it functionally equals[17] the listings. We have separate medical listings for SSI childhood disability claims.

In all cases under Titles II and XVI, including SSI childhood disability claims, we cannot find that a claimant is disabled if drug addiction or alcoholism is a "contributing factor material to" the determination of disability. This means that, if we find that the claimant is disabled, we must still deny the claim if we determine that the claimant would not be disabled if he or she stopped using drugs or alcohol.[18] An ALJ may ask for your opinions about what medical findings would persist or what limitations a claimant would still have if he or she stopped using drugs or alcohol.

---

[17] The policy of functional equivalence applies only to children (individuals under age 18) and only in the SSI program.
[18] Although the Act refers to "drug addiction" and "alcoholism," SSA's interpret this terminology to include any "substance use disorder" defined in the latest edition of the American Psychiatric Association's *Diagnostic and Statistical Manual of Mental Disorders*.

Determining Initial Disability for All Title II and Adult Title XVI Cases

The Sequential Evaluation Process

We have extensive regulations and other rules that interpret the provisions of the Act described above and instruct our ALJs and other adjudicators on how to determine whether a claimant is disabled or still disabled. The rules interpreting the basic definition of disability for adults provide a five-step *sequential evaluation process* that we use to determine whether a claimant is disabled. We use different sequential processes to determine initial eligibility of children under Title XVI and whether beneficiaries continue to be disabled (*Continuing Disability Review*, or CDR, and redeterminations of the disability of individuals who qualified for SSI as children when they reach age 18).

The sequential evaluation process requires the adjudicator to follow the steps in order, and at each step either make a decision, in which case the evaluation stops, or decide that a decision cannot be made at that step. When the ALJ determines that a decision cannot be made at a given step, he or she goes on to the next step(s) until a decision can be made. 20 CFR 404.1520 and 416.920.[19]

Note that for each of the first four steps described below, we explain that the ALJ may stop and make a decision. However, with some exceptions,[20] ALJs generally do not make their decisions at the hearing. ALJs generally issue a written decision some time after the hearing. ALJs generally ask for information relevant to all of the steps of the sequential evaluation process at the hearing. The description below explains the steps that an ALJ follows when making disability decisions.

---

[19] "20 CFR" is a reference to Title 20 of the *Code of Federal Regulations* (CFR). The CFR is a compilation of all federal regulations, and Title 20 contains SSA's regulations. Regulation section numbers that start with the number "404" are Title II regulations; those that start with the number "416" are for Title XVI. See the List of References at the end of this handbook for more information about our regulations and other rules.

[20] The most common exception is under a rule we have that allows an ALJ to announce at the hearing that he or she has found that the claimant is disabled. ALJs cannot announce denial decisions at the hearing.

STEP 1:   Is the claimant engaging in substantial gainful activity?[21]

Substantial gainful activity (SGA) is work that: (a) involves doing significant physical or mental activities; and (b) is usually done for pay or profit, whether or not a profit is realized. SGA is most often measured by gross monthly earnings. When countable monthly earnings are above a prescribed amount, which increases each year, the claimant is generally considered to be engaging in SGA. Self-employed individuals are engaging in SGA when they perform significant services in a business, work comparable to unimpaired individuals, or work which is worth the prescribed monthly SGA amount. Since the basic definition of disability is "inability to engage in any substantial gainful activity," we find that a claimant who is actually doing SGA is "not disabled" regardless of the severity of his or her impairment(s).

STEP 2:   Does the claimant have a "severe" impairment?

The ALJ will generally consider two issues at this step: whether the claimant has a "medically determinable impairment" and, if so, whether it is "severe."[22] As we have already noted, the Act requires that the claimant show the existence of an impairment by medically acceptable clinical and laboratory diagnostic techniques, which we often refer to as "objective" medical evidence.

The word "severe" is a term of art in SSA's rules. An impairment or a combination of impairments is "severe" if it significantly limits a claimant's ability to do one or more basic work activities needed to do most jobs. Abilities and aptitudes necessary to do most jobs include physical functions, such as walking, standing, sitting, lifting, pushing, pulling, reaching, carrying, handling, seeing, hearing, and speaking. They also include mental functions, such as understanding, carrying out and remembering simple instructions; using judgment; responding appropriately to supervision, co-workers, and usual work situations; and dealing with changes in a routine work setting. 20 CFR 404.1521 and 416.921.[23]

---

[21] 20 CFR 404.1574, 404.1575, 416.974, and 416.975 provide evaluation guides for determining whether work is SGA.
[22] There is no requirement to establish a medically determinable impairment that results in blindness under Title XVI.
[23] Note that a person with a physical impairment may have a limitation in a "mental" function. For example, persistent pain may interfere with a person's "mental" ability to concentrate. Partly for this reason, you may be asked to comment on a claimant's mental limitation even if you have a specialty in an area of somatic medicine. Moreover, if you are a physician, we expect that you have the training to comment to some extent on issues involving mental disorders.

The threshold for determining that an impairment is "severe" is low. Our rules explain that an impairment is not "severe" if it is only a slight abnormality which has no more than a minimal effect on a claimant's ability to do basic work activities. SSR 85-28.[24] Also, even if none of the claimant's impairments considered separately is "severe," the ALJ must consider whether the claimant's combination of impairments is "severe." Under agency rules, "medically determinable impairments" must be established by symptoms, signs, and laboratory findings, although in practice SSA may find that there is a medically determinable impairment based only on signs *or* laboratory findings. Note that it is not necessary to establish a specific diagnosis to show the existence of a medically determinable impairment. There need only be objective medical evidence demonstrating *some* medical condition to cross this threshold in the rules.

Symptoms are the claimant's own description of his or her physical or mental impairment. Such statements alone are not enough to establish that there is a medically determinable physical or mental impairment. There must also be objective medical evidence; i.e., signs or laboratory findings. (In Title XVI child cases, we will accept as a statement of a symptom(s) the description given by the person who is most familiar with the child, such as a parent, other relative, or guardian, if the child is unable to adequately describe his or her symptom(s).)

Signs are anatomical, physiological, or psychological abnormalities which can be observed apart from the claimant's symptoms. Signs must be shown by medically acceptable clinical diagnostic techniques. Psychiatric signs are medically demonstrable phenomena that indicate specific psychological abnormalities; e.g., abnormalities of behavior, mood, thought, memory, orientation, development, or perception. They must also be shown by observable facts that can be medically described and evaluated.

Laboratory findings are anatomical, physiological, or psychological phenomena which can be shown by the use of medically acceptable laboratory diagnostic techniques. Some of these diagnostic techniques include chemical tests, electrophysiological studies (electrocardiogram, electroencephalogram, etc.) medical imaging studies (such as x-rays), and psychological tests.

If the claimant does not have a medically determinable impairment, or if the claimant's medically determinable impairment(s) is not "severe," the

---

[24] "SSR" stands for "Social Security Ruling," a type of sub-regulatory rule that ALJs and our other adjudicators must follow. See the List of References at the end of this handbook for the title of this SSR and a list of important SSRs that you may need to consult.

claimant is not disabled and the analysis stops. If the claimant has at least one "severe" medically determinable impairment or a number of non-severe impairments that are severe when considered in combination, the ALJ goes to the next step.

> **STEP 3:**   Does the claimant have an impairment(s) that meets or medically equals a listed impairment in the Listing of Impairments?

The ALJ will find that the claimant is disabled when the objective medical and other findings associated with the claimant's medically determinable impairment(s) satisfies all of the criteria for an impairment described in the Listing of Impairments set out in Appendix 1, Subpart P of Part 404 of our regulations (the listings)[25] and meets the duration requirement. Disability may also be established when the claimant has an impairment or a combination of impairments with findings that do not meet the specific requirements of a listed impairment, but are medically equivalent in severity to the findings of a listed impairment and meet the duration requirement.

The Listings describe, for each "body system," medically determinable impairments and associated findings that we consider severe enough to prevent an adult from doing "any gainful activity"[26] regardless of his or her age, education, or work experience. Most of the listed impairments are permanent or expected to result in death. For some listings, we state a specific period of time for which the impairment(s) will meet the listing.[27] For all others, the evidence must show that the impairment meets the duration requirement; that is, that it has lasted or can be expected to last for a continuous period of at least 12 months. 20 CFR 404.1525 and 416.925.[28]

The Listing of Impairments is in two parts. Part A contains 14 body systems, with listings that apply to individuals age 18 and over. We may also use some listings in Part A to evaluate impairments in individuals under age 18 if

---

[25] We print the listings only in Part 404 (the Title II regulations) to save space in the CFR. They also apply to Title XVI.

[26] Note that this is a stricter standard from the standard in the basic definition of disability for adults, "any substantial gainful activity." The listings describe a higher level of severity because they do not consider the vocational factors of previous work experience, age, and education that are considered at the last step of the sequential evaluation process.

[27] For example, some cancer listings specify that an individual will be considered to be under a disability for a specified minimum period of time, such as 12 months, 18 months, or 24 months depending on the specific type of cancer.

[28] Unrelated severe impairments cannot be combined to meet the 12-month duration requirement. 20 CFR 404.1522 and 416.922.

the disease processes have a similar effect on adults and children. Part B contains 15 body systems, with listings that apply <u>only</u> to individuals under age 18.

Each body system section of the listings is also in two parts: a general introduction and specific impairment listings. The introductory text includes definitions of key concepts used in that section, and may also include substantive rules, such as requirements for specific medical findings to establish the existence of a listed impairment. Regardless of whether the medical findings needed to support an impairment are provided in the introductory text or elsewhere in the listing, the existence of an impairment covered by a listing must be established by medical evidence consisting of signs, symptoms, and laboratory findings.

The specific listings follow the introduction in each body section, after the heading "Category of Impairment." An impairment(s) is said to *meet* a listing when the evidence shows that the findings in a specific listing and any additional requirements in the introductory text are satisfied. A medical diagnosis alone is insufficient to meet a listing.[29]

Agency rules also provide for the possibility of "medical equivalence" with a specific listing because the Listing of Impairments does not include every possible impairment or combination of impairments a person could have or every possible medical finding that would indicate an inability to do any gainful activity even for impairments that are included in the listings. To find that an impairment is medically equivalent to a listed impairment, the findings associated with the impairment(s) must be at least of equal medical significance to the required criteria. If the claimant's specific impairment is not listed, the ALJ will compare the findings for the claimant's impairment with the listed impairment most like, or most analogous to, the claimant's impairment to decide whether the claimant's impairment is medically equal. If the claimant has more than one impairment, and none of them meets or medically equals a listed impairment, the ALJ will compare the findings associated with all of the claimant's impairments with those for closely analogous listed impairments. If the findings related to the claimant's impairments are at least of equal medical significance to those of a listed impairment, the ALJ will find that the claimant's impairment is *medically equivalent to* the analogous listing, or that it *medically equals* that listing. 20 CFR 404.1526 and 416.926.

---

[29] As you become familiar with the listings, you will note that there are some listings that are met simply by having a confirmed diagnosis of a particular disorder, such as non-mosaic Down syndrome—listing 10.06 for adults. However, even in these circumstances we must have objective medical evidence in the case record that establishes the diagnosis.

You will frequently be asked whether you think a claimant's impairment(s) meets or medically equals a listing. You must be prepared to identify listings that are appropriate to the claimant's impairment(s); and either to identify the evidence in the case record that shows that the impairment(s) meets or medically equals a specific listing, or to explain why it does not.

If the claimant has an impairment(s) that meets or medically equals a listing and meets the duration requirement, the ALJ will find that the claimant is disabled and the analysis stops. If not, the ALJ will go on to the next step of the sequential evaluation process.

Residual Functional Capacity (RFC)

If the claimant is not engaging in SGA and has at least one severe impairment that does not meet or medically equal a listing, the ALJ must assess the claimant's RFC before going on to step 4. The RFC assessment is a description of the physical and mental work functions the claimant can still perform in a work setting on a sustained basis despite his or her impairment(s).

RFC is the *most* that the claimant can still do despite the limitations caused by his or her impairment(s), including any related physical or mental symptoms, such as pain, fatigue, shortness of breath, weakness, or nervousness. In order to assess the claimant' RFC, the ALJ may ask you to give your opinion regarding the claimant's functional limitations and restrictions caused by medically determined impairments. If the claimant has more than one medically determinable impairment, the ALJ must consider limitations from *all* of the claimant's impairments, including limitations from any medically determinable impairment that is not "severe."[30]

You will frequently be asked your opinion about claimants' functional abilities, limitations, and restrictions. The ALJ's assessment of a claimant's RFC will not rely solely on your testimony. The ALJ will base his or her findings on all of the relevant medical and other evidence, including your testimony.[31] 20 CFR 404.1545 and 416.945. The ALJ will specify what information he or she wants you to testify about. Since you will not have

---

[30] As you saw under step 2, the agency's definition of "severe" is based on work functioning. Therefore, an impairment that is not "severe" might still cause some slight or minimal limitations in functioning, and those limitations might affect the claimant's ability to do some jobs or job functions.

[31] Other relevant evidence can include the claimant's own statements and the statements of other people who know the claimant.

examined the claimant, it will be especially important that you explain your opinion based on the information in the case record and your medical expertise.

There are two important additional agency policies about RFC you must know:

- First, RFC is generally what an individual can still do on a "regular and continuing basis," 8 hours a day, for 5 days a week, or an equivalent work schedule-that is, in a work setting.[32]

- Second, RFC considers only the effects of the claimant's medically determinable impairment(s). By rule, the ALJ cannot consider the claimant's age, sex, body habitus,[33] or overall conditioning when determining RFC, but only limitations that result from documented medically determinable impairments.

See SSR 96-8p.

The ALJ evaluates the claimant's ability to meet the physical, mental, sensory, and other requirements of work. The ALJ considers physical abilities, including: exertional activities (e.g., sitting, standing, walking, lifting, carrying, pushing, and pulling); postural activities (e.g., stooping, climbing); manipulative activities (e.g., reaching, handling); vision; the physical aspects of communication (e.g., hearing, speaking); and environmental factors (e.g., tolerance of temperature extremes or dusty environments). The ALJ will also consider mental functions (e.g., understanding and remembering instructions of various complexities, concentrating, getting along with coworkers and the public, responding appropriately to supervision, and responding to changes in the workplace). Of course, the ALJ will ask you to provide your opinions only about functioning that is within your area of training and expertise.

---

[32] In rare cases, the ALJ may ask for your opinion about functioning the claimant can do in a part-time setting. However, unless the ALJ specifies otherwise, you should assume that you are being asked for your opinion about how the claimant can function for 8 hours a day, 5 days a week, and on a sustained basis. If you are not sure, you should ask the ALJ before providing your opinion.

[33] Note, however, that SSA may consider obesity to be a medically determinable impairment. See, e.g., SSR 02-1p, cited in the List of References at the end of this handbook.

STEP 4:   Can the claimant do any past relevant work?

After assessing RFC, the ALJ decides whether the claimant is able to do any *past relevant work* (PRW), either as the claimant actually performed it or as it is generally performed in the national economy. The term "PRW" is generally defined as the work the claimant performed at the SGA level within the last 15 years (or before certain ending dates specified in our rules) and includes only jobs that lasted long enough for the claimant to learn to do them.

The ALJ will make this determination by comparing the claimant's RFC with the requirements of these jobs. If there is PRW that the claimant can still do, the claimant is not disabled and the analysis stops. If the claimant cannot do any PRW, or does not have any PRW, the ALJ will continue to the last step. You should never comment on whether you believe a claimant can do his or her PRW, even if you are asked.

STEP 5:   Can the claimant do other work?

If the ALJ finds the claimant can no longer do any PRW, or the claimant does not have any PRW, the ALJ must finally consider whether the claimant can make an adjustment to other work, which exists in significant numbers in the national economy, at the last step of the sequential evaluation process. The ALJ must consider the claimant's RFC, and the vocational factors of age, education, and past relevant work experience. The ALJ will use a complex set of agency rules, which include special rules in Appendix 2 of Subpart P of Part 404 (called the *Medical-Vocational Guidelines*, but often referred to as *the grid rules* or *the grids*). The ALJ will often call on another expert witness, called a *vocational expert* (VE), to provide testimony regarding whether work exists that an individual with a particular RFC would be able to do. Again, you should never comment on whether you believe a claimant can work, even if you are asked.

At this last step of the sequential evaluation process, the ALJ must decide whether the claimant is disabled. If the claimant can make an adjustment to other work, he or she is not disabled. If the claimant cannot, he or she is disabled.

NOTE: In cases where there is medical evidence of drug addiction or alcoholism (DAA), the ALJ may be required to also determine whether the DAA is a contributing factor that is "material" to the determination of disability. In these cases, the ALJ must also determine whether the claimant would still be disabled if he or she stopped using drugs or alcohol.

Therefore, the ALJ may ask you for your opinions about changes in medical findings and in physical or mental functional limitations (or both) that might occur if the claimant stopped substance use. If the evidence in the case shows that the claimant has DAA, you should be prepared to answer these kinds of questions and, wherever possible, to cite evidence in the case record that supports your opinion, such as evidence from a period of nonuse.

Determining Initial Disability under Title XVI for Individuals under Age 18 (SSI Childhood Cases)

For Title XVI disability purposes, a "child" is an individual who has not attained age 18. As we have already noted, Title XVI provides a different statutory definition of disability for children than for adults, based on "marked and severe functional limitations." The sequential evaluation process for children who seek SSI is different from the process for adults. The standard of disability for children who seek SSI is stricter than the standard of disability for adults. SSA regulations provide that the child's impairment(s) will be found to result in "marked and severe functional limitations" if it is of *listing-level severity*; that is, for a child to be found disabled, his or her impairment(s) must meet or medically equal a specific listing, or "functionally equal the listings" (see below). The child's impairment must also meet the same duration requirement as in the adult standard.

The three steps in the SSI childhood sequential evaluation process are:

Step 1: Is the child engaging in substantial gainful activity?

The term SGA has the same meaning for children as for adults.

- If yes, the ALJ will find that the child is not disabled.

- If no, the ALJ goes to step 2.

Step 2: Does the child have a "severe impairment or combination of impairments"?

For a child, the definition of a "severe" impairment is essentially the same as for adults except that, instead of referring to "basic work-related activities," the definition for children refers to "functional limitations." Therefore, a "severe impairment(s)" for a child is more than a slight abnormality or a combination of slight abnormalities that causes more than minimal functional limitations considering appropriate functioning for the child's age. 20 CFR 416.924(c). Whenever we consider a child claimant's functioning, we must consider it in comparison to children of the same age who do not have impairments.

- If the child does not have a medically determinable impairment(s), or if the impairment(s) is not severe, the ALJ will find that the child is not disabled.

Medical Expert Handbook

- If the child has a severe impairment, the ALJ goes to step 3.

Step 3: Does the child's impairment(s) meet or medically equal a listing, or functionally equal the listings?

The rules for determining whether an impairment(s) meets or medically equals the criteria of a specific listing are the same for children as for adults. As already noted, in evaluating whether the impairment(s) of a child meets or medically equals a specific listing, the ALJ will first consider Part B of the Listings; if the child's impairment(s) does not meet or medically equal an impairment in that part, the ALJ will consider whether there is an appropriate listing under Part A that the impairment(s) could meet or medically equal.   20 CFR 416.925(b)(2) and 416.926.

- If the child's impairment(s) meets or medically equals a listing, and satisfies the duration requirement, the ALJ will find that the child is disabled.

- If the impairment(s) does not meet or medically equal any specific listing, the ALJ will determine whether it *functionally equals the listings*.

Functional equivalence to the listings is a concept <u>used only in evaluating disability for persons under age 18 in Title XVI cases</u>. Unlike "meets" and "medical equivalence," the determination is not made by reference to specific listings or any other provisions within the Listing of Impairments; it is a standard of disability based on "listing-level severity." Our rules further define this term as requiring *marked* limitations in two of six domains of functioning or *extreme* limitation in one. Our regulations define the domains as broad areas of functioning intended to capture all of what a child can or cannot do. They are: (1) acquiring and using information; (2) attending and completing tasks; (3) interacting and relating with others; (4) moving about and manipulating objects; (5) caring for yourself; and (6) health and physical well-being. 20 CFR 416.926a.

We also define the severity terms "marked" and "extreme" for functional equivalence in our rules. 20 CFR 416.926a(e). The definitions are provided in a variety of different ways, such as in descriptive terms and in terms of scores on standardized tests.

In assessing whether the child has "marked" or "extreme" limitations, the ALJ must consider the functional limitations from all medically determinable impairments, including any impairments that are not "severe." 20 CFR 416.926a(a). The rules also require consideration of the "interactive and cumulative effects" of the child's impairment or multiple impairments in any and all affected domains. For example, while it is obvious that multiple impairments can have effects in more than one domain, the rules provide that a single impairment may have effects in more than one domain. Likewise, combinations of impairments need not have effects in multiple domains; in some cases, the combination of impairments may have an effect in only one domain. These principles, the domains, and other important information you must know if you testify at hearings involving SSI child claimants are described in more detail in 20 CFR 416.924a and 416.926a of the regulations and in SSRs 09-1p through 09-8p.[34]

In assessing whether a child has limitations, the ALJ will determine how appropriately, effectively, and independently the child performs activities compared to other children of the same age who do not have impairments. We provide guidance about, and examples of, typical and atypical functioning in each of the domains for children in four age groups[35] in 20 CFR 416.926a(g) through (l) and SSRs 09-3p through 09-8p. If you testify in SSI childhood disability claims, you must be familiar with these rules and guidance; however, you should also provide your own pediatric expertise.

Note: As you have already seen, we use the term "severe" in our sequential evaluation processes for adults and children. As you become more familiar with our program, you will notice that we also use the term "marked" in several rules, especially in some listings and in the policy of functional equivalence.[36] Our rules specify that the *phrase* "marked and severe functional limitations" that is used to define the standard of disability in the Act for children claiming SSI benefits does not have the same meaning as the *separate terms* "marked" and "severe" we use in other rules. 20 CFR 416.902.

---

[34] See the List of References at the end of this handbook.

[35] Newborns and young infants (birth to attainment of age 1), older infants and toddlers (age 1 to attainment of age 3), preschool children (age 3 to attainment of age 6), school-age children (age 6 to attainment of age 12), and adolescents (age 12 to attainment of age 18). We also have rules for adjusting chronological age for prematurity. See 20 CFR 416.924b.

[36] For example, we use the term "marked" in the mental disorders and immune system disorders listings for adults and children.

Determining Continuing Disability

In addition to adjudicating appeals involving a claimant's initial entitlement to disability benefits, ALJs also adjudicate claims involving appeals of determinations that individuals who were previously awarded disability benefits are no longer "disabled." There are two basic types of cases in this category.

- From time to time, we review the continuing disability of both adults and children under Titles II and XVI.[37] We refer to these cases as *continuing disability reviews* (CDRs) or "cessation" cases.

- Title XVI also requires that we redetermine the disabilities of individuals who qualified for SSI as children when they reach age 18 using the adult rules for initial disability claims. We refer to these cases as *age-18 redetermination* cases.

In these types of cases, the DDS will have already determined that the individual's disability ended on a specific date. The ALJ then considers whether the individual's disability ended on that date, at a later date, or not at all. In some—but not all—cases, the ALJ will consider whether the individual has become disabled again even if the disability did end in the past. The ALJ will give you instructions, and you will be asked questions, appropriate to the issues of the specific case.

We conduct CDRs for adults and children. In both cases, we use different sequential evaluation processes than in initial claims for benefits, because the Act contains different standards for these reviews. 20 CFR 404.1594, 416.994, and 416.994a. The primary difference is that there generally must be evidence showing medical improvement in the individual's condition from the more recent of the date he or she was first found disabled or the last time we found that the disability continued. There are few differences between the opinions you will be asked to give in these cases and the opinions you are asked to give in cases involving initial applications for benefits.

---

[37] We review cases at frequencies ranging from as little as 6 months up to about 7 years depending on the probability that the individual's impairment(s) will improve to the point of non-disability. We do not send all individuals' cases to the DDS for a medical review. In many cases, we determine through a questionnaire we call a "mailer" that the individual's disability continues.

Medical Expert Handbook

CDRs and Medical Improvement

The Act provides that we generally cannot find that an individual's disability has ended unless we have evidence showing that:

- The impairment(s) upon which we last found him or her to be disabled or still disabled has medically improved, [38]

- The medical improvement is "related to the ability to work" in the case of adults, [39] *and*

- The individual is not disabled under the basic definition of disability.

To determine whether medical improvement has occurred, the ALJ will look only at the impairment(s) the individual had at the time of our most recent favorable disability decision; that is, either our initial decision that the individual was disabled or, if more recent, our last determination that the individual was still disabled. We call this the *comparison point decision* (CPD). The ALJ will compare the medical severity of the CPD impairment(s) at the time of the DDS's cessation determination to the severity of those impairments at the time of the CPD. 20 CFR 404.1594(b)(7), 416.994(b)(1)(vii), and 416.994a(b)(1). Medical improvement is any decrease in the medical severity of those CPD impairments as shown by the signs, symptoms, and laboratory findings. 20 CFR 404.1594(c)(2), 416.994(b)(2), and 416.994a(c). [40]

We have complex rules defining what the term "related to the ability to work" means. Even if there has been medical improvement related to the ability to work, the ALJ will find that an adult's disability continues if the adult has an impairment(s)—including any new impairment(s) that was not present at the time of the CPD— or a combination of impairments that meet the basic definition of disability; that is, if he or she is unable to engage in SGA. Similarly, an ALJ will find that a child whose impairment(s) meets or medically equals a listing or functionally equals the listings (i.e., that results in "marked and severe functional limitations") is still disabled even if there

---

[38] There are certain specific and very limited exceptions to the requirement for showing medical improvement. See 20 CFR 404.1594(d) and (e), 416.994(b)(3) and (4), and 416.994a(e) and (f).

[39] There is no corresponding provision for children under SSI.

[40] For further guidance on medical improvement in cases involving children, see also SSR 05-03p.

has been medical improvement in the CPD impairment(s). Suffice it to say that an ALJ may ask for your opinions about issues such as the following:

- What the signs, symptoms, and laboratory findings associated with a claimant's impairments were *at the time of the CPD*.

- What the signs, symptoms, and laboratory findings associated with the CPD impairments were (if any) *at the time the DDS said that disability ended or at a later date*.

- Whether the individual's CPD impairment(s) met or equaled a listing at the time the DDS said that disability ended or at a later date.[41]

- Whether all of the individual's impairments, including any new impairment(s) in addition to the CPD impairment(s), met or medically equaled a listing at the time the DDS said that disability ended or at a later date.

- The individual's functional limitations at the time the DDS said that disability ended or at a later date based only on the CPD impairments or based on all of the individual's impairments.

As you can see, these questions are very similar to the questions you are asked to give opinions about in initial adult and child disability claims. However, in these cases, the ALJ will ask you to give your opinions only about specific impairments the claimant has or had, and will specify dates for which you should provide your opinions.

Age -18 Redeterminations

Title XVI of the Act requires that we "redetermine" the eligibility of individuals who were eligible for an SSI payment as a child when they reach age 18. The Act specifies that we must use the rules we use when we determine initial disability in adults, and not the medical improvement review standard we use in CDRs. Under our regulations, we use the adult sequential evaluation process to evaluate disability in initial adult claims, except that we do not use step 1 (Is the claimant engaging in SGA?).   20 CFR 416.987. In these cases, you will not need to distinguish CPD impairments from all current impairments, as in CDRs. The ALJ will ask you

---

[41] In some cases, the ALJ may ask you for an opinion about whether the impairment(s) met or equaled a listing that we no longer have either because we have removed or revised it. If that is the case, the ALJ will provide you with the necessary information you need to answer the question.

the same kinds of questions that he or she would ask in any initial adult claim for disability benefits.

Interrogatories

As we have already noted, we may ask you to respond in writing to specific written questions referred to as *interrogatories*. You may receive interrogatories from the ALJ, but you may also receive interrogatories from hearing office staff before a case is assigned to an ALJ for a hearing. If you receive interrogatories before a hearing, the ALJ may or may not ask you to also appear and testify at the hearing.

An ALJ may also send you interrogatories that were posed by the claimant or the claimant's representative. The ALJ must approve any interrogatories proposed by a claimant or representative. You should never answer interrogatories submitted directly to you from the claimant or his or her representative, and you should send your responses to interrogatories only to the ALJ. The ALJ and his or her staff will ensure that the claimant and his or her representative receive a copy.

Usually, the interrogatories will be in the form of a questionnaire. You may type or legibly write your responses directly on the questionnaire if space permits. If you need more space to answer a question, attach separate sheets of paper with your responses. You should answer all questions completely. It is especially important that you explain and support your responses with references to specific medical findings and other evidence you received from the hearing office. Identify the reports in which they are contained. All correspondence between you and the ALJ will become part of the official case record.

If you have a question about any of the interrogatories, you should request clarification from the ALJ (or the Hearing Office Chief Administrative Law Judge if the case is not yet assigned to a particular ALJ) in writing. If you cannot answer a particular question or cannot answer it completely, because of conflicts in the evidence or because the evidence is incomplete, you should respond by explaining why you cannot answer the question. If possible, you should also provide an opinion and recommendation to the ALJ about what evidence he or she could obtain to resolve the conflict or complete the record.

If the interrogatories relate to new medical evidence the ALJ received after you testified or responded to other interrogatories, you should state whether the new evidence changes any of your prior responses and why.

Note that in all cases, the ALJ will submit the questions and your responses for review to the claimant's representative (if the claimant has a representative) with a copy to the claimant (or just to the claimant if unrepresented). The claimant has the right to request a supplemental hearing or to produce other information to rebut any of your responses.

Other Medical Considerations

Mental Impairments in Adults

In addition to extensive information in the introductory text of the mental disorders "body system" in the listings (section 12.00, Mental Disorders), the agency has separate regulations specifically for the evaluation of mental disorders in adults. 20 CFR 404.1520a and 416.920a. These regulations require the ALJ to specify the symptoms, signs, and laboratory findings that establish the existence of a medically determinable mental impairment(s).

If the claimant has a mental impairment(s), the ALJ must rate the functional limitations in the same four broad functional areas that appear in the "paragraph B" criteria of the adult mental disorders listings: activities of daily living; social functioning; concentration, persistence, or pace; and episodes of decompensation. This *psychiatric review technique* (technique) is applied to make the threshold determination of severity with regard to a mental impairment. While the listings provide measures to determine whether an impairment imposes listing-level limitation in each domain,[42] the technique requires the ALJ to rate the domains on a multi-point scale.[43] The technique provides a five-point scale for the first three domains: none, mild, moderate, marked, and extreme. For the fourth domain (episodes of decompensation), the scale is: none, one or two, three, and four or more.

After the ALJ rates the degree of limitation in each domain, he or she determines whether the claimant has a "severe" impairment (step two of the adult sequential evaluation process), whether the impairment(s) meets or medically equals one of the mental disorders listings (step three of the adult sequential evaluation process), and if necessary, whether to assess RFC and go on in the sequential evaluation process.

There are three other provisions of these regulations you should know:

---

[42] "Marked" limitation for meeting the requirements of a mental disorders listing in the first three paragraph B criteria. The fourth paragraph B criterion is rated by the number of episodes of decompensation, and is met with three such episodes. See section 12.00C in the introductory text of the adult mental disorders listings for a description of the paragraph B criteria and definitions of the terms we use to rate whether a mental disorder meets one of the listings.

[43] With one exception (listing 12.05C), the adult mental disorders listings describe only individual mental disorders, not combinations of such disorders. Combinations of mental disorders can medically equal mental disorders listings. The technique also requires the ALJ to consider limitations from combinations of mental impairments throughout the application of the technique.

- First, the regulations specify that we use the criteria in sections 12.00C through 12.00H when we rate severity under the scales we describe above. This includes using the same definition of the term "marked" as we use in section 12.00C.

- Second, as in the adult mental disorders listings, the ALJ must consider the extent to which a mental impairment(s) interferes with the claimant's ability to function "independently, appropriately, effectively, and on a sustained basis" and provides guidance about some of the factors the ALJ must consider in making this determination.

- Third, the regulations specify that the last point on each of the two rating scales described above "represents a degree of limitation that is incompatible with the ability to do any gainful activity."[44] As you learned in the section explaining step three of the adult sequential evaluation process (page 17), "inability to do any gainful activity" is the standard of listing-level severity for adults. *This means that an adult who has an "extreme" limitation in only one of the first three broad areas of functioning or "four or more episodes of decompensation" as defined in our rules has an impairment(s) that medically equals a mental disorders listing.*

When you testify or give written evidence in a case involving an alleged mental disorder, you should be prepared to testify about: the signs, symptoms, and laboratory findings in the case record regarding the claimant's alleged mental disorder(s); your opinion about the claimant's functional limitations in the four broad areas of functioning using the rating terms in 20 CFR 404.1520a and 416.920a *and* in more specific work-related terms in connection with an RFC assessment; and your opinion about whether any mental disorder(s) "meet" or "medically equal" a listing. If you testify in a case involving intellectual disabilities (mental retardation), you must also be familiar with instructions we have in an operating manual called the Program Operations Manual System (POMS).[45] The POMS includes guidance for determining whether "mental retardation" medically equals listing 12.05C. See POMS DI 24515.056D Evaluation of Specific Issues — Mental Disorders —Determining Medical Equivalence, available at https://secure.ssa.gov/apps10/poms.nsf/lnx/0424515056!opendocument.

---

[44] 20 CFR 404.1520a(c)(4).
[45] The entire POMs is available at http://policy.ssa.gov/poms.nsf/aboutpoms

Evaluation of Pain and Other Symptoms (20 CFR 404.1529 and 416.929)

A claimant's symptoms—such as pain, fatigue, weakness, and nervousness—are often significant to the ALJ's determination of whether a claimant is disabled. Agency policy provides that symptoms can sometimes suggest a greater severity of impairment than is demonstrated by objective medical findings alone. An ALJ evaluates both the objective medical evidence (medical signs and laboratory findings) and the testimony (statements and reports from the claimant, medical sources, and other persons), and makes a finding on the *credibility* of the claimant's complaints regarding his or symptoms and their functional effects.

The ALJ may ask for your assistance in comparing a claimant's symptoms to the other evidence in the record. If the ALJ asks you to consider the effects of a claimant's symptoms, you should consider symptoms, including symptoms from any treatment side-effects, in terms of any additional physical or mental limitations or restrictions they may impose beyond those clearly demonstrated by the objective physical or mental manifestations of the claimant's impairment(s).

Our regulations and other rules require the ALJ to consider many factors that will help him or her assess the effects of a claimant's symptoms. They include, but are not limited to: the claimant's daily activities; the location, duration, frequency, and intensity of the symptom(s); precipitating and aggravating factors; the type, dosage, effectiveness, and adverse side effects of any medication; treatment, other than medication, the claimant uses or has used for relief of the symptom(s); other measures the claimant uses or has used to relieve the symptom(s) (e.g., lying flat or sleeping on or with a board for back pain); and any other factors concerning the claimant's functional limitations and restrictions. 20 CFR 404.1529 and 416.929; SSR 96-7p.

Onset of Disability

The onset date of disability is generally the first day a claimant is disabled as defined in the Act.[46] Factors relevant to the determination of disability onset

---

[46] However, a claimant cannot be eligible for SSI payments until the month after the month of application, so the ALJ will often choose an onset on the date of the application if the claimant is disabled. Nevertheless, you should be prepared to provide testimony about what the medical records show for the entire period they cover, even if they predate the application, unless the ALJ asks you to limit your testimony to the date of the application or another specific date.

include the individual's allegations, work history, medical evidence, and any other relevant information in the case record. The ALJ may ask for your opinion about when a claimant's impairment(s) first reached a specified level of severity or caused functional limitations that the ALJ will specify. Note that in some cases, the ALJ may ask for your expert opinion about these issues for periods that precede the earliest medical evidence in the record. For example, an ALJ may ask you to give an opinion about a reasonable onset date before a disabling cancer was diagnosed, even before the claimant first sought medical help.

Duration of Disability

Duration refers to that period of time during which an individual is continuously disabled. The Social Security Act provides that, in order to be considered disabled, most impairments must have lasted or be expected to last for a continuous period of not less than 12 months or be expected to result in death.[47] The claimant need not be unable to work every single day of the 12-month period. Social Security policy recognizes that many impairments are subject to exacerbation and remission, and temporary remissions do not usually prevent claimants from meeting the "continuous period" criteria. SSA rules sometimes speak of evaluating a claimant's impairment "longitudinally"; that is, to form a picture of the person's functioning over time.

Two or more unrelated severe impairments cannot be combined consecutively to meet the duration test. For example, if an individual fractured an upper extremity in May 2005 that healed and caused no functional limitations as of November 2005, and the same individual fractured a lower extremity in October 2005 which healed and caused no further limitations as of June 2006, these impairments could not be combined to meet the 12-month test. This individual could not be found disabled even if each of these impairments was sufficiently severe to preclude work activities for each period at issue.

Also, if an individual has multiple impairments, but one or more of those impairments improves or is expected to improve within 12 months, so that the combined effect of the remaining impairments is no longer severe, the duration test is not met.

---

[47] The exception is for blindness under Title XVI. The Act does not provide a duration requirement for such cases.

Failure to Follow Prescribed Treatment

Social Security regulations and other rules provide that an otherwise disabled claimant who fails, without good reason, to follow prescribed treatment that is clearly expected to restore his or her ability to work (or in the case of a child under Title XVI to improve the impairment(s) to the point of nondisability), cannot be found disabled. The treatment must be prescribed by the claimant's own treating source; it cannot simply be a recommendation, nor can you recommend or prescribe it. An ALJ *may*, however, ask you for your opinion about the expected effect or result of treatment that a claimant's treating source has prescribed.

The ALJ may also ask you to provide information that will help him or her make a finding about whether the claimant had an acceptable reason for failing to follow prescribed treatment. Examples of such reasons include:

- Acceptance of prescribed treatment would be contrary to the teachings and tenets of the claimant's or beneficiary's religion.

- Cataract extraction for one eye is prescribed, but the loss of visual efficiency in the other eye is severe and cannot be corrected through treatment;

- The individual is unable to afford prescribed treatment which he or she is willing to accept, but for which free community resources are unavailable.

- Any duly licensed treating medical source who has treated the claimant or beneficiary advises against the treatment prescribed for the currently disabling condition.

- Surgery was previously performed with unsuccessful results and the additional major surgery is again being prescribed for the same impairment;

- The treatment is very risky for the claimant because of its magnitude, unusual nature, or other reason (e.g., organ transplant, open heart surgery); or

- The treatment involves amputation of an extremity.

Appendix 10: The Duty to Submit All(?) Evidence

Robert E. Rains
Prof. Emeritus
The Pennsylvania State University Dickinson School of Law
Carlisle, PA.

On March 20, 2015, the Social Security Administrations published in final its "All Evidence" regulations, with an effective date of April 20, 2015. 80 FR 14828-14838. The regulations go a long way toward answering the much debated question whether attorney and non-attorney representatives must submit adverse evidence in Social Security proceedings. Subject to quite limited exceptions, the answer is yes, we do. But, as an examination of the Comments and Responses in the Federal Register makes clear, significant questions and ambiguities remain. For ease of reference, I have numbered the Comments and Responses although they are not numbered in the Federal Register.

Comment and Response 1. SSA has changed its terminology from evidence that is "material" to a disability determination to evidence that "relates" to a claim. "[W]e intend for the word 'relates' to have its ordinary meaning, which is to show or establish a logical connection between two things." In turn, "evidence" is "anything you or anyone else submits to us or that we obtain that relates to your claim." Some commenters suggested that the change in terminology made the rules less clear. SSA responded that, "The issue of what is 'material' involves a legal judgment....By requiring claimants to submit all evidence that 'relates' to their disability claims, we are removing the need to make that type of judgment."

SSA's distinction between material evidence and evidence that relates to a claim is, at best, rather elusive. In the context of criminal law, the Supreme Court has found there is a duty on the prosecutor to turn over evidence that is both favorable to the accused and "material either to guilt or to punishment." *Brady v. Maryland*, 373 U.S. 83 (1963). "The requirement of materiality is a concern that the suppressed evidence might have affected the outcome of the trial." *United States v. Agurs*, 427 U.S. 97, 104 (1976). Law dictionaries fail to shed additional light on the supposed distinction. For example, Bryan Garner's *A Handbook of Basic Legal Terms* defines "material" as "having some logical connection with the consequential facts." It is difficult to imagine that evidence might relate to a claim without having the possibility of affecting the outcome of that claim or having some logical connection to a consequential fact." (See also Federal Rule of Evidence 401, defining evidence as being relevant if "it has any tendency to make a fact more or less probable than it would be without the evidence; and the fact is of consequence in determining the action.")

Significantly SSA says that "evidence of treatment for conditions other than the one alleged by the claimant could relate to the claim." Query: what does this mean for the claimant who is obviously mentally impaired but wants to proceed only on the basis of real or perceived physical limitations? Can a representative agree not to submit any mental health records or information? (See ABA Model Rule of Professional Conduct 1.2(a): "...a lawyer shall abide by a client's decisions concerning the objectives of representation and...shall consult with the client as to the means by which they are to be pursued.")

SSA asserts that it expects its adjudicators to use reasonable, good faith judgment when requesting information or evidence from a claimant. "For example, we would not require a claimant to disclose treatment for a health matter such as an abortion, if the claimant alleged disability based on a genetic disorder." (Of course, a representative might wish to disclose such evidence if the claimant's reason for the abortion was knowledge or belief that the fetus carried, or had a high probability of carrying, such a serious disorder.)

"Upon request," claimants must inform SSA of relevant facts such as that they applied for worker's compensation. Thus, if asked, a representative obviously cannot deny the existence of a WC claim of which he or she is aware, but the representative does not have to volunteer the existence of that claim. But if the representative possesses any portion of the WC file that relates to the Social Security claim, the representative would have to turn over that evidence, whether or not asked to do so. It appears that a representative who is aware of a WC claim might not wish to obtain the file of that claim.

Although the distinction between material and related evidence may be ephemeral, SSA's bottom line is clear: "... we expect claimants to exercise their reasonable, good faith judgment about what evidence "relates" to their disability claims keeping in mind, however, that the meaning of "relates" is broad and includes anything that has a logical or causal connection **whether it is favorable or unfavorable to the claim.**"

Comment and Response 2: This C & R largely reiterates the prior one. "Clarifying our rules regarding **the duty to submit all evidence** that relates to the disability claim will 'enable us to obtain more complete case records and adjudicate claims more accurately.'"

Comment and Response 3: In this C & R, SSA provides another exception to the "all-evidence" rule. "Claimants do not have to memorialize statements made to others or disclose the names of all people with personal knowledge of their claims, unless they would like us to consider that information." Moreover the final rule "requires only that claimants submit all evidence 'received' from another source in its entirety." It has been suggested that the latter limitation would permit a representative to ask treating sources to send the representative only unsigned reports which would not be considered to be "in their entirety." Then if the report were unfavorable the representative would "deep six" it, but if it were favorable, the representative would ask the treating source to sign it so it could be submitted. Such shenanigans could hardly be considered to be good faith compliance with the all-evidence rules, and could well lead to sanctions against the representative.

Query: Would a representative be required to submit an unsolicited "poison pen" letter from an ex-spouse or neighbor asserting that the claimant is a malingerer or is working under the table? What if the letter were anonymous?

The duty to submit all evidence is ongoing and "applies at each level of the administrative review process, including the Appeals Council level if (it) relates to the period which is the subject of the most recent hearing decision." Query: Why does SSA limit the rule to the administrative review process? Is SSA really trying to endorse withholding relevant evidence at the initial application stage? This seems highly doubtful.

Comment and Response 4. Here SSA explains that it has rejected a proposal from the Administrative Conference of the United States (ACUS) that it only require claimants to submit evidence in specific categories.

Comment and Response 5. SSA rejects arguments such as that requiring claimants "to submit unfavorable evidence might deter claimants from seeking medical evaluations that could lead to helpful treatment out of fear that they might have to disclose this information later in a disability claim." Not requiring submission of unfavorable evidence "would also be inconsistent with Congress's intent in enacting Section 201 of the Social Security Protection Act of 2004 (SSPA), which authorizes us to impose a civil monetary penalty on a claimant who should have come forward to notify us of changed circumstances that affect eligibility, but failed to do so." Query: Why did it take SSA over a decade to come to this conclusion under the SSPA?

"In addition, it is fair to require the disclosure of related but potentially unfavorable evidence, because claimants (or their representatives) can explain to us why they believe we should give such evidence little or no weight." This was probably standard practice for the vast majority of representatives prior to promulgation of the 2015 all-evidence regulations. The problem, of course, involves the adjudicator who will latch onto even the most dubious single piece of evidence to deny a claim.

Comment and Response 6. The process will remain "non-adversarial," (at least to the extent that it ever was).

Comment and Response 7. The all-evidence rules do not alter the SSPA's statutory standard for imposing civil monetary penalty if SSA finds that a person withheld "disclosure, of a fact which the person knows or should know is material to a determination of any initial or continuing right to…[benefits or payments]." Thus it appears that SSA in theory could not impose a civil monetary penalty for failure to disclose a fact which was related to a claim but somehow not material to that claim. What such a fact might be is difficult to imagine; no example is provided.

Comment and Response 8. The all-evidence rules do not alter SSA's duty to assist claimants in developing the record.

Comment and Response 9. SSA removed the term "relevant" "to avoid confusion with the standard for submission of evidence in this final rule, which is the submission of all evidence that 'relates' to the disability claim. Query: Could evidence be related to a claim but not be relevant to it, or vice versa?

Comment and Response 10. The rules, and their exceptions, apply equally to attorney and non-attorney representatives.

Comment and Response 11. Attorneys must comply with these rules even if the attorneys believe the rules would require them to violate their state bar ethics rules. Citing "one leading legal scholar in this area" (Robert Rains, *Professional responsibility and Social Security Representation: The Myth of the State-Bar Bar to Compliance with Federal Rules on Production of Adverse Evidence*, 92 Cornell L. Rev. 363, 390 (2007)), SSA concludes that federal law prevails here under the Supremacy Clause of the U.S. Constitution.

Very importantly, "Under this final rule, we expect all representatives (attorney or non-attorney) to inform claimants they represent that we do not permit the withholding of any evidence related to the disability claim, even if it is unfavorable." Practice Pointer: It is now sound policy to put such wording in bold in one's Representation

Agreement, and to ask the client to initial this language in the margin, in order to try to preclude subsequent unhappy surprises and battles with the client.

Comment and Response 12. SSA rejects a suggestion that it extend the attorney-client privilege to "non-authorized representatives, such as physicians, licensed clinical social workers, and other licensed health care providers." Such an extension would be inconsistent with the authorization forms claimants sign when they apply which authorize such professionals to disclose otherwise confidential information.

Comment and Response 13. SSA denies that the rule is intended to permit the government to impermissibly communicate directly with represented claimants.

Comment and Response 14. SSA has purposely adopted a more limited version of the work product doctrine than that set forth in Rule 26(b) of the Federal Rules of Civil Procedure. If a treating source sends the representative treatment notes or a written opinion, the representative is bound to submit such evidence. But, "if a representative takes notes during a discussion with a claimant's medical source, those notes are protected from disclosure as work product." In short, representatives "can fully investigate the merits of any disability claim" (assuming they can get all medical sources to discuss the claimant's condition with them either face-to-face or over the telephone—a highly improbable and likely very expensive proposition in most cases), and "they do not have to disclose the results of their investigation unless they obtain a medical record or a written opinion from a medical source."

Comment and Response 15. SSA expects claimants and hence representatives to submit all evidence received from another source "in its entirety." But this does not mean that representatives must request the entirety of all evidence that may exist. For example, a representative might request only a discharge summary from a hospital chart, rather than the entire chart. If that is the only part of the chart that the representative receives, it is all that must be submitted. Although SSA states that it is not the purpose of the rule to shift responsibility for developing the record to claimants or their representatives, nevertheless SSA also expects claimants "to respond fully to any other requests we make for information or evidence related to their disability claims."

Comment and Response 16. Evidence from another source must be submitted in its entirety "unless you previously submitted the same evidence to us or we instruct you otherwise." Representatives need not submit duplicative records, but by "duplicative," SSA means "an exact duplicate of a document in the record...." No doubt many ALJs will not wish to receive overly lengthy records such as are frequently produced by the Veterans' Administration or even partial duplicates, so it is essential that representatives communicate through their ODARs with ALJs in order that the representatives can be instructed otherwise, and that such instructions be documented as well as possible.

Comment and Response 17. SSA denies that the rules will require claimants to obtain representation; the rules do not (at least in theory) shift new burdens onto unrepresented claimants.

Comment and Response 18. SSA denies the concern expressed by some commenters that the duty to submit all evidence received from another source "will burden our adjudicators with having to review unnecessary evidence in most cases."

Paperwork Reduction Act. Finally, and most implausibly, SSA asserts that, "These rules do not create any new or affect any existing collections and, therefore do not require Office of Management and Budget approval under the Paperwork Reduction Act." Query: If these rules don't create any new or affect any existing collections," then what, exactly, do they do? Isn't that their precise purpose? Perhaps SSA is implicitly drawing a distinction between paperwork and electronic communications?

The actual regulations. Subject to all the caveats set forth above, the rules themselves are fairly straightforward. 20 CFR 404.1512(a) and 416.912(a) provide that, "You must inform us about or submit all evidence known to you that relates to your disability." Subsection (b) defines "evidence." Subsection (b)(2) describes the attorney-client and work product exceptions. Subsection (c) contains the requirement to submit "evidence in its entirety, unless you previously submitted the same evidence to us or we instruct you otherwise."

The Bottom Line. For most representatives, the all-evidence regulations should not greatly affect business as usual. Although there was a longstanding debate over the duty to submit unfavorable evidence, anecdotal information suggests that most representatives did precisely that. For the relatively few who did not, the rule is now reasonably clear: subject to quite limited exceptions, representatives must submit all evidence in their possession, in its entirety, whether favorable or unfavorable. Representatives who fail to do so risk serious sanctions from SSA.

Appendix 11:   Glossary

The following is drawn from the regulations, SSR 83-10, Social Security Handbook, POMS DI 25001.001 Medical-Vocational Terms and elsewhere in the POMS, glossaries in the Medical Expert Handbook and the Vocational Expert Handbook, and from SSA's website.

Acquiescence Rulings (AR). A type of Social Security ruling in which SSA agrees to follow a circuit court of appeals decision that is contrary to SSA policy. The ruling will be followed only in the circuit from which the decision was issued. *See* §105.

Activities of Daily Living (ADL). Include adaptive activities such as cleaning, shopping, cooking, taking public transportation, paying bills, maintaining a residence, caring appropriately for grooming and hygiene, using telephones and directories, and using a post office. *See* §12.00 C.1. of the Listing of Impairments. ADLs are evaluated not only for the mental Listings but also when assessing credibility, SSR 96-7p, and pain. 20 C.F.R. § 404.1529(c)(3)(i).

Administrative Appeals Judge (AAJ). Appeals Council judge.

Administrative Law Judge (ALJ). A neutral fact finder employed by the Office of Disability Adjudication & Review (ODAR) to determine if a claimant is entitled to benefits under the law. Most decisions are related to disability programs but ALJs decide other issues such as retirement, as well. *See* §106.

Age. Age refers to an individual's chronological age and the extent to which age affects ability to adapt to a new work situation and to work in competition with others. 20 C.F.R. § 404.1563. *See* §122. A claimant reaches a particular age the day before his or her birthday. POMS GN 00302.400.

Categories of Age:

1. Younger Person—if an individual is under age 50, the regulations provide that generally SSA does not consider that the individual's age will seriously affect the ability to adapt to new work situations. It is only when an individual is illiterate and age 45 through 49 that age affects the ability to adapt to new work situations for those under age 50.

2. Person Approaching Advanced Age—if an individual is closely approaching advanced age (50-54), SSA will consider age along with a severe impairment and limited work experience as possibly seriously affecting an individual's ability to adapt to a significant number of jobs in the national economy.

3. Person of Advanced Age—SSA considers advanced age (55-59) to be the point at which age significantly affects a person's ability to engage in substantial gainful activity. If an individual is severely impaired, of advanced age, and cannot do at least medium work, he/she may be found disabled unless the individual has skills that can be used in (transferred to) less demanding jobs that exist in significant numbers in the national economy.

4. Person Close to Retirement Age—if an individual is close to retirement age (60 or older) and has a severe impairment, he or she will be considered not able to adjust to sedentary or light work unless the individual has skills that are highly marketable.

Alcoholism or Other Drug Abuse (AODA). Also referred to as drug addiction or alcoholism (DAA). *See* 20 C.F.R. § 404.1535 and §249.

Alleged Onset Date (AOD). The date on which a claimant indicated he or she became disabled due to a physical or mental impairment. *See* §204.1.

Americans With Disabilities Act (ADA). Federal law, 42 U.S.C. § 12101, that provides remedies for discrimination against disabled people. *See* §344 and SSR 00-1c.

Appeals Council (AC). The highest level of administrative appeal, the Appeals Council reviews decisions made by ALJs. Appeals Counsel members decide if a request for review of an ALJ decision will be granted, denied, or dismissed. Located in Falls Church, VA. *See* Chapter 5.

Appointed Representative Database (ARDB). Effective January 1, 2007, in order to receive direct payment a representative must be registered on this SSA database. See §178.4.

Arduous Work. Physical work requiring a high level of strength or endurance. May be arduous if it demands a great deal of stamina such as repetitive bending or lifting at a very fast pace. Generally, physical demands are classified as heavy. *But see* §119.

Auxiliary (AUX). Other family members, usually children or spouse, to whom additional monthly benefits may be payable on the earnings record of a person entitled to Social Security benefits. *See* §435. *See also* 20 C.F.R. §§ 404.330 *ff.*

Average Current Earnings (ACE). Multiple formulas are used to calculate average current earnings, then the highest number is used. A reduction in the disabled worker's, and dependents' benefits may be made for any month the worker's total Social Security benefits, workers compensation, and, where applicable, other public disability benefits exceed 80 percent of his or her "average current earnings." Note that the SSA earnings record shows the ACE amount with the 80 percent adjustment already computed. *See* §438.

Average Indexed Monthly Earnings (AIME). The dollar amount used to calculate Social Security benefits for people who attained age 62 or became disabled (or died) after 1978. To arrive at AIME, SSA adjusts actual past earnings using an "average wage index," so claimants won't lose the value of past earnings (when money was worth more) in relation to more recent earnings. If a claimant attained age 62 or became disabled (or died) before 1978, SSA uses Average Monthly Earnings (AME). *See* §204.

Broad World of Work. Work that exists at all exertional levels. It may include skilled and semiskilled work as well as unskilled work.

Carrying. Transporting an object; usually holding it in the hands, arms, or on the shoulder.

Central Office (CO). Administrative headquarters for the Social Security Administration, located in Woodlawn, Md., a suburb of Baltimore. *See* §441.

Chief Administrative Law Judge (CALJ). Located in Falls Church, Va., the CALJ has supervisory authority over Regional Chief Administrative Law Judges, Hearing Office Chief ALJs, and ALJs.

Childhood Disability Benefits (CDB). This program provides benefits for disabled adult children (DAC) who may obtain benefits on the work record of a retired, disabled, or deceased parent. These claimants must be over age 18 and unmarried, and must become disabled before age 22. 20 C.F.R. § 404.350. Disability is determined using the rules for the regular Social Security disability program. *See* §141.

Claims Representatives (CR). Federal employees of the Social Security Administration who assist individuals in applying for Social Security and SSI benefits. They determine if the claimant meets entitlement requirements of the law and regulations. They make many of the required inputs to a nationwide database that processes claims. They are supposed to represent both the claimant's and the government's interests.

Code of Federal Regulations (CFR). The Code of Federal Regulations is a codification of the general and permanent rules published in the Federal Register by the executive departments and agencies of the federal government. The Code is divided into 50 titles that represent broad areas subject to federal regulation. Each title is divided into chapters that usually bear the name of the issuing agency. Each chapter is further subdivided in parts covering specific regulatory areas. *See* §101.

Composite Job. Work that has a blend of tasks from several different occupations. The main duties of a composite job will only be adequately described by multiple DOT occupations.

Constantly. Use of this term in the RFC or SCO means that the activity or condition occurs two-thirds or more of an eight-hour day.

Consultative Examination (CE). Medical examination at government expense. Exams may be from the individual's treating physician or independent consultative physician retained by SSA. Purpose is to obtain more detailed medical findings about the impairment; or obtain technical or specialized medical information; or to resolve conflicts or differences in findings already in the file. *See* §223.

Continuing Disability Review (CDR). Periodic reviews conducted to determine if disability continues. They may be scheduled where medical improvement was expected or unscheduled if the beneficiary or state vocational rehabilitation agency reports improvement. Formerly called Continuing Disability Investigation (CDI). *See* §480.

Controlling Date (CD). The latest date a widow(er) can be found disabled. It functions like the Date Last Insured in a regular Social Security disability case. *See* §142.

Cost of Living Adjustment (COLA). Automatic periodic (usually yearly) increases in SSA and SSI benefits based on a formula tied to cost of living increases. The increase is based on the smaller of either the Consumer Price Index as published by the Department of Labor or the yearly average Wage Index, which is based on nationwide wages. *See* §404.

Date of Death (DOD). The date shown on evidence of death record, death certificate, or statement from funeral director that an individual died. The established date of death is used to determine when benefits may be paid to survivors or when benefits should cease. *See* §380.

Date of Entitlement (DOE) to Disability (DOED). Date of entitlement establishes the date from which past due benefits will be paid:

1. Title II—Five full months after date of onset.

2. Title XVI—Date of application or date disability is established for claims filed before August 22, 1996. For claims filed on or after that date, the SSI date of entitlement is the first of the month after all requirements are met. *See* §432.

Date of Filing (DOF). The date that is used to determine when an application for benefits is received. This may be the actual date received or a date in the past in certain "protective filing date" cases. *See* §204.1.

Date First Insured (DFI). The earliest date the claimant first meets the coverage requirements for Social Security disability. *See* §§131, 205.

Date Last Insured (DLI). The date on which a claimant's coverage for disability protection expires. It applies in Title II claims only. *See* §§131, 205.

Date Last Met (DLM). Same as Date Last Insured (DLI).

Date of Onset (DOO). The date the claimant became disabled. *See* §204.1.

Deceased Wage Earner (DWE). A person who has worked under the Social Security system and has died. It is possible for surviving family member or estate to receive back benefits that were due an individual before he died. Also monthly survivor benefits may be due. *See* §380.

Detailed Earnings Query (DEQY). An SSA printout that shows earnings from each employer.

Diary Date. A scheduled reexamination date in an allowed case for evaluation of possible medical improvement. *See* §480.

Dictionary of Occupational Titles (DOT). Last updated in 1991, the *DOT* provides a brief description of more than 12,000 occupations that exist in the economy. Prepared by the Department of Labor, DOL. *See* §346.

Disabled Adult Child Benefits (DAC). *See* Childhood Disability Benefits (CDB).

Disability. The inability to perform any substantial gainful activity by reason of any medically determinable physical and/or mental impairment which can be expected to result in death or which has lasted or can be expected to last for a continuous period of not less than 12 months. *See* §102.

Disability Determination Explanation (DDE). Form used by state agency that summarizes procedural status and evidence. It contains the state agency evaluation of issues at all steps of the sequential evaluation process and includes the state agency doctors' RFC assessments. *See* §203.5.

Disability Determination Service (DDS). State agency that makes disability determinations at initial and reconsideration levels. Usually called the "state agency."

Disability Determination Service Query (DDSQ). A query of an SSA database that shows information about actions taken on a claim by the state agency at the initial and reconsideration levels.

Disability Insurance (DI). Social Security Disability Insurance program. *See* §131 for insured status requirements.

Disability Insurance Benefits (DIB). Monthly Social Security disability payments.

Disabled Individual, Worker or Child (DIWC). Disability claim under Title II of the Social Security Act.

Disabled Widow/Widower Benefits (DWB or DIWW). The disability benefits available to disabled widows and widowers of insured workers, with benefits first payable to the widow(er) at age 50. *See* §142.

DISCO DIB Earnings Record. An SSA earnings printout, the name of which stands for DIB Insured Status Computation Online. It shows yearly earnings, date first insured and date last insured but it does not show the PIA.

Drug Addiction or Alcoholism (DAA). Also referred to as alcoholism or other drug abuse (AODA). *See* 20 C.F.R. § 404.1535 and §249.

Earnings Record (ER). A history of earnings reported to SSA. The earnings are used to determine insured status for entitlement to retirement, survivors, disability and health insurance benefits and to calculate cash benefit rates. *See* §204.

Earnings Requirement. Applies only in Title II DIB cases. A DIB claimant must have worked and earned at least 20 quarters of coverage in the last 40 quarters before "onset" (equivalent to 5 of the last 10 years) and be "fully insured" to be entitled to disability benefits. SSA gives special consideration to blind claimants and claimants under the age of 31. In these situations, claimants with fewer than 20 quarters of covered work may be entitled to disability benefits. (*See* Insured Status.) *See* §131.

Education. Education is primarily used to mean formal schooling or other training which contributes to ability to meet vocational requirements, for example, reasoning ability, communication skills, and arithmetical ability. However, if an individual does not have formal schooling, this does not necessarily mean that he or she is uneducated or lacks these abilities. The term "education" also includes how well the individual is able to communicate in English. 20 C.F.R. § 404.1564. Unless there is evidence to contradict a person's statement as to the numerical grade level completed in school, the statement will be used to determine the person's educational abilities. The person's present level of reasoning, communication, and arithmetical ability may be higher or lower than the level of formal education. Evidence of this includes the kinds of responsibilities the person had when working, any acquired skills, daily activities, and hobbies, as well as the results of testing. Therefore, a person will meet the criteria for the different education levels specified in the regulations, not solely on the basis of his or her statements, but based upon all evidence pertinent to evaluating that person's educational capacities. *See* §123.

Categories of Education:

1. Illiteracy—Illiteracy means the inability to read or write. SSA considers someone illiterate if the person cannot read or write a simple message such as instructions or inventory lists, even though the person can sign his or her name. Generally, an illiterate person has had little or no formal schooling.

2. Marginal Education—Marginal education means ability in reasoning, arithmetic, and language skills which are needed to do simple, unskilled types of jobs. SSA generally considers that formal schooling at a 6th grade level or less is a marginal education.

3. Limited Education—Limited education means ability in reasoning, arithmetic, and language skills, but not enough to allow a person with these educational qualifications to do most of the more complex job duties needed in semi-skilled or skilled jobs. SSA generally considers that a 7th grade through the 11th grade level of formal education is a limited education.

4. High School Education and Above—High school education and above means abilities in reasoning, arithmetic, and language skills acquired in formal schooling at a 12th grade level or above. SSA generally considers that someone with these educational abilities can do semi-skilled through skilled work. High school education includes a General Equivalency Diploma (GED).

The criterion of "high school or graduate or more—provides for direct entry into skilled work" is met when there is little time lapse between the completion of formal education and the date of adjudication, and where the content of the education would enable individuals, with a minimal degree of job orientation, to begin performing the skilled job duties of certain identifiable occupations with their RFC.

5. Inability to Communicate in English—Since the ability to speak, read and understand English is generally learned or increased at school, SSA may consider this an educational factor. Because English is the dominant language of the country, it may be difficult for someone who doesn't speak and understand English to do a job, regardless of the amount of education the person may have in another language. Therefore, SSA considers a person's ability to communicate in English when it evaluates what work, if any, he or she can do. It generally doesn't matter in what other language a person may be fluent.

Electronic Claims Analysis Tool (eCAT). A web-based automated tool designed to document the analysis made by state agency disability adjudicators and ensure that all relevant agency policies are considered during the adjudication process. This produces a Disability Determination Explanation that documents the analysis and rationale for finding a claimant disabled or denying a claim. *See* 203.5.

Electronic Disability Folder (eDIB). SSA's online collection of documents related to a claimant's case. It is designed to replace the paper files used by SSA in the past.

Electronic Disability Guide (eDG). Part of the POMS that explains policy, process and procedural changes for electronic processing of disability claims.

Electronic Records Express (ERE). Website where claimants' representatives can upload documents to a claimant's Social Security hearing exhibit file: http://eme.ssa.gov. Registration is required before using the website for the first time. Information needed to file documents is found on the barcode provided by SSA. *See* §202.1.

Electronic Worksheet (EWS). Notes written by state agency doctors and disability examiners that summarize a claimant's medical records and explain state agency doctors' conclusions in a case. *See* §222.

Employee (EE). Under the Social Security Act there are three classes of workers who are considered employees:
1. Officers of corporations.
2. Those who are employees under the common-law test.
3. Those in four specific occupations who if they are not employees under 1 or 2 above may still be employees if certain conditions are met. Agent drivers, full-time life insurance salespersons, full-time traveling or city salespersons and home workers may be considered employees.

Employer/Employee (ER/EE). The employer/employee relationship is a term used to describe who is the employer and has the final authority to control the worker in performing his or her services, or which reserves the right to do so—the person or entity which has the sole power to hire, fire, and supervise the worker. There are a number of rules or guidelines used to determine who the employer is or if the worker is in fact not an employee but self-employed.

Entitlement (ENT). A person who meets all of the eligibility requirements for a specific type of benefit and has filed an application for those benefits. *See* §432.

Environmental Conditions. Temperature, humidity, noise, vibration, fumes, odors, toxic conditions, dust, poor ventilation, hazards, etc. *See* §265.

Environmental Restriction. An impairment-caused need to avoid one or more environmental conditions in a workplace. *See* §127.

Equal Access to Justice Act (EAJA). The Act, 28 U.S.C. § 2412(d), provides for awards of attorney fees against the federal government under certain circumstances. *See* §§760 *ff.*

Established Onset Date (EOD). The date on which medical and work information substantiates that the claimant became disabled (Title II). *See* §203.1.

Exertional Activity. One of the primary strength activities (walk, stand, sit, lift, carry, push, pull) which defines a level of work.

Exertional Capability. A capability required to perform an exertional activity. *See* §125.

Exertional Impairment. Exertional impairment affects an individual's physical abilities (strength) and impairs his/her ability to walk, stand, sit, lift, carry, push, pull. *See* 20 C.F.R. § 404.1545(b).

Exertional Level. A work classification defining the functional requirements of work in terms of the range of the primary strength activities required. 20 C.F.R. § 404.1567 sets forth the primary strength activities specifically associated with sedentary, light, medium, heavy, and very heavy levels of exertion. *See* §346.1.

Exertional Limitation. An impairment-related limitation that reduces the capacity to sit, stand, walk, lift, carry, push, or pull. (See Physical Demands.)

Expedited Reinstatement (EXR). If a beneficiary, whose benefits were terminated because of the performance of SGA, stops working after the end of the 36-month reentitlement period, that beneficiary can request "expedited reinstatement," referred to as EXR in the POMS, for 60 months after entitlement is terminated because the claimant returned to work at the SGA level. *See* 20 C.F.R. § 404.1592b and §176.3. *See* §§176.3 and 495.

Extended Period of Eligibility (EPE). A 36-month period where T-2 disability benefits can begin again without filing a new application for benefits where disability ceased due to work activity (substantial gainful activity—SGA) and the earnings subsequently fall below the SGA amount. *See* 20 C.F.R. § 404.1592a and §176.3.

Family Maximum (FMAX). The maximum amount of Social Security benefits payable on a Social Security record. The family maximum is determined according to the method of computing the PIA and the kind of benefits payable to the worker. *See* §204.

Federal Benefit Rate (FBR). The federal monthly SSI payment due an individual. The amounts are set by statute and are subject to annual increases as determined by the cost-of-living adjustments. If the individual's monthly countable income exceeds the FBR, the SSI payment may be decreased or eliminated. In many states, the state adds a supplement to the FBR. *See* §414 and §433.

Federal Record Center (FRC). A storage facility for the physical storage of past records or claims that may be needed for future use.

FICA Tax. FICA stands for "Federal Insurance Contributions Act." It's the tax withheld from salary or self-employment income that funds the Social Security and Medicare programs.

Field Office (FO). The Social Security Administration has about 1300 local offices, most of which are field offices, located throughout the country. A field office may have a branch office, that is, a secondary site that is administratively managed by the field office. At local offices, individuals can apply for a Social Security number, check on an earnings record, apply for benefits, and get information about individual and family rights and obligations under the law. The agency also has toll-free telephone service nationwide. The number is 1-800-772-1213. *See* §108.

Findings of Fact and Analysis of Evidence (FOFAE). A section of the Disability Determination Explanation form used by the state agency.

Fin Dec. At the Appeals Council a final ALJ decision after court remand is referred to as a Fin Dec. *See* §560.

Fingering. Picking, pinching, or otherwise working with the fingers primarily (rather than with the whole hand or arm as in "Handling").

Framework Decision. A decision that is not "directed" by a particular rule in Appendix 2 (Medical-Vocational Guidelines) but uses the Appendix 2 rules as adjudicative guidance.

Freedom of Information Act (FOIA). A law, along with the Privacy Act, that controls the type and scope of information that may be released and to whom it may be released. The law applies to all government agencies including SSA. The FOIA makes available to the public statement of organization, administrative procedure, policies, interpretation of law and precedent decisions that affect the public, unless they fall within one of the statute's specific exemptions.

Frequently. Use of this term in the SCO or RFC means occurs one-third to two-thirds of an eight-hour workday.

Freeze—Title II (FZ). Years wholly or partly in a period of disability that are not used in computing a Social Security benefit. The years when a person is disabled are "frozen" and not counted against them when computing their benefits.

Full Range of Work. All or substantially all of the unskilled occupations existing at an exertional level. *See* §125.

Fully Insured. One of two requirements for insured status to qualify to receive Social Security disability benefits. A claimant must have one QC for every year of age after age 21 up to the calendar year before becoming disabled, but never more than 40 QCs are required. *See* §§131, 205.

Government Pension Offset (GPO). A Social Security benefit payable to a spouse may be reduced if the spouse receives a periodic payment based on his or her own employment that was not covered under Social Security from the federal government, a state, or political subdivision of a state. Generally, Social Security benefits due the spouse will be reduced by two-thirds of the amount of their government pension. There are some exceptions to when the offset may apply.

Great Lakes Program Service Center (GLPSC). An SSA regional payment center located in Chicago. *See* §§445 and 446.

Grid. A common term used for the tables in the Medical-Vocational Guidelines found in Appendix 2 of Subpart P of Regulations No. 4. *See* §129.

HALLEX. The SSA manual used by the Office of Disability Adjudication and Review. A copy may be found on SSA's website, www.socialsecurity.gov.

Handling. Seizing, holding, grasping, turning, or otherwise working with the hand or hands. Fingers are involved only to the extent that they are an extension of the hand.

Health Care Financing Administration (HCFA). The federal agency responsible for administering Medicare. Medicare consists of hospital insurance (Part A), medical insurance (Part B), and drug coverage (Part D). HCFA sets the standards which hospitals, skilled nursing facilities, home health agencies, hospices, and other providers and suppliers of services must meet in order to receive payment for Medicare-covered services and items. HCFA contracts with organizations called carriers to administer the Medicare program.

Health and Human Services (HHS). An agency of the federal government. The Social Security Administration was a part of HHS until 1995 when the Social Security Administration became an independent agency.

Health Insurance Part B (HIB). The health insurance part of Medicare, which provides comprehensive health insurance protection to the aged and disabled. *See* §404.

Health Insurance Part D. The part of Medicare that provides drug benefit coverage.

Hearing Office Chief Administrative Law Judge (HOCALJ).

Hospital Insurance Part A (HIA). Hospital Insurance (Part A) of Medicare helps pay for inpatient hospital care, inpatient care in a skilled nursing facility, home health care, and hospice care. *See* §404.

Hypothetical Questions. Hypothetical questions, often referred to as "hypotheticals," are posed by the administrative law judges to vocational experts at Social Security hearings. The questions are phrased in terms of a hypothetical situation to elicit specific vocational information concerning possible occupations the claimant could hold. *See* §343.1.

Impairment Related Work Expenses (IRWE). The cost of certain impairment-related services and items that a disabled (but not blind) person needs in order to work can be deducted from earnings for the purposes of determining SSI payment amount and whether work is SGA, even if these items and services are also needed for non-work activities. *See* §274.

Individualized Plan for Employment (IPE). Plan developed by the individual and the state vocational rehabilitation agency under 29 U.S.C. § 722 for assisting disabled individuals to return to work.

Individualized Written Rehabilitation Program (IWRP). Former name of Individualized Plan for Employment.

In-Kind Support and Maintenance (ISM). In the SSI program, unearned income in the form of food or shelter that an individual receives from someone else. *See* §422.

Insured Status (I/S). When a claimant has the requisite number of quarters of coverage for entitlement to a Social Security (Title II) benefit. The number of quarters required for insured status is dependent upon the type of benefits sought and the age of the claimant. (*See* Earnings Requirement.) *See* §§131 and 205.

Interim Assistance Agreement (IAA). Agreement by which a claimant for SSI agrees to repay the state for assistance provided while the SSI claim is pending.

Job. A position of employment. Within a given occupational classification or job-title there may be one or thousands of jobs in a prescribed geographical area. (*See* "occupation.") *See* §346.

Limited To. Does not exceed.

Living In the Same Household (LISH). SSA pays a lump sum death benefit to the surviving widow(er) if the widow(er) was living in the same household as the worker when the worker died. *See* §423.

Master Beneficiary Record (MBR). SSA's computerized record containing a history of benefits paid on an individual's record including all auxiliaries as well as current benefits being paid.

Maximum Sustained Work Capability. The highest functional level a claimant can perform on a regular and continuing basis—sedentary, light, medium, heavy, or very heavy. *See* §121.

Medicaid (MA). Also known as Medical Assistance and Title 19 (because the law governing Medicaid is located in Title XIX of the Social Security Act), it is the joint federal and state health insurance program for disabled, elderly and those with children who meet income and asset limitations. Medicaid programs vary from state to state.

Medical Evidence of Record (MER). A claimant's medical records that have been provided to SSA.

Medical Expert (ME). A medical doctor or psychologist who at an ALJ's request provides a medical opinion about a claimant's case either in testimony or by answering interrogatories.

Medical Improvement Expected (MIE). When a person's disability is expected to improve, SSA will document the file to show MIE and diary the case for future reexamination. *See* §§480 *ff.*

Medical Improvement Not Expected (MINE). If a person's disability is not expected to improve, the case will be coded MINE. *See* §§480 *ff.*

Medical Improvement Possible (MIP). The vast majority of disability cases, which are supposed to be reviewed every three years. *See* §§480 *ff.*

Medical Re-Exam Date (MRED). If medical improvement is expected, the case will be diaried for a reexamination in the future for R. *See* §§480 *ff.*

Medical-Vocational Guidelines. Also known as the "grids," the Medical-Vocational Guidelines are tables contained in 20 C.F.R., Appendix 2, Subpart P of Regulation No. 4. They feature vocational rules that consider a claimant's age, education, prior work experience, and remaining RFC to direct or guide the decision maker to a conclusion of "disabled" or "not disabled." *See* §129.

Medicare. The federal health insurance program for people 65 years of age or older, certain younger people with disabilities, and people with permanent kidney failure with dialysis or a transplant, sometimes called ESRD (End-Stage Renal Disease).

Mental Residual Functional Capacity (MRFC). What a claimant can do in a work setting on a regular and continuing basis in spite of the claimant's mental limitations and restrictions. Mental RFC focuses on a claimant's ability to understand, carry out, and remember instructions, and to respond appropriately to supervision, coworkers, and work pressures in a work setting. 20 C.F.R. § 404.1545(c). Mental RFC assessment is done by SSA decision makers. *See* §§245-247.

Medical Source Statement (MSS). A statement from a claimant's treating source about what the claimant can still do despite the claimant's impairments. The statement should be based on the medical source's findings concerning the claimant's medical history, clinical findings, laboratory findings, diagnosis and treatment. 20 C.F.R. § 404.1513(b) and (c). *See* §221.

Mid-America Program Service Center (MAMPSC). An SSA regional payment center located in Kansas City, MO. *See* §§445 and 446.

Mid-Atlantic Program Service Center (MATPSC). An SSA regional payment center located in Philadelphia. *See* §§445 and 446.

Modernized Claims System (MCS). SSA database that contains information about Title II applications.

Modernized Supplemental Security Income Claims System (MSSICS). SSA database that contains information about SSI applications similar to the MCS for Title II claims.

Monthly Benefit Amount (MBA). The regular monthly benefit check an individual receives from SSA. *See* §433.

Net Earnings From Self-Employment (NESE). The total gross income, as computed under the income tax law, derived by an individual from all trades and businesses, less the deductions (including the allowances for depreciation) attributable to such trade or business that the person is allowed to take in computing income tax.

Never. An RFC rating that means not even once during an eight-hour day.

Nonexertional Impairment. An impairment that does not directly affect the ability to sit, stand, walk, lift, carry, push, or pull; rather, this type of impairment affects the mind, vision, hearing, speech, and use of the body to climb, balance, stoop, kneel, crouch, crawl, reach, or handle, and use of the fingers for fine activities. *See* §127.

Nonexertional Limitation. An impairment-caused limitation of function which directly affects capability to perform work activities other than the primary strength activities. *See* §127.

Northeastern Program Service Center (NEPSC). An SSA regional payment center located in Jamaica, New York. *See* §§445 and 446.

Not Present. Use of this rating in the SCO means that the activity or condition does not exist.

Number Holder (NH). Wage earner—Title II.

Numident (NUMI). SSA master file based on SSN, contains all names used by the number holder, mother and father's names, date of birth, date of death, etc.

Occasionally. Use of this term in the SCO or RFC means that the activity occurs at least once up to one-third of an eight-hour workday.

Occupation. Synonymous with the term "job title" in the Dictionary of Occupational Titles. *See* §346.

Occupational Base. The occupational base is the number of occupations, as represented by RFC, that an individual is capable of performing. These "base" occupations are unskilled in terms of complexity. The regulations take notice of approximately 2,500 medium, light, and sedentary occupations; 1,600 light and sedentary occupations; and 200 sedentary occupations. Each occupation represents numerous jobs in the national economy. (In individual situations, specific skilled or semi-skilled occupations may be added to the base.) SSR 83-10. *See* §348.

Office of Central Operations (OCO). The payment center for processing disability claims located in SSA headquarters in Baltimore, MD. *See* §444.

Office of Disability Adjudication and Review (ODAR). The part of SSA that conducts hearings on Social Security claims that have been denied. This is not the same agency that denied the initial application and the reconsideration. *See* §108.

Office of General Counsel (OGC). The part of SSA that, among other things, accepts service of process on the Commissioner of Social Security and handles litigation against the Social Security Administration. *See* §611.

Office of the Inspector General (OIG). Investigative department of SSA that handles all SSA investigations. OIG investigates allegations of fraud by beneficiaries and SSA employees. It also investigates and evaluates SSA programs.

Old-Age, Survivor and Disability Insurance (OASDI). The Social Security programs that provide monthly cash benefits to wage earners and dependents when the wage earner retires, to surviving dependents, and to disabled worker beneficiaries and their dependents.

Overpayment (OP). An overpayment is an excess payment. It is the total amount an individual received for any period which exceeds the total amount that should have been paid for that period. *See* §470.

Past Relevant Work (PRW). Work a claimant performed within the last 15 years which lasted long enough for him or her to learn the job and which was substantial gainful activity. *See* §347.

Physical Demands. Jobs classified in terms of sedentary, light, medium, heavy, and very heavy exertion as both the regulations and the Dictionary of Occupational Titles (DOT) define those terms:

1. Sedentary Work involves lifting no more than 10 pounds at a time and occasionally lifting or carrying articles like docket files, ledgers, and small tools. Although sedentary jobs involve sitting, they also require a certain amount of walking and standing to carry out job duties. Jobs are sedentary if they require occasional walking and standing, provided other sedentary criteria are met. Because sedentary occupations may require occasional standing and walking, the actual periods of standing or walking should generally total no more than about 2 hours of an 8-hour workday. Work processes in specific occupations will dictate how often and how long a claimant needs to be on his or her feet to obtain or return small articles. By its very nature, work performed primarily in a seated position entails no significant stooping. Most unskilled sedentary jobs require good use of the hands and fingers for repetitive hand-finger actions.

2. Light Work involves lifting no more than 20 pounds at a time with frequent lifting or carrying of objects weighing up to 10 pounds. Since frequent lifting or carrying requires a claimant to be on his or her feet up to two-thirds of a workday, the full range of light work requires standing or walking for a total of approximately 6 hours of an 8-hour workday. Even though the weight a claimant lifts in a particular light job may be minimal, the regulations classify a job as light work when it requires a significant amount of walking or standing—the primary difference between sedentary and most light jobs.

A job is also in this category when it involves sitting most of the time with some pushing and pulling of arm-hand or leg-foot controls requiring greater exertion than in sedentary work; e.g., mattress sewing machine operator, motor-grader operator, and road-roller operator (skilled and semi-skilled jobs in these particular instances). Relatively few unskilled light jobs are performed in a seated position. The lifting requirements for the majority of light jobs can be accomplished with occasional, rather than frequent, stooping. Many unskilled light jobs are performed in one location—in which case the ability to stand is more critical than the ability to walk. Light jobs require the use of arms and hands to grasp, hold, and turn objects. They generally do not involve the use of the fingers for fine activities to the extent required in most sedentary jobs.

3. Medium Work involves lifting no more than 50 pounds at a time with frequent lifting of objects weighing up to 25 pounds. A full range of medium work requires standing or walking for a total of approximately 6 hours in an

8-hour workday in order to meet the requirements of frequent lifting or carrying of objects up to 25 pounds. As with the requirements of light work, sitting may occur intermittently during the remaining time. In contrast to the fine precision activities of the fingers and hands required by sedentary work, medium work generally requires only use of the arms and hands to grasp, hold, or turn objects.

The full range of medium work requires both considerable lifting and frequent bending-stooping ("stooping" is a type of bending in which a person bends his or her body downward and forward by bending the spine at the waist; "crouching" is bending both the legs and spine in order to bend the body downward and forward). This activity requires flexibility of the knees as well as of the torso. However, relatively few occupations in the national economy require lifting, pushing or pulling activities from primarily a sitting position; e.g., taxi driver, bus driver, a tank-truck driver (semi-skilled jobs). In most medium jobs, the critical requirement is being on one's feet for most of the workday. An individual's ability to perform frequent lifting or carrying of objects weighing up to 25 pounds is often more critical than being able to lift up to 50 pounds at a time.

4. Heavy Work involves lifting objects weighing more than 100 pounds. If a claimant can do very heavy work, he or she can also engage in heavy, medium, light, and sedentary work. *See* §125.

Plan for Achieving Self Support (PASS). An SSI work incentive program that, if approved by SSA, allows an SSI eligible individual to set aside money and/or things he or she owns to pay for items or services needed to achieve a specific work goal without violating the SSI income or asset limitations.

Prescribed Period (PP). The period of time not exceeding 7 years and ending with a qualifying date during which a claimant may establish entitlement to disabled widow(er)s benefits. *See* §142.

Presumed Maximum Value (PMV). An SSI term used in the POMS, presumed maximum value is a regulatory cap on the amount of chargeable in-kind support and maintenance which is not subject to the value of the one-third reduction rule. The PMV for an individual equals one-third the individual SSI federal benefit rate plus $20 (the general income exclusion). *See* §424.

Presumptive Disability (PD). Presumptive Disability payments are made to a person who is initially applying for SSI based on an allegation of disability or blindness, and whose medical condition is such that it presents a strong likelihood that the person will be found disabled under SSA rules. The person must meet all nonmedical factors of eligibility. The payments continue for up to 6 months pending a formal determination of disability. If the claim is ultimately denied, SSA does not claim an overpayment.

Primary Insurance Amount (PIA). The PIA is the figure from which almost all cash benefit amounts are derived, including monthly benefits for workers, their dependents, and their survivors. The PIA is based on an individual's taxable earnings averaged over the working lifetime to yield a monthly benefit that partly replaces the earned income lost because of retirement, disability, or death. *See* §204.

Prisoner Update Processing System (PUPS). An SSA database that records prisoner information by inmate's SSN.

Privacy Act of 1974 (PA). The Privacy Act requires federal agencies to publish in the Federal Register notices of systems of records they maintain which contain personal information about individuals. Under the Privacy Act, information about an individual is generally not disclosed without the individual's consent, except as provided by that law.

Program Operations Manual System (POMS). The largest system of internal instructions used by SSA employees and by the employees of the state agencies who make disability determinations. A public version is available from SSA's website, www.socialsecurity.gov. *See* §103.

Program Policy Statement (PPS). Used to indicate that a Social Security Ruling has far-reaching importance.

Program Service Center (PSC). Program service centers are located in Birmingham, Alabama; Chicago, Illinois; Kansas City, Missouri; Jamaica, New York; Philadelphia, Pennsylvania; and Richmond, California. These offices, along with the Office of Central Operations in Baltimore, Maryland, house and service the records of individuals who are receiving Social Security benefits. *See* §445.

Protective filing date. The effective filing date of an application for benefits which is before the actual filing date pursuant to SSA regulations, 20 C.F.R. §§ 404.630, 416.340, and 416.345. *See* §204.1.

Prototype states. Ten states (Alabama, Alaska, Colorado, Louisiana, Michigan, Missouri, New Hampshire, Pennsylvania, and parts of New York and California) where SSA is experimenting with eliminating the reconsideration step.

Quarters of Coverage (QCs). Social Security credits are earned for a certain amount of work under Social Security. *See* §131.

Range of Work. Occupations existing at an exertional level. *See* §125.

Reaching. Extending the hands and arms in any direction.

Reconsideration (RECON). If a person is not satisfied with the determination on a claim, he or she may request a reconsideration and submit new evidence if available. *See* §152.

Regional Chief Administrative Law Judge (RCALJ). The head administrative law judge in one of SSA's ten regions.

Regional Office (RO). Regional SSA headquarters in one of SSA's ten regions.

Remaining Occupational Base. The occupations that a claimant is capable of adjusting to considering his or her RFC, age, education, and past work experience.

Representative Identification Number (Rep ID). The 10-character identifier SSA assigns to a representative to use in lieu of his or her Social Security number (SSN) when making changes to his or her registration information. This is the representative's ID for the Appointed Representative Database (ARDB). See POMS GN 03913.001C.

Request for Voluntary Remand (RVR). At the Appeals Council, a request from SSA's Office of General Counsel that SSA agree to ask a federal court to remand a case is referred to as an RVR. Such a request is sometimes referred to informally as an RVR by all counsel involved in a federal court case.

Residual Functional Capacity (RFC). What a claimant can do in a work setting in spite of the functional limitations and environmental restrictions imposed by his or her medically determinable impairment(s). RFC is the maximum degree to which the claimant retains the capacity for sustained performance of the physical and mental requirements of jobs. 20 C.F.R. § 404.1545. RFC assessment is done by SSA decision makers. *See* §120.

Restriction. A restriction is what a claimant should not do because of an impairment-related risk to self or others or because it would be medically inadvisable. A restriction can be exertional or non-exertional.

Retirement, Survivors, Disability Insurance (RSDI). The Social Security program that pays benefits to persons who are retired, eligible dependents of deceased workers, or disabled workers.

Selected Characteristics of Occupations Defined in the Dictionary of Occupational Titles (SCO). Companion volume to the Dictionary of Occupational Titles.

Sequential Evaluation. A multi-step process that decision makers use to determine whether a claimant is or continues to be disabled. 20 C.F.R. §§ 404.1520 and 404.1594. *See* §112.

Severe Impairment. An impairment or combination of impairments that significantly limits one's physical or mental ability to do basic work activities, the abilities and aptitudes necessary to do most jobs. Examples of basic work activities include: walking, standing, sitting, lifting, pushing, pulling, reaching, carrying, and handling; seeing, hearing, and speaking; understanding, carrying out, and remembering simple instructions; use of judgment; responding appropriately to supervision, co-workers, and usual work situations; and dealing with changes in a routine work setting. 20 C.F.R. §§ 404.1520(c) and 404.1521. *See* §114.

Significant Erosion. A considerable reduction in the available occupations at a particular exertional level. Generally, use a lower exertional rule as a framework for a decision.

Skill. Knowledge of a work activity which requires the exercise of significant judgment that goes beyond the carrying out of simple job duties and is acquired through performance of an occupation which is above the unskilled level (requires more than 30 days to learn). It is practical and familiar knowledge of the principles and processes of an art, science, or trade, combined with the ability to apply them in practice in a proper and approved manner. This includes activities like making precise measurements, reading blueprints, and setting up and operating complex machinery. A skill gives a person a special advantage over unskilled workers in the labor market. *See* §346.2.

Skill Level. A work classification whereby work is defined according to skill requirements. The requirements of the different skill levels are set forth in 20 C.F.R. Section 404.1568 as follows:

1. Unskilled Work—Unskilled work is work which needs little or no judgment to do simple duties that can be learned on the job in a short period of time. The job may or may not require considerable strength. For example, SSA considers jobs unskilled if the primary work duties are handling, feeding, and offbearing (that is, placing or removing materials from machines which are automatic or operated by others), or machine tending, a person can usually learn to do the job in 30 days, and little specific vocational preparation and judgment are needed. A person does not gain work skills by doing unskilled work.

2. Semi-Skilled Work—Semi-skilled work is work which needs some skills but does not require doing the more complex work duties. Semi-skilled jobs may require alertness and close attention to watching machine processes; or inspecting, testing or otherwise looking for irregularities; or tending or guarding equipment, property, material, or persons against loss, damage or injury; or other types of activities which are similarly less complex than skilled work, but more complex than unskilled work. A job may be classified as semi-skilled where coordination and dexterity are necessary, as when hands or feet must be moved quickly to do repetitive tasks.

3. Skilled Work—Skilled work requires qualifications in which a person uses judgment to determine the machine and manual operations to be performed in order to obtain the proper form, quality, or quantity of material to be produced. Skilled work may require laying out work, estimating quality, determining the suitability and needed quantities or materials, making precise measurements, reading blueprints or other specifications, or making necessary computations or mechanical adjustments to control or regulate the work. Other skilled jobs may require dealing with people, facts, or figures or abstract ideas at a high level of complexity. *See* §346.2.

Slight Erosion. A minimal impact in the available occupations at an exertional level. Do not use a lower level exertional rule as a framework for a decision.

Social Security Disability Insurance (SSDI). The official name of the Social Security disability program.

Social Security Ruling (SSR). Precedential decisions of the Social Security Administration, including program policy statements, Appeals Council decisions, opinions of the Office of General Counsel, etc. When SSA finds a court decision to be an accurate statement of SSA policy, SSA may also issue that decision as a Social Security Ruling. *See* §101.

Southeastern Program Service Center (SEPSC). An SSA regional payment center located in Birmingham, Alabama. *See* §§445 and 446.

Specific Vocational Preparation (SVP). Training time. The specific vocational preparation (SVP) is the amount of time required to learn the techniques, acquire information, and develop the facility needed for average performance in a specific job-worker situation. The SVP classification attaches to the specific occupation and not to the time required for a given individual to learn the techniques, etc., of that occupation. *See* §346.2.

SSDC. Concurrent claim for Social Security disability and SSI benefits.

SSI Windfall Offset. The overpayment of SSI benefits which is deducted from Title II benefits as a result of full SSI benefits being paid for a month in which a beneficiary will later receive a Social Security disability benefit payment. *See* §411.

State Agency (SA). Initial and reconsideration disability claims are processed by an agency of the state government that has a contract with the federal government to make disability decisions. *See* §151.

Substantial Gainful Activity (SGA). Involves significant physical or mental activities in a work setting and is usually done for pay or profit, regardless of whether a profit is realized. *See* §113.

a. Substantial work activity. Substantial work activity is work activity that involves doing significant physical or mental activities. Work may be substantial even if it is done on a part-time basis or if an individual does less, gets paid less, or has less responsibility than he or she had before.

b. Gainful work activity. Gainful work activity is work activity that an individual does for pay or profit. Work activity is gainful if it is the kind of work usually done for pay or profit, whether or not a profit is realized.

c. Some other activities. Generally, SSA does not consider activities like self-care household tasks, hobbies, therapy, school attendance, club activities, or social programs to be substantial gainful activity. 20 C.F.R. § 404.1572.

Summary Earnings Query (SEQY). An SSA computer query that shows a number holder's annual income reported to SSA.

Supplemental Security Income (SSI). A cash assistance program funded and administered by the federal government for low-income individuals who are aged, blind, or disabled. Authorized by Title XVI of the Social Security Act. *See* §131.

Supplemental Security Income Display (SSID). A query showing SSI information from the database known as the Supplemental Security Record (SSR).

Temporary Assistance to Needy Families (TANF). Cash assistance program serving needy families with children that is funded jointly by federal and state governments and administered by state and county departments. This program replaced AFDC in 1996.

Ticket to Work. The Ticket to Work Program provides most people receiving Social Security benefits choices for receiving employment services. Under this program SSA issues a ticket to an eligible beneficiary who, in turn, may choose to assign the ticket to an Employment Network (EN) of the beneficiary's choice to obtain employment services, vocational rehabilitation services, or other support services necessary to achieve a vocational (work) goal. The EN, if it accepts the ticket, will coordinate and provide appropriate services to help the beneficiary find and maintain employment. *See* 20 C.F.R. Part 411.

Title II (T II, T-2). Social Security benefits; retirement, survivors and disability benefits are authorized under Title II of the Social Security Act. *See* §131.

Title XVI (T XVI, T-16). Supplemental Security Income benefits are authorized under Title XVI of the Social Security Act. *See* §132.

Title XVIII (T XVIII, T-18). Medicare program. Benefits for hospital insurance and supplementary medical insurance are authorized under Title XVIII of the Social Security Act.

Title XIX (T XIX, T-19). *See* Medicaid.

Trial Work Period (TWP). A trial work period is provided as an incentive for personal rehabilitation efforts for disabled workers receiving Social Security disability benefits who are still disabled but return to work. It allows them to perform services in as many as nine months without affecting their right to benefits during the trial work period if their impairment does not improve during this period. *See* §§176.3 and 490 *ff.*

Trait. A vocationally relevant attribute or characteristic which permits a person to properly perform a work activity. Traits are relevant whether learned or innate. Traits are not skills. A musician requires both a good sense of pitch and fine finger dexterity (traits) to play a piece of music by ear without error (skill); a lab researcher may require acute vision (trait) to identify a particular bacteria found in a culture (skill); a machinist must rely on perception of size and shape (trait) to cut material within certain tolerances (skill). *See* §349.3.

Transferability of skills. An individual is considered to have skills that can be used in other jobs when the skilled or semi-skilled work activities done in past work can be used to meet the requirement of other skilled or unskilled work activities.

Transferability is most probable and meaningful among jobs in which:

1. The same or a lesser degree of skill is required;
2. The same or similar tools and machines are used; and
3. The same or similar raw materials, products, processes, or services are involved.

Social Security Ruling 82-41 and 20 C.F.R. § 404.1568(d). *See* §349.

Underpayment (UP). An amount due a person that has not been paid. Underpayments usually result from unpaid accrued benefits or unnegotiated checks. *See* §443.

United States Code (USC). The compilation of all U.S. laws organized into different "titles." The Social Security Act with which we are concerned in this book is found in Title 42 of the United States Code, which is entitled "The Public Health and Welfare." *See* §109.

Unskilled Work. Work that requires little or no judgment to do simple duties that can be learned on the job in a short period of time (i.e., 30 days or less). Generally SVP of 1 or 2 as rated in the SCO.

Unsuccessful Work Attempt (UWA). Work lasting up to six months that the claimant is forced to stop or reduce below the SGA level because of the claimant's disability. Such work is disregarded when evaluating the claimant's disability under the sequential evaluation process. *See* §176.2.

User Identification Number (User ID). The number SSA assigns to a representative to use in accessing SSA's electronic services. See POMS GN 03913.001C.

Value of the One-Third Reduction (VTR). For the SSI program, value of the one-third reduction, referred to as VTR in the POMS, is countable in-kind support and maintenance valued at one-third of the individual's or couple's Federal benefit rate (as applicable). *See* §423.

Veterans Administration (VA). A federal agency that administers programs for US veterans. *See* §211.

Vocational Adjustment. Vocational Adjustment involves an interaction of a claimant's residual functional capacity (RFC) with his or her age, education, and work experience in order to decide whether the claimant can adjust to jobs which he or she may be vocationally qualified to do. *See* §129.

Vocational Expert (VE). An expert witness who provides an opinion about vocational issues for use at a disability hearing, either in person or in answer to interrogatories. *See* §§340-349.

Vocational Factors. An individual's RFC, age, education, and work experience. SSR 83-10. *See* §129.

Wage Earner (WE). An individual working under and paying wages covered under the Social Security system.

Waiting Period (WP). Five consecutive full calendar months beginning with the earliest full calendar month throughout which the worker was under a disability and had disability insured status for benefit purposes. No T-2 benefits are paid during the waiting period. *See* §133.

Western Program Service Center (WNPSC). An SSA regional payment center located in Richmond, California. *See* §§445 and 446.

Widow or Widowers Insurance Benefits (WIB). Social Security benefits paid to a surviving spouse of a deceased worker who was insured under the Social Security program. *See* §142.

Windfall Offset. The reduction in retroactive Title II benefits equal to the amount of SSI payments a recipient would not have received had Title II been paid on time. *See* §411.

Workers Compensation (WC). State laws that ensure medical care and cash benefits to a worker injured in connection with a job, or cash benefits to dependents if the worker is killed. There is a limit on the amount of Social Security disability benefits plus worker's compensation benefits a recipient may receive. *See* §437.

Appendix 12:   Annual SSI, Medicare, COLA, SGA, TWP and Earnings for QC Amounts Since 2000

Year	Federal SSI Individual	Federal SSI Couple	Federal SSI Household of Another	Medicare Premium	COLA Percent	SGA	Blind SGA	TWP Service Month	TWP Service Mo Self Employed Hours	Earnings for QC
2000	513	769	342	45.50	2.5	700	1170	200	40	780
2001	531	796	354	50.00	3.5	740	1240	530	80	830
2002	545	817	363.34	54.00	2.6	780	1300	560	80	870
2003	552	829	368	58.70	1.4	800	1330	570	80	890
2004	564	846	376	66.60	2.1	810	1350	580	80	900
2005	579	869	386	78.20	2.7	830	1380	590	80	920
2006	603	904	402	88.50	4.1	860	1450	620	80	970
2007	623	934	415.34	93.50[1]	3.3	900	1500	640	80	1000
2008	637	956	424.67	96.40	2.3	940	1570	670	80	1050
2009	674	1011	449.34	96.40	5.8	980	1640	700	80	1090
2010	674	1011	449.34	110.50[2]	0	1000	1640	720	80	1120
2011	674	1011	449.34	115.40[3]	0	1000	1640	720	80	1120
2012	698	1048	465.34	99.90[4]	3.6	1010	1690	720	80	1130
2013	710	1066	473.34	104.90[5]	1.7	1040	1740	750	80	1160
2014	721	1082	480.67	104.90	1.5	1070	1800	770	80	1200
2015	733	1100	488.67	104.90	1.7	1090	1820	780	80	1220
2016	733	1100	488.67	121.80[6]	0	1130	1820	810	80	1260
2017	735	1103	490	134.00[7]	0.3	1170	1950	840	80	1300

[1]The basic Medicare premium beginning with 2007 is increased based on earnings. Individuals earning over $85,000 per year and couples earning over $170,000 per year pay a higher amount.

[2]In 2010 because there was no COLA, the Medicare premium for those already receiving it was frozen at $96.40 if they started receiving Medicare before 2010, $110.50 if they started receiving Medicare in 2010.

[3]In 2011 because there was no COLA, the Medicare premium for those already receiving it was frozen at $96.40 if they started receiving Medicare before 2010, $110.50 if they started receiving Medicare in 2010, and $115.40 if they started receiving Medicare in 2011.

[4]In 2012, the premium for the majority of people was $99.90. Thus, those who started receiving Medicare in 2010 or 2011 received a reduction in premium amount.

[5]From 2013 through 2015 the Medicare premium for most people was $104.90.

[6]Because there was no COLA applicable to Social Security benefits for 2016, those Social Security recipients already receiving Medicare did not have a premium increase. They paid $104.90. Those getting Medicare for the first time paid $121.80. High earners paid more.

[7]New enrollees pay $134.00. Because the Medicare premium increased more than the cost of living increased for Social Security benefits for 2017, those already receiving Medicare continued to pay what they had been paying.

Appendix 13: Memorandum: Fibromyalgia, Chronic Fatigue Syndrome, and Objective Medical Evidence Requirement for Disability Adjudication

DATE: May 11, 1998

TO:
Verrell L. Dethloff
Administrative Law Judge, OHA

FROM:
Deputy Commissioner for Disability
and Income Security Programs

SUBJECT:
Fibromyalgia, Chronic Fatigue Syndrome, and Objective Medical Evidence Requirements for Disability Adjudication (Your Memo, 01/30/98)—REPLY

Commissioner Apfel has asked me to respond to the issues raised in your memorandum dated January 30, 1998. I also have copies of your memoranda addressed to Administrative Appeals Judge Andrew E. Wakshul and General Counsel Arthur Fried, which raise essentially the same issue. This memorandum is also a response to your letters to the General Counsel and Judge Wakshul.

Your letter indicates that the Social Security Administration (SSA) needs to take a definitive position with respect to whether fibromyalgia and chronic fatigue syndrome (CFS) constitute medically determinable impairments. You requested an opinion from OGC on this issue and suggested that the Appeals Council meet en banc or schedule oral argument to resolve the issue. Although the regulations authorize the Appeals Council to hear oral argument in a case raising an important question of law or policy, the Appeals Council does not establish agency policy with respect to issues related to the evaluation of specific medical conditions. Rather, the Office of Disability establishes agency policy in such cases.

Your letter states that fibromyalgia and CFS do not constitute medically determinable impairments within the meaning of section 223 (d) (3) of the Social Security Act because there are no acceptable medical criteria by which these impairments can be diagnosed. Your letter further states that "'symptoms' only become 'signs' when a medically determinable impairment has been established, and subjective 'signs' on examination are therefore not 'objective' evidence in the absence of other objective evidence first providing a predicate for a diagnosis."

However, SSA has taken a definitive position that fibromyalgia and CFS can constitute medically determinable impairments within the meaning of the statute. As you noted in your letter, CFS was discussed in the process unification training in 1996-1997.

Although we regret that you found this discussion inadequate, the training did state clearly and unequivocally that individuals alleging CFS can be found to have a medically determinable impairment under the disability program given the presence of certain specified signs and findings. This position is consistent with the instructions in Program Operations Manual System (POMS) DI 24515.075, Disability Digest No. 93-5, and Social Security Rulings (SSRs) 96-3p, 96-4p, and 96-7p, issued on July 2, 1996, which detail our policies as to how symptoms affect determinations of the presence of a medically determinable impairment, impairment severity, and the ability to engage in sustained work activity.

Establishing the existence of a medically determinable impairment does not necessarily require that the claimant or the medical evidence establish a specific diagnosis. This is especially true when the medical community has not reached agreement on a single set of diagnostic criteria. All the Act and regulations require is that some physical or mental impairment be established through medically acceptable clinical and laboratory diagnostic techniques. In some cases, the record may not establish the diagnosis, but there will be medical signs established by medically acceptable clinical techniques that show that there is an impairment, and that there is a relationship between the findings and the symptoms alleged; i.e., that the existence of a medically determinable impairment that could reasonably be expected to produce the symptoms has been established.

As you indicated in your letter, with the publication of SSRs 96-4p and 96-7p in July 1996, we intended to emphasize the statutory standard requiring the establishment of a medically determinable impairment as a predicate to the evaluation of symptoms. However, we did not mean to imply that it is first necessary to establish a fixed diagnosis in order to find the presence of a medically determinable impairment. Rather, the medically determinable impairment is established in the presence of anatomical, physiological, or psychological abnormalities that can be objectively observed and reported apart from the individual's perceptions even in the absence of a definitive diagnosis.

Your argument based on the Rulings seems to misinterpret the explanation in Footnote 2 to SSR 96-4p, which explains our longstanding policy, consistent with 20 CFR §§ 404.1528(b) and 416.928(b), that some symptoms, when appropriately reported by a physician or psychologist in a clinical setting, can also be considered "signs" because sometimes these observations constitute "medically acceptable clinical diagnostic techniques." This is true for mental impairments in general and for such widely accepted and recognizable disorders as migraine headaches.

CFS is a systemic disorder consisting of a complex of symptoms and signs that may vary in incidence, duration, and severity. The hallmark of CFS is the presence of clinically evaluated, persistent or relapsing chronic fatigue that is of new or definite onset which cannot be explained by another diagnosed physical or mental disorder, or the result of ongoing exertion. It is not substantially alleviated by rest and results in substantial reduction in previous levels of occupational, educational, social, or personal activities. Within these parameters, CFS can exhibit a variety of symptoms and signs.

As with all claims for disability, documentation of objective physical and/or mental findings in cases involving CFS is critical to establish the presence of a medically determinable impairment. In cases in which CFS is alleged, longitudinal clinical records reflecting ongoing medical assessment and treatment from the individual's medical sources, especially treating sources, are imperative to document objective physical and/or mental findings. Every reasonable effort should be made to secure all relevant evidence in cases involving CFS to ensure appropriate and thorough disability evaluation.

For purposes of Social Security disability evaluation, one or more of the following medical signs clinically documented over a period of at least 6 consecutive months establishes the existence of a medically determinable impairment for individuals alleging disability on the basis of CFS:

episodes of clinically documented low-grade fever; palpably swollen and tender lymph nodes on physical examination; nonexudative pharyngitis; and muscle wasting with no other direct cause identification.

At this time, there are no specific laboratory findings that definitively document the presence of CFS. The results of tilt-table testing to evaluate neurally mediated hypotension may be abnormal in individuals with CFS. Nonspecific laboratory findings indicative of chronic immune system activation (e.g., slight elevations in immune complexes, depressed natural killer cell activity, or atypical lymphocytes) may be included in the evidentiary record of individuals alleging CFS, but such findings are not definitive of CFS nor are they necessarily evidence of a medically determinable impairment.

Some individuals with CFS report problems with neurocognitive functioning, including problems with short-term memory, comprehension, concentration, speech, and/or calculation. Other individuals with CFS may exhibit signs of a mental or emotional disorder, such as anxiety or depression. When deficits in these areas have been documented by mental status examination and/or psychological testing, such findings constitute medical signs that establish the presence of a medically determinable impairment.

If an adjudicator concludes that an individual has a medically determinable impairment, and the individual alleges severe fatigue on a recurring basis consistent with CFS, such fatigue must be considered in deciding whether the individual's impairment is severe. If chronic fatigue is found to significantly limit an individual's ability to perform basic work activities, a "severe" impairment must be found to exist at step 2 of the sequential evaluation process.

Although symptoms alone cannot be the basis for finding a medically determinable impairment, an individual's symptoms and the effects of those symptoms on the individual's functional abilities must be considered both in determining impairment severity and in assessing the individual's residual functional capacity.

Fibromyalgia is a disorder defined by the American College of Rheumatology (ACR) and we recognize it as medically determinable if there are signs that are clinically established by the medical record. The signs are primarily the tender points. The ACR defines the disorder in patients as "widespread pain in all four quadrants of the body for a minimum duration of 3 months and at least 11 of the 18 specified tender points which cluster around the neck and shoulder, chest, hip, knee, and elbow regions." Other typical symptoms, some of which can be signs if they have been clinically documented over time, are irritable bowel syndrome, chronic headaches, temporomandibular joint dysfunction, sleep disorder, severe fatigue, and cognitive dysfunction.

I agree with your observation that we need to do a better job of explaining our policy with respect to the adjudication of claims involving impairments like fibromyalgia and CFS. Toward that end, we have been drafting policy guidance to help adjudicators evaluate these impairments.

I trust that this explanation and clarification will assist you in applying the regulations and rulings to cases involving fibromyalgia and CFS.

Susan M. Daniels, Ph.D.

cc:
Arthur J. Fried
Andrew E. Wakshul